THE BEST AMERICAN RECIPES 2005–2006

The Year's Top Picks

from Books, Magazines,

Newspapers, and the Internet

THE BEST AMERICAN RECIPES 2005–2006

Fran McCullough

and

Molly Stevens

Series Editors

Foreword by

Mario Batali

Houghton Mifflin Company
Boston New York
2005

Visit our Web site: www.houghtonmifflinbooks.com.

ISSN 1525-1101
ISBN-13: 978-0-618-57478-0
ISBN-10: 0-618-57478-6

Book design by Anne Chalmers

Cover photographs by Jim Scherer;
Overnight Macaroni and Cheese (page 110)

Food styling by Mary Jane Sawyer

Prop styling by Colleen Gannon

Printed in the United States of America

MP 10 9 8 7 6 5 4 3 2 1

contents

foreword

BY MARIO BATALI

WITH SUBSCRIPTIONS to more than a dozen food magazines and another dozen weeklies, monthlies, and quarterlies with food opinions, food theories, and food wisdom packed into their topic-specific pages, I often think I might one day see the end of my infinite appetite for recipes, plain and simple. But I don't.

As a professional cook, I am faced with hundreds of recipes on a daily basis in each of the restaurants I work in. Some come from my own stuff, some from my staff, some from my customers, and some even from people I have never met, who want me to check out their aunt Ida's dishes. I read them all with the same enthusiasm that I read a new work by this year's hot novelist or with the same urgency I once reserved for lyrics by David Byrne, of the Talking Heads. As predictable as the format of these recipes seems, I'm still fascinated by every one. I must be a simpleton. How could something so seemingly repetitive interest someone I consider so endlessly fascinating?

Obviously I am not going to cook all of them: I have neither the time nor the appetite to give them their fair tasting ritual. In fact, when I actually experiment and cook with a completely new recipe, I rarely stray from my stable of trusted cooks and authors, let alone try something from an unknown source. On the one hand, I like big, definitive, and comprehensive books like *The Gourmet Cookbook* and *How to Cook Everything* and *The Barbecue Bible*. On the other hand, I am very comfortable with personal cookbooks like those by Alice Waters, Paula Wolfert, and Ruthie Rogers and Rose Gray from the River Café in London. So what is it that I like so much about recipes in general?

On an only slightly closer look, each recipe is actually an artifact of a specific dish in time, somewhere in some real place, in some real kitchen. Some real person actually made the dish, enjoyed it enough to want to recreate it, and then took the time to write down the ingredients and the steps of the technique. This may seem insignificant in modern times, when our world buzzes with computers, laser printers, fax machines, and e-mail providers that can zip a recipe out to the far reaches of our light-speed world. But until about forty years ago, a recipe was a true and slow-moving historical document that spoke to us on myriad levels, not only about the author but about the eaters, foragers, farmers, fishermen, and butchers who helped bring the ingredients to the kitchen. Today, the recipe seems to have changed into a quicker currency of information exchange, but in my mind it still retains its innate historical significance. As Brillat-Savarin, quoted so many times, has said, "Tell me what a man eats, and I will tell you who he is." Ambrosia salad from the suburbs in the sixties and even fondue, so hip in the seventies that it seemed almost prehistoric only ten years ago, are now back in style—a new iconography for cultural change.

Observing the differences in the recipes of 2005 from those of the 1960s is as valid a barometer of culture and progress as monitoring SAT scores, literacy rates, and family size. Where we once celebrated convenience, we now celebrate authenticity. Where we once begged for tomatoes, strawberries, and asparagus that shipped year round, we now search out heirloom or geospecific ingredients in the peak of their season. Where Chinese and Italian were entire categories, we now have Sichuan, Shanghai, Pugliese, and Tuscan. If you had suggested to Julia Child in 1973 that there would be an "all food, all the time" television network, I am certain the queen herself would have scoffed. But it has happened.

And now we are here in the front of a book of fabulous recipes collected by Fran McCullough and Molly Stevens in 2005—historical documents as relevant and important as any other group of pop-culture icons. These recipes are tasty, intriguing, and easy to make. Most important, they are mouthwatering renditions of real food made by real people in real places in the good ole U.S. of A. Reading them makes me want to go into the kitchen, dig deep into this magnificent collection, and cook some delicious food for my family.

introduction

EACH YEAR as we put these collections together, there comes a point when we want to call our friends to say, "Look what we found!" Although we see hundreds of extremely familiar recipes every year, we're delighted to report that culinary creativity is hard at work all across the country. That's the joy of this project. If we were giving a state-of-the-union report on American food, we'd say the home kitchen is still a wonderful place to find really good food, one that reflects the values of classic American cooking but also embraces new techniques, new ingredients, new ways of thinking.

We certainly couldn't have imagined we'd be serving turkey carnitas (shredded slow-cooked turkey thighs). Or chicken breasts with a crispy potato chip coating. Or chocolate and peanut butter candies dreamed up by enthusiastic football fans in Ohio. All of these things are absolutely delicious, but our original attraction to them was their novelty. We just had to try them, and as always, the proof of the pudding was in the eating (and many a pudding doesn't make the cut).

We're often asked what trends we've turned up in the course of assembling our cream-of-the-crop recipes. The standout one this year could be summed up as "get real." On the most practical level, that means not fussing endlessly in the kitchen or performing heroic feats of shopping. It also means an appreciation of good, humble food, something like a family barbecue joint's stuffed dill pickles or the boldly flavored salt-and-pepper burgers created by the late Leslie Revsin, a chef who had a real knack for straightforward recipes with huge flavor returns. It means using one of your grandmother's favorite tools, the cast-iron skillet. It means using a store-bought pie crust if it doesn't make a difference to the outcome of your pie or playing with a great convenience food like the flaky biscuits in a tube at the supermarket to make Parmesan–Poppy Seed Pull-Apart Bread (we found that one in the Harley and Davidson family cookbook).

Upscale convenience is big this year. Many of the dishes we love are based on gourmet pantry products: jarred lemon curd (a base for magnificent frozen lemon cream sandwiches) and dulce de leche (a delectable ham glaze). Even famous French chefs see the point of these handy ingredients. Jacques

Pépin has a dazzling trick for transforming canned peaches into a knockout dinner-party dessert.

A few recipes in our collection require spending some significant time in the kitchen, but in each case, we promise that the results are well worth it. One of the sexiest desserts we've tested in a long time, Dahlia Bakery Butterscotch Pie, is a big production, but it'll make you very proud and your guests ecstatic. And it comes with foolproof instructions. (We tell you if a recipe is going to be more — or less, for that matter — complicated than it appears.)

A little extra time and attention in the kitchen can yield big flavor dividends. We're happy to go the extra mile and make our own garam masala mix (the recipe in this book is stellar), for instance, or dry our own herbs in the oven. If a dish is infinitely better when it's homemade (like the ricotta in the starters chapter), we want you to know about it.

We've learned a lot of these tricks from chefs, more and more of whom are making the imaginative leap to the home kitchen, not just assuming that we'll have a *batterie de cuisine* and a prep staff ready to ladle out the homemade stock. They continue to inspire us. Two of our favorite recipes this year came from two of Boston's most lauded chefs. Jody Adams's fabulous Spaghetti with Slow-Roasted Cherry Tomatoes, Basil, and Parmesan Cheese uses easy-to-find ingredients and requires no fancy techniques or culinary exertion. Likewise, Andy Husbands's super-simple recipe for blackberries and cream takes only minutes to prepare. Hotshot Irish chef Conrad Gallagher shows us an ingenious way to cook salmon that's quick and very good. And we've even got TV food celeb Ina Garten's take on lemon roast chicken with crunchy croutons. All wonderful, and all entirely doable.

In creating this book, we frequently encountered another aspect of creativity: the tendency to rethink basic ways of approaching certain dishes. That's why we love French chef Guy Savoy's take on mac 'n' cheese: he's eliminated making the sauce and instead treats the pasta to an overnight soak in creamy milk, with spectacular results. It's not only easier, it's much, much better. Marcella Hazan's meatballs are especially intriguing because there's no tomato sauce—in place of the tomatoes, it's red peppers, cooked down into a gorgeously red, slightly sweet elixir that brings out the best in the meatballs.

Many techniques we thought were more or less written in stone have been rethought this year too. After years of filling up coolers with salty water and wrestling our Thanksgiving turkeys in and out of various brines, it seems the tide may be turning. The preeminent food scientist Harold McGee is still experimenting with methods to produce the juiciest turkey with the crispest skin, but he has ruled out brining, because it just adds water. McGee prefers to leave his bird unwrapped on the refrigerator shelf for a day or two—to dry the skin and make it crisp.

Even the basic cooking rules have changed. New rule: food scientists all across the land are urging American cooks not to rinse their chickens and turkeys so as not to spread bacteria, and their voices are just starting to be heard. Although we haven't thrown out our sifters yet, the TV gadget guru Alton Brown has us almost convinced that the food processor does a much better job, without the mess.

Sophisticated Americans have long known that vegetables shouldn't be cooked to death. But wait: this year we started to relearn what older cultures have always known: "overcooked" vegetables can be wonderful. As soon as we tasted green beans cooked for three hours—yes, three hours—we knew the pendulum had swung again. Another example of this idea is London chef Fergus Henderson's Mushy Zucchini, which takes on a whole new personality when it's very slowly stewed with butter.

Cooking vegetables long enough to bring out the full dimensions of their flavor can be considered getting real. So can the idea that you don't have to roll out a big dinner every evening. It could be just an ample bowl of hearty soup (especially since so many soups this year are made with meat, sausage, or seafood) or a really good sandwich or even something from the breakfast menu. Technically, this is supper, not dinner, but it's an old idea that seems to have a new appeal. We'd be delighted to have Eggs in Purgatory, for instance, in the evening.

Whether they're fast or slow, startlingly new or completely traditional, the recipes in this book—from chefs, backs of boxes, food magazines, cookbooks, and newspaper food sections—have one thing in common: they all taste great. They're keepers, and we know they'll work in your kitchen as they have in ours. Just so you don't overlook our very favorite recipes (and one favorite cooking tip) from this year, we've made a list, the ultimate "Look what we found!"

—FRAN McCULLOUGH
and MOLLY STEVENS

our top ten favorite recipes

PANCETTA CRISPS WITH GOAT CHEESE AND PEAR —A delightful hors d'oeuvre perfect with drinks or champagne. Slices of pancetta, the unsmoked Italian bacon, go into the oven and magically return as crisp little wafers that neatly hold the cheese and pear.

CARROT GINGER SOUP WITH LIME CRÈME FRAÎCHE —An elegant, sublimely simple soup that can be served hot or chilled. Carrots and ginger are made for each other, and adding an aromatic spiced oil that you make yourself in a couple of minutes takes this soup to another level entirely.

PONTORMO'S SALAD —A humble dish of perfectly scrambled eggs over salad greens becomes extraordinary in the hands of New York Italian chef Cesare Casella. In the moment when the two elements come together, the creamy eggs wilt the greens a bit, releasing the complex aromas of the vinaigrette. And it couldn't be simpler.

RIGATONI ALLA TOTO —Plates of rigatoni being served in trattorias all over Italy superficially resemble this one but can't hold a candle to it. We almost passed by this Italian chef's version ourselves, but the unusual touch of cream along with the sausage and wine in the dish made us look twice. Now this rustic but refined dish is our standby for a consoling winter dinner, sometimes even for a dinner party.

BRAISED GREEN BEANS WITH TOMATO AND FENNEL —This is more of a stew than a side dish, and it's one of the best vegetable dishes we've ever eaten. Three hours of cooking bring out an unexpected quality in the green beans that's breathtaking, and the other vegetables are a fine counterpoint. The dish tastes like old country cooking, with a soul-stirring depth of flavor that's mostly missing in contemporary vegetable dishes.

GRILLED MOJITO CHICKEN —The name says it all. Imagine the bright summery flavors of rum, lime, and mint on a juicy grilled chicken breast. And we love the rum-soaked grilled lime wedges that you squeeze over the chicken just before serving.

BACON AND CHEDDAR SCONES —We thought we'd seen every possible scone variation, but this one tops them all. The bacon is a completely inspired addition, and it means this scone can be a meal in itself, i.e., breakfast. The scones are also great with soups and salads or as a portable lunch.

ALMOND CAKE WITH STRAWBERRY RHUBARB COMPOTE—This gorgeous almond cake is the work of Thomas Keller, arguably the best chef in the country. It has three different sources of almond flavor and it's amazingly easy to make. A lovely strawberry rhubarb compote—or just some raspberries—on the side makes it a big-deal dessert.

BROWN SUGAR–SOUR CREAM CHEESECAKE—This is what happens when a talented southern pastry chef reinterprets New York–style cheesecake. It's creamy and dense, with the distinguishing flavor of brown sugar and a touch of molasses. We especially love the little bit of cornmeal added to the graham cracker crust for extra crunch.

GINGER LEMON ICED TEA—This refreshing, exhilarating drink from a Thai restaurant in Washington, D.C.'s Georgetown is perfect with Asian food or almost any summer repast. It's great for a backyard party, because it converts to a Bangkok Swing in a flash—just add 2 ounces each of Absolut Citron and Southern Comfort. Teetotalers and drinkers alike will be extremely happy.

BEST TIP

Pastry chef Karen Barker's brilliant solution to the wide cracks that ruin the smooth surface of so many cheesecakes: gradually reduce the oven temperature as the cake bakes (see page 250). No more cracks, and no more water baths, either.

starters

phyllo cheese straws

THESE DELICATE PASTRIES make a handsome little nibble to serve with drinks, especially when you're pouring something bubbly and bright, like champagne or Prosecco. With nothing more than a dusting of Parmesan, they're more crunch than substance, making them satisfying without being filling. We also love the fact that you can assemble them several days ahead, then refrigerate and bake before serving, or bake and store in a closed tin for several days.

makes 24 crisps

- 2 sheets phyllo dough (12 x 18 inches each; see note)
- 6 tablespoons clarified butter (see note)
- 2½ tablespoons finely grated Parmesan cheese

Preheat the oven to 375 degrees.

On a cutting board, lay out 1 sheet of phyllo, brush with the clarified butter, and sprinkle evenly with cheese. (Keep the remaining phyllo covered with a moistened tea towel.) Place the other sheet of phyllo on top of the cheese and brush it with the remaining clarified butter.

Using a sharp knife, cut the buttered phyllo sheet lengthwise into thirds. (You will have 3 long strips, each about 4 inches wide and 18 inches long.) Next cut these strips crosswise into 1½-inch-wide rectangles.

Wrap each rectangle lengthwise around a pencil or skewer. Remove the pencil or skewer and place the rolled phyllo straws on a baking sheet. Continue until all the phyllo has been rolled.

Refrigerate the phyllo straws on the baking sheet for at least 10 minutes, or until they become firm.

Bake for about 9 minutes, or until golden brown. Remove from the oven and, using a spatula, slip the straws onto paper towels to cool. The straws may be kept in a sealed tin for several days.

notes from our test kitchen

- Some phyllo comes in 9-x-12-inch sheets and not the 12-x-18-inch sheets called for here. In this case, you'll need to use 4 sheets and make 2 batches of straws. Follow the directions by sandwiching half the grated cheese between 2 buttered sheets of phyllo and cutting the sheets first lengthwise into thirds so you have long strips that are each about 3 inches wide and 12 inches long. Next cut these strips crosswise into 1½-inch-wide rectangles.
- To make clarified butter, melt 1 stick (8 tablespoons) unsalted butter over medium-low heat. When the butter is thoroughly melted, turn off the heat and skim the creamy foam from the surface. Pour the butter into a small bowl, leaving any white sediment behind. One stick will yield about 6 tablespoons clarified butter. (We sometimes simply use melted butter. The phyllo may brown a little unevenly, but the taste is the same.)
- Unless you're very quick with rolling and shaping, the phyllo may start to dry out as you go. Use any extra clarified butter to brush drying edges to keep them from becoming brittle.
- Place the rolls seam sides down on the baking sheet to prevent them from unfurling as they chill or bake.

SOURCE: *The Gourmet Cookbook* edited by Ruth Reichl

COOK: Laurie Colwin after Rosalea Murphy

rosemary walnuts

THIS RECIPE FIRST SURFACED in *The Pink Adobe Cookbook,* a 1980s collection from a Santa Fe restaurant of the same name. It became a kind of signature for the late Laurie Colwin, a novelist and passionate cook who had a nose for a great recipe and brought this one to a much broader audience in one of her columns for *Gourmet.* These nuts are just Laurie's kind of food: intensely flavorful, straightforward, and easy as pie — actually, easier.

It probably goes without saying that these nuts are perfect for the holidays, especially Thanksgiving. Good to serve and good to give, so you might as well make a double batch.

makes 2 cups

- 2½ tablespoons unsalted butter
- 2 teaspoons dried rosemary, crumbled
- 1 teaspoon sea salt
- ½ teaspoon cayenne pepper
- 2 cups walnut halves (about 8 ounces)

Place a rack in the center of the oven and preheat to 350 degrees.

Melt the butter in a rimmed baking sheet and add the rosemary, salt, and cayenne. Mix well. Add the walnuts, toss, and bake in a single layer for 10 minutes. Serve warm or at room temperature. The nuts will keep for 3 days at room temperature, tightly sealed.

note from our test kitchen

We think the nuts taste best warm. You can reheat them in the oven briefly just before serving.

SOURCE: *Rick & Lanie's Excellent Kitchen Adventures*
by Rick Bayless and Lanie Bayless
with Deann Groen Bayless

COOK: Rick Bayless

hickory house stuffed pickles

RICK BAYLESS IS FAMOUS for his excellent Mexican restaurants in Chicago, his TV shows, and his Mexican cookbooks. But his people aren't Mexican, they're barbecue royalty in Oklahoma. His parents, John and Levita Bayless, ran the Hickory House in Oklahoma City for thirty-seven years, making everything from scratch. One of their specialties is these amazing pickles. The minute we heard about them, we had to try them.

You can stuff celery, of course, or eggs, but stuffing a dill pickle is inspired. The stuffing itself is simple, just pimiento cheese—but made from scratch, not from a jar. These retro treats are a great choice for a backyard picnic or a summer barbecue.

serves 8

- 4 ounces American or mild cheddar cheese, grated (about 1 cup)
- 3 tablespoons mayonnaise
- 2½ tablespoons diced pimiento or roasted red pepper
- 4 3-inch-long dill pickles, split in half lengthwise

Mix the cheese, mayonnaise, and pimiento together in a bowl.

Cut a shallow V down the center of each pickle half, leaving ½ inch on either end. Scoop out the seeds and discard. Let the pickles drain cut sides down on paper towels.

Use a fork to stuff the Vs with the pimiento cheese, mounding it in the center and spreading the cheese to cover the entire cut side of the pickle. Serve the pickles on a platter.

note from our test kitchen

We beg you to use real cheddar cheese, a mild one, and pass by the American cheese.

tip

To dress up the pickles, Bayless suggests sprinkling them with snipped fresh chives, chopped scallions, or chopped fresh parsley.

SOURCE: *Wife of the Chef* by Courtney Febbroiello

COOK: Courtney Febbroiello

manchurian dip

A LITTLE SWEET, A LITTLE GARLICKY, a little fiery, this exotic-tasting dip looks innocent enough, like glorified ketchup. But it packs an addictive punch. It's great with beer and barbecue and other lusty comestibles. We like to serve it with drinks before an Indian meal, homemade or takeout.

A good sturdy chip is the right vehicle, as are raw cauliflower florets. The *Washington Post* came up with an excellent dipper suggestion: grilled paneer, the creamy fresh cheese that's found in Indian markets and at Whole Foods Markets, among other sources. Cut the paneer into 3/4-inch cubes and sear them on all sides in a skillet lightly brushed with oil. Stick a toothpick in each one and serve warm.

makes 2 quarts

- 1 large carrot, peeled and coarsely chopped
- 1 small green chile pepper, seeded and coarsely chopped
- 1 medium red onion, coarsely chopped
- 2 large celery ribs, coarsely chopped
- 1 large bunch cilantro, including stems, coarsely chopped
- 10 medium garlic cloves, peeled
- 1 tablespoon vegetable oil
- 2 cups ketchup
- 1/4 cup soy sauce
- 1 tablespoon sugar
- 1 teaspoon chili powder or 1/2 teaspoon cayenne pepper
- Salt and freshly ground black pepper

In a food processor, combine the carrot, chile pepper, onion, celery, and cilantro. Add the garlic and pulse until blended.

Heat the oil in a medium saucepan over medium-high heat. Put the pureed vegetables in the pan and heat through, 3 to 4 minutes. Add the ketchup and soy sauce and cook for 10 minutes more. Reduce the heat to medium-low.

When the sauce starts to thicken, add the sugar, chili powder or cayenne, and salt and pepper to taste. Serve warm for the best flavor or at room temperature. The dip will keep in the refrigerator for up to 1 week; reheat gently before serving.

note from our test kitchen

Two quarts is a lot of dip, so this recipe is good for a party. If that's too much, just make half the recipe.

SOURCE: *Party Dips!*
by Sally Sampson

COOK: Chris Schlesinger

roasted red pepper dip with pomegranate molasses

THIS TERRIFIC DIP based on roasted red peppers, walnuts, and sweet-and-tart pomegranate molasses is a variation on *muhammara* (which means "brick-colored"), a traditional dish from the eastern Mediterranean. Since Paula Wolfert first published the recipe in 1994, *muhammara* has morphed into a chef's specialty all across the land. We particularly like this easy version from Chris Schlesinger, a Boston chef devoted to intense flavors.

One big advantage of this dip is that you can make it up to two days ahead (or longer)—the flavors will only improve. The obvious dipping companion is the traditional Mediterranean one: toasted pita crisps (see note). You can also use broken-up pieces of lavash, the Armenian cracker bread.

makes about 2 cups

- 1 tablespoon olive oil
- 1 Spanish onion, chopped
- 2 garlic cloves, minced
- 1 tablespoon light brown sugar
- 1 tablespoon ground cumin
- 2 red bell peppers, roasted, peeled, and seeded (see note)
- 1 cup walnuts, toasted (see note)
- 3 tablespoons fresh flat-leaf parsley leaves, plus more for garnish
- Juice of 1 lime
- 2 tablespoons pomegranate molasses (see note)

Heat a large skillet over medium-high heat. When it's hot, add the oil. Add the onion, garlic, brown sugar, and cumin and cook, stirring, until the onion is slightly caramelized, about 10 minutes. Transfer to a food processor, add the remaining ingredients, and process until smooth.

Transfer to a serving bowl, cover, and refrigerate for at least 1 hour and up to 2 days to let the flavors develop. Serve at room temperature, garnished with parsley leaves.

notes from our test kitchen

- Pomegranate molasses is available at Middle Eastern markets and some gourmet shops. Or you can make your own. To make your own pomegranate syrup, start with 4 cups pomegranate juice with no added sugar or flavorings. Bring it to a steady boil in a saucepan over high heat. Decrease the heat to maintain a steady, slow bubbling, and cook, stirring occasionally with a wooden spoon. After 20 to 30 minutes the juice will have started to thicken and will be reduced by about half. When it's done, you'll be able to dip a spoon in and remove it covered with syrup, which should take its time sliding off. You'll have about 2 cups syrup, which will keep for about 6 months in the refrigerator.
- To make pita crisps, slit the breads crosswise into 2 circles and cut the circles into wedges. Brush lightly with olive oil and toast on a baking sheet in a 350-degree oven for about 5 minutes, or until golden.
- To roast the peppers, put them directly over the gas flame on your stovetop, turning until the skins are blackened. (If you don't have a gas stovetop, you can do this under the broiler, but they need careful tending.) Put the blackened peppers in a plastic bag, and twist closed; let them sweat for about 10 minutes. The skins will slip right off.
- To toast the walnuts, arrange them in a single layer on a baking sheet and toast in a 350-degree oven, stirring occasionally, until they begin to smell good, about 10 minutes.
- We're glad to see the instruction to heat the pan *before* adding the oil. Chefs do this more or less automatically but it's not a habit with the rest of us. Doing it this way gives you a better cooking surface and is better for the pans, too.
- We've found that this dip keeps for 1 week in the refrigerator and improves each day.

SOURCE: www.tastycentral.com

COOK: Roy Finamore

homemade ricotta

ONE TASTE OF THIS CREAMY, snowy-white fresh cheese and you won't wonder why we've included this recipe in a chapter of first courses. Instead, your mind will be racing with possibilities. Probably our favorite way to serve homemade ricotta is on a pretty platter, generously drizzled with the best extra-virgin olive oil, seasoned with sea salt and fresh cracked pepper, and accompanied by slices of good bread. You can also shower the ricotta with herbs or other spices (the Middle Eastern spices sumac and Aleppo pepper are particularly nice). Or try adding dollops to a green salad or an antipasto platter. The options are endless.

makes about 1½ cups

- 1 quart whole milk
- 1 cup heavy cream
- 1 scant teaspoon coarse salt
- 2 tablespoons white vinegar

Rinse a saucepan with cold water (for easier cleanup). Have ready a strainer lined with dampened cheesecloth and set in a bowl that's deep enough so the strainer doesn't touch the bottom of the bowl.

Pour the milk and cream into the saucepan. Add the salt. Bring to a simmer over medium heat.

When the milk is simmering, turn off the heat and pour in the vinegar. Leave it alone for about 1 minute. Then start to stir slowly and gently. The milk will start separating into curds and whey (milky liquid); you are looking for the whey to become clearish, which will take about 1 minute of stirring. Once this happens, pour the mixture into the strainer. Lift the strainer out of the bowl and pour out the whey. Set the strainer back in the bowl and let the cheese drain for 15 minutes (or longer if you want a denser cheese). The ricotta is ready to serve now, but you can also refrigerate it, covered, for up to 5 days.

notes from our test kitchen

- A stickler for authenticity could argue that this isn't real Italian ricotta, because real ricotta is made with the whey of sheep's milk left over from making pecorino cheese and without cream. But this is a great way to get a very ricotta-like cheese with ordinary supermarket ingredients.
- Use any leftover homemade ricotta as you would ordinary ricotta. It also makes a wonderful breakfast drizzled with a little honey and dusted with ground cinnamon or nutmeg.

SOURCE: *The Armenian Table* by Victoria Jenanyan Wise

COOK: Victoria Jenanyan Wise

marinated yogurt cheese balls

THESE LITTLE CHEESE BALLS are delightful, with a garlicky dill dressing that's spiked with Aleppo pepper, the mellow Middle Eastern spice. Unless you've tasted a yogurt cheese ball, you may have difficulty imagining them. On the plate, they look like the little mozzarella balls called *bocconcini,* but in the mouth they're a lot more complex and delicate in both flavor and texture.

This is an easy recipe to put together once you have the drained yogurt. You'll need to start a day ahead.

Yogurt cheese balls can be an appetizer on their own, part of an appetizer table, or a tasty garnish for a salad.

serves 6

- 2 cups yogurt cheese (see note)
- 6 tablespoons extra-virgin olive oil
- 2 garlic cloves, pressed
- 2 teaspoons chopped fresh dill
- 1 teaspoon Aleppo pepper (see note)
- 1 tablespoon chopped fresh chives
- Lavash (Armenian cracker bread) or other crackers for serving

Divide the cheese into 13 portions and roll each into a walnut-size ball. Set the balls so they do not touch on a plate lined with paper towels. Cover loosely with paper towels and refrigerate for 4 to 6 hours, or until firm.

Mix together the olive oil, garlic, dill, and Aleppo pepper in a small bowl. Transfer the balls to a deep dish or a high-lipped platter in a single layer. Pour the oil mixture over the balls, cover loosely with plastic wrap, and refrigerate for at least 2 hours or up to 1 week.

Serve at room temperature with chives sprinkled over the top, accompanied by lavash or crackers.

notes from our test kitchen

- To make the yogurt cheese, use 3 cups Greek yogurt or Middle Eastern labne, which are thicker than regular yogurt because they're already drained (you'd have to spend a long time draining regular yogurt before you even started the recipe). Total by Fage is a good brand that is nationally distributed. Add 1½ teaspoons salt, mix well, and drain in a coffee filter inside a colander placed in a bowl. Let drain overnight in the refrigerator, or until it's firm.
- To make your own drained yogurt, a 2- to 4-hour process, start with 1 quart yogurt. Check the label to make sure there's no guar gum in it, because that will keep it from draining properly. Line a colander with a double layer of cheesecloth, allowing plenty to drape over the sides. Set the colander in a bowl; the bottom of the colander needs to be well above the bottom of the bowl to catch the whey. Spoon the yogurt into the colander and set aside at room temperature to drain until you have 3 cups of drained yogurt, 2 to 4 hours. You can store the drained yogurt, tightly covered in the refrigerator, for up to 1 week.
- Aleppo pepper, an earthy, mild red pepper, is sold in Middle Eastern markets and some gourmet shops. It keeps for a long time in the refrigerator. You can also mail order it from Dean & DeLuca (800-221-7714). Paula Wolfert, the Mediterranean food authority, says you can substitute 3 parts Hungarian paprika plus 1 part crushed red pepper flakes.

SOURCE: Zingerman's Deli store flyer
COOK: Ari Weinzweig

cream cheese–stuffed piquillo peppers

PIQUILLO PEPPERS are arguably one of Spain's greatest culinary treasures. These mildly piquant, smoky-sweet peppers are hand-harvested in northern Spain, then slow-roasted over wood fires, hand-peeled and -seeded (never rinsed!), and packed in jars and cans. Authentic piquillos are recognizable by their triangular shape with a slightly curved point, their small size (about 2 inches long), and the small black specks of charred skin left from the wood-roasting. Given their shape, piquillos make an ideal pouch to hold a spoonful of savory filling. In Spain, you'll find them stuffed with all sorts of meats, seafood, and cheese, but the one we love best is this domestic version from Zingerman's Deli in Ann Arbor, Michigan, which uses fresh cream cheese and a bit of garlic. With a recipe as straightforward as this, be sure to use the best cream cheese and olive oil. As the Zingerman's motto goes, "You really *can* taste the difference."

makes about 16 stuffed peppers

- 1 small (7.75 ounce) jar Spanish piquillo peppers (see notes)
- 5 ounces good cream cheese (see note), at room temperature
- 3 tablespoons extra-virgin olive oil
- 1 garlic clove, minced
- Coarse sea salt and freshly ground black pepper

With your hands, gently lift open the stem end of one of the peppers, being careful not to poke through the flesh. Using a spoon, carefully stuff a small spoonful of cream cheese inside. The cheese should fill the pepper's cavity but not be falling out the open end (a scant teaspoon should do). Continue until all the peppers have been filled.

Heat the broiler to high. Arrange the peppers in a glass baking dish. Pour 1 tablespoon of the olive oil over the top and sprinkle with the garlic. Broil until the cheese is soft and bubbly, 12 to 15 minutes (see note).

Meanwhile, pour the remaining 2 tablespoons olive oil onto a warm serving platter (preferably a white platter to show off the contrast between the crimson peppers and the green-gold olive oil). Arrange the broiled peppers on the platter. Season with salt and pepper to taste. Serve warm.

notes from our test kitchen

- Jars of piquillo peppers can generally be found in gourmet food stores specializing in Mediterranean products. You can also mail-order them from places like Zingerman's (www.zingermans.com) and La Tienda (www.tienda.com). We suggest you buy more than a few jars, since you'll soon become addicted to their flavor.
- Some brands pack 12-ounce jars of piquillo peppers. If this is the case, use a bit more cheese.
- If you're lucky enough to shop at Zingerman's Deli, you can buy their fresh Creamery Cream Cheese. If not, shop for the best, freshest, most natural cream cheese you can find, ideally one made without gums and stabilizers. If all you can find is the mass-produced stuff (i.e., Philadelphia brand), consider substituting 5 ounces fresh goat cheese (at room temperature) for the cream cheese.
- Depending on the strength of your broiler, the peppers may be ready in much fewer than 12 minutes. In our kitchen, it takes closer to 8 or 9 minutes for the cheese to become soft and bubbly and the peppers to begin to brown. So stand nearby and keep a close watch. If you leave them too long under the broiler, you risk scorching them.

source: *Bon Appétit*
story by Sarah Tenaglia
cook: Sarah Tenaglia

pancetta crisps with goat cheese and pear

Prepare to be ambushed at the kitchen door when you emerge with a tray of these elegant crisps. Happily, they take little time to prepare, so you may want to make double the amount you think you'll need. We find that each guest can easily devour two or three without pause.

makes 16

16 thin slices pancetta (see note)
Freshly ground black pepper
16 teaspoons fresh goat cheese (from a 5-ounce log), at room temperature
2 very ripe small pears, halved, cored, and cut into 1/4-inch-thick slices
Fresh thyme leaves

Preheat the oven to 450 degrees.

Place the pancetta slices in a single layer on a large rimmed baking sheet. Sprinkle with pepper. Bake until golden, about 10 minutes. Using a spatula, slide the pancetta crisps onto a platter. Top each with 1 teaspoon of the goat cheese and 1 pear slice. Sprinkle with thyme and serve.

notes from our test kitchen

- Thinly sliced pancetta really is best here; otherwise the crisps will be heavier and heartier than they should be. This means avoiding the presliced packaged stuff, because it tends to be a bit thick.
- These crisps are best served soon after making, while the pancetta is still warm. Take care that it's not piping hot, however, or the cheese will melt.

SOURCE: *The Gourmet Cookbook* edited by Ruth Reichl

COOK: Metta Miller

la brea tar pit chicken wings

VERY OFTEN THE BEST RECIPES in food magazines actually come from readers. That's true of this one, from a Boston reader of *Gourmet*. Why would you mix soy sauce, red wine, and sugar? We can't imagine how she came up with this idea, but we love it, and we think you will too. The wings come out sticky (hence their name) and deeply lacquered — sweet, savory, and the talk of the party.

These are about as far from Buffalo wings as you can get, yet they have a lot of the same appeal. Chicken wings are always finger food, and that means good times. They're easy on the host, too.

serves 12

- 4 pounds chicken wings, split at the joint and wing tips discarded
- 1 cup soy sauce (see note)
- 1/2 cup dry red wine
- 1/2 cup plus 1 tablespoon sugar
- 1/4 teaspoon ground ginger

Place a rack in the center of the oven and preheat to 400 degrees.

Arrange the wings in a single layer in a large roasting pan. Combine the remaining ingredients in a small saucepan and stir over medium-low heat until the sugar is dissolved. Pour evenly over the wings.

Bake for 45 minutes. Turn the wings over and bake until the sauce is thick and sticky, 1 hour more or a little longer. Serve hot with plenty of napkins.

notes from our test kitchen

- Unless you use good soy sauce, you'll be disappointed with the results. We recommend Kikkoman, the favorite of *Fine Cooking*'s test panel. Cheap soy sauces have additives like caramel coloring and corn syrup — the flavor won't be there. Whatever brand you buy, read the label to be sure it says "naturally brewed."
- If you can find packages of drumettes — the big, meaty first joint of the chicken wing — you can save yourself the trouble of splitting the joint and clipping off the tips of the wings. Then this recipe will take only about 5 minutes of prep time.

SOURCE: *New York Times*
STORY BY Amanda Hesser
COOK: Amanda Hesser

olive oil–poached shrimp with lemon anchovy mayonnaise

POACHING SHRIMP IN OLIVE OIL renders them more tender and flavorful than any other cooking method we've tried, but maintaining the right poaching temperature on the stovetop requires finesse. So we were thrilled to find this recipe, in which you slide the pan of shrimp and olive oil into a very low oven and it takes care of itself. As the shrimp cook, you have time enough to make the boldly flavored dipping sauce. Anchovies add the right punch to the lemony sauce.

serves 4

- 1 pound medium shrimp, peeled and deveined
- 1/2 cup plus 2 tablespoons extra-virgin olive oil
- Sea salt
- 4 anchovy fillets (see note)
- 1 garlic clove, peeled
- 1 large egg yolk
- 1 tablespoon fresh lemon juice
- 1/3 cup plus 2 tablespoons vegetable or peanut oil
- Grated zest of 1 lemon

Preheat the oven to 225 degrees.

Place the shrimp in a sauté pan or a casserole just large enough to hold them in a single layer. Toss with 1/2 cup of the olive oil and season with salt to taste. Put the pan in the oven and poach the shrimp in the oil, turning and basting occasionally, until just cooked through, about 25 minutes.

Using a mortar and pestle, pound the anchovies and garlic to a paste. Scrape into a medium bowl. Add the egg yolk and lemon juice and whisk to a slurry. Whisking rapidly, add the vegetable or peanut oil and remaining 2 tablespoons olive oil a few drops at a time, until the mixture is emulsified and thickened (see note). Fold in the lemon zest. Spoon into 4 small serving bowls.

To serve, remove the shrimp from the oil and divide among 4 plates. Serve each plate of shrimp with a bowl of the mayonnaise for dipping.

notes from our test kitchen

- If you'd rather serve this as a passed appetizer, leave the tails on the shrimp. This makes it easier for your guests to pick them up and dip them in the sauce. If the tails are removed, or if they come off while you're peeling the shrimp, offer small forks or toothpicks.
- Be sure to shop for anchovy fillets packed in extra-virgin olive oil. The kind packed in soybean or cottonseed oil won't do. And don't even think about using anchovy paste; its flavor is far inferior.
- Instead of whisking in the oil by hand, you can mash the anchovies and garlic in the mortar (or in a small bowl using a fork), transfer the mixture to a blender or food processor, and add the oil a few drops at a time with the motor running.
- You can save the olive oil left from poaching the shrimp and use it to sauté (or poach) shrimp and other seafood. Strain it and keep it covered in the refrigerator for up to 2 weeks.

SOURCE: *The Good Cook* by Anne Willan

COOK: Anne Willan

pancetta and fennel tart

THINK OF THIS AS a more tempting, sexier version of that cocktail party workhorse, quiche Lorraine. For hors d'oeuvres, let the tart cool to room temperature and cut it into thin wedges. For a sit-down first course, serve generous slices warm from the oven. You could also add a side salad and turn this into a satisfying lunch or light supper. For a lighter tart, Anne Willan suggests using half cream, half milk. We love it best with all crème fraîche.

serves 6 to 8

- 1 9½-inch tart shell (*recipe follows*)
- 1 tablespoon unsalted butter
- 7 ounces pancetta, diced
- 1 medium fennel bulb, trimmed, halved, and thinly sliced
- ½ teaspoon fennel seeds
- Salt and freshly ground black pepper
- 2 large eggs
- 1 cup heavy cream or crème fraîche

To partially bake the tart shell, butter or grease a 9½-inch tart pan with a removable base. On a lightly floured surface, using a lightly floured rolling pin, roll out the tart dough until it is 2 inches larger than the tart pan. Transfer the dough to the prepared pan and press it well into the corners, taking care not to stretch it. With your fingers, press the dough evenly up the sides of the pan and neaten the rim. Prick the base of the tart shell with a fork so it cooks more evenly and does not develop air pockets as it bakes. Chill the tart dough until it is very firm, 15 to 30 minutes (for quick results, put it in the freezer).

Preheat the oven to 425 degrees and set a baking sheet on a low rack to heat.

Trim a round of aluminum foil or parchment paper about 2 inches larger than the diameter of the pan and crumple it to make it more pliable. Press it into the tart shell, pushing it down into the corners. Fill it three-quarters full of dry beans or rice to hold the base flat. Bake the tart shell on the preheated baking sheet until the dough is brown around the edges and firm enough to hold its shape, about 15 minutes. Remove the tart pan, still on the baking sheet, from the oven and lift out the foil and beans. Lower the oven to 375 degrees, return the tart pan on the baking sheet to the oven, and continue baking until the bottom of the pastry is dry, 5 to 10 minutes more. Remove and set aside on a cooling rack while you prepare the filling. Leave the oven on.

To make the filling, melt the butter in a large skillet over medium heat and fry the pancetta, stirring often, until lightly browned, 5 to 7 minutes. Stir in the fennel, fennel seeds, and salt and pepper to taste. Cover and cook over low heat, stirring often, so the fennel softens and cooks in its own juices, until it is very tender and lightly browned, 15 to 20 minutes. Spread the filling in the tart shell.

Whisk together the eggs and the heavy cream or crème fraîche in a bowl. Season to taste with salt and pepper (remembering that the pancetta can be quite salty). Pour the egg mixture into the tart shell. Bake until the filling is set and lightly browned, 30 to 35 minutes. Serve warm or at room temperature.

note from our test kitchen

Let the tart sit for at least 20 minutes before serving. If you refrigerate it, be sure to let it come to room temperature before serving.

white wine pastry dough

ANNE WILLAN BRILLIANTLY SUBSTITUTES dry white wine for the water in this pâte brisée, which makes the dough easy to mix and roll and adds flavor. You can also make the pastry with cold water.

makes one 9½-inch tart shell

- 1¾ cups all-purpose flour
- 8 tablespoons (1 stick) unsalted butter
- 1 large egg yolk
- ½ teaspoon salt
- 3 tablespoons dry white wine or cold water, plus more if needed

Sift the flour onto a work surface and make a well in the center. Pound the butter to soften it slightly (see note) and put it in the well with the egg yolk, salt, and wine. Work the ingredients in the well together with the fingertips of one hand, dabbing and pinching so the butter softens and is partly mixed with the yolk and wine. Using a pastry scraper or your hands, draw the flour in from the sides, mixing and cutting the ingredients together with the blade of the scraper or your fingertips.

When the butter has been mixed and cut into small chunks among the flour, start using both hands. With your fingertips, work the flour into the other ingredients until coarse crumbs form. If they are dry, sprinkle them with 1 or 2 tablespoons more wine or water. When the crumbs are sticky, press them into a ball.

Work the dough on a lightly floured surface, pushing it away with the heel of your hand and gathering it up with your fingers until it is smooth, pliable, and pulls away in one piece. Press it into a ball and wrap loosely in plastic wrap. Chill the dough until firm, 15 to 30 minutes. The dough may be refrigerated for up to 2 days, or it can be frozen.

notes from our test kitchen

- Dry white vermouth can be used in place of the white wine.
- Use a wooden rolling pin to pound the butter. Choke up on the rolling pin and give the butter a few good whacks, then fold the butter over on itself and pound it again. It is ready when it's soft and pliable enough to fold without snapping. Don't pound so long as to make it slumpy or oily.

SOURCE: *Bruce Aidells's Complete Book of Pork* by Bruce Aidells with Lisa Weiss

COOK: Bruce Aidells after Loni Kuhn

tigelle
(pancetta- and parmesan-stuffed english muffins)

YOU MIGHT CALL THIS the pork-lover's grilled cheese sandwich. Traditionally *tigelle* are served to grape pickers working in the high mountains between Emilia-Romagna and Tuscany as a fortifying snack. Surely the grape pickers' wives bake their own yeasted muffins for these sandwiches, but cooking teacher Loni Kuhn discovered that Thomas's English muffins work quite nicely. *Tigelle* are best appreciated after a day of skiing or a good long walk.

makes 32 pieces

- 2 garlic cloves, peeled
- 8 ounces pancetta, diced
- 1 cup freshly grated Parmigiano-Reggiano or good domestic Parmesan-style cheese
- 1 tablespoon chopped fresh rosemary
- 8 English muffins (preferably Thomas's), fork-split in half
- 1/4 cup lard or olive oil

With the motor running, drop the garlic through the feed tube of a food processor. Stop and scrape down the sides of the bowl and add the pancetta, Parmesan, and rosemary. Pulse until the mixture forms a paste. Spread the paste on one side of each split muffin and re-form to make 8 sandwiches. The sandwiches can be assembled and refrigerated up to 6 hours ahead.

To cook the *tigelle,* heat 1/8 inch melted lard or oil in a large skillet (preferably cast-iron) over medium heat. Add 3 or more muffins (or as many as will fit without crowding) and cook on one side until lightly browned, 3 to 5 minutes. Turn and cook on the other side until lightly browned. Drain on paper towels. Transfer to a platter and cut each into 4 wedges. Serve hot or warm, but not cool.

note from our test kitchen

When forming the *tigelle*, press the halves together with some force. After filling the muffins, squeeze them between the palms of your hands to flatten them slightly. While cooking, use a flat spatula to press down on the top muffin to ensure that you get a crisp, deeply browned outer crust.

SOURCE: *Bon Appétit*
STORY BY Dorie Greenspan
COOK: Dorie Greenspan after Jacques Drouot

eggs with foie gras and cream

THE INSPIRATION FOR THIS DISH came from Jacques Drouot, the manager of the legendary Le Dôme restaurant in Paris, and the idea is quintessentially French, both luxurious and decadent. If you have a real truffle, of course it's celestial. But if you don't, use a foie gras pâté with truffles in it or add a few drops of truffle oil to the cubes of pâté or mousse.

What makes this dish is the (again very French) touch of fresh tarragon. We can think of all sorts of occasions to serve it: a birthday breakfast, as the centerpiece of brunch, or a post-midnight supper on New Year's Eve.

serves 4

- 1 4-ounce slice foie gras pâté or mousse, cut into 4 pieces
- 4 large eggs
- Salt and freshly ground black pepper
- 4 tablespoons whipping cream
- Thin slices of black truffle, cut into slivers (optional)
- 1 1/2 teaspoons chopped fresh tarragon
- 1 1/2 teaspoons chopped fresh flat-leaf parsley
- 2 slices firm white sandwich bread, toasted, buttered, and quartered

Lightly butter four 4-ounce ramekins or soufflé dishes. Cut each piece of pâté or mousse into 4 cubes. Divide the cubes among the prepared dishes. Crack 1 egg into each dish, keeping the yolks whole. Sprinkle with salt and pepper. Drizzle 1 tablespoon cream over each egg. Sprinkle the truffle slivers over, if using. Sprinkle with the tarragon and parsley. Cover each dish tightly with foil (see note).

Fill a large skillet with water to a depth of 1/2 inch. Bring to a simmer over medium heat. Add the ramekins. Cook until the egg whites are firm and the yolks are still runny, about 8 minutes.

Remove the ramekins from the water. Remove the foil and wipe the ramekins dry. Serve the ramekins warm on small plates with the toasts.

note from our test kitchen

You can skip covering the ramekins with foil and bake them. Put them in a baking dish filled with hot water to come halfway up the sides. Bake at 400 degrees for about 12 minutes, or until the whites are firm and the yolks runny.

soups

SOURCE: *The Blue Course*
by the Point Reyes Farmstead Cheese Company
COOK: The Giacomini Family

asparagus soup with blue cheese crumbles

ALTHOUGH THIS BUTTERY SOUP IS DELICIOUS even made with out-of-season asparagus, it really shines when you make it with local asparagus in spring. The bright green of the soup means you haven't overcooked it and it still has all its delicate flavor. The blue cheese crumbles are a surprise; they melt into the soup and take it to another level.

Because the source of the recipe is a cheese company, it recommends using its own very good Original Blue cheese, which is available nationwide. If you can't find it, look for Maytag Blue—you don't want a really strong blue cheese here. The blue cheese crumbles at the supermarket are too salty and flavorless.

serves 4

- 8 tablespoons (1 stick) butter
- 1 large onion, sliced
- 1 large leek (white and light green parts only), thinly sliced and well washed
- 8 ounces potatoes, peeled and cubed
- 6 cups low-sodium chicken broth
- 1½ pounds asparagus, woody ends snapped off, chopped
- Salt and freshly ground black pepper
- ⅔ cup (4 ounces) mild blue cheese, crumbled

Melt the butter in a large saucepan over medium heat. Add the onion and cook, stirring, for 1 to 2 minutes. Add the leek and continue cooking until the onion is soft.

Add the potato cubes and broth. Bring to a boil, reduce the heat to a simmer, and cook until the potatoes are tender, about 10 minutes. Add the asparagus and cook until just tender but still bright green, 4 to 5 minutes.

Remove from the heat and puree to a smooth texture in a food processor. Return the soup to the saucepan and heat gently. Season to taste with salt and pepper.

To serve, pour into warm bowls and top with the blue cheese crumbles.

notes from our test kitchen

- If you cook the soup too long, it will change color dramatically, to a dull olive khaki, and it will taste like canned asparagus. If you have leftovers, be careful when reheating them.
- Puree the soup right in the pot using an immersion blender and save yourself from having to clean the food processor.

SOURCE: Gang e-mail
COOK: Chef Bobo (Robert Surles)

calhoun school cream of cauliflower soup

WE DON'T KNOW how Chef Bobo got his nickname, but we do know that he's a French chef who taught at the French Culinary Institute, ran his own catering business, worked as Derek Jeter's personal chef, and was then hired by an elite private school on Manhattan's Upper West Side to revitalize the school lunch program. And boy, did he succeed. Chef Bobo's creative approach to nutritious, boldly flavored meals has students devouring everything in the lunch line, including cauliflower and rutabaga. His cauliflower soup was the most-requested recipe by school parents, who were amazed that their cauliflower-hating children suddenly began to ask them to make it. We knew we had to try it.

This soup is creamy and luxurious without being too rich. Simmering the cauliflower in a small amount of broth turns it sweet and mellow—something even those who don't like cauliflower will love.

serves 4 to 6

- 2 tablespoons olive oil
- 1 medium onion, chopped
- 5 cups cauliflower florets
- 2 cups vegetable broth (see note)
- 1/2 teaspoon ground coriander (see note)
- Salt and freshly ground black pepper
- 1 cup milk
- 2 tablespoons minced fresh flat-leaf parsley or chives for garnish

Heat the oil in a large saucepan over medium-high heat. Add the onion and cook until translucent and just beginning to turn golden, about 7 minutes. Immediately add the cauliflower and stir it into the onions.

Add the broth, coriander, and salt and pepper to taste. Bring to a boil and lower the heat to a simmer. Simmer until the cauliflower is tender and easily cut with a knife, 25 to 30 minutes.

If using a blender, ladle the soup into the blender until about two-thirds full and blend until smooth. Repeat with any remaining soup. If using an immersion blender, blend the soup right in the saucepan. Once all the soup is blended (it should be quite thick), pour it back into the saucepan.

Add the milk to the soup until it has a nice, creamy consistency. Adjust the seasonings and ladle into warm bowls. Garnish each bowl with a pinch of parsley or chives and serve.

notes from our test kitchen

- We sometimes use chicken broth in place of vegetable broth for a deeper flavor.
- The coriander is just an accent here and not at all discernible in the final taste. For a stronger flavor, go ahead and double the amount. Taking the time to toast and grind whole coriander seeds before adding them to the soup will also provide a huge return in flavor.
- For the luxury version, you can substitute cream or half-and-half for some or all of the milk.
- This recipe can easily be doubled, and like many soups, it can be made in advance and held for a day or two in the refrigerator.

SOURCE: *Simply Elegant Soup*
by George Morrone with John Harrisson

COOK: George Morrone

carrot ginger soup with lime crème fraîche

THIS YEAR WE SAW a number of recipes highlighting carrots and ginger, a made-in-heaven couple, and this exhilarating version stole our hearts. George Morrone, a San Francisco chef with a passion for soup, created it in Los Angeles in the 1980s, when he was trying to entice beautiful people to the table with exciting food that wouldn't expand their waistlines. Two elements make Morrone's soup different from other carrot ginger soups: the ginger oil with turmeric, which is both an ingredient and a garnish, and lime crème fraîche, which pulls all the flavors together.

You can serve the soup hot or cold. Note that you need to make the ginger oil the day before you prepare the soup; it will take less than 5 minutes.

serves 4

GINGER OIL

1 cup canola oil
2 tablespoons ground ginger
1½ tablespoons ground turmeric

CARROT-GINGER SOUP

2½ tablespoons olive oil
1 white onion, thinly sliced
1 small garlic clove, minced
1 small jalapeño, seeded and thinly sliced
1 teaspoon peeled grated fresh ginger
4 large carrots (about 1 pound), peeled and sliced
4 cups chicken broth or vegetable broth
Salt and cayenne pepper

LIME CRÈME FRAÎCHE

½ cup crème fraîche
Zest and juice of 1 lime
1 tablespoon minced fresh cilantro
Salt

GARNISH

12 sprigs cilantro
Freshly cracked black pepper

TO MAKE THE GINGER OIL:

Combine all the ingredients in a small bowl. Carefully whisk together and pour into a small saucepan. Bring to a simmer over medium-high heat and then return to the bowl. Refrigerate overnight to infuse the oil with the flavor. The following day, carefully ladle off the yellow ginger oil and store in a bottle or other airtight container. Discard the solids. The oil will keep in the refrigerator almost indefinitely.

TO MAKE THE SOUP:

Heat the olive oil and 1 tablespoon of the ginger oil in a saucepan over medium heat. Add the onion, garlic, jalapeño, and ginger and cook for about 5 minutes, or until translucent; do not let brown. Add the carrots and cook for 5 minutes more. Add 3 cups of the broth and simmer for 20 minutes, or until the carrots are tender. Transfer the soup to a blender or food processor and puree in batches until smooth. Pass through a fine-mesh strainer into a clean saucepan. Reheat the soup, adjusting the consistency with the remaining 1 cup broth as needed, and season to taste with salt and cayenne pepper.

TO MAKE THE CRÈME FRAÎCHE:

Put the crème fraîche in a small bowl. Mince the lime zest and add to the crème fraîche with the juice and cilantro. Season to taste with salt and whisk until combined. Refrigerate.

To serve, pour the soup into warm bowls and drizzle each serving with 1 teaspoon of the ginger oil. Diagonally drizzle about 1 tablespoon of the crème fraîche across each bowl in the opposite direction (you'll have some left over). Place 3 cilantro sprigs across each bowl and sprinkle with pepper.

notes from our test kitchen

- The ginger oil is a wonderful condiment to have on hand, and since it keeps forever in the fridge, you might want to consider making a double batch. It's great over grilled fish, chicken, or vegetables.
- Confession: we didn't strain our smooth puree and the consistency was fine.

SOURCE: *1,000 Italian Recipes* by Michele Scicolone

COOK: Michele Scicolone

tuscan bean and mushroom soup

IF YOU HAVE A PANTRY well stocked with things like canned beans, rice, and dried mushrooms, you can pull together this comforting soup without a special trip to the market, when you're snowbound or just too tired to go out. Dried porcini mushrooms give the soup an earthy, almost smoky flavor, and white beans and Arborio rice make it hearty enough for a main course. We like to round out the meal with a green salad and a taste of good Italian cheese.

serves 8

- 1/2 ounce dried porcini mushrooms
- 1 cup warm water
- 2 medium carrots, peeled and chopped
- 1 medium onion, chopped
- 1 cup peeled, seeded, and chopped fresh or canned tomatoes
- 1 celery rib, chopped
- 1/4 cup chopped fresh flat-leaf parsley
- 6 cups homemade meat broth or chicken broth, or a mix of half store-bought broth and water (see note)
- 3 cups drained cooked dried or canned cannellini or great northern beans
- 1/2 cup medium-grain rice, such as Arborio
- Salt and freshly ground black pepper

Soak the mushrooms in the warm water for 30 minutes. Remove the mushrooms and reserve the liquid. Rinse the mushrooms under cold running water to remove any grit, paying special attention to the stems, where soil collects. Chop the mushrooms coarsely. Strain the mushroom-soaking liquid through a paper coffee filter into a bowl and reserve.

In a large pot, combine the mushrooms and the strained soaking liquid, the carrots, onion, tomatoes, celery, parsley, and broth. Bring to a simmer. Cook until the vegetables are tender, about 20 minutes.

Add the beans, rice, and salt and pepper to taste. Cook until the rice is tender, about 20 minutes, stirring occasionally. Serve hot or warm.

notes from our test kitchen

- Michele Scicolone makes her meat broth from a combination of beef bones, veal shoulder, chicken parts, and vegetables and simmers it for 3 hours. Any good-tasting broth works equally well here. If it's low-sodium store-bought, we don't bother using half water.
- With the addition of both beans and rice, this soup can get quite thick, especially if it sits. It's a good idea to have a little extra broth on hand to thin it to your liking. Water will work as well; just be sure to check the seasoning.

SOURCE: *Stonewall Kitchen Harvest*
by Jim Stott, Jonathan King, and Kathy Gunst

COOKS: Jim Stott, Jonathan King, and Kathy Gunst

roasted mushroom-leek soup with crispy pancetta

WE'VE LONG BEEN SCOUTING for a superb mushroom soup recipe, so we rejoiced when we found this one. The secret is roasting the mushrooms and leeks in a hot oven before adding any broth, which concentrates their flavor and gives the soup a deep, woodsy, almost meaty taste.

The soup is the creation of the owners and founders of Stonewall Kitchen in York, Maine, the well-known producers of first-rate preserves and condiments, who know a thing or two about fresh, seasonal ingredients. They suggest a mix of mushrooms, including shiitake, cremini, button, and portobello, but they encourage you to go with what looks best in your market. If you choose a different assortment, no problem; just be sure to use a good variety and a total of about 1½ pounds. The better the mushrooms are, the better the soup will taste.

serves 8

- 8 ounces button mushrooms, stem ends trimmed, cut in half if large
- 6 ounces cremini mushrooms, stem ends trimmed
- 6 ounces portobello mushrooms, coarsely chopped to match the size of the other mushrooms
- 3½ ounces shiitake mushrooms, stem ends trimmed (see note)
- 3 leeks (white parts only), cut in half lengthwise, well washed, and cut into 1-inch pieces
- 1 large red or Vidalia onion, chopped into 1-inch pieces
- 1½ tablespoons chopped fresh thyme or ½ teaspoon dried, crumbled
- 3 tablespoons olive oil
- Salt and freshly ground black pepper
- ¼ cup dry red or white wine
- 5 cups chicken broth or vegetable broth
- About ¼ cup heavy cream (optional)
- 6 thin slices (about 2 ounces) pancetta

Place a rack in the center of the oven and preheat to 400 degrees.

In a large roasting pan, toss the mushrooms, leeks, onion, thyme, 2 tablespoons of the oil, and salt and pepper to taste until well combined. Roast for 45 minutes, tossing the vegetables once or twice as they cook. Transfer to a large bowl and immediately deglaze the hot roasting pan with the wine and then the broth (see note). Working in batches, puree the vegetables with the broth in a food processor or blender. Pour the pureed soup into a large soup pot and add the cream, if using. Taste for seasoning and add salt and pepper if needed. The soup can be made 1 day ahead up to this point.

Heat the remaining 1 tablespoon oil in a medium skillet over low heat. Add the pancetta and cook, turning frequently, until crisp, 5 to 10 minutes. Drain on paper towels and, using your hands, break the pancetta into 1-inch pieces.

To serve, reheat the soup until simmering. Serve sprinkled with several pieces of crisp pancetta.

notes from our test kitchen

- When trimming shiitake mushrooms, be sure to remove the entire stem, flush with the cap. Shiitake stems remain tough and fibrous even when cooked and pureed.
- You can easily make this vegetarian — even vegan — if you wish by using vegetable broth and omitting the cream. Obviously, you'll need to skip the pancetta garnish. If you miss the crunch, sauté a few handfuls of small croutons in olive oil and scatter these over each bowl.
- Red wine will give the soup a deeper, meatier profile, while white wine will keep it lighter and sharper. If you're using vegetable stock, stick with white wine.
- If the roasting pan cools too much to deglaze (meaning there's no sizzle when you add the wine and broth), put the pan over one or two burners to heat it up. The idea is to have the liquid simmer so you can scrape up any browned bits remaining from roasting the mushrooms.

tip

In her book *Wild Mushrooms*, Cynthia Nims reminds us that mushrooms are "like delicious little sponges," and if we rinse them to clean them, they will soak up quantities of water, which in turn dilutes their flavors and ruins their texture. Nims wisely suggests better methods: a soft-bristled pastry brush to flick away dirt and debris or (our favorite) a paper towel, dry or damp, depending on how dirty the mushrooms are. Only as a last resort should you use water, and then only for the quickest rinse or dip. If you like having single-use gadgets in your kitchen, cookware stores do sell baby-soft mushroom brushes. We also know some cooks who use the softest-bristled toothbrushes.

SOURCE: *Coastal Cooking with John Shields* by John Shields

COOK: John Shields after Moors Restaurant

cape cod portuguese kale soup

WHEN YOU GO ALL THE WAY to the tip of Cape Cod, you'll find a strong Portuguese presence from the old fishing days. There are Portuguese restaurants and even a bakery, and a soup like this one is almost always on the menu. It's a combination of beans, kale, the beautifully spiced Spanish chorizo, and potatoes, jazzed up with garlic and red wine vinegar.

This particular recipe comes from the legendary Moors family restaurant in Provincetown. You can freeze any leftovers or just make half the recipe if you're not serving a lot of people. This is a sturdy soup, good for fortifying against fierce weather and other challenges.

You need to soak the beans a day ahead, and in fact the soup tastes better if it's made a day or two ahead as well, which makes it a great option for entertaining.

Serve with crusty bread and sweet butter.

serves 8 to 10

- 1 cup dried small white beans
- 3 tablespoons olive oil
- 1 large onion, diced
- 1 tablespoon chopped garlic
- 12 cups chicken broth or vegetable broth
- 1 pound spicy Spanish chorizo sausage or kielbasa, cut into 1/4-inch-thick slices
- 1 pound kale, washed, stemmed, and coarsely chopped
- 3 cups cubed potatoes
- 1 tablespoon salt
- Freshly ground black pepper to taste
- 2 tablespoons red wine vinegar, plus more to taste

Soak the beans in cold water overnight. Drain and set aside.

Heat the oil in a heavy-bottomed pot over medium heat. Sauté the onion for 3 minutes. Add the garlic and sauté for 1 minute more. Add the beans and the broth. Bring to a boil and reduce the heat to a simmer.

Add the chorizo or kielbasa and cook gently for 1 hour. Add the remaining ingredients and continue cooking for 1 hour more, stirring often.

Adjust the seasonings and serve.

tip

For a *Washington Post* article, Renée Schettler spent hours testing homemade chicken stocks and came up with a good formula. You need 5 pounds of chicken (necks and backs especially, but the carcass of a rotisserie chicken works too, and that accounts for about 1 pound). Cover the chicken with water and bring to a boil. Boil for 3 minutes. Stir once, then dump the contents into a colander in the sink, washing away the scum and fat that you usually have to patiently skim off. Rinse the chicken, wipe out the pot, and this time add 4 quarts water to the chicken, plus a pinch of salt. You can add carrots, onions, a clove, parsley, celery—or nothing at all. Bring to a simmer and simmer gently over medium-low to low heat, so that just a single bubble escapes every now and then. Simmer for 1½ hours and strain.

SOURCE: *An Exaltation of Soups* by Patricia Solley

COOK: Patricia Solley

bride's soup from turkey

A BRIDE'S SOUP is supposed to sustain her through the wedding night's exertions. This lovely pale orange soup is just right: mellow and delicious enough to provoke an appetite, no garlic to offend, and full of nourishing beef broth. There's no cream to weigh it down, and yet it has a creamy quality, from the bulgur. The base is a *lot* of onions, cooked gently in butter for a long time. The red lentils and bulgur supply a little heft, and the dried mint provides a delicate high note.

Good as it is, the soup has a tragic background. The legend says it's the creation of Ezo, a breathtakingly beautiful Turkish woman born in 1909 who was sent away to Syria as a bride after a disastrous first marriage in which she was beaten. In an effort to please her mother-in-law in her second marriage, she created this soup. After dying of tuberculosis, she became a Snow White–type folk heroine, and her soup continues to be a favorite in her native land.

serves 8 generously

- 6 tablespoons (3/4 stick) butter
- 3 medium onions, finely chopped
- 2 teaspoons paprika
- 1 1/2 cups red lentils, picked over and rinsed
- 3/4 cup fine-grain bulgur wheat
- 10 cups (2 1/2 quarts) beef broth or vegetable broth
- 3 tablespoons tomato paste
- 1/4 teaspoon cayenne pepper or crushed red pepper flakes
- 2 tablespoons dried mint leaves
- Lemon slices and small fresh mint leaves or parsley leaves for garnish

Melt the butter in a large pot over low heat. Sauté the onions until golden, about 15 minutes. Stir in the paprika, then the lentils and bulgur, to coat them with butter. Add the broth, tomato paste, and cayenne or red pepper flakes and stir to combine.

Bring the soup to a boil over medium-high heat, reduce the heat to low, and simmer until the bulgur is soft and creamy, about 1 hour.

Crumble the dried mint between your palms into the soup. Stir the soup and remove it from the heat. Let it rest for 10 minutes, covered.

Ladle the soup into warm bowls and garnish each portion with a lemon slice and 1 or 2 leaves of mint or parsley.

notes from our test kitchen

- If you can't find any dried mint, which tastes quite different from fresh mint, you can use the trick on page 113 to dry the fresh. If your mint is the hothouse kind from a supermarket packet, it may not have the depth of flavor of garden mint, so you may need a little more.
- We found ourselves yearning for an even creamier touch in this soup and added some grated sheep cheese to one bowl and some whole-milk yogurt to another. Both were excellent, and crumbled sheep's milk feta is good, too.
- There's usually enough salt in the broth to carry the soup, but taste it before you serve it; it may need a little salt or even some freshly ground pepper.

SOURCE: *Roma*
by Julia della Croce

COOK: Julia della Croce

lentil soup with sausage

THIS HEARTY SOUP was discovered in a casual Roman trattoria where politicians from all over Italy hang out and eat the unassuming fare that strongly resembles home cooking. We're so used to a different kind of lentil soup, the ham-bone or ham-hock style, that this robust bowlful with its Italian sausage, fresh sage and marjoram, and lots of garlic seems like a breath of fresh air.

The soup can serve as an evening meal in itself. A salad with Italian-style greens—arugula or radicchio—and some good crusty Italian bread with a wedge of Italian cheese are all you need to call it dinner.

serves 6

- 1½ cups brown lentils, picked over and rinsed
- 10 cups water
- Sea salt
- 1 8-inch sprig fresh sage or 2 bay leaves
- 3 tablespoons extra-virgin olive oil
- 5 sweet Italian sausage links, removed from casings and crumbled
- 1 medium onion, chopped
- 4 garlic cloves, minced
- 3 tablespoons chopped fresh flat-leaf parsley
- 2 teaspoons chopped fresh marjoram or 1 teaspoon dry marjoram, crumbled
- 1 cup tomato puree or tomato sauce
- Freshly ground black pepper

Put the lentils in a large pot and add the water, 1 tablespoon salt, and the sage or bay leaves. Bring to a boil. Immediately reduce the heat and simmer for 15 minutes.

Meanwhile, heat the oil in a large skillet over medium-low heat. Add the sausage and sauté until brown on the outside but still pink inside, about 8 minutes.

Reduce the heat to low and stir in the onion, garlic, parsley, and marjoram. Sauté until the onion is translucent, about 4 minutes. Stir in the tomato puree or sauce.

Add the sausage mixture to the lentils and mix well. Simmer for 5 minutes more to marry the flavors. Remove the sage or bay leaves, taste for salt, and season with pepper to taste. Serve hot.

SOURCE: *Food & Wine*

COOK: **Maggie Pond**

chickpea soup with chorizo and smoked paprika

WE FOUND THIS RECIPE in the "Fast" section of the magazine, and sure enough, you can make the soup in less than half an hour. It's sturdy enough to be supper, with some bread and a salad, and delicious enough to be memorable. If you can manage to keep some Spanish chorizo on hand, along with a few cans of chickpeas in the winter, you can have a pantry soup that's smoky, a little spicy, and so good you'll make it more than once a season.

Maggie Pond, the soup's creator, is chef at César, the Spanish restaurant next door to Chez Panisse in Berkeley. The very Spanish flavors of smoked paprika and chorizo are what give her soup its evocative, warm personality.

serves 6

- 1 medium link Spanish chorizo (5 ounces), quartered lengthwise and thinly sliced crosswise (see note)
- 2 19-ounce cans chickpeas, drained
- 1/2 cup water
- 1/4 cup extra-virgin olive oil
- 2 medium carrots, peeled, halved lengthwise, and thinly sliced
- 1 medium onion, finely chopped
- 1 garlic clove, thinly sliced
- 3 tablespoons tomato paste
- 1 1/2 teaspoons Spanish smoked paprika (Pimentón; see note)
- 1/4 teaspoon cayenne pepper
- 4 cups beef broth or low-sodium beef broth
- 1 teaspoon sugar
- Crusty bread for serving

Cook the chorizo in a small skillet over medium-high heat until lightly browned and most of the fat has been rendered, 3 to 4 minutes. Drain the chorizo on paper towels.

In a food processor, puree half the chickpeas with the water until smooth.

Heat the oil until shimmering in a soup pot. Add the carrots, onion, and garlic. Cover and cook over medium heat until softened, about 5 minutes. Add the chorizo, tomato paste, paprika, and cayenne and cook, stirring, for 1 minute.

Add the broth and sugar along with whole and pureed chickpeas and bring to a boil. Simmer over medium heat until the vegetables are tender, about 10 minutes. Ladle the soup into warm deep bowls and serve with the bread.

notes from our test kitchen

- Be sure to get Spanish, not Mexican, chorizo for this recipe. The Spanish sausage is hard; the Mexican one is soft. Spanish chorizo is appearing in many supermarkets now; otherwise, look for it in Hispanic markets.
- Not all brands of canned chickpeas contain 19 ounces—look for the Goya brand.

tip

Pimentón, the Spanish smoked paprika, is a staple in our kitchens, and we urge you to try it. It's available in some gourmet shops or by mail from www.thespanishtable.com. If you want to make the soup without it, you can substitute 1 teaspoon regular paprika mixed with 1/2 teaspoon ground chipotle chiles for a similar smoky taste.

portuguese tomato soup

ALTHOUGH EMERIL is completely identified with New Orleans, he comes from a Portuguese family, and this is one of their standby dishes. The recipe comes from northern Portugal, where they specialize in sausage—one of Emeril's favorite things in the world. The soup is kicked up in the usual Lagasse style with three kinds of pork—bacon and two types of Portuguese sausages — plus a lot of red onion and cilantro. And there's a secret ingredient: Emeril's Original Essence, a spice blend now available in most supermarkets.

This is a rich, hearty soup, great on a winter day. The recipe serves 12, but half a recipe works well, too.

serves 12

4 bacon slices, diced
1 pound linguiça sausage, half finely chopped, half sliced 1/4 inch thick (see note)
1 pound chouriço sausage, half finely chopped, half sliced 1/4 inch thick (see note)
2 cups finely chopped red onions
1 tablespoon plus 1 teaspoon Emeril's Original Essence
2 tablespoons minced garlic
1/2 teaspoon crushed red pepper flakes
8 cups chopped seeded tomatoes
6 cups chicken broth
2 Turkish bay leaves (see note)
Salt and freshly ground black pepper
1/2 cup finely chopped fresh cilantro
Crusty bread for serving

Cook the bacon in a medium pot over medium heat for about 2 minutes. Add the sausages and cook with the bacon until browned, about 5 minutes more. Add the onions and Essence and cook, stirring often, until the onions are softened, about 5 minutes. Add the garlic and crushed red pepper and cook until fragrant, about 30 seconds. Add the tomatoes, chicken broth, and bay leaves and stir to combine.

Bring to a boil, reduce the heat to low, and simmer for about 30 minutes. Season with salt and pepper to taste. Stir in the cilantro, ladle into warm soup bowls, and serve with crusty bread.

notes from our test kitchen

- Portuguese linguiça and chouriço, delicious as they are, can be hard to find. If you can't find them, just substitute an equal amount of Spanish chorizo.
- Turkish bay leaves are far superior in flavor to California bay leaves; their ends are rounded, not pointed. They are the ones generally used by the major spice companies.

cold buttermilk soup

THE ART OF EATING, M.F.K. Fisher's omnibus book, has been published in a new fiftieth-anniversary edition. For at least that long, people have been enjoying this lovely cold shrimp soup with its buttermilk base. Fisher says it belongs in the category of "Things I Do Not Mention Gastronomically." That's because when she let on that it's made with mashed shrimp and—*eeeew*—buttermilk, the very same people who happily ate it would wince, gag, and hurry away. We've had the same reaction at our table, especially to the buttermilk news.

People do, however, love it for its deeply refreshing quality and its delicate taste, which is slightly Scandinavian. It's an excellent soup for the cook when the weather is blazing. If you buy cooked shrimp, there's no cooking at all: you just chop a little and mix things together and let the flavors marry while you have a drink with your friends.

serves 6

- 1½ pounds shrimp, cooked and chopped
- ½ medium cucumber, seeded and finely diced
- 1 tablespoon minced fresh dill
- 1 tablespoon mustard (ball park or Dijon)
- 1 teaspoon salt
- 1 teaspoon sugar
- 1 quart buttermilk

Mix together everything but the buttermilk in a medium bowl, mashing the shrimps a bit with a fork. Stir in the buttermilk and mix thoroughly. Chill thoroughly to allow the flavors to develop.

note from our test kitchen

We like to garnish each bowl with some snipped dill and a single shrimp cut in half lengthwise and butterflied.

salads

SOURCE: *New York Times Magazine*
STORY BY Jason Epstein
COOK: Alice Waters

alice waters's coleslaw

COLESLAW IS SOMETHING we can't imagine living without. What would we serve at cookouts, with slow-cooked barbecue, or with anything fried—especially chicken? But sadly, too many recipes lather on the mayonnaise and spoon in so much sugar that the slaw ends up a goopy, overly sweet mess. Leave it to Alice Waters to come up with a formula that highlights the refreshing spicy-sweet flavor of the cabbage. The accents of jalapeño, lime juice, and cilantro add a sophisticated zip, but this is still just the thing to serve with fish sticks.

serves 8 to 12

- 1 medium green cabbage (about 3 pounds), outer leaves removed
- 1/2 small red onion, cut in half through the stem, and thinly sliced
- 1 cup loosely packed fresh cilantro leaves, coarsely chopped
- 1 large jalapeño, seeded and finely chopped
- 3–4 tablespoons fresh lime juice
- 3–4 tablespoons red wine vinegar
- 1/4–1/3 cup olive oil
- 1 1/2 teaspoons Maldon or other sea salt, plus more to taste
- 1/2 teaspoon freshly ground black pepper, plus more to taste
- Large pinch of sugar, or more to taste

Quarter the cabbage through the core; cut out the core. Cut the quarters crosswise in half and, using a sharp knife, finely shred. Place the shredded cabbage in a very large bowl or pot (you'll have about 5 1/2 quarts). Add the onion, cilantro, and jalapeño to the cabbage. Toss to mix. Sprinkle with the lime juice, vinegar, oil, salt, pepper, and sugar, and toss to coat.

Let the slaw sit for 1 hour, tossing occasionally. Drain. Taste and adjust the seasonings. Wait another hour before serving at room temperature.

note from our test kitchen

Maldon sea salt, the darling of many cooks and chefs, is esteemed for its soft, flaky crystals, which add a pleasing crunch to many dishes. The texture dissipates as soon as the salt dissolves into a dish, making it nearly impossible to distinguish. When making this coleslaw, we just use any clean-tasting, coarse-grain sea salt. Kosher salt will also do. Since Maldon salt crystals are bigger than those of kosher or table salt, they take up more room in a measuring spoon. If substituting another kind of salt, start with 1 teaspoon and add more to taste.

spare your knives

As a famous chef reminded us this year (we think it was John Ash), don't use the sharp blade of your knife to scrape prepped vegetables off the chopping board, which will dull the blade and may even damage it. Use the other edge of the knife or a pastry scraper.

SOURCE: *Cooking in the Lowcountry from the Old Post Office Restaurant* by Jane and Michael Stern and Philip Bardin

COOK: Philip Bardin

boston lettuce salad with toasted almonds and ginger croutons

PHILIP BARDIN HAS BEEN THE CHEF and co-owner of the famous Old Post Office Restaurant in South Carolina's lowcountry since the late 1980s. His salad dates back even further. It's extremely simple but elegant, and when you include the ginger croutons, it's a knockout.

Bardin's idea is to create a flower on each plate, with perfect Boston lettuce leaves as the petals. Inside each petal is a scattering of warm toasted almonds, with walnut oil, raspberry vinegar, and lemon juice drizzled over.

The ginger croutons are great with lots of different salads, especially curried chicken salad. You want the ginger to be chopped as fine as possible; the food processor can do this well.

serves 4

GINGER CROUTONS

1 cup finely chopped peeled fresh ginger, fibrous pieces removed (from about 6 inches of gingerroot; see note)
1 teaspoon fresh lemon juice
6 thin slices French bread
Olive oil

SALAD

2 heads Boston lettuce
1/2 cup slivered almonds, freshly toasted in the oven and still warm (see note)
Juice of 1 lemon
Walnut oil
Raspberry vinegar
Freshly ground black pepper

TO MAKE THE GINGER CROUTONS:

Place the ginger in a small bowl and add the lemon juice. Stir well.

Preheat the oven to 350 degrees.

Cut the bread slices in half to yield 12 slices. Rub with the ginger, scrape off any excess, and place the bread on a baking sheet. Drizzle the olive oil over the top of each slice and bake until brown around the edges, 7 to 10 minutes. Let stand at room temperature for 10 minutes before serving.

MEANWHILE, MAKE THE SALAD:

Wash the large lettuce leaves in the sink or a large bowl filled with ice water, being careful not to tear them. Any sand will sink to the bottom. Dry the leaves thoroughly.

Arrange the leaves flower style on four large plates. Put a pinch of toasted almonds in the pocket of each lettuce leaf.

Splash the lemon juice over the salads. A very light drizzle of walnut oil is next, followed by light dashes of raspberry vinegar and pepper.

Place 3 ginger croutons on each plate and serve.

notes from our test kitchen

- Scrape the ginger off the bread slices once you've rubbed them or it will be overpowering. You can also skip the chopped ginger and just brush the bread slices lightly with ginger juice, now available in small bottles (or make your own according to the tip on page 53).
- To toast the almonds, arrange them in a single layer on a rimmed baking sheet and toast in a 350-degree oven until they are lightly browned and smell good, about 8 minutes.

SOURCE: *Aroma*
by Mandy Aftel and Daniel Patterson

COOKS: Mandy Aftel and Daniel Patterson

crisp vegetable salad with ginger vinaigrette

ESPECIALLY IN THE WINTER MONTHS, we often crave a salad full of crisp, refreshing textures and bright, clean flavors. This one answers that yearning. Grating a hunk of ginger to make ginger juice provides a mildly pungent, wonderfully fragrant vinaigrette that elevates the mix of thinly sliced cabbage, fennel, radish, apple, and cilantro. It's a great start or accompaniment to a rich meal.

We like to double the amount of vinaigrette to keep some on hand for other uses. The authors tell us that ginger vinaigrette also goes well with grilled vegetables, especially eggplant and scallions, and steamed bok choy.

serves 8

GINGER VINAIGRETTE

- 2 tablespoons champagne vinegar
- 1 tablespoon fresh ginger juice (see tip)
- Salt
- 1/4 cup fruity olive oil

SALAD

- 4 cups napa cabbage, thinly sliced (about 1/4 head)
- 2 cups finely shaved fennel (1 medium bulb)
- 1 1/2 cups thinly sliced celery (3–5 ribs)
- 1 1/2 cups thinly sliced radishes (about 1 bunch)
- 1 1/2 cups thinly sliced green apple (about 1 large)
- 1/2 bunch fresh cilantro, coarsely chopped (including tender stems; about 1/2 cup)
- Salt and freshly ground black pepper

TO MAKE THE VINAIGRETTE:

Combine the vinegar and ginger juice in a small bowl. Dissolve a few pinches of salt in the liquid. Slowly whisk in the olive oil. Taste and add more salt as necessary.

TO MAKE THE SALAD:

Combine the cabbage, fennel, celery, radishes, green apple, and cilantro in a large bowl. Season with salt and pepper, then pour over three quarters of the vinaigrette. Toss well. Ginger can vary considerably in strength, so you might not need all of the vinaigrette. Adjust the seasonings, add more or all of the vinaigrette if needed, and serve.

note from our test kitchen

If you have a mandoline slicer, now is the time to use it. If not, do your best to slice the vegetables and apple as thin as possible. The closer to shaved you can get them, the better the salad will be.

tip

To make ginger juice, according to Mandy Aftel and Daniel Patterson, the authors of *Aroma*, grate an unpeeled chunk of ginger on the largest-holed side of a four-sided grater and then use your hands to squeeze the juice through a strainer to remove any ginger pieces. When shopping for ginger, choose pieces with shiny, smooth skin; wrinkled and dull pieces are old and will have a weaker flavor.

SOURCE: *The Big Book of Backyard Cooking* by Betty Rosbottom

COOKS: Vicki and Steve Caparulo

grilled caesar salad

GRILLED SALAD? That was our first response, but once we tried it, we wondered why no one had thought of it before. Quartering a head of romaine and lightly charring it over a hot grill adds a pleasant, smoky sweetness to the salad. Although it doesn't have the coddled eggs and croutons of a classic Caesar, the creamy, garlicky dressing is close enough to earn it the moniker.

This is an especially handy starter if you've got the grill fired up for the main course.

serves 4

DRESSING

- 3 large garlic cloves, peeled
- 3/4 cup mayonnaise (regular or low fat)
- 2 tablespoons grated Parmesan cheese, preferably Parmigiano-Reggiano
- 4 canned anchovy fillets rolled with capers (see note)
- 2 tablespoons extra-virgin olive oil
- 1 tablespoon fresh lemon juice
- 1 teaspoon Worcestershire sauce
- 1 teaspoon Dijon mustard

SALAD

- 1/4 cup extra-virgin olive oil
- 2 medium garlic cloves
- 1/4 teaspoon kosher salt
- 1 medium (1–1 1/4 pound) head romaine lettuce, 8–9 inches long (see note)
- 1/4 cup grated Parmesan cheese, preferably Parmigiano-Reggiano
- Freshly ground black pepper

TO MAKE THE DRESSING:

Pulse the garlic in a food processor or blender until minced. Add the mayonnaise, cheese, anchovies, oil, lemon juice, Worcestershire, and mustard and process until smooth. The dressing can be made 2 hours ahead and kept, covered, in the refrigerator. Bring to room temperature 15 minutes before using.

TO MAKE THE SALAD:

Whisk together the oil, garlic, and salt in a small bowl. Set aside for 15 minutes to let the flavors develop. Remove and discard any outer bruised leaves from the romaine. Quarter the lettuce lengthwise and set aside.

Oil a grill rack and arrange it 4 to 5 inches from the heat source. Prepare a hot fire in the grill. Lightly brush the cut sides (including the stalk and leaves) of each lettuce quarter with the garlic-scented oil. Grill the lettuce quarters cut sides down until lightly browned, about 2 minutes. The leaves should be very slightly charred but still hold their shape.

Arrange the lettuce quarters cut sides up on four dinner plates. Brush some of the dressing over and under the leaves of each quarter, then drizzle each serving with a little more dressing. Divide the Parmesan among the lettuce, and season each salad with a generous amount of pepper. Serve, passing any extra dressing in a small bowl.

notes from our test kitchen

- If you can't find anchovies rolled around capers, add a few capers to the mix. Either way, shop for anchovies packed in olive oil. Anything else is inferior.
- Make this only when you can find tall, robust heads of romaine in the market. Tired-looking lettuces wrapped in plastic and shipped across the country won't hold up as well.
- If the lettuce appears sandy, do your best to rinse the quarters under running water or dunk them in a large bowl of cold water. Then take the time to let them dry cut sides down on towels for a good while. Excess water will create flare-ups on the grill.

SOURCE: *From Tapas to Meze* by Joanne Weir

COOK: Joanne Weir after Nabih

cucumber and feta salad with dill and mint

JOANNE WEIR was one of the first generation of authors to introduce Americans to such Mediterranean delights as tapenade, harissa, skordalia, and baba gannouj, so we were delighted to see her groundbreaking 1994 cookbook revised and re-released.

Among Joanne's favorite recipes in the book—and ours—is this marvelous Egyptian salad.

serves 6

- 8 ounces feta cheese (see note)
- 2 tablespoons extra-virgin olive oil
- 1 1/2 tablespoons fresh lemon juice
- Salt and freshly ground black pepper
- 1 large cucumber, peeled, seeded, and cut into 1/2-inch dice
- 1 small red onion, cut into 1/4-inch dice
- 1 tablespoon chopped fresh mint, plus sprigs for garnish
- 1 tablespoon chopped fresh flat-leaf parsley
- 1 tablespoon chopped fresh dill, plus sprigs for garnish
- 6 lemon wedges
- Pita bread, warmed (see note)

Crumble the feta coarsely into a bowl and toss it together with the oil, lemon juice, and salt and pepper to taste. Add the cucumber, onion, mint, parsley, and dill.

Place on a serving plate and garnish with sprigs of dill and mint and the lemon wedges. Serve with the warm pita bread.

notes from our test kitchen

- Since feta plays a starring role here, shop for a high-quality one. Greek, French, Israeli, and Bulgarian feta are generally good bets.
- To warm pita bread, wrap it in foil and heat in a 350-degree oven for about 10 minutes.

SOURCE: *Guy Savoy: Simple French Recipes* by Guy Savoy

COOK: Guy Savoy

green bean salad with cream

WE FALL IN LOVE with certain recipes every year and can't stop making them. This is one of those, a salad that requires only a 10-minute prep. The beans are cooked just to the point of crisp tenderness, then chilled and combined with the simplest imaginable dressing—crème fraîche, lemon, and shallot, with some chives on top. Every time we see tender green beans beckoning to us at the market, we think, "What about that Guy Savoy recipe?"

As Savoy points out, the dressing is easier to make than a vinaigrette and can be used for lots of different salads, including potato salad.

serves 4

Salt
1¼ pounds tender green beans or haricots verts, trimmed
Juice of 1 lemon
Freshly ground black pepper
1 shallot, minced
½ cup crème fraîche
1 small bunch fresh chives

Bring a large pot of salted water to a boil, add the beans, and cook for 6 to 8 minutes, or until tender but still slightly crisp. Drain and rinse under cold running water. Refrigerate until ready to serve.

Combine the lemon juice and salt and pepper to taste in a medium bowl. Stir well to dissolve the salt. Stir in the shallot and crème fraîche. Refrigerate the dressing until ready to serve.

Just before serving, combine the beans with the dressing. Arrange on individual serving plates and garnish with chive sprigs.

note from our test kitchen

We sometimes chop the chives and sprinkle them over the salad; chives with snipped dill is also a good idea.

SOURCE: *Bon Appétit*
STORY BY Anna Pump
COOK: Anna Pump

fresh green peas and sugar snaps in sesame dressing

TWO KINDS OF PEAS cooked together give you an intense, just-off-the-bush pea flavor. Here they're combined with an Asian dressing of toasted sesame oil, soy sauce, and rice vinegar, which takes them right out of the English-garden category. These zingy flavors are tempered with a little brown sugar, which brings out the sweetness of the peas even more. The salad is a good match for grilled salmon or other fish.

You can cook the peas and make the dressing a couple of hours ahead, but they need to be kept separate until just before serving. Once you toss everything together, the salad shouldn't sit around, or it will become soggy.

serves 4

- 3 cups fresh shelled peas (from 3 pounds peas in pods; see note)
- Kosher salt
- 12 ounces sugar snap peas, trimmed
- 2 tablespoons unseasoned rice vinegar
- 1 tablespoon soy sauce
- 1 tablespoon toasted sesame oil
- 1 tablespoon (packed) brown sugar
- 1/2 teaspoon freshly ground black pepper

Cook the peas in a saucepan of boiling salted water until almost tender, about 1½ minutes. Add the sugar snaps and boil for 30 seconds more. Drain, rinse under cold water, and drain again. Transfer to a large bowl.

Whisk together the remaining ingredients and 1 teaspoon salt in a small bowl. The dish can be prepared up to 2 hours ahead to this point. Let the peas and dressing stand separately at room temperature.

Pour the dressing over the peas and toss to coat. Season to taste with salt and pepper, if needed, and serve at room temperature.

notes from our test kitchen

- We rarely see truly fresh peas in the market, so we usually use frozen ones instead. Frozen petite peas work very well. A 10-ounce package will give you 2 cups of peas, so you need two packages. You don't need to defrost the peas before cooking them.
- If there are any pea shoots around, chop them and make a wreath of them around a mound of the salad.

SOURCE: *The Olive and the Caper* by Susanna Hoffman

COOK: Susanna Hoffman

greek radish salad

AN ANTHROPOLOGIST who has been working in Greece off and on for thirty years, Susanna Hoffman has completely immersed herself in the culture, its people, and their food. She notes that radishes, the base of this salad, were so adored by the ancients that golden replicas of them were offered to the sun god, Apollo. Turnips (cast in lead) and beets (in silver) were also offered, but gold was reserved for radishes.

This is an amazing salad, with its pickled onions and creamy feta cheese balancing the beautiful radishes. It's a good choice for a buffet, since there are no greens to wilt. Look for farmers'-market-quality radishes, still crisp and with a modest bite. Old supermarket radishes won't be pleasant here at all, and besides, you'll want to save the tender green radish leaves, which are delicious.

serves 4 to 6

- 4 large bunches radishes, preferably with leaves
- 1/4 teaspoon salt
- Pinch of freshly ground black pepper
- 4 ounces feta cheese, coarsely crumbled
- 1/2 cup Pickled Red Onions (*recipe follows*)
- 1 tablespoon red wine vinegar
- 3 tablespoons fruity olive oil

Trim off the tops and root ends of the radishes, reserving the tender young leaves. Cut the radishes into thin rounds and set aside. Wash the leaves and pat them dry.

Spread the radish slices and leaves, if using, on a platter. Sprinkle with the salt and pepper, top with the cheese, then spread the onions over all. Sprinkle the vinegar over the top, generously drizzle oil over all, and serve right away.

note from our test kitchen

Feta cheese comes from everywhere these days, but look for real Greek feta, which is increasingly available. Other options include Israeli, Bulgarian, and French feta.

pickled red onions

A QUICK, EASY PICKLE that's great in sandwiches or salads.

makes 3 cups

- 2 medium red onions, halved and very thinly sliced
- 1 cup red wine vinegar
- 1 cup water
- 2 tablespoons sugar
- 1 bay leaf

Place the onions in a medium bowl and set aside.

Combine the remaining ingredients in a small nonreactive saucepan and bring to a boil over high heat to dissolve the sugar. Stir and pour over the onions.

Set aside to cool and marinate for at least 30 minutes. Use right away or cover and store in the refrigerator for up to several weeks. Remove the bay leaf before using.

SOURCE: *New York Times Magazine*
STORY BY Amanda Hesser
COOK: Amanda Hesser

beet salad with horseradish and fried capers

THIS SENSATIONAL SALAD gets its power from fried salt-packed capers. They fluff up in the hot olive oil like the curled-up flower buds they are, producing a crunchy outer shell that's a salty complement to the fine balance of sweet beets, horseradish, and Dijon mustard. You can use regular bottled brined capers, but they don't open up in the same way and give the full explosion of flavor. The capers are also delicious with vegetables, fried seafood, and fish and in a Caesar salad.

Don't be scared off by the word *fry;* this is shallow-frying in a small saucepan with just a little oil, and it's a great trick to have up your sleeve.

serves 4

- 1½ pounds small beets, trimmed and scrubbed
- 5 tablespoons olive oil, plus more for frying the capers
- 2 tablespoons salt-packed or brined capers
- 1 tablespoon Dijon mustard
- 1½ tablespoons horseradish, or more to taste
- 1 tablespoon white wine vinegar
- 1 tablespoon sour cream
- Sea salt
- 1 garlic clove, crushed

Preheat the oven to 350 degrees.

Place the beets on half of a large piece of aluminum foil. Drizzle with 1 tablespoon of the oil. Fold the foil over the beets and seal the edges. Lay the package on a baking sheet and place it in the oven. Roast until the beets are tender, 45 to 60 minutes. (Test by poking a fork through the foil into a beet.) Remove from the oven. Be careful when opening the foil; steam will race out. Peel the beets while they're still warm, then slice into wedges and place in a bowl.

Soak the salt-packed capers in water for 10 minutes. Drain, rinse, then pat dry. If using brined capers, drain and pat dry. Pour ½ inch oil into a small saucepan over medium-high heat. When the oil is hot enough to toast a bread crumb in 30 seconds, add the capers. Be careful; the oil may sputter. Fry until the capers fluff up and begin to brown on the edges, 30 to 60 seconds. Drain on paper towels.

Whisk together the mustard, horseradish, and vinegar in a small bowl. Whisk in the remaining 4 tablespoons oil, followed by the sour cream. Pour half of the dressing over the beets and mix. Taste, adding more dressing or salt, if needed. Rub a platter with the crushed garlic, discard the garlic, and then spoon the beets onto the platter, sprinkle with the fried capers, and serve.

notes from our test kitchen

- Salted capers are available in Italian markets and many gourmet shops and supermarkets. They keep almost forever, so buy them when you see them.
- We love the touch of the crushed garlic clove on the platter. This really adds something; it's like those 1950s salad recipes that asked you to rub the wooden bowl with a garlic clove.

SOURCE: *Good Housekeeping*
STORY BY *Good Housekeeping* staff
COOK: *Good Housekeeping* staff

soppressata and roma bean salad with pecorino

GREEN BEAN SALADS fall into the category of dishes we deem "useful," meaning they're easy to throw together and reliably tasty. Unfortunately, useful dishes can suffer from overexposure, until some crafty cook breathes new life into the idea. And that's exactly what we've got here: green bean salad with a makeover. Instead of regular string beans, the recipe calls for the broad, flat Roma beans (green beans are fine, too), thin strips of soppressata (a better version of salami), sharp arugula, and a lemony dressing.

When you first toss this salad, you may think there's too much lemon, too little oil, and altogether not enough dressing. But one of those kitchen miracles happens and the small amount of dressing stretches to coat all the ingredients. It's thanks to the bit of fat from the soppressata, which blends with the dressing and makes everything just right. If you're still not satisfied when you taste the salad, just add a splash of olive oil.

serves 4 as main course (see note)

- 1¼ pounds Roma (broad) beans or green beans, trimmed
- 1 lemon
- 2 tablespoons extra-virgin olive oil
- ¼ teaspoon salt
- ⅛ teaspoon coarsely ground black pepper
- 2 bunches arugula (about 4 ounces each), tough stems discarded (see note)
- 4 ounces thinly sliced soppressata or Genoa salami, cut into ½-inch-wide strips
- 1 hunk (about 2 ounces) pecorino Romano cheese

If the Roma beans are very long, cut them crosswise into 2½-inch lengths. Bring 1 inch water to a boil in a 12-inch skillet over high heat (see note). Add the beans and return to a boil. Reduce the heat to low and simmer until crisp-tender, 6 to 8 minutes. Drain the beans. Rinse with cold running water to stop the cooking, and drain again.

Meanwhile, grate ½ teaspoon lemon zest and squeeze 2 tablespoons lemon juice. Combine these in a large bowl. Whisk in the oil, salt (see note), and pepper.

Add the beans, arugula, and soppressata or salami to the dressing and toss to coat. Spoon the salad onto a platter. Using a vegetable peeler, shave thin strips of pecorino Romano to top the salad. Serve.

notes from our test kitchen

- Green bean salads, especially this one, make a fine addition to bountiful summer buffets, in which case it will serve 6 to 8.
- We are in the habit of salting the water before cooking any green vegetable—it improves their texture and color—so we do that here, adding a teaspoon or so of salt to the water.
- The 1/4 teaspoon salt refers to fine-grain table salt. If you cook with coarse salt, as we do, you'll need a bit more. As with any dish, taste for seasoning, adding more as you see fit. We think this salad tastes best with another good shot of freshly ground black pepper.
- If your arugula is almost all leaves with few woody stems (like the baby arugula sold in many markets), you won't need the full 8 ounces. Figure on closer to 5 or 6 ounces.
- If you make this salad ahead, wait to add the arugula until just before serving.

SOURCE: *Frank Stitt's Southern Table*
by Frank Stitt

COOK: Frank Stitt

fig and peanut salad with arugula and mint

THIS SALAD PROVIDES one of those "Eureka!" experiences in the kitchen. The combination is unusual, but the ingredients harmonize delightfully. The crunch of the peanuts contrasts with the softness of the figs, and the sweet and peppery greens, fruity raspberry vinegar, and biting fresh mint create a pleasing play of flavors.

Frank Stitt, the creative genius behind this handsome salad and the chef-owner of Highland's Bar and Grill in Birmingham, Alabama, suggests serving it before a main course of grilled lamb or pork. We'd be happy to have it before just about anything.

serves 4

- 12 ripe black, brown, or green figs
- 1 shallot, finely minced
- 1 scallion, finely chopped
- 8 mint sprigs, 4 finely chopped, 4 left whole
- 1 tablespoon raspberry vinegar
- 1/4 cup peanut oil (see note)
- Coarse salt and freshly ground black pepper
- 1 bunch arugula, trimmed, washed, and dried
- 1 head Bibb lettuce, cored, washed, and dried
- 3/4 cup raw peanuts, toasted (see note and tip)

Cut off the fig stems and discard. Slice each fig crosswise into 4 or 5 slices and set aside.

Combine the shallot, scallion, chopped mint, and vinegar in a small bowl. Whisk in the oil and season with salt and pepper to taste.

Toss the greens with the vinaigrette in a large bowl. Arrange the salad on four plates and top with the figs and peanuts. Garnish with the mint sprigs.

notes from our test kitchen

- The peanut oil used here is a neutral-tasting oil. Avoid toasted or roasted peanut oil, which would be overpowering. You can also use a mild extra-virgin olive oil.
- Look for raw peanuts in the bulk bin at a natural foods store. Commercially roasted peanuts are not the same and won't be as good.

tip

Toasting raw nuts brings out their flavor and improves their texture. Here's how Frank Stitt tells us to do it: Spread the nuts on a rimmed baking sheet and bake in a 350-degree oven, shaking the pan from time to time, until aromatic and lightly browned, 10 to 15 minutes. Keep a close eye on the nuts, as they can burn quickly.

SOURCE: *O magazine*
STORY BY Susan Chumsky
COOK: Michel Nischan

watermelon, arugula, and toasted almond salad

THIS GORGEOUS SUMMER SALAD comes from Michel Nischan, a New York City chef with a well-earned reputation for coming up with new ways to intensify the pure flavors of fresh ingredients. The reduction of fresh watermelon juice and cider vinegar that serves as the base for the dressing makes the salad unique (and staggeringly delicious). We can't resist its sweet-tangy flavor, and we also love its deep rose color. Indeed, if you're the kind of cook who enjoys picture-perfect dishes, you'll have a good deal of fun here. Each individually plated salad starts with a square slab of watermelon. It's topped with a tangle of dressed arugula dotted with toasted almonds and sliced spring onion and drizzled with the colorful watermelon dressing.

The watermelon reduction needs time to cool, so be sure to plan ahead. You can also make the reduction a day or two in advance and store it in the refrigerator until you're ready.

serves 6

- 1½ cups chopped seedless watermelon, plus six 3-inch squares (see note)
- 1 spring onion or large scallion, thinly sliced, white and green parts separated
- ¼ cup extra-virgin olive oil
- ¼ cup cider vinegar
- ¼ teaspoon salt
- ⅛ teaspoon freshly ground black pepper
- 3 ounces baby arugula leaves
- ½ cup sliced almonds, toasted (see note)

To make the dressing, puree the 1½ cups watermelon until smooth in a blender or food processor. Strain through a sieve to make 1 cup juice. Sauté the white part of the onion or scallion in 1 teaspoon olive oil in a small saucepan over medium heat until soft, a few minutes. Add the watermelon juice and vinegar and bring to a boil over medium-high heat. Lower the heat and simmer until reduced to about 3 tablespoons, stirring occasionally, 20 to 25 minutes. Pour into a small bowl to cool. Once cool, whisk in the remaining oil, salt, and pepper.

Arrange the watermelon squares on chilled salad plates. Combine the arugula, almonds, and onion or scallion greens in a large bowl. Add 2 tablespoons of the dressing and toss gently. Top the watermelon squares with the salad. Drizzle with the remaining dressing and serve immediately.

notes from our test kitchen

- The 3-inch squares of watermelon should be about 1 inch thick, but there's no need to get out your ruler. In fact, we invite you to play around with shapes (wedges and diamonds) and dimensions to suit your mood.
- To toast the almonds, arrange them in a single layer on a rimmed baking sheet and toast in a 350-degree oven until they are lightly browned and smell good, about 8 minutes.
- We love the vegetarian cook Peter Berley's dessert idea of serving watermelon wedges with sprinkles of fleur de sel, the most delectable of sea salts. Maldon sea salt, the crunchy pyramid-shaped crystals from England, will also give the watermelon a lift. For this salad, sprinkle the salt on each slab of watermelon just before setting the arugula on top.

SOURCE: *Quick & Easy Thai* by Nancie McDermott

COOK: Nancie McDermott

pink grapefruit salad with toasted coconut and fresh mint

AS A PEACE CORPS VOLUNTEER in the countryside of Thailand for three years, Nancie McDermott fell in love with Thai food. She has spent the years since making Thai cuisine accessible to American cooks. This unusual salad (called *yum some-oh* in Thai) is tart, sweet, hot, spicy, and crunchy. You serve it with small cups of lettuce and spoons, so diners can scoop a little salad into the lettuce. It's more like a relish than a salad, an appealing counterpoint to grilled fish or chicken.

serves 4

- 3 tablespoons shredded dried coconut, sweetened or not (see note)
- 2 tablespoons fresh lime juice
- 2 tablespoons fish sauce
- 1 tablespoon sugar
- 2 cups bite-size chunks peeled and sectioned pink grapefruit or pomelo
- 1/2 cup coarsely chopped fresh mint or cilantro
- 2 tablespoons dried shrimp, coarsely chopped, or 2 tablespoons coarsely chopped roasted salted peanuts (optional; see note)
- 1 tablespoon coarsely chopped shallot
- 2 teaspoons finely chopped fresh hot green chile or crusted red pepper flakes
- Leaves of Boston or Bibb lettuce

Toast the coconut in a small dry skillet over medium-high heat for 3 to 4 minutes, tossing often, until most of it turns a rich, soft brown. Turn out into a saucer to cool.

Combine the lime juice, fish sauce, and sugar in a medium bowl and stir well to dissolve the sugar and form a smooth sauce. Add the grapefruit or pomelo, mint, toasted coconut, dried shrimp or peanuts (if using), shallot, and chile, and toss gently to combine well. Transfer to a serving platter with the lettuce leaves on the side and serve at room temperature.

notes from our test kitchen

- Unsweetened dried coconut is usually found in natural food stores.
- We urge you to include either the dried shrimp or the peanuts for their tasty crunch.

SOURCE: *The Tomato Festival Cookbook* by Lawrence Davis-Hollander

COOK: Lawrence Davis-Hollander adapted from Chris Prosperi

tomato couscous salad

THIS CHEERFUL SALAD makes a fine addition to a dinner from the grill or a bucolic summer picnic. It's quicker and less fussy to prepare than a standard potato or pasta salad, and it features a refreshing combination of zesty tomato dressing with fresh tomatoes and a bracing amount of chopped parsley. It's better when made a couple of hours before serving.

The recipe comes from Chris Prosperi, an astonishingly energetic and innovative young chef in central Connecticut. In addition to running Metro Bis restaurant, cowriting a food column for the local paper, offering regular cooking classes, and appearing on TV and radio, Chris markets a line of his own salad dressings. As a bonus, this recipe gives the formula for his popular tomato salad dressing.

serves 4

- 1 cup couscous
- Salt
- 2 cups boiling water, or less (see note)
- 1 tablespoon extra-virgin olive oil
- 1 cup diced tomato (1/4-inch pieces; see note)
- 1/2 cup chopped fresh parsley
- 1–3 tablespoons fresh lemon juice
- 2–3 dashes Tabasco sauce
- 1/2 cup Metro Bis Tomato Salad Dressing (*recipe follows*)
- Freshly ground black pepper

Mix the couscous with 1 teaspoon salt in a large bowl. Add the boiling water and the oil. Cover and let stand for 10 minutes.

Lightly fluff the couscous with a fork, then add the tomato, parsley, 1 tablespoon of the lemon juice, the Tabasco, and the dressing. Stir gently with the fork. Check the seasonings and, if necessary, adjust by adding salt, pepper, Tabasco, lemon juice, or more dressing to taste.

Cover and refrigerate for at least 2 hours or up to 6 hours (see note). Before serving, check the seasonings and adjust with salt, pepper, or lemon juice as needed.

notes from our test kitchen

- For a fluffier, lighter salad, we like to use a bit less boiling water to reconstitute the couscous. We've found the most reliable ratio to be 1½ cups boiling water to 1 cup couscous.
- As much as we think of this as a summer salad, you can make it in the off-season using cherry or grape tomatoes.
- The texture of tomatoes deteriorates when refrigerated for any length of time, so if you're planning on chilling the salad for the full 6 hours, it's best not to add them (especially if they are truly fine, ripe summer tomatoes) until just before serving.

metro bis tomato salad dressing

THIS ALL-PURPOSE DRESSING is equally good on pasta salads, grain salads, and tossed greens.

makes 2 cups

- 1 cup tomato juice
- 1/4 cup red wine vinegar
- 1 small onion, chopped (about 1/2 cup)
- 1 tablespoon Dijon mustard
- 1–2 teaspoons sugar
- 1/2 cup extra-virgin olive oil
- Salt and freshly ground black pepper

Combine the tomato juice, vinegar, onion, mustard, and 1 teaspoon of the sugar, and the oil. Add salt and pepper to taste. Process for 1 minute to mix well.

Taste and add the additional sugar or more salt and pepper as needed. Process until combined, about 15 seconds. Serve or store in a covered jar in the refrigerator for up to 2 weeks.

SOURCE: *The Pastry Queen*
by Rebecca Rather and Alison Oresman

COOK: Paula Disbrowe

wild rice and chickpea salad

PEOPLE SIMPLY ADORE this big grain- and bean-filled salad. It's based on nutty, crunchy wild rice, but so many elements are at play here—smoked ham, raisins, curry powder, chickpeas, hot sauce, honey, cumin—that you just have to take another bite and then another to taste all the wonderful flavors.

The salad works virtually anywhere—at a picnic, at a dinner party, on a buffet table, at a potluck supper. Another bonus: you serve it at room temperature. We've yet to serve it without being asked for the recipe.

serves 6

- 1½ cups wild rice, preferably organic
- 1 tablespoon kosher salt, plus more to taste
- 2½ tablespoons fresh lemon juice
- 2 tablespoons red wine vinegar
- 2 tablespoons Dijon mustard
- 1 tablespoon honey
- 1 tablespoon ground cumin
- 1 teaspoon curry powder
- Pinch of cayenne pepper
- ¼ cup extra-virgin olive oil
- 1 15-ounce can chickpeas (garbanzos), drained and rinsed
- 8 ounces smoked ham, diced (see note)
- 8 small scallions (white and light green parts only), thinly sliced
- ¼ cup golden raisins
- Freshly ground black pepper
- Hot pepper sauce

Fill a large saucepan three-quarters full of water and bring to a boil. Add the wild rice and salt and simmer over medium heat until the rice is tender but still firm to the bite, about 45 minutes. Drain and rinse under cold water.

Meanwhile, whisk together the lemon juice, vinegar, mustard, honey, cumin, curry powder, and cayenne in a large bowl. Add the oil and whisk until combined.

Add the chickpeas, ham, scallions, raisins, and wild rice and toss well. Season to taste with salt, pepper, and hot pepper sauce. Serve at room temperature. The salad can be refrigerated overnight. Bring it to room temperature and toss before serving.

notes from our test kitchen

- If you can't find wild rice, you can use Uncle Ben's Long Grain & Wild Rice in a box, minus the seasoning packet.
- You can substitute dried cranberries for the golden raisins.
- The ham makes the salad a bit sturdier, but the dish is fine—and vegetarian—without it.
- While convenient, the method of mixing the salad dressing directly in the bowl and then adding the other ingredients makes it difficult to adjust the amount of dressing if you need to. Instead, we recommend putting only about ½ cup of mixed dressing in the bowl and adding more gradually after tossing the salad.

SOURCE: *Stalking the Green Fairy* by James Villas

COOK: James Villas

greek potato salad with olives and feta cheese

FOOD WRITER JAMES VILLAS found this unusual potato salad on the tiny Greek island of Aegina, where he'd gone for lunch to taste a particular taverna's legendary stuffed lamb, spit-roasted in a wood-burning oven. The lamb turned out to be served for dinner only, so Villas and his friends had to make do with cold lamb from the night before, which arrived with this memorable potato salad.

The salad combines a lot of fresh, light ingredients—scallions, cucumber, mint, oregano, lemon—with very small red potatoes, which aren't nearly as starchy as the usual potato-salad potatoes. The feta is creamy and salty, and there's more salt from the olives and capers. As long as you rinse the capers well, the salad won't be too salty.

Serve this with a border of frisée and cherry tomatoes. It's delicious with grilled lamb, chicken, or sausages.

serves 6

- 3 pounds very small red potatoes
- Salt
- 8 ounces Greek feta cheese (see page 107 for a note on feta), crumbled
- 1/2 medium cucumber, peeled and cut into thin rounds
- 1/2 green bell pepper, coarsely chopped
- 4 scallions (white and 2 inches of green parts only), coarsely chopped
- 12 brine-cured Greek olives, pitted
- 2 tablespoons minced fresh mint
- 1 tablespoon chopped fresh oregano or 1/2 teaspoon dried, crumbled
- 1 tablespoon capers, rinsed
- Freshly ground black pepper
- 1/2 cup Greek or Italian extra-virgin olive oil
- Juice of 1 lemon
- Frisée lettuce
- 12 cherry tomatoes

Scrub the potatoes lightly and place in a saucepan with salted water to cover. Bring to a boil, reduce the heat to medium, cover, and cook for about 10 minutes, or until they can just be pierced with a fork. Drain the potatoes, cut in half or in slices, place in a large bowl, and let cool.

Add the feta, cucumber, bell pepper, scallions, olives, mint, oregano, capers, and pepper to taste and toss lightly.

Whisk the oil and lemon juice in a small bowl until well blended. Pour over the salad and toss gently but thoroughly.

Arrange the frisée around the edge of a large salad bowl, mound the salad in the middle, arrange the tomatoes around the edge, and serve.

SOURCE: *New York Times*
STORY BY Matt Lee and Ted Lee
COOK: Cesare Casella

pontormo's salad

JACOPO PONTORMO, a sixteenth-century Italian court painter, ate regally when he dined with the Medicis, but on his own was said to prefer a salad topped with scrambled egg. This story fascinated Cesare Casella, the chef-owner of Beppe, a Manhattan trattoria, and he set out to create a scrambled egg salad worthy of Pontormo.

Pontormo would have been lucky indeed. This is a fabulous salad, one you can make in 10 minutes, start to finish. Scrambled egg salad may sound bizarre, but it's a brilliant combination. The eggs warm the dressing and the herbs while wilting the greens a bit. It's a flawless balance of flavors and textures. It makes a light meal for supper or for brunch or lunch.

If you have pancetta, the unsmoked Italian bacon, in the refrigerator, you can whip up this salad anytime.

serves 4

- 1½ teaspoons red wine vinegar
- 1½ teaspoons balsamic vinegar
- 1½ teaspoons red wine
- Salt and freshly ground black pepper
- ¼ cup extra-virgin olive oil
- 4 cups mixed salad greens, in bite-size pieces
- 1 tablespoon mixed dried herbs, such as tarragon, rosemary, sage, basil, and/or oregano
- 3½ ounces pancetta, cut into 1-inch-wide strips
- 6 large eggs

Whisk together the vinegars and wine in a small bowl. Whisk in ½ teaspoon salt and ¼ teaspoon pepper, followed by 2 tablespoons of the oil. Place the salad greens in a large bowl and pour the dressing over, tossing thoroughly to coat.

Heat the remaining 2 tablespoons oil, herbs, and pancetta in a large skillet over medium heat, stirring, until the fat has rendered and the pancetta begins to crisp, 5 to 7 minutes.

Remove the pan from the heat and crack the eggs into it, on top of the pancetta and herbs. Stir the eggs with a whisk to scramble them. Return the pan to low heat for 1 minute, but remove before the eggs become completely dry. Season with salt and pepper to taste. Spread the contents of the pan over the greens and toss to mix. Serve immediately.

SOURCE: *The Spiaggia Cookbook*
by Tony Mantuano and Cathy Mantuano

COOK: Tony Mantuano

spiaggia salad dressing

SPIAGGIA, WHICH MEANS "BEACH" IN ITALIAN, is a Chicago restaurant devoted to authentic regional Italian cuisine. Its cooks use a lot of truffles in season, and in their signature two-vinegar salad dressing they also use truffle oil, which contributes great flavor and aroma. The secret ingredient is not truffle oil, however; it's butter.

Butter in salad dressing? We had to try it. It's browned butter, actually, and it's a fine foundation for the truffle flavor. You'd think it would congeal, but not at all; you're not even aware that it's there.

The vinaigrette is great with greens or a mushroom salad, but it also works well as a dressing for warm shellfish and seafood dishes.

makes 1 cup

- 2 tablespoons unsalted butter
- 2 tablespoons sherry vinegar
- 2 tablespoons balsamic vinegar
- Sea salt
- 1/2 cup extra-virgin olive oil
- 2 tablespoons truffle oil (see note)

Melt the butter in a small saucepan over medium heat. Cook to a nutty brown color, until the foam subsides, 4 to 6 minutes. Remove from the heat and let cool to room temperature, about 20 minutes.

Meanwhile, combine the vinegars and salt to taste in a small bowl. Drizzle in the cooled brown butter and then the oils, whisking until the dressing is well blended. Season with salt to taste.

The dressing will keep for up to 1 week in the refrigerator, tightly sealed. Return to room temperature and whisk before serving.

note from our test kitchen

Real truffle oil costs serious money. Don't fall for the cheap chemical version.

breakfast and brunch

SOURCE: *The Tex-Mex Cookbook*
by Robb Walsh

COOKS: Cynthia and Libby Perez

migas especiales con hongos

IT'S TRADITIONAL IN AUSTIN, TEXAS, to go to Las Manitas for breakfast and order migas, a fine dish of eggs, cheese, and fried tortillas (*migas* means "crumbs" in Spanish). Cynthia and Libby Perez, the owners of the restaurant, don't like it when people describe their food as Tex-Mex, but that's what it is, and deliciously so.

The Perez version of migas is a little different from usual ones; it has lots of mushrooms, and the cheese is Monterey Jack, not cheddar, as with most other recipes. There's a ranchero sauce that goes on top, and you'll want to serve some refried beans on the side along with some warm tortillas.

serves 2

2 tablespoons vegetable oil, plus more if needed
2 tortillas, cut into 1/2-inch-wide strips
2 cups sliced button mushrooms
1 garlic clove, minced
4 large eggs, beaten
1/2 cup grated Monterey Jack cheese
1/2 cup Ranchero Sauce (*recipe follows*)
Warm tortillas for serving

Heat the oil in a small skillet over medium-high heat. Fry the tortilla strips, stirring, for a few minutes until crisp. Remove from the pan and drain on paper towels.

Add the mushrooms and garlic to the skillet and cook for 5 minutes, or until the mushrooms are cooked through and any moisture released has evaporated. Reduce the heat to medium and add a little more oil if necessary to keep the eggs from sticking.

Pour the eggs over the mushrooms and cook, scraping from the bottom. When they are nearly set, add the tortilla strips and the cheese and cook until the cheese melts. Divide the eggs between two plates and top each with 1/4 cup sauce. Serve with the warm tortillas.

note from our test kitchen

A lot of vegetarians go to Las Manitas, so they don't fry the tortillas in lard. But we often do. Olive oil would be another good choice.

ranchero sauce

- 1 $14^{1}/_{2}$-ounce can peeled tomatoes
- $^{1}/_{2}$ can (about 7 ounces) water
- 1 medium garlic clove, minced
- 3 medium serrano chiles, stems removed

Bring the tomatoes and water to a boil in a medium saucepan over medium-high heat. Add the garlic and chiles. Remove the pan from the heat and let the sauce cool.

Puree the sauce in a blender for 2 to 3 minutes, or until it's as smooth or chunky as you like. The sauce will keep, tightly covered in the refrigerator, for 1 week.

SOURCE: *Rocco's Italian American*
by Rocco DiSpirito and Nicolina DiSpirito
with Nina Lalli

COOKS: Rocco and Nicolina DiSpirito

eggs in purgatory

IF YOU DON'T ALREADY HAVE a version of this traditional southern Italian dish of eggs poached in a spicy tomato sauce in your repertoire, now's your chance to add it. It's an example of how resourceful home cooks can make a satisfying meal with only a few ingredients. Why the name? Our best guess is that it's because the eggs are suspended in the hot, but not hellishly hot, sauce. However you interpret it, it's a great breakfast dish, especially after a big night. The spicy sauce and eggs together seem to have restorative powers. It also makes a fine supper when the cupboard's nearly bare.

serves 4

- 1/4 cup extra-virgin olive oil
- 5 garlic cloves, peeled and smashed
- 2 teaspoons crushed red pepper flakes, plus more for serving
- 2 teaspoons red wine vinegar
- 2 28-ounce cans whole peeled tomatoes, with the liquid
- 5 fresh basil leaves, 2 whole, 3 torn by hand
- 2 teaspoons salt
- 8 extra-large eggs, at room temperature (see note)
- Grated Parmigiano-Reggiano
- Toast

Preheat the oven to 425 degrees (see note).

Heat the oil in a large skillet over medium heat. Add the garlic. Stir, crushing the garlic with the edge of a spoon, until it is very light brown and tender and has broken down significantly. Add the red pepper flakes and vinegar. Add the tomatoes and liquid, the 2 whole basil leaves, and the salt to the pan. Bring to a boil, then reduce the heat and simmer for 45 minutes to 1 hour, stirring occasionally to make sure it does not stick. The tomatoes should break down. You may help them along by pushing down on them with the edge of the spoon. Reduce the heat if the sauce begins to boil.

Pour the sauce into a shallow casserole large enough to hold all the eggs without crowding. Smooth out the sauce and crack the eggs on top. Bake for about 10 minutes, or until the whites are cooked and the yolks remain runny.

Top with the cheese, red pepper flakes to taste, and the remaining torn basil leaves. Spoon out the eggs and sauce, being careful not to break the yolks, and serve with toast.

notes from our test kitchen

- Use whatever size eggs you like. If they are small, however, expect them to bake more quickly.
- Unless your oven is incredibly slow to heat, you can wait to preheat it until the sauce is about halfway cooked.
- Gently squeezing the tomatoes with your hands as you put them into the pan will help them break down more readily. Do so carefully, though, so they don't spurt all over. Wearing an apron or an old shirt is a good idea.

SOURCE: *New York Times*
STORY BY **Mark Bittman**
COOK: **Mark Bittman**

swedish pancakes

THESE ADORABLE LITTLE PANCAKES have a light, airy texture. Because they're sweeter and richer than regular flapjacks, they don't need all the butter and syrup we usually slather on. Instead, serve a stack with a dusting of confectioners' sugar. If you want to gussy things up, offer your favorite preserves and/or a little yogurt or sour cream. You can even turn Swedish pancakes into a novel dessert by topping them with whipped cream.

The Swedes have a special griddle pan for making the pancakes all the same size. Fortunately, a tablespoon measure works just fine.

serves 4

- 3 large eggs, separated
- 1/4 cup sugar
- Pinch of salt
- 1 cup milk (see note)
- 3/4 cup all-purpose flour
- 3 tablespoons melted butter, plus more for cooking
- Confectioners' sugar for dusting

Beat the yolks in a medium bowl with the sugar and salt. Add the milk and flour alternately, stirring gently after each addition, to form a thin, smooth batter. Stir in the melted butter. The batter can be covered and refrigerated at this point for up to a day.

Beat the egg whites with an electric mixer until they hold stiff peaks. Gently fold them into the batter; do not worry about fully incorporating them.

Heat a cast-iron or nonstick skillet or griddle over medium-high heat; when a drop of water skips across it before evaporating, it's ready. Melt some butter in the pan, and, using a tablespoon, scoop up a bit of batter and pour it into the pan. Cook as many pancakes at once as will fit comfortably, turning them when they are brown. The total cooking time is less than 5 minutes per pancake.

Serve immediately, sprinkled with confectioners' sugar.

notes from our test kitchen

- We use whole milk.
- Having the eggs and milk at room temperature prevents the melted butter from separating from the batter.
- Once you add the flour to the batter, do not stir any more than necessary to combine the ingredients or the pancakes will be tough and heavy.
- Be careful not to overbeat the whites (they should be smooth and glossy, not dry or clumpy), which makes them difficult to fold into the batter.
- Don't be shy with the butter when cooking the pancakes. They should cook quickly, over fairly high heat, in plenty of butter.

tip

BANANA PANCAKES

In *Bon Appétit,* Chef Bill Rohling of the Old Rittenhouse Inn on Lake Superior tells how to make banana pancakes. Just top each pancake before you flip it with 4 banana slices, then flip. The bananas will caramelize a bit as the pancakes cook on the other side.

SOURCE: *Rick & Lanie's Excellent Kitchen Adventures*
by Rick Bayless and Lanie Bayless
with Deann Groen Bayless

COOK: Bob Hoogstoel

bob's dutch baby

DUTCH BABIES ARE PUFFY OVEN PANCAKES related to popovers, and they come from the American Northwest, not Holland. But when Rick Bayless and his daughter, Lanie, went traveling all over the world looking for good food, they found this recipe in Holland, courtesy of a Dutch friend. It's a far cry from the usual Dutch baby in a skillet, good though that is.

This dish bakes in a dramatic bowl shape, which you then fill with seasonal fruit, drizzle with syrup, and garnish with confectioners' sugar. It's a pretty amazing sight for a special breakfast, as on Mother's Day or a birthday. The fruit can be anything from strawberries to mixed berries to peaches and nectarines. Rick Bayless suggests serving it with dollops of lightly sweetened whipped cream or yogurt before dusting with the sugar.

serves 4 generously

- 5 tablespoons unsalted butter
- 3/4 cup all-purpose flour
- 3/4 cup milk
- 3 large eggs
- 1/2 teaspoon salt
- 3 cups diced fresh fruit
- Confectioners' sugar for dusting
- Syrup, such as maple or blueberry, for serving

Place a rack in the upper third of the oven and preheat to 450 degrees.

Put the butter in a 12-inch skillet with an ovenproof handle. Set in the oven for 5 minutes to melt the butter completely—it's OK if it begins to brown.

While the butter melts, put the flour in a large bowl. Add the milk, eggs, and salt. Beat until smooth, using a whisk, large spoon, or hand-held electric mixer.

Pour the batter into the hot pan and return to the oven. Bake for 15 to 20 minutes, or until the sides are puffed up and dark golden brown. Remove from the oven. Loosen the Dutch baby from the sides and bottom of the skillet, then slide onto a serving plate. Pile the fruit in the center and sprinkle with confectioners' sugar. Cut into wedges. Pass warm syrup to pour on top.

note from our test kitchen

- The Dutch baby is also great in winter, made with mixed berries and diced mango.

SOURCE: *Health*
STORY BY Maureen Callahan
COOK: Maureen Callahan

english muffin strata with tomato, sausage, and fontina

As common as English muffins are, we had never given much thought to using them in recipes—that is, until this year, when they seemed to turn up everywhere. And why not? They offer a nice chewiness and a touch of sweetness, and they become wonderfully crunchy when toasted. Here they provide the basis for a cheerful breakfast casserole crowded with sausage, red onion, mushrooms, basil, tomato, and two kinds of cheese.

For a holiday breakfast, assemble the ingredients before you go to bed and then slide the dish into the oven in the morning. Because strata contains eggs, sausage, and bread, it is a complete meal on its own, but a little fruit salad is a welcome accompaniment.

serves 9

- 8 ounces turkey Italian sausage (see note), casings removed
- 2 teaspoons olive oil
- 2 cups coarsely chopped portobello mushroom caps, gills removed
- 1 cup thinly sliced red onion
- 3/4 cup low-fat milk (see note)
- 8 large eggs
- 4 large egg whites
- 3/4 teaspoon kosher salt
- 1/2 teaspoon freshly ground black pepper
- 4 whole wheat English muffins, split, toasted, and cut into 1/2-inch cubes
- 3/4 cup (3 ounces) grated fontina cheese
- 1/3 cup thinly sliced fresh basil
- 2 plum tomatoes (about 1/4 pound), thinly sliced
- 1/2 cup freshly grated Parmesan cheese

Cook the sausage in a large nonstick skillet over medium-high heat for 6 minutes, or until browned, stirring to crumble. Remove from the skillet, drain well, and set aside.

Heat 1 teaspoon of the oil in the skillet over medium heat. Add the mushrooms and sauté until lightly browned, about 5 minutes. Remove from the skillet with a slotted spoon and set aside.

Heat the remaining 1 teaspoon oil in the skillet over medium-high heat. Add the onion and sauté until softened, about 5 minutes.

Combine the milk, eggs, egg whites, salt, and pepper in a large bowl, stirring well with a whisk.

Coat a 13-x-9-inch baking dish with nonstick cooking spray. Spread the English muffin cubes evenly in the bottom of the dish. Top with the sausage, mushrooms, onion, and fontina cheese. Sprinkle with the basil. Pour the egg mixture evenly over the top. Cover with plastic wrap and chill for 2 hours or overnight.

Preheat the oven to 325 degrees.

Uncover the baking dish. Arrange the tomato slices in a single layer on top and sprinkle with the Parmesan. Bake until set, about 40 minutes (see note). Serve warm.

notes from our test kitchen

- If turkey sausage is not your thing, make this with regular pork Italian sausage. The casserole won't have the same low-fat profile, of course. You can also use whole milk and butter for the pan (in place of nonstick cooking spray).
- A nonstick skillet is essential if you hope to get away with the scant amount of olive oil used for sautéing. If you don't have a large one, you'll need to add more olive oil to prevent the mushrooms and onions from sticking and charring.
- To get the proper texture, split English muffins with a fork. Halving them with a knife won't give you the nooks and crannies that turn so marvelously crunchy when the muffins are toasted.
- We found that the casserole can take closer to 1 hour and 10 minutes to set, so allow time for this.

SOURCE: *New York Times Magazine*

STORY BY Jonathan Reynolds

COOK: Jonathan Reynolds

new england spider cake

DON'T WORRY: this is a breakfast semi-corn bread sans spiders—*spider* is a colloquial name for the cast-iron skillet it's baked in. What's especially unusual about this cake is that it indulges in a cup of cream, delivered right into its center before it goes into the oven. It's not unlike the creamy corn bread favored by novelist Marjorie Kinnan Rawlings and popularized by Marion Cunningham, but it has less cornmeal and more flour.

People *love* spider cake. It's worth buying a 12-inch cast-iron skillet if you don't already own one to make this breakfast treat for your overnight guests or your sweetie or your kids. It's a creamy, corny meal in itself, with some juice and coffee or tea.

serves 8

- 2 cups milk
- 4 teaspoons white vinegar
- 1 cup all-purpose flour
- 3/4 cup yellow cornmeal, preferably stone-ground
- 3/4 cup sugar
- 1/2 teaspoon baking soda
- 1/2 teaspoon salt
- 2 large eggs
- 2 tablespoons butter
- 1 cup heavy cream

Preheat the oven to 350 degrees.

Combine the milk and vinegar in a bowl and set aside to sour. In another bowl, combine the flour, cornmeal, sugar, baking soda, and salt. Whisk the eggs into the soured milk. Stir into the dry ingredients and set the batter aside.

Melt the butter in a 12-inch cast-iron skillet and pour in the batter. Pour the cream into the center and slide the skillet into the oven. Bake until golden brown on top, about 45 minutes. Slice into wedges and serve warm.

notes from our test kitchen

- You can use 2 cups buttermilk instead of souring the regular milk.
- People are going to want to put something on the spider cake, whether butter and honey, jam, or just butter, so be prepared. But it's perfect on its own.

tip

If spider cake inspires you to buy a cast-iron skillet, you'll need to season it when it comes out of the box (unless you buy a preseasoned one). Here's how Sharon Kramis and Julie Kramis Hearne, the authors of *The Cast Iron Skillet Cookbook*, tell us to treat a new skillet: Scrub the pan thoroughly with mild detergent to remove the layer of wax meant to keep it from rusting. Dry. Coat the pan lightly with vegetable shortening, such as Crisco, inside and out. Place the pan upside down on a baking sheet on a rack in the middle of the oven. Bake for 1 hour at 350 degrees. Make sure you have the fan on, as the pan will smoke. Turn off the heat and let the pan cool completely in the oven. Use a newly seasoned pan only to fry bacon or other fatty foods. After a few uses, it will develop its own nonstick patina. Remember never to wash a cast-iron pan with soap; just hot water. If you need to scrub it, use coarse salt and never anything metal.

SOURCE: *The Berry Bible* by Janie Hibler

COOK: Janie Hibler

raspberry almond coffeecake

HERE'S A CHARMING ALTERNATIVE to the usual coffeecake: a low, buttery cake with a whiff of almond, studded with red raspberries, sprinkled with a few chopped almonds, and modestly glazed. It's sweet, moist, and delicate, and it calls for a strong cup of coffee or pot of tea. You use frozen raspberries, which means you can make this year round.

Marcona almonds are large, flat Spanish almonds prized for their delicate sweet flavor, almost juicy interior, and satisfying crunch. Referred to as the queen of almonds, they are available in specialty stores and some supermarkets or on-line and come either raw or fried and sprinkled with sea salt. For snacking, fried Marcona almonds can't be beat. If you haven't tasted them, use this as an excuse to buy a big bag. You can also make this coffeecake with regular almonds (see note).

serves 10

COFFEECAKE

- 8 tablespoons (1 stick) unsalted butter, melted (warm, not hot)
- 2 large eggs (see note)
- 1¼ cups sugar
- 1 teaspoon almond extract
- 1½ cups self-rising flour
- 1½ teaspoons baking powder
- 1 pint (2 cups) frozen raspberries
- 2 tablespoons coarsely chopped Marcona almonds (see notes)

GLAZE

- ¼ cup confectioners' sugar
- 1 tablespoon cream or milk
- ¼ teaspoon almond extract

TO MAKE THE COFFEECAKE:

Preheat the oven to 350 degrees. Grease a 10-inch springform pan.

Put the melted butter, eggs, sugar, and almond extract in a large bowl and beat well. Add the flour and baking powder and stir until smooth. Spread two thirds of the batter in the bottom of the pan. It will be very thick, so you will have to use the back of a spoon or your fingers. Sprinkle the raspberries over the top.

Using a teaspoon, drop the remaining batter over the berries as evenly as possible—the berries will not be completely covered—and sprinkle with the chopped almonds. The batter will rise as it cooks, covering most of the berries.

Bake for 40 to 45 minutes, or until a toothpick inserted in the center of the cake comes out clean. Cool in the pan for 5 minutes.

TO MAKE THE GLAZE:

Stir the confectioners' sugar, cream or milk, and almond extract together until smooth in a small bowl and drizzle over the warm cake. Remove the sides of the pan and serve the cake warm or at room temperature.

notes from our test kitchen

- Marcona almonds are sold both raw and fried and salted. If you buy the latter, use them as they are; otherwise lightly toast them as follows. Arrange them in a single layer on a rimmed baking sheet and toast in a 350-degree oven until they are lightly browned and fragrant, about 10 minutes.
- In place of Marcona almonds, you can use whole or slivered regular almonds. Toast them the same way.
- It helps if the eggs are close to room temperature. If they are right out of the refrigerator, they will harden the melted butter.

tip

Marcona almonds have been imported to the United States only as of the twenty-first century. Traditionally fried in olive oil and sprinkled with sea salt, these crunchy, sweet nuts are excellent with drinks or sherry. Unfortunately, many of the Marcona almonds imported today are fried in olive oil and then packed in sunflower oil, which dramatically detracts from their flavor and health benefits. You can also find commercial brands of Marcona almonds that have been fried in peanut oil, which, although a step up from sunflower oil, is still inferior to olive oil.

Our recommendation is to buy raw Marcona almonds and fry them yourself. (Pour about 1/4 inch extra-virgin olive oil into a skillet and fry them, stirring, over medium-high heat until toasty. Remove with a slotted spoon and sprinkle with sea salt.) Order Marcona almonds from www.tienda.com or www.spanishtable.com.

SOURCE: *Bon Appétit*

STORY BY Kristine Kidd

COOK: Kristine Kidd

rosemary and mustard breakfast sausages

WHILE THERE'S NOTHING WRONG with breakfast sausage links, they are made immeasurably better when you slip them from their casings and season them with sautéed onion, fresh rosemary, and whole-grain mustard. In no time at all you've turned something ordinary into something quite special. Make these sausage patties the day before, and all you do in the morning is pop them in the oven while the coffee's brewing. Any late sleepers will be lured from their slumbers.

makes 12

- 1 tablespoon olive oil
- 1 medium onion, finely chopped
- 1 teaspoon chopped fresh rosemary, plus sprigs for garnish
- 1 14-ounce package breakfast sausage links, casings removed
- 2 teaspoons whole-grain mustard
- Freshly ground black pepper

Heat the oil in a small skillet over medium-high heat. Add the onion and chopped rosemary and sauté until golden, about 10 minutes. Transfer to a medium bowl. Add the sausage, mustard, and a generous amount of pepper. Mix gently. Form into twelve 2-inch-wide patties. Arrange the patties on a rimmed baking sheet. The sausages can be made 1 day ahead and chilled.

Place a rack in the lowest position in the oven and preheat to 500 degrees.

Bake the sausages until just cooked through, about 6 minutes. If the sausages have not browned, broil them for 2 minutes. Transfer them to paper towels to drain, then arrange on a platter. Garnish with the rosemary sprigs and serve.

notes from our test kitchen

- Depending on what else you're serving, count on each person eating 2 or 3 sausage patties.
- Not all breakfast sausage is sold in 14-ounce packages. Buy as close to this amount as you can get. If you find breakfast sausage without casings, that will save you a step.

main dishes

main dishes

sizzled haloumi sandwiches with lime on a summer-day salad

HALOUMI, THE SALTY, mint-flecked sheep's milk cheese of Cyprus, has long been a favorite in England, but it's just beginning to reach our shores. If you've taken a bite of it cold, you may hate it. It's one of those cheeses that squeak, and it's quite rubbery. But Marlena Spieler knows exactly what to do with it, and here it becomes the heart of a great salad–open-faced-sandwich plate. The combination of hot cheese and lime juice is heady. You can serve the sandwiches without the salad.

Look for haloumi in Middle Eastern markets, or substitute panela cheese from a Mexican market.

serves 4

- 1 head Butter, Boston, or Bibb lettuce, trimmed and separated into leaves
- 1 mild white onion, thinly sliced crosswise
- 4 tablespoons extra-virgin olive oil
- 1 teaspoon white wine vinegar
- 3 large ripe tomatoes, cut into wedges
- Salt and freshly ground black pepper
- 1/2 baguette, cut diagonally into twelve 1/2-inch-thick slices
- 12 ounces haloumi, cut into 1/2-inch-thick slices
- 2 limes, cut into wedges (or about 2 tablespoons fresh lime juice)
- Pinch of dried oregano

Preheat the broiler.

Toss together the lettuce and onion in a large bowl, then dress with 2 tablespoons of the oil and the vinegar. Divide among four plates and garnish each with the tomato wedges. Sprinkle the salads with salt and pepper and set aside.

Brush the baguette slices with some of the oil, place on a baking sheet, and broil lightly on both sides. Set aside.

Arrange the haloumi on a baking sheet and brush with some oil. Broil on one side until browned in spots, then remove. Turn over each slice of cheese and place on top of a toast. Brush with oil again and broil until hot and lightly browned in spots.

Place 3 toasts on each salad and squeeze lime juice over the haloumi, letting a little drip down onto the salad. Sprinkle with oregano and serve immediately.

SOURCE: *The Tomato Festival Cookbook* by Lawrence Davis-Hollander

COOK: Jody Adams

spaghetti with slow-roasted cherry tomatoes, basil, and parmesan cheese

JODY ADAMS, the award-winning chef-owner of Rialto restaurant in Cambridge, Massachusetts, and the author of *In the Hands of a Chef,* is best known for her bold interpretations of traditional Mediterranean dishes. When we heard that this was one of her favorite meals to cook at home, we took note.

Now that we've made it countless times ourselves, we can see why. In the summer months, when local cherry tomatoes are at their peak, there's no better way to do them justice than slow-roasting them to concentrate their natural sweetness and caramelize their fresh juices. In the off-season, when all we can find are the ordinary supermarket varieties, this technique transforms them into a rich-tasting, sweet tomato "sauce." Spaghetti and red sauce never looked or tasted so good.

serves 4

- 1/4 cup extra-virgin olive oil, plus about 1/4 cup for roasting
- 1 large white onion, cut into 1/2-inch dice
- 6 garlic cloves, smashed and peeled
- 18 fresh basil leaves, plus 1/4 cup cut into thin ribbons (see note)
- 1/8 teaspoon crushed red pepper flakes
- 48 ripe cherry or grape tomatoes, rinsed and dried (see note)
- 3 teaspoons kosher salt
- 2 teaspoons sugar
- 1 pound spaghetti
- 2 cups lightly packed arugula (see note)
- 1/2 cup finely grated Parmesan cheese

Preheat the oven to 250 degrees.

Heat 1/4 cup of the oil in a large skillet over medium heat. Add the onion and garlic and cook, stirring occasionally, until tender, about 5 minutes. Remove from the heat. Add the whole basil leaves and red pepper flakes and stir well.

Toss the tomatoes with 1 teaspoon of the salt and the sugar and place in a roasting pan (see note). The pan should be large enough to hold them in a single layer. If they won't fit, use another roasting pan and more oil. Spoon the onion mixture over the tomatoes. Add enough oil to come halfway up the tomatoes.

Roast until the tomatoes are tender but not falling apart, about 3 hours. Stir once, gently, during the roasting. You can roast the tomatoes up to 6 hours ahead of time.

Bring a large pot of water with the remaining 2 teaspoons salt to a boil. Add the spaghetti and stir constantly until the water returns to a boil. Cook until the pasta is al dente, about 7 minutes.

Meanwhile, heat the tomatoes with the onions and oil in a large saucepan over low heat. When the pasta is done, drain it and transfer to the saucepan with the tomatoes. Add the arugula. Toss well. Add the basil ribbons and toss again.

Serve immediately in warm shallow bowls with Parmesan sprinkled over the top.

notes from our test kitchen

- It's best to wait to cut the basil into thin ribbons until just before you're ready to add it to the sauce. Cut up in advance, the basil will darken. See the tip.
- If you haven't bought a fresh jar of crushed red pepper flakes in a while, add an extra pinch; the heat mellows over time.
- You may have tomatoes that are smaller than the ones called for here. An easier way to measure is by volume: figure 2 heaping pints of tomatoes.
- If you can't find any good-tasting arugula, substitute baby spinach.
- Ideally, the roasting pan should accommodate the tomatoes in a relatively snug single layer; if they are spread too far apart, you'll need to add too much oil to come halfway up the sides of the tomatoes.

tip

According to Anne Willan in *The Good Cook*, thin slicing is better than chopping for leaves like basil, arugula, and lettuce, because it's less likely to bruise them. Begin by separating the leaves from the stem (or from the head in the case of lettuce). Wash and dry them thoroughly. Then stack the leaves neatly and roll the pile tightly —imagine rolling up a big fat cigar. Using a large chef's knife, slice across the roll to make fine or coarse strips.

SOURCE: *Italian Easy*
by Rose Gray and Ruth Rogers

COOKS: Rose Gray and Ruth Rogers

tagliatelle with crème fraîche and arugula

IN THE TIME IT WOULD TAKE to extol the virtues of this remarkable recipe, you could nearly have dinner on the table. Aside from a little zesting (zip-zip with a Microplane grater) and squeezing a couple of lemons, there's really nothing to it. Stir together the lemon and crème fraîche, chop the arugula, boil up the pasta, toss the whole thing together, top with cheese, and presto, a spectacular meal. The tart lemon balances the rich cream, the arugula adds freshness, and the resulting pasta is about as sexy and sublime as you could want dinner to be. This also makes an elegant first course for a more elaborate meal.

This streamlined recipe comes from the dynamic duo behind London's phenomenally successful River Café. Known for cooking with imagination and panache, Rose Gray and Ruth Rogers set out to show us that first-rate food doesn't have to be an ordeal to prepare. You'll hear no argument from us!

serves about 4 (see note)

- Salt
- 2 lemons
- 5 ounces arugula leaves
- 5 ounces Parmesan cheese
- 1 cup crème fraîche
- Freshly ground black pepper
- 1 pound fresh egg tagliatelle (see note)

Bring a large pot of salted water to a boil.

Finely grate the lemon zest and squeeze the juice from both lemons. Coarsely chop the arugula. Grate the Parmesan.

Put the crème fraîche in a medium bowl, stir in the lemon juice and zest, and season with salt and pepper.

Cook the tagliatelle in the boiling water until al dente, drain, and return to the pot. Pour the crème fraîche sauce over it and add the arugula and half the Parmesan. Toss to combine.

Serve immediately with the remaining Parmesan.

notes from our test kitchen

- If you're serving this as a main course, expect 1 pound fresh pasta to serve 4; as a starter course, figure 6.
- Tagliatelle are long, flat, fresh egg noodles. Imagine fettuccine but a bit wider. Fresh tagliatelle can be hard to find. You have several options. You can make your own pasta. Or find another fresh pasta shape that you like—keeping in mind that wide, flat noodles are best for creamy sauces. Since traditional Italian dried pastas do not contain eggs, you won't get the same silky texture using dried, but it will still be quite good. We sometimes make this with those big bags of wide egg noodles and love the way it comes out.

SOURCE: *Cooking New American* by the editors of *Fine Cooking*

COOK: Daphne Zepos

fusilli with feta and lemon caper pesto

WE'RE THE FIRST TO ADMIT that we often overlook fusilli, the familiar corkscrew-shaped pasta. Maybe it's because it shows up so often on low-rent salad bars drenched in bad vinaigrette. Or maybe its whimsical shape seems too childish for serious cooking. But here's a recipe that reminds us exactly what makes fusilli one of the great pasta shapes of all time—pestolike sauces cling beautifully to the little spirals, and any vegetables get nicely tangled up with the noodles so nothing sinks to the bottom of the bowl.

Aside from the fresh spinach and the feta, everything in this dish is pretty much a pantry staple, so this is an ideal weeknight supper. In the time it takes to cook the pasta, the tangy, lemony pesto sauce comes together in the blender (or in a mortar if you're so inclined). Once the pasta is cooked, a little of the cooking water goes into the pesto to thin it to a creamy consistency.

The recipe comes from Daphne Zepos, a world-renowned cheese expert at New York City's Artisanal Cheese Center. Not surprisingly, given what she does for a living, Zepos stresses the importance of using only good feta for this dish.

serves 3 or 4

PASTA

- Kosher salt
- 8 ounces fusilli
- 1 bunch fresh spinach (10 ounces), stems cut off, leaves washed well but not dried

PESTO

- 1 small garlic clove, or to taste
- 2–3 anchovy fillets, rinsed and patted dry
- 1 tablespoon capers (preferably salt-packed), soaked briefly and rinsed
- 1 1-inch-long strip lemon zest, minced
- 2 tablespoons crumbled feta
- 1/4 cup coarsely chopped fresh flat-leaf parsley
- 2–3 fresh basil leaves (optional)
- 1 tablespoon fresh lemon juice
- 1/4 cup extra-virgin olive oil
- Salt and freshly ground black pepper

- 2/3 cup crumbled feta (4 ounces)

TO MAKE THE PASTA:

Bring a pot of water to a boil and add the salt and pasta. Cook until al dente. Reserve about 1/2 cup of the cooking water, then drain the pasta. Don't wash the pot.

Meanwhile, put the wet spinach in a large skillet over medium heat. Add a dash of salt, cover, and cook for 3 to 4 minutes, or until the spinach wilts but is still bright green. Remove the pan from the heat, keeping the lid on.

TO MAKE THE PESTO:

Put all the ingredients except the feta in a blender and blend until the pesto is creamy. Or add the ingredients one at a time to a mortar, pounding with the pestle until well mashed and blended before adding the next ingredient. Thin the pesto with the reserved cooking water to get the consistency of runny cream; you probably won't need the entire 1/2 cup.

Return the pasta to the pot. Add the spinach (drain any liquid left in the pan) and the pesto, stirring well to coat the pasta. Stir in the 2/3 cup feta and serve immediately.

notes from our test kitchen

- This makes a light supper if there are four people at the table. We're more apt to make it when there are only three of us.
- Buy feta only in bricks or wedges, and stay away from the precrumbled or flavored ones. Feta from Greece, France, Israel, and Bulgaria tends to be reliably good.

SOURCE: *Four Seasons Pasta* by Janet Fletcher

COOK: Janet Fletcher after Paul Bertolli

double spinach fettuccine with butter and parmesan

NO GIMMICKS, no extra steps, no exotic ingredients—just a straightforward dish of spinach fettuccine tossed with fresh spinach, sweet butter, and Parmesan. And we're not talking about mild-tasting, prewashed baby spinach but the real stuff—dark crinkly leaves with good earthy flavor. You drop the spinach into the boiling pasta pot at the last minute, so the leaves cook along with the noodles and everything is done at once.

If you don't have a good source of fresh spinach fettuccine, you can substitute plain fresh pasta. The dish won't be quite as spinachy, but it will be really good.

serves 4 to 6

- Salt
- 1 pound fresh spinach fettuccine (see above)
- 1½–2 pounds fresh spinach (not baby spinach), thick stems removed
- 5 tablespoons unsalted butter, cut into 10 pieces
- Freshly ground black pepper
- ⅔ cup freshly grated Parmesan cheese

Bring a large pot of salted water to a boil over high heat. Add the pasta and boil until it is about 1 minute shy of al dente.

Add the spinach and stir it down into the pot to wilt.

When the spinach is completely wilted, scoop out and reserve 1 cup of the cooking water, then drain the pasta and spinach and return them to the warm pot. Add the butter and salt and pepper to taste, then toss well. Add ½ cup of the cheese and toss again, moistening with some of the reserved pasta water as needed.

Divide among warm bowls, topping each serving with some of the remaining cheese. Serve immediately.

SOURCE: *Rome, at Home* by Suzanne Dunaway

COOK: Suzanne Dunaway

rigatoni alla toto

TOTO IS AN AFFORDABLE TRATTORIA in the center of Rome that turns out unassuming and delicious meals like this meaty pasta. Make it when you're craving something soothing and satisfying that won't tax you. It's one of those beautifully adaptable dishes that are quick enough for a weeknight yet elegant enough for your best company. While the creamy sauce simmers, you can have the salad made, the table set, and the wine uncorked.

serves 4

- 3 tablespoons extra-virgin olive oil
- 1 small onion, finely chopped
- 1 pound sweet Italian sausage, with or without fennel, casings removed
- 1 cup dry white wine
- A few fresh basil leaves
- Pinch of ground fennel seed, if using plain sausage (see note)
- 1 1/2 cups heavy cream
- Salt
- 1 pound rigatoni
- 1/2 cup grated Parmigiano-Reggiano

Heat the oil in a large skillet over medium heat. Add the onion and cook until translucent, 3 to 4 minutes. Add the sausage, brown it on all sides, then add the wine and cook for 1 minute. Add the basil, ground fennel (if using), and cream and simmer over low heat for 20 minutes, or until the sausage is cooked through.

Meanwhile, bring a large pot of salted water to a boil. Cook the rigatoni in the boiling water until al dente. Drain well and toss with the sauce. Serve immediately with the Parmigiano-Reggiano.

note from our test kitchen

Grind whole fennel seed by crushing it with a mortar and pestle or by chopping it on a cutting board with a large knife.

SOURCE: *Simple French Recipes for the Home Cook* by Guy Savoy

COOK: Guy Savoy

overnight macaroni and cheese

THE EPONYMOUS GUY SAVOY, a three-starred Michelin Paris restaurant, is an essential stop for globe-trotting gourmands. Like all great chefs, Savoy is always asked for uncomplicated recipes for home cooks—but unlike almost all the rest of them, he really does cook this way.

Take macaroni and cheese, for instance, a dish the French are quite partial to. In Savoy's hands, there's no cream sauce, nutty Gruyère replaces cheddar, the pasta is presented in a thin layer, and the top is gloriously crisp. All this is accomplished by simplifying the recipe and giving the pasta an overnight soak in cream and milk. You spend 10 minutes putting it together and bake it when you're ready to serve it. We guarantee raves for this elegant, sophisticated mac and cheese, still luxurious but with a delicate texture.

More like a gratin than a casserole, it makes a great light supper when paired with a salad. To make it the grand centerpiece of a heartier meal, double the recipe. We also love it as a luxurious side dish for steaks and roasts.

serves 4

- Salt
- 8 ounces elbow macaroni
- 1 1/4 cups milk
- 2 cups heavy cream
- 1 cup grated Gruyère or Emmental cheese
- Freshly ground black pepper

The day before you plan to serve the gratin, bring a large pot of salted water to a boil. Add the macaroni and cook for 4 minutes, or until very al dente. Drain and cool under cold running water.

Combine the milk, cream, and 1/2 cup of the cheese in a large bowl. Toss in the pasta and mix well. Season with salt and pepper to taste. Cover with plastic wrap and refrigerate for 24 hours. The pasta will absorb the milk mixture and expand.

When ready to serve, bring the macaroni mixture to room temperature.

Preheat the oven to 400 degrees.

Place the pasta in a 2-quart baking dish. Sprinkle the remaining 1/2 cup cheese on top. Bake for 15 to 20 minutes, or until golden and crusty. Serve immediately.

notes from our test kitchen

- Choose a good imported pasta made of durum wheat, which will be less pasty and have more character.
- The degree to which the macaroni absorbs the milk-and-cream bath varies greatly. If there seems to be a great deal of creamy milk in the pasta mixture when you're ready to bake it, pour it off and measure it. You can return 1/2 cup to the pasta, but any more will make it too wet.

SOURCE: *Eleanora's Kitchen*
by Eleanora Russo Scarpetta with Sarah Belk King

COOK: **Eleanora Russo Scarpetta**

neapolitan spaghetti pie

THIS IS PERHAPS the ultimate homey Italian dish, one you'd never see on a restaurant menu. Leftover pasta is tossed with a lot of eggs, soppressata, mozzarella, pecorino, and a little cream to make a rustic southern Italian pasta pie that's a particular hit with kids. Scarpetta's mother used to make the pie in a skillet on top of the stove and flip it to crisp the pasta on both sides. The oven method here is easier—in fact, this is one of the easiest recipes in the book.

Scarpetta notes that the pie is a good buffet item and also travels well, which makes it a great party dish. You can even make it up to 5 days ahead and reheat it or serve it at room temperature.

serves 10 to 12

- Light olive oil (see note)
- 6 large eggs, lightly beaten
- 1/4 cup heavy cream
- 1 pound dry-aged or processed whole milk mozzarella, grated (see note)
- 12 ounces hot soppressata sausage, cut into 1/4-inch dice
- 1 cup (1/4 pound) finely grated pecorino cheese
- 1 teaspoon dried parsley (optional; see tip)
- Salt to taste
- 1/2 teaspoon freshly ground black pepper, plus more to taste
- 6 cups cooked spaghetti (from 1 1/4 pounds dried pasta)

Preheat the oven to 375 degrees.

Brush the bottom and sides of a 10-inch round (3-inch-deep) cake pan with the olive oil. Line the bottom of the pan with parchment paper and set aside.

Combine everything but the spaghetti in a large bowl and stir well. Add the pasta and stir to combine. Pour the mixture into the prepared pan.

Cover the pan with foil and bake for 40 minutes. Remove the foil and bake for 20 minutes more, or until lightly browned and crisp.

Cool on a rack for about 10 minutes. Run a knife around the edge of the pan to loosen the pie. Invert to unmold, discarding the parchment paper. Place a plate or platter on top of the pie, and invert again. Cut into wedges and serve warm or at room temperature.

notes from our test kitchen

- You can use regular olive oil, of course, instead of light.
- The tasty handmade mozzarella sold in brine or water is too wet to grate for this dish. In an Italian market you may find dry-aged mozzarella; if not, use supermarket mozzarella.

tips

Frying cooked pasta is a great way to use leftovers. In an article in the *Washington Post,* Renée Schettler explained her method. She heats a cast-iron skillet until it is hot but not smoking, adds a little olive oil, and puts in the already sauced pasta (it must be cold or the insides will turn gummy), in clumps if necessary. She cooks it over medium-high heat for at least 2 minutes, or until it is crisp and golden brown, then flips it, in clumps if it's a thick pasta like penne. She cooks it on the other side for about 3 minutes, transfers it to a plate, and sprinkles it with sea salt. It can be topped with more warmed sauce or a couple of cooked eggs, or just served by itself.

Commercial dried parsley is tasteless, but Eleanora Scarpetta is right: home dried has considerable flavor. You can dry almost any green herb at home, including mint, celery, and basil. Tear off the leaves, rinse, and dry thoroughly. Or spread them out on a baking sheet and let them air-dry for 8 hours or overnight. Dry them in a 350-degree oven for 5 to 10 minutes, or until they're crumbly but not brown. You can also dry them more or less instantly in the microwave on the glass turntable on high for 2 to 3 minutes. Hothouse herbs won't be as flavorful as garden herbs, so you may need to use more than a recipe states.

SOURCE: *Food & Wine*
STORY BY Paula Wolfert
COOK: Paula Wolfert

musa's eggplant and lentil stew

BECAUSE COOKBOOK AUTHOR Paula Wolfert has traveled so extensively in the Mediterranean, especially the eastern Mediterranean, and observed thousands of the best cooks plying their trade, it's hard to surprise her. But Musa, the chef at Çiya, a restaurant on the Asian side of Istanbul, astonished her with his repertoire. His food is basic but complexly flavorful and inventive. It's peasant cooking in the hands of a master.

His eggplant and lentil stew is a good example. It's a traditional summer vegetarian meal blessed with a little pomegranate molasses. Layered so the vegetables retain their own flavors and textures, it cooks slowly, without stirring, and it's better if allowed to mellow for a few hours before serving. We've never tasted anything quite like it.

serves 6

- 1 1½-pound long narrow eggplant
- Salt
- ½ cup lentils
- ⅔ cup extra-virgin olive oil
- 1 medium onion, finely chopped
- 2 medium tomatoes, chopped
- 2 long green chiles, such as Anaheims, seeded and coarsely chopped
- 4 medium garlic cloves, minced
- 2 tablespoons chopped fresh mint leaves
- 1 tablespoon tomato paste
- ¼ teaspoon crushed red pepper flakes
- ¼ cup pomegranate molasses (see note)

Partially peel the eggplant so it has lengthwise stripes, then cut it lengthwise into 4 slices. Score each slice on one side in a crosshatch pattern. Cut each slice crosswise into 3 pieces and set on a rimmed baking sheet. Sprinkle with salt and let stand for 1 hour.

Meanwhile, cover the lentils with 2 inches of water in a small saucepan and bring to a boil. Reduce the heat to medium and simmer until tender, about 15 minutes. Drain the lentils.

Coat a small enameled cast-iron casserole with 1 tablespoon of the olive oil. In a medium bowl, toss the onion with the tomatoes, chiles, garlic, mint, tomato paste, red pepper, and 2 teaspoons salt.

Rinse the eggplant and pat dry. Spread ½ cup of the vegetable mixture in the casserole and top with half of the eggplant. Cover with half of the lentils and half of the remaining vegetable mixture. Top with the remaining eggplant, lentils, and vegetables.

Pour the remaining olive oil around the side and over the vegetables, then drizzle with the pomegranate molasses.

Bring the stew to a boil. Reduce the heat to low, cover, and cook until the eggplant is very tender, about 1½ hours. Serve hot, warm, or at room temperature. The stew will keep for 2 days in the refrigerator and its flavor will improve. Bring it to room temperature; if you're serving it warm or hot, reheat it very gently.

note from our test kitchen

Look for pomegranate molasses at Middle Eastern markets. If you can't find it, don't substitute regular molasses. Instead, use the note on page 9 to make pomegranate syrup and just cook it down further into molasses.

pastuccia

(baked polenta with sausage and raisins)

SOME OF THE TASTIEST illustrations of authentic Italian country cooking are the savory polenta casseroles that resourceful cooks fill with all sorts of goodies, from cooked greens and cheese to meats and mushrooms. We can't get enough of this one, made with meaty sausage, salty pancetta, and plump golden raisins. The combination brings out the natural sweetness of the cornmeal, and we're suckers for the way the top comes out all browned, with crunchy bits poking through.

Pastuccia makes a comforting meal accompanied by a mixed salad or green vegetable. You can also serve the pie as a hearty first course (enough for 8 to 10).

serves 6

- 2 tablespoons olive oil or lard, plus more olive oil for drizzling
- 4 ounces pancetta, diced (see note)
- 12 ounces sweet Italian sausage, with or without fennel, casings removed and meat crumbled
- 2 cups polenta (see tip)
- Salt
- About 4 cups boiling water
- 1 cup golden raisins, plumped in hot water and drained
- 3 large egg yolks
- Freshly ground black pepper

Preheat the oven to 375 degrees. Oil or butter a 10-inch-long gratin dish, 12-inch pie dish, or 9-x-12-inch baking dish.

Heat the oil or lard in a large skillet over medium heat. Add the pancetta and sausage and sauté until cooked through but not crisp, 7 to 8 minutes. Remove from the heat.

Combine the polenta and 1 teaspoon salt in a large bowl. Gradually whisk in enough boiling water to make a very thick batter. Add the raisins, three fourths of the pancetta and sausage, the egg yolks, and pepper to taste and mix well. Pour into the prepared dish. Top evenly with the remaining pancetta and sausage, and drizzle with a little olive oil.

Bake until the top is golden and the pancetta and sausage are crisp, about 40 minutes. Transfer to a rack and let cool for 10 minutes, then serve.

note from our test kitchen

Sliced pancetta is too thin to make proper dice. If your market can't cut the slices 1/4 inch thick, you'll want to buy a single chunk and slice and dice it yourself.

tip

Joyce Goldstein notes that the word *polenta* originally referred to porridge made from almost any grain. Today the term is used to describe dishes made from cornmeal. The best polenta is hulled and stone-ground. It comes in fine, medium, and coarse, with medium being the best all-purpose grind. Avoid instant polenta: it lacks the hearty texture of true polenta. The brands that Goldstein recommends are Golden Pheasant, Giusto's, and Molino Sobrino from La Morra. You'll get the sweetest corn flavor from freshly ground polenta. Avoid any polenta that looks as though it's been on the shelf for too long.

SOURCE: *Go Fish*
by Laurent Tourondel and Andrew Friedman
COOK: Laurent Tourondel

foil-baked cod with ginger, orange, and cumin

EVEN THOUGH LAURENT TOURONDEL is one of New York's most highly acclaimed seafood chefs, his fish cookbook avoids "cheffy" preparations requiring long lists of ingredients in favor of straightforward recipes that we make at home on a regular basis. In fact, at first glance, some of his recipes appear so disarmingly plain that we wonder how they could possibly be anything other than ordinary. Tourondel's genius lies in his ability to combine everyday ingredients to create dishes with flavors that soar, and this foil-baked cod is a prime example. The fish steams inside the individual foil packets so that it comes out infused with the taste of orange, ginger, and cumin and swimming in a delicious sauce.

With the spinach cooked along with the cod, this makes a light meal on its own. If there are bigger appetites at your table, offer steamed potatoes or rice on the side. Tourondel likes to serve the fish directly in the aluminum foil because of "the cool, funky look." If you'd rather, slide the fish, spinach, and juices into shallow bowls.

serves 6

- 1½ teaspoons grated fresh ginger
- Juice of 1 orange
- 3 tablespoons olive oil
- 4 cups spinach, tough stems removed, well rinsed
- Fine sea salt and freshly ground black pepper
- 6 5- to 6-ounce cod fillets, preferably Atlantic cod
- ½ teaspoon cumin seeds, toasted (see note)
- ¼ teaspoon crushed red pepper flakes

Preheat the oven to 375 degrees.

Stir together the ginger, orange juice, and olive oil in a small bowl. Set out six 12-x-20-inch rectangles of aluminum foil.

Put some spinach in the center of each piece of foil and season it with salt and pepper. Season the fish with salt and pepper, and lay 1 piece on each bed of spinach. Drizzle the ginger-orange mixture over the fish. Divide the cumin and red pepper flakes among the fillets. Wrap the foil around the fish twice to form a tight package, pressing down on the edges to seal it.

Bake the parcels directly on the baking racks (see note) until the fish is firm and opaque, about 18 minutes. Remove the packages from the oven and place them on plates. Cut them open with a knife and serve.

notes from our test kitchen

- Toast cumin seeds by placing them in a small skillet over medium-low heat. Shake the pan and toast until fragrant and slightly darkened, a few minutes.
- Used in place of cumin, rosemary pairs beautifully with the bright flavors of orange and ginger.
- Putting the packets on baking sheets will slow down the cooking.

tips

In *Food & Wine,* Stephanie Lyness revealed a few of her flavoring tricks for steaming food in foil: add chopped herbs or thinly sliced garlic, onion, or tomatoes, which will steam along with the main ingredient. Precook hard vegetables, such as carrots, before adding them to the pouch. Drizzle over a little olive oil or add a teaspoon of butter for flavor. Splash on wine or citrus juice; it will combine with any liquid the food gives off to make a sauce.

Very fresh cod can be tough and chewy, says British fish guru Rick Stein in *Rick Stein's Complete Seafood.* Most of us won't have the problem of dealing with very fresh cod, but if you do, keep it a day or two before cooking so its enzymes will have a chance to tenderize it.

SOURCE: *Take 6 Ingredients* by Conrad Gallagher

COOK: Conrad Gallagher

broiled salmon with tomato salsa

CONRAD GALLAGHER, a young Michelin-starred Irish chef, presents a brilliant technique that turns out perfectly cooked salmon in almost no time at all. Aside from mixing up a little fresh salsa, you just brush thin slices of salmon with a cilantro-flecked mayonnaise and run them under the broiler, until golden and crispy on the surface and just warmed inside.

For an extra kick, add half a finely chopped chile pepper to the salsa. Serve with a tossed salad and some good bread. It also makes a fine brunch dish.

serves 4 to 6

- 1/4 heaping cup chopped fresh cilantro
- 1 red onion, finely chopped
- 4 plum tomatoes, peeled, seeded, and diced
- Juice of 1 lemon
- Salt and freshly ground black pepper
- 1/2 cup mayonnaise
- 1 1 1/4-pound salmon fillet, skinned and thinly sliced (see note)

To make the salsa, mix 2 heaping tablespoons of the cilantro with the onion, tomatoes, and lemon juice in a medium bowl and season with salt and pepper to taste. Set aside for 30 minutes to allow the flavors to develop.

Preheat the broiler. Lightly brush a rimmed baking sheet with olive oil.

Mix the remaining 2 tablespoons cilantro and the mayonnaise in a small bowl and season with salt and pepper to taste. Arrange the salmon slices on the baking sheet so they overlap. Spread the cilantro mayonnaise on top of the salmon. Broil until the mayonnaise is bubbling and lightly golden and the salmon has just warmed through, 30 seconds to 1 minute.

Serve the salmon and salsa at once on warmed plates (see note).

notes from our test kitchen

- We aim for $^1/_4$- to $^1/_3$-inch-thick slices of salmon. Anything thicker will take longer to cook. It may help to slice the salmon at an angle, like smoked salmon.
- It helps to have a very hot broiler so that you can practically flash-cook the fish. If not, expect it to take closer to 2 minutes.
- When you serve the salmon, the slices will flake apart. Indeed, Chef Gallagher recommends flaking the fish and combining it with the salsa, but we prefer to leave the salmon in larger bits and spoon the salsa on top. A spatula works well to lift the cooked salmon from the baking sheet. You can also present the whole dish on a buffet and let people flake off as much as they like.

SOURCE: *Kinkead's Cookbook* by Bob Kinkead

COOK: Bob Kinkead

scandinavian salmon stew with mushrooms and dill

KINKEAD'S BILLS ITSELF as Washington, D.C.'s premier seafood restaurant, and with reason. Chef Bob Kinkead presents his food in such an ordinary-person way that you know it's going to work in your kitchen, too. That's the case with this sublime salmon stew, which he created to use leftover trimmings of salmon fillets.

There are four kinds of onion flavor in this chowder: onion, shallots, leek, and chives. As in so many good chowder dishes, a little smoky bacon works magic. The stew is rich but not overwhelming, and it's hard to imagine a better meal to come home to after a cold winter's day outdoors. The only caveat is that you can't make it ahead.

serves 6

- 12 ounces salmon fillets (preferably Atlantic), skinned and pin bones removed
- 3 cups fish stock or 2 cups clam juice (see note)
- 1/4 cup dry white wine
- 3 bacon strips
- 3 tablespoons butter
- 12 button mushrooms, quartered (about 2 cups)
- 2 shallots, minced (about 1/4 cup)
- 2 cups heavy cream
- 2 Yukon Gold or other waxy potatoes, peeled and diced (about 2 cups)
- 1 small yellow onion, finely diced (about 1 cup)
- 1 small leek (white part only), well washed and minced
- 1 teaspoon sea salt, plus more to taste
- 1/2 teaspoon cracked white pepper, plus more to taste
- 2 tablespoons chopped fresh dill
- 2 tablespoons chopped fresh chives for garnish

Cut the salmon into 2-x-1/2-x-1/2-inch pieces and refrigerate. Combine the fish stock or clam juice and wine in a medium saucepan and reduce by one third over medium heat. Cook the bacon in a skillet over medium-high heat until crispy. Transfer to paper towels to drain. Add 1 tablespoon of the butter to the bacon fat. Add the mushrooms and half of the shallots and sauté until well browned, 3 to 4 minutes or longer. Transfer to a bowl.

Combine the reduced wine mixture and cream in a large saucepan and bring to a boil over high heat. Add the potatoes and cook for about 5 minutes, or until tender. Strain out the potatoes and return the cream mixture to a boil to reduce further.

Melt the remaining 2 tablespoons butter in a large saucepan over medium-high heat. Add the onion, leek, and remaining shallots and cook until softened, just a few minutes. Stir in the mushroom mixture, bacon, potatoes, and reduced cream mixture. Add the salmon. Reduce the heat to medium and simmer for 1 minute. Add salt and white pepper. Stir in the dill.

Divide the stew among six warm soup plates, garnish with chives, and serve.

note from our test kitchen

If you choose the clam juice option, you may find that you don't have enough liquid. Just add some water, as much as 1 cup.

SOURCE: *Food & Wine*
STORY BY Ratha Tep
COOK: Daniel Orr

hoosier chicken with potato chip crust

DANIEL ORR is a well-known peripatetic chef who made his name in New York City, but his heart remains in Hoosier country, where his family still lives. For Independence Day, he likes to be home in Indiana, whipping up great summer food that's based on classics with a sophisticated twist.

We're nuts about anything that includes potato chips as an ingredient (not to mention mayonnaise), so we were captivated by this recipe. The five-spice powder is an intriguing addition. This is ideal picnic or backyard food. The chicken travels well, since it's good either warm or at room temperature. You can also thinly slice the chicken and serve it over salad greens.

serves 8

- 1/2 cup mayonnaise
- 2 teaspoons pure chile powder (such as ancho)
- 1 teaspoon five-spice powder
- 1 teaspoon finely grated lemon zest
- 1 teaspoon coarsely ground black pepper
- Kosher salt
- 2 1/2 pounds thin chicken cutlets (see note)
- 1 5 1/2-ounce bag potato chips, finely crushed
- 3 tablespoons unsalted butter

Preheat the oven to 225 degrees.

Mix the mayonnaise, chile powder, five-spice powder, lemon zest, pepper, and a generous pinch of salt in a medium bowl. Add the chicken and turn to coat.

Spread the potato chips on a sheet of wax paper. Coat the chicken with the crumbs, pressing them to adhere.

Melt 1 tablespoon of the butter in a large skillet over medium-high heat. When the foam subsides, add one third of the chicken cutlets and cook, turning once, until browned and cooked through, about 5 minutes.

Transfer the chicken to a baking sheet to keep warm in the oven while you cook the remaining cutlets in the remaining butter. Serve warm or at room temperature.

note from our test kitchen

Sometimes you see chicken cutlets in the meat case at the supermarket and sometimes you don't. If you can't find them, get boneless chicken breasts and pound them a bit flat. With a good sharp knife, cut through the cutlets horizontally, trying to keep them as even on both sides of the cut as possible. This is a lot easier than it sounds.

SOURCE: *Fine Cooking*
STORY BY Jennifer Martinkus and Derrin Davis
COOKS: Jennifer Martinkus and Derrin Davis

crispy chicken breasts stuffed with spinach and goat cheese

IF WE HAD A NICKEL for every time we are lured into making a dish because of a tempting photograph only to find that the real deal doesn't come close, well, we'd have a mighty big pile of nickels. Eternally hopeful, we keep trying, and every so often we find a recipe that is as appealing—or more so—in reality as it appeared on the page. The crisp, juicy chicken breasts oozing a cheesy filling won us over.

The recipe takes a little time—the filling must cool before the breasts are stuffed, and the chicken needs to chill after breading—but the instructions make it a cinch.

serves 4

FILLING

2 tablespoons olive oil
1 cup finely chopped shallots (6–8 medium shallots)
8 ounces fresh spinach, stemmed and chopped (7 lightly packed cups)
1/4 cup dry white wine
3 1/2 ounces fresh goat cheese, crumbled
1/4 teaspoon kosher salt
1/4 teaspoon freshly ground black pepper

CHICKEN

4 large boneless, skinless chicken breast halves (8–9 ounces each)
3/4 cup all-purpose flour
2 large eggs
1 1/2 cups fresh bread crumbs
Kosher salt and freshly ground black pepper
2/3 cup olive oil

TO MAKE THE FILLING:

Heat the oil in a large skillet over medium to medium-low heat. Add the shallots and cook slowly until softened and aromatic, 8 to 10 minutes. Increase the heat to medium and add the spinach (in batches, if necessary) and wine. Cook, stirring frequently, until the spinach is wilted and the liquid has evaporated, 3 to 4 minutes. Remove from the heat and stir in the goat cheese, salt, and pepper. Let cool to room temperature.

TO STUFF THE CHICKEN:

If the chicken breasts have tenderloins attached, remove them and save for another use. Trim and pat the breasts dry.

To make a pocket on the thicker side of each breast, cut into the breast with a sharp boning or utility knife about 1/2 inch from one end. Create a pocket, slicing to within about 1/4 inch of the other side (see note).

Stuff each breast with about one quarter of the filling, distributing it evenly throughout the pocket and to the ends. Press on the top of each breast to close the pocket.

Line up three wide shallow dishes. Fill the first with the flour. In the second, whisk the eggs. In the third, toss the bread crumbs with 1/2 teaspoon salt and 1/2 teaspoon pepper.

Season the breasts generously on both sides with salt and pepper. Dredge 1 breast well in the flour, shaking off any excess. Dip it into the eggs, turning to coat evenly, and then dredge it in the bread crumbs, pressing to make sure the crumbs adhere evenly. Gently shake off any excess. Set on a plate and repeat with the other breasts. Refrigerate for at least 5 minutes and up to 3 hours to let the breading set. Discard any leftover flour, eggs, or crumbs.

Preheat the oven to 350 degrees.

Heat the oil in a heavy 10-inch nonstick skillet over medium-high heat. When it is very hot, carefully add 2 of the breasts and cook until golden brown, about 3 minutes per side. If the oil gets too hot, reduce the heat to medium. Transfer the breasts to a baking sheet. Repeat with the remaining 2 breasts.

Bake until the chicken and filling reach 165 degrees on an instant-read thermometer, about 15 minutes. Serve immediately.

notes from our test kitchen

- When making the pocket, be sure to start cutting on the fatter side of the breast, making an opening that runs lengthwise down the breast.
- A slotted metal spatula is the best tool for turning and moving the chicken breasts. Tongs can damage the golden crust.

SOURCE: *Barefoot in Paris* by Ina Garten

COOK: Ina Garten

lemon chicken with croutons

WE'VE SEEN ALL MANNER OF RECIPES for roast chicken served on a bed of toasty bread cubes. One of the best of these, a golden roasted chicken presented over a generous serving of olive oil–toasted croutons that soak up the savory juices, comes from the Barefoot Contessa, Ina Garten. What elevates it above the others is the bright flavor of lemon. Before roasting, you stuff the chicken with two quartered lemons. As the chicken roasts, the juices from the lemons and the bird combine to create the most delicious pan drippings ever—exactly what you want to sop up with those crunchy croutons.

serves 3 or 4

- 1 4- to 5-pound roasting chicken
- 1 large yellow onion, sliced
- Good olive oil
- Kosher salt and freshly ground black pepper
- 2 lemons, quartered (see note)
- 2 tablespoons unsalted butter, melted
- 6 cups 3/4-inch bread cubes (from 1 baguette or round boule; see note)

Preheat the oven to 425 degrees.

Take the giblets out of the chicken (discard or save for another use) and rinse the chicken inside and out. Remove any excess fat and check for any leftover pinfeathers. Toss the onion with a little oil in a small roasting pan. Place the chicken on top of the onion and sprinkle the inside of the cavity with salt and pepper. Place the lemons inside the chicken (see note). Pat the outside of the chicken dry with paper towels, brush it with the melted butter, and sprinkle with salt and pepper. Tie the legs together with kitchen string and tuck the wing tips under the body of the chicken.

Roast for 1 1/4 to 1 1/2 hours, or until the juices run clear when you cut between the leg and the thigh. Cover with foil and allow to sit at room temperature for 15 minutes. (The onions may be burned around the edges of the pan, but the flavor is still good.)

Meanwhile, heat 2 tablespoons olive oil in a large skillet until very hot. Reduce the heat to medium-low and sauté the bread cubes, tossing frequently, until nicely browned, 8 to 10 minutes. Add more olive oil, as needed, and sprinkle with 1/2 teaspoon salt and 1/4 teaspoon pepper. Place the croutons on a serving platter. Slice the chicken and place it, plus all the pan juices, over the croutons. Sprinkle with salt and serve warm.

notes from our test kitchen

- Smaller, thin-skinned lemons are best here. (If Meyer lemons are in season, this would be a wonderful use for them.) If you have trouble fitting all 8 lemon quarters into the bird, just put any leftover wedges in the roasting pan with the onion.
- If we have fresh herbs on hand, we like to tuck a few sprigs into the chicken with the lemons. Try it with thyme, rosemary, or parsley.
- We like the tangy flavor and chewiness of sourdough bread for making the croutons.

tip

Most American poultry recipes begin like this one: "Wash [or rinse] the chicken [or duck or turkey]." But a growing number of experts, including the food science guru Harold McGee, believe that rinsing spreads bacteria all over the place, whereas cooking destroys it. Journalist Kim Severson, writing in the *New York Times*, reported that Linda Harris, a microbiologist at University of California at Davis, and other microbiologists have been trying to get American cooks to stop rinsing poultry since the 1990s. Jacques Pépin agrees, maintaining that rinsing washes away some of the flavor. For the best skin and flavor, McGee says, the bird should be as dry as possible and air-dried uncovered in the fridge, ideally for a couple of days.

The flavor argument is usually the one that convinces us, and we don't mind skipping an unnecessary step.

SOURCE: *Bon Appétit*
STORY BY **Cheryl and Bill Jamison**
COOKS: **Cheryl and Bill Jamison**

grilled mojito chicken

THE MOJITO, a highly quaffable Cuban concoction of rum and mint, has been the hottest cocktail around for a while now. But leave it to the grilling experts Cheryl and Bill Jamison to translate those flavors into a zippy marinade for grilled chicken. As good as this chicken is, what we love most is the rum-soaked grilled lime wedges that you spritz over it just before serving.

The Jamisons recommend keeping with the tropical theme by grilling sliced pineapple (see page 230) to serve with the chicken. And to drink with it? Why, ice-cold mojitos, of course!

serves 6

- 3/4 cup fresh lime juice
- 1/2 cup plus 2 tablespoons light rum
- 6 tablespoons mint syrup (see note)
- 1 tablespoon vegetable oil
- 1/2 cup finely chopped fresh mint
- 1 tablespoon coarse or kosher salt
- 6 chicken breast halves with skin and bones (about 5 pounds)
- 3 large limes, quartered lengthwise
- Fresh mint sprigs

Whisk together the lime juice, 1/2 cup of the rum, mint syrup, oil, chopped mint, and salt in a small bowl or large measuring cup. Place the chicken in a resealable bag. Pour the marinade over the chicken and seal the bag. Turn the bag over several times to distribute the marinade. Chill for 4 hours, turning twice.

Place the lime quarters in a shallow bowl. Pour the remaining 2 tablespoons rum over, tossing to coat. Let stand at room temperature.

Prepare a medium-hot grill. Remove the chicken breasts from the marinade and grill until cooked through, about 15 minutes per side. Transfer to a platter.

Grill the limes until soft and slightly charred, about 5 minutes. Garnish the platter with the mint sprigs. Squeeze the grilled limes over the chicken and serve.

notes from our test kitchen

- Mint syrup is often found with coffee, tea, and hot cocoa in the supermarket.
- Bone-in chicken breasts can take some maneuvering to cook properly. If they are extremely plump, be sure to grill the thicker part over the hottest area of the fire. If the breasts are truly enormous, we sometimes find it helps to stand them on their sides for a bit, so the heat goes directly to the thickest part. Either way, don't be a slave to the suggested cooking time. Every grill is different.
- The best doneness test for chicken is to slide an instant-read thermometer into the thickest part. When it reads 160 to 165 degrees, the chicken is done. You can also cut into a breast to see that there's no sign of pink.

SOURCE: Eat Turkey advertisement and www.eatturkey.com

COOK: Dean Thomas

turkey carnitas on mesclun greens with tangerine vinaigrette

ON OCCASION WE FIND OURSELVES drawn to a new recipe solely because it seems too original to be true. While this approach often leads to gastronomic disaster, sometimes our culinary curiosity pays off and we discover a great new dish. Turkey thighs simmered in olive oil until falling-apart tender and then shredded approximate the richness of the traditional Mexican pork dish carnitas. We still find it odd to add milk, cola, and soy sauce to the simmering turkey, but it turns out every time with just the right balance of sweetness and saltiness, and not the least bit greasy.

If you cook the turkey ahead, rewarm it in a low oven or a microwave on low before adding it to the salad.

serves 6

TURKEY

- 2 pounds turkey thighs (see note)
- Salt and freshly ground black pepper
- 2 cups olive oil
- 1 tangerine, quartered
- 2 garlic cloves, peeled
- 1/2 cup whole milk
- 1/4 cup tamari soy sauce (see note)
- 1/4 cup cola

TANGERINE VINAIGRETTE

- 1 bunch scallions, finely chopped
- 1 large jalapeño, seeds and membranes removed, minced
- 2 tablespoons sugar
- Grated zest and juice of 2 tangerines
- 1/4 cup rice wine vinegar
- 1 tablespoon tamari soy sauce
- 1/2 cup olive oil

SALAD

- 16 ounces mesclun greens, washed and drained
- 3 medium avocados, pitted, peeled, and sliced into wedges
- Blue corn tortilla strips for garnish (optional)

TO MAKE THE TURKEY:

Remove the skin from the turkey thighs and cut out the bones; don't worry about keeping the shape of the thighs. Season with salt and pepper. Heat the oil in a large saucepan over low heat. Add the turkey (see notes). Slowly simmer for 45 minutes, or until the turkey is golden brown and very tender.

Add the tangerine, garlic, milk, soy sauce, and cola. Simmer for 15 minutes more. Remove the turkey from the liquid and drain thoroughly. Discard the liquid and the tangerines and garlic. Using two forks, shred the turkey. Keep warm.

MEANWHILE, MAKE THE VINAIGRETTE:

Whisk together the scallions, jalapeño, sugar, tangerine zest and juice, rice wine vinegar, and soy sauce in a medium bowl. Whisking, slowly incorporate the olive oil. Pour into a medium saucepan and warm gently.

TO ASSEMBLE THE SALAD:

Toss the mesclun greens and avocado slices with the warm vinaigrette in a large bowl. Place the greens in the center of warm plates and top with the shredded turkey. Garnish with the tortilla strips, if desired.

notes from our test kitchen

- If you can find boneless, skinless turkey thighs, you'll save yourself some trouble.
- Tamari refers to a slightly thicker-style soy sauce made without wheat; it is often less salty than regular soy sauce. You can substitute regular soy sauce here, as long as it's naturally brewed. Do not use "lite" or low-sodium soy sauce.
- Ideally, the turkey should be submerged in the olive oil. We find that it helps to cut each of the thighs into 2 or 3 large pieces so they fit more snugly in the saucepan.
- The idea is to simmer the turkey slowly in the oil, not to let the oil get so hot that it deep-fries the meat. You'll want to stay close by to keep an eye on the temperature.

SOURCE: *Bon Appétit*
STORY BY Jamie Purviance
COOK: Jamie Purviance

barbecued tri-tip with caramelized red onions

IF YOU'VE NEVER HEARD OF A TRI-TIP, you probably don't live in California, where this inexpensive but reliably tasty cut from the beef sirloin is an old favorite. On the East Coast, it's sometimes called beef triangle, and it's worth asking for. A small flat roast with a slightly triangular shape, it can be a bit tougher than other beef roasts, so it needs to be sliced thin, as it is here.

Jamie Purviance, a master griller, suggests making this for the Fourth of July. We normally shy away from recipes with three different parts, but don't worry, all of them are simple, and you can make both the onions and the barbecue sauce ahead. You might want to make a double recipe of barbecue sauce and serve some on the side with the meat.

serves 8

CARAMELIZED RED ONIONS

- 2 tablespoons butter
- 2 tablespoons olive oil
- 2 1/2 pounds red onions (about 4 medium), halved and thinly sliced
- 2 teaspoons balsamic vinegar
- 1/2 teaspoon kosher salt
- 1/4 teaspoon freshly ground black pepper
- 1/4 cup chopped fresh chives

RED WINE BARBECUE SAUCE

- 1 tablespoon olive oil
- 1 large garlic clove, minced
- 1/4 teaspoon ground cumin
- 1/4 teaspoon chipotle chile powder (see note)
- 1/3 cup dry red wine
- 1/2 cup ketchup
- 1 tablespoon cider vinegar
- 1 tablespoon soy sauce
- 1/8 teaspoon liquid smoke

TRI-TIP

- 1 teaspoon garlic powder
- 1 teaspoon salt
- 1/2 teaspoon freshly ground black pepper
- 1 1/2–1 3/4 pounds tri-tip beef roast (1–2 roasts), trimmed of all but 1/4 inch fat
- 2 tablespoons olive oil

TO MAKE THE ONIONS:

Melt the butter with the oil in a large nonstick skillet over medium heat. Add onions and cook until deep golden brown, stirring frequently, about 30 minutes. Stir in the vinegar, salt, and pepper. Remove from the heat. The onions can be made up to 1 day ahead and refrigerated. Rewarm before serving. Stir in the chives.

TO MAKE THE BARBECUE SAUCE:

Heat the oil in a medium saucepan over medium heat. Add the garlic, cumin, and chipotle powder and cook, stirring, for 1 minute. Add the wine and simmer for 2 minutes. Stir in the remaining ingredients and simmer for 2 minutes more. The sauce can be made and refrigerated up to 2 days ahead.

TO MAKE THE TRI-TIP:

Preheat the grill to medium. If using a charcoal grill, the coals should be white-hot. Mix the garlic powder, salt, and pepper in a small bowl. Brush both sides of the tri-tip with oil and sprinkle with the garlic powder mixture, pressing it in to adhere. Grill the tri-tip for 5 minutes per side. Reduce the heat to medium-low, or if using a charcoal grill, move the meat to the cooler side of the grill.

Cover and grill, brushing with barbecue sauce and turning every 10 minutes, for about 30 minutes more, or until a thermometer inserted into the thickest part of the meat registers 125 to 130 degrees for medium-rare.

Transfer the tri-tip to a cutting board and let rest for 10 minutes. Cut the meat crosswise into very thin slices and arrange them on a platter. Surround with the caramelized onions and serve.

notes from our test kitchen

- Trader Joe's often has tri-tips in the cold case.
- You can find chipotle chile powder in some large supermarkets and gourmet specialty shops, or order it from penzeys.com.

SOURCE: *The Simpler the Better* by Leslie Revsin

COOK: Leslie Revsin

salt and pepper burgers

FEW COOKS CAN PULL OFF enticing recipes with easy-to-find ingredients, few steps, and dynamite results as well as the late Leslie Revsin, a widely acclaimed food writer and chef.

We love burgers as much as the next carnivore, and we agree with her that you don't need secret spices and special sauces to achieve a great one. Here, patties of ground beef are studded with cracked black peppercorns and then cooked in a blazing hot skillet (cast iron works best if you have it). The burgers come out juicy and perfectly seasoned, with a jolt of black pepper. The finishing touch of a quick buttery sauce of Worcestershire and mustard makes ketchup unnecessary, but we won't blame you if you go for both.

serves 4

- 2 teaspoons black peppercorns
- 1¾ pounds ground beef (preferably chuck)
- 4 kaiser rolls
- 1 teaspoon kosher salt
- 2 tablespoons butter
- 1 tablespoon Worcestershire sauce
- 2 teaspoons Dijon mustard

Place the peppercorns on a kitchen towel and fold the towel over them to cover. Crack with a meat mallet or the back of a small skillet. Form the beef into four 1-inch-thick burgers. Sprinkle one side of each with peppercorns and press in lightly.

Split and toast the rolls; keep warm. Sprinkle the salt over the bottom of a large heavy skillet over high heat. When hot, add the burgers peppered sides down and cook until crusted on the bottom, about 3 minutes. Turn and cook for 3 minutes more for medium-rare. Remove from the heat.

Set the burgers on the roll bottoms. Melt the butter in the hot skillet (see note) and stir in the Worcestershire sauce and mustard. Spoon half the sauce over the burgers and the rest over the cut sides of the tops. Cover the burgers with the tops and serve.

notes from our test kitchen

- A large cast-iron skillet is ideal here, if you have one. If not, choose the heaviest skillet you own.
- If you prefer your burgers medium or even medium-well, lower the heat a bit and keep cooking for 3 to 5 minutes more. You can also slide the pan into a 375-degree oven to finish cooking.
- After the burgers are done, it's best to add the butter to the skillet off the heat. It will melt with the residual heat and not burn. If it doesn't seem hot enough, just put it back over the heat.

tip

According to Chef John Folse in his momentous *Encyclopedia of Cajun & Creole Cuisine,* a great hamburger starts with ground beef that contains 15 to 20 percent fat. Like Leslie Revsin, Folse agrees that the fewer ingredients added to the meat, the better the burger. He also reminds us to handle the meat as little as possible so the burger maintains its juiciness and flavor.

SOURCE: *Marcella Says . . .*
by Marcella Hazan with Victor Hazan
COOK: Marcella Hazan

spicy beef meatballs with red bell peppers

NOW THAT MARCELLA HAZAN and her husband, Victor, have left their home in Venice and moved to America, what appears on their table every evening has changed with the geography, as good food always does. Marcella became intrigued with a number of foods at American markets, from avocados to jalapeños. It's her contention that some of these foods fit well with classic Italian foods, and jalapeño is definitely on the list, for its fragrance and its mellow heat.

Here she uses jalapeño with meatballs in an unusual sauce—not the usual tomato, but one made with red bell peppers. You can change the sauce to suit yourself. If you cook the peppers just a little, about 10 minutes, then they'll hold their shape on the plate. Cook them longer, and you have a very good sauce. Either way, the meatballs are wonderful.

serves 4

- 4 meaty red bell peppers
- 1/2 cup chopped onion
- Chopped jalapeño (2–3 tablespoons, or to taste)
- 2 tablespoons chopped fresh flat-leaf parsley
- 2/3 cup torn fresh bread crumbs (the soft, crustless part of a slice of bread)
- 2/3 cup whole milk
- 1 pound ground beef chuck
- 1 large egg
- Fine sea salt
- 1 1/2 cups fine, dry unflavored bread crumbs
- 1/4 cup extra-virgin olive oil

Cut the bell peppers lengthwise along the creases, remove the stems and seeds, and remove the tough skin with a swivel vegetable peeler. Cut the peppers into strips about 1/2 inch wide.

Put the onion, jalapeño, and parsley in a large bowl and mix well. Soak the torn bread crumbs in the milk in a small bowl. As soon as the bread is saturated with the milk, squeeze it out gently in your hand and add it to the onion mixture, working it in until combined. Add the ground chuck, egg, and salt to taste, kneading the mixture very gently with your hands.

Spread the dry bread crumbs on a plate. Pull off a piece of the meat mixture about the size of a very small egg and shape it in your hands into a ball, being careful not to squeeze it hard. Roll the meatball in the dry bread crumbs. Pull off another piece of the meat mixture and repeat the procedure until you have used all of it and the balls have all been rolled in bread crumbs.

Heat the oil in a 12-inch skillet over high heat. When the oil is hot, add the meatballs. Brown them to a dark color on one side, then turn them and brown the other side. Do not turn them more than once. If the meatballs do not fit into the pan in a single uncrowded layer, brown them in batches. When you have browned them all, put all the meatballs back into the skillet.

Add the peppers with a little bit of salt. Turn the contents of the pan over, using a wooden spoon and a light touch, reduce the heat to low, and cover the pan. You have a choice of how long to continue cooking. When the peppers are tender enough to put a fork through, about 10 minutes, they'll hold their shape. Or you can continue cooking until they melt into a sauce, about 10 minutes more or longer. When the peppers are done to taste, transfer the contents of the pan to a warm platter and serve at once.

notes from our test kitchen

- Jalapeños can range from very hot to very bland. The only way to tell, even within the same batch at the market, is to snip off the point and touch the flesh to your tongue. If there's not much heat at all, you may need a serrano pepper instead, or simply use more jalapeño.
- You can make the meatballs up to 3 days ahead, and we think the flavor improves the longer they sit in the refrigerator. Bring them to room temperature before gently reheating over medium-low heat. If you make them ahead, the jalapeño's heat will develop a bit as they sit, so you may want to add the lesser amount.

SOURCE: *Food Arts*
COOK: Aglaia Kremezi

greek meatballs with walnuts, almonds, and prunes

THESE OVAL BEEF MEATBALLS get their rich flavor from a mix of onion, parsley, ground nuts, lemon, and Aleppo pepper (a mild Middle Eastern pepper). In a two-step cooking technique, the meatballs are first roasted at high heat to brown the tops and then simmered in a mix of red wine, broth, and vinegar. They turn out tender, juicy, and bathed in a lip-smacking sweet-tangy broth. The walnut-stuffed prunes that simmer along with the meatballs are a bonus. This unusual recipe originated on the Greek island of Syros, in the heart of the Cyclades, and comes to us by way of Aglaia Kremezi, one of the foremost authorities on Greek food.

Serve with rice, orzo, or another grain so as not to waste the juices. Any leftovers make amazing meatball sandwiches.

serves 4

- 20 pitted prunes
- 20 walnut halves
- 1 pound lean ground beef
- 1 cup finely minced onion
- 1/2 cup fresh parsley leaves, finely chopped, plus sprigs for garnish
- 1/2 cup almonds, ground
- 1/2 cup walnuts, ground
- 1/3 cup pine nuts
- 1/3 cup bread crumbs, toasted
- 1 teaspoon Aleppo pepper (see note) or 1/4 teaspoon crushed red pepper flakes
- Salt
- 1/2 cup olive oil
- 1 large egg, beaten
- 3 tablespoons fresh lemon juice
- 1 cup chicken broth
- 2/3 cup dry red wine
- 2 tablespoons red wine vinegar
- Freshly ground black pepper

Preheat the oven to 450 degrees.

Stuff each prune with a walnut half and set aside (see note).

Combine the ground beef, onion, parsley, almonds, walnuts, pine nuts, bread crumbs, Aleppo pepper or crushed red pepper, 1/2 teaspoon salt, 1/3 cup of the olive oil, the egg, and the lemon juice in a large bowl. Using your hands, gently work the mixture to combine. Shape the mixture into 12 oval meatballs and arrange in a 13-x-9-inch baking dish. The meatballs can be made ahead to this point and refrigerated, covered, for several hours.

Brush the tops of the meatballs with the remaining oil. Bake for 15 minutes. Remove from the oven and reduce the temperature to 400 degrees.

Arrange the stuffed prunes among the meatballs. Pour the broth, wine, and vinegar over the top. Bake for 20 minutes more. Turn the oven off, baste the meatballs with the pan juices, and let them rest in the oven for 5 minutes.

To serve, place 3 meatballs and 5 stuffed prunes on each plate. Sprinkle with pepper. Spoon the pan juices around and garnish with the parsley sprigs.

notes from our test kitchen

- If the prunes are very soft, you may have trouble stuffing the walnuts inside them. If it's easier, use your thumbs to peel open the prunes like a book and then wrap them around the walnuts.
- Aleppo pepper, an earthy mild pepper, is sold in Middle Eastern markets and some gourmet shops. For more on where to buy Aleppo pepper and how to make a substitute, see the notes on page 13.
- To check the meatballs for doneness, insert an instant-read thermometer into the center of a meatball in the middle of the pan; it should read 165 degrees.
- The meatballs may throw off a good deal of fat as they cook, so after plating them, we like to tilt the baking pan and skim off the surface fat before spooning the pan juices onto the plates.

SOURCE: *The Cast Iron Skillet Cookbook* by Sharon Kramis and Julie Kramis Hearne

COOKS: Sharon Kramis and Julie Kramis Hearne

tamale pie

WE'VE BEEN LOOKING FOR a good tamale pie for a long time now, and this recipe really does it justice. The cast-iron skillet is the classic one-dish cooking and serving vehicle. Other notable features are a good balance of spices, canned chili (!—but it works), corn kernels, fire-roasted tomatoes, and a rich corn-bread topping. This is great Super Bowl fare, and first-rate comfort food anytime.

The corn-bread topping has its own touch of chili powder and corn kernels. Try it on its own (see note, page 144). It's moist and won't crumble because of the sour cream, half-and-half, and a fair amount of butter.

serves 8

CORN-BREAD TOPPING

- 1 cup stone-ground yellow cornmeal (preferably Bob's Red Mill)
- 1 cup all-purpose flour
- 1 1/2 teaspoons baking powder
- 1/2 teaspoon baking soda
- 1/2 teaspoon salt
- 1/2 teaspoon chili powder
- 2 large eggs
- 1/2 cup sour cream
- 1 cup half-and-half
- 6 tablespoons (3/4 stick) butter, melted and slightly cooled
- 2/3 cup fresh or frozen corn kernels, defrosted and drained if frozen

FILLING

- 1 pound lean ground beef
- 2 teaspoons ground cumin
- 2 teaspoons chili powder
- Salt and freshly ground black pepper
- 1 white onion, diced
- 2 garlic cloves, minced
- 2 14 1/2-ounce cans Muir Glen fire-roasted crushed tomatoes
- 2 14 1/2-ounce cans hot or mild chili
- 1/2 cup fresh or frozen corn kernels, defrosted and drained if frozen
- 2 tablespoons diced green chiles (optional)
- 2 cups grated sharp cheddar cheese

- Sour cream for serving
- 1/4 cup chopped fresh cilantro for serving

TO MAKE THE TOPPING:

Whisk together the cornmeal, flour, baking powder, baking soda, salt, and chili powder in a large bowl.

Whisk together the eggs, sour cream, half-and-half, 4 tablespoons of the melted butter, and the corn in a medium bowl. Add the egg mixture to the cornmeal mixture and stir until just combined. Do not overmix. Set the batter aside along with the remaining melted butter.

TO MAKE THE FILLING:

Preheat the oven to 400 degrees.

Heat a 10-inch cast-iron skillet over medium-high heat (see note). Add the ground beef, cumin, chili powder, and salt and pepper to taste and cook, stirring occasionally, until the beef is browned. Transfer to a plate.

Reduce the heat to medium. Add the onion and garlic to the skillet and cook, stirring occasionally, until the onion is softened but not browned, about 5 minutes.

Return the beef to the skillet. Add the tomatoes, chili, corn, and green chiles, if using.

Sprinkle the cheese over the top. Pour the corn bread batter over the top of the cheese, spreading it evenly with a spatula. Transfer the skillet to the oven and bake for 15 minutes.

Remove the skillet from the oven and drizzle the remaining melted butter over the top. Return to the oven and bake until the top is nicely browned and a toothpick inserted in the center comes out clean, 15 to 20 minutes. Remove from the oven and let stand for 10 minutes. Cut into wedges and serve with the sour cream and cilantro.

notes from our test kitchen

- To make just the corn bread, preheat the oven to 400 degrees. Generously butter an 8- or 10-inch cast-iron skillet (or round baking dish) and pour in the batter. Bake for 10 minutes. Remove from the oven and pour the remaining 2 tablespoons melted butter over the top. Return to the oven and bake for about 10 minutes more, or until golden brown and a toothpick inserted in the center comes out clean. Cool on a rack. Cut into wedges and serve. (You can also add fresh herbs or 2/3 cup grated cheddar cheese to the batter.)
- Instead of the cast-iron skillet, you can use a regular large skillet to prepare the filling up to the point of sprinkling the cheese on top. Then pour the filling into a 3-quart casserole, scatter the cheese over, and pour the corn-bread topping on top.
- The tamale pie is just as good as leftovers as it is the first time around.

SOURCE: *Washington Post*
STORY BY Renée Schettler
COOK: Sally Schneider

spiced skirt steak

NOT ALL STEAKS, even the very expensive ones, deliver truly beefy, satisfying flavor. Skirt steak, the steak that's used for fajitas, always does. This thin, accordion-like flap of meat provides great flavor when it's grilled. It's best cooked quickly and over high heat, which makes it a great weeknight dish.

Here it's given a warm, peppery, but subtle spicing with a quick rub. The prep time is virtually instant and the cooking time minimal. The steak needs to rest for 10 minutes after it's cooked, and in the meantime you can put together a salad and whatever else you'd like to serve with it.

serves 4

- 1/4 cup coarsely ground black pepper (or half black and half white)
- 1 tablespoon ground allspice
- 1 tablespoon ground coriander
- 1 1 1/2- to 2-pound skirt steak, about 1 inch thick
- Vegetable oil
- Salt

Preheat the grill or heat a large skillet over medium-high heat.

Combine the pepper, allspice, and coriander in a small bowl.

Pat the steak dry. Rub the steak with just enough oil to barely coat it. Season on both sides with salt to taste, then sprinkle a little of the spice mixture evenly over the surface and using your fingers, rub so that the spices and oil form a sort of paste.

Grill or sear the steak, turning once, until cooked to the desired degree of doneness, 1 to 2 minutes per side for medium-rare. Transfer to a cutting board and let rest for at least 10 minutes.

Carve the steak, against the grain, into thin slices. Serve immediately.

note from our test kitchen

We especially like the black-and-white pepper mix.

SOURCE: *The Gourmet Cookbook* edited by Ruth Reichl

COOK: *Gourmet* staff

brisket à la carbonnade

CARBONNADE, the Belgian beef stew with beer, was a big hit in the 1960s. Back then, beef still tasted very beefy, with lots of deep, rich flavor. Now meat with that wonderful flavor is hard to come by, but brisket always delivers. So we were especially pleased to find this slow-cooked recipe, with the brisket tucked into a blanket of beery onions with the inspired touches of balsamic vinegar and a porcini bouillon cube.

Make the carbonnade a day or two ahead and it will taste even better. If you can find the thick end of the brisket (aka the nose, thick cut, or point), so much the better. That end has a little more fat, so the meat will be more succulent. But the more commonly available thin flat brisket will be good here, too.

serves 8

- 1 3½–4 pound brisket, trimmed of excess fat
- Salt and freshly ground black pepper
- 2 tablespoons olive oil
- 2 pounds onions, halved lengthwise and thinly sliced lengthwise (about 6 cups)
- 1 Turkish bay leaf or ½ California bay leaf
- 1 12-ounce bottle beer (not dark)
- 1 tablespoon balsamic vinegar
- 1 dried porcini bouillon cube (less than ½ ounce) or 1 beef bouillon cube, crumbled

Place a rack in the center of the oven and preheat to 350 degrees.

Pat the brisket dry and sprinkle with ¾ teaspoon salt and ½ teaspoon pepper. Heat the oil in a 6- to 8-quart wide, heavy ovenproof pot over medium-high heat until hot but not smoking. Brown the meat well on all sides, about 10 minutes total. Transfer to a platter.

Add the onions and bay leaf to the fat in the pot and cook over medium heat, stirring occasionally, until the onions are golden, 10 to 12 minutes. Remove from the heat and transfer half the onions to a bowl. Set the brisket over the onions in the pot, then top with the remaining onions. Add the beer, vinegar, and bouillon cube. The liquid should come halfway up the side of the meat; if it doesn't, add water. Bring to a boil.

Cover the pot and braise in the oven until the meat is fork tender, 3 to $3^1/2$ hours. Let the meat cool in the sauce, uncovered, for 30 minutes.

Transfer the brisket to a cutting board. Skim off any fat from the sauce, remove the bay leaf, and season with salt and pepper. Slice across the grain and serve with the sauce.

note from our test kitchen

To make the brisket up to 2 days ahead, which we advise, finish cooking it and let the meat cool in the sauce. Cover the meat with wax paper, then the lid, and refrigerate. To serve, remove any solid fat on the surface of the meat, slice the meat across the grain, and arrange in a shallow baking pan. Spoon the sauce over the meat and reheat, covered, in a 325-degree oven for 45 minutes.

SOURCE: *All About Braising* by Molly Stevens

COOK: Molly Stevens

zinfandel pot roast with glazed carrots and fresh sage

POT ROAST IS ONE of the homiest suppers you could ever set before your friends and family, but this one is a dinner-party rendition, with a gorgeous garnish of glazed carrots—and parsnips too, if you like—flecked with herbs. If you're used to thinking of sage only with pork or poultry, this pot roast will be an eye-opener. As with all such dishes, leftovers the next day are even better.

serves 8

POT ROAST

- 1 3½- to 4-pound boneless beef chuck roast, preferably top blade roast
- Coarse salt and freshly ground black pepper
- 2 tablespoons extra-virgin olive oil
- 1 large yellow onion, coarsely chopped
- 1 carrot, peeled and coarsely chopped
- 1 celery rib, coarsely chopped
- 2 garlic cloves, peeled and smashed
- 1 cup Zinfandel or other robust dry red wine
- 1 cup beef broth, veal broth, or chicken broth
- 3 large (3- to 4-inch) leafy fresh sage sprigs
- 2–3 6- to 8-inch leafy fresh flat-leaf parsley sprigs
- 8–10 black peppercorns

GARNISH

- 1½ pounds small to medium carrots, peeled, or ¾ pound each carrots and parsnips, peeled (see note)
- 1 tablespoon unsalted butter
- 1 tablespoon extra-virgin olive oil
- Coarse salt and freshly ground black pepper
- 1 tablespoon red wine vinegar
- 2 tablespoons chopped fresh sage
- 2 tablespoons chopped fresh flat-leaf parsley
- Pinch of sugar

TO MAKE THE POT ROAST:

Place a rack in the lower third of the oven and preheat to 300 degrees.

If the meat isn't already tied, use kitchen string to tie it into a neat, snug shape. Season the beef all over with salt and pepper. Heat the oil in a large Dutch oven or other braising pot (a 5-quart one works well) over medium heat. Add the beef and brown it on all sides, turning it with tongs as you go, about 18 minutes total. Remove the beef and set it aside on a large plate or dish. If there are any charred bits in the pot, remove them with a damp paper towel but leave behind any tasty-looking drippings.

Return the pot to medium-high heat and add the onion, carrot, celery, and garlic. Season lightly with salt and pepper. Cook, stirring often, until just starting to brown, about 5 minutes. Pour in the wine, scrape the bottom with a wooden spoon to loosen any browned bits, and boil to reduce the wine by about half, about 6 minutes. Add the broth, return to a boil, and boil to reduce by about one third, 5 minutes more. Return the meat to the pot, along with any juices it has released, and add the sage, parsley, and peppercorns. Cover with a piece of parchment paper, pressing down so that it nearly touches the meat and the edges of the paper overhang the pot by about an inch. Set the lid in place.

Transfer the pot to the oven and braise at a gentle simmer, turning the roast once halfway through braising, until fork-tender, about 3 hours. Peek under the lid after the first 10 to 15 minutes to check that the liquid isn't simmering too vigorously; if it is, reduce the temperature by 10 or 15 degrees.

MEANWHILE, MAKE THE GARNISH:

Cut the carrots into sticks by cutting them crosswise in half, then cutting the halves lengthwise into sticks about 3 inches by 1/2 inch. This typically means cutting the thicker tops into quarters and the skinnier tips in half. If using parsnips, remove any woody cores before cutting them into sticks. Set aside.

Remove the pot from the oven. Lift the beef out with tongs or a sturdy spatula, set on a platter to catch the juices, and cover loosely with foil to keep warm. Strain the braising liquid into a medium saucepan, pressing down on the solids to extract as much liquid as possible. Let the braising liquid settle, then spoon off and discard as much fat as you easily can with a wide spoon. Measure out 1/2 cup of the liquid for glazing the carrots and set the rest aside in a warm spot.

Melt the butter with the oil in a large skillet over medium-high heat. When quite hot, add the carrots (and parsnips, if using), season with salt and pepper, and cook briskly, shaking or stirring them, until lightly glazed and browned in spots, about 8 minutes. Add the 1/2 cup braising liquid, cover partially, reduce the heat to medium, and simmer until tender but not at all mushy, 6 to 8 minutes. Uncover, raise the heat, and bring back to a boil. Add the vinegar, sage, parsley, and sugar and cook until the liquid is reduced to a glaze, about 1 minute. Season with salt and pepper to taste.

Heat the remaining braising liquid over medium-high heat, and boil for 1 or 2 minutes to concentrate its flavor. Taste. You may not need to add any salt or pepper, but do so if the liquid is lacking in flavor.

Remove the strings from the roast. For a platter presentation, arrange the carrots (and parsnips, if using) around the pot roast. Alternatively, carve the roast into 1/2-inch-thick slices and arrange the slices on dinner plates along with the carrots (and parsnips, if using). Spoon a bit of sauce over the meat and serve immediately. Pass any remaining sauce at the table.

note from our test kitchen

You can speed things up by using the tiny carrots sold in bags, but be sure to choose the organic ones, which are much tastier than ordinary ones.

herb- and pistachio-stuffed veal pot roast

This rich, elegant pot roast, with its subtle notes of fennel, mushroom, lemon, and pistachio, was very good the first night we made it. But the big revelation came the next evening when we heated up the leftovers. The roast was even more meltingly tender, with a silken sauce so delectable that it begged for plenty of bread to catch every last drop. We've never seen such a dramatic example of the benefits of making a pot roast ahead.

serves 4 to 6

PISTACHIO PESTO

- 1/2 cup unsalted lightly toasted pistachios, chopped
- 1/2 cup packed fresh basil leaves
- 1/4 cup chopped fresh chives
- 2 tablespoons chopped fresh mint leaves
- 1 tablespoon coarsely chopped poached or toasted garlic (see note)
- Finely grated zest of 1 large lemon
- 3/4 cup extra-virgin olive oil
- 1 tablespoon fresh lemon juice
- Salt and freshly ground black pepper

VEAL

- 1 3-pound well-trimmed boneless veal shoulder roast (ask the butcher to trim it; see note)
- Salt and freshly ground black pepper
- 3 tablespoons olive oil
- 4 ounces pancetta or bacon, cut into large dice
- 2 cups chopped white or yellow onions
- 2 cups chopped button mushrooms
- 1 1/2 cups chopped fresh fennel or 2 teaspoons fennel seeds
- 2 teaspoons chopped garlic
- 2 cups chicken broth
- 1 1/2 cups medium-bodied white wine
- 3/4 cup heavy cream
- 2 tablespoons finely chopped fresh parsley leaves
- 1 tablespoon finely grated lemon zest

TO MAKE THE PESTO:

Combine everything but the salt and pepper in a blender or a food processor and puree until smooth, stopping a few times to scrape down the sides. Season with salt and pepper to taste. The pesto can be made ahead and stored, covered, in the refrigerator up to 5 days or in the freezer for up to 6 months.

TO PREPARE THE VEAL:

Preheat the oven to 350 degrees.

Unroll the meat, carefully removing any netting or strings that may be wrapping it, and spread the pesto mixture liberally on the inside. Roll the meat back up tightly and rewrap with the netting or tie with string. Season the roast liberally with salt and pepper.

Heat the oil in a Dutch oven or heavy pot large enough to hold the roast and brown the roast well on all sides over high heat. Remove the roast from the pot and set aside.

Pour off all but 2 tablespoons of the fat in the pot and add the pancetta or bacon, onions, mushrooms, fennel, and garlic. Sauté over medium heat until the vegetables are softened and just beginning to color, 3 to 4 minutes. Add the broth and the wine and bring to a boil. Add the veal, cover the pot, and braise in the oven for about 1½ hours, or until the veal registers 155 degrees on an instant-read thermometer.

Transfer the meat to a cutting board and cover loosely with foil. Carefully strain the liquid into a bowl, pressing down on the solids. Wipe out the pot and return the liquid to it. (Or strain the liquid into a clean pot if you don't mind washing two pots.)

Add the cream, bring to a boil, and cook over high heat for about 5 minutes, or until the liquid is reduced and is as thick as a light sauce. Remove from the heat, stir in the parsley and lemon zest, taste the sauce, and season with salt and pepper if you think it needs it.

If you're making the roast ahead, as we suggest, let the veal cool in the sauce. Cover with wax paper, then the lid, and refrigerate. To serve, remove any solid fat from the surface of the meat, remove the netting or string, slice thickly, and arrange the slices in a shallow pan. Spoon the sauce over and reheat, covered, in a 325-degree oven until warmed through, about 40 minutes.

To serve right away, remove the netting or string from the veal and slice thickly. Serve with the hot sauce spooned over it.

notes from our test kitchen

- We couldn't find veal shoulder at the market, only veal leg. Our butcher assured us it would work as well, and he was right.
- To poach garlic, which takes away its harsh edge, separate the cloves but don't peel them. Place them in a small saucepan and cover with 1/2 inch cold water. Bring to a boil, then drain. Cover with 1/2 inch water again, bring to a boil, and drain. Rinse the garlic cloves in cold water. Remove the garlic skins and keep the cloves, tightly covered, in the refrigerator for up to 10 days.
- The pistachio pesto is wonderful on pasta.

SOURCE: *Everything Tastes Better with Garlic* by Sara Perry

COOK: Sara Perry

garlic-studded pork tenderloin with mojo

WHAT'S MOJO, YOU SAY? Pronounced "*mo*-ho," it's a zesty table sauce traditionally served over pit-roasted pork. This orange-lime version sauces a Cuban-style miniature pork roast. You treat pork tenderloin to a flavor boost the day before it's roasted, dipping slivers of garlic in a cumin and oregano spice mix, then plunging them deeply into the meat. As it roasts, the intense aroma of cumin, oregano, and garlic is irresistible.

A very appealing aspect of the recipe is that so much can be done ahead—making the mojo, prepping the roast the day before you cook it. The pork cooks quickly, in just 20 minutes. That makes it right for an effortless weekday dinner party, a challenge for any cook.

serves 6 to 8

MOJO

- 2 1/2 tablespoons chopped garlic (about 6 medium cloves)
- 1/2 teaspoon firmly packed grated lime zest
- 3 tablespoons fresh lime juice
- 1/4 teaspoon firmly packed grated orange zest
- 2 tablespoons fresh orange juice
- 3/4 teaspoon ground cumin
- 1/2 teaspoon salt
- 1/2 cup extra-virgin olive oil
- Freshly ground black pepper
- 1 tablespoon minced fresh cilantro

PORK

- 1 large pork tenderloin (about 2 pounds) or 2 smaller tenderloins (see note)
- 2 teaspoons dried oregano
- 1/2 teaspoon ground cumin
- 1/2 teaspoon kosher salt
- 1/2 teaspoon freshly ground black pepper
- 2–3 medium garlic cloves, cut into slivers

TO MAKE THE MOJO:

Blend the garlic, lime zest, lime juice, orange zest, orange juice, cumin, and salt in a blender until the garlic is finely chopped. With the machine running, slowly add the oil in a thin stream until emulsified. Transfer to a small bowl, season to taste with pepper, and stir in the cilantro. The mojo can be made up to 4 days ahead, covered and refrigerated. Bring to room temperature before serving.

TO MAKE THE PORK:

If necessary, fold the narrow end of the tenderloin back toward the center so the roast has an even thickness. Secure with kitchen string or toothpicks.

In a small bowl, combine the oregano, cumin, salt, and pepper. Using a mortar and pestle or the back of a spoon and a bowl, stir and crush together the ingredients until the oregano is well crushed. Toss the garlic slivers in the spice mixture. Using the point of a paring knife, poke deep slits in the roast and insert the garlic slivers. Rub the remaining spice mixture over the meat. Wrap the roast in foil and refrigerate for at least 2 hours or overnight.

Place a rack in the center of the oven and preheat to 475 degrees.

Take the meat from the refrigerator, unwrap, and place it on the rack in a roasting pan. Roast for 20 minutes, or until an instant-read thermometer inserted into the middle of the thickest end of the pork reads 140 to 145 degrees. Remove from the oven and let the roast rest, uncovered, for 5 minutes. (The residual heat will raise the meat's internal temperature another 5 degrees.) To serve, cut into 1/2-inch-thick slices and serve with the sauce.

notes from our test kitchen

- Pork tenderloins vary quite a bit, depending on where you live. In the Midwest and rural areas, they're often quite large. In some markets, a whole tenderloin can be less than a pound. If you have only svelte tenderloins to work with, tie two of them together with kitchen twine, or get the butcher to do it. Or cook them side by side and check their temperature at 15 minutes.
- We like Sara Perry's idea of freezing a cooked roast and taking it to the butcher, still frozen, to be thinly sliced. That way you can serve little sandwiches for 10 to 12 brunch guests. Make the mojo and have it in a bowl to drizzle onto 2-inch bakery rolls stuffed with the roast pork.
- Leftover mojo? Perry loves a warm bowl of tiny hot potatoes sauced with zesty mojo. Yum!

SOURCE: www.nimanranch.com

COOKS: Olivier Said, Maggie Pond, and James Mellgren

spanish pork loin sandwiches with alioli and arugula

SANDWICHES WERE EVERYWHERE this year—grilled, pressed, double-deckered, and so on—but these indescribably good ones topped our chart. The recipe comes from César, a great tapas place in Berkeley, California, started by Chez Panisse alums and conveniently located right next door. They tell us that the roasted pork loin makes a great meal on its own, and we agree that it does, but it's the sandwiches that really rocked our world.

There are a few components to this recipe—the brine, the spice rub, and the alioli (Spanish-style garlic mayonnaise)—but the preparation can be spread out over a couple of days, and the results are worth every second you put into it. The brining process takes 2 days, so you'll need to be thinking ahead anyway.

makes 6 to 8 sandwiches, with leftovers

BRINE

- 3 cups water
- 2 1/2 cups honey
- 1 yellow onion, coarsely chopped
- 1 garlic head, halved crosswise
- 1 bunch rosemary, cut into 1-inch lengths
- 2 tablespoons salt
- 2 tablespoons mustard seeds
- 2 tablespoons black peppercorns
- 2 tablespoons crushed red pepper flakes
- 1 bay leaf
- Pinch of freshly ground nutmeg
- 6 cups ice

- 1 center-cut boneless pork loin (about 4 pounds)
- 1/2 cup extra-virgin olive oil
- 3 tablespoons Moruño Spice (page 158)
- 3–4 baguettes
- 2–3 garlic cloves, halved
- Alioli (page 159)
- Salt
- 2 cups loosely packed arugula leaves

TO BRINE THE PORK:

Combine all the ingredients except the ice in a large saucepan over medium-high heat and heat to dissolve the honey and infuse the spices. Place the ice in a large glass bowl. Pour the brine mixture over the ice. When the ice has melted, add the pork. Cover and cure in the refrigerator for 2 days.

To roast the pork, preheat the oven to 425 degrees.

Mix together the oil and the Moruño spice in a small bowl. Remove the pork from the brine and discard the brine. Pat the meat dry and rub it all over with 1/4 cup of the oil mixture.

TO COOK THE PORK:

Preheat a cast-iron skillet over medium-high heat for 5 minutes. Sear the meat for about 2 minutes on each side. Transfer to the oven and roast until the internal temperature is 135 degrees, about 30 minutes. Remove the loin from the skillet and let rest for 20 minutes, then slice into thin medallions.

To assemble, cut the baguettes into 10-inch lengths and then slice them in half lengthwise, leaving a hinge. Rub the inside of the bread with the cut side of the garlic. Spread the alioli over the bread. Layer the pork medallions on the bread, drizzle with the remaining 1/4 cup oil mixture, sprinkle with salt, and top with arugula leaves. Serve.

note from our test kitchen

You can also roast the pork 1 to 2 days in advance, let it cool to room temperature, cover tightly, and refrigerate. To serve, let it sit at room temperature for a bit before slicing and making sandwiches.

moruño spice

THIS KEEPS FOR WEEKS in a covered jar. Use it as a spice rub for other meats and as a seasoning for stews and sautés.

makes about 1 1/4 cups

- 1/2 cup cumin seeds
- 1/4 cup coriander seeds
- 1 tablespoon black peppercorns
- 1/4 cup salt
- 1/4 cup Pimentón (Spanish smoked paprika; see note, page 43)
- 1 tablespoon paprika
- 2 teaspoons cayenne pepper

Toast the cumin and coriander in a small, dry skillet over medium heat, stirring often, until lightly browned, about 5 minutes. Using a spice grinder or clean coffee grinder, grind them to a powder, along with the peppercorns. Transfer to a small bowl, add the salt and remaining spices, and mix well.

alioli

ALIOLI IS THE ZESTY garlic mayonnaise from the Catalonia region of Spain. Besides being a killer sandwich spread, it makes a fine dip for vegetables. Or add a dollop to fish and chicken off the grill.

makes about 2 cups

- 2 garlic cloves, peeled
- 1/2 teaspoon salt
- 2 large egg yolks
- 1/2 teaspoon water
- 1/4 cup extra-virgin olive oil
- 3/4 cup peanut oil
- Juice of 1 lemon
- 1/2 teaspoon red wine vinegar (see note)
- 1/2 teaspoon sherry vinegar (see note)

Using a mortar and pestle (see note), pound the garlic and salt together until it is a smooth, creamy paste.

In a food processor or in a bowl using a whisk, process or beat together the egg yolks and water until smooth. With the processor running or while continuously whisking, slowly pour in the oils, a few drops at first until the mixture emulsifies, and then in a slow, steady stream. You can add more water if the mixture becomes too thick. Add the lemon juice and vinegars. Mix in the garlic paste until smooth. The *alioli* can be kept in a tightly covered container in the refrigerator for up to 4 days.

notes from our test kitchen

- In place of a mortar and pestle, you can use a knife to smash the garlic and salt into a creamy paste. Start by mincing the garlic. Then add the salt and continue mincing and flattening the garlic with the broad side of your knife. The garlic will break down into a paste as you go.
- If you don't have both red wine vinegar and sherry vinegar in your pantry, use all of one or the other.

SOURCE: *Bruce Aidells's Complete Book of Pork* by Bruce Aidells with Lisa Weiss

COOK: Bruce Aidells

oven-roasted ribs with coffee molasses marinade

A SPICY COFFEE-MOLASSES MARINADE provides the perfect bitter, almost smoky counterpoint to the juicy pork ribs, and it creates a gorgeous mahogany sheen. It also doubles as a dipping sauce. While oven-roasted ribs will never be as exquisitely tender as those cooked on an authentic outdoor pit barbecue, they come awfully close, and the flavor can't be beat. Besides, they only take 1½ to 2 hours in your oven and save you the trouble of tending an outdoor grill for hours.

Bruce Aidells, the wizard behind this recipe and the true king of meat, tells us that this marinade would be good on beef short ribs or even prime rib, but we can't imagine anything better than what it does for the meaty spareribs.

serves 6

MARINADE

- 1 cup strong brewed coffee
- ½ cup mild molasses
- ½ cup red wine vinegar
- ¼ cup Dijon mustard
- ¼ cup soy sauce
- 1 tablespoon Worcestershire sauce
- 1 tablespoon Tabasco, or other hot sauce
- 1 cup coarsely chopped red onion
- 2 tablespoons chopped shallot or scallions

- 2 slabs St. Louis–style spareribs (about 2½ pounds each), or 2 slabs spareribs (about 3 pounds each) or 3 slabs back ribs (about 1½ pounds each; see tip)

TO MARINATE THE RIBS:

Combine the marinade ingredients.

Put the ribs in a deep dish or resealable plastic bag and pour the marinade over. Turn the ribs to coat them, cover, and refrigerate for 16 to 30 hours.

Preheat the oven to 350 degrees.

Remove the ribs from the marinade and let the excess drip off. Reserve 1 cup of the marinade and transfer it to a small saucepan to use as a dipping sauce. Reserve the remaining marinade to use as a basting sauce.

Put the ribs fat sides up on a rack over a roasting pan (see note). Roast until the meat begins to pull away from the bones, 1½ to 2 hours, basting every 20 minutes with the marinade reserved for basting.

Meanwhile, bring the marinade reserved for sauce to a boil over high heat. Reduce the heat and simmer for 3 minutes. Set aside to serve as a dipping sauce for the ribs.

Once the ribs are tender, if you want to brown and caramelize the surface, preheat the broiler. Broil the ribs 3 to 4 inches from the heat until they bubble and brown, 2 to 3 minutes. (You may also brown the ribs directly over a charcoal or gas grill.) Serve with the dipping sauce.

notes from our test kitchen

- Fat side up means bone side down.
- The drippings from these ribs can make quite a mess. For easier cleanup, line your pan with heavy-duty foil or a silicone baking liner (no matter how gunked up the baking liner gets, it wipes right off).
- Be sure not to taste (or serve) the reserved marinade until you have simmered it for at least 3 minutes, because it has been in contact with the raw pork.

tip

In his *Complete Book of Pork*, Bruce Aidells explains the different kinds of pork ribs. Spareribs, his outright favorite, come from the pork belly once the bacon has been removed. Slabs of regular spareribs have one wide, thick end that includes the breast bones, a cartilaginous part of the pig with no real meat. St. Louis–style spareribs have been trimmed to remove these unwanted breast bones so the slabs are more regular and rectangular in shape. St. Louis–style spareribs are preferable, but if you can only find ordinary spareribs, Aidells suggests trimming away the thicker breast bones yourself before marinating and roasting them. A meaty slab of St. Louis–style ribs should weigh at least 2 pounds; 2½ pounds is better.

Back ribs, sometimes called baby back ribs, come from the back of the pig. They're what is left when a butcher cuts away a pork loin from the bones. Back ribs are leaner and have much less meat than spareribs, making them daintier to serve but less succulent to eat. Figure 1 pound of back ribs per person and about ¾ pound of spareribs per person.

SOURCE: *Esquire*
COOK: Francine Maroukian

green chili with pork and poblanos

THIS HEARTY GREEN CHILI, or *chili verde*, gets all its flavor from the combination of chiles (poblanos, green chiles, and jalapeños), a few tomatillos, and a handful of diced celery. We love the way it's not all mucked up with spices, so the sweet, smoky flavor of the chiles and the richness of the pork come through. The addition of a single potato (peeled and grated) thickens the stew just enough.

If you have the good fortune to live near a market that sells a good selection of Mexican ingredients, shopping for this chili will be a cinch. While you can roast and peel your own poblanos and use fresh tomatillos in place of canned, it's a lot easier if you can find the good canned stuff. If there's no good market nearby, consider mail-order at a place like Kitchen Market (888-HOT-4433; www.kitchenmarket.com).

serves 4

- 3 tablespoons olive oil
- 2 large yellow onions, chopped (about 2 cups)
- 1/2 cup diced celery
- 3 jalapeños, minced (see note)
- 5 garlic cloves, minced
- 2 pounds boneless pork shoulder, cut into 1/2-inch cubes and blotted dry (see note)
- 2 1/2 teaspoons Mexican oregano
- 2 1/2 cups chicken broth
- 1 small potato, peeled and grated (about 1/2 cup)
- 4 canned tomatillos, pureed (about 1/4 cup)
- 1 teaspoon coarse or kosher salt
- 2 large canned roasted poblano chiles, cut into 1/2-inch strips (about 1 cup)
- 3/4 cup canned green chiles, chopped
- 1 avocado, pitted, peeled, and finely chopped
- 2 ripe plum tomatoes, seeded and finely chopped

Heat the olive oil in a large stockpot over moderate heat. Add the onions, celery, jalapeños, and garlic, and cook, stirring occasionally, until the celery is softened, about 10 minutes. Add the pork and oregano and cook, stirring frequently, until the pork loses its color, 8 to 10 minutes. Add the broth, potato, tomatillos, and salt and bring to a boil. Reduce the heat and cook, partially covered, for $1^1/2$ hours, stirring occasionally. Add the poblano and green chiles and cook, stirring frequently, until the pork is tender, 30 to 45 minutes more. Ladle into warm serving bowls and top with the avocado and tomato.

notes from our test kitchen

- You can control the heat of the chili by removing the seeds from the jalapeños or leaving them in. Left in, the seeds of 3 fresh jalapeños can make this quite spicy. If your palate is more on the timid side, remove the seeds from 1 or 2 of the jalapeños. We encourage you to leave some in; it wouldn't be a proper chili without a little bit of heat.
- If you're having trouble finding 2 pounds boneless pork shoulder, look for boneless country-style ribs. They are cut from the shoulder and are often easier to find.

SOURCE: *Food & Wine*
COOK: Grace Parisi

dulce de leche–glazed ham

JUST WHEN WE THOUGHT there was nothing new to do to a ham, along came this recipe. A lot of Americans know dulce de leche only as that new flavor from Häagen-Dazs, but this wonderful Latin caramelized milk has a lot of other possibilities in the kitchen. Here it's used to make a glaze for the ham, and its sweetness is tempered by two kinds of mustard and a little garlic and cayenne. Any remaining glaze goes into the drippings, which are particularly flavorful because the ham is roasted on a bed of onion, producing a slightly sweet and succulent gravy.

This recipe serves a crowd. If you have leftovers, reheat them in a little of the gravy. Leftovers also make great sandwiches.

serves 12

- 1/2 cup dulce de leche (see note)
- 6 tablespoons Dijon mustard
- 2 tablespoons whole-grain mustard
- 1 large garlic clove, minced
- 1/4 teaspoon cayenne pepper
- 1 1/4 cups chicken broth
- 1 10-pound bone-in smoked ham
- 1 medium onion, thinly sliced

Preheat the oven to 375 degrees.

Whisk together the dulce de leche, mustards, garlic, and cayenne in a small saucepan. Whisk in 1/4 cup of the broth.

Trim the skin off the ham, leaving a 1/4-inch layer of fat. Score the fat in a shallow crosshatch pattern. Spread the onion slices in a large roasting pan. Set the ham on top and add 1/2 cup of the remaining broth. Cover the ham with parchment paper, then cover the roasting pan with foil. Roast the ham for 1 1/4 hours.

Remove the foil and parchment and brush the ham with all but 1/4 cup of the dulce de leche glaze. Roast the ham for 1 hour more, or until nicely glazed all over. Transfer the ham to a cutting board and let rest for at least 15 minutes.

Meanwhile, pour the pan drippings into a small saucepan and skim off as much of the fat as possible. Set the roasting pan over two burners. Add the remaining 1/2 cup broth and cook, scraping up any browned bits from the bottom and sides of the pan.

Pour the deglazed liquid into the saucepan. Whisk in the remaining 1/4 cup dulce de leche glaze and bring to a boil. Transfer the gravy to a warmed gravy boat. Thinly slice the ham and serve with the gravy.

note from our test kitchen

Dulce de leche can be found in many gourmet shops, some supermarkets, and Mexican markets.

tip

Since you'll have leftover dulce de leche, you might want to try Grace Parisi's idea of swirling it into whipped cream—or whipping them together—and putting a dollop over anything chocolate. If the dulce de leche is too firm to mix easily, warm it a bit first in the microwave or stick the jar in a saucepan of hot water.

SOURCE: *Food & Wine*
STORY BY Charlotte Druckman
COOK: Mario Batali

lamb braised in milk with garlic and fennel

WHEN WE HEARD Mario Batali describe this dish as "absolute poetry," we admit that we were tempted to roll our eyes. But one taste of this exquisite braise was all it took for us to see exactly what he meant. We can't remember ever tasting lamb as tender, sweet, and flavorful as this. The trick is slowly simmering the chunks of lamb in an indecent amount of milk and heavy cream, subtly seasoned with garlic, fennel seeds, parsley, and rosemary. Once the lamb is fork-tender, the braising liquid gets cooked down and blended into a luscious, creamy sauce. The recipe is based on one from the chef's latest book, *Molto Italiano*.

The braised lamb can be made ahead and refrigerated overnight. Reheat it gently before serving.

serves 8

- 3 garlic cloves, minced
- 1 cup chopped fresh flat-leaf parsley
- 2 teaspoons fennel seeds
- 1/2 cup extra-virgin olive oil
- 4 pounds boneless lamb shoulder, trimmed and cut into 2-inch pieces
- Salt and freshly ground black pepper
- 1 quart milk (see note)
- 1 1/4 cups heavy cream
- 2 fresh rosemary sprigs

Using a chef's knife, chop the garlic with the parsley and fennel seeds to form a coarse paste. Heat the olive oil in a large enameled cast-iron casserole over medium heat (see note). Add the garlic paste and cook until fragrant, about 1 minute. Increase the heat to medium-high and add half the lamb pieces. Cook, turning, until lightly browned all over. Transfer the lamb to a bowl and season with salt and pepper. Repeat the process with the remaining lamb.

Add 1/2 cup of the milk to the casserole and cook over high heat for 2 minutes, stirring to scrape up any browned bits. Add the remaining 3 1/2 cups milk, the cream, rosemary, and seared lamb and its juices. Bring to a simmer, then reduce the heat to low. Cover and cook, stirring occasionally, until the lamb is tender, about $1^1/_4$ hours.

Using a slotted spoon, transfer the lamb to a bowl; discard the rosemary. Boil the milk mixture over high heat, stirring occasionally, until reduced to 4 cups, about 10 minutes. Working in batches, puree the hot milk mixture in a blender. Return the sauce to the casserole, add the lamb, and simmer over low heat until warmed through. Season with salt and pepper and serve.

notes from our test kitchen

- This unabashedly rich dish is no place for low-fat milk.
- If you don't have the right-size enameled cast-iron casserole (aka Dutch oven), choose your heaviest-gauge saucepan with a tight-fitting lid. Watch the heat carefully so that the liquid simmers but never boils.
- We had a little trouble when we cooked the garlic-fennel paste first and then seared the lamb on top of it, because the bits of garlic tended to burn. A good solution is to begin by searing the lamb pieces in the oil over medium-high heat. Then, just before each batch of lamb is lightly browned, add half the garlic-fennel paste, stir it around a bit with the lamb until it becomes fragrant, and spoon the lamb into the bowl and continue.
- After removing the lamb from the pot and before boiling the braising liquid, you may want to skim off some of the fat from the surface of the liquid. Don't worry about removing all of it.
- Be cautious when blending the hot liquid. Always vent the lid to let the steam escape by leaving it open a crack or removing the center plug. Then hold the lid in place with a thick kitchen towel.

SOURCE: *Indian Home Cooking*
by Suvir Saran and Stephanie Lyness

COOK: Suvir Saran after Hemant Mathur

tandoori lamb chops

TANDOOR-COOKED LAMB CHOPS are almost always terrific, but we assumed they wouldn't work in a home oven. We first tried this version at Devi, Suvir Saran's Indian restaurant in Manhattan, where the chops are cooked in a real tandoor oven. They don't taste quite the same at home, but they still have their haunting flavors of sweet spices and their wonderful crust, the result of an overnight marinade and a finishing touch of melted butter.

The flavors are so complex that it's hard to believe these chops are not difficult to make. We like them best grilled, which enhances the crust factor, but they're also excellent roasted in a very hot oven. Because you have to start them a day ahead, they're great for fuss-free entertaining.

serves 4

- 2 pounds rib lamb chops, 1–1½ inches thick
- 8 medium garlic cloves, ground very fine or minced to a paste
- 1 3-inch piece fresh ginger, peeled and minced very fine or ground to a paste (see note)
- 1 tablespoon paprika
- 1 tablespoon Garam Masala (*recipe follows*)
- 1 tablespoon toasted cumin seeds (see note), coarsely ground
- 1 teaspoon salt
- ½ teaspoon cayenne pepper
- ¼ teaspoon ground mace
- ¼ teaspoon ground nutmeg
- ¾ cup plain yogurt, drained in a cheesecloth-lined strainer or a coffee filter for 2 hours (see note)
- ¼ cup malt vinegar (see note)
- Juice of 1 lemon
- 2 tablespoons canola oil
- 3 tablespoons melted butter

Cut 3 or 4 deep slashes in each of the chops.

Mix all the remaining ingredients except the oil and butter in a bowl (not plastic) large enough to hold the chops. Add the chops and toss to coat with the marinade. Put the chops and marinade in a large resealable plastic bag and refrigerate overnight.

When ready to cook, preheat the oven to 550 degrees (see note) or light the grill.

Add the oil to the bag with the chops and reseal. Massage the bag between your hands to oil the chops.

To roast the chops in the oven, put a rack over a foil-lined baking pan. Remove the chops from the marinade and arrange the chops on top. Roast for 20 minutes, then remove from the oven and let rest for 5 minutes. Drizzle with the melted butter, then return to the oven for 10 minutes more for medium-rare.

To grill the chops, remove them from the marinade and grill for 5 minutes per side. Let rest for 5 minutes off the grill. Brush with the butter and grill for 5 minutes more on each side for medium-rare.

notes from our test kitchen

- Lean chops are the best option here; the ones from New Zealand are leaner than American lamb.
- Toast the cumin seeds in a small dry skillet over medium heat, stirring often, until lightly browned, 2 to 3 minutes.
- The easiest way to deal with the ginger is to scrape the skin off with a spoon (easier than peeling with a vegetable peeler or a knife) and then cut it up and grind it in a food processor.
- You can save yourself a step by using Greek yogurt or Middle Eastern labne, which are already drained. In 2 hours, 3/4 cup yogurt will reduce to about 1/2 cup when drained, so just use 1/2 cup.
- Markets with some British products often carry malt vinegar, the traditional vinegar for fish and chips. If it's not around, just use a good organic cider vinegar.
- Many home ovens won't go as high as 550 degrees. Just use the highest temperature on yours and alter the cooking time accordingly.

garam masala

IF YOU CAN'T FIND THIS SPICE MIX elsewhere, make your own, which will be infinitely better. Suvir Saran's is especially fragrant and complex.

makes about 3/4 cup

- 1/3 cup coriander seeds
- 1/4 cup cumin seeds
- 1 heaping tablespoon green cardamom pods
- 1 heaping tablespoon black peppercorns
- 1 cinnamon stick, broken into pieces
- 2 teaspoons whole cloves
- 1 whole dried red chile
- 2 bay leaves
- 1/8 teaspoon ground mace

Combine everything but the mace in a medium skillet over medium heat and toast, stirring constantly, until the cumin seeds turn uniformly brown, 4 to 5 minutes. Grind to a powder in a spice grinder. Stir in the mace and store in an airtight container for up to 4 months.

side dishes

SOURCE: *The Breath of a Wok* by Grace Young and Alan Richardson

COOK: Grace Young

stir-fried garlic lettuce

One of the most beautiful and inspired cookbooks of the year was *The Breath of a Wok.* Grace Young's stories and recipes make us want to set off in pursuit of *wok hay,* the special taste of wok-cooked food. But if the wok itself is too much to tackle, Young gives us permission to stir-fry in a skillet, as her parents did when they emigrated from China to San Francisco.

Choosing a recipe from this collection was no easy feat, and we landed on this lettuce because of its refreshing crunch, sweetness, and ease of preparation. Chopped-up hearts of romaine are quickly stir-fried with smashed garlic cloves until the leaves are barely tender and still bright green. When serving, don't leave the whole garlic cloves behind in the wok; they are also delicious.

Young tells us that the Cantonese word for lettuce sounds like the words for "growing fortune," which makes this an auspicious dish to serve for the lunar New Year.

serves 4

- 1 tablespoon Shaoxing rice wine (see note) or dry sherry
- 1 tablespoon soy sauce
- 3/4 teaspoon sugar
- 1/2 teaspoon salt
- 2 tablespoons vegetable oil
- 5 medium garlic cloves, smashed and peeled
- 1 pound hearts of romaine lettuce, cut crosswise into 1-inch-wide pieces
- 1 teaspoon sesame oil (see note)

Combine the rice wine or sherry, soy sauce, sugar, and salt in a small bowl.

Heat a 14-inch flat-bottomed wok over high heat until a bead of water vaporizes within 1 to 2 seconds of contact. Swirl in the vegetable oil, add the garlic, and stir-fry for 5 seconds. Add the lettuce and stir-fry for 1 to 2 minutes, or until it is just limp. Stir the sauce, swirl it into the wok, and stir-fry for 30 seconds to 1 minute more, or until the lettuce is just tender and still bright green. Remove from the heat, drizzle on the sesame oil, and serve.

notes from our test kitchen

- Shaoxing (sometimes spelled Shoah Hsing) is a well-aged Chinese rice wine. Amber-colored, it has a higher-than-average alcohol content (close to 18 percent) and tastes and smells more like dry sherry than wine made from grapes. In its place, use dry sherry, not sake or any other wine.
- Use roasted or toasted sesame oil, not the neutral-tasting cold-pressed oil, and definitely not the hot, spicy version. Choose one made from pure roasted sesame seeds and not blended with other oils. Young recommends the Kadoya brand. Sesame oil should be stored in the refrigerator, where it will keep for up to 1 year.
- If you wash the lettuce, do your best to dry it thoroughly. The oil will splatter terribly if the lettuce is still wet.
- If you don't have a 14-inch flat-bottomed wok, make this in your largest skillet.

SOURCE: *New York Times*
STORY BY Mark Bittman
COOK: Charles Phan

bok choy with shiitakes

IF YOU'RE LOOKING FOR AN EXCITING SIDE DISH to perk up a steak, roast pork, poultry, or seafood, look no further. Once you've chopped the bok choy and trimmed the mushrooms, the actual cooking takes only minutes—less than the time it takes for people to find their seats. The recipe comes from Charles Phan, the talent behind the wok at San Francisco's wildly popular Slanted Door restaurant. We're so enamored with the balance of sweet, sour, and salty flavors and the way the meaty shiitakes play off the tender bok choy that we sometimes make this into a meal by spooning it over a bowl of steamed rice. If you do the same, expect it to serve only 2.

serves 4

- 2 tablespoons neutral oil, such as corn or canola
- 1 tablespoon minced garlic
- 4–6 heads baby bok choy or 1/2 head large bok choy, leaves and stems separated and stems coarsely chopped
- 10 small shiitake mushrooms, caps only, left whole
- 1 teaspoon sugar
- 1/2 cup chicken broth or water, plus more if needed
- 2 tablespoons Asian fish sauce

Heat a wok or large skillet over high heat and add the oil. When the oil smokes, add the garlic. Stir once and add the bok choy. Cook for 1 to 2 minutes, or until it just begins to brown. Stir and add the shiitakes and sugar.

Cook, stirring occasionally, for 1 to 2 minutes. Add the chicken broth or water and fish sauce. Cook, stirring, until the bok choy is tender. Add a bit more broth or water if necessary—the mixture should not dry out entirely. Serve immediately.

notes from our test kitchen

- Test a piece of bok choy stem before taking it from the heat. The stem should be tender throughout.
- If you want to double the recipe, cook this in batches. Overcrowding the wok or skillet will cause the vegetables to steam, and they won't have the same texture and good flavor.

SOURCE: *Bon Appétit*
STORY BY Diane Rossen Worthington
COOK: Diane Rossen Worthington

roasted broccoli florets with gremolata

WHAT A GREAT WAY TO SERVE BROCCOLI! First you roast it with a little olive oil until it's crisp-tender and just browned at the edges, then you splash it with fresh lemon juice. Most other cooks would be happy at this point, but Diane Worthington tops it all with a variation on gremolata, the traditional garnish for osso buco: lemon zest, shallot, and crunchy golden bread crumbs.

Better yet, this way of cooking broccoli is fast and easy. You can make the gremolata up to 4 hours before you serve the broccoli. And roasting the florets in the oven makes the entire prep a cakewalk.

serves 6

- 4 tablespoons olive oil
- 1 shallot, chopped
- 1/2 cup coarse fresh bread crumbs made from crustless French bread
- 2 teaspoons grated lemon zest
- Salt and freshly ground black pepper
- 2 pounds broccoli, stems removed, tops cut into 2-inch-long florets
- Juice of 1/2 lemon or more to taste

Heat 1 tablespoon of the oil in a heavy medium skillet over medium-high heat. Add the shallot and sauté until beginning to brown, about 2 minutes. Add the bread crumbs and toast until golden, stirring frequently, about 3 minutes. Transfer the mixture to a small bowl. Mix in the lemon zest and season to taste with salt and pepper. You can make the gremolata up to 4 hours ahead.

Preheat the oven to 425 degrees.

Toss the broccoli with the remaining 3 tablespoons oil in a large bowl. Sprinkle with salt and pepper and toss to coat. Spread the florets out on a large rimmed baking sheet. Roast until the stems are crisp-tender and lightly browned, about 20 minutes. Sprinkle with the lemon juice. Transfer to a serving bowl or platter. Sprinkle with the gremolata and serve.

SOURCE: *The Big Book of Backyard Cooking* by Betty Rosbottom

COOK: Betty Rosbottom

artichokes with pecorino, black pepper, and olive oil

WE DON'T USUALLY THINK of artichokes being an easy dish, but this one really is. The prep is minimal, then you toss the artichokes into boiling water for about 25 minutes. Pluck them out and let them drain while you make the world's easiest sauce to pour into the artichokes' hearts. Then at the table, you pull off the leaves and dip them into the rest of the sauce. After all the leaves have been eaten, the hearts will be nicely seasoned.

The trick, of course, is to use the really good stuff; such simple food lives or dies by the quality of its few ingredients. So choose an excellent pecorino (we like the Fulvi brand), a fine, heady, extra-virgin olive oil, and freshly cracked pepper. That's it.

The artichokes make great companions for grilled meats, such as steaks or chops. And they make a great casual first course, too.

serves 4

- 4 medium artichokes (about 8 ounces each)
- 1/2 cup fruity extra-virgin olive oil
- 6 tablespoons grated pecorino Romano cheese
- Cracked or coarsely ground black pepper
- Kosher salt

Bring a large pot of water to a boil over medium-high heat. Meanwhile, prepare the artichokes. Cut off and discard the stems so they'll sit upright without wobbling. Place each artichoke on its side and, using a sharp knife, cut off and discard about 3/4 inch of the top. Using scissors, trim and discard the sharp tips from the artichoke leaves.

Place the artichokes in the boiling water. Cover and leave the lid slightly ajar. Cook until the bases are tender when pierced with a knife and the leaves around the base can be pulled off easily, 25 to 30 minutes. Remove and drain the artichokes upside down on a plate for 5 minutes.

Meanwhile, make the sauce. Mix together the olive oil, cheese, 1 teaspoon pepper, and 1/4 teaspoon salt in a small bowl. Taste and add more salt and pepper if needed.

To serve, arrange 1 artichoke upright on each of four salad plates. Spread the leaves open and, using a spoon, scoop out the fuzzy center chokes. Salt and pepper the cavities, then spoon 1 tablespoon of the sauce into each artichoke. Divide the remaining sauce among four small ramekins or bowls and place beside the artichokes on the salad plates. Serve.

note from our test kitchen

- Tuscan or Provençal oils are good choices here.

SOURCE: *O, The Oprah Magazine*
STORY BY Laurie Winer
COOK: Govind Armstrong

roasted carrots, pearl onions, and wild mushrooms with tarragon

IF YOU'RE LOOKING FOR an unusual, elegant side dish for Thanksgiving dinner, try this one from Los Angeles chef Govind Armstrong. Wild mushrooms and fresh tarragon put a new face on carrots and onions. A mix of different varieties of mushrooms gives a more complex flavor. The vegetables are first roasted with lots of thyme sprigs, then sauced.

There's a little fussing to do here, as one might expect for a dish with so many subtle flavors.

serves 8

- Kosher salt
- 1 1/2 pounds pearl onions (see note)
- 2 1-pound bags baby carrots
- 16 large fresh thyme sprigs
- 2 tablespoons extra-virgin olive oil
- 3/4 teaspoon freshly ground black pepper
- 8 ounces mixed wild mushrooms (cremini, shiitake, oyster)
- 2 tablespoons butter
- 1/2 cup chicken broth
- 2 tablespoons sherry vinegar
- 2 tablespoons chopped fresh tarragon leaves

Bring a large pot of salted water to a boil. Add the onions. Cook for 2 minutes, then drain and cool. Trim the stem and root ends and slip off the skins.

Preheat the oven to 450 degrees.

Place the onions and carrots on separate rimmed baking sheets. To each pan, add 8 thyme sprigs, 1 tablespoon olive oil, 1/2 teaspoon salt, and 1/4 teaspoon pepper. Toss until the vegetables are coated evenly. Roast for 25 minutes, tossing the vegetables several times, until lightly caramelized and slightly tender; cool. Discard the thyme sprigs. The vegetables can be made up to 3 hours ahead and held at room temperature.

Quarter the cremini mushrooms, remove the stems from the shiitakes, and slice the oyster mushrooms. Melt the butter in a large skillet over high heat. Sauté the mushrooms until tender, about 4 minutes. Add the carrots, onions, broth, and vinegar. Cook, tossing, until heated through, 3 to 4 minutes. Add the tarragon, 1/4 teaspoon salt, and the remaining 1/4 teaspoon pepper, toss, and serve.

note from our test kitchen

To speed this recipe along, use frozen pearl onions, which means you can ignore the first step. Just defrost the onions completely and pat them dry before continuing.

SOURCE: *Washington Post*

COOK: Ed Bruske after Anna del Conte and Corby Kummer

braised green beans with tomato and fennel

ONE OF THE COOKING TRENDS we're happiest about is the resurrection of slow-cooked vegetables, and no single member of the kingdom benefits more from this treatment than green beans. While we'll always appreciate the crisp-tender goodness of summer's freshest (and skinniest) specimens, nothing beats the pleasure of digging your fork into a helping of sumptuously tender braised beans. Sure, they turn drab and limp, but oh, man, one taste can make you weak in the knees.

Cooks from the American South and Italy were never brainwashed by the French blanch-and-shock method and have always known that long-cooked vegetables are best. The inspiration for this recipe comes from Anna del Conte, the Italian food historian and cookbook author, and it has both Italian (the fennel and tomato) and southern (the bacon) accents. The only liquid is tomato juice and whatever juices the beans give off, which become concentrated and intensely flavorful. When we say slow-cooked, we mean slow—the beans simmer gently for 3 full hours.

serves 6 to 8

- 2 tablespoons bacon drippings or olive oil
- 1 medium yellow onion, thinly sliced
- 1 pound green beans, trimmed (see note)
- 1 $14\frac{1}{2}$-ounce can diced tomatoes, with the liquid
- 2 thick slices bacon, diced, or 1 ham hock
- 1 teaspoon freshly ground fennel seeds (see note)
- $\frac{1}{2}$ teaspoon salt
- Freshly ground black pepper

Heat the bacon drippings or oil in a heavy pot or Dutch oven with a tight-fitting lid over medium heat. Add the onion and cook, stirring occasionally, until tender, about 5 minutes. Add the beans, tomatoes with juice, bacon or ham hock, fennel, salt, and pepper to taste and bring to a simmer.

Cover, reduce the heat to very low, and simmer gently until tender, about 3 hours, stirring and tasting the beans occasionally. Season with salt and pepper to taste. Serve warm.

notes from our test kitchen

- The best beans for braising are mature ones, long and thick, not the skinny haricots verts. Save those for the quick dip in boiling salted water.
- To grind fennel seeds, use a mortar and pestle or chop the seeds with a large chef's knife. Since they cook for so long, it's okay to leave them coarsely ground. The preground stuff won't give you the same flavor.
- If you like a kick to your food, go ahead and add a generous amount of coarsely ground black pepper. It will play nicely with the other flavors.
- These beans are just as good made ahead. Gently reheat them before serving.

tip

In his *Washington Post* article, Ed Bruske summarized research that Corby Kummer, one of the country's most authoritative food writers, published in the *Atlantic Monthly*. Flavor compounds take a long time (hours, even) to develop. Indeed, flavor does not necessarily fade with color; the two are governed by distinctly different compounds. In addition, green beans contain a fibrous substance, lignin, also found in wood, hemp, and linen, which can be hard to digest unless fully cooked.

SOURCE: *The Whole Beast* by Fergus Henderson

COOK: Fergus Henderson

mushy zucchini

ST. JOHN, Fergus Henderson's London restaurant, has become a mecca for serious eaters from all over the world. What they love about Henderson's cooking is his astonishing ability to take the most common thing and transform it into something extraordinary. Very often the transformations involve bits of a pig that are usually dismissed by other cooks—tails, snouts, trotters. But Henderson is equally inventive with something as ordinary and even boring as zucchini. In his hands it becomes a succulent treasure, not an undercooked holdover from some health craze. When you eat this dish, you feel you're tasting real zucchini for the first time, that its true spirit has finally been released. Lovers of al dente vegetables, beware—your days are numbered.

serves 6

- 8 tablespoons (1 stick) unsalted butter
- 4 garlic cloves, minced
- 1 pound zucchini, trimmed and sliced into rounds a little thicker than 1/3 inch
- Sea salt and freshly ground black pepper

Melt the butter in a large skillet over low heat and sweat the garlic, making sure it doesn't brown or burn. Add the zucchini, season carefully with salt and pepper, and toss to coat. Cover and continue the gentle cooking, stirring occasionally.

After 15 minutes, uncover. When some of the zucchini slices start to break, binding the whole together, check the seasoning and serve.

SOURCE: *New York* magazine
STORY BY Rob Patronite
COOK: Andrew Feinberg

roasted brussels sprouts with walnuts and pecorino

NO MORE WRINKLED NOSES when people hear you're serving Brussels sprouts—they'll be begging for more. Properly cooked Brussels sprouts are sweet, nutty, and full of good flavor. In this preparation, from Franny's restaurant in Brooklyn, they're also anointed with olive oil and given a good roasting. The walnuts and pecorino are perfect counterpoints. Look for fresh Brussels sprouts on their long stalks in the fall at the farmers' market.

serves 4

- 1/2 cup walnuts
- 24 Brussels sprouts, cut in half
- Extra-virgin olive oil
- Salt and freshly ground black pepper
- Squeeze of fresh lemon juice
- Aged pecorino Toscano for topping

Preheat the oven to 350 degrees.

Toast the walnuts on a rimmed baking sheet for about 10 minutes, or until they smell toasty; set aside. Crumble them when they're cool enough to handle.

Turn the oven up to 450 degrees.

Toss the Brussels sprouts in a bowl with enough olive oil to coat each sprout, 2 to 3 tablespoons. Season with salt and pepper to taste.

Arrange the sprouts in a single layer on the baking sheet and roast for about 20 minutes, or until fork-tender and some of the leaves have become crunchy.

Let the sprouts cool on the baking sheet, then toss in a large bowl with the walnuts. Drizzle liberally with olive oil, add a squeeze of lemon, and season with salt and pepper.

Shave some of the pecorino on top and serve warm.

SOURCE: *Daniel's Dish* by Daniel Boulud

COOK: Daniel Boulud

spaghetti squash roasted with sage and bacon

MANY COOKS ARE FAMILIAR with this golden winter squash, whose flesh cooks up into strands like noodles, and most recipes we know call for steaming and saucing the squash as if it were pasta. Daniel Boulud thinks spaghetti squash has more going for it than its novel appearance, and he proves his point with this elegant side dish. Roasting the squash concentrates its mild, sweet flavor, which is accented by savory bacon, onion, garlic, and sage. This is an unexpected and reliable side dish for roast meats and poultry from autumn through winter.

serves 4 to 6

- 2 tablespoons extra-virgin olive oil
- 1/4 pound country-style bacon, cut into 1/4-inch cubes (see note)
- 1 cup thinly sliced white onion
- 2 garlic cloves, thinly sliced
- 2 sprigs fresh sage, stemmed and coarsely chopped, plus a few more sprigs for garnish
- 2 medium spaghetti squash (2–3 pounds each), halved lengthwise and seeded
- 1 tablespoon unsalted butter
- Salt and freshly ground black pepper

Place a rack in the center of the oven and preheat to 350 degrees.

Heat the oil in a large roasting pan over medium heat. Add the bacon and cook until lightly browned. Drain off half the fat. Add the onion, garlic, and chopped sage, tossing to combine. Place the squash halves on top, cut sides down, and cover the pan with foil. Bake until tender, 50 to 60 minutes.

Using a fork, scrape out the pulp in long strands. Return the pulp to the roasting pan. Add the butter, season with salt and pepper, and toss to combine. Serve immediately, decorated with a few sage sprigs.

note from our test kitchen

You can leave the bacon out if you like.

tips

In her enormously helpful *Field Guide to Produce*, Aliza Green explains that the larger the spaghetti squash, the thicker its fibers. For a more delicate dish, stick with two smaller squashes. If you like the thicker, noodle-shaped strands, go for one large (5- to 6-pound) squash. Beyond that, purchase only rock-hard squash; any soft spots indicate bruising or spoiling. Choose winter squash with matte rather than shiny skin, and store in a cool, dark place.

SOURCE: *Home Plate Cooking*
by Marvin Woods and Virginia Willis

COOK: Marvin Woods

tomatoes stuffed with bacon and corn bread

STUFFED AND BAKED TOMATOES launched a strong comeback this year, and of all the versions we tried, this one from a young southern chef won our hearts. There's just something impossible to resist about the combination of bacon, corn bread, and tomatoes bound together with a little mayonnaise. While these are best in the summer made from truly ripe, locally grown tomatoes, the dish is also a good way to salvage well-traveled supermarket tomatoes. Feel free to play around with the seasonings, trying different herbs, such as parsley or basil, and adding some freshly grated Parmesan.

serves 8

- 4 large ripe tomatoes
- 2 cups crumbled corn bread (see tip)
- 1/2 cup mayonnaise
- 6 slices bacon, cooked until crisp and crumbled
- 2 scallions, chopped
- 2 sprigs fresh thyme, leaves chopped
- Coarse salt and freshly ground black pepper

Preheat the oven to 350 degrees. Coat a baking dish with nonstick cooking spray (see note).

Halve the tomatoes horizontally with a serrated knife. Using a spoon, carefully scoop out the pulp and reserve.

Combine the tomato pulp, corn bread, mayonnaise, bacon, scallions, and thyme in a medium bowl. Season with salt and pepper to taste.

Spoon the corn bread mixture into the tomato shells. Transfer the stuffed tomatoes in a single layer to the prepared baking dish. Bake until heated through, about 20 minutes. Serve.

notes from our test kitchen

- In place of nonstick cooking spray, we like to brush the pan with olive oil. It adds a nicer flavor.
- Depending on the size of the tomatoes, these may take an extra 8 to 10 minutes to cook through. We like them best when the mayonnaise is good and bubbly but the tomato shells haven't started to burst.

tip

Corn bread intended for stuffing should be a bit drier than most, and this Buttermilk Corn Bread from *The Gourmet Cookbook* is just that. (Even though it's meant for stuffing, the corn bread still makes good eating, especially warm from the oven and slathered with butter.) Whisk together 1 cup all-purpose flour, 3/4 cup yellow cornmeal, 1 1/2 teaspoons baking powder, 1/2 teaspoon baking soda, and 1/2 teaspoon salt in a large bowl. Whisk together 1 cup well-shaken buttermilk, 2 large eggs, and 4 tablespoons (1/2 stick) melted butter in another bowl. Add the wet ingredients to the dry and stir until just combined. Spread the batter evenly in a buttered 8-inch square pan and bake on the center rack of a 425-degree oven until golden, about 25 minutes. Cool in the pan.

SOURCE: *Bon Appétit*

STORY BY Zov Karamardian

COOK: Zov Karamardian

spinach and roasted red pepper gratin

NOTHING AT ALL WRONG with creamed spinach, but we love this Mediterranean-style gratin, which includes three different cheeses, leeks, and red bell peppers. It's also beautiful, with red bell pepper strips peeking through a creamy green field. More roasted red pepper strips on top make it a festive holiday choice.

Because you can make it a day ahead and it travels so well, this is a fine party dish. For vegetarians, it's substantial enough to be a mainstay on a buffet table.

serves 8

- 4 10-ounce bags fresh spinach leaves
- 3 red bell peppers
- 1½ tablespoons butter
- 1½ tablespoons olive oil
- 3 medium leeks (white and pale green parts only), thinly sliced and well washed (about 3 cups)
- 1 large shallot, chopped (about ¼ cup)
- 3 garlic cloves, minced
- 1 cup whipping cream
- 4 large eggs
- 1 cup part-skim ricotta cheese
- ½ cup grated Swiss cheese
- ¼ cup grated Parmesan cheese
- 1½ teaspoons salt
- ½ teaspoon freshly ground black pepper

Heat a large nonstick skillet over medium-high heat. Working in batches, about 10 cups at a time, sauté the spinach in the dry skillet until bright green and wilted, about 2 minutes per batch. Transfer the spinach to a strainer. Squeeze the spinach dry; roll in a kitchen towel to remove the excess water.

Char the peppers directly over a gas flame or under the broiler until blackened on all sides. Enclose in a paper bag and let stand for 10 minutes. Peel, seed, and slice the peppers into ¼-inch-wide strips.

Melt the butter with the oil in a large heavy skillet over medium heat. Add the leeks, shallot, and garlic and cook until soft, about 5 minutes. Remove from the heat.

Whisk together the cream and eggs in a large bowl. Whisk in the cheeses, salt, and pepper. Stir in the spinach, two thirds of the roasted pepper strips, and the leek mixture. If you're making the dish a day ahead, cover it and refrigerate. Bring to room temperature before proceeding.

Preheat the oven to 350 degrees.

Generously butter a 13-x-9-inch baking dish. Transfer the spinach mixture to the prepared dish. Bake the gratin until a knife inserted into the center comes out clean, about 50 minutes. Arrange the remaining red pepper strips decoratively over the top of the gratin and serve.

note from our test kitchen

We happened to have some small basil leaves around when we made this dish and impulsively tossed in a few torn leaves. We liked it.

butternut squash and pecan gratin with goat cheese

THIS HANDSOME GRATIN pairs tender, sweet slices of butternut squash with tangy fresh goat cheese and toasted pecans. The flavors of fall make it a welcome substitute for sweet potatoes at Thanksgiving. Or dress up an ordinary dinner of roast pork or chicken by serving it on the side. We also find it satisfying enough as a light supper along with a big salad.

serves 6 to 8

- 2 tablespoons unsalted butter
- 1 yellow onion, finely chopped
- 2 garlic cloves, minced
- 2 cups heavy cream
- 2 teaspoons kosher salt
- 1/2 teaspoon freshly ground black pepper
- 2 1/2 pounds butternut squash, peeled, seeded, and cut into 1/4-inch-thick slices
- 1 1/2 cups pecans, toasted and coarsely chopped (see note)
- 4 ounces fresh goat cheese, crumbled
- 3 tablespoons chopped fresh flat-leaf parsley for garnish

Preheat the oven to 350 degrees. Generously butter a 13-x-9-inch gratin dish.

Melt the butter in a large skillet over medium-high heat. Add the onion and cook, stirring, until lightly browned, about 5 minutes. Add the garlic and cook for 1 minute. Add the cream, salt, and pepper and bring to a boil. Add the squash and 3/4 cup of the pecans and return to a boil. Reduce the heat and simmer gently for 5 minutes (see note).

Transfer half the squash mixture to the prepared gratin dish. Dot with half the goat cheese. Cover with the remaining squash mixture and sprinkle the remaining goat cheese over the top. The gratin can be assembled several hours before baking, covered, and left at room temperature for up to 1 hour or refrigerated for 3 to 4 hours. Return to room temperature before baking.

Place the gratin dish on a sturdy baking sheet. Bake until the squash is very tender, the cream is mostly absorbed, and the top is golden, about 45 minutes. Remove from the oven and sprinkle with the remaining 3/4 cup pecans and the parsley. Let rest for 10 minutes before serving.

notes from our test kitchen

- For a truly tender gratin, we like to simmer the squash and cream together for about twice the amount of time the recipe calls for, closer to 10 minutes. The squash slices may fall apart some when you transfer them to the gratin dish, but the result will be more sumptuous.
- To toast the pecans, spread them in a single layer on a rimmed baking sheet. Bake in a 350-degree oven, shaking the pan occasionally, until they smell toasty, about 10 minutes.

tips

Real Simple offers this helpful advice for buying and storing butternut squash. Choose a squash that feels heavy for its size. Shiny or slightly green skin indicates an underripe squash. Look for dull cream- or caramel-colored skin. Do not refrigerate butternut squash, or it will become mealy. Store in a cool, dark place for up to a month.

Amy Goldman, author of *The Compleat Squash,* cautions us against winter squash that may have been harvested while immature. If you can pierce the skin with your thumbnail, the squash will improve a lot if you keep it in a cool place for 2 to 3 weeks.

SOURCE: *Fine Cooking*
STORY BY Jacques Pépin
COOK: Jacques Pépin

pommes fondantes
(skillet-roasted potatoes)

THE ENGLISH TRANSLATION OF THIS DISH, "skillet-roasted potatoes," doesn't do it justice. The literal translation, "melting potatoes," may sound wacky, but it does give you a sense of the creamy texture that you get when you cook potatoes this way. The technique is a classic French one (this recipe comes from the legendary Jacques Pépin, after all), whereby potatoes are simmered in broth until just tender. At that point, you press down on them one by one to crack them open, which allows them to absorb even more broth, giving them their melting texture and savory flavor. Once cracked, the potatoes continue to cook until all the broth has evaporated and they begin to sizzle and turn all crispy brown on the outside.

In the classic version, the potatoes are first trimmed into neat little ovals. Thankfully, Jacques has come up with a method that requires no peeling or fussy trimming, only shopping for the right potatoes—baby Yukon Gold or Red Bliss. Anything larger than 1¾ inches in diameter won't work. A nonstick skillet is essential so the potatoes don't stick to the pan as the liquid evaporates.

serves 4 to 6

- 2 pounds baby Yukon Gold or Red Bliss potatoes (20–25 potatoes, 1½–1¾ inches in diameter)
- 2 cups homemade or low-sodium chicken broth, plus more if needed
- 2 tablespoons good extra-virgin olive oil
- 1 tablespoon unsalted butter
- 1 sprig fresh rosemary
- 1 teaspoon kosher salt (less if the broth is salty)
- 1–2 tablespoons thinly sliced fresh chives
- Fleur de sel or other sea salt for serving (optional; see note)

Trim any eyes or damaged areas from the potatoes and wash well in cold water. Arrange as many potatoes as will fit in a single layer in a 10-inch nonstick skillet (there should be a little room to spare; save any extra potatoes for another use). Add the broth, oil, butter, rosemary, and salt. Bring to a boil over high heat. Reduce the heat to medium, cover the pan but leave the lid ajar, and boil until the potatoes are tender when pierced with a fork, about 20 minutes (see note). The liquid should still halfway surround the potatoes; if it doesn't, add more broth or water until it does.

Remove the pan from the heat and press on each potato with a metal 1/4-cup measuring cup just until it cracks open. Set the pan over medium-high heat and cook, uncovered, until all the liquid has evaporated and the potatoes have browned on one side, about 10 minutes. Gently turn the potatoes and brown the other side, 4 to 5 minutes.

Remove the pan from the heat and let the potatoes rest for 5 minutes before transferring them to a serving platter. Sprinkle with the chives and serve immediately, passing the fleur de sel at the table, if using.

notes from our test kitchen

- Be sure there's a little wiggle room in the pan. Once the potatoes are tender, you need to be able to flatten them slightly and still have them all fit.
- Be careful not to overcook the potatoes. If they are too soft, they will mash, not crack, when you press on them.
- When cracking open the potatoes, press gently but steadily. It may take a few potatoes to get the sense of how much pressure to apply. You want to crack open the skin, but the potatoes should hold together. Don't push so hard that you crush them.
- The little sprinkle of the crunchy French sea salt fleur de sel is a welcome finishing touch, but not essential. For more on fleur de sel, see page 249.

SOURCE: *A Year in a Vegetarian Kitchen* by Jack Bishop

COOK: Jack Bishop

drunken pinto beans with charred onions and chiles

YOU MAY KNOW JACK BISHOP as one of the cast on the hugely popular PBS television show *America's Test Kitchen*. What you may not know is that every night after work he cooks dinner for his mostly vegetarian family. As a result, the recipes Bishop comes up with must be quick to assemble using convenient ingredients, and, more important, they must satisfy his (and his family's) very discriminating palates.

These spicy beans (named "drunken beans," or *frijoles borrachos*, from the beer added to turn them into a brothy stew) are both quick to prepare and flavorful. To give the dish its toasty flavor, Bishop, who is part of a team known for carefully fine-tuning every recipe in order to achieve perfection, recomends cooking the onions and chiles over medium-high heat so that they char, almost burn in spots. Use as much chile as you can tolerate; the dish should be spicy.

The broth carries a lot of the flavor, so serve the beans over rice.

serves 6 (or 3 or 4 as a main dish)

- 2 tablespoons extra-virgin olive oil
- 2 medium onions, chopped
- 1–2 medium jalapeño or serrano chiles, seeded if desired to reduce heat, and minced
- 1 12-ounce bottle beer (see note)
- 2 15-ounce cans pinto beans, rinsed and drained
- 1 tablespoon fresh lime juice
- 2 tablespoons minced fresh cilantro leaves
- Salt

Heat the oil in a large skillet over medium-high heat until shimmering. Add the onions and chiles and cook, stirring occasionally, until browned, 8 to 10 minutes.

Add the beer and bring to a boil. Stir in the beans and simmer until the flavors meld, about 10 minutes. (The beans should be juicy but not swimming in liquid.) Stir in the lime juice, cilantro, and salt to taste. Serve, or refrigerate in an airtight container for 1 to 2 days and reheat.

notes from our test kitchen

- Choose a medium-weight beer with a flavor you enjoy. We like Corona, but use what you have on hand.
- Pinto beans are traditional here, but we also like to make this with black beans. Even white beans work well.

SOURCE: *I'm Just Here for More Food* by Alton Brown

COOK: Alton Brown

grits soufflé

WE WERE A LITTLE STARTLED by the idea of making a soufflé out of grits, but it's masterful. Basically this is a grits casserole, with garlic, two cheeses (cheddar and Parmesan), and lots of butter, but the foamy egg preparation takes the grits to a whole new, sophisticated level. Don't get scared off by the soufflé idea. TV food guru Alton Brown makes it foolproof. You'll end up with a gorgeous high-rise dish that's very impressive and tastes even better. Brown likes to heat up the leftovers and enjoy them for breakfast—a great idea. We didn't have any leftovers, however.

The only secret of this dish is to make it with real stone-ground grits, not instant and not supermarket.

serves 4 to 6

- 4 tablespoons (1/2 stick) unsalted butter
- 1/2 cup grated Parmesan cheese (not shredded)
- 2 cups water
- 1/2 cup stone-ground grits (see note)
- 2 garlic cloves, minced
- 1/8 teaspoon salt
- 3 large egg yolks
- 1 1/2 cups grated cheddar cheese
- 1/4 teaspoon cayenne pepper
- 4 large egg whites
- 1 tablespoon warm water
- 1/4 teaspoon cream of tartar

Place a rack in the center of the oven, remove any racks on higher shelves, and preheat to 375 degrees. Peel back the wrapper on the butter and, holding it like a big lipstick, thoroughly grease a soufflé dish, being especially careful to grease the corners. Put the rest of the butter aside.

Add the Parmesan and cover the dish tightly with plastic wrap. Shake to coat the entire interior with cheese; dump out and reserve any excess. Refrigerate the soufflé dish.

Place the water, remaining butter, grits, garlic, and salt in a medium saucepan and bring to a boil over medium heat. Reduce the heat to low and simmer, partially covered, until the grits are almost done, 10 to 15 minutes, depending on their coarseness.

Place the egg yolks in a large metal bowl and beat until light in color and slightly thickened.

Remove the grits from the heat and add them to the yolks little by little. Add the cheddar, the reserved Parmesan, and the cayenne.

Beat the egg whites, warm water, and cream of tartar in a large grease-free bowl with an electric mixer, starting on low and moving gradually to high, until you have medium peaks.

Remove the soufflé dish from the refrigerator. Add one fourth of the egg foam mixture to the grits base. Continue to add the foam by thirds, folding it in very gently with a rubber spatula. Turn the batter into the prepared dish.

Place the soufflé dish in the oven on a disposable pie tin and bake for about 45 minutes, or until the soufflé has risen and is browned on top. Serve immediately.

note from our test kitchen

Great grits can be ordered from www.hoppinjohns.com. They should be stored in the freezer, where they'll keep for many months.

tip

We heard a Bounty commercial this year that advocated putting garlic cloves in the microwave for 15 seconds (wrapped in paper towels, of course) to facilitate peeling. It works for us, though it slightly cooks the garlic. Be careful when you retrieve the cloves from the microwave; they're extremely hot.

SOURCE: *Low Carb 1-2-3*
by Rozanne Gold with Helen Kimmel, M.S., R.D.

COOK: Rozanne Gold

whole wheat couscous with cumin

IN HER LOW-CARB BOOK, Rozanne Gold is more or less cooking with one hand tied behind her back (the carb hand). So we were curious to see what she'd come up with. Gold's recipes are always reliably good, but we got excited about one in particular: this whole wheat couscous with a dose of cumin seeds. Gold also adds chicken fat (you can also use duck fat, if you have it), which is hardly a staple in most households, but it adds a lot of complexity to an extremely simple dish. Butter will do just fine, however.

If you haven't tried whole wheat couscous, you should—we think it's a great weeknight side dish, with a flavor all its own. This much cumin might overwhelm the ordinary couscous that's much more widely available.

If you're wondering about the carb count, it's about 14 grams per serving, once you've subtracted the fiber. Not low carb, but much lower than comparable side dishes, such as potatoes or pasta.

serves 6 to 8

- 1 tablespoon cumin seeds
- 1½ cups water
- Salt
- 1 cup whole wheat couscous
- Freshly ground black pepper
- 2 tablespoons chicken fat or unsalted butter, at room temperature

Toast the cumin seeds in a small nonstick skillet over medium-high heat stirring constantly, until toasted and crispy, 2 to 3 minutes. Set aside.

Pour the water into a saucepan and add some salt. Add 1 teaspoon of the toasted cumin seeds and bring to a boil. Reduce the heat and add the couscous. Stir until the liquid is absorbed but the couscous is still moist, 2 to 3 minutes. Remove from the heat. Cover the saucepan and let stand for 3 minutes.

Fluff the couscous with a fork and add salt and pepper to taste. Transfer to a warm bowl and stir in the chicken fat or butter until incorporated. Sprinkle with the remaining 2 teaspoons toasted cumin seeds and serve.

SOURCE: Goodness Gardens fresh sage package
COOK: Brian Murphy

sage applesauce

WE WERE WONDERING what to do with some leftover fresh sage when we noticed this recipe on the back of the package. Tart green applesauce seasoned with maple syrup, sage, and black pepper sounded interesting. In fact, this is a terrific, just slightly sweet companion for any kind of pork (think ham, pork chops, roast pork, sausages), or roast turkey, for that matter. The applesauce is cooked with the apple skins intact. You toss them out later, after straining the applesauce, but they contribute a lot of flavor and character to the sauce.

serves 2 generously

- 2 large Granny Smith or other tart green apples
- 2 tablespoons maple syrup
- 1 tablespoon water
- Pinch of black pepper
- 1 teaspoon finely chopped fresh sage

Core the apples but leave the skins on. Cut into ½-inch cubes. Bring the apples, syrup, and water to a boil in a medium saucepan. Reduce the heat to low and simmer for 15 minutes. Strain the applesauce, discarding the skins. Add the pepper and sage. Let stand at room temperature for 30 minutes to develop the flavors before serving.

SOURCE: **Sur la Table cooking school handout**

COOK: **Jennifer Armentrout**

spiced cranberry sauce

EACH YEAR, no matter how hard we try, a few great recipes manage to elude us. Fortunately, the truly worthy ones seem to resurface one way or another. For instance, this popular cranberry sauce first appeared in *Fine Cooking*, and then a year later the editors of the magazine took it on the road for a series of Thanksgiving cooking classes.

We think of this as cranberry sauce with a difference. While it still looks and tastes very much like the old standard, there's something special about it. The magic comes from the star anise, which lends an exotic, fragrant note without overpowering the sauce.

As with most cranberry sauces, this can be made ahead and kept refrigerated until the big day.

makes about 2½ cups

- ½ cup ruby port
- ½ cup water
- ¾ cup sugar
- 2 whole star anise
- Pinch of salt
- 12 ounces fresh or frozen cranberries
- 1 teaspoon finely grated orange zest

Combine the port, water, sugar, star anise, and salt in a medium saucepan. Bring to a boil over medium-high heat, stirring to dissolve the sugar. As soon as the mixture reaches a boil, remove it from the heat, cover, and let stand for 20 minutes to infuse the star anise into the liquid. Meanwhile, pick through the cranberries for stems, rinse them well in a colander, and drain.

Return the liquid to a boil over medium-high heat and add the cranberries. When the mixture again returns to a boil, reduce the heat to a simmer and cook, occasionally stirring gently, until most of the berries have popped open and the sauce has thickened slightly, 8 to 10 minutes. Discard the star anise. Stir in the orange zest and let the sauce cool to room temperature. If not using the same day, refrigerate for up to a week (return the sauce to room temperature before serving).

notes from our test kitchen

- Star anise is a hard, reddish brown, star-shaped spice about as big as a quarter. Shop for it at an Asian market or in the spice department of a well-stocked gourmet store. It's best if you can find the star-shaped pods intact, not broken into pieces.
- Be sure to remove all the star anise before letting the sauce cool. Once the sauce thickens, the spice is difficult to fish out.

SOURCE: www.wegmans.com

COOK: Wegmans Staff

avocado and hominy relish

IF YOU PASS OVER the cans of hominy in the Latin section of your supermarket because you don't know what to do with them, here's a great place to start. Hominy (sometimes labeled *pozole* or *posole*) refers to corn kernels (white or yellow) from which the hull and germ have been removed so that only the tender, starchy part remains. Typically used in stews (the most famous being a hearty pork stew called posole), hominy kernels have a sweet corn flavor and a soft, pleasing texture.

With the combination of avocado, bell peppers, lime juice, and onion, this zippy relish is a close cousin to fresh salsa. The hominy bulks it up enough to make it an ideal side dish for just about anything off the grill or as part of a buffet of other bold dishes.

serves 4

- 1½ teaspoons olive oil
- 1 15-ounce can white hominy or *pozole* (see note), rinsed and drained
- 1 medium red or yellow bell pepper, cored, seeded, and cut into medium dice
- 1 medium green bell pepper, cored, seeded, and cut into medium dice
- 1 medium avocado, pitted, peeled, and cut into medium dice
- ½ medium red onion, cut into medium dice
- 1 jalapeño, seeded and minced
- 2 tablespoons chopped fresh cilantro
- Juice of 1 lime

Heat the oil in a large skillet over medium heat until very hot (see note). Add the hominy and sauté, stirring frequently, until just heated through, about 1 minute. Transfer to a large bowl. Add the remaining ingredients and toss together. Serve. The relish can be made several hours ahead and kept refrigerated. The lime juice will prevent the avocado from browning.

notes from our test kitchen

- Wegmans recommends Goya brand hominy, which is labeled *pozole*. If you can't find Goya, shop for any brand without a lot of additives.
- Given the small amount of oil called for in the recipe ($1^1/_2$ teaspoons), a nonstick skillet makes the most sense. We like to add a few drops more oil (closer to $1^1/_2$ tablespoons) and give the hominy a chance to brown a bit. It makes the relish even more appealing.

SOURCE: *The Rosengarten Report* by David Rosengarten

COOK: David Rosengarten after Grandma Hitchcock

grandma hitchcock's creamy mustard sauce for ham

BE IT THE HOLIDAYS or just a gathering of friends and family, few things sustain a crowd better than a magnificent baked ham. But what to serve with it is always the question—or used to be, until we discovered this amazing mustard sauce. It's an old-fashioned boiled dressing that hits a perfect sweet, sharp, and creamy harmony.

This mustard sauce can be served warm or at room temperature, which makes it ideal for a buffet. It will thicken some as it cools but still taste great. We recommend serving a bowl of sauce on the side or passing it at the table, so guests can spoon on as much as they like. Expect folks to ask for seconds.

makes about 2½ cups

- ¼ cup Colman's Mustard powder
- ½ cup sugar
- 2 teaspoons salt
- ½ teaspoon freshly ground black pepper
- ½ cup white vinegar
- 2 cups heavy cream
- 4 large egg yolks, beaten

Combine the mustard, sugar, salt, and pepper in a saucepan. Add the vinegar and whisk to blend well.

Add the cream and egg yolks to the saucepan, place over low heat, and cook, stirring, until thickened and smooth. Serve.

note from our test kitchen

Store any leftover mustard sauce in the refrigerator for 1 to 2 days. It will thicken up like a mayonnaise and makes an unbelievably good spread for ham sandwiches.

tip

According to David Rosengarten, the cardinal sin when cooking a ham, no matter what kind, is heating it at too high a temperature for too long. The secret is a low oven temperature—275 degrees—until it reaches an internal temperature of 135 degrees, which can take as long as 6 hours. Let the ham rest for 15 to 30 minutes before carving.

breads

SOURCE: *Washington Post*
STORY BY Lisa Yockelson
COOK: Lisa Yockelson

better biscuits

WE TAKE OUR HATS OFF to baker Lisa Yockelson, who has made dozens and dozens of biscuits in pursuit of the ultimate light, airy one. These are the kind that elude most cooks: tall, moist, and delectable. Although any biscuit tastes better warm and Yockelson advises serving them right out of the oven, these are still delicious several hours later, at room temperature.

If you want to make everyone at your table very happy, this is the way to do it.

makes about 11 biscuits

- 2 cups all-purpose flour
- 2 1/4 teaspoons baking powder
- 2 tablespoons sugar
- 1/2 teaspoon cream of tartar
- 1/4 teaspoon baking soda
- 1/4 teaspoon salt, preferably fine sea salt
- 8 tablespoons solid vegetable shortening (or 4 tablespoons shortening and 4 tablespoons butter), cut into pieces
- 3/4 cup buttermilk
- Melted butter or whole milk to glaze the unbaked biscuit tops (optional)

Preheat the oven to 400 degrees.

Whisk together the flour, baking powder, sugar, cream of tartar, baking soda, and salt in a large bowl. Add the shortening pieces and, using a pastry blender or two knives, cut the fat into the flour until it resembles small bits and flakes.

Shake the buttermilk, pour it over the mixture, and, using a wooden spoon, stir just until a dough forms. The dough should come together but still be slightly moist. Using your fingertips, lightly knead the dough in the bowl 3 or 4 times.

Turn the dough onto a lightly floured work surface. Roll or pat the dough until it is 1 inch thick. Using a 2-inch round cutter, cut out biscuits. Transfer the biscuits on a spatula to an ungreased baking sheet, spacing them about 2 inches apart. Lightly press together the scraps and cut a few more biscuits. Do not rework the dough, or it will be tough.

Brush a little melted butter or milk, if using, on top of each biscuit, taking care not to let it drip down the sides (which would prevent the biscuit from rising as high).

Transfer the biscuits to the oven and immediately increase the temperature to 425 degrees. Bake for 15 to 20 minutes, or until golden and high. Cool on a rack for 2 minutes and serve warm.

note from our test kitchen

- If you'd prefer not to use shortening, try to find good lard, which has the same baking qualities. Another option is the trans fat–free palm oil shortening from Spectrum, which can be found in natural foods stores.

SOURCE: *Nightly Specials* by Michael Lomonaco

COOK: Michael Lomonaco

savory chipotle chile muffins

WE HARDLY EVER SEE SAVORY MUFFINS, so we were delighted to encounter this recipe. The muffins get a southwestern spin from the smoky chipotle chile and cumin, and a little cornmeal gives them just the right texture as well as a nice taste.

These aren't breakfast muffins, though they'd be great with eggs and chorizo, but are intended for the bread basket at lunch or dinner. They're a natural with barbecue or chili, soup, or salad. Just be sure to serve them warm.

makes 15 muffins

- 1½ cups milk
- 6 large eggs
- 5 tablespoons unsalted butter, melted
- 2 tablespoons chipotle chiles in adobo sauce, blended to a puree
- 2 cups all-purpose flour
- ½ cup cornmeal
- 1 tablespoon plus 1½ teaspoons baking powder
- 1 tablespoon ground cumin
- 1 teaspoon fine sea salt
- 1 teaspoon freshly ground black pepper

Preheat the oven to 425 degrees. Grease a 15-cup muffin tin or two 8-cup tins.

Beat the milk, eggs, butter, and chipotle puree together in a medium bowl until smooth.

Stir together the remaining ingredients in another medium bowl to combine well. Pour in the milk mixture, stirring to incorporate and avoid lumps.

Pour the batter into the muffin tin(s), filling each cup three-quarters full.

Bake the muffins until they rise and are golden brown, about 35 minutes.

Transfer the muffins to a napkin-lined basket and serve warm from the oven.

notes from our test kitchen

- We like to keep a can of chipotles in adobo in the pantry as well as chipotle puree in the refrigerator. It keeps almost forever. To make the puree, dump the contents of a can into the food processor and process until you have a rough puree.
- You can add 1 tablespoon sesame seeds or 3 tablespoons chopped pecans to the batter. The pecan version is wonderful.
- Cut the recipe in half if you're not serving a crowd.

SOURCE: *The Pastry Queen*
by Rebecca Rather with Alison Oresman

COOK: Rebecca Rather

bacon and cheddar scones

WHEN WE READ that these tempting scones were the best-selling scone ever at Rather Sweet Bakery & Café, a funky, popular eatery in Fredericksburg, Texas (the heart of Texas hill country), we knew we had to give them a try. They're buttery and tender beyond belief, but what makes them truly distinctive is that they're studded with salty smoked bacon, shreds of sharp cheddar cheese, and a generous dose of black pepper. For non-Texans, Rebecca Rather suggests adding 2 teaspoons freshly ground black pepper, which will still give quite a kick. But at her bakery, Rather increases it to a full tablespoon (coarsely ground, please) to satisfy her customers' tastes. Sometimes she ups the ante by adding two chopped and seeded fresh jalapeños as well. We leave that decision to you.

These hearty scones make a great breakfast on their own, or pair them with scrambled eggs and a bowl of fruit for a real feast. Since they're savory and not at all sweet, we love serving them for lunch and dinner. Just one turns a bowl of soup into a wholesome supper.

makes 8 or 10

- 3 cups all-purpose flour
- 1 tablespoon baking powder
- 2 teaspoons freshly ground black pepper
- 1 teaspoon salt
- 8 tablespoons (1 stick) chilled unsalted butter, cut into small cubes
- 1½ cups grated cheddar cheese
- 10 slices bacon, cooked until crisp and cut into 1-inch pieces
- 4 scallions (white and green parts), thinly sliced
- ¾–1½ cups buttermilk
- 1 large egg
- 2 tablespoons water

Preheat the oven to 400 degrees.

Using a mixer with the paddle attachment, combine the flour, baking powder, pepper, and salt. With the mixer running, gradually add the butter, mixing until the dough is crumbly and there are flour-butter bits about the size of small peas. Add the cheese and mix until just blended. (This can also be done by hand. Stir together the flour, baking powder, pepper, and salt in a large bowl. Gradually cut in the butter with a pastry blender or two knives until the mixture resembles small peas. Stir in the cheese.)

Add the bacon, scallions, and 3/4 cup buttermilk. Mix by hand just until all the ingredients are incorporated. If the mixture is too dry, add the remaining buttermilk, 1 tablespoon at a time, until the dough is pliable and can be formed into a ball. Stir as lightly and little as possible.

Place the dough on a lightly floured work surface. Pat it into a ball. Using a well-floured rolling pin, flatten the dough into a circle about 8 inches wide and 1/2 inch thick. Cut the dough into 8 or 10 wedges.

Whisk the egg and water in a small bowl. Brush each wedge with the egg wash. Place the scones on an ungreased baking sheet and bake for 18 to 20 minutes, or until golden brown and no longer sticky in the middle. Serve warm.

notes from our test kitchen

- You may also swap out the cheddar for Swiss, Monterey Jack, or any semisoft grating cheese. Whichever cheese you use, don't buy the pregrated stuff. Its flavor is inferior.
- Rebecca Rather recommends apple-smoked bacon for these, but any good bacon will do—thin or thick, as long as it's cooked crisp.
- For a richer scone, substitute heavy cream for half of the buttermilk.
- These are best served warm but may be kept in an airtight container for several hours or overnight.

SOURCE: *Joan Nathan's Jewish Holiday Cookbook* by Joan Nathan

COOK: Joan Nathan after Rose Zawid

onion–poppy seed rolls

COOKBOOK AUTHOR and Jewish cooking authority Joan Nathan remembers getting these golden spiral rolls from bakeries on the Lower East Side. Unlike many traditional bakery creations, however, they're straightforward enough to make at home. The dough is similar to a challah—rich with eggs and lightly sweetened—and is filled with diced onion, poppy seeds, and a bit of salt, rolled up jelly-roll fashion, and cut into pinwheels. Tucked into muffin tins, the rolls pop up nicely during baking to reveal their filling. We like to put a basket on the table for Saturday night dinner or any holiday.

makes 12 rolls

- 1 scant tablespoon (1 package) active dry yeast
- 1½ teaspoons plus ½ cup sugar
- About ¾ cup lukewarm water
- ¼ cup plus 3 tablespoons vegetable oil
- 3 large eggs
- 1½ teaspoons fine salt
- 4–4½ cups all-purpose flour
- ½ medium onion, diced
- 2 tablespoons poppy seeds
- ½ teaspoon coarse salt

Dissolve the yeast and 1½ teaspoons of the sugar in the lukewarm water in a large bowl.

Whisk ¼ cup of the oil into the yeast mixture, then beat in 2 of the eggs, 1 at a time, with the remaining ½ cup sugar and the fine salt. Gradually add the flour. When the dough holds together, it is ready for kneading. (You can also use a mixer with a dough hook for both the mixing and kneading.)

Turn the dough onto a floured work surface and knead until smooth. Clean the bowl and grease it, then return the dough to the bowl. Cover with plastic wrap and let the dough rise in a warm place for 1 hour, or until it almost doubles in size. The dough may also rise in an oven that has been warmed to 150 degrees and turned off.

Punch down the dough, cover, and let rise again in a warm place for 30 minutes more. Roll out the dough on a lightly floured surface to a rectangle about 12 x 18 inches or as thin as you can.

Sprinkle the onion, poppy seeds, and coarse salt over the dough, leaving a 1-inch border along the edges.

Using a pastry brush, paint the border of the dough with some of the remaining 3 tablespoons oil. Then roll the dough up from the long side like a jelly roll. The dough will be very malleable. Pinch the ends closed.

Oil a 12-cup muffin tin with the remaining oil.

Using a dough cutter (see note), cut the dough into at least 12 rounds and place the rolls in the tins, cut sides up. Mix the remaining egg with a little water and brush over the rolls. Let rise for 30 minutes more.

Meanwhile, preheat the oven to 350 degrees.

Bake for 20 to 25 minutes, or until golden. Remove from the oven and serve warm.

note from our test kitchen

If you don't have a dough cutter (also called a bench scraper), cut the dough with a chef's knife.

SOURCE: *Saveur*

STORY BY Megan Wetherall

COOK: Maite Marijon

bolos do caco
(madeiran griddle cakes with garlic parsley butter)

BASKETS OF THESE FLAT, moist griddle cakes are served at restaurants and festivals all across the Portuguese island of Madeira. A bit of mashed sweet potato added to the dough makes them nicely chewy and slightly sweet, and the griddle cooking crisps the outside. Think English muffins gone rustic. Split and slathered with a zesty garlic parsley butter and served hot off the griddle, they make an inspired alternative to ordinary garlic bread.

In Madeira they are baked on hot stone slabs or tiles. At home, you can bake them on a griddle or in a cast-iron pan.

makes 6

GRIDDLE CAKES

- 1 pound white-fleshed sweet potatoes, peeled and halved (see note)
- 1 1/2 tablespoons (2 packets) active dry yeast
- 1/4 cup lukewarm water
- 3 3/4 cups all-purpose flour
- 4 teaspoons salt
- 3/4 cup room-temperature water
- 1–2 tablespoons vegetable oil

GARLIC PARSLEY BUTTER

- 16 tablespoons (2 sticks) butter, at room temperature
- Leaves of 1/4 bunch fresh flat-leaf parsley (about 1/4 cup)
- 6 garlic cloves, minced
- Salt

TO MAKE THE GRIDDLE CAKES:

Put the sweet potatoes in a deep pot, cover with cold water, and bring to a boil. Boil over medium-high heat until soft, 30 to 35 minutes. Drain well (see note) and pass through a potato ricer or food mill into a large bowl. Set aside to cool.

Dissolve the yeast in the lukewarm water in a small bowl and let stand until foamy, about 5 minutes.

Stir the yeast mixture into the potatoes. Add the flour (see note), salt, and room-temperature water (see note). Mix until a soft, tacky dough forms. Transfer the dough to a clean bowl, cover with plastic wrap, and set aside in a warm place to rise until doubled in size, about 30 minutes.

Transfer the dough to a lightly floured work surface and knead until smooth, 7 to 10 minutes. Divide the dough into sixths and shape into six 6-inch disks. Transfer the disks to a parchment-lined baking sheet dusted with flour, setting them at least 1 inch apart. Lightly dust the disks with flour, loosely cover with plastic wrap, and set aside in a warm place to rise for 45 minutes.

Heat a griddle over medium heat until hot, then brush with a thin film of oil. Working in batches, transfer the disks to the griddle without deflating them and cook until deep golden brown on each side, 3 to 5 minutes per side. Transfer the cakes as they are done to a wire rack to cool.

TO MAKE THE GARLIC PARSLEY BUTTER:

Combine all the ingredients in a small bowl by mashing with a fork or small wooden spoon.

To serve, split the cakes in half, slather the insides with the garlic parsley butter, and reassemble the halves. Reheat the cakes on the griddle over medium heat. Quarter and serve warm.

notes from our test kitchen

- If you can't find white-fleshed sweet potatoes, use regular russet potatoes.
- It's essential to drain the potatoes well before ricing. If the potato flesh seems waterlogged, return it to the empty pot and place it over low heat, shaking once or twice, for 1 to 2 minutes to dry out.
- We recommend adding the last of the flour a bit at a time until the dough reaches a soft, slightly tacky consistency. This will take into account the slight variation in moisture content of various potatoes; you may not need to add all the flour.
- If you're using unsalted butter, don't be timid when adding salt to the garlic parsley butter. With salted butter, only add a pinch.
- Any leftover garlic parsley butter can be used on other bread or rolls.

SOURCE: *A Blessing of Bread* by Maggie Glezer

COOK: Maggie Glezer after Ofra Sadeh

egyptian cheese rolls

IMAGINE A SORT OF homespun cheese-filled croissant and you'll have *rarif al rarif,* or Egyptian cheese rolls. Rectangular and buttery, they aren't as delicate or flaky as their French equivalent, but they are wonderfully tender, with a handsome golden exterior. They're at least twice the size of most dinner rolls and great in the bread basket for a big feast, but we recommend cutting them in half. They're a fine morning pastry, too.

Making them takes some time, but once you get the hang of it, you can move right along. We find it easiest to spread the process out over two days, refrigerating the rolls overnight before baking.

The traditional cheese for these rolls is a fresh salty Israeli cheese called *brinza.* Mexican queso fresco is a good facsimile. If that's unavailable, Monterey Jack works well, as long as you season it with a little salt.

makes 8 large rolls

- 1 teaspoon instant yeast
- About 3¾ cups bread flour
- 1¼ cups warm water
- Salt
- 1 teaspoon sugar
- 2 tablespoons vegetable oil
- 8 tablespoons (1 stick) unsalted butter, at room temperature (see note)
- 8 ounces queso fresco or Monterey Jack cheese
- Chopped fresh mint or other fresh herbs (optional)
- 1 large egg, beaten
- Sesame seeds for sprinkling (optional)

Whisk together the yeast and 1¼ cups of the flour in a large bowl, then whisk in the warm water until smooth. Let stand uncovered for 10 to 20 minutes, until it begins to ferment and puff up slightly.

Whisk 2 teaspoons salt, the sugar, and the oil into the yeast mixture until smooth. With your hands or a wooden spoon, stir in the remaining 2½ cups flour all at once. When the mixture forms a shaggy ball, scrape it out onto your work surface and knead it until it is well mixed, fairly smooth, and firm. Soak the mixing bowl in hot water to clean it and warm it for rising the dough. This dough does not require much kneading—it just has to come together and be fairly smooth. It is stiff, though, so you will have to use some force to knead it. If the dough is too firm to knead, add a tablespoon or two of water; if it seems too wet, add a few tablespoons of flour. The dough should feel firm and stick to itself easily but not to the work surface.

Place the dough in the warmed clean bowl and cover it with plastic wrap. Let the dough rise until it has at least doubled in size, 2 to 2½ hours.

Do not punch the dough down. On a lightly floured work surface, dusting with flour as needed, roll out the dough into a thin 16-inch square. Smear it with half the butter. Fold the dough into thirds like a business letter, rotate it a quarter of a turn, and fold it into thirds again. Return the dough to the bowl, cover, and let it relax for 30 minutes (in the refrigerator if your kitchen is warm). Repeat the rolling out, buttering, and folding, using the remaining 4 tablespoons butter. Let the dough relax again for 30 minutes, or, for the flakiest rolls, refrigerate it for an hour or two to cool down.

Generously butter a 13-x-9-inch baking pan. Cut the cheese into eight 4-inch wide blocks.

Roll out the dough again into a 16-inch square. Cut the square in half, then cut each piece into four equal rectangles, each 8 x 4 inches. Divide the cheese among the centers of the dough rectangles, sprinkling with salt (if using Monterey Jack) and/or the chopped herbs, if using. Fold the sides of each dough rectangle over the cheese, then shape the piece into a neat cylindrical bundle, making sure that the cheese is completely enclosed. Place seam sides down in the pan, making 2 even rows.

Cover the pan well with plastic wrap. The rolls can be refrigerated for up to 24 hours at this point. Let the rolls rise until tripled in size, about 2 hours (or up to 3 hours if the rolls have been refrigerated).

Meanwhile, place a rack in the lower third of the oven and remove all the racks above it. Preheat the oven to 400 degrees.

When the rolls have tripled and remain indented when gently pressed with your finger, brush them with the beaten egg and sprinkle with the sesame seeds, if using. Bake for 30 to 40 minutes, turning the pan halfway through baking, until nicely browned. Transfer to a wire rack to cool before serving.

notes from our test kitchen

- Be sure the butter is soft enough to spread easily on the dough. It's best to leave it at room temperature for several hours before using.
- The dough can be tough to roll out because it's so stiff. If you're having trouble getting the square to its full dimensions, stop and take a 5- to 10-minute breather (leaving the dough rolled out). The dough will relax and be willing to stretch farther when you return.
- If your kitchen is too warm, or if at any time the butter starts to get oily and ooze from the dough, transfer the whole thing to the refrigerator and let it cool.

SOURCE: *Harley and Davidson Family Recipes* by Margo Manning and Carol Lange

COOKS: Davidson's great-grandson and his wife

parmesan–poppy seed pull-apart bread

IF YOU'RE A CONVENIENCE-FOOD PHOBE, this recipe will send you straight into recovery. It's amazing how those cylinders of biscuit dough at the supermarket can be transformed into something so scrumptious and homemade-tasting. The trick is to buy the flaky biscuits; other varieties won't give you the same effect.

The agents of the transformation are a little onion, a little butter, a little Parmesan, some poppy and celery seeds, and dill. The biscuits rise in the oven to make a pull-apart bread to partner with soups or salads. If you want a "homemade" bread that goes together in moments and is great with soups and salads, try it.

serves 6

- 3 tablespoons butter, melted
- 1 tablespoon minced onion, sautéed in a little more butter
- 1 tablespoon poppy seeds
- 1/4 teaspoon celery seeds
- 1 10 1/2-ounce package prepared flaky biscuit dough (in the dairy section at the supermarket)
- 1/4 cup grated Parmesan cheese
- 1 1/2 teaspoons dried dill

Preheat the oven to 400 degrees.

Melt the butter in a 9-inch round pan. Sprinkle the onion, poppy seeds, and celery seeds over the butter. Cut each biscuit into 4 pieces. Put the Parmesan and the dill in a plastic bag. One at a time, shake the biscuit pieces in the bag and then arrange in the pan. Sprinkle the remaining cheese-dill mixture over the top.

Bake for 15 to 18 minutes, or until golden brown on top. Turn onto a serving platter and serve hot.

desserts

desserts

SOURCE: *The Fearless Chef*
by Andy Husbands and Joe Yonan
COOK: Andy Husbands after his mother

hot blackberries and cream

WE'RE ALWAYS DELIGHTED when chefs return to their mother's recipes. This unfussy dessert comes from a lauded Boston chef, Andy Husbands. Growing up in the Pacific Northwest, where the berries grow plumper, juicier, and more prolifically than just about anywhere, Husbands remembers his mother folding together sour cream and fresh berries, dusting the top with brown sugar, and popping the dish under the broiler. As the berries release their juices into the cream, the sugar caramelizes into a crunchy sweet topping. We're guessing the lime zest is a little flourish of the chef's, but we're not complaining. It's just right.

Husbands advises making this only in the summer, when blackberries are at their prime, but we confess that we've broken down and made it off-season and still loved the results. For a variation, follow the same formula using fresh blueberries and crème fraîche.

serves 4

- 1 cup sour cream, at room temperature
- 1 tablespoon sugar
- Finely grated zest of 1 lime
- 1/2 teaspoon ground cinnamon
- 1 pint fresh blackberries, washed and well drained
- 1/2 cup lightly packed light or dark brown sugar

Place the broiler rack in the lowest possible position, so that it is at least 6 inches from the top element, and heat the broiler.

Combine the sour cream, sugar, lime zest, and cinnamon in a small bowl. Gently fold in the blackberries and transfer to a small gratin dish. Sprinkle the brown sugar on top.

Broil until the brown sugar melts and caramelizes, 1 to 3 minutes, turning the dish halfway through so the top browns evenly but does not burn. Serve hot.

SOURCE: *Jacques Pépin Fast Food My Way* by Jacques Pépin

COOK: Jacques Pépin

caramelized peaches

WE DON'T THINK OF CHEFS like Jacques Pépin rummaging through their pantries for a can of peaches, but that's the unlikely base for this delectable dessert. Instead of draining off the heavy syrup the peaches are packed in, Pépin uses it to make an unusual caramel cream sauce. But wouldn't it be even better made with fresh peaches in season? Surprisingly, no. William Grimes of the *New York Times* loved this dessert so much he thought he'd do Pépin one better and make it with fresh fruit—still good, but not better.

If you can manage to keep some pound cake in the freezer along with some pistachios, you can whip up this charming dessert on the spur of the moment.

serves 4

- 1 29-ounce can peaches in heavy syrup
- 1/2 cup heavy cream
- 1 tablespoon cognac
- 1 tablespoon fresh lemon juice
- 1–2 tablespoons water, if needed
- 4 1/2-inch-thick slices brioche or pound cake
- 2 tablespoons coarsely crushed pistachios

Drain the peaches, reserving the syrup, and pour the syrup into a skillet. Cook over high heat until the syrup is reduced and turns into caramel, 9 to 10 minutes, shaking the pan near the end so the caramel doesn't burn around the edges.

Add the peaches to the caramel and stir in the cream. Bring to a boil, stirring occasionally, to melt the caramel and combine it with the cream. Boil for 1 to 2 minutes, then transfer to a bowl and cool. Stir in the cognac and lemon juice and add the water if the sauce is too thick. Cover and refrigerate until serving time.

Just before serving, toast the brioche or pound cake slices and place a slice on each of four dessert plates. Arrange 2 peach halves on top of each slice and coat with the sauce. Sprinkle the peaches with the pistachios.

notes from our test kitchen

- If you have no pistachios, substitute chopped toasted almonds.
- Because the dessert tastes best when the caramelized peaches are well chilled, make them early on the day you plan to serve it.

SOURCE: *Inspired by Ingredients*
by Bill Telepan and Andrew Friedman

COOK: Bill Telepan

berry clafouti with crème fraîche

EVERYWHERE WE LOOKED this year we saw versions of clafouti ("kla-foo-*tee*"), the homey, custardy French dessert that seems to have taken America by storm. Of the several recipes we tried, this was our favorite, possibly because it features this year's dairy darling, crème fraîche, which adds another memorable level of flavor.

Because there's so little batter compared to most clafoutis, the fruit really shines here. You want fully ripe, local berries. Tristar strawberries have a long season, and you may be able to find some at the farmers' market to pair with August's blackberries and the last of the blueberries. If you'd perversely like to make this dish in winter, however, you can: use frozen wild blueberries and fresh raspberries, which seem to suffer less from being hauled long distances than other berries do.

serves 6

- 2 large eggs
- 1/3 cup sugar
- 3 tablespoons all-purpose flour
- 1/2 vanilla bean, split lengthwise and soft seeds scraped out and reserved (see note)
- Pinch of salt
- 1/3 cup plus 3 tablespoons crème fraîche
- 1/3 cup milk
- 1 1/2 pints mixed berries (hulled and quartered strawberries, blueberries, raspberries, and/or blackberries)
- 1 1/2 teaspoons confectioners' sugar

Preheat the oven to 400 degrees.

Whisk the eggs and sugar together in a medium bowl until frothy. Add the flour, vanilla seeds, and salt and whisk to combine.

Whisk 1/3 cup of the crème fraîche with the milk in a separate bowl and then whisk into the batter.

Coat a 10-inch nonstick ovenproof skillet with nonstick cooking spray or butter. Pour one third of the batter into the pan. Bake until just set, about 5 minutes, then remove from the oven. Top with 1 pint of the berries and then the remaining batter. Return the skillet to the oven and bake until the batter has puffed up, 20 to 25 minutes.

Remove the skillet from the oven and let the clafouti cool for 10 minutes, then slide a thin knife or spatula around the edge to loosen it. Place a large plate upside down over the pan; flip to release the clafouti onto the plate. Invert again onto another plate so that the berries are on top. Set aside.

Whip the remaining 3 tablespoons crème fraîche with the confectioners' sugar in a small bowl. Cut the clafouti into 6 wedges. Serve each wedge of clafouti with some of the remaining berries and a dollop of the crème fraîche mixture.

notes from our test kitchen

- Vanilla beans can be hard to find, but you can use 1 teaspoon vanilla extract instead.
- We like to serve clafouti right out of the skillet, skipping the flipping process and saving an extra plate to wash.

SOURCE: *Hallelujah! The Welcome Table* by Maya Angelou

COOK: Maya Angelou

banana pudding

SOME OF THE WORLD'S great literary spirits are also naturals in the kitchen. Maya Angelou is among the best of cooks, and her feasts are legendary among those lucky enough to have partaken.

In her cookbook, all the recipes are grounded in stories from her own life. When she was a young and unsophisticated woman, Angelou was seeing an older man, who restricted their trysts to a particular day of the week at his house. One afternoon she gets the day wrong and runs smack into a rival, a married woman. The man insists that his relationship with this other woman is based on the banana pudding she brings him once a week and that once Angelou tastes the pudding she'll understand. The pudding turns out to be mediocre. Angelou walks out forever, and on the way home buys the fixings for this very fine version.

This is the wonderful, consoling dessert you wish your grandmother made. If you leave it in plain sight in the kitchen, you're likely to find people hanging over it with spoon in hand.

serves 8

- 1/3 cup plus 5 tablespoons sugar
- 1/3 cup cornstarch
- Pinch of salt
- 3 cups milk
- 8 large eggs, separated
- 3 tablespoons butter
- 1 tablespoon vanilla extract
- 3 cups vanilla wafer cookies (about 1 box)
- 4 ripe bananas, peeled and thinly sliced
- 1/2 teaspoon cream of tartar

Place a rack in the center of the oven and preheat to 350 degrees.

Combine 1/3 cup of the sugar, the cornstarch, and salt in a large saucepan. Stir until blended, then stir in the milk. Cook over medium heat until thickened, stirring constantly. Boil for 1 minute, then remove from the heat.

Whisk the egg yolks in a small bowl. Whisk in 1/2 cup of the hot milk mixture until blended. Pour the yolk mixture into the pan and cook over medium heat, stirring, for 2 minutes. Remove from the heat and stir the butter and vanilla into the custard.

Place half the vanilla wafers in a shallow 2-quart casserole. Top with layers of half the banana slices and half the custard. Repeat the layering, ending with the custard.

Beat the egg whites and 1/4 cup (4 tablespoons) of the remaining sugar in a large bowl with an electric mixer on low speed until frothy. Add the cream of tartar and increase the speed to medium. Gradually beat in the remaining 1 tablespoon sugar and beat just until the whites hold stiff peaks.

Immediately spoon the meringue over the hot custard, taking care that it touches all sides of the baking dish.

Bake for 10 minutes, or until the top is lightly browned. Remove from the oven and cool for 1 hour. Refrigerate, covered with plastic wrap, for at least 4 hours before serving.

SOURCE: *Baking at Home with The Culinary Institute of America*
COOKS: CIA Baking and Pastry Arts staff

mango mousse

MANGO AND RUM: what could be more delectable? In this mousse, rum, preferably dark rum, is used to soften the gelatin. A meringue base considerably lightens things and gives the mousse a gorgeous satiny texture.

It's hard to imagine an easier homemade dessert for a crowd, especially if you use canned mango puree. We like to double the recipe to make a big bowl to serve 16.

serves 6 to 8

- 1 large mango (see note)
- 1 packet powdered unflavored gelatin
- 1/4 cup light or dark rum or water
- 2 cups heavy cream
- 1/2 cup sugar
- 2 large egg whites
- Grated lime zest for garnish

Peel the mango and cut the flesh away from the pit. Puree the mango in a food processor or blender until completely smooth. You should have about 1 1/2 cups. Transfer to a large bowl.

Sprinkle the gelatin over the rum or water in a small bowl and stir to break up any clumps. Let the gelatin soften for about 2 minutes. Heat the softened gelatin in the top of a double boiler over barely simmering water (or in a heatproof bowl set over a pot of barely simmering water). Otherwise, place in the microwave on low for about 20 seconds, or until the granules melt and the mixture is clear (see note).

Whip the cream in a chilled deep bowl until it starts to thicken. Gradually add 1/4 cup of the sugar while whipping the cream to medium peaks.

Beat the egg whites on low speed in the clean bowl of a stand mixer fitted with the whisk attachment or in a large bowl with a hand-held mixer until they are foamy. Increase the speed to high and gradually add the remaining 1/4 cup sugar while beating. Continue to beat on high speed until the meringue holds medium peaks.

Stir the melted gelatin into the mango puree. Using a spatula, fold the whipped cream into the mango puree until evenly blended. Add the meringue in 2 additions, folding in just until blended.

Pipe or spoon the mousse into six 6-ounce molds (see note). Refrigerate for at least 3 hours and up to 24 hours. Garnish with the lime zest just before serving.

notes from our test kitchen

- Mangoes are variable in flavor. We opted to make the mousse with canned Alfonso mango puree from India, available at all Indian markets. Alfonsos are, according to aficionados, the best mangoes in the world (they're not sold fresh in the United States), but that's not to say you won't find a truly wonderful mango at your market. If you use the canned puree, a 425-gram can will give you the 1½ cups of puree you need; use an 850-gram can to double the recipe. Canned puree is already sweetened, so cut the amount of sugar in half and use the ¼ cup sugar with the egg whites, not the cream.
- Unless you have help in the kitchen or you're extremely speedy, the gelatin may start to set up before you've finished whipping the cream and the meringue, so it's a good idea to mix it into the mango puree as soon as it's melted.
- We like to make the mousse in a large glass bowl. Presented this way, the recipe will easily serve 8.
- Instead of the lime zest, we like to garnish the bowl of mousse with a ring of chopped pistachios.
- Ginger cookies are an ideal companion for the mousse. Leftovers are delicious over gingerbread or diced mangoes with blueberries. The mousse keeps for at least 48 hours in the refrigerator.

grilled pineapple with butter rum sauce

WHENEVER WE MAKE THIS, someone always begs for just a bit more sauce to drizzle over his or her ice cream. It's not that we're stingy with it, it's that this sauce is so good. Not only is pineapple and rum a match made in heaven, but you'll love the way the fruit's tropical sweetness and refreshing texture play against the warm sauce and cool ice cream. Grilling the pineapple caramelizes its sugars, making it taste even sweeter. We've even skipped the pineapple and just served the sweet, buttery sauce with ice cream and been quite happy.

If it's not grilling season, broil the slices until warmed through and beginning to caramelize. If you want to do all the cooking outdoors, cook this sauce by putting the pan right on the grill (or make it ahead on the stove and reheat it while you grill the pineapple).

serves 8

- 8 tablespoons (1 stick) unsalted butter
- 1 cup lightly packed brown sugar
- A pinch each of ground nutmeg, cinnamon, and allspice
- 1/2 cup Myers's or other dark rum
- 8 1-inch-thick slices very ripe fresh pineapple, cored if not totally soft in the center
- Vanilla ice cream for serving (optional)

Cook the butter, brown sugar, spices, and rum in a small saucepan over medium heat, stirring, until the sugar is dissolved and the butter melted. Bring to a simmer and cook for about 10 minutes more, stirring occasionally, until the sauce is slightly syrupy and coats the back of a spoon. Keep warm.

Heat the grill, making sure it's clean, and brush or spray it with a touch of oil so the pineapple doesn't stick. Grill the pineapple slices until warmed through and caramelized, about 10 minutes per side.

Serve immediately, in rings or chunks, with the warm sauce and ice cream, if you like.

frozen lemon cream sandwiches

LET'S FACE IT, our pantries are changing—for the better. With higher-quality ingredients available in jars, cans, boxes, and tubs, it's easier than ever to get things like real crème fraîche, jarred lemon curd, and buttery Dutch cookies, the three key ingredients in this impressive-looking dessert. Combining lemon curd and crème fraîche to make a filling for a frozen sandwich is a brilliant conceit. Once frozen, the pale yellow filling remains soft and creamy, with a flavor that is slightly sweet and a little tangy, with a bright shot of lemon.

serves 6

- 1 7-ounce container crème fraîche, chilled
- 1/4 cup lemon curd (see note)
- Finely grated zest of 1 lemon
- 12 crisp butter waffle cookies (see note)
- 1/4 cup finely chopped unsalted pistachios

Line a small baking sheet with wax paper.

Beat the crème fraîche, lemon curd, and lemon zest in a small chilled bowl with a hand-held mixer until firm peaks form.

Arrange half the cookies on the baking sheet and spoon the lemon cream onto the centers, letting it ooze gently to the edges. Top with the remaining cookies, pressing down very gently. Transfer the baking sheet to the freezer and freeze until the sandwiches are firm, at least 4 hours.

Spread the nuts on a plate and roll the edges of the sandwiches in them. Serve at once. The cookies can be frozen in an airtight container for up to 1 week.

notes from our test kitchen

- *Food & Wine* staffers recommend Wilkins & Sons Tiptree Lemon Curd as "the creamiest, most lemony" brand they tried. Surprisingly, it's less expensive than other brands. Most well-stocked supermarkets carry it, or find it at Todaro Brothers, (877) 472-2767.
- Jules Destrooper Crisp Butter Wafers are available in the fancy cookie section of most supermarkets. They are best, since they don't become brittle when frozen.

SOURCE: *Dallas Morning News*
COOK: **Bernice Fraze**

crisp lemon mint cookies

EACH YEAR AROUND HOLIDAY TIME, the *Dallas Morning News* hosts a huge cookie contest, but this was the first year that Bernice Fraze, a retired government employee and an enthusiastic home baker, entered. Banking on tradition, Bernice dug out her grandmother's old recipe for crisp lemon cookies and made one small change: she added fresh mint. The change proved enough to catch the judges' attention, and Bernice won a first-place ribbon.

These drop cookies are crisp, light, and lemony with a hint of fresh mint.

makes 2 dozen

- 8 tablespoons (1 stick) unsalted butter, at room temperature
- 3/4 cup sugar
- Grated zest of 1 lemon
- 1 large egg yolk, at room temperature
- 1 teaspoon lemon oil or 1 tablespoon lemon extract
- 3/4 cup all-purpose flour
- 1 tablespoon finely chopped fresh mint

Place two racks near the center of the oven and preheat to 350 degrees. Butter two baking sheets or line with parchment paper.

Cream the butter and sugar in a large bowl with an electric mixer on high speed until smooth and fluffy (see note). Switching to low speed, add the lemon zest, yolk, and lemon oil or extract and mix to combine. Add the flour, 1/4 cup at a time, and mix well, scraping the sides of the bowl after every addition. Add the mint and mix well.

Drop the dough by heaping teaspoonfuls onto the prepared sheets, about 2 inches apart. Bake for 12 to 15 minutes, or until lightly browned, rotating the sheets halfway through baking. Watch carefully near the end of the baking time to prevent overbrowning. Cool on the baking sheets for 5 to 10 minutes. Transfer to a wire rack to cool completely before serving.

note from our test kitchen

For a bigger mint flavor, add the mint to the butter and sugar while creaming. This will extract more of the herb's essential oils (and flavor).

SOURCE: *Nesting*
by Ame Mahler Beanland and Emily Miles Terry

COOK: Margie Beiser Lapanja
after Dorismarie Welcher

cowboy cookies

MARGIE LAPANJA ONCE OPENED A BAKERY just to sell these cookies, and we can see why. Tender, sweet, and hearty, they are practically as big as Texas, which may be their birthplace, and they have it all—oats, chocolate chips, and coconut—in great abundance. In our experience, they bring out the inner cowboy in everyone who bites into them.

You can halve the recipe or make a full batch and freeze extras.

makes 4 dozen

- 1½ cups (3 sticks) margarine, at room temperature (see note)
- 2 cups light brown sugar, packed
- 2 cups sugar
- 4 large eggs
- 2 teaspoons vanilla extract
- 1 teaspoon salt
- 4 cups unbleached all-purpose flour
- 1 teaspoon baking powder
- 2 teaspoons baking soda
- 4 cups old-fashioned oats
- 2 cups chocolate chips
- 1 cup shredded coconut, sweetened or unsweetened
- 1 cup chopped nuts

Preheat the oven to 350 degrees. Line two baking sheets with parchment paper.

Cream the margarine and sugars in a large bowl with an electric mixer until fluffy. Add the eggs, vanilla, and salt and beat well.

Whisk together the flour, baking powder, and baking soda in a large bowl. Gradually mix into the margarine mixture with a sturdy wooden spoon. Stir in the oats until the dough comes together. Finally, stir in the chocolate chips, coconut, and nuts.

Scoop out the dough with a 2-ounce ice cream scoop and drop onto the prepared sheets, about 2 inches apart. Press the tops of the dough mounds slightly with a spoon. Bake for 7 to 12 minutes, rotating the baking sheets halfway through, until the cookies are light golden with tiny cracks on the tops. Transfer to a wire rack to cool completely.

notes from our test kitchen

- We much prefer butter to margarine.
- Our first choice for nuts is pecans; walnuts are second.

source: *The King Arthur Flour Cookie Companion* by King Arthur Flour
cooks: The bakers at the King Arthur Flour Company

almond crisps

We never tire of these old-fashioned almond-scented brown-sugar cookies. Judging by their delicate texture and neat appearance, you'd think they were rolled and cut out with a cookie cutter. Instead, they are the easiest kind of drop cookies. Studding each cookie with a pair of roasted salted almonds keeps them from being too plain and lends a pleasing salty edge to them.

makes 2½ dozen cookies

- 8 tablespoons (1 stick) unsalted butter, at room temperature
- ¼ cup packed light brown sugar
- 2 tablespoons sugar, plus more for flattening the cookies
- ½ teaspoon salt
- 1 tablespoon water
- 2 teaspoons almond extract
- 1¼ cups unbleached all-purpose flour
- ½ cup roasted salted whole almonds

Place two racks near the center of the oven and preheat to 325 degrees.

Cream the butter, sugars, salt, water, and almond extract in a medium bowl with an electric mixer or a wooden spoon. Add the flour, stirring to make a stiff dough.

Drop the dough by teaspoonfuls onto ungreased baking sheets (or parchment-lined for easy cleanup) about 2 inches apart. Flatten to a ¼-inch thickness with the bottom of a drinking glass dipped in sugar (see note). Top each cookie with 2 almonds, pressing them in gently.

Bake the cookies for 17 minutes, rotating the sheets halfway through baking, until browned around the edges. Cool on the baking sheets for 5 minutes. Transfer to a wire rack to cool completely.

notes from our test kitchen

- The 1 tablespoon water is not a misprint. This little bit helps moisten the dough so it comes together.
- Before dipping the drinking glass in sugar to flatten the cookies, the King Arthur bakers recommend wiping it with a wet paper towel. This moistens the glass just enough. You will probably need to moisten the glass only for the first cookie; the sugar will cling to the glass on its own after that.

tip

Who ever would have imagined that a leftover Pringles canister would be of use in the kitchen? *The King Arthur Flour Cookie Companion* came up with the novel idea of using these foil-lined cardboard tubes to ship cookies (if they are about 2½ inches in diameter). Rinse and dry the canister and then wrap it with a sheet of decorative gift-wrapping paper (this helps disguise the fact that you were eating Pringles in the first place). Place a wadded-up paper towel at each end for cushioning and seal the top with plastic wrap before snapping on the lid.

SOURCE: *The Weekend Baker* by Abigail Johnson Dodge

COOK: Abigail Johnson Dodge

chocolate chip–brownie double-deckers

WHO SAYS WE CAN'T HAVE IT ALL? If you have a tough time choosing between superfudgy, chewy brownies and buttery chocolate chip cookies, then these are for you. A bottom layer of intensely chocolatey brownies (which Dodge calls "prescription-strength brownies") and a layer of sugary, slightly crisp chocolate chip cookies make them the best of both worlds.

The technique of melting the butter in a saucepan and then adding all the other ingredients has two advantages. It keeps the layers incredibly moist, and it means fewer bowls to wash afterward.

These don't last long if they are anywhere near folks who love chocolate.

makes 2 dozen 2-inch squares

CHOCOLATE CHIP LAYER

- 12 tablespoons (1 1/2 sticks) unsalted butter
- 1 cup firmly packed light brown sugar
- 1 1/2 cups all-purpose flour
- 1/2 teaspoon baking soda
- 1/4 teaspoon salt
- 1 large egg
- 1 teaspoon vanilla extract
- 1 cup semisweet chocolate chips

BROWNIE LAYER

- 12 tablespoons (1 1/2 sticks) unsalted butter, cut into 6 equal pieces
- 3/4 cup unsweetened Dutch-process cocoa powder, sifted if lumpy
- 1 1/2 cups sugar
- 1/4 teaspoon salt
- 2 large eggs
- 1 1/2 teaspoons vanilla extract
- 3/4 cup all-purpose flour

Place a rack in the center of the oven and preheat to 325 degrees. Lightly grease a 13-x-9-inch baking pan.

TO MAKE THE CHOCOLATE CHIP LAYER:

Melt the butter in a medium saucepan over medium heat, stirring occasionally. Remove from the heat and add the brown sugar. Whisk until no lumps remain. Set aside to cool. (You can make the brownie layer while it cools, if you like.)

Combine the flour, baking soda, and salt in a small bowl until well blended. Once the butter mixture has cooled, add the egg and vanilla to it and whisk until blended. Stir in the flour mixture with a rubber spatula until blended. Stir in the chocolate chips. Set aside.

TO MAKE THE BROWNIE LAYER:

Melt the butter in a medium saucepan over medium heat, stirring occasionally. Remove from the heat and add the cocoa powder. Whisk until smooth. Add the sugar and salt and whisk until blended. Add the eggs 1 at a time, whisking after each addition just until blended. Whisk in the vanilla. Sprinkle the flour over the chocolate mixture and stir with a rubber spatula just until blended.

Scrape the brownie batter into the prepared baking pan and spread evenly with a rubber spatula.

Drop large scoops of the chocolate chip dough over the brownie batter and spread evenly with the rubber spatula. Bake until a toothpick or cake tester inserted in the center comes out with small, gooey clumps of brownie sticking to it, about 40 minutes. Don't overbake or the brownie won't be fudgy. Transfer the baking pan to a wire rack to cool completely.

Using a bench scraper or a knife, cut into 2-inch squares. The cooler the double-deckers are, the cleaner the cutting will be, but these fudgy treats will always leave some sticky crumbs on the knife.

note from our test kitchen

The double-deckers may be made ahead and frozen for up to 1 month. After cooling and cutting, wrap them tightly in plastic and freeze. They take only about 20 minutes to thaw and even taste great partially frozen.

triple-chocolate cranberry oatmeal cookies

CHOCK-A-BLOCK with three kinds of chocolate chips, bits of fresh cranberries, and chewy oats, these cookies please grownups and kids alike. The decorative drizzle of melted chocolate dresses them up for the holidays. Because they keep well, they're great for packing into a pretty box and giving away—that is, if you can bear to part with them.

makes about 30

- 1 cup all-purpose-flour
- 1/2 teaspoon baking soda
- 1/2 teaspoon ground cinnamon
- 1/4 teaspoon salt
- 10 tablespoons (1 1/4 sticks) unsalted butter, at room temperature
- 1/2 cup sugar
- 1/2 cup packed light brown sugar
- 1 large egg
- 1 teaspoon vanilla extract
- 1 cup old-fashioned oats
- 1/2 cup semisweet chocolate chips
- 1/2 cup milk chocolate chips
- 1/2 cup white chocolate chips
- 1/2 cup coarsely chopped fresh or frozen cranberries
- 2 ounces milk chocolate or white chocolate, chopped, for drizzling

Place a rack in the center of the oven and preheat to 350 degrees. Line two large rimmed baking sheets with parchment paper.

Whisk the flour, baking soda, cinnamon, and salt in a medium bowl until well blended.

Beat the butter and both sugars in a large bowl with an electric mixer until smooth. Beat in the egg and vanilla. Add the flour mixture and oats and stir until blended. Stir in all the chocolate chips and the cranberries.

Drop the dough by rounded tablespoonfuls onto the prepared sheets, 2 inches apart. Bake the cookies, one sheet at a time, until the edges are light brown, about 16 minutes. Cool on the baking sheets for 5 minutes. Transfer to a wire rack to cool completely.

Stir the chopped milk chocolate or white chocolate in the top of a double boiler over barely simmering water (or in a heatproof bowl set over a pot of barely simmering water) until melted and smooth. Using a small spoon, drizzle the melted chocolate over the cookies in a zigzag pattern.

The cookies can be made 2 days ahead and stored in an airtight container at room temperature.

notes from our test kitchen

- Depending on your interpretation of "rounded tablespoonfuls," you may end up with closer to 2 dozen cookies. We sometimes do.
- Even though chopped chocolate melts better than chips (see tip), we occasionally cheat and use chips. The drizzle won't be quite as delicate, but it will work. You can also skip the drizzle altogether if that's more your style.
- For extra credit, melt a little of both white and dark chocolate for drizzling.

tip

In *Bon Appétit*, pastry chef and cookbook author Elinor Klivans explains why it's best to use chopped chocolate and not chocolate chips for melting and drizzling. Because chocolate chips are designed to hold their teardrop shape during baking, they don't melt as evenly as plain chopped chocolate.

SOURCE: *The Village Baker's Wife* by Gayle and Joe Ortiz with Louisa Beers

COOKS: Gayle and Joe Ortiz

raspberry walnut brownies

AT THE BUSTLING Gayle's Bakery & Rosticceria in Capitola, California, these killer brownies are legendary. The bakers at Gayle's like to rotate the selection in their case, but anytime these gooey, chocolatey gems disappear, regular customers become frantic.

The key is to underbake the brownies slightly so they remain dense. It would be a sin to let them dry out in the oven. A little bit of raspberry jam helps keep them moist and lends only a hint of berry flavor. For full-on raspberry brownies, see the tip that follows.

This recipe bears the signature of a professional bakery in its liberal use of bowls and utensils. Plus there's a chocolate–cream cheese icing that elevates these into the realm of serious stuff. But one taste and you'll be convinced that they are worth every minute of your efforts.

makes twenty-five 2-x-3-inch brownies

BROWNIES

- 9 ounces unsweetened chocolate, cut into 1/2-inch pieces
- 16 tablespoons (2 sticks) plus 1 tablespoon unsalted butter
- 1/4 cup raspberry jam (see note)
- 2 teaspoons vanilla extract
- 6 large eggs
- 3 cups sugar
- 1 1/2 cups all-purpose flour
- 1/4 teaspoon salt
- 1 1/2 cups walnuts, toasted and finely chopped (see note)

ICING

- 4 ounces bittersweet chocolate
- 8 tablespoons (1 stick) unsalted butter, at room temperature
- 2 ounces cream cheese, at room temperature
- 2 1/3 cups confectioners' sugar

Place a rack in the center of the oven and preheat to 325 degrees. Grease a 15-x-10-inch glass baking pan (see note) with a little butter.

TO MAKE THE BROWNIES:

Melt the chocolate in the top of a double boiler over barely simmering water (or in a heatproof bowl set over a pot of barely simmering water). Melt all the butter in a separate saucepan. Add the melted butter to the melted chocolate, stirring continuously until smooth. Stir in the raspberry jam and vanilla.

Beat the eggs in the bowl of a stand mixer fitted with the whisk attachment or in a large bowl with a hand-held mixer for 1 minute. With the mixer on high, slowly add the sugar and beat for 10 minutes, or until light and thickened.

Combine the flour and salt and place them in a sifter (see note). If you used a stand mixer, transfer the whipped eggs to a large bowl for easier folding. Sift the flour and salt into the egg mixture, folding it in with a rubber spatula in 4 additions. Fold in the chocolate mixture, then the walnuts.

Pour the brownie batter into the prepared pan. Bake for 25 to 30 minutes, checking the progress as the brownies bake, until a toothpick inserted in the center comes out almost clean. Overbaking makes them dry. Cool in the pan on a wire rack.

TO MAKE THE ICING:

When the brownies are completely cool, melt the chocolate in the top of a double boiler over barely simmering water (or in a heatproof bowl set over a pot of barely simmering water). Let cool.

Beat the butter and cream cheese with an electric mixer on medium speed until smooth. Beat in the confectioners' sugar and melted chocolate. Spread the icing evenly over the brownies. Cut into 2-x-3-inch rectangles to serve. These will keep for 1 to 2 days if tightly wrapped and refrigerated. Return to room temperature to serve.

notes from our test kitchen

- Either seedless or regular raspberry jam works fine.
- A sieve makes a fine sifter for the flour and the salt; shake it back and forth or tap the side with your hand to coax the flour through.
- To toast the walnuts, put them on a rimmed baking sheet in a 350-degree oven and bake, shaking the pan occasionally, until they smell toasty and are beginning to darken, 10 to 12 minutes.
- If you don't have a 15-x-10-inch baking pan, use a 13-x-9-inch one, and bake the brownies a bit longer.

tip

For fresh raspberry brownies, Gayle Ortiz omits the jam and nuts and presses one half-pint basket of fresh raspberries into the batter after pouring it into the pan. Make sure the berries are fully immersed in the batter. Bake as directed.

SOURCE: *Saveur*

STORY BY Sarah Bir

COOK: Sarah Bir

peanut butter buckeyes

COLLEGE FOOTBALL FANS may already know the story, but we didn't. The Ohio State University mascot is the buckeye, the inedible nut of the Ohio buckeye tree. In honor of their mascot, OSU fans make these peanut butter and chocolate confections to take to tailgates. Word has it that serious boosters even serve them on their Christmas buffets.

You enrobe the sweet, creamy peanut butter centers in a thin shell of semisweet chocolate. Leave a little of the peanut butter peering through, so they resemble their namesake nuts, which are a glossy dark brown with a light circular patch. The candies may remind you of a Reese's cup, but they have a lot more peanut filling. One friend we served them to wouldn't stop talking about them for weeks.

Buckeyes are good at room temperature or chilled. We even like them straight from the freezer.

makes about 30

- 2 cups sifted confectioners' sugar
- 3/4 cup smooth peanut butter
- 4 tablespoons (1/2 stick) unsalted butter, melted (see note)
- 1/2 teaspoon vanilla extract
- 1/4 teaspoon salt
- 6 ounces semisweet chocolate chips
- 1/2 teaspoon vegetable shortening

Line two baking sheets with wax paper.

Put the confectioners' sugar, peanut butter, butter, vanilla, and salt in a medium bowl and beat well with a wooden spoon. Roll the peanut butter mixture into 1-inch balls and transfer to a prepared baking sheet in a single layer. Freeze until firm, 15 to 20 minutes.

Melt the chocolate and shortening in the top of a double boiler over barely simmering water (or in a heatproof bowl set over a small pot of barely simmering water), stirring often. Remove the pot and bowl together from the heat.

Working with about 6 peanut butter balls at a time, insert a toothpick into the center of a ball and dip about three quarters of the ball into the melted chocolate, leaving about a 3/4-inch circle of peanut butter visible at the top. Twirl the toothpick between your finger and thumb to swirl off excess chocolate, then transfer to the other baking sheet, chocolate side down. Slide out the toothpick and repeat the dipping process with the remaining peanut butter balls and chocolate, reheating the chocolate if necessary.

Freeze the buckeyes until firm. Smooth out the toothpick holes left in the peanut butter. Buckeyes keep well sealed in a cool place for up to 1 week and up to 2 weeks in the refrigerator. Serve at room temperature or chilled.

note from our test kitchen

- Combining the ingredients while the melted butter is still warm makes it easier to stir. Otherwise, the peanut butter filling can be rather stiff. You may find it easier to abandon the wooden spoon after the initial mixing and work it with your hands until well blended.

SOURCE: *Food & Wine*
STORY BY Mitchell Davis
COOKS: Naomi Duguid and Jeffrey Alford

breton butter cake

KOUIGN AMANN (pronounced "kween-yah-*mahn*"), a sugary version of puff pastry from Brittany, is arguably one of the world's greatest cakes. (The name comes from the heart of Brittany, where Breton, a Celtic tongue related to Welsh, is still spoken.) As the layers of yeasted dough, butter, and sugar bake, they become a flaky pastry that is sweet and buttery inside and crackly and caramelized on top and around the edges. Cookbook authors Naomi Duguid and Jeffrey Alford have come up with an easy version by using store-bought bread dough or pizza dough. It may not be entirely authentic, but it is entirely heavenly.

Serve this warm after dinner with a sip of port or for afternoon tea. The cake can be kept at room temperature overnight, but it's best eaten the day it's made. Refrigerating will make it stale.

serves 6

- 1 pound frozen bread dough or pizza dough, thawed
- 8 tablespoons (1 stick) chilled butter, cut into 16 slices, plus 1 tablespoon melted butter (see note)
- 3/4 cup plus 2 tablespoons sugar

Roll out the dough on a lightly floured work surface into a rough 8-x-12-inch rectangle. Cover with plastic wrap and let rest for 25 minutes. Lightly flour the rolling pin and roll out the dough to a 14-x-18-inch rectangle. Cover with plastic wrap and let rest again for 25 minutes.

Butter a 9-inch cast-iron skillet. Flour the work surface.

Roll out the dough as thinly as possible, keeping a rectangular shape. Scatter 5 slices of the butter over two thirds of the dough and sprinkle with 1/4 cup of the sugar. Fold the bare third of dough into the center and fold in the opposite side, like folding a letter (see note). Dust with flour and roll out again as thinly as possible, retaining the rectangular shape. Top with another 5 slices of butter and 1/4 cup of the sugar, folding, dusting with flour, and rolling out the dough again as before. Repeat the process one last time, using the remaining 6 slices of butter and 1/4 cup of the sugar, folding and rolling it out as thinly as possible.

Fold in the corners of the dough to make a slightly round shape and transfer it to the prepared skillet. With a sharp knife, make six 2-inch-long cuts all the way through the dough in a starburst pattern. Cover the dough with plastic wrap and let rise for 45 minutes.

Place a baking stone or baking sheet in the lower third of the oven and preheat to 450 degrees.

Brush the dough with the melted butter and sprinkle with the remaining 2 tablespoons sugar. Put the skillet on the stone or baking sheet and bake for 25 minutes, or until richly browned on top. With a spatula, transfer the cake to a large plate and let rest for 30 minutes. Cut into wedges and serve.

notes from our test kitchen

- Use salted, not unsalted, butter.
- This is best made on a day or at a time of day when the kitchen remains cool, so the butter between the layers does not melt, which is important to producing the flaky layers. If you have air conditioning, use it to cool the kitchen. You can also slide the dough in and out of the refrigerator between rolling, but this can become vexing.
- After you roll out the dough, scatter the butter and sugar over it, and fold it like a letter, it's best to turn the dough 90 degrees before rolling again. This way you are not always rolling in the same direction and the butter layers become more evenly distributed.
- The more you work a yeasted dough, the more resilient it becomes. If you find that the dough is becoming too elastic and refuses to roll out, cover it loosely with plastic wrap and let it rest for 15 to 20 minutes before continuing. This will relax the dough and make it easier to roll out.
- If you don't have a well-seasoned cast-iron skillet, use a regular cake pan. The cake may come out with less crunchy caramelized edges, but it will still be tasty.

SOURCE: *Favorite Recipes from 10 Years of Fine Cooking* by *Fine Cooking*

COOKS: Johanne Killeen and George Germon

triple caramel cake

TRUE GOODNESS NEVER GOES OUT OF STYLE. The minute we tasted this cake, we knew why the editors of *Fine Cooking* chose it as one of a handful of favorite recipes in ten years. The cake looks like a plain bundt cake with a nice caramel drizzle, but its flavor and texture are out of this world. You start by making a creamy caramel sauce. One third of it goes into the batter to make the cake incredibly moist, one third is drizzled over the top as a chewy caramel glaze, and the final third is folded into whipped cream to make a marbled topping for each slice. This is a terrific holiday dessert.

serves 10 to 12

- 3 cups heavy cream
- 2½ cups sugar
- 12 tablespoons (1½ sticks) unsalted butter, at room temperature
- 4 large eggs, at room temperature
- 2 cups unbleached all-purpose flour
- 1½ teaspoons baking powder
- Pinch of salt

Slowly bring 2 cups of the cream to a boil in a medium saucepan (see note). Reduce the heat and keep at a bare simmer.

Put 1 cup of the sugar in a heavy medium saucepan over medium heat. Leave undisturbed until the sugar begins to melt and darken. Gently shake the pan to distribute the sugar and to keep it from burning. When all has melted and the caramel is a very dark amber, remove from the heat. Carefully add the hot cream, stirring constantly with a wooden spoon. Don't worry if the caramel hardens; it will melt as the sauce boils. Return the pan to the heat and keep the sauce at a gentle boil for about 5 minutes, stirring constantly. Set aside for at least 30 minutes, stirring often, until the sauce is cool. Measure 1 cup of the caramel to add to the cake batter and refrigerate the rest.

Place a rack in the lower third of the oven and preheat to 325 degrees. Grease and flour a 12-cup bundt pan.

Cream the butter and remaining 1½ cups sugar in a large bowl with an electric mixer until fluffy. Add the eggs 1 at a time, beating until each one is incorporated before adding the next. Sift together the flour, baking powder, and salt into a bowl. Gently but thoroughly fold the dry ingredients into the butter mixture alternately with the reserved 1 cup caramel, beginning and ending with the dry ingredients.

Pour the batter into the prepared pan and bake until a skewer inserted in the center comes out clean, 35 to 40 minutes. Cool on a wire rack for about 10 minutes and then unmold and cool completely on the rack. Bring the remaining caramel sauce to room temperature. When the cake is cool, glaze it by drizzling half of the remaining caramel sauce over the top.

Whip the remaining 1 cup cream until it holds firm peaks. Fold in the last third of the caramel gently, leaving streaks visible. Serve with the cake.

notes from our test kitchen

- You can make the caramel sauce ahead; just reheat it to room temperature before using.
- Be sure to use at least a 2-quart saucepan for making the caramel. Otherwise, it may well boil over when you add the warm cream.
- The cake is best the day it is made. It can also be wrapped tightly in plastic wrap (before glazing) and kept at room temperature overnight.

SOURCE: *Los Angeles Times*

COOK: **Roxana Jullapat**

hazelnut–brown butter cake

SOMEHOW THIS AMAZING CAKE manages to be light like a meringue, rich, and buttery all at once. The secret is slowly browning the butter with a split vanilla bean until the butter turns toasty and aromatic. The batter contains very little flour, relying instead on ground hazelnuts and confectioners' sugar to thicken it, so it ends up nicely crunchy. Beaten egg whites give the cake its loft.

The remarkable recipe comes from Roxana Jullapat, the pastry chef at the popular West Hollywood restaurant Lucques, and customers go crazy for it. At the restaurant, Jullapat garnishes the slices with a sprinkle of fleur de sel (the delicately crunchy sea salt) and caramel ice cream. It's also good on its own.

serves 10

- 12 tablespoons (1 1/2 sticks) butter (see note)
- 1 vanilla bean
- 5 ounces skinned hazelnuts, toasted (see tip)
- 1 1/3 cups confectioners' sugar
- 1/3 cup all-purpose flour
- 5 large egg whites
- 1/4 cup sugar
- Fleur de sel for serving (optional; see note)
- Caramel ice cream for serving (optional)

Place an 8-inch skillet over low heat and add the butter. Cut the vanilla bean in half lengthwise. Scrape the seeds out and add the seeds and bean to the butter. When the butter turns a golden brown, 15 to 20 minutes, remove from the heat. Remove and discard the vanilla bean and transfer the butter to a bowl to cool.

Place a rack in the center of the oven and preheat to 350 degrees. Spray a 10-inch cake pan with nonstick cooking spray and line the bottom with parchment paper.

Grind the hazelnuts with the confectioners' sugar in a food processor. Place the ground nuts in a large bowl. Add the flour and stir until well combined.

Beat the egg whites and sugar in a large bowl with an electric mixer until stiff peaks form. Fold the whites into the nut mixture. Fold in the room-temperature brown butter.

Pour the batter into the prepared pan. Bake until a skewer inserted in the center comes out clean, about 1 hour. Cool on a wire rack for 10 minutes, then run a sharp knife around the edge and unmold onto a serving platter. Sprinkle each serving of cake with a little fleur de sel and accompany with a scoop of caramel ice cream, if desired.

notes from our test kitchen

- We use unsalted butter and add a pinch of salt to the batter. Salted butter will also work.
- Fleur de sel is considered by many the queen of sea salts. Its grains are small flake-like crystals with a delicate crunch. As its name suggests, fleur de sel comes from France, where it is harvested by skimming the salty foam from the surface of seawater. You can find fleur de sel at gourmet stores or online at www.saltworks.us or www.zingermans.com.

tip

In *Pie,* Ken Haedrich explains how to skin and toast hazelnuts. Preheat the oven to 350 degrees. Spread the hazelnuts on a large rimmed baking sheet and toast until the skins blister and the nuts look golden brown, 10 to 12 minutes. Immediately pour the nuts onto a clean kitchen towel, fold the towel over, and let cool for 1 minute. Then vigorously rub the nuts in the towel to remove the skins. Don't worry about any small bits of skin that won't come off.

The folks at the Hazelnut Council in Washington State tell us that Turkish hazelnuts are easier to skin than domestic nuts, so if you have a choice, Turkish are the ones you want.

brown sugar–sour cream cheesecake

EVERY NOW AND AGAIN we come across a cookbook that takes us weeks (if not months) to choose from, and *Sweet Stuff* is just such a book. Karen Barker is the James Beard Award–winning pastry chef at Magnolia Grill (the restaurant that she owns with her husband, chef Ben Barker) in Durham, North Carolina. She takes familiar desserts and joyfully revitalizes them. This cheesecake, for instance, has the standard elements of any New York–style cheesecake, but Barker adds a few down-home southern accents.

A bit of cornmeal in the graham-cracker crust adds a delightful crunch. Then the cream cheese filling is sweetened with molasses and brown sugar, and a bit of peach brandy or bourbon goes into the sour cream topping.

Barker also introduced us to a novel way of baking cheesecake. She eliminates the nuisance of a water bath (hallelujah!) and instead has us lower the oven temperature at 20-minute intervals. This descending heat keeps the cake smooth, satiny, and completely crack-free.

serves 12

CRUST

- 1 1/2 cups graham cracker crumbs
- 1/2 cup yellow cornmeal, preferably stone-ground
- 2 tablespoons sugar
- 6 tablespoons (3/4 stick) unsalted butter, melted

FILLING

- 1 1/2 pounds cream cheese, at room temperature
- 8 tablespoons (1 stick) unsalted butter, at room temperature
- 1 1/4 cups lightly packed light brown sugar
- 2 tablespoons molasses
- 2 teaspoons vanilla extract
- 1/2 cup sour cream
- 1/4 cup heavy cream
- 4 large eggs

TOPPING

- 1 1/2 cups sour cream
- 2 tablespoons lightly packed light brown sugar
- 1 1/2 tablespoons peach brandy, bourbon, or orange juice

TO MAKE THE CRUST:

For a gas oven, place the rack on the bottom; for an electric one, place it in the center. Preheat the oven to 350 degrees. Butter a 10-inch springform pan, line the bottom and sides with parchment paper, and butter the parchment paper.

Combine the graham cracker crumbs, cornmeal, sugar, and melted butter in a bowl. Mix with a fork until the crumbs are evenly moistened. Press the crumbs into the bottom and 1/2 inch up the sides of the pan (see note). Bake for about 8 minutes, or until the crust just starts to pick up a bit of color around the edge. Remove from the oven and cool. Leave the oven on.

TO MAKE THE FILLING:

Combine the cream cheese, butter, and sugar in the bowl of a mixer fitted with the paddle attachment or in a large bowl with a hand-held mixer and mix until very smooth, scraping down the sides as necessary. Add the molasses and vanilla and mix. Add the sour cream and mix. Add the heavy cream and mix just to blend in. Add the eggs 1 at a time, and mix just to incorporate. Scrape the bowl, making sure the filling is well mixed. Pour it into the prepared crust.

Bake at 350 degrees for 20 minutes and then turn the oven down to 300 degrees. Bake for 20 minutes more and turn the oven down to 250 degrees. Bake for 20 minutes more and turn the oven to low (or 225 degrees). Continue baking until the cake looks set around the edges but just a bit jiggly in the very center (see note).

MEANWHILE, MAKE THE TOPPING:

Whisk together the sour cream, brown sugar, and peach brandy or other liquid.

As soon as the cake is done, remove it from the oven and turn the oven up to 350 degrees. Slowly and evenly pour the sour cream topping over the cake. You can use an offset spatula to help spread it into an even layer.

Bake for 3 minutes, or until the topping is just set. Cool completely on a wire rack. Refrigerate for several hours or overnight before serving.

notes from our test kitchen

- For tamping down the pie crust, Karen Barker recommends using the bottom of a metal 1/4-cup measuring cup. This produces a smoother, more compact crust than you can get using your fingers.
- The timing for the final baking interval in the low oven differs widely from one oven to another. The only way to be sure is to nudge the cake and check that the sides are set and the center is just jiggly. We find this takes anywhere from 20 to 40 minutes at the low setting.
- When you return the oven temperature to 350 degrees and pour on the topping, the topping may take longer than 3 minutes to set. How long depends on how quickly your oven reheats. Don't leave the cake in too long, however; you want the topping to barely set, usually 5 to 10 minutes.

tips

Karen Barker offers a helpful set of precautions for avoiding the cracks that plague cheesecake makers:

- Have all your ingredients at room temperature.
- Don't overbeat the filling. Beating incorporates air, which causes the cake to expand, subsequently contract, and thus crack.
- Once the eggs are added, beat until just combined.
- Lining the sides and bottom of the pan with parchment will prevent the cake from clinging to the sides of the pan as it cools, which can cause cracking.
- Overbaking is the most common cause of cheesecake cracks.
- Allow the cake to cool completely on a wire rack before refrigerating.
- And finally, if despite all these precautions the surface cracks, decorate it with berries!

SOURCE: *Bouchon* by Thomas Keller with Jeffrey Cerciello

COOK: Thomas Keller

almond cake with strawberry rhubarb compote

LOTS OF PEOPLE THINK Thomas Keller is the best chef in America, and anyone who has dined at the French Laundry restaurant in Napa or Per Se in New York City might agree. Although he made his name in the world of haute cuisine, Keller also loves simple food—and that's what this almond cake is. It gets a triple-almond whammy from almond paste, sliced almonds, and amaretto.

You don't need to serve it with the strawberry rhubarb compote, but it's a wonderful companion and so easy to make that you really ought to try it. If strawberries and rhubarb aren't in season, serve the cake with some fresh raspberries and a dollop of whipped crème fraîche.

serves 8

- 7 ounces almond paste
- 1/4 cup sugar
- 8 tablespoons (1 stick) unsalted butter, cut into small pieces and chilled
- 2 tablespoons honey
- 3 large eggs
- 2 tablespoons amaretto, plus additional for brushing
- 1/3 cup all-purpose flour, sifted
- Kosher salt
- 1/3–1/2 cup sliced almonds, toasted (see note)
- Confectioners' sugar for dusting
- Strawberry Rhubarb Compote (recipe follows)
- 1/4 cup crème fraîche, whipped to soft peaks

Preheat the oven to 350 degrees. Butter the bottom of an 8-inch round cake pan and butter and flour its sides. Line the bottom with parchment paper.

Cream the almond paste and sugar in the bowl of a stand mixer or in a large bowl with a hand-held mixer. Start on low speed to break up the almond paste, then increase the speed to medium for about 2 minutes, or until the paste is broken into fine particles. Add the butter and mix for 4 to 5 minutes, or until the mixture is light in color and airy, scraping down the sides as necessary. It's important to mix it long enough, or the cake will have a dense texture. Mix in the honey, then add the eggs 1 at a time, beating until each one is incorporated before adding the next. Add the amaretto, flour, and a pinch of salt and mix just to combine.

Scrape the batter into the prepared pan and smooth the top. Bake for about 25 minutes, or until the cake is golden and springs back when pressed. Transfer to a wire rack to cool.

Invert the cooled cake onto the rack, remove the parchment paper, and invert the cake again so that the top is once again facing upward. Brush the top of the cake with amaretto and sprinkle with the almonds. Dust with confectioners' sugar. The cake will keep, well wrapped, at room temperature for 2 days.

Cut the cake into 8 wedges and serve with the compote and a dollop of whipped crème fraîche.

notes from our test kitchen

- You can buy tiny bottles of amaretto at the liquor store; they're useful to have on hand.
- To toast the almonds, put them on a rimmed baking sheet in a 350-degree oven and roast, shaking the pan occasionally, just until they smell toasty, 8 to 10 minutes.

strawberry rhubarb compote

- 1 pound strawberries, rinsed and hulled
- 1 pound rhubarb, trimmed
- 1 lemon
- 3/4 cup sugar

Select about 4 ounces (3/4 cup) of the smallest strawberries. Cut them lengthwise into quarters and set aside.

Cut the remaining strawberries into halves or quarters, so that they're roughly the same size. Place them in a medium saucepan.

With a paring knife, pull away and discard the strings that run the length of the rhubarb stalks. Cut the stalks into 3/4-inch pieces and add to the saucepan.

Use a fine grater or a Microplane to zest the lemon. Add 1 teaspoon of the zest to the pan. Squeeze 1 tablespoon juice from the lemon and add to the pan. Add the sugar and stir to coat the fruit.

Cook over medium-high heat, stirring often to dissolve the sugar. By the time the sugar has dissolved, the fruit will have released a lot of juice. Boil for about 4 minutes to reduce the liquid somewhat, then reduce the heat and simmer for 2 minutes more, or until the rhubarb is soft. Don't worry if some of the rhubarb falls apart.

Remove from the heat and stir in the reserved strawberries. Cool to room temperature, then refrigerate in a covered container until cold. Any extra compote will keep for 2 weeks and is delicious for breakfast, especially with crème fraîche.

tip

Alton Brown, the TV cooking equipment guru, says sifters are passé. It's much easier and more efficient to put the dry ingredients in a food processor and whiz them together in a few pulses. We're keeping our sifters for the moment, but if we pass a year without using them, they're history.

dahlia bakery butterscotch pie

HERE'S A SHOWSTOPPING DESSERT that your guests will talk about for weeks. Imagine a crisp, flaky pie crust filled with rich butterscotch pudding, topped with sliced bananas and a poof of whipped cream, and dusted with crunchy salty sweet pistachio brittle.

The recipe comes from Seattle chef Tom Douglas and his colleague, Shelley Lance. At Dahlia Bakery they make individual butterscotch pies or tarts. At home we make one large pie and carry it proudly to the table. To make your life easier, the various components (pie shell, filling, and brittle) can all be made in advance and assembled just before serving.

serves 6

Extra-Flaky Pie Crust (page 259; see note)

FILLING

- 11 tablespoons (1 stick plus 3 tablespoons) unsalted butter
- 1⅔ cups firmly packed dark brown sugar
- 1⅓ cups hot water
- ¼ cup cornstarch
- 2 tablespoons plus 2 teaspoons all-purpose flour
- Scant ½ teaspoon salt
- Scant 1 cup whole milk
- 4 large egg yolks
- 1 tablespoon vanilla extract

PISTACHIO BRITTLE

- 1 cup shelled natural (undyed) pistachios
- 3 tablespoons water
- ¾ cup sugar

GARNISH

- 2–3 medium ripe bananas, peeled and sliced
- Whipped cream (see note)

TO MAKE THE PIE CRUST:

If making one 9-inch pie, flatten the dough into a disk and wrap in plastic. If making individual pies, divide the dough into 6 equal balls. Flatten into ½-inch-thick disks and wrap in plastic. Refrigerate until firm enough to roll, about 1 hour. Get out one 9-inch pie dish or six 1-cup individual pie dishes.

Working with 1 piece of chilled dough at a time, using a floured rolling pin, roll the dough into a circle large enough to line the pie on a sheet of lightly floured wax paper. Invert the dough over the pan, center it, and peel off the paper. Gently tuck the dough into the pie dish, without stretching it, and sculpt the edge so it is slightly higher than the rim. Place in the freezer while you line the other pie dishes, if using.

Place a rack in the center of the oven and preheat to 400 degrees. Line the pie plates with aluminum foil and pour in enough dried beans to reach the top.

Bake the pie shells for 15 minutes to set the crust. Remove the foil and the beans and, with a fork, prick the bottom of the pastry in several places. Reduce the oven temperature to 375 degrees and continue baking until the pastry is golden brown and fully baked, 15 to 17 minutes. If the crust starts to puff up during baking, deflate it with a fork. Cool on a wire rack.

TO MAKE THE FILLING:

Melt the butter in a heavy large saucepan over medium to medium-high heat, stirring a few times. Continue to heat until brown flecks begin to appear on the bottom of the pan. Add the brown sugar and continue to cook over medium-high heat, stirring constantly, for 2 minutes. Carefully stir the water into the saucepan; be prepared to step back away from the spattering. Remove from the heat.

Combine the cornstarch, flour, and salt in a medium bowl (see note). Gradually whisk in the milk. Add the milk mixture to the saucepan and return to medium-high heat, whisking constantly, until it reaches a boil. Reduce the heat slightly and cook, whisking constantly, for 3 minutes. The mixture will be very thick. Remove from the heat.

Whisk the egg yolks in a small bowl. Gradually whisk 6 or 7 tablespoons of the hot butter mixture into the yolks to temper them. Stir the tempered yolks into the saucepan. Return to the heat and continue to cook over medium heat, stirring constantly, for 2 minutes. Remove from the heat and pour into a bowl. Whisk in the vanilla. Press a piece of plastic wrap against the filling, without any gaps or air pockets, to keep a skin from forming. Cool to room temperature on a wire rack. Refrigerate for at least 4 hours or overnight.

TO MAKE THE PISTACHIO BRITTLE:

At least 1 hour before serving, lightly oil a piece of aluminum foil and place it on a baking sheet. Arrange the pistachios close together in a single layer in the center of the sheet and set aside.

Combine the water and sugar in a heavy small saucepan over medium heat and stir constantly until the sugar dissolves, about 2 minutes. Increase the heat to high and stop stirring. Heat, swirling the pan from time to time instead of stirring, until the mixture is light golden brown, 7 to 8 minutes. Slowly pour the mixture over the pistachios, taking care to cover all of them. Set the baking sheet aside and let cool completely. Break the brittle into pieces (see note). Place the pieces in a food processor and process into fine crumbs.

TO ASSEMBLE AND GARNISH THE PIES:

Smooth the filling by stirring gently, then spoon some into each pie shell, leaving room around the outside for the banana slices. Tuck some banana slices here and there around the filling. Put a generous dollop of whipped cream on top, then sprinkle with the pistachio brittle. Serve at once.

notes from our test kitchen

- We use a store-bought 9-inch pie shell for prebaking as described above. The amount of filling needed is the same.
- To avoid lumps, sift the cornstarch into the flour and salt.
- You'll have much more pistachio brittle than you need for this dessert. What we like to do is grind only a few handfuls and break the rest into shards to serve as a candy treat.
- To top the pies or pie, whip about 1 cup of heavy cream lightly sweetened with 2 to 3 tablespoons of granulated or confectioners' sugar.

extra-flaky pie crust

makes 1 single crust or enough for six 1-cup pies

- 1 cup all-purpose flour
- 2/3 cup cake flour
- 1 tablespoon sugar
- 1/2 teaspoon salt
- 4 tablespoons (1/2 stick) chilled unsalted butter, cut into 1/4-inch pieces
- 5 tablespoons chilled vegetable shortening, cut into pieces
- 1/4 cup cold water

Put the flours, sugar, and salt in a food processor. Add the butter and pulse several times to cut it in. Fluff the mixture with a fork, lifting it up from the bottom of the bowl. Scatter the shortening over the flour and pulse 5 or 6 times. Fluff the mixture again. Drizzle half the water over the flour mixture and pulse 5 or 6 times. Fluff the mixture and sprinkle on the remaining water. Pulse 5 or 6 more times, or until the dough starts to form clumps. When it reaches this point, transfer the dough to a large bowl.

Using your hands, pack the dough as you would a snowball. Knead the ball 2 or 3 times. Put it in the center of a piece of plastic wrap and flatten it into a disk about 3/4 inch thick. Wrap in the plastic and refrigerate until firm enough to roll out, at least 1 hour or overnight. Roll out as directed in the recipe.

tips

Ken Haedrich offers a helpful hint for what to do if you don't have cake flour. Substitute 1/4 cup cornstarch for 1/4 cup of the all-purpose flour. Sift the cornstarch into the flour, then proceed.

To keep the pie shell from getting soggy, Ken Haedrich recommends painting the bottom of the crust with a beaten egg white as soon as it's baked. Then return the crust to the oven to bake the egg white into a hard finish, about 2 minutes.

SOURCE: Cooking school handout
COOK: Pam Anderson

silky pumpkin pie

COOKBOOK AUTHOR PAM ANDERSON is known for her down-to-earth recipes that always work, and this pie is no exception. At first glance it looks rather ordinary—no fancy flourishes or gimmicky twists—but every time we serve it, guests declare that it's the best pumpkin pie they've ever had.

It's hard to say exactly what makes it so astoundingly good, but we think it's because the spices are added with a light hand, so you can actually taste the sweet earthiness of the pumpkin. The other winning characteristic is the dense, velvety texture. Partially baking the pie shell before filling means you can bake the filling at a lower temperature than usual, which keeps it from curdling or getting at all rubbery.

By using a combination of frozen butter, shortening, and cream cheese, Anderson creates a foolproof crust that comes together in a food processor and is a dream to roll out.

makes one 9-inch pie

DOUGH

- 1 cup plus 2 tablespoons bleached all-purpose flour
- 1 tablespoon sugar
- 1/2 teaspoon salt
- 4 tablespoons (1/2 stick) unsalted butter, cut into 1/2-inch pieces and frozen until solid
- 2 ounces cream cheese, cut into 1/2-inch chunks and frozen until solid
- 2 tablespoons vegetable shortening, cut into 1/2-inch pieces and frozen until solid
- 3 tablespoons ice water

FILLING

- 1 15-ounce can pumpkin (not pie filling)
- 1/2 teaspoon salt
- 1 teaspoon ground ginger
- 3/4 teaspoon ground cinnamon
- 1/4 teaspoon ground allspice
- 1/8 teaspoon ground nutmeg
- 1 14-ounce can sweetened condensed milk
- 1 cup evaporated milk
- 2 large eggs plus 2 large egg yolks
- Whipped cream for garnish (optional)

TO MAKE THE DOUGH:

Pulse the flour, sugar, and salt in a food processor to combine. Add the butter and toss with a fork to coat with the flour mixture and break up any stuck-together cubes. Pulse 4 times, 1 long second each time. Break up the cream cheese and shortening pieces and add to the flour mixture; toss to coat. Pulse until the fats are the size of peas and fine gravel, another 4 or 5 long 1-second pulses. Transfer the mixture to a medium bowl. Add the water and stir with a rubber spatula until small clumps form, adding a few more drops of water only if necessary. Gently press the clumps together to create a cohesive ball. Wrap the dough ball in plastic and press into a thick disk. Refrigerate for at least 1 hour or up to 2 days.

Put the dough on a lightly floured work surface and roll into a 14-inch round. Fold the dough in half, transfer it to a 9-inch pie plate, and unfold it into the pan. Trim the dough to a ½-inch overhang and roll this under with your fingertips so that it's flush with pan lip. Flute the edge (make sure the dough stays fully on the rim of the plate to minimize shrinkage during prebaking). Refrigerate for at least 1 hour.

Place a rack in the lowest part of the oven and preheat to 400 degrees.

Line the dough with a double sheet of heavy-duty foil and bake until the edges have started to turn golden, about 20 minutes. Remove the foil and return the pan to the oven until the pie shell loses its raw appearance and is lightly browned, about 5 minutes more. Remove the pie shell from the oven and turn the oven down to 300 degrees.

MEANWHILE, MAKE THE FILLING:

Combine the pumpkin, salt, ginger, cinnamon, allspice, and nutmeg in a medium saucepan. Heat over medium-low to medium heat just to blend the flavors, about 5 minutes, stirring occasionally. Add the condensed and evaporated milks and whisk to combine; cook until heated through. Put the eggs and yolks in a medium bowl and whisk to blend. Whisk the pumpkin mixture into the eggs, a spoonful at a time at first to warm the eggs gently; whisk well to get a silky filling.

Pour the warm filling into the warm pie shell; you'll have extra filling, which you can pour into individual ovenproof custard cups and bake alongside the pie (see note). Bake until a thin-bladed knife inserted in the center of the filling comes out clean, 30 to 40 minutes; check the custard cups after 15 to 20 minutes. Let cool on a wire rack and then refrigerate. Serve at room temperature or chilled, with a dollop of whipped cream, if you like.

note from our test kitchen

Save the extra filling you baked in the custard cups (you'll have 2 or 3) for a kitchen treat or serve them as children's desserts at Thanksgiving.

tip

In her book *The Good Cook,* Anne Willan explains that disks of pastry should be wrapped loosely in plastic wrap when put in the refrigerator to chill. If too tightly wrapped, the dough tends to sweat, which means it will be sticky when you start to roll it.

SOURCE: *The Village Baker's Wife*
by Gayle and Joe Ortiz with Louisa Beers
COOK: Johanne Killeen

fresh fig crostata

FRESH FIGS ARE AVAILABLE only for a few months in the fall. We can think of no better way to honor them than by baking them up into a crostata —a rustic, freeform fruit tart. As the figs bake, their juices meld with the sprinkling of cinnamon sugar until they become soft and caramelized.

makes one 10-inch tart

- 2 tablespoons superfine sugar (see tip)
- 1/4 teaspoon ground cinnamon
- 12 fresh figs (about 12 ounces), stemmed
- 1 disk Crostata Dough (*recipe follows*)
- Confectioners' sugar for dusting

Place a rack in the center of the oven and preheat to 450 degrees.

Combine the sugar and cinnamon in a small bowl. Cut the figs in half vertically.

Place the dough on a lightly floured work surface and roll it out into a freeform 11-inch circle. Transfer the dough to a small baking sheet and sprinkle with 1 tablespoon of the cinnamon-sugar mixture.

Starting in the center, cover the dough with a starburst of figs, placing them skin sides down and leaving a 1 1/2-inch border around the edge. Sprinkle the remaining cinnamon sugar over the figs.

In a casual fashion, bring the edges of the dough up, letting it slightly drape over the outer edge of the fruit. Press down on the dough where the sides form a corner at the bottom, being careful not to mash the fruit.

Bake for 20 to 25 minutes, or until the crust is golden and the figs are soft and slightly caramelized. Cool on the baking sheet on a wire rack for about 10 minutes. Dust with confectioners' sugar and serve warm.

note from our test kitchen

If you have a baking stone, preheat it in the oven for baking the crostata.

crostata dough

makes enough for 2 crostatas

- 16 tablespoons (2 sticks) chilled unsalted butter
- 2 cups all-purpose flour
- 1/4 cup superfine sugar (see tip)
- 1/2 teaspoon salt
- 1/4 cup ice water

Cut the butter into 1/2-inch pieces and return it to the refrigerator.

Place the flour, sugar, and salt in a food processor and pulse several times to combine.

Add the butter and toss carefully once or twice with your hands to coat it with flour mixture. Pulse 15 times, or until the butter pieces are the size of small peas. With the processor running, add the ice water all at once through the feed tube. Process for about 10 seconds, stopping before the dough becomes a solid mass.

Divide the dough in half and place each half on a sheet of plastic wrap, pressing any loose particles into the mass of dough. Gently form each into a 7-inch disk.

Seal the dough with the plastic wrap and refrigerate for at least 1 hour. The dough may be refrigerated for up to 2 days or frozen for up to 2 weeks. To use frozen dough, thaw overnight in the refrigerator. Roll out as directed in the recipe.

tip

Superfine sugar is sold in the baking aisle of most supermarkets. It also goes by the name of bar sugar, because it's what bartenders use to make mixed drinks. If you don't have a box on hand, here's a tip from Abigail Johnson Dodge, author of *The Weekend Baker*. Pulse regular granulated sugar in food processor until it's finely pulverized. Measure the sugar for the recipe after processing.

SOURCE: www.aboutpeanuts.com

COOK: Unknown

southern peanut pie

TRADITIONAL IN VIRGINIA and the Carolinas, peanut pie deserves to be better known in other parts of the country. As the pie bakes, the salty, roasted peanuts rise to the top of the sweet filling, so you get a contrast of crunchy and gooey. Peanut pie devotees like to say that it's like pecan pie, only better. And we'd be hard pressed to disagree.

Top each slice with a scoop of vanilla ice cream or a puff of whipped cream.

makes one 9-inch pie

- 3 large eggs
- 1/2 cup sugar
- 1/4 teaspoon salt
- 1 1/2 cups dark corn syrup
- 4 tablespoons (1/2 stick) butter, melted (see note)
- 1/2 teaspoon vanilla extract
- 1 1/2 cups chopped roasted peanuts (see note)
- 1 9-inch unbaked deep-dish pie shell

Place a rack in the center of the oven and preheat to 375 degrees.

Beat the eggs until just foamy in a large bowl. Add the sugar, salt, corn syrup, butter, and vanilla. Continue to beat until thoroughly blended. Stir in the peanuts. Pour into the pie shell (see note). Bake until the filling is set, 50 to 55 minutes. Serve warm or cool.

notes from our test kitchen

- Since the peanuts add plenty of salt to this pie, we recommend unsalted butter.
- Use plain salted roasted peanuts here. Not unsalted, and certainly not honey-roasted.
- Just before putting the pie in the oven, lightly drag a fork across the surface to distribute the peanuts evenly.
- Check for doneness by giving the pie a jiggle. The filling should be just set.
- This pie tastes best when it's had a chance to cool. It's even good straight from the fridge. If it is sliced while still warm, the filling will run out.

SOURCE: *Pure Chocolate*
by Fran Bigelow with Helene Siegel

COOK: Fran Bigelow

milk chocolate sorbet

IF YOU'RE THINKING of passing over this recipe because you don't have an ice cream maker or don't feel like hauling it out, stop right here. We discovered quite by accident that this silky-smooth sorbet freezes nicely on its own, no churning required. If you have an electric ice cream maker at the ready, by all means use it. The texture will be even dreamier.

A little bit of dark unsweetened chocolate underscores the creamy, sweet character of the milk chocolate.

makes about 1 quart

- 1/2 cup sugar
- 3 cups water
- 1 pound plus 6 ounces milk chocolate, finely chopped (see tip)
- 2 ounces unsweetened chocolate, finely chopped (see tip)
- 1/2 teaspoon vanilla extract

Combine the sugar and water in a heavy medium saucepan. Bring to a simmer over medium-high heat.

Remove from the heat and add the chocolates. Let stand for 1 minute to melt the chocolates. Stir until completely smooth. Stir in the vanilla.

Set aside to cool further until warm to the touch. Pour into a blender and cover tightly. Blend on high speed until smooth, about 1 minute. Pour into a bowl. Press a piece of plastic wrap against the surface, without any gaps or air pockets, to keep a skin from forming. Set aside to cool for about 30 minutes, or until the mixture is just room temperature (see note). If it sits too long, it will become too thick to churn, so keep a watchful eye.

Freeze in an ice cream maker following the manufacturer's directions.

note from our test kitchen

Unless you have a professional-grade electric ice cream maker (one with a built-in compressor freezer, not one that requires prefreezing a liner), it's best to transfer the cooled mixture to a plastic container and let it freeze on its own without churning. The convenient hand-cranked ice cream freezers that don't require ice work only if the mixture is well chilled. Luckily, the texture of this sorbet doesn't suffer at all from lack of churning.

tip

It should come as no surprise that Fran Bigelow, a world-class chocolatier who runs Fran's Chocolates in Seattle, stresses the importance of buying the very best chocolate when making desserts. Bigelow explains that inferior chocolate will produce inferior results, no matter how good your technique or formula. She encourages us to read labels and purchase only pure chocolate. Sugar, cocoa, butter, vanilla, and lecithin are the only other allowable ingredients. Eschew all chocolates listing vegetable fats as an ingredient. Recommended brands are Callebaut, Valrhona, El Rey, Michel Cluizel, and Scharffen Berger, most of which are available in gourmet stores and over the Internet.

SOURCE: *The Compleat Squash* by Amy Goldman

COOK: Amy Goldman after Daniele Gespert

pumpkin eggnog ice cream

THE COMPLEAT SQUASH is much more than a cookbook. It's a passionate tribute to all manner of Cucurbitaceae (the extended family of squash), with special attention to the history and importance of heirloom varieties. We were a little surprised, then, to find in the dessert section a recipe using plain old canned pumpkin, but when Amy Goldman said it was the best ice cream she's ever had, we knew we had to try it. And we are very glad we did. The ice cream has an outrageously creamy texture, and it's not too sugary, so the natural sweetness of the pumpkin comes through. Consider serving it for Thanksgiving in place of pie.

makes 1 quart

- 2 cups heavy cream
- 2/3 cup milk
- 1/2 cup sugar
- 3 large egg yolks, lightly beaten
- 1 teaspoon pumpkin pie spice
- 1 teaspoon vanilla extract
- 1 1/2 cups canned pumpkin (not pie filling)
- 1 tablespoon dark rum

Combine the cream, milk, and sugar in a medium saucepan and cook over low heat, stirring constantly in a figure-eight to distribute the heat. When the mixture is warm, add about 1 cup of it to the beaten yolks to temper them so they don't curdle; then pour the egg mixture into the pan and continue cooking, stirring constantly, until the mixture coats the back of the spoon, about 10 minutes.

Strain the mixture into a bowl and whisk in the pie spice and vanilla. Cool to room temperature before adding the pumpkin and rum. Refrigerate until chilled. Freeze in an ice cream machine following the manufacturer's directions.

notes from our test kitchen

- One small can of pumpkin will give you $1\frac{1}{2}$ cups.
- Be sure to buy plain pumpkin puree and not pumpkin pie filling. If in doubt, read the ingredients label.
- Because there are only 3 egg yolks in this recipe (some ice cream recipes call for as many as 8), it won't thicken as much as some. Don't worry, it will still freeze to the right consistency.

SOURCE: *The Gourmet Cookbook* edited by Ruth Reichl

COOK: Michel Richard

cheesecake ice cream

LEAVE IT TO A EUROPEAN CHEF to think creatively about that quintessential American supermarket food product, cream cheese. While most people's minds run to cheesecake, bagels, and spreads, the French expat chef Michel Richard came up with this indecently good ice cream. It has a remarkably luxurious texture as well as a rich, slightly tart taste, like a faintly lemony cheesecake.

There's no custard to fuss with, so the ice cream goes together in less than 5 minutes. It's so unusual that it's hard to imagine it could be such child's play to make.

In early summer, when local strawberries are at their prime, think of strawberry cheesecake ice cream (see note), which might cost you all of another 5 minutes' prep time.

makes about 1 quart

- 8 ounces cream cheese, at room temperature
- 3/4 cup sugar
- 1/8 teaspoon salt
- 1 cup milk
- 1 tablespoon fresh lemon juice
- 1/2 cup heavy cream
- 1/2 teaspoon vanilla extract

Combine everything but the cream and vanilla in a blender and blend until smooth. Transfer to a bowl and stir in the cream and vanilla. Cover the bowl with plastic wrap and refrigerate for at least several hours for the flavors to develop.

Freeze the mixture in an ice cream maker following the manufacturer's directions. Transfer to an airtight container and freeze until ready to serve (it will keep for 1 week). Let the ice cream soften for 5 minutes before serving.

notes from our test kitchen

- Don't use whipped cream cheese or low-fat cream cheese—you want the real thing here.
- To keep the ice cream fresh, put a layer of plastic wrap directly over the surface before freezing or refreezing.
- To make strawberry cheesecake ice cream, add a pint (12 ounces) of ripe strawberries, hulled and coarsely chopped, to the ingredients in the blender.

drinks

SOURCE: *Washington Post*
STORY BY Walter Nicholls
COOK: Aulie Bunyarataphan

ginger lemon iced tea

WE'VE HAD GINGER LEMONADE and lemonade–iced tea drinks, but none as winning as this very gingery, lemony concoction. The black tea brings the flavors into focus and makes the drink especially refreshing. It's a good foil for spicy food.

At Bangkok Joe's, Aulie Bunyarataphan's restaurant in the Georgetown section of Washington, D.C., she serves an alcoholic version known as a Bangkok swing: just add 2 ounces of Absolut Citron and 2 ounces of Southern Comfort to each tall glass.

serves 8

- 8 cups water
- 1 medium (about 4 ounces) gingerroot, smashed and cut into chunks (about 3/4 cup chunks)
- 3 black or Lipton tea bags
- 1 cup sugar
- 1/2 cup fresh lemon juice
- Ice
- Lemon wedges and/or slices of fresh ginger for garnish

Bring the water, ginger, and tea bags to a gentle boil in a medium saucepan over medium heat. Simmer for 15 minutes. Add the sugar and lemon juice and stir until the sugar is dissolved. Remove from the heat and strain the tea into a bowl or pitcher, discarding the solids.

Set aside to cool slightly. Cover and refrigerate until completely chilled, at least 2 to 3 hours. Serve over ice with the lemon wedges and slices of ginger.

note from our test kitchen

This recipe makes a weak tea. That's desirable if you're going to add alcohol, which can turn strong tea bitter. If you'd like it stronger, just add another bag or two.

SOURCE: *Star Palate*
edited by Tami Agassi and Kathy Casey
COOK: Liz Smith

watermelon twist

WE'LL HAVE WHAT LIZ SMITH IS HAVING . . . That would be this giddy, essence-of-summer cocktail that's somewhere between a margarita, a vodka tonic, and one of those great Mexican fruit juice drinks. We were particularly enthralled with the salt-and-pepper rim on the glasses.

The only problem with this drink, which is easy to make, is that it also goes down very easily, especially on a hot day. It's definitely not a cooler, so you might want to warn your thirsty guests.

serves 4

3 cups seeded and cubed watermelon
Sea salt
Freshly ground black pepper
4 shots of vodka or gin
2 limes, halved

Liquify the watermelon in a blender; if it seems too pulpy, you may need to strain it.

Mix the salt and pepper in a saucer. Moisten the rims of chilled martini glasses or other stemmed glasses, then dip in the salt and pepper to frost the rims.

For each drink, fill a cocktail shaker with ice, then mix 3 ounces (6 tablespoons) of the watermelon juice with 1 shot vodka or gin and the juice of half a lime. Shake vigorously, then strain into the chilled glass and serve.

SOURCE: *The Encyclopedia of Cajun & Creole Cuisine* by John Folse

COOK: John Folse

good morning mimosa

IS IT ANY SURPRISE that New Orleans would be the source for a less innocent version of the classic brunch drink the mimosa? John Folse, an authority on all things Cajun and Creole, spikes the standard combination of orange juice and champagne with a bit of orange liqueur, giving the drink a deeper flavor and a little more punch. They don't call that town the Big Easy for no reason!

makes 2 drinks

- 4 ounces orange juice
- 2 tablespoons orange liqueur (see note)
- 12 ounces champagne

Chill two champagne glasses. Combine 2 ounces orange juice and 1 tablespoon liqueur in each glass. Fill with champagne and serve.

note from our test kitchen

Use Grand Marnier or Triple Sec for the orange liqueur.

SOURCE: *Santé*
COOK: **Robert Larcom**

margaria

WE WERE THRILLED to find this refreshing drink that uses two of our favorite ingredients, pomegranate juice and tequila. The colorful cocktail is the signature drink of 15 Ria, a restaurant located in the Washington Terrace Hotel in D.C. Get it: marga-*ria*?

serves 1

Ice
3 ounces tequila, preferably Jose Cuervo
1 ounce Triple Sec
2 splashes pomegranate juice (see note)
1 splash fresh lime juice
Lime wedge for garnish

Fill a cocktail shaker halfway with ice. Add the tequila, Triple Sec, and pomegranate and lime juices, and shake. Strain into a chilled 8-ounce glass. Garnish with a lime wedge.

notes from our test kitchen

- Pomegranate juice is available in many supermarkets in the bottled juice section or with the produce. Pom is the most popular brand.
- We prefer silver tequila in a margarita—or margaria, as the case may be—because its lighter character blends best with the fruit juices. You should use what you like.

SOURCE: *Party Drinks!* by A. J. Rathbun

COOK: A. J. Rathbun after Mrs. Robert S. Allison

sparkling apple cocktail

FORGET TRENDY GREEN APPLE MARTINIS served in swanky martini bars by ultrahip mixologists. This apple cocktail comes from a much more innocent time, and it slides down pretty darn innocently too. Cocktail authority and poet A. J. Rathbun found the formula in a 1940s book entitled *Cocktail Guide and Ladies' Companion,* where it's touted as the secret behind lively quilting parties. We may not host our own quilting parties, but we do appreciate the way a good cocktail can add sparkle to any gathering.

We'd be remiss not to warn you that these drinks pack a wallop. If you're looking for something a little less potent, cut back on the amount of applejack and add more of the harmless sparkling cider.

serves 10

- Ice
- 1 750-milliliter bottle nonalcoholic sparkling cider
- 1 750-milliliter bottle applejack
- Apple slices for garnish (optional)

Fill a large pitcher with ice cubes.

Add the cider to the pitcher until it reaches the halfway mark. Add the applejack until the pitcher is full. Stir with a large spoon. Pour into highball glasses and serve. If you're feeling adventurous, garnish each glass with an apple slice.

notes from our test kitchen

- Look for sparkling apple cider with the juices and mixers.
- Applejack is apple brandy.

SOURCE: *The Pat Conroy Cookbook*
by Pat Conroy with Suzanne Williamson Pollak

COOK: Pat Conroy after Reverend William Ralston

mount vernon christmas punch

CERTAIN OCCASIONS DEMAND a big bowl of boldly spiked punch, but we don't see many good recipes. The best formulas seem to be passed down from at least a few generations back, and that's exactly where this powerful concoction comes from. Apparently it was served at Mount Vernon at Christmastime, when the George Washington family must have had hordes of visitors—or very strong constitutions. A single batch makes nearly 4 gallons, and it's pretty much straight booze, with the exception of a bit of sweet tea and the juice from the jar of maraschino cherries. The miraculous thing, however, is the way all the alcohols blend into something dangerously smooth. We recommend finding some of those small punch cups to serve it in, and you'll want to use a real punch bowl. Pat Conroy suggests decorating the bowl with an ice ring. It helps keep the punch cold, and it's very pretty floating around. Make one by filling a bundt pan halfway with water and the cherries (pour the cherry juice into the punch) and freezing.

The punch is best when made a week ahead. As the alcohols meld, their flavors mellow.

serves a crowd

- 1 quart strong brewed English Breakfast tea, sweetened
- 1 gallon good bourbon
- 1 gallon sherry (see note)
- 1 quart sweet vermouth
- 1 pint best-quality Jamaican rum
- 1 pint yellow or green Chartreuse (see note)
- 4 bottles champagne, or more to taste
- 12 lemons, each cut into 4 wedges
- 1 quart maraschino cherries, without stems but with their juice (see note)

Combine the tea, bourbon, sherry, vermouth, rum, and Chartreuse in a large bowl. The punch can be made ahead up to this point.

When it's time to serve the punch, add the champagne—as much as you wish. Add the lemon wedges and cherries and juice, and serve.

notes from our test kitchen

- If 4 gallons seems like too much, the recipe is easily scaled back.
- We use a medium-dry sherry, but cream sherry would work as well.
- Pat Conroy prefers green Chartreuse, but you can use either.
- Don't forget to pour in the maraschino cherry juice; it helps sweeten the punch.
- If you're timid about this punch, try adding ginger ale to soften it. You can also substitute ginger ale for the champagne if you like.
- Conroy offers a great idea for leftover punch: add a little soda water and an orange slice for a terrific old-fashioned.

SOURCE: *Sweet Serendipity*
by Stephen Bruce with Brett Bara

COOK: Stephen Bruce

serendipity's fr-r-rozen hot chocolate

NEW YORK CITY'S LEGENDARY SERENDIPITY almost defies description: part restaurant, part boutique, all wrapped in a glam fantasy atmosphere. A visit to Serendipity makes adults feel like kids and makes kids feel all grown up.

The most notorious item is this slushy, creamy, chocolatey goodness. Jackie O used to share one of these frosty treats with John-John and Caroline. As first lady, she once requested the recipe so it could be served at a White House gala, but the formula was such a highly guarded secret that the request was denied.

Now Serendipity's owners have published a cookbook to celebrate the restaurant's fiftieth anniversary. We were shocked to learn that the frozen hot chocolate is nothing more than a blend of melted chocolate, store-bought hot cocoa mix, milk, and ice. We suspect that much of its magic comes from the way it is served at the restaurant—in an enormous goblet, loaded with whipped cream and chocolate shavings and festooned with colored straws for sharing. Because it's made with milk and not ice cream, this is actually much lighter than a classic chocolate milkshake.

makes enough for 1 giant goblet (about 1 quart)

- 6 1/2-ounce pieces of a variety of your favorite chocolate (see note)
- 1 1/2 tablespoons sugar
- 2 teaspoons store-bought hot chocolate mix
- 1 1/2 cups milk (see note)
- 3 cups ice
- Whipped cream for serving
- Chocolate shavings for serving

Chop the chocolate into small pieces and melt it in the top of a double boiler over barely simmering water (or in a heatproof bowl set over a pot of barely simmering water), stirring occasionally. Add the sugar and hot chocolate mix, stirring constantly until thoroughly blended. Remove from the heat, slowly add 1/2 cup of the milk, and whisk until smooth (see notes). Cool to room temperature.

Combine the remaining 1 cup milk, the chocolate mixture, and the ice in a blender. Blend on high speed until the mixture is smooth and has the consistency of a frozen daiquiri. Pour into a giant goblet and top with the whipped cream and chocolate shavings. Serve with spoons or straws—or both!

notes from our test kitchen

- You really can use any kind of chocolate bar to make this: semisweet, milk, Hershey's, or the fanciest European bars. Avoid anything with fillings or nuts. We like bittersweet.
- We wouldn't dream of using anything but whole milk for this.
- Warming the 1/2 cup of milk in the microwave makes it blend more easily into the chocolate.
- Use a sturdy wire whisk to mix the melted chocolate, hot chocolate, and sugar. It's the best way to get it smooth.

credits

Phyllo Cheese Straws. From *Patrick O'Connell's Refined American Cuisine* by Patrick O'Connell. Copyright © 2004 by Patrick O'Connell. Reprinted by permission of Little, Brown and Co., Inc.

Rosemary Walnuts. From *The Gourmet Cookbook* edited by Ruth Reichl. Copyright © 2004 by Condé Nast Publications. Reprinted by permission of Houghton Mifflin Company.

Hickory House Stuffed Pickles. From *Rick & Lanie's Excellent Kitchen Adventures* by Rick and Lanie Bayless with Deann Groen Bayless. Copyright © 2004 by Rick Bayless. Reprinted by permission of Stewart, Tabori, & Chang.

Manchurian Dip. From *Wife of the Chef* by Courtney Febbroiello. Copyright © 2003 by Courtney Febbroiello. Used by permission of Clarkson Potter/ Publishers, a division of Random House, Inc.

Roasted Red Pepper Dip with Pomegranate Molasses. From *Party Dips!* by Sally Sampson. Copyright © 2004 by Chris Schlesinger. Reprinted by permission of Harvard Common Press.

Pomegranate Molasses. Reprinted with permission from *Pomegranates* by Ann Kleinberg. Copyright © 2004 by Penn Publishing, Inc., in association with Ten Speed Press, Berkeley, CA, www.tenspeed.com.

Homemade Ricotta. Originally published on www.tastycentral.com. Copyright © 2004 by Roy Finamore. Reprinted by permission of Roy Finamore.

Marinated Yogurt Cheese Balls. Originally published as Yogurt Balls Marinated in Garlic Dill Oil with Aleppo Pepper, in *The Armenian Table: More than 165 Treasured Recipes That Bring Together Ancient Flavors and 21st-Century Style* by Victoria Jenanyan Wise. Copyright © 2004 by Victoria Jenanyan Wise. Reprinted by permission of St. Martin's Press, LLC.

Cream Cheese–Stuffed Piquillo Peppers. Originally published as Baked Stuffed Piquillo Peppers, in *Zingerman's Guide to Good Eating* by Ari Weinzweig. Copyright © 2003 by Ari Weinzweig. Reprinted by permission of Houghton Mifflin Company.

Pancetta Crisps with Goat Cheese and Pear by Sarah Tenaglia. Originally published in *Bon Appétit*. Copyright © 2004 by Condé Nast Publications. All rights reserved. Reprinted with permission.

La Brea Tar Pit Chicken Wings. From *The Gourmet Cookbook* edited by Ruth Reichl. Copyright © 2004 by Condé Nast Publications. Reprinted by permission of Houghton Mifflin Company.

Olive Oil–Poached Shrimp with Lemon Anchovy Mayonnaise by Amanda Hesser. Originally published as Shrimp with Anchovy Mayonnaise, in the *New York Times*. Copyright © 2004 by the New York Times Co. Reprinted with permission.

Pancetta and Fennel Tart. From *The Good Cook* by Anne Willan. Copyright © 2004 by Anne Willan. Reprinted by permission of Stewart, Tabori, & Chang.

Tigelle. From *Bruce Aidells's Complete Book of Pork* by Bruce Aidells with Lisa Weiss. Copyright © 2004 by Bruce Aidells. Reprinted by permission of HarperCollins Publishers.

Eggs with Foie Gras and Cream. Originally published in *Bon Appétit*. Copyright © 2004 by Dorie Greenspan. Reprinted by permission of Dorie Greenspan.

Asparagus Soup with Blue Cheese Crumbles by the Giacomini Family. From *The Blue Course* by the Point Reyes Farmstead Cheese Company. Copyright © 2004 by the Giacomini Family. Reprinted by permission of Point Reyes Farmstead Cheese Company.

Calhoun School Cream of Cauliflower Soup by Robert Surles. Copyright © 2004 by Robert Surles. Reprinted with permission.

Carrot Ginger Soup with Lime Crème Fraîche. From *Simply Elegant Soup* by George Morrone with John Harrisson. Copyright © 2004 by George Morrone and John Harrisson. Reprinted by permission of Ten Speed Press, Berkeley, CA, www.tenspeed.com.

Tuscan Bean and Mushroom Soup. From *1,000 Italian Recipes* by Michele Scicolone. Copyright © 2004 by Michele Scicolone. Reprinted by permission of Wiley Publishing, Inc., a subsidiary of John Wiley & Sons, Inc.

Roasted Mushroom-Leek Soup with Crispy Pancetta. From *Stonewall Kitchen Harvest* by Jim Stott, Jonathan King, and Kathy Gunst. Text copyright © 2004 by Jim Stott, Jonathan King, and Kathy Gunst. Used by permission of Clarkson Potter/Publishers, a division of Random House, Inc.

Cape Cod Portuguese Kale Soup. From *Coastal Cooking with John Shields* by John Shields. Copyright © 2004 by John Shields. Used by permission of Random House, Inc.

Bride's Soup from Turkey. Originally published as Bride Soup, in *An Exaltation of Soups* by Patricia Solley. Copyright © 2004 by Patricia Solley. Used by permission of Three Rivers Press, a division of Random House, Inc.

Lentil Soup with Sausage. From *Roma* by Julia della Croce. Copyright © 2004 by Julia della Croce. Used by permission of Chronicle Books LLC, San Francisco. Visit www.chroniclebooks.com.

Chickpea Soup with Chorizo and Smoked Paprika by Maggie Pond. Originally published as Garbanzo Soup with Chorizo and Smoked Paprika, in *Food & Wine*. Copyright © 2004 by Maggie Pond. Reprinted by permission of Maggie Pond.

Portuguese Tomato Soup. Originally published as Portuguese Tomato and Sausage Soup, in *Emeril's Potluck* by Emeril Lagasse. Copyright © 2004 by Emeril's Love of Food Productions, LLC. Reprinted by permission of William Morrow, a division of HarperCollins Publishers.

Cold Buttermilk Soup. From *The Art of Eating, 50th Anniversary Edition* by M.F.K. Fisher. Copyright © 2004 by M.F.K. Fisher. Reprinted with permission of Wiley Publishing Inc., a subsidiary of John Wiley & Sons, Inc.

Alice Waters's Coleslaw. Copyright © 2004 by Alice Waters. First published in the *New York Times Magazine*. Reprinted by permission of the New York Times Agency.

Boston Lettuce Salad with Toasted Almonds and Ginger Croutons by Philip Bardin. From *Cooking in the Lowcountry from the Old Post Office Restaurant* by Jane and Michael Stern with recipes by Philip Bardin. Copyright © 2004 by Jane and Michael Stern and Philip Bardin. Reprinted by permission of Rutledge Hill Press.

Crisp Vegetable Salad with Ginger Vinaigrette. Excerpted from *Aroma* by Mandy Aftel and Daniel Patterson. Copyright © 2004 by Mandy Aftel and Daniel Patterson. Used by permission of Artisan, a division of Workman Publishing Co., Inc., New York. All rights reserved.

Grilled Caesar Salad by Vicki and Steve Caparulo. From *The Big Book of Backyard Cooking* by Betty Rosbottom. Copyright © 2004 by Vicki and Steve Caparulo. Used by permission of Chronicle Books LLC, San Francisco. Visit www.chroniclebooks.com.

Cucumber and Feta Salad with Dill and Mint. From *From Tapas to Meze* by Joanne Weir. Copyright © 2004 by Joanne Weir. Reprinted by permission of Ten Speed Press, Berkeley, CA, www.tenspeed.com.

Green Bean Salad with Cream. From *Guy Savoy: Simple French Recipes* by Guy Savoy. Copyright © 2004 by Guy Savoy. Reprinted by permission of Stewart, Tabori, & Chang.

Fresh Green Peas and Sugar Snaps in Sesame Dressing by Anna Pump. Originally published in *Bon Appétit*. Copyright © 2004 by Anna Pump. Reprinted by permission of Anna Pump.

Greek Radish Salad. First published as Radish Salad with Pickled Onions and Feta Cheese, in *The Olive and the Caper* by Susanna Hoffman. Copyright © 2004 by Susanna Hoffman. Used by permission of Workman Publishing Co., Inc., New York. All rights reserved.

Beet Salad with Horseradish and Fried Capers by Amanda Hesser. First published in the *New York Times Magazine*. Copyright © 2004 by the New York Times Co. Reprinted with permission.

Soppressata and Roma Bean Salad with Pecorino. Originally published in *Good Housekeeping*. Copyright © 2004 by *Good Housekeeping*. Reprinted by permission of *Good Housekeeping*.

Fig and Peanut Salad with Arugula and Mint. Excerpted from *Frank Stitt's Southern Table* by Frank Stitt. Copyright © 2004 by Frank Stitt. Used by permission of Artisan, a division of Workman Publishing Co., Inc., New York. All rights reserved.

Watermelon, Arugula, and Toasted Almond Salad by Michel Nischan. Originally published in *O, the Oprah Magazine*. Copyright © 2004 by Michel Nischan. Reprinted by permission of Michel Nischan.

Pink Grapefruit Salad with Toasted Coconut and Fresh Mint. From *Quick and Easy Thai* by Nancie McDermott. Copyright © 2004 by Nancie McDermott. Used by permission of Chronicle Books LLC, San Francisco. Visit www.chroniclebooks.com.

Tomato Couscous Salad. From *The Tomato Festival Cookbook* by Lawrence Davis-Hollander. Copyright © 2004 by Lawrence Davis-Hollander. Reprinted by permission of Storey Publishing LLC.

Wild Rice and Chickpea Salad by Paula Disbrowe. From *The Pastry Queen* by Rebecca Rather and Alison Oresman. Copyright © 2004 by Rebecca Rather. Reprinted by permission of Ten Speed Press, Berkeley, CA, www.tenspeed.com.

Greek Potato Salad with Olives and Feta Cheese. From *Stalking the Green Fairy* by James Villas. Copyright © 2004 by James Villas. Reprinted by permission of Wiley Publishing Inc., a subsidiary of John Wiley and Sons, Inc.

Pontormo's Salad by Cesare Casella. Originally published in the *New York Times*. Copyright © 2004 by Cesare Casella. Reprinted by permission of Cesare Casella.

Spiaggia Salad Dressing by Tony Mantuano. From *The Spiaggia Cookbook* by Tony Mantuano and Cathy Mantuano. Copyright © 2004 by Tony and Cathy Mantuano. Used by permission of Chronicle Books LLC, San Francisco. Visit www.chroniclebooks.com.

Migas Especiales con Hongos by Cynthia and Libby Perez. From *The Tex-Mex Cookbook* by Robb Walsh. Copyright © 2004 by Robb Walsh. Used by permission of Broadway Books, a division of Random House, Inc.

Eggs in Purgatory by Rocco DiSpirito. From *Rocco's Italian American* by Rocco DiSpirito. Copyright © 2004 by Spirit Media, LLC. Reprinted by permission of Hyperion. Available wherever books are sold.

Swedish Pancakes by Mark Bittman. Originally published in the *New York Times*. Copyright © 2004 by the New York Times Co. Reprinted with permission.

Buttermilk Pancakes with Caramelized Bananas by Bill Rohling. First published in *Bon Appétit.* Copyright © 2004 by Bill Rohling. Reprinted by permission of Bill Rohling.

Bob's Dutch Baby by Bob Hoogstoel. From *Rick & Lanie's Excellent Kitchen Adventures* by Rick Bayless and Lanie Bayless with Deann Groen Bayless. Copyright © 2004 by Rick Bayless, Lanie Bayless, and Deann Groen Bayless. Reprinted by permission of Stewart, Tabori, & Chang.

English Muffin Strata with Tomato, Sausage, and Fontina by Maureen Callahan. Copyright © 2004 by *Health.* Reprinted by permission of *Health.* For subscriptions please call 1-800-274-2522.

New England Spider Cake by Jonathan Reynolds. First published in the *New York Times.* Copyright © 2004 by the New York Times Co. Reprinted with permission.

Raspberry Almond Coffeecake. From *The Berry Bible* by Janie Hibler. Copyright © 2004 by Janie Hibler. Used by permission of William Morrow, a division of HarperCollins Publishers.

Rosemary and Mustard Breakfast Sausages by Kristine Kidd. First published in *Bon Appétit.* Copyright © 2004 by Condé Nast Publications. All rights reserved. Reprinted by permission.

Sizzled Haloumi Sandwiches with Lime on a Summer-Day Salad. From *Grilled Cheese* by Marlena Spieler. Copyright © 2004 by Marlena Spieler. Used by permission of Chronicle Books LLC, San Francisco. Visit www.chroniclebooks.com.

Spaghetti with Slow-Roasted Cherry Tomatoes, Basil, and Parmesan Cheese by Jody Adams. From *The Tomato Festival Cookbook* by Lawrence Davis-Hollander. Copyright © 2004 by Lawrence Davis-Hollander. Reprinted by permission of Storey Publishing.

Tagliatelle with Crème Fraîche and Arugula. From *Italian Easy* by Rose Gray and Ruth Rogers. Copyright © 2004 by Rose Gray and Ruth Rogers. Used by permission of Clarkson Potter/Publishers, a division of Random House, Inc.

Fusilli with Feta and Lemon Caper Pesto by Daphne Zepos. Originally published in *Cooking New American* by the editors of *Fine Cooking.* Copyright © 2004 by Daphne Zepos. Reprinted by permission of Daphne Zepos.

Double Spinach Fettuccine with Butter and Parmesan. From *Four Seasons Pasta* by Janet Fletcher. Copyright © 2004 by Janet Fletcher. Used by permission of Chronicle Books LLC, San Francisco. Visit www.chroniclebooks.com.

Rigatoni alla Toto. From *Rome, at Home* by Suzanne Dunaway. Copyright © 2004 by Suzanne Dunaway. Used by permission of Broadway Books, a division of Random House, Inc.

Overnight Macaroni and Cheese. Originally published as Macaroni and Cheese in *Simple French Recipes for the Home Cook* by Guy Savoy. Copyright © 2004 by Guy Savoy. Reprinted by permission of Stewart, Tabori, & Chang.

Neapolitan Spaghetti Pie by Eleanora Russo Scarpetta. From *Eleanora's Kitchen* by Eleanora Russo Scarpetta with Sarah Belk King. Copyright © 2004 by Eleanora Russo Scarpetta. Reprinted by permission of Broadway Books, a division of Random House, Inc.

Musa's Eggplant and Lentil Stew by Paula Wolfert. Originally published in *Food & Wine.* Copyright © 2004 by Paula Wolfert. Reprinted by permission of Paula Wolfert.

Pastuccia. From *Italian Slow and Savory* by Joyce Goldstein. Copyright © 2004 by Joyce Goldstein. Used by permission of Chronicle Books LLC, San Francisco. Visit www.chroniclebooks.com.

Foil-Baked Cod with Ginger, Orange, and Cumin. From *Go Fish* by Laurent Tourondel and Andrew Friedman. Copyright © 2004 by Laurent Tourondel and Andrew Friedman. Reprinted by permission of Wiley Publishing, Inc., a subsidiary of John Wiley & Sons, Inc.

Broiled Salmon with Tomato Salsa. First published as Gratinated Salmon with Vegetable Salsa, in *Take 6 Ingredients* by Conrad Gallagher. Copyright © 2004 by Conrad Gallagher. Reprinted by permission of Kyle Books.

Scandinavian Salmon Stew with Mushrooms and Dill. From *Kinkead's Cookbook* by Bob Kinkead. Copyright © 2004 by Bob Kinkead. Reprinted by permission of Ten Speed Press, Berkeley, CA, www.tenspeed.com.

Hoosier Chicken with Potato Chip Crust by Daniel Orr. Originally published in *Food & Wine*. Copyright © 2004 by Daniel Orr. Reprinted by permission of Daniel Orr.

Crispy Chicken Breasts Stuffed with Spinach and Goat Cheese by Jennifer Martinkus and Derrin Davis. Originally published as Crispy Stuffed Chicken Breasts with Spinach and Goat Cheese, in *Fine Cooking*. Copyright © 2004 by Jennifer Martinkus and Derrin Davis. Reprinted by permission of Jennifer Martinkus.

Lemon Chicken with Croutons. From *Barefoot in Paris* by Ina Garten. Copyright © 2004 by Ina Garten. Reprinted by permission of Clarkson Potter/Publishers, a division of Random House, Inc.

Grilled Mojito Chicken by Cheryl and Bill Jamison. Originally published as Mojito Marinated Chicken Breasts, in *Bon Appétit*. Copyright © 2004 by Cheryl and Bill Jamison. Reprinted by permission of Cheryl and Bill Jamison.

Turkey Carnitas on Mesclun Greens with Tangerine Vinaigrette by Dean Thomas. Originally appeared in an Eat Turkey advertisement and on www.eatturkey.com. Copyright © 2004 by Dean Thomas. Reprinted by permission of the National Turkey Federation.

Barbecued Tri-Tip with Caramelized Red Onions by Jamie Purviance. Originally published in *Bon Appétit*. Copyright © 2004 by Jamie Purviance. Reprinted by permission of Jamie Purviance.

Salt and Pepper Burgers. From *The Simpler the Better* by Leslie Revsin. Copyright © 2004 by Leslie Revsin. Reprinted by permission of Wiley Publishing, Inc., a subsidiary of John Wiley & Sons, Inc.

Spicy Beef Meatballs with Red Bell Peppers. From *Marcella Says...* by Marcella Hazan with Victor Hazan. Copyright © 2004 by Marcella Polini Hazan and Victor Hazan. Reprinted by permission of HarperCollins Publishers.

Greek Meatballs with Walnuts, Almonds, and Prunes by Aglaia Kremezi. First published as Baked Meatballs from Syros with Walnuts, Almonds, and Prunes, in *Food Arts*. Copyright © 2004 by Aglaia Kremezi. Reprinted by permission of M. Shanken Communications, Inc.

Tamale Pie. From *The Cast Iron Skillet* by Sharon Kramis and Julie Kramis Hearne. Copyright © 2004 by Sharon Kramis and Julie Kramis Hearne. Reprinted by permission of Sasquatch Books.

Spiced Skirt Steak by Sally Schneider. First published in and excerpted from *A New Way to Cook* by Sally Schneider. Copyright © 2004 by Sally Schneider. Used by permission of Artisan, a division of Workman Publishing Co., Inc., New York. All rights reserved.

Brisket à la Carbonnade. From *The Gourmet Cookbook* edited by Ruth Reichl. Copyright © 2004 by Condé Nast Publications. Reprinted by permission of Houghton Mifflin Company.

Zinfandel Pot Roast with Glazed Carrots and Fresh Sage. From *All About Braising: The Art of Uncomplicated Cooking* by Molly Stevens. Copyright © 2004 by Molly Stevens. Used by permission of W. W. Norton & Company, Inc.

Herb- and Pistachio-Stuffed Veal Pot Roast. From *John Ash Cooking One on One* by John

Ash with Amy Mintzer. Copyright © 2004 by John Ash. Used by permission of Clarkson Potter/Publishers, a division of Random House, Inc.

Garlic-Studded Pork Tenderloin with Mojo. From *Everything Tastes Better with Garlic* by Sara Perry. Copyright © 2004 by Sara Perry. Used by permission of Chronicle Books LLC, San Francisco. Visit www.chroniclebooks.com.

Spanish Pork Loin Sandwiches with Alioli and Arugula by Olivier Said, Maggie Pond, and James Mellgren. Originally published as Pork Loin Bocadilla in *César: Recipes from a Tapas Bar* by Olivier Said and James Mellgren with Maggie Pond. Copyright © 2003 by Olivier Said and James Mellgren. Reprinted by permission of Ten Speed Press, Berkeley, CA, www.tenspeed.com.

Oven-Roasted Ribs with Coffee Molasses Marinade. From *Bruce Aidells's Complete Book of Pork* by Bruce Aidells. Copyright © 2004 by Bruce Aidells. Used with permission of HarperCollins Publishers.

Green Chili with Pork and Poblanos by Francine Maroukian. Originally published as Chili Verde in *Esquire*. Copyright © 2004 by Francine Maroukian. Reprinted with permission of Francine Maroukian.

Dulce de Leche–Glazed Ham by Grace Parisi. Originally published in *Food & Wine*. Copyright © 2004 by *Food & Wine*. Reprinted with permission.

Lamb Braised in Milk with Garlic and Fennel by Mario Batali. First published in *Food & Wine*. Copyright © 2004 by Mario Batali. Reprinted with permission of Mario Batali.

Tandoori Lamb Chops by Suvir Saran. Originally published as Gael's Tandoori Lamb Chops in *Indian Home Cooking* by Suvir Saran and Stephanie Lyness. Copyright © 2004 by Suvir Saran and Stephanie Lyness. Used by permission of Clarkson Potter/Publishers, a division of Random House, Inc.

Stir-Fried Garlic Lettuce by Grace Young. From *The Breath of a Wok* by Grace Young and Alan Richardson. Recipes copyright © 2004 by Grace Young. Reprinted by permission of Simon & Schuster Adult Publishing Group.

Bok Choy with Shiitakes by Charles Phan. Originally published in the *New York Times*. Copyright © 2004 by Charles Phan. Reprinted by permission of Charles Phan.

Roasted Broccoli Florets with Gremolata by Diane Rossen Worthington. First published in *Bon Appétit*. Copyright © 2004 by Diane Rossen Worthington. Reprinted by permission of Diane Rossen Worthington.

Artichokes with Pecorino, Black Pepper, and Olive Oil. From *The Big Book of Backyard Cooking* by Betty Rosbottom. Copyright © 2004 by Betty Rosbottom. Used by permission of Chronicle Books LLC, San Francisco. Visit www.chroniclebooks.com.

Roasted Carrots, Pearl Onions, and Wild Mushrooms with Tarragon by Govind Armstrong. First published in *O, the Oprah Magazine*. Copyright © 2004 by Govind Armstrong. Reprinted by permission of Govind Armstrong.

Braised Green Beans with Tomato and Fennel by Ed Bruske. First published in the *Washington Post*. Copyright © 2004 by Ed Bruske. Reprinted by permission of Ed Bruske.

Mushy Zucchini. From *The Whole Beast* by Fergus Henderson. Copyright © 2004 by Fergus Henderson. Reprinted by permission of HarperCollins Publishers.

Roasted Brussels Sprouts with Walnuts and Pecorino by Andrew Feinberg. Originally published in *New York*. Copyright © 2004 by Andrew Feinberg. Reprinted by permission of Andrew Feinberg.

Spaghetti Squash Roasted with Sage and Bacon. Originally published as Spaghetti Squash Roasted with Sage, in *Daniel's Dish* by Daniel Boulud. Copyright © 2004 by Daniel Boulud. Reprinted by permission of Filipacchi Publishing.

Tomatoes Stuffed with Bacon and Corn Bread

by Marvin Woods. From *Home Plate Cooking* by Marvin Woods and Virginia Willis. Copyright © 2004 by TRENI. Reprinted by permission of Turner South. A Time Warner Company. All rights reserved.

Buttermilk Corn Bread by the staff at *Gourmet.* From *The Gourmet Cookbook* edited by Ruth Reichl. Copyright © 2004 by Condé Nast Publications. Reprinted by permission of Houghton Mifflin Company.

Spinach and Roasted Red Pepper Gratin by Zov Karamardian. Originally published in *Bon Appétit.* Copyright © 2004 by Zov Karamardian. Reprinted by permission of Zov Karamardian.

Butternut Squash and Pecan Gratin with Goat Cheese. From *Gratins: Savory and Sweet Recipes from Oven to Table* by Tina Salter and Catherine Jacobes. Copyright © 2004 by Tina Salter and Catherine Jacobes. Reprinted by permission of Ten Speed Press, Berkeley, CA, www.tenspeed.com.

Pommes Fondantes by Jacques Pépin. Originally published in *Fine Cooking.* Copyright © 2004 by Jacques Pépin. Reprinted by permission of Jacques Pépin.

Drunken Pinto Beans with Charred Onions and Chiles. From *A Year in a Vegetarian Kitchen* by Jack Bishop. Copyright © 2004 by Jack Bishop. Reprinted by permission of Houghton Mifflin Company.

Grits Soufflé. Originally published as Gritty Soufflé, in *I'm Just Here for More Food* by Alton Brown. Copyright © 2004 by Alton Brown. Reprinted by permission of Stewart, Tabori, & Chang.

Whole Wheat Couscous with Cumin by Rozanne Gold. From *Low Carb 1-2-3* by Rozanne Gold with Helen Kimmel, M.S., R.D. Copyright © 2004 by Rozanne Gold. Reprinted by permission of Rodale Press, Inc.

Sage Applesauce by Brian Murphy. Copyright © 2004 by Goodness Gardens. Reprinted with permission.

Spiced Cranberry Sauce by Jennifer Armentrout. First published in a *Fine Cooking*/Sur la Table handout. Copyright © 2004 by Jennifer Armentrout. Reprinted by permission of Taunton Press.

Avocado and Hominy Relish by the staff at Wegmans Food Market. Originally published as Avocado and Pozole Relish, on www.wegmans.com. Copyright © 2004 by the staff at Wegmans Food Market. Reprinted by permission of Wegmans Food Market.

Grandma Hitchcock's Creamy Mustard Sauce for Ham. Originally published in *The Rosengarten Report.* Copyright © 2004 by David Rosengarten. Reprinted by permission of David Rosengarten.

Better Biscuits by Lisa Yockelson. Originally published as Buttermilk Biscuits, in the *Washington Post.* Copyright © 2004 by Lisa Yockelson. Reprinted by permission of the Choate Agency, LLC.

Savory Chipotle Chile Muffins. From *Nightly Specials* by Michael Lomonaco and Andrew Friedman. Copyright © 2004 by Michael Lomonaco and Andrew Friedman. Recipes copyright © 2004 by Michael Lomonaco. Reprinted by permission of William Morrow, a division of HarperCollins Publishers.

Bacon and Cheddar Scones by Rebecca Rather. Originally published as Apple Smoked Bacon and Cheddar Scones in *The Pastry Queen* by Rebecca Rather and Alison Oresman. Copyright © 2004 by Rebecca Rather. Reprinted by permission of Ten Speed Press, Berkeley, CA, www.tenspeed.com.

Onion–Poppy Seed Rolls. From *Joan Nathan's Jewish Holiday Cookbook* by Joan Nathan. Copyright © 2004 by Joan Nathan. Used by permission of Shocken Books, a division of Random House, Inc.

Bolos do Caco by Maite Marijon. First published in *Saveur.* Copyright © 2004 by *Saveur.* Reprinted with permission.

Egyptian Cheese Rolls. First published as Rarif al Rarif, in *A Blessing of the Bread* by Maggie Glezer. Copyright © 2004 by Maggie Glezer. Used by permission of Artisan, a division of Workman Publishing Co., Inc., New York. All rights reserved.

Parmesan–Poppy Seed Pull-Apart Bread. From *Harley and Davidson Family Recipes* by Margo Manning and Carol Lange. Copyright © 2005 by Margo Manning and Carol Lange. Reprinted by permission of Ten Speed Press, Berkeley, CA, www.tenspeed.com.

Hot Blackberries and Cream. From *The Fearless Chef* by Andy Husbands and Joe Yonan. Copyright © 2004 by Andy Husbands. Reprinted by permission of Adams Media Corporation.

Caramelized Peaches. From *Jacques Pépin Fast Food My Way.* Copyright © 2004 by Jacques Pépin. Reprinted by permission of Houghton Mifflin Company.

Berry Clafouti with Crème Fraîche by Bill Telepan. From *Inspired by Ingredients* by Bill Telepan and Andrew Friedman. Copyright © 2004 by Bill Telepan. Reprinted by permission of Simon & Schuster Adult Publishing Group.

Banana Pudding. From *Hallelujah! The Welcome Table* by Maya Angelou. Copyright © 2004 by Maya Angelou. Used by permission of Random House, Inc.

Mango Mousse. From *Baking at Home with The Culinary Institute of America* by CIA Baking and Pastry Arts staff. Copyright © 2004 by the Culinary Institute of America. Reprinted by permission of Wiley Publishing, Inc., a subsidiary of John Wiley & Sons Inc.

Grilled Pineapple with Butter Rum Sauce by Park Kerr. First published in *Cooking New American* by the editors of *Fine Cooking* magazine. Copyright © 2004 by Park Kerr. Reprinted by permission of Park Kerr.

Frozen Lemon Cream Sandwiches by Grace Parisi. Originally published in *Food & Wine.* Copyright © 2004 by *Food & Wine.* Reprinted with permission.

Crisp Lemon Mint Cookies by Bernice Fraze. Originally published in the *Dallas Morning News.* Copyright © 2004 by the *Dallas Morning News.* Reprinted with permission.

Cowboy Cookies by Margie Beiser Lapanja. Originally appeared as Margie's Cowboy Cookies, in *Goddess in the Kitchen* by Margie Beiser Lapanja. Copyright © 1998 by Margie Beiser Lapanja. Used by permission of Margie Beiser Lapanja. Visit www.margielapanja.com.

Almond Crisps. From *The King Arthur Flour Cookie Companion* by the Bakers at the King Arthur Flour Company, Inc. Copyright © 2004 by the King Arthur Flour Company, Inc. Reprinted by permission of the Countryman Press, www.countrymanpress.com.

Chocolate Chip–Brownie Double-Deckers. From *The Weekend Baker: Irresistible Recipes, Simple Techniques, and Stress-Free Strategies for Busy People* by Abigail Johnson Dodge. Copyright © 2005 by Abigail Johnson Dodge. Used by permission of W. W. Norton & Company, Inc.

Triple-Chocolate Cranberry Oatmeal Cookies by Elinor Klivans. Originally published in *Bon Appétit.* Copyright © 2004 by Elinor Klivans. Reprinted by permission of Elinor Klivans.

Raspberry Walnut Brownies by Gayle and Joe Ortiz. From *The Village Baker's Wife* by Gayle and Joe Ortiz with Louisa Beers. Copyright © 2004 by Gayle and Joe Ortiz. Reprinted by permission of Ten Speed Press, Berkeley, CA, www.tenspeed.com.

Peanut Butter Buckeyes by Sara Bir. Originally published in *Saveur.* Copyright © 2004 by Sara Bir. Reprinted by permission of Sara Bir.

Breton Butter Cake by Naomi Duguid and Jeffrey Alford. Originally published in *Food & Wine.* Copyright © 2004 by Naomi Duguid and Jeffrey Alford. Reprinted by permission of Naomi Duguid and Jeffrey Alford.

Triple Caramel Cake by Johanne Killeen and George Germon. Originally published in *Favorite Recipes of 10 Years of Fine Cooking.* Copyright © 2004 by Johanne Killeen and George Germon. Reprinted by permission of Johanne Killeen and George Germon.

Hazelnut–Brown Butter Cake by Roxana Jullapat. Originally published in the *Los Angeles Times*. Copyright © 2004 by the *Los Angeles Times*/TMS Reprints.

Brown Sugar–Sour Cream Cheesecake. From *Sweet Stuff* by Karen Barker. Copyright © 2004 by Karen Barker. Reprinted by permission of the University of North Carolina Press.

Almond Cake with Strawberry Rhubarb Compote. Excerpted from *Bouchon* by Thomas Keller. Copyright © 2004 by Thomas Keller. Used by permission of Artisan, a division of Workman Publishing Co., Inc., New York. All rights reserved.

Dahlia Bakery Butterscotch Pie. From *Pie* by Ken Haedrich. Copyright © 2004 by Tom Douglas and Shelley Lance. Reprinted by permission of Harvard Common Press.

Silky Pumpkin Pie by Pam Anderson. Copyright © 2004 by Pam Anderson. Reprinted with permission.

Fresh Fig Crostata by Johanne Killeen and George German. First published in *Cucina Simpatica* by Johanne Killeeen and George German. Copyright © 1991 by Johanne Killeen and George German. Reprinted by permission of HarperCollins Publishers.

Southern Peanut Pie. Originally published on www.aboutpeanuts.com. Copyright © 2004 by Virginia Carolina Peanut Promotions. Reprinted by permission of Virginia Carolina Peanut Promotions.

Milk Chocolate Sorbet by Fran Bigelow. From *Pure Chocolate* by Fran Bigelow with Helene Siegel. Copyright © 2004 by Fran Bigelow. Used by permission of Random House, Inc.

Pumpkin Eggnog Ice Cream. From *The Compleat Squash* by Amy Goldman. Copyright © 2004 by Amy Goldman. Used by permission of Artisan, a division of Workman Publishing Co., Inc., New York. All rights reserved.

Cheesecake Ice Cream by Michel Richard. From *The Gourmet Cookbook* edited by Ruth Reichl. Copyright © 2004 by Condé Nast Publications. Reprinted by permission of Houghton Mifflin Company.

Ginger Lemon Iced Tea by Aulie Bunyarataphan. Originally published in the *Washington Post*. Copyright © 2004 by Aulie Bunyarataphan. Reprinted by permission of Aulie Bunyarataphan.

Watermelon Twist by Liz Smith. From *Star Palate: Celebrity Cookbook for a Cure* edited by Tami Agassi and Kathy Casey. Copyright © 2004 by Documentary Media LLC. Reprinted by permission of Liz Smith.

Good Morning Mimosa. From *The Encyclopedia of Cajun & Creole Cuisine* by John Folse. Copyright © 2004 by John Folse. Reprinted by permission of John Folse.

Margaria by Robert Larcom at Myriad Restaurant Group. First published in *Santé*. Copyright © 2004 by Myriad Restaurant Group. Reprinted by permission of Myriad Restaurant Group.

Sparkling Apple Cocktail. Originally published as Don't Just Stand There, in *Party Drinks!* by A. J. Rathbun. Reprinted by permission of Harvard Common Press.

Mount Vernon Christmas Punch. From *The Pat Conroy Cookbook: Recipes of My Life* by Pat Conroy with Suzanne Williamson Pollak. Copyright © 2004 by Pat Conroy. Used by permission of Doubleday, a division of Random House, Inc.

Serendipity's Fr-r-rozen Hot Chocolate. From *Sweet Serendipity* by Stephen Bruce with Brett Bara. Copyright © 2004 by Stephen Bruce. Reprinted by permission of Universe Press.

index

A

B

C

D

E

F

G

H

I

K

L

M

N

O

P

Q

R

S

T

V

W

Y

Z

THE B·E·S·T AMERICAN SERIES®

THE BEST AMERICAN SHORT STORIES® 2005

Michael Chabon, guest editor, Katrina Kenison, series editor. "Story for story, readers can't beat the *Best American Short Stories* series" (*Chicago Tribune*). This year's most beloved short fiction anthology is edited by the Pulitzer Prize–winning novelist Michael Chabon and features stories by Tom Perrotta, Alice Munro, Edward P. Jones, Joyce Carol Oates, and Thomas McGuane, among others.

0-618-42705-8 PA $14.00 / 0-618-42349-4 CL $27.50

THE BEST AMERICAN ESSAYS® 2005

Susan Orlean, guest editor, Robert Atwan, series editor. Since 1986, *The Best American Essays* has gathered the best nonfiction writing of the year and established itself as the premier anthology of its kind. Edited by the best-selling writer Susan Orlean, this year's volume features writing by Roger Angell, Jonathan Franzen, David Sedaris, Andrea Barrett, and others.

0-618-35713-0 PA $14.00 / 0-618-35712-2 CL $27.50

THE BEST AMERICAN MYSTERY STORIES™ 2005

Joyce Carol Oates, guest editor, Otto Penzler, series editor. This perennially popular anthology is sure to appeal to crime fiction fans of every variety. This year's volume is edited by the National Book Award winner Joyce Carol Oates and offers stories by Scott Turow, Dennis Lehane, Louise Erdrich, George V. Higgins, and others.

0-618-51745-6 PA $14.00 / 0-618-51744-8 CL $27.50

THE BEST AMERICAN SPORTS WRITING™ 2005

Mike Lupica, guest editor, Glenn Stout, series editor. "An ongoing centerpiece for all sports collections" (*Booklist*), this series has garnered wide acclaim for its extraordinary sports writing and topnotch editors. Mike Lupica, the *New York Daily News* columnist and best-selling author, continues that tradition with pieces by Michael Lewis, Gary Smith, Bill Plaschke, Pat Jordan, L. Jon Wertheim, and others.

0-618-47020-4 PA $14.00 / 0-618-47019-0 CL $27.50

THE BEST AMERICAN TRAVEL WRITING 2005

Jamaica Kincaid, guest editor, Jason Wilson, series editor. Edited by the renowned novelist and travel writer Jamaica Kincaid, *The Best American Travel Writing 2005* captures the traveler's wandering spirit and ever-present quest for adventure. Giving new life to armchair journeys this year are Tom Bissell, Ian Frazier, Simon Winchester, John McPhee, and many others.

0-618-36952-X PA $14.00 / 0-618-36951-1 CL $27.50

THE BEST AMERICAN SCIENCE AND NATURE WRITING 2005

Jonathan Weiner, guest editor, Tim Folger, series editor. This year's edition presents another "eclectic, provocative collection" (*Entertainment Weekly*). Edited by Jonathan Weiner, the author of *The Beak of the Finch* and *Time, Love, Memory*, it features work by Oliver Sacks, Natalie Angier, Malcolm Gladwell, Sherwin B. Nuland, and others.

0-618-27343-3 pa $14.00 / 0-618-27341-7 cl $27.50

THE BEST AMERICAN RECIPES 2005–2006

Edited by Fran McCullough and Molly Stevens. "Give this book to any cook who is looking for the newest, latest recipes and the stories behind them" (*Chicago Tribune*). Offering the very best of what America is cooking, as well as the latest trends, time-saving tips, and techniques, this year's edition includes a foreword by celebrated chef Mario Batali.

0-618-57478-6 CL $26.00

THE BEST AMERICAN NONREQUIRED READING 2005

Edited by Dave Eggers, Introduction by Beck. In this genre-busting volume, bestselling author Dave Eggers draws the finest, most interesting, and least expected fiction, nonfiction, humor, alternative comics, and more from publications large, small, and on-line. With an introduction by the Grammy Award–winning musician Beck, this year's volume features writing by Jhumpa Lahiri, George Saunders, Aimee Bender, Stephen Elliott, and others.

0-618-57048-9 PA $14.00 / 0-618-57047-0 CL $27.50

THE BEST AMERICAN SPIRITUAL WRITING 2005

Edited by Philip Zaleski, Introduction by Barry Lopez. Featuring an introduction by the National Book Award winner Barry Lopez, *The Best American Spiritual Writing 2005* brings the year's finest writing about faith and spirituality to all readers. This year's volume gathers pieces from diverse faiths and denominations and includes writing by Natalie Goldberg, Harvey Cox, W. S. Merwin, Patricia Hampl, and others.

0-618-58643-1 PA $14.00 / 0-618-58642-3 CL $27.50

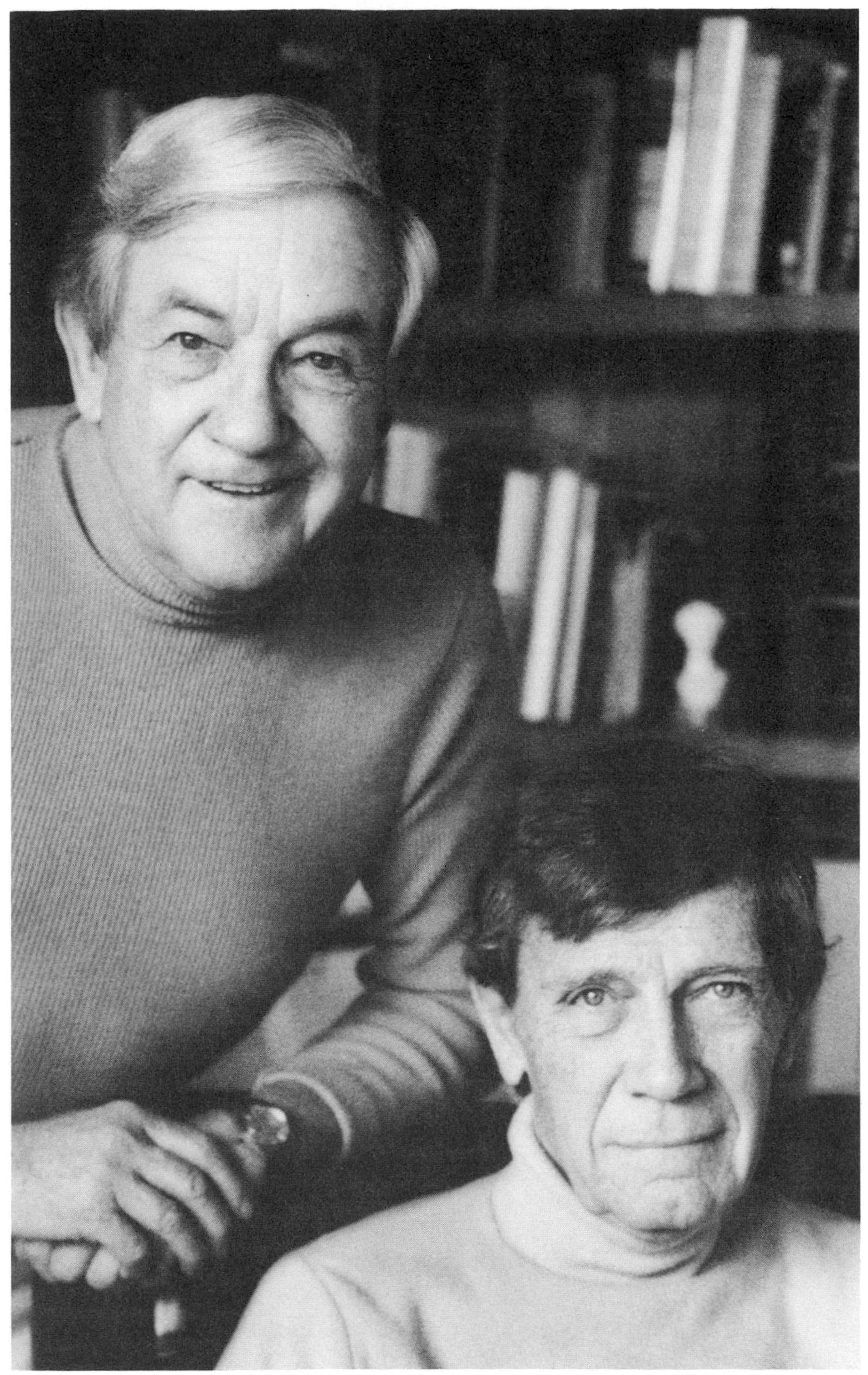

Jerome Lawrence and Robert E. Lee. Photo copyright by Stathis Orphanos.

Selected Plays of

JEROME LAWRENCE and ROBERT E. LEE

SELECTED PLAYS OF

EDITED BY
Alan Woods

FOREWORD BY
Norman Cousins

OHIO STATE UNIVERSITY PRESS
Columbus

See p. 579 for further rights information.

Library of Congress Cataloging-in-Publication Data

Lawrence, Jerome. 1915–
[Selections]
Selected plays of Jerome Lawrence and Robert E. Lee / edited by Alan Woods.
p. cm.
Includes bibliographical references.
ISBN 0-8142-0646-8 (alk. paper)
I. Lee, Robert Edwin, 1918–1994. II. Woods, Alan. 1942–
III. Title.
PS3523.A934A6 1995
812′.54—dc20 94-15894
CIP

Text and jacket design by Donna Hartwick.
Type set in Caslon 540 by Huron Valley Graphics, Inc., Ann Arbor, Michigan.
Printed by Cushing-Malloy, Inc., Ann Arbor, Michigan.

The paper in this book meets the guidelines for permanence and durability of the Committee on Production Guidelines for Book Longevity of the Council on Library Resources. ♾

9 8 7 6 5 4 3 2 1

Contents

Foreword

Great playwrights are both teachers and social philosophers. They open the minds of people to important truths, enabling them to make useful connections with their fellow human beings. They put people in close touch not only with their own time but with past events that tend to lose reality in the history books. They help people to banish the terrors that disfigure life and to deal with their inner fears. Finally, they help people to come into more genuine possession of the joys of living.

Those qualities are quintessentially characteristic of the work of Jerome Lawrence and Robert E. Lee. They fulfill their obligation to entertain but they also enable people to leave the theatre feeling better about belonging to the human species than when they arrived. They transmit their own deep belief in the possibilities of human betterment—and they do this as storytellers and not as sermonizers. They don't superimpose; they share. When the curtain goes up on a Lawrence and Lee play, the theatregoer can expect an adventure in transformation, for Lawrence and Lee have discovered a way of transmitting their enthusiasm, concerns, apprehensions, and the possibilities of a more just social order without spotlights or special effects.

As human beings, Jerry and Bob are constantly involved in the drama of the surrounding world. The slightest vibrations are picked up on their antennae. They respond to whispers and not just to explosions. They are constantly on the lookout for the obscure ingredients that go into the making of great events. To paraphrase Winston Churchill, their work hangs on the hinges of history. And they are as involved in the human situation as are any of their characters.

Their success as collaborators is no accident. I have seldom known two human beings who are better suited intellectually, emotionally, and spiritually to the challenge of creative partnership. Each contributes different colors to achieve a rainbow effect over their stage. Their respect for each other has not wavered over half a century. The way they communicate with each other is one of the wonders of the world. The train of thought started by one has hardly begun to move when tracks are already being laid down by the other. Even more important perhaps than their joint creativity is their joint moral and social imagination. They have an instant and instinctive reaction to injustice—and the greater the effort of the perpetrator to conceal or justify the wrongdoing, the greater their skill in holding him to accounts. The result is that you feel connected to the injustice unless you do something about it.

Jerome Lawrence and Robert E. Lee are evolutionists—not in the sense of the central theme of their *Inherit the Wind*, but in the Jeffersonian sense. That is, they are constantly making the case for human perfectibility. Not for perfection but for the capacity of human beings to ascend to ever-higher levels of individual and collective growth. Like Hammerstein and Rodgers, they give a common touch to elegant ideas; they love the theatre and they satisfy the love of people for it. But they are first and foremost sensitive and compassionate thinkers, locked into the human procession with all its glory and pain, and determined to use their combined skills to advance that procession even as they make people proud to be part of it.

This collection of a cross section of their plays is long overdue and establishes them not just as important social critics but as architects and innovators—architects who know something about the design of a good society; innovators whose understanding of cause and effect enables them to define new causes and to produce remarkable new effects.

Norman Cousins

General Introduction

Jerome Lawrence and Robert E. Lee's partnership as dramatic writers, after five decades, serves as a reminder of the strength once possessed by the American theatre. The playwrights' joint work, represented by the plays in this volume, typifies the years in which the commercial theatre served as an arena for ideas of substance, presented through highly professional collaborations among writers, performers, directors, producers, and audiences. Lawrence and Lee's work recalls the achievements of that period before financial and other considerations reduced the commercial theatre to its current overwhelming reliance on lavishly entertaining spectacles.

Lawrence and Lee's plays were (and are), with one notable exception, intended for the commercial theatre: a professional, profit-making business enterprise. When successful, the plays reaped large profits for producers, performers, and playwrights alike. Perhaps for that reason, and others to be explored below, the plays of Lawrence and Lee have received little scholarly attention. Yet in sheer number of performances, audiences, and productions, the commercial theatre far outweighs the experimental art that receives the lion's share of scholarly criticism. As I have argued elsewhere,[1] the popular commercial theatre provides a rich source for comprehending the audience of the past in its broadest range. For that reason alone, Lawrence and Lee's work deserves examination.

But Lawrence and Lee are more than just popular commercial playwrights. At their most successful, their plays have become classics of the modern stage, far outlasting those "hits" by many other contemporary playwrights, which disappear after their initial Broadway run and subsequent productions in community, academic, and regional theatres. Lawrence and Lee's plays survive because they deal with ideas and provide more than an evening's entertainment: they provide food for thought as well, dealing with some of the major conflicts of our time.

Jerome Lawrence and Robert E. Lee have collaborated on more than twenty produced plays and musicals, several hundred radio and television scripts, and numerous films. Eight stage plays have been chosen for this selection of their work. Each represents at least one facet of their work that will be explored in greater length in the introductions to each play's text.

Three of these plays (*Inherit the Wind*, *Auntie Mame*, and *First Monday in October*) were commercial successes on the Broadway stage, while one (*The Night Thoreau Spent in Jail*) was a landmark success in the regional theatre movement.

The remaining four included in this volume had varying degrees of success in the commercial theatre. *Only in America* had a short life in New York but ran more than a year in Los Angeles. *Diamond Orchid* was a success in academic theatre after its premature Broadway closing. *The Gang's All Here* had a respectable run in New York without financial success but has been widely produced in the following years, its theme of political corruption remaining always current. *A Call on Kuprin*, despite high praise from most reviewers, is the only piece in this anthology that was unsuccessful commercially in its original production and has had little life since. The various reasons for its failure to attract an audience permit a different glance at aspects of the commercial theatre.

Lawrence and Lee routinely have used history to comment on contemporary events: both *Only in America* and *The Night Thoreau Spent in Jail* take actual figures from the history of the United States in order to reflect on topics ranging from racism and anti-Semitism to nonviolent civil disobedience. *Inherit the Wind* and *The Gang's All Here* take historic events (the Scopes "Monkey Trial," the corruption in the presidency of Warren G. Harding) and fictionalize them to allow the playwrights greater freedom in drawing modern parallels. In *Diamond Orchid*, the career of Evita Peron in post–World War II Argentina inspired Lawrence and Lee to create a fictional piece exploring the nature of demagoguery.

Two of the plays are dramatizations from fiction. *Auntie Mame*, taken from the best-selling sketches published in 1955 by Patrick Dennis, gave Lawrence and Lee the chance to celebrate the freedom of the individual, while noting—comically, to be sure—the need to maintain that freedom vigilantly. *A Call on Kuprin*, freely drawn from a 1959 novel by Maurice Edelman (then a member of the British Parliament), uses the Soviet-American space competition to explore questions of patriotism and the role of the scientist in the modern world.

First Monday in October is unique in this collection in that it forecast the future when it was first produced: what would happen, the play asks, if the first female Supreme Court justice were to be an archconservative in conflict with a politically liberal senior justice? Recent American history has proven much of *First Monday in October* to be prophetic—indeed, many drama editors termed the play "history before it happens."

The plays included here, then, are examples of the work of Jerome Lawrence and Robert E. Lee. As I hope to demonstrate, they are extremely well-crafted pieces. Responses to their initial productions have more to do with the nature of the commercial American theatre, its mode of production, and audience tastes than with the merits of particular scripts. This introduction will examine the lives and careers of Jerome Lawrence and Robert E. Lee, then explore the context of the American commercial theatre during their most active years, the period from the mid-1950s through the mid-1970s. Finally, I will attempt to explore some of the reasons for the lack of scholarly and critical examination of Lawrence and Lee's work: why this anthology represents the first attempt to explore the range and nature of their collaboration.

Both Jerome Lawrence and Robert E. Lee were born and educated in northeastern Ohio, Lawrence in Cleveland on 14 July 1915, Lee some thirty miles west in Elyria on 15 October 1918. Ohio has served as a base for many of their later dramatic works, providing settings, origins for characters, and general backgrounds. Both men went to college in central Ohio, and both began individual careers in radio while in school. Lawrence became a Phi Beta Kappa graduate of Ohio State University in Columbus, where he won campus playwriting contests three times, wrote for the student newspaper as a columnist and drama critic (although not of his own plays), and gained radio experience by writing for the university station. He also acted extensively while a student and saw his first published play appear nationally in *Six Anti-Nazi Plays*.[2] Lawrence worked briefly for newspapers in Wilmington and New Lexington, Ohio, before moving into network radio on the West Coast as a writer and director.

Robert Lee's college education came at Ohio Wesleyan University in Delaware, Ohio, where he majored in astronomy and was active in the drama program. Before attending Ohio Wesleyan, he won a precollege summer scholarship at the school of speech at Northwestern University. Lee's deep voice got him continuous work as an announcer at radio stations in Columbus and Cleveland, and he was widely known as "Radio's Youngest Announcer": "I used to do all the big band remotes. . . . I really said 'Let's swing and sway with Sammy Kaye' more times than anybody else—his band used to have eight originations from Cleveland, and I did all of them."[3]

The two never met in Ohio, nor did their trails cross when each wrote and directed at KMPC in Beverly Hills, although at different times. Their careers paralleled in the late 1930s and early 1940s, with Lawrence writing and directing radio programs for CBS in both Hollywood and New York, while Lee was writing and directing on both coasts for the advertising agency Young and Rubicam, often at CBS.

By the early 1940s, Lawrence and Lee knew of each other's work; indeed, each had friends suggest that they meet. The meeting eventually took place at Colbee's Restaurant in the CBS New York headquarters building during January 1942, just after Pearl Harbor. The two decided to form a partnership and immediately began writing radio scripts together. Their first working session, at a Howard Johnson's in Manhattan with the pair writing on yellow pads, resulted in a script, "Inside a Kid's Head," produced on the experimental radio program, *Columbia Workshop*. "Inside a Kid's Head" was later widely anthologized in print.[4] The team's second joint script, "Brownstone Front," didn't carry the "Lawrence and Lee" credit: the sponsor of the *Manhattan at Midnight* series was a client of Young and Rubicam where Lee was still employed, so the script was credited to "Jerome Lawrence and Ulysses S. Grant."

The team of Lawrence and Lee succeeded so quickly with these and a number of other radio plays that by the spring of 1942, having completed other assignments—Lee at Young and Rubicam, Lawrence at CBS (where he was a writer on the wartime series *They Live Forever*)—they drove west to set up business in Los Angeles. Lawrence had been working on a proposed radio series about Amelia Earhart with publisher George Palmer Putnam, Earhart's widower. Putnam formed a partnership with the two writers and an editor, "Cap" Palmer (no relation), setting up offices in Hollywood as Lawrence, Lee, Palmer, and Putnam.

By the middle of 1942, World War II claimed the writers: in July, both went to Washington, D.C., as expert consultants to the secretary of war and became two of the founders of the worldwide network of the Armed Forces Radio Service, originating such programs as *Mail Call*, *Yarns for Yanks*, and contributing to *Command Performance*. They wrote and directed the major radio commemorations of World War II, including the official Army-Navy programs for D-Day, Victory in Europe Day, and Victory over Japan Day.

In what little spare time they could find, the partners also began writing for the live theatre. Their first effort, the comic *Madhouse on Madison*, was abandoned as too frivolous for the war years. Their second, *Top of the Mark*, took a more serious tone. Following a platoon through the war and ending with a reunion in San Francisco after the war's end, it treated serious social and political issues in the manner of their later successes. Despite support from such figures as playwright Marc Connelly, *Top of the Mark* was never produced. Connelly brought the play to agent Harold Freedman, a dominant figure in the commercial theatre of the day, who was impressed enough to take on Lawrence and Lee as clients. Freedman sent the play to the Theatre Guild,[5] whose cofounder, Theresa Helburn, wanted to discuss the play with the authors personally by telephone. By this time, however, both Lawrence and Lee were in uniform: Lawrence, a staff sergeant, was in Casablanca as a radio correspondent, en route to the Fifth Army Mobile Radio Station in Italy. Lee, an Air Force cadet stationed in Los Angeles with the Armed Forces Radio Services unit, was (as he put it), "guarding a cannon, protecting the Fox lot from enemy invasion."

Lee told Helburn the team couldn't work on the play until after the war. By that point, their interest (as well as that of the Theatre Guild) in *Top of the Mark* had waned. The play remains unproduced, while the promising connection with the Theatre Guild was never renewed.

Lawrence and Lee's first produced Broadway playscript was the book for the musical *Look, Ma, I'm Dancin'!* The team had met Hugh Martin, the composer of *Best Foot Forward* (1941) and the film *Meet Me in St. Louis* (1944), who was working on an idea for a musical with Jerome Robbins as a starring vehicle for comedienne Nancy Walker. (Walker had been a hit in a supporting role in *Best Foot Forward.*) Lawrence and Lee were asked to write a sample scene, about members of a traveling ballet troupe crowded into a single Texas hotel room. The writers accepted the task casually, turning out the scene within a week. To their delight, Oliver Smith and Richard Dorso, who were to produce the show, hired them to do the musical's book.

Elated, the team returned to New York to write the show, taking an apartment on Fifty-second Street between Fifth and Sixth Avenues, the block then known as Jazz Alley. But the production failed to materialize. Lawrence and Lee were still writing radio scripts, working at this point on the highly successful *Favorite Story* (starring Ronald Colman), *The Frank Sinatra Show*, and *Hallmark Playhouse*, among others. Lee eventually returned to Los Angeles to marry Janet Waldo, a radio actress then best known for playing Corliss Archer. As soon as Lawrence decided *Look, Ma, I'm Dancin'!* would never be produced and also returned to Los Angeles, the show was read by producer-director George Abbott, who took the project over and put it into rehearsal. Lawrence and Lee crossed the country again.

Look, Ma, I'm Dancin'!, starring Nancy Walker with Harold Lang and Herbert Ross in the cast, opened at the Adelphi Theatre in New York on 29 January 1948. The show traced the fortunes of an itinerant ballet company bankrolled by a beer heiress (Walker), who insisted on performing—turning into a comically bumbling ballerina in the process. With direction by Abbott and choreography by Robbins, *Look, Ma, I'm Dancin'!* garnered positive reviews and enthusiastic audiences. But it was what Lawrence termed "a nervous hit." Despite being housed in a large theatre away from Times Square, *Look, Ma, I'm Dancin'!* was among Broadway's top grossing hit musicals through the end of April 1948. An unusually hot May and June resulted in the box office figures dropping by more than fifty percent in those days before air conditioning, and the show closed on 11 July. (The heat also closed Rodgers and Hammerstein's *Allegro* and the long-running *Brigadoon*; the season's biggest hit, *High Button Shoes*, survived the heat wave.)[6] *Look, Ma, I'm Dancin'!* made a modest profit, however, and firmly established Nancy Walker as a star Broadway comic.

Look, Ma, I'm Dancin'! received a great deal of publicity, including a feature spread in *Life* magazine;[7] Lawrence and Lee's satirical thrust at Texas engendered a tongue-in-cheek response from one *Time* magazine reader, who threatened to cancel the company's "passports to Texas" because of the show's comic mockery of that state.[8]

Lawrence and Lee returned to their radio careers, continuing with the task of writing, directing, and producing 299 broadcasts of notable musical theatre works for the weekly series *The Railroad Hour* between 1948 and 1954, including the scripts and lyrics for sixty original musicals. Their next stage collaboration was *Inherit the Wind*, which would not be produced until 1955. With its success, first at Margo Jones's Theatre '55 in Dallas and shortly thereafter on Broadway, the partners moved firmly into the commercial theatre. Their timing was excellent: radio drama disappeared as a mass medium in the mid-1950s, buried by the competitive form of television. By then, however, Lawrence and Lee had become fixtures of the Broadway theatre scene and of the "road," the touring commercial theatre outside New York.

The partners wrote almost exclusively for the live theatre from 1955 through the late 1970s, with occasional projects for television and film being adaptations of their stage plays. Thus their 1956 Broadway musical, *Shangri-La*, hardly a utopia in its accident-prone Broadway production, had a far more salubrious presentation on television's *Hallmark Hall of Fame* in 1961. The film of *Auntie Mame* was an almost verbatim transfer of their stage play and remains vastly popular on videocassette into the 1990s. Notable films were also made of *Inherit the Wind* and *First Monday in October*. Their most recent collaboration, *Whisper in the Mind*, opened in October 1990 at Arizona State University in Tempe. *Whisper in the Mind* examines scientific rationalism and the power of the mind through Benjamin Franklin's confrontations with Dr. Anton Mesmer in 1784. As with many of their earlier works, *Whisper in the Mind* uses historic sources, adding fictional elements as a means to discuss contemporary concerns.

Lawrence and Lee's longevity as a writing team rests on the two partners' personal compatibility and on their careful nurturing of the collaborative process. The two have complementary personalities and interests: Lee, for example, is fascinated by how things work and possesses a photographic memory. Lawrence has been tirelessly active in professional associations, writers' conferences, symposia, and countless efforts aimed at national and international communication, joining delegations of writers on visits to the Soviet Union and the People's Republic of China in the 1960s and 1970s in efforts to encourage freedom of speech. Both teach (Lee at the University of California, Los Angeles, and Lawrence at the University of Southern California), lecturing extensively at colleges and universities across North America and at theatrical conferences and festivals.

From their earliest meetings in 1942, the two have avoided any set pattern of composition: one does not transcribe while the other dictates, the popular notion of how a writing partnership functions. (Lawrence and Lee's essay "Which One Can't Spell?"[9] explores some of the misconceptions about the collaborative process.) Rather, both write, discuss, revise, and, most importantly, read aloud. That both had theatrical performance experience is crucial; while neither writer pretends to high acting ability, they read all dialogue aloud, listening for words or phrases that sound false or are inappropriate to individual characters and situations. As Lawrence said, "When a play is really working, we become identified with the people we're writing about. We can easily play the roles of advocates in creating the dialogue. This way, the characters, if well fleshed-out, sit down alongside us and help us write the plays."[10] Lee adds, "Did Jerry write this? Did I write that? The point is, neither of us did. The play is really working when the character, whom we imagined, says, 'I've got to say this.' "

Most important for the collaborative process, the playwrights adopted what they term "the U.N. Veto" at the beginning of their partnership. "The whole theory is, either one of us has the absolute right to say 'no' . . . but then has the obligation to make his negative a positive, by coming up with something better—that the other will say yes to," Lawrence has explained. Both have written projects on their own, usually because the other wasn't fired by the idea—that was the case, for example, with Lawrence's one-act play, *Live Spelled Backwards . . .* (1966),

Lee's dramatization of John Reed's *Ten Days That Shook the World* (1973) and his chancel drama, *Sounding Brass* (1975).

Prose pieces are produced differently. "It's kind of impossible to do them jointly," according to Lee. The partners instead often write magazine articles and books separately. Lee authored *Television: The Revolution* in 1943, accurately forecasting that medium's future, while Lawrence published *Actor: The Life and Times of Paul Muni* on his own in 1974.

For articles published under the joint byline, the team collaborates on revisions after one has produced a first draft. "Then the other helps punch it up, changing. . . . So we're each other's editors," Lawrence says. In the period of their greatest activity in radio, during the run of *The Railroad Hour*, the partners often wrote (and directed) individual shows separately, although the writing credit was always to the partnership.

One result of their working pattern is that neither Lawrence nor Lee can identify which one originated lines, situations, or characters, except for rare instances. Perhaps their most quoted line of dialogue from *Auntie Mame*, for example, is Mame's "Life is a banquet and most poor sons-of-bitches are *starving* to death." Neither remembers who wrote it. Lee thought at first that the line came from Patrick Dennis's published book. But when asked for permission to quote it in books of popular quotations, Dennis pointed out that he first encountered the line in the original draft of Lawrence and Lee's play, "though he wished he had written it."

Similarly, the genesis for the plays, when not directly commissioned—as were *Auntie Mame* and *A Call on Kuprin*—remains lost in the collaborative process. Typical is Lawrence's description of starting work on *First Monday in October*: "One of us called the other and said, 'What would happen if there was a woman on the Supreme Court?' " *The Night Thoreau Spent in Jail* was a rare exception: the initial idea was Lawrence's. He roughed out an outline and began writing, using Thoreau's imagined trial of himself as the organizing point, but hit a snag. Lee came up with the idea of fluid, almost cinematic structure, "time awash," which solved the problem; so the play, originally to be Lawrence's sole work, became a collaborative effort.

The actual process of writing has varied with technology. When the partnership began in 1942, the writers used yellow legal pads, sometimes with Lee writing in his own shorthand; the writers then typed drafts from their handwritten copy. Over the years, they used whatever mechanical aids were available, speaking dialogue into tape recorders, transcribing the results on manual then electric typewriters, up to their present use of word processors linked by modems and fax machines.

Technology has permitted them to work together although geographically separated. Through much of the 1960s, Lawrence was based in New York, while Lee lived in Southern California. They worked over the telephone, meeting face-to-face only occasionally on one coast or the other.[11] More recently, with both in the

Los Angeles area but separated by some thirty miles of freeway, computer technology provides the link.

Whatever the equipment used, however, the process of writing, editing, and honing—what Lee terms "writing with an eraser"—has remained remarkably constant, as has the constant production of plays for all media, resulting in the enormous body of work, both realized and unrealized, of which this anthology represents only a fraction in a single form, the live theatre.

The commercial theatre world to which Lawrence and Lee aspired in the late 1940s and joined with such success in the mid-1950s, was to vanish by the early 1970s. When Lawrence and Lee became active, the "Broadway" theatre in New York City was the center of a national theatrical business: plays and musicals were developed during tryout tours (usually on the East Coast), then opened in New York. Successes toured across the North American continent after their Broadway runs, often for several years. Theatres in cities of even modest size provided venues for tours, termed the "road" in show business jargon, often with large subscription audiences. The Hartman Theatre in Columbus, Ohio, for example, offered its audiences eighteen touring productions in the 1947–48 season, when *Look, Ma, I'm Dancin'!* opened in New York.[12] Even moderately successful shows could, at least in the 1940s and early 1950s, recoup part of their investment on tour, billed as recent Broadway hits.

Stage stars—most notably such luminous figures as Alfred Lunt and Lynn Fontanne, Katharine Cornell, Maurice Evans, and Helen Hayes—routinely alternated seasons in New York with year-long tours of the road. The road tours in turn fueled the commercial theatre in New York: newspapers in such cities as Indianapolis, Columbus, and Pittsburgh regularly chartered "show trains" from railroads, taking hundreds of residents into New York for a weekend of sightseeing and theatregoing, often to see the same performers they had seen in touring productions at home.[13] Commercial theatre was a truly national one during this period: while centered in New York, its major stars and productions were visible across the continent.

Costs were low enough in the late 1940s that a production could recoup its investment in several months, rather than the several years that became necessary by the mid-1970s. Highly successful hits typically ran for a season or two; multiyear runs, although not unknown (*Tobacco Road* racked up seven years in the 1930s, while both *Oklahoma!* and *Life with Father* ran throughout the decade of the 1940s), were extremely rare. The relatively short runs of successes suggests that the audience was finite: after a season or so, the New York audience—even augmented as it certainly was by tourists and show trains—was exhausted. With runs for all but the most runaway hits limited, producers kept costs low in order to have some chance of repaying backers' investments.

Lower production costs, relatively rapid recovery of those production costs, and the possibility of high profits from adding a road tour to the Broadway run, all combined to create a high degree of activity in the commercial theatre: in the 1948–49 season, for example, seventy-six productions appeared in the commercial theatre. By 1955–56, the total had dropped to fifty-six; only twenty-nine productions constituted Broadway's 1988–89 theatrical season.[14]

The high level of production in the late 1940s and early 1950s also helped foster the existence of a professional theatre community based in New York: producers, directors, performers, and writers, all regularly working in the live theatre, and all collaborating on projects for production. By the mid-1950s, the theatre community—including performers, stagehands, designers, and so forth, was estimated to stand at twenty thousand people.[15] Jerome Lawrence and Robert E. Lee became part of that theatrical scene at a time when collaboration was normal, rather than exceptional, and when many of the theatre's workers regarded the creation of plays and musicals as the work of skilled craftspeople. Such collaborations were once common in the theatre, as Richard Hummler pointed out in *Variety*, the show business weekly.[16] Hummler is correct in finding such collaboration a function of "a more pragmatic and overtly commercial . . . era, when scripts were tailored more precisely for the marketplace, and for mass acceptance, than they are today."[17] While multiple authors are common in both commercial cinema and television, as Hummler writes, the common practice in those media is for writers to work separately on successive drafts. The true partnership process employed by Lawrence and Lee has become a rarity, as the modes and processes of theatrical production have changed to focus on the individual playwright, now nurtured through grants, workshops, and nonprofit theatrical venues. In the collaborative theatre community of the late 1940s and early 1950s, getting the show right for the individual star performer, or for the director/producer, was paramount, and with less attention paid to the theatre's "art" than became the case in later years.

Lawrence and Lee's most active years in the professional theatre are those of the theatre's most productive years, in terms of sheer activity at the very least, during the post–World War II period. As the plays in the present anthology make clear, the great activity of those years often resulted in masterworks of the theatre as well. Lawrence and Lee's contemporaries include Arthur Miller, Tennessee Williams, William Inge, Leonard Bernstein, Lerner and Loewe, Frank Loesser, the later works of Rodgers and Hammerstein, and the early works of Stephen Sondheim.

Although we tend to remember a period's theatre by the plays and their writers, and the major performers who attracted the audience, an integral part of the commercial American theatre's community were the producers, directors, and designers—the artists who created the physical productions. The commercial theatre in the 1940s and 1950s supported a number of major talents in each area. Producers such as Herman Shumlin, Kermit Bloomgarden, David Merrick, Griffith and Prince, Fryer and Carr, Robert Whitehead, Roger L. Stevens, George Abbott—all maintained permanent offices and mounted productions each season, often supported by "angels": the wealthy who regularly backed productions as a somewhat risky but always glamorous investment.[18] A major designer would work constantly; in the 1956–57 season alone, for example, Oliver Smith designed the scenery for four Broadway productions in addition to his work on *Auntie Mame.*[19]

The final component of the commercial theatre community was, of course, its audience. The theatregoing audience of the period consisted of people who attended with some regularity and saw more than just the major successes each season. Such an audience was sophisticated and experienced, discerning judges of talent in both the performance and writing of plays. Part of the high quality of the commercial theatre during the decades immediately following World War II is undoubtedly due to the presence of a regular and knowledgeable audience. That audience, and the activity that surrounded a theatre community in which large numbers of writers, performers, and production workers could make a living without needing constantly to seek employment in film and television, enabled the commercial American theatre to reach levels not attained before or since.

The regular theatre audience has, in large part, disappeared in New York City, as the city's population has fragmented into discrete communities. As Thomas Disch puts it in an examination of the decline of the commercial theatre, the "melting pot has been replaced by a mosaic, the separate components of which regard one another with apathy or contempt."[20]

By the mid-1960s, much of the creative energy of the Broadway theatre had dissipated. A new generation of playwrights was emerging, as the first of the generation born during the Depression and the early years of World War II reached maturity. But with the exception of Edward Albee, whose first full-length play, *Who's Afraid of Virginia Woolf?*, burst on the Broadway scene in 1962, many of the younger playwrights were produced not on Broadway, but in the burgeoning off-Broadway and off-off-Broadway theatre. As always in a commercial venture, costs underlay the shift: the Broadway theatre's steadily increasing costs in the early 1960s fostered steady increases in the prices charged for tickets. Increasing costs made theatregoers less willing to see plays other than those touted as hits by critics; increasing ticket prices also helped to scatter the regular theatre audience. By 1975, a small comedy such as *Same Time, Next Year* cost almost $154,000 to produce and charged $11 for the best tickets; in 1956, a similar comedy, *The Loud Red Patrick*, had cost $45,000 to produce and its best seats cost $5.75.[21] Increasing production costs also helped to kill off the touring theatre across North America. By the mid-1960s, the commercial American theatre was an industry in sharp decline, beset by apparently intractable problems.[22]

One response to the contracting American theatre was the establishment of professional regional theatres, intended to ensure that theatrical performances were available even if the commercial theatre no longer could supply enough productions to keep local theatres filled regularly. The Hartman Theatre in Columbus, mentioned above, housed only seven productions in the 1967–68 season and then closed permanently.[23] Founded at least in part as a response to the disappearance of the "road," those regional theatres frequently were established as nonprofit entities, intended as cultural institutions on the same level as art museums or symphony orchestras. The history of the nonprofit regional theatre movement of the 1960s and 1970s has been well documented and needs no repetition here.[24] One aspect of the regional theatre movement, in which Lawrence and Lee played seminal roles, does bear some discussion, however, as it provided a model for later developments.

Lawrence and Lee founded the American Playwrights Theatre in 1965 in hopes of bypassing the harshly commercial conditions then beginning to dominate the Broadway stage. Headquartered at Ohio State University, the American Playwrights Theatre (APT) created the first truly national theatrical production mechanism seen in the United States since a brief but intense period of activity by the American National Theatre and Academy (ANTA) in the late 1940s.[25] The APT provided original scripts by established playwrights to member theatres, who were in turn offered the exclusive rights to produce the scripts. In its fifteen-year history, the APT offered twelve scripts, nine of which received productions from member theatres.[26]

The most successful play in APT's history was Lawrence and Lee's own *The Night Thoreau Spent in Jail*, with more than two thousand performances at APT member theatres during its first two years alone.[27] By the end of the 1970s, the regional professional theatre had become so well established that the pattern of professional production changed: no longer were most commercial theatre plays and musicals rehearsed in New York, then tried out for several weeks in cities on the East Coast before opening on Broadway, the standard practice of earlier years. Now, many productions originated in nonprofit regional theatres and were either moved intact to the Broadway stage, as was the case with the 1990 winner of the Tony Award for best play, Frank Galati's adaptation of *The Grapes of Wrath*,[28] or were given new (and often more elaborate) physical productions before being transferred. Lawrence and Lee adopted that practice with *First Monday in October*, first presented at the nonprofit Cleveland Play House in 1975 before its 1977 commercial production at the Kennedy Center in Washington, D.C., and its 1978 move to Broadway, Los Angeles, and Chicago.

The team of Jerome Lawrence and Robert E. Lee has been active longer than any of their contemporaries other than Arthur Miller. Alone among theatre writers of the 1950s and 1960s, Lawrence and Lee moved freely—and successfully—from serious drama to comedy to musical comedy.

Despite their range and large body of work, Lawrence and Lee have not been the subject of much scholarly attention. Each of their plays was critically reviewed when first produced, of course, and new productions continue to gather reviews and publicity. Lawrence and Lee themselves have been frequently interviewed over the course of their careers. Accordingly, an enormous amount of printed material is available documenting the team's career.[29] The plays have not received a similarly extensive assessment, however. Given their success, such a lack seems odd. Some possible reasons for the critical silence suggest themselves, however, and may help to put these popular playwrights into closer perspective.

First, although Lawrence and Lee's major successes were popular with audiences and were highly praised by most of the New York reviewers, in several instances influential critics failed, on a first viewing, to recognize the playwrights' contributions. Lawrence and Lee were fortunate to have major stars in their first five Broadway productions, which also misled some of the reviewers. *Look, Ma, I'm Dancin'!* was regarded as a satisfactory vehicle for a new star, but there was little recognition of the structure and wit of the musical's book. Critical reaction to the other plays is discussed in detail below, in introductions to each text. Although positive, reviewers tended to focus on the productions rather than on the playwrights' contributions (with several notable exceptions). As the original reviews are widely available, either through microform editions of the *New York Times* or the collected volumes of *New York Theatre Critics Reviews*, later researchers find little to encourage further exploration of the plays.

A further reason for the silence regarding Lawrence and Lee's plays, ironically enough, is that they are too well crafted to attract the attention of major academic scholars of drama. The playwrights' penchant for fictionalizing historical events and characters in the interest of examining social issues frequently led careless reviewers to dismiss the plays as mere transcriptions of historic documents. That was especially the case with *Inherit the Wind* and *The Gang's All Here*: observers often congratulated Lawrence and Lee for including speeches and incidents that the playwrights had, in fact, created themselves.

Such responses were mistaken. Although *Inherit the Wind*, *Diamond Orchid*, and *The Gang's All Here* were based on actual events, Lawrence and Lee created what they have termed "factual fiction or fictional fact," inventing dialogue, characters, and incidents that do not exist in any public record. In *Only in America*, the team developed a plot based in part on Harry Golden's life, incorporating many of his pithy sayings while inventing more of their own.

Lawrence and Lee succeed in capturing the spirit of their subjects so well that often observers remain unaware of their contribution. Reviewers were unaware that many of the incidents and lines in *Auntie Mame* were not in Patrick Dennis's book but were created by the playwrights; in *Only in America*, Harry Golden received credit for proverbs minted by Lawrence and Lee. Supreme Court Justice William O. Douglas praised the writers for having the good sense to include Clarence Darrow's "famous speech" beginning "Progress has never been a bargain" in *Inherit the Wind*; Darrow never gave such a speech. "He could have said it," the playwrights observe, "he might have said it, he *should* have said it." But he didn't—the speech is the result of Lawrence and Lee's creative fictionalization of the Scopes trial.

The playwrights' very success in capturing the spirit of the characters and the events they choose to dramatize has thus worked against them. In every play, the partners are self-effacing: there is no readily apparent Lawrence and Lee style in structure or in diction. Instead, each play has a style appropriate to the dramatic action and character. This lack of an easily identifiable style makes the work of Lawrence and Lee difficult to categorize and makes it even more difficult to undertake critical analyses based on primarily literary concerns.

Finally, Jerome Lawrence and Robert E. Lee explore ideas, but do so in plays that either were enormously successful or which had limited Broadway runs. Perversely, either result can lead to dismissal by scholarly critics. The plays that were not box office smashes rarely are even read, while the major successes often still are regarded as star vehicles—certainly the fate of *Inherit the Wind*, *Auntie Mame*, and *First Monday in October*—despite the plays' continuing to hold the stage after more than three decades and after cast changes made the scripts' merits obvious belatedly even to the few initially negative New York reviewers.[30]

Lawrence and Lee's plays are linked by thematic concerns, however, even if dramatic structure and style vary individually from script to script. Throughout the plays included in this anthology, several themes remain constant. In all, the right of the individual to personal fulfillment and the expression of an individualized approach to life is explored—and frequently celebrated, as in *Auntie Mame*, *Only in America*, and *The Night Thoreau Spent in Jail*. In *Diamond Orchid*, the effects of societal oppression of individual development are explored, while in *Inherit the Wind*, *The Gang's All Here*, *A Call on Kuprin*, and *First Monday in October* the degree to which the individual can, should, or must exercise those rights is debated.

Individual rights often force characters to defy authority, always nonviolently, another constant theme running throughout the plays. That conflict is treated both comically, as in Mame's defiance of the Upsons and Mr. Babcock in *Auntie Mame* and Harry Golden's calm assertion of minority rights in *Only in America*, or more seriously, with Thoreau's incarceration in *The Night Thoreau Spent in Jail* or Kuprin's willingness to forego his own freedom so that his niece can escape in *A Call on Kuprin*.

Two of the plays published here present darker variations of the same themes. In *The Gang's All Here*, Hastings's lack of personal integrity and vision leads to governmental corruption; only when Hastings himself becomes aware of the widespread effect of his own failings can he redeem himself and set corrective forces in motion. In *Diamond Orchid*, Felicia's greed and her capacity for self-delusion is clearly shown to be a result of the crushing force exerted by a rigid and rapacious class system externally imposed. Alone among Lawrence and Lee's leading characters, Felicia never comes to self-knowledge. Although her final speech as she dies provides the audience with enough information ultimately to understand the character, Felicia herself never seems to understand that she has perpetuated the abusive patterns that created her implacable ambition. And the final scene in *Diamond Orchid*, with its implication that the social forces that created Felicia will produce new Felicias continually, suggests a less optimistic view of the world than is present in the other plays.

It is significant, of course, that the pessimism of *Diamond Orchid* is rare among the plays of Lawrence and Lee. While the playwrights are passionately involved with the ideas that motivate their plays, the plays celebrate the human potential for positive action and demonstrate their authors' optimistic belief that injustices can be overcome, that society's problems can be overcome. Just as Justices Dan Snow and Ruth Loomis attain a clearer understanding of, and sympathy for, their philosophical opposites in *First Monday in October*, most of Lawrence and Lee's characters learn and grow in the course of their plays. The ending of *Inherit the Wind*, with Drummond's weighing—and finding equal—Darwin's *Origin of the Species* and the Bible, provides the paradigm for Lawrence and Lee's plays. Issues are fully debated, and a new, more humane synthesis usually results.

In reaching those syntheses, Lawrence and Lee fully utilize the resources of the live theatre. The sheer theatricality of their plays, again varying according to subject matter, provides another constant in the work. The rapid whirlwind of Auntie Mame's personality, for example, is reflected in the structure of her play, composed of many fast-paced scenes with dizzying changes of scenery and costumes.[31] The orgiastic revival meeting vividly creates the atmosphere of intolerant religious bigotry in *Inherit the Wind*, while the fluid time and space of *The Night Thoreau Spent in Jail* mirrors Thoreau's dream-like examination of the sources of his moral stance in that play.

Lawrence and Lee's theatricality is present in smaller scenes as well. The interactions of the Supreme Court justices screening a pornographic film in *First Monday in October*, staged with the most minimal of stage devices, precisely encapsulates their conflicts, and Harry Golden's rehearsing the children in *Only in America* captures the essence of the character's response to racial prejudice. Similar instances could be cited from the other plays gathered here; in each case, Lawrence and Lee have found a theatrical metaphor that epitomizes the dramatic situation or conflict they wanted to address. Their choices of dramatic structure and the visual imagery of the stage precisely mirror the larger concerns of each play.

Jerome Lawrence and Robert E. Lee have supplied the American theatre with a string of major works stretching through much of the last half century. Through their founding of the American Playwrights Theatre, they provided a model for the development of new plays by the regional theatre movement, then in its fledgling state. As teachers of young playwrights (in addition to their university bases in California, both have taught in many other universities across the country and overseas at the Salzburg Seminar in American Studies), they have been instrumental in encouraging and developing new writers and in helping to provide a forum for their work. Both Lawrence and Lee have been highly active in encouraging international cooperation, leading ventures involving writers of different societies. Their major achievement, however, lies in their passionate belief that the theatre must be of consequence and must deal with ideas and issues of social significance. Their plays demonstrate how playwrights can write of major issues with passion, wit, and grace, avoiding the overtly didactic. The selected plays of Jerome Lawrence and Robert E. Lee collected here also demonstrate forcefully the achievements of the commercial American theatre during its period of greatest achievement, in the decades following World War II, and point to the establishment of new patterns of theatrical production with *The Night Thoreau Spent in Jail.*

As master craftsmen, Lawrence and Lee provide superb models in the plays printed here. This selection of their work provides a sampling of the range and breadth of their interests and concerns, as their collaboration continues actively on the fiftieth anniversary of their joint work.

Notes

1. "Emphasizing the Avant-Garde: An Exploration in Theatre Historiography," in *Interpreting the Theatrical Past: New Directions in the Historiography of Performance*, ed. Bruce McConachie and Thomas Postlewait (University of Iowa Press, 1989), 166–76.

2. "Laugh, God!" in *Six Anti-Nazi One-Act Plays* (New York: Contemporary Play Publications, 1939).

3. Robert E. Lee, interviewed by the author, 28 December 1988, Malibu, California. Unless otherwise indicated, all direct quotations from Jerome Lawrence and Robert E. Lee are from this interview, a transcript of which is available at the Jerome Lawrence and Robert E. Lee Theatre Research Institute, The Ohio State University.

4. Some of the anthologies include Eric Barnouw, ed., *Radio Drama in Action* (New York: Farrar and Rinehart, 1945); Edwin Duerr, ed., *Radio and Television Acting* (New York: Rinehart, 1950); Ernest H. Winter, ed., *Happenings* (Toronto: Thomas Nelson and Sons, 1969); R. K. Sadler, T. A. S. Hayllar, and C. J. Powell, *Bring the House Down* (Sidney and New York: John Wiley and Sons Australasia Printing, 1976).

5. The Theatre Guild, founded by Lawrence Langner, Theresa Helburn, Phillip Moeller, Helen Westley, and Rollo Peters in 1919, was the single most prestigious producing organization in the American commercial theatre through the mid-1950s. Best known for its early association with playwrights Eugene O'Neill and George Bernard Shaw, the Guild offered regular subscription series both in New York and in major cities across North America. Its history is amply documented in Norman Nadel's *A Pictorial History of the Theatre Guild* (New York: Crown, 1969). An account of its most productive period is in Roy S. Waldau's *Vintage Years of the Theatre Guild* (Cleveland: Case Western University Press, 1972).

6. Box office figures are taken from the weekly listings of Broadway productions in issues of *Variety*, 4 February 1948 through 15 July 1948.

7. 23 February 1948.

8. 15 March 1948, p. 23.

9. *Theatre Arts* (June 1958): 63–65.

10. *W*, 31 October7–November 1975, p. 8; clipping in Billy Rose Theatre Collection, New York Public Library Research Center at Lincoln Center.

11. Whitney Bolton, "Lawrence and Lee Long Lasting Team," *New York Morning Telegraph*, 25 October 1966; clipping in Billy Rose Theatre Collection, New York Public Library Research Center at Lincoln Center.

12. Scrapbooks and business records in the Hartman Theatre Collection, Lawrence and Lee Theatre Research Institute, The Ohio State University.

13. One such show train, led by then–Columbus mayor Frank Lausche, allowed an onstage announcement of Melvyn Douglas's absence from a performance of *Inherit the Wind* to be turned into a celebration rather than an excuse for disappointed audience members to request refunds. The story is amusingly recounted in Tony Randall and Michael Mindlin's *Which Reminds Me* (New York: Delacorte Press, 1989), 33–34.

14. Season figures for 1948–49 from *Variety* (4 June 1975), p. 59; 1988–89 figures from *Variety* (31 May–7 June 1989), p. 72.

15. Brooks Atkinson, *Broadway*, rev. ed. (New York: Macmillan, 1974), 432.

16. "Anybody here remember collaboration? Once common practice, now defunct," *Variety* (28 December 1988–3 January 1989), pp. 39, 42.

17. Hummler, p. 39.

18. Marguerite Cullman's autobiography, *Occupation: Angel* (New York: W. W. Norton & Company, 1963) supplies a light-hearted account of the role of investors during the 1940s and 1950s.

19. Smith designed the musical *Candide* (opening 1 December 1956), *A Clearing in the Woods* (10 January 1957), *Visit to a Small Planet* (7 February 1957), and a revival of the hit musical *Brigadoon* at City Center (27 March 1957); details from Louis Kronenberger, ed., *The Best Plays of 1956–1957* (New York: Dodd, Mead & Company, 1957).

20. Thomas M. Disch, "The Death of Broadway," *The Atlantic*, 267 (March 1991): 98.

21. *Variety*, 14 March 1975, p. 161; 3 October 1956, p. 83.

22. William Goldman's *The Season: A Candid Look at Broadway* (New York: Harcourt, Brace and World, 1969) provides a detailed look at the 1967–68 commercial theatre season in New York, included extended analyses of the business of theatre.

23. Scrapbooks and financial records, Hartman Theatre Collection, Lawrence and Lee Theatre Research Institute.

24. See, for example, Julius Novick, *Beyond Broadway: The Quest for Permanent Theatres* (New York: Hill & Wang, 1969), and Joseph W. Zeigler, *Regional Theatre: The Revolutionary Stage* (Minneapolis: University of Minnesota Press, 1973).

25. The history of ANTA in its formative years under the executive directorship of Robert Breen remains to be written. During its greatest activity, ANTA produced experimental works in its own Broadway theatre, sponsored national conferences, sent professional actors and directors throughout the country, and provided literary and promotional support to its members nationwide.

26. David Ayers, letter, 10 February 1981; typescript in American Playwrights Theatre Collection, Lawrence and Lee Theatre Research Institute.

27. The production is fully documented in Laurence E. Fink, "From Thought to Theatre: Creation, Development, and Production of *The Night Thoreau Spent in Jail* by Jerome Lawrence and Robert E. Lee" (master's thesis, Ohio State University, 1988).

28. Galati's adaptation was first produced by the Steppenwolf Theatre on 17 September 1988 at the Royal-George Theatre in Chicago. With many of the Chicago actors, *The Grapes of Wrath* opened at the La Jolla Playhouse near San Diego on 9 May 1989; that production played in repertory for some dozen performances at the Royal National Theatre in London beginning June 22, 1989. *The Grapes of Wrath* opened at the Cort Theatre on Broadway on 22 March 1990, closing on 2 September 1990.

29. A full bibliography of published material by and about the playwrights is available in

Mark Winchester's "Jerome Lawrence and Robert E. Lee: A Classified Bibliography," *Studies in American Drama 1945 to the Present*, 7:1 (1992), 88–160.

30. John Chapman, reviewer for the *New York Daily News*, did eventually recognize Lawrence and Lee's contributions to *Auntie Mame* in print, as discussed below in the introduction to that play's text.

31. Both Rosalind Russell, the first Mame, and Eve Arden, who played the role in the West Coast company, recount amusing stories about the frantic action backstage during performances. Rosalind Russell and Chris Chase, *Life Is a Banquet* (New York: Random House, 1977), 193–94; Eve Arden, *Three Phases of Eve* (New York: St. Martin's Press, 1985), 127–28.

While this volume was in production, Robert E. Lee passed away after several years of ill health. Both Jerome Lawrence and Robert E. Lee were involved in each step of the preparation of this anthology, and I deeply regret that Bob will not see the finished volume. The anthology is dedicated to his memory, and to the achievements of the fifty-two year collaboration between Lawrence and Lee.

Alan Woods

INHERIT
THE
WIND

Introduction

Indignant at thought control, rampant in America and in many parts of the world in the era of the McCarthy "witch-hunts," Lawrence and Lee searched in the early 1950s for "a parallel, a parable from history to help bring some light to the present." They found in the 1925 Scopes Trial a jumping off place to express in dramatic form their passion for the right to think freely. They were inspired by Maxwell Anderson's technique of using dramatic and poetic license in his re-creation of the aftermath of the Sacco-Vanzetti case in his 1935 drama, *Winterset*,[1] and his use, in the 1933 *Mary of Scotland*, of fictionalizing history by writing scenes that never actually happened.

Lawrence and Lee's agent, Harold Freedman, tried all through 1953 and most of 1954 to interest a Broadway producer or director in *Inherit the Wind*, but all refused it. Only when Margo Jones discovered it was the play born on a living stage at Theatre '55 in Dallas.[2] Actor J. Frank Lucas was imported from Houston to play Drummond with a large cast of Dallas professional and community actors, and *Inherit the Wind* opened on 10 January 1955.[3] Immensely popular with audiences, it was called a "new play of power, humanity and universal truth" by Dallas reviewer John Rosenfield.[4]

Now the play attracted the attention of New York producers, all of whom had previously rejected it. Producer-director Herman Shumlin took on the project, with Jones serving as associate-producer. Shumlin recast the play, luring the veteran stage and film actor Paul Muni out of retirement to play Drummond. A well-known Broadway character actor, Ed Begley, was cast as Brady, and Hornbeck provided Tony Randall with his first major stage role. Shumlin put the play into immediate rehearsal, and opened it in New York on 21 April 1955 after a brief tryout in Philadelphia.[5]

The play was an instant success, with Muni's spectacular performance in the lead receiving particular praise. Muni was returning to the Broadway stage after an absence of six years; it had been longer since he'd made an American film, so his successful reappearance was doubly significant. Although the acting and the power of Shumlin's production received most of the attention, some of the reviewers realized the strength of the script that brought Muni back to the stage. John Chapman termed the play "one of the most exciting dramas of the last decade, magnificently written by Jerome Lawrence and Robert E. Lee."[6] William Hawkins termed it "a tidal wave of a drama."[7]

Other responses were less enthusiastic, notably that of Lewis Funke in the influential *New York Times*: "[Lawrence and Lee] have bucked one of the great hurdles of the theatre. History already written is lacking in suspense and suspense is one of the vital elements of theatrical sustenance. . . . The consequence is a play that is only intermittently compelling. . . . nothing has been spared to frame and make this play live. The trouble is that it does not live sturdily enough."[8] Funke's assessment was later countermanded by the *Times*'s senior critic, Brooks Atkinson, who praised the authors for "their ability to resolve their thesis in terms of dramatic conflict between two giants" and in a review of a later production called it "One of the most stirring plays in recent years . . . bursting with vitality. Literature of the stage."[9]

Among the other critics, Walter Kerr in the *New York Herald Tribune* accused the authors of "fairly random" structure that led to "a kind of block-print melodrama." Kerr had nothing but praise for the acting and directing, calling Muni's performance "a dazzling, and in every way delightful, tour de force" and noting that "an enormous company stirs and buzzes under Herman Shumlin's sharply focused direction."[10]

The opinions of Kerr and Funke were in the minority, and had little effect on *Inherit the Wind*'s success. Indeed, Kerr's signature was on the Donaldson Award certificate awarded to *Inherit the Wind.* (It also garnered the Outer Critics' Circle Award for best play and later won the London Critics' Award for Best Foreign Play of the Year.) Yet it is the initial reviews from Funke and Kerr, representing the two major daily papers in New York at the time, that are discovered when researchers return to the original press notices. That the *New York Times* critic exerts enormous influence over the commercial theatre has been a point of much controversy since the late 1960s.[11] The opinions of reviewers for the *Times* also loom much larger in historical research than they perhaps should, in large measure due to the *Times*'s ready availability through microforms in libraries everywhere as well as to the paper's high reputation.

The worth of *Inherit the Wind* has been established, of course, by the play's continued successes and constant production since the mid 1950s. In addition to a successful film version and two television adaptations,[12] *Inherit the Wind*, in its theatrical version, has been translated into more than thirty-three languages. The play has also survived misguided (and illegal) efforts to update it. Adrian Hall adapted the text for a 1981 production at the Trinity Square Repertory Theatre, cutting the Rachel-Cates romance and adding an audio-visual prologue linking the Scopes trial to renewed efforts in the 1970s by Creationists to ban or restrict the teaching of evolution theory. Hall's efforts were praised by Robert Brustein in the *New Republic*, who regarded the play itself as "dated and melodramatic" and concluded that "Hall's editing is so effective that you are well into the last act before you begin to question the quality of the text."[13]

Other reviewers were less impressed by Hall's additions. The *Boston Herald American* review concluded, "The Trinity production has a prologue designed to bring the meaning of the play closer to the concerns of a 1981 audience. . . . one wonders if it is really necessary in this new production of a play that had the whole country talking in its own day."[14] The reviewer for the *Providence Journal* noted, "Where do these visions and this version leave *Inherit the Wind*? Pretty much as it was, an entertaining and well-devised play that does not hammer its points over the head unduly."[15]

Efforts to "improve" *Inherit the Wind* simply reaffirmed what New York audiences and newspaper reviewers learned in 1955 when Paul Muni developed a tumor in his eye and had to leave the cast of the play. Although Muni had been given much of the credit for the play's success, Melvyn Douglas replaced Muni and was equally successful on Broadway and later in a year-long tour of the United States and Canada. The play's sound construction allowed a different interpretation of the lead, and Douglas was highly praised. Walter Kerr noted that Douglas was "content to build the role a shade more quietly than Muni did," while John Chapman called Douglas's work "an individual performance by an able and thinking actor."[16] Indeed, Douglas late in his life credited *Inherit the Wind* with breaking his Hollywood image of a charming, but lightweight, comedian.[17]

The reviews of this play in its continuous production during the past thirty-six years have been enthusiastically positive, and its continuing relevance praised worldwide. In the late 1980s and early 1990s, the play has been staged in actual courthouses; in 1991, the Scranton Public Theatre performed it in Philadelphia's City Hall in commemoration of the two hundredth anniversary of the Bill of Rights, with posters proclaiming "The Right to Think."[18] American reviews through the years can be summed up by Norman Nadel's summary comment in the Scripps-Howard newspapers: "A masterpiece. This is the test: to see a play one, twice, three times. And each time to leave the theatre as deeply moved, as lifted up, as magnificently entertained. And as convinced that it is one of the truly great American dramas of this century."[19]

Inherit the Wind's appeal derives not only from the issues it raises, still hotly debated in the contemporary United States, but in the careful structure the playwrights created. Drawing upon the historic Scopes trial, Lawrence and Lee fictionalize the characters, giving their dramatic creations clearer motivations and personalities than the actual figures had. The fictionalization also permits them to simplify historic action and combine characters: the drama's Bert Cates is defended only by Henry Drummond, while the real Clarence Darrow led a three-lawyer defense team for John Scopes, including Dudley Field Malone and Arthur Garfield Hays.

The play builds slowly from the opening scenes on the square in Hillsboro. There are actually two opening scenes: the first, with Melissa and Howard, was performed in Dallas but was cut from the Broadway version. The Melissa-Howard sequence humorously establishes the conflict between Creationists and Evolutionists, as Melissa's horrified response to Howard's taunt that "your old man's a monkey" parallels the community's reaction to Bert's teaching. The

Broadway production opened with Rachel's visit to the jail, followed by the townspeople gathering to welcome Brady, slowly filling the stage to create a spectacular cheering throng when Brady arrives. The choice of the town square as setting allows the authors to introduce the characters either in groups or singly, while simultaneously creating the bustling atmosphere of a small town preparing for an event as exciting as a county fair. The large cast (twenty-two in Dallas, almost tripled to sixty-five for Broadway) also helps set the background of the town's reaction to the issues to be discussed in the trial.

Lawrence and Lee also use that scene to introduce the major characters—Brady with the stage tumult of singing and processions, Drummond with the *coup-de-théâtre* that ends the scene. Hornbeck is introduced as the ironic commentator on the action, serving throughout the play to point up the inconsistencies in Brady's position. Equally important is the figure of Rachel, who functions as the town's surrogate: her growth in understanding from the first scene, in which she begs Bert to recant, to the play's final scene, when she movingly presents the case for intellectual freedom, is the emotional and intellectual arc of the play.

The second scene moves directly to the trial. *Inherit the Wind* is, of course, primarily a courtroom drama, and the entire play leads to the Brady-Drummond confrontation. Lawrence and Lee break up the trial itself, however, with important and revelatory scenes: the prayer meeting, for example, vivifies the traditionalists' viewpoint, rising to a climax with Reverend Brown's cursing his own daughter. The epic confrontation between Brady and Drummond forms the climax of the play itself, with Brady's defeat shown in the theatrically and dramatically effective sequence of Brady pounding the air with his fists, reciting, with fervent hammer-blows, the names of the books of the Old Testament, then retreating into impotent infancy in the arms of his wife.

If the emotional climax of *Inherit the Wind* is at the end of the second act, the intellectual climax occurs in the beginning of the third. In Drummond's "Golden Dancer" speech, the motivation of the lawyer is revealed, and the credo by which he lives—which is, in many ways, the point of the play—made clear. The notion of intellectual freedom is reinforced by Rachel later in the act.

Lawrence and Lee brilliantly dramatize Brady's loss of power and respect through his aborted prepared speech and his physical collapse that follows, including his incoherent babbling of his decades-long, bottled-up, undelivered presidential inaugural address. Drummond's rebuke of Hornbeck after the news of Brady's death reiterates the balance and fairness the play demands, as does the final statement of Lawrence and Lee's drama: Drummond's weighing of the Bible and Darwin's *Origin of the Species* and slapping them together, side by side, into his briefcase. Typically, as master theatrical craftsmen, Lawrence and Lee make that final point visually, describing it in the stage directions, not through dialogue. Throughout *Inherit the Wind*, they have found ways to make their point vividly theatrical. The play's continued life in performance attests to their accomplishment.

Notes

1. "*Inherit the Wind*: The Genesis and Exodus of the Play," *Theatre Arts* (August 1957): 33, 94.

2. Margo Jones's initial contacts with the playwrights and *Inherit the Wind* are detailed in Jerome Lawrence's *Actor: The Life and Times of Paul Muni*, 2d ed. (New York: Samuel French, 1983), 317–18. The Theatre in Dallas changed the digits of its name annually, reflecting Jones's interest in new drama.

3. A full account of the Dallas production is given in Helen Sheehy's *Margo: The Life and Times of Margo Jones* (Dallas: Southern Methodist University Press, 1989), 252–56.

4. John Rosenfield, "'Inherit the Wind': Arena Stage's Finest Hours," *Dallas Morning News*, 11 January 1955, p. 12. It should be noted that Rosenfield's headline refers to the Dallas theatre's staging pattern, not to the Arena Stage company of Washington, D.C.

5. Accounts of the casting, rehearsal, and opening of *Inherit the Wind* are in Sheehy, pp. 256–59, and Lawrence, *Actor*, pp. 319–27. Lawrence provides a detailed description of Muni's involvement.

6. "*Inherit the Wind* Is a Splendid Drama of Ideas, Superbly Acted," *New York Daily News*, 22 April 1955, as reprinted in *New York Theatre Critics Reviews* (abbrev. *NYTCR*) 16 (1955): 322.

7. " 'Play Builds '55 Moral On Darwin," *New York World-Telegram and the Sun*, 22 April 1955; rpt. *NYTCR* 16 (1955): 323.

8. "Theatre: Drama of the 'Monkey Trial,' " *New York Times*, 22 April 1955; rpt. *NYTCR* 16 (1955): 323.

9. "New Lead: Old Part," *New York Times*, 25 September 1955, sec. 2, p. 1; "Drama on Coast," *New York Times*, 23 March 1958, sec. 2, p. 1.

10. "Theater: *Inherit the Wind*," 22 April 1955; rpt. *NYTCR* 16 (1955): 324.

11. William Goldman in *The Season* (New York: Bantam Books, 1970), 81–94, discusses the power of the *New York Times* at length. Similar assessments of the power of the *Times* theatre critic appear in Richard Hummler's description of a conflict in 1989 between playwright David Hare and Frank Rich, then critic for the *Times*; see Hummler, "Ruffled Hare Airs Rich Bitch," *Variety*, 15 November 1989, pp. 1, 5, and Geoffrey Stokes, "The Secret Rupture," *Village Voice*, 28 November 1989, pp. 37–39.

12. The motion picture, with Spencer Tracy, Fredric March, and Gene Kelly, was produced and directed by Stanley Kramer and released by United Artists in 1960. Melvyn Douglas and Ed Begley acted in the *Hallmark Hall of Fame* production on NBC-TV in 1965 directed by George Schaefer. The 1988 NBC-TV production starred Jason Robards and Kirk Douglas with a script by John Gay, which made some major changes in the original work. At Douglas's prodding, Brady became a Jimmy Swaggert-type evangelist. Although the play and Robards won Emmy Awards in 1989, the original playwrights were less than enthusiastic.

13. *The New Republic*, 25 April 1981, 21, 24.

14. *Boston Herald American*, n.d.; clipping in the Billy Rose Theatre Collection, New York Public Library.

15. *Providence Journal*, n.d.; clipping in the Billy Rose Theatre Collection, New York Public Library.

16. Walter F. Kerr, "Theater: '*Inherit the Wind*,' " *New York Herald Tribune*, 19 September 1955; John Chapman, "New Actor in a Big Role," *New York Daily News*, 25 September 1955; clippings, *Inherit the Wind* Scrapbook, Lawrence and Lee Collection, Billy Rose Theatre Collection, New York Public Library.

17. Melvyn Douglas and Tom Arthur, *See You at the Movies: The Autobiography of Melvyn Douglas* (Lanham, Md.: University Press of America, 1986), 184–86.

18. *Time* magazine listed the production as particularly noteworthy in its "Critics' Voices" column. *Time*, 21 October 1991, 24.

19. Norman Nadel, "On the Aisle —— 'Monkey Trial' of 1925 Makes Thunderous Drama," *Columbus (Ohio) Citizen*, 27 June 1955, n.p.; clipping, *Inherit the Wind* Scrapbook, Lawrence and Lee Collection, Billy Rose Theatre Collection, New York Public Library.

FOREWORD

Inherit the Wind is not history. The events which took place in Dayton, Tennessee, during the scorching July of 1925 are clearly the genesis of this play. It has, however, an exodus entirely its own.

Only a handful of phrases have been taken from the actual transcript of the famous Scopes trial. Some of the characters of the play are related to the colorful figures in that battle of giants: but they have life and language of their own—and, therefore, names of their own.

The greatest reporters and historians of the century have written millions of words about the "Monkey Trial." We are indebted to them for their brilliant reportage. And we are grateful to the late Arthur Garfield Hays, who recounted to us much of the unwritten vividness of the Dayton adventure from his own memory and experience.

The collision of Bryan and Darrow at Dayton was dramatic, but it was not a drama. Moreover, the issues of their conflict have acquired new dimensions and meaning in the years since they clashed at the Rhea County Courthouse. So *Inherit the Wind* does not pretend to be journalism. It is theatre. It is not 1925. The stage directions set the time as "Not too long ago." It might have been yesterday. It could be tomorrow.

Lawrence & Lee

EDITOR'S NOTE

This text of *Inherit the Wind* is the Dramatists Play Service acting edition originally published in 1958, with blocking directions reflecting a simplified touring production removed. Two lines in the Drummond-Brady confrontation in act 2, slightly altered by the playwrights for the 1991 Philadelphia production, are printed here for the first time.

The original text was published by Random House (New York) in 1955; that version reflects the Broadway staging of Herman Shumlin. Some of the stage directions in the present version are drawn from the Random House text.

Lawrence and Lee have also published a revised text, through Dramatists Play

Service. The 1986 revised version creates a two-act text by continuing the first act through the original act 2, scene 1, and beginning the second act with the original act 2, scene 2. In this version, therefore, the first act ends with Drummond's "All motion is relative. Perhaps it is *you* who have moved away—by standing still," while the second act opens with Brady questioning Howard in court.

Inherit the Wind is also available in a mass-market Bantam paperback edition, first published in 1960, with almost two and a half million copies in print. It has also been translated into more than thirty languages.

CAST

Inherit the Wind opened in New York at the National Theatre on 21 April 1955. It was produced by Herman Shumlin in association with Margo Jones, and directed by Mr. Shumlin. The scenery was designed by Peter Larkin, costumes by Ruth Morley, and lighting by Feder, with Terese Hayden as the assistant director. The cast included:

RACHEL BROWN	Bethel Leslie
MEEKER	Robert P. Lieb
BERTRAM CATES	Karl Light
MR. GOODFELLOW	Salem Ludwig
MRS. KREBS	Sara Floyd
REV. JEREMIAH BROWN	Staats Cotsworth
CORKIN	Fred Herrick
BOLLINGER	Donald Elsom
PLATT	Fred Miller
MR. BANNISTER	Charles Thompson
MELINDA	Mary Kevin Kelly
HOWARD	Eric Berne
MRS. LOOMIS	Rita Newton
HOT DOG MAN	Howard Caine
MRS. McCLAIN	Margherita Sargent
MRS. BLAIR	Ruth Newton
ELIJAH	Charles Brin
E. K. HORNBECK	Tony Randall
HURDY GURDY MAN	Harry Shaw
TIMMY	Jack Banning
MAYOR	James Maloney
MATTHEW HARRISON BRADY	Ed Begley
MRS. BRADY	Muriel Kirkland
TOM DAVENPORT	David Darrid
HENRY DRUMMOND	Paul Muni
JUDGE	Louis Hector
DUNLAP	Fred Miller
SILLERS	Fred Herrick
REUTERS' MAN	Edmund Williams
HARRY Y. ESTERBROOK	Perry Fiske

Townspeople, hawkers, reporters, jurors, spectators, played by: Lou Adelman, Joseph Brownstone, Clifford Carpenter, Michael Constantine, Michael Del Medico, James Greene, Ruth Hope, Sally Jessup, Julie Knox, Patricia Larson, Michael Lewin, Evelyn Mando, Sarah Meade, Gian Pace, Richard Poston, Jack Riano, Gordan Russell, Carroll Saint, Robert Shannon, Maurice Shrog.

Inherit the Wind was produced prior to its Broadway run at the Forrest Theatre, Philadelphia, opening on 31 March 1955.

Inherit the Wind was first presented at the Dallas Theatre '55 on 10 January 1955, directed by Margo Jones. The scenery and lighting were designed by James Pringle. The cast included:

HOWARD .... Joe Walker
MELINDA .... Dolores Walker
RACHEL BROWN .... Louise Latham
MR. MEEKER .... Michael Dolan
BERTRAM CATES .... Harry Bergman
GEORGE SILLERS .... John Maddox
MRS. KREBS .... Sadie French
MR. DUNLAP .... San Brunstein
WORKMAN .... Tommy Wright
REVEREND JEREMIAH BROWN .... Gilbert Miller
MR. BAGLEY .... Joe Parker
HAWKER .... Joan Breymer
SALESLADY .... Harriet Slaughter
ELIJAH .... Eddie Gale
E. K. HORNBECK .... James Field
ORGAN GRINDER .... Oscar Wilson, Jr.
MATTHEW HARRISON BRADY .... Edward Cullen
SARAH BRADY .... Kathleen Phelan
THE MAYOR .... Charlie West
HENRY DRUMMOND .... J. Frank Lucas
RADIO MAN .... Eddie Gale

Time: Summer. Not too long ago.
Place: A small town.

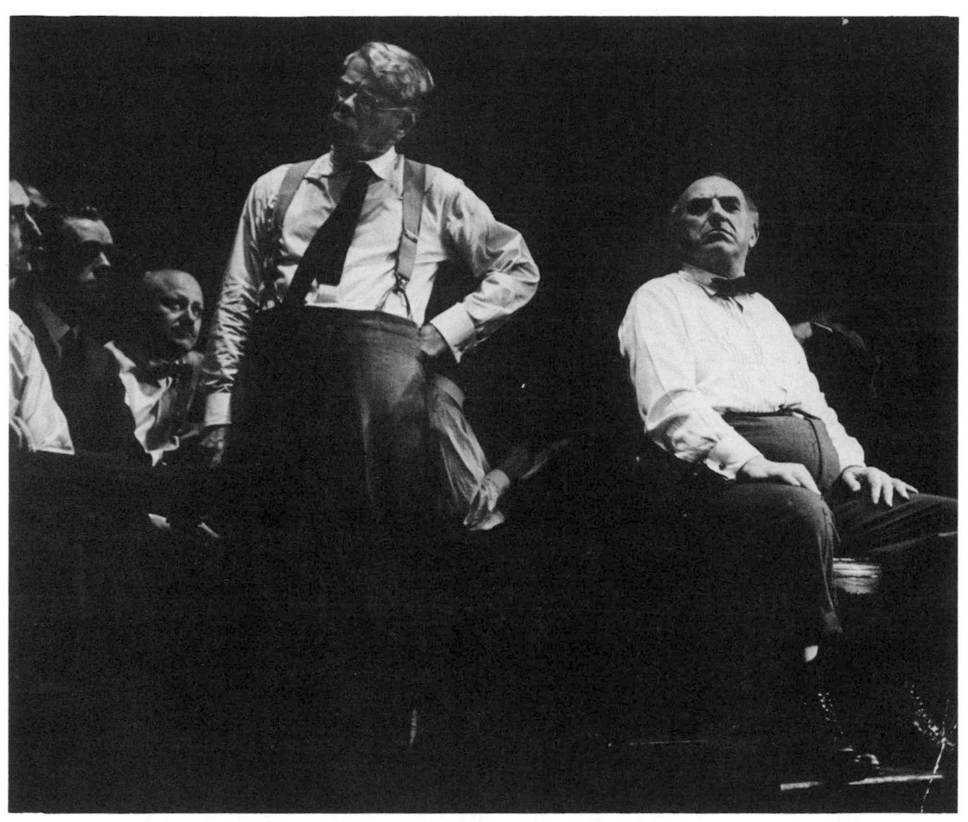

Paul Muni and Ed Begley Sr. in *Inherit the Wind,* New York, 1955. Photo by Staats Cotsworth. Jerome Lawrence and Robert E. Lee Collection, Lawrence and Lee Theatre Research Institute, The Ohio State University.

Louis Hector (as Judge) and Paul Muni in *Inherit the Wind* (photo taken from behind jury box), New York, 1955. Photo by Staats Cotsworth. Jerome Lawrence and Robert E. Lee Collection, Lawrence and Lee Theatre Research Institute, The Ohio State University.

INHERIT THE WIND

ACT ONE

SCENE 1

In and around the Hillsboro Courthouse. The foreground is the actual courtroom, with jury box, judge's bench and a scattering of trial-scarred chairs and counsel tables. On a raked level above it are the courthouse square, Main Street, and the converging streets of the town. This is not so much a literal view of Hillsboro as it is an impression of a sleepy, obscure country town about to be vigorously awakened.

It is important to the concept of the play that the town is visible always, looming there, as much on trial as the defendant. The crowd is equally important, so the court becomes an arena.

It is an hour after dawn on a July day that promises to be a scorcher. Howard, a boy of thirteen, wanders onto the courthouse lawn. He is barefoot, wearing a pair of his pa's cut-down overalls. He carries an improvised fishing pole and a tin can. He studies the ground carefully, searching for something. A young girl's voice calls from offstage.

MELINDA. (*Calling sweetly.*) How-ard . . . ! (*Howard, annoyed, turns and looks toward the voice. Melinda, a healthy, pig-tailed girl of twelve, skips over to him.*) Hello, Howard. (*Howard is disinterested, continues to search the ground.*)

HOWARD. 'Lo, Melinda.

MELINDA. (*Making conversation.*) I think it's gonna be hotter'n yesterday. That rain last night didn't do much good.

HOWARD. (*Professionally.*) It brought up the worms. (*Suddenly he spots one in the lawn. Swiftly he grabs for it and holds it up proudly.*) Lookit this fat one! (*He chases her.*)

MELINDA. (*Shivering.*) How can you touch 'em? It makes me all goose-bumpy! (*Howard dangles it in front of her face. She backs away, shuddering.*)

HOWARD. What're yuh skeered of? *You* was a worm once!

MELINDA. (*Shocked.*) I wasn't neither!

HOWARD. You was so! When the whole world was covered with water, there was nuthin' but worms and blobs of jelly. And you and your whole family was worms!

MELINDA. We was not!

HOWARD. Blobs of jelly, then.

MELINDA. Howard Blair, that's sinful talk! I'm gonna tell my Pa and he'll make you wash your mouth out with soap!

HOWARD. Ahhh, your old man's a monkey! (*Melinda gasps. She turns indignantly and runs off. Howard shrugs in the manner of a sapient man-of-the-world, rising and looking after her.*) 'Bye, Lindy. (*Rachel enters. She is 22, pretty, but not beautiful. She wears a cotton summer dress. She carries a small composition paper suitcase. There is a tense, distraught air about her. She may have been crying. She looks about nervously, as if she doesn't want to be seen. When she sees Howard, she hesitates, then she scurries across to the courthouse area in the hope that the boy will not notice her. But he does see Rachel, and watches her with puzzled curiosity. Then as he exits, he addresses the worm, dangling it in the air.*) What do you wanta be when you grow up? (*He goes off. Rachel stands uncertainly in the courthouse area. Unsure, she looks about.*)

RACHEL. (*Tentatively calling.*) Mr. Meeker . . . ?

MEEKER. (*A little irritably.*) Who is it? (*After a pause, Mr. Meeker, the bailiff, enters. There is no collar on his shirt, his hair is tousled, and there is still a bit of shaving soap on his face, which he is wiping off with a towel as he enters.*) Why, hello, Rachel. 'Scuse the way I look. (*He wipes the soap out of his ear. Then he notices her suitcase.*) Not goin' away, are you? Excitement's just startin'.

RACHEL. (*Earnestly.*) Mr. Meeker, don't let my father know I came here.

MEEKER. (*Shrugs.*) The Reverend don't tell me his business. Don't know why I should tell him mine.

RACHEL. I want to see Bert Cates. Is he all right?

MEEKER. Don't know why he shouldn't be. I always figured the safest place in the world is a jail.

RACHEL. Can I go down and see him?

MEEKER. Ain't a very proper place for a minister's daughter.

RACHEL. I only want to see him for a minute.

MEEKER. Sit down, Rachel. I'll bring him up. You can talk to him right here in the courtroom. (*Rachel sits. Meeker starts out, then pauses.*) Long as I've been bailiff here, we've never had nothin' but drunks, vagrants, couple of chicken thieves. (*A little dreamily.*) Our best catch was that fella from Minnesota that chopped up his wife; we had to extradite him. (*Shakes his head.*) Seems kinda queer havin' a schoolteacher in our jail. (*Shrugs.*) Might improve the writin' on the walls. (*Meeker goes out. Nervously, Rachel rises, puts suitcase on bench, is about to sit again. Bert Cates enters followed by Meeker. Cates is a pale, thin young man of twenty-four. He is quiet, shy, well-mannered. Rachel and Cates face each other expressionlessly, without speaking. Meeker pauses in the doorway.*) I'll leave you two alone to talk. Don't run off, Bert. (*Meeker goes out. Rachel and Cates look at each other. There is tension between them, as if they want to rush into each other's arms.*)

RACHEL. Hello, Bert.

CATES. Rache, I told you not to come here.

RACHEL. I couldn't help it. Nobody saw me. Mr. Meeker won't tell. (*Troubled.*) I keep thinking of you, locked up here—

CATES. (*Trying to cheer her up.*) You know something funny? The food's better than the boarding house. And you'd better not tell anybody how cool it is down here, or we'll have a crime wave every summer.

RACHEL. (*Indicating suitcase.*) I stopped by your place and picked up some of your things. A clean shirt, your best tie, some handkerchiefs.

CATES. Thanks.

RACHEL. (*Rushing to him.*) Bert, why don't you tell 'em it was all a joke? Tell 'em you didn't mean to break a law, and you won't do it again!

CATES. (*Breaking away from her.*) I suppose everybody's all steamed up about Brady coming.

RACHEL. He's coming in on a special train out of Chattanooga. Pa's going to the station to meet him. Everybody is!

CATES. Strike up the band.

RACHEL. Bert, it's still not too late. Why can't you admit you're wrong? If the biggest man in the country—next to the President, maybe—if Matthew Harrison Brady comes here to tell the whole world how wrong you are—

CATES. You still think I did wrong?

RACHEL. Why did you do it?

CATES. You know why I did it. I had the book in my hand, Hunter's *Civic Biology*. I opened it up, and read my sophomore science class Chapter 17, Darwin's *Origin of the Species*. (*Rachel starts to protest.*) All it says is that man wasn't just stuck here like a geranium in a flower pot; that living comes from a *long* miracle, it didn't just happen in seven days.

RACHEL. There's a law against it.

CATES. I know that.

RACHEL. Everybody says what you did is bad.

CATES. It isn't as simple as that. Good or bad, black or white, night or day. Do you know, at the top of the world the twilight is six months long?

RACHEL. But we don't live at the top of the world. We live in Hillsboro, and when the sun goes down, it's dark. And why do you try to make it different? (*He turns away. Rachel crosses to bench, opens suitcase, gets the shirt, tie, and handkerchiefs from the suitcase.*) Here.

CATES. Thanks, Rache.

RACHEL. Why can't you be on the right side of things?

CATES. Your father's side. (*Rachel starts to close suitcase preparing to leave. Cates stops her.*) Rache—love me! (*They embrace. Meeker enters with a long-handled broom.*)

MEEKER. (*Clears his throat.*) I gotta sweep. (*Rachel breaks away and hurries off.*)

CATES. (*Calling, wanting to say "I love you."*) Thanks for the shirt! (*Meeker, who has been sweeping impassively, now stops and leans on the broom.*)

MEEKER. Imagine. Matthew Harrison Brady comin' here. I voted for him for President. Twice. In nineteen-hundred, and again in oh-eight. Wasn't old enough to vote for him the first time he ran. But my Pa did. (*Turns proudly to Cates.*) I *seen* him once. At a Chautauqua meeting in Chattanooga. (*Impressed, remembering, booming it.*) The tentpoles shook! (*Cates moves nervously.*) Who's gonna be your lawyer, son?

CATES. I don't know yet. I wrote to that newspaper in Baltimore. They're sending somebody.

MEEKER. (*Resumes sweeping.*) He better be loud.

CATES. (*Picking up the shirt.*) You want me to go back down?

MEEKER. No need. You can stay up here if you want.

CATES. (*Going toward the jail.*) I'm supposed to be in jail; I'd better be in jail! (*Meeker shrugs and follows Cates off. The lights fade. Lights go up full on town scene. Mrs. Krebs enters, crossing the stage. Mr. Goodfellow enters, unlocks door to his haberdashery store.*)

MR. GOODFELLOW. Warm enough for you, Mrs. Krebs?

MRS. KREBS. The Good Lord guv us the heat, and the Good Lord guv us the glands to sweat with.

MR. GOODFELLOW. I bet the Devil ain't so obliging.

MRS. KREBS. I don't intend to find out. (*The Reverend Jeremiah Brown, a gaunt, thin-lipped man, strides on, looks around scowling.*)

MR. GOODFELLOW. Good morning, Reverend.

BROWN. 'Morning.

MRS. KREBS. 'Morning, Reverend.

BROWN. Mrs. Krebs. (*Sees banner has not been hung, calls off.*) Where's the banner? Why haven't you raised the banner?

SILLERS. (*Enters followed by Phil, another workman. They carry a canvas banner between them.*) Paint didn't dry till just now.

BROWN. See that you have it up before Mr. Brady arrives. (*Cooper enters, greet Mrs. Krebs.*)

SILLERS. Fast as we can do it, Reverend.

BROWN. We must show him at once what kind of a community this is . . .

SILLERS. Yes, Reverend. Come on, Phil. Hep. (*They cross to court house, where they proceed to hang banner, which says: "Read your Bible."*)

MRS. KREBS. Big day, Reverend.

BROWN. Indeed it is. Picnic lunch ready, Mrs. Krebs?

MRS. KREBS. Fit'n for a king.

BOLLINGER. (*Running on, carrying a trumpet.*) Station master says old Ninety-four's on time out of Chattanooga. Brady's on board all right. (*Dunlap and Bannister enter, greet the Reverend.*)

COOPER. The minute Brady gets here, people are gonna pour in. Town's gonna fill up like a rain barrel in a flood.

GOODFELLOW. That means business. (*Mrs. Loomis and her daughter Melinda enter with a lemonade pitcher and lemonade stand. They proceed to set it up.*)

COOPER. You bet.

BANNISTER. Where they gonna stay? Were we gonna sleep all them people?

MRS. KREBS. They got money, we'll sleep 'em.

DUNLAP. Looks like the biggest day for this town since we put up Coxey's Army.

HOWARD. (*Bolting on.*) Hey! Ted Finney's got out his big bass drum. And you ought to see what they done to the depot. Ribbons all over the rainspouts.

MELINDA. (*At the lemonade stand.*) Lemonade! Lemonade! (*Mrs. Blair enters, looking for Howard.*)

SILLERS. (*Who, with Phil, has finally raised the banner over the court house door, calls out to the Reverend.*) It's all ready, Reverend! (*All focus on the banner over the courthouse. Applause, cheers. Bollinger blows a fanfare on his trumpet.*)

HOT DOG MAN. (*Enters as banner cheer dies down. He sells his hot dogs from box he carries.*) Hot dogs. Get your red hots. Hot dogs.

MRS. McCLAIN. (*Carrying a shopping bag full of frond fans.*) Get your fans, compliments of Maley's Funeral Home, 35 cents.

MELINDA. Lemonade! Lemonade!

MRS. BLAIR. (*Who has spotted her son.*) Howard! Howard!

HOWARD. (*Racing to her.*) Hey, Ma, this is just like the County Fair. (*E. K. Hornbeck enters. He is a newspaperman in his middle thirties, who sneers politely at everything including himself. His clothes, those of a sophisticated city dweller, contrast sharply with the attire of the townspeople. As he wanders down through the crowd, he looks around with wonderful contempt. He makes his way down by Mrs. Krebs. He is unaware of her as she spots him as an out of towner and a prospective roomer.*)

MRS. BLAIR. (*To Howard.*) Now you settle down and stop running around, and pay some attention when Mr. Brady gets here. Spit down your hair. (*Howard spits in her hand, and she pastes down a cowlick.*) Hold still! (*Howard breaks away. Elijah enters. He carries a wooden vegetable crate full of books, which he hawks in a shrill screeching voice.*)

ELIJAH. Buy a Bible, your guide book to eternal life. Buy a Bible!

HOT DOG MAN. Hot dogs! Get your red hots. Hot dogs!

MRS. McCLAIN. (*Has also spotted Hornbeck as a prospective customer, moves to him.*) Want a fan? Compliments of Maley's Funeral Home, 35 cents.

HORNBECK. I'd die first. (*Mrs. McClain turns from him in a huff.*)

MRS. KREBS. (*To Hornbeck.*) You're a stranger, aren't you, Mister? Want a nice clean place to stay?

HORNBECK. I had a nice clean place to stay, Madam, and I left it to come here.

MRS. KREBS. You're gonna need a room.

HORNBECK. I have a reservation at the Mansion House.

MRS. KREBS. Oh? (*She sniffs.*) That's all right, I suppose, for them as *likes* having a privy practically in the bedroom. (*She turns away from him. He tips his straw hat to her.*)

HORNBECK. The unplumbed and plumbing-less depths. Ahhh, Hillsboro, Heavenly Hillsboro, the buckle on the Bible belt. Hallelujah! (*The Hot Dog Man and Elijah converge on Hornbeck from opposite sides.*)

HOT DOG MAN. (*Thrusting a hot dog on a bun at Hornbeck.*) Hot dog?

ELIJAH. (*Same business with Bible.*) Buy a Bible?

HORNBECK. (*Up-ends his suitcase and sits on it.*) Now that poses a pretty problem. Which is hungrier—my stomach or my soul? (*Buys hot dog.*) My stomach. (*Hot Dog Man accepts money from Hornbeck and moves off.*)

ELIJAH. (*Miffed.*) What are you? An evolutionist? An infidel? A sinner?

HORNBECK. (*Munching on hot dog.*) Of course I am. Isn't everybody?

ELIJAH. Buy a Bible. (*Hornbeck spies the Organ Grinder and his monkey who have entered during the preceding. Gleefully, Hornbeck greets the monkey with outstretched arms.*)

HORNBECK. Grandpa! Welcome to Hillsboro, sir. Tell me, have you come to testify for the defense or for the prosecution? (*The monkey, oddly enough, doesn't answer.*) No comment, eh? That's fairly safe. But I must warn you, sir, you can't compete with all these monkey-shines!

MELINDA. (*She holds out a penny, which the monkey takes.*) Look! He took my penny!

HORNBECK. Now how could you ask for better proof than that? There's the father of the human race!

TIMMY. (*A boy of fifteen or sixteen, comes running on breathlessly.*) Train's coming! I seen the smoke 'way up the track! (*Timmy dashes off. The crowd mills around excitedly. Brown, fearing for his well-planned reception, jumps onto the platform and takes control.*)

BROWN. All the members of the Bible League, get ready. Let us show Mr. Brady the spirit with which we welcome him to Hillsboro! (*The crowd lets out a mighty cheer. Mrs. Blair blows a note on her pitch-pipe.*)

MRS. BLAIR. (*Singing.*)
We're marching to Zion—

ALL. (*Taking up the song.*)
—Beautiful, beautiful Zion.

(*The crowd marches off after Mrs. Blair, singing.*)
We're marching upwards to Zion,
The beautiful city of God.

(*Hornbeck picks up his suitcase, and moves through the crowd. Even the Organ Grinder leaves his monkey tied to the hurdy gurdy and joins the departing crowd.*)

HORNBECK. Amen! (*To the monkey.*) Shield your eyes, monk, you are about to meet the mightiest of your descendents. A man who wears a cathedral for a cloak and a church spire for a hat, whose tread has the thunder of the legions of the lion hearted.

CROWD. (*Offstage, singing.*)
Let those refuse to sing
Who never knew our God
But children of the Heavenly King
But children of the Heavenly King
Shall shout their joys abroad.
We're marching to Zion (*etc.*)

(*Mr. Goodfellow, the storekeeper, emerges from his establishment.*)

HORNBECK. Hey, you're missing the show.

GOODFELLOW. Somebody's got to mind the store.

HORNBECK. May I ask your opinion, sir, on the subject of evolution?

GOODFELLOW. Don't have any opinions. They're bad for business. (*Offstage a cheer. Then a thumping drum and trumpet into "Gimme That Old Time Religion."*)

SINGING. (*Off.*)

Gimme that old time religion,
Gimme that old time religion,
Gimme that old time religion,
It's good enough for me.

It was good enough for father,
It was good enough for father,
It was good enough for father,
And it's good enough for me.

It was good for the Hebrew
children,
It was good for the Hebrew
children,
It was good for the Hebrew
children,

HORNBECK. Sound the trumpet, beat the drum! Everybody's come to town to see your competition, monk. Alive and breathing in the county cooler—a high school-teacher, wild, untamed.

(*Matthew Harrison Brady enters, a benign giant of a man. He basks in the cheers and the excitement, like a patriarch surrounded by his children. He is gray, balding, paunchy, an indeterminate sixty-five. He is followed by Mrs. Brady. The Mayor, running on ahead of Brady, shows him to the platform which Brady and his wife mount. The rest of the Brady party and the townspeople rush on.*)

ALL. (*Singing as they enter.*)

And it's good enough for me.

Gimme that old time religion,
Gimme that old time religion,
Gimme that old time religion,
It's good enough for me.

BROWN.

It is good enough for Brady!

ALL. (*Singing.*)

It is good enough for Brady,
It is good enough for Brady,
And it's good enough for me.

(*Wild cheer and trumpet. Brady and Mrs. Brady stand on the platform. Brady seems to carry with him a built-in spotlight. So Mrs. Brady—pretty, fashionably dressed, a proper "Second Lady" to the nation's "Second Man"—seems always to be in his shadow. This does not annoy her. Sarah Brady is content that all her thoughts and emotions should gain the name of action through her husband. Brady removes his hat and raises his hand. Obediently, the crowd falls to a hushed anticipatory silence.*)

BRADY. Friends—and I can see most of you are my friends, from the way you have decked out your beautiful city of Hillsboro— (*There is a pleased reaction, and a spattering of applause. When Brady speaks, there can be no doubt of his personal magnetism. Even Hornbeck, who slouches contemptuously, is impressed with the speaker's power, for here is a man to be reckoned with.*) Mrs. Brady and I are delighted to be among you! (*Brady takes his wife's hand and draws her to his side, then mops his brow.*) I could only wish one thing: that you had not given us *quite* so warm a welcome! (*Brady removes his alpaca coat. The crowd laughs. Brady beams. Mrs. McClain hands him a frond fan. Brady takes it.*) Bless you. (*He fans himself vigorously.*) My friends of Hillsboro, you know why I have come here. I have not come merely to prosecute a lawbreaker, an arrogant youth who has spoken out against the Revealed Word. I have come because what has happened in a school room of your town has unloosed a wicked attack from the big cities of the North!—an attack upon the law which you have so wisely placed among the statutes of this state. I am here to defend that which is most precious in the hearts of all of us: the Living Truth of the Scriptures! (*Applause and emotional cheering.*)

PHOTOGRAPHER. Mr. Brady. A picture, Mr. Brady?

BRADY. I shall be happy to oblige! Sarah . . .

MRS. BRADY. No, Matt. Just you and the dignitaries.

BRADY. You are the Mayor, are you not, sir?

MAYOR. I am, sir. (*Photographer kneels and focuses on Brady.*)

BRADY. (*Extending his hand.*) My name is Matthew Harrison Brady.

MAYOR. Oh, I know. Everybody knows that. I had a little speech of welcome ready, but somehow it didn't seem necessary.

BRADY. I shall be honored to hear your greeting, sir. (*The Mayor clears his throat and takes his speech from his pocket.*)

MAYOR. Mr. Matthew Harrison Brady, this municipality is proud to have within its city limits the warrior who has always fought for us ordinary people. The lady folks of this town wouldn't have the vote if it wasn't for you fightin' to give 'em all that suffrage. Mr. President Wilson wouldn't never have got to the White House and won the war if it wasn't for you supportin' him. And, in conclusion, the Governor of our state . . . (*His hand is raised.*)

PHOTOGRAPHER. Hold it! (*The camera clicks.*) Thank you. (*Ladies enter with first picnic table. They push their way through the crowd. They are followed by Mrs. Krebs, who is carrying a large bowl of potato salad, which she now places on table. Mrs. Brady is disturbed by the informality of the pose.*)

MRS. BRADY. Matt, you didn't have your coat on.

BRADY. Perhaps we should have a more formal pose. Who is the spiritual leader of the community?

MAYOR. That would be the Reverend Jeremiah Brown.

BROWN. (*Stepping forward.*) Your servant and the Lord's.

BRADY. The Reverend at my left, the Mayor at my right. (*The Reverend mounts platform. Stiffly, they pose.*) We must look grave, gentlemen, but not too serious. Hopeful, I think is the word. We must look hopeful. (*Brady assumes the familiar pose. The camera clicks.*)

PHOTOGRAPHER. (*As the crowd murmurs approval.*) Thank you. (*Ladies now enter with second table. Mrs. Krebs moves to second table and proceeds to prepare a heaping plate of food for Brady.*)

MAYOR. (*Refers to last page of his undelivered speech.*) And in conclusion, the Governor of our state has vested in me the authority to confer upon you a commission as Honorary Colonel in the State Militia. (*Wild cheering and applause as he hands the certificate to Brady.*)

BRADY. (*Savoring it.*) "Colonel Brady." I like the sound of that.

BROWN. We thought you might be hungry, Colonel Brady, after your train ride—

MAYOR. So the members of our Ladies' Aid have prepared a buffet lunch.

BRADY. Splendid, splendid, I could do with a little snack.

BANNISTER. (*An eager beaver.*) You know, Mr. Brady—I mean *Colonel* Brady, all of us here voted for you three times.

BRADY. I trust it was in three separate elections. (*Big laugh from crowd. Tom Davenport, a crisp, businesslike young man, crosses to Brady, offers his hand.*)

DAVENPORT. Sir, I'm Tom Davenport.

BRADY. (*Beaming.*) Of course, Circuit District Attorney. (*Putting his arm around Davenport's shoulder.*) We'll be a team, won't we, young man? Quite a team. (*Spies the picnic tables. The sight of food is a magnetic attraction for Brady.*) Ah, what a handsome repast! What a challenge it is to fit on the old armor again. (*Mrs. Krebs hands him the plate of food. He takes it graciously and starts to add more to the already heaping plate.*) To test the steel of our truth against the blasphemies of science, to stand forth—

MRS. BRADY. Matthew, it's a warm day. Remember the doctor told you not to overeat.

BRADY. (*Adding one more heaping spoonful to his plate.*) Don't worry, Mother, just a bite or two. (*Brady has helped himself to some chicken. Rachel enters with napkins, which she proceeds to arrange on table.*) Who among you knows the defendant? Cates. Is that his name?

DAVENPORT. Well, we all know him, sir.

MAYOR. Just about everybody in Hillsboro knows everybody else.

BRADY. But can someone tell me, is this fellow Cates a criminal by nature?

RACHEL. (*Almost involuntarily.*) Bert isn't a criminal—he's good, really— (*The crowd, which up until now has kept up a steady buzz of conversation, suddenly becomes quiet. All eyes focus on Rachel. Rachel seems to shrink from the attention. She starts out.*)

BRADY. Wait, my child. Is Mr. Cates your friend?

RACHEL. I can't tell you anything about him—

BROWN. (*Fiercely.*) Rachel. (*To Brady.*) My daughter will be pleased to answer any questions about Bertram Cates.

BRADY. Your daughter, Reverend? You must be proud indeed. (*He takes her by the arm.*) Now, how did you come to be acquainted with Mr. Cates?

RACHEL. (*Suffering.*) At school. I'm a schoolteacher too.

BRADY. I'm sure you teach according to the precepts of the Lord.

RACHEL. I try. My pupils are only second graders.

BRADY. Has Mr. Cates ever tried to pollute your mind with his heathen dogma?

RACHEL. Bert isn't a heathen— (*Distraught, she looks from Brady to her father.*)

BRADY. (*Sympathetically.*) I understand your loyalty, my child. This man, the man in your jailhouse, is a fellow schoolteacher. Likeable, no doubt. And you are loath to speak out against him before all these people. (*Brady takes her arm, still carrying his plate. He moves her easily away from the others.*) Think of me as a friend, Rachel. And tell me what troubles you. (*They reach exit and, barely visible to the audience, talk quietly.*)

BANNISTER. Who's gonna be the defense attorney?

DAVENPORT. We don't know yet. It hasn't been announced.

MAYOR. (*Turning to Mrs. Brady at the table.*) Well, whoever he is, he won't have much chance against your husband, will he, Mrs. Brady? (*Crowd laughs.*)

HORNBECK. I disagree.

MAYOR. Who are you?

HORNBECK. E. K. Hornbeck, of the Baltimore *Herald*.

BROWN. (*Can't quite place the name but it has unpleasant connotations.*) Hornbeck? Hornbeck?

HORNBECK. I am a newspaper man, bearing news. When this sovereign state determined to indict the sovereign mind of a less than sovereign schoolteacher, my editor decided there was more than a headline here. The Baltimore *Herald*, therefore, is happy to announce that it is sending *two* representatives to "Heavenly Hillsboro"—the most brilliant journalist in America today— (*Tipping his hat.*) myself. And the most agile legal mind in the world today—Henry Drummond. (*This name is like a whipcrack. Hornbeck moves easily to the picnic tables.*)

MRS. BRADY. (*Stunned.*) Drummond—

BROWN. Henry Drummond, the agnostic?

BANNISTER. I heard about him. He got them two Chicago child-murderers off, just the other day.

BROWN. A vicious, godless man. (*Blithely, Hornbeck, having inspected the food, chooses a drumstick. He waves it jauntily toward the astonished party.*)

HORNBECK. A Merry Christmas and a jolly Fourth of July! (*Munching the drumstick, he gets his suitcase and exits. Brady and Rachel, having left the scene, have missed this significant disclosure. There is a stunned pause.*)

DAVENPORT. (*Genuinely impressed.*) Henry Drummond for the defense. Well.

BROWN. Henry Drummond is an agent of darkness. We won't allow him in this town.

DAVENPORT. I don't know by what law you can keep him out.

MAYOR. I could look it up in the town ordinances.

BROWN. I saw Drummond once. In a courtroom in Ohio. A man was on trial for a most brutal crime. Although he knew and admitted the man was guilty, Drummond was perverting the evidence to turn the guilt away from the accused and on to you and me—and all of society.

MRS. BRADY. Henry Drummond. Oh, dear me. (*Davenport comforts her.*)

BROWN. I can still see him. A slouching hulk of a man, whose head juts out like animals'. You look at his face and you wonder why God made such a man. And then you know God didn't make him. He is a creature of the devil—perhaps even the devil himself. (*Melinda utters a frightened cry.*)

MELINDA. Mama! (*Turns and buries her head in her mother's skirts. Brady and Rachel return to the scene. Rachel has a confused and guilty look. Brady's plate has been scraped clean, only the fossil of the chicken-leg remains. Brady looks around at the ring of faces, which have been disturbed by Brown's description of the heretic Drummond.*)

MRS. BRADY. Matt—they're bringing Henry Drummond for the defense.

BRADY. (*Pale.*) Drummond— (*The townspeople are impressed by the impact of this name on Brady.*) Henry Drummond—!

BROWN. We won't allow him in town.

MAYOR. I think maybe the Board of Health—

BRADY. No! I believe we should welcome Henry Drummond. (*Astonished reaction from the crowd.*)

MAYOR. Welcome him?

BRADY. If the enemy sends its Goliath into battle, it magnifies our cause. Henry Drummond has stalked the courtrooms of this land for forty years. Where he fights, headlines follow. The whole world will be watching our victory over Drummond. If St. George had slain a dragonfly, who would remember him? (*Cheers and pleased reaction from the crowd. Mrs. Blair steps to Mr. Brady and offers him a plate.*)

MRS. BLAIR. Would you care to finish up the pickled apricots, Mr. Brady?

BRADY. (*Taking plate.*) It would be a pity to see them go to waste.

MRS. BRADY. Matt, do you think—?

BRADY. Have to build up my strength, Mother, for the battle ahead. (*Brady munches thoughtfully.*) Now what will Drummond do? He'll make us forget the lawbreaker and put the law on trial. But we'll have the answer for Mr. Drummond, right here in some of the things this sweet young lady has told me.

RACHEL. But, Mr. Brady, I—

BRADY. A fine girl, Reverend, a fine girl.

BROWN. Rachel has always been taught to do the righteous thing.

BRADY. I'm sure she has— (*Melinda brings him a paper cup of lemonade, curtsies.*) Thank you. A toast then, a toast to tomorrow. (*Rachel unseen moves off.*) To the beginning of the trial and the success of our cause. A toast, in good American lemonade. (*Brady downs his drink. The crowd cheers and applauds.*)

MRS. BRADY. Mr. Mayor, it's time now for Mr. Brady's nap. He always likes to nap after a meal.

MAYOR. We have a suite ready at the Mansion House. I think you'll find your bags already there.

BRADY. Very thoughtful, considerate of you.

MAYOR. If you'll come with me—it's only across the square. . . .

BRADY. Oh, and I want to thank all the members of the Ladies Aid for preparing this nice little picnic repast.

MRS. KREBS. It was our pleasure, sir.

BRADY. And if I just seemed to pick at my food, I didn't want you to think I didn't enjoy it. But you see, we had a box lunch on the train.

ALL. (*Singing as they exit.*)
It is good enough for Brady,
It is good enough for Brady,
It is good enough for Brady,
And it's good enough for me.

Gimme that old time religion,
Gimme that old time religion,
Gimme that old time religion,
It's good enough for me.

(*As the stage clears, the singing fades out. The lights go down slowly on the town set. Lights come up. Again we see a portion of the courthouse. Hornbeck enters. He looks around, tries a perch on the window ledge. Rachel enters. Distressed, she doesn't notice Hornbeck.*)

RACHEL. (*Calling out.*) Mr. Meeker? Mr. Meeker . . . (*She calls down toward the jail.*) Bert, can you hear me? Bert, you've got to tell me what to do! I don't know what to do— (*She turns and sees Hornbeck.*)

HORNBECK. I give advice at remarkably low hourly rates. Ten per cent off to unmarried young ladies, special discounts to the clergy and their daughters.

RACHEL. What are you doing here?

HORNBECK. I'm inspecting the battlefield—the night before the battle. Before it's cluttered with the debris of journalistic camp-followers. (*She starts off.*) Tell me—why do you want to see Bert Cates? What's he to you, or you to him? Can it be that both beauty and biology are on our side? (*She starts off again.*) Wait. (*She stops.*) There's a piece from my newspaper, perhaps you might like to see it. Just arrived from that wicked modern Sodom and Gomorrah—Baltimore. (*Fishing a folded sheet of newspaper out of his pocket, he offers it to her. He pulls out an apple and polishes it on his sleeve.*) Not the entire edition, of course. No Happy Hooligan, Barney Google, Abe Kabibble; merely the part worth reading—E. K. Hornbeck's brilliant little symphony of words. You should read it. (*Rachel starts to read.*) My typewriter's been singing a sweet, sad song about the Hillsboro heretic, B. Cates, boy-Socrates. Latter-day Dreyfus. Romeo with a biology book. I may be rancid butter, but I'm on your side of the bread.

RACHEL. (*Looking up, surprised.*) This sounds as if you're a friend of Bert's.

HORNBECK. As much as a critic can be a friend to anyone. (*Watching her read, he takes another bite out of his apple, then offers it to her.*) Have a bite? (*Rachel shakes her head.*) Don't worry. I'm not the serpent, little Eva. This isn't from the Tree of Knowledge. You won't find any in the orchards of Heavenly Hillsboro. Birches, beeches, butternuts. A few ignorance bushes. No Tree of Knowledge.

RACHEL. Will this be reprinted here?

HORNBECK. In the "Weekly Bugle"? Or whatever they call the leaden stuff they blow through the local linotypes. I doubt it.

RACHEL. It would help Bert if people here could read this. (*She appraises Hornbeck, puzzled. He takes a bite out of his apple.*) You don't seem like the kind of person who'd write an article like this. You seem so—

HORNBECK. Cynical? That's my fascination. I do hateful things, for which people love me, and loveable things for which they hate me. I am the friend of enemies, the enemy of friends. I am admired for my detestability. I am both Poles and the Equator, with no Temperate Zones in between.

RACHEL. You make it sound as if Bert is a hero. I'd like to think that, but I can't. A schoolteacher is a public servant: I think he should do what the law and the school board want him to. If the superintendent comes to me and says, "Miss Brown, you're to teach from Whitley's Second Reader," I don't feel I have to give him an argument.

HORNBECK. Ever give your pupils a snap quiz on existence?

RACHEL. What?

HORNBECK. Where we are, where we came from, where we're going?

RACHEL. All the answers to those questions are in the Bible.

HORNBECK. (*With a genuine incredulity.*) *All?!* You feed the youth of Hillsboro from the little truck-garden of your mind?

RACHEL. I think there must be something wrong in what Bert believes, if a great man like Mr. Brady comes here to speak out against him.

HORNBECK. Matthew Harrison Brady came here to find himself a stump to shout from. That's all.

RACHEL. You couldn't understand. Mr. Brady is the champion of ordinary people, like us.

HORNBECK. Wake up, Sleeping Beauty. The ordinary people played a dirty trick on Colonel Brady. They ceased to exist. Time was when Colonel Brady was the hero of the hinterland. Water-boy for the great unwashed. But they've got inside plumbing in their heads these days. There's a highway through the backwoods now; and the trees of the forest have reluctantly made room for their leafless cousins, the telephone poles. Henry's Lizzie rattles into town, and leaves behind the Yesterday-Messiah—standing in the road alone, in a cloud of flivver dust. The boob has been de-boobed. Colonel Brady's virginal small-towner has been *had* . . . By Marconi. And Montgomery Ward. You sure you don't want a bite? Awful good.

(*Hornbeck strolls out of the courtroom and onto the town square; the lights dissolve. Rachel goes off into the darkness. The store fronts glow with sunset light. Goodfellow pulls the shade in his store window and locks the door. Mrs. McClain crosses, fanning herself wearily.*)

GOODFELLOW. Gonna be a hot night, Mrs. McClain.

MRS. McCLAIN. I thought we'd get some relief when the sun went down. (*Hornbeck watches as the Organ Grinder comes on idly with his monkey. Melinda enters, attracted by the melody which tinkles in the twilight. She dances to the music, gives the monkey a penny and watches them exit. Melinda is alone, back to the audience. Hornbeck, silent and motionless, watches. The faces of the buildings are now red with the dying moment of sunset. A long, ominous shadow appears across the buildings, cast from a figure approaching offstage. Melinda, awed, watches the shadow cast on the courthouse. Henry Drummond enters, carrying a valise. He is hunched over, head jutting forward, exactly as Brown described him. The red of the sun behind him hits his slouching back, and his face is in shadow. Melinda, backing away from the shadow on the courthouse, bumps into Drummond, turns and looks at Drummond, full in the face.*)

MELINDA. (*Terrified.*) It's the Devil! (*Screaming with fear, Melinda runs off. Hornbeck crosses slowly toward Drummond, and offers his hand.*)

HORNBECK. Hello, Devil. Welcome to Hell. (*Drummond turns, peers at Hornbeck, recognizes him, shakes hands with him. Hornbeck takes his valise. As they start to move, three men come out of the drug store and watch them as they go off. The lights fade slowly.*)

CURTAIN

ACT ONE
Scene 2

The Courthouse. A few days later. The shapes of the buildings are sharply etched in the background, as if Hillsboro itself were on trial. The court is in session, fans are pumping. The humorless judge sits on his bench; he has a nervous habit of flashing an automatic smile after every ruling. Cates sits with Drummond at the counsel table. Brady sits grandly at the prosecution table with Davenport. He fans himself with benign self-assurance. Hornbeck is sitting right of the Judge as if on a window ledge. Rachel, tense, is among the spectators. The Reuters' man sits at the Reporters' table with three other Reporters. Meeker is in his chair. Bannister is on the witness stand. Davenport is examining him.

DAVENPORT. Mr. Bannister, do you attend church regularly?

BANNISTER. Only on Sundays.

DAVENPORT. (*Crossing to his seat at Brady's table.*) That's good enough for the prosecution. Your Honor, we will accept this man as member of the jury. (*Bannister rises and starts toward the jury box.*)

JUDGE. One moment, Mr. Bannister. You're not excused.

BANNISTER. (*A little petulant.*) I wanted that there front seat in the jury box. (*Judge waves him back. Bannister sits in witness chair.*)

DRUMMOND. (*Rising.*) Well, hold your horses, Bannister. You may get it yet!

JUDGE. Mr. Drummond, you may examine the venireman.

DRUMMOND. Thank you, your honor. Mr. Bannister, how come you're so anxious to get that front seat over there?

BANNISTER. Everybody says this is going to be quite a show. (*Spectators laugh.*)

DRUMMOND. I hear the same thing. Ever read anything in a book about Evolution?

BANNISTER. Nope.

DRUMMOND. Or about a fella named Darwin?

BANNISTER. Can't say I have.

DRUMMOND. I'll bet you read your Bible.

BANNISTER. Nope.

DRUMMOND. How come . . . ?

BANNISTER. I can't read.

DRUMMOND. Well, you are fortunate. He'll do. (*Bannister turns toward the Judge, poised.*)

JUDGE. Take your seat, Mr. Bannister. (*Bannister races to the jury box as if shot from a gun, and sits in the front row seat, beaming.*) Mr. Meeker, will you call a venireman to fill the twelfth and last seat on the jury?

BRADY. Your Honor, before we continue, will the court entertain a motion on a matter of procedure?

JUDGE. Will the learned prosecutor state the motion?

MEEKER. Jesse H. Dunlap. You're next, Jesse.

BRADY. It has been called to my attention that the temperature is now 97 degrees Fahrenheit. (*He mops his forehead with a large handkerchief. Dunlap goes to witness stand.*) And it may get hotter! (*There is laughter. Brady basks in the warmth of his popularity.*) I do not feel that the dignity of the court will suffer if we remove a few superfluous outer garments.

JUDGE. Does the defense object to Colonel Brady's motion?

DRUMMOND. (*Askance.*) I don't know if the dignity of the court can be upheld with these galluses I've got on.

JUDGE. Well—we'll take that chance, Mr. Drummond. Those who wish to remove their coats may do so. (*With relief, all except the Judge takes off their coats and loosen their collar buttons. Drummond removes his coat, drapes it over back of his chair—as does Brady. Drummond wears wide, lavender suspenders. The spectators react.*)

BRADY. (*With affable sarcasm.*) Is the counsel for the defense showing us the latest fashion in the great metropolitan city of Chicago?

DRUMMOND. I'm glad you asked me that. I brought these along special. (*He cocks his thumbs in the suspenders.*) It just so happens I bought these galluses at Peabody's General Store in *your* home town, Mr. Brady. Weeping Water, Nebraska. (*Drummond snaps the suspenders jauntily. There is amused reaction at this. Brady is nettled: this is his show, and he wants all the laughs. The Judge pounds for order.*)

JUDGE. Let us proceed with the selection of the final juror. (*Dunlap is a rugged, righteous-looking man.*)

MEEKER. State your name and occupation.

DUNLAP. Jesse H. Dunlap. Farmer and cabinet-maker.

DAVENPORT. Do you believe in the Bible, Mr. Dunlap?

DUNLAP. (*Vigorously, almost shouting.*) I believe in the Holy Word of God. And I believe in Matthew Harrison Brady! (*There is strong applause, and a few scattered "Amens" from spectators.*)

DAVENPORT. This man is acceptable to the prosecution.

JUDGE. Very well. Mr. Drummond?

DRUMMOND. (*Quietly, without rising.*) No questions. Not acceptable.

BRADY. (*Annoyed.*) Does Mr. Drummond refuse this man a place on the jury simply because he believes in the Bible?

DRUMMOND. Well, if you can find an Evolutionist in this town, you can refuse him!

BRADY. Your Honor, I object to the Defense Attorney rejecting a worthy citizen without so much as asking him a question.

DRUMMOND. (*Agreeably.*) All right, I'll ask him a question. (*Saunters over to Dunlap with deliberate slowness.*) How are you?

DUNLAP. Kinda hot.

DRUMMOND. So am I. Excused. (*Dunlap looks at Judge, confused as Drummond crosses back to his table and sits.*)

JUDGE. You are excused from jury duty, Mr. Dunlap. You may step down. (*Meeker waves Dunlap back and he joins the spectators, a little miffed.*)

BRADY. (*Rises, seriously.*) I object to the note of levity which the counsel for the defense is introducing into these proceedings.

JUDGE. The bench agrees with you in spirit, Colonel Brady.

DRUMMOND. (*Rising angrily.*) And *I* object to all this damned "Colonel" talk. I am not familiar with Mr. Brady's military record.

JUDGE. Well—he was made an Honorary Colonel in our state militia. The day he arrived in Hillsboro.

DRUMMOND. The use of this title prejudices the case of my client: it calls up a picture of the prosecution, astride a white horse, ablaze in the uniform of a militia colonel, with all the forces of right and righteousness marshalled behind him.

JUDGE. Well, what are we to do?

DRUMMOND. Break him. Make him a Private. I have no serious objection to the honorary title of "Private Brady." (*There is a buzz of reaction. The Judge gestures for the Mayor to come over for a hurried, whispered conference.*)

MAYOR. Well, we can't take it *back*—! (*There is another whispered exchange. Then the Mayor steps gingerly toward Drummond.*) By—by authority of—well, I'm sure the Governor won't have any objection—I hereby appoint you, Mr. Drummond, a temporary Honorary Colonel in the State Militia.

DRUMMOND. (*Rises, shaking his head, amused.*) Gentlemen, I don't know what to say. It is not often in a man's life that he attains the exalted rank of "Temporary Honorary Colonel."

MAYOR. (*Shaking hands.*) It will be made permanent, of course, pending the arrival of the proper papers over the Governor's signature. (*Meeker leads Sillers to the witness stand.*)

DRUMMOND. (*Looking at the floor.*) I thank you.

JUDGE. Colonel Brady. *Colonel* Drummond. You will examine the venireman.

MEEKER. State your name and occupation.

SILLERS. George Sillers. I work at the feed store.

DAVENPORT. Tell me, sir. Would you call yourself a religious man?

SILLERS. I guess I'm as religious as the next man. (*Brady rises. Davenport immediately steps back, deferring to his superior.*)

BRADY. In Hillsboro, sir, that means a great deal. Tell me, do you have any children, Mr. Sillers?

SILLERS. Not as I know of. (*The crowd titters.*)

BRADY. If you had a son, Mr. Sillers—or a daughter, what would you think if that sweet child came home from school and told you that a Godless teacher—

DRUMMOND. Objection! We're supposed to be choosing jury members! The prosecution's denouncing the defendant before the trial has even begun!

JUDGE. Objection sustained. (*The Judge and Brady exchange meaningless smiles.*)

BRADY. Mr. Sillers. Do you have any personal opinions with regard to the defendant that might prejudice you on his behalf?

SILLERS. Cates? I don't hardly know him. He did buy some peat moss from me once, and paid his bill.

BRADY. Mr. Sillers impresses me as an honest, God-fearing man. I accept him.

JUDGE. Thank you, Colonel Brady. *Colonel* Drummond?

DRUMMOND. Mr. Sillers, I just heard you say that you were a religious man. Tell me something. Do you work at it very hard?

SILLERS. Well, I'm pretty busy down at the feed store. My wife tends to the religion for both of us.

DRUMMOND. In other words, you take care of this life, and your wife takes care of the next one?

DAVENPORT. Objection.

JUDGE. Objection sustained.

DRUMMOND. Tell me, Mr. Sillers, while your wife was tending to the religion, did you ever happen to bump into a fella named Charles Darwin?

SILLERS. Not till recent.

DRUMMOND. Well, from what you've heard about this Darwin, do you think your wife would want to have him over for Sunday dinner? (*Drummond nudges Sillers with his elbow.*)

BRADY. (*Rising.*) Your honor, my worthy opponent seems to me to cluttering the issue with hypothetical questions—

DRUMMOND. I'm doing *your* job, Colonel.

DAVENPORT. (*Leaping up.*) The prosecution is perfectly able to handle its own arguments.

DRUMMOND. Look, I've just established that Mr. Sillers isn't working very hard at religion. Now, for your sake, I want to make sure he isn't working at evolution.

SILLERS. (*Simply.*) I'm just working at the feed store.

DRUMMOND. This man's all right. Take a box seat, Mr. Sillers. (*Sillers starts toward jury bench.*)

BRADY. I am not altogether satisfied that Mr. Sillers will render impartial judgment in this trial—

DRUMMOND. Out of order. The prosecution has already accepted this man.

BRADY. I want a fair trial.

DRUMMOND. So do I!

BRADY. Unless the state of mind of the members of the jury conforms to the laws and patterns of society—

DRUMMOND. Conform! Conform! What do you want to do—run the jury through a meatgrinder, so they all come out the same?

DAVENPORT. (*Rising.*) Your Honor!

BRADY. I've seen what you can do to a jury. Twist and tangle them. Nobody's forgotten the Endicott Publishing case—where you made the jury believe the obscenity was in their minds, not on the printed page. It was immoral what you did to that jury. Tricking them. Judgment by confusion. Think you can get away with that here?

DRUMMOND. All I want is to prevent the clock-stoppers from dumping a load of medieval nonsense into the United States Constitution.

JUDGE. This is not a Federal court.

DRUMMOND. (*Slapping his hand on the table.*) Well, dammit, you've got to stop 'em somewhere. (*The crowd breaks out in disapproval. The Judge beats with his gavel.*)

JUDGE. Gentlemen, if you please, you are *both* out of order. The court rules that the jury has been selected. (*Brady lets his arms fall, and bows with benign acceptance.*) Owing to the lateness of the hour and the unusual heat, the court will be recessed until ten o'clock tomorrow morning. (*Judge raps the gavel, and the court begins to break up. Then the Judge notices a slip of paper, and raps for order again.*) Oh. The Reverend Brown has asked me to announce that there will be a prayer meeting tonight on the courthouse lawn, to pray for justice and guidance. You are all invited.

DRUMMOND. Your Honor. I object to this commercial announcement.

JUDGE. Commercial announcement?

DRUMMOND. For Reverend Brown's product. Why don't you announce that there will be an Evolutionist Meeting?

JUDGE. I have no knowledge of such a meeting.

DRUMMOND. That's understandable. It's bad enough that everybody going into the courthouse has to walk underneath a banner that says "Read your Bible." Your Honor, I want that sign taken down. Or else I want another one put up. Just as big, just as big letters—saying, "Read your Darwin."

JUDGE. (*Furiously.*) Colonel Drummond, you are out of order. The court stands recessed. (*The Judge bangs his gavel, and fuming, exits. With the Judge's exit, the formality of the courtroom is relaxed. There is a feeling of relief as spectators and jurors adjust their sticky clothes, and start to move off, talking excitedly. The jurors leave. Spectators move out, talking loudly. Mayor rushes to Brady to help him on with his coat.*)

MAYOR. Let me help you with your coat, Colonel Brady.

BRADY. Thank you, Mayor.

MAYOR. Exciting day, sir.

DAVENPORT. I felt by and large it went well, don't you, Colonel?

BRADY. Fine, fine. Nothing to worry about. (*Hornbeck wanders off.*)

REUTERS' REPORTER. Who'll be your first witness tomorrow, Colonel?

BRADY. You'll see.

MRS. BLAIR. Would you autograph my fan, Mr. Brady?

BRADY. Mrs. Brady has autograph cards.

DUNLAP. Bless you, Mr. Brady, for what you're doing.

BROWN. You're coming to us for supper tonight, Colonel, in the Sunday School room, and afterwards, naturally, we'll expect you at our prayer meeting.

BRADY. Yes. Fine, excellent.

MRS. BRADY. They sent over some mail from the Mansion House. These letters will gladden your heart, Matt. (*Brady and his wife exit. Brown turns to Rachel who has lagged behind waiting for a chance to talk to Cates.*)

BROWN. Rachel!

RACHEL. (*Not moving.*) Yes, Father. (*Brown exits.*)

MAYOR. (*To Davenport.*) I don't know if it's legal what I did about the "Colonel" business.

DAVENPORT. Don't worry. You won't get hit by a thunderbolt.

MAYOR. Sometimes I don't know—I just don't know.

(*Noise of crowd exiting now fades out completely. In marked contrast to the adulation that has surrounded Brady, nobody even comes near Drummond. He packs his brief in a tattered leather case. Rachel moves toward Bert. They stand face to face wordlessly. Both seem to wish the whole painful turmoil over. Suddenly Rachel darts to Drummond.*)

RACHEL. Mr. Drummond. You've got to call the whole thing off. It's not too late. Bert knows he did wrong. He didn't mean to. And he's sorry. Now why can't he just stand up and say to everybody: "I did wrong. I broke a law. I admit it. I won't do it again." Then they'd stop all this fuss, and—everything would be like it was. (*Drummond looks at Rachel, not unkindly.*)

DRUMMOND. Who are you?

RACHEL. I'm—a friend of Bert's.

DRUMMOND. How about it, boy? Getting cold feet?

CATES. I never thought it would be like this. Like Barnum and Bailey coming to town.

DRUMMOND. We can call it off. You want to quit?

RACHEL. Yes!

CATES. People look at me as if I was a murderer. Worse than a murderer! That fella from Minnesota who killed his wife—remember, Rache?—half the town turned out to watch 'em put him on the train. They just stared at him as if he was a curiosity—not like they *hated* him! Not like he'd done anything really wrong! Just different!

DRUMMOND. There's nothing very original about murdering your wife.

CATES. People I thought were my friends look at me now as if I had horns growing out of my head.

DRUMMOND. You murder a wife, it isn't nearly as bad as murdering an old wives' tale. Kill one of their fairy-tale notions, and they call down the wrath of God, Brady, and the state legislature.

RACHEL. You make a joke out of everything. You seem to think it's all so funny!

DRUMMOND. Lady, when you lose your power to laugh, you lose your power to think straight.

CATES. Mr. Drummond, I can't laugh. I'm scared.

DRUMMOND. Good. You'd be a damned fool if you weren't.

RACHEL. (*Bitterly.*) You're supposed to be helping Bert, and every time you swear you make it worse for him.

DRUMMOND. (*Honestly.*) I'm sorry if I offend you. But I don't swear just for the hell of it. You see, I figure that language is a poor enough means of communication as it is. So we ought to use all the words we've got. Besides, there are damned few words that everybody understands.

RACHEL. You don't care anything about Bert! You just want a chance to make speeches against the Bible!

DRUMMOND. I care a great deal about Bert. I care a great deal about what Bert thinks.

RACHEL. Well, I care about what the people in this town think about *him.*

DRUMMOND. Can you buy back his respectability by making him a coward? (*He spades his hands in his hip pockets.*) I understand what Bert's going through. It's the loneliest feeling in the world—to find yourself standing up when everybody else is sitting down. To have everybody look at you and say, "What's the matter with him?" I know. I know what it feels like. Walking down an empty street, listening to the sound of your own footsteps. Shutters closed, blinds drawn, doors locked against you. And you aren't sure whether you're walking toward something—or just walking away. . . . (*He takes a deep breath, then turns abruptly.*) Cates, I'll change your plea and we'll call off the whole business—on one condition. If you honestly believe that you committed a criminal act against the citizens of this state and the minds of their children. If you honestly believe that you're wrong and the law's right. Then the hell with it. I'll pack my grip and go back to Chicago, where it's a cool hundred in the shade.

RACHEL. Bert knows he's wrong! Don't you, Bert?

DRUMMOND. Don't prompt the witness.

CATES. What do you think, Mr. Drummond?

DRUMMOND. I'm here. That tells you what I think. Well, what's the verdict, Bert? You want to find yourself guilty before the jury does?

CATES. (*Quietly, with determination.*) No, sir. I'm not gonna quit.

RACHEL. (*Protesting.*) Bert—!

CATES. It wouldn't do any good now, anyhow. If you'll stick by me, Rache—well, we can fight it out! (*Rachel shakes her head, bewildered, tears forming in her eyes.*)

RACHEL. I don't know what to do; I don't know what to do—!

CATES. (*Half kneeling beside her.*) What's the matter, Rache?

RACHEL. I don't want to do it, Bert; but Mr. Brady says—I—

DRUMMOND. What does Mr. Brady say?

RACHEL. They want me to testify against Bert!

CATES. (*Stunned.*) You can't—!

MEEKER. Bert, I don't mean to hurry you; but we hafta close up the shop. (*Cates is genuinely panicked.*)

CATES. Rache, some of the things I've talked to you about are things you just say to your own heart. If you get up on the stand and say those things out loud—

Don't you understand? The words I've said to you—softly, in the dark—just trying to figure out what the stars are for—or what might be on the back side of the moon!—don't—

MEEKER. Bert—

CATES. They were just questions, Rache: I was just asking questions! If you repeat those things on the witness stand, Brady'll make 'em sound like answers. And they'll crucify me! (*Meeker touches Bert's arm. Bert pulls away and almost runs off.*)

DRUMMOND. What's your name? Rachel what?

RACHEL. Rachel Brown. Can they make me testify?

DRUMMOND. I'm afraid so. It would be nice if nobody ever had to *make* anybody do anything. But—Don't let Brady scare you. He only *seems* to be bigger than the law.

RACHEL. It's not Mr. Brady. It's my father.

DRUMMOND. Who's your father?

RACHEL. The Reverend Jeremiah Brown. (*Drummond whistles softly through his teeth.*) I remember feeling this way when I was a little girl. I used to wake up at night, terrified of the dark. I'd think sometimes that my bed was on the ceiling, and the whole house was upside down; and if I didn't hang onto the mattress, I might fall outward into the stars. (*She shivers a little, remembering.*) I wanted to run to my father, and have him tell me I was safe, that everything was all right. But I was always more frightened of him than I was of falling. It's the same way now.

DRUMMOND. (*Softly.*) Is your mother dead?

RACHEL. I never knew my mother. (*Distraught.*) Is it true? Is Bert wicked?

DRUMMOND. Bert Cates is a good man. Maybe even a great one. And it takes strength for a woman to love such a man. Especially when he's a pariah in the community.

RACHEL. I'm only confusing him. And he's confused enough as it is.

DRUMMOND. The man who has everything figured out is probably a fool. College examinations notwithstanding, it takes a very smart fella to say "I don't know the answer!" (*Drummond puts on his hat, touches the brim of it as a gesture of good-bye, and goes slowly off.*)

CURTAIN

Paul Muni in *Inherit the Wind,* New York, 1955. Gift of Edward A. Wright. Jerome Lawrence and Robert E. Lee Collection, Lawrence and Lee Theatre Research Institute, The Ohio State University.

Melvyn Douglas in *Inherit the Wind*, touring production, Shubert Theatre, Detroit, 1956. Program files, Lawrence and Lee Theatre Research Institute, The Ohio State University.

ACT TWO

SCENE 1

The courthouse lawn. The same night. The oppressive heat of the day has softened into a pleasant summer evening.

Sillers and Dunlap, in work-clothes, are hammering at the makeshift platform, getting it ready for the prayer meeting. Sillers glances up at the "Read Your Bible" banner.

SILLERS. What're we gonna do about this sign?

DUNLAP. The Devil don't run this town. Leave it up. (*Brady enters, followed by four reporters. Hornbeck brings up the rear, he alone is not bothering to take notes. Apparently this informal press conference has been in progress for some time, and Brady is now bringing it to a climax.*)

BRADY. —and I hope that you will tell the readers of your newspapers that here in Hillsboro we are fighting the fight of the Faithful throughout the world! (*All write. Brady eyes Hornbeck, leaning lazily, not writing.*)

REUTERS' MAN. (*British accent.*) A question, Mr. Brady.

BRADY. Certainly. Where are you from, young man?

REPORTER. London, sir. Reuters News Agency. (*The sound of people humming softly the hymn, "Revive Us Again."*)

BRADY. Excellent. I have many friends in the United Kingdom.

REUTERS' MAN. What is your personal opinion of Henry Drummond?

BRADY. I'm glad you asked me that. I want people everywhere to know I bear no personal animosity toward Henry Drummond. There was a time when we were on the same side of the fence. He gave me active support in my campaign of 1908—and I welcomed it. (*Almost impassioned, speaking at writing tempo, so all the reporters can get it down.*) But I say that if my own *brother* challenged the faith of millions, as Mr. Drummond is doing, I would oppose him still. (*Dunlap pounds.*) I think that's all for this evening, gentlemen. (*The reporters move away in a knot of discussion. Brady crosses to Hornbeck.*) Mr. Hornbeck, my clipping service has sent me some of your dispatches. (*Humming quietly, the townspeople continue to gather.*)

HORNBECK. How flattering to know I'm being clipped.

BRADY. It grieves me to read reporting that is so—biased.

HORNBECK. I'm no reporter, Colonel. I'm a critic. (*Rev. Brown and Mrs. Brady enter slowly.*)

BRADY. I hope you will stay for Reverend Brown's prayer meeting. It may bring you some enlightenment.

HORNBECK. It may. I'm here on a press pass, and I don't intend to miss any part of the show.

BRADY. Good evening, Reverend. How are you, Mother?

MRS. BRADY. The Reverend Brown was good enough to escort me.

BRADY. Reverend, I'm looking forward to your prayer meeting.

BROWN. You will find our people are fervent in their belief.

MRS. BRADY. I know it's warm, Matt; but these night breezes can be treacherous. And you know how you perspire. (*She takes a small kerchief out of her handbag and tucks it around his neck. He laughs a little.*)

BRADY. Mother is always so worried about my throat.

BROWN. (*Consulting his watch.*) I always like to begin my meetings at the time announced.

BRADY. Most commendable. Proceed, Reverend. After you. (*Brown mounts the few steps to the platform. Brady follows him, loving the feel of the board beneath his feet. This is the squared circle where he has fought so many bouts with the English language, and won. The townspeople, still humming, take their places for the prayer meeting. The prayer meeting is motion picture, radio, and tent show to these people. To them, the Reverend Brown is a combination Milton Sills and Douglas Fairbanks. He grasps the railing and stares down at them sternly. Brady is benign. He sits with his legs crossed, an arm crooked over one corner of his chair. Brown is milking the expectant pause. Just as he is ready to speak, Drummond comes in and stands at the fringe of the crowd. Brown glowers at Drummond. The crowd is still humming.*)

BROWN. Brothers and sisters, I come to you on the Wings of the Word. The Wings of the Word are beating loud in the treetops! The Lord's Word is howling in the Wind, and flashing in the belly of the Cloud!

MRS. KREBS. I hear it!

ELIJAH. I see it, Reverend!

BROWN. And we *believe* the Word!

ALL. We believe!

BROWN. We believe in the Glory of the Word!

ALL. Glory, Glory! Amen, amen! (*Rachel enters. The townspeople have heard the Reverend tell this story countless times, and they love it. They have familiar responses, which they make—with minor variations—at each telling. The prayer meeting builds as if it were a concerto—with Brown's narration providing the solo melody, and the answers of the townspeople forming a well-orchestrated counterpoint. The tone at the beginning is subdued, almost pastoral, but the voices and faces contain the seed of the frenzy which will burst forth later on.*)

BROWN. Hearken to the Word! (*He lowers his voice.*) The Word tells us that the World was created in Seven Days.

ALL. Amen.

BROWN. In the beginning, the earth was without form, and void. And the Lord said, "Let there be light!" And there *was* light!

ALL. Praise the Lord! (*The humming now stops completely.*)

BROWN. And the Lord saw the Light and the Light saw the Lord, and the Light said, "Am I good, Lord?" and the Lord said, "Thou art good!"

ELIJAH. (*Deep-voiced, singing.*) And the evening and the morning were the first day!

VOICES. Amen, amen!

BROWN. (*Calling out.*) The Lord said, "Let there be Firmament!" And even as He spoke, it was so! And the Firmament bowed down before Him and said, "Am I good, Lord?" And the Lord said, "Thou art good!"

ELIJAH. (*Singing.*) And the evening and the morning were the second day!

VOICES. Amen, amen!

BROWN. (*With mounting tempo.*) On the Third Day brought He forth the Dry Land, and the Grass, and the Fruit Tree! And on the Fourth Day made He the Sun, the Moon, and the Stars—and He pronounced them Good!

VOICES. Amen.

BROWN. On the Fifth Day He peopled the sea with fish. And the air with fowl. And made He great whales.

MRS. LOOMIS. Hallelujah!

BROWN. And He blessed them all. (*Pauses, then gravely.*) But on the morning of the Sixth Day, the Lord rose, and His eye was dark, and a scowl lay across His face. (*Shouts.*) Why?

ALL. Why?

BROWN. Why was the Lord troubled?

ALL. Why? Tell us why! Tell us the troubles of the Lord!

BROWN. (*Dropping his voice almost to a whisper.*) He looked about Him, did the Lord; at all His handiwork, bowed down before Him. And He said, "It is not good—

ALL. (*Moan.*) Oh.

BROWN. It is not enough—

ALL. (*Moan.*) Oh.

BROWN. It is not finished.

ALL. (*Moan.*) Oh, Lord!

BROWN. I . . . shall . . . make . . . Me . . . a . . . *Man*!" (*The crowd bursts out into an orgy of hosannahs and waving arms.*)

ALL. Glory! Hosannah! Bless the Lord who created us!

MRS. KREBS. (*Throwing herself to the ground. Shouting out.*) Bow down! Bow down before the Lord!

ELIJAH. Are we good, Lord? Tell us! Are we good?

BROWN. (*Answering triumphantly.*) The Lord said, "Yea, thou art good! For I have created ye in My Image, after My Likeness! Be fruitful, and multiply, and replenish the Earth, and subdue it!"

ELIJAH. (*Deep-voiced, singing.*) The Lord made Man master of the Earth . . . !

ALL. Glory, glory! Bless the Lord!

BROWN. (*Whipping 'em up.*) Do we believe?

ALL. (*In chorus.*) Yes!

BROWN. Do we believe the Word?

ALL. (*Coming back like a whip-crack.*) Yes!

BROWN. Do we believe the Truth of the Word?

ALL. Yes!

BROWN. (*Pointing a finger toward the jail.*) Do we curse the man who denies the Word?

ALL. (*Crescendo, each answer mightier than the one before.*) Yes!

BROWN. Do we cast out this sinner in our midst?

ALL. Yes! (*Each crash of sound from the crowd seems to strike Rachel physically, and shake her. The prayer meeting has passed beyond the familiar bounds into an area of orgiastic anger.*)

BROWN. Do we call down hellfire on the man who has sinned against the Word?

ALL. (*Roaring.*) Yes!

BROWN. (*Deliberately shattering the rhythm, to go into a frenzied prayer, hands clasped together and lifted heavenward.*) O Lord of the Tempest and the Thunder! O Lord of Righteousness and Wrath! We pray that Thou wilt make a sign unto us! Strike down this sinner, as Thou didst Thine enemies of old, in the days of the Pharaohs! (*All lean forward, almost expecting the heavens to open with a thunderbolt. Rachel is white. Brady shifts uncomfortably in his chair, this is pretty strong stuff, even for him.*) Let him feel the terror of Thy sword! For all eternity, let his soul writhe in anguish and damnation—

RACHEL. *No!* (*She rushes to the platform.*) No, Father. Don't pray to destroy Bert! (*As she falls to her knees in front of platform.*) No, no, no . . . !

BROWN. Lord, we call down the same curse on those who ask grace for this sinner—though they be blood of my blood and flesh of my flesh! (*The townspeople are shocked. Some bow their heads, some turn away, unable to watch.*)

BRADY. (*Rising, grasping Brown's arm.*) Reverend Brown, I know it is the great zeal of your faith which makes you utter this prayer! But it is possible to be overzealous, to destroy that which you hope to save—so that nothing is left but emptiness. (*Brown turns.*) Remember the wisdom of Solomon in the Book of Proverbs—(*Softly.*) "He that troubleth his own house . . . shall inherit the wind." (*He makes a gesture with his open hand to indicate nothingness: the empty air, the brief and unremembered wind. Brady leads Brown to chair on platform and sits him down. Brown seems dazed, shaken. Benignly, Brady turns to the townspeople.*) The Bible also tells us that God forgives His children. And we, the Children of God, should forgive each other. (*Rachel slips off.*) My good friends, return to your homes. The blessings of the Lord be with you all. (*Slowly the townspeople move off, singing and humming "Go, Tell It On the*

Mountain." As the crowd starts to move off, there are murmurs of "Thank you, Colonel Brady." When the crowd has almost cleared, Rev. Brown steps off platform to Mrs. Brady. Brady joins them in front of platform and motions them off. Brady and Drummond are left alone on stage.) We were good friends once. I was always glad of your support. What happened between us? There used to be a mutuality of understanding and admiration. Why is it, my old friend, that you have moved so far away from me?

DRUMMOND. All motion is relative. Perhaps it is *you* who have moved away—by standing still. (*The words have a sharp impact on Brady. For a moment, he stands still, his mouth open, staring at Drummond. Then he takes two faltering steps backward, then moves off. Drummond stands alone. Slowly the lights fade on the silent man. The curtain falls momentarily.*)

CURTAIN

ACT TWO
SCENE 2

The courthouse, two days later. It is bright midday, and the trial is in full swing. The Judge is on the bench, the jury, lawyers, officials and spectators crowd the courtroom. Howard, the thirteen-year-old boy, is on the witness stand. He is wretched in a starched collar and Sunday suit. The weather is as relentlessly hot as before. Brady is examining the boy, who is a witness for the prosecution.

BRADY. Go on, Howard. Tell them what else Mr. Cates told you in the classroom.

HOWARD. Well, he said at first the earth was too hot for any life. Then it cooled off a mite, and cells and things begun to live.

BRADY. Cells?

HOWARD. Little bugs like, in the water. After that, the little bugs got to be bigger bugs, and sprouted legs and crawled up on the land.

BRADY. How long did this take, according to Mr. Cates?

HOWARD. Couple million years. Maybe longer. Then comes the fishes and the reptiles and the mammals. Man's a mammal.

BRADY. Along with the dogs and the cattle in the field: did he say that?

HOWARD. Yes, sir. (*Drummond is about to protest against prompting the witness, then he decides it isn't worth the trouble.*)

BRADY. Now, Howard, how did *man* come out of this slimy mess of bugs and serpents, according to your—"Professor"?

HOWARD. Man was sort of evoluted. From the "Old World Monkeys." (*Brady slaps his thigh.*)

BRADY. (*To Jury.*) Did you hear that, my friends? "Old World Monkeys"! According to Mr. Cates, you and I aren't even descended from good American monkeys! (*There is laughter from spectators. Brady turns back to Howard.*) Howard, listen carefully. In all this talk of bugs and "Evil-ution," of slime and ooze, did Mr. Cates ever make any reference to God?

HOWARD. Not as I remember.

BRADY. Or the miracle He achieved in seven days as described in the beautiful Book of Genesis?

HOWARD. No, sir. (*Brady stretches out his arms in an all-embracing gesture.*)

BRADY. Ladies and gentlemen—

DRUMMOND. Objection! (*Rising.*) I ask that the court remind the learned counsel that this is not a Chautauqua tent. He is supposed to be submitting evidence to a jury. There are no ladies on the jury.

BRADY. Your Honor, I have no intention of making a speech. There is no need. I am sure that everyone on the jury, everyone within the sound of this boy's voice, is moved by his tragic confusion. He has been taught that he wriggled up like an animal from the filth and muck below! (*Continuing fervently, the spirit is upon him.*) I say that these Bible-haters, these "Evil-utionists," are brewers of poison! And the legislature of this sovereign state has had the wisdom to demand that the peddlers of poison—in bottles—(*Turns and points at Cates.*) or in books—clearly label the products they attempt to sell! (*There is applause from the spectators. Howard gulps. Brady points at the boy.*) I tell you, if this law is not upheld, this boy will become one of a generation, shorn of its faith by the teachings of Godless science! But if the full penalty of the law is meted out to Bertram Cates, the faithful the whole world over, who are watching us here, and listen to our every word, will call this courtroom blessed! (*Applause from the spectators. Even one of the jury members is moved to applaud, but is stopped by his neighbors. Dramatically, Brady moves to his chair. Condescendingly, he waves to Drummond.*) Your witness, sir. (*Brady sits. Drummond rises, slouches toward the witness chair.*)

DRUMMOND. Well, I sure am glad Colonel Brady didn't make a speech! (*Nobody laughs. The courtroom seems to resent Drummond's gentle ridicule of the orator. To many, there is an effrontery in Drummond's very voice—folksy and relaxed. It's rather like a harmonica following a symphony concert.*) Howard, I hear you say that the world used to be pretty hot.

HOWARD. That's what Mr. Cates said.

DRUMMOND. You figure it was any hotter then than it is right now?

HOWARD. Guess it musta been. Mr. Cates read to us from a book.

DRUMMOND. Do you know what book?

HOWARD. I guess that Mr. Darwin thought it up.

DRUMMOND. (*Leaning on the arm of the boy's chair.*) You figure anything's wrong about that, Howard?

HOWARD. Well, I dunno—

DAVENPORT. (*Leaping up, crisply.*) Objection, Your Honor. The defense is asking that a thirteen-year-old boy hand down an opinion on a question of morality!

DRUMMOND. (*To the Judge.*) I am trying to establish, Your Honor, that Howard—or Colonel Brady—or Charles Darwin—or anyone in this courtroom—or *you*, sir—has the right to *think*!

JUDGE. Colonel Drummond, the right to think is not on trial here.

DRUMMOND. (*Energetically.*) With all respect to the bench, I hold that the right to think is very much on trial! It is fearfully in danger in the proceedings of this court!

BRADY. A *man* is on trial!

DRUMMOND. A thinking man! And he is threatened with fine and imprisonment because he chooses to speak what he thinks.

JUDGE. Colonel Drummond, would you please rephrase your question.

DRUMMOND. Let's put it this way, Howard. All this fuss and feathers about Evolution, do you think it hurt you any?

HOWARD. Sir?

DRUMMOND. Did it do you any harm? You still feel reasonably fit? What Mr. Cates told you, did it hurt your baseball game any? Affect your pitching arm? (*He punches Howard's right arm playfully.*)

HOWARD. No, sir. I'm a leftie.

DRUMMOND. A southpaw, eh? Still honor your father and mother?

HOWARD. Sure.

DRUMMOND. Haven't murdered anybody since breakfast?

DAVENPORT. Objection.

JUDGE. Objection sustained. (*Drummond shrugs.*)

BRADY. Ask him if his Holy Faith in the scriptures has been shattered—

DRUMMOND. When I need your *valuable* help, Colonel, you may rest assured I shall humbly ask for it. Howard, do you believe everything Mr. Cates told you?

HOWARD. (*Frowning.*) I'm not sure. I gotta think it over.

DRUMMOND. Good for you. Your pa's a farmer, isn't he?

HOWARD. Yes, sir.

DRUMMOND. Got a tractor?

HOWARD. Brand new one.

DRUMMOND. You figure a tractor's sinful, because it isn't mentioned in the Bible?

HOWARD. (*Thinking.*) Don't know.

DRUMMOND. Moses never made a phone call. Suppose that makes the telephone an instrument of the Devil?

HOWARD. I never thought of it that way.

BRADY. (*Rising, booming.*) Neither did anybody else! Your Honor, the defense makes the same old error of all Godless men! They confuse material things with the great spiritual realities of the Revealed Word! (*Turning to Drummond.*) Why do you bewilder this child? Does Right have no meaning to you, sir? (*Brady's hands are outstretched, palms upward, pleading. Drummond stares at Brady long and thoughtfully.*)

DRUMMOND. (*In a low voice.*) Realizing that I may prejudice the case of my client, I must say that "Right" has no meaning to me whatsoever! (*There is a buzz of reaction in the courtroom.*) *Truth* has meaning—as a direction. But one of the peculiar imbecilities of our time is the grid of morality we have placed on human behavior: so that every act of man must be measured against an arbitrary latitude of right and longitude of wrong—in exact minutes, seconds, and degrees! (*He turns to Howard.*) Do you have any idea what I'm talking about, Howard?

HOWARD. No, sir.

DRUMMOND. Well, maybe you will. Some day. Thank you, son. That's all. (*Pleasantly Drummond musses the boy's hair, then crosses back to his chair and sits.*)

JUDGE. The witness is excused. (*He raps his gavel, but Howard remains in the chair, staring goop-eyed at his newly-found idol. There is a low murmur of mixed amusement and indignation.*) We won't need you any more, Howard: you can go back to your pa now. (*Two raps from the Judge's gavel bring Howard back to reality. He rises, runs to his seat—pausing to grin at Drummond, who smiles back.*) Next witness.

DAVENPORT. Will Miss Rachel Brown come forward, please? (*Rachel rises unsteadily and crosses to witness stand. She moves quickly, as if wanting to get the whole thing over with. She looks at no one. Cates watches her with a hopeless expression:* Et tu, Brute. *Meeker swears her in perfunctorily. She sits.*)

BRADY. Miss Brown. You are a teacher at the Hillsboro Consolidated School?

RACHEL. (*Flat.*) Yes.

BRADY. (*Indicating Cates.*) So you have had ample opportunity to know the defendant, Mr. Cates, professionally?

RACHEL. Yes.

BRADY. (*With exaggerated gentleness.*) Is Mr. Cates a member of the spiritual community to which you belong?

DRUMMOND. (*Rises.*) Objection! I don't understand this chatter about "spiritual communities." If the prosecution wants to know if they go to the same church, why doesn't he ask that?

JUDGE. Uh—objection overruled. (*Drummond slouches, disgruntled. Cates stares at Rachel disbelievingly, while her eyes remain on the floor. The exchange between Drummond and the Judge seems to have unnerved her, however.*) You will answer the question, please.

RACHEL. (*Confused.*) I did answer it, didn't I? What was the question?

BRADY. Do you and Mr. Cates attend the same church? (*There are satisfied chuckles from the townspeople at this minor magnanimity.*)

RACHEL. Not any more. Bert dropped out two summers ago.

BRADY. Why?

RACHEL. It was what happened with the little Stebbins boy.

BRADY. Would you tell us about that, please?

RACHEL. The boy was eleven years old, and he went swimming in the river, and got a cramp, and drowned. Bert felt awful about it. He lived right next door, and Tommy Stebbins used to come over to the boarding house and look through Bert's microscope. Bert said the boy had a quick mind, and he might even be a scientist when he grew up. At the funeral, Pa preached that Tommy didn't die in a state of grace, because his folks had never had him baptized— (*Cates, who has been smoldering through this recitation, suddenly leaps angrily to his feet.*)

CATES. Tell 'em what your father really said! That Tommy's soul was damned, writhing in hellfire!

DUNLAP. (*Jumping up and shaking a fist at Cates.*) Cates, you sinner! (*The Judge raps for order. Finney jumps up, holds Dunlap back. The spectators are vehement in their disapproval of Cates. But the scientists—Aaronson, Keller, and Page—sit in quiet embarrassment. There is confusion in the courtroom.*)

CATES. Religion's supposed to comfort people, isn't it? Not frighten them to death!

JUDGE. (*Pounding gavel loudly.*) We will have order, please! (*The commotion subsides. Drummond tugs Cates back to his seat.*)

DRUMMOND. Your Honor, I request that the defendant's remarks be stricken from the record. (*He sits. The Judge nods.*)

BRADY. But how can we strike this young man's bigoted opinions from the memory of this community? (*Brady turns, about to play his trump card.*) Now, my dear. Will you tell the jury some more of Mr. Cates' opinions on the subject of religion?

DRUMMOND. (*Leaps up.*) Objection! Objection! Objection! Hearsay testimony is not admissible.

JUDGE. The court sees no objection to this line of questioning. Proceed, Colonel Brady. (*Drummond sinks back, disgusted.*)

BRADY. Will you merely repeat in your own words some of the conversations you had with the defendant? (*Rachel's eyes meet Bert's. She hesitates.*)

RACHEL. I don't remember exactly—

BRADY. (*Helpfully.*) What you told me the other day. That presumably "humorous" remark Mr. Cates made about the Heavenly Father. (*Low gasps of outrage from spectators.*)

RACHEL. Bert said— (*She stops.*)

BRADY. Go ahead, my dear.

RACHEL. (*Pathetically.*) I can't—

JUDGE. May I remind you, Miss Brown, that you are testifying under oath, and it is unlawful to withhold pertinent information.

RACHEL. Bert was just talking about some of the things he'd read. He—he—

BRADY. Were you shocked when he told you these things? Describe to the court your innermost feelings when Bertram Cates said to you: "God did not create Man! Man created God!" (*There is a flurry of reaction. Loud outrage from the spectators. Judge gavels for quiet.*)

DRUMMOND. Objection!

RACHEL. Bert didn't say that! He was just joking. What he said was: "God created Man in His own image—and Man, being a gentleman, returned the compliment." (*Hornbeck guffaws and pointedly scribbles this down. Another outburst from the spectators. Judge gavels them quiet. Drummond sits throwing a wry smile at Cates. Brady is pleased. Rachel seems hopelessly torn.*)

BRADY. Go on, my dear. Tell us some more. What did he say about the holy state of matrimony? Did he compare it with the breeding of animals?

RACHEL. No, he didn't say that— He didn't *mean* that. That's not what I told you. All he said was— (*She opens her mouth to speak, but nothing comes out. An emotional block makes her unable to utter a sound. Her lips move wordlessly.*)

JUDGE. Are you ill, Miss Brown? Would you care for a glass of water? (*Meeker gets water glass from Judge's table, passes it to Brady who offers it to Rachel. She refuses it. Rachel's head is lowered. She seems on the brink of collapse.*)

BRADY. Under the circumstances, I believe the witness should be dismissed.

DRUMMOND. And will the defense have no chance to challenge some of these statements the prosecutor has put in the mouth of the witness?

CATES. (*To Drummond.*) Don't plague her. Let her go.

DRUMMOND. (*Pauses, then sighs.*) No questions.

JUDGE. For the time being, the witness is excused. (*Reverend Brown comes forward to help his daughter from the stand. His demeanor is unsympathetic as he escorts her from the courtroom. There is a hushed babble of excitement.*) Does the prosecution wish to call any further witnesses?

DAVENPORT. Not at the present time, Your Honor.

JUDGE. We shall proceed with the case for the defense. Colonel Drummond.

DRUMMOND. Your Honor, I wish to call Dr. Amos D. Keller, (*Keller rises.*) head of the Department of Zoology at the University of Chicago. (*Keller steps forward.*)

BRADY. Objection.

DRUMMOND. On what grounds?

BRADY. I wish to inquire what possible relevance the testimony of a *Zoo*-ology professor can have in this trial.

DRUMMOND. (*Reasonably.*) It has every relevance! My client is on trial for teaching Evolution. Any testimony relating to his alleged infringement of the law must be admitted!

BRADY. Irrelevant, immaterial, inadmissible.

DRUMMOND. (*Sharply.*) Why? If Bertram Cates were accused of murder, would it be irrelevant to call expert witnesses to examine the weapon? Would you rule out testimony that the so-called murder weapon was incapable of firing a bullet?

JUDGE. I fail to grasp the learned counsel's meaning.

DRUMMOND. Oh. (*He makes exaggerated gestures, as if explaining things to a small child.*) Your Honor, the defense wishes to place Dr. Keller on the witness stand, so that he may explain to the gentlemen of the jury exactly what the evolutionary theory is. How can they pass judgement on it if they don't know what it's all about?

BRADY. I hold that the very law we are here to enforce excludes such testimony! The people of this state have made it very clear that they do not want this *zoo*-ological hogwash slobbered around the schoolrooms! And I refuse to allow these agnostic scientists to employ this courtroom as a sounding board, as a platform from which they can shout their heresies into the headlines! (*Spectators applaud.*)

JUDGE. Colonel Drummond, the court rules that zoology is irrelevant to the case. (*The Judge flashes his customary mechanical and humorless grin. Puzzled, Keller sits.*)

DRUMMOND. Agnostic scientists! Then I call Dr. Allen Page— (*Page rises. Drummond stares straight at Brady.*) Deacon of the Congregational Church—and professor of geology and archeology at Oberlin College.

BRADY. (*Dryly.*) Objection!

JUDGE. Objection sustained. (*Again, the meaningless grin. Page sits.*)

DRUMMOND. (*Astonished.*) In one breath, does the court deny the existence of zoology, geology and archeology?

JUDGE. We do not deny the existence of these sciences; but they do not relate to this point of law.

DRUMMOND. (*Fiery.*) I call Walter Aaronson, (*Aaronson rises.*) philosopher, anthropologist, author! One of the most brilliant minds in the world today! Objection, Colonel Brady?

BRADY. (*Nodding, smugly.*) Objection. (*Aaronson sits.*)

DRUMMOND. (*Intensely.*) Your Honor! The Defense has brought to Hillsboro—at great expense and inconvenience—fifteen noted scientists! The great thinkers of our time! Their testimony is basic to the defense of my client. For it is my intent to show this court that what Bertram Cates spoke quietly one spring afternoon in the Hillsboro High School is no crime! It is incontrovertible as geometry in every enlightened community of minds!

JUDGE. In *this* community, Colonel Drummond—and in this sovereign state—exactly the opposite is the case. The language of the law is clear; we do not need experts to question the validity of a law that is already on the books. (*Drummond, for once in his life, has hit a legal roadblock.*)

DRUMMOND. (*Scowling.*) In other words, the court rules out any expert testimony on Charles Darwin's *Origin of Species* or *Descent of Man*?

JUDGE. The court so rules. (*Drummond is flabbergasted. His case is cooked and he knows it. He looks around helplessly. He strides angrily to his table and starts to pack his briefcase. As he crosses, spectators whisper excitedly at the turn of events. Drummond suddenly stops packing.*)

DRUMMOND. (*There's a glint of an idea in his eye.*) Would the court admit expert testimony regarding a book known as the Holy Bible?

JUDGE. (*Hesitates, turns to Brady.*) Any objection, Colonel Brady?

BRADY. If the counsel can advance the case of the defendant through the use of the Holy Scripture, the prosecution will take no exception!

DRUMMOND. Good! (*With relish.*) I call to the stand one of the world's foremost experts on the Bible and its teachings— (*All peer off, trying to see who Drummond's "surprise witness" may be.*) Matthew Harrison Brady! (*There is an uproar in the courtroom. The Judge raps for order. Brady is stunned.*)

DAVENPORT. Your Honor, this is preposterous!

JUDGE. (*Confused.*) I—well, it's highly unorthodox. I've never known an instance where the defense called the prosecuting attorney as a witness.

BRADY. Your Honor, this entire trial is unorthodox. If the interests of Right and Justice will be served, I will take the stand.

DAVENPORT. (*Helplessly.*) But Colonel Brady— (*Buzz of awed reaction. The giants are about to meet head on. The Judge raps the gavel again, nervously.*)

JUDGE. The court will support you if you wish to decline to testify—as a witness against your own case. . . .

BRADY. (*With conviction.*) Your Honor, I shall not testify *against* anything. I shall speak out, as I have all my life—on behalf of the Living Truth of the Holy Scriptures!

JUDGE. Uh—Mr. Meeker, you'd better swear in the witness, please . . . (*Drummond moistens his lips in anticipation. Brady moves to the witness stand in grandiose style. Meeker holds out a Bible. Brady puts his left hand on the book, and raises his right hand.*)

MEEKER. Do you solemnly swear to tell the truth, the whole truth, and nothing but the truth, so help you God?

BRADY. (*Booming.*) I do.

MRS. KREBS. And he will! (*Spectators agree. Brady sits, confident and assured. His air is that of a benign and learned mathematician about to be quizzed by a schoolboy on matters of short division.*)

DRUMMOND. Am I correct, sir, in calling on you as an authority on the Bible?

BRADY. I believe it is not boastful to say that I have studied the Bible as much as any layman. And I have tried to live according to its precepts.

DRUMMOND. Bully for you. Now, I suppose you can quote me chapter and verse right straight through the King James Version, can't you?

BRADY. There are many portions of the Holy Bible that I have committed to memory. (*Drummond crosses to counsel table and picks up a copy of Darwin.*)

DRUMMOND. I don't suppose you've memorized many passages from the *Origin of Species?*

BRADY. I am not in the least interested in the pagan hypotheses of that book.

DRUMMOND. Never read it?

BRADY. And I never will.

DRUMMOND. Then how in perdition do you have the gall to whoop up this holy war against something you don't know anything about? How can you be so cocksure that the body of scientific knowledge systematized in the writings of Charles Darwin is, in any way, irreconcilable with the spirit of the Book of Genesis?

BRADY. Would you state that question again, please?

DRUMMOND. Let me put it this way. (*He flips several pages in the book.*) On page nineteen of *Origin of Species*, Darwin states— (*Davenport leaps up.*)

DAVENPORT. I object to this, Your Honor. Colonel Brady has been called as an authority on the Bible. Now the "gentleman from Chicago" is using this opportunity to read into the record scientific testimony which you, Your Honor, have previously ruled is irrelevant. If he's going to examine Colonel Brady on the Bible, let him stick to the Bible, the Holy Bible, and only the Bible! (*Approval with amens and applause from spectators. Drummond cocks an eye at the bench.*)

JUDGE. (*Clears his throat.*) You will confine your questions to the Bible. (*Davenport sits smugly. Drummond slaps shut the volume of Darwin.*)

DRUMMOND. (*Not angrily, crossing to his table.*) All right. I get the scent in the wind. (*He tosses the volume of Darwin on the counsel table.*) We'll play in *your* ball park, Colonel. (*He searches for a copy of the Bible, finally gets Meeker's. Without opening it Drummond scrutinizes the binding from several angles.*) Now let's get this straight. Let's get it clear. This is the book that you're an expert on? (*Brady is annoyed at Drummond's elementary attitude and condescension.*)

BRADY. That is correct.

DRUMMOND. Now tell me. Do you feel that every word that's written in this book should be taken literally?

BRADY. Everything in the Bible should be accepted, exactly as it is given there. (*Medium loud "amens" from spectators. Drummond looks askance toward the "amen" corner.*)

DRUMMOND. (*Leafing through the Bible.*) Now take this place where the whale swallows Jonah. Do you figure that actually happened?

BRADY. The Bible does not say "a whale," it says "a big fish."

DRUMMOND. (*Finds the place in the Bible, shows it to Brady.*) Matter of fact, it says "a great fish"—but it's pretty much the same thing. What's your feeling about that?

BRADY. I believe in a God who can make a whale and who can make a man and make both do what He pleases!

SPECTATORS. Amen, amen!

DRUMMOND. (*Turning sharply to the Court Recorder.*) I want those "Amens" in the record! (*He wheels back to Brady.*) I recollect a story about Joshua, making the sun stand still. Now as an expert, you tell me that's as true as the Jonah business. Right? (*Brady nods, blandly.*) That's a pretty neat trick. You suppose Houdini could do it?

BRADY. I do not question or scoff at the miracles of the Lord—as do ye of little faith.

DRUMMOND. Have you ever pondered just what would naturally happen to the earth if the sun stood still?

BRADY. You can testify to that if I get you on the stand. (*There is laughter from the spectators.*)

DRUMMOND. If they say that the sun stood still, they must've had a notion that the sun moves around the earth. Think that's the way of things? Or don't you believe the earth moves around the sun?

BRADY. I have faith in the Bible!

DRUMMOND. You don't have much faith in the solar system.

BRADY. (*Doggedly.*) The sun stopped.

DRUMMOND. Good. (*Level and direct.*) Now if what you say factually happened—if Joshua halted the sun in the sky—that means the earth stopped spinning on its axis; continents toppled over each other, mountains flew out into space. And the earth, arrested in its orbit, shriveled to a cinder and crashed into the sun. How come they missed *this* tidbit of news?

BRADY. They missed it because it didn't happen.

DRUMMOND. It must've happened! According to the laws of nature. Or don't you believe in nature, Colonel? Would you like to ban Copernicus from the classroom, along with Charles Darwin? Pass a law to wipe out all the scientific development since Joshua. Revelations—period!

BRADY. (*Calmly, as if instructing a child.*) The laws of nature were born in the mind of the Heavenly Father. He can change them, cancel them, use them as He pleases. It constantly amazes me that you apostles of science, for all your supposed wisdom, fail to grasp this simple fact. (*Drummond, shaking his head, flips a few pages in the Bible.*)

DRUMMOND. Listen to this: Genesis 4–16. "And Cain went out from the presence of the Lord, and dwelt in the land of Nod, on the East of Eden. And Cain *knew his wife!*" Where the hell did *she* come from?

BRADY. Who?

DRUMMOND. Mrs. Cain. Cain's wife. If, "In the beginning" there were only Adam and Even, and Cain and Abel, where'd this extra woman spring from? Ever figure that out?

BRADY. (*Cool.*) No, sir. I will leave the agnostics to hunt for her. (*Laughter from spectators.*)

DRUMMOND. Never bothered you?

BRADY. Never bothered me.

DRUMMOND. Never tried to find out?

BRADY. No.

DRUMMOND. Figure somebody pulled off another creation, over in the next county?

BRADY. The Bible satisfies me, it is enough.

DRUMMOND. It frightens me to imagine the state of learning in this world if everyone had your driving curiosity. (*Drummond is still probing for a weakness in Goliath's armor. He thumbs a few pages further in the Bible.*) This book now goes into a lot of "begats." "And Aphraxad begat Salah; and Salah begat Eber" and so on and so on. These pretty important folks?

BRADY. They are the generations of the holy men and women of the Bible.

DRUMMOND. How did they go about all this "begatting"?

BRADY. What do you mean?

DRUMMOND. I mean, did people "begat" in those days about the same way they get themselves "begat" today?

BRADY. The process is about the same. I don't think your scientists have improved it any. (*Laughter from spectators.*)

DRUMMOND. In other words, these folks were conceived and brought forth through the normal biological function known as *sex.* (*Gasp of shock from Mrs. Blair and Mrs. McClain, and a sputter of hush-hush reaction through the court. Howard's mother clamps her hands over the boy's ears, but he wriggles free.*) What do you think of sex, Colonel Brady?

BRADY. In what spirit is this question asked?

DRUMMOND. I'm not asking what you think of sex as a father, or as a husband. Or a Presidential candidate. You're up here as an expert on the Bible. What's the Biblical evaluation of sex?

BRADY. It is considered "Original Sin."

DRUMMOND. (*With mock amazement.*) And all these holy people got themselves "begat" through "Original Sin"? (*Huge reaction from outraged spectators. Brady does not answer. He scowls and shifts his weight in his chair.*) All this sinning make 'em any less holy?

DAVENPORT. Your Honor, where is this leading us? Where does it have to do with the State versus Bertram Cates?

JUDGE. Colonel Drummond, the court must be satisfied that this line of questioning has some bearing on the case.

DRUMMOND. (*Fiery.*) You've ruled out all my witnesses. I must be allowed to examine the one witness you've left me in my own way!

BRADY. (*With dignity.*) Your Honor, I am willing to sit here and endure Mr. Drummond's sneering and his disrespect. For he is pleading the case of the prosecution by his contempt for all that is holy.

DRUMMOND. I object, I object, I object.

BRADY. On what grounds? Is it possible that something is holy to the celebrated agnostic?

DRUMMOND. *Yes*! (*His voice drops, intensely.*) The individual human mind. In a child's power to master the multiplication table there is more sanctity than in all your shouted "Amens!" "Holy, Holies!" and "Hosannahs!" An idea is a greater monument than a cathedral. And the advance of man's knowledge is more of a miracle than any sticks turned to snakes, or the parting of waters! But are we now to halt the march of progress because Mr. Brady frightens us with a fable? (*To the jury, reasonably.*) Gentlemen, progress has never been a bargain. You've got to pay for it.

Sometimes I think there's a man behind a counter who says, "All right, you can have a telephone; but you'll have to give up privacy, the charm of distance. Madam, you may vote; but at a price; you lose the right to retreat behind a powder-puff or a petticoat. (*Pointing to the sky.*) Mister, you may conquer the air; but the birds will lose their wonder, and the clouds will smell of gasoline!" (*Thoughtfully, seeming to look beyond the courtroom.*) Darwin moved us forward to a hilltop, where we could look back and see the way from which we came. But for this view, this insight, this knowledge, we must abandon our faith in the pleasant poetry of Genesis.

BRADY. We must *not* abandon faith! Faith is the important thing!

DRUMMOND. Then why did God plague us with the power to think? Mr. Brady, why do you deny the *one* faculty which lifts man above all the other creatures on the earth: the power of his brain to reason? What other merit have we? The elephant is larger, the horse is stronger and swifter, the butterfly more beautiful, the mosquito more prolific, even the simple sponge is more durable! (*Wheeling on Brady.*) Or does a *sponge* think?

BRADY. I don't know. I'm a man, not a sponge. (*There are a few snickers at this, the crowd seems to be slipping away from Brady and aligning itself more and more with Drummond.*)

DRUMMOND. Do you think a sponge thinks?

BRADY. If the Lord wishes a sponge to think, it thinks.

DRUMMOND. Does a man have the same privileges that a sponge does?

BRADY. Of course.

DRUMMOND. (*Roaring, for the first time: crossing and stretching his arm toward Cates.*) *This man wishes to be accorded the same privilege as a sponge! He wishes to think!* (*There is applause from the scientists. The sound of it strikes Brady exactly as if he had been slapped in the face. Even the faithful are beginning to doubt the infallibility of their champion.*)

BRADY. But your client is wrong! He is deluded! He has lost his way!

DRUMMOND. It's sad that we aren't all gifted with your positive knowledge of Right and Wrong, Mr. Brady. (*Drummond strides to Dr. Page, and takes from him a rock, about the size of a tennis ball. Drummond weighs the rock in his hand as he saunters back toward Brady.*) How old do you think this rock is? (*Davenport rises about to object.*)

BRADY. (*Intoning.*) I am more interested in the Rock of Ages, than I am in the Age of Rocks. (*A couple of die-hard "Amens." Drummond ignores this glib gag.*)

DRUMMOND. Dr. Page of Oberlin College tells me that this rock is at least ten million years old.

BRADY. (*Sarcastically.*) Well, well, Colonel Drummond! You managed to sneak in some of that scientific testimony after all. (*Drummond opens up the rock, which splits into two halves. He shows it to Brady.*)

DRUMMOND. Look, Mr. Brady. These are the fossil remains of a pre-historic marine creature, which was found in this very county—and which lived here millions of years ago, when these very mountain ranges were submerged in water.

BRADY. I know. The Bible gives a fine account of the flood. But your professor is a little mixed up on his dates. That rock is not more than six thousand years old.

DRUMMOND. How do you know?

BRADY. A fine Biblical scholar, Bishop Usher, has determined for us the exact date and hour of the Creation. It occurred in the Year 4,004 B.C.

DRUMMOND. That's Bishop Usher's opinion.

BRADY. It is not an opinion. It is literal fact, which the good Bishop arrived at through careful computation of the ages of the prophets as set down in the Old Testament. In fact, he determined that the Lord began the Creation on the 23rd of October in the Year 4,004 B.C. at—uh, 9 A.M.!

DRUMMOND. That Eastern Standard Time? (*Laughter.*) Or Rocky Mountain Time? (*More laughter.*) It wasn't daylight-saving time, was it? Because the Lord didn't make the sun until the fourth day!

BRADY. (*Fidgeting.*) That is correct.

DRUMMOND. (*Sharply.*) That first day. Was it a twenty-four-hour day?

BRADY. The Bible says it was a day.

DRUMMOND. There wasn't any sun. How do you know how long it was?

BRADY. (*Determined.*) The Bible says it was a day.

DRUMMOND. A normal day, a literal day, a twenty-four-hour day? (*Pause. Brady is unsure.*)

BRADY. I do not know.

DRUMMOND. What do you think?

BRADY. (*Floundering.*) I do not think about things that . . . I do not think about!

DRUMMOND. Do you ever think about things that you *do* think about? (*There is some laughter. But it is dampened by the awareness throughout the courtroom, that the trap is about to be sprung.*) Isn't it possible that first day was twenty-five hours long? There was no ways to measure it, no way to tell! *Could* it have been twenty-five hours? (*Pause. The entire courtroom seems to lean forward.*)

BRADY. (*Hesitates—then.*) It is . . . *possible* . . . (*Gasp of shock from spectators. Many spring to their feet. Drummond's got him. And he knows it! This is the turning point. From here on, the tempo mounts. Drummond is now fully in the driver's seat. He pounds his questions faster and faster.*)

DRUMMOND. Oh. You interpret that the first day recorded in the Book of Genesis could be of indeterminate length.

BRADY. (*Wriggling.*) I mean to state that the day referred to is not necessarily a twenty-four-hour day.

DRUMMOND. It could have been thirty hours! Or a month! Or a year! Or a hundred years! Or *ten million years!* (*Davenport is able to restrain himself no longer. He realizes that Drummond has Brady in his pocket. Red-faced, he leaps up.*)

DAVENPORT. I protest! This is not only irrelevant, immaterial—it is *illegal!* (*The courtroom is a storm of impassioned, arguing voices. The Judge pounds for order, but the emotional tension will not subside.*) I demand to know the purpose of Mr.

Drummond's examination! What is he trying to do? (*Both Brady and Drummond crane forward, hurling their answers not at the court, but at each other.*)

BRADY. I'll tell you what he's trying to do. He wants to destroy everybody's belief in the Bible, and in God!

DRUMMOND. You know that's not true. I'm trying to stop you bigots and ignoramuses from controlling the education of the United States! And you know it! (*Arms out, Davenport pleads to the court, but is unheard. The Judge hammers for order.*)

JUDGE. (*Shouting.*) I shall ask the bailiff to clear the court, unless there is order here.

BRADY. How dare you attack the Bible? (*Spectators start to quiet.*)

DRUMMOND. The Bible is a book. A good book. But it's not the *only* book.

BRADY. It is the revealed word of the Almighty. God spake to the men who wrote the Bible.

DRUMMOND. And how do you know that God didn't "spake" to Charles Darwin?

BRADY. I know, because God tells me to oppose the evil teachings of that man.

DRUMMOND. Oh, God speaks to you.

BRADY. Yes.

DRUMMOND. He tells you exactly what's right and what's wrong?

BRADY. (*Doggedly.*) Yes.

DRUMMOND. And you act accordingly?

BRADY. Yes.

DRUMMOND. So you, Matthew Harrison Brady, through oratory, legislation, or whatever, pass along God's orders to the rest of the world! (*Laughter begins.*) Gentlemen, meet the "Prophet From Nebraska!" (*Brady's oratory is unassailable, but his vanity—exposed by Drummond's prodding—is only funny. The laughter is painful to Brady. He starts to answer Drummond, then turns toward the spectators and tries, almost physically, to suppress the amused reaction. This only makes it worse.*)

BRADY. (*Almost inarticulate.*) I— Please— !

DRUMMOND. (*With increasing tempo, closing in.*) Is that the way of things?

BRADY. No.

DRUMMOND. God tells Brady what is good!

BRADY. No.

DRUMMOND. To be against Brady is to be against God! (*More laughter.*)

BRADY. (*Confused.*) No, no! Each man is a free agent—

DRUMMOND. Then what is Bertram Cates doing in the Hillsboro jail? (*Applause from scientists and more townspeople.*) Suppose Mr. Cates had enough influence and lung power to railroad through the State Legislature a law that only *Darwin* should be taught in the schools!

BRADY. Ridiculous, ridiculous! There is only one great Truth in the world—

DRUMMOND. The Gospel according to Brady! God speaks to Brady, and Brady tells the world! Brady, Brady, Brady, Almighty! (*Drummond bows grandly. The crowd laughs.*)

BRADY. The Lord is my strength—

GOODFELLOW. (*Giggling.*) It is kinda funny.

MRS. KREBS. (*Plaintively.*) What's the matter with him?

DRUMMOND. What if a lesser human being—a Cates, or a Darwin—has the audacity to think that God might whisper to *him*? That an un-Brady thought might still be holy? Must men go to prison because they are at odds with the self-appointed prophet? (*Brady is now trembling so that it is impossible for him to speak. He rises, towering above his tormentor—rather like a clumsy, lumbering bear that is baited by an agile dog.*) Extend the Testaments! Let us have a Book of Brady! We shall hex the Pentateuch, and slip you in neatly between Numbers and Deuteronomy! (*The court is in an uproar with arguments and laughter. Brady is almost in a frenzy.*)

BRADY. (*Reaching for a sympathetic ear, trying to find the loyal audience which has slipped away from him.*) My friends— Your Honor— My Followers— Ladies and Gentlemen—

DRUMMOND. The witness is excused.

BRADY. All of you know what I stand for! What I believe!

JUDGE. You are excused, Colonel Brady.

BRADY. I believe, I believe in the truth of the Book of Genesis! (*Beginning to chant.*) Exodus, Leviticus, Numbers—

DRUMMOND. Your Honor, this completes my testimony. The witness is excused.

BRADY. Deuteronomy, Joshua, Judges, Ruth, First Samuel—

JUDGE. Court is adjourned until ten o'clock tomorrow morning.

DAVENPORT. Your Honor, I want to speak to you about striking all this from the record. (*They are out.*)

BRADY. Second Samuel, First Kings, Second Kings— (*Pounding the air with his fists.*) Isaiah, Jeremiah, Lamentations, Ezekiel, Daniel, Hosea, Joel, Amos, Obadiah, Jonah, Micah, Nahum, Habakkuk, Zephaniah— (*Brady beats his clenched fists in the air with every name. All exits completed. Brady and Mrs. Brady are left alone on stage. Still erect on the witness stand.*) Haggai, Zechariah, Malachi . . . (*His voice trails off. He sinks, limp and exhausted into the witness chair. Mrs. Brady looks at her husband, worried and distraught with helpless anger.*)

MRS. BRADY. Matt— (*There is distant laughter from offstage.*)

BRADY. They're laughing at me, Mother!

MRS. BRADY. (*Unconvincing.*) No, Matt. No, they're not!

BRADY. I can't stand it when they laugh at me! (*Mrs. Brady stands beside and behind her husband, putting her arms around the massive shoulders and cradling his head against her breast.*)

MRS. BRADY. (*Soothing.*) It's all right, baby. It's all right. (*Mrs. Brady sways gently back and forth, as if rocking her husband to sleep.*) Baby . . . Baby . . . !

CURTAIN

Paul Muni and Ed Begley Sr. in *Inherit the Wind,* New York, 1955. Print files, Lawrence and Lee Theatre Research Institute, The Ohio State University.

ACT THREE

The courtroom, the following day. The lighting is low, somber. The stage is empty except for Brady, Drummond, and Cates.

Drummond and Cates sit, waiting for the jury to return. Drummond leans back in a meditative mood. Cates, the focus of the furor, is resting his head on his arms. Brady sits at his table, eating a box lunch. He is drowning his troubles with food, as an alcoholic escapes from reality with a straight shot. Hornbeck enters, bows low to Brady.

HORNBECK. Afternoon, Colonel. Having high tea, I see. (*Brady ignores him.*) Is the jury still out? Swatting flies and wrestling with justice—in that order? (*Brady continues eating, ignoring Hornbeck. Hornbeck crosses to Drummond. Cates lifts his head.*) I'll hate to see the jury filing in; won't you, Colonel? I'll miss Hillsboro—especially this courthouse: a melange of Moorish and Methodist. It must have been designed by a congressman. (*Hornbeck smirks at his own joke, then lies down on second row of spectator chairs, and pores over a newspaper. Neither Cates nor Drummond has paid the slightest attention to him.*)

CATES. (*Staring straight ahead.*) Mr. Drummond. What's going to happen?

DRUMMOND. What do you think is going to happen, Bert?

CATES. Do you think they'll send me to prison?

DRUMMOND. They could.

CATES. They don't ever let you see anybody from the outside, do they? I mean—you can just talk to a visitor—through a window—the way they show it in the movies?

DRUMMOND: Oh, it's not as bad as all that. When they started this fire here, they never figured it would light up the whole sky. A lot of people's shoes are getting hot. But you can't be too sure. (*Brady rises majestically from his debris of paper napkins and banana peels, and goes off.*)

CATES. *He* seems so sure. He seems to know what the verdict's going to be.

DRUMMOND. Nobody knows. (*He tugs on one ear.*) I've got a pretty good idea. When you've been a lawyer as long as I have—a thousand years, more or less—you get so you can smell the way a jury's thinking.

CATES. What are they thinking right now?

DRUMMOND. (*Sighing.*) Some day I'm going to get me an *easy* case. An open-and-shut case. I've got a friend up in Chicago. Big lawyer. Lord how the money rolls in! You know why? He never takes a case unless it's a sure thing. Like a jockey who won't go in a race unless he can ride the favorite.

CATES. You sure picked the long shot this time, Mr. Drummond.

DRUMMOND. Sometimes I think the law *is* like a horse race. Sometimes it seems to me I ride like fury, just to end up back where I started. Might as well be on a merry-go-round, or a rocking horse . . . or . . . (*He half-closes his eyes. His voice is far away, his lips barely move.*) Golden Dancer. . . .

CATES. What did you say?

DRUMMOND. That was the name of my first long shot. Golden Dancer. She was in the big side window of the general store in Wakeman, Ohio. I used to stand out in the street and say to myself, "If I had Golden Dancer I'd have everything in the world that I wanted." (*He cocks an eyebrow.*) I was seven years old, and a very fine judge of rocking horses. (*He looks off again into the distance.*) Golden Dancer had a bright red mane, blue eyes, and she was gold all over, with purple spots. When the sun hit her stirrups, she was a dazzling sight to see. But she was a week's wages for my father. So Golden Dancer and I always had a plate glass window between us. (*Reaching back for the memory.*) But—let's see, it wasn't Christmas; must've been my birthday—I woke up in the morning and there was Golden Dancer at the foot of my bed! Ma had skimped on the groceries, and my father'd worked nights for a month. (*Re-living the moment.*) I jumped into the saddle and started to rock— (*Almost in a whisper.*) And it *broke*! It split in two! The wood was rotten, the whole thing was put together with spit and sealing wax! All shine, and no substance! (*Turning to Cates.*) Bert, whenever you see something bright, shining, perfect-seeming—all gold, with purple spots—look behind the paint! And if it's a lie—show it up for what it really is! (*A Radio Man comes in, lugging an old-fashioned carbon microphone. The Judge, carrying his robe over his arm, comes on and scowls at the microphone.*)

RADIO MAN. (*To Judge.*) I think this is the best place to put it—if it's all right with you, Your Honor.

JUDGE. There's no precedent for this sort of thing.

RADIO MAN. You understand, sir, we're making history here today. This is the first time a public event has ever been broadcast.

JUDGE. Well, I'll allow it—provided you don't interfere with the business of the court.

RADIO MAN. Thank you, sir! (*The Radio Man starts to string his wires. The Mayor hurries on, worried, brandishing a telegram.*)

MAYOR. (*To Judge.*) Merle, gotta talk to you. Over here. (*He draws the Judge aside, not wanting to be heard.*) This wire just came. The boys over at the state capitol are getting worried about how things are going. Newspapers all over are raising such a hullaballoo. The boys are beginning to feel nervous. After all, November ain't too far off, and it don't do any of us any good to have any of the voters gettin' all steamed up. Wouldn't do no harm to just let things simmer down. (*The Radio Man reappears.*) Well, go easy, Merle. (*Tipping his hat to Drummond as he hurries off.*)

RADIO MAN. (*Crisply, into the mike.*) Testing 1—2—3—4—5. (*Judge exits. Drummond rises.*) Testing 1—2—3—4—5. (*Signals to assistant offstage. Drummond crosses to the microphone.*)

DRUMMOND. (*To the Radio Man.*) What's that?

RADIO MAN. An enunciator.

DRUMMOND. You going to broadcast?

RADIO MAN. We have a direct wire to WGN, Chicago. As soon as the jury comes in, we'll announce the verdict. (*Drummond takes a good look at the microphone.*)

DRUMMOND. Radio! God, this is going to break down a lot of walls.

RADIO MAN. (*Hastily.*) You're—you're not supposed to say "God" on the radio.

DRUMMOND. Why the hell not? (*The Radio Man looks at the microphone, as if it were a toddler that had just been told the facts of life.*)

RADIO MAN. You're not supposed to say "Hell," either.

DRUMMOND. (*Sauntering back to his chair.*) *This* is going to be a barren source of amusement! (*Brady re-enters and crosses ponderously to the Radio Man.*)

BRADY. Can one speak into either side of this machine? (*The Radio Man starts at this rumbling thunder, so close to the ear of his delicate child.*)

RADIO MAN. (*In an exaggerated whisper.*) Yes, sir. Either side. (*Brady attempts to lower his voice, but it is like putting a leash on an elephant.*)

BRADY. Kindly signal me while I am speaking, if my voice does not have sufficient projection for your radio apparatus. (*A voice offstage is heard yelling loudly, "Jury's comin' back in." Suddenly the air is charged with excitement as the spectators scurry expectantly back to their seats, talking noisily. Meeker enters, reaches up for the gavel and raps it several times.*)

MEEKER. Everybody rise. (*Everybody rises. The Judge enters.*) Hear ye, hear ye. Court will reconvene in the case of the State versus Bertram Cates. (*The court sits. Meeker waves jury on. They enter, faces fixed and stern, and take their seats.*)

CATES. (*As the jury files in, whispers to Drummond.*) What do you think? Can you tell from their faces? (*Drummond is nervous, too. He squints at the returning jurors, drumming his fingers on the table top. Cates looks around, as if hoping to see Rachel—but she is not there. His disappointment is evident. The Radio Man has received his signal from offstage, and he begins to speak into the microphone. Spectators are chattering excitedly.*)

RADIO MAN. (*Low, with dramatic intensity.*) Ladies and gentlemen, this is Harry Y. Esterbrook, speaking to you from the courthouse in Hillsboro, where the jury is just returning to the courtroom to render its verdict in the famous Hillsboro Monkey Trial case. The Judge has just taken the bench. And in the next few minutes we shall know whether Bertram Cates will be found innocent or guilty. (*The Judge looks at him with annoyance, waving to him to stop. Gingerly the Radio Man aims his microphone at the Judge and steps back. Spectators quiet. There is hushed tension all through the courtroom.*)

JUDGE. (*Clears his throat.*) Gentlemen of the Jury, have you reached a decision?

SILLERS. (*Rising.*) Yeah. Yes, sir, we have, Your Honor. (*Meeker crosses down to Sillers and takes a slip of paper from him. Silently, he crosses to the Judge's bench, gives Judge verdict note and crosses to his chair. All eyes following the slip of paper. The Judge takes it, opens it, raps his gavel.*)

JUDGE. The jury's decision is unanimous. Bertram Cates is found guilty as charged! (*There is tremendous reaction. Some cheers, applause. "Amens." Some boos. Brady is pleased. But is not the beaming, powerful, assured Brady of the Chautauqua tent. It is a spiteful, bitter victory for him, not a conquest with a cavalcade of angels. Cates stares at his lap. Drummond taps a pencil. The Radio Man talks rapidly, softly into his microphone. The Judge does not attempt to control the reaction.*)

RADIO MAN. Did you hear that, friends out there in radio land? Bertram Cates has been found guilty as charged. I can tell you the confusion here is simply unbelievable and now the next voice you hear will be that of the Judge actually pronouncing sentence.

HORNBECK. (*In the manner of a hawker or pitchman.*) Step right up, and get your tickets for the Middle Ages! You only *thought* you missed the Coronation of Charlemagne!

JUDGE. (*Raps his gavel. The noise quiets down.*) The prisoner will rise, to hear the sentence of this court. (*Drummond looks up quizzically, alert.*) Bertram Cates, I hereby sentence you to—

DRUMMOND. (*Sharply.*) Your Honor! A question of procedure!

JUDGE. (*Nettled.*) Well, sir?

DRUMMOND. It is not customary in this state to allow the defendant to make a statement before sentence is passed? (*The Judge is red-faced.*)

JUDGE. Colonel Drummond, I regret this omission. In the confusion, and the—I neglected— Uh, Mr. Cates, if you wish to make any statement before sentence is passed on you, why, you may proceed. (*Clears throat again. Cates rises.*)

CATES. (*Simply.*) Your Honor, I am not a public speaker. I do not have the eloquence of some of the people you have heard in the last few days. I'm just a schoolteacher.

MRS. BLAIR. Not any more you ain't!

CATES. (*Pause. Quietly.*) I *was* a schoolteacher. (*With difficulty.*) I feel I am . . . I have been convicted of violating an unjust law. I will continue in the future, as I have in the past, to oppose this law in any way I can. I— (*There is a buzz of resentment from the spectators. Cates isn't sure exactly what to say next. He hesitates, then sits down. There is a crack of applause from scientists. Brady is fretful and disturbed. He's won the case. The prize is his, but he can't reach the candy. In his hour of triumph, Brady expected to be swept from the courtroom on the shoulders of his exultant followers. But the drama isn't proceeding according to plan. The gavel again. The court quiets down.*)

JUDGE. Bertram Cates, this court has found you guilty of violating Public Act Volume 37, Statute Number 31428, as charged. This violation is punishable by fine and/or imprisonment. (*He coughs.*) But since there has been no previous violation of this statute, there is no precedent to guide the bench in passing sentence. (*He flashes the automatic smile.*) The court deems it proper— (*He glances at the Mayor.*) to sentence Bertram Cates to pay a fine of— (*He coughs.*) one hundred dollars. (*The mighty Evolution Law explodes with the pale puff of a wet firecracker. There is a murmur of surprise through the courtroom. Brady is indignant. He rises, incredulous.*)

BRADY. Did your honor say one hundred dollars?

JUDGE. That is correct. (*Trying to get it over with.*) This seems to conclude the business of the trial—

BRADY. (*Thundering.*) Your Honor, the prosecution takes exception! Where the issues are so titanic, the court must mete out more drastic punishment—

DRUMMOND. I object!

BRADY. To make an example of this transgressor! To show the world—

DRUMMOND. Just a minute. Just a minute. The amount of the fine is of no concern to me. Bertram Cates has no intention whatsoever of paying this or any other fine.

MRS. BLAIR. Well, let him go to jail then. (*Low, brief mutter of approval from spectators.*)

DRUMMOND. He would not pay it if it were a single dollar. We will appeal this decision to the supreme court of this state. Will the court grant thirty days to prepare our appeal?

JUDGE. Granted. The court fixes bond at . . . five hundred dollars. I believe this concludes the business of this trial. Therefore, I declare this court is adjourn—

BRADY. (*Hastily.*) Your Honor! (*He reaches for a thick manuscript.*) Your Honor, with the court's permission, I should like to read into the record a few short remarks which I have prepared—

DRUMMOND. I object to that. Mr. Brady may make any remarks he likes—long, short or otherwise. In a Chautauqua tent or in a political campaign. Our business in Hillsboro is completed. The defense holds that the court shall be adjourned.

BRADY. (*Frustrated.*) But I have a few remarks—

JUDGE. And we are all anxious to hear them, sir. But Colonel Drummond's point of procedure is well taken. I am sure that everyone here will wish to remain after the court is adjourned to hear your address. (*Brady lowers his head slightly, in gracious deference to procedure. The Judge raps his gavel.*) I hereby declare this court is adjourned, sine die. (*There is a babble of confusion and reaction. Hornbeck promptly crosses to Meeker and confers with him in whispers.*)

HAWKER. Eskimo Pies. Get your Eskimo Pies! (*Judge raps with his gavel.*)

JUDGE. (*Projecting.*) Quiet! Order in the—I mean, your attention, please. (*The court quiets.*) We are honored to hear a few words from Colonel Brady, who wishes to address you— (*The Judge is interrupted in his introduction by Meeker and Hornbeck. They confer sotto voce. The babble of voices crescendos.*)

HAWKER. Get your Eskimo Pies! Cool off with an Eskimo Pie! (*Brady preens himself for the speech, but is annoyed by the confusion. Hornbeck hands the Judge several bills from his wallet, and Meeker pencils a receipt. The Judge bangs the gavel again.*)

JUDGE. We beg your attention, please, ladies and gentlemen! Colonel Brady has some remarks to make which I am sure will interest us all. (*Brady stretches out his arms, in the great attention-getting gesture.*)

BRADY. My dear friends . . . ! Your attention, please! (*The bugle voice reduces the noise somewhat. But it is not the eager, anticipatory hush of olden days. Attention is given him, not as the inevitable due of a mighty monarch, but grudgingly and resentfully.*) Fellow citizens and friends of the unseen audience. From the hallowed hills of sacred Sinai, in the days of remote antiquity, came the law which has been our bulwark and our shield. Age upon age, men have looked to the law as they would look to the mountains, whence cometh our strength. And here, here in this — (*The Radio Man approaches Brady nervously.*)

RADIO MAN. Excuse me, Mr.—uh, Colonel Brady—would you . . . uh . . . step a little closer to the enunciator . . . ?

BRADY. Here?

RADIO MAN. Fine. (*Brady, helped by Radio Man, steps to Davenport chair. Radio Man crosses back to his microphone. In this momentary lull, the audience has slipped away from him again. Even Mrs. Brady, trying to quiet people, is turned away from her husband. Brady's vanity and cussedness won't let him give up, even though he realizes this is a sputtering anticlimax. By God, he'll make them listen.*)

(*Simultaneously.*)

BRADY. (*Red-faced, his larynx taut, roaring stridently.*) As they would look to the mountains whence cometh our strength. And here, here in this courtroom we have seen vindicated— (*A few people leave. He watches them desperately, out of the corner of his eye.*) We have seen vindicated—

RADIO MAN. (*After an offstage signal.*) Ladies and gentlemen, our program director in Chicago advises us that our time here is completed. Harry Y. Esterbrook speaking. We return you now to our studios and "Matinee Musicale."

(*Radio Man takes the microphone and goes off. This is the final indignity to Brady, he realizes that a great portion of his audience has left him as he watches it go. Brady brandishes his speech, as if it were Excalibur. His eyes start from his head, the voice is a tight, frantic rasp. Mrs. Brady is trying to quiet people.*)

BRADY. From the hallowed hills of sacred Sinai . . . (*He freezes. His lips move, but nothing comes out. Paradoxically, his silence brings silence. The orator can hold his audience only by not speaking.*)

GOODFELLOW. Look at him!

MRS. BRADY. (*Spinning around, with terror.*) Matt—

JUDGE. Meeker, quick! (*There seems to be some violent, volcanic upheaval within Brady. His lower lip quivers, his eyes stare. Very slowly, he seems to be leaning toward the audience. Then, like a figure in a waxworks, toppling from its pedestal, he falls stiffly, face forward. Meeker springs forward, catches Brady by the shoulders and breaks his fall. The sheaf of manuscript, clutched in his raised hand, has scattered in mid air. The great words flutter innocuously to the courtroom floor. There is a burst of reaction. Mrs. Brady screams.*)

DAVENPORT. Get a doctor! (*Mrs. Brady rushes to his side.*)

MRS. BRADY. Matt! Dear God in Heaven! Matt! (*Drummond, Hornbeck and Cates watch, silent and concerned. The silence is tense.*)

MRS. McCLAIN. (*Wailing.*) O Lord, work us a miracle and save our Holy Prophet! (*Rudely, Meeker pushes her back.*)

MEEKER. (*Contemptuously.*) Get away! (*Crisply.*) Elijah, give us a hand here. Get him across the street to Doc's office. (*Elijah and Meeker lift Brady in the chair with difficulty and begin to carry him out. A strange thing happens. Brady begins to speak in a hollow, distant voice—as if something sealed up inside of him were finally broken, and the precious contents spilled out into the open at last.*)

BRADY. (*As he is carried out, in a strange, unreal voice.*) Mr. Chief Justice, Citizens of these United States. During my term in the White House, I pledge to carry out my program for the betterment of the common people of this country. As your new President, I say what I have said all of my life . . . (*The crowd tags along, curious and awed. Only Drummond, Cates and Hornbeck remain, their eyes fixed on Brady's exit.*)

DRUMMOND. How quickly they can turn. And how painful it can be when you don't expect it. I wonder how it feels to be Almost-President three times—with a skull full of undelivered inauguration speeches.

HORNBECK. Something happens to an Also-Ran. Something happens to the feet of a man who always comes in second in a foot-race. He becomes a national unloved child, a balding orphan, an aging adolescent who never got the biggest piece of candy. Unloved children, of all ages, insinuate themselves into spotlights and rotogravures. They stand on their hands and wiggle their feet. Split pulpits with their pounding! And their tonsils turn to organ pipes. Show me a shouter and I'll show you an Also-Ran. A might-have-been. An almost-was.

CATES. (*Softly.*) Did you see his face? He looked terrible. . . . (*Meeker enters. Cates turns to him. Meeker shakes his head: "I don't know."*)

MEEKER. I'm surprised more folks ain't keeled over in this heat. (*He picks up Brady's speech from floor.*)

HORNBECK. He's all right. Give him an hour or so to sweat away the pickles and the pumpernickel; to let his tongue forget the acid taste of vinegar victory. Mount Brady will erupt again by nightfall, spouting lukewarm fire and irrelevant ashes. (*Cates shakes his head, bewildered. Drummond watches him, concerned.*)

DRUMMOND. What's the matter, boy?

CATES. I'm not sure. Did I win, or did I lose?

DRUMMOND. You won.

CATES. But the jury found me—

DRUMMOND. What jury? Twelve men? Millions of people will say you won. They'll read in their papers tonight that you smashed a bad law. You made it a joke!

CATES. Yeah. But what's going to happen now? I haven't got a job. I'll bet they won't even let me back in the boarding house.

DRUMMOND. Sure, it's gonna be tough, it's not gonna be any church social for a while. But you'll live. And while they're making you sweat, remember—you've helped the next fella.

CATES. What do you mean?

DRUMMOND. You don't suppose this kind of thing is ever finished, do you? Tomorrow it'll be something else—and another fella will have to stand up. And you've helped give him the guts to do it!

CATES. (*With new pride in what he's done.*) Mr. Meeker, don't you have to lock me up?

MEEKER. They fixed bail.

CATES. You don't expect a schoolteacher to have five hundred dollars.

MEEKER. (*Jerking his head toward Hornbeck.*) This fella here put up the money.

HORNBECK. (*With a magnanimous gesture.*) With a year's subscription to the Baltimore *Herald*, we give away—at no cost or obligation—a year of freedom. (*Rachel enters, carrying a suitcase. She is smiling, and there is a new lift to her head. Cates turns and sees her.*)

CATES. Rachel!

RACHEL. Hello, Bert.

CATES. (*Indicating her suitcase.*) I don't need any more shirts. I'm free—for a while anyway.

RACHEL. These are *my* things, Bert. I'm going away.

CATES. Where are you going?

RACHEL. I'm not sure. But I'm leaving my father.

CATES. Rache . . .

RACHEL. Bert, it's my fault the jury found you guilty. (*He starts to protest.*) Partly my fault. I helped. (*Rachel hands Bert the orange book.*) This is your book, Bert. (*Silently, he takes it.*) I've read it. All the way through. I don't understand it. What I do understand, I don't like. I don't want to think that men come from apes and monkeys. But I think that's beside the point. (*Drummond looks at the girl admiringly.*)

DRUMMOND. That's right. That's beside the point.

RACHEL. Mr. Drummond, I hope I haven't said anything to offend you. (*He shakes his head.*) You see, I haven't really thought very much. I was always afraid of what I might think—so it seemed safer not to think at all. But now I know. A thought is like a child inside our body. It has to be born. If it dies inside you, part of you dies, too! Maybe what Mr. Darwin wrote is bad. I don't know. Bad or good, it doesn't make any difference. The ideas have to come out—like children. Some of 'em healthy as a bean plant, some sickly. I think the sickly ideas die mostly, don't you, Bert? (*Bert nods yes, but he's too lost in new admiration for her to do anything but stare. He does not move to her side. Drummond smiles, as if to say: "That's quite a girl!" The Judge walks in slowly.*)

JUDGE. (*Quietly.*) Brady's dead. (*They all react.*)

DRUMMOND. I can't imagine the world without Matthew Harrison Brady.

CATES. What caused it? Did they say? (*Dazed, the judge goes off, without answering.*)

HORNBECK. Matthew Harrison Brady died of a busted belly. (*Drummond slams down his briefcase. Glowers at Hornbeck.*) Be frank! Why should we weep for him? He cried enough for himself! The national tear duct from Weeping Water, Nebraska, who flooded the whole nation like a one-man Mississippi! You know what he was: a Barnum-bunkum Bible-eating bastard! (*Drummond rises, fiercely angry.*)

DRUMMOND. You smart-aleck! You have no more right to spit on his religion than you have a right to spit on my religion! Or my lack of it!

HORNBECK. (*Askance.*) Well, what do you know! Henry Drummond for the defense—even of his enemies!

DRUMMOND. (*Low, moved.*) There was much greatness in this man.

HORNBECK. Shall I put that in the obituary?

DRUMMOND. Write anything you damn please.

HORNBECK. How do you write an obituary for a man who's been dead thirty years? "In Memoriam—M. H. B." Then what? Hail the apostle, whose letters to the Corinthians were lost in the mail? Two years, ten years—and tourists will ask the guide, "Who died here? Matthew Harrison Who?" (*A sudden thought.*) What did he say to the minister? It fits! He delivered his own obituary! (*Hornbeck finds the Bible.*) Here it is: his book! (*Thumbing hastily.*) Proverbs, wasn't it?

DRUMMOND. (*Quietly.*) "He that troubleth his own house shall inherit the wind: (*Turns to Hornbeck.*) and the fool shall be servant to the wise in heart." (*Hornbeck looks at Drummond, surprised. He snaps the Bible shut, folds his arms and crosses slowly toward Drummond, his eyes narrowing.*)

HORNBECK. Well, well, Colonel Drummond! We're growing an odd crop of agnostics this year!

DRUMMOND. (*Evenly.*) I'm getting damned tired of you, Hornbeck.

HORNBECK. Why?

DRUMMOND. You never pushed a noun against a verb except to blow up something.

HORNBECK. That's a typical lawyer's trick: accusing the accuser!

DRUMMOND. What am I accused of?

HORNBECK. I charge you with contempt of conscience! Self perjury. Kindness aforethought! Sentimentality in the first degree.

DRUMMOND. Why? Because I refuse to erase a man's lifetime? I tell you Brady had the same right as Cates: the right to be wrong! (*Turns away.*)

HORNBECK. "Be-Kind-To-Bigots" Week. Since Brady's dead, we must be kind. God, how the world is rotten with kindness!

DRUMMOND. A giant once lived in that body. But Matt Brady got lost. Because he was looking for God too high up and too far away.

HORNBECK. You hypocrite! You fraud! (*With a growing sense of discovery.*) You're more religious than *he* was! (*Drummond doesn't answer.*) Excuse me, gentlemen. I must get me to a typewriter and hammer out the story of an atheist—who believes in God! (*He slaps his straw hat on his head and goes off.*)

CATES. Colonel Drummond.

DRUMMOND. Bert, I am resigning my commission in the State Militia. I hand in my sword!

CATES. Doesn't it cost a lot of money for an appeal? I couldn't pay you . . .

DRUMMOND. I didn't come here to get paid. (*Putting on his hat.*) Well, I'd better get myself on a train.

RACHEL. There's one out at five-thirteen. Bert, you and I can be on that train, too!

CATES. (*Smiling, happy.*) I'll get my stuff!

RACHEL. I'll help you. (*They start off. Rachel remembers her suitcase, runs back for it. Cates clasps Drummond's arm.*)

CATES. (*As he runs off with Rachel, calling over his shoulder.*) See you at the depot! (*Drummond is left alone on stage. Suddenly he notices Rachel's copy of Darwin on the table, calls off.*)

DRUMMOND. Say—you forgot— (*But Rachel and Cates are out of earshot. He rotates the volume in his hand, this one book has been the center of the whirlwind. He is about to put it into his briefcase when he notices the Bible at the edge of the Judge's bench. He picks up the Bible in the other hand, looks from one volume to the other, balancing them thoughtfully as if his hands were scales. He half smiles, half shrugs. Then Drummond resoundingly slaps the two books together, side by side, jams them into his briefcase, neither one on top. Slowly, he climbs to the level of the empty town square, leaving as he arrived, alone, off to fight another battle.*)

CURTAIN

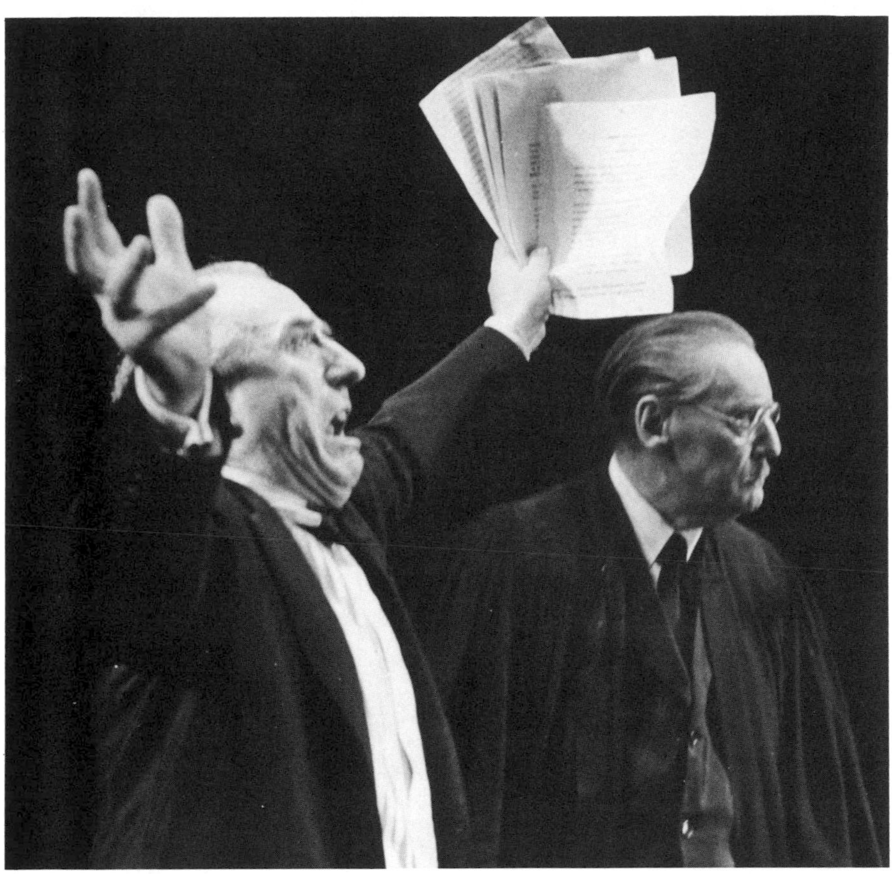

Ed Begley Sr. and Louis Hector in *Inherit the Wind,* New York, 1955. Photo by Arthur Cantor. Artist files, Lawrence and Lee Theatre Research Institute, The Ohio State University.

AUNTIE MAME

Introduction

Lawrence and Lee's second theatrical triumph came with their dramatization of Patrick Dennis's collection of comic vignettes, *Auntie Mame,* which opened on Broadway eighteen months after *Inherit the Wind.* Published in 1955, the book was an immediate best-seller, and the rights for a dramatic version were quickly snapped up by producers Robert Fryer and Lawrence Carr, who approached Rosalind Russell to play the title role. Russell, after many years as a film star, had returned to the stage triumphantly in the musical *Wonderful Town* (produced by Fryer) in 1953.

Auntie Mame was a roaring success. With a huge cast, multiple sets, and constant costume and wig changes for the star, it settled into a long run at the Broadhurst Theatre, generating four simultaneously touring companies in North America. The play was produced in more than a dozen foreign countries. Oddly enough, however, the play itself was initially discounted by some reviewers. Rosalind Russell's frenetic comic performance was lavishly praised, and she appeared on numerous magazine covers. The adaptation was praised as well, but again there were negative reactions. John Chapman termed it "an unstuck montage,"[1] while Richard Watts, Jr., observed, " '*Auntie Mame*' actually isn't very much of a play. It doesn't really try to be anything save a brightly superficial and shrewdly fabricated theatrical concoction replete with gags."[2] Brooks Atkinson was even harsher in the *New York Times*: "*Auntie Mame* would be a major crisis without [Rosalind Russell]."[3]

Despite those views putting the play's success squarely on Rosalind Russell's capable shoulders, her replacements in the Broadway company of *Auntie Mame* also succeeded, as did the stars of several touring productions. Lawrence and Lee's play proved far more effective than had first been apparent to a handful of the reviewers. John Chapman, critic for the New York *Daily News*, was eventually moved to muse in print:

> Did it ever occur to you that a critic could be wrong once in a while? It has to me.
>
> For example, take the night of Oct. 31, 1956, when "Auntie Mame" opened. While admitting that I had one wonderful time, I wrote, "The only reason for seeing the comedy is Rosalind Russell. . . . "
>
> My apologies to the adapters of Patrick Dennis' novel, Jerome

> Lawrence and Robert E. Lee. They must have wrought better than I thought, for "Auntie Mame" is actress-proof. Anybody could play it, and almost everybody has.[4]

Even Atkinson of the *Times* reversed his negative views of *Auntie Mame* after seeing Beatrice Lillie play the role.[5] His initial criticism of the playwrights brought an immediate response from the writer, poet, and editor Louis Untermeyer, who criticized Atkinson's "intemperate attack" on Lawrence and Lee and defended their work: "In adapting a book which, while entertaining, was formless and rather repetitious, Jerome Lawrence and Robert E. Lee resolved the twofold problem of retaining the comic spirit of the book and giving it a structural unity."[6]

Auntie Mame, like *Inherit the Wind*, has clearly stood the test of time: both the original comedy and its musical incarnation, *Mame*, remain in constant production.[7] Why the negative responses to the initial performances in 1956? In part, some reviewers overreacted against what was the most anticipated production of the season. The book had been a major best-seller (Russell describes seeing "a garden of those books" when she sailed to Europe after signing the contract to play Mame).[8] Morton DaCosta, the director, had done the hit comedy *No Time for Sergeants* the previous season; Russell was herself a major attraction. The play had been phenomenally successful on its pre-Broadway tour. All factors were in place for reviewers to disparage the work as not up to expectations.

In addition, *Auntie Mame* defied the traditional structure of a comedy: it does not proceed with the logical causality of a well-made play, build to a climax in the middle of the second act, or rely upon sexual innuendo for much of its humor. Rather, Lawrence and Lee adopted the episodic structure of the book—a string of unconnected stories about the title character in roughly chronological order—to the stage. The play has the structure of a musical comedy (as several reviewers noted)[9] and, indeed, was translated to the musical format by Lawrence and Lee some ten years later. *Auntie Mame* thus defied the reviewers' expectations of its genre: many simply proved unable to appreciate the playwrights' achievement in successfully dramatizing Patrick Dennis's best-seller. Once the play achieved classic status, reviewers were able to articulate Lawrence and Lee's achievement. Edward Hayman's review of a 1987 Detroit production is typical of later notices:

> Nobody ever has accused Jerome Lawrence and Robert E. Lee's modern classic comedy *Auntie Mame* of being a well-made play. It tumbles through its 25 scenes in the same carefree way its title character, who is still reigning Queen of the Free Spirits in our American dramatic literature, tumbles through her life. . . .
>
> But, as the Hilberry Theatre's robust revival demonstrates, *Auntie Mame* is more than a facile artifact of a bygone Broadway. It comes to us, after more than 30 years of almost constant production, with its heart beating as strong as ever.[10]

Lawrence and Lee were signed to fashion a stage version of *Auntie Mame* after Patrick Dennis had attempted it but found himself unable to leave out anything from his work.[11] Although the book's episodic structure provided the play's basic concept, the dramatization is a free one. Lawrence and Lee compressed the action severely, left out several key episodes from the book that emphasize Mame's sexuality, and freely invented both lines and situations—most notably Mame's famous remark to Gooch, "Life is a banquet, and most poor sons-of-bitches are *starving* to death! Live!" (act 2, scene 6). A closer look at Lawrence and Lee's handiwork puts to rest the notion that the play is a loosely structured shambles: the piece is carefully crafted.

Take, for example, the first act. In the first eleven scenes, Lawrence and Lee provide a whirlwind of activity, taken from the first three chapters of Dennis's original. The action covers at least a full year: Patrick's father drops dead during the first scene on 15 October 1928, while the sequence ends at Christmas after the stock market crash of 1929, although to fit in all the events that take place after the crash (which happens in scene 7) an additional year seems likely. Neither the script nor the production stresses the passage of time, however. The effect of placing all of the events in December compresses the action, creating a smooth flow from Patrick and Norah's arrival (on 1 December) to Mame's engagement to Beau on Christmas Eve. In Dennis's book, Patrick and Norah arrive at Mame's in the midst of a wild party on 1 July. By shifting the arrival to December, Lawrence and Lee focus on the holiday season, giving a sound structure to the piece.

Compression is also evident in the act's final three scenes at Peckerwood. In the original, Mame and Patrick visit Peckerwood after her marriage to Beau (in chapter 4). The visit is an extended one: Mame avoids a fox hunt by actually spraining her ankle and is disgraced when Sally Cato manages to have Mame cause a pileup of horses.[12] The sidesaddle fox hunt then follows, with the significant difference that Patrick, the book's narrator, also rides to the hounds so that he can describe the hunt. Lawrence and Lee's theatrical version, with the Burnside family watching the "hunt" taking place in the theatre's auditorium, provides the comic climax to the act, finding a vividly dramatic way to present the event.

The playwrights also found a solution to the difficulty of Patrick's growing up through the collage effect during the first four brief scenes of the second act. Mame and Beau's honeymoon travel bridges several years, permitting the substitution of an older actor for the young Patrick. The transition, including Beau's fondness for photography and his falling off the Matterhorn, have no counterpart in the Dennis book, in which Beau dies after thirteen months of married bliss by being kicked in the head by a Central Park horse.[13] The major change from the book in the play's second act, however, is the expansion of Agnes Gooch's role and influence.

Lawrence and Lee's Gooch is much more pivotal to the plot, and naive, than the book's mousy secretary. Dennis's Gooch is far more sexually voracious, especially after a drink or two.[14] Lawrence and Lee chose not to dramatize Dennis's chapter 6, which deals with the pregnant Gooch (and marries her off to one of Patrick's St. Boniface teachers). By placing Gooch's downfall later in Patrick's life, the playwrights again compress the action. Gooch's continued presence in the play provides a linkage between events that are discrete in the book. Mame suffers from a head cold in the book and therefore sends Gooch to the party with O'Bannion. Lawrence and Lee's decision to have Patrick bring Gloria to meet Mame, thus necessitating her getting rid of O'Bannion, connects the Upson family events (chapter 8 in the Dennis book) with Mame's care for Gooch, as well as demonstrates concretely Mame's concern for Patrick's well-being. (Mame's care for Gooch also foreshadows her support of the Epstein home for refugee Jewish children next door to Upson Downs in Montebank.)

The riotous party sequence (act 2, scene 10), the comic climax of the second act, has no direct counterpart in Dennis's vignettes, in which the Upsons demonstrate their boorishness and prejudice in Mountebank during a joint visit by Mame and Patrick. The party setting also provides a marvelously theatrical closure, echoing the party in the beginning of the first act, with many of the same characters present. Lawrence and Lee introduce Pegeen into the scene; only her name and Irishness are taken from Dennis's chapter 10. The flaming drinks, the appearance of Mame's galley proofs, Gloria's tale of ping-pong woe—all are original to the play. The scene ties together a number of different plot strands in a highly efficient and effective manner.

A number of other changes from the book to the play have the same purpose—to link disparate episodes together. Thus Lindsay Woolsey, for example, is Mame's suitor from the beginning of the play, her publisher, and her second husband in the play. In the original, he appears only as her publisher in chapter 5. Patrick's nurse, Norah, is packed off to Ireland with a pension in Dennis's chapter 4; she remains a devoted member of Mame's household throughout the play.

Equally significant are those episodes from the book that do not appear in the play. Mame's visit to St. Boniface with the pregnant Gooch is cut. So too are Mame's escapades with Patrick's fraternity brothers (Dennis's chapter 7), her disastrous care for English war refugees (chapter 9), and the vampirish Maddox sisters' attempt to ensnare Patrick (chapter 10, except for the character of Pegeen). Other than an obvious need to streamline and compress the action, those sections would have undermined the play's careful structure. Dennis's Mame is much more sexually promiscuous than Lawrence and Lee's character, which is a major point of chapter 7. The dreadful English children of chapter 9 have no connection with Patrick, pulling the narrative in an entirely new direction, while omitting the Maddoxes permits the far more theatrically effective contrasting of the commonsensical Pegeen with empty-headed Gloria.

In transferring Patrick Dennis's popular sketches to the stage, Lawrence and Lee crafted a tightly structured theatrical work. In act 1, the arrival of Young Patrick saves Mame from a life of dilettantism and hedonism; in act 2 the coin is flipped as she saves Patrick from Babbittry, bigotry, a life "locked up in a safe-deposit box."

The rapidly paced action, multiple settings, and large cast give the impression of a loosely knit series of scenes. That impression is false: *Auntie Mame* may not be a causally logical, well-made play conforming to the conventions of the mid-1950s, but its action is as carefully structured and linked through character relationships as any comedy of its period.

NOTES

1. "The Wonderful Rosalind Russell Is a Blessing to '*Auntie Mame,*' " *Daily News* (New York), 1 November 1956; rpt. *New York Times Critics Reviews* (abbrev. *NYTCR*) 17 (1956): 230.

2. "The Triumph of Rosalind Russell," *New York Post*, 1 November 1956; rpt. *NYTCR* 17 (1956): 232.

3. "Theatre: Roz Russell," *New York Times*, 1 November 1956; rpt. *NYTCR* 17 (1956): 229.

4. "Some Matters of Opinion," *New York Sunday News*, 15 June 1959, sec. 2, p. 1.

5. Brooks Atkinson, "B. Lillie as Mame," *New York Times*, 8 June 1958, sec. 2, p. 1.

6. Letter, *New York Times*, 18 November 1956, sec. 2, p. 3.

7. The film version of *Auntie Mame*, also directed by Morton DaCosta and with Russell and Peggy Cass repeating their stage performances, was released by Warner Brothers in 1958. The film has become something of a cult object; the 10th Street Cinema in New York ran it as a regular midnight feature, as did the Tiffany Theatre on the Sunset Strip in Los Angeles for many years, with patrons coming dressed as their favorite characters. The entire audience would recite the on-screen dialogue in unison. The videocassette release continues to break sales and rental records; it was third on the Book-of-the-Month Club's popularity chart as recently as 1991.

8. Rosalind Russell and Chris Case, *Life Is a Banquet* (New York: Random House, 1977), 189.

9. Tom Donnelly, "Theater: Masterpiece of Rozzle-Dazzle," *New York World-Telegram and the Sun*, 1 November 1956, p. 22; Jerry Gaghan, "Auntie Mame Scores Smash Hit," unidentified clipping (Philadelphia), *Auntie Mame* Scrapbook, Billy Rose Theatre Collection, New York Public Library. Burr, "Legit Tryout: *Auntie Mame*," *Daily Variety*, 25 September 1956, even described the comedy as "the funniest legit musical of recent seasons" (*Auntie Mame* Scrapbook).

10. Edward Hayman, " 'Auntie Mame' starts at the Hilberry," *Detroit News*, 7 December 1987; production file, Jerome Lawrence and Robert E. Lee Theatre Research Institute, The Ohio State University.

11. According to Robert E. Lee, Dennis produced "a 320-page first act" before abandoning the project (interview, 28 December 1988).

12. Patrick Dennis, *Auntie Mame* (New York: Vanguard Press, 1955), 78–83.

13. Dennis, 92.

14. Dennis, 106–9.

Foreword

Having had nothing to do with writing the play *Auntie Mame,* it is easy for me to be quite detached and objective about it. And I can say, right along with the critics and the thousands of people who have seen it, that it makes a wonderfully entertaining evening in the theatre.

If you are looking for a conventional little play suitable for the Freshman Frolic or the church basement—the sort of thing summarized in the catalogues of dramatic publishers as "Comedy; one interior; modern dress; three acts; four men; five women"—keep right on looking because *Auntie Mame* isn't it.

Like Mame herself, *Auntie Mame* is in no way conventional as a play. Nor could it be, because my novel, *Auntie Mame,* from which the play is derived, isn't even a novel, really. It is, instead, a couple of dozen episodes that take place in a couple of dozen localities over a couple of dozen years. I can't quite label it myself, but the matchless Rosalind Russell, who originated the role of Mame, who *is* Mame, calls this offering "a revue without music," and her definition is better than any I can supply. Both novel and play are freaks, then—but such *popular* freaks that their lavish eccentricities cannot be entirely despised.

Not every episode in my book is in the play. To get them all in—not that every one is worth dramatizing—would require passing out box luncheons, blankets, and tooth brushes to a rough-and-ready audience of slavish theatregoers weaned on Eugene O'Neill and the Ring Series. But an astonishing number of the episodes in the book *are* in the play; enough so that the casual reader is convinced that every word of the novel has been translated to the stage. If that isn't catching the "spirit" of a book, I don't know what is.

And Jerome Lawrence and Robert E. Lee have gone yet a step further in their dramatization, for they have caught—far better than I—the moments of heartbreak that are also in *Auntie Mame* and placed them on the stage so deftly that, between the guffaws and giggles, snickers and snorts, there are audible sobs and visible tears at each and every performance. That is what I meant to do in the novel and, I am afraid, failed. To me, comedy is measured not only by its laughs, but by its tears. With every pratfall the heart should also ache. In this play it does, and I still cry just as hard when I drop into the Broadhurst Theatre now as I did on the night the play was out in Wilmington. Two handkerchiefs are par for the course.

But enough of the clown longing to play Hamlet. To quote from *Hamlet* itself,

"The play's the thing something, something, something the king." And here it is, a warm, rich, sprawling, unorthodox comedy that I am proud and happy to have inspired.

Patrick Dennis

All the sick-rooms in America—and a large proportion of the well-rooms—are strewn with copies of Patrick Dennis's remarkable novel *Auntie Mame.* It is not easy to pinpoint the lady's hypnotic fascination, but there is a fiercely familiar quality about her. Something of her determination to do, be, and see everything in human experience burbles in everyone's blood stream.

Perhaps Mame is a symbol of this century. Since the time Mr. Coolidge started getting his shirts laundered on Pennsylvania Avenue, anyone truly perceptive could absorb more interesting stimuli in an hour than a Victorian aunt might encounter in a month of bank holidays. From all the recent miracles of communication and mobility, a new kind of human being has emerged: the *multi-person.* And because Mame is the multi-person personified, we could no more squeeze her into a single set than a single snapshot could portray the limitless panorama of her life and adventures. In his novel, Patrick Dennis vaguely nodded in the direction of the Aristotelian unities. We determined to toss Mr. Aristotle's pronunciamentos squarely in the ash can. We deliberately set out to design an entertainment that had the scope and ubiquity to match Mame's multi-personality.

Dramatizing *Auntie Mame* was an interesting challenge, because everybody agreed on one thing: it was impossible. Of course it is, in terms of conventional theatre. But we are very lucky: we have unconventional audiences. And, we hope, unconventional readers.

Every work for the theatre requires producers with taste, a director with resourcefulness and insight, a designer with playwright's blood, and a player who knows that it requires an equal part of hard work and ham to create that luminescence Noel Coward calls "star quality." *Auntie Mame* has had all these in Fryer and Carr, Morton DaCosta, Oliver Smith, and the unforgettable Rosalind Russell.

At one point, five companies of *Auntie Mame* were running simultaneously as a galaxy of other superstars followed: Greer Garson, Constance Bennett, Eve Arden, Beatrice Lillie, Sylvia Sidney, Shirl Conway, Conchita Montes as *Tia Mama* in Spain, Lilebel Ibsen (Henrik Ibsen's granddaughter) as *Min Fantastiske Tante* in Norway.

Ten years later we had the joy of turning *Auntie Mame* into the musical *Mame*—with Jerry Herman's melodically incomparable music. During a five-year run on Broadway and later on the stages of the world, a parade of star-ladies included: Angela Lansbury, Celeste Holm, Ginger Rogers, Janis Paige, Ann Miller, Jane Morgan, Susan Hayward, Juliet Prouse, Elaine Stritch, Janet Blair, Joan Brickhill, Patrice Munsel, Gretchen Wyler, Jan Clayton, Giselle MacKenzie, twice for Sylvia

Pinal in Mexico City, two separate companies in Tokyo plus the musical stars of a dozen other capitols.

For Mame Dennis Burnside life has indeed been a banquet.

Lawrence & Lee

Editor's Note

Two versions of *Auntie Mame* have been published: the hardcover Vanguard (New York) edition of 1957, and the acting edition published by Dramatists Play Service in 1960. The text printed here combines the two. The Dramatists Play Service text simplifies the complicated scenic production designed for the Broadway run, reducing the number of sets required by relocating act 1, scenes 4 and 5, in the living room of the Beekman Place apartment. The two versions have minor variations in lines, most often to accommodate the reduced scenery and, in other cases, to tighten the script. This edition restores the original scenic plan but retains the cuts (and the expanded telephone switchboard scene [act 1, scene 9]) of the Dramatists Play Service version.

Those theatres looking for a simpler version of the play for performance are advised to seek out the Dramatists Play Service text. As the spectacular nature of the physical production and the many costume changes for Rosalind Russell as Auntie Mame were much remarked upon when *Auntie Mame* opened on Broadway, it was felt best to present the text as originally performed.

Beatrice Lillie as Auntie Mame, London, 1958. Photo by Houston Taylor. Jerome Lawrence and Robert E. Lee Collection, Lawrence and Lee Theatre Research Institute, The Ohio State University.

CAST

Auntie Mame opened in New York at the Broadhurst Theatre on 31 October 1956. It was produced by Robert Fryer and Lawrence Carr, and directed by Morton DaCosta. The production was designed by Oliver Smith. The play is based on the novel by Patrick Dennis. The cast included:

NORAH MULDOON .... Beulah Garrick
PATRICK DENNIS, as a boy .... Jan Handzlik
ITO .... Yuki Shimoda
VERA CHARLES .... Polly Rowles
OSBERT .... Chris Alexander
RALPH DEVINE .... Grant Sullivan
BISHOP ELEFTHAROSES .... William Martel
M. LINDSAY WOOLSEY .... John O'Hare
AUNTIE MAME .... Rosalind Russell
MR. WALDO, a paper hanger .... Geoffrey Bryant
MR. BABCOCK .... Robert Allen
AL LINDEN, the stage manager .... Wally Mohr
A THEATRE MANAGER .... William Martel
ASSISTANT STAGE MANAGER .... Duane Camp
A MAID .... Kip McArdle
A LEADING MAN .... Paul Lilly
LORD DUDLEY .... Walter Riemer
A CUSTOMER .... Kip McArdle
A CUSTOMER'S SON .... Barry Towsen
MR. LOOMIS, a floor-walker .... Chris Alexander
BEAUREGARD JACKSON PICKETT BURNSIDE .... Robert Smith
COUSIN JEFF .... William Martel
COUSIN FAN .... Nan McFarland
COUSIN MOULTRIE .... Frank Roberts
SALLY CATO MACDOUGAL .... Marian Winters
EMORY MACDOUGAL .... Barry Blake
MOTHER BURNSIDE .... Ethel Cody
FRED, a groom .... Paul Lilly
SAM, another groom .... James Field
A HUNTSMAN .... Chris Alexander

DR. SHURR, a vet .... Geoffrey Bryant
PATRICK DENNIS, a young man .... Robert Higgins
AGNES GOOCH .... Peggy Cass
BRIAN O'BANNION .... James Monks
GLORIA UPSON .... Joyce Lear
DORIS UPSON .... Dorothy Blackburn
CLAUDE UPSON .... Walter Klavun
PEGEEN RYAN .... Patricia Jenkins
MICHAEL DENNIS .... Jan Handzlik

and a great many friends of AUNTIE MAME

Auntie Mame was produced prior to its Broadway run at the Playhouse, Wilmington, Delaware, opening on 24 September 1956; at the Forrest Theatre, Philadelphia, opening on 2 October 1956; and at the National Theatre, Washington, D.C., opening on 16 October 1956.

The action of the play takes place in Auntie Mame's Beekman Place apartment and various other locations in which she becomes involved during a period of years from 1928 to 1946.

Auntie Mame

ACT ONE

Scene 1

A projection appears on the curtain. It is a blow-up of a legal document: A voice on the P.A. speaks the words along with the projection:

"LAST WILL AND TESTAMENT

I, Edwin Dennis, being of sound mind and body, do hereby bequeath to my only son, Patrick, all my worldly possessions. In the event of my demise, I direct our faithful servant, Norah Muldoon, to deliver Patrick to my sister and next-of-kin, Mame Dennis, at 3 Beekman Place, New York City. The expenses of his upbringing shall be supervised by the Knickerbocker Bank as trustee, with the full power to keep that crazy sister of mine from doing anything too damned eccentric."

Behind this document, music begins to sound a trifle fey and Disney-esque.

"Since I keep myself in splendid physical condition through daily workouts at the Chicago Athletic Club, I am confident that these provisions will not go into force or effect for many years. I hereby affix my hand this fourteenth day of October, in the year 1928.

Signed:
EDWIN DENNIS"

There is a startled, eyebrow-lifting figure in the music, and the will slides out of sight, to be followed by a newspaper clipping, which reads:

"CHICAGO TRIBUNE—OCTOBER 15, 1928
BUSINESSMAN DROPS DEAD IN
STEAMROOM OF CHICAGO ATHLETIC
CLUB"

(*No voice on the headline.*)

ACT ONE
SCENE 2

Buzzing of a door bell, as the lights come up behind the scrim. Silhouetted in the foyer of the Beekman Place apartment are the stiff and uncomfortable figures of Norah Muldoon and Patrick, aged 10.

Norah tentatively presses the doorbell. From the interior of the apartment we hear laughter and the muffled gaiety of a fairly well-oiled party. The foyer is decorated in the gaudy Chinoiserie of the late Twenties.

NORAH. (*Looking around uncomfortably.*) It's like the ladies' restroom in the Oriental The-ay-ter.

YOUNG PAT. (*Clutching on to Norah's hand in terror.*) You're not scared, are you, Norah?

NORAH. Of course not, and don't you be, Patrick. Norah's here to look after you. (*She refers to a slip of paper in her trembling hand.*) Number 3, Beekman Place. This is where the lawyer told us to come. We're only doing what he told us. Of course we're not scared, child. (*They are drinking in the strangeness of their surroundings, and do not notice the door as it opens. Ito, a diminutive Japanese houseman, pads out unheard.*)

ITO. You want? (*Norah jumps. Patrick grasps Norah's hand more tightly.*)

NORAH. Glory be to God! I'm Miss . . . that is, I'm Norah Muldoon. And I've been sent by this boy's father—God rest his soul—to bring young Patrick here to live with his aunt, Miss . . . (*She glances again at the slip of paper.*) a Miss Mame Dennis, her name is. (*Ito studies Norah, then young Patrick—still clinging to Norah.*)

ITO. (*With sudden resolve.*) Must be mistake. No want little boy today. (*Ito starts to slam the door, but Norah puts her foot in it.*)

NORAH. But I sent the wire from Chicago myself, saying we'd arrive at 6 o'clock today.

ITO. Not important. Boy here, house here, Madam here. You come in. You wait. I fetch. (*Turns.*) Madam having affair now. (*Ito starts to usher them into the noisy interior of the apartment. Young Patrick looks warily at Norah.*)

YOUNG PAT. Norah, do you think we ought to?

NORAH. We've got no choice, Paddy. We've got no place to go. Come, child.

ACT ONE
SCENE 3

Young Pat and Norah go through the door, and the wall of the foyer breaks away, revealing a cross-section of Mame's Beekman Place apartment. A dozen or more people are milling about at the inebriated apex of a cocktail party. There is apparently a dining room off right, and a bar off left. The guests are continuously crossing back and forth between the hors d'oeuvres and the wet stuff.

Upstage center is a curved staircase which ascends to a bedroom area. Norah and Young Pat look about them, baffled by the milling confusion.

GIRL. Oh, Alex, you're simply *murdering* me! (*The apartment is homey as a Shinto shrine—low tables, low sofas, and high guests. Among the guests are a man who looks very much like Alexander Woollcott; a man who looks very much like Robert Benchley; Ralph Devine, a muscular educator; Osbert, a besandaled mystic; an orthodox Lithuanian Bishop; M. Lindsay Woolsey; and other typical cocktail party habitues of the late Twenties. Vera Charles, a famous British actress from Pittsburgh, is holding forth in the center of the room. Ito motions Norah and Pat to a bench, where they sit uncomfortably. There is a cheery panel behind them, depicting a Japanese nobleman disemboweling himself with a Samurai sword. Ito scurries out of sight, in search of Auntie Mame.*)

VERA. Mame's been trying to lure me into the daylight for months!—Birds, and the trees and all of that horrible nature business that I can't stand 'til five o'clock in the afternoon.

NORAH. Motheragod, the halls of hell!

RALPH DEVINE. Go on, Vera, go on.

VERA. Well, darling, I couldn't tell you why I ever let Mame persuade me—but Daphne had persuaded Mame that a fling into modern dance would tone her up. And you'll never believe—

RADCLIFFE. (*A He-type She, entering.*) Well, God knows if they want Maude killed professionally, they've sent the poor slob to the right place.

VERA. Radcliffe!

NORAH. White Slavers!

RADCLIFFE. I told her from the start—

VERA. Really, Radcliffe!

RADCLIFFE. Sorry, darling. Didn't realize you were still on.

VERA. Anyway, there we were barefooted, in our camisoles on Daphne's lawn—squatting and unsquatting. Osbert, darling, you really should speak to Daphne. Of course, *I* managed beautifully—I was grace personified—but it damn near killed Mame.

OSBERT. Daphne's whole theory of modern dance is based on challenging the pelvis.

VERA. Mame was challenged all right. She had to go to Swami Paramanda for a month to push her pelvis back where it was. (*Lowering her voice.*) Don't, for heaven's sake, mention to Mame that I mentioned this. You know, I adore her, but in a camisole—well!!! (*Mame enters, down the stairs.*)

AUNTIE MAME. I'll get the maid started, Ito. Ring up Bonelli and tell him to get out here with some more gin. (*Auntie Mame's hair is bobbed very short with straight bangs above her slanting brows; a long robe of embroidered golden silk floats out behind her. She wears tiny gold slippers twinkling with jewels, and jade and ivory bracelets clatter on her arms. Her long fingernails are lacquered a delicate green. An almost endless bamboo cigarette holder hangs languidly from her bright red mouth. She crosses to Norah and looks at her with an expression of bemused surprise.*) Oh dear, the Employment Bureau didn't tell me you were bringing a child with you. Well, no matter. He looks like a nice little boy. And if he misbehaves, we can always toss him into the river. (*All laugh, except Norah and Young Pat.*) I guess you know what's expected of you—just a little light slavery around the place.

NORAH. I'm prepared to *buy* my way out. I'll give you my life savings if you'll let this child and me escape from this nest of thieves and slavers! (*Auntie Mame reacts with sad incredulity, then plucks at the sleeve of a distinguished man wearing a goatee.*)

AUNTIE MAME. Dr. Fuchtwanger—just in time. You'd better get this woman on your couch in a hurry.

NORAH. I'm not that kind of a woman, mum. All I'm looking for is a Miss Mame Dennis who's supposed to live at Number 3, Beekman Place.

AUNTIE MAME. (*Calling.*) Ito, oh, Ito! (*Ito comes on.*) Ito, where have you been? Show this woman the kitchen and get her started on the glasses.

ITO. Oh, Missy Dennis, this not dishwashing lady.

AUNTIE MAME. Oh, I'm so sorry. (*Shrugs.*) Then I must have invited you. What would you like to drink?

NORAH. Did you not get my telegram? I'm Norah Muldoon.

AUNTIE MAME. (*Gasps.*) No! That's not possible. The wire said December first. That's tomorrow. This is November 31st.

NORAH. (*Balefully.*) No, mum. 'Tis the first, God curse the evil day.

AUNTIE MAME. That's ridiculous. Everyone knows "Thirty days hath September, April, June and Nov" . . . Oh, God! (*Dramatically she enfolds Young Pat in her arms.*) But, darling! *I'm* your Auntie *Mame*! (*Baffled, Young Pat submits to Auntie Mame's effusive embrace. She turns toward her guests, lifting her voice.*) Quiet, quiet, everybody. I have an important announcement to make. This is *my little boy*. (*There are reactions of surprise, pleasure and a few raised eyebrows.*) Oh, he's not really *my* little boy. He's my brother's son. From Chicago. (*She sniffs.*) My poor late brother. (*Norah crosses herself. There are some sympathetic clucks and one hiccup.*) This little tyke. In all the whole wide world, I'm his only living relative. And he's my only living relative. (*She stoops down and embraces him again.*) That's all we have, just each other, my little love. (*There are a few moist eyes at this touching scene. Then Mame looks at Young Pat quizzically.*) What's your—(*Recovers.*) What am I going to call you, dear?

YOUNG PAT. Pat. Patrick Dennis.

AUNTIE MAME. I know the Dennis part, darling, and from now on you must call me "Auntie Mame." Now, how would you like a mart—? Is it your bedtime? Heavens, it can't be. Do you want the—ah, powder room, darling? Or food? Food, that's it! You must be famished. You run right along in there and help yourself to the caviar—(*Young Pat starts toward the inside room. She calls after him.*) After that you can go upstairs and read a book or something.

RALPH DEVINE. (*Approaching Mame.*) Oh, Mame! You're not going to let that child *read*? Taste life second hand!

AUNTIE MAME. Ralph, do you think you could work little Patrick into one of your advanced study groups?

RALPH DEVINE. Yes, I think there just might be an opening. (*Young Pat returns, munching a deviled egg.*)

AUNTIE MAME. (*To Young Pat.*) Where've you been going to school, dear?

YOUNG PAT. Chicago Boys' Latin.

RALPH DEVINE. (*With a hollow laugh.*) Uh-huh. Where they build a wall of dull encyclopedias around the id!

YOUNG PAT. The id?

RALPH DEVINE. See? Doesn't even know a simple two-letter word. That's John Dewey for you.

AUNTIE MAME. (*Explaining to Young Pat.*) Shake hands with Mr. Devine, Patrick. He runs a school down in the Village where they do all sorts of advanced things. Perhaps we'll enroll you there.

YOUNG PAT. (*Eagerly, shaking hands with Ralph.*) Is it a military school? Do they wear uniforms? (*Ralph Devine looks appalled.*)

RALPH DEVINE. In my school, young man, we don't wear *any*thing.

AUNTIE MAME. It's heaven. (*Norah is shocked, but Ito tugs her out of the room, up the stairs. The party begins to bubble again. Mame draws Young Pat aside.*) Now, these are a lot of your Auntie Mame's most intimate friends; I don't know all their names, but you can just circulate and you'll hear the most fascinating conversation. Oh, I'm sorry you missed the cast of *Blackbirds*, but they had to leave early.

YOUNG PAT. Who's he? (*He indicates the bearded patriarch, in mitred cap and jeweled robes, impassively eating stuffed celery.*)

AUNTIE MAME. That's a Lithuanian Bishop. Doesn't speak a word of English. Stimulating man. (*They come into the circle where Vera Charles is holding forth.*) Vera? Vera, this is my little boy. Patrick! I want you to meet a star. One of the great ladies of the theatre, and your Auntie Mame's dearest friend, Vera Charles.

YOUNG PAT. Hello.

VERA. How do you do.

AUNTIE MAME. She just *loves* little boys.

VERA. (*Distastefully.*) Yes. (*Ito helps the Bishop into his cape. Auntie Mame moves toward him.*)

AUNTIE MAME. Oh, Bishop, do you have to run? I'm so sorry. We certainly enjoyed your conversation. Too bad nobody else here spoke Lithuanian. Such a darling—and so worldly for a man of God. (*The Bishop exits. Auntie Mame crosses back to Young Patrick, who had been listening to Vera. Auntie Mame takes his hand and draws the boy away.*) Isn't she scintillating, darling? Now I want you to meet—

YOUNG PAT. Auntie Mame, what's "nymphomania"?

AUNTIE MAME. It's very simple. Nymphomania is— (*Crosses to table, takes out pad and pencil.*) I'll tell you what we're going to do. Every time you hear a word you don't understand, just take this pad and pencil and write it down. Later on Auntie Mame will explain it to you. (*Young Pat moves to take down words.*) Oh, the adventure of molding a new little life.

OSBERT. Goodbye, Mame, I've got to fly.

AUNTIE MAME. Goodbye, Osbert, darling. I'll see you on Tuesday. Don't catch cold. (*Osbert exits. She notices Young Pat writing.*) Are you enjoying yourself, dear?

YOUNG PAT. I guess so.

AUNTIE MAME. I imagine it's a little confusing—after Chicago and everything.

YOUNG PAT. I guess so, ma'am.

AUNTIE MAME. Uh-uh.

YOUNG PAT. I mean Auntie Mame.

AUNTIE MAME. (*Crosses to Ralph Devine.*) Oh dear, this is tougher than talking with the Lithuanian Bishop. (*Ralph Devine looks analytically at Young Pat.*)

RALPH DEVINE. You know why. The poor little fella's a mass of inhibitions. Send him to me. Won't be a repression left after the first semester.

AUNTIE MAME. Consider him enrolled.

RALPH DEVINE. Good. Give his libido a good shaking up, that's what we'll do. Incidentally, Mame, how's *your* libido these days?

AUNTIE MAME. Stirred, but not shaken.

RALPH DEVINE. Who's the lucky man?—still Lindsay Woolsey?

AUNTIE MAME. (*Airily.*) Among others.

RALPH DEVINE. Well, I wouldn't mind being one of the others that he's among.

AUNTIE MAME. You're a naughty boy, Ralph, but you have lovely muscles.

RALPH DEVINE. Well, I don't mean to drink and dash—but I don't want to be late for my rubdown. (*Ralph Devine departs athletically. Vera is carried across in a prone position, with Ito at one end and Lindsay supporting the great actress's feet. Vera is out stone-cold.*)

ITO. Guest room again, Missy?

AUNTIE MAME. No—no, the coats are in there. Dump her in my room. And, Ito, get that God-awful dress off her.

ITO. (*Grinning.*) Me tuck her in. (*He giggles as they carry her up the stairs.*)

YOUNG PAT. Is the English lady dead, Auntie Mame?

AUNTIE MAME. She's not English, darling. She's from Pittsburgh.

YOUNG PAT. She *sounded* English.

AUNTIE MAME. When you're from Pittsburgh, you've got to do something. Now, read me the words you didn't understand.

YOUNG PAT. (*Clearing his throat, reads with difficulty.*) Free-love. Stinko. Hotsy-Totsy Club. Bath-tub gin. Karl Marx. (*He looks up innocently.*) Is he one of the Marx Brothers?

AUNTIE MAME. No, dear.

YOUNG PAT. (*Resuming.*) Narciss-iss-istic. Lys-iss-istrata. Lesbian. Son-of-a - - - (*Deftly she rips the pad out of his hands.*)

AUNTIE MAME. My, my, what an eager little mind. (*She rips the page from the pad.*) You won't need some of these words for months and months. (*Lindsay Woolsey comes down the stairs.*)

LINDSAY. Well, I suppose the new arrival means you can't have dinner with me tonight.

AUNTIE MAME. You're so understanding, Lindsay.

LINDSAY. Displaced by the younger generation!

AUNTIE MAME. Not at all. Not at all.

LINDSAY. I suppose this means I'll be seeing you even less.

AUNTIE MAME. *More*, Lindsay, more. We'll be taking the little lad to the zoo and the aquarium—and we'll be dropping in your office and you can show him how you publish books. We'll be together almost constantly—the three of us.

LINDSAY. Yeah. That's exactly what I had in mind. (*Lindsay exits. The party is thinning out now. Between leave-takings Auntie Mame tries to make her new little visitor seem at home.*)

AUNTIE MAME. Well, now, there's so much we have to discover about each other. I never had a live little boy around the place before. I did mean to have your bedroom all fixed up for you. A friend of mine is coming in to redo the sculpture room into a nursery—well, it's not really a sculpture room, darling, but a sculptor-friend of mine stayed in it for about six months. Such talented fingers, but what he did to my bust—uh—that's the head you know. Anyway he's going to redo the room for you with bunnies all over everything. (*A Man approaches Auntie Mame. He is supporting a Woman who is completely stoned.*)

MAN. 'Night, Mame. Thanks. (*He extends his hand.*)

AUNTIE MAME. Goodnight, Charles. (*The Girl begins to pass out.*) Watch it, Edna.

MAN. (*As he staggers out with his companion.*) We're already late for Clifton's party. (*They go.*)

AUNTIE MAME. Give Clifton my love. Tell him I'm sorry to miss him, but to ring me up next week some time. (*To Young Pat.*) Now, let's sit down for one minute and really get to know each other. (*As they sit on bench.*) What did you think of the conversation of the party?

YOUNG PAT. Some of it was a little over my head.

AUNTIE MAME. Good heavens, child, didn't your father ever talk to you?

YOUNG PAT. Hardly ever. I only saw him at breakfast time.

AUNTIE MAME. Well, what did he say then?

YOUNG PAT. He usually said, "Pipe down, kid, the old man's hung."

AUNTIE MAME. Amen. (*Turning to Young Pat.*) What did you do in Chicago for *fun*?

YOUNG PAT. Well, Norah took me to the movies every Saturday afternoon. And I played parchesi with the doorman once in a while—until he got fired.

AUNTIE MAME. Oh dear. Didn't they ever do anything cultural for you in Chicago? (*Waving it away.*) Never mind. (*She pats his cheek.*) Ahhh, your Auntie Mame is going to open doors for you, Patrick—doors you never even dreamed existed! What times we're going to have! (*She rises and crosses to a table, snapping off the overhead light.*) Now, what on earth did I do with that will? (*Searching through a random stack of papers in the drawer.*) It's here some place. (*Reading from a blue-backed document.*) Five pounds Beluga caviar, get hair done—this can't be it— (*She turns it over.*) Oh, yes, this *is* it. (*Auntie Mame returns to sit beside Young Pat on the bench, and leafs through the legal document.*) Your father says you're to be reared as a Protestant. Well, I've no objection to that. (*She gazes off at the ceiling, drawing on her cigarette.*) Though it would be a shame to deprive you of the exquisite mysteries of the Eastern religions. (*She turns to him.*) Where did you go to church, darling?

YOUNG PAT. The Fourth Presbyterian.

AUNTIE MAME. You mean to say there are *four* Presbyterian churches in a place like Chicago? Well, no matter. I guess we can scrounge around and find some sort of Presbyterian Church in the neighborhood. (*She continues to flip through the document.*) Now there's a lot of fol-de-rol about the Knickerbocker Bank and some Mr. Babcock who's been appointed your trustee. (*She slaps the will down on her lap, annoyed.*) Well, I see what that means. *I* have the responsibility, and your trustee has the authority.

YOUNG PAT. I saw a movie once about a trustee.

AUNTIE MAME. Oh?

YOUNG PAT. There was a big prison break, and the trustee saved the warden's daughter.

AUNTIE MAME. This isn't the kind of a trustee that lives in a prison dear. As a rule. (*She mouths the name disdainfully.*) Mr. Babcock. (*Her nostrils dilate slightly.*) We'll tackle him in our own good time. (*Tosses the will on the floor.*) Now, tell me, Patrick. Is your Auntie Mame anything like you expected?

YOUNG PAT. No, ma'am. The only picture I ever saw of you was with a shawl and a rose between your teeth. Like a Spanish lady. It's in my suitcase that's coming. (*Auntie Mame smiles reminiscently, then seriously:*)

AUNTIE MAME. But didn't your father ever *say* anything—*tell* you anything—about me, before he died?

YOUNG PAT. Yes, ma'am.

AUNTIE MAME. Well, what was it? (*Young Pat gulps.*) Come now, my little love. You must always be perfectly frank with your Auntie Mame.

YOUNG PAT. (*Takes a deep breath, and blurts it out.*) Well, my father said since you're my only living relative, beggars can't be choosers. But to be left in your hands was a fate he wouldn't wish on a *dog*!

AUNTIE MAME. (*Evenly.*) That bastard. (*Dutifully, Young Pat reaches for the pad and starts to write down the strange word. She glances at the boy and speaks sweetly.*) That word, dear, was "Bastard." (*She takes the pad and pencil from Young Pat, and prints in virulent block letters.*) B-A-S-T-A-R-D— (*Magnificently she hands him the pad.*)—And it means *your late father*!

THE LIGHTS FADE

ACT ONE
SCENE 4

The foyer of Auntie Mame's apartment, two weeks later. A Paperhanger, atop a ladder, is putting some finishing touches on the wild, neocubist wallpaper which he has just hung. He comes down the ladder, looking at his handiwork suspiciously. Norah comes on and makes a little gasp at the sight of the bizarre walls.

NORAH. What is it?

PAPERHANGER. It's wallpaper. But don't look at me. I didn't pick it out, I only pasted it on. Why, is it upside-down?

NORAH. No more than everything else around here, I guess. You haven't seen the boy, have you?

PAPERHANGER. Saw a kid go out 'bout a hour ago.

NORAH. Sendin' him all over the city alone. "He's got to discover New York for himself" says she. "You can't go with him, Norah. We want him to turn out to be independent, don't we?" Independent! He'll turn out to be dead under some truck.

PAPERHANGER. I've got an order here to redo a couple of bedrooms. Can I get in?

NORAH. (*Sarcastically.*) At two o'clock! Why, you'll be lucky to get in by five. She's still sleepin'.

PAPERHANGER. Well, I'll get started in the other bedroom then.

NORAH. Oh, you can't go in there, either!

PAPERHANGER. Why not? She ain't sleeping in two bedrooms, is she?

NORAH. Oh, no. It's the first lady of the American the-ay-ter out cold in the guest room.

PAPERHANGER. Again! What's she do, live here?

NORAH. Miss Charles don't live here. She drinks here and she does her passin' out here. It's a wonder to me their blood hasn't turned to vinegar. Two weeks I've been here and they've had thirteen cocktail parties.

PAPERHANGER. Only thirteen in two weeks!

NORAH. They had to call one off. The bootlegger couldn't come that day. (*Young Pat dashes on, clear across the apron of the stage, and through the door, heading toward the stairs. He carries a model airplane—an approximation of the Spirit of St. Louis.*) Thank God you're safe.

YOUNG PAT. Where's Auntie Mame? I've got to show her something.

NORAH. Your Auntie Mame's still asleep.

PAPERHANGER. (*Unrolling an outrageously garish length of wallpaper—the motif of a bloodshot eye.*) This'll wake her up.

ACT ONE
SCENE 5

The lights come up—faintly—on Auntie Mame's plush bedroom. She is reclining on a huge bed, with a sleeping mask over her eyes. Young Pat bursts in the door.

YOUNG PAT. (*Excitedly.*) Auntie Mame! Auntie Mame! (*Auntie Mame is shocked into jangling wakefulness. She sits upright in bed and clutches the mask from her face.*)

AUNTIE MAME. (*Confused.*) What is it? What happened?

YOUNG PAT. I've got something to show you. (*He opens the venetian blinds and a shaft of bright afternoon sunlight hits Auntie Mame squarely in the face. She reels back against *the pillow.*) Look! (*Young Pat spins the airplane. Auntie Mame watches it with fascinated horror.*)

AUNTIE MAME. My God! *Bats!* (*Young Pat attempts to show her his new toy, proudly.*)

YOUNG PAT. See? It's got a rubber-band motor, and I whittled the body out of balsa-woods, and— (*Auntie Mame gestures him away, closing her eyes and holding her aching head.*)

AUNTIE MAME. Please, darling—your Auntie Mame's hung. (*Young Pat is deeply hurt by this. It's Chicago all over again. Quietly he takes the airplane and starts off.*)

YOUNG PAT. (*Softly.*) Oh, sure, Auntie Mame. (*Suddenly Auntie Mame realizes what she has done. Peeking through her fingers, she braves the sunlight and calls to the boy.*)

AUNTIE MAME. Patrick. Patrick, come back. (*Young Pat stops at the far side of the room, turns.*) You know, I really am interested in all your projects. But you've got to admit it's a bit surprising for Auntie Mame to find Mr. Lindbergh in her bedroom before breakfast. (*She squints at the light.*) Child, how can you *see* with all that light? (*Obligingly, Young Pat crosses downstage and pulls an imaginary venetian blind a hair closed. The lights come down just a mite.*) That's better. Now be a perfect angel and ask Ito to bring me a very light breakfast: black coffee and a sidecar. And you might ask him to fix something for your Aunt Vera. I think I hear her coming to in the guest room. (*Young Pat starts toward the kitchen obediently.*) First—come and give your Auntie Mame a good morning kiss. (*Young Pat starts to run toward her.*) Gently, dear. Gently. (*Young Pat kisses her tenderly on the cheek.*) That was lovely, darling. You'll make some lucky woman very happy some day. (*Gingerly Auntie Mame takes the airplane model and winds the propeller tentatively.*) You know, I really am fascinated by aviation. I never knew before they did it all with rubber bands. (*The telephone rings insolently. This affects Auntie Mame like a dentist's drill at the nape of her neck. Young Pat picks up the phone.*)

YOUNG PAT. (*Into the phone.*) Hello? Miss Dennis—yes, she's here. Who's calling, please? (*Pause.*) Hold the wire. (*To Auntie Mame, covering the mouthpiece.*) It's Mr. Babcock—from the Knickerbocker Bank. (*Auntie Mame takes the phone, pressing the receiver to her chest.*)

AUNTIE MAME. Oh, my God, I've been dodging him for days. (*Realizing what she's done, she speaks sweetly.*) Oh, hello, Mr. Babcock! How nice to hear your voice at long last. (*Young Pat is attentive, knowing that he is at issue here.*) I, too, am looking forward with anticipation to meeting *you*. (*She listens.*) Oh, the little lad is fine. Just fine. And he, too, can't *wait* to meet you. (*Young Pat shrugs indifferently. Auntie Mame covers the mouthpiece, and speaks hoarsely to Pat.*) Hurry my tray, dear. Auntie needs fuel. (*Young Pat exits. Auntie Mame turns back to the phone.*) Please *do* stop by, Mr. Babcock—*any*time. (*She goes pale.*) In how many minutes? (*Flustered.*) Yes, Fifty-seventh Street *is* right in my, uh, "neck-of-the-woods." "Spitting distance." How vivid. (*Pause.*) Come right along. Then you can join me for breakfa—*tea*! (*Nodding.*) Number Three, Beekman Place. Right away. (*She puts down the phone. She lets out a plaintive yell.*) Vera! VERA! Get in here! (*The door to the adjoining bedroom is opened fumblingly, and Vera staggers in, heading for the bed. Vera's evening gown looks as if it had *been slept in, which it has. She still wears a totally discouraged orchid. She has one shoe on, and her hair and make-up are a mess.)*

VERA. (*Wobbly and incoherent.*) Did you call me, darling?

AUNTIE MAME. (*Getting up.*) I'm about to be attacked by the Knickerbocker Bank.

VERA. (*Falling onto the bed.*) That's lovely. Why in hell did that Japanese sandman let me sleep in my best Lanvin?

AUNTIE MAME. He tried to get it off you, but you bit him. Patrick's trustee is on his way over here.

VERA. It's ruined. Absolutely ruined.

AUNTIE MAME. Some hideous creature who's coming here to thwart all the plans I've made for the boy's cultural enlargement!

VERA. (*Incredulously.*) He's coming here—in the middle of the night? (*Vera, half rising, blinks at the partially opened blinds.*) My God, that moon's bright. (*She falls right back down again.*)

AUNTIE MAME. Oh, don't be silly, Vera. Don't you realize—some horrible man is descending like a vulture to rob me of my child?

VERA. Mame, you're being *ut*terly hysterical.

AUNTIE MAME. I've got to make the right impression. You have no idea how conservative the Knickerbocker Bank is; it's so conservative they don't pay any interest at *all.* (*Vera rises, hazily, slapping herself in the face to waken herself.*)

VERA. All right. Let's get organized. What time is it? What *day* is it? (*Vera picks up a clock and looks at it in horror.*) Blessed mother of Maude Adams. I was due at the Theatre Guild an hour ago.

AUNTIE MAME. You can't desert me in my predicament, Vera. Look at my face. What on earth am I going to wear?

VERA. How am I going to face the Theatre Guild? The way I look I couldn't even understudy a witch in "Macbeth."

AUNTIE MAME. (*Hurrying to the closet.*) That's just like you, Vera! Here my life is about to be blown to bits—and all you can think of is your career! (*Auntie Mame starts hauling clothes out of a closet frantically and dumping them on the bed. She pulls out one very flashy dress, beads and spangles, and holds it up in front of herself appraisingly.*) Will this make me look like a Scarsdale matron? (*Vera squints at her, disbelieving.*)

VERA. Have you ever been to Scarsdale? (*Young Pat enters with a small breakfast tray on which there are a cup of coffee and a side-car.*)

YOUNG PAT. Good afternoon, Auntie Vera.

VERA. Yes, dear. (*Vera takes the side-car and pours it straight down.*) Do the Jane Cowl routine. You know, conservative dress, madonna-like hair do.

AUNTIE MAME. Madonna-like hair do. That's it. A switch. A switch.

VERA. Have you got one?

AUNTIE MAME. Dozens. (*She pulls out an array of switches, that puts a rainbow to shame.*)

VERA. My God, don't you ever throw anything away?

AUNTIE MAME. Who knows when I may go back to one of these colors?

VERA. If you kept your hair natural the way I do, you wouldn't need—

AUNTIE MAME. If I kept my hair natural the way you do, I'd be bald. Pick out the one nearest to mine.

VERA. (*Picking out the black one and tossing it on the bed.*) Try this. And you need a dress—like the one I wore when I played Lady Esme in "Summer Folly." (*Mame takes a lovely green frock from the pile.*) Oh, that's stunning.

AUNTIE MAME. Isn't it? It's my new Maggie Rouf. But I've never had it on yet. And I'll be damned if I'll put five hundred dollars on my back for that awful man. (*An idea.*) A suit! A suit! That'll do. (*Picks up the switch.*) Help me braid this switch so it looks like a halo.

VERA. (*Protesting.*) I've got to get over to the Guild!

AUNTIE MAME. Vera, you can't desert me! (*Vera helps Auntie Mame reluctantly.*)

VERA. *You* should be helping *me*. Do you want me to *lose* this part? (*Vera is braiding Auntie Mame's switch furiously, then drops it. Auntie Mame puts one end of the switch in her mouth and braids it herself.*) It's this lovely, lovely play where everybody thinks out loud and it runs four-and-a-half hours. It's called "Strange—" (*She can't remember the title, and gropes for it.*) "Strange Inter—Inter—Inter"

AUNTIE MAME. (*Helpfully.*) "Course?"

VERA. For God's sake, no. They're opening in Boston. I do hope Lawrence and Terry don't think I'm too British for the part. They'll probably give it to that Lynn what's-her-name.

AUNTIE MAME. Ouch! (*Mr. Babcock appears in the foyer and rings the door buzzer.*) Not already! (*Calls.*) Ito,—answer the door!

VERA. I've got to get out before he gets in!

AUNTIE MAME. Well, I can't leave him standing in the foyer like a Fuller Brush man.

VERA. What do you want me to do, fly out the chimney?

AUNTIE MAME. Oh, Vera, for heaven's sake—

VERA. (*Grandly.*) You can't expect me to appear before my public looking as if I'd been slept in!

AUNTIE MAME. Really, Vera—one banker doesn't make a matinee. (*Pinning the braid hastily.*) All right. Wait here, I'll get rid of him in five minutes—I promise.

VERA. Mame, you just don't understand the responsibility of being in the public eye. (*Babcock, in the foyer, is getting impatient. He presses the door buzzer again. Auntie Mame starts out and her braid topples into her face.*)

AUNTIE MAME. (*Turns urgently to Young Pat.*) Patrick. Make Mr. Babcock feel right at home, just like Auntie Mame taught you.

YOUNG PAT. Sure, Auntie Mame. (*Auntie Mame pushes Vera out the door with a shove in the derriere.*)

VERA. (*Protesting.*) But the Theatre Guild.

AUNTIE MAME. (*The other hand is struggling with the switch.*) What am I going to do with this *God damned halo*?????

ACT ONE
SCENE 6

The lighting cross-fades to the foyer and the redecorated downstairs. Mr. Babcock is punching the door buzzer a little irritably. He is conservative to the very inlays of his molars, with all the personality of a steamroller wearing a vest. Ito scurries to the door, carrying a feminine nightgown on a hanger. He opens the door.

ITO. You want?

BABCOCK. Babcock is the name. Miss Dennis is expecting me.

ITO. Okay. You come in. I take coat. (*Ito starts to help Babcock off with his coat, but cannot manage it while carrying the negligee. He gives the negligee to Babcock who holds it awkwardly. Ito starts off with Babcock's coat and muffler, leaving the banker holding the negligee.*) You sit.

BABCOCK. Say—! (*Ito takes the negligee from the slightly ruffled Babcock and scampers off giggling. Young Pat comes down the stairs and greets Mr. Babcock with unaffected composure.*)

YOUNG PAT. Mr. Babcock?

BABCOCK. That's right, Sonny.

YOUNG PAT. We've been expecting you. (*He offers his hand.*) My name is Patrick Dennis.

BABCOCK. (*Shaking the boy's hand.*) Fine, fine.

YOUNG PAT. Please sit down, Mr. Babcock. My Auntie Mame will be right down. She's having trouble with her halo. (*Recovers.*) She'll be right down.

BABCOCK. Fine, fine. (*They look at each other, realizing they have absolutely nothing to communicate.*) Well, you look like a bully little chap. Yes, sir, a bully little chap.

YOUNG PAT. You look very bully, too, Mr. Babcock.

BABCOCK. (*Clears his throat.*) Yes. Well, you seem to be taking all this like a regular little soldier. Oh, say, I have a boy just about your age up in Darien. We'll have you up soon, and Junior can show you his cigar-band collection.

YOUNG PAT. (*Politely.*) That would be swell. (*Babcock slaps his knees and rises impatiently.*) Would you care for a martini, Mr. Babcock?

BABCOCK. No, thank you. (*He breaks off, startled, as he sees the hari-kari painting.*) Maybe you'd better order me one, Sonny.

YOUNG PAT. (*Wheeling the portable bar to the right.*) Dry or extra dry? (*Babcock is about to reply, but stops open-mouthed to watch Young Pat as he takes a martini glass with great finesse, breathes in it and dries it snappily with a cocktail towel. The boy holds the glass up to the light and squints through it approvingly.*) Please sit down. (*Babcock's mouth has sprung open, and apparently he's not going to reply.*) I'll make 'em like I do for Mr. Woollcott. (*From an ice bucket, he drops some cubes into a pitcher; then he pours in a great quantity of gin and stirs.*) Stir—never shake. Bruises the gin. (*Babcock nods mechanically. Young Pat uncorks the vermouth, pours a smidgeon into the glass, swills it around by rotating the stem then empties it completely.*) Would you care for an olive? Auntie Mame says olives take up too much room in such a little glass! (*Babcock shakes his head, his jowls flapping, and takes the glass. The Banker takes one sip, then turns to see Auntie Mame coming down the stairs demurely—complete with braided coronet and all the aplomb of a Scarsdale matron being played by Jane Cowl. She blanches at Young Pat's alcoholic gambit, but makes a lightning recovery. Young Pat wheels the bar back into place.*)

AUNTIE MAME. (*Grandly.*) Why, Mr. Babcock, what an honor it is to have you in our little home. (*She draws him aside, confidentially.*) Though I wonder if it makes the best first impression on a sensitive young mind to see you drinking during business hours.

BABCOCK. (*Floundering indignantly.*) But—but *he*—

AUNTIE MAME. (*Patting his arm reassuringly.*) Don't you worry, I won't breathe a word to the Knickerbocker Bank. (*Babcock puts down the drink on table, and tries to slide it out of sight, behind him. He can't quite figure out how he has been put on the defensive.*)

BABCOCK. Now, just a minute. Where did that youngster learn to mix a—

AUNTIE MAME. (*With dignified hauteur.*) Mr. Babcock, Knowledge is power! (*This stops him.*)

BABCOCK. (*Clears his throat.*) That, Miss Dennis, is exactly what I am here for. To discuss this youngster's education. His *proper* education.

AUNTIE MAME. (*Offering a dish.*) Nuts?

BABCOCK. No, thank you.

AUNTIE MAME. *Do* sit down, Mr. Babcock. (*They do. Mr. Babcock finds himself uncomfortably close to the floor on the Japanese settee. Auntie Mame sits opposite him, and Young Pat sits on the ottoman between them. He looks back and forth from one speaker to the other as his fate is being decided.*)

BABCOCK. (*Very business-like.*) Now. All the money this little fella's "Dad" left him is in good, steady bonds. So he never has to worry where his next meal is coming from. Unless—um—the Bolshevikis take over the government. Or the Democrats get back in.

AUNTIE MAME. Jelly beans?

BABCOCK. (*Taking one.*) Now I'm sure you agree that it's high time this little shaver was enrolled in some institution of learning.

YOUNG PAT. (*Brightly.*) Oh, I'm already—

AUNTIE MAME. Now—now. Let Mr. Babcock talk, dear.

BABCOCK. Now, I've gone to, uh, some pains to, uh, gather information on a number of the better boys' schools in town. (*He brings list from inside coat pocket.*)

AUNTIE MAME. Personally, I prefer co-educational schools.

BABCOCK. (*Shocked.*) What do you mean?

YOUNG PAT. (*Helpfully.*) Co-educational means when boys and girls go—

BABCOCK. I know, I know. (*Clears his throat.*) First on my list is the Buckley School, which is known to be splendid.

AUNTIE MAME. Have you considered a school down in the Village run by a Mr. Ralph Devine? It's wonderfully progressive and—

BABCOCK. (*Holding up a hand as if directing rush-hour traffic.*) Your late brother was very specific in his will. He said *conservative* schooling. (*Consulting his list.*) Now, the Browning School gives a boy the basics. Three years of Latin— (*While Babcock is speaking, Vera appears at the top of the stairs behind him. She gesticulates vigorously to Mame, who is facing her. Babcock looks up.*)

AUNTIE MAME. (*Covering.*) That's enough candy, dear. Not you, Mr. Babcock. Have as much as you like. (*Quickly.*) Have you thought of the Dalton School? It's right up—

BABCOCK. No, no. That one is a *li*ttle too experimental. (*He digs out several pamphlets.*) We must choose a school which is both exclusive and restricted.

AUNTIE MAME. (*Gritting her teeth.*) Exclusively *what* and restricted to *whom*?

BABCOCK. Want to keep the riffraff out of this lad's life—(*Mame is about to explode.*)

AUNTIE MAME. Mr. Babbitt—

BABCOCK. Bab*cock*.

AUNTIE MAME. Yes. Uh—exactly who decides which is riff and which is raff?

BABCOCK. Now, Miss Dennis, unless we can agree on some proper school here in Manhattan, we shall have to consider an institution such as *my* alma mater, St. Boniface, up in Massachusetts.

AUNTIE MAME. No, no, that's too far away! Have you thought of the Ethical Culture School—that's just across town?

BABCOCK. I'd like to keep that west-side influence out of the boy's life as much as possible. (*Auntie Mame stands, icily, indicating that the interview is over.*)

AUNTIE MAME. It was very good of you to come, Mr. Babcock.

BABCOCK. But we haven't arrived at any conclusions.

AUNTIE MAME. Haven't we?

BABCOCK. Well, what school is it going to be?

AUNTIE MAME. You name the school of your choice, and Patrick and I will know exactly what to do.

BABCOCK. (*Strongly.*) I'd say Buckley.

AUNTIE MAME. Then *bully* for Buckley.

BABCOCK. Well— (*This has been easier than he thought it would be.*) For a minute there, I thought we were going to have a little friction. (*He chortles.*) But I'm glad to see you're actually a fine, sensible woman. I'll make out a check to the Buckley School and you can take him down and register him.

AUNTIE MAME. (*Sweetly.*) Whatever you say. Well, it's so nice of you to— (*Vera, with a scarf tied around her head like a peasant babushka, comes down stairs and plods across the room. She is wearing Auntie Mame's new Maggie Rouf and dragging Auntie Mame's best mink on the floor behind her.*)

VERA. (*In a thick accent.*) Floor all scrubbed, Fraulein Dennis. Clean yoost like in old country. I go now, get lamb chops, two bottles milk for boy.

AUNTIE MAME. (*Between her teeth.*) Pick up my coat.

YOUNG PAT. Goodbye, Auntie Vera.

VERA. (*Back in her own voice.*) 'Bye, kid. (*There is a big take from the already bewildered Babcock, as Vera scoots out the front door, on her way to the Theatre Guild. Auntie Mame turns innocently back to Babcock.*)

AUNTIE MAME. You were saying, Mr. Babcock?

THE LIGHTS FADE

ACT ONE
SCENE 7

The panels of the living room have been switched and the furnishings have been redressed, as much as time will allow. The wallpaper is now modern.

The phone rings. The Paperhanger is coming down his ladder, looks around at his handiwork, shakes his head. Ito enters from the foyer, carrying a chart.

PAPERHANGER. Phone's ringin'. (*He goes out to kitchen. Ito puts down the chart on table, facing upstage, and picks up the phone.*)

ITO. (*Into phone.*) Missy Dennis residence. Stock Broker? Missy Dennis not here, you call back next month some time. (*He listens.*) Missy Dennis say anybody who call servant dirty bastard is dirty bastard. (*He puts down the phone, smiling happily. Norah enters in a hat and coat, her arms full of groceries.*)

NORAH. (*To Ito.*) Now, where've *you* been?

ITO. Missy Dennis send me 'cross ocean. Staten Island. Bring back body.

NORAH. What body?

ITO. For boy.

NORAH. (*Reading cover on chart.*) "The Physiological Anatomical Medical Supply Company." What in the name of St. Brigid is it?

ITO. Missy say boy gotta know inside like outside. (*He flips over the cover, revealing a skeleton.*)

NORAH. Oh, the poor man. Nothin' but a liver, God rest his soul. (*She crosses herself.*)

ITO. (*Starting up stairs with chart.*) Missy say put in boy's room.

NORAH. I dare ya. There's not an inch of space left up there.

ITO. I make space. I put white mice your room. (*He giggles.*)

NORAH. (*As she goes into kitchen.*) Put 'em in your own pagoda, ya heathen! (*Auntie Mame and Lindsay come in the foyer. They are loaded down with packages and boxes. Auntie Mame is aglow with excitement and decked out in furs, but Lindsay is getting a little tired of this maternal bit. They come into the apartment.*)

AUNTIE MAME. What a day! What a lovely, lovely day!

LINDSAY. What a day is right. On our feet for five hours—no lunch. Why don't they put a bar in F.A.O. Schwartz? I haven't even had a chance to call my office. I might have been bought out by Knopf.

AUNTIE MAME. Stop complaining, Lindsay. Fix yourself a drink. And then we can open the parcels. I can't wait to see Patrick's face when he sees all these lovely things.

LINDSAY. Mame! When are we going to have a day, an hour, a minute—some time to ourselves?

AUNTIE MAME. Time! Lindsay, don't you realize I've had to make up for Patrick's ten neglected years in a matter of months. (*Picking up a brightly colored book.*) Dr. Giselle says it's practically an impossibility.

LINDSAY. Does Dr. Giselle also happen to mention that what a child needs is a father?

AUNTIE MAME. Now, Lindsay—

LINDSAY. (*Pressing on.*) You know there are a lot of women in this town who think I'm a reasonably good catch. I'm reasonably successful; you've admitted yourself that I'm reasonably attractive, I'm reasonably . . .

AUNTIE MAME. Oh, Lindsay, that's the trouble. You're "reasonably" everything. You're reasonably in love with me, and we'd be reasonably happy. But that's not enough. Besides, how can I be a wife? I'm too busy being a mother. (*The door bell buzzes.*)

LINDSAY. There was Coué, Dada, Nature Foods, modern dance—

AUNTIE MAME. Oh, you think Patrick is a *phase*—

LINDSAY. Well, frankly, I do. (*Babcock bursts in.*)

BABCOCK. Where is she? Where is that madwoman? Where is that irresponsible, deceitful Bohemian Delilah? (*Lindsay tries to protest, through the entire following scene—but never succeeds in getting more than a word in edgewise.*)

LINDSAY. Now just a minute, Sir—

AUNTIE MAME. (*With a hollow hauteur.*) Why, Mr. Babcock, whatever do you mean?

BABCOCK. You know damned well what I mean. Why, you're no more fit to raise a child than Jezebel! (*Auntie Mame, concerned, rushes forward.*)

AUNTIE MAME. Patrick! Something's happened to my little love!

BABCOCK. You're damn right someth—Come in here, you little heathen! (*He drags Young Pat into the room. Young Pat huddles in an overcoat, with apparently nothing on underneath.*)

AUNTIE MAME. Patrick—what's wrong? (*Before the boy can answer, Babcock thunders on.*)

YOUNG PAT. Well, he came over to my school—

BABCOCK. I'll tell you what's wrong. I was doing my conscientious duty. I dropped by the Buckley School to check on the kid's academic standing. And what did I find? He isn't even registered. Never has been. So I've been hunting in every low, half-baked school for the feeble-minded in this town. And finally I found him—in the lowest of them all.

AUNTIE MAME. Mr. Devine is a progressive educator. He uses the same theory as Bertrand Russell does in England—

BABCOCK. I walk into that so-called "institution of learning"—and what do I find? A whole school-room of 'em—boys, girls, teacher—romping around, stark naked! Bare as the day they were born!

AUNTIE MAME. I can assure you that the students under Mr. Devine's care were engaged in healthful, broadening pursuits.

BABCOCK. Broadening. (*Turns to Young Pat.*) Show 'em what you were doing when I broke into the place. Go ahead—show 'em!

YOUNG PAT. We were just playing fish families.

BABCOCK. "Fish families!"

YOUNG PAT. It's part of constructive play.

BABCOCK. Listen to this.

YOUNG PAT. Well, we do it just after Yogurt Time. Mrs. Devine and all the girls crouch down on the floor under the sun lamps—and they pretend to be lady-fishes, depositing their eggs in the sand. Then Mr. Devine and all the boys do what gentlemen fish do.

AUNTIE MAME. What could be more wholesome or natural?

BABCOCK. Natural! It might be natural for a sardine! (*To Lindsay.*) Would you put a boy of yours in a school like that?

AUNTIE MAME. Mr. Babcock. I consider your behavior most undignified.

BABCOCK. Undignified! At least I'm wearing a vest.

AUNTIE MAME. Making a scene. Causing what might well be a traumatic experience for this child.

BABCOCK. (*Holding up a hand.*) Look, I know how you can twist things around. So I'm getting out of this combination nudist-camp-opium-den, before you make *me* look like the vice-president in charge of free love!

AUNTIE MAME. (*Righteously covering Pat's ears.*) Mr. Babcock. Not in front of the B-O-Y! (*Babcock goes toward the exit, turns threateningly.*)

BABCOCK. Tomorrow morning, I, me, *personally*—I'm taking this kid off to boarding school myself. I'm placing him in St. Boniface Academy and he's going to stay there. The only time you'll get your depraved hands on him is Christmas and summer and I wish to God there was some way to prevent that.

YOUNG PAT. (*Running to Auntie Mame.*) Auntie Mame. Do I have to? Do I?

AUNTIE MAME. (*Frantically.*) Please, Mr. Babcock—I'll do whatever you say. If you'll only let the child stay near me.

BABCOCK. Not on your life! He goes, and he goes tomorrow.

LINDSAY. Now let's be reasonable about this—

BABCOCK. I'm going to turn this kid into a decent, God-fearing Christian if I have to break every bone in his body.

AUNTIE MAME. If you'll give me another chance—

BABCOCK. I wouldn't give you the time of day, after the dirty doublecross you pulled on me.

AUNTIE MAME. (*Pleading in real desperation.*) Mr. Babcock, he's all I have, he's my life.

BABCOCK. You have him ready by 8 o'clock *sharp*. And, kid, you'd better be wearing knickers! (*He exits.*)

YOUNG PAT. I want to stay with you, Auntie Mame. I don't want to go to that old St. Bony Face.

AUNTIE MAME. Hush, my little love. I'm sure St. Boniface is really very nice. Now, go upstairs and get ready for dinner and we'll talk about it later. (*She watches as Pat climbs the stairs.*) Lindsay, Lindsay, what am I going to do?

LINDSAY. (*Honestly concerned.*) Don't worry, Mame. I'll help you. I'll get the kid back some way.

AUNTIE MAME. (*Crying.*) I just don't think I can bear it. I just don't—

LINDSAY. Mame, I've never seen you cry before . . . (*Lindsay tries to comfort her. The doorbell jabs insistently and we hear the strident voice of Vera in the outside hall.*)

VERA. (*From off.*) Mame, are you in there?

AUNTIE MAME. Oh, I just couldn't take anything else today!

VERA. It's urgent, it's vital, it's *dire*! (*She hurries on stage.*) Have you talked to your stock broker? (*She looks at the unhappy Mame.*) Yes. I can see you have.

LINDSAY. What about her stock broker?

VERA. Don't you know? He's called me half a dozen times, trying to locate both of you.

LINDSAY. (*Paling slightly.*) What happened?

VERA. Oh, nothing—except that nothing's worth anything any more! (*Phone rings.*)

LINDSAY. Don't you worry, Mame. I'm sure this is only something temporary. It can't possibly affect people like you and me—who have a lot of solid stuff like Bank of the United States. (*Ito scampers in from kitchen to answer the phone. He covers the mouthpiece, then speaks blandly to Auntie Mame.*)

ITO. Missy Dennis. Stock broker want to say hello before he jump out of the window. (*Lindsay grabs phone.*)

LINDSAY. (*Into phone.*) How bad is it, Arthur? (*The blood drains from his face.*) Everything? (*He can hardly say it.*) Atwater-Kent, too???????? (*Slowly he puts down the telephone, stunned.*) Mame, I'm afraid you're wiped out. We *all are.*

VERA. (*Philosophically.*) And everybody said I was such a fool, spending all my money at Tiffany's.

AUNTIE MAME. Who gives a damn about money? I've lost my child!

VERA. What?

LINDSAY. Patrick's trustee is sending him away to school.

VERA. Oh, Mame, darling—I know how you must feel.

AUNTIE MAME. Do you?

VERA. Well, not exactly, of course. I've never *had* a child. But, after all, I'm an actress, I can imagine. (*Abruptly, business-like.*) Now look—I've got everything worked out for you—I've got the perfect solution for all your problems. I'm going to tell Brock he simply *has* to give you a part in my new play. It opens Thanksgiving in New Haven.

AUNTIE MAME. No, thanks, Vera, I don't want your charity, I don't want anything but—

VERA. No, no, darling. It isn't charity, I want you in it. Besides, Patrick's trustee is sure to let Patrick come back when he finds out you've settled down into something steady like acting.

AUNTIE MAME. Do you really think so, Vera?

VERA. Oh, I know he would. Don't you agree, Lindsay?

LINDSAY. Well—

AUNTIE MAME. Oh, but you're so right, Vera. And if he didn't, I'd be earning the money to fight him. About $500 a week to start, don't you think? And then there'll be a raise—

VERA. Mame, it'll only be a bit—at the end of the last act. (*Persuasively.*) But it'll be like old times! Think of the fun we had trouping together in "Chu-Chin-Chow."

AUNTIE MAME. I accept, I accept. Vera, your heart is from Tiffany's too. Oh, I can't wait to hear the overture!

VERA. Mame—this is a drama. Serious drama. I play the part of a Balkan Princess who—

AUNTIE MAME. (*To Lindsay.*) I was in the front line of the chorus and Vera was behind me.

VERA. Behind you! If I'd been behind you, I'd have kicked you in the behind, you.

AUNTIE MAME. (*Sings illustratively.*)
"I'm a Chu Chu Girl from Chu-Chin-Chow.
And how!"
(*Clicks tongue.*)
"And how!"
(*Clicks tongue.*)

VERA. (*Pushes Mame into the back row.*)
"I'd love to chin and chew with you."

AUNTIE MAME. (*With elaborate gestures.*)
"And turn the skies to blue with you."

VERA. (*Showing her how it was really done.*)
"And turn the skies to blue with you."

AUNTIE MAME. That's it!

BOTH. (*Harmonizing.*)

"And twenty-three skidoo with you!
Chee-chee! Choo-Choo! Chow-Chow!"

(*Click tongues.*)

"And how!"

(*Click tongues.*)

"And how! And how!"

(*Hilariously they fall into each other's arms. Mercifully the lights fade on the two Sing-Song Girls.*)

ACT ONE
SCENE 8

The stage of the Shubert Theatre, New Haven. Reverse angle.

STAGE MANAGER. Set up for Act Three, Scene Two. And quiet on stage. There are still critics out there—I hope.

MAID. (*Off.*) I can't find my feather duster.

STAGE MANAGER. Props! Get 'em their feather dusters. Lemme have a work light, Bob. (*The work light comes on. The Theatre Manager rushes backstage. He is a splenetic man with glasses and a cigar, bred by the Shuberts.*)

THEATRE MANAGER. (*Pointing upstage to the theatre audience behind the house curtain.*) Look, half the audience out there has gone home, and the other half has gone to sleep. Does this play ever *end*????

STAGE MANAGER. We're almost set, Mr. Unger. (*The Assistant Stage Manager comes out with a prop bench. Norah hurries on.*)

NORAH. Miss Dennis ain't ready.

THEATRE MANAGER. Who the hell is Miss Dennis?

STAGE MANAGER. She plays Lady Iris.

THEATRE MANAGER. Shh—!

NORAH. (*Starting off.*) She wants more time to arrange her accessories.

STAGE MANAGER. (*Exploding.*) She's had two and a half acts to arrange her damned accessories.

THEATRE MANAGER. Get that curtain up—and if that Dennis dame ain't ready— (*He clamps the cigar in his teeth.*) —*I'll* play Lady Iris.

STAGE MANAGER. Lights. Kill the work light. Take it up, Bob. (*The audience for this play-within-a-play is presumed to be at extreme upstage. The work light goes off. The curtain, upstage, rises and we see footlights shining directly into our faces. The business of the play, therefore, is directed upstage; but the asides in the following are given downstage, to the actual theatre audience. The Maid and Butler dust furiously. Everything that he dusts, she dusts again immediately afterwards.*)

MAID. What do you suppose is happening now, Meadows, in the conservatory?

BUTLER. It is all over, Perkins. It is done with! We have lost the master—and, worse than that, the master has lost himself.

MAID. But love burns bright in this house tonight, Meadows!

BUTLER. And we shall all be consumed in the flames!

MAID. Don't be ridiculous, Meadows. Tonight we are living a legend. There is a *princess* beneath this roof, and every room vibrates with the fragrance of this fragile royal flower!

BUTLER. And our master is drugged by the heady perfume.

MAID. (*Quickly, resuming her dusting.*) Hush, Meadows. They are coming now! (*The Maid and Butler scurry off. From the opposite side, Vera and her Leading Man enter dramatically. Vera is svelte and statuesque, and her Leading Man is more of a matinee idol than is absolutely necessary. He always seems about to speak, but never manages to get a line out—Vera has seen to that; she also does a polished job of upstaging the poor guy.*)

VERA. But, Rrrreginald, tew dew sech a thing—tew desh oaf tewgethaw lake thisss—would be med; quate enchantingly med. (*Auntie Mame comes into the wings in flaming red. Norah is helping her as she does last minute primping. On her wrists are clanging bell bracelets. An uncomfortable actor in tails stands alongside of Mame. He plays the part of Lord Dudley.*)

AUNTIE MAME. Oooooooh, Lord Dudley. Your flahterry is enough to turn a young girl's head! (*There is a tinkling of bells. Vera touches her coiffeur, and begins again.*)

VERA. Naow, Rreginald, it would be medness. Ay belung tew one wuld, yew tew anothah. It's bettah thet we paht now; now whale we cheddish this ecstasy we've known. (*Vera moves regally toward the wings, then speaking away from her audience, but so we can hear clearly, she drops all affectation and speaks in good clear Pittsburgh.*) What the hell have you got back there—reindeer? (*She wheels upstage toward her own audience and instantaneously resumes her Mayfair elegance.*) This is gudbay, Rreginald. Ay heah the othahs coming. (*The Others sweep on, led by Auntie Mame on the arm of an embarrassed stage Lord. Around her wrists are the bracelets we have seen—and heard—before: fashioned from large silver Siamese temple bells. With every gesture, she drowns out the dialogue. Vera glares at her with all the loving kindness of the Apache Kid on the warpath.*)

AUNTIE MAME. (*As she enters; with an uninhibited stage laugh.*) Ooooooh, no mahr champagne, Lord Dudleh, or I shall forget myself altogethah! (*She makes a sweeping gesture and the bells clang like New Year's Eve.*)

VERA. (*Frigidly poking Mame in the back with her elbow.*) Ay've sumthing tew tale yew ull. Ay'm nut gaowing to meddy Rrrreginald after ull. May place is at haome with Prince Alexiss. Ay must gaow beck—beck to *muy* wuld. (*Reginald looks crushed. Auntie Mame, on a sudden Stanislavsky impulse, pats his arm comfortingly. The effect is as subtle as the passing of a fire-engine. Reginald steps out of reach. Vera turns to Auntie Mame, with a look that would paralyze the average Bengal tiger.*) Lady Irrriss. Would yew be gude enough to rrring for my wrrrap!

AUNTIE MAME. Certainly, Princess. (*She curtseys deeply; the bells peal deafeningly. A Footman hands Auntie Mame the wrap, folded. It is a voluminous chinchilla. As Auntie Mame advances to Vera, Vera turns toward us and mutters menacingly.*)

VERA. And get rid of those goddamn cow-bells! (*Flustered, Auntie Mame tries to muffle the bells in the coat as Vera turns with a gracious wave toward her audience.*)

AUNTIE MAME. Do let me help you, Princess. (*She puts the cape over Vera's shoulders upside-down, the hem at her neck, the collar sweeping the floor.*)

VERA. Thank yew, Lady Iris. (*An awful look comes over her face as she realizes the cape is upside down. She points down her back to the collar. Auntie Mame engages in a brief but unsuccessful battle with the chinchilla. Vera decides to get off and quick.*) Gudbay, gudbay. I shall always feel a deep attechment for you ull! (*As Vera sweeps off, Auntie Mame's outstretched hand mysteriously remains connected to the small of Vera's back, so that she is tugged along toward the exit. The bells keep clanging. Vera grunts, over her shoulder.*) Let go. For God's sake, *let go*!

AUNTIE MAME. (*Helplessly wailing.*) I can't let go. I'm caught. *I'm stuck!* (*There is some less than amiable thrashing as the two women try to disentangle themselves.*)

STAGE MANAGER'S VOICE. (*Off, frantic.*) Curtain! Bring down the curtain! (*There is the anaesthetic lowering of velour, cutting off the ribald laughter and cat-calls.*) Places for curtain calls! (*The Actors make a formal line facing upstage, but Auntie Mame is still enmeshed with Vera.*)

VERA. You amateur! (*The curtain rises, and All bow graciously to the audience upstage. The curtain comes down.*)

AUNTIE MAME. (*Miserable.*) I was only trying—

VERA. Ruining my beautiful play with your goddam Swiss-bell-ringing act!

AUNTIE MAME. But, Vera, they're the only bracelets I have left— (*The curtain goes up again for a second curtain time. More bows. Vera flings off the encumbrance of the chinchilla and Auntie Mame. She does this with such violence that Auntie Mame is catapulted forward into what seems to be a solo curtain call. The applause is thunderous.*)

VERA. That's enough! (*The curtain falls again. The Stage Manager comes on, wild-eyed.*)

STAGE MANAGER. That's enough! Strike the set! Work light!

VERA. (*Wheeling on Mame.*) Why did you do this to me? Why?

AUNTIE MAME. (*Honestly distraught.*) I was only trying to *make* something out of Lady Iris—give her some character . . .

VERA. You scene-stealing society bitch! (*Turns her back on Auntie Mame.*) Oh, God. And there were Critics out there. We're ruined. We're all ruined. (*As she goes off.*) Ruined. Ruined. (*She's gone. The others in the cast avoid Auntie Mame as if she had a touch of leprosy.*)

AUNTIE MAME. I was only trying to—I was only— (*They're all gone now—and just the bare work lights and a box remain on the empty stage. Auntie Mame sinks down, alone and dismal. Young Pat comes hesitantly toward Auntie Mame, pausing at the edge of the circle of light.*)

YOUNG PAT. I thought you were very good, Auntie Mame. Everybody noticed you.

AUNTIE MAME. Oh, my little love. How did you get to New Haven?

YOUNG PAT. Ito brought me up.

AUNTIE MAME. But how could he drive you up when I've already sold the car?

YOUNG PAT. (*Brightly.*) Oh, he didn't drive; we hitch-hiked!

AUNTIE MAME. But Mr. Babcock thinks you're in that horrible school—

YOUNG PAT. (*Patting her shoulder.*) It's all right, Auntie Mame. It's Thanksgiving vacation.

AUNTIE MAME. (*Looking around the stage forlornly.*) Is it? (*He comes to her and puts his arm around her tenderly.*)

YOUNG PAT. Can I be your escort? Can I take you back to your hotel?

AUNTIE MAME. (*Tears in her eyes.*) You can take me all the way back to New York. Oh, Patrick. Are you ashamed of your Auntie Mame?

YOUNG PAT. I'm *proud* of you. Nobody liked the stinky old play at all until you came in. (*Young Pat kisses her lightly on the cheek. Then he takes a step back, bows slightly from the waist, offering his arm.*) Lady Iris? (*She smiles in spite of her dejection, rises, takes his arm.*)

AUNTIE MAME. Chahmed, Lord Dudley! (*She makes an Edwardian gesture. They start off together, and she hugs him close as . . .*)

THE LIGHTS FADE

ACT ONE
SCENE 9

Telephone switchboard. Buzzing in darkness. We see Auntie Mame wrestling with the plugs. Several are already in place.

AUNTIE MAME. Widdicombe, Gutterman, Applewhite, Bibberman and Black—good morning. One moment, I'll connect you with Mr. Gutterman. (*She plugs.*) Widdicombe, Gutterman, Applewhite, Bibberman and Black, good— Yes, Mr. Bibberman, I'll get you Mr. Applewhite. (*She crosses two plugs, one from each board to the other.*) Widdicombe, Gutterman, Applewhite, Bibberman and Black. Good morning. Long distance— (*She plugs.*) Mr. Widdicombe, I have your San Francisco call. (*She plugs.*) Yes, Mr. Bibberman. (*Innocently.*) Oh, did I give you Mr. Gutterman instead of Mr. Applewhite? I'm sorry, Mr. Bibbercome—uh, Bibberbib. (*She pulls down a plug from one side, and starts to put it in the other side. But there is already a plug in the hole she wants to put it in. She pulls down the offending plug from the hole with her other hand and holds it up, addressing it as if it were a person.*) Mr. Applewhite, what were you doing in that hole with Mr. Gutterman? (*She now has two plugs, one in each hand. Forgetting where they are supposed to go, she thrusts one plug in her bodice to free her hand for another call. She puts up another plug.*) Mr. Widdicombe, I'll try to connect you with San Francisco. Now let me see. . . . (*She starts rearranging the plugs at random, sticking one plug in her mouth.*) Mr. Bibberbip is in there and Mr. Gutterwipe is talking to—. (*The board is going crazy now. She is plugging and unplugging frantically now. Buzz.*) Oh, there you are, Mr. Applewhite. Yes, sir. (*She dials.*) Eldorado 5-2121. Yes, sir. Hold on, Mr. Widdicombe. I'll find San Francisco. (*Buzz.*) Widdicombe, Gutterman, Applewhite. Oh! Supervisor? I did? (*She pushes a key.*) I'm afraid you gave me a wrong number, sir. There is *no* Applewhite 5-, Mr. Eldorado. (*The frantic buzzing continues.*) I don't know what I did with San Francisco. I'll tell you what I *can* do. I can get you Pittsburgh if it's a clear day. (*A particularly insistent buzz. Auntie Mame has managed to knit the plugs together, but extricates one and plugs it in.*) Hello? Oh, hello, Mr. Black. Long time no hear. What? What's that? Tired? No, I'm not tired. Fired? (*A wail.*) Whyyyyy??????

THE LIGHTS FADE

ACT ONE
SCENE 10

A roller-skate counter at Macy's. "Silent Night" is playing peacefully against the cacophony of people assailing the roller-skate counter. But there is no clerk behind the counter.

SHOPPER. (*Calling angrily.*) Floor walker! Do I have to wait until New Year's to straighten out these roller skates? (*Mr. Loomis, a carnation wearing a man, is trying to mollify the customers.*)

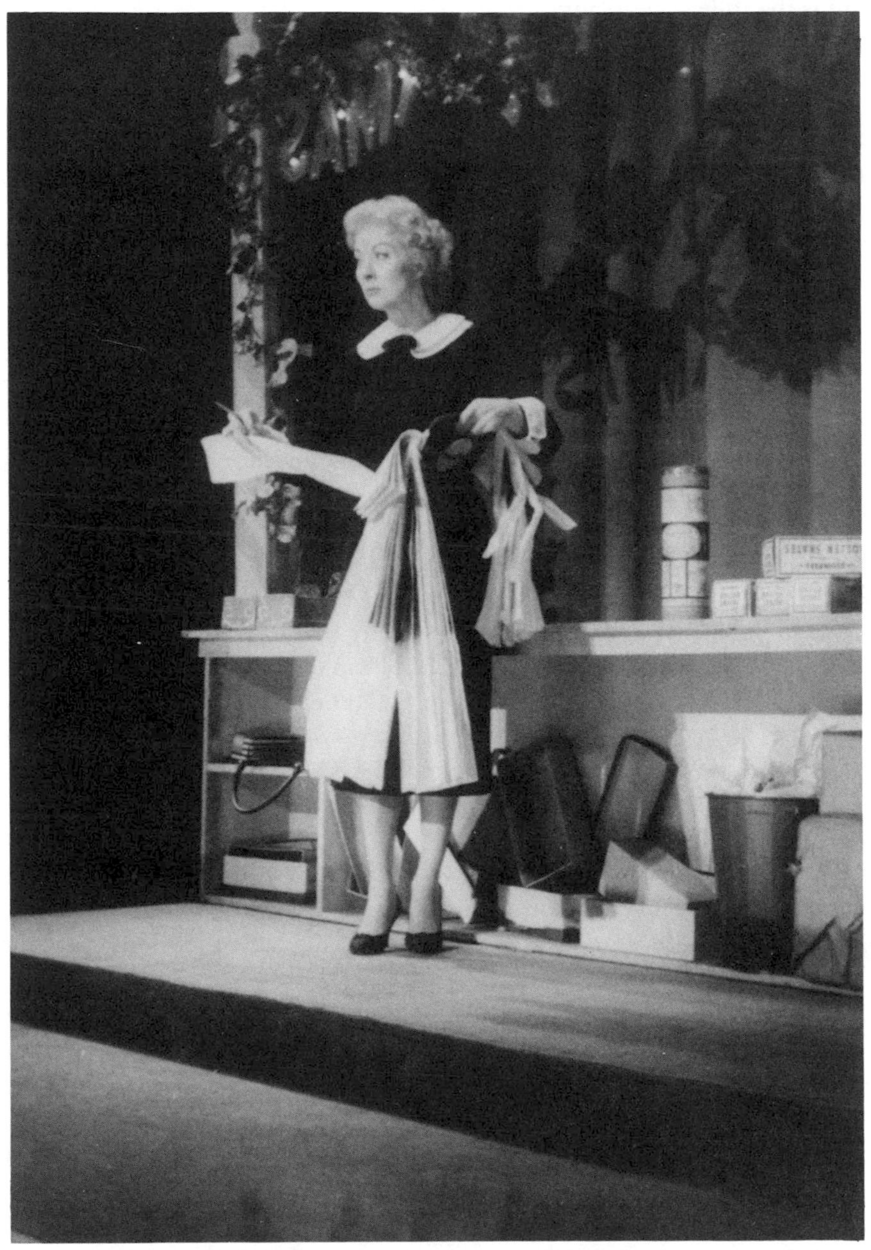

Greer Carson in *Auntie Mame,* New York, 1957. Photo by Jerome Lawrence. Jerome Lawrence and Robert E. Lee Collection, Lawrence and Lee Theatre Research Institute, The Ohio State University.

LOOMIS. If you'll just be patient, Madam, I'm certain our roller-skate lady will be here momentarily. (*Raising his voice, sing-song to "Silent Night."*) Roller-skate lady. Where is the roller-skate lady?

SHOPPER. Your stupid clerk sent me two left roller skates. Does Macy's think my kid has two left feet—is that what you think?

LOOMIS. Perhaps we'd better take this up the with Complaint Department. If you'll just step this way, Madam. (*The Shopper storms off with Loomis.*) Christmas. God deliver us. (*Auntie Mame enters with a Woman. Auntie Mame is carrying a Tinker Toy box and a sales book.*)

WOMAN. Clerk, clerk. Am I ever going to get out of here? All I want are these roller skates.

AUNTIE MAME. I don't know how I got over there in Tinker Toys. (*Calling rather plaintively.*) Mr. Loomis? Would you help me with this sales slip, please? (*Auntie Mame opens the sales book. This is the most bedraggled sales book in the history of retailing-selling. Carbons, tissues spill out in hectic disarray. Auntie Mame turns back to her customer.*) Oh, Mrs. Jennings, why don't you let me send these to you C.O.D.! Then you won't have to pay any money at all!

WOMAN. Well, I would eventually—

AUNTIE MAME. Don't you worry your head about it, Mrs. Jennings. I'll take care of everything. (*Up.*) Never mind, Mr. Loomis. (*She scribbles a slip.*)

WOMAN. Now just a minute—

AUNTIE MAME. Here's your slip now. See? You don't even have any bundles to carry. (*The Woman goes off.*) Oh, I just love C.O.D. (*During the above, a fine-looking Southern gentleman comes on. This is a hell of a guy; you can tell it from the genuineness of his smile. He's rosy-cheeked, with steel-grey hair. His camel's-hair coat and Cavanaugh hat indicate a cozy opulence. This is Beauregard Jackson Pickett Burnside. Auntie Mame turns to him. Reflexively, her eyelids flutter slightly.*)

BEAU. (*In a deep musical Southern drawl.*) Ma'am, would you be good enough to assist me in ordering twenty-four pairs of those fine-looking roller skates?

AUNTIE MAME. (*Taken aback.*) Twenty-four! My, what a proud father you must be!

BEAU. (*Chortles.*) Oh, they're not my children, ma'am; I'm a single gentleman. But a lot of little tykes at the Oglethorpe Orphanage—just outside of Savannah—are gonna pop their eyes out when this package arrives. (*He reaches in his pocket for a roll of bills which would choke a mastodon.*) Now, how much does that come to, little lady? (*Auntie Mame, fumbling with the sales book, looks at the roll of bills dismayed.*)

AUNTIE MAME. You want to pay? *Cash*?

BEAU. Oglethorpe Orphanage, R.F.D. 2, Savannah, Georgia. (*Auntie Mame starts to write, then stops and looks around like a trapped animal.*)

AUNTIE MAME. Are you sure you wouldn't rather have these go C.O.D.?

BEAU. (*Laughs heartily.*) Now, what would those little nippers think if their Uncle Beau sent 'em a Christmas present *co*-llect on *de*-livery.

AUNTIE MAME. Mr. Loomis—?

BEAU. (*He is now most gallant.*) If it would be any aid to you, ma'am, I suppose I could *take* the package with me.

AUNTIE MAME. Oh, no. That's worse. (*She looks around as if she were admitting former membership in the Communist Party.*) You see, I haven't worked here very long. And the only kind of sales slip I know how to make out is C.O.D.

BEAU. Well, now. Maybe I can be of some assistance, little lady. I've got a passing familiarity with *fi*-nancial matters. (*He comes behind the counter and takes the sales book out of her hands and starts to write up the order. This gives Auntie Mame a chance to size up Beau, with some admiration.*)

AUNTIE MAME. You'd better not come back here.

BEAU. First you gotta get your dupli*cates* and tripli*cates* straightened out elsewise Mr. Macy won't have any way of knowin' what you sold.

AUNTIE MAME. That's why they have all that tissue-paper!

BEAU. First the name— (*Writes.*) Beauregard Jackson Pickett Burnside.

AUNTIE MAME. That's a long name to get on such a little slip. (*Beau writes with amazing efficiency, and Auntie Mame peeks over his shoulder. Mr. Loomis comes on. He rises to his full five feet five.*)

LOOMIS. Miss Dennis, may I inquire what is going on here?

AUNTIE MAME. (*Floundering.*) Well, Mr. Loomis, this nice gentleman simply offered to—

BEAU. This little lady—Miss Dennis, is that your name?—she was having a mite of trouble making out my sales slip for a couple of dozen roller skates—

LOOMIS. (*Frigidly.*) Was there something *unusual* about the order?

AUNTIE MAME. Yes. He wants to pay *cash*!

LOOMIS. (*Incredulously.*) Am I to understand that a Macy's employee doesn't know how to make a *cash sale*?????

AUNTIE MAME. I'm a whiz at C.O.D.'s. You can see— (*Mr. Loomis seizes the sales book and leafs through it in amazement.*)

LOOMIS. Miss Dennis, this sales book is a shambles. You are obviously incompetent to dispense merchandise. You will report to personnel immediately for your dismissal.

BEAU. (*Trying to gloss over the matter.*) Now, she was just doin' the best she knew how. . . .

LOOMIS. Well, it's not good enough for the R. H. Macy Company! (*Loomis starts off, still leafing through the sales book.*) Good heavens, it'll take auditing a week to straighten out this mess. (*Beau follows, protesting.*)

BEAU. Now, you listen here to me, sir. I feel entirely responsible for bringing about this unfortunate misunderstandin'. (*Auntie Mame gets her purse from under the counter and starts off in the opposite direction. Thinking of a moneyless Christmas up ahead, she is sad and dispirited. Suddenly she remembers something and calls across to Beau as he disappears on the tail of Mr. Loomis.*)

AUNTIE MAME. (*Calling.*) Don't forget the roller skates for those little nippers. (*Sniffs, then belligerently.*) Get 'em at Gimbels!!!!! (*The Shoppers drift off and lighting on the Macy's area fades. Behind the crowd Auntie Mame has slipped on a somewhat threadbare cloth overcoat. We hear a legato disconsolate "Deck the Halls" as a spot follows Mame, downhearted and desolate.*)

ACT ONE
SCENE 11

The Beekman Place Apartment lights up softly. Some of the furnishings and expensive hangings are gone. There is a Christmas tree. Young Pat is just finishing decorating it. Moving continuously from the previous scene, Auntie Mame walks into the apartment, stands looking at Young Pat and the grubby little tree. Young Pat turns and sees her.

YOUNG PAT. Auntie Mame! Gee, I didn't expect you home so soon.

AUNTIE MAME. Well, they kinda gave me my Christmas vacation a little bit early. But I'm glad, really. Because now it fits with *your* vacation—and we won't have to miss even a day together.

YOUNG PAT. How do you like the tree? I decorated it myself. Aren't you surprised? (*Auntie Mame sinks down on an ottoman and involuntarily her hand covers her face.*)

AUNTIE MAME. It's beautiful, dear, it's simply beautiful. (*She chokes up. Young Pat, fully aware of her low spirits, determines to cheer her up. He reaches behind the tree for an oblong jeweler's package.*)

YOUNG PAT. I'm going to give you your Christmas present right now. You don't even have to wait till Christmas morning. (*He hands it to her.*) Here. Open it. (*Really speechless, Auntie Mame unwraps the tissue.*)

AUNTIE MAME. Patrick! Where did you get the money?

YOUNG PAT. Mr. Leavitt at the Pawn Shop gave me a very good price for my microscope and my hockey stick.

AUNTIE MAME. Patrick!

YOUNG PAT. I was getting kinda tired of microbes. (*Auntie Mame opens the package and holds up a rhinestone bracelet in excellent taste. She shakes her head, with dazed happiness.*)

AUNTIE MAME. Oh, my.

YOUNG PAT. They're not *quite* diamonds.

AUNTIE MAME. Oh, darling, that's the most beautiful bracelet I've ever owned. (*She kisses him.*)

YOUNG PAT. Wiggle it! (*She does. No sound.*) See. It doesn't make any noise. I told the man you had to have a quiet one—for when you go on the stage again. (*She puts it on. He helps her fasten the clasp.*) And when you wear it with your mink coat—why nobody will ever know you work at Macy's!

AUNTIE MAME. I've given up Macy's, dear. And my mink coat is down at Mr. Leavitt's with your hockey stick. (*Auntie Mame gets up and shakes the depression as if she were discarding a garment. Calling.*) Norah! Ito! If we're going to have Christmas, let's have it all the way around. (*She goes to a drawer and takes out several small boxes. Norah and Ito come on, Ito drawing on his house coat.*)

ITO. Yes, Missy Dennis? (*Auntie Mame hands each of them a package. She hands a suit box to Young Pat.*)

AUNTIE MAME. Merry Christmas, everybody.

NORAH. But it isn't until Tuesday, mum.

ITO. Missy Dennis get mixed up with calendar again. Not Christmas yet.

AUNTIE MAME. Well, we *need* it now—so let's go ahead and have it. (*They start to unwrap their packages eagerly.*) I did want to pay you some of your back salary, but—

NORAH. Now, not another word about it, mum. You know we wouldn't think of leavin' you.

ITO. (*Cheerfully.*) No place else get job anyhow. (*Ito lifts out an inexpensive wrist watch.*) Ohhhhh.

AUNTIE MAME. It isn't seventeen jewels, Ito—but I'm not sure that time is worth all that decoration these days.

ITO. Thank you, Missy. (*Norah opens a box of perfume, cologne and bath salts, unscrews and smells each one.*)

NORAH. It's so French-smellin'! I'll be the most aromatic thing on Beekman Place. (*Young Pat has been wrestling with the suit box. Now he has it open and he holds up a pair of long pants.*)

YOUNG PAT. Golly! Long pants! At last. (*Eagerly.*) Can I try 'em on, Auntie Mame? Right now?

AUNTIE MAME. Right now. (*Young Pat dashes upstairs. Ito and Norah exchange glances, then decide to speak.*)

NORAH. Well, we got a little present for you, too, mum—Ito and me. Now I hope you're not gonna be angry for what we done.

AUNTIE MAME. Just what is it you have done?

NORAH. (*Blurts it out.*) Well, Ito had a bit of money put by—and so did I—for a rainy day, you might say. But we both figgered it couldn't get much wetter than it is right now.

ITO. We pay grocery and butcher bill. (*He hands her a whole sheaf of bills speared on a nail.*) Now Mr. Schultz no give nasty looks with lamb chops. (*Auntie Mame sinks to the ottoman in unbelieving gratitude. She stares at the spiked bills, which look like a ragged miniature Christmas tree.*)

AUNTIE MAME. (*Moved deeply.*) You're both so dear to me. I'll pay you back some day—if I ever can. You know I will. (*Norah comes toward her, gently.*)

NORAH. You're a lovin' woman, mum. You're odd, but you're *lovin'*! And all we wish is you could find a *man*. As wonderful and lovin' and fine a gentleman as you are a fine lady. (*Thinking.*) Whatever happened to that nice Mr. Lindsay Woolsey? He was a dear soul.

AUNTIE MAME. He *was* a dear man, Norah. But I sent him away. I said no so many times when I had money, I couldn't say yes when I went broke. (*At this moment, Young Pat comes down the stairs, bursting with pride in his first long pants. He beams.*)

YOUNG PAT. Look! (*Auntie Mame rises and crosses to the landing, where he stands—almost as tall as she is.*)

AUNTIE MAME. Besides, I have my own fine gentleman, Norah. (*She holds up her wrist.*) Who buys me diamonds. (*Smiling.*) Or "almost" diamonds. (*In apparent high spirits, Auntie Mame moves blithely to the radio and snaps it on.*) What we need now is some music—some Christmas carols! (*The radio squeals a little, as she spins the dial through some spot announcements—finally coming to rest on a choral version of "Deck the Halls with Boughs of Holly." Auntie Mame starts to sing, and directs the others to join in with her—which they do enthusiastically, joining hands and dancing in a circle.*)

ALL. (*Singing.*)
"Deck the halls with boughs of holly,
Fa-la-la-la-la—la-la-la-la
'Tis the season to be jolly,
Fa-la-la-la-la—la-la-la-la."

(*Auntie Mame begins to break up. She turns away from the others, trying to conceal her tears. This ain't no season for her to be jolly. Young Pat, Norah and Ito rally around trying to comfort her.*)

YOUNG PAT. (*Hugging her.*) Don't cry, Auntie Mame! Please don't cry.

AUNTIE MAME. (*Trying to dry her tears.*) Oh, hell, we don't even have any Kleenex! (*But Norah offers her apron to Auntie Mame, and she uses it to wipe away the tears. The doorbell chimes. Norah scampers toward the kitchen, and Ito starts for the door. Auntie Mame turns to Ito.*) If that's Santa Claus, tell him we've already had it. (*Ito ushers in the rubicund but apologetic figure of Beauregard Burnside. He takes over in a generous and expansive way, hardly giving anyone else an opportunity to speak.*)

BEAU. Ma'am, you don't know how happy I am to see you.

AUNTIE MAME. (*Uncertainly.*) Well, I . . .

BEAU. (*Doffing his wide-brimmed hat.*) Little Lady, do you know I've been skittlin' all over town trying to find you. Do you realize there are ninety-seven Dennises in the Man-hattan *Di*-rectory? And I was beginning to worry you *might* live in that place over there called "Brooklyn."

AUNTIE MAME. But why did you . . . ?

BEAU. I came to apologize. I told 'em right out it was all their fault, those Macy folk. A lady with your charm and refinement should have an executive position with a lot of hired help to rassle with all them pesky writin' and figurin' details. (*He starts toward the door.*) Will you excuse me a second, ma'am, while I skittle out and pay that cab driver so he can go home to his family?

AUNTIE MAME. (*Stunned.*) You left a taxi meter running—in the middle of the depression? (*Beau raises his hand in a benediction.*)

BEAU. Ma'am, when you're in oil, a stock-market crash is somebody else's noise. (*Auntie Mame is non-plussed.*) And if you wouldn't consider me *pre*-sumptuous, I'd be most honored if you'd let me squire you out to dinner tonight.

AUNTIE MAME. No, thank you, we're just having a Christmas celebration, and I can't leave my little family.

BEAU. Ma'am, I like that. I like a woman who has feelin's about family. Why, I've got practically every kind of relative invented. You oughta come down Georgia-way and meet 'em all one day. You'd just love Peckerwood.

AUNTIE MAME. Peckerwood? Who's Peckerwood?

BEAU. Why, that's the name of my little ol' plantation. (*He turns and takes in Pat, Norah and Ito in an expansive gesture.*) Bring your little family along to dinner, ma'am; the more the merrier! (*Auntie Mame is still spinning from the speed of all this.*)

AUNTIE MAME. But I'm not really dressed. . . .

BEAU. (*At the door.*) You look just fine to me, ma'am. A little powder on your nose, and you're just fine. I'll tell that taxi to wait. (*They all look at each other in excited bewilderment.*)

YOUNG PAT. He's nice—I like him!

AUNTIE MAME. Shh!

NORAH. Marry him, mum! The minute he asks you!

AUNTIE MAME. Norah, for God's sake!

YOUNG PAT. What's his name, Auntie Mame? You don't even know his name.

AUNTIE MAME. (*Wisely.*) Yes, I do. Family, we are about to break bread with Beauregard Jackson Pickett Burnside! (*Norah and Ito laugh delightedly. Swiftly, Auntie Mame goes into action.*) Norah, get your coat. Ito, change your jacket. Where's my bag? (*She powders her nose as everyone flies around getting ready to go out.*) Patrick, wear your scarf—it's cold outside. (*Norah comes on in a scrubby cloth coat, carrying a corsage. She hands it to Auntie Mame.*)

NORAH. I was going to give you this wee thing at dinner.

AUNTIE MAME. (*She pulls an ornament off the tree and pins it on Norah's coat.*) Here's one for you, too. (*Young Pat appears in overcoat and muffler, and races for the door.*)

YOUNG PAT. (*Excitedly.*) Come on! We hadn't ought to keep Mr. Burnside waiting! (*Ito returns in a black alpaca coat.*)

ITO. (*Beaming.*) Me never believe in Santa Claus. Me beginning to change mind.

AUNTIE MAME. Well, I never expected Santa Claus to have a Southern accent. (*They all tear out the door, Auntie Mame bringing up the rear.*)

ANNOUNCER. (*Through the radio.*) Merry Christmas from Manny, Moe and Jack, your credit clothiers.

AUNTIE MAME. (*Magnanimously, in a rich Southern accent.*) Merry Christmas to you-all, Manny, Moe and Jack! And a happy little ole New Year! (*She exits after the others, and the lights fade.*)

ACT ONE
SCENE 12

There is drippy Southern music. We bleed through the scrim to the picturesque tableau of the white-columned portico of the Burnside Mansion at Peckerwood, with the aristocracy of Oglethorpe County posed gracefully on the lawn awaiting the arrival of Auntie Mame. The scrim parts, and the stage comes alive with a twittering crowd of Southern belles and Georgia gentlemen, all dressed in Sunday best. A few wide white steps lead up to a veranda and a twin-leafed practical door. The front area is the lawn of Peckerwood, filled with bluegrass and bluebloods.

This is a gathering of the clan to give the o.o. to Uncle Beau's Yankee girlfriend. The tone is roughly the same as that with which General Sherman was received in Atlanta seventy years before.

Prominent in the crowd is Cousin Jefferson Davis Clay Pickett, who booms like the cannons at Fort Sumter.

Cousin Fan, a fussy, insecure poor relative, emerges and twitters ineffectually around the veranda.

COUSIN JEFF. Must be somethin' mighty special about this Dennis woman if'n Beau skittles her all the way down here from New York City. (*Turns to the veranda.*) Mornin', Cousin Fan.

COUSIN FAN. Peculiar mornin', Cousin Jeff. *Mighty* peculiar. Is it generally known that Beau and his lady friend have a *child* with 'em? (*There are gasps, and a general reaction of shocked astonishment.*)

COUSIN JEFF. No-o-o-o!

COUSIN FAN. Don't think it's what you're thinkin'. The boy's thirteen, and Beau's only known her since Christmas. (*There is an air of disappointment at this. Cousin Fan sniffs.*) Besides—she hain't even *met* Mother Burnside yet. (*There is an eager reaction among the clan.*)

COUSIN JEFF. Ho-ho. Seems as if we're all right on time to see the fireworks.

COUSIN FAN. Well, you all know what a delicate *di*-gestive system Mother Burnside has. (*She rolls her eyes upwards. Jeff turns confidentially to his wife.*)

COUSIN JEFF. Ho-ho. When she gets riled, ain't nobody in the State of Georgia—maybe in the whole Confederacy—can outburp Mother Burnside. (*The genteel chit-chat freezes suddenly as Sally Cato MacDougal floats in. She carries a parasol. This is a peaches-and-cream Southern belle. Every eye is on her. She is followed by her grubby little brother, Emory, who is about Young Pat's age.*)

SALLY CATO. Well, now—!

COUSIN JEFF. Why, Sally Cato MacDougal!

SALLY CATO. Hello, Jeff honey.

COUSIN FAN. Didn't rightly 'spect you to be comin' round for the doin's.

SALLY. (*Dripping sweetness.*) Why, however could I manage to stay away when our own dear Beau is bringin' his little Yankee friend back down here to Peckerwood? Why, I wouldn't feel like a true daughter of the South if I didn't ooze out all the hospitality that's just simmerin' in my inners!

COUSIN JEFF. You're a big-hearted woman, Sally Cato.

SALLY. (*Fluttery.*) Well, now, jus' because Beauregard and me been engaged since grammar school, don't mean I refrain from wishin' him and his new-found friend every happiness. (*Young Pat comes running on. He is slightly Lord Fauntleroyed. He stops short when he sees the crowd of people.*)

YOUNG PAT. My Auntie Mame—Miss Dennis, I mean—she says she'll be here in just a minute. (*Sally Cato smiles lovingly at Young Pat.*)

SALLY. Well now—what a lovable, genteel little gentleman. (*She calls to her brother gutterly.*) Emory, come on over here. (*Back to Pat.*) You and my little brother are gonna get along like a pair of colts in a pasture. I can just tell. (*She hits Emory with her parasol. Then flutters among the guests. Emory sullenly faces Young Pat.*)

EMORY. What's your name, Yankee boy?

YOUNG PAT. Patrick Dennis.

EMORY. If ya gimme a dime, I'll take you down to my shanty and show ya my dirty pitchas.

YOUNG PAT. Maybe I'd better not—right now. (*Making conversation.*) Your sister's nice.

EMORY. (*Incredulous.*) *Nice?!* You're plumb crazy. They teach ya to spell up there, Yankee boy?

YOUNG PAT. Sure.

EMORY. (*Lowering his voice.*) My sister is a B-I-T-C-H. (*There is a clatter and rumble from within the portals of Peckerwood. Mother Burnside's gravelly baritone is raised in acid invective.*)

MOTHER BURNSIDE'S VOICE. (*Off.*) Where's my soda tablets? What son of a no-good-hound-dog stole my soda tablets?

BEAU'S VOICE. (*Also from off.*) They're right in your lap, Maother. (*All turn as Beau pushes a wheelchair onto the verandah; in the wheelchair sits Mother Burnside, a beady-eyed imperious woman built along the lines of a General Electric refrigerator. Dressed all in black, she looks like a cross between Caligula and a cockatoo. Everybody proffers a tentative greeting.*)

MOTHER BURNSIDE. Beauregard, when you gonna trot out that New York filly? (*Her beady eyes scan the assemblage contemptuously.*) All I can see around here is *family.*

ALL. Mornin', Mother Burnside.

MOTHER BURNSIDE. (*Suddenly brightens.*) 'Ceptin' you, Sally Cato. Still paintin' your finger-nails?

SALLY. You're lookin' cute as a bug, Miz Burnside. (*Mother Burnside burps.*) Well, welcome home, Beau-darlin'!

BEAU. (*Uncomfortably.*) Hello there, Sally Cato.

MOTHER BURNSIDE. (*To Beau, wagging her head.*) When we got peaches right here, ripe for the pickin', I can't see why any man would go hankerin' after some *Northern* alligator pear. (*She clasps a hand to her stomach, as if a gastritic eruption were about to take place.*)

BEAU. (*Worried.*) Now, now, Mama—let's keep our hominy grits goin' the right way! (*He calls off.*) Mame? Mame-honey, we're all out here, waitin' for you.

AUNTIE MAME'S VOICE. (*From off. Calls, Southern as a candied yam.*) Ah'm comin', Beau-sugah. Ah'm just bustin' to meet yoah sweet little old mothah! (*Mame swirls on, wearing a hoopskirt and looking very much like Scarlett O'Hara. She stops, with a little faked gasp.*)

BEAU. Mother, may I present Miss Mame Dennis? (*Auntie Mame falters only for a fraction of a second, then advances and takes Mother Burnside's leathery hand.*)

AUNTIE MAME. I don't mind sayin', Miz Burnside, you're everything I ever expected and quite a bit more. (*Mother Burnside burps.*)

BEAU. (*Waving across the lawn.*) And these are all my kinfolk. That's my cousin, Jefferson Davis Clay Pickett; his wife; Cousin Fan; Aunt Euphemia; Uncle Moultrie; Lizzie Beaufort—you'll get to know 'em all. You'll all be first-namin' each other soon as we pour another gallon o' bourbon into the punch bowl! (*Beau exits.*)

AUNTIE MAME. I cain't tell you how chowmin' it is to meet all of you-all! (*This doesn't sound quite right to her, but she carries it off nicely. Sally swoops up, taking Mame's hands with a gush of affection.*)

SALLY. And I'm Sally Cato MacDougal. I could just tell from the first *instant* I set eyes on you that we was gonna be the *closest* of bosom friends, Mame. May I call you Mame?

AUNTIE MAME. Please do.

SALLY. You call me "Sally Cato," heah?—All my most intimate friends *do.* (*Several glances are exchanged. Auntie Mame is completely taken in.*)

AUNTIE MAME. Why, that's awfully kind of you, Sally Cato.

SALLY. Was it *horses* brought you and Beauregard together?

AUNTIE MAME. (*Blankly.*) Horses?

SALLY. Well, I can't imagine Beau even *lookin'* at a lady who wasn't practically *bawn* on a horse.

AUNTIE MAME. (*Laying it on.*) Oh, I just love riding. Up in New York hardly a day goes by that I don't have the sadd—the *boots* on. Up every morning at the crack of noon for a brisk canter through Central Park.

SALLY. Well, now—that settles it. Here I've been wrackin' my poor brain tryin' to figure out what *special* I could do to let you know how I feel about your bein' down here. And what could be better than a *hunt*!

AUNTIE MAME. (*Paling a little.*) A hunt???

SALLY. (*Raising her voice.*) Listen, evabodeh! Beauregard's gone and *surprised* us all. It seems Miz Dennis here is a prominent North'n horsewoman.

AUNTIE MAME. (*Trying to put the brakes on this.*) Well, I wouldn't say *prominent*—No—I'm not prominent.

SALLY. (*Barreling on.*) So natcherly, we'll have to have a hunt! Dawn, tomorrow morning! And evabody's invited! (*She turns brightly to Auntie Mame.*) Won't we have the lark, all of us—at sunup—leapin' over those hedges, jumpin' over those river gaps, the hounds yappin' around those boulders—(*Auntie Mame steadies herself against one of the columns.*) I tell you, Mame, every eye in this county is going to be on you tomorrow mornin'!

AUNTIE MAME. (*Thinking fast.*) If I'd only *known*. You see, I didn't bring down any of my ridin' togs.

SALLY. Don't you worry, Mame child. I've got *dozens* of things you could wear. What's your shoe size? (*Mame tries to draw her feet under her skirt.*)

AUNTIE MAME. (*Lying.*) Three-B.

SALLY. Marvelous. Same as I wear. I can even fit you out with boots.

AUNTIE MAME. (*Weakly.*) I don't know if Beau would want me to—

SALLY. (*Barreling on.*) You *do* ride astride, Mame dear?

AUNTIE MAME. (*A hopeful gleam in her eyes.*) No—No. Side-saddle—always. Daddy, the Colonel, insisted that I learn it. He said it was the only way for a true lady to ride. So graceful. Silly of him, of course, because *nobody* rides side-saddle these days, but it's the only way I know how. (*She sighs, pleased with herself.*)

SALLY. (*Purring.*) Now, isn't that grand! I just happen to have a little old side-saddle that'll do you *fine*. (*Beau comes out, carrying a trayful of punch glasses. Graciously he passes them around to the guests.*)

BEAU. Refreshment, ladies? (*Mame drinks a whole punch-cup at one gulp.*)

SALLY. Beau darlin', we're having ourselves a hunt! At dawn tomorrow! And you want to hear somethin' fantastic? Your sweet little Yankee girl is gonna ride side-saddle.

BEAU. I won't allow it! It's too dangerous.

SALLY. But, darling, she's insisted.

BEAU. Well, anything Mame says she can do, she can do. I tell you—this is an amazing woman. (*Mame quickly downs a second drink.*)

SALLY. Oh, Mame sugah—I'm just going to *hold my breath* until dawn tomorrow.

AUNTIE MAME. Do that, honey.

THE LIGHTS FADE

ACT ONE
SCENE 13

The lighting makes a transition. It is not quite dawn. In the distance a grumpy rooster crows. The set has not been changed.

A spotlight picks up the area of the Dutch window and the door. Behind the Dutch window, Mame is dressing, with the aid of a couple of unseen dressers on their knees. Young Pat is seated at the bench just outside the window. Auntie Mame keeps poking her head out of the window to talk to Young Pat, as she is dressing. Young Pat has a book in his hand.

AUNTIE MAME. Stop looking at the pictures and read it to me, darling. I'm listening. (*Young Pat turns to the opening page.*)

YOUNG PAT. "How to Ride a Horse." (*She is struggling to get into a pair of borrowed riding boots. Young Pat begins to read.*) It says you should always get on a horse from the left side.

AUNTIE MAME. *Your* left side or the *horse's* left side?

YOUNG PAT. It doesn't say. Listen to this. (*He reads.*) "Whenever a rider approaches a strange mount"—I guess that means the horse—"he should fix the animal in the eye with a masterful gaze. For a horse can detect the slightest indication of trepidation." (*He breaks off.*) What's "trepidation?"

AUNTIE MAME. That's what your Auntie Mame's got a bad case of right now. Go on, dear, go on.

YOUNG PAT. "The horse is extremely sensitive . . . "

AUNTIE MAME. Where??????????

YOUNG PAT. There are some peachy pictures in this book about how to jump over fences. It says you should *lean.*

AUNTIE MAME. If anybody does any leaning, it's gotta be the horse. (*Auntie Mame tries vainly to pull on one of the boots. After a painful groan, she stops, closes her eyes and mutters something inarticulately under her breath.*)

YOUNG PAT. What did you say, Auntie Mame?

AUNTIE MAME. I'm not talking to you, my little love. I'm talking to God. (*She emerges in riding skirt and the flapping boots only half on. She can hardly walk.*) I think Sally Cato left a foot in this one.

YOUNG PAT. (*Rising.*) I'll help you. (*Auntie Mame sits on the bench and Pat tries to shove the boot on.*)

AUNTIE MAME. So this is what they call "dying with your boots on."

YOUNG PAT. (*Sympathetically.*) Why are you going through all this, Auntie Mame?

AUNTIE MAME. Darling, if I can only snag you an Uncle Beau, all our problems will be solved. (*She makes a wistful half-smile.*) Besides, there's one other extremely minor, relatively unimportant little old thing: I happen to be in love with him. (*Young Pat laughs happily.*)

YOUNG PAT. Has he asked you anything yet?

AUNTIE MAME. (*Shaking her head.*) No. But he wouldn't have brought us down here—if he didn't intend to.

BEAU. (*From off.*) Are you dressed yet, Mame, honey? (*Young Pat quickly hides the book behind his back.*)

AUNTIE MAME. Oh, yes, Beau, darlin'. (*He enters, resplendent in a red riding habit. He has several cameras draped about his neck.*) Oh my, how handsome you look.

BEAU. (*Focusing camera.*) Likewise, Mame. Hold it! (*Auntie Mame strikes a fancy pose. He snaps a picture.*) You are now immortalized in cell-you-loid. (*He turns to Young Pat.*) Would you excuse us for a second, young fella? There's something I want to talk to your Auntie Mame about.

YOUNG PAT. (*Obligingly.*) Oh, sure. (*He scoots out.*)

BEAU. (*Taking a deep breath.*) Mame, what I've got to say, I've got to say fast, afore that huntin' horn blows. And talk fast is somethin' that don't come easy to a south'n gentleman.

AUNTIE MAME. Then talk slow, Beau darlin'—I can listen fast. (*Beau takes her hand.*)

BEAU. I consider myself a very lucky man. It was luck that made me smell oil when I was walkin' across that soy bean patch Cousin Marvin left me. And it was just pure dumb Georgia luck that roller-skated us together last Christmas.

AUNTIE MAME. (*Hanging on every word.*) I feel that same way, Beau, dear. Go on.

BEAU. Mame, honey . . . what I want to ask you is— (*He is beginning to get red-faced.*) Would you . . . Could you . . . ? That is, *might* you . . . (*She turns away coyly. The hunting horn sounds blatantly off. Beau reacts like a fireman who has heard the bell. He drops Mame's hand abruptly.*) To the hounds! (*He bolts off eagerly. Mame is left alone.*)

AUNTIE MAME. Hounds! Sons-of-bitches. (*Her shoulders sag as the lights fade. Mame exits in the momentary darkness. The lighting makes the full transition to rosy dawn. The scene is still Peckerwood, but bathed in a lovely early morning glow.*)

ACT ONE
SCENE 14

The red-coated huntsman comes on and blows another blast on the hunting horn.

Beau and Cousin Jeff come on, ready for the hunt.

BEAU. (*Taking a deep breath of morning air.*) Can't wait to get on the trail of that fox. We *got* a fox, ain't we, Jeff?

JEFF. Had to use that spare one we was keepin' in the cellar of the ice-house. He's a mite moth-eaten, but he'll do. (*Sally Cato comes on, assured in her riding habit. She crosses to Beau and fiddles with his ascot.*)

SALLY. Beau darlin'—now ain't you just the *handsomest* little old thing.

BEAU. (*Embarrassed.*) Aw-w-w, Sally Cato. (*Turns, searching.*) Hope we got Mame a nice piece of horse-flesh.

SALLY. (*Patting Beau's lapel cozily.*) Don't you worry one minute 'bout your sweet little ole Northern gal. I puhsonally picked her mount. I've seen to it that she's gonna be took care of just fine. (*She smiles at him with every tooth in her head.*)

BEAU. You're a big-hearted woman, Sally Cato. (*There is a gentle whinny off. Beau crosses, calling to the grooms.*) Hold her steady, boys! (*Reaches in his pocket.*) I got a lump of sugah for you, Brown Beauty old girl! (*He goes off, and we hear him mounting—the creak of leather and pawing in the gravel.*) Hup-hup. Atta girl! (*Sally Cato slaps her whip on the ground and laughs. Auntie Mame comes out of the house, followed by Young Pat. She's putting up a brave front, and he is still reading from the book, instructing her. She actually manages to smile at Sally Cato as she tries to fake the walk and stance of an experienced horsewoman.*)

AUNTIE MAME. Mornin', Sally Cato.

SALLY. (*Sweetly.*) Mornin', Mame dear. How unusual you look. (*Calls off.*) You can bring up Miss Dennis' horse now, boys. (*Back to Mame.*) He's the most special thing in mah stable; evahbody talks about him. What an exhilaratin' day we're gonna have. (*She starts off toward the mounting block offstage. The hounds and the Hunters have all crossed over, too.*)

AUNTIE MAME. Just a minute, Sally Cato—Wouldn't my horse like it if I called him by his name? What's his name?

SALLY. (*Smiling.*) Lightnin' Rod. (*Sally Cato goes off. Auntie Mame looks struck.*)

GIRL. (*Entering.*) Mawnin', Miss Dennis. (*She skips.*)

AUNTIE MAME. Mawnin'! Mawnin'! (*Auntie Mame imitates the girl's skip.*)

YOUNG PAT. (*Concerned.*) Auntie Mame—could you maybe—sprain your ankle—quick?

AUNTIE MAME. (*Grimly.*) I've got to go through with it. I can't be a disgrace to Beau in front of all his people. (*There is a fierce whinnying off, and wild stomping. Two Grooms back onto the stage in panic; One has his upstage hand hidden in his coat. There is a babble of voices onstage and off.*)

VOICES. Ho! Rein him up. Stand clear of that horse, boy. Steady, steady! (*Auntie Mame stares off, horrified.*)

AUNTIE MAME. (*Dry-throated.*) That—that—that horse's name isn't—Lightnin' Rod?

GROOM. (*Nods, portentously.*) Lightnin' Rod. (*Again, the offstage horse thunders a whinny and paws the gravel.*)

AUNTIE MAME. (*Swallows.*) Maybe if I gave him a lump of sugar, it would— (*The Groom lifts up his bandaged hand.*)

GROOM. I wouldn't try it if I was you, Ma'am. (*Mame kisses Pat goodbye, then edges toward the offstage animal, trying to stare it down.*)

AUNTIE MAME. (*Muttering to herself.*) "Fix the animal in the eye with a masterful gaze—" (*She goes off like Sidney Carton en route to the guillotine. There is more pawing and whinnying, accompanied by shouts and grunts, as she presumably manages to get aboard the horse. Young Pat watches with horrified fascination. Cousin Fan helps on the bloodthirsty figure of Mother Burnside, who has a pair of field glasses. She sits in a rocker.*)

MOTHER BURNSIDE. (*Looking down toward where the animal is stomping.*) Naow that is what I call a spirited animule! (*Auntie Mame off, lets out a fading scream, as the horse hoofs gallop away. Mother Burnside waves a dirty old lace handkerchief, delightedly.*) Goodbye, Yankee Girl! (*The Huntsman's horn sounds off, and the hunt is evidently in progress. Mother Burnside glues the field glasses to her eyes. She rocks delightedly through the following. Emory dashes on. Young Pat watches tip-toe. Emory rushes up to him and grabs his arm.*) Hey, Yankee Boy! I seen 'em side-saddlin' up Lightnin' Rod. Your aunt ain't plannin' to ride him, is she?

YOUNG PAT. Plannin'? Look!

EMORY. Kee-ripes. Look at 'em go.

YOUNG PAT. Auntie Mame! Fall off! Fall off! (*The sound of the progressing hunt comes from three staggered speakers on the balcony rail. We hear stereophonically the yapping of the dogs and the pounding of horses' hooves and the occasional bleat of the Huntsman's horn. Mother Burnside's field glasses follow the action, and she rocks vigorously and chortles with grisly good humor, punctuated by burps.*)

MOTHER BURNSIDE. Cleared the first hedge-row and not a broken leg yet! Look at 'em go! What's she coming back this way for? That fool Yankee girl's got 'em goin' in circles. (*Young Pat, Emory, Cousin Fan, Mother Burnside and two of the Grooms are watching in fascinated horror.*) Get out of my flower-garden. Keep them damn horses out of my bouganvilla. Look out fer that yar flood wall.

YOUNG PAT. Lean, Auntie Mame—lean! (*Cousin Fan and Young Pat cover their eyes—then peek out, fearing the worst.*)

MOTHER BURNSIDE. Gol dang if that Yankee gal didn't sail right over it! NO HANDS!

GROOM. She's passin' everybody!

MOTHER BURNSIDE. She's passin' the Mastuh of the Hounds! (*She puts down the glasses angrily.*) Mighty bad form, passin' the Mastuh! (*The glasses go up again, and sweep along, following the action.*)

YOUNG PAT. She's passin' the dogs!

MOTHER BURNSIDE. (*Astounded.*) Mother of Jefferson Davis, she's passin' the Fox! (*Mother Burnside rocks as if she herself were in the saddle. Off, we hear the wheezing of a Model-A Ford approaching at top speed, honking, and screeching of brakes. There is a car-door slam off, and the Vet rushes on. He has a gun in a holster, and his face is livid with rage.*)

VET. (*Roaring accusation.*) Miz Burnside! Is that hawse out thar Lightnin' Rod???

MOTHER BURNSIDE. (*Delighted.*) Suah looks like it. (*To the Vet.*) But we won't need a hawse doctah around here today. We're going to need the othah kind!

VET. (*Thundering.*) Plain premeditated *murdah*, that's what it is! (*He points toward the progressing fox hunt, which has apparently zig-zagged several times across the field of vision from the portico. Suddenly Mother Burnside stops rocking and leans forward. Now all the Watchers freeze, staring dead front in horror. The sound of hoofs, hounds and cries grows louder, as if the hunting party were advancing straight upon them.*)

MOTHER BURNSIDE. (*Shrieks.*) That damn Yankee Girl is leadin' 'em straight into the livin' room! (*But it is a near miss. All eyes swing toward offstage the opposite side from which the hunt departed, but the same side on which the Vet's car is parked. The noise of the approaching hunt grows louder still. Young Pat covers his eyes. Cousin Fan shrieks. Mother Burnside braces one leg against the railing.*)

VET. (*Screaming, his arm raised.*) Watch out—my flivvah's parked in back of them begonia bushes! That's caounty property! That's—

GROOM. Rein her in! (*There's a mighty crash of hoofs against glass and tin; there is the outraged "Ah—oo-gah" of an old Ford horn, which subsides into a dying gasp.*)

YOUNG PAT. (*Cries out.*) Auntie Mame!!!!! (*Almost as if hurtled onto the stage, Auntie Mame staggers forward. She is windblown and disheveled. In one hand she has a broken steering wheel from the Vet's car. She is holding something in her other hand, but it is hidden behind the folds of her skirt.*)

MOTHER BURNSIDE. What happened to the fox?

AUNTIE MAME. (*Holding aloft the limp furpiece that was once a fox.*) Trampled to death! (*The Others from the hunt begin to pour on, babbling with astonishment, congratulating the dazed Auntie Mame. Beau rushes up to her.*)

BEAU. Are you all right, Mame-honey????? When I saw that crazy hawse crash into that car, and you flyin' through the air— (*Auntie Mame lamely holds up the steering wheel.*)

AUNTIE MAME. If I hadn't grabbed hold of this, I'd be in North Carolina! (*Sally Cato comes on uncertainly. But everybody is gathered around Auntie Mame admiringly.*)

JEFF. Soo-*pub* hawse-woman! Pufeckly soo-*pub*!

VET. (*Turning on Sally Cato.*) Sally Cato MacDougal, as County veterinarian, Ah *commanded* you two years ago to have that crazy Lightnin' Rod destroyed. Why, she oughta have her name read outta every huntin' pack in the who' county.

BEAU. (*Turning his back on Sally Cato and swelling with pride close to Auntie Mame.*) Everybody—ah want you to meet my little *YANKEE VALKYRIE*! (*They embrace. The Vet shakes his fist at Sally Cato. Auntie Mame is blushing prettily at the flood of compliments.*)

JEFF. What a seat that woman has! What a magnificent *seat*! (*Auntie Mame glances back with a startled take. Then she touches the back of her skirt to see if it's torn there.*)

BEAU. (*Stretching out his arms.*) Listen, evahbodeh! I have an important announcement to make to you-all! This magnificent Diana-of-the-Chase is gonna become Mrs. Beauregard Jackson Pickett Burnside! (*Auntie Mame tosses the fox to Sally Cato like a bridal bouquet.*)

SALLY. Emory, come on home!

EMORY. (*Happily.*) Hot damn! Mah sistah's gonna bust a gut! (*He skeedaddles off, following his sister.*)

MOTHER BURNSIDE. Well, what are you-all standin' around for??? Skittle yo' selves into the house and we'll all have a *glass* o' *whiskey*! Come on. (*Cousin Fan helps Mother Burnside off. All congratulate the beaming Beau and the beat-up but victorious Auntie Mame as they file into the house. Nobody's paying much attention to Young Pat, and he hangs back unnoticed. All the guests have gone inside now. Beau takes Auntie Mame's hand.*)

BEAU. Ah'll make you happy, Mame-honey. For a honeymoon, we'll take a year off and go clean around the world! Just you and me. (*He embraces her. Young Pat, hearing this, slips farther downstage, feeling very much alone. Auntie Mame starts to go in the house with Beau but suddenly she glances back and sees Young Pat.*)

AUNTIE MAME. You go in the house, darlin'. I'll be there in just a minute. (*Crossing quickly to him, sympathetically.*) Patrick, my little love—

YOUNG PAT. (*Softly.*) Congratulations, Auntie Mame. (*She takes Young Pat's hand and leads him to the bench. She sits, holding him, though he hangs back a bit.*)

AUNTIE MAME. Your Auntie Mame's in love—and very, very happy.

YOUNG PAT. I won't see you for a long time.

AUNTIE MAME. But, darling, you'll be busy at school. And I'll write you every day. I promise. And I'll be back with you before you even know it. Now come on in the house and we'll have some breakfast. And let me see you smile. I haven't gone yet. Up! Up! That's my boy. (*Pat manages a small smile and starts to go. He stops and turns to Auntie Mame who is on her way inside.*)

YOUNG PAT. Can I ask you just one question? (*She nods.*) How did you stay on that horse?

AUNTIE MAME. It was just like the bracelet in New Haven: I got stuck. (*She reaches behind her, confidentially.*) But at the other end! (*They laugh warmly, and Auntie Mame gives Patrick a big hug and they go into the house together.*)

CURTAIN

ACT TWO

SCENE 1

In the darkness we hear an uncertain blend of ex-boy-sopranos singing the "Saint Boniface Fight Song":

BOYS' VOICES. (*Unseen, singing.*)
"Fight, fight, fight for Saint Boniface, Boniface!
We will win for Saint Boniface, Boniface!
Carry the ball over the line!
Show 'em what we can do!
Fight, fight, fight for Saint Boniface Blue!"

As the music fades, the lights come up on:

A study room at Saint Boniface Academy, stage right. Young Pat is seated at a study table wearing a beanie. He looks taller and older, but this is the same lad who gave Auntie Mame's life a purpose and direction in Act One. But somehow the ingenious charm of childhood seems to have worn off a bit. There is a trace of cockiness and conceit about Young Pat now, and occasionally he shows a faint resemblance to a Mr. Babcock who has been shrunk in the laundry. Young Pat is checking over a letter he has written.

YOUNG PAT. (*Reading.*) "To Mrs. Mame Burnside, American Express, Cairo. Dear Auntie Mame. It's wonderful to get your letters every day. Thank you for the chop-sticks you sent from Yokohama. They sure come in handy. I guess you and Uncle Beau are enjoying the world all right—and vice versa." (*He makes an insertion in long hand.*) Ha, ha—joke. (*He continues reading.*) "Mr. Babcock says if I work hard here at Saint Boniface he will enroll me at Rumson University, which is Mr. Babcock's alma mater. He says I'll be very lucky if I'm admitted—considering everything." (*He turns the page over to read the other side.*) "I plan to spend the holidays again with the Babcocks in Darien. Junior Babcock and I have swell times there, and I have met the kids from practically all the best families in Connecticut. (*As the lights fade, we hear a haunting muezzin cry, and the right half of the traveler curtain closes in front of Young Pat's study room.*)

ACT TWO
SCENE 2

The action is continuous, as the spot hits stage left, revealing:

The Pyramids. This is an inset, with levels, suggesting the slope of the Great Pyramid.

We find Uncle Beau, in a pith helmet and wearing a garland of Leicas and light meters. He has climbed above Auntie Mame to shoot down at her as she studies Young Pat's letter. She is garbed in a fetching camel driver's outfit from Russek's, and scowls slightly as she reads aloud.

AUNTIE MAME. (*Reading.*) "Junior Babcock and I have swell times there, and I have met the kids from practically all the best families in Connecticut." (*She calls up to Beau.*) Oh dear, Beau—I have a feeling we should be getting back.

UNCLE BEAU. (*Fiddling with his camera.*) Just one more shot.

AUNTIE MAME. Home, I mean. I feel Patrick needs me.

UNCLE BEAU. Move a little to the right, Mame darlin'. I'm gettin' too much Pyramid and not enough you.

AUNTIE MAME. Beau. I do wish you'd stop climbing up on things. It makes me so nervous.

UNCLE BEAU. Remember the higher you go, the more interesting the shot. Now, look natural. (*Auntie Mame strikes a Vogue-cover pose, and puts on a frozen smile.*) Oh, that's just fine. (*He clicks the picture, fussing inexpertly with the camera.*) You know, Mame, I think that's gonna turn out even better than the one of you standing by the old Moulmein Pagoda, looking eastward to the sea.

AUNTIE MAME. Now you come down from there. (*As he does, she takes his arm affectionately.*) Little did I think when I married you that I was getting such a wonderful photographer, too. (*Lightly.*) Oh, did you remember to put film in the camera this time?

UNCLE BEAU. I sure did! (*He opens the camera to make sure, and the entire roll of exposed film unreels itself in the bright Egyptian sunlight.*) Dang! (*The lights fade on the Pyramid area, stage left. In the momentary darkness we hear the strains of the Rumson University alma mater.*)

ACT TWO

Scene 3

GLEE CLUB. (*Singing off.*)
"O Rumson U., dear Rumson U.,
To thee we'll e'er be staunch and true.
E'en when our college days are through,
We'll remember you, Rumson U."

The lights come up on the area stage right.

A dormitory room at Rumson University. The action is continuous.

Several years have passed, and for the first time we see Patrick Dennis, the young man. He lounges casually at a typewriter, with text books littering the desk in front of him. However, he is engaged in the happy pastime of writing another letter to his Auntie Mame. He wears a beanie blazoned with the Rumson "R." He has matured into a remarkably handsome, intelligent and personable young man. There's only one trouble: he knows it. Pulling the letter from the typewriter, Patrick reads.

PATRICK. (*Reading.*) "To Mrs. Beauregard Jackson Pickett Burnside, care of American Express, Zurich, Switzerland. Dear Auntie Mame. I think it's great that you and Uncle Beau are getting an eighth honeymoon on your eighth anniversary. Everybody here was certainly impressed with the statue of the laughing Buddha you sent me from Siam: It was a bit large, however, to get through the door of the dorm. If you decide to go on that caravan to Baghdad, don't let them give you a camel named 'Lightnin' Rod.' Rumson U. is not as dull and denominational as you thought. Miss Pritchard's finishing school is nearby and it's overflowing with the prettiest debutantes you ever saw. Since you came and spent my last vacation with me, I have grown several more inches, my voice has changed several more times—and you may not recognize what my glands have done to me. (*He turns the page over.*) Give Uncle Beau a kiss for me; I'm sure he will enjoy it more coming from you since I've been shaving almost daily now and my beard tickles. (*A thought occurs to him and he pencils an insert into the letter.*) . . . or so the debs tell me. (*He chuckles at his own joke, then continues reading.*) Say 'Hi' to the Matterhorn for me. Your loving nephew, Patrick." (*The lights fade. From off, we hear some hyperbolic yodeling.*)

ACT TWO
SCENE 4

The Matterhorn. The levels which represented the Pyramids have been redressed and masked to depict an Alpine glacier.

Uncle Beau is actually out of sight amid the peaks high above Auntie Mame, who is decked out in a stunning fur parka, and reads Patrick's letter. Again, the action is continuous.

AUNTIE MAME. (*Reading.*) Glands . . . Debutantes! (*She calls up to Uncle Beau who is out of sight above.*) Beau, I have a feeling that Patrick's right on the brink of something.

UNCLE BEAU. (*Offstage.*) Just a little higher and I think this is gonna be the best shot yet! Mame honey, do you mind stepping back a bit? (*Auntie Mame looks over her shoulder and down behind her. From the expression on her face, we know it is a sheer drop of half-a-mile straight down. She calls up to Beau, sweetly.*)

AUNTIE MAME. I'd rather not.

UNCLE BEAU. Don't you never mind—I'll skittle up a might.

AUNTIE MAME. Please, Beau, no higher.

UNCLE BEAU. Remember, honey, the high shots are the best. (*Auntie Mame starts to protest, but we see an ice-axe being lowered from above.*) Take this, honey. Pesky thing keeps gettin' in my way.

AUNTIE MAME. (*Taking it, gingerly.*) No! Hang on to the other end, dear, for your balance.

UNCLE BEAU. (*Offstage. Calling down.*) Don't you worry, Mame—I'm as sure-footed as a mountain goat. Hold it—just like that! Steady—wait'll I re-focus. (*Again Mame strikes a pose, while Beau yodels blithely. But suddenly the yodel resolves into a thin, fading scream, which reverberates down the glacier.*)

AUNTIE MAME. (*Tentatively.*) Beau???? (*The other end of the rope drops with limp significance. Auntie Mame looks up, horrified.*) Beau!!!!! (*The lights fade quickly. Melancholy voices from backstage hum "Massa's in the Cold, Cold Ground," with a wistful yodel in counterpoint.*)

ACT TWO

Scene 5

The Beekman Place apartment.

There are dustcovers over some of the chairs. Lindsay, who is graying nicely into a sort of Manhattan Ronald Colman, adjusts a Dictaphone. Vera, who is now somewhere between forty and death, has not aged at all—due to the diurnal ministrations of Charles of the Ritz.

VERA. (*Looking at Lindsay skeptically.*) What's that thing supposed to be, Lindsay?

LINDSAY. A Dictaphone.

VERA. She'll never use it. You've lugged all this junk in here for nothing.

LINDSAY. Vera, she can't go on living in a vacuum. Mame's always got to have a project!

VERA. She's got a project. Now she's the tragedy queen, and she's having fun being miserable. All she's done for two years is wander around Europe, re-visiting the places she's been with Beau. Eight times she climbed that lousy Matterhorn—to toss rose petals down the glacier.

LINDSAY. Well, she must have loved him. (*Vera starts to take off some of the dustcovers.*)

VERA. Let's get some more of these dustcovers off—the place looks like a morgue. (*Lindsay helps her.*)

LINDSAY. You know, Vera, I'm a coward—I should've gone to the boat to meet her. (*Vera is prowling for a drink. The door buzzer rings. Lindsay crosses to open the door for Agnes Gooch, a dowdy owl-eyed secretary who slouches in the foyer, with a shorthand pad under her arm.*)

VERA. (*At bar.*) I haven't seen her since I dragged myself over for the funeral. Wasn't it just like Mame to keep him till I got there? (*Looking at the label of the lone bottle.*) Southern Comfort. Oh, well.

LINDSAY. (*At the door, to Gooch.*) Oh, yes—come in.

VERA. (*Turning from the bar, expectantly.*) Mame!? (*Gooch schlumps into the apartment.*) My God, she can't have changed *that* much!

GOOCH. (*In a flat, nasal drone.*) I'm from Speed-o.

VERA. (*Blankly.*) What?

LINDSAY. I called this secretarial service. I want to show Mame we really mean business, let her know I'm really serious about this thing. (*Turning to Agnes.*) Your name is . . . ?

GOOCH. Agnes Gooch.

LINDSAY. Now, Miss Gooch, you'll be taking dictation from Mrs. Burnside—and she's a pretty fast talker.

GOOCH. Oh, Speed-o won't let anybody out who can't do at least 100 words a minute. (*She lowers her eyes modestly.*) I'm over 200.

VERA. You're not! Well, if Mame does any dictating—which I doubt—it'll be sprinkled with French, Egyptian, Japanese and four-letter words.

GOOCH. (*After a moment's thought.*) I'm afraid I'm not your girl. (*Gooch starts to leave, but Lindsay moves to stop her.*)

LINDSAY. Please stay, Miss Gooch. This should be an interesting experience for you. Mrs. Burnside will pour out a flood of words and ideas, and you must soak them all up. You'll be her . . . (*He gropes for the word.*) Her *sponge*! (*Gooch looks at Lindsay askance. Vera throws up her hands.*)

VERA. Oh, Lindsay, how can Mame write a book? She can't even sit still long enough to write a post-card.

LINDSAY. (*Leading Gooch toward the desk.*) I've got somebody to help her. (*He glances at his watch.*) Oh, good Lord, I told the fellow to be here at three o'clock.

VERA. (*Interested.*) What fellow?

LINDSAY. Miss Gooch, you're on salary as of right now. (*Auntie Mame and Patrick appear in the foyer. She is in black, heavily veiled, and Patrick wears his Ivy League best. They have been chatting warmly. Patrick presses the buzzer three times.*)

AUNTIE MAME. Why are you ringing, Patrick? Don't you have a key?

PATRICK. Of course. I forgot. (*Within the apartment, Lindsay springs into excited action.*)

LINDSAY. Three buzzes—that's the signal! (*He herds Vera and Gooch out the door.*) Come on—we're going to surprise her.

VERA. Oh, you're acting like a school boy. (*Lindsay comes back for Gooch, who has started toward the foyer door.*)

LINDSAY. You too! (*He pulls her off. Patrick ushers Mame in, just as the others vanish. They are carrying parcels.*)

PATRICK. Welcome home, Auntie Mame. (*Auntie Mame looks about the room with a dramatic remoteness.*)

AUNTIE MAME. Dear old Beekman Place. It's so loyal. No matter how far I go, it just sits here and waits for me. You know, I rather expected Vera at the boat.

PATRICK. I wouldn't let her come. I wanted to be alone with you. (*They hug.*)

AUNTIE MAME. Patrick, my little Patrick. Now open your presents. Oh, Patrick, every time I see you, you get taller and more grown up. (*Patrick tears open a package and is baffled as he takes out a pair of Bavarian leather walking shorts. Auntie Mame holds them up against him. With a grin Patrick remembers a similar gift of many years before.*)

PATRICK. Golly, short pants—at last! Can I try 'em on right now, Auntie Mame? Right now? (*They both laugh—but Auntie Mame's attitude changes instantly as Vera and Lindsay burst into the room. She drops the pants and strikes a mournful pose.*)

LINDSAY. Surprise! Surprise, Mame!

VERA. Surprise, darling—welcome home! (*Auntie Mame is now Duse, playing the Tragic Muse for the benefit of Vera.*)

AUNTIE MAME. (*Kissing Vera lightly on the cheek.*) Vera, dear. And staunch, stalwart Lindsay. How good of you both to rally 'round this bereft old woman. (*The others exchange glances.*)

PATRICK. Doesn't she look great?

LINDSAY. Mame, you look marvelous.

VERA. (*Eyeing the widow's weeds suspiciously.*) How can you tell? Mame, couldn't you have gone to *purple* by now?

LINDSAY. Mame, I haven't seen you since the Huns took Rome. Oh, no, it was when the Bears took Wall Street.

AUNTIE MAME. Oh, Lindsay, that day was nirvana compared to what I've been through since. If only I'd jumped off the Matterhorn after him.

PATRICK. (*Crossing to the bar.*) Now, now, Auntie Mame—what you need is a good stiff drink.

AUNTIE MAME. No, no, no, Patrick. There is no barbiturate for my grief. I've given up alcohol completely. I haven't touched a drop since that St. Bernard brought me back to life. (*She becomes aware of the dictating machine and the typewriter.*) What's that?

LINDSAY. Well, that's your Dictaphone and this is your typewriter. (*Gooch comes out of hiding and plods flat-footedly to her place at the desk. Auntie Mame looks at the secretary blankly.*)

AUNTIE MAME. And what's *that*?

GOOCH. I'm your "sponge"!

LINDSAY. (*Clears his throat to spring his surprise.*) These are the tools of your new trade. You're going to write a book, Mame, and I'm going to publish it.

AUNTIE MAME. (*Waving away the paraphernalia, including Agnes.*) Oh, Lindsay, don't be ridiculous. The way I feel, I can hardly read a book, let alone write one.

LINDSAY. (*Convincingly.*) All I want you to do is put your *self* on paper. Your memoirs.

PATRICK. Nobody's had a more exciting life than you, Auntie Mame. Done more things. I think it'd be terrific.

VERA. And think of all the fascinating people you've known. Like me.

LINDSAY. And it'll take your mind off things.

AUNTIE MAME. (*Suspiciously.*) Oh, I see—this is some kind of a conspiracy.

LINDSAY. No, no—

AUNTIE MAME. Some trumped-up occupational therapy, like leathercraft, or hooking rugs.

LINDSAY. I swear to you, it'll be a fascinating book. Why, it can easily be a best-seller. Mame, you'd be doing *me* a favor.

AUNTIE MAME. (*Starting to pace, intrigued.*) My memoirs. My memoirs. Patrick, you forgot my drink.

PATRICK. There's only Southern Comfort.

AUNTIE MAME. Anything, dear, just make it a double. (*She peels off some of the crepe, dumping it in Gooch's lap.*) What a lovely, lovely idea. I see it in two volumes, don't you, Lindsay? Boxed, like Proust.

LINDSAY. Let's get something to bind first. Remember, Mame, writing isn't easy—it means at least six months of gruelling concentration.

AUNTIE MAME. (*Her eyes lighting up.*) Let me see, let me see. (*Gooch takes her pad and poises her pencil like a female Boswell.*) "Chapter One, Page One!" (*Gooch writes furiously.*) Well, I'll be damned! This isn't so difficult, Lindsay. (*To Gooch, puzzled.*) What are you writing?

GOOCH. (*Reading back her shorthand by rote.*) "Chapter One, Page One, well, I'll be damned, this isn't so difficult, Lindsay, what are you writing"

VERA. She *is* fast.

PATRICK. (*Handing the drink to Mame.*) Atta girl, Auntie Mame—you're off and running.

AUNTIE MAME. (*To Patrick.*) Oh, Patrick, do you really think I should? You heard Lindsay. After all, it'll take up all my time, and I really came home just to be with you.

PATRICK. You can't exactly be with me. No women allowed in the dorm.

AUNTIE MAME. I keep forgetting. You're all grown up now. You don't need me any more. (*Gooch is still taking every word down in frantic shorthand. Auntie Mame looks toward Lindsay.*) How do I turn her off? (*She resumes pacing.*) Now, where was I? The most important thing is to have a good beginning.

VERA. Is she supposed to start right this minute?

LINDSAY. Why don't you wait for your collaborator? He's on his way over here right now. (*There is a blank pause.*)

AUNTIE MAME. Collaborator?

LINDSAY. (*Backing water.*) Well, after all, you're only an ama— you're not a professional writer, and naturally I thought you'd want as much help as we could . . . (*Lindsay sees that this is completely the wrong tack. He puts on his most winning and gracious publisher's air.*) Mary Lord Bishop over at my office lined up this young man who's done a great deal of work with women authors, and . . .

AUNTIE MAME. (*With smoldering indignation.*) You don't trust me to write my own life myself! My God, who else could write it? (*She turns to Vera with a hollow laugh.*) He wants to give me a ghost!

LINDSAY. Not a ghost. More of an editor.

AUNTIE MAME. Who? Maxwell Perkins?

LINDSAY. Well, not quite. I haven't met this chap, O'Bannion, myself, but . . .

AUNTIE MAME. What did you say his name was?

LINDSAY. Brian O'Bannion. He's a . . .

AUNTIE MAME. O, God, deliver me. I can see him now—one of those beery, loose-mouthed Irish tenors.

LINDSAY. Mary says he's a very good poet. Wrote a volume called "The Wounded Tulip."

AUNTIE MAME. Probably pansy.

LINDSAY. Now, Mame.

AUNTIE MAME. Do you think I'm going to let some moon-eyed versifier mess up my memoirs with a lot of miserable Irish wit? (*The doorbell buzzes. Patrick crosses to the foyer door and opens it. He converses in hushed tones with the visitor. Auntie Mame rails on against Lindsay and his editorial notions.*) I'll bet you don't give Willa Cather a low-comedy Irishman to tell her how to punctuate! Some funny-paper Jiggs out of Lady Gregory who . . .

PATRICK. Auntie Mame. There's a gentleman to see you. Mr. O'Bannion. (*Auntie Mame looks toward the doorway as O'Bannion enters. He is about thirty-five, tall, and very thin. He has white skin and hair as black as coal—short and very curly. His eyes are turquoise blue, rimmed with thick, black lashes. He wears a sportcoat of tweedy homespun with big suede patches at the elbows and a dirty trench coat is slung over his shoulder. O'Bannion shifts his weight gracefully in the doorway and gives Auntie Mame a slow, sad smile, parting a fine set of choppers. His intense blue eyes seem to reach out and caress her.*)

O'BANNION. (*Mellifluously.*) Miss Bishop said it might not be amiss if I happened to drop by. (*O'Bannion half closes his eyes.*) You're Mrs. Burnside, of course. I could sense the aura of creative vitality about you. (*Vera, Lindsay and Gooch swing their respective gazes slowly from the newcomer to Auntie Mame.*)

AUNTIE MAME. (*Swallowing, a little flustered.*) Won't you come in, Mr. O'Bannion? We were just talking about you. (*He comes into the room like a graceful cat, slithering around the furniture with a kind of pelvis movement that is vaguely imitative of an electric eel. Lindsay, Vera and Gooch watch, fascinated by the crackling chemistry between O'Bannion and Auntie Mame.*) So awfully kind of you—a really renowned poet—to bother with my childish little scribblings. (*He gives her the old hot-eye again and she clears her throat nervously. As she crosses to him, she takes off her coat, dropping it behind her.*) Tell me, do you think that you and I can ever get any place? (*Quickly.*) With the book, I mean. (*O'Bannion takes Auntie Mame's hand in both of his and turns on that slow, sad smile again.*)

O'BANNION. I feel that you and I are going to create something beautiful! (*The poet draws Auntie Mame closer to him, kissing her hand. She turns her back to the audience, and we see that her "widow's weeds" are virtually backless; and somewhere around the fifth lumbar vertebra there is a livid heliotrope flower.*)

THE LIGHTS FADE

ACT TWO
SCENE 6

In the darkness we hear an ancient Gaelic lullaby, sung touchingly by unseen male voices.

VOICES. (*Offstage singing.*)
"Tu ra loora lay,
A loora lay,
A toora loora lay;
Tu ra loora lay,
A loora lay,
A toora loora lay."

The Beekman Place apartment—refurnished and refurbished as a literary atelier. The wall panels have been reversed, to become impressive bookcases. A bust of Dickens adorns the niche by the spiral staircase. Brian O'Bannion reclines on a leathery loveseat. To say he has made himself at home is a gross understatement; he is wearing a lush quilted dressing gown, and lounges with half-closed eyes, one forearm dramatically crooked over his meditative forehead.

Agnes Gooch sits like a flat-chested owl at her typewriter. Intensely she pounds away at a manuscript, the stethoscope of a Dictaphone dangling from her ears. Apparently what she hears stirs the spirit of Proserpina in her otherwise vacuous vitals. Occasionally a little "coo" of excitement escapes her lips, prompted by what is coming through the earphones. Her eyes sparkle and she types furiously with vicarious delight, jumping up and down with her feet under the desk.

O'BANNION. (*Annoyed.*) Please, please—Miss Gooch! How can I court the Muse with all that clackety-clackety?

GOOCH. I'm just taking off what Mrs. Burnside dictated. (*O'Bannion makes a deprecating gesture, waving aside anything that Auntie Mame has dictated as unimportant.*) But everything Mrs. Burnside dictates is so wonderful, it makes me all goose pimply. Why, when I listen to all the things she's done, and think of all the things I haven't done, I just want to go out and start trying everything and seeing everything and being everything—just like she has!

O'BANNION. I'm not sure the human race is ready for this book. (*Grandly.*) But it is *I* who shall clothe the naked incidents in poetry and symbolism. (*He glances at his watch and calls off insolently.*) Norah! Ito! It's time for my nectar. (*Norah enters from the kitchen, her hands on her hips, and sizing up O'Bannion.*)

NORAH. What's that of yours it's time for, your majesty?

O'BANNION. My nectar, my nectar!

NORAH. (*Sarcastically.*) In exactly what part of Ireland is it, me bucko, where you drink "nectar"?

O'BANNION. (*Laying it on, airily.*) I come from that part of the Green Isle that has no latitude, nor longitude, and the leprechauns play in the twilight mist . . .

NORAH. You know, you're just about four bricks short of a full load! (*Norah goes off disgustedly. The telephone rings and Agnes answers it.*)

GOOCH. (*Into phone.*) Mrs. Burnside's residence. No, she isn't here—she's out on the moors. (*Pause.*) *The moors.* (*She listens again.*) Maybe you'd better talk with Mr. O'Bannion. (*Gooch gets up from her desk and carries the telephone on a long cord to the recumbent O'Bannion.*) It's that Mr. M. Lindsay Woolsey. He says it's important. (*Grandly O'Bannion takes the telephone from the servile secretary, who trembles with excitement at the instant their hands brush.*)

O'BANNION. (*Into phone.*) O'Bannion here. How are you, Lindsay? (*He listens.*) The moors? Oh, that's what we call the terrace where I send her to meditate when the fog is crawling up from the Queensborough Bridge. (*He listens again.*) I can't put her on, but I'll be happy to give her another message. (*This probably nettles Lindsay, but O'Bannion continues with his attitude of bland mastery of the situation.*) I'll tell her. But of course she'll be at your party tonight—I'm bringing her. Goldwyn? Samuel Goldwyn? (*He listens; this boy can smell a buck.*) Well, if he's interested, he'll have to buy our book sight unseen! (*He hangs up. Auntie Mame enters, looking like a Brontë with a long plaid muffler around her throat.*)

O'BANNION. (*Eagerly.*) Alana, Samuel Goldwyn's coming to the party tonight. And we're to be at Lindsay's a half-hour early to tell him the story.

AUNTIE MAME. Dear Lindsay!—how good of him. Goldwyn's perfect for my story. After all, it *is* the American "Wuthering Heights." (*Gooch comes forward, apologizing for living. In one hand she has a stack of manuscript as thick as the New York telephone directory, and in the other hand she has two pages.*)

GOOCH. (*Indicating the thick sheaf of pages.*) Here's what you dictated, Mrs. Burnside . . . (*And indicating the two sheets.*) . . . and here's what Mr. O'Bannion edited.

AUNTIE MAME. Oh. Thank you, Agnes. Now Mr. O'Bannion and I are going to work for a little bit. Why don't you do whatever it is you *do* do to relax?

GOOCH. Oh, thank you, Mrs. Burnside. I think I'll just fix myself a Dr. Pepper. (*Gooch takes a glass from the bar and goes off to the kitchen. She looks moon-eyed at O'Bannion as she exits. The moment she is gone, O'Bannion tries to nuzzle Auntie Mame, but deftly she slips away from his embrace.*)

O'BANNION. You glorious creature!

AUNTIE MAME. Brian—please—we're supposed to be working.

O'BANNION. Every time I come within ten feet of you, you reject me. How can we make music, until our lutes are in tune?

AUNTIE MAME. Well, after we finish the book, we can tune our lutes.

O'BANNION. We're not collaborating in the fullest sense of the word. (*Amorously.*) Alana, collaborate with me!

AUNTIE MAME. Brian, really!

O'BANNION. You're a block of ice, and we're supposed to be writing of burning passion and hot blood.

AUNTIE MAME. But I'm only eleven years of age in this part of the book.

O'BANNION. But *mature*—mature for eleven!

AUNTIE MAME. Brian, we've got to get to work.

O'BANNION. (*Sighs.*) All right, slave-driver. Where were we? (*Auntie Mame, relieved, examines the two pages which are the total of O'Bannion's editing.*)

AUNTIE MAME. Still on chapter two. It's not going very fast, is it? It took us a month-and-a-half on chapter one.

O'BANNION. But what a chapter.

AUNTIE MAME. What a month-and-a-half. (*Fending him off.*) Please, Brian, I cannot concentrate when you're doing things like that.

O'BANNION. Sorceress!

AUNTIE MAME. Besides, it takes Agnes no time at all to knock off a Dr. Pepper. (*Wishing the whole thing were over.*) How long do you think it's going to take us to finish the book?

O'BANNION. Flaubert spent thirteen years on "Madame Bovary."

AUNTIE MAME. How did she stand it?

O'BANNION. Read me our last sentence. (*Auntie Mame reaches for the top page on the thick stack of manuscript, and reads.*)

AUNTIE MAME. (*Reading.*) "My puberty in Buffalo was drab."

O'BANNION. No, no! It has no majesty! "Drab" is such a drab word.

AUNTIE MAME. How right you are, Brian. It has no afflatus. (*Gooch enters from the kitchen, pouring a Dr. Pepper into a highball glass. Auntie Mame looks at her and gets an idea.*) What about "bleak"?

O'BANNION. (*Testing it.*) Bleak . . . bleak! How bleak was my puberty! Bleak Buffalo. Hear how those two words cling to each other—like a man and a woman, locked in each other's arms! Listen to the words sing!

GOOCH. (*Enraptured.*) How bleak was my puberty! (*Auntie Mame glares at Gooch, who melts away into the kitchen.*) I'm sorry. (*As soon as Gooch is out of sight, O'Bannion goes to work again, kissing Auntie Mame helter-skelter.*)

O'BANNION. "Bleak." Oh, God, let me caress that talent! Where is it hidden, that germ of genius, *where* is it?

AUNTIE MAME. Brian, please— (*She glances at the page of edited manuscript.*) I'm worried about something. Coccamaura. I wonder if the general public is going to understand all this symbolism. (*She reads.*) "Like an echo from the caves of Coccamaura, I came forth whilst Deirdre wept cool tears." Wouldn't it be simpler to say, "On the day I was born, it rained in Buffalo"?

O'BANNION. Drab, drab, drab!

AUNTIE MAME. It's drab, but it's clear.

O'BANNION. Clarity! How beauty is obscured by clarity.

AUNTIE MAME. All right, Brian, just what is it you want to say?

O'BANNION. (*Fumbling.*) Well, it's quite obvious— (*Suddenly he makes an extravagant gesture.*) We're drying up! We need inspiration! Get out the Yeats, the Synge, the Joyce! It's poetry time!

AUNTIE MAME. (*Wearily.*) Again??? (*Auntie Mame takes a thin volume from the table. Although she is bored with this poetry ritual, she accepts it as a part of the eccentric trappings of authorship. Resignedly she slips to the floor with O'Bannion and they lie head to head, their feet extending in opposite directions. With dutiful concentration she begins to read.*)

"The lyre and lute
Are mute, are mute.
And gray is the grave where my lover lies;
Where my lover lies,
Where my lover lies,
Mute, mute, mute."

(*Gooch comes from the kitchen, stepping over them.*)

GOOCH. I rinsed out the glass.

AUNTIE MAME. Aren't you neat, Agnes? (*Gooch plods back into the kitchen.*)

O'BANNION. Glorious! Glorious! More! More! (*Auntie Mame turns to another poem. Patrick appears in the hallway and lets himself in. Auntie Mame and O'Bannion are so wrapped up in their "work" that they do not hear the sound of Patrick coming in. She reads.*)

AUNTIE MAME.

"Bright bleeds the blood of the broken rose,
And my loins leap up to utter passion's feckless cry.
My loins cry out for thee,
O love!
O love!—"

(*O'Bannion has been acting out the imagery on Auntie Mame's neck and ear; Patrick clears his throat.*) Oh, hush, Agnes.

PATRICK. (*Coolly.*) Auntie Mame— (*Auntie Mame and O'Bannion spring up from the floor. Auntie Mame is a little flustered.*)

AUNTIE MAME. Why, Patrick—what are you doing home from school?

PATRICK. I had something very important I wanted to talk with you about—but if you're busy . . .

AUNTIE MAME. (*Covering quickly.*) Oh, Brian and I were just working—on the book.

PATRICK. I'll bet that's going to be some book.

AUNTIE MAME. This is my nephew, Patrick; this is my collaborator, Mr. Brian O'Bannion. (*The two nod to each other with the cordiality of Ben Gurion encountering Nasser.*)

PATRICK (*Glumly.*) We've met. Auntie Mame, I wonder if I could talk to you a little bit—alone. It's rather personal—and rather important.

AUNTIE MAME. Why, of course, my dear. If you don't mind, Brian—? (*O'Bannion, somewhat wounded, decides to make an exit.*)

O'BANNION. (*Starting up the staircase.*) It's quite all right. I was just going up to my room—to change. (*Raising his voice.*) Pay no attention to me. Don't anybody pay attention to me at all! (*He exits grandly up the stairs.*)

PATRICK. To his *room*! Is he *living* here?

AUNTIE MAME. Why, of course, darling. There was nobody in the sculpture room. And since we're working together literally day and night—so to speak . . .

PATRICK. (*Primly.*) It looks very cozy.

AUNTIE MAME. For a moment there you sounded exactly like somebody from the Knickerbocker Bank.

PATRICK. Please get O'Bannion out of here. Right away.

AUNTIE MAME. I beg your pardon?

PATRICK. I don't want him in this house.

AUNTIE MAME. Aren't you taking a rather imperious tone? Mr. O'Bannion is my colleague.

PATRICK. Colleague, my foot! Gloria would never understand that you and this Irish phoney are . . .

AUNTIE MAME. Gloria? Who's Gloria? (*Patrick takes a deep breath.*)

PATRICK. Auntie Mame, listen to me. (*He takes her shoulders.*) I've met a girl. I've been going with her for several months.

AUNTIE MAME. Oh?

PATRICK. She's—well, she's a very special girl. I guess I should have told you about her before. I would have, but I knew you were all tied up with your book and . . . (*Significantly.*) . . . everything. And until now, it wasn't really definite.

AUNTIE MAME. What's definite now?

PATRICK. Gloria's *the* girl, that's what's definite. And you're going to meet her. Tonight.

AUNTIE MAME. I hope you didn't leave her sitting in the car.

PATRICK. I dropped her off at her girl friend's. Bunny Bixler's on Park Avenue. She wanted to get spruced up before she met you.

AUNTIE MAME. (*Nervously.*) Well—I'd better do some sprucing up of my own.

PATRICK. (*Starting toward the foyer door.*) I'll bring Gloria back in about ten or fifteen minutes, okay?

AUNTIE MAME. (*A little flustered.*) I'll have my face all organized. (*From off, we hear O'Bannion's voice at the top of the stairs.*)

O'BANNION. (*Calling.*) Mame, where did Ito hide my white tie? (*Patrick stops dead in his tracks, pointing his finger toward the sound of the voice.*)

PATRICK. Wait a minute. If *he's* still in the house, I'm not going to bring Gloria back here.

AUNTIE MAME. May I inquire why?

PATRICK. Gloria happens to be a very sensitive and well-brought-up girl. And I don't want you flaunting your new flames and your old peccadilloes in front of her.

AUNTIE MAME. (*Freezing.*) Then why bring her here at all?

PATRICK. (*Getting angry himself.*) You want to know the truth? I've been trying to avoid it. But she wanted to meet you.

AUNTIE MAME. So you just dropped by to make sure I was all scrubbed up and presentable for inspection! Is that it?

PATRICK. (*Suffering.*) No, no, Auntie Mame. (*Pleading.*) Just for five minutes tonight will you try to act like a normal human being? Then I won't make any more demands on you. Gloria's from good stock—and she just doesn't have to know about all your airy-fairy friends from Fire Island; or your Irish friend upstairs. I'd just rather my little Glory didn't know about a lot of things that ordinary mortals simply don't have to know about. (*There is a deathly pause.*)

AUNTIE MAME. (*With quiet intensity.*) Should she know that I think you've turned into one of the most beastly, bourgeois, babbity little snobs on the Eastern seaboard, —or will you be able to make that quite clear, without any help from me? (*This is the first time in Patrick's entire life that Auntie Mame has really let him have it with both barrels. He is stunned. He looks at her for a moment, then turns on his heels and starts out.*)

PATRICK. All right. Just forget about the whole thing. (*Auntie Mame realizes it would be fatal to let him go out in this mood.*)

AUNTIE MAME. Patrick—bring your girl here. I won't let her get the wrong impression, I promise. (*They look at each other.*)

PATRICK. (*With a warm smile.*) Thanks, Auntie Mame. (*He goes out. Auntie Mame begins to pace, chewing on the knuckle of her index finger. From upstairs we hear O'Bannion's untrained Irish baritone singing, "I'll Take You Home Again, Kathleen." At this sound, Auntie Mame really looks worried: how is she going to get him out of here?*)

AUNTIE MAME. (*Calling up the stairs.*) Brian . . . (*O'Bannion breaks off in mid-song, and appears at the head of the stairs in full dress shirt and trousers—but no tie or coat yet.*)

O'BANNION. (*From the head of the stairs.*) Yes, Alana? Why aren't you getting dressed? We can't keep the Goldwyns waiting.

AUNTIE MAME. (*With difficulty.*) Would you mind awfully if I didn't go to the party with you tonight?

O'BANNION. (*Affronted.*) You want me to go *alone*? I wouldn't think of it!

AUNTIE MAME. But—something came up . . .

O'BANNION. (*Imperiously.*) Hurry and get dressed, Alana. I'm *not* goin' to that party alone! (*He turns on his heel and goes back into his upstairs bedroom. Gooch plods out of the kitchen and whines at Auntie Mame.*)

GOOCH. Mrs. Burnside, if there's nothing else you wanted me for, I just thought I'd turn in.

AUNTIE MAME. Agnes, I wonder— (*Auntie Mame starts pacing around Agnes.*)

GOOCH. (*Getting nervous at Auntie Mame's perusal.*) Mrs. Burnside, is anything wrong?

AUNTIE MAME. Agnes! You're coming out.

GOOCH. (*Clutching the sides of her dress.*) Where?

AUNTIE MAME. (*Yanking off Agnes' glasses.*) Why, Agnes, you have lovely eyes. Take those glasses off and leave them off *forever.*

GOOCH. But I can't see anything out of my right eye.

AUNTIE MAME. Then look out of the left one. (*Auntie Mame points to Agnes' shoes.*) What do you call those things?

GOOCH. Orthopedic oxfords.

AUNTIE MAME. Kick 'em off. (*Gooch, baffled, complies. Auntie Mame pulls her dress tight around the midriff.*) My goodness, Agnes—you do have a bust. Where on earth have you been hiding it all these months?

GOOCH. (*Getting worried.*) Mrs. Burnside—

AUNTIE MAME. (*Positively.*) Take off your clothes.

GOOCH. (*With a proper little gasp.*) Mrs. Burnside! There's a man in the house!

AUNTIE MAME. Don't be a goose, Agnes, get those clothes off and keep them off. (*Agnes peels out of her clothes and stands trembling in a shapeless white slip. Mame calls off.*) Norah! Ito! Come on in here, we've got some work to do! (*Norah and Ito hurry in from the kitchen.*)

GOOCH. (*Cringing.*) I don't have a very clear picture of what's going on.

AUNTIE MAME. (*Briskly.*) Agnes, I'm sending you to that party tonight with Mr. O'Bannion. (*Gooch looks thunder-struck and begins to get the shakes.*)

GOOCH. Oh, I couldn't. I'm too nervous. (*Auntie Mame strides to the bar and pours a stiff slug of Irish whiskey for Agnes.*)

AUNTIE MAME. This'll calm you down.

GOOCH. But spirits do the most terrible thing to me. I'm not the same girl.

AUNTIE MAME. What's wrong with that? (*She forces the jigger on Gooch. The Secretary starts to drink, then hesitates.*)

GOOCH. Will it mix with Dr. Pepper?

AUNTIE MAME. (*Emphatically.*) He'll love it. Drink! (*Agnes drinks. Before the liquor hits bottom, Auntie Mame is slapping Agnes' cheeks.*) Oh, Agnes, for God's sake, close your pores! We really should do something about that skin. A good physic would work wonders, but I guess it's too late in the day to start that. (*She turns crisply to the servants.*) Norah, go upstairs, drag out that sexy Patou velvet! Ito, get out all my cosmetics: the face creams, the lipsticks, the eyebrow pencils! (*Ito scampers up the stairs delightedly.*)

ITO. You see, me be Charlie of the Ritz! (*Auntie Mame starts to drag Agnes up the stairs, but Agnes hangs back, holding onto the bannister.*)

GOOCH. (*A coward to the core.*) Mrs. Burnside, I think I know what you want me to do, and I'm not a bit sure I want to do it!

AUNTIE MAME. Agnes, where's your *spine*? Here you've been taking my dictation all these weeks, and you don't get the message of my book! *Live!*—that's the message!

GOOCH. (*Still hanging back, as if she didn't know what the word meant.*) Live?

AUNTIE MAME. Yes! Life is a banquet, and most poor sons-of-bitches are *starving* to death! Live! (*Intoxicated, partly by the liquor, partly by Auntie Mame's enthusiasm, Agnes decides to let herself go as she charges up the stairs.*)

GOOCH. (*Hypnotized.*) Live! Live! Live!

THE LIGHTS FADE

ACT TWO

SCENE 7

The Beekman Place apartment, a half hour later.

As the lights come up, the room is empty. Then Ito scampers down the spiral stairs, giggling giddily. He disappears into the kitchen.

Next Norah hurries down the stairs, gathering up some of Gooch's discarded clothing.

NORAH. (*Muttering.*) The whole house has gone nuts. (*Shaking her head as she goes off.*) She'll never make a silk purse out of *that* sow's ear! (*Now Auntie Mame appears at the head of the stairs. She turns back as Agnes calls to her from off.*)

GOOCH'S VOICE. (*Calling from off.*) Mrs. Burnside, I can't *breathe*!

AUNTIE MAME. Fine! If you can breathe, it isn't tight enough. (*Auntie Mame starts down the stairs, carrying a fur wrap. She looks at her watch. Under her breath:*) Oh, God. (*Glancing nervously toward the outside door, she takes several glasses toward the bar, straightening up for Gloria's imminent arrival. In the manner of a grand duke, O'Bannion comes down the stairs in his full dress regalia.*)

O'BANNION. (*Startled.*) And why aren't you ready?

AUNTIE MAME. (*Turning to face O'Bannion.*) Now, Brian, you're going to have to understand. I'm not going to the party tonight.

O'BANNION. (*Splenetically.*) Then *I'm* not going either! (*Stamping his foot.*) I'm not, I'm not, I'm *not*!

AUNTIE MAME. You can use the Dusenberg. And I've got a date for you!

O'BANNION. Who? (*Slightly mollified.*) Vera?

AUNTIE MAME. Certainly not. You couldn't trust Vera. (*Going to the foot of the stairs and calling up.*) Agnes—?

O'BANNION. Agnes! You certainly can't expect me to be seen at a fashionable party with that— (*Haughtily.*) Would you ask Toscanini to lead a harmonica band? I'm staying right here!

AUNTIE MAME. Now, Brian.

O'BANNION. You don't appreciate me. I'm a minstrel without a lute—

AUNTIE MAME. Not those lutes again.

O'BANNION. (*Throwing himself on the sofa and kicking his heels like a petulant infant.*) I won't take Agnes to the party! I won't, I won't, I won't, I won't. (*Gooch starts down the stairs.*)

AUNTIE MAME. (*Coaching.*) Head up! Shoulders back! Tummy in! That's right! Tonight, Agnes, you're the Queen of Rumania! (*Gooch looks almost regal. O'Bannion's jaw drops.*)

O'BANNION. Well! (*O'Bannion gives her the old hot-eye; then offers Gooch his arm, and she takes it.*)

GOOCH. (*Transported.*) Hotcha. (*In the outer hallway, Patrick and Gloria appear. Patrick starts to use his key to let himself in, then thinks better of it and presses the door buzzer. Auntie Mame jumps.*)

AUNTIE MAME. Quick, Brian. Hang these furs on the Gooch. Hurry! (*She hesitates for a moment, then crosses to the door with some misgivings. She opens the door and greets Patrick and Gloria.*)

PATRICK. (*As if he were presenting the Kimberly diamond.*) Auntie Mame, this is Gloria. Gloria Upson. And this is my Auntie Mame. Mrs. Burnside.

GLORIA. (*Extending a limp hand.*) I cahn't tell you how pleased I am to make your acquaintance. (*Gloria is lovely, tanned, pleasant, but without real warmth. There is something wrong with this girl—you can't quite put your finger on it—a kind of ersatz composure, a mail-order chic. When she talks, there seems to be novocaine in her upper lip.*)

AUNTIE MAME. Come in, children, come in. There are some friends here I want you to meet.

PATRICK. (*Bristling.*) Auntie Mame, you promised— (*But Auntie Mame is completely composed as she ushers them into the living room.*)

AUNTIE MAME. This is my secretary, Miss Gooch. My good right hand, my Boswell, you might say. (*With an appropriate gesture.*) This is Miss Upson, and my nephew Patrick. (*Gooch's eyes light up at the sight of Patrick.*)

GOOCH. Oh, can this be the helpless little infant you found in a basket on your doorstep?

AUNTIE MAME. (*Indicating the resplendent O'Bannion.*) And this is Agnes' *date.* What's your boy-friend's name, Agnes? O'Bannion, wasn't it? (*Patrick breathes a sigh of relief at his aunt's deft recovery.*)

O'BANNION. (*Curtly.*) We'll be on our way. Good night.

GLORIA. I cahn't tell you how pleased I am to have made your acquaintance, Mr. O'Bannion. (*Turning to Gooch.*) And Miss Boswell. (*O'Bannion and Gooch go out.*)

AUNTIE MAME. (*Taking Gloria's hands.*) Patrick says you're very special to him; that means you're very special to me, too.

GLORIA. (*Looking about, vacuously.*) My! What a stunning apartment. Don't tell me you've read all these books, Mrs. Burnside!

AUNTIE MAME. Well, not all of them. Do sit down, dear. Can I get you something? A cognac, or a Drambuie—

PATRICK. Would you like another hot chocolate, honey?

GLORIA. Oh, not a *thing*. On our way to Bunny's, Patrick and I just stuffed ourselves at Howard Johnson's. (*Gloria laughs musically.*) And do you know what your silly nephew did? He talked French to the waiter. Imagine anybody talking French to a waiter at a Howard Johnson's! (*She nudges him playfully.*) Show-off.

AUNTIE MAME. If nobody minds, I think *I'll* have something. (*She pours herself a brandy; her face is troubled by her first appraisal of the girl—but she's determined to keep an open mind.*) You're at school, dear?

GLORIA. I'm an Upper Richmond Girls School girl.

AUNTIE MAME. How did you get that lovely tan so early in spring?

GLORIA. Oh, I played hookey for a couple of weeks. Mums and Daddums and I went down to our place in Fort Lauderdale. We have a place in Fort Lauderdale.

PATRICK. While she was gone, it was the longest two weeks in my life. And yet—it's the funniest thing, Auntie Mame—when Gloria and I are together, we don't really do much of anything. I mean, we don't even talk—I'm just so busy staring at her.

GLORIA. Silly.

AUNTIE MAME. Have you chosen your major yet, dear?

GLORIA. (*Blankly.*) Chosen my major?

AUNTIE MAME. What courses are you taking at college?

GLORIA. Oh, just a general sort of liberal arts thing. You know, English Lit and like that. Upper Richmond's top-hole. Really top-hole.

AUNTIE MAME. How did you two ever get acquainted?

GLORIA. Oh, Uncle Dwight introduced us.

AUNTIE MAME. Uncle Dwight?

PATRICK. That's Mr. Babcock.

AUNTIE MAME. Oh, yes.

GLORIA. He's not really my uncle. But he's been a real close friend of the family ever since I was a little girl with braces on my teeth.

AUNTIE MAME. Someday I'd like to meet "Mums and Daddums."

PATRICK. Oh, we don't want to bother you with a lot of family stuff.

GLORIA. Naturally, we'll expect you at the wedding.

AUNTIE MAME. (*Pale.*) The wedding?

PATRICK. I told you it was definite, Auntie Mame.

GLORIA. We've decided on a September wedding. It's lovely, just lovely then at the Church of the Heavenly Rest—that's right near our place in Mountebank.

AUNTIE MAME. September. Dear me. Tell me,—just where is Mountebank.

GLORIA. Right above Darien. You'll love it. It's the most restricted community in our part of Connecticut.

AUNTIE MAME. I'll get a blood test. (*Patrick knows a storm cloud when he sees one, and he's determined to get his girl out before the downpour.*)

PATRICK. If we hurry, we could still catch the last couple of dances at the country club.

AUNTIE MAME. I hate to have you rush off. (*But Gloria doesn't care about sticking around here; she smiles synthetically, and stiff-arms a handshake.*)

GLORIA. I cahn't tell you how pleased I am to have made your acquaintance.

PATRICK. (*Halfway to the door.*) I'll drop you a note and let you know what's happening.

AUNTIE MAME. Do that! (*Gloria goes out. Patrick turns.*)

PATRICK. (*Lowering his voice.*) Isn't she a dream?

AUNTIE MAME. Oh, yes—yes, she is . . . Did I pass inspection?

PATRICK. You were great, Auntie Mame. Really top-hole. (*Patrick goes out. Auntie Mame stands alone, a little dazed—and not at all sure that what has just happened has really happened.*)

AUNTIE MAME. (*With a semi-bitter bemusement.*) Why did I ever buy him those long pants?

THE LIGHTS FADE

ACT TWO
SCENE 8

The Beekman Place apartment again; no changes. The lighting indicates that it is early morning of the following day. Norah comes downstairs, carrying a breakfast tray containing juice and a raw egg in an egg cup.

Ito, in a chauffeur's uniform, hurries on. They meet in the center of the apartment.

ITO. (*Confused.*) Missy say go to garage, get Dusenberg—we drive to Connecticut today—very important. I go to garage. No Dusenberg.

NORAH. And it's his majesty's breakfast I've got here. Only there's not a smell of that O'Bannion in the place. You suppose he's gone for good, God bless the day?

ITO. Me no know what to do. Got road map to Mountebank. Got uniform. No Dusenberg.

NORAH. That Mr. Lindsay always has a car or two. (*She hands Ito the egg cup.*) The glorious thing is that O'Bannion's gone. You can have his raw egg. I'll drink his nectar. (*But they stop abruptly as Gooch staggers on from outside. The strap of her evening dress is askew, her hair is tangled and she has a definite 'out all night' air about her.*)

ITO. What happen, Missy Gooch?

GOOCH. I *lived*! (*She seems hypnotized as she walks straight across stage.*)

NORAH. What kind of party was that?

GOOCH. Oh, we never got to that party. Brian said he was going to take me for a drive. But we parked.

ITO. Where Dusenberg now, Missy Gooch?

GOOCH. Brian dropped me off here—and said he was driving due west. (*Looks around, panicky.*) Where's Mrs. Burnside?

ITO. She put on face—get ready for trip to Connecticut.

GOOCH. I've got to see her before she goes.

NORAH. Is anything wrong, Miss Gooch?

GOOCH. I did just what she told me. I lived! I've got to find out what to do *now*!!! (*Ito and Norah look at each other significantly, as Gooch shuffles off.*)

THE LIGHTS FADE

ACT TWO
SCENE 9

The patio of the Upsons' home in Mountebank. Late afternoon. A portable roll-on bar is left. A bench, also on wheels, is center, backed up by an Early American wagon wheel. Before the lights come up, the prattle of extroverted chickadees informs us that we have reached the apotheosis of exurbia. The sunlight of a late spring afternoon slants across the little flagstone heaven where the Upsons take their ease. Mr. Upson is carrying out the bar stools—Early American; and Mrs. Upson enters with trays of hors d'oeuvres—also Early American, which she places on a table. The Upsons are a hearty, well-padded couple, enormously pleased with themselves and their way of life.

MRS. UPSON. Well, I just think it's a very good match for our little Gloria, that's what I think. (*Mrs. Upson is fluttering nervously about, prettying up the patio. She is a*

Walter Klavun, Rosalind Russell, and Dorothy Blackburn in *Auntie Mame,* New York, 1956. Photo by Arthur Cantor. Jerome Lawrence and Robert E. Lee Collection, Lawrence and Lee Theatre Research Institute, The Ohio State University.

rosy, flaccid woman who thinks Walter Lippman makes tea. Mr. Upson is loud and square as the basement of a Masonic temple. He thinks Walter Lippman is a socialist.)

MR. UPSON. (*Lifting up his paraphernalia on the bar.*) I still can't see why Dwight didn't want us to meet the aunt.

MRS. UPSON. I guess we never would have if she hadn't phoned. I thought it was only my duty to ask her to buzz up here. Besides, I was dying to get a look at her.

MR. UPSON. Where is she now?

MRS. UPSON. She's up in the guest-room changing again.

MR. UPSON. She certainly brought enough clothes.

MRS. UPSON. And they're expensive ones, Claude. I looked at the labels.

MR. UPSON. Why, I'll bet she's even better fixed than Dwight figures. (*Mrs. Upson purses her lips, a little worried.*)

MRS. UPSON. I hope it's all right to have the cocktail hour here on the patio. I don't want her to think we live like gypsies.

MR. UPSON. You show me a gypsy that lives like we do. (*He chortles with self-satisfaction.*)

MRS. UPSON. Now, Claude Upson, you be *genteel* in front of Mrs. Burnside!

MR. UPSON. (*Belligerently.*) God damn it, I'm always genteel! (*From inside the house, we hear Auntie Mame call out in her most Connecticut manner.*)

AUNTIE MAME'S VOICE. (*From off.*) Yoo-hoo!

MRS. UPSON. Oh, that must be she. (*She raises her voice.*) We're out here on the patio, Mrs. Burnside. (*Auntie Mame, stunningly dressed for spring-in-the-country, starts through the doorway onto the patio, but suddenly loses footing.*)

AUNTIE MAME. Oops! (*The Upsons react with concern.*) Oh dear—I'm always tripping over that *adorable* little hooked rug.

MRS. UPSON. Do be careful; we'd feel awful if you had an accident.

MR. UPSON. (*Jovially.*) Don't you worry. I've got plenty of personal liability insurance.

AUNTIE MAME. (*Blithely.*) Well, then, let's bring on more hooked rugs!

MR. UPSON. Now, there's one thing we oughta know right off. You do take a little nip now and then?

AUNTIE MAME. (*Smiling prettily.*) On festive occasions.

MR. UPSON. (*Blandly.*) Good, I'll have an Upson daiquiri ready in a minute. (*Auntie Mame would rather have vermouth and Castoria, but she indicates her pleasure at the prospect.*)

AUNTIE MAME. (*Glancing around the patio.*) Oh, Mrs. Upson, I can't get over how much thought you've given every detail of your house.

MRS. UPSON. We've done everything we could to make it seem like a little bit of authentic Colonial America.

AUNTIE MAME. And how well you've succeeded! Those adorable miniatures in the powder room of John Quincy Adams.

MRS. UPSON. Well, I said to the decorator from Altman's—

AUNTIE MAME. Altman's? I would have said Sloane's. Solid Sloane's!

MRS. UPSON. (*Giggling.*) Don't you have an *eye*, though. *Downstairs* is Sloane's. Upstairs is Altman's!

MR. UPSON. (*Looking up from his bar chores.*) I'll bet you didn't notice our sign-post out by the driveway . . . ?

AUNTIE MAME. But I *did*! I did! What a divine name you've chosen for your place. (*Trying to recall.*) "Upson . . . "

UPSONS. (*Together.*) "Downs!"

AUNTIE MAME. I'll bet *you* thought that up, Mrs. Upson.

MRS. UPSON. Oh, no. It was Claude. I'm just a homebody. Claude's the clever one. (*Mr. Upson laughs.*) I'm so delighted to see we have the same tastes. I know you're just going to adore the wedding we've planned for the children.

AUNTIE MAME. (*Wetting her lips.*) Now, about the wedding. Don't you think, Mrs. Upson, that . . .

MR. UPSON. Hold it! Hold it! Let's forget the last names right off. After all, we're practically family, aren't we? I just want to be plain Claude.

MRS. UPSON. And I'm Doris.

AUNTIE MAME. "Doris." I've always loved the name of Doris. Not too coy and not too chic. Sort of bitter-sweet.

MR. UPSON. What do we call you?

AUNTIE MAME. All my intimate friends call me just plain Mame.

MRS. UPSON. How lovely. (*Trying to get on Auntie Mame's level.*) Old-fashioned—and yet modern, too. Mamie.

AUNTIE MAME. (*Correcting.*) Mame.

MR. UPSON. (*Pouring a daiquiri and handing it to her.*) Well, Mamie old girl, here's your poison. I make my daiquiris with a secret ingredient I learned from this native down in Havana, Cuba. You'll never guess what the secret ingredient is—but I'll say *this* much. There's no sugar in a Claude Upson daiquiri. (*She sips it.*)

AUNTIE MAME. And yet it's so *sweet*. What *ever* do you use? Chocolate ice cream?

MR. UPSON. (*Guffawing.*) Sa-a-y, that's rich. Did you hear that, Doris? Chocolate ice cream. (*He puts a bear-like hand on Auntie Mame's shoulder.*) Since we're practically relatives, I'm going to let you in on my little secret, *honey*.

AUNTIE MAME. I beg your pardon?

MR. UPSON. Strained honey—that's the secret ingredient. (*He chortles.*) Of course, I use quite a little rum, too! (*Mame points playfully into her glass and in a hail-fellow-well-met mood. Mrs. Upson goes to table and comes over with trays of canapes.*)

MRS. UPSON. Now, I made these especially for you, dear.

AUNTIE MAME. (*Taking a canape.*) Don't they look delicious, though. Mm-m-m-mm-mm-*mm*! (*She takes a bite.*) What *are* they?

MRS. UPSON. Well, I take two cans of tuna fish and put them through the meat-grinder, then add clam juice and peanut butter. It's a recipe I cut out of the "Ladies Home Journal." (*She proffers the other tray.*) These others are just plain jack cheese and chutney. (*Mrs. Upson steers Auntie Mame to a bench. Surreptitiously, Mame tosses the hors d'oeuvre over the patio wall.*) Now, sit you down right here, Mamie. There's something *special* I have to show you. (*She deposits trays and pulls out a photo album.*)

AUNTIE MAME. (*Gleefully.*) Baby pictures. Of Gloria?

MRS. UPSON. Oh, the whole family, more or less. (*They start to leaf through the album.*)

AUNTIE MAME. (*Pointing to one snap.*) On a bear rug! Isn't that precious? (*Mame tosses her drink over her shoulder when Mrs. Upson isn't looking.*)

MRS. UPSON. (*Giggling.*) Better not ever let Patrick see *that* one! That's Miss Tuthill—little Glory's first school teacher. I think the light was hurting her eyes. (*She turns another page.*) And here's Gloria when she was a flower girl at Muriel Puce's wedding.

AUNTIE MAME. What's she eating?

MRS. UPSON. Oh, those are the braces on her teeth.

MR. UPSON. All right, all right—that's enough of the girly-girly talk. I figure while we've got Mamie here, we oughta tell her what the plans are. (*He sits beside Mame, his fat paw around her shoulder.*)

AUNTIE MAME. Plans?

MR. UPSON. For Patrick's career. Dwight Babcock and I have it all worked out. He came to me, and he said "Claude"—he always calls me Claude—

MRS. UPSON. (*Confidentially to Auntie Mame, crowding her from the opposite side.*) When they're together, it's "Dwight and Claude, Claude and Dwight"—that's all you hear.

MR. UPSON. Yup! Yup! Yup! Now, when the kiddies get back from their honeymoon. I want Patrick to take his choice. With my connections, I can slip him into a berth on Madison Avenue, or a seat on the Stock Exchange.

AUNTIE MAME. A seat *and* a berth!— (*Auntie Mame practically bumps noses with Mrs. Upson. Mr. Upson notices her glass is empty.*)

MR. UPSON. Say, you're a fast drinker, Mamie! But don't you worry—I made plenty.

AUNTIE MAME. Oh, I don't think— (*Mr. Upson takes her glass and crosses to the bar.*)

MRS. UPSON. You don't happen to like gin, do you, Mamie?

AUNTIE MAME. (*Whispers.*) I adore it.

MRS. UPSON. After dinner, I'll get the cards and we'll have a little game.

MR. UPSON. Now we come to the problem of what to give the kiddies for a wedding present. And I've got that all settled, too. Here's my idea, Mamie. Why don't we get together, you and I, and buy the newlyweds *that*! (*He stares dead-front. Auntie Mame follows his gaze, but doesn't see anything.*)

AUNTIE MAME. What?

MR. UPSON. (*He takes her arm and leads her down center.*) Why, that lot—right next door. Wouldn't that make a wedding present, though? We could take down this wall here so that their patio would come smack up against ours. You couldn't tell where one left off and the other began!

AUNTIE MAME. So you wouldn't really be losing a daughter: you'd be gaining a patio!

MR. UPSON. But we've got to move fast. Some people are bidding on the property. (*He lowers his voice.*) The *wrong* kind.

AUNTIE MAME. Oh?

MR. UPSON. Fella named Epstein. A-bra-ham Epstein.

AUNTIE MAME. (*Enthusing.*) The cellist? How lucky you are. All that lovely music right next door! And she's a darling. One of the nicest—

MRS. UPSON. (*Confidentially.*) I guess maybe you don't understand quite how it *is* up here, Mamie. But this section is restricted only to our property line. So we feel we have an obligation to make sure that—well—*you* know.

MR. UPSON. Tell you what I'll do, Mamie. I'll have my broker make a bid—and when it goes in escrow we'll just divvy it up, fifty-fifty. You won't have to worry about a thing. (*Auntie Mame plants her glass on the bar with an irritated precision that is only a hint of the emotion repressed within her.*)

AUNTIE MAME. (*Too quietly.*) My, you've thought of everything, haven't you! Laid out Patrick's career—planned the wedding—even chosen my wedding gift. Well, I guess there's only one thing left for me to do. (*She crosses back between the Upsons.*)

MR. UPSON. What's that, Mamie?

AUNTIE MAME. Give an intimate little family dinner! (*Auntie Mame looks archly from one to the other, the lights begin to fade.*)

MRS. UPSON. Lovely, lovely.

MR. UPSON. Mamie, you're top-hole!

THE LIGHTS ARE OUT

ACT TWO
SCENE 10

The Beekman Place apartment. The room is undergoing another metamorphosis, and any previous decor would seem definitely mid-Victorian. The panels have been reversed to display some Fauvist outrages. The furniture looks like a geometrist's nightmare. But presiding over this transformation is a trim redhead named Pegeen Ryan, who is crisp and businesslike as she arranges the abstract ashtrays and the Twenty-First-Century objets d'art.

At first, Pegeen is bustling about the apartment alone. Then Agnes Gooch enters. She, too, has been transformed by the miracle of maternity. There is no doubt about it; the Gooch is six months pregnant. Her pelvis protests at every step as she crosses wordlessly to the kitchen. Neither Gooch nor Pegeen pays the slightest attention to the other. Patrick, in dinner dress, appears in the foyer and lets himself in. His nervousness gives way to amazement as he enters and takes in the new decor.

PATRICK. What's going on?

PEGEEN. Face-lifting. (*She sizes up Patrick, not uncritically.*) You must be the heir-apparent. The "Little Love."

PATRICK. (*Wandering around the room.*) Are you the new decorator? Did you do all this?

PEGEEN. (*Grins.*) For money. (*Ito enters in livery, carrying the bare skeleton of a futuristic sofa.*) Right here, Ito. That's fine. (*Ito puts down the sofa at Pegeen's direction.*)

PATRICK. What are you made up for, Ito? Where's my aunt?

ITO. Missee dress now. (*He goes off to kitchen. Pegeen gathers up some cushions and places them on the bench, which is just a few inches from the floor.*)

PATRICK. What's that?

PEGEEN. It's a sofa. Danish Modern. You find it every place except Denmark. Your aunt made it very explicit: she said she didn't want a sofa that sat around singing "Nearer My God To Thee."

PATRICK. Yeah, but do *you* like it?

PEGEEN. She's not paying me to like it. If she told me she wanted a tombstone for a coffee table, I'd get her a tombstone for a coffee table. And it would be a *good* tombstone. But that doesn't mean I'm going out to buy one for myself.

PATRICK. You should have told my aunt that.

PEGEEN. I did.

PATRICK. You know, you're the first *honest* interior decorator she's ever had, Miss - - -?

PEGEEN. Pegeen Ryan. Unincorporated.

PATRICK. (*Shaking her hand, pleasantly.*) Hi.

PEGEEN. Hi. (*But Patrick is restless again. He glances toward the head of the stairs.*)

PATRICK. Where is she? Where's my aunt?

PEGEEN. You already asked that.

PATRICK. Did I?

PEGEEN. Relax. People get married every day.

PATRICK. (*Nervously.*) I'm not getting married every day. I'm getting married three weeks from Tuesday.

PEGEEN. (*Tossing it off.*) Congratulations.

AUNTIE MAME. Patrick—! (*He turns and sees Auntie Mame starting down the stairs. She is really dressed to the hilt, in a gold hostess gown. Both she and Patrick start speaking at once.*)

PATRICK. Auntie Mame, what's the idea of all this?

AUNTIE MAME. (*Anticipating his protest.*) Now, Patrick, I don't want to hear a word out of you. I simply had to drive up to Mountebank. Doris insisted!

PATRICK. Oh, that part's all right—they adore you. (*Casting a dubious eye around the room.*) But why did you have to change—?

AUNTIE MAME. (*Innocently.*) Really, I'm so relieved. Now, I've tried to make everything special for tonight, and to give the Upsons as cozy a time as they gave me. (*Patrick nods vaguely.*)

PEGEEN. (*Suddenly.*) Oh! I forgot the horror! (*Pegeen darts off, but Auntie Mame calls after her.*)

AUNTIE MAME. Don't say that, Pegeen. It gives a surge and flow to the whole room.

PATRICK. You mean there's more? (*Auntie Mame addresses Patrick eagerly.*)

AUNTIE MAME. It's divine. Wait till you see it! Damndest thing I ever bought! (*She parts her skirt, revealing chic slacks underneath.*)

PATRICK. (*Wincing at her profanity.*) Uh—Auntie Mame, I don't suppose it's really necessary to say this—but with Gloria's folks, I hope you won't let your language get too—well, too *vivid.*

AUNTIE MAME. I won't use one teensy-weensy son-of-a-bitch all evening.

PATRICK. Good. And one other little thing. Politically, I guess you gathered they're on the conservative side.

AUNTIE MAME. I'm only wearing Republican clothes.

PEGEEN. (*Calling from off.*) Could somebody give me a hand with the ladder?

AUNTIE MAME. Patrick, be a little gentleman and help Pegeen, will you?

PATRICK. (*Agreeably, as he exits.*) Yeah. Sure. (*Agnes Gooch emerges from the kitchen, munching a canape.*)

AUNTIE MAME. Musn't nibble on the hors d'oeuvres, Agnes. You'll get fat.

GOOCH. I'm sorry, Mrs. Burnside. I try to do exactly what you say. You're so wonderful. Nobody else would have taken me in in my hour of need. I'll never be able to thank you.

AUNTIE MAME. Oh, twaddle—I'm the grateful one. You've given me a new interest—someone to look after, now that I'm losing Patrick.

GOOCH. I wish I had somebody to look after.

AUNTIE MAME. You will, dear, you will. (*Gooch is dragging herself up the stairs as Patrick backs through the door, helping Pegeen with the ladder. He doesn't see the pregnant secretary, who stops halfway up the stairs to watch. Pegeen is carrying a tasteful but bizarre mobile.*)

PATRICK. (*To Pegeen.*) Where do you want me to set this up?

PEGEEN. Right where you are is fine. (*Patrick unfolds the ladder, and Pegeen starts up it to hang the mobile in place. Patrick looks at it warily.*)

PATRICK. What's that supposed to be, anyway?

AUNTIE MAME. (*Quickly.*) You don't like it?

PATRICK. Well, it might be a little avant-garde for the Upsons.

AUNTIE MAME. (*Decisively.*) Pegeen, take it right down. I want everything to be absolutely perfect for Patrick. (*Pegeen hesitates at the top of the ladder.*)

GOOCH. (*From halfway up the stairs.*) *I* think it's very unusual. (*Patrick wheels around as if he'd been stabbed.*)

PATRICK. What the hell is Agnes doing here???

AUNTIE MAME. (*Innocently.*) Where else would she be in her friendless condition?

PATRICK. This is one thing the Upsons simply will not understand.

AUNTIE MAME. We don't have to talk about it. Maybe they won't notice.

PATRICK. Won't notice! (*Agnes whimpers on the staircase. In the outer hallway Mr. and Mrs. Upson and Gloria appear and ring the buzzer.*) (*Panicked.*) My God—they're here!

PEGEEN. (*From the ladder.*) Help me get this thing down!

PATRICK. (*Hastily.*) No, no—leave it up! Just get the ladder out of here!

AUNTIE MAME. Norah—Ito—somebody, answer the door.

GOOCH. (*Helpfully, starting down the stairs.*) I'll get it. (*Patrick leaps toward the staircase to block her.*)

PATRICK. Oh, no you don't!

AUNTIE MAME. Now, now, Agnes, Patrick is right. (*Firmly.*) I want you to go upstairs and stay there.

GOOCH. What'll I *do*, Mrs. Burnside?

AUNTIE MAME. *Sleep*, Agnes! Knit! Read Dr. Gesell. (*The door buzzes again, a little more impatiently. With painful slowness, Gooch starts up the stairs again. As Pegeen folds the ladder and disappears with it, Ito scampers out of the kitchen and opens the door for the Upsons. Auntie Mame extends her hands in greeting.*) Welcome, welcome to the Burnside fireside!

MR. UPSON. Good to see you, Mamie! You don't look a day older. (*He laughs.*)

AUNTIE MAME. Doris—and little Glory! How I've been looking forward to this evening.

GLORIA. (*The well-bred robot.*) I cahn't tell you how pleased I am to see you again. (*This time, Auntie Mame turns the tables and gives Gloria the stiff-arm. Mrs. Upson looks around, a little baffled by the decor.*)

MRS. UPSON. My!

PATRICK. Hi, everybody. Glory.

AUNTIE MAME. Do sit down. (*The Upsons settle down in the furniture, with some difficulty. Mrs. Upson, who is no channel swimmer, finds herself with her knees high in the air and her buttocks in the nap of the rug.*) Are you perfectly comfortable down there, Doris?

MRS. UPSON. Oh, it's so *interesting*!

AUNTIE MAME. Now, I know you're all just perishing for something to drink after that long drive down the parkway. (*Calling.*) Ito, bring in the punch!

PATRICK. Punch? (*Mr. Babcock has appeared in the outer hallway, and rings the buzzer. Ito comes out of the kitchen, carrying a tray with a dozen or so curious, torch-shaped glasses. At the sound of the buzzer, he passes the tray with the punch bowl and glasses to

Norah, who has entered behind him. Ito scampers to the door and admits Babcock. Norah passes glasses to each guest. In counterpoint to Mr. Babcock's entrance, Gloria looks up at the mobile, quizzically.)

GLORIA. What's that *thing*?—hanging there?

PATRICK. (*Without affectation.*) It's an abstraction. Non-representational.

GLORIA. (*Girly-girly to Auntie Mame.*) Mrs. Burnside, how'm I ever going to stop this nephew of yours from using such big words?

MR. UPSON. (*As he spies Mr. Babcock in the door.*) Dwight!

MR. BABCOCK. Claude! (*Mr. Upson tries to get up to shake hands, but is having some difficulty getting out of the low furniture.*)

AUNTIE MAME. How good of you to come, Mr. Babcock. (*Norah has put the silver tray down on the bar, and Auntie Mame is ladling out drinks into the torch-like glasses. Norah and Ito exit to kitchen. Mr. Babcock, moving to shake hands with Mr. Upson, crashes into the mobile.*)

MR. BABCOCK. Ooops.

AUNTIE MAME. Oh dear, we'll have to raise that. (*Calling.*) Pegeen, would you bring back the ladder? (*She stops Mr. Upson from drinking.*) Won't you sit down, Mr. Babcock? Now, they're almost ready—the specialité de la maison. (*Pegeen re-enters with the ladder.*) I'm afraid you'll have to get that a little higher, dear; it's getting in people's hair. (*Pegeen sets up the ladder and climbs up to adjust the mobile.*) Oh, I want you all to meet Miss Pegeen Ryan.

MRS. UPSON. Are you the aircraft Ryans?

PEGEEN. Afraid not—just the brick-laying Ryans.

AUNTIE MAME. Claude, I'm not going to tell you one thing that's in these drinks—because all the ingredients are secret. (*She takes a long Japanese kindling-match from the table.*) Now hold still! (*She sets fire to the drink in Mr. Upson's hand.*)

MR. UPSON. (*A little stunned.*) Well, what do you know! (*Auntie Mame moves from guest to guest, igniting the drinks.*)

AUNTIE MAME. The trick is to drink them up fast, before all the alcohol burns away. (*Auntie Mame lights another drink for Pegeen on the ladder.*)

PEGEEN. I feel like Miss Liberty. (*Patrick seems a little surprised that Auntie Mame has included Pegeen in the party, but he doesn't say anything. Each of the guests holds his drink at arm's length. They make abortive attempts to bring the glasses close to their faces, but the heat makes them thrust the torches away again.*)

AUNTIE MAME. A dear friend of mine who may drop in later calls this "The Flaming Mame."

PATRICK. (*Tensing up again.*) Who? Who? Who's dropping in later?

AUNTIE MAME. Just family, Patrick. (*Patrick looks a little like the Captain of the Titanic just after he talked to the boiler room. Mrs. Upson makes an attempt to sip her drink, but withdraws suddenly—and bats at her eyebrows as if trying to extinguish a small conflagration.*) Why, don't be an old 'fraidy-cat, Doris! There's nothing to be scared of; we're fully covered by fire insurance. (*She slaps Mr. Upson on the shoulder, knowing he will appreciate the wisdom of this.*) Now, are we all lit?

PATRICK. (*Restlessly.*) Mr. Upson, wouldn't you be happier if I fixed you a daiquiri?

MR. UPSON. No, no, son. Not for a minute. Your Auntie fixed this for me, and I'm going to drink it. Why it looks just *fine.* (*Norah and Ito come out from the kitchen bearing an elaborate tray of hors d'oeuvres.*)

GLORIA. (*Nibbling on one of the hors d'oeuvres.*) Oh, this is spicy! Try one of the little striped ones, Mums. (*Delightedly Ito and Norah pass "the little striped ones" to all the guests. Deftly Auntie Mame declines.*)

MR. BABCOCK. Say, these *are* tasty.

MRS. UPSON. (*To Auntie Mame.*) What are they, dear?

AUNTIE MAME. Just plain old pickled rattlesnake. (*The process of mastication ceases instantly. Gloria goes into a paroxysm of coughing. Helpfully Auntie Mame tries to force one of the flaming drinks into Gloria's hand.*) Why, it's pure protein. And before they marinate them, they *always* remove the fangs. (*Glancing at Babcock's drink.*) Mr. Babcock, you've gone out! (*The perfect hostess, she moves to relight his drink.*)

MR. BABCOCK. (*Waving her aside.*) Don't bother, Mrs. Burnside. (*Auntie Mame looks hurt.*)

MRS. UPSON. Mamie dear, with the wedding only three weeks away, I've just got to decide. Would you say six bridesmaids?

GLORIA. Muriel Puce had eight.

AUNTIE MAME. Then I'd say let's keep up with the Puces. (*The unseen bedroom door opens and Agnes Gooch waddles down the stairs. Patrick turns the color of skim milk. Auntie Mame addresses Gooch as if she were a puppy who had just been indiscreet on a new carpet.*) Agnes, I told you to *stay in your room*!

GOOCH. (*Whining helplessly.*) But, Mrs. Burnside, it's a quarter past eight. And you told me . . .

AUNTIE MAME. (*Quickly.*) I told you to *take your pills* at a quarter past eight.

GOOCH. But my calcium pills are in the kitchen.

PATRICK. Auntie Mame! (*Gooch painfully makes her way down the stairs and all eyes are on her. It would be easier to conceal an elephant in Bergdorf's window. No effort is made to introduce or explain Agnes, which makes the pause all the more painful and telling.*)

MR. UPSON. (*Leaning over to Mr. Babcock, confidentially.*) Is that a member of the family?

MR. BABCOCK. Damned if I know.

MR. UPSON. It's a member of *some*body's family.

AUNTIE MAME. (*Making the best of it.*) Doris, I'd like you to meet my secretary. She's a little bit—she's not quite her*self* at the moment.

MRS. UPSON. (*Warmly, to the Gooch.*) Now, we know all about these *women's* things, don't we! (*Sympathetically.*) What's your name dear?

GOOCH. (*Simpers.*) Gooch.

MRS. UPSON. (*Taking her arm.*) You sit right over here beside me, Mrs. Gooch. (*Auntie Mame and Patrick exchange a glance. When Gooch sits in this modern furniture she really spreads. The furniture is so low, that she sprawls completely flat.*) A little expectant mother always makes me feel weepy. I remember when I was carrying Gloria.

GLORIA. Oh, Mummy. (*Agnes reaches over and takes a canape from tray.*)

AUNTIE MAME. (*Warning.*) Now, now, Agnes—

MRS. UPSON. Remember, Mamie—she's eating for two. (*Turns back to Gooch.*) And what does *Mr.* Gooch do?

GOOCH. Oh, my father passed on.

MRS. UPSON. Oh, no, I mean your husband. (*Gooch lets out a protracted wail. Both Patrick and Auntie Mame have descended on her and are helping her out of the sofa from either side.*)

AUNTIE MAME. (*Singing it out.*) Calcium time! Pegeen! (*With Pegeen's help, the Gooch is steered off into the kitchen. Patrick turns back to face the guests, sweating.*)

PATRICK. You know, there's one thing about my Auntie Mame. She's big-hearted; whenever anybody's in trouble, she— (*The doorbell buzzes. Patrick jumps. Ito goes to the door, opens it, and ushers in Vera Charles, dripping foxes, as usual.*)

AUNTIE MAME. (*Effusively.*) Vera!

VERA. Mame, darling. Like an opening night—without critics! Heaven! (*Mrs. Upson nudges Mr. Upson.*)

MRS. UPSON. (*Lowering her voice somewhat, excitedly.*) Claude! Claude! That's Vera Charles, the famous actress, just as sure as I'm sitting here.

AUNTIE MAME. Mr. and Mrs. Upson, Miss Upson, Mr. Babcock—I want you to meet my dearest friend, Vera Charles.

MRS. UPSON. (*Under her breath.*) I told you, Claude, I told you! (*Vera quickly senses that this is a matinee house.*)

VERA. (*Turning it on.*) How do you do. I'm so charmed to meet you, all of you.

GLORIA. (*Rushing up.*) Miss Charles, I've just got to tell you how I *adored* you in "Reflected Glory."

VERA. (*With a frozen smile.*) Did you, dear? That was Tallulah Bankhead.

AUNTIE MAME. Vera, can I persuade you to have a drink?

VERA. Oh, yes. Anything but rum! I've just been at the most Godawful party, and all they had were daiquiris—made with honey yet!! (*She makes a grimace and pours herself a tumbler of straight Scotch. The doorbell chimes and Ito ushers in the slightly grayed but still muscular figure of Ralph Devine.*)

AUNTIE MAME. Ralph Devine! You're a *dream* to come. (*Patrick turns away with a cramp in his solar plexus.*)

PATRICK. Oh, God.

AUNTIE MAME. Doris, you were considerate enough to show me the pictures of your little Gloria's school teachers—Miss Tuthill and all that mob—and I thought you'd like to meet Patrick's very *first* school teacher here in New York.

RALPH. (*Blandly.*) Why, Mame, don't you have a picture of me?

AUNTIE MAME. (*Easily.*) Not one we could show in mixed company. (*There are some eyebrows cocked at this, but Ralph floats effortlessly among the guests for introductions. He wears a skin-tight jersey sport shirt which is open at the neck not quite to the navel. He looks at Mr. Babcock curiously.*)

RALPH. Say, haven't we met somewhere before?

MR. BABCOCK. (*Studying him narrowly.*) I don't recognize the *face*.

PATRICK. Auntie Mame, I thought it was just going to be family tonight.

AUNTIE MAME. But you don't want the Upsons to think we don't have any friends. After all, these are the people who helped raise you. (*Glancing up at Pegeen, who seems to be having trouble with the mobile.*) Are you having trouble, Pegeen? (*Turning.*) Patrick, why don't you give her a hand? (*Patrick starts up the ladder to help Pegeen. When he gets to the top, he is in fairly close juxtaposition to Pegeen, and Gloria is not very much pleased.*)

PEGEEN. (*Nearly losing her balance.*) Ohhhhhhh! (*Patrick throws his arms around her, to keep her from falling. She grins at him.*) Thanks, Lochinvar.

PATRICK. (*Smiling back.*) Courtesy of the house.

PEGEEN. I'm okay. You've got troubles enough of your own.

PATRICK. Don't I, though?

GLORIA. (*Indignant.*) Well, that's a pretty picture, I *must* say! (*Vera decides it's time for her to go on, and she takes center stage, as usual.*)

VERA. Yes. Isn't it? Ladies and gentlemen, I want to propose a toast. (*She lifts her glass toward Pegeen and Patrick at the top of the ladder.*) To this lovely young couple, as they start up the ladder of life together.

PATRICK. (*Coming down the ladder hastily.*) No, no, Auntie Vera—*this* isn't Gloria, *that's* Gloria. (*Vera turns and finds herself staring straight into the frozen visage of Gloria Upson.*)

VERA. Pity. (*Vera downs her Scotch. The door buzzer rings. Ito moves to the door. Pegeen has succeeded in hanging the mobile, but is too fascinated by this three-ring circus to descend from her grandstand seat atop the ladder. Lindsay comes in, carrying a thick manila envelope.*)

AUNTIE MAME. (*Crossing to greet him.*) Lindsay, Lindsay—that's what we've needed—calm, reasonable you.

LINDSAY. (*Smiling proudly.*) I hope I'm not crashing in on anything, Mame, but I couldn't wait. I had to bring it right over.

AUNTIE MAME. What is it? (*Pleased, Lindsay hands her the envelope.*)

LINDSAY. Be careful—the ink's still wet. (*Auntie Mame draws out of the envelope the galley proofs of her book.*)

AUNTIE MAME. My book!

LINDSAY. Mame, you'll have to correct these galleys; it's your last chance to change your life.

AUNTIE MAME. (*Jubilantly waving the galleys.*) Look, everybody! I'm in print—just like Fannie Hurst! (*Vera crosses to Auntie Mame and takes some of the galleys from her, looking at them interestedly.*)

PATRICK. Congratulations, Auntie Mame. (*Patrick crosses to Auntie Mame and she puts her arm around him warmly.*)

AUNTIE MAME. Darling, I hope you don't mind, there is a lot in here about you. (*She hands him a fistful of the galleys.*)

MR. UPSON. Well, this seems to be quite a day for you, Mamie.

MRS. UPSON. An authoress! Well!

GLORIA. Patrick, you old meanie!—Why didn't you tell us your auntie was literate.

RALPH. (*Crossing to Auntie Mame.*) Am I mentioned in your book, Mame?

AUNTIE MAME. Mentioned! You're *exposed*! (*She hands him some of the galleys to peruse. In fact, everybody is busy going through the galleys, except the Upsons and Mr. Babcock, who seem definitely on the outside and nonparticipants in this activity.*)

VERA. You know, I've been to so many wonderful parties here, Mame, now I'm going to find out how they all ended.

PATRICK. (*Laughing warmly as he reads one of the galleys.*) Hey, I'd almost forgotten about the time we got locked in the Mummy Room at the Metropolitan. (*He flips to another galley.*) And the time you got Miss Earhart to give me a flying lesson. (*He laughs.*) Boy, I had no talent for that! (*He flips to another galley. Warmly.*) And here's all about the roller skates. And Uncle Beau. And that Christmas when we were so broke . . . (*They laugh reminiscently. Suddenly Gloria claims the center of attention.*)

GLORIA. Mrs. Burnside, you could practically write a whole book about what happened to *me*. (*But through the babble of conversation, Auntie Mame didn't quite hear what Gloria said.*)

AUNTIE MAME. I beg your pardon, Gloria?

GLORIA. I said, you could practically write a whole book about what happened to me. (*Everybody quiets down to listen to Gloria's narrative, which she dramatizes athletically.*) Bunny Bixler and I were in the semi-finals—the very semi-finals, mind you—of the ping-pong tournament at the club, and this *ghastly* thing happened. We were both playing way over our heads, and the score was 29–28, and we had this terrific volley, and I ran back to get this really terrific shot . . . (*She runs back, demonstrating with an imaginary ping-pong paddle—then stops like Lady Macbeth.*) . . . and I *stepped* on the ping-pong ball! Just squashed it to nothing! And then Bunny and I went to the closet of the game room to get another ping-pong ball, and the closet was *locked*! Imagine! So we had to call the whole thing off. It was ghastly, just ghastly! (*There is another dazed pause. Vera screws a fresh drink into Auntie Mame's numbed hand, and turns her attention back to the galleys. Mame takes a long drink. Patrick comes over and takes a drink from the same glass.*)

MR. UPSON. (*With a forced chuckle.*) But it *is* amusing!

MR. BABCOCK. Yes. It is amusing.

VERA. It's hilarious!

AUNTIE MAME. (*Startled.*) *What* is?

VERA. (*Deep in the galleys.*) Your story.

LINDSAY. And the most important thing, Vera, is that she did it all by herself. There isn't an Alana or a Coccamaura in the whole book. (*Agnes enters from the kitchen—Vera, whose joints have now been loosened by an alcoholic oiling, crosses to the Upsons.*)

VERA. (*Confidentially.*) You know, you'll never believe this, Mr. Upjohn, but Lindsay got this Irish slob—Brian . . . what was his name? Oh, it doesn't matter . . . to come here and live with Mame till she got the book finished. Of course, he didn't do a damn thing except— (*She breaks off, fortunately.*) Mame, my hat's off to you! (*Agnes Gooch has been lured to the galleys, and her voice cracks as she makes an emotional announcement from the staircase.*)

GOOCH. (*Ecstatically.*) I'm so proud! The whole last chapter is about *me*! (*She reads.*) "Fighting the Stigma of the Unwed Mother!" (*She flattens out on the stairs to read. Now the Upsons and Babcock are shocked to the marrow.*)

MR. BABCOCK. (*Trying to soothe the irate Upsons.*) Claude, as soon as we get him away from the aunt, everything's going to be fine.

VERA. (*Reading galleys.*) Why, Patrick, I never realized how many times you unzipped me and put me to bed! (*There is much good-natured laughter at this but Mr. Upson takes on a righteous tone.*)

MR. UPSON. (*Standing, piously.*) Now, just a moment. We have some *young* people here.

PATRICK. (*Trying to gloss it over.*) Well, sir, I only did it when Miss Charles passed out! (*This, of course, makes it worse: the Upsons are certain that Auntie Mame's apartment is a den of iniquity.*)

GLORIA. Patrick, how can you defend people who—who—

PATRICK. (*Acidly.*) Who've never played ping-pong???

GLORIA. (*Haughtily to Patrick.*) I certainly hope when we're married you won't invite people like *this* to our house?

PATRICK. *Who* is coming to our house? Muriel Puce and Bunny Bixler?

GLORIA. (*Regally.*) What's wrong with Muriel Puce?

PATRICK. Nothing, not a damned thing! Except she's got the I.Q. of a dead flashlight battery!

GLORIA. *WELL!*

VERA. (*Dramatically.*) Lindsay, it's marvelous. Mame's going to make a fortune from this book!

LINDSAY. She sure as hell will. But not for herself. Mame's assigned all of her royalties to the Epstein Home in Mountebank.

RALPH DEVINE. (*Interested.*) Epstein, the cellist?

MR. UPSON. What? What's that about Mountebank?

VERA. Can't the Epsteins afford their own home?

AUNTIE MAME. No, Vera, they're not going to *live* there. They're building a home for Refugee Jewish Children. (*There is a warm and favorable reaction from Mame's group.*)

MR. UPSON. (*Frigidly.*) Are you ready, Doris?

MRS. UPSON. I've been ready for quite a long time.

MR. UPSON. Come, Glory. We have a long way to go. (*He starts herding them toward the foyer door.*)

BABCOCK. Claude, please! Claude! (*Shaken, Babcock strides back into the room. He explodes vehemently directly at Auntie Mame.*) For nine years, Mame Dennis Burnside, I've done everything I could to protect this boy from your cockeyed, idiotic nincompoopery! But this is the limit. Now you've ruined everything—all my plans for this boy's future— (*Patrick is turned away and Auntie Mame reaches with her eyes to see how he has taken all of this.*)

AUNTIE MAME. (*To Babcock.*) *Your* plans, *your* plans! You have the bill-of-fare, and you're shouting orders for everybody. (*Lowers her voice.*) But did it ever occur to you that this boy might be hungry for something that you never even heard of? (*Softening.*) When Patrick walked into my life—a frightened little boy hanging onto Norah's hand—it was love at first sight. For nine years I've tried to open some windows in his life. (*She turns on Babcock.*) Now all you want to do is shut him up in some (*She reaches for the appropriate word.*) —some safe deposit box. Well, I won't let you do that to my little one! (*She stops abruptly, distantly.*) No, he's not little any more. And he's not mine. But he's not yours either, Mr. Babcock. I doubt very much that Patrick will allow you to settle him down in some dry-veined, restricted community. Make him an Aryan from Darien!—and marry him off to a girl with *braces on her brains*! (*Auntie Mame stands there, breathless, triumphant. Babcock exits. Lindsay crosses to Mame, narrowing his eyes slightly.*)

LINDSAY. Mame, did you deliberately *plan* all this?

AUNTIE MAME. (*Looking at him innocently.*) Don't be ridiculous, Lindsay. You know Patrick always makes all his own decisions. (*Patrick looks at his aunt with a crooked smile; Auntie Mame, ever the hostess, takes the center of the room with a tray of canapes.*) Rattlesnake, anyone?

PATRICK. (*To Mame.*) Thank you, Lady Iris.

AUNTIE MAME. Charmed, Lord Dudley.

THE LIGHTS FADE

ACT TWO
SCENE 11

Immediately following Auntie Mame's party, we hear the choral voices singing a bizarre variant on Rimsky-Korsakoff's "Song of India."

AUNTIE MAME'S VOICE. Oh, Sahib, Sahib, will you help me with this cablegram, please? Oh, where am I?

INDIAN VOICE. Punjab, India.

AUNTIE MAME'S VOICE. June 28, 19—. What year is it?

INDIAN VOICE. 1946. (*Exactly as at the beginning of the play, there is a projection on the scrim. Auntie Mame's voice is heard over the loudspeaker as the words unfold.*)

AUNTIE MAME. (*Voice off.*) Mr. and Mrs. Patrick Dennis, 224 East 50th Street, New York. Dear Patrick and Pegeen. Arriving from India June 31st. Please meet me Beekman Place apartment. Uncle Lindsay off on Safari with Maharani. Means nothing. Coming back to pick up nylons, Nescafe, Kleenex, and dentures for Maharani. Will explain why when I see you, because cable rates are ninety rupees per word and obviously only a damned fool would be silly enough to waste all the money on a long cablegram that went on and on and on and on. (*Her voice fades as the projection fades. We bleed through the scrim to see Patrick and Pegeen pacing in the Beekman Place apartment. The scrim flies. A tiger skin, some elephant tusks and some packing boxes are scattered about.*)

PATRICK. (*Calling off.*) Auntie Mame, what are you doing in there?

AUNTIE MAME. (*Entering like an Indian Princess in a flowing green-blue sari.*) Just giving Michael his presents, dear. (*Michael comes on holding turban.*)

MICHAEL. Look, Dad! (*To Auntie Mame.*) Which is the front, Auntie Mame?

AUNTIE MAME. Let me do it for you, my little love. (*She puts the turban on him.*) There. Now Salaam to your mother, Michael—like Auntie Mame just taught you. (*Michael bows.*) Ahhh, very good, Sahib.

PEGEEN. That's not a real sword is it?

MICHAEL. It's a scimitar.

AUNTIE MAME. (*Looking at her watch.*) Oh, dear! "Bell darwazay pair carr-ay ahn."

PATRICK. That's what I always say.

AUNTIE MAME. In Hindustani, that means "The water oxen are waiting at the gate." Of course, *my* ox is waiting at Idlewild. Pan American Flight 100 for Karachi. (*Crosses back to Michael.*) Oh, Michael, if I could only show you India! The splendor, the mystery, the elephants in the streets.

PATRICK. Now, Auntie Mame.

AUNTIE MAME. I know. I shouldn't even bring up the possibility of Michael's going to India with me.

MICHAEL. But Auntie Mame said she'd love to have me, she said so right in there.

PEGEEN. It's ridiculous. I wouldn't hear of it.

MICHAEL. (*He turns to his father.*) Dad?

PATRICK. Now look, it's out of the question completely. You heard your mother. (*Michael wheels on his mother.*)

MICHAEL. (*Earnestly.*) You know what your trouble is, Mom? You don't live, live, LIVE! Life is a banquet, and most poor sons-of-bitches are starving to death! (*Pegeen grabs Michael and clamps her hand over his mouth, and holds him protectively. Auntie Mame and Patrick exchange a significant glance. Patrick crosses toward Michael and Pegeen. Pegeen knows that in this family you live it up to the hilt—and there's no sense in trying to resist. Helplessly, Pegeen nods and lets Michael go. Patrick steers him into the erratic but inspiring custody of Auntie Mame.*)

PEGEEN. (*A little helplessly.*) One thing you've got to understand. School begins the day after Labor Day. He's got to be back by then.

AUNTIE MAME. (*Vaguely.*) Naturally. Of course. Labor Day. That's sometime in November, isn't it?

PATRICK. (*Firmly.*) The first week in September, Auntie Mame.

MICHAEL. (*Taking Mame's hand.*) Don't you worry, Dad, I'll be back by Labor Day.

AUNTIE MAME. Labor! Oh, the problem of labor in India is gargantuan.

MICHAEL. What's "gargantuan," Auntie Mame?

AUNTIE MAME. On the plane, Michael, I'll give you a pad and pencil, and you can write down all the words you don't understand. (*Auntie Mame draws Michael toward the stairs and they start climbing.*) Come, darling, I've been out all morning shopping for your travelling gear. Let's try things on. (*Pegeen throws up her hands.*) Oh, I'm going to open doors for you. Doors you never dreamed even existed. (*Michael looks up at Auntie Mame adoringly, as they continue to climb, slowly, slowly, their eyes to the mountain tops.*)

PEGEEN. My God, she's the Pied Piper!

AUNTIE MAME. Oh, what times we're going to have, my little love. What vistas we're going to explore together. First we're going to see the Taj Mahal, which is one of the Seven Wonders of the World— (*They go off together toward that adventure of life, and we know what a banquet it is going to be for both of them.*)

CURTAIN

For curtain calls, Norah and Ito come out with trays of champagne glasses. Then the entire cast stream in through the foyer door, each taking a champagne glass and toasting the audience. Young Patrick-Michael reaches for champagne, but Pegeen gently slaps his hand and gives him a glass of milk instead. Once they are all on, they turn their glasses and toast toward the steps, down which Auntie Mame comes, and bows like an Indian Princess.

THE GANG'S ALL HERE

Introduction

The Gang's All Here continued Lawrence and Lee's use of fictionalized historic events to comment on contemporary American society. The events surrounding the nomination and presidency of Warren G. Harding gave the playwrights a base to explore the political processes by which the nation selects presidents.

In the late 1950s, the effects of advertising and the electronic media upon politics were already apparent, while the popular Dwight D. Eisenhower's presidency was marred by charges of corrupt underlings. Lawrence and Lee were interested in writing "about the Presidency. Not about a president, or the president, but about the man, the office, the father-image, the godhead we send to 1600 Pennsylvania Avenue. Write about the 'public solitude' this man faces, the problems he grapples with, personal, emotional, moral, spiritual."[1]

President Harding provided the perfect vehicle for such an examination. According to the popular historical view of Harding, he was an amiable hack politician, totally devoted to following the Republican party line in his native Ohio, where he had served as lieutenant governor from 1903 to 1905 and had been elected United States senator in 1914. A strikingly handsome man, Harding's potential was spotted early in his career by Harry M. Daugherty, a former state legislator active in Republican party politics. When the 1920 Republican party national convention in Chicago split evenly between the candidacies of General Leonard Wood, former chief of staff of the United States Army, and Governor Frank O. Lowden of Illinois, "fifteen men in a smoke-filled room"[2] seized upon Harding as the party's nominee. Harding then swept the general election of 1920 by the largest plurality to that date, in part because he conducted the campaign from his Marion, Ohio, front porch, where his utterances could be carefully controlled.[3]

Harding, therefore, provided an ideal base for Lawrence and Lee's purposes: not only was his a candidacy based on image rather than accomplishment or record, his presidency provided an object lesson in corruption by the cronies of the chief executive. From scandal in the Veterans' Bureau to the Teapot Dome oil leases, Harding's subordinates in the federal government and the influence-peddling "Ohio Gang" are notorious for rapacious greed at the public's expense.[4] Harding's Ohio roots as a newspaperman in Marion doubtless also appealed to the Ohio-born playwrights, who knew the territory intimately.

As had been the case with *Inherit the Wind*, however, Lawrence and Lee chose to use Harding's history only as source material, and to write a fictive drama. They continued to prefer the freedom to stray from the actual facts. As they noted in response to a negative evaluation by historian M. R. Werner, "If we put the actual Warren G. Harding on the stage, audiences would throw rocks at the actors and jeer the authors who could dream up such outrageous fiction."[5]

The playwrights began by changing names, Harding becoming Griffith P. Hastings. But there were numerous similarities to the real-life president and first lady: Harding referred to his wife, Florence Kling Harding, as "the Duchess"; the political savvy and dominance Frances Hastings displays in the drama reflect the popular image of Mrs. Harding's influence over her husband. Hastings and Harding share a love of poker and of evenings spent with cronies over drinks and cards.

The supporting cast of cronies in Lawrence and Lee's play have fairly exact historic parallels as well. Walter Rafferty reflects Charles Daugherty's personality and experience, while Doc Kirkaby (an osteopath) is similar to Harding's actual White House physician, Doc Sawyer (a chiropractor), in not being a regular M.D. Senator Joshua Loomis, the secretary of the interior who signs away oil leases, doubles Senator Albert Fall; Charles Webster's role in the corrupt Veterans' Bureau reflects Harding's appointee to the real Veterans' Bureau, Charles R. Forbes. The jovial Axel Maley of the play is a fictionalized version of Daugherty's sidekick, Jess Smith, who committed suicide in 1923 before his Ohio bank accounts (in a bank run by Daugherty's brother) could be examined.

Aspects of other figures from history are borrowed for characters in the drama. The righteous Arthur Anderson, for example, combines elements of Harding's secretary of state, Charles Evan Hughes, and the moral incorruptibility of Secretary of Commerce Herbert Hoover. Political boss Higgy has the physical traits of Pennsylvania boss Boise Penrose, although there is little other similarity.

Lawrence and Lee also freely borrowed events from the Harding administration. The basement poker den that concludes the first act reflects both the infamous "little green house on K Street," center for the Ohio Gang's graft, and the house that Daugherty and Smith shared on H Street, where Smith eventually died. Hastings's physical attack on Rafferty at the end of act 2, scene 1, is based on an anecdote reported anonymously by Adams, which has a furious Harding attacking Veterans' Bureau chief Forbes.[6] Harding had a reputation as a ladies' man, having ensconced a Marion girl in New York with their illegitimate daughter after his election to the Senate. And Lawrence and Lee's fictional president dies, as did Harding, in a hotel room in San Francisco at the end of a grueling lecture tour. Although Harding died of thrombosis following a heart attack and a bout of pneumonia, widespread rumors at the time attributed his death variously to suicide or to a mercy killing by Mrs. Harding to avoid scandal.[7]

The playwrights also freely created new material, characters, and scenes in their treatment of the historic record, both for theatrical effect and to emphasize their interpretation of the basic story. Thus the character of Bellingham is added as a foil for the corrupt Rafferty and his cronies and a hopeful alternative to the cynical view of political power that the play otherwise presents. Hastings's surprise nomination is far from the fact of Harding's announced candidacy, while Harding appears to have been a more active president than his fictional counterpart. The presence of Arthur Adams in San Francisco, providing a final example of Hastings's vacillation over his culpability and setting up the following scene with Rafferty is also invented, as is the Hastings-Rafferty clash itself. That final confrontation provides the play's clearest statement of the conflict between corrupt self-interest and the public good. It also proves the catalyst for Hastings's choice of suicide.

The playwrights also invented the president's statement to the press, along with the naive young reporter, John Boyd. Hastings's interaction with Boyd serves a double purpose in the script. Not only does Boyd supply the heroic view of Hastings held by the general public, otherwise kept offstage or reported through recorded crowd noises, the scene also shows Hastings functioning as a kindly newspaper editor, gently guiding an inexperienced reporter facing a momentous event. The last action Hastings accomplishes prior to his suicide, therefore, echoes his own tragedy: being thrust into circumstances beyond his capabilities.

Lawrence and Lee intended their drama to be a cautionary tale to an audience who, in the autumn of 1959, was facing the first stages of a presidential campaign. With a universally praised Melvyn Douglas as Hastings, a solid supporting cast led by E. G. Marshall as Rafferty, and generally favorable reviews, *The Gang's All Here* had all the elements for a successful run. The two most influential New York reviewers, Brooks Atkinson of the *New York Times* and Walter Kerr of the *Herald Tribune*, were both positive, Atkinson calling the play "extraordinarily interesting in the theatre," while Kerr summed up his review with " 'The Gang's All Here' is lively, interesting, colorful showmanship, however noble its motives, and I suggest you join the gang."[8]

The Gang's All Here, however, didn't find its audience. During its first seven weeks on Broadway, it played to more than 80 percent of capacity each week. Beginning with Thanksgiving week, attendance began a rapid decline, sinking to less than 40 percent during Christmas week. Although business increased slightly after the Christmas holidays, the production was closed on 23 January 1960, without recouping any of its $150,000 investment.[9]

Any Broadway production's box-office draw can be due to a wide range of reasons, many unfathomable. In the case of *The Gang's All Here*, several factors can be identified in hindsight, even though definitive causes must remain problematical. Perhaps most decisive was the mood of the country—after eight years of the Eisenhower presidency, audiences were unwilling to contemplate governmental corruption. While the Eisenhower administration had included its share of graft, there were not sufficiently strong parallels between the venality of the play's politicians and contemporary government officials to excite general interest. The *Variety* review of the Philadelphia tryout engagement found no contemporary application of the play's action, for example.[10]

The New York reviewers also all identified the play as being a thinly veiled dramatization of the Harding administration, and then focused on the actual history. The play's central message was thereby missed: if it is only a retelling of Harding's personal tragedy, the playwrights' larger indictment of a government run by cronies relying on popular opinion goes unperceived and misunderstood. Paradoxically, Melvyn Douglas's performance as Hastings also skewed the play in performance. The brilliance of Douglas's characterization made it difficult for reviewers to notice the social criticism that frames the story of the hapless senator from Ohio. While theatrically effective, Douglas's acting unbalanced the drama.

Finally, producer Kermit Bloomgarden, along with Lawrence and Lee, may simply have presented the play too early in the political season. *The Gang's All Here* opened before the presidential campaign of 1960 got well under way, during the period when fresh candidates were presenting fresh and hopeful images. While the 1960 campaign was not noted for the electorate's cynicism, unlike more recent contests, the pragmatic realities of the Kennedy-Nixon race did not exist in the autumn of 1959. Perhaps significantly, Gore Vidal's *The Best Man*, a political drama that opened in the spring of 1960, was more commercially successful. Its depiction of political maneuvering during a party convention is neither less cynical nor more dramatic than in *The Gang's All Here*. Vidal's play also includes fictionalized portraits of more contemporaneous politicians (including Melvyn Douglas as a thinly veiled Adlai Stevenson). Its success was clearly due to its timing, suggesting that the early closing of *The Gang's All Here*, in addition to the other factors identified above, had as much to do with when it was presented as with its dramatic effectiveness.[11]

Consequently, *The Gang's All Here* has not had the tours, film adaptations, and constant production enjoyed by *Inherit the Wind* and *Auntie Mame*. Even so, *The Gang's All Here* remains frequently produced in regional academic and community theatre, particularly during presidential election seasons. In Washington, D.C., the play was produced during the 1960 campaign by Arena Stage. Zelda Fichandler reported that the play "did wonderful business," and noted that, while "some of the overtones came from the political vibrations in the air of Washington at election time," the "chief pull came from the human dilemma the play so eloquently captures."[12] And Robert E. Lee directed the play at the University of California, Los Angeles, during the 1971 campaign with the entire theatre turned into a convention hall, a style of presentation widely used by other theatre groups since.

As the concept of a president elected by his looks and image loses its exclusive identification with Warren G. Harding, the play's larger message, and the achievement of the playwrights in presenting the ramifications of such an election, have become clearer. *The Gang's All Here* retains a hold in the repertory, its effectiveness having overcome the misperception by its first reviewers of its themes and important message.

Notes

1. Jerome Lawrence and Robert E. Lee, "The Gang Is Almost Here," typescript, Lawrence and Lee Collection 8:10, Jerome Lawrence and Robert E. Lee Theatre Research Institute, The Ohio State University.

2. The famous phrase derives from an interview Daugherty gave to the *New York Times*, 21 February 1920; as cited by Samuel Hopkins Adams, *Incredible Era: The Life and Times of Warren Gamaliel Harding* (Boston: Houghton Mifflin, 1939), 130.

3. Adams provides a useful account of the version of Harding's career generally accepted when Lawrence and Lee were writing *The Gang's All Here*. Daugherty's role is reinforced by his self-serving memoir, *The Inside Story of the Harding Tragedy*, in collaboration with Thomas Dixon (1932; rpt. Boston and Los Angeles: Western Islands, 1975). Andrew Sinclair provides a revisionist view in *The Available Man: The Life behind the Masks of Warren Gamaliel Harding* (New York: Macmillan, 1965), attempting to demonstrate that Harding was far more manipulative and in control than earlier believed. Although interesting, Sinclair's interpretation was not available to the playwrights; the vast majority of Harding's papers seen by Sinclair were not accessible to researchers at the time Lawrence and Lee were writing the play.

4. Charles L. Mee, Jr., provides an entertaining popular summary of corruption during the Harding administration in *The Ohio Gang: The World of Warren G. Harding* (New York: M. Evans, 1981). A fictionalized account supplies a major subplot for Gore Vidal's *Hollywood: A Novel of America in the 1920's* (New York: Random House, 1990).

5. Jerome Lawrence and Robert E. Lee, unpublished letter to the *New York Herald Tribune*, 8 November 1959, typescript, Lawrence and Lee Collection 8:10, Lawrence and Lee Theatre Research Institute.

6. Adams, p. 297. The incident purportedly took place in the White House in the winter of 1923, after Forbes had been forced to resign during the growing scandal.

7. See Sinclair, pp. 286–87, and Adams, pp. 378–84, for thorough discussions of the rumors, their sources, and their probabilities.

8. Brooks Atkinson, "Theatre: Political Play," *New York Times*, 2 October 1959, rpt. *New York Theatre Critics Reviews* (abbrev. *NYTCR*) 20 (1959): 292; Walter Kerr, "First Night Report: '*The Gang's All Here*,'" *New York Herald Tribune* 2, October 1959, rpt. *NYTCR* 20 (1959): 291. Frank Aston of the *New York World-Telegram and the Sun* and Richard Watts, Jr., of the *New York Post* were similarly praising; John Chapman of the *New York Daily News* and John McClain of the *New York Journal American* praised the production and performance while finding flaws with the play; Robert Coleman of the *New York Daily Mirror* wrote the only entirely negative notice. All these reviews are reprinted in the *NYTCR* 20 (1959): 289–91.

9. Box office figures are taken from weekly charts in *Variety*, 7 October 1959 through 27 January 1960. The high grosses in the first seven weeks most likely reflect the popularity of the play with theatre party brokers; the sudden slump in the eighth week suggests that the show had exhausted its advance sale and theatre party sales at that point.

10. Waters, "Show Out of Town," *Variety*, 16 September 1959, p. 56.

11. Douglas makes the same point in comparing the success of *The Best Man* with the failure of *The Gang's All Here*, presenting the Lawrence and Lee play entirely in terms of its relevance to events in the Eisenhower administration. Melvyn Douglas and Tom Arthur, *See You at the Movies: The Autobiography of Melvyn Douglas* (Lanham, Md.: University Press of America, 1986), 197–200.

12. Zelda Fichandler, typescript (to Robert E. Lee), 15 November 1960; Lawrence and Lee Collection 8:11, Lawrence and Lee Theatre Research Institute.

Foreword

Once every four years we get a chance to make history. We go into a voting booth, close the canvas curtain behind us, pull a lever or make an X, and the consequences of what we do will be remembered as long as the English language is spoken or written.

That time is almost here again. The Presidential hopefuls are making their shy denials, and the hyperthyroid campaign Barnums are kicking up a preconvention ruckus. The political air has the brittle snap of first-night anticipation. The box office is already open for America's greatest quadrennial show, and the follow spot is preparing to seek the man who will go to 1600 Pennsylvania Avenue.

In *The Gang's All Here* we are trying to catch some of the high excitement and drama of a convention year. We are looking at another convention, an imaginary one. We are examining a White House–bound human being, also imaginary. We are taking a long look at the men who surround a President, the cronies who can become more powerful than kings.

Inauguration Day is much simpler than a Coronation at Westminster Abbey. Yet it makes a phenomenal change in the man who says "So help me God." Many of our Presidents have been rocketed into the White House with almost no preparation. Often they arrive with a hopeless misconception of what is expected of them. How does it feel to stand alone in the Chief Executive's office for the first time?

Our play is not about *a* President, or *the* President, but about the Presidency itself: the father image, the godhead we send to Washington. The great American legend is that every boy can grow up to be President. But what happens to the man-boy? What happens, in particular, if he should never have been elected in the first place; if he sweeps in on his good looks, his "Hail! Hail! The Gang's All Here" personality?

We have stripped any partisan label from our central character. Our politicos are either Republicans or Democrats—it does not matter which. The cigar butts in the caucuses of both parties smell pretty much the same. And the stench of expediency is no more fragrant around a donkey than an elephant.

Is "government by crony" inevitable? We burden our Presidents with such responsibility that only a genius can comprehend the job, and only an archangel can perform it. Hence, we are governed by appointees. Who can blame a man in the White House for choosing people he *knows* to be near him? Prime question: what kind of people does he know?

If Griffith P. Hastings of our play happens to resemble, in part, a President during the rememberable past, he also combines traits of many Presidents. For us to deny that the character is drawn from one President in particular, is perhaps as foolish as for anybody else to insist that he *is* one President in particular.

We ask the playgoer's permission to set us free from the restraint of *mere* facts. We hope you will see on the stage people you can identify, not with remote names in books and newspapers, but with the forces we feel shape Twentieth-Century democracy, small d.

If the man we fondly X'd in a voting booth turns out to be a struggling incompetent, whose fault is it? The President's? Not if he really tries, and gains each day in self-knowledge. It's too easy to blame the gang around him, because opportunists are always waiting to fill any governmental vacuum. Perhaps the real trouble lies in our own reluctance to think about history except on that November Tuesday. When we push aside the little canvas curtain and leave the voting booth, the show isn't over. That's when the big curtain is going up.

Lawrence & Lee

(This article, by the playwrights, appeared in the New York *Herald Tribune* on 27 September 1959, the Sunday before the play's New York opening.)

EDITOR'S NOTE

Two editions of *The Gang's All Here* appeared in 1960: a hardcover version, published by World (Cleveland and New York), and an acting text, published by Samuel French, Inc. The two have only minor differences.

The two-act version published here for the first time was prepared by Jerome Lawrence and Robert E. Lee for the present anthology. The first act in the original version ended with the present act 1, scene 2; the second act opened with the present act 1, scene 3 (the poker party), and ended with the present act 2, scene 1. The original act 3 is now the final scene of act 2. Some transitional dialogue has been altered by the playwrights, who have also made additional minor changes throughout. This text of *The Gang's All Here* represents the playwrights' final version of the text.

CAST

The Gang's All Here opened in New York at the Ambassador Theatre on 1 October 1959. It was produced by Kermit Bloomgarden Productions, Inc., in association with Sylvia Drulie, and directed by George Roy Hill. Scenery and lighting were designed by Jo Mielziner, with costumes by Patricia Zipprodt. The cast included:

WALTER RAFFERTY	E. G. Marshall
JOSHUA LOOMIS	Bernard Lenrow
CHARLES WEBSTER	Paul McGrath
TAD	Bill Zuckert
HIGGY	Howard Smith
JUDGE CORRIGLIONE	Victor Kilian
DOC KIRKABY	Fred Stewart
FRANCES GREELEY HASTINGS	Jean Dixon
GRIFFITH P. HASTINGS	Melvyn Douglas
COBB	Edwin Cooper
MAID	Anne Shropshire
BRUCE BELLINGHAM	Arthur Hill
ARTHUR ANDERSON	Bram Nossen
AXEL MALEY	Bert Wheeler
LAVERNE	Yvette Vickers
RENEE	Alberta MacDonald
PIANO PLAYER	John Harkins
JOHN BOYD	Clay Hall

The Gang's All Here was produced prior to its Broadway run at the Forrest Theatre, Philadelphia, opening on 10 September 1959.

ACT ONE

Scene 1: Two hotel rooms in Chicago. Past midnight during a political convention.

Scene 2: The Executive Suite, 1600 Pennsylvania Avenue, Washington, D.C.
Scene 3: A basement room on L Street in Washington.

ACT TWO

Scene 1: The Executive Suite.
Scene 2: The Presidential Suite of a hotel in San Francisco.

Bernard Lenrow, E. G. Marshall, Fred Stewart, Bert Wheeler, Melvyn Douglas, and Paul McGrath in *The Gang's All Here,* New York, 1959. Jerome Lawrence and Robert E. Lee Collection, Lawrence and Lee Theatre Research Institute, The Ohio State University.

THE GANG'S ALL HERE

ACT ONE

SCENE 1

On a scrim: a fast succession of photos of the time, 1920, and of the convention.

Over it, a tape of the delegates, late at night, casting their votes for the nomination of the President. The gavel pounds, and the voice of the Chairman pleads for attention.

CHAIRMAN'S VOICE. Before adjourning for the night, the chair appeals to every delegate to this great convention to break the deadlock between the distinguished General Simpkins and the Honorable Governor of Massachusetts. If we don't, we may all be here till Election Day. On the seventeenth ballot tomorrow morning, *please* let's nominate the next President of the United States so we can all go home! (*Gavel again.*) Convention stands adjourned until nine-thirty a.m.

Lights come up on a hotel room, on a raised level. It is thick with cigar smoke. People are milling around; delegates are trying to crowd in. Prominent in the group are Webster, Higgy, Doc, Ax, the Judge, and Rafferty, who has his back to the audience at the start. Ax's job is keeping people out of the room, but he is not doing it very effectively.

WEBSTER. (*Accusingly, to Tad.*) You never called for the Ohio count!

TAD. It wouldn't 'a made any difference, would it?

DOC. At least we'd know where they stand.

AX. Ask Walt.

HIGGY. Where is Walter?

RAFFERTY. (*Turning front.*) I'm here.

AX. Waddya think, Walt?

RAFFERTY. I think there must be a faster way to pick a President.

CORRIGLIONE. And better!

WEBSTER. Fine. Let's re-write the Constitution. But not tonight. (*The telephone on the table rings shrilly. Webster grabs it, answers.*) Yes? Who's calling from Philadelphia? (*All are puffing on cigars or cigarettes, and the blue smoke ascends into the light. Tad takes off his coat, to be in shirt-sleeves like the others, except the Judge. The heat of this July night is more than thermal.*) All right, I'll take it. (*He stretches the phone cord for some scant privacy. To Doc.*) Keep counting! (*Taut, into phone.*) This is Charlie Webster. Hell, no, you didn't wake me up. We may be here all night. And we've agreed not to leave this room until we settle on a candidate. (*Quietly, Rafferty slips out of the room. He walks down into a lower hotel room. He loosens his tie, settles into a chair and begins playing solitaire. In the upper smoke-filled room, a Bellboy appears in a doorway with several yellow envelopes.*)

BELLBOY. Three telegrams for Mr. Charlie Webster.

HIGGY. Somebody give the kid a half a dollar. (*Webster motions for somebody to take care of it; Tad crosses and pays the boy. But Higgy has the telegrams in his hand.*) Want me to read these to you, Charles?

WEBSTER. (*Grabbing the telegrams, quickly.*) Let me have those.

HIGGY. (*Shrugs.*) Certainly, Charles.

AX. (*To Doc.*) Did you figure in those five Nebraska votes? (*Doc nods, and continues counting. Higgy moves out of the room, goes to another area, dimly lit, and begins phoning, his hulking back to the audience. Tad follows him.*)

WEBSTER. (*Scanning the telegrams as he talks.*) Whatever deals we have to make will not affect our commitments to you. (*Almost shouting into the phone.*) We're not desperate. Why should we be desperate? (*Closes his eyes.*) Go ahead, I'm listening. (*Webster listens, nodding. The counting has fallen into an ominous silence. The Delegates crane over Doc's shoulder to see the totals.*) Those are excellent suggestions. I'm writing them all down. (*He's not writing a damn thing.*) And we feel very friendly toward your people too. Same to you. (*He hangs up.*) Son-of-a-bitch. All he wants is the dome of the Capitol. (*Webster is aware that Doc's totals have caused the ominous silence.*) Well?

DOC. The Governor still needs seventy-three votes. (*This is bad news for Webster. He is dead with weariness.*)

WEBSTER. What do you think, Walt? (*No answer.*) Walt? Walt? Where the hell is Rafferty? (*They all shrug. Nobody saw him leave. Webster clicks the phone urgently.*) Operator. Get me Walter Rafferty's room. No! I don't want room information. (*To the others.*) What the goddam hell is his room number?

AX. 1026.

WEBSTER. (*Into phone.*) 1026—and fast! (*The lights come up on a hotel room at stage level, downstage center and Left. Walter Rafferty is seated in the armchair, playing solitaire on the back of a suitcase. This is a lean, Cassius-looking man—a professional politico of the Enlightened Twenties. He turns up the cards idly, but he is biting hard on the stem of a rakish cigarette holder. Joshua Loomis hurries in, clicking the door shut behind him. An amiable Senator with the drawl of the big ranch country, he seems baited and tired.*)

LOOMIS. The whole hotel is going crazy. What the hell are you doing, Walt?

RAFFERTY. Waiting.

LOOMIS. (*Fixing himself a drink at the table.*) Well, I can't wait much longer. The oil boys from San Antonio rented me a seven-room suite on the top floor. There are so many people up there trying to see me, I can't even get in.

RAFFERTY. I've got room for you, Senator. For you—and all your votes.

LOOMIS. (*Takes list from coat pocket.*) Here's a midnight count of how many delegates have switched horses since adjournment.

RAFFERTY. (*Looks up from the cards, his eyes half-closed.*) The Governor is seventy-three votes short of the nomination and the General needs eighty-two.

LOOMIS. Eighty-one. I can't stay uncommitted all night. When are you going to spring our boy?

RAFFERTY. Just relax. (*The phone rings. Rafferty leans over and picks up the receiver.*)

LOOMIS. If that's San Antonio, I don't want to take it.

RAFFERTY. (*Into phone.*) Yes?

WEBSTER. (*From the upstairs room.*) Walt? Charlie Webster.

RAFFERTY. Hello, Charlie.

LOOMIS. Don't tell Charlie Webster I'm here.

WEBSTER. You by yourself?

RAFFERTY. No. Josh Loomis just dropped in.

LOOMIS. You son-of-a-bitch.

WEBSTER. Why did you leave?

RAFFERTY. I had to go to the can.

WEBSTER. We've got a can up here.

RAFFERTY. Some things I like to do by myself.

WEBSTER. I've got to see you.

RAFFERTY. (*Affably.*) Come right on down, Charlie. (*He hangs up the phone. Webster slams down his phone and makes his way out of the upper room. Others follow, and gradually the lights fade on that area.*)

LOOMIS. I don't want to talk to Webster. I'm having enough trouble with my people. Some of them think the offers from his Governor are as sweet as we can get.

RAFFERTY. Don't be a damn fool, Josh. You gonna settle for a handful of post offices when you can have everything?

LOOMIS. Do I get Interior? Positively?

RAFFERTY. (*Resuming his game of solitaire.*) Sometimes you have to ask for one thing to get another.

LOOMIS. What are you going to give yourself?

RAFFERTY. Oh, the Justice Department, eventually.

LOOMIS. (*Nervously.*) Nobody's going to get anything if you don't start moving.

RAFFERTY. When enough palms are sweating, Josh, we'll trot our dark horse out of the stable.

LOOMIS. Does the horse know about it?

RAFFERTY. Not yet.

LOOMIS. Isn't that a little risky?

RAFFERTY. You know him, you've played enough poker with him. Let me handle it. (*He stops playing with the cards, and chews on the cigarette holder.*) I've been waiting eight years for tonight. I'm not going to spoil it by rushing. (*Charlie Webster appears in the doorway. He is the State Chairman from Massachusetts, manager of his*

Governor's campaign. Webster might be mistaken for a banker or a successful corporation executive. But his granite face is worried and the pin-stripe suit is wrinkled with sleeplessness. Rafferty greets him heartily.) Come on in, Charlie.

WEBSTER. (*Entering.*) Well, Senator Loomis, has Walt convinced you to swing your votes over to the Governor?

LOOMIS. (*Cautiously, sitting.*) He's been working on me.

WEBSTER. Good. Senator, I've gone over your suggestions very carefully. The Governor will do his best to get favorable legislation for your people. And you'll have a post office at practically every cactus bush. (*Higgy enters, followed by Tad. Higgy is a sagging mountain of a man who speaks with the distinctive diction of New Jersey. Tad, a jittery delegate in shirt sleeves, has borrowed attention by attaching himself to the mighty Higgins. Webster looks at the new arrivals distastefully. Rafferty flops down on the bed and tilts his straw hat over his face, seeming to be asleep.*)

TAD. We've been waiting in your suite, Senator. We didn't know you were down here.

LOOMIS. (*Uneasily.*) Good evening, gentlemen. Mr. Higgins, I didn't expect to have the campaign managers for the Governor and for the General both paying me a call. Quite an honor.

HIGGY. Honor, hell. I'm giving you one last chance to climb on the General's bandwagon.

LOOMIS. Oh? Has the General decided to make some promises?

HIGGY. General Simpkins makes only one promise, to ride up Pennsylvania Avenue and get off at the White House. That's a damn sight more than his Governor'll ever do. (*Massachusetts and New Jersey glare at each other.*)

LOOMIS. Do you suppose the General will be riding on horseback, or in a limousine?

HIGGY. What difference does it make?

LOOMIS. Well, oats are going out and oil is coming in.

WEBSTER. (*Sitting in the chair above the table, leaning across it urgently.*) Senator Loomis, we've got to have a decision tonight. This deadlock is dangerous. A complete stranger could slip in—some grass roots amateur with nobody behind him but the people. What do you say, Senator?

LOOMIS. My instructions are to wait and see what developments occur. (*As Loomis starts to leave, he meets Doc and the Judge in the doorway, followed by Ax.*) Good evening, Doctor Kirkaby, Judge Corriglione. Mr. Maley. (*Loomis escapes. Doc is a dry realist with a county-seat sense of humor. Judge Corriglione still has a few shreds of the judicial mien, despite a lifetime of losing battles between his conscience and expediency.*)

DOC. (*Crossing to Webster.*) Did you land him, Charlie?

WEBSTER. Without Loomis, where do we stand?

DOC. Oh. The Governor still needs seventy-three votes. (*Webster paces. Higgy sits on the bed.*)

WEBSTER. (*Taking the list from Doc.*) All right. Here's what we do. Tomorrow morning, stuff the balcony, get professional cheer leaders. We'll march in and whoop up a demonstration they'll never forget! We'll drag out those seventy-three votes!

JUDGE. So that's how we get a President. Like a touchdown at a football game.

WEBSTER. My God, the Governor's almost in!

AX. I knew a girl once who was almost a virgin.

HIGGY. Face it, Charles. Your Governor's been screwed.

WEBSTER. Your goddam General is eighty-one votes short of the nomination. Where do you think those votes are coming from?

HIGGY. (*Drawing on his cigar.*) Eventually, Charles, they're coming from you. (*He rises to face the Judge.*) When are you gonna unglue those votes you control, and give 'em the man they want? The man our worthy opponents would have run if they'd been smart enough to get him! Simpkins! General Simpkins!

DOC. This convention wouldn't nominate General Simpkins if you stuck a saber up his ass and called him Teddy Roosevelt.

HIGGY. You come to me with your little poop of a Governor of Massachusetts—

WEBSTER. (*Heatedly.*) He's a good administrator!

HIGGY. (*Fetches an envelope out of the pocket of his coat, and carelessly tears the canceled stamp off the corner as he speaks.*) Here's what I want you to do, Charles. Make me a list of the men in public life who got there just because they were good administrators. Write 'em on the back of this stamp. (*He tosses the torn stamp to Webster, then moves to the door like Moby Dick through a swarm of pilot fish.*) You smart alecks can sit here all night if you want to. As soon as I pry loose a couple more favorite sons, you gentlemen may be knocking on the door of *my* suite. (*Higgy goes out. There is an uncertain pause. Suddenly Tad starts to the door.*)

TAD. I'm going along with Higgy.

WEBSTER. (*Desperately.*) And how many crumbs do you think you'll get from the fat boy's table?

TAD. What the hell are you gonna do? Pick a name out of a hat?

JUDGE. Look, gentlemen, there's a point where you have to stop compromising.

WEBSTER. Are you going to make a speech, Judge?

JUDGE. Yes! A short one. For fifteen minutes can we consider the possibility of nominating the best man?

DOC. Your boy got eleven and a half votes on the fourteenth ballot.

TAD. God help us. Not another college professor.

JUDGE. At least Arthur Anderson is a statesman; not just a vote catcher.

WEBSTER. Judge Corriglione. You have not yet arrived in that appointive marble heaven called the Supreme Court, where elections only happen to other people.

JUDGE. All I'm asking, Charlie, is how crazy is it to think that the interests of the country and the interests of the party aren't too far apart?

TAD. My money's on the General. (*He crosses toward the door again, but Rafferty stops him.*)

RAFFERTY. Tad! (*When Rafferty wants attention, he gets it. He is the politician's politician—and when he talks, everybody listens. He has a shrewd sense of pause and timing, an earthy eloquence which would be meaningless on a platform but which is brilliant in a smokefilled room. Rafferty gets up from the bed, saunters downstage and seems to be peering out an imaginary window.*)

AX. What are you doing, Walt.

RAFFERTY. (*Taking a deep breath.*) I'm smelling Chicago. (*He leans forward and scans the street eleven stories down.*) I'm looking for something, too. And I don't see it. Not one solitary soldier boy. (*He twists a fresh cigarette into the holder.*) I do see a young lady who seems to be in an interesting line of work. (*Drawn by the same curiosity, Webster, the Judge, Doc, and Ax join Rafferty at the window. They look down appreciatively.*)

AX. Why doesn't that cop pick her up?

DOC. He just did.

RAFFERTY. Like hell. She picked *him* up.

TAD. (*Shrugs and heads for the door again.*) I'm sleepy and I'm hungry. I'm going back to my caucus and recommend the General.

RAFFERTY. (*Roaring.*) That street down there is *hollering* at you! The General's a soldier and everybody's sick of soldiers, including the soldiers themselves. The cops are sick of being cops. They don't want to run in the "ladies of the evening"—they want to spend the night with them. (*He strides impatiently from one delegate to another.*) Four years ago, could we have seen that much of a woman's leg? Fashions change. In politics, too. Four years ago, it was very smart to have the brain showing. But the people who make the X's this November will want a clean-shaven gent with lots of his own hair on top. Everybody's fed up with heroes and angels; they want to come back down here where the good times are. (*A pause. Then he sits on the arm of a chair and speaks with a storyteller's intensity.*) I want to tell you something. About eight years ago, I had a startling experience. I was walking down the path in back of the Hotel McKinley in Wilmont, Ohio. I saw a man coming up the path toward me. Forty feet away. But even at that distance, I could see there was something special about him. The power of his walk, the silver majesty of his head. And the eyes—the kind of eyes that seem to be looking directly at you, even if you're 'way at the edge of a crowd. And I said to myself, "Walt Rafferty, you'd better find out who that fella is—because he's got what people vote for. He could be anything—even President of the United States."

JUDGE. Well, who was it?

RAFFERTY. (*Rising and crossing to the phone.*) Operator, let me have Suite 517, please.

WEBSTER. (*Worried.*) What are you doing, Walt?

RAFFERTY. Hello, Frances. Hope I didn't wake you. May I speak to your husband?

WEBSTER. (*Fast.*) You're acting strictly as an individual, not for any of us.

RAFFERTY. Don't wet your pants. Everything's going to be— (*Into phone.*) Hello, Griff?

TAD. (*Puzzled.*) Griff?

RAFFERTY. Do I have the honor of addressing Senator Griffith P. Hastings? (*They all start talking at once.*)

WEBSTER. (*Angrily.*) If you think you're going to take over this convention— (*The Judge rises, worried.*)

TAD. I can stay awake as long as any of you.

RAFFERTY. (*Covering the mouthpiece.*) Shut up, everybody! (*There is a sullen silence. Rafferty speaks blandly into the phone.*) Griff, some of the boys are up here in Room 1026— No, Griff, it's not a poker game. (*The Judge groans.*) We just wanted to— well, get your point of view on a few things. We're a long way from a decision, but some of us here have been thinking of you as a possibility. (*He listens, frowns.*) Now, Griff. Wait a minute. (*Another pause. He turns his back to the group.*) I don't see how you can refuse a thing like this without even talking it over.

WEBSTER. Save me from the shy violets.

TAD. I saw Hastings make a speech once.

JUDGE. *Saw* him make a speech?

TAD. He didn't say a damned thing, but he sure looked great.

RAFFERTY. (*Hanging up the phone.*) He's not interested.

WEBSTER. That's a smart act to play, Walt. How long did you rehearse it?

RAFFERTY. This late at night Keith's is closed.

DOC. Y'ask me, it's lucky for everybody he doesn't want it. We wouldn't be electing Hastings, we'd be crowning that wife of his Queen of the United States.

AX. Yeah. Queen Pain-in-the-Ass the First! (*They laugh.*) It's bad enough dames've got the vote—the next thing you know they'll want to run for office! (*Rafferty signals subtly for Doc to lead an exodus.*)

DOC. (*Getting the message, pulling on his coat.*) I'm going out and get some food.

WEBSTER. Call Room Service.

DOC. I said food. Not those wooden sandwiches. There's a chop suey joint just off Michigan Boulevard. They give a cup of wanton soup—with an olive in it. Very dry.

TAD. I gotta check with my caucus.

DOC. (*Ushering out Tad and the Judge.*) We can do some figuring while we're eating.

TAD. Who're you guys gonna try now?

JUDGE. Does anybody have a phone number on Rutherford B. Hayes?

WEBSTER. (*Turns in the doorway.*) Coming, Walt?

RAFFERTY. (*Leans back thoughtfully in his chair, his hands clasped behind his head.*) Charlie, you don't like chop suey.

WEBSTER. (*Closes the door and comes slowly back into the room. These are two king makers of the party; this is a duel by lamplight.*) What does the "P" stand for?

RAFFERTY. Huh?

WEBSTER. Griffith *P.* Hastings. "President"?

RAFFERTY. That's everybody else's middle name.

WEBSTER. He's the Senate champ, isn't he? Holds the all-time record; hardly ever makes a roll call, never introduced a bill.

RAFFERTY. Yep, he's a good party man. Never forgets a face. Never forgets a friend. (*Pause.*) Charlie, a long time ago, in the city of Athens, there was a Golden Age. Everybody had everything. And the statesman who ran the show was a fella named Pericles. The school books say he looked like a god on Olympus. But with no Pericles, there wouldn't have been a Golden Age for anybody.

WEBSTER. Goddamn it, Walt, if we can just find those seventy-three votes.

RAFFERTY. I've got them. I can get them.

WEBSTER. (*Turning.*) How?

RAFFERTY. Josh Loomis and Griff Hastings are old poker buddies.

WEBSTER. You two-faced bastard! Have you had Loomis in your pocket all along, keeping your mouth shut till you could be king maker? You want to be Higgy?

RAFFERTY. I'm prettier than Higgy. And much easier to do business with.

WEBSTER. What do you want?

RAFFERTY. I just want you to add a four-letter word to your Governor's patriotic aspirations.

WEBSTER. What?

RAFFERTY. Vice. I think he'd make a splendid candidate for *Vice*-President.

WEBSTER. Absolutely not.

RAFFERTY. Charlie, with no effort at all you can lose Ohio.

WEBSTER. Are you working with me or against me?

RAFFERTY. I'm just working.

WEBSTER. For Hastings? He turned you down.

RAFFERTY. (*Rising and crossing to Webster.*) Charlie, I have elected three Senators and God knows how many Congressmen with one sure-fire technique: They all didn't want it so much they were *sure* to get in.

WEBSTER. Hastings can be Vice-President.

RAFFERTY. Sorry, Charlie. (*He crosses to the desk, picks up the phone.*)

WEBSTER. Walt, the Governor's a man of impeccable reputation.

RAFFERTY. Well?

WEBSTER. I've heard some stories about Hastings.

RAFFERTY. Oh?

WEBSTER. Pretty much of a ladies' man, isn't he?

RAFFERTY. They can vote now. The ladies like a ladies' man.

WEBSTER. Yeah. If he's married, with a family, all the trimmings.

RAFFERTY. Griff's married.

WEBSTER. What about the trimmings?

RAFFERTY. Queen Victoria's dead, Charlie.

WEBSTER. Your Senator doesn't make those periodic visits to New York to call on Queen Victoria. She's got a kid, hasn't she?

RAFFERTY. Queen Victoria?

WEBSTER. Damn it, Walt. Is it true?

RAFFERTY. Is what true?

WEBSTER. I don't want to find out about any illegitimate child three weeks before Election Day.

RAFFERTY. None of it's true. Take my word for it.

WEBSTER. I believe you. Because you'd be taking one helluva chance if it were true. And if I leave the Governor sitting in the Vice-Presidential outhouse—

RAFFERTY. (*Putting down the phone, sitting on the desk.*)—what does Charlie Webster get?

WEBSTER. Cabinet?

RAFFERTY. Or equivalent.

WEBSTER. What does that mean? (*Rafferty doesn't answer.*) Can I name it?

RAFFERTY. For example?

WEBSTER. The Veterans' Bureau?

RAFFERTY (*He is thoughtful, then nods.*) You can have it.

WEBSTER. Will Hastings approve it?

RAFFERTY. If I say so, your grandmother can be Ambassador to Mexico.

WEBSTER. (*Crossing, thoughtfully.*) All right. Now, can we pull it off?

RAFFERTY. (*With sudden energy.*) If we stay up all night and work like hell, we can.

WEBSTER. What about Doc and the Judge?

RAFFERTY. Don't worry about them. That's my job. Just hang on to the Governor's votes. (*Knock. Rafferty crosses and opens the door for Frances Greeley Hastings. She is a handsome woman, a small-town patrician for whom Washington is simply an enlarged county seat. Waiting is painful for her, and she has had to wait too much of her life.*)

FRANCES. Mr. Rafferty.

RAFFERTY. Why, Mrs. Hastings.

FRANCES. (*She comes in, reacting to the intensity of the cigar smoke.*) I was under the impression that a meeting of delegates was in progress. (*Rafferty and Webster exchange glances.*)

RAFFERTY. (*Closing the door.*) It's only a recess. With the bad news Griff gave us on the phone, some of the boys had to go out and get braced up.

WEBSTER. Sit down, Mrs. Hastings.

RAFFERTY. Frances, you know Charlie Webster.

FRANCES. We met at the banquet of the National Grange, two years ago. (*She sits.*)

WEBSTER. (*Impressed.*) Yes.

FRANCES. I understand, Walter, that you just made the Senator a very flattering offer. (*There is a pause. Rafferty looks at Webster.*)

RAFFERTY. Did we, Charlie? (*Another pause.*)

WEBSTER. I think we can rally the entire party behind your husband, Mrs. Hastings. If he chooses.

FRANCES. What about your Governor, Mr. Webster?

WEBSTER. He'll take second place on the ticket.

FRANCES. Oh?

WEBSTER. He's already agreed.

FRANCES. And the General?

RAFFERTY. He just lost the war.

FRANCES. What commitments are involved?

RAFFERTY. None.

WEBSTER. None whatsoever.

FRANCES. (*Taking a deep breath.*) Mr. Webster, I have no admiration for women who impose themselves on the political careers of their husbands. I consider myself only a watcher. But hardly a *disinterested* watcher. (*Turning to Rafferty.*) Walter, you know him. I believe you should nominate him for one reason—he's the best man for the job. And not on the basis of any desperation, or any deals, or any favors promised.

WEBSTER. (*Quickly.*) Oh, no deals, Mrs. Hastings. We don't work that way. Not in this party.

FRANCES. Then get together all the leaders of the principal delegations and go to him and tell him it's his patriotic duty to accept.

RAFFERTY. (*Interrupting.*) There's no time, Frances. We'll be caucusing all night. It'll take three, maybe four ballots tomorrow to clinch this thing.

WEBSTER. (*Going to the phone.*) You want me to go talk to him? What's that room number?

FRANCES. He's not there. He went out for a walk by the lake front. (*With conviction.*) Whatever decision is made will be entirely his. (*She turns to Webster.*) You see, my husband is a modest man— (*She breaks off, realizing that Webster is no longer looking at her, but at a figure in the doorway. There's no doubt who he is: the shock of silver hair, the penetrating eyes, the bearing of an emperor. But Griffith P. Hastings shatters this aura of majesty as soon as he opens his mouth in private conversation.*)

HASTINGS. I got outside the hotel, took one breath of fresh air, and I realized what the Duchess was up to. (*He ignores his wife, who moves between the beds. Hastings comes in.*) Give me a cigar, will you Walt? When I breathe smoke, I'd just as soon it was my own. (*Rafferty hands him a cigar. Hastings bites off the end.*) Hello, Charlie. Why don't *you* run for President? I'll vote for you.

WEBSTER. (*Hands Hastings matches.*) Here you are, Senator.

FRANCES. (*Taking a step forward.*) Griffith, if you're embarrassed by our discussing this without you—

HASTINGS. Nobody gets embarrassed in politics, Duchess. You get elected or you don't get elected; but you don't get embarrassed. (*Examining the cigar studiously.*) Were you serious about that phone call, Walt?

RAFFERTY. Absolutely.

HASTINGS. You want me for a sacrifice play? A bunt to shortstop so the General can get home? I'm willing to do that—if you guarantee I won't get stuck with the nomination.

FRANCES. Griffith doesn't mean that, gentlemen.

HASTINGS. You want to be First Lady, Frances? Go ahead, I'll give you a divorce and you can marry General Simpkins. (*Turning to the others.*) The Duchess would make a hell of a First Lady. She's got the stomach for it.

RAFFERTY. Funny thing; I thought every school boy in America wanted to be President.

HASTINGS. Then get a school boy.

RAFFERTY. Griff, listen to me. Have I ever steered you wrong?

HASTINGS. Couple of times. (*He lights his cigar and grins.*) Nothing serious.

RAFFERTY. You've trusted me through most of your political career.

HASTINGS. (*Simply.*) All of it.

RAFFERTY. Well, trust me now. I'm not going to feed you a lot of patriotic swill. It's as simple as this: the party wants you, the party needs you.

WEBSTER. That's right, Senator.

HASTINGS. (*For the first time, he is completely serious.*) For God's sake, Walt, I don't know how to be President!

RAFFERTY. Who does? Do you think any backwoods lawyer, or country storekeeper, or half-drunk Civil War General knew any more about it than you do?

HASTINGS. Damn it, Walt, don't sell me. I like the Senate. It's the greatest club in the world. "Senator Hastings"! It's got a nice sound to it. But "President Hastings" scares the bejezus out of me. (*Looking around.*) You got a bottle around here any place?

RAFFERTY. Help yourself.

HASTINGS. (*Ignoring it.*) In the Senate, up on Capitol Hill, it's like being in a band. You've got ninety-five other fellas tooting the melody along with you. But the President's way out there in front, all by himself—playing solo.

RAFFERTY. You won't be alone. You can have your friends with you. The band plays on!

HASTINGS. (*Crossing to sit at table.*) What makes you think I could get elected?

RAFFERTY. The man we name tonight in this room automatically moves into 1600 Pennsylvania Avenue. (*Pause.*) Griff, Griff, when you're sitting on a rocking chair on the front porch of the White House, everybody in the country is going to relax, breathe easy again! That's what they need, Griff. They need you!

HASTINGS. What about the other candidates?

RAFFERTY. They've erased each other. We've got a blank slate.

HASTINGS. How can I expect anybody to go into a voting booth and do what I wouldn't do? I wouldn't vote for me. Not for President.

RAFFERTY. You know what'll happen? Some dark horse can stampede the convention—God knows who. Maybe somebody without your integrity, somebody who wants the office for purely selfish reasons. Only one person can stop that. You.

HASTINGS. (*At the window.*) Four years I'd be apologizing for getting myself stuck where I don't belong. I hate apologizers.

RAFFERTY. I guess I was wrong. Go back to Wilmont, Griff. Set type. Write editorials about widening Center Street. To hell with the country.

HASTINGS. (*He looks distantly out the window. He seems to be thinking how much of his private life would vanish in the hot Presidential spotlight.*) It's so bright up there. You can't even let your beard grow.

RAFFERTY. Lincoln did.

HASTINGS. I mean over a weekend.

WEBSTER. There is one question we'd like to ask you, Senator. It's more or less a standard question that we ask all candidates.

HASTINGS. Well?

WEBSTER. Is there anything in your life that might cast reflection on the party? Or the country?

FRANCES. (*Icily.*) That seems a peculiar question to ask a United States Senator.

RAFFERTY. You don't have to answer that, Griff.

HASTINGS. Why not? I think it's a good question. I want a few minutes to think.

RAFFERTY. (*Gestures to Webster.*) We'll be out in the hall. (*Rafferty and Webster go out and close the door. Frances looks at her husband's back.*)

FRANCES. Griffith. (*She circles above the table to the right. He puts down his cigar and crosses left.*)

HASTINGS. I've got to think, Duchess.

FRANCES. If you're worried about personal problems, *our* personal problems . . .

HASTINGS. (*Ironically.*) What personal problems? We've got the perfect marriage.

FRANCES. There's no reason why people shouldn't believe that. Griffith, you don't think it's just two men out there asking you to be President—it's the whole country!

HASTINGS. If I only had time to sleep on it.

FRANCES. This is the one night in your life to stay awake, to know what's going on. You still can't see it, can you? You still don't know who wears your clothes.

HASTINGS. (*Takes off his coat and holds it up to her.*) This coat belongs to a country newspaper editor who had good enough friends to get himself elected to the United States Senate. This coat does not belong to the President of the United States. (*He tosses the coat over the back of the chair. He sits, and she crosses above the table.*)

FRANCES. All my life I've been hearing that speech. Griffith, you said you didn't have any business in county politics. You said you didn't know how to be a State Legislator. You didn't think you could run the newspaper, you said the same thing about the newspaper! And see how wrong you were.

HASTINGS. (*Scowls.*) Duchess, this thing is different. A President has to be special. Everything he does and says is important. Hell, I was born unimportant. It's the only talent I've got.

FRANCES. I don't believe that. Neither do you. (*Her voice softens.*) The October before we were married, you and I climbed to the top of Mount Wilmont. Remember?

HASTINGS. (*A short laugh.*) "Mighty Mount Wilmont. Highest point in the County. One hundred ten feet above sea level."

FRANCES. Up there, we looked back over the town, and I told you it was *your* town, it could be your town, and you could bid for the newspaper, and we could make it the most important daily in Southeastern Ohio, and we *did*! And we were happy then, they were good years, working together, weren't they, Griffith?

HASTINGS. I had a railroad ticket in my inside coat pocket that day. You didn't know that, Duchess. I'd paid my final week's rent at the boarding house. I meant to tell you I was leaving Wilmont to take a job in a land office in Denver. But I didn't go. Because of something that happened between you and me. And it hasn't happened often enough since then, has it, Frances? You gave me the feeling I was quite a guy. Quite a guy. (*He tries to embrace her. She pulls away.*)

FRANCES. Of course I did. I still do. Do you expect me to keep proving it to you?

HASTINGS. (*With a ghost of a smile.*) It might help.

FRANCES. This isn't just a matter of a man and a woman touching each other. Or not touching. Or how we happen to get along as husband and wife. You shouldn't even be thinking about that now. It has nothing to do with how successful we've been—*you've* been—politically. (*He turns away. She pursues him.*) They're holding a door open for you. All you have to do is walk in.

HASTINGS. You make it sound like the easiest job in the world to say yes to the toughest job in the world. (*She stops.*)

FRANCES. Is it me? I'll go away. It'll be less difficult for you if I'm not around.

HASTINGS. Oh, Christ, Frances—without you I couldn't do it at all. (*He throws up his hands.*) Hell, I can't do it with a heavenly choir and a team of professional Saints. I can't. I just can't do it.

FRANCES. (*Angry.*) What right do you have to say you can't do it? How can you deny the country and the people who believe in you? And me? And for what? For the sake of some— (*She gropes for the word.*) —of some momentary appetite.

HASTINGS. If *you* had a little more appetite once in a while—

FRANCES. *I* didn't make things this way. *I* don't have a lover in some back alley apartment . . .

HASTINGS. Get off my back, Frances! (*He moves away, and she moves after him.*)

FRANCES. That's the only thing that's stopping you, isn't it? Isn't it?

HASTINGS. Damn it, stop hammering at my head about that! We made a deal. We're not going to talk about it. It's over.

FRANCES. If it's over, let it *be* over.

HASTINGS. (*Strides right and puts on his coat.*) You really want this, don't you, Frances? Why?

FRANCES. Not for myself. For you. It's a chance to make your life really *mean* something. (*Defeated, she sits on arm of chair.*) But we'll forget about it. I'll never mention it again. (*Hastings is touched by his wife's emotion. He's given her a ragged time, and he knows it. He snaps his fingers nervously, wishing that this decision had fallen to somebody else, anybody else. Then with a gambler's sudden air of recklessness, he goes to the door and opens it. Rafferty and Webster hurry in.*)

RAFFERTY. Well, Griff? What's the answer?

HASTINGS. I'm a poker player. You deal me a royal flush, at least I'm going to pick up the cards. (*This is a signal for jubilant action. Rafferty claps Hastings on the back, Webster pumps his hand. Frances is between the beds, silent, watching with stunned disbelief.*)

RAFFERTY. Great, Griff. Charlie, get on the phone!

WEBSTER. Congratulations, Senator! We'll shake up that convention.

(*Webster rushes to the phone, jiggling it impatiently. Rafferty paces, waving his hands, the general before the battle.*)

WEBSTER. Operator! Operator, find me the head sign painter at the Coliseum! I don't care if you have to get him out of bed. What the hell is that Philadelphia number?

RAFFERTY. Gotta get Doc and the Judge back here; dig up some public stenographers, and a platoon of bellboys.

(*Doc, Ax, and the Judge burst into the room, excitedly.*)

DOC. Walt, what the hell has happened?

WEBSTER. Plenty!

DOC. It's all over the hotel that Higgy made a deal.

RAFFERTY. Not with us. (*Tad enters, followed by Higgy.*)

TAD. Higgy's picked up enough votes to kill your chances dead, Charlie.

HIGGY. Charles, out of Christian charity, I've come back to offer your poor disappointed Governor the Vice-Presidency.

WEBSTER. That's very interesting, Higgy. You're just in time. (*To Hastings, who has been standing quietly.*) Senator, this is the Honorable James J. Higgins of New Jersey.

RAFFERTY. Higgy, I'd like you to shake hands with our party's nominee—and the next President of the United States: Griffith Pericles Hastings. (*Higgy glances toward Hastings with disbelief and pained indignation. The smart operator has just outsmarted himself. Hastings, with an air of genuine grandeur, extends his hand to the dumfounded Higgy. The lights fade. In the darkness we hear the tumult of voices echoing in the convention hall. Again and again the Gavel pounds.*)

CHAIRMAN'S VOICE. (*Booming.*) Illinois yields the floor to the delegation from the State of Massachusetts. (*There is a crest of excited reaction.*)

WEBSTER'S VOICE. The Great Commonwealth of Massachusetts wishes to change its vote and casts a unanimous ballot for the distinguished Senator from the Buckeye State—Griffith P. Hastings! (*The cheers are deafening. There is a wild, impromptu chorus of "Beautiful Ohio," which fades away into awed silence. Projections of Washington's Monument and the Capitol dome appear impressionistically on the cyclorama.*)

HASTINGS' VOICE. I do solemnly swear.

JUSTICE'S VOICE. That I will faithfully execute.

HASTINGS' VOICE. That I will faithfully execute.

JUDGE'S VOICE. The office of the President of the United States.

HASTINGS' VOICE. The office of the President of the United States.

JUDGE'S VOICE. And will, to the best of my ability—

HASTINGS' VOICE. And will, to the best of my ability—

JUDGE'S VOICE. Preserve, protect, and defend the Constitution of the United States.

HASTINGS' VOICE. Preserve, protect, and defend the Constitution of the United States.

JUSTICE'S VOICE. So help me God. (*Pause.*)

HASTINGS' VOICE. (*Softly.*) So help me God. (*The music strikes in with "Hail to the Chief," full at first, then fading to background.*)

ACT ONE
SCENE 2

The upstairs sitting room of the Presidential apartment in the White House. March 4 of the following year. It is midafternoon. In the distance, we still hear the military band playing "Hail to the Chief." There are several medium-sized packing cases on the floor. There are tall doors down right and left; the right ones lead to the corridors of the White House, the left ones to other rooms of the private suite. Near the door at right is a panel of buzzers. Cobb, the Chief Steward, enters from the right. He is dignified, graying, immaculately dressed. He has none of the mannerisms of a butler, more those of a diplomat. Frances follows him, wearing a long fur cape, a flowered hat, and carrying a muff. She is tremendously impressed, but is trying to conceal it. She moves to a chair, placing her hat and coat on the chair.)

COBB. This is the Executive Suite, Mrs. Hastings. I hope you'll find it comfortable. Your private rooms are through here. (*He indicates to the left, then calls off to the right.*) Don't let the van leave. Here are some more boxes to go.

FRANCES. These are *my* packages. The President's.

COBB. (*Crosses and presses one of the buttons on the panel.*) I'll have them opened immediately. (*A maid enters. Cobb indicates the boxes, which she starts to open. From off, there is a flurry of activity—voices and applause.*)

FRANCES. The President's coming. Hurry. May I call on you for anything we may need?

COBB. You can summon me, or anyone in the household, by using these buzzers.

FRANCES. (*Coming to sofa.*) Thank you. Will you tell all your people, please, that we have only one task, really. To make certain the President is comfortable here.

COBB. Yes, Mrs. Hastings. (*The Maid unwraps an ornate footstool.*)

FRANCES. (*To Cobb.*) Put it right here. (*She points in front of the chair.*) It's my husband's favorite stool. He loves to rest his feet on it. I made the petit point myself. (*Indicating the other boxes.*) I'll take care of those. (*The Maid exits. Cobb crosses to the right.*)

COBB. (*Calling offstage.*) Right in here, Mr. President. (*Hastings enters. He is wearing a swallowtail coat, striped pants, and he carries a silk top hat and a black topcoat. The ride up Pennsylvania Avenue, the brisk March air, the stimulus of the cheers and applause seem to have had an almost chemical effect on Hastings. His cheeks are glowing, his eyes brighter; he actually seems taller than before. Cobb nods, then goes out, to leave the new President and First Lady alone for the first time.*)

HASTINGS. (*Over his shoulder to Cobb, tardily, preoccupied.*) Oh, thank you. Thank you. (*Frances opens her mouth to speak, but stops, realizing that her husband is in a kind of baffled and wondering reverie. Slowly, he walks around the room. He looks at the Great Seal of the United States, embossed on the back of a chair. He touches it tentatively, as if it might break or vanish. Frances is silent, sensing that this is a thunderous moment in her husband's life. Hastings notices a colorful painted plate on a side table, picks it up, turns it over. He reads the inscription on the back, almost reverently.*) "To President and Mrs. A. Lincoln. From H.R.M. Victoria." (*He replaces the plate, hardly believing what he is saying.*) Frances, we're going to live here. Those people today, along the streets cheering, they want me, Frances. They really want me. I don't know why they voted for me. I wonder if *they* know. But I'm going to do a job for them. I'm not scared any more. I'm not even worried. Well, I'm a little worried. But it's going to be fine. Everything's going to be fine.

FRANCES. And your address was splendid, Mr. President.

HASTINGS. (*With a little laugh.*) When I was a Senator, it would have just been a speech. Now it's an address. (*He has crossed and embraced her.*) Damn, my feet hurt. During that parade I thought they were going to make me stand the whole four years. (*He sits on the couch and takes off one shoe. His eyes light on the footstool.*) Oh my God, Frances, look what they've got here. A monstrosity just like you knitted for me back home. (*Cobb enters in time to overhear this. Frances, embarrassed, moves upstage.*)

COBB. Mr. President, may I welcome you on behalf of the housekeeping staff. My name is Cobb. I'm the Chief Steward.

HASTINGS. (*Making the name stick.*) Cobb. C-o-b-b. I've met so many people today, I've been using an old politician's trick: when somebody tells you who he is, you write his name across his forehead. (*With a grin.*) Cobb, you might ask the people around here not to wash their faces for a few days. (*Hastings laughs. Cobb smiles, and picks up Hastings' hat and coat from the couch. Frances is unpacking the cartons.*)

COBB. Sir, a member of the interim office staff is standing by with a schedule for the rest of the day.

HASTINGS. (*Rubbing his foot.*) Fine. Fine. Send him in. Let's get it over with.

COBB. Yes, sir. (*Cobb goes out. Frances begins pacing, casting sidelong glances at her husband's shoeless foot.*)

FRANCES. Griffith, these people are really seeing you for the first time, aren't they? Later on, I think it would be nice if you "unbend" a little. But this first day is so important. Just remember who you are. That's all I ask.

HASTINGS. (*Writing on his own forehead.*) Look. "John Quincy Adams." (*Frances moves back and forth between the packing cases and the desk, where she puts various personal effects. Hastings massages his foot. But at the sound of a knock, he puts on his shoe and begins lacing it up.*) Come in. (*Bruce Bellingham enters. There is a quiet confidence about him. He is in his mid-thirties, good-looking, and wouldn't be caught dead wearing his Phi Beta Kappa key. Bellingham has several pages of typed memoranda and a telegram in his hand.*)

BELLINGHAM. Mrs. Hastings, Mr. President. May I submit today's calendar? And I knew you'd want to see this telegram at once.

HASTINGS. (*Taking the telegram.*) Now wait a minute. Who are you?

BELLINGHAM. I'm sorry. I should have introduced myself. My name is Bellingham.

HASTINGS. Bellingham.

BELLINGHAM. I'm part of the inter-administration liaison staff.

HASTINGS. Every four or eight years, you get four to eight days' work—that the idea? (*Bellingham nods. Hastings smiles.*) Not what I'd call a steady job.

BELLINGHAM. Just a short strip of adhesive tape between administrations. (*Both men laugh.*)

HASTINGS. (*Scanning the telegram.*) Damn!

FRANCES. Is anything wrong, Griffith?

HASTINGS. (*Folding the wire and stuffing it in his vest pocket.*) Nothing. (*To Bellingham.*) O.K. Roll out the schedule.

BELLINGHAM. Four-thirty—tea for the Inaugural party; Five-fifteen—reception for the Supreme Court Justices and the senior members of Congress; Six—reception for the Diplomatic Corps; Six-forty-five—international press representatives; Seven—greetings to the White House staff—that can be very brief; Seven-oh-five—leave for the Inauguration Banquet; Eight-twenty-five—dessert at the second Inauguration Banquet at the Willard.

HASTINGS. (*Wryly.*) Eight-forty-five—leave for Ford's Theatre.

FRANCES. (*Reaching for the paper.*) I'll handle the schedule.

HASTINGS. (*Taking the memorandum from her.*) Don't try to drive the flivver, Duchess. (*Offended, she moves to the boxes. To Bellingham.*) Just keep me headed in the right direction and I'll be there.

BELLINGHAM. Mr. Arthur Anderson has asked to see you as soon as possible, privately.

HASTINGS. Fine. Make it early next week.

BELLINGHAM. He's waiting outside, sir.

HASTINGS. Oh? I guess you'd better send him in.

BELLINGHAM. Yes, sir. (*Bellingham goes out. Hastings turns to Frances, worried. Frances crosses to the desk with more things.*)

HASTINGS. I figured Anderson was one Cabinet post we had all locked up. (*Knock.*) Come in. (*Anderson enters, carrying a brief case. He is proper, stiff, incapable of informality of any kinds. Brilliant without being witty, dignified without real warmth, even his good manners cannot wholly conceal his contempt for ineptitude.*)

ANDERSON. Mr. President, please forgive my intrusion.

HASTINGS. (*Crosses to shake hands with him.*) Glad to see you, Mr. Secretary. You know my wife?

ANDERSON. I have already had that honor.

HASTINGS. Sit down, Mr. Secretary.

ANDERSON. I'll be as brief as possible. (*He sits on the sofa.*) Sir, we are confronted with an urgent foreign policy decision. (*Frances starts removing the contents of the last box. She cannot avoid eavesdropping when such important matters are at stake.*)

HASTINGS. (*Sitting.*) You didn't waste much time getting your feet wet in the State Department mud puddle, did you?

ANDERSON. I came down right after the first of the year for a briefing. This morning, the American Ambassador in Tokyo was handed a communication which calls for an entirely new policy on the Mandated Islands.

HASTINGS. The Mandated Islands.

ANDERSON. Our treaty commitments do not make it clear whether an island under mandate is, in fact, under military protectorate.

HASTINGS. Yes. You know, in the Senate I was mainly concerned with domestic issues. Now let's cut this right down to the bone; what's the gist of the problem, as you see it?

ANDERSON. This new challenge makes it imperative that we issue an immediate and definitive declaration of the American position.

HASTINGS. Well, what do you think, Mr. Secretary?

ANDERSON. To me, a mandate is meaningless unless it is implemented. The issue is the extent of the implementation.

HASTINGS. If that's how you feel, I want you to know I'm one hundred per cent behind you. Go ahead and make a statement.

ANDERSON. Mr. President, the decision should be yours.

HASTINGS. (*Taking a deep breath, rising and moving to right center.*) Well, here's what we'll do. We'll get a committee to make a study of the whole picture.

ANDERSON. There have been two reports by previous bipartisan committees.

HASTINGS. Oh? What'd they say?

ANDERSON. The two committees were diametrically opposed. (*He removes the two hefty reports from his briefcase.*)

HASTINGS. Tell me, Mr. Anderson. Arthur. What's the *right* thing to do?

ANDERSON. My recommendations would, I am afraid, run directly counter to the promises made during the recent campaign. (*A pause.*)

HASTINGS. What would happen if we didn't do anything?

ANDERSON. I don't know, sir.

HASTINGS. Well, leave it with me. The basic stuff. I'll get back to you as soon as I can. (*Anderson hands him the two thick reports.*) Don't they have a digest, a condensation of these things?

ANDERSON. These *are* the condensations, Mr. President.

HASTINGS. (*Nods.*) Fine. Fine. Thank you.

ANDERSON. (*Starts out.*) I'll be waiting for your decision, sir.

HASTINGS. Good. Thank you. Fine.

ANDERSON. (*Nodding a good-bye.*) Mrs. Hastings. (*He goes out.*)

HASTINGS. (*Standing at his desk, troubled.*) I'm off to a great start.

FRANCES. (*Reasonably.*) Griffith, you can't be expected to be an authority on all these matters. So you have assistants who are knowledgeable. Like Mr. Anderson. Or anybody else you choose.

HASTINGS. If I can understand them.

FRANCES. At the newspaper, did you set all the type yourself? In the Senate, did you read every word in the Congressional Record? Of course you didn't. Nobody does. Griffith, a great many people are going to help you. We're all going to help you. (*Frances goes off with her coat and hat. The new President leafs through the reports, scowling. He is a painfully slow reader, and digesting a typewritten page is an agony for him.*)

BELLINGHAM. (*Re-enters with a sizeable stack of mail.*) Here's the important mail, sir. The wires and cablegrams are on top. We've screened out the purely congratulatory stuff.

HASTINGS. (*Takes the correspondence, glances at it, then transfers it to the desk, where an impressive mountain of reading matter is piling up.*) Thank you, thank you, Mr. Bellingham. I'll get right at it, as soon as— (*He looks at the schedule on desk.*) Tell me, where's this "Tea for the Inaugural Party"? It's past four-thirty.

BELLINGHAM. That's going on right now, in the East Room. (*Frances comes back in.*)

HASTINGS. Is that where the boys are? Down there with all that marble, drinking tea? Why don't we ask 'em up here?

BELLINGHAM. It's a party of several hundred people.

HASTINGS. Not everybody. Just a few close friends.

FRANCES. Don't you want a little rest, Griffith?

HASTINGS. Rest, hell. I want to see somebody I can talk to. (*To Bellingham.*) You know Senator Loomis? On sight?

BELLINGHAM. Yes, sir.

HASTINGS. Ask him to get some of the boys together—Walt, and Ax, and the Judge. Have 'em bring their teacups ups here. (*Bellingham nods and starts out.*) One other thing—

BELLINGHAM. Yes, Mr. President?

HASTINGS. Does "tea" mean . . . tea?

BELLINGHAM. Whatever refreshments are required can probably be made available.

HASTINGS. (*Measuring him.*) Maybe you ought to stay longer than four days. (*Abruptly.*) Just a minute. What does— (*He breaks off, digs the folded telegram out of his pocket and studies it.*) What exactly does "quid pro quo" mean?

BELLINGHAM. It means a horse trade, Mr. President. I scratch your back, you scratch mine.

HASTINGS. That's what I thought. (*Looking at wire.*) Why the hell doesn't he say that? You got any plans after this "interim" business?

BELLINGHAM. Well, I'm on a loan from the Commerce Department. I'm a consultant over there. It's Civil Service, purely nonpolitical.

HASTINGS. If I can make an arrangement with your boss, would you consider coming over here? Wouldn't be Civil Service, of course. (*Bellingham is too Washington-wise to turn handsprings at the suggestion of a Presidential appointment.*) Think about it.

BELLINGHAM. I will, sir. (*He goes out respectfully.*)

FRANCES. Liquor? Griffith, you're asking that young man to break the law. And *you* can't break the law—you're the President!

HASTINGS. I need a drink. And I think you could use one, too, Duchess.

FRANCES. Well, maybe I could. But as First Lady, I think I should abstain.

HASTINGS. Swell. You can abstain for both of us. (*He puzzles over the telegram.*)

FRANCES. (*Crossing toward him.*) You want to tell me who the telegram's from?

HASTINGS. Samuel Cavendish.

FRANCES. (*Above table.*) And he's turned down the Cabinet appointment.

HASTINGS. (*Hands her the telegram.*) No, damn it. He's accepted. How do you talk to a man who's worth eight hundred million dollars? What do I call him? "Sam"? I promised Treasury to Josh Loomis.

FRANCES. Well, just be glad you won't have anyone like Mr. Loomis in your Cabinet. (*She puts telegram on table.*)

HASTINGS. (*Irked.*) *Senator* Loomis.

FRANCES. Why don't you give a Cabinet post to that young man you've known nearly five minutes—Mr. Bellingham?

HASTINGS. What's wrong with him?

FRANCES. Perhaps nothing. But you don't know a thing about him. You've got to be more cautious now, Griffith.

HASTINGS. (*He gets up.*) I like him! I happen to like him! That's the way I work. That's the way I am. You're not going to change me now. (*Cobb enters with the tea wagon. There are two bottles of bourbon on the bottom shelf of the cart. Following Cobb and the tea cart.*) Medicinal?

COBB. *Bonded* medicinal.

FRANCES. (*Disapprovingly, she starts off.*) I'll be in here dressing, if you need me. (*She goes out, but Hastings doesn't realize she's gone.*)

HASTINGS. You don't have to stay, Cobb. This bunch knows how to get a cork out of a bottle. (*He chortles amiably.*)

COBB. Yes, Mr. President. (*Cobb leaves discreetly. Hastings pours himself a short drink and downs it, straight. Braced, he looks around the room, realizing for the first time that he is alone. He tries to fight off the feeling of fright at the pinnacle on which he finds himself.*)

HASTINGS. Frances? (*He crosses to the door. It is almost a moment of panic.*) Fellas? Where is everybody? (*He notices the whiskey bottle and glass where he left them on the desk. He crosses quickly, picks them up, and with the sleeve of his morning coat he wipes off the circle left by the moist glass. He stands, miserable, like an unwelcome guest in his own house.*) Frances???

LOOMIS' VOICE. (*From the hallway.*) I guess we're supposed to go right on in. (*With relief, Hastings crosses to greet Loomis, who enters, carrying a teacup in one hand.*)

HASTINGS. Josh!

LOOMIS. Now this is what I call a real special privilege. Congratulations, Mr. President. (*They shake hands warmly.*)

HASTINGS. Thanks, amigo. (*Rafferty, Webster, and Doc enter. They are subdued and impressed by the occasion and the surroundings. Hastings makes an extra effort to make them feel comfortable.*) Come on in, fellas. I've been waiting for you. (*There seems to be a new barrier of formality between the Gang and Hastings. Each waits for the President to speak first.*) Walt! Did you ever think we'd make it?

RAFFERTY. It's a great day, Mr. President.

HASTINGS. (*Claps Rafferty on the shoulder, then extends his hand to Doc and Webster.*) Charlie. Doc.

WEBSTER. Mr. President.

DOC. (*With an inclination of his head, almost as if to royalty.*) Mr. President. (*Judge Corriglione appears in the doorway, and stops, genuinely awed. Hastings calls to him.*)

HASTINGS. Come on in, Judge. Pull up a bench.

JUDGE. (*Coming in.*) I hope we aren't imposing on you, Mr. President.

HASTINGS. Imposing! I invited you up here, didn't I? (*Addressing them all.*) Starting now, let's forget this "Mr. President" stuff. I've been "Griff" all these years, don't put any "Misters" between us, now. (*In the doorway, Hastings spots a short, bubbly little man whose face has the mobility of a clown's, and who darts about with almost annoying good spirits. This is Axel Maley. The President shouts a greeting to him.*) Ax! Join the party. But if you call me "Mr. President," I'll kick you right back into the middle of Ohio!

MALEY. (*Hesitates. Then he decides to take a chance and his face lights up.*) Hi ya, Prez. (*Everybody laughs.*)

HASTINGS. What do you think of the White House, Ax?

MALEY. It's got the Wilmont County Courthouse beat all hollow. And say, you even made the front page of your own newspaper. (*There is more laughter at this, and the stiffness begins to subside.*)

HASTINGS. (*Clapping him on the shoulder.*) Damn it, Ax, it's good to see you. I wasn't sure I could laugh in this suit of clothes! (*Crossing to the tea cart.*) Now. What'll you have?

WEBSTER. Tea, I suppose.

HASTINGS. (*Slyly, he pulls out two bottles from beneath the tea cart.*) I don't imagine anybody's interested in bourbon? (*There is hearty approval. Maley waltzes to the President's side, putting his teacup daintily on the cart.*)

MALEY. No sugar in mine, please! (*Everybody laughs. Hastings pours. Judge has not offered his teacup; Hastings smiles at him warmly.*)

HASTINGS. Come on, Judge. None of this gang is going to report you to the Bar Association.

JUDGE. (*Crossing.*) Well, all right. A short one. Thank you, Mr. President.

MALEY. (*Lifting his cup.*) Gentlemen. To them as is in and them as is out. Especially us as is in. (*Everybody laughs and starts to toast. But Rafferty stops them.*)

RAFFERTY. No. Wait a minute. (*He looks around the room at each face with that sense of drama he used so well in the smoke-filled room.*) I want to propose a toast. To the only man in this room. (*Facing Hastings.*) Because all of us here are just extensions of you, Griff. Extra eyes, extra minds, extra hands. Any time you need us in the next four years—

WEBSTER. Eight years, Walt! Eight! (*The others affirm this.*)

RAFFERTY. Any time in the bright and glorious years ahead— (*Rafferty moves deliberately to the panel of buzzers.*) Whenever you need any of us, we'll be a finger tip away. (*Indicating the buzzers, as if each were marked.*) Doc. Charlie. Josh. The Judge. Axel Maley, Esquire. (*Pointing to the bottom button.*) Your humble servant, Walter Rafferty. (*He lifts his cup in a toast.*) Gentlemen. The President of the United States.

GANG. The President. (*They drink. It is a solemn moment.*)

HASTINGS. (*Moved.*) Thank you, boys. I didn't expect to feel this good today. I don't know whether it's the words or the schnapps! (*Frances enters in her Inauguration gown.*)

RAFFERTY. Why, Frances, what a beautiful gown. (*They all turn to look at her.*)

HASTINGS. Look what can happen to a country editor these days: winds up married to the First Lady.

FRANCES. (*A little embarrassed at the attention.*) I'm glad you like it.

HASTINGS. I'd better like it. For what that cost, we could've bought a used linotype machine! You'll wear it once and they'll stick it in the Smithsonian. Sit down, fellas, sit down. (*They begin to make themselves more comfortable. Loomis settles easily on to the sofa. Maley has taken a bottle from the tea cart and is ready to pour refills.*)

MALEY. What are you worried about money for, Prez? (*He indicates Loomis with his cup.*) Just have your Secretary of the Treasury here print you up a bushel-basketful of thousand-dollar bills. (*Everybody chuckles at this, except Hastings.*)

HASTINGS. (*Pained.*) Josh, a hell of a thing has happened. I feel terrible about it.

RAFFERTY. What?

HASTINGS. (*Turns to his Campaign Manager with irritation.*) I thought we had these Cabinet appointments all nailed down. And Josh was supposed to be my Secretary of Treasury.

RAFFERTY. (*Blandly.*) That's right. As soon as your Senate buddies say O.K.

HASTINGS. Well, look at this wire. (*Handing him the telegram.*) Cavendish accepted. You told me this was just a gesture because he plunked a hundred thousand into the campaign kitty. Do you expect me to pitch an old friend like Josh in the ash can, just to pay off a campaign debt?

RAFFERTY. (*He is thoughtful.*) Let me see that Cabinet list.

HASTINGS. Here. (*He fishes a sheet of paper from an inside pocket, then turns to Loomis.*) I don't know what to say, Josh. I'm embarrassed.

LOOMIS. (*Getting up.*) Naturally I'm disappointed, amigo, but Cavendish is one of the smartest men in the country. He'd have to be to pile up all that money.

HASTINGS. How'm I going to do this job with a bunch of walking bankbooks and carnation-wearing diplomats?

FRANCES. You promised to surround yourself with the best minds.

HASTINGS. Aren't there any good minds who also know how to speak Ohio? My friends happen to be worthy and bright. Am I supposed to say: "Thank you, goodbye, go home"?

RAFFERTY. None of us did what we did because we expected anything out of it.

HASTINGS. I want the Cabinet *I* want. Not what somebody things would look good in a history book.

RAFFERTY. (*Drawing out a pencil.*) Well, maybe we can do a little juggling.

FRANCES. Griffith, why don't you save these decisions for a regular business day when there aren't so many pressures? Now I think we should excuse ourselves. There's an Inaugural Ball—two of them, in fact. (*Rafferty scribbles something on the list and hands it back to Hastings.*)

HASTINGS. Can we make this change?

RAFFERTY. (*Nods.*) I'll fix it so there aren't any ruffled feelings.

HASTINGS. (*Enthusiastically.*) Now you're talking. Everybody, meet my Secretary of the Interior! What about it, Josh?

LOOMIS. (*With a modest laugh.*) What can I do? I've been drafted.

VOICES. Congratulations, Mr. Secretary. Good luck, Josh. Take good care of Interior.

HASTINGS. Hell, we'll get all the good poker players away from the Senate. (*Crossing to Rafferty.*) Better watch out, Walt, we'll take all your money.

RAFFERTY. I'm out of the picture. Tomorrow morning I'll be on a train to Columbus.

HASTINGS. (*Shocked.*) What's that?

RAFFERTY. I'm going back home. I've got a law practice.

HASTINGS. But you're my Postmaster General.

RAFFERTY. What do I know about stamps? I'm a lawyer.

HASTINGS. I thought it was all settled.

RAFFERTY. I said I'd consider it. I didn't say I'd accept it.

HASTINGS. You just told me that any time I needed you—

RAFFERTY. Pick up a phone. I can be here overnight. The trains are still running.

HASTINGS. (*Pleading.*) You can't leave me, Walt.

RAFFERTY. A hundred other guys are better qualified for Postmaster General.

HASTINGS. You've got to stay right here in Washington.

RAFFERTY. Doing what?

HASTINGS. (*Fishes into his pocket for the Cabinet list and examines it again.*) We're not really committed on the Justice Department, are we?

RAFFERTY. No.

HASTINGS. That's where I want you, Walt. As my Attorney General.

RAFFERTY. That's a tremendous responsibility, Griff.

HASTINGS. You can handle it. My God, you did a brilliant job on the campaign. You've got to stay. I need you. (*Pause. Everything is going precisely as engineered, but Rafferty and his Cohorts are playing it with skillful innocence.*)

RAFFERTY. Well, I'm a poker player, too. I'll play whatever cards you deal me.

HASTINGS. (*Shakes Rafferty's hand warmly.*) Thank you, Walt. (*Pacing up and down.*) Well, it's not gonna be so lonesome around here, Duchess. Say, what about Charlie?

WEBSTER. (*Hastily.*) Oh, Walt's already suggested me for a little job at the Veterans' Bureau. I'll just be off in a corner some place, doing my job.

HASTINGS. (*Crossing to Maley in front of sofa.*) And we're not going to leave the Honorable Axel Maley out in the cold, are we?

MALEY. Don't worry, Prez. As long as Walt's got a warm office, *I* won't freeze. (*Bellingham enters, carrying brief case. He pauses at the door.*)

BELLINGHAM. Excuse me, Mr. President, the Supreme Court Justices are beginning to arrive.

DOC. Any Supreme Court Justices in here?

MALEY. Dog-gone, I forgot my robes!

HASTINGS. (*Goes quickly behind the desk.*) Just a minute, I want to make some changes in this Cabinet list. (*Glancing up.*) Say, I want you boys all to meet Mr. Bellingham. He may be working with us. Ax, pour him a little orange pekoe.

MALEY. Tea, Mr. Bellingham?

BELLINGHAM. Thank you.

MALEY. (*Crossing to the tea cart.*) You do? Around here, if you really want tea, you'd better ask for bourbon.

HASTINGS. (*Has been searching the drawers of the desk, looking for a pencil. Suddenly he stops. Soberly.*) Say, look what I found. (*He holds up a half-empty bottle of ink-like medicine.*) I guess it belongs to my honorable predecessor.

BELLINGHAM. (*Crosses to Hastings.*) I'll see that it's forwarded to him.

HASTINGS. (*He is still studying the bottle.*) I knew the man was sick, but when I sat beside him in that limousine, all the way down Pennsylvania Avenue—God that was a long trip!—he didn't say a word. It was like riding in a hearse beside the body. (*He unscrews the cap and tastes the medicine from his finger tip. It's bitter.*) Is this stuff "President Juice"? The poor bastard.

COBB. (*Enters.*) Excuse me, Mr. President, the Supreme Court Justices are all here.

RAFFERTY. Come on, boys, we'd better go. (*The Gang moves to leave, but Hastings speaks quickly to stop them.*)

HASTINGS. Wait a minute. This is the first time I'm really going out there on my own. Not just waving, I mean, or reading off a paper. The parade's over. Now I've got to start waiting on the customers. (*Simply.*) If any of you say prayers, or have friends who know how to say prayers, ask them to mention me a couple of times, just in passing. I'll be grateful.

RAFFERTY. Sure, Griff.

JUDGE. (*Genuinely.*) I'll light a candle for you, Mr. President.

HASTINGS. Thanks, Judge, I'll need it. (*He is the bluff "good fellow" again.*) See? Nothing to worry about. Not a damn thing to worry about. Because I've got my friends with me! Thanks for coming, boys. Remember, the key's always under the front mat. Of course, there may be a dozen Secret Service men standing on it. (*Laughing, Doc, Loomis, Webster, Corriglione, and Rafferty go out. Maley steps to the doorway.*)

MALEY. (*Winking at the President, as he leaves.*) Say, if you ever get a parking ticket in this town, I know the Chief of Police. See you, Prez. (*The President chuckles as Maley leaves.*)

BELLINGHAM. Excuse me, sir, but we can't get too far behind schedule.

HASTINGS. (*Crossing crisply to the desk.*) Mr. Bellingham, I want to announce a couple more cabinet appointments. Today.

FRANCES. (*Concerned.*) Griffith, I'd like to talk to you before you do anything.

HASTINGS. What's the protocol? Can I release them straight to the press, or does the Senate want the news ahead of the newspapers?

BELLINGHAM. The releases can be concurrent.

HASTINGS. Fine. I've persuaded Walt Rafferty to accept the Attorney Generalship. And Senator Loomis will head up the Department of Interior.

FRANCES. Mr. Bellingham, the President will send you a written memorandum when and if he decides who his Cabinet is going to consist of.

HASTINGS. Frances, I don't know what language you speak. But I just said, in English, that Walt Rafferty and Josh Loomis are going to be in my Cabinet. You're not the whole damned Senate, you don't have to pass on them. For the sweet love of God, will you try to be on my side? (*Bellingham is embarrassed. Hastings softens.*) Duchess, we've got to spend four years in this place. Together. Let's try to put on a decent show for the people.

FRANCES. (*Going to the window.*) Whatever you say, Griffith.

BELLINGHAM. (*Clearing his throat.*) Is that all, Mr. President?

HASTINGS. Just see to it the new Cabinet nominations are in the papers tonight.

BELLINGHAM. (*Picking up his brief case.*) I'll send out the press release immediately, and prepare the necessary papers to go up to the Hill.

HASTINGS. Good. Thank you.

BELLINGHAM. Any further details can be handled by my successor.

HASTINGS. Your successor! I want you to stay. (*There is a pause. Bellingham wets his lips, and looks squarely at Hastings.*)

BELLINGHAM. I'm sorry, sir. I can't.

HASTINGS. Why not? Don't you approve of my friends? (*Confronting him.*) O.K., they're not Princeton professors. But they're good guys. You'll get on with them. Or maybe you're on the other side of the political fence.

BELLINGHAM. I voted for you, sir. I live over in Arlington, where they let people vote.

HASTINGS. Then you're going to stay.

BELLINGHAM. (*With polite evasion.*) The Justices are waiting for you, Mr. President.

HASTINGS. (*Angrily.*) O.K., Mr. Interim! You can strap up your fancy brief case and leave any time you want to. I don't know anything about you anyhow. Hell, there's ten thousand like you in Washington.

BELLINGHAM. Yes, sir. (*He starts out.*)

HASTINGS. Bellingham. (*Bellingham turns. Hastings studies him. He wants this man. He respects him, and needs him. It will be a major personal victory if he can persuade Bellingham to stay. Slowly.*) Take your pick. You can go back to the Commerce Department and write memos nobody reads. Or you can stay here, and help me do a job. Help me *try* to do a job. (*Bellingham is wavering. Rafferty comes into the room.*)

RAFFERTY. Hey, I've got nine beards down in the Oval Room. They're getting a little restless! (*Rafferty looks from the President to Bellingham. The younger man stares at the old political hand, whose cocksure attitude says: "I own the White House."*)

BELLINGHAM. I'll stay, Mr. President.

HASTINGS. Good! (*Hastings crosses to Bellingham.*) Say, what's your first name?

BELLINGHAM. Bruce.

HASTINGS. (*Between them.*) Bruce, shake hands with Walt. You're on the same team! (*Bellingham and Rafferty look at each other. They do not shake hands. Hastings goes back to the desk and picks up Anderson's heavy digests. He crosses back to the two men. Rafferty reaches out his hand to take the books, but the President gives them to Bellingham.*) Say, will you read through these things and tell me what to do? (*Taking a deep breath, the President offers his arm to Frances and they start out, Frances looking back at the silent duel in the room behind her. Rafferty and Bellingham stand facing each other, not moving. The air between them has a warmth approaching Absolute Zero as the lights narrow on them.*)

(*In the black.*)

INTERVIEWER'S VOICE. Mrs. Hastings, our readers want to know what it really feels like to be the President's wife. (*Projection: White House.*)

FRANCES' VOICE. Well, the White House is just one of millions of American homes. Our home life isn't too different from the average, normal husband and wife . . . (*Projection: Frances & Hastings, glaring at each other.*)

INTERVIEWER'S VOICE. Do you very often give advice to your husband?

FRANCES' VOICE. Well . . . now and then. (*Projection: Frances arguing with Hastings.*) Since women have the vote now, I like to think that they chose me as First Lady just as Griffith was elected President. (*With a modest little laugh.*) By a landslide. . . .

INTERVIEWER'S VOICE. And what a landslide that was! On important decisions, Mrs. Hastings, do you think the President is influenced by what you tell him? (*Projection: Hastings head down, hands clamped over his ears.*)

FRANCES' VOICE. I think he tries to get the best advice he can. But his decisions are his own. He's the Captain of the ship. That's the President's job, isn't it?! (*Projections: Throughout Frances' speech, a succession of cuts of Hastings, conferring with Bellingham, Rafferty, Anderson. He is increasingly confused.*)

INTERVIEWER'S VOICE. Are you getting used to our Washington summers?

FRANCES' VOICE. Oh, the President loves the heat. (*Projection: Hastings collapsed in chair with fan, armpits of his shirt sopped with sweat.*) And he thrives on his work. (*Projections: [1] Hastings shaking hands with top-hatted dignitaries. [2] Hastings seated, wearing Indian headdress and with a midget on his lap.*)

INTERVIEWER'S VOICE. And what do you and President Hastings do together when you have a night off at the White House? (*Projection: Frances standing alone by mantel, thinking.*)

FRANCES' VOICE. Together? Oh, I suppose the President does pretty much what any American husband usually does when he has a night off. . . . (*Black. Laughter from poker players. Lights up on Poker Party.*)

ACT ONE
SCENE 3

The basement of a house on L Street in Washington. Six months later. This is a poker-game room, which is mostly below ground level of a rather musty old Victorian house. Through the dormer windows, high in the room, we see the looming presence of the Capitol dome, ablaze with light. At the upper right, descending directly toward the audience, is a staircase, which is outside the room itself. At the foot of the stairs is the only entrance to the room—a heavily bolted door. It is after midnight on a mild September night. There is a large circular poker table down center, with appropriate green felt. An overhead fixture casts a tight circle of light around the players. Down right is a side table loaded with glasses, ice buckets, mixers, and fifths of bourbon, Scotch, and rye. Down left is an overstuffed chair. The Judge is sitting on the arm, away from the poker party, leafing through a blue-backed legal document. His place at the table is vacant. At back, in the shadows, is a scarred upright piano. Five men sit around the table, intent on their cards. The players are Rafferty, Maley, Webster, Doc, and Loomis. All are in shirt sleeves except Doc, who wears a brigadier general's uniform. They are deep in the end-game of a hand of draw poker.

LOOMIS. (*Shoving forward a stack of chips.*) Ten and raise you ten.

WEBSTER. Ten and ten better.

LOOMIS. What if Griff doesn't come tonight?

RAFFERTY. He'll be here. (*Doc looks at his cards with disgust and tosses them down. He rises from the table and crosses toward the liquor.*)

MALEY. Why don't you take off your coat, Doc?

DOC. It's against Army regulations.

LOOMIS. That's for colonels on down, boy. Show me where it says in the manual that a brigadier general can't play poker in his shirt sleeves.

MALEY. He's just jealous, Doc, 'cause they didn't give him no uniform over at Interior. (*Smirking.*) But I'll tell you who really got gypped! Poor old Walt! All those policemen under him, and the whole FBI, and they don't even give him a *badge*!

RAFFERTY. Play cards, Ax.

MALEY. Oh, sure, sure. I stay. I always stay. (*Rafferty glances thoughtfully toward Corriglione, then turns his attention back to his own cards. Loomis and Rafferty measure each other across the table.*)

WEBSTER. (*Laying down his cards.*) Two pair, ten high.

RAFFERTY. Three jacks. (*He takes in the pot.*)

WEBSTER. Do you realize that's a week's salary for the head of the Veterans' Bureau?

LOOMIS. I ache for you, boy.

RAFFERTY. Shall we deal you in this time, Judge?

JUDGE. Not yet.

RAFFERTY. Speed it up, will you? We want that ready for Griff to sign when he gets here.

LOOMIS. How about you, Doc? You in? (*Doc nods affirmatively.*)

MALEY. If I was the President's personal physician, like certain people in this room, I'd prescribe him a few hands of draw every night.

DOC. Same prescription I give myself. Not my fault if he won't take the medicine.

LOOMIS. I'll tell you what's wrong with Griff: he's got a severe case of Frances Greeley Hastings. (*Shaking his head.*) With half the country female—and some of 'em even pretty—he had to marry the Duchess!

RAFFERTY. What makes you an authority on marriage?

LOOMIS. Being a bachelor, I know everything about it. A fella on a river bank has a better seat for a drowning than a guy out there in the water going under.

DOC. (*Snorts.*) Washington is full of great men, and the women they married when they were very young. (*He sits at the poker table.*)

LOOMIS. Anybody got jacks or better?

WEBSTER. I'll open. (*He tosses in a chip. All stay.*)

LOOMIS. Cards, gents?

MALEY. I got a great hand here. But if nobody minds, I'd like four new cards. (*Loomis deals four cards to Maley, who lets out a gurgle of delight as he picks up each one.*) Oh! Well! How about this! My, my, my! (*He tosses in his cards.*) I'm out! (*Rafferty and Webster have also taken cards. Now Rafferty cuts the deck, but holds the second half of it in mid-air as he sees the Judge coming toward the table. All attention turns to the Judge.*)

JUDGE. (*Tossing the legal document onto the table in front of Rafferty.*) I never saw that. I didn't read it. (*He steps away.*)

RAFFERTY. All right. You didn't read it. What do you think of it. (*Pause. Corriglione doesn't answer.*)

LOOMIS. Is it legal?

JUDGE. If you can get the President to sign it, it's legal. Declare war, and murder is legal. (*Corriglione puts his hand on Rafferty's shoulder.*) Walt. Why don't you hold up a bank? A nice, clean, straightforward felony, with a gun in your hand.

RAFFERTY. Is that humor, Your Honor?

JUDGE. I've gone along on a lot of things, you know that. But this one scares me.

RAFFERTY. Why?

JUDGE. How can you justify signing these oil reserves over to Interior?

RAFFERTY. Who's going to ask a question like that?

JUDGE. A grand jury. A Congressional Committee. Anybody who suspects malfeasance.

RAFFERTY. There isn't going to be any malfeasance.

JUDGE. Then what do you want this executive order for?

RAFFERTY. What do you care, Judge? You never read it.

JUDGE. Why do you keep asking me to these parties? (*He turns to get his hat and brief case.*)

DOC. You're a helluva poker player.

LOOMIS. Sit down, Corriglione. We'll deal you in.

JUDGE. No. Thank you, no. (*He crosses to the door.*) I haven't got the guts to play that kind of poker. (*Judge Corriglione unbolts the door and leaves the room without another word. We see him climbing up the stairs to the ground level, his shoulders slumped. Rafferty crosses to the door and passes the heavy bolt again, locking it. As Maley deals, Loomis picks up the legal document and weighs it in his hand.*)

LOOMIS. What if the President asks our friend Mr. Bruce Bellingham to boil this down into three pungent paragraphs?

RAFFERTY. Bellingham won't see it. Because you'll get it back from Griff tonight. Signed. (*Returns to his chair and sits.*)

WEBSTER. Why does Griff keep Bellingham in the top drawer?

RAFFERTY. He reads. He's a pair of glasses. Don't worry, Charlie. Nobody in politics stands still. Any day now you'll find Mr. Bellingham in the waste basket.

MALEY. There's them as is in, and them as is out.

RAFFERTY. Axel, tell our friends what you found out about Mr. Bruce Bellingham.

MALEY. (*Beaming.*) A big fat fascinating nothing.

DOC. What good is that?

MALEY. For eighteen months he was some place; and *nobody*—but nobody—knows where.

LOOMIS. You think he was in prison?

RAFFERTY. We'll find out.

WEBSTER. Griff ought to know about this.

RAFFERTY. When you draw an ace, Charlie, you don't stick it in your hatband. (*Throwing in his cards.*) I'm out. (*He gets up and walks over to the piano.*) We having any entertainment for Griff tonight?

MALEY. The La Reve Sisters are coming over.

DOC. Who're *they*?

MALEY. It's a dancing and singing act. They dance, mostly. I got 'em from that club on K Street where they serve very old ginger ale. (*Intermittently Rafferty pokes one finger at the piano, thinking. Webster and Loomis compare hands. Loomis takes in the pot.*)

WEBSTER. Whatever happened to that girl Griff used to see all the time in New York, when he was a Senator?

MALEY. Claire Jones?

LOOMIS. She was a pretty one. Too bad he had to give her up.

DOC. Bedfellows make strange politics.

MALEY. How about something fancy this time? Spit in the ocean? Or deuces, treys, and one-eyed queens wild? (*All look at him dourly.*) O.K., straight draw. (*Hastings appears at the top of the stairs and starts to descend. His hat brim is turned down over his face, and he has turned up the collar of his topcoat to help conceal his identity. Hastings knocks. The Players look at each other questioningly. Maley springs to the door, and speaks through it, with his hand on the bolt.*)

MALEY. Who is it?

HASTINGS. (*Through the door.*) Mr. John Smith. (*They all know who "Mr. John Smith" is, and they spring up, pushing back their chairs as Maley unlocks the door eagerly, and swings it open. Rafferty strikes a welcoming chord on the piano. Doc goes to the bar. Hastings enters, takes off his hat and tosses it across the room into the easy chair.*) I'm home! (*Rafferty helps him off with his coat, and we get a good look at the President. This is not quite the same man we saw before. The hair is a touch whiter, the face creased with a few more lines of responsibility, but he seems to be riding now on nervous energy. The members of the Gang, although still showing deference for his office, seem much more cozy with him than they were six months before. There is a warm interchange of greetings. Rafferty takes Hastings' coat and hat, putting them atop the piano.*)

MALEY. We're very glad you could come, Mr. Smith! Everything's ready, Mr. Smith.

HASTINGS. (*Crosses to the green felt table and touches it affectionately.*) Out of the mausoleum and back to the green pastures! Hi ya, Doc, Josh, Charlie.

RAFFERTY. Charlie, crack out a fresh pack for the head man.

LOOMIS. We've been missing you, amigo.

HASTINGS. Do you know how many times I've wanted to come to these shindigs? But every fifteen minutes something comes up that makes it impossible for the country to stay in business! (*He sits. Doc has been fixing a stiff highball for the President; he hands it to him.*) I'd better not. There's tomorrow morning. (*He waves it away. But Doc insists.*)

DOC. This is a prescription. A gargle. But swallow it.

HASTINGS. (*He smiles, then shrugs.*) Doctor's orders! (*They all drink with him.*)

WEBSTER. Now that Mr. Smith is here, we've crossed over to the good stuff.

MALEY. I got this in New York from a very distinguished bootlegger.

HASTINGS. While you fellas have been taking each other's money, I've been closed for three-and-a-half hours with Arthur Anderson, the British Ambassador, and twenty State Department ginks who have sitting muscles made out of cast iron. I got Arthur Anderson in the men's room so he could tell me what it was all about, and he got me so confused I forgot to go the toilet! (*They all laugh. Maley goes to the bar for a bottle, which he brings back to the table.*) I suppose some place there's a book that gives you the facts on all this stuff. But who's got time to read a book? Hell, I shouldn't bellyache about it. (*Getting up.*) Let's play poker! (*He gets up and goes to the head of the poker table.*)

WEBSTER. (*Handing Hastings an unopened pack of cards.*) Never been touched by human hands.

HASTINGS. Why, thank you, Charlie. How've you been? Taking good care of the veterans?

WEBSTER. Doing my best.

HASTINGS. Taking good care of Charlie?

WEBSTER. Haven't won a hand yet tonight.

HASTINGS. Well, the sucker just got here and the evening's young! Who's the banker?

RAFFERTY. What do you need?

HASTINGS. Oh, five hundred for a starter. (*Maley has "freshened" the President's drink with about four fingers of straight bourbon and placed the glass in front of him on the poker table. Anticipating the game, Hastings sips from it, not realizing it is a new drink.*)

MALEY. You ought to give 'em the slip more often, Prez.

HASTINGS. (*As he deals.*) It's a neat trick, shaking the Secret Service boys. With my hat brim turned down, and my coat collar turned up so nobody'll recognize me, every step of the way I feel like Mata Hari. (*He picks up his own hand and taps the cards emphatically on the table.*) Why? A butcher goes home at night, he forgets all about hindquarters of beef. And the next morning he's a better butcher. My barber doesn't spend the whole night shaving people. If he did, I'd have one less ear! (*All have picked up their hands, arranged their cards, and are studying them.*) Are we playing jacks or better? Who's got 'em? (*All pass until Rafferty.*)

RAFFERTY. (*Clears his throat.*) I'll open. (*He pushes in some chips. Everybody stays.*)

HASTINGS. Let's make this a respectable pot, boys. (*Putting in a stack.*) This is the first chance I've had to raise the Attorney General. (*Looks around the table at the others, who are taking their cue from Rafferty. The President feigns a Southern accent.*) Now don't let mah little ole blue chips get lonely! (*Everybody stays except Loomis, who moistens his lips, so that we sense he has four aces. He tosses in his cards.*)

LOOMIS. I'm out.

HASTINGS. Tough, Josh. Better luck next time.

LOOMIS. Sure.

RAFFERTY. I'll stay.

HASTINGS. Cards? (*He hands out draws.*) What the hell is there about a piece of pasteboard that *feels* so good in your fingers. (*With euphoria from every pore.*) You get around a table with people you like, and once in a while you get a hand you like, and it's almost something physical—like holding five beautiful women.

MALEY. Kee-ripes! He's got five queens! I'm getting out of here.

HASTINGS. (*Beaming at his hand.*) I'll play along with these. (*Reactions from all the Players: the President has a good hand.*)

RAFFERTY. (*Tossing in some chips.*) Into the pat hand.

HASTINGS. Bunch of hot shots here. O.K., sports. (*He raises considerably. He loves the quiet tension which hovers in the air around the table. Webster throws in his cards, glances at Rafferty with an expression which says, "I just threw away one helluva hand."*) Water too deep for you, Charlie?

MALEY. (*Throwing in his cards.*) I can't bluff this gang with a pair of sixes. (*He gets up and goes for the cigars.*)

DOC. (*Matching the bet.*) *I* can still swim.

RAFFERTY. (*Pushing in his chips.*) Call.

HASTINGS. (*Showing his cards.*) Ten high straight. (*Doc has a flush, but Rafferty's eyes tell him to throw it in. He does.*)

RAFFERTY. (*Showing his cards.*) Couple of more kings out of work.

HASTINGS. (*Chortles happily and pulls in the pot.*) Why can't I get this lucky in the market? Where'd you dig up those tips you gave me, Ax? You got a broker in the Kremlin?

RAFFERTY. (*Innocently.*) Yeah, Ax. We all got stung.

MALEY. I was a bull when I should have been a bear. (*He passes out cigars.*) Gentlemen, compliments of yesterday's Cuban Government. (*They all light their cigars. Doc shuffles the second deck.*)

HASTINGS. During the campaign, I had the cockeyed idea that Cabinet meetings would be like this: a box of cigars in the middle of the table; we'd read over the mail together; then we'd deal out who-does-what, have a drink or two, and call it a day. No such luck. Your deal, Charlie. (*Maley replaces the cigars, then trots back to Hastings' elbow and refills his glass. The President is now on his third highball, but apparently doesn't realize it, nor does he show any signs of intoxication. Hastings cuts, Webster deals, and everybody antes in.*)

LOOMIS. (*Taking the cards, clears his throat.*) Why don't we have a Cabinet meeting right now, for about fifteen seconds?

RAFFERTY. Hell, don't bother Griff with any business. Unless it's damned important.

LOOMIS. (*Reaches back into the pocket of his coat, which is draped over the chair behind him.*) You know I wouldn't do that, amigo. (*Fumbling.*) We've got a little foul-up over at Interior—you know, one of those blamed duplications, with everybody steppin' on everybody else's toes. (*Shrugs.*) There's just one way to clear up the whole thing. A little old executive order. (*He tosses the blue-backed legal document to Hastings, who scowls at it.*)

HASTINGS. Don't make me read anything.

LOOMIS. Well, I've been over it pretty careful. (*Hastings is browsing gloomily through the paper. Loomis affects a sudden change of heart, and tries to take back the document. Doc, embarrassed, rises quickly and crosses to the bar for a drink. Maley is pouring drinks at the table.*) I'm an ornery bastard, pestering you on your night out. Forget about it. (*Maley crosses to the bar. Rafferty stops the nervous Loomis from grabbing the paper.*)

RAFFERTY. I've read it. It's all right. Corriglione went over it, too.

HASTINGS. Oh? What did the Judge say?

RAFFERTY. It's legal. Read it if you want to. We'll wait for you. (*Rafferty uncaps pen and holds it for Hastings. Hastings laughs a little at this, then riffles to the last page and prepares to write his name. But something in the document seems to catch his eye, and he turns back to the preceding page. Each Watcher holds his breath. The President seems uneasy. He knows he shouldn't be signing a "blank check" in this cursory fashion. But he sees the poker hand, face down on the table. Then he looks across the table thoughtfully at Loomis.*)

HASTINGS. Josh. If you were President, and I asked you to sign this, would you do it?

LOOMIS. (*A moment's pause.*) I scarcely think I'd be inclined to question an old friend's judgement. (*A breath more of hesitation. Then Hastings quickly scrawls his name, and grins as he passes the paper back to the relieved Loomis. Maley returns to his seat at the table.*)

HASTINGS. At least this Administration accomplished something today.

RAFFERTY. I thought for a minute you were going to call in Cavendish for a consultation. (*There is the nervous laughter of relieved tension.*)

WEBSTER. I wonder if old Stone Face can play poker. (*Doc wanders back to his seat.*)

LOOMIS. Don't ask me to teach him.

MALEY. Whenever I play with millionaires, they always set a ten-cent limit.

HASTINGS. That's why they're millionaires. (*They all laugh. Hastings and the rest of the Gang are examining their cards. Higgy appears at the top of the outside staircase, and *seems even fatter as he waddles carefully down the narrow stairs. He knocks at the door. Maley and Rafferty exchange glances.*)

MALEY. The girls wasn't supposed to be here until one o'clock.

HASTINGS. Girls?

MALEY. (*Crosses to the door. His hand on the bolt, speaking through the door.*) Laverne, honey? (*Higgy doesn't answer.*) Renee? (*Again, a pause. Maley looks baffled. Hastings, who has been looking at his cards, suddenly pushes back his chair and rises.*)

HASTINGS. Hell, it's that cable from Downing Street.

RAFFERTY. Who knows you're here?

HASTINGS. Only Bruce. Let him in. (*As the door swings open, the bulbous Higgy enters.*)

HIGGY. Gentlemen. Good evening, Mr. President. (*Hastings is puzzled, but he assumes Higgins has been invited. The Players look at the New Jersey Politician as if he were Friday roast beef at a convent. Safely in the door, he looks around the room with malign good humor.*) How ya been? (*Loomis tucks the signed paper back in his coat pocket. Higgy plunks his hat on the bar and turns to Hastings.*) You remember me, Mr. President?

HASTINGS. Of course—New Jersey.

RAFFERTY. What are you doing out of Camden, Higgy?

HIGGY. I sent you a change-of-address card, Mr. Rafferty; maybe the Postmaster General isn't up to the level of the rest of the Cabinet.

HASTINGS. If you've come to play poker, play poker.

HIGGY. (*He floats.*) I'll just watch. (*Smoothly.*) It would represent a change of policy for this Administration to deal me in. (*Rafferty gives Higgy a disintegrating look. Higgy doesn't disintegrate. A little uncomfortably, the game proceeds; but Higgy, over their shoulders, glancing at several of the hands, is a source of irritation. The following conversation lies against a counterpoint of desultory betting. Doc opens. All stay. Webster deals the cards. Maley clutches his cards to his chest as Higgy peers over his shoulder.*)

DOC. (*Staring straight at Higgy's belt buckle.*) Rumor is rampant, Higgy, that you will not even be entered this year in the Atlantic City beauty contest.

HIGGY. I've left New Jersey. Y'see, I caught a little chill at the convention. And when I got home, even Asbury Park began to feel like Alaska.

MALEY. There's them as is in, and them as is out. (*Tossing in his cards.*) I'm out.

HIGGY. Oh, I'm not "out." I'm a District of Columbia citizen now. Nice place, isn't it? Although the summers *do* get warm. (*Studying Webster's cards thoughtfully as Webster bets.*) Now I wonder, Charles, if your hand is as strong as you think it is.

HASTINGS. Mr. Higgins, poker is the order of business; if you're not going to play, what can we do for you?

HIGGY. I was thinking maybe I could do something for you, sir, and for the boys here.

RAFFERTY. Such as?

HIGGY. In my new job as investigator for the Hearn Committee I'm being asked to do something that just pains me. Anybody got a light? (*Webster passes a lighter to*

Higgy without enthusiasm.) Thanks, Charles. (*Kindling his cigar.*) I wonder if you realize how interested Senator Hearn is in everything you gentlemen are doing. (*The Gang is very still.*)

HASTINGS. What about Senator Hearn?

HIGGY. Well, his subcommittee might bump into some very colorful information; and then again, it might not. (*Admiring the lighter as he gives it back to Webster.*) Hmmm, eighteen carets! Was this a gift from a grateful veteran?

HASTINGS. (*Irked.*) Mr. Higgins, we came here to play poker.

HIGGY. So did I. (*With piety.*) And all of us being dedicated to good, clean, honest government—

RAFFERTY. Griff, the Reverend Higgins is the gentleman who once offered to sell Jersey City to Manhattan for fifteen cents.

HASTINGS. What's he selling now?

HIGGY. Not a thing, Mr. President. I've just got a taxpayer's healthy curiosity about certain administrative departments. The Veterans' Bureau, for example.

WEBSTER. (*Rising irritably.*) Anything you want to know about the Veterans' Bureau, just come to me. My files are open at any time to any authorized agency, including the Hearn Committee.

HIGGY. Quit bluffing. I've seen your hand.

HASTINGS. (*Rising, indignantly, to Higgy.*) Get the hell out of here.

HIGGY. Mr. President, I thought I was doing the Administration a service by coming to you before I reported to Senator Hearn.

HASTINGS. If you mean to imply any reflection on my friends, I won't even dignify your insolence by asking for an apology!

HIGGY. O.K. O.K., sir. I came here because I feel sorry for these poor sons-of-bitches you call your friends. They're gonna get hung higher than the Washington Monument.

RAFFERTY. Go home, Higgy. Your mother's barking for you.

MALEY. (*A little nervously.*) Walt, maybe we shouldn't oughta—

RAFFERTY. Go home, Higgy! (*He holds the door open. Higgy resumes his insolent pleasantry.*)

HIGGY. (*In the doorway.*) You've got my phone number, Walter. (*Higgy lumbers up the stairs. Rafferty slams and bolts the door. There is a pause. Hastings has held his cards, waiting for the game to get started again. Now he throws down the hand violently, and the cards splatter.*)

HASTINGS. Damn it all! Where can I go? I try to get away from the yapping and the yelling and Frances trying to sweat me into a suit of silver armor. I want to play cards with my friends! (*He weaves unsteadily to the armchair and sits.*) And this cockroach comes crawling out of the woodwork. (*He kills off half the drink in his hand.*)

MALEY. (*Pointing to the chips.*) You're lucky tonight, Prez. Don't quit while you're winning.

RAFFERTY. Who could have told Higgins you were here?

HASTINGS. Nobody knows. I didn't tell anybody, except Bruce. He doesn't even know Higgins.

RAFFERTY. Doesn't he? (*The President is feeling his drinks now. Bellingham hurries down the outside stairs.*)

MALEY. Play cards, Prez. Don't think about anything. Not tonight. Play cards. (*Hastings doesn't react. Maley speaks with forced brightness.*) Say, did you hear the one about the Siamese twins on their honeymoon? And one of 'em turned to the other one and said— (*Bellingham knocks at the door. Nobody moves. The knock is repeated. Maley dances to the door.*)

MALEY. Girls?

BELLINGHAM. (*Through the door.*) It's Bellingham.

MALEY. Aw, nuts! (*He looks back into the room for instructions. The Poker Players are mute.*)

HASTINGS. Let him in. (*Maley passes the bolt and opens the door. Bellingham enters and crosses directly to the President. He takes an envelope from his pocket and offers it to Hastings, who stares at it.*)

BELLINGHAM. I brought this directly from the decoding room, Mr. President. It's from Downing Street. The Prime Minister still has a number of questions.

HASTINGS. The Prime Minister will have to wait until tomorrow.

BELLINGHAM. It's already "tomorrow" in London.

HASTINGS. Well, London can go on our time for a change. Tell 'em that, and tell me something. Did you ever meet a fat boy from New Jersey, named Higgins?

BELLINGHAM. Yes, sir.

HASTINGS. Did you tell him I was here tonight?

BELLINGHAM. I got the impression Mr. Higgins was an old friend, someone who knew all of you intimately.

LOOMIS. I know my dentist intimately. But I don't want to have my teeth drilled at a poker party.

BELLINGHAM. All right. I told Higgins.

HASTINGS. (*To Bellingham.*) When I tell you I'm going some place, I don't want to read about it in the *New York Times* before I get there.

BELLINGHAM. Mr. President, Higgins has been pestering me for weeks. At first, I didn't pay any attention to him—

DOC. Would somebody please explain to Mr. Bellingham that the most common bird in the political zoo is the goofus who was flying north when everybody else was flying south? When it finally dawns on this birdbrain that he's flapping in the wrong direction, he finds out all the good nests are gone. And what does he do then? Craps all over everything.

MALEY. Yeah. Politics is for the birds.

BELLINGHAM. Mr. Higgins is hinting at some pretty damaging things. Not about you, sir, but about some of the people in this room. (*Webster gets to his feet, indignantly.*)

RAFFERTY. He's lying.

BELLINGHAM. Then somebody'd better shut him up. But if he's telling the truth— (*Hastings crosses to the side table. He takes a fresh bottle of bourbon, and empties some of it into his glass. He then pours a drink for Bellingham.*)

HASTINGS. Ax. Right now would be a very good time for you to make a joke.

RAFFERTY. Griff, if you believe the blathering of that paranoic fat boy, you better get yourself another Attorney General.

HASTINGS. Sit down, Walt.

RAFFERTY. Put Mr. Bellingham in! He seems so hot on justice. We came down to Washington because you said you *had* to have us. You dragged us out of some pretty high-paying private practices. I don't know what Mr. Interim was dragged away from. And some of us are pretty curious, by the way.

HASTINGS. (*To Bellingham.*) Bruce, how many drinks have you had this evening?

BELLINGHAM. None.

HASTINGS. You've got some catching up to do. (*Hands Bellingham a glass.*) Haven't you heard about "All Work and No Play"? (*Starts away, then wheels back, angrily.*) Drink it! What do you want to be a troublemaker for? We're gonna play poker together. Whose deal is it? Give Bruce a hand! You're all gonna like him as soon as you start taking his money! (*The President starts to pick up his splattered cards. As he bends over to get some that have fallen to the floor, he seems to teeter on the edge of nausea.*) I don't feel exactly great, Doc. You got something in your little black bag you can give me?

DOC. I'm not sure—

HASTINGS. (*Grabbing Doc by the shoulder roughly and spinning him around.*) "You're not sure"! What the hell kind of doctor are you, Doc? You oughta see the stack of letters I've got on my desks from the A.M.A.! Every damned M.D. in the country is yelling bloody murder because the President's personal physician is a chiropractor! (*Softening quickly, clapping Doc on the shoulder like an old comrade at arms.*) I'll stick by ya. Don't you worry, Doc. I'll stick by ya. I'll stick by ya. (*During the above, Laverne, Renee, and the Piano Player come down the steps.*)

LOOMIS. Come on, amigo. We've got a nice deck of Bicycles all warmed up. (*Laverne knocks: three raps, then two.*)

MALEY. Here comes some medicine for ya, Prez. (*He scurries to the door.*) Laverne? Renee? (*The girls giggle. Hastings sinks into his chair at the poker table. Maley opens the door and ushers in the La Reve Sisters and the Piano Player. The girls are jazzy flappers. Laverne has a very sincere bustline and she's a talker. Renee is a shapely pair of legs surmounted by a sloe-eyed, vacuous face.*) Fellas, these are the La Reve Sisters.

LAVERNE. I'm Laverne.

RENEE. And I'm Renee.

LAVERNE. La Reve means "The Dream." It's French.

DOC. Piano player, let's have some music. (*Piano Player crosses to the piano, plays.*)

MALEY. Take off your coats, girls, and make yourself at home.

RAFFERTY. Let's turn off some of these lights. (*Webster switches off the main lights. The girls take off their coats and are bespangled and gartered.*)

MALEY. (*Leading Laverne by the arm toward Hastings.*) Girls, I want you to meet Mr. Smith. He's the guest of honor. (*The girls, who know exactly what is expected of them, push out a coy greeting.*)

LAVERNE. Pleased to meet you, Smitty.

RENEE. Ooooo, he's cute.

LAVERNE. Say! Did anybody ever tell you that you look almost exactly like—

RAFFERTY. Yeah. Everybody tells him. Don't they, Smitty?

RENEE. He *does* look exactly like—

MALEY. (*Puts his arm around Renee and pulls her aside.*) Shut up, honey. (*Aloud.*) Ain't they knockouts? Renee ain't got much upstairs, but what a staircase!

LAVERNE. (*To Hastings.*) You want to dance, big boy?

HASTINGS. (*His eyes on Bellingham, sensing his disapproval.*) Sure, sure! Why not?

LAVERNE. Say, you are cute. (*Hastings begins to dance awkwardly, still looking at Bellingham. Webster and Loomis move the poker table and clear the chairs. Over Hastings' shoulder, pointing to Doc.*) Renee, why don't you dance with that one? (*To Hastings.*) Renee's always had a "push" for soldier boys. (*Renee twirls among Doc, Rafferty and Maley. She chatters to Hastings as they dance.*) We call ourselves the La Reve Sisters, but we're not actually sisters. In this business, it's not blood that counts, it's talent. (*Bellingham crosses to the door, chagrinned by this demonstration. Hastings sees him leaving.*)

HASTINGS. (*Shouting.*) Hey! Hey, you! (*The President's raised voice stops Bellingham.*) Where do you think you're going, Mr. Bellingham? Don't you like the company? (*Bellingham looks away. The President bellows at him furiously.*) Look at me! (*The Piano Player stops playing. All other activity in the room freezes.*) What's the matter? You want me to act as if I'd already been stamped on a fifty-dollar bill?

LAVERNE. Just try to have a good time, honey.

HASTINGS. (*Pulling her up onto the poker table, using a chair as a step.*) I'll show you how to have a good time! (*He shouts.*) Music!! Loud music! (*Atop the poker table, Hastings and Laverne start to dance with violent energy. Bellingham watches, staring up at Hastings with a wondering dismay and pity. Hastings stops dancing and thunders down at him over the honky-tonk music.*) Stop looking at me like that. You hear me? I don't want you around. I don't want you around the White House! I don't want you around my life! Get out! Get out! (*Bellingham turns to leave, but a violent drunken gesture by Hastings makes Laverne lose her balance and fall from the table. She screams. Webster and Doc break her fall. Hastings looks around at his gang.*) Get out! (*The stage light falls away except for a single spot burning down on the stunned Hastings. The whimpering of Laverne is covered by:*

Loud, full military band, coda of: HAIL, HAIL, THE GANG'S ALL HERE.)

CURTAIN

ACT TWO

SCENE 1

On the scrim is a huge projection of the White House, the white columns looming like bars of a prison.

The music of happy Christmas tunes: "Jingle Bells," "Deck the Hall"; and a projection of the huge Christmas Tree on the White House lawn.

A single phone starts ringing insistently. Nobody answers it. Then a projection of an empty chair beneath the Presidential seal. Phones start ringing all over the White House, from varying perspectives. Over the loudspeakers we hear a White House Operator. The calls are punctuated by the buzzes and clicks of the incoming calls.

OPERATOR'S VOICE. White House. One moment. I'll connect you with the Security Chief. —White House. Mr. Bellingham is no longer here. He can be reached at the Senate Office Building. —White House. The Press Secretary is busy. Will you hold the line, please? —White House. I'm sorry, Senator. No calls are being put through to the President's office. All his appointments have been canceled for the day. Thank you, sir. —I can give you the Press Secretary now. Thank you for waiting. —White House. Yes, Long Distance? We've been unable to reach the President. Will you ask Mexico City to try Secretary Anderson at the State Department? National 2-100. —White House. Mrs. Hastings is out of the city for the Christmas holidays. She's expected back tomorrow. I'll give you the Appointment Secretary. —White House. One moment. I'll connect you. —White House. I'm sorry, Mr. Maley. The President still hasn't returned. I'll leave word how many times you've called. As soon as he comes in. (*The Voice and the buzzes begin to fade.*) White House. We are unable to reach the President. I'll report that you called, Mr. Secretary. (*The light on the scrim fades as it rises.*)

The sitting room of the Presidential apartment in the White House. It is early in January of the following year. The gloom of twilight makes the room seem more tired and cheerless than before. A Christmas tree rises in the corner and some impersonal Christmas decorations are hung around the room. Frances enters, wearing furs, and carrying an ample handbag, which she treats protectively. Cobb follows her in, carrying a traveling case. Frances goes behind the desk and pulls off her gloves with hurried impatience, as if there is a great deal for her to do. She calls toward the inner rooms.

FRANCES. Griffith?

COBB. The President isn't here, Mrs. Hastings.

FRANCES. Where is he?

COBB. I don't know, Madam. He left at seven-fifteen this morning. Alone. Except for the driver and the Secret Service people.

FRANCES. Where did he go?

COBB. The staff was not informed. He didn't expect you back until tomorrow.

FRANCES. (*Picking up the phone.*) Central, get Walter Rafferty for me. (*To Cobb.*) These decorations should be removed. The holiday season is over.

COBB. Yes, Mrs. Hastings.

FRANCES. As I came in, I noticed Mr. Bellingham downstairs.

COBB. He's been waiting all afternoon to see the President.

FRANCES. The President left instructions that he doesn't want to see Mr. Bellingham.

COBB. He was told that.

FRANCES. (*Into phone.*) Hello. Walter? Just a moment. (*Covering the mouthpiece.*) Mr. Cobb, tell Mr. Bellingham that in the President's absence I will see him. (*Cobb nods and goes out. Frances continues to talk into phone.*) Walter, I came back from Wilmont a day early. I have to see you immediately. It concerns your friend, Axel Maley. (*She draws some deposit slips out of her purse.*) While I was home, one of the officers of the Gibraltar Bank gave me some rather startling information. I can't tell you on the phone, Walter. It's something I've got to show you in person. (*Pause.*) No, I haven't told Griffith. Where is he, do you know? (*Knock.*) Just a moment. (*Calling.*) Will you wait, please? (*Into phone.*) Not here, not at the White House. All right, I'll meet you there as quickly as I can. (*She hangs up, then quickly puts the deposit slips back into her purse.*) Come in.

BELLINGHAM. (*Enters.*) Thank you for seeing me, Mrs. Hastings.

FRANCES. I'm afraid you're wasting your time. The President just won't see you.

BELLINGHAM. Then may I talk to you for a few minutes?

FRANCES. Why?

BELLINGHAM. I need your help.

FRANCES. In connection with your work for the Hearn Committee?

BELLINGHAM. I think Senator Hearn would fire me if he knew why I'm here.

FRANCES. (*Rising.*) Bruce, I don't know what happened between you and the President, or why he let you go. But I do know you've hurt him very much by going to work for a man who's trying to smear him.

BELLINGHAM. That's not what he wants to do, Mrs. Hastings. But he's accumulated some pretty terrifying facts about men close to the President. The President's got to know about them.

FRANCES. Is that why you're here?

BELLINGHAM. Somebody's got to tell him.

FRANCES. Does it occur to you that other people are looking after the President's welfare?

BELLINGHAM. Then please persuade him to listen to me.

FRANCES. I'll try. But later. Not today. I'll call you at your office. (*Picking up her purse from the desk.*) Now, if you'll excuse me, I have to leave for an appointment outside the White House. (*Resignedly Bruce crosses with Frances toward the door, but Hastings enters. He seems preoccupied, depressed.*)

HASTINGS. (*To Bellingham, with quiet bitterness.*) Get out.

BELLINGHAM. Mr. President.

HASTINGS. Just get out. (*He dumps his coat on a chair.*)

FRANCES. Bruce is my guest. He came here to see me.

HASTINGS. (*Turns to Frances.*) What are you doing back from Wilmont, Duchess? Couldn't you take the Greeleys, even with Christmas ribbons?

FRANCES. (*Pointedly.*) I haven't been at the Greeleys.

HASTINGS. Oh?

FRANCES. I've been trying to reach you all day, Griffith. Where have you been?

HASTINGS. Out at the Navy Hospital. (*He draws a bottle of medicine from his pocket. It is ink-like and remarkably similar to his predecessor's.*) If those doctors had any brains, they'd know this stuff isn't going to do any good.

FRANCES. You're not sick?

HASTINGS. President juice. That's all this is. The doctors are very disappointed in me. I'm all right. But don't let it out that I've been at the Navy Hospital all day. (*He sits on the sofa.*) The stock market'll go down eleven points. And we can't afford it.

FRANCES. You mustn't be sick, Griffith. Don't even joke about it. (*The phone rings. Frances picks it up.*) Hello? No, no. You've got to wait for me, Walter. I'm coming right now. (*She hangs up.*)

HASTINGS. What does Walt want?

FRANCES. We can talk about it later. (*She starts to go.*) Griffith, I think you should listen to Mr. Bellingham.

BELLINGHAM. Mr. President—

HASTINGS. I don't want to hear any more from you. Come back in a few years, Mr. Interim. You can help shoe in a new President.

BELLINGHAM. Give me five minutes. Then throw me out if you want to.

FRANCES. Please, Griffith.

HASTINGS. O.K. Five minutes. (*He takes out his watch and puts in on the desk.*)

FRANCES. I'll be back almost immediately.

BELLINGHAM. (*Waits for Frances to leave and then addresses Hastings with businesslike intensity.*) Mr. President, may I speak to you as if you were still an editor and I'm bringing you a news story?

HASTINGS. Go ahead.

BELLINGHAM. The day after I left my desk here, Senator Hearn offered me a job with his committee. I turned him down, because I knew all he wanted was to pick my brains. But I changed my mind. I took the job because I thought I could help you.

HASTINGS. How?

BELLINGHAM. Higgins wasn't bluffing. He *knows*!

HASTINGS. Knows what? *What* does he know!?

BELLINGHAM. My God, Mr. President, don't *you* know?

HASTINGS. You want to talk to me like a newspaperman? O.K.! But there's one thing I insist on as an editor. I want to know the *reliability* of the source. I wouldn't believe Higgy if he told me January first was New Year's Day!

BELLINGHAM. Then believe me.

HASTINGS. Who are you? For eighteen months, nobody knew where you were. Walt says you were in jail. Is that true? Do you want to tell me where you were?

BELLINGHAM. I'll tell you what I wasn't doing, Mr. President. I wasn't stealing a million dollars a month from the Veterans' Bureau. I didn't have my fingers up to the shoulders in bootleg graft, like your Department of so-called Justice!

HASTINGS. Answer my questions.

BELLINGHAM. All right. I'll tell you what I was doing, and I'm ashamed of it, because I was running away. (*He speaks quietly, his face turned away from the President.*) I joined an order.

HASTINGS. What?

BELLINGHAM. I was a novice, in a place way off in the mountains, where you give up your life; you even give up your name. I was "Brother Pacificus." I went there because I thought they could teach me some kind of faith. But faith isn't something you can learn; it's something that happens to you. (*Bellingham's tone becomes bitterly back-to-earth, as he tosses his brief case on the table.*) Back in Washington, at least I've been part of the human race. Not a very proud part. I think I'd rather be a jackal, or a self-respecting typhoid germ.

HASTINGS. Idealism was last year. They voted it out.

BELLINGHAM. It's not idealism to recognize a fact.

HASTINGS. Give me a fact.

BELLINGHAM. All right. (*Graphically, gesturing around the room.*) This is the Veterans' Hospital outside Louisville, Kentucky, a site chosen by the Honorable Charles Webster because of its proximity to that great American institution, the Kentucky Derby. (*Drawing a door in the air with his forefingers.*) Through this door come in the bed sheets and blankets and bandages for the somewhat bent tin soldiers who didn't duck quite quickly enough. Let's just look at the bed sheets. Here they come, clean and cool and fresh, and God, how they're needed! But Mr. Webster's inspector—carefully schooled in what he's expected to do—opens up a package of two hundred, looks at the top sheet— (*Bellingham pantomimes examining a sheet, finding something wrong with it.*) "Oh! Oh! This sheet is torn! Can't allow our boys to sleep on defective merchandise! Condemn the whole carload!" Mind you, that sheet really *was* torn, the *top* sheet! But the other hundred and ninety-nine in every batch were the best bed sheets money could buy, and the government paid for them, two dollars and ten cents apiece. But thirty cents a sheet is the *most* you can expect to get for "Condemned Merchandise." And who just *happens* to buy them at a fraction of cost? The original manufacturer! (*With an expansive gesture of mockery.*) He's delighted! He can shut off his power, lay off his help, and keep sending the same carload back to the same Veterans' Hospital so that the same inspector can mark down the same bed sheets and keep carting them back to him. Perpetual motion! And every time around, the government pays the full price for every sheet!—while the aching bastards in the wards sleep on bare mattresses and bed springs. Naturally, this manufacturer is making enough profit to afford a few Christmas presents. And in Mr. Webster's office, it's Christmas almost every week!

HASTINGS. I don't believe it.

BELLINGHAM. (*Confronting him.*) Senator Hearn does. Because he has a locked file containing invoices, bills of lading, swatches from marked sheets that the government has bought as many as twenty-five times, and sworn affidavits from three inspectors who got scared.

HASTINGS. If this is so damned well documented, why hasn't that headline-crazy Senator issued some subpoenas?

BELLINGHAM. There's one piece missing. He's trying to trace down where the money goes. Do you suppose Mr. Rafferty can supply any information on this subject?

HASTINGS. As an investigator, you mean?

BELLINGHAM. No, sir, that is *not* what I mean.

HASTINGS. Damn it, Walt is my best friend. I appointed him to hunt down exactly this kind of immorality in government.

BELLINGHAM. I only want to say that Mr. Rafferty has not been living in a monastery.

HASTINGS. (*Picking up the phone.*) Get Walter Rafferty for me. (*He slams down the phone.*)

BELLINGHAM. I guess you haven't been hearing what everybody in Washington is saying. . . .

HASTINGS. (*Almost belligerently.*) What?

BELLINGHAM. That George Washington couldn't tell a lie—but Griffith Hastings can't tell a liar.

HASTINGS. Just forget the easy jokes. In anything as big, as new, as the Veteran's Administration, people make mistakes. Honest mistakes. We'll get them cleaned up. Walt will.

BELLINGHAM. Mr. President. Do you know about the "honest mistake" called "the fish bowl"?

HASTINGS. What does that mean?

BELLINGHAM. Once a week some joker from the Justice Department makes a business trip to Manhattan. He takes a hotel room, different hotel every week. Correction: he takes *two* hotel rooms, adjoining. On a table in the center of one room he puts a fish bowl. The door to the hallway is unlocked, and the fisherman sits in the next room with his eye at the keyhole. At fifteen-minute intervals, assorted gentlemen drop by, each depositing a thousand fish into the bowl. The eye behind the keyhole checks off the names on a list, and makes sure none of the fingers are sticky. Curiously enough, Senator Hearn has a man on the same floor with a lovely view of the elevator; not only is he making a list, he's taking pictures. To the surprise of nobody, this Photo Album turns out to be the "Who's Who" of the Alcoholic Beverage Profession. Can you guess how many of these fish bowl regulars have been indicted by your Justice Department? Not one!

HASTINGS. If Senator Hearn has a list of lawbreakers, why doesn't he do something about it? He doesn't have to wade through an indictment, he can call a cop on the corner.

BELLINGHAM. He doesn't care about a few bootleggers or the character who checks off the list; he wants to know where the money's going. There seems to be a welfare fund for building a playground and rest home for retired Army and Navy officers at Key West, but there isn't any such place at Key West.

HASTINGS. Does Pacificus mean "Peaceful"?

BELLINGHAM. That's right, sir.

HASTINGS. How the hell did you ever get a name like that? (*Abruptly, Frances hurries into the room. She is nervous and excited. Rafferty is at her heels, and he too seems disturbed and indignant.*)

RAFFERTY. Frances is all steamed up, Griff, and obviously there's something here that we'll have to look into.

HASTINGS. I've been trying to get you, Walt. We've got some housecleaning to do.

RAFFERTY. I've trusted Ax the same as you have!

HASTINGS. What's this got to do with Ax?

FRANCES. (*Pulling the deposit slips out of her purse.*) Look at these, Griffith.

RAFFERTY. Just a minute, Frances. Let's not discuss this in front of Senator Hearn's messenger boy.

HASTINGS. We're going to do a lot of discussing in front of him. You might as well get used to it. (*He takes the deposit slips.*)

FRANCES. Mr. Maley has on deposit at the Gibraltar Trust in Wilmont more than one million, six hundred thousand dollars. (*Hastings glances quickly at Bellingham. His eyes widen. Is this the missing piece of the puzzle?*)

HASTINGS. Holy God!

FRANCES. How can a man making eight thousand dollars a year accumulate—

HASTINGS. We've got to sit Ax down right away, and have him tell us where all this came from! (*He indicates the deposit slips.*)

RAFFERTY. I just found out about it twenty minutes ago from Frances. It's as much a shock to me as it is to you.

FRANCES. We tried to get Mr. Maley on the telephone, but there wasn't any answer.

HASTINGS. I want Ax here, in this room, with a complete explanation. Not tomorrow. Not Monday. Now! Bruce, find him. Get him over here. (*Bellingham starts toward the door.*)

RAFFERTY. (*Crosses to phone.*) All right, if you're in such a big rush, I'll put some of the boys from the Department on it.

BELLINGHAM. I'll find him. (*He goes off.*)

HASTINGS. (*Calling after Bellingham.*) The Weldon Park. Look downstairs in the billiard room.

FRANCES. Has Mr. Maley said anything to you, Walter, about speculations?

RAFFERTY. I guess Ax has been doing pretty well in the market.

HASTINGS. Not if he takes his own tips.

RAFFERTY. Chances are the money isn't even his. Ax is a pretty public-spirited gent. I know he's treasurer or trustee for some welfare fund or other.

HASTINGS. *What* fund?

RAFFERTY. (*Goes to desk humidor for cigar.*) Oh, that thing for retired Army-Navy officers at Key West.

HASTINGS. (*With a sinking feeling.*) God, not Ax! Not poor, funny little Ax . . . !

RAFFERTY. Stop worrying about it. We'll get Ax straightened around.

HASTINGS. I want a complete list of his business transactions. What stocks was Ax in?

RAFFERTY. Some oils. And we all had a nice little gain on one new issue— (*He clips his cigar.*) Universal Hospital Supply. Were you in on that, Griff?

HASTINGS. I hope to hell not. Were you?

RAFFERTY. I may have been.

HASTINGS. Charlie Webster's your boy, Walt. You wanted him in the Veterans' Bureau. And if there's any stink over there, *you* can help explain it.

RAFFERTY. You've been listening to that jail bird again.

HASTINGS. *What* jail bird?

RAFFERTY. That Bellingham.

HASTINGS. If that's a sample of the accuracy of your information, you're in trouble, Walt. You and Charlie Webster and I had better get this settled, before the newspapers settle it for us.

RAFFERTY. Oh, Charlie's off on vacation. Didn't anybody tell you?

HASTINGS. Get him back.

RAFFERTY. I don't know if we can. He's on a boat.

FRANCES. *What* boat?

RAFFERTY. How should I know *what* boat? Charlie's been working pretty hard. He needed a little rest.

HASTINGS. Where was he going? Bermuda? The Bahamas? Cuba?

RAFFERTY. Greece, I think.

HASTINGS. (*Outraged.*) Greece! He could see a few ruins right in his own office.

RAFFERTY. Look, Griff, this is the same as any other business. We all have to blink once in a while at a padded expense account, or if somebody sticks an office stamp on a letter to his girl.

HASTINGS. (*Brandishing the deposit slips.*) This is one helluva lot of two-cent stamps.

RAFFERTY. What are you, Griff, an old lady or a practical politician? (*His manner is easy and persuasive.*) Why do you think I got into politics? I like it. I like the game. So do you. It's better than poker. And the green felt runs all the way from the White House lawn to the valleys of California. When the table's as big as that, you don't play penny ante.

FRANCES. But this isn't a poker game, Walter. You're supposed to be working for the people.

RAFFERTY. Swell. I'll serve the people. And I'll do it the way it's always been done, the way the people, if they're honest, *expect* it to be done. (*Holding up a cigar.*) A cigar manufacturer is also serving the public. And if he's smart, he can turn an awful lot of tobacco leaves into thousand-dollar bills. Bravo! More power to him.

HASTINGS. There's a moral consideration—

RAFFERTY. In *politics*? Who are you—some dime-in-the-platter backstreet preacher? Don't give me that "morality" noise. That's for the hicks, the holy old ladies, and the softies buying cemetery plots at a thousand per cent markup. You think this country was built on the Twenty-third Psalm? Hell, it came out of nerve and salesmanship and gut-tearing competition. How do you think old Cavendish got his eight hundred million? In a Sunday School?

HASTINGS. I happen to know that Sam Cavendish is a deeply religious man.

RAFFERTY. He can afford morality. He's rich enough. I'm not. Neither are you. The "land of plenty" for everybody except the politician, who sticks his head through the hole in the canvas and lets the goddamned free press sling mud balls at him. He can't run his business like a business, because it's never *his* business. It belongs to the blessed American public that doesn't give a hoot in hell until some poor bastard gets his pinky caught in the cash register! Name me a job that demands more and pays less than serving the American taxpayer. The Customers' Man can screw 'em blind on the Big Board. That's O.K. The Oil Boys can simmer the fat out of the ground, the Real Estate Sharps can bank a six-month million—everybody gets rich except the poor ass of a "Public Servant." And you've got the gall to scream because a few of your friends are smart enough to do exactly what everybody else in the country is doing.

HASTINGS. How much have you been hiding from me? How much are *you* involved?

RAFFERTY. About as much as you are.

HASTINGS. Nobody with any respect for the Presidency will believe I'm personally mixed up with a thing like this.

RAFFERTY. Oh? Did you ever know a whore house where the madam was a virgin?

HASTINGS. No more clever answers, Walt. I'm calling you.

RAFFERTY. Don't call me, Griff. You can't win this pot.

HASTINGS. I want to know if my Attorney General is a thief. (*Rafferty is lighting a cigar, and we do not know at once how this accusation has affected him. Suddenly he flings down the burning match and approaches Hastings with controlled wrath.*)

RAFFERTY. Don't used such graphic language with me, Mr. President! You wouldn't be in this room—you'd never have gotten your muddy shoes in the Senate cloak room—if it weren't for me!

HASTINGS. I never asked for this job.

FRANCES. I was there, in the room, when you begged him to take the nomination. Everybody in the party wanted him!

RAFFERTY. They wanted him like hell! I shoved him down the throat of that convention, like pushing a goof pill down a bucking horse's gullet, while it was biting my hand. I had to fight for every half vote. I had to buy and sell and bargain and crawl on my belly to the delegations from Nebraska and Oregon and Utah, who didn't know Griffith P. Hastings from Fatty Arbuckle!

HASTINGS. "My humble servant"! You did me such a favor heading up the Justice Department where you could look out for your whole rotten gang!

RAFFERTY. *Our* gang, Mr. President. The gang that makes up your margins in the stock market. The gang that knows enough about your private life to retire you from public life forever.

HASTINGS. Don't threaten me! I'll demand your resignation.

RAFFERTY. When the President starts accusing the Cabinet, it's the *brain* accusing the *fingers*! The head versus the right hand!

FRANCES. If thy right hand offend thee, cut if off!

RAFFERTY. And bleed to death? We won't let you do that to yourself, Griff!

HASTINGS. I have a right to expect my appointees to conduct themselves as honorable men!

RAFFERTY. When the saints come marching in, I strongly recommend that they take over the Federal Government. Until such time, the taxpayers will have to be content with human beings who are imperfect, who make mistakes, who may occasionally be swayed by "enlightened self-interest."

HASTINGS. (*Crosses to desk telephone.*) That's a fancy name for Grand Theft!

RAFFERTY. Don't force me to do what I don't want to do, Griff. But if old friends start denouncing old friends, it could become a national pastime. It wouldn't make me happy to have you pick up a newspaper and read, not on the front page, inside somewhere, innuendos, a little hint or two—about a girl in an apartment on Gramercy Park, who entertained distinguished visitors. *A* distinguished visitor. (*Hastings becomes rigid. Frances is pale; she glances from her husband to Rafferty, then back again.*)

HASTINGS. (*Putting down the phone.*) I'll deny it.

FRANCES. *We'll* deny it.

RAFFERTY. As a good newspaperman, Griff, you know that's the best way to spread a rumor. Deny it, and it goes on the front pages. They'll wheel out the eighty-four-point type they've been saving for the Second Coming! "*No* White House Love Nest!" (*An inspiration.*) Tell you what you can do. Hire some third-rate novelist to write a book—to prove that the President is not the father of Claire Jones' illegitimate child! (*Hastings, infuriated, leaps at Rafferty and seizes him by the throat.*)

HASTINGS. You son-of-a-bitch! You dirty son-of-a-bitch! (*Hastings struggles with Rafferty, his hands still around his throat. Frances screams. Bellingham comes in, white-faced.*)

BELLINGHAM. Mr. President— (*Hastings continues to struggle with Rafferty until Bellingham pulls them apart. The President is trembling, his voice is husky with emotion.*)

HASTINGS. Well? Where's Ax? Why didn't you bring him back with you?

BELLINGHAM. The police are in his room. And a squad from the Fire Department. They were too late. (*With hardly any voice.*) Ax Maley stuck a revolver in his mouth and blew out the back of his head. (*Hastings is stunned with grief. He sinks to the sofa in utter disbelief. Somehow there is the sense that the death of his old friend is his own death as well.*)

THE LIGHTS FADE

ACT TWO
SCENE 2

On the scrim: a projection of the Golden Gate bridge, then crowds look up adoringly. The President's voice over a public address system is coming to an oratorical climax.

HASTINGS' VOICE. So, my friends in this magnificent city by the Golden Gate, let us march forward together. With daring, seasoned by reasonable caution, with hearts ready to climb mountain tops, yet with feet planted solidly in the valleys of practicality, let us stand shoulder to shoulder in quest of our inevitable destiny.

(There are Cheers and Applause, the honking of Klaxons. A Band plays "Hail to the Chief." As the Curtain rises, the background sky is a colorful stream of confetti, serpentine, and American flags. The effect fades away as the Lights come up.)

A hotel room in San Francisco, high above Union Square. It is the following summer. This is the sumptuous sitting room of the best suite in the hotel. The decor is Louis Quinze, baroque, golden, and chandelier-ridden. A balcony upstage overlooks the square. In the center of the room is a huge brocade couch. There are several large upholstered chairs and a gilt French phone. The afternoon sun floods across the room warmly. Bellingham is on the balcony, looking down at the activity in the square below. Frances is seated in a chair, listening to the cheers, but staring into the distance. Her voice has a weary, wistful quality.

FRANCES. When he's up on a platform speaking to everybody, he doesn't seem much different. But when he comes back to our hotel suite, in city after city, I see how old he looks, what it's doing to him. My God, it seems like a hundred years since that hotel room in Chicago, when I pushed him to take the nomination. You know—I never imagined it would be anything like this.

BELLINGHAM. (*Coming in from the balcony.*) Why hasn't he said anything?

FRANCES. He's running away. That's the only reason for this endless speaking tour.

BELLINGHAM. What's he running away from? Is he still afraid of the stories Rafferty can start? I know how painful this is for you, Mrs. Hastings, but plenty of presidents have survived attacks on their personal lives. It wasn't so long ago half the country was singing a jingle about Grover Cleveland: "Ma, Ma, where's my Pa? Gone to the White House, ha, ha, ha." But they elected him. Twice!

FRANCES. Bruce, I'm not afraid of any personal scandal. *I'm* not frightened—I've told him that. He's really running away because he can't face the fact that his friends have done this.

BELLINGHAM. He's got to face it. He's got to speak out. I had to beg Senator Hearn for the chance to come to San Francisco. The Senator was ready to issue subpoenas last Friday. The President can be impeached!

FRANCES. Can they impeach him for trusting old friends?

BELLINGHAM. Old friends are fine. For lodge meetings and class reunions. But "Government by Crony" can destroy him!

FRANCES. Bruce, what can he do? He blames himself so much, he can't get the words out.

BELLINGHAM. Get somebody else to speak for him. Somebody he can trust.

FRANCES. Arthur Anderson is here in San Francisco. I invited him. I've convinced Griffith he has to see him.

BELLINGHAM. Good.

FRANCES. Perhaps he'll take the Secretary into his confidence. I don't know. If he doesn't, I don't know what else to try. (*Unsteadily, she crosses to the cabinet.*) Would you care for something to drink?

BELLINGHAM. No, thank you.

FRANCES. If you don't mind. (*Frances takes a decanter of whiskey from the cabinet and awkwardly pours herself a shot, spilling some. She drinks quickly, almost painfully. Bellingham watches with quiet surprise; he's never seen her take a drink before. There are voices in the hall. Frances dabs at the spilled liquor with her handkerchief.*)

HASTINGS' VOICE. (*From off, heartily.*) All right, fellas, the Secret Service is relieved for the day. You lucky bums can go inspect the Barbary Coast. Give me a full report. (*There is laughter from the hallway. Hastings comes into the room, stops short at the sight of Bellingham.*)

HASTINGS. Bruce! (*Whereas the President's hair was silver before, now it is completely white. But this, and the other ravages of the year, seem to have given him even greater stature. He has the majesty of a man who has just been cheered by thousands of people. Some strands of serpentine and confetti still cling to his coat. He is glad to see Bellingham, but he senses the purpose of this unexpected visit.*) What are you doing in San Francisco?

BELLINGHAM. (*Shaking hands with Hastings.*) You're looking very well, Mr. President.

HASTINGS. Sure, there's nothing like shaking hands with a few thousand strangers to put a man in shape. (*He lifts a strand of confetti from his shoulder and dangles it.*) You've got to be careful in a town where there are lots of Italians. You don't know if they're throwing confetti or spaghetti. (*Hastings laughs.*) That's Ax's joke. I know, Duchess. There never was such a person as Axel Maley. I only read about him in the funny papers. (*Suddenly, to Bellingham.*) Look, by God, this is lucky! Arthur Anderson's coming up in a minute. I tell you, I've got a guardian angel that sent you here to translate for me!

FRANCES. You'll be able to talk more freely with Secretary Anderson if you're alone.

BELLINGHAM. She's right, sir. (*Frances exits.*)

HASTINGS. Sure, sure. How about a drink? (*He crosses to the cabinet, bracing himself for what Bellingham has to tell him.*) O.K., Bruce. What's the news?

BELLINGHAM. They're trying to whitewash everything except the White House.

HASTINGS. Why doesn't that damn Senator you work for stay in the Senate Office Building and answer his mail? (*He gets highball glasses.*)

BELLINGHAM. He may be the best friend you've got.

HASTINGS. Hearn? He never did me any favors. Two things this country could do without: Prohibition and Senate Investigating Committees. (*He reaches for a bottle, holding it up appraisingly. He calls off.*) Duchess, the maid's been nipping at the Scotch again. (*He pours two drinks, long and straight, then hands one to Bellingham.*) I sent Doc out to fill a prescription. But this medicinal alcohol isn't exactly Haig and Haig Pinch. (*The two men look at each other. Hastings lifts his glass in a toast.*) To happier days. (*They drink.*) When was the last time I saw you? At the funeral? (*Bellingham nods.*) The Duchess says I shouldn't have gone. How could I not go? He was my friend. Didn't Shakespeare say something like that: "Every man's death diminishes me."

BELLINGHAM. It wasn't Shakespeare, and it isn't true. Ax Maley, alive, diminished all of us.

HASTINGS. I looked down into the casket and just one thing kept running through my mind: "There's them as is in and them as is out." Poor, sweet little guy.

BELLINGHAM. You have no idea what Axel Maley did to you, Mr. President.

HASTINGS. I know damn well what he did.

BELLINGHAM. And what some of your other friends have done.

HASTINGS. What does that mean?

BELLINGHAM. (*Drawing a photostat from his pocket. Frances, who has been listening, comes back into the room.*) On September fourteenth last year, you signed an executive order—

HASTINGS. I've signed a thousand executive orders. (*He crosses to Bellingham and takes the photostat, turning the pages of it quickly, searchingly.*)

BELLINGHAM. This one was unique. It was a very special favor for a very special friend. It allowed Secretary Loomis to give away—literally *give away*—government oil lands to private individuals for personal profit.

HASTINGS. I never signed such an order! (*He pales as he reads it.*) I never *understood* I was signing such an order.

BELLINGHAM. I believe that, sir, but nobody else will. To Senator Hearn this is evidence that the President himself is criminally involved.

FRANCES. (*Softly.*) Oh, God.

BELLINGHAM. There are ten thousand oil wells on government land, gushing money into private pockets, including Mr. Loomis'. It's no secret from anybody except the public. And it's not going to be a secret from them much longer. (*Hastings sits. The confetti-majesty vanishes like paper in a fire.*) But you can still take decisive action, Mr. President. I told Hearn you're not part of this. He'll only believe it if you clear the record yourself. Admit that you've been sold out by your friends.

FRANCES. Let Secretary Anderson say the words. You authorize him.

BELLINGHAM. After Hearn lets loose his blast, anything you say will only sound defensive. Rafferty and Loomis can only stay afloat by hanging on to you. If you don't cut free, you'll sink with them.

HASTINGS. I'm tired.

FRANCES. Of course you're tired. You haven't eaten all day. I'll order you something.

HASTINGS. No.

FRANCES. What would you like? A steak, some chops?

HASTINGS. No, nothing heavy. Some soup, maybe.

FRANCES. Bruce?

BELLINGHAM. No, thank you. (*Frances goes out. Slowly Hastings raises his head, looks at Bellingham.*)

HASTINGS. Bruce. What am I going to do? (*Without a trace of self-pity.*) Back in Wilmont, once a year, they used to take the brightest kid from the junior class at the high school and make him Mayor for a Day. They'd stick a couple of phone books under him so he could reach the fountain pen. For twenty-four hours he'd run the town. But the next morning, the *real* mayor would always come back and straighten out the mess. (*With a wistful laugh.*) Wouldn't it be great if tomorrow they sent me back to 11A? (*He picks up book from the side-table and hands it to Bellingham.*) Hey, did you ever read this?

BELLINGHAM. (*Looking at the title on the spine.*) "A Boy's Lives of the Presidents."

HASTINGS. (*Taking the book from him, leafing through it.*) I've been reading about this Martin Van Buren. The way I see it, the country would have been just as well off if he'd stayed in Albany. You wouldn't call him a great President, would you?

BELLINGHAM. I suppose if a President has five minutes of greatness in four years he's doing fine.

HASTINGS. (*Smiling.*) That Millard Fillmore—he had about thirty seconds! (*He laughs, then sobers.*) What are they going to say about me in a book like this—fifty years from now? (*Bellingham is silent.*) Down there, after the speech, everybody wanted to shake hands with me. But they aren't shaking hands with a man. More of a monument. When a fella gets to be President, he has to swear off being a man. They make him into a breathing statue. A nice, shiny, hand-shaking statue—like the King of England. Ask *him*. Ask him what a peach of a job it is. (*Thoughtfully, moving to the center of the room.*) No, it's different. They leave the Kings to shake hands with the old ladies, while some other fella sits at the head of that long table and answers the questions. And if he gives the wrong answers they shoo him out and shoo somebody else in. And the King goes right on shaking hands as if nothing happened. That's pretty smooth. But the poor bastard who gets *this* job has to shake hands and know the answers, too. And worst of all, he's stuck. (*Eyes moist.*) *I* can't quit, Bruce. Who the hell can I turn in my resignation to? God? (*The telephone rings. Hastings picks it up, a little impatiently.*) Yes. (*He listens.*) I guess so. All right, send him up. (*Slowly he hangs up the telephone.*) Arthur Anderson is on his way up in the elevator.

BELLINGHAM. I'd better go.

HASTINGS. Stay! Please stay.

BELLINGHAM. I'm the enemy. (*As he stares at the President, his gaze softens.*) Not really. I'm leaving the Hearn Committee.

HASTINGS. Good. Get out of politics. Smart boy.

BELLINGHAM. No, sir. I'm not going to run away again. Somebody in politics has to give a damn. And I give a damn. (*He shakes hands with the President and starts to leave.*)

HASTINGS. (*Stopping him.*) Bruce. (*Bellingham turns.*) I never really wanted to fire you.

BELLINGHAM. (*Softly, meaningfully.*) Mr. President. I never really quit. (*A soft smile passes between the men. Bellingham goes out. Frances enters.*)

FRANCES: Your soup will be up in just a few moments, dear. (*There is a knock at the door. Frances starts to go, but realizes her husband is tortured with uncertainty. She tries to give him what strength she can.*) Griffith, it's not as if you had to make a decision. Do you understand—there's only one thing you can do. Don't even think about me, or what they might say about us personally. It doesn't matter. (*Hastings just stares at her. There is another knock.*) I'll leave you alone with Arthur Anderson.

HASTINGS. (*Suddenly desperate.*) No, Frances. Stay here.

FRANCES. (*She wants to remain, as a mother wants to be with her child in a time of pain or sorrow, but she knows it will only weaken him.*) I'd stay, I'd do anything, if I thought I could help. But I can't. (*She goes off. The President straightens himself, and manages to put on some of the bluff, extroverted manner.*)

HASTINGS. (*Calling.*) Come in. Come in, Mr. Secretary. (*Arthur Anderson comes into the room. Despite the forbidding formality, he is trying to be kindly. They shake hands.*)

ANDERSON. How are you, Mr. President?

HASTINGS. Fine, Arthur, Fine. Sit down, uh—Arthur. (*Anderson sits.*) It was very good of you to come all the way across the country like this—on such short notice.

ANDERSON. From the urgency of the request, I gathered it was on a matter of major importance.

HASTINGS. Well, yes, I suppose you could put it that way. (*He picks up a newspaper, clutching it in his fists, trying to find a way to say what must be said. He squeezes the paper so hard, his knuckles are white.*) How was the trip out?

ANDERSON. Warm. But endurable.

HASTINGS. Glad you're here, Arthur. Glad you're here. Now. Let's get right down to the core of things. (*He reaches for the book as something to hang on to, another means for delaying what he dreads to say.*) I've been reading a lot of history lately. Government. Political science. Lives of the Presidents. Mr. Secretary, I've made mistakes. But *all* of them made mistakes.

ANDERSON. (*Even the antiseptic Anderson is touched by this. He now speaks with some awkwardness.*) Would you care to be more specific about anything, Mr. President?

HASTINGS. (*Unable to look directly at Anderson.*) Yes. Let's take one of these Presidents. What does this man do if he has based his entire political life on the reliability of friends? And if these friends—this is just imaginary, you understand—if they turn out to be unworthy of the confidence he's put in them. (*Hastings' confession peters out. He's looking at the floor; Anderson is unable to watch Hastings.*)

ANDERSON. Such a man would need to call on the deepest resources of his greatness.

HASTINGS. (*Tossing the book on the table. Exploding.*) I don't understand all this talk about greatness! I didn't get elected because I was going to be some kind of one-man government. I can't do this job by myself. You've got to have faith. In the people around you. I've got faith in you, Arthur.

ANDERSON. Let me help you, Mr. President. If I can.

HASTINGS. All right, Arthur. Here's what I want you to do. (*He takes a deep breath.*) I want you to— I want you to— (*He breaks off and tries again.*) I want you to—

ANDERSON. Yes, sir?

HASTINGS. (*His whole body is taut. He touches his stomach, doubling over slightly, in genuine pain.*) Frances! Frances! (*Anderson moves to help him, but the President waves him away. Frances enters quickly. Hastings sits, his head in his hands.*)

FRANCES. Yes?

HASTINGS. Frances, I seem to be— Why don't you phone up Doc Kirkaby to bring over some of those white pills? I—

FRANCES. Yes, dear. (*She goes out quickly.*)

HASTINGS. My stomach tightens up and I can't think. Arthur, will you be at your hotel?

ANDERSON. The St. Francis.

HASTINGS. Fine. Fine. I'll call you a little later and we'll go over these things point by point.

ANDERSON. I'll be waiting for your call. (*Anderson starts to leave, then stops, concerned.*) I know a very good internist here; would you like me to call him?

HASTINGS. No, no. The General's right down the hall. He'll take care of it. (*Frances re-enters, nodding for Anderson to leave. Anderson goes out. Hastings seems a little dazed; he hasn't fully realized that the Secretary has left. He calls after him.*)

HASTINGS. Thank you, Arthur! (*He repeats numbly to himself.*) Thank you.

FRANCES. Dr. Kirkaby is on this way. He says you're to lie down immediately. Why don't you undo that collar, Griffith? It's too tight.

HASTINGS. It's nothing. Don't worry, I feel fine. Fine! (*Sighs.*) I won't kid you, Duchess. I feel God-awful! (*He catches her hand.*) I didn't tell him. (*Frances looks at him, wordlessly. There is a knock at the door.*)

FRANCES. Come in, Doctor.

DOC. (*Enters. His uniform looks as if he had pulled it on hastily. He carries a black medical satchel, which he puts down on the coffee table.*) What seems to be the trouble, Griff? (*He crosses to the chair, bends over the President, and takes his wrist.*)

FRANCES. The trouble is you won't take care of yourself, Griffith. You haven't had a bite to eat all day.

DOC. (*Feeling Hastings' forehead.*) You don't seem to have a fever, boy.

HASTINGS. It's like somebody's made a fist inside of me and won't let go.

FRANCES. Where? Where is the pain?

DOC. (*Poking his own stomach.*) I get the same kind of thing, Griff. When you're traveling, you've gotta expect it. It's the different water, and all that. I'll tell you what. Why don't I get some of the newspaper boys together for a few rounds of poker? That'll relax your stomach muscles.

FRANCES. Is that what you call a prescription, "Doctor"?

HASTINGS. No poker, Doc. Thanks. Not now.

DOC. I better call a specialist. When you don't want to play poker, you're sick. I got a medical directory in my room.

FRANCES. If people will let you rest. And if you get some food.

DOC. Let's not take any chances. I'll be right back. (*He starts out, not taking his medical satchel. He stops short.*) Walt! (*Rafferty comes in jauntily, claps Doc on the shoulder as they pass in the doorway. Frances is shocked. Hastings sits up. But Rafferty is feeling his way. He studies the President, trying to gauge how much Hastings may have disclosed to Anderson.*)

HASTINGS. Who pushed the button for you?

RAFFERTY. (*Pleasantly.*) We're old friends, Griff. My responses are automatic.

DOC. (*Sensing the tension, he slips out of the room.*) I'll get the medical directory. (*He leaves.*)

RAFFERTY. I was a little hurt to find out you'd sent for Anderson without even consulting me. Naturally I was on the next train. Did you and Secretary Anderson have a nice chat?

HASTINGS. Are you worried, Walt? Are you sweating?

RAFFERTY. (*Twisting a cigarette into the holder.*) No.

HASTINGS. What did you come for?

RAFFERTY. I've traveled three thousand miles and you don't even ask me to sit down.

HASTINGS. Tell me how you're serving the public, Walt. I'm damned interested.

RAFFERTY. (*Seemingly relaxed, lighting the cigarette.*) We've had differences. But we've had a lot of years together. How many poker hands have we played, Griff? A thousand? Five thousand? How many fifths of bourbon have we put away? We've been good for each other, haven't we? You used to ask my advice. Sometimes you'd even take it.

HASTINGS. I'm listening.

RAFFERTY. There's a little mix-up with Josh, a little minor confusion over at Interior about some leases.

HASTINGS. (*Picking up the photostat.*) Some oil leases.

RAFFERTY. Could be. Probably a bookkeeping error. But we've got a two-party system and the other boys might not look at it that way. However, there's a very simple solution. When the Hearn Committee starts making its big noise, we simply explain who was the author of the whole plan, who drew it up, who approved it, who recommended it for your immediate action. Just name the name.

HASTINGS. Who?

RAFFERTY. The Judge. Corriglione.

HASTINGS. I hope you've got a return ticket, Walt. (*A new power seems to be rising inside of Hastings.*)

RAFFERTY. Now, just a minute, Griff. This is a simple way. The best way. I've been giving this a lot of thought.

HASTINGS. I know damn well you have.

RAFFERTY. This way nobody'll get hurt.

HASTINGS. Except Corriglione.

RAFFERTY. What're you going to do? I like him. I've always liked him. But, Griff, don't play a gypsy fiddle for the Judge. (*In Hastings' code, the betrayal of friends is almost unthinkable. He turns on Rafferty with the power of a man who has just discovered a truth he can fight for, and a lie he can fight against. Outraged, he flings a mocking but belated indictment at his Attorney General.*)

HASTINGS. O.K., Walt. What'll we do next?

RAFFERTY. What?

HASTINGS. Something really big. Not just oil or booze or bed sheets. You want a power project to play with? Help yourself. How about grabbing off a National Park for your front yard?

RAFFERTY. If you want to talk realistically, fine. (*He rises.*)

HASTINGS. I'm being realistic! We're playing on the world's biggest poker table, aren't we? Let's make this a respectable pot.

RAFFERTY. Don't be a damn fool, Griff.

HASTINGS. You certainly aren't scared, are you, Walt? We've got plenty of friends left to hang. That's the normal way of doing business. Isn't that what made this country: "I'm for me and the hell with everybody else." Who'll we get rid of now? How about *you*? Are you expendable, Walt?

RAFFERTY. (*Defensively.*) Everything your Attorney General has done as been legal—with the blessing, approval, and signature of your Majesty, Griffith the First!

HASTINGS. This sort of thing? (*He tosses the photostat aside, mocking Rafferty's tone.*) Penny ante! What about your big triumph of nerve and salesmanship—manufacturing a President of the United States? Don't be modest. Take the credit, Walt. And while you're at it, take credit for the illegitimate child, too. Because you and everybody who voted for me were the parents of a bastard. A bastard idea—that anybody can be President. (*A waiter enters with a rolling table. A silver soup tureen and service is atop it.*)

FRANCES. I'll take it. That's all. (*She wheels table. Waiter leaves.*)

RAFFERTY. They've never sent a President to a federal penitentiary. Do you want to make history?

HASTINGS. I haven't done anything dishonest.

RAFFERTY. Say that. Somebody may believe you. (*He draws a key ring out of his pocket and begins to detach one key with studied casualness.*) Suppose I invite your friend Senator Hearn to inspect my safe-deposit box. Did you ever wonder why Ax Maley's will has never been probated? I've stopped it. To protect you. (*He fingers the key.*) His will is right behind this key. His entire seven-figure estate, however acquired, goes to his dear friend and benefactor, Griffith P. Hastings.

HASTINGS. (*He looks at Rafferty, almost as if he were seeing him for the first time. He speaks with great calm and certainty.*) Walt, I haven't made very many suggestions during my term in office, but I suggest that you *do* take Senator Hearn to your safe-deposit box. Show him anything you like.

RAFFERTY. Do you want to be impeached? Is that what you want?

HASTINGS. Walt, you're out. Out of the Administration. Out of my life.

RAFFERTY. You're not that stupid. Almost, maybe. But not quite. You're not going to throw me out. Even in that sleeping little mind of yours, you can imagine what could happen.

HASTINGS. Yes. I know what's going to happen. Everybody is going to see us. Exactly as we are. Both of us. And maybe we've done the country a favor, Walt. Maybe people will make sure nothing like this ever happens again. Oh, I suppose there'll always be plenty of Walt Rafferty's around. But I pray to God that there'll never be another Griffith P. Hastings. (*Pause.*) Good-bye, Walt.

RAFFERTY. Frances! Don't let him be a damned fool.

FRANCES. Good-bye, Walter.

RAFFERTY. (*He goes to chair, gets his hat, then turns.*) Before you torpedo the boat, Griff, just remember: everybody sinks together. The saints and the sons-of-bitches. And a halo is no life preserver! (*Exits.*)

FRANCES. He won't do anything.

HASTINGS. Yes, he will.

FRANCES. Then don't let him! Fight him!

HASTINGS. How can I? He'll wreck more than just one man. Much more.

FRANCES. (*She is on the verge of tears. Hurriedly, she makes an excuse to go off.*) Lie down, dear. I'll get you a pillow. (*She exits. Alone on the stage, Hastings closes his eyes. Then he looks up, his fists clenched, searching for support.*)

HASTINGS. Dear Jesus. (*As he lowers his head, he sees Doc's medical satchel on the coffee table. Without any visible emotion, Hastings crosses quickly to it, glancing over his shoulder to make certain Frances isn't coming. He looks at the labels of several bottles, and finally finds one small bottle, which seems to be what he's looking for. He puts it in his jacket pocket and crosses to the phone as Frances enters with a bed pillow, which she places on chair. Into phone.*) This is the President. I want the newsmen sent up here. All of them. The whole press staff. All the correspondents. Everybody. Right away. (*Hastings hangs up and turns to Frances. He extends his arms, palms up, helplessly. She comes to him. They embrace.*)

FRANCES. I did this to you.

HASTINGS. Like hell. I wanted to be President, too. I never made it. I only got elected.

FRANCES. I wish we were back in Wilmont.

HASTINGS. Why?

FRANCES. It's home.

HASTINGS. I don't mind hotel rooms. I like them. (*He lets Frances go.*) Something happens to a man in a hotel room. The bellboy raises the window, and puts the key on the dresser, and you're free. If you spill something, *they've* got to clean the rug. No matter what happens, all you've got to do is pay for it. The great American monument to irresponsibility. (*There is a knock at the door.*)

HASTINGS. (*Letting his wife go.*) Come in. (*John Boyd enters. He is alone, an open-faced young man fresh out of journalism school. He is scared stiff.*)

BOYD. They called the press room, sir.

HASTINGS. Well, where are all the fellas?

BOYD. Secretary Anderson gave them the slip, and they all went out to try to find him, and get a story out of him. They told me to just stay there and answer the phone. (*Blurting it.*) I'm John Boyd, *Sacramento Bee.* It sure is an honor meeting you, Mr. President. (*Correcting his own copy, quickly.*) *Surely* is an honor.

HASTINGS. Well, Mr. Boyd, I've got a statement to make. You can pass this on to the old hands when they get back from finding out that Arthur Anderson doesn't have anything to tell them. (*Boyd hurriedly digs some folded copy paper and a pencil from his pocket and stands with school-boy attentiveness.*) The President has just accepted the resignation of the Attorney General—no, that's too damned polite—I have just *demanded* the resignation of the Attorney General of the United States, Mr. Walter Rafferty.

BOYD. (*He is writing, but suddenly stops, shocked by the enormity of the story. He glances for a telephone.*) I'd better call Mr. Hudson. He's the political reporter on the *Bee*. I just answer phones. I've only been on the paper a couple of months.

HASTINGS. (*Crosses to him, and clasps a hand on his shoulder.*) Keep writing.

BOYD. Yes, sir.

HASTINGS. Rafferty. Two f's.

BOYD. Yes, sir.

HASTINGS. The President also requests Senator Hearn to make special inquiry into an executive order transferring certain government oil lands to the administration of Secretary Loomis. (*Obviously the boy is far behind. Hastings takes the paper and pencil out of his hands.*) What have you got? (*Glances at the paper, and then starts writing on it himself.*) Don't write "the's" and "and's." Put down the important words. Demand Hearn Investigate Loomis! (*He hands the paper and pencil back. This has taken an enormous toll of energy. He sinks to the couch, leaning his head back a little.*) The President also directs that Charles Webster, former head of the Veterans' Bureau, be extradited to stand trial for grand theft and betrayal of the public trust. (*Closing his eyes.*) Oh. The President wishes to reaffirm his complete confidence in his good friend, Judge Cesare Corriglione. (*He opens his eyes, looks over at the boy, realizing the young man's confusion. Slowly, he spells the name.*) C-o-r-r-i-g-l-i-o-n-e. (*Boyd stops writing, and looks up, expecting more.*) You got it?

BOYD. Yes, sir.

HASTINGS. Well, when I was an editor, that would have been enough for a story. (*Frances has filled the soup bowl and puts it on the table beside the big chair.*)

BOYD. Thank you, sir. Thank you, Mr. President. (*Boyd stops, turns, then wipes his hand across his suit and tentatively holds it out to the President. Hastings smiles and offers his hand. The boy crosses and shakes it. There is a look of real admiration in the boy's face. He almost runs out of the room. Frances crosses to Hastings.*)

HASTINGS. For the first time, I felt like a President of the United States. For about forty-five seconds. Well, that's fifteen seconds better than Millard Fillmore.

FRANCES. (*She takes his hand, touches his face.*) I'm proud of you. I'm very proud of you.

HASTINGS. (*Staring after the departed Boyd.*) Frances, I can't let school kids read in a history book that the President of the United States was a criminal. (*His hand touches the outside of his jacket pocket.*) Frances, do me a favor. Get me my robe, will you?

FRANCES. Of course. (*She moves quickly toward the other room. He watches her. The instant she's out of sight, he rises, reaches into his pocket, takes out the bottle, uncaps it, and dumps the contents into the soup. He thrusts the empty bottle back into his pocket. Slowly he stirs the soup, staring at it. Then he takes a spoonful, then another, increasing the tempo. Frances re-enters, carrying a gold brocade dressing gown. She helps him off with his jacket and into the dressing gown. He continues to sip the soup.*) Griffith, that should be piping.

HASTINGS. No. This is fine. Frances, sit down.

FRANCES. (*Takes his coat and puts it on the couch.*) I'm going to call down and ask them—

HASTINGS. (*Urgently.*) Frances, sit down.

FRANCES. There's some toast on the cart. I could break it into croutons.

HASTINGS. Frances!

DOC. (*Enters, with an open medical directory in his hands.*) Say, I got the number of this specialist. A Dr. Lenfelder. They say he's the best. (*Hastings tips up the soup bowl and finishes it entirely. Doc and Frances watch him. Hastings hands the empty soup bowl to Frances.*)

HASTINGS. (*With a faint smile.*) Don't take him away from the sick people. (*He sinks into the chair.*) I feel fine now, General. (*The full light of the sunset is on his face.*)

DOC. You sure, boy?

HASTINGS. I haven't felt this good in a long time. Had to have some food, that's all. Can't run the Lizzie without some gas in the tank.

DOC. Yeah. Well, if you need me—

HASTINGS. Frances'll call.

DOC. (*Crossing to get his satchel.*) Griff. Get some rest if you can.

HASTINGS. I'll try.

DOC. So long, boy. (*Doc goes out. Now the pretense falls away and Hastings sags a little, closing his eyes.*)

FRANCES. (*Worried.*) What's the matter, dear?

HASTINGS. (*With an effort, he opens his eyes, speaking against the pressure of time.*) Frances, I haven't been feeling great, off and on. Arthur Anderson knows. Doc'll swear to it. So if anything happens to me, it won't be too much of a surprise.

FRANCES. (*Sitting on the footstool next to him.*) I'm not listening to you. You haven't been taking care of yourself, that's all.

HASTINGS. (*Insistently.*) Afterward, don't let them do an autopsy.

FRANCES. An autopsy!!???

HASTINGS. Make sure.

FRANCES. Don't say that. Don't even think that.

HASTINGS. (*Suddenly alarmed.*) What did you do with my jacket? (*She rises and crosses toward it.*) Take the bottle out of the pocket. Get rid of it. (*Confused, Frances follows his directions. But when she sees the empty bottle, she freezes.*) Don't let Doc know where I got it. He'd feel bad.

FRANCES. (*As the realization strikes her.*) God. Oh, God! (*Frances starts to rush toward the outside door to call after Doc, but Hastings stops her, commandingly.*)

HASTINGS. Frances! (*She stops. He reaches out his hand, weakly. The dying light of the sun is on his face.*) Don't spoil my chance to be on a two-cent stamp! (*She hesitates, then slowly turns and crosses back. She sinks to her knees and embraces him. He closes his eyes and there is a moment of peace: perhaps he has been able to save the dignity of the high office he never wanted.*)

CURTAIN

ONLY
IN
AMERICA

Introduction

Only in America, Jerome Lawrence and Robert E. Lee's second script produced on Broadway during the fall of 1959, was their first work to explore the life and work of an actual living person: Harry Golden, author of the book of essays that provided the play with its title and some of its incidents. Paradoxically, Lawrence and Lee invented most of the events and action in *Only in America,* taking more liberty with the real Golden's life and career than they had with that of Warren G. Harding in *The Gang's All Here.*

Only in America did not succeed in New York. With Nehemiah Persoff playing Harry Golden, it ran only twenty-eight performances. Several of the New York reviewers were harshly negative in evaluating the play, while only one of the seven New York newspapers printed a wholly positive notice. Robert Coleman, in the *Daily Mirror,* summed up the play as "swell theatre," while Brooks Atkinson commented, "As painters of [Golden's] portrait, Mr. Lawrence and Mr. Lee have caught a good likeness. But they are not able to add much of their own." Walter Kerr of the *Herald Tribune,* the most negative of the reviewers, termed the piece "overstuffed, and seriously overripe."[1] Waters of *Variety* had foreshadowed the later reviews in his response to the play's out-of-town opening in Philadelphia: "Subject to tightening and directorial reorganization, it should have a comfortable success. Or, in a classic phrase, it needs work. . . . there is little conflict or tension, although the adapters have caught the Golden tone and character remarkably."[2]

Harry Golden's book, which provided the ostensible source for Lawrence and Lee's play, had been an immediate success when published in 1958.[3] Golden published his personal monthly, the *Carolina Israelite,* from his adopted hometown of Charlotte, North Carolina. The short essays, editorials, and personal musings in the book were drawn from the *Carolina Israelite,* founded in 1942. The book contains no narrative whatsoever. Lawrence and Lee's earlier book dramatization, *Auntie Mame,* at least drew from its source a chronological structure organized around young Patrick's life story; *Only in America* had nothing similar.

Lawrence and Lee turned to Golden's own life, freely creating for theatrical effect. The drama, for example, has Golden arriving in Charlotte and renting the house in order to establish his newspaper. His wife, Kate, remains in New York to be near their son, Bobby, hospitalized with muscular dystrophy, as well as to keep her job. The real Harry Golden went to Charlotte in 1941 to accept a job selling advertising and writing editorials for the *Charlotte Labor Journal,* later moving to the

Charlotte Observer. He began publishing the *Carolina Israelite* on the side in 1942. Golden and his wife, Genevieve (nicknamed "Tiny"), had four sons; their youngest, Peter, was born brain damaged in 1938, and was institutionalized until his death in 1957. The pair were amicably separated before Golden went to North Carolina, a separation that was legally formalized in 1961.[4]

The details of Golden's life, therefore, were freely modified by the playwrights. (And, as they note at the beginning of the script, "The character of Harry Golden is based on Harry Golden. All the other people of the play are fictional. . . .") Lawrence and Lee focused on Golden's character for the drama's connective structure, using a strategy similar to that they had employed in dramatizing *Auntie Mame*. The play thus follows Golden through a series of episodes, each selected to demonstrate various facets of his personality and social views.

The playwrights sound a couple of their major themes in the first act. The centrality of race relations, both for the actual Harry Golden and his theatrical doppleganger, is emphasized not only by Helen's hiring, but by the juxtaposition of the threatening telephone call from the Ku Klux Klan with Jed's seeking help for his jailed older brother, Melchior.

The first act also contains the first hints of coming changes, both social and political, in the Old South. Helen's description of her college training at Cornell sharply contrasts with her parents' experiences and work. In his confrontation with Birnbaum, Harry presents his vision of assimilation as Jewish immigrants move from ghettos into the professions and businesses, stressing the need for tolerance. And the Whitmore scene provides Golden with the opportunity to state clearly his perception of the coming societal changes and his desire to be a witness and commentator.

Humor is derived from Harry's explanation of Yiddish terms and phrases to the Southerners, while, predictably, the Southerners mispronounce Yiddish. While the humor is obvious, it is very much in keeping with Golden's own writing. The joke on defining *zoftig* in the first scene, and the following exchange:

> FRED: My wife's a Presbyterian.
> HARRY: One of the Ten Lost Tribes.

are taken directly from Golden's book.[5] In the latter instance, Lawrence and Lee condense a three-page essay into two lines.

In addition to the elements of necessary plot (what Harry is doing in Charlotte, why his wife is not with him, what kind of paper the *Carolina Israelite* is to be), the first act thoroughly establishes Harry's personality. His swatting out ideas with a broom handle as if it were a baseball bat, the use of a barrel for "pickling" ideas into essays, the affability and easy charm he demonstrates in his relations with all other characters—all are carefully set out. Golden's monologues are, for the most part, the only text reworked directly from the Golden book of essays, apart from occasional humorous exchanges such as cited above. Otherwise, the dialogue is wholly invented, much as are the characters and situations.

Act 2 reinforces the image of Golden presented in the first act and introduces new conflict: Harry's hidden status as an ex-convict. The first sequence in the act demonstrates Harry's acceptance into the community. Again, Lawrence and Lee use juxtaposition effectively, following the make-believe bus-riding scene with Harry's summons before the state legislative committee. As the following scene with Kate Golden demonstrates, the playwrights link Harry's fear that his past will be revealed with the "red-baiting" tactics employed by the House Committee on Un-American Activities and Senator Joseph McCarthy in the late 1940s and early 1950s. Their concern for freedom of expression, which had provided much of the impetus for *Inherit the Wind* earlier in the decade, received direct expression in the hearing scene, especially in the examination of Dr. Leota Patterson. Senator Martin Claypool's dogged discovery of subversive behavior and activity, although eventually ridiculed, epitomizes as well the playwrights' convictions regarding legislative witch hunts.

Golden's testimony, drawn heavily from the book's section four, "The Vertical Negro,"[6] serves to break the tension created by Dr. Patterson's interactions with the committee. The act ends, however, with the confrontation between Golden and Whitmore—but delays the revelation of Harry's past when Whitmore backs away from forcing Harry to make his confessional statement.

The past is revealed, of course, in the third act, but only after the publication of *Only in America* is a huge success. Again, the playwrights have fictionalized the actual events for dramatic purpose: Golden revealed his past himself to Judith Crist of the *New York Herald Tribune* after anonymous letters were sent to his publisher and to the New York papers.[7] Golden apparently had little thought of fleeing—by the time he returned to Charlotte from New York, an outpouring of support nationwide (similar, but not identical, to that dramatized in the play) had already taken place.

Lawrence and Lee, then, shaped and focused Harry Golden's life to suit their dramatic ends. They discarded the actual Golden's personal life, creating a new and wholly supportive theatrical wife to replace Golden's estranged wife, suppressing Golden's three healthy sons—adults by the time the play was produced—in the process. Changing Golden's life and the reason he relocated to Charlotte served the same dramatic purpose, as did omitting the fact that Golden subsidized the *Carolina Israelite* for most of its existence.

Lawrence and Lee chose to emphasize Golden's personality and his socially progressive views. Although obviously their play could have been about Golden's struggle to establish the *Carolina Israelite* or about the vicissitudes of his personal life, they selected his significance as a southern writer committed to racial justice and equality. Harry Golden as a force for social change is the focus for the dramatization of *Only in America*, and each of the elements of the play centers on either the ways in which he worked for social change or on his warmly sentimental humor and evocations of life in the Jewish immigrant community of New York's lower East Side in the early years of the century.

The result is a gently sentimental play; *Only in America* lacks the high drama of

Inherit the Wind or the clear-cut distinction between moral authority and political corruption of *The Gang's All Here*. Rather, it reflects the folksy humor of Harry Golden himself. Indeed, as several of the reviews of the New York production pointed out, Lawrence and Lee caught Harry Golden's personality perfectly. Why, then, did the play not attract an audience in New York?

Harry Golden himself provides one answer: the play focused too fully on Golden: "My own opinion, now that I may indulge in postmortems, is that people would not pay $6.90 [the top ticket price] to watch a make-believe Harry Golden when for $2 at a Hadassah meeting they can hear the real Harry Golden with luncheon thrown in. In short, there was too much of me in the play, not enough of the times or of Charlotte or of the issue."[8] Golden also mentions that Herman Shumlin, the play's producer-director, wanted to replace Nehemiah Persoff in the role of Golden, a view that both Lawrence and Lee agreed with many years later, saying that Persoff "wasn't quite, quite right" for the role.[9] Lawrence and Lee had urged Paul Muni to play the role; but the retired actor, fearing his ability to memorize was gone, refused.[10]

The opening night performance of *Only in America* appears to have been rocky; the *Variety* reviewer observed, "The trouble probably goes deeper than the script. Perhaps the cast . . . was thrown off balance when several of the obvious laugh lines failed to ignite, for until the very end the performance seemed strangely stilted and mistimed. What appeared to be tense, exaggerated direction may have been simply the instinctive, panicky tightening-up of rattled actors."[11] Opening night nerves aside, *Only in America* remained a character study, without the added excitement of suspense. The social conflict the Civil Rights movement was to crystallize had not yet become a critical element in American society: racial equality was an issue still comfortably distant from most Northerners in 1959.

Significantly, the 1960–61 West Coast production of *Only in America*, with Herschel Bernardi as Harry Golden, was a major success. Opening at the Ivar Theatre in Hollywood on 25 December 1960, it ran nearly a year, touring throughout Southern California after its initial stand. California reviewers praised the work, citing the playwrights for having "judiciously arranged" the scenes, and having "an inherent knack for selecting dramatic material."[12] Away from the commercial pressures of the Broadway theatre, which by the late 1950s was beginning its transformation into mostly a tourist spectacle, and after the Civil Rights movement had begun, *Only in America* was able to reach its audience.

Notes

1. All reviews are dated 20 November 1959, and all are reprinted in *New York Theatre Critics Reviews* (abbrev. *NYTCR*) 20 (1959). Robert Coleman, "'Only in America' Swell Show," *New*

York Daily Mirror, p. 227; Brooks Atkinson, "Theatre: Only in America," *New York Times*, p. 226; Walter Kerr, "First Night Report: '*Only in America*,'" *New York Herald Tribune*, p. 225.

2. Waters, "Show Out of Town: *Only in America*," *Variety*, 28 October 1959, p. 64.

3. Harry Golden, *Only in America* (Cleveland and New York: World Publishing, 1968).

4. The details of Golden's life are taken from his autobiography, *The Right Time* (New York: G. P. Putnam's Sons, 1969).

5. Golden, *Only in America*, 277–79.

6. Golden, *Only in America*, 121–162.

7. Judith Crist, "Golden, Best Seller Author, Reveals His Prison Past," *New York Herald Tribune*, 19 September 1958, pp. 1, 11. The episode is treated in Golden's *The Right Time*, pp. 349–58, written many years after the play. In 1958, Lawrence and Lee received permission from both Crist and Golden to use this material.

8. *The Right Time*, 368.

9. Lawrence and Lee, interview, 28 December 1988. See also Golden, *The Right Time*, 366–67.

10. Jerome Lawrence, *Actor: The Life and Times of Paul Muni*, 2d ed. (New York: Samuel French, 1983), 364.

11. Hobe, "Show on Broadway: *Only in America*," *Variety*, 25 November 1959, p. 70.

12. Harold Hildebrand, "'Only in America' at Ivar," *Los Angeles Examiner*, 29 December 1960, sec. 2, p. 6; David Bongard, "'Only in America' at Ivar," *Los Angeles Herald-Express*, 27 December 1960, sec. C, p. 4.

Foreword

In November of 1959 the play we wrote of *Only in America,* based freely on Harry Golden's life and work, was presented at the Cort Theatre in New York. The fact that it didn't run as long as *Abie's Irish Rose* or *Life With Father* is beside the point. It was one of the happiest experiences of our theatrical lives, because we got to know the remarkable Harry Golden and became, in effect, part of his family.

The play did run, however, for almost a year on the West Coast, to great critical and audience salvos. It starred Herschel Bernardi, who later wore the beard of Tevya nightly in *Fiddler on the Roof* on Broadway.

How do you make a play out of a book of essays? We didn't. We turned to the man himself. Harry put on drama the moment he hitched up his suspenders in the morning. This was the deceptive thing about him. He seemed relaxed, calm, easy-going; even Harry tended to see himself as a reflection in Walden Pond. Actually, he was sort of a rocket-propelled blimp, driven by enormous restlessness and an appetite for the unusual.

Harry had an astonishing gift of insight, not in fragmentary glimpses, but through a panoramic window. He saw a universe entire, with moons and matzoh-balls revolving around each other in Cartesian precision. Everybody didn't agree with the Golden vista, but almost everybody got a chuckle out of it.

We had a strange experience when we flew to Charlotte and saw for the first time Harry's combined office and living quarters on Elizabeth Avenue. We had already put on paper, entirely from imagination, a description of the play's principal set: an interbellum frame house, with a wide veranda, a lamppost in the front yard and spirea bushes hugging the steps. When the car pulled up in front of the house, there was the set of our play, exactly as we had pictured in our minds. If we had been closer to Duke University, we would have reported it as proof of ESP.

Coming away from Charlotte and our happy conversations there, we made some preliminary notes. We have just dug out these basic points, key phrases which helped us to define and illuminate the work at hand:

> The generosity of the human spirit is greater than its selfishness.
>
> Prejudice and narrowness can be conquered with laughter more effectively than with solemnity or rancor or force.
>
> Be yourself, your blessed self. Don't be an amateur gentile (or, if

you're a gentile, don't be an amateur Jew!) If you're a black, don't be an amateur white man.

Make all the world your province. There can be upheavals in tiny towns like Athens or Bethlehem. Or Charlotte, North Carolina.

The great and the powerful are usually circumscribed by the fact that they are surrounded by momentous consequences. The unknown man is more free to light candles in the dark places of the world. Little men are often the cause of the great and powerful figures of history—who, in themselves, are simply effects. The idea-ridden child is father of the genius.

One rational anomaly is worth ten million Prussian conformists.

A doer doesn't have to carry a yardstick. He has no responsibility to measure the precise results of his doing. Historians can do this for him a few centuries later.

We live in an era of fear. The so-called prudent man of our century rarely sticks his neck out. He tries to protect himself by hiding even the originality of his own thinking behind the mass of other people surrounding him. He thinks this is the way to survival; but the man who is really interested in surviving himself is no less interested in the survival of others as well.

A happy oyster only gets eaten. But the irritated oyster sometimes produces a pearl. To us, Harry Golden was the creative irritant. If the South is America's oyster, Harry was its grit of sand, which helps make the South bring forth pearls of great price.

Lawrence & Lee

(This essay was originally published in the *Carolina Israelite*, January–February 1967.)

Editor's Note

Only in America was published by Samuel French, Inc., in 1960. That text, which reflects the Broadway production, is reprinted here, with some changes. Most notably, the playwrights have deleted a minor character from the final scene. Other changes are minor, consisting mostly of deleting detailed directions for stage movement.

Cast

Only in America opened in New York at the Cort Theatre on 19 November 1959. It was produced and directed by Herman Shumlin. The scenery was designed by Peter Larkin, with costumes by Ruth Morley and lighting designed by Tharon Musser. William Barnes was production assistant. The cast included:

HELEN CHENEY .... Lynn Hamilton
HERBERT LOOMIS .... Martin Huston
MRS. ARCHER-LOOMIS .... Enid Markey
HARRY GOLDEN .... Nehemiah Persoff
FRED .... Daniel Keyes
WES .... Howard Wierum
RAY .... Wayne Tippet
TELEPHONE MAN .... Alan Alda
I. BIRNBAUM .... Ludwig Donath
JED .... Josh White, Jr.
VELMA .... Dinnie Smith
LUCIUS WHITMORE .... Sheppard Strudwick
BALTHASAR .... Jerry Wimberly
CALVIN .... David Baker
RUTH-ELLA .... Charlotte Whaley
KATE GOLDEN .... Shannon Bolin
HERSHEY M. STODDARD .... Edwin Whitner
CHAIRMAN .... Vincent Gardenia
STATE SENATOR CLAYPOOL .... Harry Holcombe
DR. LEOTA PATTERSON .... Flora Campbell
LEGISLATOR .... Laurens Moore
STENOTYPIST .... Edmund Williams
BILL DRAKE .... Don Fellows
YOUNG MAN .... Norris Borden

Only in America was produced prior to its Broadway run at the Forrest Theatre, Philadelphia, opening on 20 October 1959.

THE PLACE: Charlotte, North Carolina, and the State Capitol at Raleigh.
The time is the 1940's and 1950's.
The play is in three acts. Act II takes place five years after Act I.

The character of Harry Golden is based on Harry Golden. All the other people of the play are fictional and unrelated to any persons, living or dead, integrated or segregated.

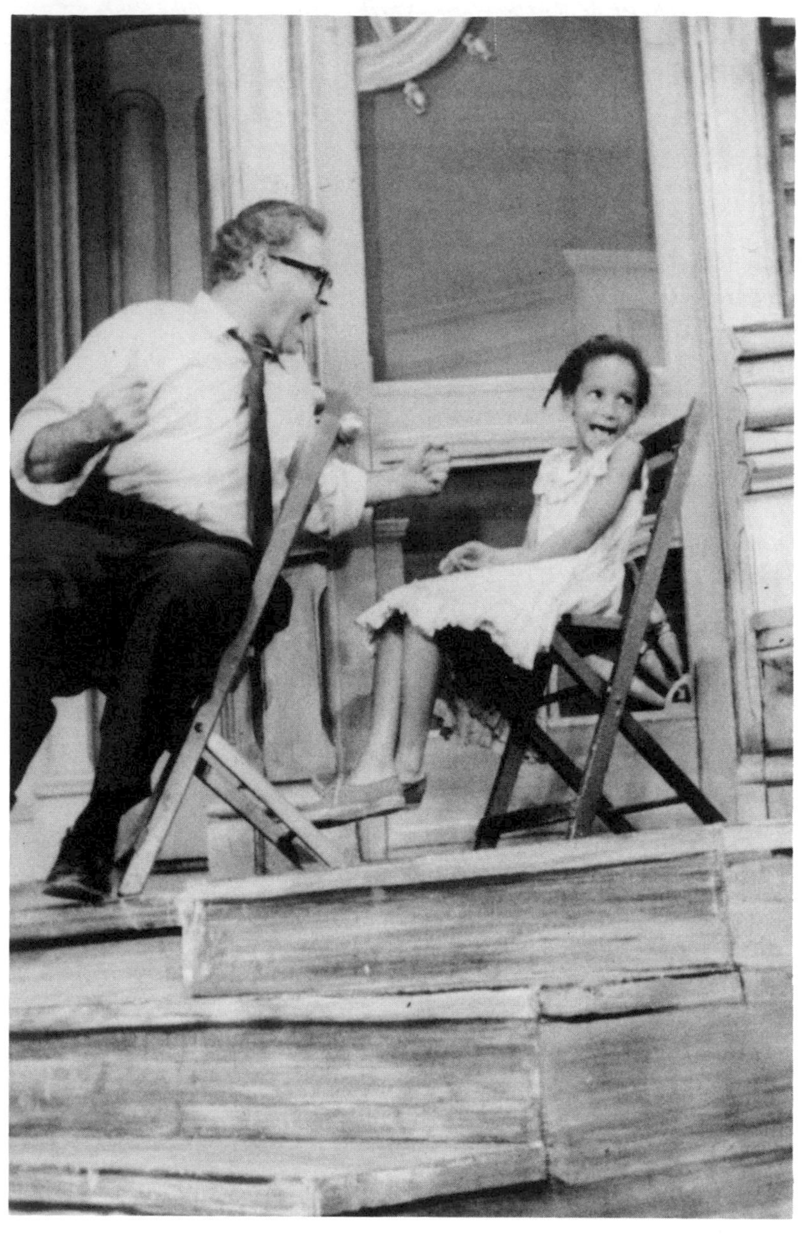

Nehemiah Persoff and Charlotte Whaley in *Only in America*, New York, 1959. Jerome Lawrence and Robert E. Lee Collection, Lawrence and Lee Theatre Research Institute, The Ohio State University.

Only in America

ACT ONE

The house which is going to be the office of the CAROLINA ISRAELITE. It is a pre–World War One white wooden house, with a broad furbelowed veranda. There is a parlor-sitting-room with expansive windows facing out on the street, and the downstage wall is cut away to reveal the interior. This parlor area is a jog in the floor plan, so that it projects far downstage. Three steps lead down from the veranda to the street level. It is a well-travelled street, residential, but adjacent to the business district of Charlotte, North Carolina. The background is an impression of the city itself: prosperous, bustling, proud, increasingly industrial but still retaining some of the quiet elegance of the plantation era. Right of the house is a climbable telephone pole. A white-barked birch tree twists its branches over the roof-top. The parlor is sparsely furnished: an overstuffed sofa and a skinny bridge lamp. There is a framed lithograph on the wall of General Robert E. Lee, slightly askew. Nailed to the post at the head of the steps is a sign reading: "TO LET." Through a well-worn screen door, we see a small entry-hall and stairs leading to bedrooms above. The parlor is through an arch from the entry. A grubby patch of lawn at the side of the house, slopes up to some spirea bushes. Before the Curtain rises, we hear the sound of a lawn mower, being pushed in short, irritable strokes. The inside of the house is concealed by a scrim painted to represent siding.

It is mid-afternoon of a spring day.

As the Curtain rises, we see Helen Cheney, an attractive black woman in her mid-twenties, on her hands and knees, scrubbing the floor of the veranda with a brush. Herbert Loomis, a gangling white boy of 15, is mowing the difficult side yard and not enjoying it at all. He stops, leaning wearily on the lawn mower.

HERBERT. Helen, is there any beer in the ice box?

HELEN. There isn't any ice box. (*Mrs. Archer-Loomis has hurried on during Herbert's speech. She wears a flowered dress, a large hat, and she is tugging at some freshly-laundered white gloves. She is portly but energetic, and is valiantly fighting the battle of trying to preserve the illusion of the late 30's from the disadvantage point of the mid-50's. She is in a hurry.*)

MRS. ARCHER-LOOMIS. Did the gentleman show up yet, Helen?

HELEN. (*Rising.*) No, ma'am.

MRS. ARCHER-LOOMIS. I do hope that veranda's dry enough for the new tenant to walk across.

HELEN. I'll run a dry-mop over it, Miz Archer-Loomis. (*She goes inside to get mop.*)

MRS. ARCHER-LOOMIS. You call that thirty-five cents' worth of lawn-mowing, Herbert? Shoulda got a nigra boy to do it. (*Helen comes out with mop.*) He'd've made it look like the puttin' green at the country club, and only cost me fifteen cents.

HERBERT. Are you kiddin', Aunt Henrietta? You can't give a homely girl a haircut and expect her to come out pretty. (*Pointing down emphatically.*) This lawn is a homely girl.

MRS. ARCHER-LOOMIS. That the kind o' sass they teach you in high school? (*Turning to Helen.*) Helen, I did want to get a look at the new tenant before he moved in. But he took the place sight-unseen—so I took *him* sight-unseen.

HERBERT. (*Looking at his watch.*) Aunt Henrietta, it's two-thirty. I only agreed to work 'til two-thirty.

MRS. ARCHER-LOOMIS. Oh, don't let me stretch you into overtime. (*Herbert leaves with the lawn mower.*) If I wait around any longer, I'll be frowned-upon late for my Immortal Books meeting. Now, Helen, here's the gentleman's name. (*Crosses to Helen, gives her slip of paper.*)

HELEN. Yes, ma'am.

MRS. ARCHER-LOOMIS. And don't breathe a word about the previous tenants.

HELEN. No, Miz Archer-Loomis. What's your Immortal Book for this month?

MRS. ARCHER-LOOMIS. "How to Stop Worrying and Start Living." I've been so frazzed, I haven't even had a minute to read it! (*Mrs. Archer-Loomis hurries off. Helen goes into the house and starts scrubbing the floor. Harry Golden enters. Herbert, whistling, comes out from behind the house. Harry is in his late forties, somewhat paunchy and unpressed. He wears horn-rimmed glasses with a sort of owlish good humor. He is carrying a worn briefcase and a battered portable typewriter. He consults a folded newspaper, searching for a house address.*)

HERBERT. That's it.

HARRY. I have an appointment to meet Mrs. Archer-Loomis.

HERBERT. Ain't here. Go on up the steps. The colored girl can show you around.

HARRY. Thank you. Thank you, son.

HERBERT. (*Warningly.*) Good luck, Mister. (*Herbert backs off.*)

HARRY. Same to you. (*Harry knocks on the screen door.*)

HELEN. Door's open. (*As Harry opens the screen door, the scrim flies, revealing the inside of the house. Harry looks about the entry hall, then goes through the archway into the parlor, where Helen is still on her knees.*) You're Mr. Golden? (*Harry nods. Helen gets up, puts pail in kitchen.*)

HARRY. I'm a little late. I'm out of the habit of carrying a watch. (*Crossing up to behind sofa, addressing the picture on the wall.*) General Lee! Good afternoon!

HELEN. (*Re-enters, takes mop to closet. Harry looks into kitchen.*) Try not to see the clutter. There's been nobody livin' here since— (*She cuts off discreetly.*) For a spell.

HARRY. (*Looking at his folded newspaper.*) One thing I didn't understand in this ad. It says: "Semi-Completely Furnished." Just what does that mean?

HELEN. Well—

HARRY. (*Has put bag on sofa table.*) Never mind. I think I get the idea. (*Puts typewriter down.*) Just so it doesn't rain on the inside and the outside at the same time.

HELEN. It's a good house, Mr. Golden.

HARRY. I guess the movers didn't get here yet? I've got some office furniture on the way.

HELEN. No, sir.

HARRY. (*Goes to Helen, taking out bills.*) I suppose Mrs. Loomis will want a month's rent in advance.

HELEN. That's Mrs. *Archer*-Loomis. With a hyphen. She's very particular about that hyphen.

HARRY. Ohhh. Do you suppose I'll qualify as a tenant for a hyphenated landlady?

HELEN. I think you'll do fine, Mr. Golden. (*Harry hands her the bills.*) I'll make out a receipt. (*She gets paper and pencil out of the drawer. Harry sits on sofa. A loose downstage leg slips off, and the couch lurches. Harry rises and puts leg back in place.*) Maybe I ought to explain what "Semi-Completely Furnished" means.

HARRY. I think it's just been vividly demonstrated.

HELEN. Here's your receipt. (*She hands him the receipt. He notices a ring she is wearing.*)

HARRY. Is that a college ring?

HELEN. Yes.

HARRY. Where'd you go to college?

HELEN. (*Takes off apron.*) I went to Cornell. They sent me up there on a state scholarship.

HARRY. Oh? That must come in very handy in the floor-scrubbing line. (*An idea hits him.*) Can you type?

HELEN. (*Puzzled.*) Yes.

HARRY. You see, I'm starting a business here, and I'm going to need some help.

HELEN. What kind of business will you be running?

HARRY. I'm in the writing business. But running a business? No, I don't want to "run" a business. I'd like to "walk" a business. Or "sit down" a business, you know what I mean? I've been running for so long, I want to settle down for a change. Settle *myself* down. (*He smiles a little and crosses to Helen.*) How would you like to work as my secretary?

HELEN. Mr. Golden. Nobody has a Negro secretary in Charlotte.

HARRY. Well, you can make me the exception! How about it?

HELEN. I'll have to think.

HARRY. (*Easily.*) Okay. Take your time. Think it over. (*Outside, Fred enters. Fred is a little man with an easy air of a southern handyman. He wears an open shirt and work-pants, generously spattered with paint drippings. He loves to putter. He carries a kit of tools. He goes up to the veranda stairs and starts fussing with the "To Let" sign.*)

HELEN. Key's in this table drawer. The same one works the front and the back. The handy man'll get rid of that barrel on the porch.

HARRY. Fine.

HELEN. (*Starts to leave. She is moved by Harry's offer. She pauses at the screen door.*) Mr. Golden, whether I do it or I don't, thank you for asking me.

HARRY. What's your name?

HELEN. Helen—Helen Cheney.

HARRY. Let me know. (*Helen goes out into the porch.*)

FRED. Mrs. Archer-Loomis told me to take the sign down. Do I still do it?

HELEN. The new tenant's inside. (*Helen exits as the Moving Men start on, pushing a roll-top desk on a dolly. Wes is the dean of moving-men. He is in his mid-forties, portly, red-faced. He wears an old open vest and unpressed pants, which bulge out below his waist-line. Ray is the younger of the two, a fresh young man in his mid-twenties, always looking toward Wes for advice and help. He wears a peaked cloth cap, and workclothes. He has a refreshing ingenuousness in his manner.*)

WES. Easy, easy. That's it. (*They move the desk to a stop near the foot of the stairs.*)

FRED. (*As he removes the "To Let" sign.*) Hi, Ray, Wes.

WES. (*Taking a delivery order from his vest pocket.*) Afternoon, Fred. Got a delivery here for Mr. H. Golden. (*Harry has been poking his head into the kitchen. Now he hears the moving men outside and starts toward the screen door.*)

FRED. (*Gesturing inside.*) She got 'im in!

RAY. I'll be damned. He's really movin' in.

WES. Maybe he just don't care.

FRED. Either he just don't care, or he just don't know.

HARRY. (*Comes out onto the porch.*) Good afternoon, gentlemen. (*Jumps off porch.*) Now there is a *desk*! (*He pats it.*) I've go no use for those modern desks, you know what I mean? Flat-chested, skinny-legged. Give me a desk with a belly on it. A nice zoftig desk.

FRED. What's that—"zoftig"?

HARRY. Well, you tell a girl she's *fat*, that's an insult. But if a girl has just enough, in the right places— (*He pantomimes in mid-air.*)

FRED. That's zoftig?

HARRY. That's zoftig. It's Yiddish.

WES. Your end in first.

RAY. I take it you're a gentleman of the Jewish persuasion? (*Wes and Ray roll desk into house.*)

HARRY. Nobody persuaded me. I woke up one morning, born, and there I was—Jewish!

FRED. My wife's a Presbyterian.

HARRY. One of the Ten Lost Tribes.

FRED. No kiddin'. You know, we've got some Jewish people here in Charlotte. Where you from?

HARRY. New York City. We've got some Jewish people there, too. (*Fred starts down the steps, carrying the sign.*) Say, you're not going to throw away that sign, are you?

FRED. No. Might need it. This is the third time in eleven months I've put it up and took it down again.

HARRY. You're not going to need it for a while. Say, I can use this barrel. Bring it in the house, will you? (*Harry takes the sign and moves through the screen door into the entry hall. The Moving Men have now set the desk upright in the parlor.*)

WES. Where do you want this?

HARRY. Right over here. Against the wall.

FRED. (*Doubtfully follows instructions.*) An empty barrel? In the parlor? (*Harry picks up the small table and puts it against the back wall.*)

HARRY. Say! I'm not interfering with your union, am I?

WES. In the liftin' business you take any help you can get.

HARRY. (*The desk is now in place.*) That's fine. Perfect. (*Still has "To Let" sign in his hand.*) Tell me something. Why has this house had such a rapid turnover? (*There is a dead pause. Ray takes the plunge.*)

RAY. Well, the Carruthers family is perfectly easy to explain. They was passin'.

HARRY. What?

RAY. Colored folks passin' for white. Way I understand it, Miz Archer-Loomis started gettin' these 'nonymous letters.

HARRY. Anonymous letters! Uh huh! Speak to me of tenant number two.

WES. Anything I know about Miss Velma is second, third hand. There were complaints about a commercial establishment in a residential area.

HARRY. What *kind* of commercial establishment?

WES. Miss Velma ran a —Massage Parlor.

HARRY. Is Massage Parlor, by any chance, a euphemism!?

FRED. If that's Yiddish for whorehouse, it was a euphemism.

RAY. You won't be bothered none by Velma's old clients. After her, Doc was here for almost six months.

HARRY. Doc. Why did he leave?

FRED. Oh, he didn't exactly leave. (*A pause.*) He hung himself. (*Harry looks from Fred to Wes. Wes looks at a spot on the ceiling above the desk where the hook used for the "deed" still remains. All look at it. A pause.*)

WES. Maybe you'd like the desk in a slightly different location?

HARRY. Why?

FRED. (*With admiration.*) You really don't mind, do you?

HARRY. (*Shrugs.*) Well, they've all moved out, haven't they? Where I was brought up, on the lower East Side of New York, when a new family moved into a place, it was very rare for the old family to move out. They'd just *accumulate*. Well, I'd better get busy. (*Takes paper out of bag.*)

WES. There's more stuff. We'll bring it right in.

HARRY. I've got work to do. (*The Moving Men go off. But Fred lingers, watching curiously as Harry opens up a battered portable typewriter. With satisfaction, he pushes up the roll-top and centers the typewriter on the open desk. He takes a sheet and spins it into the typewriter. He looks at the blank page thoughtfully. Fred watches all this with interest. Since there is no chair at the desk, Harry starts to type standing up. As he is typing, Wes re-enters with the swivel chair. Wes slips the swivel chair under Harry, who settles down into it without looking up and without missing a click at the typewriter. Ray enters with file cabinet.*)

RAY. (*As he is in the door.*) Say, where do you want I should put—

FRED. (*Imperiously.*) Sshhhhhhh!! (*Ray takes file, puts it in corner. They all watch, impressed. Harry pulls the page out of the typewriter, swings around in the swivel chair, realizing for the first time that he has an audience.*)

WES. You're a writer?

HARRY. Maybe.

FRED. So that's how you do it? You just sit down and *do* it!

RAY. Whadja write?

HARRY. Just an idea.

RAY. What is it?

HARRY. (*He decides the best explanation is to read it.*) "While the blond, blue-eyed Anglo-Saxons were wandering around Britain naked, painting themselves blue and eating berries, we Jews already had diabetes." (*He looks from one face to the next. There is absolutely no reaction. Harry shrugs, crosses to barrel and tosses the sheet into the barrel.*)

FRED. Don't let all those words go to waste. (*He starts to reach into the barrel to take out the page of paper.*) Lemme take this home and show it to my wife. It'll be something to talk about.

HARRY. (*Stopping him.*) No, no—I don't want this for a waste-basket. The *opposite*—a "Save-Basket," maybe. When I write things, what I'll do is I'll toss 'em in this barrel to pickle for a couple of weeks. Then I'll pull 'em out, and if they still taste pretty good, maybe I'll make 'em into a little newspaper.

WES. A newspaper? We already got two dailies here in Charlotte.

HARRY. This won't be a daily.

RAY. A weekly? (*Harry shakes his head.*)

FRED. (*Askance.*) A monthly?

HARRY. (*Thinks, looking at the barrel.*) *Some* months.

FRED. But the other papers'll beat you to all the news and the gossip.

HARRY. I'm not going to have any news or gossip.

WES. Then what's to write about?

HARRY. Life. I believe in it. Life is a tremendous thing, and it goes on all the time.

FRED. I'll subscribe!

HARRY. (*Touched, shaking his hand.*) Thank you. You're my first subscriber. How many publishers have a subscription list before the paper even has a name?! (*He turns toward Wes, points.*)

WES. (*Backs up a step.*) We'll wait and see how Fred likes it.

HARRY. (*Amiably.*) Fine. (*Wes and Ray start to leave. There is a warm feeling growing among the four men.*) Starting a paper is like having a baby. Calls for a libation. (*Picks up bottle.*) I'm a little short on glasses, but this stuff disinfects itself.

FRED. (*Takes the bottle.*) What do you say when somebody has a baby in that Yiddish?

HARRY. Mazel tov.

FRED. (*Toasting the bottle.*) Mazel tov. (*He drinks and passes the bottle to Wes.*)

WES. (*Not quite pronouncing it.*) Mazel tov. (*He takes a swig and passes the bottle.*)

RAY. Mazel *toff.* (*He drinks, passes the bottle back to Harry.*)

HARRY. Thank you, gentlemen.

FRED. Good luck. (*Fred goes out screen door, the Moving Men follow. Ray salutes Harry, Harry returns it. Fred has picked up his tool box. All go down steps and start off. Harry has picked up the barrel and puts it above desk, gets an idea, runs out on porch.*)

HARRY. Gentlemen, I think I've got a name for the new baby. A combination of you-all and me. "The Carolina Israelite." (*There is an absolutely blank reaction from the Three Men.*) Fred, want to cancel your subscription? (*Wes looks at Fred, who shrugs a little sheepishly, as the LIGHTS fade.*)

(*As the LIGHTS come up, it is a bright morning. A muscular Lineman is peering up at the telephone pole. He carries coils of wire looped and telephone test equipment. He also has a new phone ready to install. He adjusts his heavy leather belt and starts to climb the pole. He wears sun-tan work-clothes and is deeply tanned himself. Helen is onstage. She has brought in some books, a red baseball cap, and a framed picture of Kate. She places the books and the picture atop the desk. She puts the cap on the sofa, and goes out. Herbert comes on simultaneous with Helen's action. He is sucking on a coke bottle. He gawks up at the Lineman, who is halfway up the pole.*)

HERBERT. Hey, watcha doin', puttin' that telephone back in again?

LINEMAN. No, I'm greasing a car, can't you tell? (*The Lineman goes out of sight at the top of the pole. Herbert goes to steps, sits, watches Lineman. Harry comes downstairs. He is in his shirt-sleeves and looks as though he just got up. He goes to his desk and starts to open the top drawer when Helen re-enters, pushing a small rolling typewriter table on which a second hand standard sits, with a stack of mimeographed sheets and blank envelopes alongside. There is also a Charlotte phone book.*)

HELEN. Good morning, Mr. Golden.

HARRY. (*Opens drawer, then notices the picture of Kate. He picks it up and looks at it.*) Morning, Helen. I have no idea what time it is. Are you early or am I late?

HELEN. It's just past nine. I got some more things out of the packing box. I hope I did right.

HARRY. Oh, sure. Fine, Helen. Sure. (*He notices the cap and looks at it with amusement.*) Where did you find this?

HELEN. In the bottom of the crate. Did you want it out?

HARRY. Yeah, sure! This is my *thinking* cap. (*Gets bottle and glass from drawer.*) I know it's foolish. But I think it helps me concentrate.

HELEN. I took the liberty of fixing you some coffee. How do you take it?

HARRY. Coffee? This early in the morning? (*He pours himself a drink, and downs it with relish.*) Hahhh! Y'know the best drink is the first one in the morning. It crashes down like an avalanche! (*Putting glass down.*) Now coffee. *Now* it can find its way! (*Helen goes into the kitchen. He calls after her.*) Black! (*Harry scratches his head.*) You should pardon the expression.

LINEMAN. This is 323. Give me a test on this line will ya? (*At the sound of the Lineman's voice, Herbert rises and goes to pole.*) I don't know if it's a party line or a business phone. What does the order say? (*Harry takes the baseball cap, which he cocks on the side of his head. He seems to be deep in thought.*) There's a squawk on this circuit. Give me a new pair, will ya? (*Harry has crossed to the closet to get a broom. Herbert climbs up pole to get a look in the window. Harry grips the broom as if it were a baseball bat. Taking a wide-legged stance, he makes several passes over an imaginary home plate, as if he were a batter waiting for a good pitch. Helen enters from the kitchen, and looks puzzled. She is carrying a coffee cup and saucer. Harry looks at her a little abashed, as he almost hits her with the broom.*)

HARRY. (*Grinning.*) Don't worry. I'm not going to hit you. This is the way I like to *warm up*. When I have to bat out a few ideas, you know what I mean? (*He pantomimes this. Helen crosses to desk—puts coffee down. Harry waves his bat again, speculatively, waiting for the imaginary whoosh of another pitch.*) Naw. Let it go. What I want is an idea I can slam into a home run. (*He grips the broom more tightly and his eyes light up.*) Here it is. Maybe this is the one. (*He takes a roundhouse swing and rushes to the typewriter. Helen crosses to her own typewriter. Quietly, she continues her own secretarial duties. Herbert is incredulous at what he has seen inside. And when he sees Helen at the typewriter, he is really floored. Mrs. Archer-Loomis comes on, but stops short as she sees Herbert staring unashamedly into the window.*)

MRS. ARCHER-LOOMIS. (*Sharply.*) Herbert! (*Herbert jumps down from the pole, crosses to his aunt with a pained attitude.*) Did the Loomises rear you to be a peeping Tom?

HERBERT. You told me you wanted me to see what was going on.

MRS. ARCHER-LOOMIS. Never! Never did I instruct you to goop in the front window. What did you see?

HERBERT. Aunt Henrietta, you've done it again. You know what he's doing in there? Playing baseball. By himself. In the parlor. With a broom.

MRS. ARCHER-LOOMIS. So he's peculiar. Just so I don't have any more colored people passing for white. And that can't happen, because I found out in the morning mail, he's not only respectable, he's biblical.

HERBERT. Biblical?

MRS. ARCHER-LOOMIS. I got this invitation to subscribe to the Israelite Something-or-other. That means he's Jewish, so certainly he can't be— (*She breaks off.*) He couldn't be *both*, could he? (*She starts up the stairs.*) Oh, Herbert, if your uncle weren't dead, I'd give him a piece of my mind. Leaving me *this* thing instead of something simple like a few hundred shares of I.B.M.!

HERBERT. Maybe you shouldn't've thrown out Miss Velma.

MRS. ARCHER-LOOMIS. What do *you* know about Miss Velma?

HERBERT. Don't be so square, Aunt Henrietta. She didn't send out mimeographed invitations. But word got around. (*Herbert backs off. Mrs. Archer-Loomis knocks on the door.*)

HARRY. (*Unrolling the page from his typewriter.*) Come in. It's unhooked.

MRS. ARCHER-LOOMIS. (*She enters, full of "Welcome Wagon" grace. Back in the corner, Helen has stopped typing, and Mrs. Archer-Loomis doesn't notice her right away.*) Mr. Golden? (*Harry rises and doffs his baseball cap with a smile.*) I'm sorry I was away for the weekend at Chapel Hill, and wasn't able to greet you personally. I'm Mrs. Archer-Loomis.

HARRY. (*Warmly.*) With the hyphen. Of course! It's a pleasure. (*They shake hands. Harry takes her to couch.*) Sit down, sit—oh— (*She starts to sit on left end of couch; he pulls her to the right, then crosses to steady it. Mrs. Archer-Loomis sits carefully, sees Helen at typewriter and is shocked.*) I hope it didn't inconvenience you, my hiring Miss Cheney?

HELEN. (*Rises and nods guardedly to her former employer. She begins to gather up the stamped envelopes from the typewriter table and to stack them into a box. Lineman starts down pole. Quietly.*) Mr. Golden, I— I'll take these down to the post office, so they'll get right off. (*Tactfully, she starts toward the door.*)

HARRY. Fine. (*He picks up the broom.*) Say, will you get somebody to cut off the *broom* part of this broom—you know what I mean? All I want is the handle. (*Helen is a little puzzled, but she takes the broom and goes out quickly.*)

MRS. ARCHER-LOOMIS. Mr. Golden, I'm quite surprised to find Helen working for you.

HARRY. Why? She was working for you.

MRS. ARCHER-LOOMIS. But as a domestic. In the South, the nigra is *never* hired in a *professional* capacity. (*Lineman is down. Crosses behind house.*)

HARRY. Well, suppose she wears an apron? Would that help?

MRS. ARCHER-LOOMIS. Oh, Mr. Golden, I don't understand you. When we talked on the phone, I gathered you might be a married man, with a family.

HARRY. I am.

MRS. ARCHER-LOOMIS. Then they'll be coming here to live with you?

HARRY. No. Not right away. (*He hands her the picture.*) This is Kate.

MRS. ARCHER-LOOMIS. She's very pretty. How sad that you're separated.

HARRY. Only geographically.

MRS. ARCHER-LOOMIS. Mr. Golden. I haven't had a chance to make any inquiries into your antecedents.

HARRY. My ancestors? Well, the Mayflower beat us to this country. However, I am descended from a long line of Kibitzers and Schnorrers.

MRS. ARCHER-LOOMIS. Are those old European families?

HARRY. The oldest.

MRS. ARCHER-LOOMIS. I'm glad to hear that. But, Mr. Golden, what I *would* like to know is why your—

HARRY. Why my wife isn't here? We have a son in the hospital up in New York. We think they have the best doctors for treating muscular dystrophy.

MRS. ARCHER-LOOMIS. Oh, I'm sorry to hear about that.

HARRY. My wife can't be too far away from Bobby. But she'll be down to visit—maybe to stay—if the paper works out.

MRS. ARCHER-LOOMIS. About your paper. Is it going to be *cultural*?

HARRY. I'm not sure. Depends on what you mean by culture.

MRS. ARCHER-LOOMIS. Everybody knows what culture is. For instance, we had a season of light opera that was *very* cultural. It lost eight thousand dollars.

HARRY. Oh. If losing money is culture, meet the champ.

MRS. ARCHER-LOOMIS. I intended to subscribe to your paper, Mr. Golden. (*Both rise.*) But, frankly, I'm quite bothered about some of the things I've seen here. It seems to me you're more radical than biblical. (*The Lineman has come to the door and knocks.*)

HARRY. Come in.

LINEMAN. (*Entering.*) Phone company. Got an instrument for you.

HARRY. Help yourself.

LINEMAN. (*Wagging the instrument.*) Where do you want this thing?

HARRY. On the desk.

LINEMAN. You'll have to drill a hole in the side of it.

HARRY. Why?

LINEMAN. For the cord. So you can roll down the cover.

HARRY. Oh, no. This desk is always going to be open for business. Like an all-night hamburger joint. (*The Lineman shrugs and goes to work. He puts down tool kit, moves barrel a few feet, starts to work.*)

MRS. ARCHER-LOOMIS. I'll be leaving.

HARRY. (*Follows her out onto the veranda.*) I want you to know, Mrs. Archer-Loomis, that I hold absolutely no prejudice against you, even though you are a member of a persecuted minority.

MRS. ARCHER-LOOMIS. (*Totally baffled.*) What minority am *I* a member of?

HARRY. Landlords—and landladies—the most unpopular people in all history! All over the world, millions of tenants are just waiting for the roof to cave in or the plumbing to explode. Anything! Just so it means trouble for the poor landlord! (*Smiling.*) But I'm the minority's minority. Some of my best friends are landlords. And, I hope, landladies. (*Even in spite of herself, Mrs. Archer-Loomis is falling under the sway of the Golden charm. Harry takes her fingers and bows, with a trace of the grand manner. Helen enters, carrying the broom handle, minus the straw. At the sight of Helen, the thawed Mrs. Archer-Loomis quickly ices over again. She hurries down the steps, ignoring the *girl completely. She goes off. Jed, a thirteen-year-old Negro boy, comes on, carrying the "To Let" sign, the back of which has been freshly painted.*)

HELEN. Here's your broom. What's left of it.

HARRY. (*Taking it.*) Thank you, Helen. (*He crosses into the parlor-office, weighing the broom handle in his hands. Takes a few practice swings. The Lineman is still hard at work. Helen goes up steps.*)

JED. Delivery from Tryon Street Sign Company.

HELEN. I'll take it. (*She comes down steps and takes the sign and initials the receipt. Jed gives up the sign with reluctance, still staring at it curiously.*)

JED. This "Carolina Israelite"—that the same kind of Israelite that old King Pharaoh chased through the Red Sea?

HELEN. It's been a long chase.

JED. I didn't know they got all the way to Carolina. (*Lineman starts to put wire around desk. Jed goes off impressed, still looking back over his shoulder, puzzled.*)

HELEN. (*Calling.*) Your sign's here, Mr. Golden. (*Harry puts broom in closet, comes out onto the veranda, takes the sign and reads it proudly.*)

HARRY. They did a nice job. (*He flips sign over. Helen enters house, crosses to her table.*) Well, got to get the shingle up. (*He hangs sign on post, steps back to admire it.*)

LINEMAN. (*Dials.*) Franklin 5–6624. Give me a ring back on this, will ya, honey? (*Hangs up.*)

HARRY. (*Enters house.*) Finally I know how a brand new dentist feels. Now all I need is a waiting room full of cavities. (*PHONE rings; Lineman answers.*)

LINEMAN. O.K. You're in business. (*Hangs up.*)

HARRY. (*Sits.*) Fine. (*Harry starts to bring the phone toward him, but the cord is very short, and only goes a foot or so from the desk.*) Say, how about a little more stretch on this thing? So I could sit on the sofa and call.

LINEMAN. (*Looks at ceiling.*) A long cord? Not in *this* house! (*He goes out and the screen door slams. Harry's eyes drift subtly toward the ceiling.*)

HARRY. There's been plenty of tzouris around here.

HELEN. Plenty.

HARRY. How do you know what tzouris means?

HELEN. Well, there was a Jewish boy in my Psychology Seminar at Cornell; and when he flunked the final, he sang, "Nobody knows the Tzouris I've seen." (*Harry laughs.*)

HARRY. Tell me. After Ithaca, how come you wandered back into the land of Egypt?

HELEN. Well, the South may be Egypt, Mr. Golden—but the North isn't quite the Promised Land. When you've got half-a-dozen kid brothers and sisters, and folks who need you, what good is Ithaca? When I came home, I brought my father a store-made suit; and my mother a dress that nobody'd ever worn before, not ever. I was seventeen when I left Charlotte; and in all my life I'd never seen my father except in overalls. And I'd never seen my mother, except in an apron. (*She breaks off, apologetically.*) I'm sorry. I'll get on with the work.

HARRY. No. Tell me. What does your father do?

HELEN. He's a janitor. And my mother works in people's kitchens. When I was a kid, playing around outside, a car would pull up and the people would say, "Tell Nettie not to come tomorrow. And tell Jim the key is under the front mat. We're going to Florida." And Nettie is your mother and Jim is your father—and those people in the car don't even know you have a last name.

HARRY. (*After a thoughtful pause.*) Miss Cheney.

HELEN. Yes, sir?

HARRY. Those people who drove down to Florida—did they come back with a nice deep tan?

HELEN. I suppose so.

HARRY. That's a pretty neat trick: to think in one direction while your skin's going in the other. (*They both laugh a little. Then Harry makes a decision.*) Helen, I want you to take a letter. (*Promptly she reaches for her pad.*) We may not send this out right away. But let's see how it sounds. (*He paces as he talks.*) "Dear Possible Advertiser, Wherever You Are—" (*Helen is dutifully taking this down, although she looks a little askance at this beginning.*) "This letter is about a new kind of paper. It's actually a very *old* kind of paper—what might be called a 'personal journal.' The opinions in it will be my opinions. And I hope—" (*He breaks off.*) "I hope—" How'm I going to tell people what this paper is going to be like? *I'm* not sure. But without any advertisers, there can't be any paper to find out about. You know what I'm trying to do, Helen? Make a pig-in-a-poke kosher! I'm crazy. Clean off my rocker. Who's going to cough up a Confederate uniform button to somebody who's saying what nobody wants to hear? Maybe I am crazy. But maybe I'm not! If I can sneak in a few laughs—just a few—maybe I can get a few advertisers—just a few. (*Doubtfully.*) Maybe. (*Mr. Birnbaum, who has entered during the above, is a conservatively dressed merchant, slightly balding, nervous, but with a discipline to keep his tension in check, except for occasional outbursts. He goes up the steps, looks at the sign and shakes his head. He raps importantly on the screen door. Birnbaum has scoured his speech clean from any trace of an immigrant's accent.*) Come in. (*Birnbaum walks in. Harry crosses to him pleasantly, extends his hand.*) My name's Harry Golden.

BIRNBAUM. (*There is no pleasantness in him.*) Birnbaum. I. Birnbaum. (*Shakes hands, takes off hat.*) I am a committee of one representing several Jewish merchants in Mecklenberg County.

GOLDEN. Fine.

BIRNBAUM. What are you trying to do to us, Mr. Golden?

HARRY. Sit down, Mr. Birnbaum. (*Birnbaum begins to search his pockets.*) You looking for something? Cigar? (*Birnbaum shakes his head.*) Cigarette?

BIRNBAUM. (*Finds what he's looking for.*) Tums! (*Harry sits in his swivel chair to wait to find out the reason for Birnbaum's visit. Birnbaum pops a Tum into his mouth.*) I got your circular. Why, Mr. Golden? *Why* would anybody come to Charlotte, North Carolina, and start a newspaper for the Jews? Mr. Golden, do yourself a favor. Do *me* a favor.

HARRY. Yes?

BIRNBAUM. *Go home!*

HARRY. (*Searching his memory.*) Isaac Birnbaum—the Dixie Dry Goods Store—"Exclusive but not Expensive." As a matter of fact, I was just writing you a letter.

BIRNBAUM. Please! Not another letter. (*He takes another Tum, his last.*)

HARRY. Make a note of that, Helen. (*Turning back to Birnbaum.*) I'd like to have you meet my secretary, Miss Cheney.

BIRNBAUM. (*Glances over and sees Helen at the typewriter. He reaches for another Tum, but realizes they're all gone. Then he sinks back, closing his eyes.*) Oh, God! Mr. Golden, you're probably a nice fella, trying to make a dollar. A crazy way to make a dollar, but fine. I personally have been in Charlotte thirty years. A lifetime I have been trying to build myself a comfortable business. (*Helen exits to kitchen.*) A *Charlotte* business. A Carolina business. Not a *Jewish* business. And now you come in here like a bulldozer to wreck everything.

HARRY. (*He is a little bit stopped. Is Birnbaum making sense? Uncertainly, takes bottle from drawer.*) I—I certainly didn't come here to make trouble for anybody. (*Trying to ease the tension.*) How about a schnapps? (*He pours a drink.*)

BIRNBAUM. No, never, not during business hours.

HARRY. (*Lifting the glass.*) L'cheim. (*Birnbaum gestures in mid-air as if the man is crazy. Harry drinks.*) I'll tell you, Mr. Birnbaum, you remind me of a story from the old country. Once a lion escaped from a travelling circus. Thousands of people were running through the streets frantically. An old man with a beard asked, "What's all the excitement about?" They yelled: "A wild lion is loose!" And the old man asked, "Is that *good* for the Jews, or *bad* for the Jews?"

BIRNBAUM. What you're doing is bad for the Jews!

HARRY. Why?

BIRNBAUM. Because it *calls attention*! (*He lowers his voice, more reasonably.*) I'll tell you frankly. About my own son, Leslie. He was born Leonard Birnbaum. Today he is legally Leslie Burns. At first—I won't deny it—I felt bad about this. But he's in medical school now. And when Leslie goes out to practice, he'll be a *regular* doctor, not just a Jewish doctor! (*Helen re-enters.*)

HARRY. He's crazy. Even the Pope has a Jewish doctor. (*Mr. Birnbaum can't answer this, and is apparently getting some gastric distress. His Tums gone, he throws the empty wrapper on the floor, looks in his pockets.*) Helen, see if you can find our guest an Alka-Seltzer. (*Helen goes out to the kitchen.*)

BIRNBAUM. How can I make you understand?

HARRY. Mr. Birnbaum. I saw it every day on the East Side of New York, when I was a kid. The Immigrants would get off the boat with long, full beards. And the first thing they bought was a razor. Everybody wanted to be like the goyem—fast! But today, a doctor with a beard is *automatically* a specialist!

BIRNBAUM. The struggle will not be so hard for Leslie Burns!

HARRY. Maybe, maybe. But the way I see it—who needs an amateur gentile?

BIRNBAUM. (*Rises and shakes his fist at Harry.*) Haven't you heard about anti-Semitism?

HARRY. I'm against it! But how about the anti-Semite? A sick man. Who knows—maybe his teeth hurt. (*He shakes his head sadly.*) What a loss to Leslie. A beautiful name like Birnbaum. "Pear Tree"! Absolutely beautiful. There's nothing wrong with a name like Burns. It's very nice, if you wrote "My Heart's in the Highlands," you know what I mean? Take "Goldberg." "Golden Mountain." In Italian, it's "Monte d'Oro"! Or "Rosenfeld"—"Field of Roses"! For a name, what could be lovelier?

BIRNBAUM. (*Hopelessly.*) Is this the kind of thing you're going to put in this paper?

HARRY. Possible.

BIRNBAUM. Who's interested besides the Jews—and the Jews aren't interested!

HARRY. Well, I'm going to write about a lot of things. I've got some new ideas about the South.

BIRNBAUM. (*Muttering.*) He's got ideas about the South!

HARRY. I suppose it's foolishness to ask if the Dixie Dry Goods would take an ad.

BIRNBAUM. Absolutely not! Under no circumstances! I refuse to— (*He breaks off, glances toward the kitchen. His attitude changes.*) I *will* take an ad. On one condition. Don't write about the Shvartze. About the black man, don't stick your neck out, Mr. Golden. Because you're sticking *my* neck out, too. You've got nothing to lose.

HARRY. I've got a neck. (*He speaks without ire, but with intense conviction.*) Mr. Birnbaum, I believe very strongly that "Let us not stick our necks out" is the watchword of the ghetto! And I do not believe in ghettoes: white, black, Puerto Rican or Jewish!

BIRNBAUM. Maybe you had a happier childhood than I did. My name is Isaac. And it is hard to forget the kids yelling at me, "Hey, Ikey! Ike! Ike!"

HARRY. How many of those kids grew up and put stickers on their windshields: "I like Ike"?

BIRNBAUM. (*Throwing his hands in the air.*) On top of everything, he's a Republican! (*Starts for door.*)

HARRY. (*Follows him.*) Wait. The next time you see Leslie, I want you to tell him about a friend of mine. He also changed his name. But now he's sorry. Because he figures that come judgment day, when the whole human race is lined up, getting their passports stamped for the final excursion, one of three Jewish fellas is going to be in charge: Jesus, Marx, or Freud! (*Helen has entered. Harry takes Alka-Seltzer from her, and offers it to Birnbaum.*) Alka-Seltzer? (*Birnbaum takes Alka-Seltzer and downs it in a gulp, burps, hands Harry the glass and goes off.*) You'd better fix one for me, too. (*The lights fade.*)

(*There is a lighting transition to night. The light from a street lamp throws sharp shadows along the veranda and down the empty street. The stage is deserted. There is no light in the parlor-office and all is quiet inside the house. Jed, the young Negro boy, comes on. He is very much distraught. He hesitates, looking at Harry's sign. Suddenly, with resolution, he dashes up the steps, is about to knock, then hesitates. Hearing footsteps down the street, fear overtakes him. He backs down the steps and runs off. Herbert enters on his way home from the movies, whistling and finishing up the dregs of a sack of popcorn. Velma enters. Her hair is getting tired of being dyed, but she was really a knockout about twelve years ago. She still has a good many charms on the voluptuous side. Harry would definitely call her zoftig. She crosses in a sort of "Remembrance of Things Past" mood, staring at Harry's house—particularly up at the second story. Herbert watches her pass with a glint of recognition in his eye. Velma stops in front of the house, shifts her hips into "at ease" position, and looks about warmly. Herbert takes a few steps toward her.*)

HERBERT. Hi, Miss Velma. (*Velma looks at him with a detached disdain.*) When did you get back in town? I was talking to the hardware salesman, who said you were workin' in Raleigh.

VELMA. (*Her eyes narrowing.*) I don't want any trouble with you, kid.

HERBERT. Miss Velma, whatcha got against me?

VELMA. If I even answer you, they'll say I'm contributing to the delinquency of a minor. (*She looks back at the house fondly.*) I always like to visit houses where I used to live. I like to know if the people living in 'em now are happy. (*Dreamily.*) I can almost hear the girls laughing, and the victrola playing. (*On first step.*) It's crazy, but I can even smell the cigar smoke. (*Tentatively, craning her neck a little as if she were going to stare in the front window, Velma goes tiptoe up the steps to the veranda. Suddenly she sees for the first time the sign by the screen door: "The Carolina Israelite." She is incredulous.*) Holy God, it's a church! (*Inside, the telephone starts ringing and Velma jumps as if it were a burglar alarm. She hurries down the steps and exits without even a fare-thee-well to Herbert, who saunters off. After the second ring, a lamp is turned on in the stairwell and Harry appears on the staircase, dressed in robe and slippers. He tightens the belt on his robe. As he comes through the archway into the parlor-office, he flips light switch. Bridge lamp goes on. The telephone continues to rasp insistently.*)

HARRY. (*Picking up the phone.*) Hello? Kate? Oh, excuse me, I was expecting a long distance call. (*Pause.*) Yes, this is Harry Golden. (*Pause.*) Well, I'm both—the editor *and* the publisher. (*He rubs his eyes.*) Well, I'm glad you got our first issue—and it's very nice of you to call me and— (*Whatever is coming through the telephonic earpiece seems to waken Harry like a splash of cold water.*) Oh, you didn't like it. (*Apparently a rabid tirade is coming over the telephone now, and Harry tries several times to get a word in edgewise, politely—but without success.*) You have a right to whatever opin— (*He listens.*) I don't expect everybody to agree with—. Yes—. Well—. But— (*Finally Harry just gives up and listens for quite a while. Harry makes an amiable response to a sharp question.*) I'm still here. Just let me know when you want me to say something.

(*Pause.*) Am I *supposed* to be scared? (*Pause.*) Sure I know what K.K.K. means. (*Getting down to business.*) Listen, you dopey bastards! If you put a bomb under my veranda, you'll make me into a Hebrew Nathan Hale. I'm a nobody. You guys want to make me into a *somebody*. Swell. When can I expect you? I'll put a light on the porch. (*Pause.*) Are you still there? (*Pause. There has evidently been a click from the other end.*) Hello? Hello? (*He holds the telephone at arm's length, looking at it with a shrug. He hangs up the telephone as if it were a little bit dirty, then wipes off his hand on his pajama leg.*) Boom! (*Addressing the phone.*) Please, boys, don't do it. It shouldn't happen to Mrs. Archer-Loomis. (*The phone rings. Harry picks it up and assumes he is still talking to K.K.K.*) Go ahead, Kleagle. Oh, New York. Yes, I'm ready for my call. (*As the party finally answers at the other end, Harry rises with excitement.*) Kate? Kate, I woke you up. (*Brief pause.*) I tried to get you earlier, but the lines were tied up. No, no, no, nothing's wrong. Everything's just fine. I'm a success; the Ku-Klux-Klan wants to kill me. (*He listens.*) Kate, the paper came out today. I sent you the very *first* copy. I think you'll like it. I hope you'll like it. *I* like it, Kate. I agree with everything the guy says! (*He listens.*) Who knows? After paying the printer, I've got forty dollars and seventy-five cents left—cash money. (*He softens.*) How's Bobby? (*Pause. Looking down as he listens.*) Yeah. I know. Sure. I'll be up—maybe week after next. Kate, if the paper works, you can run right out and buy a railroad ticket. (*He listens.*) All right. No promises. What? (*Pause.*) Oh, sure. They've got an A. & P. here, a Piggly-Wiggly, everything but hot pastrami. And I wash the dishes every Thursday. Go back to sleep, Kate. Happy dreams. (*Slowly he hangs up the telephone—with affectionate contrast to the previous time. In fact Harry's reaction to the telephone instrument itself is always conditioned by the person with whom he's talking. Jed appears again. He seems to have mustered his courage. He takes a deep breath, then bolts up the steps to the veranda. Jed pounds urgently at the door. Harry scowls thoughtfully.*) Are they here already? (*He crosses his fingers, and goes out into the entry hall. Harry flicks on the porch lights, and Jed freezes. Harry squints through the screen.*) Who is it?

JED. 'Scuse me, sir. I don't have no business wakin' people up this hour of the night. But I noticed you was connected with the Israelites—and maybe you can help me!

HARRY. (*Opens door.*) Come on in. (*Jed takes two steps in, stops. Harry moves him in, closes door.*) What's your trouble?

JED. It's my brother Melchior. He's in jail again. And if somebody don't bail him out, they're going to give 'im sixty days on the road gang.

HARRY. What's he done? What's he in for?

JED. Melchior ain't done nothin'. No crime. He's my big brother. He's real strong.

HARRY. What's your name?

JED. Jed! It's Jedediah, really—only everybody calls me "Jed." Just like they call Melchior "Mel." Melchior's one of the wise men in the Bible.

HARRY. How come you wanted to see *me*, Jedediah?

JED. (*Hesitantly.*) The Israelites—they was top experts at gettin' people freed from bondage—Egypt, and like that! And since you're connected with the Israelites, I thought—well, you oughta know how to get somebody outta jail.

HARRY. (*Rubs his forehead thoughtfully.*) Oh? Yeah. Sure. I'm a top expert. What charges they got against him?

JED. Disturbin' the peace. He hit a bus driver. (*Harry whistles. Jed crosses to Harry.*) Mel didn't feel like sitting in the back of the bus. And the driver made a fist at him, and Mel made a fist back, and Mel's fist accidentally got in the driver's face.

HARRY. What's the bail?

JED. Forty dollars.

HARRY. (*Laughing at the irony of it.*) Forty dollars. Pretty expensive bus ride.

JED. Mel just cares too much.

HARRY. (*Reaching for envelope with money.*) And this time he cared forty dollars worth. Couldn't he have cared 20 dollars worth? Oh, what the hell. Here. (*Handing him the money.*)

JED. I didn't expect *you* to—I just thought maybe you could *know* somebody—and make a phone call. (*He looks at Harry wonderingly.*) You must be *rich.*

HARRY. (*Gives him the money.*) Oh, sure.

JED. I don't even know your name.

HARRY. Cornelius Vanderbilt. (*Rises, arm around Jed, leads him to door.*) And don't worry— (*Opens door. Jed and Harry come on the porch.*) I'll get along. I'll sell a railroad.

JED. (*As he goes down steps.*) Thank you, sir. We'll pay you back. Honest. Thanks! Thanks, Mr. Vanderbilt. (*Harry shrugs. The lights fade.*)

(*It is a sunshiny afternoon. Fred is painting base of steps. Helen is drinking milk from a carton.*)

FRED. What time's Mr. Golden gettin' back, Helen?

HELEN. You never know. When he goes downtown to hunt for advertisers, it sometimes takes him three hours to get three blocks.

FRED. I never saw a man like to talk to people the way he does. He talks to everybody.

HELEN. Better'n that, he listens to everybody. If talking were advertising, this'd be the *Saturday Evening Post.*

FRED. You know, a lot of people feel kinda upset about you workin' here.

HELEN. I know. How do you feel?

FRED. Well, I don't know. My wife says I'm adjustin' to it. She thinks maybe I'm gettin' over-adjusted.

HARRY. (*Enters in a happy mood.*) Hello, Fred. How's the painting business. (*Up steps.*)

FRED. Fine, Mr. Golden.

HARRY. (*Goes in. Helen follows.*) Helen, I got two new advertisers. Little ones. But every inch counts. (*Fred finishes, goes off.*)

HELEN. That'll make up for the Shelby Rolling Mills.

HARRY. Where did they go?

HELEN. Letter's on your desk. They "regretted" to cancel their advertisement. On the advice of their attorney.

HARRY. That's the same kind of "regret" we got from the Electric Company. Maybe I ought to send a box of candy to the Bar Association.

HELEN. Melchior was here again. He says he just can't remember the words you told him to say when he's riding a bus.

HARRY. If he forgets, tell him silence is stronger than a left hook.

HELEN. A committee of ladies from the Richmond Street Prayer Circle came by to announce that this month you're their *project*.

HARRY. Project? What are they going to do to me?

HELEN. They're going to pray for you.

HARRY. Well, that can't hurt, can it? (*Peering into the barrel.*) Well, Helen, how about getting out a newspaper?

HELEN. Same way we did the first issue?

HARRY. Why not? Seemed to work all right, y'know what I mean? (*Harry puts cigar in mouth, lifts the barrel, and dumps the contents haphazardly onto the floor in front of the sofa.*) I hope we let 'em pickle long enough! (*As he goes through the pages.*) A long piece, then a short piece. A serious piece, then a funny piece—we should be so lucky! Helen, separate the long ones from the short ones.

HELEN. (*Eagerly.*) Yes, Mr. Golden.

HARRY. Boy, I struck out swinging on this one. (*He crumples it. She retrieves it. He studies another item.*) I hope the printer can read my typing better than *I* can. Ah. Here's a starter: "Never Die on Friday."

HELEN. Why?

HARRY. It spoils everybody's weekend.

HELEN. We've got a lot of short ones this time.

HARRY. Good. They're harder to write. (*Studying another sheet.*) "What Every Temple Wants: A Blond Rabbi." (*Shrugging.*) Maybe. What else have we got here? (*He reads another.*) "The Shadkhan always carried an umbrella."

HELEN. What's a—"Shadkhan"?

HARRY. Ohh—a professional friend of the family. A marriage broker. On the Lower East Side, marriages weren't made in heaven: they were made under the shadkhan's umbrella. If the girl was 18, she'd ask the shadkhan, "What does he look like?" At the age of 25 she'd ask, "What does he do for a living?" At the age of 35 she'd ask, "WHERE IS HE!?" (*He searches through some more pages.*)

HELEN. (*Puzzling over the end of one sheet.*) What kind of punctuation do you want at the bottom of this page?

HARRY. Read it.

HELEN. (*Reading.*) "The big social event on the lower east side of New York was a wedding or a bar."

HARRY. Huh? Oh—Mitzvah. There's another page. (*On his knees, he reaches for another page, which he seizes on with an air of discovery.*) "A wedding or a Bar *Mitzvah*." (*Hands it to Helen.*)

HELEN. What's that?

HARRY. A once-in-a-lifetime birthday party. (*Reflectively.*) Ahhh, Helen—so many things start happening to a boy when he's thirteen. A whisker breaks through, his glands start to murmur to him. And on the Saturday nearest his thirteenth birthday, the skinny little kid, who looks as if he couldn't crack a walnut, stands up in front of the whole congregation and says: "Today I am a Man!" (*Unobtrusively, Helen starts taking shorthand notes.*) But on Saturday night, you never saw celebrations like those weddings and Bar Mitzvahs in the old days. Such music, such food! And the poor Bar Mitzvah kid stood there in his blue serge suit—that itched—and had to shake hands with two hundred people he never saw before. And everybody gave him a fountain pen so he could write out a prescription as a doctor fifteen years later. (*Smiling as he thinks back.*) But there was one big headache. Gate-crashers! Young fellas on the Lower East Side used to gather on a street corner and say, "Let's go to a wedding"—like today they'd say, "Let's go to a movie." It wasn't too tough to get in. You put on your good suit and picked out the celebration that smelled the best. By the time the *invited* guests arrived, with a fountain pen or a wedding present, all the food was gone! (*He chuckles to himself.*) They tried everything. A hat-check fee. You didn't wear a hat. "Show your invitation." "I left it home." Finally they licked it. They hired a couple of bruisers from the district Tammany Club. When you came to the door, one of these fellas would smile very politely and say, "Whom do you know, the bride or the groom?" You'd take a guess and say, "The bride." Wham!—they picked you up by the collar: "Get outta here, you bum, this is a Bar Mitzvah!" I wish I had that in the story.

HELEN. You have. I'll type it up later.

HARRY. Well, thank you, Cornell. (*Picks up another piece.*) Here's one: "Aaron Burr accomplished what most men dream of all their lives: to be convicted of adultery at the age of eighty." (*Whitmore enters.*) Here's a shortie, an in-betweener: "Cato's cure for a hangover—raw cabbage leaves." I wonder if it works. I'll have to take a drink sometime and find out. (*Whitmore climbs the veranda steps and knocks.*) If you're an advertiser, come on in. If you aren't, we don't need any! (*Lucius Whitmore enters. He is a distinguished-looking man, with white hair. He walks in an almost military manner, ramrod stiff. His clothing is rich and well-tailored, but there is no dandyism about him. No one can doubt that he is an aristocrat in the oldest and best Southern tradition. He has a copy of the "Carolina Israelite" folded under one arm. Whitmore takes off his hat as he comes into the room, discovering Harry on his hands and knees, shuffling through pages of manuscript on the floor. At the sight of Whitmore, whom she recognizes, Helen takes a step back.*)

WHITMORE. I'm not exactly an advertiser. But I *am* associated with some of them. (*Harry gets up. Helen gathers some papers, picks up coat, clips, exits into kitchen.*)

HARRY. (*Smiling a little sheepishly.*) Excuse me for shouting at you. (*He extends his hand.*) I'm Harry Golden.

WHITMORE. (*Taking his hand, studying him.*) Lucius Whitmore.

HARRY. (*Recognizing the name.*) Oh!

WHITMORE. I apologize for disturbing you.

HARRY. (*With a little laugh.*) Well, this isn't exactly the way they get out the Atlanta "Constitution." (*Glancing at the floor, littered with countless scraps.*) Do you know what I mean?

WHITMORE. (*Only the faintest trace of a smile crosses his face.*) I should have telephoned for an appointment, Mr. Golden.

HARRY. No, no—that's never necessary. (*Pleased, he notices a copy of the paper under Whitmore's arm. Squats, gathers papers from floor.*) You've got a copy of the paper. I'm honored.

WHITMORE. Yes. (*Opens the slim paper and turns through its pages easily.*) I'm legal counsel for Roger Lundy, who runs the Fuel Oil Company on South Tryon Street.

HARRY. I just saw him this morning. He took out an ad. Quite a guy—knows Shakespeare. How often do you run across a fuel-oil distributor who can quote *Coriolanus*?

WHITMORE. I've advised him *not* to take that advertisement. (*There is a dead pause. Harry rises.*) However, you made a very favorable impression on Mr. Lundy; and he asked me to meet you before he acted on my advice.

HARRY. Well, here I am. Look me over. I have very sound teeth.

WHITMORE. Mr. Golden, I have a responsibility to protect my clients.

HARRY. Protect them from what? Do I look like Sherman marching to the sea? Mr. Whitmore, I need your clients. A column inch or two from some of them will get this stuff off the floor and into a printing press. (*Picks up last few papers from floor.*) Y'see, I am not a "gentleman publisher." Don't confuse me for a minute with Marshall Field. You know how he happens to own the Chicago Sun-Times? One day his wife said, "Honey, will you run down to the corner and buy me a newspaper?"

WHITMORE. (*Laughs.*) I find your paper vastly amusing. But, Mr. Golden, I don't *agree* with what you're writing. I don't oppose your paper. But when you ask my clients to *endorse* it, that's a rather different matter.

HARRY. Are you saying the free American press is controlled by its advertisers? I realize I'm pretty small potatoes to get so *noble* about this—but I just don't believe it.

WHITMORE. May I sit down?

HARRY. (*Gesturing to sofa.*) Please.

WHITMORE. (*Sitting; Harry puts papers on sofa table.*) You know, we've had visitors from the North before—people who come here for a few days, even a few weeks, then scurry back North, experts on the Southern problem.

HARRY. (*Simply.*) I'm living here, Mr. Whitmore. Permanently.

WHITMORE. Yes. That interests me. (*Scowling, troubled.*) We have another kind of visitant, who wants to throw matches into the brush, just to see it blaze.

HARRY. So you've had some strangers here with matches in their pockets. Does that mean you want to keep everybody else out?

WHITMORE. Certainly not. We have new businesses coming from the North every week.

HARRY. Ah! You welcome the dollars, but you're worried about the ideas! Why? Is there anything in my paper about Pappy chasing his daughter-in-law around the barn? Who's writing all those plays and novels about how sick the South is? The Southern boys! Who made incest look like the Confederacy's favorite indoor sport? Nobody from Nantucket! (*Whitmore has heard enough and starts to speak; Harry goes on.*) Do you know why I came to the South? (*Harry moves to the window.*) Because the next great story in America is happening here, right here. Right outside this window. The shifting of a whole social order. Sure, down here you still have the beautiful white-pillared mansion on the hill at twilight—twenty-seven rooms and one bath. But the plumber's coming! And now a tractor chugs up that hill, and it doesn't care who drives it. What a story! I want to talk about it in a paper of my own! Do you want to stop me?

WHITMORE. I'll advise Mr. Lundy at the Fuel Oil Company— (*He rises.*) to think it over. (*Goes out the screen door.*)

HARRY. (*Sighs, calls after Whitmore and follows him out onto the porch.*) Mr. Whitmore, are you by any chance the attorney for the Shelby Rolling Mills?

WHITMORE. Why, yes, I am.

HARRY. And the Catawba Light and Power?

WHITMORE. Yes.

HARRY. (*With a hopeful twinkle.*) While the fuel oil company is "thinking it over," will you see if the rolling mill and the electric light company could maybe "think it over" too? (*This amuses Whitmore. He smiles, pats Harry on the shoulder and goes down the steps. Harry is quite happy as he watches Whitmore go off. Harry re-enters the house, taking a cigar and matches from his shirt pocket. As he strikes the match, Helen enters from the kitchen.*)

HELEN. How'd it go?

HARRY. Maybe I've made a friend, Helen. If somebody'd give me a fountain pen, I think I could say: "TODAY I AM A MAN!" (*He puts the lighted match to his cigar, as*)

CURTAIN

ACT TWO

The office. But it is five years later and there have been many changes: a lot of circulation files, a swing (or a hammock) on the veranda, a rug on the floor, a new leather couch. An air of prosperity prevails. On the wall are pictures flanking Robert E. Lee: Adlai Stevenson and Chief Justice Warren.

At Rise: Fred is just hanging up two new ones: Einstein and Sandburg. Helen is at the desk, going through a huge stack of mail.

FRED. You know, from the way they sign their names, I'd think Einstein was Sandburg and Sandburg was Einstein. (*Watching Helen.*) Those all new subscriptions?

HELEN. Most of them.

FRED. I can remember five years ago when he only had *one* subscriber. (*He goes out door, leaving it ajar. Mrs. Archer-Loomis hurries on. Goes up steps.*) Looking for Mr. Golden?

MRS. ARCHER-LOOMIS. Well, I am, and I'm not.

FRED. He ain't in. Helen's there. (*Mrs. Archer-Loomis knocks, enters house. Helen rises. Fred exits.*)

HELEN. Can I help you, Miz Archer-Loomis?

MRS. ARCHER-LOOMIS. Where's Mr. Golden, Helen?

HELEN. He's making a speech at the Thursday Afternoon Merchants' Association. He's the guest of honor.

MRS. ARCHER-LOOMIS. I'm relieved he's not here. Because what I want to do is sort of a surprise. You know he's coming to talk to our Immortal Books Group next Wednesday—on the Old Testament. (*Sits.*) After all, that *is* an immortal book, isn't it? And I felt I just had to have something appropriate-proper to serve for the dessert-coffee. (*She unfolds a copy of "The Carolina Israelite."*) So I want to have one of those Hebraic delicacies he's always writing about. Helen, what's a bagel?

HELEN. Well, I really don't know exactly. It's kind of a hard doughnut. Like a little wheel.

MRS. ARCHER-LOOMIS. A wheel? And you eat it?

HELEN. You eat it with lox. (*They stare at each other blankly.*)

MRS. ARCHER-LOOMIS. What are lox?

HELEN. I don't know that, either. (*She studies the paper again.*)

MRS. ARCHER-LOOMIS. Oh, dear. Helen, do you know what a blintz is or something else called a knishe?

HELEN. Maybe I could find out.

MRS. ARCHER-LOOMIS. (*Rises.*) Do try, Helen. Do it secretly—so I can surprise him at the party. I just don't want to have to fall back again on pineapple upside-down cake. (*She has walked to the screen door, starts to leave but stops as she hears voices. Harry and Birnbaum have entered during above speech.*)

BIRNBAUM. Harry, what a speech you gave. You didn't offend anybody!

MRS. ARCHER-LOOMIS. (*Starts for the kitchen.*) I've got another source of information.

HARRY. What was to worry about, Ike?

MRS. ARCHER-LOOMIS. I'll go out the back way. (*She is gone. Helen follows her into the kitchen.*)

BIRNBAUM. I'll be perfectly frank. When the Merchants' Association invited you to speak, I started to shake.

HARRY. (*They are now below the steps.*) Imagine! My mother couldn't speak a word of English—and now the leading merchants of Charlotte, North Carolina, take time out to listen to her son! What a wonderful country! It could only happen in America!

BIRNBAUM. A favor. (*Quickly he reaches in his pocket and hands Harry three one-dollar bills.*) Here. Kindly enter a subscription for my son Leslie.

HARRY. You told me he reads the paper.

BIRNBAUM. Yah. My copy. I'm ashamed. Is this any way for one business man to treat another?

HARRY. (*Laughs, takes money, fishes out a scrap of paper and a pencil stub.*) Let's see—that's Leslie Burns—

BIRNBAUM. (*Proudly.*) M.D., University Hospital, Columbus, Ohio.

HARRY. It's done. (*Up steps.*)

BIRNBAUM. If you've got a minute, stop in the store later in the day. (*Mrs. Archer-Loomis starts on.*) Harry, what size shirt do you wear? Never mind. We've got sizes. (*Harry is in door.*)

MRS. ARCHER-LOOMIS. (*Takes Birnbaum's arm.*) Tell me, Mr. Birnbaum, what is a bagel? And one other thing, what is a lox? (*They are gone.*)

HARRY. (*He has taken a small package from his pocket. He addresses the pictures on the wall.*) Gentlemen, it's a pleasure to have you here for what they always call "this auspicious occasion." It was five years—or thirty-one issues ago—that this barrel went to work for me. (*He is now facing the barrel.*) As publisher of the Carolina Israelite, I wish to take this occasion to thank the barrel. (*He bows to the barrel.*) Also the poor schlemiel who fills it up. (*He is taking on more and more of the mock pomposity of an after-dinner speaker. Helen enters and is watching this curious ceremony from the kitchen door. She is intrigued, but doesn't let Harry know that she is watching him.*) In token of my esteem, Mr. Golden, I want to present you, Mr. Golden, with this solid gold-plated wrist watch—which we hope to hell you take off when you get in the bath-tub. (*He hands the jeweler's box toward a non-existent recipient. Now, Harry dances over to the position of the recipient and accepts the watch with his other hand.*) You shouldn't have done it. Sir, I am deeply touched. What can I say? There's no sense in saying anything foolish. And if it's any good, I'd better get it on paper for the next issue. That barrel can't type worth a damn! (*Puts watch case down, puts watch on. Helen applauds. Harry is a little sheepish about it.*) Oh, Helen. I've been meaning to get a watch for a long time. And I figured I might as well make the most of it, you know what I mean?

HELEN. I know what you mean. Mazel tov.

HARRY. (*Straps the wrist watch onto his wrist. Exuberantly, hand behind back.*) You want to know what time it is, Helen? Ask me what time it is.

HELEN. What time is it?

HARRY. (*Looks at the watch, and his expression goes somewhat blank. He shakes his wrist a little, and holds the watch up to his ear.*) Oh, you gotta *wind* these things! (*Helen laughs.*)

HELEN. How does it feel to be a success, Mr. Golden?

HARRY. (*There is a pause.*) Is that what I am? I never thought of it that way. A success.

HELEN. (*Goes to desk, picks up mail.*) Look at all these subscriptions; you've passed seventeen thousand—including Mrs. Roosevelt! You're zooming!

HARRY. (*Shrugs.*) "Zooming."

HELEN. So enjoy.

HARRY. I'm enjoying. Helen, I'm going to let you in on a little secret I haven't even told myself. (*Whitmore comes down the street.*) I think now maybe Kate can come down and live here permanently.

HELEN. That's wonderful.

HARRY. And there'll be enough money to send her up to New York to see Bobby in the hospital, just the way she does now.

WHITMORE. (*Knocks on screen door.*) Harry! Are you in there, Harry?

HARRY. (*Comes out on porch, shakes Whitmore's hand.*) Lucius! How are you? Come on in; have a drink.

WHITMORE. I don't think so. (*Helen picks up envelopes and letter opener from desk and goes into kitchen.*)

HARRY. (*Sees copy of paper Whitmore carries. Pretends to be shocked.*) "The Carolina Israelite"! You don't believe the stuff that guy writes, do you?

WHITMORE. I see "that guy" doesn't approve of what the School Board is doing.

HARRY. Only of what it's *not* doing!

WHITMORE. Where do you want to talk? It's something important.

HARRY. It's cooler out here. (*Indicates to Whitmore to sit.*)

WHITMORE. (*Sitting on the swing.*) You know, Harry, most people in this town don't agree with you, but we respect you. Why can't the people up North show the same kind of understanding for the way we Southerners feel?

HARRY. I'm a Southerner too, Lucius.

WHITMORE. (*This touches him. He slaps the side of Harry's leg.*) You damned Tar-Heel! Harry, when that second Supreme Court decision came through, we all tried to act as if we didn't even hear it.

HARRY. I hate to hear an alarm clock go off, but I don't stay in bed all day.

WHITMORE. The alarm clock ringing in *our* ears, Harry—we *can't* shut it off. We've been sitting in that School Board meeting day after day, painfully agreeing with each other. Seven of us on that Board—and every one solid for separate and equal. But I'm a lawyer, Harry. And I know you never get a real verdict unless you've got somebody speaking up for the other side. I look around the room at that School Board meeting, and all I see is myself. We all think alike.

HARRY. (*Leans against door frame.*) I know what you mean. It's the difference that makes the difference. They've got the same trouble over in Israel. No Shiksas! (*Whitmore looks blankly at Harry.*) I'll explain it to you later.

WHITMORE. Fine. Now. Eli Severn's moving out of Mecklenberg County. There'll be a special election to fill his place.

HARRY. Who's your candidate?

WHITMORE. (*Giving Harry a long look.*) You.

HARRY. (*Genuinely incredulous and moved.*) You want *me* to run for the School Board?

WHITMORE. No, Harry. We want you *on* the School Board. If you agree to be the candidate, there'll be no opposition.

HARRY. Thank you, Lucius. I can't tell you how much I thank you.

WHITMORE. (*Picks up his briefcase and rests it across his knee, as if the whole matter were settled.*) You're going to be very valuable to us, Harry. Everybody on the Board agrees to that.

HARRY. Why do you want me? You don't like my ideas.

WHITMORE. I don't want integration. But when you keep getting the same wrong answer month after month, it's time to let somebody else help us try to add up the figures.

HARRY. (*Turning to Whitmore.*) What would I be? A perpetually dissenting minority. What good is that?

WHITMORE. If that's how you feel, what good are these pieces you write? (*He waves the paper.*) I'm offering you a chance to get in there where the fight's going on! Sit with us, say "NO" all day if you have to—but sweat it out with us.

HARRY. I thank you. I thank all the members of the Board. But I can't do it.

WHITMORE. Think about it.

HARRY. Lucius, I don't know how to get votes. Can you see me kissing babies? I'd scare the daylights out of 'em. All right, around the belt buckle I look like William Jennings Bryan. Is that going to get me elected?

WHITMORE. You don't have to turn into a politician, Harry; we're handing this to you—all tied up with a shiny blue ribbon.

HARRY. (*Helplessly.*) I can't.

WHITMORE. Why?

HARRY. (*Lifting his voice, unconvincingly.*) Well, I've—I've got the paper to get out. And I've got certain—obligations—I've—

WHITMORE. What kind of reasons are those?

HARRY. It's impossible—it's just impossible—

WHITMORE. Harry, don't ask me to believe you're the same as all the others. Are you just a carpetbagger with a typewriter?

HARRY. Lucius—

WHITMORE. Are you just a fancy talker, Harry? We thought you'd like to put some of that talking into *doing*! (*Harry turns away.*) It's true to form! Precisely true to form. Like all the rest of the Yankee-yellers, the short-term experts, you're afraid to stick your neck out! (*Picks up hat, puts it on.*) You've had us fooled, because you lived right here inside our City Limits—and you made us laugh. But that doesn't really make you much different from the ones who spit at us from a safe distance. (*Whitmore tosses aside his copy of the newspaper. Without a farewell, he starts down the steps of the veranda, his whole face taut with indignation. Every epithet has hit Harry like a blow in the face. He has maintained silence with great difficulty, and it is not until Whitmore has moved some distance from the house that Harry finally calls to him.*)

HARRY. Lucius. (*Whitmore stops, turns back.*) Please. Come back. There are a couple of things I guess you've got to know about. In the house, if you don't mind. (*Whitmore goes up steps and enters house. Harry closes door. Helen enters from the kitchen.*) Helen. (*Harry reaches into his pocket for a dollar bill.*) Here, I want you to go to that tobacco store at the far end of town—Riordan's—and get me four Antonio y Cleopatra cigars.

HELEN. You got some this morning, Mr. Golden.

HARRY. Well, I need some more. Besides, I want to patronize this fellow. (*Helen takes the money and goes out the front door, a little mystified. She crosses the veranda, goes down the steps and exits. Whitmore sits on the sofa. Harry goes to Whitmore.*) There's a very good reason why I can't be a member of your School Board. It's something that happened a long time ago. But it happened. And I've kidded myself into thinking I'd never have to tell anybody.

WHITMORE. I'm not asking you to tell me anything.

HARRY. (*Turns.*) I've *got* to. Because I can't stay here or keep publishing the paper if Lucius Whitmore—or anybody else—believes what you just said to me on the porch. (*He takes a deep breath.*) I can't run for political office, because—in 1929, I was sentenced to five years in the Federal Penitentiary. (*There is a long pause.*) I was young, I was working with a small brokerage firm. Maybe you've forgotten how things were in the twenties. Playing the stock market was a national pastime—one big joy-ride—with everything going up, up, up. I was out to make a killing along with everybody else. (*The memory is painful.*) A smart-aleck kid like me didn't even take the trouble to buy the stock half the time. It was all on paper. They'd be calling back tomorrow morning to sell it anyway, and buy something else again, and sell *that* a few hours later. So you just juggled figures on the back of an envelope. I got caught. Nobody got hurt from what I did. I made sure of that. I had to sell my house, everything we had, to settle the accounts. What I did was wrong, it was illegal; I didn't try to wriggle out of it. I pleaded guilty and that was it. When it was all over, I went around from one job to another. But I was always bumping into people, y'know what I mean—people who knew, people who remembered. So I got out of New York, went on the road for a promotional firm, helping put out those special anniversary editions of newspapers, things like that. And one of the places I came for a few days was Charlotte. (*He smiles a little distantly.*) I liked it. One day I said to Kate, "I want to go to Charlotte and take a chance on myself." I wouldn't let Kate come with me. What if the whole thing blew sky-high? So Kate hung on to her job—and I moved down here to do the only thing I really wanted to do: start my own paper. I was a damn fool. How can you hide in public? Every time I've opened the mail, every time I've picked up the telephone, the thought has crossed my mind: maybe this is it, maybe this is yesterday catching up with me. Somebody saying right out loud: "Harry Golden is an ex-con." (*He laughs a little. Whitmore looks down.*) Isn't it funny that the guy who finally spills the beans about Harry Golden—is Harry Golden? Do you want a drink? I need one. (*He crosses to desk, starts to pick up bottle.*)

WHITMORE. (*Not looking at Harry.*) I'm sorry, Harry. I'm sorry you had to tell me. (*Rises, goes toward screen door.*) I'm sorry I had to know. (*Whitmore goes through door, down steps and exits. Harry moves on to the porch, looks after the departed Whitmore. He makes a silent effort to call Whitmore. He picks up the paper Whitmore has tossed aside, crumples it in his hands, and the lights fade.*)

(*It is the next morning. Some Negro children come on, Indian-file. They are lugging battered folding chairs. In the dark, Helen places purse on file then goes to desk; when the lights come up she is at the desk, dusting. Ten-year-old Balthasar, the ringleader, is on first. Followed by Ruth-Ella, who is seven and Calvin, who is a dynamic six.*)

BALTHASAR. Now, I'm goin' to do the talkin'. Is that clear? Answer yes or no.

CALVIN. Yes, but I'm goin' to be the driver.

BALTHASAR. You hush up, Calvin. You're lucky I even let you come! (*Helen, who has heard the children, comes out on the veranda.*) We wondered if we could see Mr. Golden.

HELEN. What's all this stuff for?

CALVIN. Gonna be a bus, Aunt Helen.

RUTH-ELLA. We're gonna make a bus.

HELEN. Calvin, what's Ruth-Ella got in her mouth?

CALVIN. Only a penny.

HELEN. Spit it out in Aunt Helen's hand!

RUTH-ELLA. (*Spits it out.*) I'm going to give it to the bus driver.

HELEN. (*Puts coin in Ruth-Ella's hand.*) Ruth-Ella, we don't eat money.

BALTHASAR. Can Mr. Golden help us bus-ridin' practice?

HELEN. Certainly not. Bal, you get all this junk out of here.

BALTHASAR. He helped my big brother. Told him just what to say, what not to say. We want to learn too.

HELEN. When I get home tonight, *I'll* be the bus driver.

CALVIN. Aw, girls ain't ever bus drivers. *I'll* be the bus driver.

BALTHASAR. (*Turns to Calvin.*) We gotta have a bus driver who's the right color. Calvin, where'd you park your brains?

HELEN. (*Turns, sees Harry who came down steps during speech above.*) Oh, good morning, Mr. Golden.

BALTHASAR. Please, can't you help us, Mr. Golden? We drug these chairs nine blocks.

RUTH-ELLA. (*Jumping up and down.*) I wanta ride the bus! I wanta ride the bus!

HARRY. (*Coming out on the porch.*) What's going on out here?

HELEN. Nothing you have to think about, Mr. Golden.

HARRY. Why not? I'd rather think about anything than what I've been thinking about. So you drug these chairs nine blocks, huh? All right. Where's the bus?

HELEN. Mr. Golden, you don't have to do this.

HARRY. Can't expect me to go around drivin' busses unless there's a bus to drive! Now this is the bus. Right up here. Come on! (*The children line up their chairs on the veranda, with the swing representing the back seat of the bus.*)

KIDS. (*Ad-lib.*) Oh, boy, we're going to make a bus.

HENRY. Now, the big white bus driver sits here. All right, anybody who wants to ride this heah bus, line yo'selves up down there. (*Harry is play-acting a tough, white Southern bus driver, with a thick accent. Calvin and Balthasar line up. Helen takes Ruth-Ella down steps. Ruth-Ella jumps to the front of the line. Helen goes to the back.*) All aboard. Step lively. (*Ruth-Ella steps up to the top step and hands Harry the penny she has been holding. Harry looks at it critically.*) What yo' givin' me, little girl? This is only a penny. The fare's a dime.

RUTH-ELLA. It's a *pretend* dime.

HARRY. Oh? Well, you're just lucky this is a *pretend* bus! (*He raises his voice.*) Colored folks to the *rear*! (*Ruth-Ella quickly sits in the chair directly behind Harry. He turns and glares at her.*) How's your hearin', little girl?

RUTH-ELLA. I kin hear.

HARRY. Then you must be from Chicago. I said to the *back* of the bus.

RUTH-ELLA. I—What should I say?

HARRY. (*Gently, as himself.*) I paid my dime and I'd like to sit in this empty seat.

RUTH-ELLA. I paid my dime and I'd like to sit in this empty seat.

HARRY. (*The tough bus driver again.*) Who taught you to say that?

RUTH-ELLA. You did.

HARRY. Not me! I'm the big white bus driver! (*Ruth-Ella laughs.*) All right! Climb aboard!

BALTHASAR. (*Scampers up the steps.*) Here's my dime.

HARRY. What's your name?

BALTHASAR. Bal.

HARRY. What kind o' name is that?

BALTHASAR. Short for Balthasar. He was one of the Three Wise Men.

HARRY. Ohhhh, you've got a brother named Melchior.

BALTHASAR. Yes, sir.

HARRY. He's that wise man does all this thinkin' after it's too late. Back! Back! Back o' the bus. (*Balthasar sits to left of Ruth-Ella. Harry sees this and rises.*) What yo' sittin' in that seat fo'? That's a white folks' seat!

BALTHASAR. I paid my dime and I'd like to sit in this empty seat. (*He gulps.*) Please.

HARRY. (*Becoming himself again.*) That please is good. Keep it in. (*Now as the bus driver he returns to his seat.*) We got a schedule to meet. Get on up here, get aboard! (*Calvin boards the imaginary bus, dropping a fare in pantomime. He stands between Balthasar and Ruth-Ella. Harry points to a pretended sign above the swing, which represents the rear of the bus.*) You see that sign, little boy? (*Pointing at air.*) "This section for members of the Colored Race." Now where you gonna sit?

CALVIN. (*Turns to look.*) I don't see no sign.

HARRY. (*Now his voice becomes so reasonable that all—even Helen—wonder whether he is speaking as himself or as the imaginary bus driver. However, the Southern accent remains.*) Now, we poor bus drivers don't wanta make trouble fo' you. Why you-all wanta make trouble fo' us poor bus drivers? Disturbin' the peace, gettin' all tangled up with the policeman and the law. What's so special about these heah front seats, when you-all got a section all reserved *just fo' you*—in the back of the bus? (*Begins to shepherd them to seats on the swing.*) (*Balthasar and Calvin sit on the swing, puzzled. Ruth-Ella sits on Calvin's lap.*) That's fine! (*Harry walks away to the end of the veranda, turns, and looks at them. The persuasive bus driver turns into the angry Harry Golden.*) What are you doing sitting back there????!! (*They jump with surprise. The accent is gone now. Harry is frank and forceful.*) Are you going to let some molasses-lipped bus driver wheedle you out of your seats? Come back here! (*Ruth-Ella and Balthasar return to their seats. Calvin hangs back.*)

HELEN. (*To Calvin.*) Now you listen to what he says!

CALVIN. I'm listenin'. But which one is he *now*?

HARRY. If anybody gives you an argument, just say one simple sentence. What're you going to say?

ALL. I paid my dime and I'd like to sit in this empty seat.

HARRY. And the *louder* they yell at you, the *softer* you're going to answer!

ALL. (*Whisper.*) I paid my dime and I'd like to sit in this empty seat.

RUTH-ELLA. Please.

HARRY. When you talk soft like that, you make it awful hard for anybody to say you're disturbin' the peace. Here's your penny back. (*Gives Ruth-Ella her penny. Herbert enters during the above speech, carrying a telegram.*)

HERBERT. Telegram for you, Mr. Golden.

HARRY. (*Taking it.*) Why, thank you, Herbert.

HERBERT. It's from Raleigh. (*Harry starts to open it.*) Miss Foley down at the

Western Union office was bug-eyed while she was pasting it up. I'm not supposed to know, but it's from the Governor of North Carolina. (*Harry's face clouds as he reads the telegram.*) I'll stick around, in case you want to sent a reply.

HARRY. (*Disturbed.*) No, not right now. Thanks, Herbert. (*Herbert goes out, glancing back at Harry. Harry turns back toward door, deep in thought. He becomes aware that Helen and all the kids are looking at him.*) I think you better put this bus back in the garage. (*Goes into house.*)

HELEN. Run along home now, you kids. (*The kids fold their chairs, go down the steps, and exit during the following dialogue.*)

CALVIN. I'm going to be the bus driver now. Only it's not going to be a bus, it's going to be a space machine.

RUTH-ELLA. Will we have to sit in the back of the space machine?

BALTHASAR. Going to the moon costs fifteen cents, but you can sit anyplace you please. (*They are gone.*)

HELEN. (*Goes into the office, sees Harry who is seated on the sofa re-reading the telegram.*) Is there something I can do?

HARRY. (*Vaguely, not looking at her.*) No, no.

HELEN. (*A step in.*) Is anything wrong?

HARRY. (*He reads the telegram.*) "The Governor requests your appearance before a State Legislative Committee at the Capitol building in Raleigh on 12 May to express your views concerning the crisis in education in North Carolina."

HELEN. That's good, isn't it? You'll have a chance to tell them some of your ideas. (*Helen crosses to her typewriter, picks up pad.*) Do you want to dictate a reply?

HARRY. No. Go home, Helen. We're not going to work today.

HELEN. What is it, Mr. Golden?

HARRY. It's something I can't tell you about, but I'm scared.

HELEN. (*She puts down pad on typewriter table, picks up purse, and starts out. She turns and decides to say something.*) Mr. Golden. Were you scared when you hired me?

HARRY. Of course not.

HELEN. I was. With a scrubbing brush down there on the floor, I was safe. But sitting at a typewriter, I'm a target. I've got a job only a white person is supposed to do. Every morning, coming to work, walking down the sidewalk, I've been scared. But the minute I come through that screen door, I feel better because I know you're not afraid. But, Mr. Golden, if you're scared, what am I going to do?

HARRY. (*He is too moved to answer. Rises.*) I'll see you tomorrow. (*Helen pauses for a second, turns, goes out door and exits. Harry goes to the phone on his desk and dials.*) Operator, would you get me New York City, please. Mrs. Harry Golden, Eldorado 5–1072. (*The lights fade.*)

(*As the lights come up Harry is at the sofa. Kate is seated in the swivel chair. She is a quiet, thoughtful woman, handsome, firm, but with some tragedy in her face. Her greying hair is neat. She wears a simple traveling suit. It is night and only the lights inside the office are on.*)

HARRY. I should have shaved.

KATE. I've seen your whiskers. (*He picks up telegram.*) That's the fiftieth time you've read that telegram. (*She takes it from him.*)

HARRY. It doesn't change. God, it's good to see you sitting in that chair. Being with you six times a year is a hell of a way to run a marriage. I was a louse to let you come all the way down here.

KATE. What are you so worried about, Harry? This isn't a subpoena. It's an invitation from the governor, that's all.

HARRY. Hah! An invitation with teeth in it. Kate, somebody in Charlotte knows.

KATE. Are you sure?

HARRY. I'm sure. And when I get into that committee room in Raleigh, what if somebody stands up and asks me point blank: "Mr. Golden, where were you for five years?" Then everybody'll know.

KATE. Harry, when are you going to settle down to some nice, safe, steady job? Like getting yourself shot out of a cannon at the circus.

HARRY. You don't think I should go?

KATE. You'd be crazy to go. You want some excuses? I'll give you a hundred. Harry, for once in your lifetime be unavailable!

HARRY. I've certainly been unavailable as a husband.

KATE. Am I complaining? Look! Every time I start feeling sorry for myself, or for you, I just think how much better it is to have you doing the work you want to do, that you ought to do. (*She puts wire on desk, goes to Harry.*) Do you remember saying to me, "Kate, I want to do something crazy. I want to start a paper where I can write anything I think. And print it." Now you're doing it. You've done it. Are you going to throw it all over?

HARRY. No. You're absolutely right, Kate. I'll send a wire. I don't have to give any reason. I don't have to give any explanation. I'll just say I won't come. (*Puts telegram blank in typewriter. Pause. He slaps the desk.*) I can't do it. I'd never be able to use this typewriter again. I wouldn't be able to write one word. Kate, if I were a cotton farmer, it would be different. But what's my line of goods? What do I wrap in bales to sell? Ideas, beliefs, opinions. (*Kate turns to look at Harry.*) What kind of a fourteen-carat coward would I be if I refused to say out loud at the State Capitol what I say every day here at my typewriter?

KATE. I don't want you to get hurt.

HARRY. (*Rises.*) If not getting hurt were the acid test of human behavior, who would even get born?

KATE. Harry, I think I'd better stay for a while.

HARRY. If you said that to me the day before this wire came, I'd have leaped in the air and danced a kazotsky. The whole 192 pounds! But how can I let you come live in a house with a bomb under the veranda? (*He goes to her.*) Kate, when you love somebody, you want to bring her good things. And if you can't, you want to run.

KATE. So you ran. I let you run. I wanted you to run. Because, Harry, I knew what would happen to you, coming home from a job as a night clerk in a hotel, or from no job at all. I watched you one night when you thought I was asleep, looking at a receipt for a light bill *I* paid. And I never wanted you to have that look on your face again. Harry— (*Takes his hand.*) you had to go away. I think I know why better than you do. But now all I want is for you to keep doing your work.

HARRY. I've got to go to Raleigh, Kate. I'd better have a statement prepared in advance.

KATE. You can't go down to that legislative hearing. (*Rises, crosses to him, takes arms.*) Harry, do you realize what's happening in other states? They call people like you, so they can destroy them, people who were born here, important educators suddenly fired in the middle of a term. Ministers ripped out of pulpits they've held maybe twenty-five years. Imagine what they can do to you!

HARRY. (*Embraces her.*) It's a risk I've got to take! I've got to, Kate.

KATE. (*Touches shirt.*) Who does your laundry, Harry?

HARRY. Three different places. A different one each week. They're all advertisers.

KATE. Well, they're eating up your shirts. Maybe it'll be different here in North Carolina. You've made a lot of friends. Some of them might be at the hearing.

HARRY. I know one of them will be. He's the chief counsel for the legislative committee. A man named Lucius Whitmore.

KATE. If he's a friend of yours, maybe there isn't too much to worry about.

HARRY. That's right, Kate. There's not a damn thing to worry about. Who the hell is Harry Golden? A big shot? A front page headline? What can they take away from me anyhow? This business? When people drop in here, the first thing they ask is: "Harry, how's business?" What can I answer them? It's like making love to a woman. Even when it's bad, it ain't bad. (*They laugh together. The lights fade and the curtain is lowered for 30 seconds.*)

The scene is a Legislative hearing room in the State Capitol in Raleigh. The action is played in front of a drop which has the effect of mahogany paneling. There are executive-type chairs all around a long and impressive table, and the leather upholstery is trimmed with brass buttons. A dignified panel of Legislators, including Martin L. Claypool and the Chairman sit at the table, playing with pencils. Lucius Whitmore at the far end. A Stenographer is in the shadows behind him, working a stenotype machine. Harry and Kate and Dr. Leota Patterson are waiting in the background. Harry is in a pressed blue suit. Dr. Patterson is an attractive business-like woman in her mid-thirties. Kate is trying to appear calm. Giving testimony in the witness chair at the center of the table is Hershey M. Stoddard, a too-meticulous Carolina educator.)

STODDARD. And to me it is patently apparent that integration in the Northern States has been an utter failure.

CHAIRMAN. (*Leans forward.*) We're not talking about the North, Mr. Stoddard. The Governor has designated this committee to find *some* way to keep schooling our young people and still comply with what is known as the "law of the land."

STODDARD. There's only one solution. Private schools. For every white child in the state. It will be costly, of course. However, I have prepared a blueprint for a massive transfer to private educational facilities, as proposed in the Claypool Plan. (*He hands over a portfolio, which is passed down the table to the Chairman.*)

CHAIRMAN. We'll put this in the record. (*He glances at his colleagues.*) Mr. Whitmore?

WHITMORE. No questions, Mr. Chairman.

CHAIRMAN. Senator Claypool?

CLAYPOOL. No. No. No questions.

CHAIRMAN. Thank you, Mr. Stoddard.

STODDARD. Thank *you*. (*Rises.*) Thank you for hearing me, gentlemen. Uh—I might only add that I would consider it a patriotic duty and a privilege to expand immediately the facilities of the Stoddard School—of which I am proprietor and headmaster. (*Harry, in the background, clears his throat, re-crosses his knees and glances at Kate. Stoddard nods to the committee and exits.*)

CHAIRMAN. (*Leaning toward Claypool beside him.*) Who's next on that list, Martin? (*Claypool hands a list to the Chairman, who examines it.*) Dr. Leota Patterson, is she here? (*Dr. Patterson rises and crosses toward the witness chair. The entire Committee, being Southern gentlemen, rise until Dr. Patterson has seated herself.*) Thank you for coming, Dr. Patterson. Lucius?

WHITMORE. (*Studies a dossier in front of him. He scowls, and there seems to be much more tension in the air surrounding this witness than there was with Mr. Stoddard. Slowly.*) Would you be so good as to tell us the position you hold at the present time, Doctor?

PATTERSON. (*Tight-throated.*) I am the executive secretary of Better Schools, Incorporated, of North Carolina.

CHAIRMAN. The name would imply that you don't think the schools of North Carolina are very good.

PATTERSON. I don't think anything is so perfect, Mr. Chairman, that it cannot be improved.

WHITMORE. Dr. Patterson, do you oppose the system: "Separate and Equal."

PATTERSON. There is no such system. Separate, yes. Equal, no.

CHAIRMAN. (*Nettled, leans in.*) This "Doctor" business. You're certainly not an M.D., are you? Or a lady dentist?

PATTERSON. I have a Ph.D. from Columbia. My B.A. and M.A. are from the University of North Carolina.

WHITMORE. I have some articles here by Dr. Patterson which would indicate that she is a passionate partisan of integration. Do you care to correct me, Doctor?

PATTERSON. (*Wetting her lips.*) I think every intelligent person in the South is in favor of integration. (*There is a buzz of reaction at this.*) Some people think it should begin yesterday, some think it should begin a thousand years from now.

CHAIRMAN. (*Coolly.*) I take it you belong to the "yesterday" school?

PATTERSON. (*Simply.*) Today will be soon enough.

CLAYPOOL. Whatever we have to do will be done gradually. Gradually.

PATTERSON. (*Leans forward.*) It seems to me the job of this committee is to carry out the law of the land, to implement it—not to evade it.

CLAYPOOL. (*Getting hot under the collar.*) Now see here, Miss or Doctor, or whatever you call yourself, nobody asked you to come here and tell us what our job is.

PATTERSON. I am here at the specific invitation of the Governor. My views and the objectives of my organization have been set forth in detail. Copies are on your desk. Or possibly in your wastebaskets. (*Legislator gives papers to Claypool. There is a high-voltage charge of hostility in the room, unrelieved by any humor. Claypool fishes out several pages from his briefcase.*)

WHITMORE. Dr. Patterson—

CLAYPOOL. (*Interrupting.*) Now just a minute! *Here's* something that isn't in my wastebasket! (*He brandishes the papers at the witness as if they were Excalibur.*) I have here a list of organizations with which you have been associated. The "Inter-Faith Educational Improvement Association," which was on the Attorney General's list in 1954 as a "subversive" or so-called "front" organization.

PATTERSON. (*Heatedly.*) The designation was false! Some of the leading citizens of the South were members!

CLAYPOOL. That's beside the point. (*Rises.*) You were a member, and it was cited by the Attorney General.

PATTERSON. Is it your intention to discredit me, publicly, so that I won't be able to continue my work? (*She looks at Whitmore.*)

WHITMORE. We merely wish to establish pertinent truths so this committee can evaluate your recommendations.

CLAYPOOL. (*Flipping a page.*) I find that you are a subscriber to the following publications: *The Nation. The New Republic.*

PATTERSON. (*Breaking in, rising.*) I also subscribe to the Charlotte *Observer* and the *Carolina Israelite*! (*Harry puts his hand over his eyes, wishing he could dig a hole in the floor. Kate clutches his arm.*) Not to mention the *Christian Science Monitor*! (*Harry looks up, beaming; the bullet just missed him! Dr. Patterson sits. Claypool sits.*)

CHAIRMAN. If no one has any further questions, I think we should thank the Doctor for her trouble and excuse her from this session.

WHITMORE. I have nothing further.

CHAIRMAN. Senator Claypool?

CLAYPOOL. (*Curtly.*) That's all.

CHAIRMAN. That will be all, Dr. Patterson.

PATTERSON. (*Rising.*) I understood that I was asked here to express my opinion on the Claypool plan.

CHAIRMAN. (*Rapping.*) That will be all, Dr. Patterson.

PATTERSON. (*Frustrated, looks at Whitmore.*) But I have certain evaluations—

CHAIRMAN. (*Definitely.*) We shan't detain you any further. (*Men sit.*) Thank you. (*Dr. Patterson, almost in tears, looks at Whitmore. Whitmore looks down, then sits. She *hurries off. The Chairman confers rather ominously with the Legislators on either side of him, consulting their individual notes. They come to a whispered conclusion, and the Chairman looks about the room.*) Is Mr. Golden in the Committee Room? Mr. Harry Golden? (*Harry pats Kate's hand, then crosses to the witness chair uncomfortably, avoiding Whitmore's eyes. Whitmore, too, avoids looking directly at Harry.*) You are Mr. Harry Golden, Editor and Publisher of the *Carolina Israelite*?

HARRY. I plead guilty. (*There are some chuckles at this. But the Chairman is a little square. Harry sits.*)

CHAIRMAN. Mr. Golden, this is not a courtroom. You have been called to Raleigh to give us your viewpoint on—uh, the question facing us.

HARRY. Mr. Chairman, I *do* have something to suggest. But I'm not sure you're going to like it. My idea would completely replace the Claypool Plan, which you're now considering.

CHAIRMAN. You have a concrete proposal?

HARRY. Oh, yes. And it's so new, gentlemen, it isn't even in your wastebaskets yet! (*Some skeptical glances are exchanged around the table.*) I call it the Vertical Negro Plan.

CLAYPOOL. I beg pardon? What was the word?

HARRY. "Negro."

CLAYPOOL. No, no—the other word.

HARRY. Vertical. I've noticed a curious thing here in the South. There's never any segregation problem when everybody's standing up, you know what I mean? The White and the Negro stand at the same supermarket counter; pay phone and light bills to the same clerk; and stand at the same drugstore counters. It's only when the Negro "sets" that the fur begins to fly. (*One of the Legislators laughs a little at this, and the Chairman raps his gravel.*) Now, I have no blueprints that I want to put into the record. (*He gestures toward the papers and exhibits lying on the conference table.*) Just one simple little amendment— Provide only *desks* in all the public schools—*no seats*! The desks should be those "standing-up" jobs, like the old-fashioned bookkeeping desks. This may be a blessing in disguise. The kids aren't learning to read sitting down—maybe they'll learn how to read standing up. (*The Legislators chuckle at this, then glance at one another a little sheepishly. The Chairman starts to bring down the gavel for order, then realizes he'd be silencing himself.*)

CHAIRMAN. All right, Mr. Golden. You made us laugh. Even I laughed. Now, do you have anything serious to propose?

HARRY. (*Innocently, spreading out his hands.*) I couldn't be more serious! Now take the movie theatres in Charlotte. A Negro can't buy a ticket. A couple of months ago there was a revival of the Laurence Olivier *Hamlet*, and some Negro school teachers wanted to see it. How did they work it? One Saturday afternoon, they asked some white friends to lend them two of their little children. Holding these white children by the hand, they were nursemaids. Nobody tried to stop them. "Come right in. Sit right down." What kind of segregation is this? (*Warming to his theme.*) How simple it would be—the White Baby Plan. Borrow a white baby, go anywhere, sit anywhere!

Eventually there could be a factory to manufacture White babies of plastic. The dolls, of course, should all have blonde curls and blue eyes. (*There is some unwilling laughter scattered through Harry's speech.*)

CLAYPOOL. (*Slams his fist on the table.*) This is absurd!

HARRY. Of course it is!

CHAIRMAN. Are you finished now, Mr. Golden?

HARRY. One last thing, which may prove to be the most practical plan of all. The Golden "Out-of-Order" Plan. I want you to imagine— (*Harry gets up from the chair and demonstrates.*) Here is a drinking fountain, marked "For Whites Only." And over here— (*He crosses several steps.*) —is a fountain clearly marked "For Colored Only." Now. I have a friend who's the manager of a Five and Ten Cent Store in Charlotte, and at my suggestion, he cut off the water in that White fountain— (*He points toward it.*) and put up a sign, "Out-of-Order." A White customer comes up—and he's hot and he's thirsty—and he looks over there and sees the *Colored* drinking fountain, and he decides to take the plunge. (*Dramatizing this, pantomiming it.*) He leans over and takes his drink, and he swallows it. And is he surprised! Nothing happens to him! It's plain old H-2-O. After a while, everybody is drinking this segregated water. There hasn't been a single complaint yet. As I see it, gentlemen, the real key to the plan is to keep the "Out-of-Order" sign up for at least two years. We've got to do this thing *gradually*.

CLAYPOOL. (*Slaps his hand on the table and rises indignantly.*) Mr. Chairman! (*Harry sits.*) When I want to hear jokes, I'll tune in Bob Hope on the television! I think all of you should know who this man *is*—this man who asks us to laugh at the most dangerous problem of the century! (*Harry holds his breath. Here it comes.*) May I ask Mr. Golden a few *personal* questions?

CHAIRMAN. Go ahead, Martin. (*Harry is hanging tightly to the arms of the chair.*)

CLAYPOOL. Mr. Golden, my family settled in Winston-Salem in the year 1731. May I inquire how long your people have been North Carolina residents?

HARRY. I came here in 1655—

CLAYPOOL. Huh?

HARRY. —with the Indigo Trade. (*The Legislators are quietly stunned by this.*) The merchants who brought the colors and the dyes from the West Indies—in sailing ships!—the men who turned the cotton from the fields of North Carolina into rainbows!—they were Israelites, and so am I.

CLAYPOOL. Are you telling us you were born here in North Carolina?

HARRY. No, sir. I was born on the Lower East Side of New York City—which is not an enemy power.

CLAYPOOL. Specifically! Where were you? What did you do? Before you came to Charlotte?

HARRY. (*Wets his lips.*) A lot of things; a lot of different jobs.

CLAYPOOL. This man isn't going to tell you anything about himself! I feel it is my duty to expose— (*Kate rises slowly.*) Harry Golden to the full light of public scrutiny—

HARRY. (*Closes his eyes, and reaches into his inside coat pocket for a folded sheet of paper on which he has typed a statement. Softly, a little hopelessly.*) Mr. Chairman—

CLAYPOOL. (*But he overrides Harry's quiet protest.*) —And reveal exactly the manner of person he is!

HARRY. Please! Will the committee allow me to read a statement I have prepared—

CLAYPOOL. (*Breaking in, emphatically.*) No, sir! What this man has *already* said should be stricken from the record.

HARRY. (*Stands, holding the statement in front of him. He tries to keep his hands from shaking.*) Mr. Chairman, in all fairness, I think I should have the opportunity—

CHAIRMAN. (*Silences this byplay with a rap of the gavel.*) You will have a chance to reply, if that seems necessary, Mr. Golden.

CLAYPOOL. (*Taking a deep breath.*) I have documentary proof that Harry Golden is a rabble-rousing radical! (*Harry is a little dazed at this; it's certainly not what he expected. He sits. Kate sits.*)

CHAIRMAN. Would the Senator care to mention anything specific?

CLAYPOOL. Gladly. I quote from a recent issue of this man's newspaper. (*Claypool brandishes a newspaper.*) Listen to this. How this man defames one of the most sacred of our nation's symbols. I'm quoting. (*He reads.*) "I wish the Bald Eagle had not been chosen as the representative of our country; he is a bird of bad moral character; like those among men who live by sharping and robbing, he is generally poor and often very lousy." (*He points toward Harry.*) There's the man that wrote that.

HARRY. (*Smiles and shrugs. Clearing his throat.*) It's a pretty good hunk of material. If the Senator will turn the page, he'll see that's a quote from a prominent Philadelphia subversive, Benjamin Franklin.

CLAYPOOL. (*There is some laughter and embarrassed confusion. But Claypool is caught off-balance only momentarily.*) The Devil's Advocate always quotes Scripture. (*Flamboyantly, stretching out his arms.*) It is my conviction that this man is a subversive himself.

CHAIRMAN. Martin, you've got to stop calling everybody who doesn't agree with you a subversive.

CLAYPOOL. All right! Pick up the telephone: call the Kremlin; get a commissar to tell us how to run the North Carolina schools. (*Sits and sulks.*)

CHAIRMAN. (*Turns to Harry.*) We'll be happy to hear your statement now, Mr. Golden.

HARRY. Oh. Oh. No, no, no—I really didn't have anything further to say.

CHAIRMAN. Any other questions, gentlemen? (*He looks around the table.*) Mr. Whitmore?

WHITMORE. (*Seems to be debating within himself. Now he reaches a decision. He gets up slowly.*) There is one question I feel I must ask Mr. Golden. (*There is a pause, which seems interminable to Harry. He throws a quick glance toward his wife.*) This committee is examining a crisis in education. And I think we're entitled to know your educational background. (*Harry relaxes a little; this isn't the big question—yet.*) You are a graduate of what school, Mr. Golden?

HARRY. P.S. 20, New York City.

WHITMORE. Do you hold any academic degree?

HARRY. My diplomas are some well-stamped library cards.

WHITMORE. You have a secretary in your office, Mr. Golden?

HARRY. Yes, sir.

WHITMORE. She is a member of what race?

HARRY. The human race.

WHITMORE. She is a nigra, is she not?

HARRY. My secretary is Colored, yes.

WHITMORE. And what school did she attend?

HARRY. Miss Cheney went to Cornell.

WHITMORE. How does it happen that you, coming from that great liberal state of New York, were not able to receive the same educational benefits which were accorded a Colored girl who answers your telephone and types in your office?

HARRY. Well, the generosity of the great State of North Carolina granted Miss Cheney a scholarship to attend any university *outside* the great State of North Carolina.

WHITMORE. Would you call this arrangement "separate and equal"?

HARRY. I'd call it damned foolishness. I'm one of the few Tar Heels who's getting any benefit out of this noble investment in out-of-state education. Most of the Negro students you export to Northern Universities never come back here to buy so much as a Coca-Cola.

CLAYPOOL. Fine. We're rid of them!

HARRY. What about the illiterate brothers, the sick fathers, who aren't going any place, least of all to M.I.T.?

WHITMORE. (*Getting angry.*) This has no relevance—

HARRY. No *relevance*! We talk about education, but what are we educating them *for*? To make tomorrow *richer*! And instead you're impoverishing yourselves!

WHITMORE. We know what we're doing!

HARRY. (*Rises.*) Do you? How do you know whether the child you didn't educate might have grown up to discover a cure for something which might some day save your life?

WHITMORE. (*He is furious. The paper trembles in his hand.*) There is one further question I should like to ask the witness. Mr. Golden— (*Kate rises slowly. The two men look into each other's faces. There is a tense pause.*)

CHAIRMAN. Yes, Mr. Whitmore?

WHITMORE. (*Conquering his anger, he turns toward his chair and speaks slowly.*) Nothing. My question is not pertinent to this hearing. (*He sits. Harry shakes his head, hardly believing what has happened. The Chairman raps his gavel with a tone of finality.*)

CHAIRMAN. If there is no objection, the committee will recess for lunch until two o'clock. (*Turning toward Harry on the stand.*) That will be all, Mr. Golden. (*Men, except Whitmore, rise to exit.*) Thank you for coming to Raleigh.

HARRY. That's all?

CHAIRMAN. That's all. (*The Chairman and the Committee Members rise and begin to disperse. Kate rises. Harry slowly tears up his "prepared statement." He shreds it into very small pieces; then he shoves them into his side pocket. Harry is like Daniel having been excused from the lion's den. He crosses toward Whitmore, who is busily sorting some papers for his briefcase. Harry approaches Whitmore, who looks up from his papers, then reaches out his hand to Harry, palm up.*)

WHITMORE. You've got some waste paper in your pocket, Harry. (*Kate goes to Harry. Harry pulls the shreds of his "prepared statement" out of his coat pocket, and hands the pieces to Whitmore. Whitmore, with a faint smile, tosses the bits of paper into a wastebasket beneath the table.*)

CURTAIN

ACT THREE

The office. As the curtain rises we see a new employee—but not a new character—at the typewriter. She is busily pounding out address stickers. The new employee is Velma, but she is known to her less-than-intimates as Miss Killigrew. Fred, the handyman, is putting a fresh coat of paint on the porch railing. There is an air of busy and pleasant activity about the whole place. Bill Drake comes down the street. His attire is crisp and Edwardian, but his crewcut marks him as a stranger to Charlotte. He seems intelligent and perceptive. He is carrying a slim attache case. He is studying the surroundings with the air of a man who isn't seeing quite what he expected to see. Fred looks at him with moderate curiosity as he goes up the veranda steps.

FRED. Hiya!

DRAKE. How are you? (*He crosses to the screen door and raps on it. Velma goes to the front door, taking a quick look at herself in a vanity mirror.*)

VELMA. (*Sweetly.*) I'm coming. (*She opens the door and seeing how handsome Drake is, cannot help appraising him in the "old manner." She steps out on porch.*) Ohhh. Good afternoon.

DRAKE. I'd like to see Mr. Golden. I'm afraid I don't have an appointment.

VELMA. (*Musically.*) Well, come in, come in. (*Drake comes in through the screen door and into the entry hall. For one preoccupied moment she makes a turn to lead him up the stairs, goes up two steps, then recovers.*) Oh! (*Comes quickly down steps to Drake.*) I don't know much about his appointments. You see, I'm new here. But he said he'd be back from town about fifteen minutes ago. May I help you in any way? I mean, did you want to subscribe, or buy advertising, or something like that?

DRAKE. No. I just want to talk to Mr. Golden.

VELMA. (*A little blankly.*) Oh. (*She continues to stare at Drake, which makes him a little uncomfortable. He fidgets, picks up a copy of the newspaper which is lying on the sofa, and begins to leaf through it. She goes to typewriter table, sits. Harry comes down the street. Birnbaum is with him, and they have apparently been having a friendly discussion.*)

HARRY. Ike, you worry too much. Every year things get better. Look what we've got now: Chocolate matzohs!

BIRNBAUM. (*Laughs, feels Harry's rumpled suit.*) Harry, you need a new suit. I want you to come down to the store. Pick out anything you want. On the house.

HARRY. For you I'm not even a business deduction.

BIRNBAUM. Consider it a gift from Leslie. In honor of he's now beginning his second year of residency.

HARRY. No. But thank you, thank Leslie.

BIRNBAUM. We've got a new suit with *all* the miracle fibres. So new you never have to press it.

HARRY. (*Shrugs.*) I never pressed the old one.

BIRNBAUM. (*Waving as he goes off.*) I'll put one aside. And you—wear it in good health.

HARRY. (*Has climbed steps, then sees Fred, who has been painting the railing.*) Fred, you're not painting that *again*!

FRED. Well, I had a little free time on my hands. My wife says that since I've been working around here, once in a while I almost remind her of Edward R. Morrow.

HARRY. Really? (*Fred takes a cigarette from behind his right ear, puts it in the corner of his mouth and lets it dangle.*) In living color! (*Laughs and goes into the house.*) Miss Killigrew, anything happen? (*He sees Drake as he comes into the parlor-office. Drake rises.*) Oh, hello.

VELMA. This gentleman wishes to see you.

DRAKE. (*Smiles and extends his hand to Harry. They shake as Velma begins to type, one-finger style.*) I'm Bill Drake.

HARRY. (*Blank for a second, then remembers.*) Oh, yes, from the publishing house in New York. What brings you to Charlotte?

DRAKE. Harry Golden.

HARRY. (*He is a little disturbed by this.*) Oh. I was honored by your offer on the phone, you know what I mean? (*Outside, Fred completes his work and goes off. Harry is the gracious but nervous host.*) Would you like a cigar? (*Drake shakes his head.*) I guess you met Miss Killigrew. (*He indicates Velma.*) She's helping out while my regular secretary is on vacation. (*Velma nods, and gives Drake a little-too-warm smile.*)

DRAKE. We said hello.

HARRY. (*He wants to talk to Drake privately, so he crosses to his desk and takes a sheet of paper from above the typewriter. To Drake.*) Sit down. Miss Killigrew, you said you've had experience collecting delinquent accounts, so why don't you make a couple of calls for me?

VELMA. (*Takes paper out of typewriter, puts it aside and goes to Harry.*) Oh, I'd be happy to.

HARRY. (*Handing her the list.*) Just say that you happened to be in the neighborhood.

VELMA. (*Looking at the list.*) I'll be very tactful. (*Has looked at list.*) Oh, I know most of these gentlemen personally.

HARRY. Well, then you can do it all on a nice friendly basis. (*Velma goes out the door, down the steps, and off.*) She just started working here today, but she seems to have very good connections. (*A sudden thought.*) Can I give you a drink? A little bourbon?

DRAKE. Maybe later. Mr. Golden, when I phoned you, why did you say "No" to a book?

HARRY. (*After a little pause.*) Well, various reasons. Various reasons. A book with my name on it—maybe my picture on the back cover, the way they do with books—no, I don't think so.

DRAKE. I don't understand, Mr. Golden.

HARRY. Well, a book is something *special*, you know what I mean? All my life, a book has meant something very personal to me. Almost as personal as friends. I have a respect, a reverence, for a book! (*Picks up a book from above typewriter.*) With a newspaper, if you say something stupid, there's always the next issue. But a book—there it is, in libraries, in the card index! All over the world, people read books!

DRAKE. (*Smiling a little ruefully.*) If you were in my business for two weeks, you'd be amazed how many books there are that people *don't* read.

HARRY. If this is going to be a book nobody reads, why publish it? (*Puts book on desk.*)

DRAKE. All I want you to do, Mr. Golden, is go through your back issues, select your favorite pieces, and let us put them between covers.

HARRY. Look—Carl Sandburg is for books. Thomas Wolfe is for books. Santayana is for books. But who am I?

DRAKE. Well, there was a very proper intellectual named Henry Ward Beecher, making a great deal of noise about abolition a hundred years ago; but his sister, who boiled his eggs for him, wrote a book. And that started the explosion.

HARRY. (*With half a smile.*) Please—we don't talk about that down here.

DRAKE. (*Taking a small clipping from his pocket.*) The way I heard about you—I saw this little item in one of the New York papers—what you said before a committee of the Carolina Legislature.

HARRY. (*Frowns a little.*) I wish that hadn't hit the wire services. (*Drake is silent, watching him. Harry moves about with increasing nervousness.*) Mr. Drake, I haven't got time to fool around with a book. The newspaper takes up most of my time. All of it. You people up there don't want to bother about me. (*Drake studies the man, trying to read the real motive behind his reticence.*)

DRAKE. (*After a pause.*) I'll take that drink now.

HARRY. Sure, sure. (*He goes to desk, pours two shots. Drake takes a glass and speaks with gentle irony.*)

DRAKE. To silence? (*Pause.*) To darkness? To hiding? (*Neither of the men drinks. Harry has been moved by Drake's words.*)

HARRY. Mr. Drake. More than anything in the world, I would be proud to have the book you describe. But what if you get hurt? You, and your company?

DRAKE. It's a gamble. Particularly in *my* business, the future is always a gamble.

HARRY. For everybody. (*Staring thoughtfully into the drink.*) No. For my mother, the future was never a gamble. She had a special personal arrangement with the

Head Office. (*He smiles warmly, remembering.*) She had God, right there with her in the kitchen. She talked to Him—all the time. Actual conversations. And for anything up ahead, any plan for the future, she'd always say, "With God's help." For instance, I'd say to her, "I'm going to the library tomorrow." Quick, without a breath in between, she'd add: "With God's help!" (*He speaks hesitantly, with difficulty.*) If I should say yes, if I say "Go ahead with the book"—could you put that in the contract?

DRAKE. "With God's help"?

HARRY. "With God's help." (*Drake smiles and nods. They lift their glasses and drink as the lights fade.*)

(*In the intervening darkness, we hear a sound of pruning shears snipping a hedge. As the lights come up, it is late afternoon and long, reddish shadows fall across the veranda and the parlor-office. Herbert, in a T-shirt and soiled dungarees, is trimming the spirea bushes at the side of the house. Helen is seated in Harry's swivel chair, sorting mail. There is a considerable accumulation of it. The two moving men, Ray and Wes, come on, carrying a very feminine dressing table. Ray knocks with his foot and pushes open the door, which was ajar, with the same foot. They come through the screen door into the entry hall.*)

RAY. (*Calling out.*) Furniture delivery.

HELEN. (*Gets up from the desk to see what it is they have brought in.*) That's to go upstairs—in the bedroom.

WES. Are you *sure*? (*Helen nods affirmatively.*)

RAY. I figured they got the wrong address. This don't look like a piece of furniture for a guy that smokes cigars!

HELEN. It's for *Mrs.* Golden. It's a surprise. (*The moving men shrug, and start up the stairs with the dressing table.*) Be careful with the turn on the landing. (*Helen comes through the door and stands on the veranda, looking down the street, as if waiting for somebody.*)

HERBERT. (*Has finished trimming the bush, moves along the veranda to the steps. He sits on the top step.*) That New York train's always late. (*As he settles himself on the step.*) Boy, that spirea bush sure needed a crewcut! (*Herbert becomes as Aristotelian as he can in a dirty T-shirt.*) You know, it's interesting. Bushes sit around all winter, not doing anything, and all of a sudden they start sprouting like crazy. That's how it is with *life*!

HELEN. (*Looks at him with disbelief.*) Oh!?

HERBERT. Say, Mr. Golden sent my aunt a copy of his book—straight from the publisher in New York. It's very profound. He says— (*Dramatizing it.*) "America is on a huge breast binge." (*He repeats the following by memory, as if wanting to tell it to the fellows at school.*) "In times of great stress, the instinct is to seek the safety and comfort of a mother." So—*breasts*!

HELEN. (*Marveling sarcastically.*) You put your finger right on it, Mr. Loomis. The most profound thing in the book.

HERBERT. I'm not so sure he's right, though. When I take out girls, I don't ever think of my mother. (*Herbert moves to right of veranda as he hears the moving men come down the stairs and cross out onto the veranda. Ray starts down the steps, but Wes pauses for a word with Helen.*)

WES. When Mr. Golden gets back, tell him we read about his book in the Charlotte *News*.

HELEN. I'll tell him.

WES. He's really made it, hasn't he?

RAY. It's pretty much of an honor, movin' furniture for a *bookmaker*! (*Ray and Wes go off. Helen goes back into the house. Harry enters in jubilant spirits.*)

HERBERT. Hi, Mr. Golden. Welcome back.

HARRY. (*Starting to climb the stairs.*) How's everything been here?

HERBERT. Okay. Say, my aunt let me read part of the book you sent her. It's great. I like it better than *Ivanhoe*.

HARRY. (*Pats him on the shoulder.*) Herbert. Don't tell Sir Walter. (*Harry goes into the house. Carrying the bushel basket, Herbert goes off. To Helen, who is doing the floor.*) Don't you remember? You were promoted.

HELEN. (*Rises.*) You only mind when the floor is *all* you can do. (*Harry plunks down his bag on the sofa.*) Welcome back, Mr. Golden.

HARRY. (*En route, he waves casually to the picture gallery.*) Glad to see ya, boys.

HELEN. Is Mrs. Golden really coming down?

HARRY. Next Sunday. She's quit her job. And I've ordered plane tickets for every Saturday so she can keep on visiting Bobby.

HELEN. Everything's ready here. They brought the dressing table. And I saw that the big closet was all cleared out.

HARRY. That's fine. (*He goes to his suitcase and opens it. It is piled high with copies of "Only in America."*)

HELEN. How did it go in New York? Was it exciting?

HARRY. Exciting. They gave me a luncheon. A cocktail party. A literary tea, yet. A lot of writers were there. *Real* writers. Helen, the kind of sandwiches they serve at a literary tea—you could get four of 'em in a shot glass. (*Helen laughs. He takes six books out of his suitcase.*) Did you get your copy?

HELEN. It's wonderful. Did everybody want your autograph?

HARRY. At least three people. I'm a literary lion. I've got a confession to make, Helen. I went around to all the book stores—Doubleday, Brentano's, Scribner's, Macy's—just to see the books stacked on the tables. "There's Harry Golden—right between William Faulkner and Fanny Hurst!" What a feeling!

HELEN. (*Goes to her desk.*) Everybody in town is talking about your book.

HARRY. (*Goes to desk.*) You know, I sent out complimentary copies to a lot of people here in Charlotte. What if I sent a book to everybody who might have bought it? (*Sits in swivel chair, picks up a letter.*) Anyway, I told the publishers if they had a lot of copies left over, I'd try to take them off their hands—give 'em away with every news subscription, or something. (*Holding up the letter.*) Here's somebody who wants to know if his March–April issue got lost in the mail. He should know! The March–April issue is still in the barrel, and here it is a quarter to June! (*He glances at a few more pieces of mail in a desultory fashion.*) We've got to get an issue out, Helen. So I'll have the time clear when Kate comes down. (*He puzzles over one envelope, studying the postmark.*) "Personal." Do I know anybody in Ogunquit, Maine? (*He opens it and takes out a letter and a newspaper clipping. He flips to the signature.*) It's from your replacement.

HELEN. My replacement?

HARRY. When you were on vacation, I hired this girl—she only worked a few days. (*He begins to laugh, as he reads the newspaper clipping.*) Holy Moses! (*He hands Helen the clipping.*) I sent her out to collect some advertising bills. And that's when the phone started to ring! You think women are gossips? Twenty guys called me: "Harry, I see you've got an old friend working for you. Ha, ha, ha!" I had to let her go, even though she collected every penny.

HELEN. (*Studying the clipping.*) This is just a society item about a wedding. (*She reads.*) "The bride is the former Miss Velma Killigrew of the North Carolina Killigrews."

HARRY. (*Reading from the letter.*) "I have recently been married to a wonderful man here in New England. When the society editor asked me about my past, I just said what came into my head. I hope you won't be offended."

HELEN. (*Reading from the clipping.*) "The bride was graduated from finishing schools in the Carolinas, and for the past several years has been associate editor of the *Carolina Israelite.*"

HARRY. How was I to know that Velma was *Velma*? (*He spreads out his arms, with palms-up innocence. Helen laughs.*) I should have suspected: even before I told her, she knew exactly where the bathroom was.

HELEN. What are you going to do about it?

HARRY. What am I going to do about it? I'm going to send her a wedding present. Autographed! (*Gets copy from desk, signs it.*) "Congratulations to my former associate—a whiz at circulation." Here's her address; see that she gets this. (*Gives it to Helen. Harry swings around in swivel, looks at barrel.*) Well, let's get to work. (*He crosses to barrel. Helen picks up pad and pencil. He leans over barrel, calling down into the bottomless well.*) Hello-o-o, down there! (*Harry picks one item out of the barrel.*) Here's one we can use. "Cleopatra was a call girl." Hmmm. Might be all right surrounded by strong ads. (*Drops it back in barrel.*) Go home, Helen. There isn't enough here to paste up a layout. Getting a book published sure interferes with writing. (*He puts a sheet into the typewriter.*) I'll have to play a little night baseball. A double header. (*He types one word and the phone rings. He picks it up.*) Hello. Oh, I'm fine, Lucius. To tell you the truth, I'm working. Lunch? Whenever you say. Tomorrow's fine. Good night, Lucius. (*He puts the telephone down, then picks it up and lays it aside.*) If I'm going to get any work done tonight, I've got to disconnect myself from the outside world.

HELEN. (*Going toward the door.*) Don't work too hard.

HARRY. Helen, if it weren't for work, all you could do is have a good time. And wouldn't that be hell? (*Helen goes out. He pounds on the typewriter as the lights fade.*)

(*As the lights come up it is early morning. Kate comes on, goes up the steps, and knocks on the door. She opens the door and goes in; she calls up the stairs.*)

KATE. Harry? (*She starts into the living room and sees Harry slumped over his desk. She puts down her bag and crosses quickly to his side and shakes his shoulder.*) Harry! Are you all right, Harry?

HARRY. (*Apparently he has been in an almost comatose sleep; suddenly he is fully awake.*) Kate! (*Rises and takes her in his arms.*) You're actually here! What time is it? I'm so happy; everything's ready for you. I can't tell you how happy I am! (*Kate looks at him with almost tears in her eyes. She is trying to tell him something, but it simply won't come out.*) Why didn't you wire me—or phone? I would have met your train.

KATE. I flew. I tried to call you from La Guardia. The line was busy.

HARRY. (*Looks over at the phone, picks up the receiver and places it back in the cradle. Puts on his glasses that he had taken off during the fade-out.*) I had the phone off the hook.

KATE. So I thought everybody must be trying to call you, and I wanted to be with you.

HARRY. Something's happened to Bobby.

KATE. No.

HARRY. What's wrong, Kate?

KATE. (*This indicates to her that he doesn't know what has happened. There is a tense pause. Harry is painfully awake now. He looks straight at his wife. She hands him a copy of the New York Herald-Tribune.*) This was on the stands at ten-thirty last night. All the other papers must have it by now.

HARRY. It finally happened.

KATE. I called the paper. They said there had been an anonymous letter. They said the story had been thoroughly checked out, and they had to print it.

HARRY. Sure—it's news. On the front page yet. "Author of ONLY IN AMERICA revealed as ex-convict." That's it. That's the end.

KATE. No it's not, Harry.

HARRY. I feel like old Sophocles. On his eightieth birthday he said "Thank God it's over." This'll kill the book. And the paper, too, that's dead.

KATE. Why is it dead?

HARRY. What can I put in the next issue? Can I make jokes about this? Who's going to believe, or even laugh, when they read anything I write from now on? (*Puts paper on bag.*) Damnit, it's all my fault. I've been asking for it, really asking for it. Every issue the circulation got bigger and I kept puffing up my chest. Harry Golden is a big man! An influence! And I couldn't resist the temptation to be in a library.

KATE. Don't blame yourself.

HARRY. I should have done what my mother always said: spit three times and say: "Kein ahora"—"You shouldn't have so much good luck it kills you." But I forgot.

KATE. Harry—

HARRY. It's very simple. We have no problem. Just get the hell out, that's all.

KATE. Now listen to me, Harry. You're not going to walk out, slam the door and leave all this behind.

HARRY. Why should I embarrass these people by staying here? Make 'em feel like damned fools because they trusted me? Boy, will the K.K.K. have an ox-roast! (*He goes to desk, puts cover on typewriter.*)

KATE. Where'll we go, Harry?

HARRY. California. Alaska. Maybe the moon. You can go to the moon now. The only trouble is, when you come out of the door, you're on the lawn in front of the Hayden Planetarium. And I'd better send back these autographed pictures so they won't ever embarrass the donors. (*He has placed closed typewriter on the floor and now rolls down the cover of the desk. It slams hard. He stands for a moment, touching the desk with affection. Then he turns and starts for the stairs.*) I'll grab a few more things upstairs. (*The phone rings.*) Don't answer it.

KATE. But it might be somebody—

HARRY. Don't answer it. (*He disappears up the stairs. Kate looks helplessly at the phone as it continues to ring. Jedediah enters. Goes up the steps and knocks on the door urgently.*)

JED. (*Calling.*) Mr. Golden!

KATE. (*Calling up the stairs.*) Harry, somebody's at the door.

HARRY'S VOICE. Who is it?

JED. It's Jed, Mr. Golden. Jedediah. I've got to talk to you. (*There is a slight pause, then Harry comes down the stairs carrying two shirts and a shaving kit. He opens the door and steps out.*) Sir, they got Mel down at the Sheriff's office. There was a ruckus out back of the Shelby plant last night, they think Mel did it. He wasn't even there!

HARRY. (*Flatly.*) What am I supposed to do?

JED. I just come to you, Mr. Golden—*natural.*

HARRY. You're a damned fool, Jedediah! When are you going to learn? Who's going to tend to you the way you look out for your no-good brother? (*Goes in the house, to the sofa, puts shirts and kit into suitcase. Jed follows him.*)

JED. (*Flashing.*) He ain't no-good! (*Corrects himself.*) He's *not* no-good, I mean. He's just big, and he cares too much.

HARRY. (*Bitterly.*) Well, tell him to *stop caring*! (*Jed is stunned, he backs away uncertainly.*) And, Jedediah.

JED. Sir? (*Kate watches this, anxious, but motionless.*)

HARRY. You're a big boy, now. Take some of that advice yourself! (*Jed cannot believe this is Harry Golden speaking to him. He goes out the screen door onto the porch. Harry follows the boy out on the porch.*) Jedediah.

JED. Yes, sir?

HARRY. Go to a lawyer named Lucius Whitmore. Tell him I said to get Melchior out of trouble. Tell him it's a favor for an old friend, who used to live in Charlotte. (*Jed, totally baffled, moves off. Harry takes a deep breath and goes back into the house. He meets Kate's silent eyes.*) Jedediah doesn't read the *New York Herald-Tribune*. (*Harry begins to put the stuff from the overnight kit into his big suitcase. The telephone, which stopped ringing during the above, now starts to jangle again. Harry shakes his head, gets coat.*) Why answer? What's to say? (*He picks up his own suitcase and then takes Kate's.*) You would have liked it here, Kate.

KATE. Where are we going, Harry?

HARRY. Away. Just away. If there's no plane soon, there'll be a train—or a bus. I'll wire Helen from wherever we are. She'll wind up things.

HERBERT. (*Rushes on excitedly, bounding up the steps, carrying about fifteen telegrams. Knocking.*) Telegrams! (*He comes into the house.*) Wow! Have you been getting a lot, Mr. Golden. Down at the telegraph office they said they never got so many wires in one night for one person. Real interesting!

HARRY. What's "real interesting," Herbert?

HERBERT. Your life. You must have had a real interesting life.

KATE. I'll take them for Mr. Golden. (*Herbert goes to Kate and hands her the stack of wires. Kate starts to open them.*)

HARRY. I don't want to look at any of this stuff now, Kate. I just want to leave.

HERBERT. Leave! Holy Toledo! You're not moving out, are you? My Aunt's gonna bust her corset! (*Harry starts to move toward the door again. Kate has opened a telegram.*)

KATE. Wait! This one's from Carl Sandburg. Listen. "The People, Yes. Harry Golden, Yes."

HARRY. (*Moved, pauses a moment. Then turns to go again.*) Come on, Kate. (*Harry goes out onto the porch, Kate following him. Herbert, stunned, sinks to the couch. Harry, carrying the bags, comes down the steps. Kate hesitates on the veranda. Fred comes on. He is deeply concerned.*)

FRED. Mr. Golden! I was drivin' along to work in my car, and I heard what they were sayin' about you on the radio. And I turned right around in the street and come over here.

HARRY. You can get a ticket for that, making a U-turn. They'll put you in jail.

FRED. You'd still keep me on your mailing list, even if they did, wouldn't you? (*The phone rings.*)

HARRY. (*Puts bag down, holds out hand.*) I'll say goodbye, Fred. It's been good knowing you; you're a helluva man with a paintbrush!

FRED. You can't do that! (*Harry picks up bag, comes down steps.*) Why, before you came to town, I didn't have anything to talk to my wife about. But since you've been here, we even *argue*.

HERBERT. (*During the above, has answered the telephone. He comes out the screen door.*) Mr. Golden, there's a long-distance call for you. From Chicago, Illinois.

HARRY. Tell 'em they got the wrong number. (*Helen enters. Goes to Harry.*) Helen, I'm glad you're here. (*Helen starts to speak but Harry continues.*) You've never been one for asking questions, so please don't start now. I want you call the printer and cancel our standing order. Tell the paper company to forget the new shipment. If you'll get a few of my personal things together, I'll write you our address—when we have one. And the circulation files—hell, you might as well burn them.

HELEN. (*Takes a step toward Harry.*) No, Mr. Golden. I won't do that. And maybe you'll fire me for what I've just done. (*She crosses to base of steps.*) Hello, Mrs. Golden. (*She speaks with a pride and a certainty which we have not seen in her before.*) I took quite a lot on myself this morning, Mr. Golden—early this morning when I heard. I thought maybe you'd be packing bags or something like that. And I didn't think I could stop you by myself. (*Birnbaum and Whitmore hurry on, Birnbaum still tying his necktie.*) So I went down to the corner store and phoned up Mr. Whitmore and Mr. Birnbaum. (*Goes up steps to Kate.*) I had to, Mrs. Golden. He mustn't leave.

WHITMORE. Harry. I had an idea we were having lunch today. Mrs. Golden, it's good to see you. (*The phone rings. Herbert answers it.*)

BIRNBAUM. (*Takes a suitcase and the typewriter from Harry and puts them on the porch.*) Harry. A little squib in a newspaper! How can this change the fine relationship we've had since the first minute you walked into this town? (*He gives a modifying shrug.*) All right. The *second* minute. (*Harry looks from one face to another, still bewildered, but unconvinced.*)

HERBERT. (*Into phone.*) Would you mind telling me who's calling from Philadelphia? (*Ray and Wes come on carrying a chiffonier. Wes steps to below Kate.*)

WES. Here's the last of the new stuff for Mrs. Golden. So you can surprise her. (*Suddenly he sees Kate, and his face falls.*) Unless you're Mrs. Golden.

KATE. (*Pleasantly.*) I'm surprised.

RAY. (*Picks up the chiffonier and starts up the steps.*) I was in jail once. For U-turnin' the movin' truck. It was nothing. (*Goes into house and up the stairs carrying the chiffonier.*)

WHITMORE. Harry, I want you to meet me at the Lawyer's Club at 12:30. We'll have a table right up front, where we can say hello to everybody. *Both* of us.

HARRY. You all know. And it doesn't seem to make any difference! I don't understand it!

WHITMORE. Harry. You haven't been reading your own paper. We need you in Charlotte. You may be the best Christian we've got.

Norris Borden, Ludwig Donath, Enid Markey, Martin Huston, Nehemiah Persoff, Sheppard Strudwick, Shannon Bolin, Lynn Hamilton, Daniel Keyes, Wayne Tippit, and Howard Wierum in *Only in America,* New York, 1959. Jerome Lawrence and Robert E. Lee Collection, Lawrence and Lee Theatre Research Institute, The Ohio State University.

HARRY. (*He goes up the veranda steps.*) Kate, we can stay! We don't have to go. All my life I've been thinking of myself as a member of a minority group. And I've been wrong. (*He turns to all the others, projecting.*) I'm a member of the biggest majority group in the world—the people who make mistakes! A member! Hell, I'm on the Board! (*Almost a whisper.*) Thanks. Thank you.

MRS. ARCHER-LOOMIS. (*Rushes on, calling as she comes in.*) Mr. Golden! Mr. Golden! Oh, Mr. Golden! (*She crosses to Harry.*) I have the most gratifying news. The Genealogy Secretary of the United Daughters of the Confederacy has made a most heartwarmin' discovery. My Great-great-grandfather Archer was married to Rebecca Levinson—an *Israelite*!

HARRY. (*This strikes even Harry as funny. He spreads out his arms in a gesture of welcome.*) Lanzman!

MRS. ARCHER-LOOMIS. And naturally we're not going to give the slightest ripple on the water notice to— (*Suddenly she sees the suitcases and lets out a little started gasp.*) Herbert!

HERBERT. Now, Aunt Henrietta!

HELEN. It's all right, Mrs. Archer-Loomis. They're coming, not going.

WHITMORE. Twelve-thirty for lunch, Harry?

HERBERT. Come on, Aunt Henrietta. I'll walk you home. (*He takes Mrs. Archer-Loomis' arm.*)

MRS. ARCHER-LOOMIS. Goodbye, Mr. Golden! Mrs. Golden! 'Bye! (*Mrs. Archer-Loomis and Herbert go off. Whitmore and Birnbaum start off.*)

BIRNBAUM. Wait a minute, Lucius! (*To Kate.*) Glad you're here, Mrs. Golden. (*They go off.*)

WES. We'll be seeing you, Mr. Golden! (*Ray gives Harry a vigorous salute; Harry returns it. They go off. Harry stands on the veranda, looking at Kate.*)

HARRY. (*With a feeling of genuine wonder.*) Kate! I almost just made my biggest mistake, y'know what I mean? I almost quit believing in life. It's a tremendous thing, and it goes on all the time! (*An idea is forming in his mind.*) I'd better get busy. I've got work to do! (*Resolutely he goes into the house, puts down the bag, flings open the rolltop desk. He pulls off his coat, tosses it over the swivel chair. He sees the baseball cap where Helen has left it. He puts it on, grasps the stick and take the familiar baseball stance—eager to wallop a new notion into a home-run.*)

CURTAIN

A CALL ON KUPRIN

Introduction

A Call on Kuprin was the second play Jerome Lawrence and Robert E. Lee drew from a published book; like *Auntie Mame* before it, it was entirely fictional. Ironically enough for playwrights who had specialized in creating fictional versions of actual events, *A Call on Kuprin* wound up being overwhelmed by an actuality undreamt of at the time of its creation. The play also continued Lawrence and Lee's conviction that ideas surmount political and social interests, concerns raised earlier by *Inherit the Wind*, *Only in America*, and *The Gang's All Here*.

Both *The Gang's All Here* and *A Call on Kuprin* suffered from being produced on Broadway at the wrong time. *The Gang's All Here* had been a few months premature in presenting political concerns before its audience was ready to contemplate politics. Two years later, the timing for *A Call on Kuprin* turned out to be prophetically unfortunate.

A Call on Kuprin was commissioned by Robert E. Griffith and Harold Prince, the Broadway producers who had, by 1961, a string of mostly successful musicals to their credit. The play was based on a book by Maurice Edelman.[1] The novel opens with the successful launching of a cosmonaut into space—at a time well before manned space flight had happened. Lawrence and Lee dramatized the novel; George Abbott—a frequent collaborator with Griffith and Prince on such musicals as *The Pajama Game*, *Damn Yankees*, *New Girl in Town*, and *Fiorello!*—joined the project as the director. Abbott was also an old acquaintance of Lawrence and Lee, having directed their first Broadway production, *Look, Ma, I'm Dancin'!* Problems emerged quickly with *A Call on Kuprin*, beginning with casting, which rapidly became difficult because of timing.

The play was scheduled for very late in the 1960–61 season. Lawrence recalled that Abbott wanted to go right into production in the spring: "He was sick to death of swimming and playing golf in Florida, . . . George wanted to go right away."[2] According to Carol Ilson, Harold Prince also was willing "to risk a late season opening. . . . he went into production immediately. . . . Prince felt he had too good a play to wait till fall."[3] The spring opening meant that Henry Fonda, who was approached to play Smith, the lead, was unavailable; so was Richard Widmark; so were a number of other leading men. Abbott cast Jeffrey Lynn, a well-respected performer who never reached the status of a major star, in the part. Both Lawrence and Lee felt that Lynn was miscast and that the play suffered as a result.

Current events upstaged the play in a wholly unpredictable way. While playing its pre-Broadway tryout at Philadelphia's Forrest Theatre in early May 1961, the play was scooped by the Soviet Union's successful launch of Yuri Gagarin as the first human in space. The Soviet Union's stunning coup in space travel doomed *A Call on Kuprin*. By the time the production reached the Broadhurst Theatre in New York three weeks later, it looked dated: a space program able to launch a cosmonaut but unable to retrieve him (as in the play) was patently behind the times as the Soviets both launched and retrieved Gagarin.

Although the play was praised in its Philadelphia tryout—the *Variety* reviewer terming it an "exciting play with plausible action and characters and plenty of fine suspense"[4]—*A Call on Kuprin* split the New York reviewers.[5] Four reported positively, with Howard Taubman writing a rave response in the *New York Times*. The remaining three reviewers were critical, sometimes harshly so. The split nature of the reviews, combined with the lessened status of the *Times* reviewer,[6] worked against the production's finding an audience. So did its timing: opening at the very end of the theatrical season, *A Call on Kuprin* needed to generate significant audience interest to survive the traditionally lessened attendance during the summer months. In 1961, the regular New York theatregoing audience shrank during the hot vacation months, while tourists tended not to patronize new productions which had not yet established a national reputation.

Virtually all the reviewers regarded *A Call on Kuprin* as either a thriller or a melodrama, and most mentioned the elaborate physical production provided by Donald Oenslager, Abbott's rapidly paced direction, and spectacular performances from George Voskovec as Kuprin and Eugenie Leontovich as his aged mother. The New York reviewers parted company, however, on the effectiveness of the script.

Taubman's rave included, in its opening paragraph, fulsome praise for Lawrence and Lee, saying that "their new play . . . is not only contemporary and tautly suspenseful but also says something of vast importance."[7] John McClain, in the *Journal American*, called the play "well-conceived, acted, and magnificently produced" and "a thoughtful and engrossing narrative, forcefully told and beautifully embroidered. I believe we are ready for a good suspense story, after all these years and I, for one, enjoyed myself immensely."[8] Robert Coleman thought that the playwrights didn't "begin to build true suspense until the middle of the second act," but concluded his review by noting that the play "packs a wallop when it gets up steam."[9] Richard Watts, Jr., found the piece "steadily effective" and "a workmanlike, interesting and intelligent melodrama."[10]

Frank Aston, writing in the *New York World-Telegram and the Sun*, raved over Eugenie Leontovich's performance but found the play itself too abstract, while John Chapman of the *Daily News* admitted that "the significance of . . . 'A Call on Kuprin,' must be over my head," terming the play a television drama.[11] Walter Kerr, in the most harshly critical review, called the play "a great deal of scenery in three acts," feeling that Oenslager's scenery was the most notable part of a script marred by predictable humor, sentimental language, and superficiality.[12]

A Call on Kuprin never found its audience and closed after twelve performances, on 3 June 1961. The play was costly to perform, receiving a large production close to the scale of the musicals on which Griffith, Prince, and Abbott usually collaborated. On Broadway, the drama required forty-six characters, played by twenty-six performers (a young Dabney Coleman, later to achieve prominence in films and television, performed five roles as various tourists and military men, both Soviet and American). Large crowd scenes opened both of the first two acts, setting up the Muscovite world of the play. The opening scene, the Ukraina Hotel lobby, established contrasts between western and Russian activities (this scene was revised and simplified for publication after the Broadway engagement). By contrast, the Gorky Park scene that opens act 2 is purely Russian, Smith being the only westerner in the action.

Lawrence and Lee use those establishing scenes to set the moods of both acts. In act 1, Smith is very much out of place, a tourist coping with a suspicious, foreign bureaucracy and caught up in the swirl of international intrigue. The foreignness of the situation is underscored by Lawrence and Lee's choice to have the Russian characters speak in Russian, not in a theatrically accented English; Smith therefore is literally helpless. He is no match for the Russian security agent, Trifonov. By act 2, Smith's relationship with Vera allows him to be comfortable in Gorky Park, even though he remains obviously a tourist who can be quizzed by passersby about American jazz and popular music. The relaxed Smith in this scene is vastly different from the frustrated foreigner who began the play.

Smith's status as the outsider, the "other," is doubled by the otherness of Madame Kuprina. Kuprin's otherworldly mother was regarded by Walter Kerr as "a patently unnecessary role."[13] Kerr appears to have missed the function Kuprina served, both in Edelman's novel and, in far more pointed ways, in Lawrence and Lee's dramatization. Not only does Kuprina function as the visible reason for Kuprin's sudden return to the Soviet Union from his Ohio university position, she is also a constant reminder of the Russian past contrasting with the Soviet present. Kuprina's imaginary servants and the invisible eavesdropping forces that she keeps at bay with her rings are imaginative echoes of the constant surveillance of both Soviets and tourists, made visible in the play by Trifonov.

Madame Kuprina's character is found in Edelman's novel, as is the basic story line, including the romantic involvement of Smith and Vera. In making a play of the novel, Lawrence and Lee of course simplified the action. As might be expected for an American dramatization, Smith becomes an American writer rather than English, and Kuprin's British sojourn at Cambridge is reset at Perkins Observatory in Delaware, Ohio, where Robert Lee had studied astronomy in the mid 1930s. Lawrence and Lee deleted entirely the novel's other protagonist, Laye-Parker, a somewhat fatuous Member of Parliament, who originates the notion of getting Kuprin to defect. Not only would a second protagonist have confused the already complex action, Edelman's underlying satire on bumbling British politicians is a secondary element in the plot, which detracts from the central conflict. Lawrence and Lee made major changes in the character of Trifonov and in subsidiary incidents in the plot, virtually all of which stem from the theatrical need to simplify and clarify the central dramatic action (even if it still remained confusing to at least one reviewer, John Chapman).

The play retains the novel's insistence that Soviet citizens can indeed be patriotic and further undercuts the situation's tendency toward melodrama by making Trifonov, the ostensible villain, not only somewhat sympathetic but also driven by patriotism. Even the suspenseful interrogation scene, which gives act 2 its climax, contains a balance: the Soviet intelligence men are not agents of an evil empire but loyal citizens attempting to protect their homeland from meddlesome spies. The point is reiterated in Miroff's moving farewell to his homeland from space in act 3,[14] in sequence and incidents not in the Edelman original.

Lawrence and Lee made two major changes from their source, one of which reveals the playwrights' interests in using the story, while the other speaks to the nature of commercially driven theatre. In the novel, Smith murders Kuprin when the scientist refuses to defect; Smith does not flee with Vera, rather escaping alone to Turkey. The drama provides a commercially far more satisfying ending: Kuprin confronts Trifonov, the security man's basic integrity is appealed to, and Smith and Vera set off for a happy life together.

The reasons Smith uses to convince Kuprin to defect are based far more on political power in the novel. In the drama, Smith appeals to Kuprin's belief in the universality of science. Kuprin restates the argument to Trifonov in the speech that provides the play's climax: "Does it matter now, that Columbus was a Genoese, working for Spain? Copernicus a Pole? Kepler a German? Einstein a wandering Jew? Today, now, who cheers because Ptolemy was an Egyptian, Archimedes a Greek? What they *thought* matters. The IDEA matters. Man is winning. Don't make us all lose!" The demand that ideas be free is Lawrence and Lee's contribution to *A Call on Kuprin*; the theme informs all their work. While the end of the Cold War and the collapse of Soviet hegemony now makes *A Call on Kuprin* a period piece, its central conflict remains timely.

Notes

1. Maurice Edelman, *A Call on Kuprin* (Philadelphia & New York: J. B. Lippincott, 1959).

2. Jerome Lawrence, interview, 28 December 1988.

3. *Harold Prince: From* Pajama Game *to* Phantom of the Opera (Ann Arbor: UMI Research Press, 1989), 60.

4. Murd, "A Call on Kuprin," *Variety*, 10 May 1961, p. 88.

5. The reviews, all dated 25 May 1961, are reprinted in *New York Theatre Critics Reviews* (abbrev. *NYTCR*) 22 (1961): 282–85.

6. Brooks Atkinson, the highly regarded *Times* reviewer, retired in 1960. Taubman, who had

been the *Times* music reviewer, replaced him. Not as universally admired as Atkinson, Taubman succeeded in dissipating much of the power of a *Times* rave during his relatively brief tenure in the position. See William Goldman, *The Season* (New York: Bantam, 1970), 82–83.

7. "Theatre: 'Call on Kuprin' Aims High, Hits Target," *The New York Times*, rpt. *NYTCR* 22 (1961): 283.

8. "Suspenseful Melodrama," *New York Journal American*, rpt. *NYTCR* 22 (1961): 282.

9. " 'Call on Kuprin' Packs Wallop," *New York Mirror*, rpt. *NYTCR* 22 (1961): 183.

10. "Two on the Aisle: An Effective Cold War Melodrama," *New York Post*, rpt. *NYTCR* 22 (1961): 284.

11. Aston, " 'A Call on Kuprin' at the Broadhurst," *New York World-Telegram and the Sun*, rpt. *NYTCR* 22 (1961): 284–85; Chapman, " 'A Call on Kuprin' an Elaborate Production of a Television Plot," *New York Daily News*, rpt. *NYTCR* 22 (1961): 282.

12. "First Night Report: '*A Call on Kuprin*,' " *New York Herald Tribune*, rpt. *NYTCR* 22 (1961): 285.

13. *Ibid.*

14. Vera's translation of Miroff's words—"Which I may never see again. Goodbye, Meadowland"—reinforces the Soviet patriotism while foreshadowing Vera's own imminent departure from Russia.

Foreword

We would like to live long enough to know what a Social Security check looks like. We hope to see our children receive their B.A.'s. And it must be an interesting feeling to be a grandfather.

We wrote the play, *A Call on Kuprin,* in an honest effort to improve the chances of realizing these simple fulfillments.

When we began shaping the play, the headlines from which it seems to spring were unwritten. But we knew that the nameless Shepards and Gagarins would inevitably leap the Van Allen belt and win Presidential handshakes or smacks on both cheeks in Red Square.

Our play may be timely but it is not topical. We are less concerned with the adventuring of Cosmonauts than with the adventuring of the scientific mind. There is one thing more dramatic than a daring exploit: that is the daring of the mind which imagines it. A few years ago, when driving through Princeton, we used to detour through side streets in the hope of seeing Albert Einstein shambling along the sidewalk or sitting on his front porch. Unfortunately, we never had the honor of paying a call on Einstein. But we have tried to project the excitement of meeting a man of similar magnitude as we pay *A Call on Kuprin.*

The most volatile propellant in our society is not chemical fuel, liquid or solid: it is gray matter. But we are not going to keep ourselves alive on this planet solely by the exercise of intellectual razzle-dazzle. We must demonstrate, as Kuprin does, our "potential for compassion."

Producers Griffith and Prince decided to call the play "An Adventure." And just as Sir Carol Reed's *The Third Man* had the giant ferris wheel of Vienna spinning around its mystery, so the maelstrom of Moscow swirls about Kuprin. This is not a cartoon Moscow of gloomy Czarists or comic Communists. *A Call on Kuprin* is a view of an authentic Moscow which is trying so desperately to leap from the twelfth century to the twenty-first.

The Soviet capital has color, vitality, humor, and danger. Donald Oenslager designed a kaleidoscope of rooftops, amusement parks, avenues and alleyways where Muscovites and Americans brush shoulders, wonder at one another, and even fall in love.

Exactly a year before the opening of this play, the Lawrence half of this play-writing team visited the Soviet Union, to gather impressions which would make the play a constructive comment on the schizoid world in which we live.

And long before Lee met Lawrence, he was traveling through space at the speed of light—optically—at the eyepiece of the world's third largest telescope. Coincidentally, Lee's mentor at Ohio Wesleyan University was a Russian, Professor Nicholas T. Bobrovnikoff, who is in some ways the inspiration for Professor V. V. Kuprin of this play. So the highways among the stars, like the boulevards of Moscow, have their basis in reality.

Conquering space means more than occupying it. The moon doesn't take orders from Moscow because there is a hammer-and-sickle flag lying in some crater, buried in moon-dust. But the flags of a hundred nations will be lying in earth-dust, highly radioactive, unless we explore not merely the weightless dark of space, but the waiting hearts and minds of our fellow human beings, wherever they were born, wherever they happen to live.

We are optimists. We hope this play will be presented at the Maly in Moscow as well as the Broadhurst in New York, for its challenge is double-edged.

Forget the Social Security checks. We want to go to those commencement exercises.

Lawrence & Lee

(This essay, titled "Hero of the Mind in Moscow," appeared in the *New York Herald Tribune* on Sunday, 21 May 1961, before the play's New York opening.)

Production Notes

This is a play about people and ideas, not scenery. It is not necessary to the concept of the play that the scenic effects be literal or abstract. They should merely be suggested.

The language differences should be treated realistically: the Russians speak Russian, the Americans speak English. Many are bilingual. Avoid like the plague broad, burlesque English-speaking Russian caricatures. It is not necessary that the actors speaking Russian sound like cosmopolitan Muscovites. But it is necessary that they speak and act with the conviction that they *are* speaking Russian. Actually, there are hundreds of dialects in the Soviet Union. Do not let yourself be tyrannized by some "Russian expert."

There are no conventional villains in this play, and the Soviet authorities should never be portrayed as such. Treat each side with humanity and the result will be reality. Even in the K.G.B. scene, these are not robots in uniform; they have senses of humor. Trifonov is an unwilling conspirator, a gentle man who would prefer to spend his time over a volume of Tolstoy in a library.

To bridge the various scenes, Russian music is suggested.

Editor's Note

A Call on Kuprin was published by Samuel French in 1962. The acting edition text, which was slightly revised from the version acted on Broadway, is currently available from Samuel French under the title *Checkmate*. It is republished here under its original title, with a few printing errors corrected and slightly simplified stage directions.

Cast

A Call on Kuprin opened in New York at the Broadhurst Theatre on 25 May 1961. It was produced by Robert E. Griffith and Harold Prince, and directed by George Abbott. The scenery and lighting were designed by Donald Oenslager, with costumes by Florence Klotz. Ruth Mitchell was production stage manager and John Allen the stage manager. The play is based on the novel by Maurice Edelman. The cast included:

HEAD INTOURIST CLERK .... Rita Karin
MR. KENDALL .... Nicholas Saunders
MRS. KENDALL .... Marie Baratoff
ASSISTANT CLERK .... Ludmilla Tchor
AMERICAN COUPLE ..... Tania Velia, Dabney Coleman
INTOURIST AIDE .... Victor Merinow
WOMAN PORTER .... Gedda Petry
HOLLOWAY .... Claude Horton
JONATHAN SMITH .... Jeffrey Lynn
NINA .... Halyna Harcourt
TOURIST GUIDE .... Edmund Shaff
TOURIST COUPLE .... Doreen Kay, Andre Pascal
TOURISTS .... Ted Vadim, Joe Ponazecki
OLD WOMAN .... Ludmilla Toretzka
FLOWER PEDDLER .... Gedda Petry
PROFESSOR TRIFONOV .... Leon Janney
SOVIET POLICEMAN .... Victor Merinow
MADAME KUPRINA .... Eugenie Leontovich
VERA KUPRINA .... Lydia Bruce
ARTHUR HARRINGTON .... John Allen
MARINE SGT. LOOMIS .... Dabney Coleman
AMERICAN AMBASSADOR .... William Swetland
CHESS BOY .... Lauri Ikonen
KVAS VENDOR .... Doreen Kay
WOMAN SWEEPING .... Ludmilla Toretzka
DRUNK .... Joe Ponazecki
JAZZ ENTHUSIAST .... Tania Velia
HER FRIENDS .... Halyna Harcourt, Edmund Shaff

BOOK PEDDLER .... Rita Karien
RUSSIAN SAILORS .... Andre Pascal, John Hirst
GUARD .... Dabney Coleman
PROFESSOR V. V. KUPRIN .... George Voskovec
SINGING GIRLS ... Halyna Harcourt, Tania Velia, Gedda Petry
COL. I. L. MAKAROV .... John Garson
K.G.B. GUARD .... Andre Pascal
SECOND K.G.B. GUARD .... Dabney Coleman
K.G.B. INTERPRETER .... Victor Merinow
GUARDS AT YALTA .... Nicholas Saunders, Dabney Coleman

A Call on Kuprin was produced prior to its Broadway run at the Forrest Theatre, Philadelphia, opening on 8 May 1961.

ACT ONE

Scene 1: A phone booth, the Ukraina Hotel, Moscow (in One)
Scene 2: A Street Corner (in One)
Scene 3: Madame Kuprina's Apartment
Scene 4: The roof-top of the U.S. Embassy, Moscow (in Two)

ACT TWO

Scene 1: Gorky Park, near the Chess Pavilion (in Two)
Scene 2: Madame Kuprina's Apartment
Scene 3: A River Bank (in One)
Scene 4: K.G.B. Headquarters

ACT THREE

Kuprin's Dacha in Yalta, on the Black Sea.

TIME: 1961

George Voskovec, Jeffrey Lynn, Lydia Bruce, and Eugenie Leontovich in *A Call on Kuprin*, New York, 1960. Jerome Lawrence and Robert E. Lee Collection, Lawrence and Lee Theatre Research Institute, The Ohio State University.

Gorky Park scene (Jeffrey Lynn and Lydia Bruce, left of center), *A Call on Kuprin*, New York, 1960. Jerome Lawrence and Robert E. Lee Collection, Lawrence and Lee Theatre Research Institute, The Ohio State University.

A Call on Kuprin

Before the opening curtain, we hear Russian music, then a Woman's Voice, speaking pleasantly, even alluringly.

WOMAN'S VOICE. Americans! Intourist invites you to see magnificent Moscow, lovely Leningrad, Yalta by the Sea: Tourist or Deluxe. Educational and Carefree!

ACT ONE

SCENE 1

A telephone booth in the lobby of the Ukraina Hotel in Moscow. This is just off the area of the bustling Intourist Bureau. It is very much like an American telephone booth, but the letters over the door spell телефон.

Jonathan Smith is standing in the glassed-in booth, desperately trying to dial a number. Smith seems a cut above the average tourist. He is in his early forties, has a sharp, sensitive face, intelligent eyes. Frustrated, Smith tries to juggle some coins in his hand, tries depositing some, tries dialing. Absolutely nothing happens. Smith hangs up the phone, searches hopelessly all around the booth for a phone book. There is none. He goes back to the phone, drops in a coin, dials Operator. Still nothing happens. He clicks the receiver.

SMITH. (*Into phone.*) Operator! Operator, can you help me? Ya Americansky. I am a friend. (*Jiggling the hook, desperately.*) Come back, come back! (*There seems to be no response. Wearily, he hangs up. Smith reaches in the coin return. Nothing. He shrugs. A Female Porter comes across, carrying some heavy luggage. Smith motions to her.*) Excuse me. Can you tell me how get a number in Moscow? Or how you dial information? Or where I can find a phone book? (*The Female Porter shrugs. She indicates that she doesn't understand English. She goes off. Smith returns to the phone, starts to search through some kopecks in his hand, shakes his head helplessly. Holloway, a lean, perpetually bemused Englishman, wearing a tweed jacket and sandals and smoking a pipe, crosses toward the Intourist Bureau. Smith sees him and comes out of the telephone booth.*) Pardon me. Are you an American?

HOLLOWAY. British. Same thing. We declared our independence from you in 1776.

SMITH. I wonder if you can help me. How do you find a phone number in Moscow?

HOLLOWAY. Oh, that's quite a trick!

SMITH. Where do they keep the phone books?

HOLLOWAY. No phone books. If you don't know somebody's number, they consider it's none of your business. (*He grins.*) Handy, isn't it? (*He extends his hand.*) My name's Holloway.

SMITH. (*Shaking hands.*) Smith.

HOLLOWAY. Pleasure. "Golloway," the Russians call me. You know they turn all their "H's" into "G's." Oh, don't mind the footwear. (*He indicates his sandals, apologetically.*) What the visiting businessman wears in Moscow.

SMITH. You're here on business?

HOLLOWAY. (*Nodding.*) Lumber. I come in every year, try to buy up plywood. But they're very sticky.

SMITH. How do you mean?

HOLLOWAY. You can't shop around. There's only one firm to deal with. Mother Russia, Incorporated. What brings you to Moscow, Mr. Smith?

SMITH. Oh, a lot of reasons. Curiosity mainly. I may be a cornball but I still believe in the Brotherhood of Man. And I want to know if it's going out of business.

VOICE. (*On P.A.*) Attention. All members of Tour A will foregather instantly at Bus Number 37.

HOLLOWAY. You Tour A?

SMITH. B.

HOLLOWAY. So'm I. That's luck.

SMITH. If you get to Moscow so often, how come you're taking a tour?

HOLLOWAY. Have to do something between bureaucrats. Can't sit in a hotel room all day staring at a fringed lamp and a chromo of a Collective Farm.

SMITH. I've got a friend in Moscow. How do I look him up?

HOLLOWAY. American?

SMITH. No, Russian. Fellow I used to know in college.

VOICE. (*On P.A.*) Tour B. Members of Tour B will foregather instantly at Bus Number 38 in front of the hotel.

HOLLOWAY. Foregathering time.

SMITH. I tried Moscow University. But they clammed up as soon as I said his name.

HOLLOWAY. They "clam" very easily here.

SMITH. There must be a way to get to him. Friend of mine even wrangled an interview with Khrushchev. And Kuprin isn't that important. Yet.

HOLLOWAY. V. V. Kuprin?

SMITH. Yes.

HOLLOWAY. You know the man? Personally?

SMITH. Sure. He was my astronomy professor in college, back in the thirties. I worked with him at Perkins Observatory in Ohio.

HOLLOWAY. You a scientist?

SMITH. Not really. I write syndicated pieces about science. "You, too, can understand the Einstein Theory"—that kind of thing. I guess I'm what you'd call a lowbrow egghead. (*He laughs, then digs into his pocket for a creased slip of paper.*) I've got an address. Kuprin's mother. It's probably no good any more. (*Holloway takes it, scowls over the paper.*) If I could just get a map of the city—

HOLLOWAY. (*He shakes his head sadly.*) Not a chance.

SMITH. You mean it's on the inside cover of the telephone book. Do you think the guide will know?

HOLLOWAY. (*Quickly.*) No, not the guide. I'll tell you; later maybe I can help you find this place.

SMITH. That's very nice of you. (*Nina the tour guide, enters. She is pretty, perky, hardly the sexless machine which is the stereotype of the Soviet Woman.*)

NINA. (*Calling.*) We are missing two members of Tour B. The bus cannot proceed until we have located— (*She breaks off, looking askance at Holloway.*) Mr. Golloway.

HOLLOWAY. (*Pleasantly.*) *Zdrasht*-veet-cheh, Nina. (*To Smith.*) Zdrasht-veet-cheh means "Hello." Nina means Nina. This is Nina.

NINA. You are *not* taking this tour again, Mr. Golloway?

HOLLOWAY. It is not Moscow which entices me, Nina—it is you.

NINA. (*Wagging a finger at him.*) I have learned a new American idiom— You, Mr. Golloway, it fits perfectly. "You are full of balonies!"

HOLLOWAY. What's the use of jamming the Voice of America?

SMITH. Our culture seeps through.

NINA. (*Turning to Smith.*) You are an American.

HOLLOWAY. His name is Smith. Nina is the Elizabeth Taylor of Intourist.

NINA. (*Suspiciously.*) Who is Elizabeth Taylor?

SMITH. A movie star.

NINA. (*Proudly.*) Oh. We see all the cinemas from America. Johnny Weissmuller. Deanna Durbin. Sonja Henie. We know, we know. (*Abruptly.*) Please to come instantly, Mr. Golloway. You are delaying the entire Tour B.

HOLLOWAY. I know it by heart. "On your right, the Bolshoi Theatre, built in 1824. Damaged by fire and restored in 1856. In summer the company rests. Approaching is Gorky Street, which is 100 meters broad—"

NINA. (*Waving him off.*) Okay. I will go home. You give the tour.

HOLLOWAY. It is not allowed. (*He exits, puffing at his pipe.*)

SMITH. (*Agreeably.*) Sorry we held you up, uh—Nina. Where do you want us to go?

NINA. (*Appraising him.*) Mr. Smeeth. I like you. (*Shaking his hand like a pump handle, Soviet-style.*) Peace and friendship.

SMITH. (*He smiles back at her.*) Peace and friendship. (*They go off together. The lights fade.*)

ACT ONE
SCENE 2

A street corner near the Antipoyevsky Pereulok. It is night. In the dark, we hear a woman's voice in a plaintive sing-song.

FLOWER PEDDLER. (*In Russian.*) Dahlias. Bright, fresh-cut dahlias. (*A street light comes on, and we see the Flower Peddler with a babushka around her head and a tray of yellow flowers on a leather strap around her neck. There is an air of mystery in the puddle of lamplight. Trifonov comes on, looking about quizzically, as if searching the lights of the apartments high up and out front. Trifonov is slight, pleasant, professorial. He wears steel-rimmed glasses and a rumpled business suit. The peddler offers him a bunch of flowers.*)

TRIFONOV. Nyet. (*He takes off his glasses and peers in an alley-way which seems to go into the darkness upstage. There is the sound of an approaching car and the flare of headlights. Trifonov moves off. The car comes to a stop, off. The car door opens, slams.*)

HOLLOWAY'S VOICE. (*Off, in Russian.*) Wait for us here. (*Smith and Holloway come on. Smith is studying the creased slip of paper, Holloway scans the buildings.*)

SMITH. Our cab driver seemed so excited.

HOLLOWAY. The whole town will be excited in a few hours. He was telling me they have another man in orbit.

SMITH. I kept hearing him say "Chelovyek."

HOLLOWAY. Man-Star. Chelovyek-Zvezda. This is a chap named Miroff. The cab driver says he's going to broadcast from up there in three languages. Goes over Moscow at 10 P.M. We'll be back in time. Now, let's see, what's that address?

SMITH. (*Reading, with difficulty.*) Antipoyevsky Pereulok. Five-A.

HOLLOWAY. Pereulok means "alley." It's around here some place.

PEDDLER. (*In Russian.*) Dahlias? Fresh-cut dahlias?

HOLLOWAY. (*In Russian, to the Peddler.*) Where do we find Antipoyevsky Pereulok? Number 5A? (*The Peddler backs away, shaking her head. Holloway turns to Smith, in English.*) They don't like us poking around the back streets.

SMITH. (*He crosses to the Peddler and points to some of the flowers.*) I'd like to buy some of these. (*He reaches in his pocket for some coins, as the Peddler wraps a bunch of dahlias eagerly in a newspaper. Smith consults Holloway.*) Is this enough? (*He is holding a large coin between his fingers. The Peddler beams.*)

HOLLOWAY. No, no. Too much. (*He fishes in Smith's palm for a smaller coin. The Peddler's face clouds over. But Smith already has the flowers.*) Here. (*He hands the Peddler a small coin. She glares at Holloway and goes off grumbling.*)

PEDDLER. (*In Russian.*) Capitalist!

SMITH. You see? Money has no meaning in the New Social Order. (*They laugh.*)

HOLLOWAY. (*Glancing upstage.*) Here's your alley—back this way. Now the trick is to find the house number. I'll wait with the cab.

SMITH. I don't know how long I'll be.

HOLLOWAY. No matter. If I don't hang onto Boris, you'll never get another taxi around here. (*The taxi horn sounds impatiently, the headlights flick off and on.*)

SMITH. Will Boris wait?

HOLLOWAY. (*He reaches into his coat pocket for a wallet.*) When I show him this. In Russia, old man, there is nothing so powerful as a document. Doesn't matter *what* document. Smallpox vaccination, driver's license, prescription for your eyeglasses. And if you have a document with a photograph like *this*! (*He flourishes it in front of Smith, who examines it under the street lamp.*)

SMITH. My God, it's you and Khrushchev!

HOLLOWAY. You know those dreadful chaps who elbow their way forward to get photographed with celebrities? Well, I'm one of them. (*He grins.*) When I flash this, Moscow is mine.

SMITH. I'm glad you were on Tour B.

HOLLOWAY. So am I. Good hunting. (*He waves jauntily to Smith, who exits, scanning the buildings. After Smith leaves, Holloway's air of frivolity suddenly turns grave, and he stares after Smith soberly. A Soviet Policeman, in uniform, comes on. He sees Holloway standing on the street corner, and he comes up to him.*)

POLICEMAN. (*In Russian.*) Let me see your papers. (*Suddenly, Holloway whips out his wallet of documents, brandishing the photograph importantly. The Policeman looks. Impressed, he steps back a pace or two, salutes. In Russian.*) Sorry, Tovareesh. A thousand apologies, Tovareesh.

HOLLOWAY. (*In Russian.*) Not at all. (*The Policeman salutes again, goes off. We hear the cab honk more insistently. Holloway crosses toward the sound, the all-powerful photograph still in his hand. He calls to the unseen cab driver.*) Patience, Boris. Remember the words of Tolstoy: "God Waits." Why should you be different? (*Holloway exits. Trifonov appears silently. He draws on a cigarette, holding it from underneath between thumb and forefinger, Russian-fashion. He looks off toward Holloway, then slowly his eyes turn toward the alley-way down which Smith has gone and he looks up at the buildings thoughtfully, puffing on the cigarette.*)

THE LIGHTS FADE

ACT ONE
SCENE 3

Madame Kuprina's apartment. There is the sound of a man's footsteps reaching the top of a long flight of stairs—then a knock on the door. In the darkness, we hear Madame Kuprina's voice.

MADAME KUPRINA. (*Calling, in Russian.*) Dmitri! (*A pause. The knock is repeated in the darkness. The voice is a plaintive old woman's, calling helplessly.*) Dmitri! (*We hear the shuffling of footsteps. Madame Kuprina pulls the cord on a lamp, and we see her for the first time. Madame Kuprina is a thin, timid old lady in a black lace dress. Yet there is a vague regality about her. The room has a musty elegance. There are plush curtains, antimacassars on the couch. A large and curious box is draped with a crocheted shawl and crowned with an arch of framed photographs. A century-old sideboard supports a rubber plant. There are several embroidered chairs and tasseled lamps. Smith is standing in a faint blue light outside the heavy oak door of the apartment. He is breathing hard, having climbed six flights of stairs. He knocks again.*) Who's there? (*She stands at the door, holding onto both the knob and the bolt protectively.*)

SMITH. (*Through the door, in English.*) I am looking for the Kuprin apartment. Are you Madame Kuprin? I mean—Kuprina? (*Madame Kuprina, still hesitating at the closed door, does not answer. She trembles slightly. There is only the thickness of the door between them, and Smith can hear her breathing. He speaks with a quiet intensity.*) I am from America. I hope you speak English. I am an old friend of Vassili's.

MADAME KUPRINA. (*She speaks for the first time in English. As if it were some legendary continent.*) From America—! (*She turns back into the apartment, and calls again.*) Dmitri! Dmitri!

SMITH. (*He speaks rapidly. This may be his only chance to make contact.*) I've brought you some flowers.

MADAME KUPRINA. (*This sign of grace touches her.*) Flowers! (*Slowly, almost dazed, she loosens the bolt and opens the door.*)

SMITH. (*He does not enter at once. They merely look at each other.*) Madame Kuprina?

MADAME KUPRINA. (*Remotely.*) I am Madame Kuprina.

SMITH. (*Relieved.*) I'm so glad you speak English. My name is Smith. (*He hands her the flowers. She takes them, with a slight inclination of the head. Then, with a wide gesture, she opens the door completely and invites him to come in.*)

MADAME KUPRINA. Entrez, monsieur. (*Smith enters. Madame Kuprina lights another lamp, and we get a better look at her. She is about 75, with white hair drawn back tightly from a wide forehead. Her black dress, buttoned to the neck, is only lightened by the white cuffs at her wrists. She clutches the flowers.*) You have news of my son?

SMITH. (*Puzzled.*) No. I knew him when I was in college. In America.

MADAME KUPRINA. Oh, yes, America.

SMITH. This is the only address I have.

MADAME KUPRINA. Allow me to offer you some refreshment.

SMITH. Thank you, no.

MADAME KUPRINA. (*Calling off.*) Tea, please. And cakes. Be quick about it, Dmitri. (*She holds out the flowers in their newspaper wrapping, but no servant appears to take them from her. Sighing, she puts them on the sideboard.*) Servants! Nothing but trouble.

SMITH. (*Cautiously.*) You still have Dmitri?

MADAME KUPRINA. Why not? I have kept all my servants.

SMITH. (*Frowning.*) Professor Kuprin told me about Dmitri. But he was an old man even when your son was a little boy.

MADAME KUPRINA. (*Nodding.*) Yes, Dmitri has been very faithful. He was my mother's servant also.

SMITH. I wonder if I could get in touch with Vassili. Could you give me his address?

MADAME KUPRINA. His address? (*The old woman begins to laugh, quietly.*) It's strange, isn't it? But I don't know where Vassili is.

SMITH. Perhaps his telephone number—?

MADAME KUPRINA. They won't tell me.

SMITH. Who won't tell you?

MADAME KUPRINA. No one. They keep it from me. (*Madame Kuprina suddenly puts her finger to her lips.*) Shhh! They are listening!

SMITH. (*Baffled.*) Who?

MADAME KUPRINA. (*Leaning forward, secretively.*) They listen to every word I say. Dmitri, all of them. They spy on me. (*She grips his arm.*) Do you see anything?

SMITH. Where?

MADAME KUPRINA. (*She gestures in the air with her arm.*) Moving.

SMITH. (*Uncomfortably, looking around the room.*) I don't see anything.

MADAME KUPRINA. (*Eyes bright.*) They are invisible! I wear these rings to keep them from reaching my vibrations. You understand?

SMITH. Yes. That's very useful.

MADAME KUPRINA. (*Holding up a cluster of rings on a bony hand.*) But it doesn't interfere with my late husband, the General, who is in the second aura. (*There is the sound of approaching footsteps, climbing the stairs. Smith is startled by the sound as if he, too, has been infected with Madame Kuprina's paranoia. The old woman hides beneath the table.*) They're coming back! (*In the blue light outside the door, we see an attractive figure of a young woman, 25 perhaps, carrying a shopping bag in one arm while she fits the door key with her free hand. She pushes the door open and enters. Seeing a visitor, she is alarmed.*)

VERA. (*In Russian.*) Who are you?

SMITH. I only speak English.

VERA. (*In English.*) Who are you?

SMITH. I'm an old friend of Professor Kuprin's, from America.

VERA. What are you doing here?

SMITH. I'm just trying to locate Professor Kuprin, that's all.

VERA. (*Trying to get him out.*) We know nothing about Professor Kuprin, we have no contact with him.

MADAME KUPRINA. Verochka?

VERA. What have you done to her?

SMITH. I didn't do anything. Just brought her flowers. Ask Dmitri.

VERA. (*Gently lifting her great aunt from beneath the table.*) Dmitri has been dead for twenty years.

SMITH. I'm sorry. I didn't understand. I'd better go.

VERA. Yes, please.

SMITH. (*Turning at the door.*) If I could just leave a message for Professor Kuprin. I have something for him from his daughter.

VERA. From Nadya?

SMITH. And his grandchildren.

VERA. You have seen them?

SMITH. Just a couple of days ago. In Princeton, New Jersey.

VERA. (*Changing her tone.*) Great Aunt. We have a visitor from abroad. From America. A friend of Vassili's.

MADAME KUPRINA. (*She looks up, as if she had never seen Smith before. She crosses, extending her hand to be kissed, regally.*) Enchanté. (*Smith takes her hand, inclines his head.*)

VERA. We do not often have guests. And never before from America. (*Suddenly, she decides to throw away her caution.*) We shall all have some tea together. I insist. Is that correct? "Shall" or "will"?

SMITH. (*A little amused.*) If you are insisting, then it is "will."

VERA. Of course. The imperative. Command. Yes? "We *will* have tea together." (*Softening, graciously.*) Please?

SMITH. Sure.

VERA. (*She starts toward the other room.*) And I can practice my English with a real American! My friends will be so jealous of me. (*She stops abruptly.*) I don't know your name.

SMITH. Smith.

VERA. Smees.

SMITH. (*Pronouncing it more carefully.*) No. Smith.

VERA. That's what I said. Smees. I am doing it wrong?

SMITH. You are doing it delightfully.

VERA. I am Vera—also Kuprina. Vassili is my cousin. (*She starts off.*) In America, everybody is studying Russian, yes?

SMITH. Not quite everybody. (*An embarrassed pause; to Madame Kuprina.*) The last time I saw your son was half-way through a chess game.

MADAME KUPRINA. (*Imparting a great confidence.*) Did you know that my son is a Prince?

SMITH. Oh?

MADAME KUPRINA. The Czar has made all of the Professors members of the nobility.

SMITH. You must be very happy.

MADAME KUPRINA. (*Shaking her head gravely.*) They haven't told you, have they? (*Barely a whisper.*) The Czar is dead.

SMITH. (*Uncomfortably.*) Oh, I *did* hear about that, yes.

MADAME KUPRINA. The new Czar is changing everything. (*As Vera re-enters with the flowers in a vase.*) Sh. We do not talk about it.

SMITH. (*Standing.*) I hope you won't go to any trouble.

VERA. Sit, sit. We want you to see that in the Soviet Union *we* have the good things of life, too, Professor Smees.

SMITH. I'm not a professor.

VERA. But you knew my cousin Vassili when he was at the university, in America.

SMITH. I was only a student then. Now I'm a writer.

MADAME KUPRINA. Writers are also nobility!

SMITH. There is no nobility in the United States.

VERA. A classless society. Exactly like ours. Does it seem a little bit like New York? With the crowds, the busses, the traffic? And can you guess what is underneath here? (*She crosses eagerly to the large box, draped with a crocheted shawl.*) We were able to get one because Vassili is so important in the government. (*Proudly, Vera unveils a TV set with about a ten-inch tube.*) Large screen! We have two hours of the television every day. Some of my things have been on the television.

SMITH. Oh, do you write, too?

VERA. (*Laughing.*) With a needle and thread. I work for the Maly Theatre, a designer.

MADAME KUPRINA. I do not like to watch the television. I think it can look at me. I am glad it is broken.

VERA. The man is coming to fix it next month. And if I am not here, you *will* let him in? Promise me, Great Aunt?

MADAME KUPRINA. No. No. (*Getting up.*) I will get the tea. (*Kissing Vera.*) I promise. (*She goes out.*)

VERA. In America, the women are very beautiful, are they not? Mrs. Smees also?

SMITH. Who?

VERA. Your wife.

SMITH. I'm not married. How is Professor Kuprin's wife? And his son?

VERA. If you should see Vassili, do not ask him about his wife and son. It is very painful to him. (*Madame Kuprina enters with the tea tray.*)

MADAME KUPRINA. Chi, chi!

VERA. (*Taking the tray.*) Thank you, Chodinka. How long are you here in Moskva?

SMITH. A few days. A week, perhaps.

VERA. To reach Vassili is very difficult.

MADAME KUPRINA. (*Suddenly alert.*) They're coming! (*There are footsteps again, mounting the stairs, and a figure appears in the blue light at the door. It is Trifonov. He pauses, then knocks on the door, softly, quickly. Vera, Smith and Madame Kuprina look at one another with uncertainty. The Old Woman whispers hoarsely.*) Dmitri?

VERA. (*She pats her Aunt's hand reassuringly, then goes to the door. In Russian, her hand on the bolt.*) Who is it?

TRIFONOV. (*In Russian.*) Professor Trifonov, from the University. (*Vera does not answer.*) Vassili has been a friend of mine for many years. (*Vera opens the door.*

Trifonov comes in with a humble air. He still speaks in Russian.) Spasebo. (*Sees Smith.*) Oh, I am disturbing? (*In English, to Smith.*) You. You are an American? (*Smith nods.*) I can tell. The haircut. The shoes. (*He crosses to Madame Kuprina and kisses her hand.*) Ah, Grashdanka Kuprina! At the University, your so-brilliant son speaks often of you. (*Nervously he pulls out a pack of White Sea cigarettes; starts to take one himself, then offers the pack around the room. All refuse.*) You have heard him speak of me? Professor Trifonov. (*There is no response. He smiles at Vera.*) I know you. Vera, is it not? Vassili says you take the most excellent care of his dear mother. (*There is a strained pause. Fumbling, Trifonov lights a cigarette. To Madame Kuprina.*) You do not mind?

VERA. This is Smees.

TRIFONOV. (*He shakes hands warmly, in the abrupt, pump-handle Soviet style.*) I beg the name again?

SMITH. S-M-I-T-H. Very unusual.

TRIFONOV. Ah, yes! Smith. You are scientific, no doubt. Like Kuprin. I am the opposite. The humanities. Associate Professor of World Literatures. At Moscow University. (*Turning to the others.*) I intrude. I know. It was my hope to find Vassili here. To say what it is not wise to say in the halls of the university. (*There is a pause. He turns quickly to Smith.*) You understand, we have complete academic freedom. However, there must be authority. Otherwise, chaos. Yes? Suddenly my lectures were cancelled. I see now my mistake. Too much formalism. Many of us have made this error. Shostakovitch, also. But now my classes are restored to me. I did not know why. (*There is genuine emotion in his voice; he is almost on the verge of tears.*) I have just found out that Dr. Kuprin spoke to the academic committee, personally, on my behalf. I would wish to die if saying thank-you to him would make embarrassment for so great a scientist. (*He turns quickly.*) I go. I go. (*He nods to each of them.*) Such an honor. You will thank Vassili for me? (*Taking Smith's hands and pumping it.*) You are close friend to Professor Kuprin?

SMITH. Many years ago.

TRIFONOV. You are, therefore, also close friend to me. I may help you perhaps in Moscow? At what hotel are you?

SMITH. The Ukraina.

TRIFONOV. It will be for me a privilege, Mr. Smith, to be at your service. You will remember me? Trifonov.

SMITH. Trifonov.

TRIFONOV. (*He darts to the door.*) Spasebo, Spasebo. Dasvahdanya. (*To Smith.*) Peace and friendship! (*Trifonov leaves quickly. Vera crosses to bolt the door.*)

VERA. (*Turning.*) Now we will have our tea.

SMITH. I'm terribly sorry. I have a taxi waiting. I think.

VERA. Oh.

SMITH. When will your cousin be coming here?

MADAME KUPRINA. (*Vaguely.*) Seychass. Seychass.

VERA. We do not know. We never know.

SMITH. (*He frowns.*) I'd like to see you again. Would you come to the theatre with me one night? You can whisper a translation to me, and I'll keep saying, "What? What?"—and we'll annoy all the people around us. (*They both laugh. Madame Kuprina looks up sharply at the unaccustomed sound.*)

MADAME KUPRINA. Laugh! That is good, Verochka. Laugh. To laugh is very stylish in Paris. (*They all laugh.*)

SMITH. What theatre?

VERA. In the summer, they are all closed. I am on vacation.

SMITH. Could we have dinner and dance?

VERA. You like to dance?

SMITH. Yes.

VERA. What night?

SMITH. Not "Seychass." Tomorrow.

VERA. The day after. Tuesday night. Where shall we meet?

SMITH. Here?

VERA. (*Quickly.*) No, no.

SMITH. My hotel, then.

VERA. That would not be wise, either. Uh—better, just outside the Novoslobodskaya Metro. By the third pillar from the left. You will remember?

SMITH. I'll find it. (*Turning to Madame Kuprina.*) Au revoir, Madame. A bientôt.

MADAME KUPRINA. (*In precise English, extending her hand.*) Until we meet again. (*Smith kisses her hand, then goes to the door. Vera passes the bolt.*)

SMITH. We didn't say what time. Eight o'clock?

VERA. Eight o'clock.

SMITH. (*He starts for the door, then turns.*) What was that fellow's name? Trifonov?

VERA. That's what he said.

SMITH. Don't you know him?

VERA. No. I never saw him before.

SMITH. But he said he was a friend of Vassili. Do you believe him?

VERA. You say *you* are a friend of Vassili. And I have never seen you before.

SMITH Yes. I see. Well—Tuesday?

VERA. Tuesday. (*Smith goes down the stairway and off. Vera watches him, the blue light on her face, the yellow lamplight behind her. The lights fade. Across a star curtain, a tiny spot of light crosses.*)

CHET HUNTLEY. (*On P.A.*) Chet Huntley, N.B.C. News, New York. The Soviets have a new entry in the space merry-go-round, and this time they may have really caught the brass ring. This one seems to be driven by atomic power and has been named the "Chelovyek-Zvezda," a hyphenation of the Russian words for "Man" and "Star." The Man-Star can apparently change altitude, direction, orbital radius, and velocity—so it can be steered to hover and soar at will. So it's much more than a man on a bullet-ride or a captive kite on the gravity string. The newest Red Star-wagon has been passing a dozen times daily over the continental United States. David?

DAVID BRINKLEY. (*On P.A.*) From Washington, no comment.

ACT ONE
SCENE 4

The rooftop of the U.S. Embassy in Moscow. There is a skyline of Moscow. A parapet, some chimney pots. On the balustrade is a radio. A young Ivy-League-ish man, Harrington, is leaning over it, listening intently to a voice from outer space.

VOICE. (*On radio, in English.*) I, Sergei Ivanovitch Miroff, a citizen of the Soviet Union and a volunteer for humanity, bring greetings to Britain and the English-speaking world. Peace to mankind. Mir Miru. (*Harrington flips off the radio as a Marine Sergeant, in dress uniform, enters, escorting Smith to the rooftop.*)

SERGEANT. Right up here, sir.

HARRINGTON. Mr. Smith? (*Smith nods. They shake hands.*) I'm Arthur Harrington. We're glad you're here.

SMITH. Thank you.

HARRINGTON. Sergeant—?

SERGEANT. The Ambassador will join you in a few minutes.

HARRINGTON. We don't usually receive a V.I.P. on the roof of the Embassy.

SMITH. V.I.P.? I think you have the wrong Smith.

HARRINGTON. We've got the right one. It was good of you to come so promptly.

SMITH. Your messenger caught up with me at the Tretyakov Gallery.

HARRINGTON. In this town it isn't always a good idea to use the telephone. Every line is a party line. (*Pointing to the sky.*) There he is.

SMITH. The Chelovyek? No. That's Arcturus. Alpha Bootes. There's no Russian in that.

HARRINGTON. We hope. Unless your friend Kuprin has been working overtime.

SMITH. How did you know Kuprin was a friend of mine?

HARRINGTON. We're in the knowing business. (*The Marine Sergeant enters, followed by the Ambassador. He is a distinguished man, with thinning grey hair.*) Oh, Mr. Ambassador. This is Jonathan Smith. (*The men shake hands.*)

SMITH. Mr. Ambassador.

AMBASSADOR. How do you like my new office? At least I get away from all those people down there.

HARRINGTON. Comrade Miroff just said "Cheerio" to London, sir.

AMBASSADOR. Yes, and every time he sails over the Potomac, he says "Hello, folks" to Washington. The Senate Foreign Relations Committee is getting goddamn nervous. Thank you for coming, Mr. Smith. We have something important to discuss with you.

SMITH. About Kuprin? Is that why I'm here?

AMBASSADOR. You've been trying to see him.

SMITH. Yes. But I haven't had much luck. (*Pointing.*) There it is! (*The three men look up, following an arc slowly across the sky.*)

HARRINGTON. The Chelovyek-Zvezda.

AMBASSADOR. Greetings, Comrade Miroff.

SMITH. I never thought human beings would get their feet so far off the ground. It's almost a sacrilege—climbing up there bodily, on a ladder of rockets.

AMBASSADOR. More than rockets this time. And your friend did it.

SMITH. I wish he hadn't. (*He laughs.*) That's a helluva thing to say, isn't it? I'm being anti-progress, like my grandfather, who was sure the Wright Brothers had offended the sparrows.

AMBASSADOR. (*Eyes to the sky.*) When I look at that thing, it scares me.

SMITH. Why?

AMBASSADOR. It could be carrying a warhead. And all Comrade Miroff would have to do is touch a button—and obliterate San Francisco. Or London.

SMITH. A warhead. I don't believe it. Kuprin is a pure scientist.

HARRINGTON. He may be pure. We don't know about the company he works for.

AMBASSADOR. Mr. Smith. Do you think a scientist can be happy in the Soviet Union?

SMITH. I'm not sure a scientist can be happy anywhere.

AMBASSADOR. Last July, Kuprin was supposed to go to Geneva, to make a speech.

SMITH. I remember. I wrote a column about it.

AMBASSADOR. He never made the speech.

SMITH. But I read it.

AMBASSADOR. Oh, the speech was delivered all right. But not by Kuprin. At the last moment, the Soviet Government wouldn't let him leave the country. From what we've been able to find out, he was practically yanked off the plane. For a very good and specific reason. They didn't think he'd come back.

HARRINGTON. It would be a big blow to the Soviets if they lost Kuprin.

AMBASSADOR. You know how important he is? What Einstein was to the atomic break-through in the U.S., that's what Kuprin is today in the U.S.S.R. But according to our best information, he's had a belly-full of bureaucracy and secrecy and the corruption of his ideas.

HARRINGTON. We're almost certain he still wants to get out of the Soviet Union.

AMBASSADOR. And if he does, by God, we're going to help him!

SMITH. What can *I* do?

AMBASSADOR. First of all, you could let Professor Kuprin know that the door is open on *our* side. We *want* him, if he wants to come. He'll be welcome in any laboratory, any facility we have.

SMITH. Why doesn't Cal Tech tell him that? Or M.I.T.?

AMBASSADOR. They have. No answer.

HARRINGTON. Apparently the letters never reached him.

AMBASSADOR. For the past year, Kuprin has been the most inaccessible man in the Soviet Union. None of our people has been able to get close to him.

SMITH. In that case, how do you expect me to reach him?

HARRINGTON. You may be the only person who can.

AMBASSADOR. It will be a great victory for us, Mr. Smith, and for our allies, if the foremost physicist in the Soviet World chooses freedom.

SMITH. That'd make a lot of headlines. But how do you ask a man to defect?

AMBASSADOR. You don't ask him. You give him a choice. And *choice* is something these people don't often have.

HARRINGTON. There's another way of looking at it. When Kuprin came back here in 1939, he was defecting from the United States.

SMITH. How do you mean?

AMBASSADOR. He'd taken out his first American citizenship papers.

SMITH. I never knew that.

HARRINGTON. Did you know he has a daughter in the States?

SMITH. Nadya? Of course. I saw her and her kids just for a couple of days ago. I brought some pictures of them for Koopy. (*He reaches into his pocket.*) They're just snapshots, but— (*Harrington and the Ambassador take the snapshots and pore over them.*)

AMBASSADOR. This is his daughter?

SMITH. Nadya Novack. That's her husband.

HARRINGTON. He's a Czech. A violent anti-Red. These snapshots may be more valuable than a weapon.

SMITH. A weapon. (*Taking back the pictures.*) I don't think I'm your man. I don't want to force anybody to do anything.

AMBASSADOR. All we ask is that you pay a call on Kuprin.

SMITH. I've been trying to do that.

AMBASSADOR. Keep at it. Get to him. Try to make him remember the reasons he wanted to become an American twenty years ago. What it's like walking along a street in some American town, compared with walking along that street down there. If Kuprin goes with you—willingly—imagine what it will do for the prestige of the West in the eyes of the World. (*Smith hesitates. The Ambassador drives harder.*) If you were a Soviet scientist and you wanted to get out, wouldn't you welcome an old friend from America, offering you the machinery to do it?

SMITH. It would depend on the machinery.

AMBASSADOR. It's all been planned. Our people have worked this out carefully. I think you'll have a good chance of success, but there's one thing you must recognize clearly. If Kuprin agrees to leave the country, you'll have a very dangerous job to do.

SMITH. I've been shot at. I was in the Army four years.

AMBASSADOR. Nobody's drafting you, Mr. Smith.

SMITH. I know. I understand. I don't see how anybody could turn down a thing like this. I'll do it. I just hope to hell I *can* do it, that's all.

HARRINGTON. If you don't mind, sir, I'd like to ask him a question or two. (*The Ambassador nods.*) How do you know this is the American Ambassador?

SMITH. You told me.

HARRINGTON. How do you know who I am?

AMBASSADOR. Let's make this easier for him, Harrington, not harder. (*To Smith.*) This is Moscow, Mr. Smith. Not Delaware, Ohio. So be careful.

SMITH. You want me to keep my mouth shut, is that it?

HARRINGTON. God, no! There's nothing more suspicious than a silent American.

SMITH. But don't make friends?

AMBASSADOR. Don't trust friends. I don't like doing business this way, but we didn't make the rules.

SMITH. All right. Suppose I get to Kuprin. He says: "Good. Fine. I want to come to America." What do I do?

AMBASSADOR. We know that Kuprin shuttles quite a bit: between the University here and a place they've given him down in Yalta. A dacha, a summer house. Right on the Black Sea.

HARRINGTON. There's a jetty. And when the tide's in, a boat can be waiting less than fifty feet from the kitchen door.

SMITH. A boat?

HARRINGTON. A dinghy.

SMITH. You want me to row him all the way to Istanbul?

HARRINGTON. There'll be a boatman. He'll get you both to a Turkish trawler. She looks like a crummy old fishing tub. But below decks, she's got a pair of 2,000 horsepower motors.

SMITH. Boy, this is out of my line. Do I contact anybody?

HARRINGTON. Just Kuprin. We'll know when you're in Yalta.

AMBASSADOR. Mr. Smith, after you leave the Embassy, you are not to come back here again. You'll be acting as one individual helping another individual.

SMITH. What if I get into trouble? With the Soviet authorities?

AMBASSADOR. We'll try to get to you before anything like that happens.

HARRINGTON. When we get down to my office, I'll brief you on the whole thing. But if there's an emergency, or if we have any change in instructions, someone will approach you and say the word "Tsushima."

SMITH. "Tsushima."

HARRINGTON. He may not even say the word. He may just have a book called "Tsushima."

AMBASSADOR. Better memorize the Russian letters so you can recognize it.

HARRINGTON. If a man shows you that book, do whatever he tells you. Exactly what he tells you.

SMITH. What does "Tsushima" mean?

HARRINGTON. It was the worst naval defeat in Russian history.

SMITH. And I'm supposed to do an encore? With a fishing trawler and a dinghy? (*He comes down to the parapet.*)

AMBASSADOR. How do you feel?

SMITH. It's like the day before the Flood—when there were the first raindrops. (*He stares up at the sky.*)

CURTAIN

ACT TWO
SCENE 1

Gorky Park. It is early evening in what seems to be a blending of Central Park and Coney Island, with a Slavic flavor all its own. Lights are coming on. People are strolling along the grass, underneath the trees, or lolling on the park benches. Everything is immaculately clean. There are litter baskets and cigarette disposals every few yards. Upstage is the Chess Pavilion, where a match is in progress. For the people outside, a metal chess board has been erected vertically, with chessmen magnetized. As each move is made within the pavilion, it is blared through the loudspeakers outside. A boy fixes the pieces on the big board. A number of chess aficionados are watching the course of the game. There is a portable bookstall, where a student riffles through the bookseller's wares. An old woman is sweeping the sidewalk with a broom made of bundled twigs.

VOICE. (*In Russian, on loudspeaker.*) Lindfors King to C-6. Gardez. (*Crowd is awed. Smith and Vera enter eating ice cream.*)

VERA. (*Indicating the cup in his hand.*) You like it? It is good?

SMITH. Best damned ice cream I ever ate.

VERA. Why do you say "damned"? Does that mean something is bad?

SMITH. Only sometimes. We use it for strong feeling. Good or bad. (*Drunk enters. He bumps into the old woman sweeping. She hits him on the backside with her broom.*)

VOICE. Bogolyubov—pawn to B-8. White Queens the Pawn. (*Applause. Cheers.*)

SMITH. What do you call this place?

VERA. Gorky Park. One of our national centers of culture and rest.

VOICE. No—no— Bogolyubov chooses to Knight his Pawn! It's shahk, shahk, shahk! (*Tremendous excitement.*)

SMITH. Does "shahk" mean check? (*Vera nods.*) This act would really pack 'em in Las Vegas.

VERA. What is Las Vegas?

SMITH. One of *our* national centers of culture and rest.

VOICE. (*Excitedly.*) Lindfors, King to D-6. Bogo Queen to G-3, check. Lindfors, King to E-6. Bogo Queen to C-7, and it's all over! (*Cheers. The crowd breaks. The chess board is carried off.*)

VERA. You think Gorky Park is damned good?

SMITH. Even better than that dance pavilion the other night.

VERA. What was wrong with the dance pavilion?

SMITH. Oh, I was crazy about it. Only time I ever heard "Chattanooga Choo-Choo" played in A-minor. (*He starts to throw his ice-cream cup on the ground.*)

VERA. No, no. That's a one ruble fine. Fifty kopeks if you throw a cigarette on the ground. (*She drops it in a litter can.*)

SMITH. (*Taking her arm.*) When do you think I'll get to see your cousin?

VERA. Today.

SMITH. Really?

VERA. (*Teasing.*) I will buy you a copy of Pravda. His picture is on page 3.

SMITH. Look, I'm only going to be here a few days. I don't have much time.

VERA. Please to be patient. (*Pulling away from his arm.*) In the Soviet Union we do not hold each other's arms unless we are married or engaged.

SMITH. Oh, I'm sorry. (*A group of young people have been watching Smith and they shove one girl forward.*)

GIRL JAZZ ENTHUSIAST. If you please—

SMITH. (*A little baffled.*) Hello. (*The boys prod her forward. Vera watches, not really approving of all this—especially since the girl is pretty cute.*)

GIRL. (*She addresses Smith in studied English.*) They wish me to speak at you because in English I have received "excellence."

SMITH. Well—congratulations.

GIRL. (*Prodded by the boys.*) You know Louis Armstrong? And Harry Jam-ess?

SMITH. Not personally. I know their music. (*The trio confers triumphantly.*)

GIRL. (*In Russian.*) He knows! He knows! (*Turning back to Smith.*) Louis Armstrong is a very cultured cornet player, yes?

SMITH. (*Smiling.*) "Harry Jam-ess" also. (*Smith puts thumb and forefinger together in the familiar "Okay" gesture. The girl is puzzled.*)

GIRL. Explain, please? What means this? (*She imitates Smith's hand gesture.*)

SMITH. It means—okay. Swell. Great. (*The light dawns on the girl. She turns to the boys, repeating the gesture.*)

TRIO. (*Enthusiastically.*) Okay! Okay! Harashaw!

GIRL. (*To Smith, in poor English.*) Excuse. You have, please, chewing gum? (*Smith shrugs apologetically. He hasn't any. But Vera is angry. She lashes out at the trio.*)

VERA. (*In Russian.*) It is undignified to beg! (*Chastised, the trio moves off.*)

SMITH. What did you say to them?

VERA. That Soviet Citizens do not have to beg. (*Smith starts to take out a cigarette. But Vera hastily reaches into her purse and pulls out a pack of White Seas, offering him one.*) Ours are stronger.

SMITH. (*He takes one of her cigarettes, offers her one of his.*) Try one of mine.

VERA. I only smoke when I'm unhappy.

SMITH. Maybe I can help you give up smoking. (*They laugh. A bookseller ap-*

proaches them with a tray full of books. Smith shrugs helplessly.) Sorry. I learned the wrong alphabet.

VERA. We have books in English. (*To the bookseller, in Russian.*) Show him something in English. (*To Smith again.*) The latest authors. The great literature from America. (*Joyfully, the bookseller comes up with a book which she offers him proudly.*)

SMITH. (*Taking the book, reading the title.*) "White Fang," by Jack London. (*Politely he nods "no" and puts it down.*)

VERA. I would like to read your books. What do you write about?

SMITH. Science mostly. Funny thing. Thinking got commercial. All of a sudden every kid wants to be a scientist instead of a baseball player. (*Two Sailors pass, little fingers intertwined.*) Are *they* engaged?

VERA. Of course not. They are comrades. They are men.

SMITH. I'm glad to hear it.

VERA. Today I went to the beauty salon. (*Then quickly.*) Oh, I should not tell a man such things. (*They sit on a bench.*)

SMITH. I didn't even know you had them in Moscow.

VERA. Before, beauty salons were very seldom. But now it is all right to individualize ourselves.

SMITH. Don't overdo it. My wife spent half her time "individualizing herself."

VERA. (*Clouded.*) You said you were not married.

SMITH. Divorced.

VERA. I'm sorry.

SMITH. I'm not. Yes, I am. But when a marriage refuses to work—well, only a damned fool keeps trying.

VERA. That's how you use "damned."

SMITH. (*Nods.*) That's the way. You're not married, are you?

VERA. (*A pause, then she speaks softly.*) No.

SMITH. Engaged? Besieged by suitors? (*She laughs, shakes her head.*) I refuse to believe you have taken vows in a political nunnery.

VERA. The man to whom I was engaged was killed in the Far East. (*Smith sobers. Unwilled tears are forming in her eyes.*) It happened to many of us. He was a technician. An engineer in China. This is a big country—also. (*Smith touches her hand, comfortingly.*) He was a very fine man. (*She tries to smile, and a tear or two spills out in the process.*) Much, much better than I was. Than I am.

SMITH. And since then?

VERA. There has been no one, because— (*She takes a deep breath, stiffening her resistance to emotion.*) because I *wanted* no one. (*Vera gets up.*) My eyes are washing away my face. You will excuse me, please?

SMITH. (*Rising.*) But you look fine.

VERA. (*Starting off.*) I will be back presently. (*She is gone. A Kvas wagon is winding among the crowd. Holloway saunters toward Smith.*)

HOLLOWAY. Zdrasht-veet-chech.

SMITH. Oh—hi!

HOLLOWAY. Missed you today. Tour B was a bloody bore. Any luck finding your friend Kuprin?

SMITH. Not yet.

HOLLOWAY. (*Smirks.*) If I were you, I'd quit looking for him, and settle for *her*. Get in the queue, old man; I'll buy you both a Kvas.

SMITH. What's Kvas?

HOLLOWAY. The Coca-Cola of the Soviet Union. Amazing stuff. Hard to describe. Tastes like dirty Schweppes, with the bubbles taken out. Two! (*A Soldier has taken his station at the entrance to the chess pavilion. Vera, coming back on, questions him.*)

VERA. (*Excitedly, running back to Smith.*) Smees! Did you see him? They say he is in there.

SMITH. Who?

VERA. My cousin. Vassili. Has he come out yet? (*The strollers from the park gather on each side of the pavilion to watch the exit of the hero and cheer him.*)

SMITH. Koopy's been in there all the time? Watching the chess match? (*Hastily, Smith hands his cup back to Holloway and rushes toward the entrance to the chess pavilion, which is elevated by a few steps. He waits eagerly for Kuprin to come out. Vera follows him, hanging back, remaining on the ground level. Holloway, stuck with the two cups of Kvas, looks at them ruefully, then gives one to the drunk.*)

HOLLOWAY. Here, my friend. Compliments of the working people of the British Empire.

DRUNK. Spaseebo. (*All the activity is concentrated on the elevated doorway from which the celebrity is now appearing. Kuprin emerges from the pavilion behind him. There are cheers. Kuprin is carefully protected by Makarov and soldiers. Kuprin looks about nervously, as if anxious to escape.*)

VOICES. Kuprin! Kuprin! (*The Soviet soldiers, like football linemen, begin to shoulder the hero out. Suddenly Smith's voice rises above the confusion.*)

SMITH. (*Calling.*) Koopy! (*The unfamiliar nickname cuts through to Kuprin's ear. He stops, turns, looks for the voice. Anonymous hands are being thrust at Kuprin. He shakes them inexpertly. Smith raises his arm and waves, desperately trying to get Kuprin's attention.*) Koopy! Here I am! Over here!

KUPRIN. (*In English.*) Who is it? (*Smith tries to push his way through, but he is blocked by spectators.*)

SMITH. (*Calling.*) I've got to see you, Koopy! It's Smith! (*A light of joyful recognition breaks on Kuprin's face, as he spots his old friend. But Kuprin is being drawn away.*)

KUPRIN. Smith! (*Vera is merely watching. Holloway rotates a dry cigarette in his mouth. Trifonov, equally engrossed, watches at the opposite side.*)

SMITH. (*Urgently.*) I want to see you! We've got to talk! (*The conversation between Smith and Kuprin is fitful, interrupted by the confusion and the distance between them.*)

KUPRIN. (*In English.*) Call me! Telephone me!

SMITH. (*Desperately.*) How? (*Conversation is hopeless. Kuprin has been whisked away. Smith shakes his head in an agony of frustration. The spectators begin to scatter.*

Several bystanders look at Smith curiously. He turns toward Vera. Angrily.) Why didn't you warn me?

VERA. I didn't want you to be disappointed.

SMITH. So we sat around and talked about my divorce and your cosmetics, while Kuprin was right on the other side of that wall? (*He gestures toward the chess pavilion.*)

VERA. (*Bewildered.*) Did I do something wrong, Smees?

SMITH. You didn't do a damn thing!

VERA. Vassili is very famous, like someone from the cinema.

SMITH. Does that mean he can't talk to his family? Or friends, who come eight thousand miles to see him?

VERA. He wants to see you. You could tell that, couldn't you?

SMITH. Then why the hell didn't you help me?

VERA. I am sorry.

SMITH. So am I. God! Women! (*Hurt and bewildered, Vera turns and runs off. Smith starts to follow. Trifonov comes up to Smith.*)

TRIFONOV. Mr. Smith. Trifonov.

SMITH. Oh, hello.

TRIFONOV. I saw what happened with Kuprin. Regrettable. Most regrettable. I do not mean to criticize. Forgive me. You are a guest in our country. But I, who am a colleague of Professor Kuprin at the University—even I do not try to shake his hand in public, or take the risk of thanking him.

SMITH. Risk? (*Unseen by Trifonov, Makarov enters and crosses alongside the guard.*)

TRIFONOV. Oh, we have complete freedom. However. When our revolution is two hundred years old like yours, we will not require the proof of dedication— (*He breaks off, unhappily.*) I am saying it badly. (*He looks around. The crowd has almost fallen away.*) You know the expression? "One critic, an individualist. Two critics, a plot." You understand?

SMITH. No, I don't believe so.

TRIFONOV. You plus Kuprin makes one plus one. (*Suddenly Trifonov sees Makarov studying him. He moves quickly and steadily away from Smith.*)

MAKAROV. (*In Russian.*) Stop! (*Makarov summons the guard to arrest Trifonov. In Russian.*) Citizen, it will be necessary to put you under protective custody. (*Three girls enter the park singing a Russian song. They are followed by two fellows.*)

TRIFONOV. (*In Russian.*) I am a professor at Moscow University. I have done nothing. (*As the Soldier examines Trifonov, the girls lower their singing and watch curiously.*)

MAKAROV. Take him to KGB headquarters.

TRIFONOV. (*In Russian.*) Please, please. (*Smith watches the proceeding, appalled. The girls and their followers shrug and continue singing as Trifonov is dragged off.*)

THE LIGHTS FADE

ACT TWO
SCENE 2

Again, Madame Kuprina's apartment. Madame Kuprina is seated in a chair, squinting over a book of catechism. Vera comes on from the kitchen, flushed with restrained excitement. She has a plate of caviar and a bottle of vodka; she checks the label and arranges the caviar, vodka and glasses on the sideboard. Then Vera surveys the room, straightening an antimacassar, smoothing the shawl which drapes the TV.

MADAME KUPRINA. (*In Russian.*) Such excitement.

VERA. (*In English.*) Speak English, Great Aunt. To practice for our guest of honor.

MADAME KUPRINA. (*In English.*) Who is coming? The President of America? (*She looks far off.*) Mr. Wilson died, did he not? Or did they shoot him? (*Vera has gone into the kitchen, so doesn't answer. Madame Kuprina gets up rather painfully, shrugs.*) Il n'y a pas de quoi. (*Vera comes back in, as Madame Kuprina surveys the sideboard.*) Caviar. And the best Vodka.

VERA. For Smees. You will be very nice to him, Great Aunt, when he comes. If he comes. I hope he will come. I left a note at his hotel. (*She glances anxiously toward the door. Madame Kuprina turns Vera's face in her hands, studying the girl with a faint trace of humor.*)

MADAME KUPRINA. You like him, Verochka?

VERA. (*Quickly, protesting too much.*) No, no, Great Aunt. He is a friend of Vassili's, and I wish him to like the Soviet Union.

MADAME KUPRINA. *I* do not like the Soviet Union. (*Smith has bounded up the stairs and appears in the Blue Light at the entrance way. He knocks.*) They are coming!

VERA. (*She quickly takes off her apron, hiding it under a chair cushion, then goes to the door.*) Smees?

SMITH. S-M-E-E-S! (*Vera unbolts the door and Smith comes in.*) Thanks for the invitation to dinner. I accept. (*With some embarrassment.*) I don't deserve it, after the way I yelled at you in the park.

VERA. But it was *my* fault.

MADAME KUPRINA. (*Clearing her throat.*) Kindly introduce me.

VERA. Mr. Smees from America. An old friend of Vassili's.

MADAME KUPRINA. Enchanté! Please take a seat. We are expecting a "guest of honor."

VERA. But this *is* the guest of honor, Great Aunt.

MADAME KUPRINA. Oh. (*Offering her hand.*) Enchanté!

VERA. But we do have the surprise.

SMITH. Chicken Kiev?

VERA. Better. Much better. (*Vera crosses to the table and pours a shot-glass full of vodka. Eagerly she hands it to Smith.*) While we wait for the surprise, will you have vodka.

SMITH. Thank you. But do you mind if I just sip it? I haven't got the Russian knack of flinging it back in one fell swoop. I have very cowardly tonsils.

VERA. Try it.

SMITH. Okay. (*He does. They applaud.*) Say, after you left the park, the strangest thing happened. I saw that little professor again. That Trifonov. And they arrested him. (*A moment of silence.*)

VERA. I told you I don't know him. I know nothing about him.

SMITH. I really felt sorry for him.

VERA. Nobody is arrested ever in New York?

SMITH. Sure. For a crime. What do you think he did?

VERA. Well—perhaps something against the People's government. Perhaps—

MADAME KUPRINA. (*Quickly.*) Vassili says do not talk. (*Kuprin appears in the blue light of the hallway. He knocks.*)

VERA. Ah. The surprise. (*Vera goes to the door and passes the bolt. Through the door, in Russian.*) Is it you?

KUPRIN. Da. (*Vera throws door open as if she were raising the curtain at a play.*)

SMITH. Koopy! (*Kuprin enters the room, and for the first time we see his private face. Even in relaxation his eyes are clouded with too much thinking. He is restive, moody, and though he makes a genuine attempt to be socially gracious, he often seems anti-social and preoccupied, even testy in his lightning-quick reactions, which contrast with long silences. Vera looks proud, seeing the happy reaction of Smith's face. But she is troubled when she turns and sees that Kuprin is not smiling. Smith takes a few steps toward Kuprin, starts to extend his hand, but stops—because Kuprin is merely staring at him.*)

KUPRIN. (*Distantly.*) Yesterday, I saw this face. And I thought, "That looks like Smith. It couldn't be. What would he be doing in Moscow?" (*He narrows his eyes.*) I didn't even get to shake your hand. (*There is a moment's hesitation. Then Kuprin puts out his hand and a smile breaks over his face.*)

SMITH. (*Shaking his hand.*) You haven't changed.

KUPRIN. Of course I have. So have you. What difference does it make?

VERA. (*Looking uncertainly from one to the other.*) I wanted to surprise you. Both! (*Kuprin nods, gives Vera a kiss on the cheek, then crosses to his mother and embraces her.*)

KUPRIN. Mamuschka.

MADAME KUPRINA. (*Stroking his face, in Russian.*) You're looking thin. You don't eat enough.

KUPRIN. (*In English.*) She says I look thin, that I don't eat enough. Actually, I have put on two kilos. (*The two men stand looking at each other, half unbelieving, as Vera gets vodka for Kuprin.*)

SMITH. (*Warmly.*) Koopy. "Koopy!" Can I still call you that, now that you're so famous?

KUPRIN. (*Waving deprecatingly.*) Famous! Mickey Mouse is also famous. What about you, Smith? What are you doing in our part of the world?

SMITH. Sightseeing.

KUPRIN. Good. It must be nice to have time to do things like that.

VERA. (*She has poured a shot glass full of vodka and presses it on Kuprin.*) Here, Cousin.

KUPRIN. (*He nods his thanks, takes the glass, raises it.*) To our guest.

SMITH. No. Let's drink to the old days. (*This has a very darkening effect on Kuprin. Silently, he downs the drink in one gulp, Russian style. Smith hesitates. Then valiantly he throws the vodka at his tonsils. He smiles, a little surprised: it wasn't too bad. Vera applauds. Kuprin stares thoughtfully at his empty glass.*)

KUPRIN. About the size of an eye-piece, isn't it? (*With a conscious effort to clown, Kuprin puts the shot glass up to his eye and squints into it.*) I can't see a damn thing. (*He looks up at the ceiling.*) What's the matter with you, Smith? You haven't opened the dome. (*The two men laugh.*)

MADAME KUPRINA. (*She looks up at the ceiling, frightened. She points.*) Yes, yes, there is something wrong with the ceiling. (*To Smith.*) What are you doing to the ceiling?

KUPRIN. It's all right, Mamuschka. We were making a joke about the days when Smith and I looked into a telescope together. The nights. No more.

SMITH. Won't they give you a telescope?

KUPRIN. They say I am "too important" now; I can't waste my time in observatories. But sometimes I get lonely for the stars. (*Dismissing his sentimentality.*) Besides, it's all radio-astronomy now. Earphones instead of eye-pieces.

SMITH. Have you ever looked through a telescope, Vera?

VERA. Oh, yes. For ten kopecks, in the park, they let you look at the moon.

KUPRIN. See? Now Vera is the astronomer in the family.

VERA. What were you doing at the observatory in America?

MADAME KUPRINA. (*A little frightened.*) Shhh. You must not ask. Vassili is not allowed to tell you what he is doing!

KUPRIN. (*Restlessly.*) Not what I am doing *now*. What Smith and I did together years ago.

SMITH. (*To Vera.*) We'd spend all night taking one shaft of starlight, peeling it apart, trying to find out what's inside. Sometimes we'd catch a glimmer of an idea.

KUPRIN. (*Snorting.*) On cold nights it was easier to catch pneumonia.

SMITH. We had a very good arrangement. Koopy got the ideas, I got the colds. (*They laugh.*)

VERA. You were very happy then, weren't you, Cousin?

KUPRIN. (*Waving the comment away.*) Ahh. Everything we remember is covered with strawberries and sour cream. (*Darkening.*) Not everything. But much.

SMITH. Koopy, did you ever try to get back?

KUPRIN. (*Gruffly.*) What?

SMITH. You must have wanted to. Did you ever try?

KUPRIN. (*A little pale.*) Where did you get an idea like that?

SMITH. It just seems logical.

KUPRIN. (*Sharply.*) Why? I have everything here. They give me everything.

SMITH. But you'd have a chance to—

KUPRIN. (*Covering quickly.*) Mamuschka, where is the chessboard? I want the chessboard.

MADAME KUPRINA. The television is hiding it.

KUPRIN. Smith. There was a chess game we never finished. How many years ago—?

SMITH. Twenty-one.

KUPRIN. Twenty-one years ago. I shall amaze you. I can remember precisely the position of every piece on that chess board. I'm bluffing? I could be. But I'm not. I do remember. I'll show you.

SMITH. We can go right on where we left off.

VERA. After dinner. Please. Not till after dinner.

KUPRIN. No. Now. (*He is getting the chessboard and chessmen from behind the TV set.*)

SMITH. (*Quietly.*) I showed up that night, Koopy, to finish the game.

KUPRIN. (*He is busy with the chess pieces, setting them up on the board.*) Let me see—had you castled? Yes, you had.

SMITH. Four-oh-five and one-half Sandusky Street. Your door was half-open. Half a loaf of bread, unwrapped, on the table.

KUPRIN. (*Still arranging the pieces, avoiding a response.*) I had your Queen's Knight. Both your Bishops.

SMITH. There were tea leaves still in the pot on the stove. Still warm. But you were gone.

KUPRIN. And my Queen was—so. (*He places the Queen squarely on the board.*) There. The chessboard is exactly the way we left it.

SMITH. *Why*, Koopy?

KUPRIN. (*He glances toward his mother, then quickly away. He lashes out at Smith. With vehemence.*) Why did I leave? Because I like to take twenty-one years to think between chess moves! That's why! (*Kuprin rubs his forehead.*) What am I shouting at you for? I'm sorry, Smith. I'm tired, I'm tired.

SMITH. Are they working you hard?

KUPRIN. I work myself hard. (*With genuine interest.*) Tell me about you.

SMITH. I write. For newspapers. I've been doing a lot of pieces about space engines. Last night I couldn't sleep. I think I figured out how your Chelovyek works.

KUPRIN. It's not "mine." It's a Soviet achievement.

SMITH. The engine is yours. It's the same energy source that's in the center of stars, isn't it? (*No answer from Kuprin.*) Some kind of extension of Bethe's formula: the helium, hydrogen, carbon 12 cycle?

KUPRIN. (*Shrugs.*) Everybody's been working on it. The British were ahead at first.

SMITH. But now you're ahead. *Way* ahead! (*Kuprin doesn't answer.*)

VERA. (*Going toward the kitchen.*) I'll go look at the chicken. (*Madame Kuprina *sits, still ostensibly engrossed in her catechism, her lips moving mechanically from time to time. But her back is stiff, and she is tense as she listens to every word that the men are saying. Occasionally she glances up when one voice or the other rises.)*

SMITH. We were at the observatory together, when I was a student, turning cranks and pushing buttons, did you have a line on this thing, even then?

KUPRIN. (*Frowning.*) Theories, theories. That's all.

SMITH. (*Leaning forward.*) But the basic ideas were in your mind? That long ago? (*Kuprin hesitates, then nods yes. Excitedly, Smith pushes back his chair and gets up.*) Say that! The concept of the stellar engine that put Miroff into space was born in the United States, in the mind of a professor at an American university. Can you imagine how that announcement would shake up the world? Think what a reception you'd get when you came home!

KUPRIN. (*As if it were a totally meaningless word.*) Home?

SMITH. I have an official invitation for you. Come back. To Delaware if you like. Or Princeton. Any laboratory you like. Any telescope. (*Vera is standing in the doorway, drawn by the intensity of the voices.*)

KUPRIN. You're crazy, Smith. You've been writing too many newspaper stories. *Reading* too many.

SMITH. When you wake up in the morning, doesn't it terrify you? The ideas that might come into your mind during the day?

KUPRIN. (*He seems to be shaking off a guilt.*) No, no.

SMITH. And what will your ideas produce, Koopy? A whole armada of space vehicles? You'll put them there, but you won't have a damn thing to say about where they go, or what they do!

KUPRIN. (*He has just been touched at the scientist's most delicate nerve. In a burst of anger, he gets up, paces, shouting. Angrily.*) These things don't have anything to do with me. I am a scientist. I do my work. I do it the best I can. The same as an old woman sweeping the streets with a broom of twigs. It's the same thing. (*An abrupt change. He stares at the floor.*) That's not true. Of course it's not. Ohhhh, Smith—what you say to me I say to myself. Not only when I get up in the morning. When I go to sleep at night. When I hope to sleep. And all night long. (*He looks up now, directly at Smith. He speaks with a painful directness.*) I think that Thomas A. Edison was the last happy inventor. There was no danger that his gramophone— (*He makes a winding-up gesture.*) could turn into an electric-chair. (*Madame Kuprina's eyes have been darting eagerly from one man to the other. She gestures to Vera, who crosses to her. Madame Kuprina whispers in Vera's ear, in Russian.*)

VERA. (*Laughs.*) Don't be ridiculous, my darling.

MADAME KUPRINA. (*She rises to her feet. In English.*) It is not ridiculous. (*She points a shaky finger at Smith.*) He is a Bolshevik! (*This absurdity breaks the tension between Smith and Kuprin. They laugh.*)

KUPRIN. Mamuschka. Smith is my friend. From the University in America.

MADAME KUPRINA. He is deceiving you. He looks too young.

KUPRIN. I was ten years older than he was then. I am still ten years older. We have invented nothing to change that.

MADAME KUPRINA. (*Still eyeing Smith with hostility.*) But he does not look intellectual.

KUPRIN. (*Laughing, he claps a hand on Smith's shoulder.*) Never mind. *I* think you are intellectual. (*Madame Kuprina sits, rigidly, still looking at Smith with distrust.*)

VERA. (*Trying to smooth things.*) Such brilliant men. You are hungry, and you do not even know it. We will eat now. (*A wall phone begins to rasp in the hallway. They all look at one another. There is a moment of tension and held breaths. Vera unbolts the door, goes out and stands in the blue light, answering the phone. Into phone, in Russian.*) Allo, allo.

MADAME KUPRINA. (*In English.*) I do not like the telephone. It listens to me.

KUPRIN. (*He drops to his haunches, almost like a child at his mother's knees. Comfortingly he pats her hand in her lap.*) It brings faraway people close. Soon I will be going to Yalta. (*Smith listens attentively.*) The phone will ring, Vera will put the receiver to your ear, and I will say "Hello, Mamuschka!"—exactly as if I were here in this room.

VERA. (*She re-enters the room, and speaks with a vague apprehension. In Russian.*) They want you, Cousin Vassili.

KUPRIN. (*Also a little apprehensive.*) Excuse me, Smith. I'm like a doctor in the United States: always on call. (*Kuprin goes out to the phone, mutters into it in Russian.*)

SMITH. (*He crosses to Vera, takes her hand. Softly, sincerely.*) Thank you, Verochka. This evening means a great deal to me.

VERA. To Vassili also.

KUPRIN. (*He hangs up the phone slowly, and comes back into the room. He looks at them helplessly.*) Did I have a briefcase?

VERA. You are not leaving?

KUPRIN. They need me. I must go immediately. (*Smith is disturbed.*)

MADAME KUPRINA. I forbid it!

VERA. Chicken Kiev. And artichokes!

MADAME KUPRINA. You must eat.

KUPRIN. I eat, Mamuschka. The chicken Kiev and the artichokes will have to wait. Like the chess game.

VERA. Twenty-one years. They will get cold.

KUPRIN. Forgive me, Smith. Something has gone wrong. (*Offering his hand.*) Smith, enjoy the Soviet Union. And perhaps, in your newspapers, you will write about the startling discovery you have made: the Russian people are also human beings. (*He goes quickly to kiss his mother.*) Dasvadanya, Mamuschka.

SMITH. (*Suddenly desperate.*) Koopy. I've *got* to see you again!

KUPRIN. (*He turns. His face darkens at Smith's imperative tone.*) I doubt if that will be possible. (*He walks past Smith to the door, and opens it.*)

SMITH. (*Urgently.*) Koopy!

KUPRIN. (*Stopping.*) Yes?

SMITH. (*Playing against time.*) I have a message for you.

KUPRIN. A message?

SMITH. From—from your daughter. From Nadya.

KUPRIN. (*Slowly, he closes the door and comes back into the room. In a thin voice.*) From Nadya. (*For a few seconds Kuprin does not speak. He sinks into a chair, and puts his hands up to his face.*)

SMITH. She sends you her love.

KUPRIN. (*A whisper.*) Her love. (*The tears spurt from his eyes onto his fingers. Madame Kuprina watches him, concerned. She grasps Vera's arm.*)

MADAME KUPRINA. Why does he make Vassili cry?

VERA. (*Comfortingly.*) Sh. Sh. It is *good* news. That is why Vassili is crying.

KUPRIN. (*Shaking off his tears. To Madame Kuprina and Vera.*) Leave me alone with Smith. Just a few moments. Please. (*Vera helps Madame Kuprina to her feet, but is reluctant to leave.*) It is all right, Mama. Verochka, get her to lie down. (*Vera helps Madame Kuprina toward the kitchen, but she is protesting as her niece guides her out of the room.*)

MADAME KUPRINA. Why does anybody want to hurt Vassili? (*They are gone. Kuprin turns quickly to Smith.*)

KUPRIN. All about Nadya. Everything. Please. Quickly.

SMITH. (*Reaching into his pocket.*) I've brought you a couple of photographs. (*He takes out some snapshots and Kuprin reaches for them eagerly. Hastily he wipes his glasses and looks at the pictures warmly.*)

KUPRIN. (*With quiet affection.*) Nadya. Nadinka. When did you see her?

SMITH. Only a few days ago.

KUPRIN. (*He holds one photo at arm's length to focus better.*) She doesn't look well. She looks thin. Does she get enough to eat? What are the children called? Yes, she really looks pale. You can see her collar-bones. Why is she wearing such high heels? I want to know everything. (*Kuprin smiles through his excitement.*) I begin to sound like my mother.

SMITH. I don't know everything. I went to see her and Novack before I left the States. They live in Princeton. A nice house. The same street where Einstein used to live.

KUPRIN. Good. More.

SMITH. Novack is doing well.

KUPRIN. (*His face clouding.*) Novack.

SMITH. I thought I might be seeing you. That's why I stopped in Princeton.

KUPRIN. That was thoughtful of you, Smith. Why doesn't she write to me?

SMITH. She did. At first.

KUPRIN. Nothing ever got through. Not even a post card. It's because of Novack. A violent man. An extremist. Does he know being so anti-Soviet means being against his children's grandfather?

SMITH. You can't blame Novack. He had a rough time in Czechoslovakia. But if it's any comfort, he and Nadya are very happy together. (*Kuprin nods, still staring at the picture.*) She's more beautiful than that. Snapshots don't do her justice. And the children, Jimmy and Penny—

KUPRIN. (*Laughing.*) "Jimmy and Penny." Such American names. The boy must be ten, and the girl almost eight.

SMITH. I don't really know. They spoke a lot about you.

KUPRIN. (*With genuine surprise, ruffling his hair with his hand.*) About me? Do they know anything about me?

SMITH. Your photograph is on the piano. Jimmy says he's going to be a scientist like his grandfather. A *real* scientist, he says, not just a political scientist like his father. Jimmy must be the hero of his school since you're so famous.

KUPRIN. And the little girl?

SMITH. Well, Penny is not so scientific.

KUPRIN. Fine. I hate women scientists. Even age eight. (*He shuffles quickly through the pictures again.*) May I keep these?

SMITH. I brought them for you.

KUPRIN. (*He scowls at the face of Novack in one of the snapshots.*) It's his fault, you know. Novack's. If it weren't for him, they could come visit me.

SMITH. You could go visit them. (*There is a pause. The thought of this is gyrating in Kuprin's mind. Then he breaks away sharply and moves toward the door.*) Come back to America with me, Koopy!

KUPRIN. (*Acidly.*) Tonight? Sorry. Can't make it. Haven't got my toothbrush.

SMITH. (*He crosses to him and turns him around forcibly, holding his shoulders.*) Koopy. Come. Live in America. Work in America.

KUPRIN. Why?

SMITH. You'll have freedom.

KUPRIN. No scientists are free any more. Not yours either.

SMITH. In America—

KUPRIN. It's no different!

SMITH. It is!

KUPRIN. Everywhere it's the same. Can science move mountains? Yes! But the politicians tell us which mountains to move.

SMITH. If you'd stayed in America—

KUPRIN. If I'd stayed in America, my Mother would be dead. They wouldn't guarantee her safety. So I came back here with my wife and son.

SMITH. Nadya doesn't even know what happened.

KUPRIN. She was a child. How do you tell a child? She was away at school. Safe in America, with friends. Then the war broke out here. (*With great difficulty.*) Mischa—and my wife— (*Pause.*)

SMITH. What happened, Koopy? Can you tell me?

KUPRIN. (*Almost angrily.*) They died! As simple as that! Mischa lived a tiny percentage of a lifetime, and he died. His mother, too. The bombs were falling. They wanted to get the women and children to safety. (*Ironically.*) So they were packed into a cattle car. And they died, like cattle.

SMITH. I'm sorry, Koopy.

KUPRIN. (*Trying to dismiss it.*) It was twenty years ago. (*Sighs.*) Oh, Smith, if we scientists really gave a damn about the human race, we'd invent a Memory Selector. Some neat little gadget with dials and transistors that would let us hold in our heads all the useful stuff, but erase the pain.

SMITH. (*With growing intensity.*) I can get you back there, Koopy. Back to America. Do you trust me? I can do it. Trust me!

KUPRIN. (*He shrieks at him.*) STOP IT! For God's sake, get your hands out of my life! (*He reaches into his breast pocket and pulls out the snapshots which he put there with such a cherished gesture earlier. He shoves them at Smith.*) Here! Here! Take these back. I don't know who these people are. I am not an American! No part of me is in America! (*Madame Kuprina appears from the bedroom. Her eyes are blazing. At arms' length, she is holding out a small pistol, pointing it at Smith. Her hand trembles. The men look at her, stunned.*)

MADAME KUPRINA. (*To Smith, in a strained, throaty voice.*) Bolshevik! You are trying to hurt my Vassili.

VERA. (*She appears at the kitchen door. In Russian.*) Great Aunt! (*Swiftly, Vera crosses to the old woman and takes the gun away from her.*)

MADAME KUPRINA. (*Continuing muttering.*) Bolshevik, Bolshevik.

KUPRIN. (*To Vera.*) Where did that come from?

VERA. It's mine.

KUPRIN. Get rid of it.

VERA. Two women, alone. When you are away at Yalta—

KUPRIN. (*Firmly, to Vera.*) Get rid of it! (*He crosses to his mother and steadies her. He seems to be speaking to himself as much as to his mother.*) When we are afraid, we are always in great danger. When we stop being afraid, we can breathe again. We can look around. We can see what is real, what is shadow. (*Kuprin moves quickly to go.*) Goodbye. (*Kuprin opens the door, then turns suddenly and comes back to shake Smith's hand. He looks down at the pictures, then grabs hold of them and takes them, patting Smith's shoulder with appreciation. Then he turns and goes.*)

THE LIGHTS FADE

ACT TWO
SCENE 3

A River Bank. Night. Merely an overturned rowboat in a spotted area, in One. There is a distant sound of accordion music.

SMITH. (*Unseen.*) Let's leave the boat here.

VERA. (*Unseen.*) I am not sure if we are allowed to be here.

SMITH. (*Unseen.*) I know a swell way to find out. (*Vera and Smith enter, in swimming-gear. Smith has a towel around his shoulders. Vera wears a loose beach robe over her bikini.*) I never thought of Moscow as swimsuit country. I guess Napoleon was here out-of-season.

VERA. You're cold.

SMITH. (*Grinning.*) Only externally. (*She sits against the boat, opening up her beach robe to put it around his shoulders.*)

VERA. We can share this. Come. Sit.

SMITH. (*Sitting close to her.*) This kind of collectivism is for me. (*He draws her closer to him, and they share the mutual warmth of their bodies. Smith kisses her lightly on the temple. This is the first time they have been so physically close, and there is an electric attraction between them.*) Aren't you afraid of me?

VERA. (*Softly.*) Of course. (*She turns quickly and looks up into his face intently.*) Now please to tell me truthfully. Am I terribly un-American?

SMITH. (*Smiling.*) Terribly.

VERA. (*She is disappointed, but she tries to conceal it.*) Good. I would not want to be an "imitation American." A substitute for somebody eight thousand miles away.

SMITH. (*Drawing her a little closer to him.*) I'm very happy with the present geographical arrangement. (*He starts to kiss her. She bends her face toward him—but just before their lips touch, she pulls away and hugs her knees with a defiant expression.*) What's the matter?

VERA. (*In a burst of Slavic contrariness.*) I do not wish to kiss you because I wish to kiss you too much! (*Her sudden move has pulled the robe from around his shoulders. He rubs his shoulders and arms. Quickly and contritely, she offers him the robe again.*) I'm sorry. (*She frowns.*) I do not understand this at all. And I do not like it when I do not understand things.

SMITH. Stop thinking.

VERA. Would you like me—would we be together, like this, if I were not my cousin's cousin?

SMITH. How? I never would have met you. I'm very grateful to Koopy.

VERA. (*Softly.*) I am grateful also.

SMITH. (*Carefully.*) Does he ever talk to you about trips he'd like to take?

VERA. Oh, yes. He loves the Crimea.

SMITH. I mean—outside the country. (*Vera is very silent and motionless.*) He was supposed to go to Geneva. Last July. Why didn't he go? Do you have any idea?

VERA. (*Angrily.*) My cousin, my cousin! "Koopy!" Vassili! Questions—only about him. Why?

SMITH. You don't have to tell me anything. What are you so damned suspicious about? (*He gets up.*) Come on, let's go back. I'll take you home.

VERA. (*She gets up, following him.*) Please. Do not be angry with me. (*She touches his back.*) You see, I am afraid to like people. I have been disappointed in so many—I would not like to be disappointed in you.

SMITH. (*He turns, looks at her. Then suddenly he holds her very close to him. Softly, over *her shoulder.*) I don't want you to be disappointed in me, either. (*He kisses her shoulder. Then, in a mutual surge of attraction, they kiss full on the lips, a long kiss. They break, look at each other with the excitement of physical discovery.*)

VERA. Again, please. (*They kiss again. Then he spreads out the robe and they lean back on the overturned boat.*)

SMITH. Verochka, I—

VERA. (*Touching his lips.*) Stop. Shhh.

SMITH. Why?

VERA. You were going to say you love me. Do not say it.

SMITH. (*Smiling.*) Censorship.

VERA. Love, love, love. It does not mean anything. It is all worn out. The word "love" I mean. We have exhausted it. Here in the Soviet Union, where we are so advanced, we have rejected love. Romantic love. The—the—the illusion that each person there is only one counterpart in the universe. Platonic mythology! Not suitable, not practical for daily life. But— (*She is clasping her shoulders with her hands, chilled in the night air. Smith pulls her down and kisses her. She softens.*) Oh, Smees. Dear, good Smees. Why should I love you more than ice cream? (*She buries her head against his chest.*) Last night, with a pencil and paper, I made a list. A catalogue. "What is Smees?"

SMITH. A catalogue?

VERA. I put down—one, two, three, four, five, six—all of your qualities. And you turned out, not better, not worse, than a hundred other men. Are you good-looking? Not especially. (*He laughs a little.*) Except your eyes. They are special. Height? Average. Not very much taller than myself. Voice? Pleasant. Intellectual? Yes and no. (*She looks into his face.*) But I could not find on the list what it is that makes me think of you, not once in a while, but all the time. Why, Smees? Why?

SMITH. (*He holds her very tightly. Very softly.*) Will you hold my arm? When we walk?

VERA. Yes. Yes. When must you leave? Tomorrow? If it is tomorrow, do not tell me.

SMITH. If I don't go tomorrow, I'll have to go the day after tomorrow. Or the day after that. Or next week. (*He kisses her hair.*) But I'll stay as long as I can. (*He turns away, troubled.*) God. Oh, God—

VERA. Why "God, oh, God"?

SMITH. I wish I could take you with me. But it would be difficult, Verochka. For you.

VERA. (*Simply.*) English is difficult. But we learn.

SMITH. (*He grasps her shoulders.*) Do you think you love me enough?

VERA. Is there a yardstick for love?

SMITH. Yes! You measure love by what you'll give up for it.

VERA. For example?

SMITH. Smoking? Would you give up cigarettes for love?

VERA. I have already.

SMITH. Vodka?

VERA. (*With an easy laugh.*) Yes.

SMITH. New dresses?

VERA. Yes.

SMITH. Television?

VERA. It doesn't work anyhow.

SMITH. Your friends? (*There is a moment's hesitation.*)

VERA. Of course. They'd be surprised, but I would.

SMITH. Your family, your Great Aunt?

VERA. (*She begins to draw away a little.*) My Great Aunt is part of the whole complex of love.

SMITH. Would you leave her? Would you give up your country to love me?

VERA. Why do you ask such questions?

SMITH. (*Pressing.*) Would you?

VERA. (*After an agonized hesitation, she answers, brushing her lips against his.*) Yes, yes, yes, yes— (*He embraces her. Then she speaks, softly, penetratingly.*) Would you give up *your* country, Smees, for me?

SMITH. (*There is a pause. He wets his lips.*) Vera, can you get permission to leave the Soviet Union? There must be some way to get out.

VERA. You did not answer *my* question.

SMITH. Can you arrange it? You've got to.

VERA. For love?

SMITH. For more than love. For safety.

VERA. Whose safety?

SMITH. Listen to me, Verochka. If Koopy goes back to America—

VERA. (*Interrupting.*) But he *cannot* go back to America. He told you that, didn't he? It is impossible.

SMITH. But he wants to go, doesn't he? I know he does. I could see it. I'm going to help him.

VERA. (*Drawing away from him.*) Is this why you came to the Soviet Union?

SMITH. It's not why I *came.*

VERA. I don't believe you. I don't believe anything you say! (*She gets up.*)

SMITH. Take Madame Kuprina! Get out of the Soviet Union. If you can.

VERA. (*With rising anger.*) You had to see "Koopy"! Your "old friend." You made him cry, with little pictures of his daughter, and his grandchildren. He trusts you. I trusted you. What am I? A door to open? A lock to be broken, so you can get to something else, reach what you really want?

SMITH. (*He takes her arms firmly.*) I want you to be safe, I don't want anything to happen to you, I want to be with you, I love you.

VERA. Get out your yardstick. How *much* do you love me? Enough to forget what you want to do to Vassili? Why can not *you* stay here? Do what you are asking me to do! Give up *your* friends, *your* vodka, *your* cigarettes, *your* country. Can you do that? (*Smith doesn't answer.*) *Can* you? (*He slings the towel around his shoulders.*

Furious, she starts off. Off, we hear the quick churning of oars, as if another boat is pulling away from shore, and the protest of disgruntled frogs. Vera sees something which alarms her. She quietly pulls Smith to a crouching position.)

SMITH. What's wrong?

VERA. (*Worried, lowering her voice.*) There was another boat. Close in. Beside ours.

SMITH. (*Concerned.*) Could they hear what we were saying?

VERA. I don't know. (*They stare at each other, trying to remember just what they said, what might have been overheard. Vera's voice falls to an anxious whisper.*) I don't know!

THE LIGHTS FADE

ACT TWO
SCENE 4

The Headquarters of K.G.B. We see three rooms, adjoining. One is a tiny waiting room, with nothing but a bench. Holloway sits there disconsolately, guarded by a Soldier. The lights come up on this area first.

HOLLOWAY. (*To the Soldier, in English.*) Since you've helped yourself to all my gear, old boy, I wonder if I could trouble you for a cigarette?

SOLDIER. (*In Russian.*) I do not speak English.

HOLLOWAY. Oh. Well, here's what I had in mind— (*He pantomimes smoking.*)

SOLDIER. (*In Russian.*) Not permitted.

HOLLOWAY. (*In English.*) Not permitted. (*Holloway thinks for a minute, then clears his throat, and pantomimes as he speaks.*) A book. I was reading a book. A book. I thought maybe you could get it back from the high—the chief—the whatever-he-is-in there— Hmmm? (*He gestures toward the middle room. The Soldier is impassive. Holloway gives up, nods resignedly.*) Not permitted. Not permitted. (*The lights come up on an Interrogation Room. It has plastered gray walls, a table with several chairs around it; all utility and no flourishes, except for the scarlet hammer-and-sickle flag. Vera sits at the table, intent on a typewritten document of several pages. Two men watch her silently. One is Makarov, the Bureau Chief. He is a Colonel, but wears civilian clothes. He is plump, balding, worried. The other is Tkachenko, an earnest, wiry interpreter. Aside from the ill-fitting double-breasted suits, Moscow-made, they could be executives of an American plumbing firm. Vera looks up from the paper. Makarov hands her an uncapped fountain pen.*)

VERA. (*Shaking her head.*) Nyet.

MAKAROV. (*In Russian.*) Do you find this dossier inaccurate?

VERA. (*In Russian.*) I cannot swear to things I do not know about. (*Her eyes are angry, her jaw is set. She waves away the fountain pen. Makarov and Tkachenko confer in worried whispers over the unsigned paper.*)

MAKAROV. (*Jerking his head toward the door, in Russian.*) See what he thinks we should do. (*Tkachenko takes the typed pages and crosses into an inner office where a man in civilian clothes is listening to the interrogation on an earphone. His back is to us, so we do not see his face. A cardboard carton containing Holloway's personal effects is on the desk in front of him.*)

TKACHENKO. (*In Russian.*) She won't sign it. (*The man takes the paper, uncaps a fountain pen, and writes a signature at the bottom of the page. As he turns to do so, we see it is Trifonov.*)

TRIFONOV. (*As he writes. With dutiful reluctance.*) Vera—Kuprina. (*He hands the paper back to Tkachenko, who crosses to the office and shows the signature to Makarov, who scowls thoughtfully. Then he studies Vera, sniffs, makes a decision.*)

MAKAROV. (*To Vera, in Russian.*) You may go. (*Tkachenko holds open the door and Vera hurries out. As she passes Holloway in the anteroom, there is a moment of semi-recognition. Makarov has crossed after her to the door of the waiting room, and watches them both intently. However, Holloway suppresses any clue in his face which might indicate he has seen Vera before. Without a word, Vera exits. Tkachenko glances at Makarov, who nods, returns to his desk.*)

TKACHENKO. (*In English.*) You will come in, please, Mr. Golloway. (*Holloway takes a deep breath and goes into the office.*) This is Colonel I. L. Makarov, who wishes to ask you a few questions.

HOLLOWAY. I have a few questions to ask the Colonel. Why do you have a soldier pick me up on the steps of my hotel? Am I under arrest? What for?

MAKAROV. (*In Russian.*) You will sit, please.

HOLLOWAY. (*He continues the pretense of not understanding the language.*) Sorry, old man. My Russian is very poor. No capiche.

TKACHENKO. (*In English.*) I will translate. Colonel Makarov says you may sit.

HOLLOWAY. I don't care to sit. Tell your Colonel I'm a British subject, a businessman. I'm here to spend Pounds Sterling for Soviet products. And this is a damned shabby way to treat a customer. Why am I here? (*The two men confer together in Russian.*)

TKACHENKO. We have information, Mr. Golloway, that you are aiding in academic corruption.

HOLLOWAY. Gentlemen. My only "academic corruption" was when I was a boy at Eton. Writing on the walls of the loo. Pure pornography. Nothing political. But surprised you chaps know about it. (*Makarov and Tkachenko confer again in Russian. Now Makarov stands, holding the paper with Vera's forged signature.*)

MAKAROV. (*In Russian.*) You know the young lady who just left here?

TKACHENKO. (*In English.*) The girl who just left here. You know her.

HOLLOWAY. Haven't had the pleasure.

MAKAROV. (*Indicating the paper, in Russian.*) I have here a sworn statement, concerning an American national named Smith.

TKACHENKO. (*In English.*) The Colonel is holding a sworn statement concerning an American national named Smith. (*Makarov continues speaking in Russian, while Tkachenko translates fragmentarily in the breaths between.*) It has been signatured by Vera Kuprin, cousin of distinguished Soviet scientist. You will kindly tell us what you know about Smith. (*Tkachenko sits, a pad and pencil ready.*)

HOLLOWAY. (*Thinking a minute.*) Smith? Smith. Well, he's got a brother. They make cough drops. Beards on both of them. Possible Cuban connections. (*The two Russians confer again.*)

TKACHENKO. (*In English.*) If you desire to be released, you will give us complete and non-fictional information about persons working in subversive network directed against Professor Kuprin.

HOLLOWAY. If you intended to release me, you'd give me back my personal effects.

TKACHENKO. (*To Makarov, in Russian.*) He wants his things. (*Makarov nods, indicates that Tkachenko should go into the next room and get them. Tkachenko crosses to the office, where Trifonov hands him the box containing Holloway's gear. He reaches up and takes out a green-bound book, which he keeps. Tkachenko crosses back into the office and puts the box on the desk in front of Makarov. Holloway starts to reach for some of the things, but Makarov stops him.*)

MAKAROV. (*In Russian.*) He gets these things back only if he names names.

TKACHENKO. (*In English.*) You get these things back only if you name names.

HOLLOWAY. I get my gear, *then* I name names. (*Makarov thinks this over, then dumps the box in front of Holloway, who notices at once that his book is missing.*) This isn't everything. I had a— (*He breaks off.*) Never mind. (*Throughout the following, Tkachenko writes. As Holloway speaks, he is stuffing his things back into his pockets, strapping on his wrist watch, counting his money and checking the contents of his wallet.*) You agree to let me go as soon as I name names? (*Makarov nods impatiently.*)

TKACHENKO. It is agreed.

HOLLOWAY. (*With a sign.*) I'll start at the beginning.

TKACHENKO. Start. (*Makarov leans over his shoulder and watches as he writes.*)

HOLLOWAY. (*Straight-faced.*) Christopher Robin. He works with— God, I feel like a swine! With Peter Sellers.

TKACHENKO. Sellers.

HOLLOWAY. With an "S."

TKACHENKO. Any Americans?

HOLLOWAY. One. Eliot.

TKACHENKO. What initials?

HOLLOWAY. *T. S.* (*In the office, Trifonov rises and crosses into the office. He has put the green-backed book into his jacket pocket. Everybody turns to look at Trifonov as he comes in.*)

TRIFONOV. (*In Russian.*) Excuse me, Colonel. He is talking foolishness. (*He picks up the paper on which Tkachenko has been writing. In English.*) I'm disappointed in you, Mr. Holloway. Do you really think we are so lacking in sophistication? T. S. Eliot. "The Wasteland." Born, St. Louis, Missouri, 1888. Correct?

HOLLOWAY. I wouldn't know.

TRIFONOV. Mr. Holloway, you are too modest about your cultural attainments. You have told the Colonel— (*Mimicking Holloway.*) "Sorry, old man, my Russian is very poor." (*He turns to Makarov.*) His Russian is about as poor as Pushkin's.

MAKAROV. (*In English, slightly Oxfordian.*) I rather gathered that.

TRIFONOV. You see, Mr. Holloway, we are concealing nothing. Why don't we sit down like friends while you tell us what you know about this fellow Smith? (*They all sit, pleasantly.*)

HOLLOWAY. I'm in the lumber business. Offices in Manchester, Leeds.

TRIFONOV. And Liverpool. We know. You actually *are* in the lumber business. And *I* actually am a Professor. My classes in World Literature are very well attended. But you and I serve our countries in other ways. Yes?

HOLLOWAY. Who am I supposed to be—the "Toothpick Pimpernel"? (*Trifonov laughs, slaps Holloway on the shoulder.*)

TRIFONOV. Ahhh, I like you, Holloway. I have long admired you.

MAKAROV. Mr. Holloway— (*He breaks off and reprimands the interpreter.*) By the way, it's *H*olloway, not *G*olloway. Huh—Huh—Holloway.

TKACHENKO. Huh—Huh—Golloway.

MAKAROV. (*Turning back to Holloway.*) I apologize. Our regular translator is on vacation at the U.N. Professor Trifonov is my lieutenant at the University, assigned to the protection of Dr. Kuprin.

HOLLOWAY. Bully.

TRIFONOV. Gentlemen, I'm going to make a confession. Whenever I find myself baffled—temporarily—I become a traitor. I say to myself, "What would I do if I were on the other side?"

HOLLOWAY. *Which* other side? Washington or Beijing? (*The Russians look at one another with weak smiles.*)

TRIFONOV. I imagine myself to be *you*, Mr. Holloway. What is my relationship to Smith?

HOLLOWAY. Smith? What Smith? There are millions of them.

MAKAROV. You were together on Tour B out of the Ukraina Hotel.

TRIFONOV. You spoke to him two days ago at Gorky Park.

HOLLOWAY. Oh, *that* Smith. Nice chap. Hardly seems like an American at all. (*They are all beginning to close in on Holloway, hammering questions at him.*)

MAKAROV. What is he doing in Moscow?

HOLLOWAY. Spending money.

TRIFONOV. What is his relationship to Kuprin's cousin?

HOLLOWAY. How the devil should I know?

MAKAROV. What is the nature of conspiracy against Professor Kuprin?

HOLLOWAY. Smith is a tourist!

MAKAROV. Your Mr. Smith is a tourist who is *not* a tourist.

HOLLOWAY. He's not "my" Mr. Smith.

MAKAROV. He is trying to obtain from Professor Kuprin scientific data which is classified secret. Is this true?

HOLLOWAY. He looks like a tourist to me.

TRIFONOV. (*Pointing his finger at Holloway.*) Smith wishes to make capital—I use the word advisedly—of an ancient friendship for Kuprin. Am I correct?

MAKAROV. You will answer, please!

HOLLOWAY. I don't know Kuprin. I don't know Kuprin's cousin. I don't know about any bloody conspiracy. If you want to ask me questions about plywood, I'll give you some fast answers. (*He stands.*) Now, why don't you let me go, so I can help make the Soviet Union the wealthiest nation in the world? (*He looks defiantly from one face to another in the ring surrounding him. Smith appears in the waiting room, a prodding Soldier behind him. Smith is fretful and disturbed. The Soldier hands a slip of paper to the Guard in the waiting room, who then knocks on the door of the office. The Soldier indicates to Smith that he should sit on the bench.*)

MAKAROV. (*In Russian.*) Come. (*The Guard enters the office. He hands Tkachenko the slip of paper.*)

TKACHENKO. (*In Russian.*) The American's here. Smith. (*Tkachenko hands the Guard a form, a pencil, and the empty cardboard box which had contained Holloway's gear. The Guard crosses to the waiting room. In the waiting room, the Soldier sets about emptying Smith's pockets.*)

SMITH. Hey.

MAKAROV. (*Glancing at his watch.*) An hour and twenty minutes ago, you telephoned Mr. Smith in room 927 at the Ukraina Hotel. You asked him to meet you at the Gay-Oo-Em Department Store.

HOLLOWAY. Why not? Is GUM off-limits?

TRIFONOV. At the shoelace counter across from the fountain.

HOLLOWAY. So?

TRIFONOV. Does this indicate anything?

HOLLOWAY. Yes. That you listen to telephone conversations.

MAKAROV. What did you wish to say to Mr. Smith that you could not say over the telephone?

HOLLOWAY. I wanted to show him where to buy a fur hat, a balalaika and a gramophone disc of Boris Goudonov.

TRIFONOV. You went out on this shopping expedition carrying only one thing. This book. (*He takes out the green-backed book. Holloway pales a little.*)

HOLLOWAY. Is there a ban on reading?

TRIFONOV. I find it curious that a man in the lumber business should be reading this particular book. (*He studies the spine of the volume thoughtfully.*) "Tsushima." (*The Russians all watch Holloway's face for a reaction. There is none.*) Would an Englishman read "Tsushima" in Russian for pleasure? When he says he doesn't even know Russian?

HOLLOWAY. Well, I'm studying.

TRIFONOV. (*Biting, incisive.*) What does "Tsushima" mean, Mr. Holloway?

HOLLOWAY. I gather it's a bit like what "Waterloo" means to the French.

MAKAROV. Or Dunkirk to the English.

TRIFONOV. Now. I am becoming a traitor again. If I were in British intelligence I might find it amusing to use "Tsushima" as a kind of code word. Logical?

HOLLOWAY. If ever I meet a chap from British Intelligence, I'll suggest it.

TRIFONOV. I say you *are* from British Intelligence. You were going to meet Smith at GUM. To show him this book. And to tell him something. What, Mr. Holloway?

HOLLOWAY. This is your fairy tale; finish it yourself.

TRIFONOV. You want to warn Mr. Smith. That he is in great danger. That the Soviet government knows precisely why he is here. To induce Professor Kuprin to disclose scientific information. You were sent, with this book as your badge, to tell him, "Stop! They know! Turn yourself into a tourist again." That was the conversation that should have taken place by the shoelaces at GUM.

HOLLOWAY. Look, have you got poor old Smith out there chewing his nails? Invite him in. See how much we've got to say to each other.

MAKAROV. Not immediately, Mr. Holloway. (*To the Guard, in Russian.*) Conduct Mr. Holloway into that office. (*The Guard escorts the reluctant Holloway toward the office.*)

HOLLOWAY. Now what? "This way to the Egress"? (*After Holloway and the Guard go through the door, Trifonov quickly gives instructions.*)

TRIFONOV. (*In Russian.*) When I buzz, drag me in here—as if I were a prisoner. (*Then Trifonov crosses quickly into the office, taking the green-backed book with him. At a nod from Makarov, Tkachenko crosses to the waiting room door and signals for Smith to be brought in. Makarov sheds his facility with English, and ostensibly leans on Tkachenko for all translation. The Guard brings Smith in, and puts the box containing his effects in front of Makarov. The Guard takes his post at the door. Smith and the Russians eye one another silently. Tkachenko crosses, takes the interrogation form from Smith.*)

SMITH. I'm a tourist. An American. I haven't done anything. (*There is no answer. Tkachenko continues reading the form which Smith has filled out. Makarov simply stares at him. Smith is growing more apprehensive.*) I don't speak any Russian. Do you speak English? Either of you? (*Silently, Tkachenko passes the form to Makarov, who merely glances at it. In the office, Trifonov and Holloway are leaning into the squawk box, watching each other.*) I don't even know where I am. Am I under arrest? What for?

TKACHENKO. Do you wish to place a telephone call to your Embassy?

SMITH. (*He hesitates.*) Not especially. First I want to know what the trouble is. (*Makarov speaks first in Russian in the following, and Tkachenko translates.*)

TKACHENKO. What is the purpose of your visit to the Soviet Union?

SMITH. A vacation.

TKACHENKO. Your *true* purpose.

SMITH. Sightseeing. (*Tkachenko translates.*)

MAKAROV. (*In Russian, chuckling.*) Did he come here to buy shoelaces?

TKACHENKO. (*Also smiling.*) Did you come here to buy shoelaces?

SMITH. I came here because your government ran an ad in the Travel Section of the *New York Times*. I read it. Here I am. Does that make me a subversive? (*The Russians merely look at him, then begin examining his effects. Smith watches nervously. In the room, Trifonov puts down the ear phone and faces Holloway.*)

TRIFONOV. Your friend Smith is disarming. (*Nodding his head.*) You know why we don't get on with the Americans? Because we like them too much. We want too much to be like them. You, Mr. Holloway, have a great advantage. The British and Americans get along splendidly because they don't really have much use for each other. (*Standing, seriously, leaning across the desk.*) You understand, Mr. Holloway. This is more than an official duty for me. I care a great deal, personally, about what happens to Kuprin. (*Holloway smiles.*) You don't believe me.

HOLLOWAY. No.

TRIFONOV. I have known Vassili thirty years. Thirty-five, almost. I have much affection for him. And if Mr. Smith did something violent—

HOLLOWAY. Americans aren't violent.

TRIFONOV. But they are. Violence is taught daily to their young. On the television. (*Holloway watches him as he takes his small steel-rimmed spectacles from a drawer and begins to assume the air of the humble, insecure professor.*) Smith is an amateur. He has not had your long experience hiding behind plywood. (*No reaction from Holloway. Trifonov stuffs the book under his belt, buttons his jacket over it.*) "Half a league, half a league, half a league onward, into the jaws of death rode the six hundred." You recall, of course, this excellent narrative ballad by Alfred Lord Tennyson? 1809–1892. How bravely your Light Brigade charged "into the cannon's mouth." A Russian cannon.

HOLLOWAY. Czarist.

TRIFONOV. Soon another blunder in the Crimea. But this time, not the "Six hundred." Only one. One man. Smith. "His not to reason why, his but to do and—" (*Trifonov shrugs. Holloway is silent. He puts on the glasses, peers at Holloway.*) You can still warn him. Go ahead, Mr. Holloway. Call out. (*Holloway is silent.*) Shout "Tsushima"!

HOLLOWAY. (*Pause.*) Why should I shout? I'm in the lumber business. (*They study each other. Trifonov wonders if he has made a wrong guess. He presses a buzzer, which sounds in the Interrogation Room. Makarov and Tkachenko have been examining Smith's personal effects with infinite detail. Smith has been watching impatiently. At the sound of the buzzer, Makarov turns to Tkachenko and mutters something quickly. Tkachenko gestures for the Guard to join him and opens the door to the office. Roughly, Tkachenko pulls Trifonov into the Interrogation Room. The Guard closes the door and remains rigidly in front of it. Behind the door, Holloway is listening on the ear phone. Smith rises.*)

MAKAROV. (*In Russian, to Smith.*) Do you know this man?

TKACHENKO. (*In English.*) You know this man? (*Trifonov seems to hold his breath, looking at Smith as if to say: "Don't give me away." He is playing the contrite, beaten little professor.*)

SMITH. (*After a pause.*) I'm not sure. I've seen a lot of people in Moscow. No, I don't think I've ever seen him. (*Trifonov seems to react gratefully. Makarov hands the dossier to Tkachenko, who reads in English.*)

TKACHENKO. This man, Professor Trifonov, was seen by you on 11th August in living quarters of Grashdanka Kuprina—number 5A Antipoyevsky Pereulok. He made deviationist statements against the University administration and the People's government. True?

SMITH. You're off your rocker.

TKACHENKO. Repeat, please.

SMITH. Rocker. You're off it. Bedbug. Crazy as a. (*Tkachenko hesitates and glances at Makarov.*) Tell your boss it's idiomatic profanity. Impossible to translate. (*Tkachenko mumbles something in Russian. Makarov nods, then turns to Trifonov.*)

MAKAROV. (*In Russian.*) Do you know this American?

TRIFONOV. (*Vehemently, shaking his head.*) Nyet! (*Trifonov turns to Smith, speaking English with an air of impassioned shame.*) I do not know you, sir, but I apologize on behalf of the peoples of the Soviet Union. You are a guest of my country. I am ashamed. (*He turns on Tkachenko.*) Is this the way we make friends? What will he say about us when he goes back to the United States? He is innocent, as I am innocent. (*He repeats the last sentence in Russian to Makarov. Makarov clicks off the switch on the squawk box and indicates for the soldier to bolt the door to Trifonov's office.*)

MAKAROV. (*After a pause, in Russian.*) Let them go.

TKACHENKO. (*In Russian.*) Both of them? (*Makarov nods. Tkachenko speaks in English.*) You may go. You are free to leave. Both. (*Eagerly, Trifonov bounces his head up and down in gratitude and darts into the waiting room, where he waits, tensely. Smith is gathering up his gear from the table.*) Thank you for voluntary co-operation.

SMITH. Oh, I love being yanked into a police car. Makes a fella feel important.

TKACHENKO. Peace and friendship.

SMITH. Swell. (*Smith crosses to the waiting room, where Trifonov is lingering, reading the green-backed book. Smith passes him, but Trifonov clears his throat. Holloway rattles the door, but Smith does not hear him.*)

TRIFONOV. Sir.

SMITH. (*Turning.*) Yes?

TRIFONOV. This is a most interesting book.

SMITH. Oh?

TRIFONOV. (*Showing him the title.*) It has significance to you?

SMITH. (*A pause.*) Yes.

TRIFONOV. (*Glancing toward the office.*) Appear casual. We are having a literary discussion.

SMITH. (*Starting off.*) Outside.

TRIFONOV. No. You must not be seen with me. (*Very low.*) Repeat quickly your instructions.

SMITH. (*Hesitates.*) I know them.

TRIFONOV. (*Gripping Smith's arm.*) Good. I was testing you. Tell them to no one. (*Glancing around again.*) Have you seen him again?

SMITH. Kuprin?

TRIFONOV. (*Hushing him quickly.*) "K!" Will "K" co-operate?

SMITH. I'm not sure. I hope so.

TRIFONOV. He is in the Crimea.

SMITH. Already?

TRIFONOV. (*Nods.*) Yalta. What will you do?

SMITH. Go to Yalta.

TRIFONOV. Correct. Do you have any questions?

SMITH. (*Thinking.*) No. Oh, will I need papers for him? When we get to Turkey?

TRIFONOV. (*Realizing.*) When you get to Turkey? (*Then covering.*) Everything will be taken care of. (*A nervous glance toward the office again.*) They suspect me only. Not you. Go. Proceed as planned. (*Smith goes out. Trifonov takes a step, seeming to follow Smith—then he pauses to watch the American disappear. Holloway rattles the locked door in the office. Trifonov silently opens the door to the Interrogation Room and stands in the doorway, nodding wisely to the others.*)

HOLLOWAY. (*Pounding on the door.*) Smith! It's a trap! TSUSHIMA! (*Makarov and Tkachenko look at Trifonov with satisfaction. Holloway, disheartened, leans his head against the locked door.*)

CURTAIN

ACT THREE

Kuprin's dacha in Yalta, a summer house at the very edge of the Black Sea. We see chiefly a large cozy room, with several comfortable chairs. There is a curtained archway to a bedroom area. The room is walled with books, except for wide windows, which face out across the porch toward the sea. The porch and the interior of the dacha are of equal importance as playing areas. Wooden steps lead up from the porch to a jetty, running out of sight. We see sea-washed pilings which support the jetty. There is an upgrade path.

It is night and the lighting in Kuprin's study is a pattern of lamplit pools. Kuprin, in casual clothes, is bending over portable telemetering equipment which is, in effect, an elaborate and intricate radio receiver, in a downstage corner of the study. Kuprin frowns as the loudspeaker regurgitates static and incoherent tones. Then he crosses to a worktable, littered with open books, scraps of sketches, typewritten reports. He picks up the telephone.

KUPRIN. (*Into telephone, in Russian.*) Kuprin. Have you got a time for the 169th transit of the Chelovyek? 34th meridian, that's close enough. (*He cocks the phone on his shoulder as he scrawls down the data which is given him. He grunts acknowledgment.*) Spasebo. (*Kuprin hangs up, crosses back to the radio, clicking off the sound. He seems disturbed. He wanders out onto the porch, clenching his hands around the wooden railing, as he looks seaward. From behind the jetty, there is the occasional "wheep" of small ships' whistles, and the jangling of a buoy, stirred by a boat's wake. A Soldier on guard duty passes along the path on his rounds. He is not much more than a shadow in the darkness. The Soldier moves up the path. Suddenly, the Guard stops, alert, and calls out a challenge in Russian.*)

SOLDIER. Who is there?

MADAME KUPRINA'S VOICE. (*Unseen, at a distance, weary.*) Dmitri! Dmitri, emportez nos baggages—vite, vite! (*Kuprin recognizes his mother's voice at once; astonished, he hurries past the Soldier as Madame Kuprina and Vera appear. Vera is holding onto the older woman's arm, and she is carrying a petit-point carpetbag.*)

KUPRIN. Mamuschka! (*He waves the Soldier away, speaking in Russian.*) It's all right. This is my mother and my cousin. (*The Soldier goes off, as Kuprin embraces them both, and takes the carpetbag from Vera.*)

VERA. (*Tensely, in English.*) Does the Guard speak English?

KUPRIN. (*In English.*) No, I'm sure not. Why?

VERA. Then speak English.

MADAME KUPRINA. (*In Russian.*) Verochka has been terrified.

VERA. (*Warningly.*) Speak *English*, Great Aunt!

KUPRIN. (*In English.*) Terrified? Why should she be terrified? (*Taking command.*) Come in the house, come in the house.

MADAME KUPRINA. (*With grandeur.*) Understand, Vassili. I have been calm. Completely calm. But Verochka wanted so much to see you. What could I do? (*They are crossing the porch. Vera enters the dacha ahead of the others, looks around the room, cautiously, warily. Madame Kuprina plucks at her son's sleeve, whispers to him.*) I tell you the truth, Vassili. I fear for the girl's sanity! (*In the doorway she turns, calls up the path imperiously.*) Dmitri! Do not forget my jewel box! (*Kuprin helps his mother into the house.*)

VERA. (*To Kuprin, softly.*) Thank God, you're safe.

KUPRIN. (*Baffled.*) Safe from what? Why didn't you let me know? How did you get here? Why didn't you telephone me?

VERA. I was afraid to use the telephone.

MADAME KUPRINA. You see, Vera? (*Gesturing toward her son.*) Here he is. He is well. (*She frowns at Kuprin.*) *Are* you well? You have a very bad color.

KUPRIN. (*With a faint smile.*) Suntan, Mamuschka. I've been working outside.

MADAME KUPRINA. I do not approve. The sun is very bad for the head. (*Vera remains almost stubbornly silent.*) You see, Vera. No one has harmed Vassili. (*Looking around the room.*) Everything is the same. Exactly as it was when we were here last summer. (*Her eyes fall on the radio. Scornfully.*) *That* is new. I do not like it.

VERA. (*She wants to say something to Kuprin alone.*) You need rest, Great Aunt. It was a long trip, Vassili. We sat up all the way to Yalta. A day and a night and a day.

KUPRIN. (*He goes to pour a short brandy for his mother.*) You are children, imagining things in the dark.

MADAME KUPRINA. Ah! Exactly what I have been telling her. (*Kuprin looks questioningly at Vera, and the set of her face tells him it is not imagination. He crosses to his mother with the brandy, and speaks soothingly.*)

KUPRIN. I am happy that you are here, Mamuschka. But you should not have taken such a long train trip.

MADAME KUPRINA. You would not believe the conditions on the train. The coach was cold. But worse, the *tea* was cold. The Czar will know about this. Verochka. Remind me, I must write a letter to the Czar.

KUPRIN. (*Handing her the cognac.*) This will warm you, Mamuschka.

MADAME KUPRINA. (*Taking it.*) Cognac! You are a good boy, Vassili. A good son. (*She pats his hand.*) I shall tell your father. (*Lowering her voice.*) I expect to speak to him tonight. The vibrations are very favorable.

VERA. (*In a low voice.*) We must get her to bed.

MADAME KUPRINA. (*With a full voice.*) "Get her to bed"! I heard that. I hear many things that you do not think I hear.

KUPRIN. (*Gently, to his mother.*) You need sleep, both of you. In a bed, not a railway coach. Tomorrow morning, sunshine. (*To Vera.*) A few days in the Crimea—

MADAME KUPRINA. The Crimea. The Crimea. (*Kuprin and Vera are helping the old woman toward the curtained archway which leads to the bedrooms. Suddenly Madame Kuprina stops, a little panicked.*) What if there is another Crimean War? What shall we do if Dmitri is conscripted? (*Kuprin leads her off. Vera, alone, lets go the facade of firmness and strength. She hears a sound, and looks outside, startled. It is the crunch of the Soldier's boots along the path again. Kuprin comes back into the room. He is scowling, thinking.*)

VERA. (*Taut.*) Has Smees been here? (*Kuprin shakes his head.*) If he comes to Yalta, you must not see him. (*She throws her arms around him, and speaks in a rush of emotion.*) Vassili, it is *my* fault. I arranged for Smees to meet you. At Gorky Park. Then at dinner. I did not know all this would happen.

KUPRIN. (*Impatiently.*) All what? What has happened?

VERA. (*In a guilty monotone.*) I was called in for questioning. They gave me a paper to sign. (*With spirit.*) But I refused! I would not sign it!

KUPRIN. What kind of paper?

VERA. To accuse Smees. (*In a flood of words.*) They wanted me to swear I knew he was trying to get scientific data from you. To take out of the Soviet Union. (*Kuprin is silent.*) I do not believe it. It could not be true. (*Hopefully.*) Is there a possibility, please, that it is not true?

KUPRIN. I don't know.

VERA. Do not see him. I am sorry I made you to meet him.

KUPRIN. Child. I met Smith when you were still learning your letters. Go to bed. Go to sleep, Verochka.

VERA. Vassili, please. Do not let anything happen to Smees.

KUPRIN. There is one Russian skill we should try to lose. We worry too well. (*She starts toward the archway.*) Verochka. (*She stops.*) I think you have fallen in love a few years too soon. (*She goes off quickly. Kuprin tests the radio again moodily, then flips it off. There is a flurry of excitement. A second Guard rushes down the path, with a rifle poised.*)

SECOND GUARD. (*Shouting toward the jetty. In Russian.*) Stop! Identify yourself!

FIRST GUARD. (*He appears at the top of the path. In Russian.*) What did you see?

KUPRIN. (*He comes out onto the porch. In Russian.*) What's the matter?

SECOND GUARD. (*In Russian.*) I thought I saw someone prowling.

FIRST GUARD. (*In Russian.*) Where?

SECOND GUARD. (*Pointing. In Russian.*) Out there.

FIRST GUARD. (*He goes up on the jetty, looks around, shakes his head. In Russian.*) I don't see anything.

FIRST GUARD. (*In Russian.*) We will check, Tovareesh Kuprin. (*The two Guards go up onto the jetty and cross out of sight. Kuprin, scowling, follows them a short distance. We hear the Soldiers' voices off, throwing challenges. Smith appears from under the jetty. He looks battered and unshaven. His coat is torn, his hand is bleeding. He glances around, then quickly crawls, army-style, into the house. Kuprin and the Guards come back and *hesitate on the porch. In Russian.*) Shall we look inside? (*Smith flattens himself against the bookcases.*)

KUPRIN. (*Shakes his head. In Russian.*) Not necessary. (*The Guards exit up the path, still searching. Kuprin comes into the house, stops short at the sight of Smith.*) I've been expecting you.

SMITH. Good. Does that mean you're ready to leave with me, Koopy?

KUPRIN. I think you've got a compulsion to suicide, Smith. What's the matter with your hand?

SMITH. You grow very sharp rocks around here.

KUPRIN. (*He glances out to make sure the Guards are gone.*) What do you think will happen to you—and to me—if they find you here?

SMITH. (*Tersely.*) You've got an appointment. At eleven o'clock. At the end of that jetty. There'll be a boat waiting. For both of us.

KUPRIN. (*Striding away from him.*) I don't want to hear about it!

SMITH. (*Pressing on.*) Out in the fog, there's a trawler. The boatman knows where. We can be in Turkish waters by sunrise.

KUPRIN. (*Shakes his head.*) Not possible. Let me do something about that hand.

SMITH. The first step is the longest. Then home. Back to the States. To Ohio, if you like.

KUPRIN. (*He gets a first-aid kit out of a drawer.*) It is not twenty-one years ago! What the hell is wrong with you, Smith? You've forgotten the most basic reality of science: the IRREVERSIBILITY OF TIME!

SMITH. You want to leave—don't you, Koopy?

KUPRIN. (*Overprotesting.*) No!

SMITH. I don't believe it.

KUPRIN. How did you get here? (*He daubs some Merthiolate on Smith's cut hand, and presses a piece of gauze against it.*)

SMITH. I came on a tour. (*Kuprin ties a handkerchief around Smith's hand.*)

KUPRIN. Fine. Be a tourist. See sights. Lie on the beach. Then fly back to America and tell Nadya that her father is completely happy.

SMITH. I can't do that, can I? Because it's a lie. (*He looks at his hand.*) Thanks.

KUPRIN. Now goodbye, Smith. Get back along the rocks before the tide comes in.

SMITH. No. I came here to help you, Koopy. To help you get away.

KUPRIN. (*Exploding.*) From what? From myself? Are you going to liberate my soul from my body? Disconnect my brain from my spinal cord, so you can take it back to your Bureau of Standards in a paper parcel?

SMITH. You don't belong here. You belong with us.

KUPRIN. Oh, the exquisite certainly of the Americans, who know precisely where everybody belongs.

SMITH. Remember how Nils Bohr got out of Nazi Germany in the belly of a bomber? Every scientist in the Free World cheered. They'll cheer you!

KUPRIN. Freedom—a generality.

SMITH. It is like hell! Why did you start to become an American citizen? (*Kuprin doesn't answer.*) I know why. Because a scientist, more than any other human being, must have the right to disagree. Even with his own findings. Even with himself!

KUPRIN. In the United States, I would be working for the military, for the government, the same as here.

SMITH. But nobody would threaten your mother or put you under house arrest if you refused. You could fish in the Mississippi River if you liked. (*Kuprin gestures him to silence. The Guard crosses down the path to the jetty. Smith waits.*) Koopy. I'm a door. I'm a passport. I'm a way out.

KUPRIN. What would I be? A renegade. In my own country, a name to be torn out of physics books. And in your country? Still a renegade. A kind of Soviet Benedict Arnold. Who would trust me in the U.S. or the U.K.? When I had turned my back so easily on the U.S.S.R.?

SMITH. You want to be told what to do all your life?

KUPRIN. At my university I am not required to sign an anti-American oath.

SMITH. When you're locked in a cage, you don't have to sign an oath that you won't run away!

KUPRIN. You have no respect for my patriotism.

SMITH. You're trying to Sovietize the world!

KUPRIN. You're trying to Americanize the world! You only believe in freedom if it has 1776 stamped on it. This is the country of my childhood, Smith. And bad as you think it may be, it is better than it was. And it can be better still. It must be. Every year we are getting to be more and more like the West!

SMITH. (*Penetratingly.*) Are you? How many people are fleeing *to* the Soviet Union? (*Kuprin is silent as the Guard paces from the jetty up the path again.*) Everybody you knew in Ohio—or their parents—or grandparents—did exactly what you really want to do! *CUT FREE*!

KUPRIN. A scientist who defects from the Soviet Union is a General who deserts. Do you realize that, Smith? I hold a rank equivalent to a General of the Red Army. And my responsibility is perfectly clear. I should call the guards back and have you arrested.

SMITH. (*Firm.*) You won't do that, Koopy. Because you want to leave. (*Kuprin shakes his head, no.*) You've wanted to leave for years. You tried to get out last July.

KUPRIN. Not true!

SMITH. Then why didn't you give your speech in Geneva?

KUPRIN. I couldn't go. (*Correcting himself, quickly.*) I decided not to go.

SMITH. Or wouldn't they *let* you go? Because you had plans, then, to leave the Soviet Union for good!

KUPRIN. (*Emotionally.*) No, no. (*Gesturing toward the jetty.*) And this plan *you* have now—it won't work. Forget about it. (*More quietly.*) Smith, I don't want you to get into trouble because of me. (*The phone rings. Kuprin crosses, picks it up.*) Ya slooshayu.

(*Smith checks his watch, then carefully moves out of the house, glancing up the path for the Guards. He jumps out onto the jetty to look for the boat. Kuprin, disturbed by what he hears, speaks briskly in Russian.*) At what time? How many degrees? I will be listening. (*He hangs up the phone and crosses to the radio. He clicks it on. We hear the sound of the Chelovyek. Warily, Smith comes back into the house.*)

SMITH. The Chelovyek? (*Kuprin, preoccupied, nods yes.*) The frequency's lower, isn't it?

KUPRIN. It's receding further into space.

SMITH. Doppler effect? (*Again Kuprin nods, and bends into the radio.*)

MIROFF'S VOICE. (*In Russian, weak, cavernous.*) I have followed all the procedures— (*All of Miroff's taped speech continuing behind the following:*)

SMITH. Is it Miroff? (*Kuprin nods. Miroff continues in Russian.*) What's he saying?

KUPRIN. (*In English, translating.*) I hope you are listening, Professor Kuprin. I wish that your eyes and your mind were in my body, so I would know what to do.

SMITH. What's wrong? (*Kuprin motions him to silence, and leans in closer, continuing to translate.*)

KUPRIN. I no longer have rotational stability. The black sky is tumbling over and over around me. (*There is a burst of static. Kuprin suddenly strides back and forth across the room, helpless, angry at himself.*)

MIROFF'S VOICE. (*In Russian.*) Neutron density: 164.7, 171.35, 180.90. (*He continues a flow of numbers in Russian, each slightly higher.*)

KUPRIN. For so many years, the power source wasn't strong enough. Now we have more power than we can control!

SMITH. What's he saying now?

KUPRIN. Instrument check.

SMITH. What happened, Koopy? (*Pause.*) What went wrong?

KUPRIN. I don't know. The most damning confession a scientist can make, isn't it? "I don't know." Before one piece of metal is welded to another, the theoretician—myself—tries to imagine every possible emergency. I travel ahead of each satellite, in my mind. "What if—?" I think over and over again: "What if—?" "What if—?" (*He breaks off, as Miroff stops counting and begins saying some words in Russian.*) Listen. (*Vera enters from the bedroom area, unseen by the men. She wears a robe and stands in the archway. Kuprin translates.*) If I fail to complete my mission, I ask— (*He breaks off. Kuprin closes his eyes. The Voice continues in Russian.*)

VERA. (*Translating softly as she crosses from archway.*) —I ask the forgiveness of my government and my friends and especially I ask your forgiveness, my dear Professor Kuprin.

SMITH. (*He turns, startled to see her.*) Vera. (*He reaches for her hand, but she slips past him to Kuprin's side. There is a burst of static and just the tone from the Chelovyek continues.*)

KUPRIN. (*Distressed.*) I never should have met Miroff. I never should have seen his face. They didn't want me to see him. I insisted. Do you know why, Smith? I read on his medical chart that he was born the same year, the same month as Mischa. (*Closing his eyes.*) Does Mischa have to die in every generation? (*The voice of Miroff continues in Russian.*)

SMITH. He's not dead. Listen.

KUPRIN. (*Translating, in English.*) I am now nearly six thousand seven hundred kilometers above the surface of the earth. I have traveled farther out into the universe than any man has ever been.

SMITH. (*A whisper.*) My God.

KUPRIN. More than a radius of the earth away from it.

SMITH. If he's in an open curve— (*The voice continues in Russian, and Kuprin translates.*)

KUPRIN. He says, "My eyes are moist, but the tears do not run down my cheeks, for there is no 'down.' " (*Another burst of static. The three lean closer into the radio to hear the fading voice.*) I missed that. A crescent. He sees a crescent of light along the Western Atlantic. But it is night in Europe. And deep night all across my beloved U.S.S.R. which— (*Kuprin breaks off, turning away from the radio. Smith looks at Vera questioningly.*)

VERA. (*Softly.*) Which I may never see again. Goodbye, Meadowland.

KUPRIN. (*He snaps off the radio, gets up and crosses toward the porch. Guiltily.*) Smith! You never killed a man, did you!

SMITH. Yes! In North Africa. During the war. I had to.

KUPRIN. But you didn't *know* the man you killed, did you?

SMITH. No.

KUPRIN. That would be easier, I think. Different. No. Not really different, in the eyes of God. If He watches such things. And if there *is* a God. (*Rapidly, in a kind of catharsis, lashing himself.*) If Miroff dies, it won't be the first. In the early experiments, they did not even have names. Or faces. Two died in the centrifuge, six inches off the ground. And how many others before Gagarin?

VERA. No, Vassili!

KUPRIN. (*In a surge of guilt.*) I admit this, Smith. You—your people are more careful with human life. I would not be responsible for what is happening tonight— (*Pointing toward the sky.*) —if we had reached Geneva. (*Vera, shocked, crosses to him, touches his lips.*)

VERA. Do not talk about it, Vassili!

KUPRIN. Smith knows! (*Facing Smith, opening his insides.*) There. Now. I say it out loud. Yes. I *did* try to leave. With Vera as my secretary, my mother to see doctors in Zurich. Oh, it was all worked out so carefully. So carefully it didn't work at all.

SMITH. Then leave with me now!

KUPRIN. (*Resignedly.*) There is no chance. Oh, Smith, do you know what my existence has been like since last July? How expertly I am "protected"? Everything I do is known. Every place I go, I am watched. Wherever I look, I see my "guardian." My jailer. Trifonov.

SMITH. (*Stunned.*) Trifonov! (*The full realization hits him. He turns to Vera.*) Holy God!

VERA. Smees—

SMITH. (*Decisively.*) We've got to go. All of us. (*He reaches toward Vera.*) We can all go together!

VERA. Oh, Smees, we cannot.

SMITH. Vera, I was so afraid I'd never see you again.

VERA. Were you afraid, Smees? I was afraid also. I am still afraid.

SMITH. Don't be afraid of someone who loves you. (*Smith embraces her. Then commandingly.*) Now, get ready.

KUPRIN. (*Remotely.*) It is not possible, Smith.

SMITH. It *is*, Koopy. You taught me: "Nothing in the universe is impossible." Improbable, maybe. A *chance*! But no event is forbidden. Back at the observatory, you told me that again and again: "ABSOLUTELY NOTHING IS IMPOSSIBLE!" (*He grips Kuprin by the shoulders.*) Is freedom worth a chance? (*Kuprin doesn't answer. The two men look at each other. Smith glances quickly at his watch. Trifonov enters slowly along the path.*)

KUPRIN. (*Abruptly.*) Verochka. Get dressed.

VERA. (*Hesitating.*) Vassili, I—

KUPRIN. Do as I say! (*Vera goes into the bedroom.*)

SMITH. I'll see if the boat's here.

KUPRIN. No! (*He starts for the jetty, but stops as he sees Trifonov.*)

TRIFONOV. Vassili Vladimorovitch, you would not like the Turkish Coast. It is oppressively hot in the summer.

SMITH. (*To Trifonov.*) "Tsushima," for God's sake! (*He starts toward Trifonov.*)

TRIFONOV. Mr. Smith. The guards are waiting. They will come when I call them. Use discretion. (*Gently.*) I do not enjoy what authority sometimes requires me to do. But I follow orders. I would prefer to live in libraries. Open a book, and let Count Tolstoy talk to me. Or listen to the songs of your so brilliant Walter Whitman. 1819–1892.

KUPRIN. What *are* your orders, Trifonov?

TRIFONOV. To protect you. (*Genuinely.*) I have infinite respect for you, Vassili. Your mind is one of the great treasures of the Soviet Union. However, if you try to leave, my instructions are explicit. (*Trifonov quietly takes out a small revolver.*)

KUPRIN. And if I don't go, if I refuse, what happens to Smith?

TRIFONOV. He will stand trial for espionage. Our courts are fair. (*Vera appears from the bedroom area. She is dressed.*)

SMITH. Vera. Stay inside. (*Vera gasps. Trifonov motions to her with the gun to come out on the porch.*)

TRIFONOV. (*In Russian.*) Over there! (*Vera crosses to Smith's side.*)

KUPRIN. What are we, Trifonov? Cave men? Are you more advanced because you are carrying a mechanized club? We are supposed to be civilized, Trifonov.

Why are we behaving like this? We are *winning*! Not *his* country, or *our* country, this man or that man. But MAN HIMSELF! All of us are *winning*!

TRIFONOV. You, your thoughts, your genius belong to the people of the Soviet Union!

KUPRIN. Who belongs to what—what difference does it make? Does it matter now, that Columbus was a Genoese, working for Spain? Copernicus a Pole? Kepler a German? Einstein a wandering Jew? Today, now, who cheers because Ptolemy was an Egyptian, Archimedes a Greek? What they *thought* matters. The IDEA matters. Man is winning. Don't make us all lose! (*Kuprin moves deliberately toward the jetty. Trifonov's gun follows him.*)

TRIFONOV. Vassili. Please do not try to leave.

KUPRIN. (*Shouting.*) I will try! And when you "follow your orders," Trifonov, you will be robbing your country, our planet, of what ideas I still have—many, many—in my head, in my notes, in the charts on those walls—meaningless to anyone but me. (*He takes a step closer to Trifonov.*) But I'll make a bargain with you. (*He gestures toward Smith and Vera.*) Let them go. And I will stay here. I will work. I will never again try to leave the Soviet Union. As your friend, I give you my word.

TRIFONOV. (*Impressed.*) As my friend!

KUPRIN. (*He crosses to Trifonov, touches his arm.*) Andrei, let them have the most priceless thing they can take to America: the knowledge that we have the potential for compassion. (*Slowly Trifonov lowers his gun.*) Go! (*Smith draws Vera toward the jetty.*)

MADAME KUPRINA. (*From within the house.*) Vassili! Vassili!

VERA. (*Turning back.*) Your mother—

KUPRIN. I will take care of her. (*Taking Vera's hand.*) We will see each other again, Verochka.

VERA. (*She is crying.*) We *will*!

SMITH. (*Taking Kuprin's hand.*) We *will*!

KUPRIN. Smith, tell them—

SMITH. I know what to tell them. The truth—about Copernicus, and Einstein, and Kuprin. Dasvadanya. (*Swiftly, Smith takes Vera along the jetty toward the waiting boat. Kuprin stares at Trifonov: will he keep his word? Very slowly, Trifonov puts the gun back in his pocket.*)

MADAME KUPRINA. (*Entering through the archway.*) Vassili! (*Kuprin crosses into the house, and takes his mother in his arms. Trifonov remains silent on the porch.*)

KUPRIN. What is it? What's wrong?

MADAME KUPRINA. I dreamed there was a war.

KUPRIN. A dream. That's all, Mamuschka. (*Quietly.*) Go back to sleep. Dream again. Dream that peace has been declared. (*From far off in the fog, we hear the cough of powerful motors revving up, then roaring away into the distance. The two Guards shout a warning in Russian, in response to the sound. But Trifonov waves them back.*)

TRIFONOV. (*Calling. In Russian.*) Nyet. Nyet. A fishing boat.

KUPRIN. Listen. Listen, Mamuschka. They are safe!

MADAME KUPRINA. (*Strangely.*) Safe? Who is safe? (*Trifonov hears this, and knows that it applies to him. Slowly, he turns and starts up the path. Kuprin waves a silent goodbye to Smith and Vera in the unseen boat. Then he turns slowly, lifts his eyes to the night sky. Above the overcast, unseen, the Chelovyek-Zvezda still circles. He raises his hand in a final salute and goodbye to the Man-Star.*)

CURTAIN

DIAMOND
ORCHID

Introduction

Casting was a problem for the Broadway production of *Diamond Orchid*. As had been the case with *A Call on Kuprin*, *Diamond Orchid* was rushed into production with a relatively inexperienced performer in the leading role (in this case, Jennifer West, who had triumphed the previous season in *Dutchman* off-Broadway). It was not a hit when it opened in New York in February 1965; a revised version (under the title *Sparks Fly Upward*) succeeded when produced at Southern Methodist University in December 1967 with a more experienced Nan Martin playing Felicia. Alexander Scourby's presence in the male lead also strengthened the latter piece.

Lawrence and Lee's preface describes the tortured path *Diamond Orchid* traveled on its way to Broadway and the problems with casting the central role. Early versions of the script suggest that the playwrights' textual difficulties lay in two central areas: the personality of Felicia/Paulita (the fictionalized Evita Peron), and the basic shape of the play. In a 1960 typescript, the play is in three acts and employs a flashback structure, both opening and closing in the plaza after the fall of the Brazo regime.[1] The central element in the first and last scenes is a crowd attempting to demolish a massive statue of Paulita. Orton appears in the first scene, preventing the statue's destruction; his efforts to explain Paulita's rise motivate the rest of the play. A chastened mob in the final scene permits the statue to be restored, understanding the need to be reminded constantly of the conditions that made Paulita's rise and the Brazo dictatorship possible.

The Paulita of the 1960 text is a harsher character than in later versions. She is far more self-conscious about her poverty, more driven to seek revenge against the aristocracy, and far more articulate about class divisions in her society. The character clearly manipulates both Orton and Brazo. While her motives are strongly visible, Paulita has fewer self-doubts and is far less sympathetic than she was to become. As Lawrence and Lee report, Vivien Leigh observed that the playwrights didn't like Paulita. Robert E. Lee later agreed: "It was quite true. And, as a matter of fact, that was a big flaw of the play. . . . We rewrote it with much more understanding, if not affection, for the role."[2]

By the 1963 version, the flashback structure had been dropped, three acts reshaped into two, and the first act of the play was close to the final version.[3] Paulita is softened, less driven, and less self-consciously political than in the earlier script. Some of the final elements of the play, missing from the 1960 text, are in place here. In the 1960 script, for example, Paulita wants to attend a reception at the

United States Embassy with Orton; the reception, hosted by Ambassador Loomis, ended the first act.[4] The 1963 text discards the reception, replacing it with the socially significant Pentecostal Ball as the aim of Paulita's ambition. The pre-Ball reception at the Casa Rivera (act 1, scene 4 in the version published here) appears for the first time in the 1963 script, as does Guzmano's speech, "You want to know the biggest number in the world? *One*! There is no number larger than one. One human being at a time," a clear statement of the playwrights' belief in the power of the individual.

Diamond Orchid's second act was more problematic. The 1963 text adds the first scene of the second act, with Brazo and Paulita in the Presidential Palace the night of his inauguration, and with Paulita teaching Brazo how to make love to a crowd. Unlike later in the final script, however, Paulita is in a negligee. Her European trip is presented through newsreels (1963 text's act 2, scene 4), a device deleted from both the Broadway version and the revision published here. The 1963 version also adds a scene for Orton in exile (act 2, scene 6), with Mama Jamas visiting to plead with him to help Paulita in her illness. The play ends with Paulita's collapse in the village church.

When produced on Broadway in 1965, *Diamond Orchid* had much the structure of the play as published here.[5] It ended, however, in Paulita's executive suite, following the scene in Guzmano's clinic. The dying Paulita, as reviewer Walter Kerr noted, "is dressed in her finery and carted limp to a public balcony."[6]

For the Dallas production, Lawrence and Lee returned to their original vision of the play, ending in the plaza as a mob destroys all traces of Brazoism, only to be stopped by Orton's vehement insistence that they accept culpability for Felicia's career. The Dallas version also adds the young girl at the end, and the pessimistic suggestion that the social conditions which created Felicia have not been resolved, that the rise to power of a strong-willed dictator can happen again.

The weakness of the play's second act as performed on Broadway was noted by several of the New York newspaper reviewers. Richard Watts, Jr., regarded the second act as "a hasty and incomplete first draft following unfortunately on an opening section filled with high dramatic promise."[7] According to John McClain, "the latter portion of the play seems to have been rather spottily constructed, with the story line jumping here and there in short, unfulfilled vignettes."[8] Many years later Jerome Lawrence said, "We made far too many cuts in *Diamond Orchid*."[9] The cuts, restored for the version published here, helped make the play's second act appear disjointed on Broadway.

Adding to *Diamond Orchid*'s problems was the central performance, as Lawrence and Lee note in their introduction. Their view is supported by New York newspaper reviewers. Norman Nadel said that Jennifer West "is equally accountable for the fiasco. The real Evita was a bad actress, and Miss West fails to make even that believable."[10] John McClain reported that "her strenuous vocal attack on some of the final scenes was enough to produce titters from the rear of the hall."[11] Kerr wrote that West "is in difficulties very quickly, breathlessly skipping past emotions, ignoring transitions, swallowing words—all in an effort to make lightning do what plain speech won't."[12]

Too many cuts and an inadequate performance in the leading role doomed *Diamond Orchid* in New York. The revised script's success in Dallas as *Sparks Fly Upward* confirms the importance of the critical response to the first performance of any play. Whether *Diamond Orchid* might have succeeded with better performances in 1965 and without the desperate cutting of dialogue to shore up weak acting that apparently took place during the out-of-town tryout cannot, of course, be determined. As printed here, *Diamond Orchid* presents Felicia as a sympathetic figure; her savagery when she finally gains power is clearly motivated by her deprivations in early life, and her drive for acceptance at any cost is also fully explored. Felicia's ability to believe in her own myth is demonstrated in several key scenes, notably as she plots Brazo's release from prison (act 1, scene 7), and as she distributes charity to the poor (act 2, scene 3).

The playwrights also provide several instances of Felicia's magnetism (act 1, scene 3, as she seduces both Brazo and Garcia; act 1, scene 7, winning over the labor leaders; the final scene of the first act, as she learns her power over the crowd). In those instances, Felicia's personality is shown in action, rather than merely being described by other characters. Indeed, one of the weaknesses of the 1960 version was precisely in this area; only one scene (the successful rally in the plaza, in the 1960 text act 2, scene 3) demonstrated the character's abilities, although her charismatic qualities were mentioned numerous times. The final version of the script does not require the performer to add unwritten dimensions to the character—Felicia is shown in action. While an individual actress might not embody Felicia's attractiveness, the attraction is provided by the lines of the text, at least in the version performed in Dallas.

Lawrence and Lee's fictionalization of the life and death of Evita Peron followed the rough outlines of Evita's career.[13] The real Eva Duarte was born illegitimately, in poverty, and made her way to Buenos Aires, where she became a radio actress. Untutored, she eventually became the mistress of Colonel Juan Peron and, after he seized power in 1945, his wife. Although she appears to have had little to do with the events of 17 October 1945, Peronist mythology eventually gave her a central role in orchestrating the crowds who forced Peron on a reluctant government. The real Eva Peron defied the Argentine elite; her conflict with the Sociedad de Beneficencia (Charitable Society) and their refusal to name her as their honorary president is reflected in Felicia's offering Mama Jamas as president of the Society for Benevolence after confronting Dona Elena (act 2, scene 2).[14] Orton is based loosely on the figure of Ernesto Sammartino, a member of the Chamber of Deputies rumored to have been an early lover of Eva who eventually escaped into exile in Uruguay. Felicia's tour of Europe parallels Evita's 1947 "Rainbow Tour," during which she was awarded the Grand Cross of Isabel the Catholic by Francisco Franco, while Pope Pius XII effectively snubbed her by presenting only a rosary at a general audience.

There was a major effort to nominate Eva Peron for the vice presidency in 1951, but her illness from cancer (along with other political concerns) led her to refuse the honor; she died from uterine cancer on 26 July 1952. Her last public appearance was at Peron's inauguration on 4 June; a brace hidden by her fur coat allowed her to stand in an open car during the inaugural parade. Evita's appearances during her last few months, heavily supported by Peron, are the source for the final scene in the Broadway version of *Diamond Orchid.*

Only Guzmano, his Nobel Prize and his back-country clinic, correspond to nothing in the life of the real Evita. Here Lawrence and Lee have freely invented, providing a clear contrast between Felicia's false charity and Guzmano's selflessness. The figure of Dona Elena is also invented, providing a single individual representing the oligarchic aristocracy in stark opposition to the *arriviste* Felicia. The playwrights' invention of a local society event to replace the American Embassy reception of the 1960 text of *Diamond Orchid* happily focuses Felicia's social ambitions.

Lawrence and Lee have compressed the time of the historic events in Eva Peron's life for theatrical economy. While based on actuality, Felicia's European tour, the first signs of her illness, and the campaign for the vice presidency are all combined skillfully into a single chronological sequence. Her rise to power is similarly condensed. Otherwise, the playwrights have been faithful to the outline of Eva Peron's career and life.

The image of Felicia/Paulita/Evita, rising to power and driven by the need to escape from grinding poverty, is a powerful one. Lawrence and Lee's dramatization of Eva Peron's life permits the playwrights to explore the nature of power and the roots of dictatorship. While *Diamond Orchid* has a far darker view of humanity than the other plays produced by the collaboration of Jerome Lawrence and Robert E. Lee, and has had correspondingly less success than their usual demonstrations of the power of the individual to effect change, it remains nonetheless a riveting exploration of the abuses of power.

NOTES

1. Jerome Lawrence and Robert E. Lee, *Diamond Orchid,* typescript (1960), Lawrence and Lee Collection 5:1, Jerome Lawrence and Robert E. Lee Theatre Research Institute, The Ohio State University.

2. Robert E. Lee, interview, 28 December 1988.

3. Jerome Lawrence and Robert E. Lee, *Diamond Orchid,* typescript, Lawrence and Lee Collection 5:3.

4. Loomis is a favorite name with the playwrights; characters, both major and minor, with that name appear in each of the other plays included in this anthology. Ambassador Loomis

disappeared from *Diamond Orchid* after revisions, making the play unique among Lawrence and Lee's published work for its lack of a Loomis.

5. The Broadway text for *Diamond Orchid* is not available; the play's structure is reconstructed here from programs for its tryout at the Shubert Theatre, New Haven (20–23 January 1965) and the National Theatre, Washington, D.C. (25 January–6 February 1965). Lawrence and Lee Collection 5:6, Lawrence and Lee Theatre Research Institute.

6. Walter Kerr, "Theater: *Diamond Orchid*," *New York Herald Tribune*, 11 February 1965, rpt. *New York Theatre Critics Reviews* (abbrev. *NYTCR*) 26 (1965): 378.

7. Richard Watts, Jr., "Two on the Aisle," *New York Post*, 11 February 1965, rpt. *NYTCR* 26 (1965): 379.

8. John McClain, "Fine Peron Story Runs Off the Rails," *New York Journal American*, 11 February 1965, rpt. *NYTCR* 26 (1965): 380.

9. Jerome Lawrence, interview, 28 December 1988.

10. Norman Nadel, "'Diamond Orchid' in the Rough," *New York World-Telegram and the Sun*, 11 February 1965, rpt. *NYTCR* 26 (1965): 379.

11. McClain, 380.

12. Kerr, 378.

13. I have drawn heavily upon Joseph A. Page's major work, *Peron: A Biography* (New York: Random House, 1983) for the historic data in the following paragraphs. Eva Peron's *My Mission in Life*, trans. Ethel Cherry (New York: Vantage, 1953) is a clear example of mythmaking in action.

14. Otelo Borroni and Roberto Vacca, *La vida de Eva Peron* (Buenos Aires: Editorial Galerna, 1970), 1:137, as cited by Page, 188–89.

FOREWORD

In the summer of 1952 (winter in South America), JL stumbled into the airport in Buenos Aires—on the day Evita Peron died. It was pure chance.

Here's an account of what happened in a letter sent to Bob and Janet Lee:

Dear Bob and Jan, August 4, 1952

I arrived here in Montevideo a few minutes ago. I didn't write you from B.A.—because it's a madhouse. I've never had such an experience in my life. I couldn't write from there because, first, they tell me letters are confiscated or censored—and suddenly, you'll find yourself slapped into jail—and second, everything's paralyzed. Even the post-office is closed, and the people are milling through the streets, mad, hypnotized, strangled, paralyzed—by a dead woman.

Let me start back at Santiago. The trip to B.A. over the Andes was something I shall never forget. We flew 19,000 feet high—right past the highest mountain in South America, 23,000 feet, so close you could touch it. I tipped my sombrero to the Christ of the Andes. Jesus, what a statue! But the whole thing was like flying over the Himalayas—even more breath-taking than the flight from Lima to Cuzco!

A few minutes before we reached Mendoza and the Argentine border, they took our cameras away. By this time it was dark, and I complained: "If anybody can invent a way to take pictures with a camera like this, in the dark, from 19,000 feet high, he'll make a fortune!" They didn't like this.

When we landed at B.A., it began. First we had to have a silent moment of prayer at the airport for the soul of the First Lady! Then you saw her picture—everywhere, EVERYWHERE! Customs was the roughest I've ever gone through. They examined every sock! Police clearance. Questions right and left.

Then into town. I lugged my own luggage through the dark and shrouded streets: every street lamp in the city is draped in black. People sobbing everywhere. People milling through the streets—a mad orgy of mourning!

At the hotel—nobody working but the owner. It was an official week of mourning—all unions were in the streets paying tribute to their Evita. Bob and Jan, it sounds dreadful; but I wouldn't have missed seeing this for anything in the world!

The whole thing was like watching Nazi Germany in the early days of

> Hitler's rise to power. And what a great play there is in this woman—(excuse me, Jan)—this *whore* who came to power. And strangely enough, she did a tremendous amount of good—so much so that two million people lined up in queues four miles long—waiting 16 hours in the cold, in the rain, through the night—just to pass her casket.
>
> I talked to people, to everybody I could who spoke English. Why did they love her so? Why did they idolize her? Because she did things for the poor. But, I said, at the expense of your freedoms! Their answers were strangely logical—"Before we had the freedom to starve, the freedom to let our children die from sickness."
>
> I can't begin to tell you everything in this letter or a dozen letters. There's a hell of a play in this, Bob, a great part for a great actress! She was a strikingly beautiful woman, was Evita. And damn smart! And, oh, do I have stories to tell you about her!
>
> Got into several scrapes with the police and the soldiers when I tried to take some pictures—and they tried to rip the film from my camera—they thought I was making fun of their solemn mourning. Nobody hurt!
>
> Montevideo is like basking in the quiet sunshine after being in the hail-storm that was B.A. The city, the country, is on an emotional tear that is impossible to conceive! If I had planned it, I couldn't have arrived there at a more dramatic moment!

JL got back to California well before Labor Day, after a stop in Rio. Bob and Janet returned home from a teaching stint at the Banff School of Fine Arts in Alberta, Canada. The first thing Bob said to JL was: "I've already begun researching her. I've got a file folder full of newspaper clips about Evita, and I'm half-way through reading her holier-than-thou autobiography."

In the months and years that followed we read and researched everything we could find about this Fascist Cinderella. We met with Fleur Cowles, who had written the best book on the Perons, *Bloody Precedent,* published in 1952, just a few months before Evita's death. It was Fleur who told us about the symbol of power Evita had worn: a lapel brooch, a gaudy orchid five inches across and seven inches long, made of pure white diamonds that cost the people of Argentina more than a quarter of a million dollars. That gave us the title of the first version of the play: *Diamond Orchid.* And we started to write.

In her book Fleur Cowles expressed what was our point of view, too. But she had met this diamond-hard flower in person, and wrote this vivid description: "I cannot obliterate the image of this woman-politico with too much power, too much rage, too many flunkies in high government places, too little opposition, too much greed, too much money; a woman too fabled, too capable, too sexless, too driven, too overbearing, too slick, too neurotic, too shy, too tense, too sneering, too diamond-decked, too revengeful, too hateful of North Americans, too ambitious—and far, far too underrated for far too long by our world."

The Dallas, then Broadway productions of *Inherit the Wind*, followed by the

New York production of *Auntie Mame*, delayed our second draft of *Diamond Orchid.* We had previously begun exploring the possibility of writing a work for the theatre on a woman evangelist like Aimee Semple McPherson. When Greer Garson replaced Rosalind Russell in the role of the non-musical Mame at the Broadhurst, she told us that she also wanted to play a fictional Aimee for the stage, and perhaps later for the flicks. So one Sunday night, when the Broadhurst was dark, we became co-explorers on this theme. Billy Graham was pack.ng them in at Madison Square Garden. Greer put on a babushka, hiding her distinctive flaming hair, and wore no make-up. Nobody recognized her as we sat in the first row of the balcony, just above the shouting preacher, studying Billy Graham's methods, his expressions, his evangelical hypnotism of the mob in the Garden.

In the cab, on our way back to her hotel, we looked at each other. A religioso evangelist, especially a female one, was not nearly as exciting as a political lady rabble-rouser. How much more dramatic and theatrical was the inverse epiphany of an Evita Peron.

We flew back to California and tackled the third draft of the play.

We wanted to hear it read aloud, and we invited two old friends for that first reading in JL's Malibu living room, Nina Foch and William Conrad. The sound of waves of the Pacific was an interesting counter-melody. The play came alive. When we finished, Nina clutched her freshly-mimeographed copy.

"May I keep this copy?" she asked. "I want to have this always, as it is—before it's fucked up by a lot of producers, directors, scenic designers, yes, *and* actors!"

We sent a copy east to our agent, Harold Freedman, who gave it first to the best producers in the business: Robert Whitehead and Roger Stevens, who decided immediately to produce it in concert with another distinguished man-of-the-theatre, Alfred de Liagre. Whitehead sent the play to Charles Laughton, who agreed to direct it, providing we could find the proper actress. "The rehearsal process," Laughton said, "is too bloody difficult. I cannot be expected also to teach some bloody amateur how to act. We must have the best actress, the very best, the most experienced."

Who?

We began following Vivien Leigh around the country (she was touring in *Battle of Angels*), offering her the fourth draft of the play, the fifth, the sixth. She was tempted.

"But," she said. "I don't think I can play this. You don't like this woman, that's the trouble. Besides, it's too rich; it should be an opera!"

Laughton took sick. Whitehead dropped the play. De Liagre agreed to go on with it, solo. He signed Jose Quintero as director; he's a Panamanian, he understood the Latin temperament. Jose joined us on what seemed like an endless search for an actress. We flew to England to talk to Dorothy Tutin. She was excited about it; she wanted to begin playing the part at Bristol Old Vic, her favorite acting home. It kept being postponed.

Our old friend Dore Schary stepped in as producer and made some cogent suggestions about the fascinating lady and her less than fascinating husband. But he, too, failed to get the play air-borne.

Then the fabled Gilbert Miller, who owned his father's Broadway playhouse, Henry Miller's, took over as producer, in concert with Roger Stevens, back where it started. We all decided to take a chance on an unknown: Jennifer West, who had done nobly in an Off-Broadway production of *Dutchman*. We surrounded her with a notable cast: Finlay Currie as a South-American Schweitzer named Guzmano, Helen Craig as Evita's mother.

Opening night on Broadway, the too-inexperienced Miss West reached a peak of hysteria: she screamed the entire part. Jose Quintero paced across the stage following the final curtain, muttering to himself: "She didn't do anything I told her; not a goddam thing."

The reviews were drab; the critics never really saw the play we wrote; it closed that Saturday night. The heads of Twentieth-Century Fox, who had bought it for a film in a pre-production deal, with accustomed "shrewdness" shelved it.

A year later, Dallas critic John Rosenfield asked us to come up with a play as a memorial to Margo Jones at Southern Methodist University. We sent him a copy of *Diamond Orchid*, some pre-Broadway cuts made in desperation restored, and re-titled: *Sparks Fly Upward*. The brilliant academic director Burnet Hobgood recruited Nan Martin and Alexander Scourby for the leads. The play again sounded as right as it had in our typewriters and at the first reading on the shores of the Pacific.

But despite the success of that production (including rave reviews) the play is rarely performed. *Evita*, the near-opera production Vivien Leigh had predicted, has been a gigantic hit, thanks to the razz-ma-tazz theatrical staging by Hal Prince. Are we bitter? A little. We're very fond of our play, what it says. And we're glad we wrote it. It's published by Dramatists Play Service and now here, to read, to be performed. Unsung though it may be.

Lawrence & Lee

EDITOR'S NOTE

Diamond Orchid is available in an acting edition, under the title *Sparks Fly Upward*, from Dramatists Play Service, who published the text in 1967. That text, revised slightly from the Broadway production, is reprinted here.

Jennifer West in *Diamond Orchid,* New York, 1965. Photo by Jerome Lawrence. Jerome Lawrence and Robert E. Lee Collection, Lawrence and Lee Theatre Research Institute, The Ohio State University.

CAST

Man is born unto trouble
As the sparks fly upward.
Job 5:7

Sparks Fly Upward opened at McFarlin Auditorium, Dallas, Texas, on 3 December 1967. It was produced as a benefit for the Margo Jones Special Fund by the University Theatre of Southern Methodist University. The production was directed by Burnet M. Hobgood, with scenery by Alan G. Leach. The cast included:

FELICIA .... Nan Martin
MAXIMILIAN ORTON .... Alexander Scourby
RADIO DIRECTOR .... Robert Dracup
RADIO ANNOUNCER .... William Shapard, Frederick Bailey
SOUND EFFECTS MAN .... Jack Robinson
STUDIO ENGINEER .... Richard Ceilley
RADIO ACTOR .... Charles H. Roberts
STUDIO EXECUTIVE .... John MacLehan
JORGE SALVADOR BRAZO .... Gene Ross
GARCIA .... William Utay
DONA ELENA RIVERA .... Eloise Swanson
DR. DOMINGO GUZMANO .... Frank Janson
BUTLER .... Jack Heifner
FOOTMEN .... David Moffatt, David Teed, John MacLehan
SOLDIERS .... John Nance, Jack Leonard, William Brenner, Milton Justice, Jack Robinson
CARLOS .... Steve Ochsenschlager
PORTERO .... Denis Adams
AGUILA .... Robert Dracup
WAITRESS .... Rozanne Gates
OLD MAN .... Jack Heifner
CAPTAIN .... Thomas Parsell
LIEUTENANT .... David Moffatt
CITIZENS .... Eva Price, Ed Price, Jan Carroll Davis, Frances Alford, Peggy Long, Gay Mallon
SOCIAL SECRETARY .... Louise Kent Kane
CLERK-TYPIST .... Lis Morris
EUGENIO .... Charles H. Roberts

CECILE .... Sharon Ulrick
CHAUFFEUR .... William Brenner
MAMA JAMAS .... Raven Hail
OLD WOMAN .... Claudia Nickerson
OLD-MAN-WITH-A-CRUTCH .... Richard Ceilley
POOR-MAN-WITH-CAP .... John MacLehan
FATHER MODESTO .... David Teed

Diamond Orchid opened in New York at Henry Miller's Theatre on 10 February 1965, It was produced by Gilbert Miller in association with Stevens Productions, Inc., and directed by Jose Quintero. Scenery and lighting were designed by David Hays, with costumes by Donald Brooks. The cast included:

MAXIMILIANO ORTON .... Bruce Gordon
PAULITA [FELICIA] .... Jennifer West
ANNOUNCER .... William Cottrell
DIRECTOR .... Leon B. Stevens
SOUND EFFECTS MAN .... John Garces
RADIO ACTOR .... Felice Orlandi
JORGE SALVADOR BRAZO .... Mario Alcalde
STUDIO EXECUTIVE .... Mel Haynes
GARCIA .... Bruce Kirby
DONA ELENA RIVERA .... Margery Maude
DR. DOMINGO GUZMANO .... Finlay Currie
NEWSCASTER .... John Armstrong
FIRST SOLDIER .... Gerald McGonagill
SECOND SOLDIER .... Borah Silver
THIRD SOLDIER .... John Garces
FOURTH SOLDIER .... James Goodnow
CARLOS .... William Cottrell
PORTERO .... Louis Guss
AGUILA .... Leonardo Cimino
OLD MAN .... Rene Enriquez
WAITRESS .... Betty Hellman
CAPTAIN .... Gerald McGonagill
LIEUTENANT .... Borah Silver
SOCIAL SECRETARY .... Patricia Jenkins
MALE SECRETARY .... John Garces
MAMA .... Helen Craig
OLD WOMAN .... Mary Bell
MAN-WITH-CAP .... Felice Orlandi
CARDINAL FRAZZINI .... Leon B. Stevens
NURSE .... Betty Hellman

SERVANTS .... John Sarno, Felice Orlandi, Rene Enrique, James Goodnow, John Armstrong

Diamond Orchid was produced prior to its Broadway run at the Shubert Theatre, New Haven, opening on 20 January 1965, and at the National Theatre, Washington, D.C., opening 25 January 1965.

THE PLACE is a Latin-American country.
THE TIME is the recent past.
The play is in two acts.

The action of the play is continuous; one scene flows into the next without interruption.

The scenic design is simple and telegraphic. The action is encircled by the skyline of a Latin-American capital, seen against a cyclorama on which the colors change to suit the hour and the mood of each scene.

The settings are not literal; they are indicated in imaginative shorthand. The people, their clothing and props are completely real, but they move with Elizabethan freedom. The city is there, part of the action, part of the mood, in all scenes except the clinic.

The entire scheme should be swift and bold.

The people of the play do not speak with even a hint of a Spanish accent. Since they are, for the most part, literate and educated men and women, the translation of their words into English does not carry with it the corruption of sounds sometimes associated with Latin-Americans using our language. They are speaking their own language, and speaking it well. When a Spanish word appears in context, it should be pronounced flawlessly. The English should be spoken with equal felicity.

Diamond Orchid

ACT ONE

Scene 1

Felicia's apartment. The ample bed seems so thoroughly slept in that it is impossible to tell whether anyone is still in it.

A man's clothes are draped over a chair, with a pair of highly polished shoes underneath. The frame of a full-length mirror stands so that anyone looking into it is facing directly into the audience.

The bedclothes move slightly; there is something alive and probably feminine hidden beneath the covers.

Orton comes into the light. He is a great lover of life and all its tastes, carnal and intellectual.

He wears a dressing gown and slippers. He takes a pack of cigarettes out of a pocket of his robe and puts one in his mouth, pats the pockets of his suit coat, and scans the room for a match.

ORTON. (*With the dry cigarette in his mouth.*) Felicia? (*No answer from the bed.*) Child, are you asleep? (*Felicia wriggles in the bed, the blankets over her head.*) Is there such a thing as a match in this establishment? (*A willowy arm reaches out from under the covers. Like a graceful white snake, the jaws of the hand close on a box of penny matches in the feminine debris on a bedside table. The arm flings the matches toward the voice. The matchbox clatters to the floor. With an effort, Orton bends down, picks it up. Lighting his cigarette.*) There's no doubt about it. You are the perfect hostess. (*He sighs, starts to pull on his trousers.*)

FELICIA. (*From under the covers, sleepily.*) What are you doing, Maxo?

ORTON. Putting on my trousers.

FELICIA. Why?

ORTON. Because I don't usually go to my office naked.

FELICIA. (*Still unseen beneath the covers.*) Why go to your office? They can make soap without you.

ORTON. I don't want them to find it out. (*She rolls over, still concealed in the bundle of blankets.*)

FELICIA. Maxo. Have you ever been in bed with a great actress? (*A short pause.*)

ORTON. (*Leaning into the mirror to look at a nick in his chin.*) Yes. Just now. (*Felicia flings off the bedclothes, and we see her for the first time.*)

FELICIA. Darling Maxo! I love you for that! (*She leaps out of bed, barefoot, in a lacy negligee, her hair loose. She takes the cigarette out of Orton's mouth so she can kiss him. Then she keeps the cigarette for herself, jumping back into bed and drawing on it, her knees tucked snugly against her compact breasts.*) But I didn't mean *me.* A *famous* actress, in the movies. Have you ever slept with one of the French ones? Or Italian? Maxo? (*He doesn't answer. He is lighting himself another cigarette.*) With the big breast-works, 'way out to here— (*She gestures.*) —like the headlights on a Rolls Royce?

ORTON. Those hot cinema sex-pots are cold bouillabaisse in bed. So I'm told. (*She laughs and watches while Orton dresses himself. Felicia may be a beautiful woman, but so static a word as "beauty" is hardly a description for her. Every attitude she takes is bright with tension. With the high wind of temperament, she can sweep across a wide range of moods. Her lack of education and refinement is not concealed by any artful veneers, it is simply unimportant. What she lacks is hidden by what she possesses: an intense vitality. She is like some scarlet fabric, whose coarse weave goes unnoticed in its blaze of color. Orton breathes heavily as he starts to put on his shoes.*)

FELICIA. (*Leaping out of bed.*) Let me do that. (*She helps him on with one shoe, and starts to tie it.*)

ORTON. (*A little surprised.*) Why, thank you, child.

FELICIA. You're surprised when I do something nice, aren't you?

ORTON. With you, I'm perpetually surprised. (*She has tied one shoe. With deliberate contrariness, she yanks the lace out of the other, dangles it in front of him. He reaches for it, but she pops into bed and toys with the shoelace.*)

FELICIA. You'd be sick of me in three days, if I were nice to you all the time. Like everybody else is. Yes-ing and bowing and running to open doors for you. Just because you're such a big, important, name-in-the-papers, rich, political fat-ass! They're all afraid of you. Except me. I'm not. (*She looks at the shoelace, debating—then tosses it to him playfully.*) I'm not afraid of you at all. (*Orton threads the lace into his shoe. She rolls over on the bed and stares at the ceiling.*) It must be marvelous to have people be afraid of you. I think that's what God must like best. Fear. It would be so much more exciting than incense, and candlesmoke, and all those hallelujahs. (*She bites her knuckle, rather sadly.*) Poor God. I feel sorry for Him: He has to go to Mass every day.

ORTON. You're lying on my necktie.

FELICIA. (*Furiously.*) You don't listen to me.

ORTON. You don't listen to *me.*

FELICIA. Of course not. The only way to endure a man is to turn him off!

ORTON. I've got a present for you.

FELICIA. (*Quickly.*) Where is it?

ORTON. (*Delighted.*) You were listening!

FELICIA. (*Jumping out of bed again.*) Give it to me now.

ORTON. (*Smoothing his rumpled necktie.*) What if there isn't any? (*Felicia grabs the shoe away from him and flings it squarely into his stomach. Orton collapses on the bed.*)

FELICIA. (*Suddenly contrite.*) Did I hurt you?

ORTON. (*Winded.*) Of course.

FELICIA. I'm sorry.

ORTON. (*Affably.*) No, you're not. You're a bad-mannered little bitch. (*Angrily she brandishes the shoe at him again. Hastily he gets up, retreating from her.*) Respect! Respect for a Senator of the Republic!

FELICIA. You *bought* your way into the Senate!

ORTON. I was freely elected.

FELICIA. You were expensively elected! You sold yourself the same way you sell your soap. (*She is stalking him around the room, while he limps in one stockinged foot.*)

ORTON. Not true!

FELICIA. You had so many pictures of yourself pasted on every shack and fence and telephone pole, of course people voted for you. So they wouldn't have to look at you any more. You and your lopsided face!

ORTON. My face is not lopsided.

FELICIA. On that pillow, when you're lying on your side, you ought to see yourself.

ORTON. Fortunately, most of the voters don't. (*She laughs, kneels, takes his foot to slip on the shoe.*)

FELICIA. (*Feeling the bottom of his foot.*) My God, you don't have any arches at all. (*Putting the shoe on his foot, tying the lace.*) My poor Maxo. A lopsided face and no arches. (*She giggles at the thought.*)

ORTON. I may drink hemlock. (*Looking at his watch.*) I had twenty things to do this afternoon. And you're the only one I did.

FELICIA. Hold your foot still, or I'll make you tie this yourself.

ORTON. I've had my exercise.

FELICIA. What's hemlock?

ORTON. You're hemlock.

FELICIA. I want to know.

ORTON. Did you ever read a book, child? Every word, clear to the very end?

FELICIA. Of course not. I may *write* a book someday. I'll read *that* one. (*Restlessly.*) Books! You give all that money for libraries. Do you think anybody looks up to see your name dug in the marble? Nobody. Kids go inside to stick gum under the chairs; the old men go in to use the urinals.

ORTON. See? I'm a public servant.

FELICIA. Like hell. You're selfish, Maxo.

ORTON. (*Amused, pulling her to his lap.*) Am I?

FELICIA. You don't know how to live. (*He kisses her, fondly.*)

ORTON. Tell me how to live.

FELICIA. You really want to know?

ORTON. From an authority.

FELICIA. First of all, get rid of your wife.

ORTON. Impossible. (*He holds her affectionately.*) In a country where the marriage vows are held so sacred. (*Orton puts another cigarette in his mouth, but Felicia snatches it as she leaps up.*)

FELICIA. You smoke too much. (*He crumples an empty pack.*)

ORTON. You're a splendid example.

FELICIA. Next you ought to get rid of that mausoleum where your wife lives. And all that junk they told you was art.

ORTON. All right, I am de-wifed, de-nicotined and de-Picassoed. Now what? (*She thinks.*)

FELICIA. Abolish the Senate.

ORTON. Put myself out of work?

FELICIA. And see that there's some justice around. (*She lights Orton's last cigarette for herself.*)

ORTON. Justice for Felicia.

FELICIA. Why shouldn't I want for myself what everybody else wants?

ORTON. You know what everybody wants?

FELICIA. You're damned right I know.

ORTON. What do you think they want?

FELICIA. They don't want to *think*, I'll tell you that!

ORTON. (*Looking around.*) Where's my briefcase?

FELICIA. (*Stalking him as he looks for the briefcase.*) If they're hungry, they want a plate of beans and a bottle of beer. And if they're not hungry, they want something *better* than beans and beer. Maybe a place to make love, without Grandma and the kids listening, and a goat peeing in the corner. You know what your trouble is, Maxo? You've forgotten how to *want*!!! What do you want, except food, and brandy, and a woman once in a while? You don't even want money.

ORTON. I've *got* money.

FELICIA. You haven't got a cigarette. (*Passionately.*) And if somebody wants a cigarette, by God, *give* it to 'im! (*She takes Orton's cigarette out of her own mouth and thrusts it back in his.*) That's justice!

ORTON. I've always wondered what it was. Now I know.

FELICIA. You don't know anything about politics. Politics is *gambling*. And nobody can be a real gambler unless he's *poor*. You lose a million pesos in the stock market, what the hell, it doesn't mean anything. But the poor peon who bets five pesos on a cockfight, there's a real gambler. If *he* loses, he doesn't eat! And he's in there, up close, where it happens, with clawing and the blood and the dirt!

ORTON. Colorful, but inaccurate. The President of our Republic doesn't gamble. Takes no chances, offends nobody. He isn't even rich: he's working on it.

FELICIA. President Sit-On-His-Ass!

ORTON. He's afraid if he stands up, somebody'll pull the chair out from under him. (*Looking around.*) What did I do with my briefcase?

FELICIA. When am I going to see you?

ORTON. Soon.

FELICIA. Tomorrow?

ORTON. Can't.

FELICIA. (*Quickly, defensively.*) Neither can I. (*Orton has his coat and briefcase, gives her a farewell peck.*)

ORTON. I'll phone you. (*He pats her chin-line as if she were a little girl. He speaks softly, fondly.*) Thank you for the siesta, child.

FELICIA. (*Furious, but quiet.*) Why do you keep calling me "child"?

ORTON. Because you *are* a child. Immature as a tadpole and delightful to be with.

FELICIA. (*In an emotional explosion.*) Then BE with me!!! (*The flood gate breaks open, the whole tide of her outrage at being so dispensable to Orton.*) You think it's any fun, being squeezed in between the soap and the Senate? When you feel like it. When YOU feel like it! What do you think I do between the time you go out that door and when I see you again? *Knit*??? My God, I go crazy, there's nothing to do!

ORTON. You can catch up on the movies—

FELICIA. I'm caught. I've seen them all. Most of them twice.

ORTON. You have your work—

FELICIA. An hour a day. Not every day, even. Forty-five minutes rehearsal, fifteen minutes on the air.

ORTON. The sponsor's happy. You're selling soap.

FELICIA. That's all you care about. Your filthy soap! And what a soap. Alkali and lilacs. I wouldn't touch the slimy stuff. I'd get leprosy first. That's the trouble with you, Maxo. Soap! You're so clean, you smell! (*He puts down his briefcase, tries to placate her.*)

ORTON. Child— (*The word slipped out involuntarily.*)

FELICIA. (*Shrieks.*) DON'T CALL ME "*CHILD*"!!! (*Orton puts his arms around her affectionately. She begins to cry, part in loneliness, more in fury at her loneliness. Orton puts a forefinger on her cheek.*)

ORTON. (*Tasting the tear.*) Salt-water. This is no river, no lake. This is a tidal-wave of emotion.

FELICIA. (*Almost begging.*) Take me *OUT*!

ORTON. I do.

FELICIA. Little hole-in-the-wall restaurants—

ORTON. Where they serve the best food outside of Paris.

FELICIA. And where nobody ever sees us.

ORTON. My chi— (*He breaks off.*) Felicia, don't you think we owe some consideration to my wife?

FELICIA. (*In growing fury.*) Your "wife"? What good is she? If she had an electric plug, you could use her to make ice cubes for drinks.

ORTON. Please—

FELICIA. You can't even stand to look at her. She's got a face like the Rio de Oro basin after a dry summer! Wife! All because fifty years ago some priest rattled off a lot of Latin in a church.

ORTON. It was a cardinal. In a cathedral. And it was 19 years ago.

FELICIA. A cardinal can't make a husband and wife. A marriage is made in a bed!

ORTON. What do you want me to do?

FELICIA. Take me someplace. To the U.S. Embassy. You're always invited to those fancy receptions.

ORTON. Totally impractical.

FELICIA. Why?

ORTON. They wouldn't understand. North Americans are very odd people: they assume a married man is sleeping with his wife.

FELICIA. All the time????

ORTON. That's what they like to think.

FELICIA. I know where I want to go. Maxo, promise you'll take me?

ORTON. Where?

FELICIA. Promise first.

ORTON. Tell me where first.

FELICIA. Sit down. (*He sits, a bit warily. She sits on his lap again.*) I want you to take me to the Liberation Ball. (*Pause.*) Please? Maxo?

ORTON. Liberation Day is four months off.

FELICIA. I'll wait.

ORTON. Why do you want to go? It's an obscenity.

FELICIA. Obscenity?

ORTON. Dancing for the poor just makes the rich feel richer. (*Felicia listens intently.*) Besides, it's a bore.

FELICIA. It wouldn't be if you took me.

ORTON. I daresay.

FELICIA. I'll change my hair. Lighter, I think. (*Piling her hair on top of her head.*) An upsweep. Like Greer Garson in that movie. And I'll wear lots of jewelry, so everybody'll notice me. I'm only thinking of *you*, Maxo. I'm only agreeing to go so you'll have a good time.

ORTON. (*Clearing his throat.*) On the way to the Ball, we'd have to stop at the Casa Rivera.

FELICIA. Why?

ORTON. Traditional. A few old friends of President Rivera drop by for a glass of champagne.

FELICIA. I thought he was dead.

ORTON. We pay our respects to his widow.

FELICIA. (*Airily.*) I don't mind. I'd like to see the inside of the Casa Rivera.

ORTON. Now how would I present you to this Queen Mother of the Republic? Let me visualize this. (*Wetting his lips.*) It is the eve of the most brilliant event of the social calendar. We are greeted by Dona Elena, who was First Lady for twelve years. I kiss her hand, she says "Welcome, Senator Orton." Now what? (*Felicia, still seated on his lap, grows tense.*) What do I say about my Greer-Garson-ized companion, rattling with rhinestones? "Dona Elena, it is my honor to grace your villa tonight with—" (*Shaking his head.*) Won't work. Frankness is the key. "I should like to present a little tramp from the back-country of the Rio de Oro who works on one of my radio programs. She is excellent company. In bed. She has a father complex. Never having met the gentleman." (*There is an instant before the lightning jumps. Felicia begins to slap Orton, hard, with both hands.*)

FELICIA. Damn you! Damn, damn, damn, damn! Damn you! Damn! (*She pauses, breathless.*)

ORTON. (*Flatly.*) Off. (*Stunned, Felicia slides off his lap. Hurt by what he has said, she goes to the corner of the room, her back to him.*) I apologize. But sometimes, to be a gentleman, a gentleman has to be something *less* than a gentleman.

FELICIA. (*Her back to him.*) I want the key. To this apartment. (*He pauses. Then slowly takes the key-ring from his pocket and twists off a single key. He holds it out in his hand.*)

ORTON. You're sure? (*She turns, merely stares at him. He drops the key into a glass jar on the side-table, and starts to go. Then he remembers something.*) Oh. Look under the bed. (*Felicia hesitates, then crosses quickly and slides a large box from beneath the bed. She lifts out a magnificent silver-fox cape.*)

FELICIA. How did it get here?

ORTON. I had it delivered while you were on the air.

FELICIA. (*Swirling it around her shoulders.*) It's beautiful, Maxo! I— (*Facing him.*) You expect me to thank you?

ORTON. It's optional.

FELICIA. (*Proudly.*) Well, I won't. You let me know what good wine tastes like—then you only let me have a sip. You give me this, but you won't take me any place I can wear it. That's no present! (*She flings the fox cape at him, it falls to the floor.*) You want me to feel poor, that's all. I hang that in my closet, and all it does is make me realize how much I *haven't* got.

ORTON. Be careful! That's *almost* the truth. And for you, child, truth is hemlock. You've got to lie, always. Not just to your enemies, to your friends. Most of all, to yourself. Because if you ever slip, and let the truth come out— (*Picking up the fur.*) God help you.

FELICIA. (*Softly.*) I don't need you, Maxo.

ORTON. (*Putting the cape around her shoulders fondly.*) That's a good girl. Lie. (*He goes out. Pause.*)

FELICIA. Maxo? (*Realizing he's gone, she shouts defiantly after him.*) Thank you, Maxo! For leaving! For good! It's wonderful—I don't have to be nice to you any more, I've got everything I want! (*She clutches the fur cape tightly about her. Alone now, her bravado is losing its starch.*) Every God-damned thing! (*Despite the fur, she shivers.*) What the hell do I need with you?

THE LIGHTS FADE

ACT ONE
SCENE 2

In the dark, at the other side of the stage, a bright little electric sign flashes on. It reads, in red letters: "SILENCIO—EN ACCION."

The lights come up on an announcer, who stands at a microphone. This is almost a documentary of a vanished art form and should be played without satire.

ANNOUNCER. So use the soap of society. When you smell the aroma of lilacs, it's Orton's. (*The announcer has been cupping his hand to his ear, to hear his own mellifluous tones. Now an offstage organist begins a soap-opera theme. A sound-effects wagon appears in the enlarged circle of light. A director, earphones on head, is throwing cues to music, sound, and actors from a script on an easel.*) And now, the concluding moments of today's suspenseful episode of . . . "Adios Romance." (*The music holds anxiously. The director cues the sound man. A speeding car roars from a record on the turntable. The announcer lowers his voice.*) Armando and Carlotta are speeding along the Camino de la Playa in Carlotta's high-powered Mercedes. Faster, faster, the powerful car plunges recklessly into the night. (*The sound man yawns, then speeds up the turntable. The drone of the car rises to a higher pitch. A bored radio actor ambles toward the microphone, a marked script in his hand. Felicia comes on and takes her stance at the microphone. She is the dedicated actress, immersed in her work. She is dressed pertly, crisply, with a satchel-bag over her shoulder. She twists a large handkerchief in one hand, and holds the script with white-knuckled intensity in the other.*)

RADIO ACTOR. (*Taking his cue from the director.*) Carlotta. (*Pause. Felicia wets her lips.*) Carlotta, don't you think you're driving a little fast? (*Felicia becomes more rigid.*) Carlotta. Answer me!

FELICIA. You don't call ninety miles an hour fast, do you, Armando? (*She forces a tense little laugh.*)

RADIO ACTOR. You're a mad-woman, Carlotta. Where are we going in this insane burst of speed? (*Felicia takes a deep breath, winding up for a dramatic reply. But the sound man deliberately jumps her cue with a hideous squeal of tires on a tight curve, at high speed. She glares at the sound man.*)

FELICIA. Anywhere! Nowhere! Speed is my love! I am in love with speed! And if you force me to live without it, I do not wish to live at all!

RADIO ACTOR. (*Calling out, tensely.*) Don't you see that old peasant with his vegetable wagon up ahead? Carlotta!!! (*The sound man simulates a tremendous crash: a series of recorded screeching, shattering, tumbling sounds. Then he reaches for the lever of a glass-crash machine, and dives for a box of broken debris which he rattles noisily. Felicia screams. The organ music hits with a dissonance, then modulates into the theme. The radio actor saunters away disinterestedly. Felicia takes out a compact and coolly fixes her make-up.*)

ANNOUNCER. (*Over the organ music.*) What will happen in the next thrilling episode of "Adios Romance"? Listen again on Monday. Until then, Orton's soap hopes your weekend will be filled with lilacs. (*The organ music rises in volume, then cuts as the "Silencio" sign is flicked off.*)

RADIO ACTOR. How are the writers going to get us out of this one? (*The radio actor tosses away his script, which flutters to the floor.*)

FELICIA. How was my scream? (*She looks around for reaction, and gets none. The radio actor drapes a coat over his shoulders and goes off. She turns to the director.*) Did you like the way I screamed? Luis? It was from inside, you could tell that, couldn't you? I really felt it.

DIRECTOR. Fine.

FELICIA. I wasn't too loud?

DIRECTOR. (*Drily.*) You were superb.

FELICIA. I'm glad. I want to be. For all those millions of people out there, wondering what's happened to me. Caring. (*The director is picking up the script pages which are scattered on the floor.*) What *does* happen? (*The director pretends not to hear her.*)

DIRECTOR. (*To the sound man.*) Get your stuff out as fast as you can. There's a public-service speech booked in here right after the news. (*The sound man collects his gear.*)

FELICIA. What time's my call on Monday?

DIRECTOR. (*Trying to sound casual.*) Oh, you're not in on Monday, Felicia. (*There is a blank moment. Then she looks pleased.*)

FELICIA. Good. I can have a long weekend. (*Thoughtfully.*) On Tuesday I suppose I'll be coming out of the anesthetic. A lot of special effects, filter, music, as I'm returning to consciousness. Send me the script, Luis, so I can *really* do a job of it.

DIRECTOR. (*Not looking at her.*) You're not in on Tuesday, either.

FELICIA. Wednesday? (*There is a pause.*)

DIRECTOR. Wednesday's the funeral.

FELICIA. (*Genuinely moved.*) Oh! Does Armando die?

DIRECTOR. No.

FELICIA. The old peasant with the cart? (*Silencio. The full import hits Felicia.*) You've killed me???!!! (*The director nods.*) You think my listeners will stand for it?

DIRECTOR. (*Rippling his fingers at her.*) Adios, Felicia. You're dead.

FELICIA. You can't kill me. I'll quit first. And I won't quit. (*A sudden idea.*) Rewrite the scripts. Armando saves me. He carries my broken body to a little wayside hospital, a handsome young surgeon falls in love with me and performs a miracle of brain surgery. My whole life passes before my eyes. My God, it could last for months!

DIRECTOR. (*Shaking his head.*) It would be like curing Camille.

FELICIA. (*With a blaze of pride.*) I'll go to work for Radio Mundo. They want me very much.

DIRECTOR. Do they want you without the lilac smell of Orton?

FELICIA. Did that flat-footed bastard order you to write me out?

DIRECTOR. (*Enjoying himself.*) No. Killing you off was my own inspiration. It's something I've been wanting to do to you, darling, for a long time. And when I heard the Senator had turned in his key to the "Ladies' Room"—

FELICIA. I'll drag you up before my union.

SOUND MAN. (*Sarcastically.*) All of a sudden she's a good union member! When we were on strike, she wouldn't carry a picket sign.

FELICIA. You think I'm a street-walker?

SOUND MAN. Yes. Except when we need somebody to walk the streets.

DIRECTOR. How the hell do you think you got this job?

FELICIA. I won it. I'm an actress! (*The director snorts.*) I'm too humble to say it. But I'm a *great* actress. Maxo says so.

DIRECTOR. Maybe you've given him a few performances the rest of us have missed. (*The sound man can't mask a guffaw at this. Felicia lets fly with her purse, swinging it like a hammer-thrower. The director ducks. The purse hits the easel, knocking it down along with the earphones.*)

FELICIA. You filthy, foul-mouthed, foul-minded—

DIRECTOR. For God's sake—

FELICIA. This fish factory! It ought to be burned down! For the good of the country, for the good of art! (*She is flailing the room with her purse, shattering one of the records on the sound-table.*)

SOUND MAN. Watch out! (*She hits the microphone and it topples to the floor.*)

FELICIA. Did I smash your lousy microphone? Good! (*She makes a mighty fling with the purse but the strap breaks and the missile goes wild. Brazo appears. He is tall, striking, in his full Colonel's uniform, topped off by an officer's cap with gold braid all over the visor. He is carrying a large leather briefcase. He is followed by a minor studio executive, who is horrified by the chaos. Weaponless, Felicia kicks at the director and sound man trying to subdue her.*)

BRAZO. Do your people always get so much realism in their performances?

STUDIO EXECUTIVE. (*Flustered.*) Not as a rule. (*Felicia's arms are pinned behind her and she is being dragged, struggling, out of the studio.*)

FELICIA. (*Seeing Brazo.*) They've killed me, they've murdered me, I'm dead, and I won't stand for it! Help me, for God's sake! (*They pull her, squirming, past the bewildered Colonel.*) Doesn't anybody around here have guts enough to help me??!

BRAZO. (*Taking command ineffectually.*) Well, now, I'd like a clarification of this situation. (*But Felicia has been dragged out, kicking, by the director and sound man.*)

STUDIO EXECUTIVE. Nothing for you to worry about, Colonel. Troublemaker. Fierce temper.

BRAZO. Oh, I could see that. I was aware of that.

STUDIO EXECUTIVE. Our apologies, Colonel. Sorry to have a distraction like this just before your broadcast.

BRAZO. Well, a Senorita in trouble— (*Chortling a little.*) After all, we *are* a nation of gentlemen. (*Staring towards the departed Felicia.*) Remarkable display of emotion, wasn't it? (*The director reappears, out of breath. Technicians are clearing the broken equipment and debris.*)

STUDIO EXECUTIVE. We'll have to get you another studio. (*Hurrying off.*) How about G? Is that clear?

BRAZO. Oh, one other matter.

DIRECTOR. Yes, Colonel Brazo?

BRAZO. I want to change the title of my address: "A Cavalryman Speaks Straight From the Saddle." One of my colleagues pointed out that might give the impression that my mouth was in the wrong part of my anatomy. (*He laughs and the director joins rather uncertainly.*) Yes. Have your announcer say: "We are happy to present Colonel Jorge Salvador Brazo, the distinguished—et cetera, et cetera—whose topic is 'A Cavalryman Speaks His Mind.'" Delete "Straight From the Saddle." Insert "Speaks His Mind." Is that clear? (*The director scribbles the change on the script.*)

DIRECTOR. Yes, sir. I'll get this approved right away.

BRAZO. It's already been approved. By me. We in the military take full responsibility for what we say. (*The director hesitates, then nods.*)

DIRECTOR. If you'll wait right here, Colonel. (*He goes off. Brazo is left alone in the studio. He notices Felicia's satchel-purse in the corner. He goes to it, picks it up, pauses, then opens it. He takes out an identification card, starts to read it.*)

STUDIO EXECUTIVE. (*Calling from off.*) We're ready now. This way, Colonel Brazo. (*Brazo slips the card back in the purse, and starts to put it in the corner where he found it. Then he changes his mind, stuffs Felicia's purse into his briefcase, and goes off, as the lights fade.*)

ACT ONE
SCENE 3

Felicia's apartment again. The bed, as always, is unmade.

It is late the same afternoon. Felicia hurries in, still fuming from her scuffle at the radio studio. Garcia, a sleepy-eyed and totally disenchanted cab driver, slouches into the room behind her, waiting for his fare.

FELICIA. You didn't have to follow me. I told you I'd bring you the money, I just misplaced my purse, that's all.

GARCIA. The last time a dame told me to "wait in the cab, she'd bring me the fare" was four and a half years ago. I'd still be waiting. (*Felicia pulls open a drawer of the bed-table and slams it shut, skims the room with her eyes.*)

FELICIA. I don't seem to have any money.

GARCIA. I don't seem to be surprised.

FELICIA. I'm terribly sorry.

GARCIA. So am I. But, lady, I like to be paid. I've got a right to be paid.

FELICIA. I like to be driven. I've got a right to be driven.

GARCIA. Don't think I'm money-mad, but how'm I supposed to support myself?

FELICIA. Go to your union. Demand a living wage from your employer.

GARCIA. Sweetheart. *You're* my employer.

FELICIA. But I lost my purse. (*He nods wearily. Oh, sure.*) I really *did* lose my purse.

GARCIA. Where's the phone?

FELICIA. What for?

GARCIA. To call the police.

FELICIA. Please. I've had an awful day.

GARCIA. So have I.

FELICIA. Be generous. You'll feel better.

GARCIA. With the Transport Workers, it's illegal to be generous. And I'm on the Grievance Committee. I'd have to bring myself up for discipline.

FELICIA. Lie.

GARCIA. *I* can lie, but the meter ain't learned.

FELICIA. (*A little desperately.*) Then—take something from this room. Anything you want. (*He shrugs, saunters around the room appraisingly. He picks up the edge of the disheveled blanket, and a thought blossoms in his mind.*)

GARCIA. *Anything*? (*Before she can answer, he presses on, with a mixture of shyness and daring.*) If you like to ride in taxicabs so much, maybe we could work out some permanent arrangement. Huh?

FELICIA. (*Hastily.*) You'd get in trouble with your union.

GARCIA. Screw the union. I'm off in half an hour. We could settle the whole thing—*friendly*! (*Starting out.*) I'll be back.

FELICIA. No!

GARCIA. I can't stay now, I'm on duty. (*He goes. Felicia sinks to her knees beside the bed, and seizes the blanket, stuffing part of it into her mouth like an infant grasping for security.*)

FELICIA. God, God, God! Did you put me here just to sleep with taxi drivers? You want me to hang a meter on my body, so much a mile, and 25 centavos a minute for waiting time? God, do you know what's wrong with you? You're stupid! (*Horrified at what she has said.*) Sweet God, dear Heavenly Father, I didn't mean to say that. I know, I know I should go to my confessor so he can go to the bishop and pray to the Saints to go to the Holy Mother so she can go to you—but I haven't got *time* for all that! (*She points her finger straight at Heaven, giving orders.*) Now, you listen to me, God. I need a miracle. (*She gets up from her knees, shakes her fist.*) MAKE

PEOPLE KNOW WHO I AM! (*Closing her eyes.*) Did you ever look down, once, at that stink-hole where you let me be born? I mean, up close? Smell it? I asked Sister Emilia at the Convent School if you ever saw me. *Me!* And she said, Yes, of course, you watched all of us, every minute, but I don't believe it. Did you bother to look at me when I was confirmed, in a patched-up white dress four of my sisters wore before me? Did you??? Maybe you couldn't see through all the dust in the summer and the mud in the winter. Go down there the next time you walk the earth; try living awhile in the beautiful back country of the Rio de Oro, see how *you* like it. (*Instantly devout again.*) I thank you, dear Heavenly Father, for letting me get out of that hellhole. I even thank you for that guitar player, that dirty little guitar player, who paid my train fare. And I thank you for bringing me my blessed protector, my Maxo— (*Breaking off bitterly.*) What was so terrible about asking him to take me to the Liberation Day Ball? (*All remnants of piety are gone.*) Maxo doesn't appreciate me. Neither do you! You don't know what you made when you made me! God damn you, God, you don't know me! (*She crumples to her knees by the bedside, terrified at her own blasphemy. She clings to the blanket again and speaks in a little-girl voice.*) Sister Emilia. Rock me. Tell God how sorry I am. (*She sways back and forth on her knees. There is a light knock. She doesn't hear it. The knock is repeated, more firmly. She stops, thinking it is the cab driver.*) Go away! You don't want to see me. I'm sick.

BRAZO. (*Unseen.*) I have something for you. (*Felicia bolts to a standing position. Looking at herself in the mirror frame, she is aghast.*)

FELICIA. I can't see anybody now.

BRAZO. I hate to leave your purse hanging on the doorknob.

FELICIA. Oh? Just a minute. (*With the blanket, she tries to scrub her face clean of the tear stains, then lets it fall to the floor. She jams a few frantic bobby pins into her hair, and looks at her chewed-up lip make-up, muttering under her breath.*) Judas Priest! (*She grabs for a lipstick, twists it, finds it empty, throws it to the floor.*) To hell with it. (*Raising her voice.*) Come in. (*Seeing the blanket on the floor.*) No—wait! (*Desperately, she flings the blanket to camouflage the unmade bed. Then she straightens to a model's pose, smooths her dress over her hips and turns toward the door.*) Won't you come in? (*Brazo enters, officer's cap in hand. His black hair is Brylcreem perfect. He bows slightly.*)

BRAZO. Senorita Jamas. (*He flicks open his briefcase, draws out the satchel-purse, hands it to Felicia.*)

FELICIA. (*A little dazed.*) Why, thank you.

BRAZO. It is my pleasure. May I present myself? Jorge Salvador Brazo. (*This is one of those rare occasions when Felicia is wordless.*)

FELICIA. How kind of you—is it General?

BRAZO. (*With arrogant modesty.*) Not yet. Colonel.

FELICIA. Colonel Brazo. How marvelously considerate. (*They stare at each other with no dislike whatsoever. She notices the ripped strap on her purse.*)

BRAZO. A scar of battle. (*She laughs.*) In the Army, we'd give you a decoration. I'll have my saddle-maker repair it for you.

FELICIA. No, no, no, it's old, I have a closet-full of them. (*Brushing back a wisp of*

Mario Alcade and Jennifer West in *Diamond Orchid,* New York, 1965. Photo by Jerome Lawrence. Jerome Lawrence and Robert E. Lee Collection, Lawrence and Lee Theatre Research Institute, The Ohio State University.

hair.) I can't imagine what you must think of me, after what you saw at the studio. I don't want you to think I'm one of those unprofessional, temperamental actresses, all fire and no control.

BRAZO. I'm the kind of man who likes to warm himself by a fire.

FELICIA. Oh? I must look terrible, no make-up, no jewelry at all.

BRAZO. Only the rich unhappy old women need jewelry.

FELICIA. (*Suddenly.*) I haven't even asked you to sit down.

BRAZO. (*Moving to a chair, sitting.*) At the radio station, you said you needed someone to help you.

FELICIA. You see, I'm the star of this radio series, so naturally I have approval of the plots. And when they showed me some of the scripts up ahead, I said: "I'd rather you killed me than ask me to do anything so unbelievable. You're killing my character." When I threatened to quit, they were frantic, naturally. But what could I do? A person must have integrity. That's all that really matters, isn't it? The *truth*!!! (*There is no Machiavellian contrivance in her version of the quarrel. She manages to convince herself that this is what happened.*)

BRAZO. (*Impressed.*) Do you know how rare it is these days to meet a woman with spirit? All our senoritas are trying to be butterflies.

FELICIA. (*With a little laugh.*) Nobody's ever accused *me* of being a butterfly. I haven't time. I'm at the studio, it seems like twenty-three hours a day. (*With intensity.*) But no matter how hard I work, I try to keep a light burning inside. A columnist on *El Popular* said I was "incandescent." Like a light, you know. I have the clipping in my scrapbook. Would you like to see it? No, that would be arrogant of me, I'm really a very humble person, I pray to the saints to keep me that way. I pray all the time. (*Brazo crosses his knees, relaxing and enjoying a conversation in which he has to put forth neither effort nor ideas. Felicia makes a sudden switch.*) I'm being rude, talking about myself, with such a famous guest.

BRAZO. Not famous. Not *really* famous.

FELICIA. You're humble, too. I've seen your picture in the paper, haven't I?

BRAZO. From time to time. But it can be uncomfortable to have your picture too much in the papers.

FELICIA. Oh?

BRAZO. Everybody knows you, and nobody knows you.

FELICIA. How profound! I've had that experience as an artist. I hold an entire nation close to my heart, I make them laugh a little perhaps, or cry. Then I step away from the microphone into the bright shadow of lonely fame. I gave an interview to one of the Sunday magazines. And that's what they called it: "The bright shadow of lonely fame." (*Moving closer to him.*) That article could have been about *you*. (*Brazo enjoys her flattery. She studies his face.*) I remember now, where I saw your picture. On the Society page; last year's Liberation Ball.

BRAZO. I'm on the permanent guest list, as chief of liaison for General De Santes.

FELICIA. You were wearing a white uniform.

BRAZO. Cavalry dress whites, yes. Mine were tailored in Madrid.

FELICIA. With all the medals. You looked splendid.

BRAZO. Thank you. I wish *you* had been there.

FELICIA. May I tell you the truth? To me, it's a bore. Worse. An obscenity.

BRAZO. (*Shocked.*) Obscenity?

FELICIA. Dancing for the poor just makes the rich feel richer.

BRAZO. It *is* a bit stiff. All those dowagers, the Society for Benevolence.

FELICIA. And that silly party at the Casa Rivera before the ball.

BRAZO. (*Impressed.*) Have you been there?

FELICIA. (*Obliquely.*) Well, it's traditional. A few special friends come by to pay their respects to Dona Elena. Oh, it's terribly stiff, terribly.

BRAZO. Well, I suppose their Society does some good work. But I've seen the way they do it.

FELICIA. Oh?

BRAZO. (*Hastily.*) *My* family never received charity. We weren't wealthy, of course, but we weren't poor. My father was in the government service. Postal department. Not a clerk—an official, understand, he had men under him. That was in Punta Australis, far to the South, very poor country, very rocky. And—(*Breaking off.*) oh, you can't be interested.

FELICIA. Believe me, I am, I am!

BRAZO. Well, the Society for Benevolence used to come around, hand out food, practically *throw* it at the poor, as if they were feeding birds.

FELICIA. No heart.

BRAZO. That's it. Even as a boy, I couldn't help feeling sorry for the way they treated the poor wretches. (*Waving away his memories.*) But *you* wouldn't know anything about such things.

FELICIA. But I do.

BRAZO. Obviously, you're aristocratic. Fine blood.

FELICIA. I used to know a girl who was very poor. (*She sinks to the floor, takes his hand so Brazo can share her compassion physically.*) From the Rio de Oro.

BRAZO. Hell's latrine—oh, forgive me—army talk.

FELICIA. That's what it is! And when this girl came to the city, she was frightfully frightened.

BRAZO. And you befriended her.

FELICIA. I tried to see things through her eyes. More than anything else, she wanted to go to the Liberation Ball.

BRAZO. How did you get her an invitation?

FELICIA. Oh, that was impossible. So we stood together, outside, on the street, with the crowd, with the police on horses, their rumps shoving us back so we could only see the chandeliers through the windows and hear the music, far off, over the lights, and the newsreels, and the women in their jewels and diamonds, and it made me furious! (*Quick change.*) For my girl-friend. I could see how much it hurt her, because she could never be a part of all that. And that's why I say it's an obscenity!

BRAZO. I wonder if you realize how few people there are with your kind of honesty. (*Felicia looks down, modestly. He kisses her hair tentatively, as if she were a virgin, which, of course, she is, in her own mind.*)

FELICIA. Colonel Brazo, you're so gentle. (*She touches the muscles of his arm, then quickly pulls her hand away as if she had never touched a man before.*) But strong. That's the true "*gentle*-man," isn't it? Tenderness and strength. Both. (*Brazo's conceit makes him flex that arm muscle almost involuntarily.*)

BRAZO. (*Suddenly.*) You must do me a great favor, Senorita Jamas. A great honor. Can I persuade you to have dinner with me tonight?

FELICIA. Impossible, Colonel. Unless you call me Felicia.

BRAZO. I shall withdraw the invitation, unless you call me Jorge. (*There is a knock. Felicia jumps up, Brazo also rises.*)

FELICIA. I can't imagine— (*Covering.*) I'm a little embarrassed. You see, I've never had a male visitor in this room before.

BRAZO. Don't worry, I'll explain, I'm here strictly in the line of service.

FELICIA. (*Tentatively, calling toward the door.*) Who is it?

GARCIA'S VOICE. (*From off.*) I was fast, wasn't I! (*The door opens and Garcia, the cab driver, enters with a sheepish and expectant grin. Then he sees Brazo.*)

GARCIA. Oh. (*Felicia simultaneously reaches for her purse and her poise.*)

FELICIA. (*The grand lady, to Brazo.*) This man is a precious jewel among cab drivers. You won't believe what he just did. He drove me home from the studio, wouldn't take any money, then volunteered to go back and try to find my purse.

BRAZO. That's very decent.

FELICIA. (*To Garcia.*) But, you see, Colonel Brazo has already done your good deed for you.

GARCIA. Yeah?

BRAZO. (*Handing money to Garcia.*) This should cover the fare.

FELICIA. Oh, I shouldn't let you.

GARCIA. (*Taking the money, crestfallen.*) Money. (*He looks at Felicia with the expression of a hungry tom-cat, who's just been kicked out of the house. He takes a pencil from a clip on his hat and writes on a slip of paper.*)

FELICIA. (*Grandly, to Garcia.*) Thank you, my dear, good man. For your *faith*.

GARCIA. I had *hope* too. (*Handing her the slip of paper.*) Here's my number. Call me when you want a ride. (*Garcia goes out.*)

BRAZO. (*Admiringly.*) That man is your slave. You have the gift of command.

FELICIA. (*Interested.*) Do I?

BRAZO. You'd make a fine officer. (*Felicia picks up the glass jar from the bedside table. Thoughtfully she rotates the key inside it.*)

FELICIA. (*Slowly.*) Will you teach me, Colonel Brazo? (*More intimately.*) Jorge?

THE LIGHTS FADE

ACT ONE
SCENE 4

A sala in the Casa Rivera, dominated by a glittering chandelier, and several paintings of the more chivalrous period of Velasquez: semi-armored Dons on white horses charging up a hill. The atmosphere is sedate elegance.

This is the home of the grande dame of the capital, the former first lady, Dona Elena, a distinguished 70 and still a classic beauty.

Orton is there, resplendent in full evening dress, a cigar in his mouth, a glass of champagne in his hand.

With his back to the audience, staring up at one of the paintings, is Dr. Domingo Guzmano, a grizzled Nobel-Prize winner. He is pure protein, like an 80-year-old piece of meat, which has been salted and left in the sun to dry. His white hair is unkempt, his knuckles large, his eyes impatient and critical. He wears an ancient and uncomfortable dinner jacket and a gnarled black tie. He holds an empty champagne glass.

DONA ELENA. How *dare* they go out on strike?

ORTON. How dare *you* drink champagne?

GUZMANO. (*Coughs huskily.*) My glass is empty, by the way. (*A servant quickly fills Guzmano's extended glass. Dona Elena glances at the old man with concern; is he getting too high?*)

ORTON. My dear Dona Elena, a General Strike isn't a revolution.

DONA ELENA. It could be! Why doesn't our President *do* something?

ORTON. He doesn't want to offend anybody.

GUZMANO. What is more offensive than a man who doesn't want to offend anybody? If I want a chicken dinner, I've got to offend a hen.

ORTON. (*Comfortingly.*) Stop worrying, Elena. How much can the Union Leaders do? Close the butcher shops, turn off the power, stop the streetcars? How many gowned ladies are going to your Liberation Ball tonight on a streetcar?

DONA ELENA. We can last longer than they can.

GUZMANO. They can live on beans. You can't. Or won't.

ORTON. Why, this house could hold out five years just on the bubbly behind the corks in the wine cellar.

GUZMANO. (*Arching his eyebrows.*) Bring on the revolution! (*They all laugh.*)

DONA ELENA. Oh, it feels good to laugh. Should I stop thinking and be silent? That's what a woman's supposed to do, isn't it?

ORTON. Were you always silent in the Presidential Palace? Never a suggestion to your husband?

DONA ELENA. Once in a great while, I asked a question. But there's no time for questions now, is there? We get the answers first! And they're the *wrong* answers!

GUZMANO. Oh, shut up, Elena. When I put a slice of tissue on a microscope slide, I don't have the goddamndest idea what I'm going to see. I know that *anything* is possible. But *you* want to write out a laundry-slip so tomorrow will come back all clean, starched, just the way you ordered it. Hell, I'd rather be dead.

ORTON. You'll outlive us all. The Nobel Prize makes you immortal.

GUZMANO. (*Sitting.*) Remember to say that at my funeral.

DONA ELENA. When we aren't here, what will people say about us? "You had so much that was good and lovely, why didn't you protect it, why did you let it slip away?"

GUZMANO. Protect *what*?

DONA ELENA. What we had in this country when my husband was alive. When there wasn't all this shouting in the streets, or smashing of windows. When people had *manners*. (*Staring up at one of the paintings.*) Gentility.

GUZMANO. The patients waiting in the rain outside my clinic don't care a noseful-of-snot about gentility. Whenever I hear this talk about running sweetly backwards to the Hapsburgs and the Hohenzollerns, I march straight to the music room and start playing Bach. Then everybody's got to shut up and listen to me for forty-five minutes. (*He grins.*)

ORTON. You can't play Bach after eight glasses of champagne.

GUZMANO. (*Closing one eye.*) At ten glasses, I become Bach himself. (*A doorbell chimes, off.*)

ORTON. I suppose that's De Santes. Importantly late.

DONA ELENA. The General can't be here. He's sending his Liaison Officer.

ORTON. Brazo? Oh, God.

DONA ELENA. Don't you like him? I'm told he's very popular.

ORTON. (*Drily.*) Horses are crazy about him.

DONA ELENA. I heard him make a speech on the radio once.

ORTON. What did he say?

DONA ELENA. I don't remember exactly.

ORTON. That's it. If Brazo had the personality of—oh, Benito Mussolini, say—or Rudolph Valentino—he could make trouble. But he hasn't got the *zip*. (*A servant enters.*)

SERVANT. (*Announcing.*) Colonel Jorge Salvador Brazo. Senorita Felicia Jamas. (*Orton, who is refilling his champagne glass, looks up, startled. Brazo enters, glittering with medals, his shoes and hair slickly shined. Felicia floats on his arm. She is transformed. Her face is pale and remote. She wears a superb white sheath, and a white lace mantilla. Her hair is a sculptured blonde pompadour. She wears no jewelry, but it is impossible to avoid looking at her. She is attempting a detached, pristine air, and, by and large, carrying it off. But this is her first venture into the high stratosphere of society. She is a little bird flying with the eagles, and she knows if she falters she can fall, or be gobbled up. Dona Elena steps forward to greet them.*)

DONA ELENA. Colonel Brazo.

BRAZO. How delightful to see you, Dona Elena. Of course you know Senorita Jamas. (*Orton chokes slightly on a sip of champagne.*)

FELICIA. (*Stiffly.*) Enchanted.

DONA ELENA. (*Scrutinizing Felicia.*) Jamas? My memory's going grey. Where did we meet? (*Brazo is puzzled. Felicia has led him to believe she was part of this coterie.*)

FELICIA. (*Playing from non-existent strength.*) There are so many important people in your life, Dona Elena, it would be immodest of me to expect you to remember.—

DONA ELENA, (*Weighing the name.*) Jamas . . .

FELICIA. (*Swiftly, trying to keep afloat.*) A very old family. From the provinces.

DONA ELENA. Oh? Perhaps my husband knew your father.

ORTON. (*Half-sarcasm, half to the rescue.*) Or mother. The Jamas family has a wide reputation, Dona Elena. I don't quite remember what for. But famous, famous. It may come to me later. (*Felicia smiles thinly at Orton—half gratitude, half "Don't you spoil this for me, you bastard!"*)

DONA ELENA. (*Without enthusiasm.*) Senorita Jamas, Colonel Brazo—may I present Dr. Guzmano, who is paying one of his rare visits to the capital.

BRAZO. Doctor.

FELICIA. Enchanted.

DONA ELENA. And Senator Orton. (*Orton and Brazo nod formally.*) (*Note: the accent is Ortón.*)

FELICIA. Oh, I know the Senator very well. (*There is an arched eyebrow moment.*)

DONA ELENA. You do?

FELICIA. By *reputation*. And I've admired his skills. Who hasn't? (*She smiles faintly. Orton's smile is equally faint. She extends her hand with angelic serenity, so that Orton is obliged to cross the entire room.*)

ORTON. (*His eyes never leaving hers.*) Enchanted.

FELICIA. (*As Orton kisses her hand.*) Can you imagine, Senator, how long I've been waiting for this moment? (*Servants bring in champagne for Brazo and Felicia, also refilling the other glasses.*)

BRAZO. (*Turning to Dona Elena.*) General De Santes was overcome with regret that he couldn't be here. This foolishness with the unions! (*Shaking his head, coining a phrase.*) But work before play, you know. Good to have a firm hand on the reins. Salud. (*They all sip at their champagne. Felicia wears an expression of listening to symphony music.*)

DONA ELENA. Does the General think he can prevent the strike?

BRAZO. (*The expert.*) Well, the Government was tardy calling on us. (*Shooting a frown at Orton.*) Very tardy. However, now that the Army is in the saddle, I can safely say there will *not* be a General Strike tonight. Not a chance.

ORTON. You're quite sure of that?

BRAZO. Positive. Why, these agitators wouldn't dare— (*Every light goes out, even the distant flow of the city skyline. Dona Elena gasps. There is a confusion of voices.*)

DONA ELENA. Candles! Bring candles! (*Servants come in quickly, lighting long tapers in candelabra, which are placed about the room. Dona Elena paces indignantly.*) There! You see? They've done it!

FELICIA. (*Impressed, crossing toward a window.*) How exciting! The whole city, all those people, and not a single light. (*The entering candles give a shimmering uncertainty, which Felicia finds delicious.*)

BRAZO. (*Putting an arm around her shoulder, protectively.*) I don't want you to be concerned, my dear.

FELICIA. I'm not. I'm loving it.

BRAZO. Where's a telephone? I've got to report to the General. (*Bowing.*) Excuse me, excuse me. (*A servant leads him out with a single taper.*)

ORTON. (*Wryly.*) How comforting to know the Army's in the "saddle."

DONA ELENA. And we get plunged into blackness, like savages!

GUZMANO. Oh, I don't mind. We're all too damned electrical.

FELICIA. (*Strangely.*) *I* think we should all be on our knees. (*They all look at the girl.*)

ORTON. On our knees?

FELICIA. Praying. For a man who could stop things like this. Someone strong—like your late husband, Dona Elena. (*Orton smiles at the shrewdness of his fledgling.*)

DONA ELENA. Isn't that what I just said, Maxo? Isn't it?

GUZMANO. You want a strong man? How about the fellow who just turned out the lights!

FELICIA. Who?

ORTON. Aguila, probably. Or maybe the butcher boy, Portero.

DONA ELENA. You see? Now our lives are being run by the butchers.

ORTON. Oh, the butcher boy's no butcher. He's too busy being head of the Butchers' Union.

DONA ELENA. Monsters!

GUZMANO. (*Riding over her.*) They feel the same way about you.

DONA ELENA. They're all alike.

ORTON. Not at all, easy to tell apart; Portero's a slab of beef, Aguila's a wasp.

FELICIA. (*Eyes bright.*) What if— (*Breaking off suddenly, with a convincing contriteness.*) Oh, no, I mustn't say what *I* think, in such distinguished company.

ORTON. But we're fascinated. *What* do you think, child? (*Though his irony is subtle, it reaches Felicia.*)

FELICIA. Well, it's just what I've learned from the most brilliant man I've ever known.

ORTON. Oh?

FELICIA. Colonel Brazo. He admires his General so much! What if General De Santes were in the President's chair—?

DONA ELENA. Our lights would be on, right now!

FELICIA. Yes!

ORTON. A wise soldier never goes into politics. He might get shot.

DONA ELENA. The General is a great patriot!

ORTON. He has bad eyesight. He can't tell his own face from the national flag.

DONA ELENA. (*Impassioned, frustrated.*) How can I wake you up? We have an enemy, right here with us! People who want to take everything away! (*Waving vaguely around the room.*) Our paintings, our music, our lives, everything we own! And if personal property isn't safe, how safe are personal thoughts? If they can take away what you live in, they can take away what you believe in. It's *their* world or *ours*. (*Guzmano stirs in the chair like an old volcano, rumbling to life again.*)

GUZMANO. Ours, theirs. Yours, mine. Civilized, savage. Right, left. North, South. East, West. God! (*Shaking his head.*) I'll tell you where there's a split in the world: between the people who have plumbing and the people who have privies. Eggs for breakfast or *nothing* for breakfast. (*Felicia sinks at the feet of Guzmano.*)

FELICIA. It's too marvelous. Am I actually sitting at the feet of the man who's done so much for humanity?

GUZMANO. "Humanity." Who the hell is *he*? José Humanity? Manuel Humanity? Never met 'em.

FELICIA. But, my dear Doctor, when I think how many millions of people you've—

GUZMANO. (*Interrupting.*) Millions? You want to know the biggest number in the world? *One*! There is no number larger than one. One human being at a time. Get rid of one case of rickets. Lance one boil on one man's back. Once in a while a woman drops twins and you cut two umbilical cords; that's as high as you have to count in medicine. Unless you're a vet. I get into that, too. Peasants and their goddam goats! (*Felicia is surprised at the earthiness of the supposedly sublime old man.*)

ORTON. (*Slyly.*) Oh, the Senorita wouldn't know about such things. (*Guzmano extends his empty champagne glass, which a servant fills.*)

DONA ELENA. How many drinks does that make, Doctor?

GUZMANO. Numbers, numbers, you put numbers on everything, then throw the things away. Trade in the human mind for a computing machine. Choose the ugly mathematical certainty over the beauty of human error.

FELICIA. Do you agree with him, Senator?

ORTON. I listen to Guzmano the way I listen to music. It's hard to argue with a good cello. (*Brazo comes in crisply.*)

BRAZO. I've just talked with the General, and it's perfectly safe for you to proceed to the Liberation Ball.

DONA ELENA. Thank God. And thank you, Colonel. (*To a servant.*) Have the cars brought around.

BRAZO. But I find myself in an embarrassing position. The General has assigned me to take personal command of the mounted guard outside the Ball, for your protection. And that seems to leave Senorita Jamas unattended. (*There is an awkward moment.*)

FELICIA. Perhaps Senator Orton would be gallant enough to escort a helpless stranger . . . ?

BRAZO. Would you be so kind, Senator? I think you'll find Senorita Jamas delightful company. (*It is Karma. Magnificently trapped, Orton nods. Brazo kisses Felicia's hand.*) Apologies, my dear. Dona Elena. Gentlemen. (*Bowing, Brazo goes off. A servant enters.*)

SERVANT. The limousines are here.

DONA ELENA. Shall we go? (*Guzmano kills off his champagne. Other servants bring wraps, furs. Felicia is brought the fox cape which Orton gave her.*)

ORTON. (*Admiring the fur.*) What exquisite taste!

FELICIA. Thank you.

ORTON. I'm going to spoil your evening, I'm afraid. Just a stuffy old Senator, after your Colonel's fertile mind and sparkling wit.

FELICIA. (*Deftly blunting the dig.*) How clever you are, Senator—to see in Jorge the same fine qualities that *I* do. (*She smiles, he looks at her askance, as the candles lead them off.*)

THE LIGHTS FADE

ACT ONE
SCENE 5

The Radio Studio. December. Six months later.

The "Silencio" sign flashes on. An announcer reads news from a fistful of teletype pages.

ANNOUNCER. —and crowds throng the beaches on both sides of the Estuary for another sweltering December weekend. (*Turning to a fresh page.*) News from the Labor Front. Another fiery clash between Portero of the Butchers' Union and Aguila of the powerful Transport and Electrical Workers. In a blistering speech today, the Wild Bull of Labor blamed Aguila for the fiasco of the General Strike last spring, claiming he ended the black-out of the city after less than 90 minutes because of quote, "Bungling cowardice in the face of military pressure." Unquote. Senor Aguila's reply to Senor Portero was not considered suitable for quotation on the air. (*Another page.*) Now, aficionados, the Jai-Alai scores. (*Two soldiers burst into the studio and point their rifles at the startled announcer. Simultaneously, the rooftops of the city along the cyclorama light up in spurts of gunfire, like lightning flashes behind the black silhouette. A cannon booms, a rocket bursts in the sky high above the buildings. There is a cataclysmic charge of horses' hooves, rivaling the Four Hundred. In the radio studio, one soldier rips the teletype pages from the announcer's hand and forces a single piece of paper on him. The announcer hesitates. The soldiers prod him with their bayonets. Sweat pouring down his face, the announcer reads into the microphone.*) Attention. An official government announcement. A peaceful revolution has just taken place and— (*The announcer hesitates, and is prodded again.*) —by the free will of the people, the Army of Justice is marching on the Presidential Palace to proclaim a new President, Jorge Salvador Brazo. (*With no enthusiasm whatsoever.*) Viva President Brazo! (*There is an offstage crash, as a door is broken in. Three more soldiers, wearing the same uniform as the first two, rush in, brandishing drawn rifles.*)

SOLDIERS. Drop your rifles! (*The first two soldiers look up, amazed, and their rifles clatter noisily to the floor. One new soldier holds the first two at bayonet point, the other new soldiers flank the baffled and terrified announcer. One soldier rips the sheet of paper from the announcer's shaking hands, crumples it, and hands him a new page, indicating with his bayonet point that the announcer should read it.*)

ANNOUNCER. (*His voice cracking with fright.*) Attention. An official government announcement. The revolution has just been overthrown. General Rafael De Santes announces the arrest of former Colonel Jorge S. Brazo. General De Santes, speaking for the government, declares that the aborted uprising had nothing whatsoever to do with the "will of the people" but was an individual act of hare-brained idiocy. Fellow citizens, return to your homes. Go to bed. Go to sleep. Long live the Republic. (*A soldier points his gun toward an offstage control room and the "Silencio" sign goes off. The announcer mops his brow. The first two soldiers casually pick up their guns, turning to the newcomers with the intimacy of barracks-buddies.*)

SOLDIER. Pepe, what happened?

2ND SOLDIER. Who knows? Some damn fool on a horse. (*Arms around each others' shoulders, they all go off together.*)

THE LIGHTS FADE

ACT ONE
SCENE 6

A room in Orton's villa. In the darkness, a match ignites into the orange-blue flame of brandy burning in a chafing dish. Orton, in a robe, sits in a tall throne-like chair at an ornately carved dining table, waiting to be served a midnight delicacy. A rich 16th-century Spanish tapestry hangs behind him.

Orton watches with satisfaction as the servant expertly bathes some crepes with flaming brandy.

ORTON. No more brandy. A drop of curaçao, and just a whisper more of the Framboise.

SERVANT. Won't it keep you awake, Senator?

ORTON. I've given up sleep. It's fattening. (*The servant spoons the crepes onto a plate, and serves Orton.*) Where's the melted butter? (*A doorbell chimes off.*)

SERVANT. Shall I answer it, Senator? Everyone else is asleep.

ORTON. If it's a gentleman, tell him he's no gentleman to ring doorbells at 1:30 in the morning. If it's a lady, a *young* lady— (*Taking a delicious bite.*) —ask her if she's hungry.

SERVANT. (*Going out.*) Yes, Senator. (*The chime repeats. Orton, alone, pours himself a brandy, swirls it in a snifter. Grandly, Felicia sweeps on, wearing a full-length mink.*)

ORTON. (*Calmly.*) What kept you?

FELICIA. You can't sleep. Of course you can't. None of us can.

ORTON. (*Coming slowly to his feet.*) Oh, I rarely sleep. I was once told that my face looks lop-sided on a pillow. That image keeps me awake nights. (*The servant appears, a question mark on his face.*) Another place-setting for the Senorita.

FELICIA. (*Pacing.*) No, no, I couldn't possibly eat, not now. (*Orton waves away the servant, who goes out.*)

ORTON. Too bad. You'd like these. Crepes Framboises. My own recipe.

FELICIA. My dear Senator Orton—

ORTON. "Senator?" When you threw shoes at me, I was Maxo.

FELICIA. I'm completely changed. Couldn't you see that? At Dona Elena's, and at the Ball?

ORTON. I saw a white angel, floating a few feet off the floor. Pristine and pure. I hardly thought you'd stick to that role for half a year.

FELICIA. It's not a role. It's my *self.*

ORTON. And what became of that little charmer who used to act on the radio?

FELICIA. (*Smiles.*) She was killed in an automobile crash.

ORTON. Killed? Or maimed into respectability?

FELICIA. She doesn't exist.

ORTON. I'll never find her again?

FELICIA. Never.

ORTON. Pity. She had a tongue like a fish-wife, but I'll miss her. (*Indicating the waiting plate.*) Do you mind? Hot, they're superlative. At room temperature, they're just drunken pancakes. (*Felicia uses the glamour of the mink coat, trying to stir up banked fires.*)

FELICIA. Please, please, go right ahead. (*He sits slowly, takes a bite.*) Senator, a man with your taste and understanding, and, and—

ORTON. Discernment.

FELICIA. That's it. Discernment. Naturally, you can see the full scope of what Brazo is trying to do.

ORTON. Exactly what *was* your colonel up to this evening?

FELICIA. An honest, democratic attempt by the Army of Justice to liberate the people! (*Orton laughs. Felicia stiffens.*) Would you have the courage to do what Jorge did?

ORTON. I've got something better than courage. Sense. And enough love for my own carcass not to climb up on a white stallion and lead a half-assed charge up the lawn of the Presidential Palace.

FELICIA. (*Jeanne d'Arc.*) Senator, lift up the telephone. It is in your power to rescue one of the greatest men of the century!

ORTON. Which century?

FELICIA. You don't know Jorge the way I do!

ORTON. I won't argue about *that.*

FELICIA. What do you think the headline's going to be tomorrow morning in "El Popular"?

ORTON. Nobody reads "El Popular" except people who can't read.

FELICIA. "Where's Brazo?" That's what it's going to say! It's a police state, where you have to lock up the opposition.

ORTON. He's a thief! He tried to steal the Presidency. He gets the same treatment as somebody who steals a car. Or a horse. (*Rising, dabbing at his lips with a napkin.*) Now that it's all over, I'll tell you where Brazo made his mistake. (*Rotating his brandy snifter.*) Oh, let me give you a cognac.

FELICIA. A Strega. (*Hardly any voice.*) What was his mistake?

ORTON. He didn't use the *new* army.

FELICIA. Jorge resents mechanization, but he accepts it. (*He pours her a Strega. She takes it, but is listening so intently she forgets to drink it.*)

ORTON. I'm not talking about tanks. I mean the "dirty overalls" army, the Labor Unions. You saw it happen. When the electrical workers go out, so do the lights. When the butchers go out, you don't eat. That's *power*! (*Felicia is silent. Orton takes three bottles, the brandy, the Strega, the Framboise, and lines them up on the table.*) Can you count to three? Here's a nation. (*Picking up one bottle at a time.*) One—the people who work, the Labor Unions. Two—the people they work for.

FELICIA. Like you.

ORTON. Like me. And three—the people with the guns.

FELICIA. (*Softly.*) Like Brazo.

ORTON. Like De Santes. Now. When you have two of these three working together—any two—you have a government. But your half-wit hero tried to make a government with just one liqueur. Not even a full bottle. (*Forcefully, he puts down the bottle of Strega.*)

FELICIA. (*Thoughtfully, touching each bottle.*) Money. The Army. The Unions. (*Wheels spinning in her head.*) You want to get rid of Jorge, don't you?

ORTON. We have.

FELICIA. No, you haven't. Your laws say there's got to be a trial. Think of the publicity that'll give him. Headlines every day, for months! Instead of getting rid of Brazo, you'll be going to work for him. As his press agent! You'll make him a national hero, is that what you want?

ORTON. (*Squinting at her, appraisingly.*) You're really quite brilliant, aren't you? And it's all instinct. Not a shred of learning. God, what a terror you'd be if you could spell.

FELICIA. (*Sweetly.*) I may do you a favor, Senator. An enormous favor.

ORTON. Now, *that* frightens me.

FELICIA. What would you think if I got him out of the country? I can do it. I'm probably the only person who can. Jorge and I will leave the country for good. (*No answer.*) And never come back. All you have to do is just let him out of jail. That's all. (*Orton lights a cigar with a silver lighter.*) Out of politics, out of the country. Forever. I promise. By my sainted mother. (*Orton merely draws on his cigar.*) No trial. No publicity. Just goodbye. (*He smokes silently.*) You don't trust me. (*Orton shakes his head. Suddenly, Felicia picks up the silver lighter, the glass of her "ladyship" is cracking.*) By God, you do it, Maxo, or I'll burn down the drapes! (*Orton's eyes light up. He takes a cigar out of his mouth. Felicia tries to recapture her grand manner.*) In the name of justice, Senator, I appeal to you as a humanitarian, as a—

ORTON. Wait. Go back! For just an instant there, I felt the vibrations of a departed friend. The tender whisper of a voice I thought was forever stilled.

FELICIA. (*Fighting to restrain her temper.*) Is there any mercy in you? Look in your heart! (*Orton is unmoved. The vulgarity bursts through.*) If it's not in your heart, look in your stomach, you strutting garbage pail, you pompous son-of-a-bitch! (*Delighted, Orton claps his hands and dances around the room.*)

ORTON. Ahhhh, there she is! Resurrected! Risen from the dead! And I was afraid she'd been mummified in mink. (*Fiercely Felicia hurls the lighter at him. He ducks, chortles.*) You're out of practice. Don't you ever throw anything at Brazo?

FELICIA. No! Because he's exactly the opposite of you. He isn't ashamed of me. He takes me places. He worships me.

ORTON. (*Indicating the coat.*) And that's an offering at your shrine?

FELICIA. (*Drawing the mink regally about her.*) A hundred and forty-four skins!

ORTON. Whose?

FELICIA. That ratty little fox of yours I gave to charity.

ORTON. It will keep some orphan warm.

FELICIA. (*A new tack, sweetly.*) Maxo, be a darling. Tell me where he is. (*Orton merely smokes, studying her.*) He's not in a hospital, is he? He wasn't hurt?

ORTON. Oh, he's safe.

FELICIA. You've got him in jail someplace, haven't you?

ORTON. Where some well-planned spontaneous uprising could set him loose? Oh, no.

FELICIA. Tell me where he is!

ORTON. Behind walls eight feet thick, thanks to the Conquistadores.

FELICIA. (*Shocked.*) Three Rivers! (*Orton's silence is verification. She's appalled.*) That's not a jail, it's a fortress. (*The edge goes out of Orton's voice; he is almost kindly.*)

ORTON. You play the sweepstakes, you lose, what can you do? Tear up the ticket. (*She turns away. He reaches for her hand.*) Let me see your hand. (*Reluctantly, she lets him take it. He examines the fingers.*) You think I don't know how your knuckles got like this? (*She pulls her hand away, looks at him defiantly.*) Stop breaking your fingernails on phone dials. Pounding on doors. It's no use.

FELICIA. (*With waning ferocity.*) Jorge has a lot of friends at the Officers' Club!

ORTON. (*Drily.*) There's nothing an ambitious colonel hates more than another ambitious colonel.

FELICIA. General De Santes loves him.

ORTON. Well, the General just kissed him with a dishonorable discharge. (*Felicia didn't know this.*) De Santes wouldn't even see you tonight, would he? (*Felicia's spirits are at the nadir.*) Would he, child?

FELICIA. Don't call me "child." I'm not a child. I'm not anything.

ORTON. If you're in love with a peacock, don't make him think he's an eagle.

FELICIA. (*Almost a monotone.*) Don't you really sleep, Maxo?

ORTON. Not much.

FELICIA. You're lucky. I have a nightmare. Every night. The same one. I dream that I'm *not*.

ORTON. Not what?

FELICIA. Not anything. In my dream, I'm a little girl. And I look at the place I'm supposed to be sitting in school, and it's empty. Then I look in my bed where I'm supposed to be lying, and it's empty. Then I start running, looking for myself. And I ask people if they've seen me, and they don't know who I am. They don't say I'm dead, or missing, or lost. They just act as if I've never been born. (*She has covered her eyes. Suddenly she looks up. She's crying.*) Make them put *me* in Three Rivers, and let him out. It's my fault. I got him to do it. My God, he's sitting in some lousy cell, blaming me for all this. You've got to get him out. Because he loves me. Remember love, Maxo? You insensitive pig! Don't you remember what it's like to love???

ORTON. Quite clearly. (*Looking at her probingly.*) Are you actually in love with Brazo?

FELICIA. (*Defiantly.*) Yes!

ORTON. More than you ever were with me?

FELICIA. Hell, yes! (*Pause. Orton sighs, puts out his cigar.*)

ORTON. (*Calls.*) Carlos!

FELICIA. (*Tense.*) What are you going to do?

ORTON. (*Playing Pilate.*) I'm going to make a mistake. But it's your mistake, child, not mine.

SERVANT. (*Entering.*) Yes, Senator?

ORTON. Call the airport and find the first flight out of the country tomorrow morning. Any direction. The further the better. Make a reservation for— (*Fishing for a name.*) for Senor and Senora Juan Martinez.

SERVANT. (*Starting out.*) Yes, Senor.

ORTON. And bring me a raincoat.

SERVANT. But it's not raining.

ORTON. That's *your* opinion. A raincoat. An old one. (*A little confused, the servant goes out. Orton calls after him.*) And make those reservations *tourist*. (*Facing Felicia.*) When I kept a stable, I had a mad horse. I couldn't bring myself to shoot him. I left the stable door open so he could run away.

FELICIA. Dear Maxo! I take back everything I said about you. I'll wash out my mouth with soap. *Your* soap.

ORTON. No commercial, please. Just a little security.

FELICIA. Security?

ORTON. To make absolutely certain that Senor and Senora Juan Martinez do not get off the plane the first place it lands, turn around, and fly straight back here again. I don't suppose this possibility even nibbled at your mind?

FELICIA. (*Piously.*) Never. I give you my word.

ORTON. I don't want your word. I want your coat.

FELICIA. (*Hugging the mink protectively about her.*) No!

ORTON. The coat. (*Orton gestures for the coat again, more firmly. Reluctantly, she lets him take it off her shoulders.*) Send me your new address, and this will be forwarded to you, fully insured, wherever you are. In exactly one month. I promise—by your sainted mother.

FELICIA. (*Petulantly.*) Why a month?

ORTON. By then, the charge of the light-headed brigade up the Presidential lawn will be half-way between stale headlines and stale history. And what feeble machinery your colonel had working for him can be dismantled.

FELICIA. (*Submissively.*) Whatever you say, Maxo.

ORTON. (*Surprised.*) Well. Blessed are the meek.

FELICIA. What do they get?

ORTON. The earth. (*He turns her face toward him.*) Presumably. You're too good for Brazo.

FELICIA. (*Steadily.*) Too good for Brazo. Not quite good enough for you. (*The servant enters with a huge, dilapidated trenchcoat.*)

SERVANT. Senator, I've made the reservations. A.L. #107, leaving Campo Robles at 7:05 in the morning. For Caracas.

ORTON. (*Taking the raincoat.*) Your ticket will be at the airport. And what papers you'll need.

FELICIA. Will Jorge be there?

ORTON. Senor Martinez will be on the plane, in the seat beside you. (*Turning to the servant.*) Wake up the chauffeur. Have him drive Senorita Jamas to her apartment.

FELICIA. No.

ORTON. You'll never get a taxi this time of night.

FELICIA. I've got one waiting. (*Orton thinks for a moment.*)

ORTON. Carlos, have the cab driver come in, I want to see him.

FELICIA. Why?

ORTON. To pay your fare home. (*The servant goes out. Affectionately, Orton drapes the oversized raincoat around Felicia's shoulders. Gently, he turns her chin so that she is facing him.*) No more door-to-door canvassing. No more frantic phone calls. Is that clear? (*She turns away, and nods.*) When you look me straight in the eye, I know you're lying. But if you seem to be lying, there's the barest chance you might be telling the truth. (*The servant and the cab driver appear. It is Garcia.*) Driver, here's a thousand pesos. (*Orton hands him some money from a drawer.*) I want you to drive the senorita directly to her apartment. No stops. Wait outside and make certain she does not leave that apartment the rest of the night. If she does, phone me immediately. (*He scrawls a phone number on a pad and hands it to Garcia.*) At six a.m. drive her directly to Campo Robles airport. You understand?

GARCIA. (*Folding the money into his pocket.*) For a thousand pesos, I can understand anything. (*He turns to go. The servant follows him out. Felicia seems completely defeated. The raincoat hangs around her like a collapsed circus tent. She looks tiny and pathetic. The hem of the coat drags on the floor as she moves to leave.*)

FELICIA. (*A whisper.*) Goodbye, Maxo. (*Without looking at him, she goes off. Orton watches her, then runs his hand across the smoothness of the fur, as if caressing a woman. He takes a fragment of the crepes framboises on his fork, but it is cold. The flavor is gone.*)

THE LIGHTS FADE

ACT ONE
SCENE 7

A basement restaurant on the Plaza. The same night, a few hours later. A neon sign reading "Cerveza" faces the street above, from which a staircase descends sharply into this all-night cafe, with dirty checkered cloths on the tables. Through an iron grill, the legs of passersby can be seen on the sidewalk above. There are intermittent late-at-night traffic sounds.

A toothless old man is mopping the floor. A sleepy-eyed waitress is clearing beer bottles from an empty table. There is a pay telephone on the wall.

Aguila and Portero are seated, each with a fratricidal contempt for the other. Aguila is the cynical up-from-the-ranks president of the Transport and Electrical Workers. He is shrewder than Portero, the bulking, husky-voiced head of the Butchers' Union.

They are not despicable men. They are opportunists.

Garcia stands with a bottle of beer, watching Felicia with the intensity of an acolyte. Felicia is going for broke. She still wears Orton's raincoat, and has tied a scarf over her head like a peasant's babushka. In the same spirit with which she played the grand lady, Felicia now casts herself as the Madame Roland of the proletariat.

Everything depends on convincing these two Labor giants, and she is feeling her way. Can she unite them? Or should she play one against the other? Her eyes dart from Aguila to Portero, then back to Aguila, who spits, leans back, crosses his arms insolently. Felicia is worried, but she tries to ignore this, lines up a coffee mug, a beer bottle and a bottle of chili sauce on the table.

FELICIA. (*Holding up the chili bottle.*) This is you. The people who work. (*To Portero.*) The Butchers. (*To Aguila.*) The Transport and Electrical Workers. (*Putting down the chili bottle, picking up the coffee mug.*) This is the people you work *for.*

PORTERO. Who's the beer bottle?

FELICIA. The military. (*Aguila spits.*) Put two of these together—any two—

you've got a government. (*Holding up the beer bottle.*) Brazo tried it alone. It didn't work. He needed *you*. He needed your strong backs.

GARCIA. (*Tasting the phrase.*) "Strong-Backs."

FELICIA. Together, you and Brazo— (*Clicking the chili sauce against the beer bottle.*) —can make a government! (*With the chili sauce and the beer bottle, she knocks the coffee mug off the table and it shatters on the floor.*) You clear the table! For a banquet, for the people who deserve to eat! (*Aguila, the intellectual, is staring at her glumly, trying to size her up. What makes the dame tick?*)

PORTERO. If the beer bottle gets in the Presidential Palace, what happens to the chili sauce?

FELICIA. (*Recklessly.*) Anything, you get anything you want!

AGUILA. (*Screwing up his face.*) From some flat-on-his-ass Colonel who can't even get himself out of jail?

FELICIA. *You're* going to get him out of jail!

AGUILA. (*Getting up.*) Jesus! Only a beef-brain like you, Portero, would even listen to this idiot.

GARCIA. (*Whispering, urgently, to Aguila.*) She has a lot of connections.

AGUILA. Sure. Below the waist. (*Patting his empty pockets.*) What time is it? I put on my clothes so fast I forgot my watch.

FELICIA. It's only a quarter past four. Plenty of time to—

AGUILA. (*To Garcia.*) Why the hell did you haul me outa bed in the middle of the night?

GARCIA. I'm a good union member. You couldn't miss this meeting. She said Portero was coming.

PORTERO. (*To Felicia.*) *You* told me Aguila was coming. (*Aguila shakes his head cynically.*)

AGUILA. Okay. We're both suckers. Come on, "good union member"—drive me home.

GARCIA. (*Proudly.*) I've already got a fare. (*Disgusted, Aguila starts up the stairs.*)

FELICIA. (*With exquisite calm.*) It's all right. It's better. Go home, go to bed, Senor Aguila. After all, there can only be *one* Minister of Labor in the cabinet of President Brazo. (*Aguila hesitates, half-way up the stairs.*) Senor Portero, *you* are the man to represent all the working people in the new government. *You* weren't to blame for the failure of the General Strike!

AGUILA. (*Brandishing his hand, proudly.*) That hand turned off every light in the city!

FELICIA. (*With skillful contempt.*) For how long? You didn't even stop the Liberation Ball. The rich people went right on dancing. The poor people made more babies.

PORTERO. They didn't have any orchestra at their damned ball.

FELICIA. Oh, yes, they did!

AGUILA. Fiddle players are all finks. You can't organize musicians.

FELICIA. If you'd had the Army—

AGUILA. We *had* the Army. On the other side! Who threw the tear gas at my boys at the power plant?

PORTERO. So you had a good cry and turned the lights back on!

AGUILA. (*Livid.*) What did you dumb hook-in-the-shank butchers do? Nothing! (*With non-sequitur suspicion.*) How does she know they had an orchestra?

FELICIA. (*Ignoring it.*) You needed Brazo!

AGUILA. He's a soldier!

FELICIA. He's a Colonel!

AGUILA. I wouldn't trust a lousy private!

FELICIA. When Brazo is in the Presidential Palace—

PORTERO. If he couldn't get there with the whole army—

FELICIA. General De Santes let him down!

AGUILA. See? The higher they go, the lousier they get! Generals! (*He spits.*)

FELICIA. (*Marveling.*) *You're* the generals, and you don't even know it! General Portero! General Aguila!

GARCIA. Major Garcia?

FELICIA. There's a *new* army. The unions. You're in command, and you don't even realize it.

AGUILA. (*Cynically.*) What do you know about unions?

FELICIA. (*Proudly.*) I'm a loyal dues-paying member of the Associated Guild of Actors!

AGUILA. (*Snorts.*) I mean a *working* union! Actors don't work!

FELICIA. Not enough. (*With irresistible authority, since she's lying.*) You want to see the shoes I wore thin, walking with a picket sign, because Radio Mundo was firing actors and hiring phonograph records?

AGUILA. (*Sniffing.*) You smell like money!

FELICIA. Is perfume only for rich people? Maybe the Strong-Backs would like to smell good. Or their wives. But what the hell are you doing for 'em? For *this* man? For this Strong-Back?

AGUILA. Portero, for once let's do something together: Let's get out of here.

FELICIA. (*With increasing tempo.*) You snivel, and beg, and put everybody out of work with strikes, so you can finally get your shoes on the carpets of the rich men's offices. And what do they give you after a thousand hours of talk? Maybe half-a-centavo an hour raise. If you're lucky. More likely fifty stitches in your head. Or a widow for a wife. (*Portero seems to be wavering. Garcia looks at her with awe and reverence. But Aguila is still unsold. She goes up a few steps toward Aguila.*) Are you important? Right now, locked up in Three Rivers, Brazo's more important than you are. Is anybody afraid of you? Who listens when you make a speech? Who claps? Who gives a damn? Brazo will make you important! You can run *more* than the truck drivers and the electrical workers. Why not? Minister of Public Power! How does that sound?

AGUILA. Who arrested Brazo? The Army! His *own local*! (*Felicia claps her hands triumphantly.*)

FELICIA. That proves it! He's fighting on your side. On *our* side. Brazo is one of us.

OLD MAN. (*With toothless enthusiasm.*) Bravo Brazo! (*The waitress applauds.*)

FELICIA. Hear that? The poor are for Brazo. Because Brazo was poorer than any of us: a naked little brat, running around in the dirt the way you did, the way I did. Tonight, Brazo was out there, risking his life for you. But you weren't with him. You let down the man who's fighting to go to work for you! (*Aguila shakes his head skeptically.*) Why shouldn't the government work for the working people? For us! For the unions! For the Strong-Backs!

WAITRESS. Yeah, why not?

FELICIA. (*Crossing to Portero, taking his arms.*) You, Portero, you're the man I can trust! You're going to be the hero tonight. People will remember the name PORTERO the rest of their lives.

PORTERO. A live Portero or a dead Portero?

FELICIA. They want to get Brazo out of the country. That's how much they're afraid of him. His plane takes off at 7:05. But if we keep him from getting on that plane—

AGUILA. How?

FELICIA. Something happens to his car along the road. How far is it from Three Rivers to the airport?

PORTERO. Oh—twenty kilometers.

GARCIA. On my meter, twenty-two.

FELICIA. (*Tempo, groping for ideas.*) Can there be an accident?

GARCIA. (*Eyes brightening.*) With a taxicab?

FELICIA. (*The idea growing.*) Bigger. A traffic tie-up. *Trucks*! Big trucks. Wide trucks. Slow trucks. Trucks with engine trouble. How many will it take to jam the airport road?

AGUILA. What would the Butcher Boy do?

PORTERO. (*Angrily to Aguila.*) Don't call me Butcher Boy!!!

FELICIA. (*Racing on, ignoring the friction.*) Get on the telephone! Pound on doors! Fill up the Plaza, like in the newsreels! You've got thousands of men in your union. Get 'em out of bed, wake up the whole damn city with the name "Brazo!"

PORTERO. That kind of thing takes time!

FELICIA. My God, you've got an hour and a half!

AGUILA. I don't know—

FELICIA. You can do it! If you've got guts enough!

AGUILA. Who pulls Brazo out of that traffic jam?

FELICIA. Can't you find a truck driver with muscle enough to smash a car window, reach in, turn the handle of a door? Maybe Senor Aguila will want to be there himself, to shake the hand of the new President! (*Unobtrusively, two military officers—a captain and a lieutenant—have entered, and stand silently at the head of the stairs, watching and listening.*)

PORTERO. (*Beginning to be sold.*) By God, we could do what we almost did the night of the strike. I'll get every member of my union in the Plaza. My "Strong-Backs." The strongest. Arc lights. Loudspeakers. And I, personally, the "Wild Bull of Labor," will— (*He breaks off, seeing that all are looking toward the top of the *stairs. Portero turns, pales at the sight of the military.*) The Butchers' Union disclaims any connection with any conspiracy of any kind. (*The two soldiers merely look.*)

FELICIA. (*With pure bravado, to the soldiers.*) Well? What do you think you can do about it? Are you going to shoot all the people who want Brazo? You'll have to shoot everybody in the country. (*The soldiers start slowly down the stairs. Felicia puts her arm protectively around Portero, challenging the officers.*) Don't try to intimidate this brave patriot. (*Pointing proudly to Aguila.*) Or my respected colleague, the head of the Transport and Electrical Workers. (*Before Aguila can protest, she races on.*) Senor Aguila has tasted your tear gas once, and he doesn't intend to taste it again.

CAPTAIN. (*Slowly, measuring her.*) We understand you tried to talk to our Commanding Officer tonight. And he wouldn't listen.

LIEUTENANT. Some of the younger officers at the Campo Marziale are very concerned about the General's hearing.

CAPTAIN. De Santes is half-deaf. But sometimes, if people make enough noise, even old saddle-face can hear. (*There's a static charge in the air. Felicia's abrupt decision is the spark which leaps the gap.*)

FELICIA. (*Taking command.*) Portero, get on the phone! Get your butchers in the Plaza. Aguila, get those trucks on the road. And Garcia, we *can* use those taxis. Hundreds of them. On every street leading into the Plaza. Sound your horns, again and again and again. Bra-zo! BRA-ZO! BRAA-ZO! (*The people in the cafe churn into action. Garcia races excitedly up the steps. Portero goes to the wall telephone. Aguila makes a shrill whistle between his fingers, then barks commands to his aides. The old man, carrying his mop like a drum-major's baton, marches in circles chanting "Brazo! Brazo! Brazo!" The waitress claps in rhythm. Outside a couple of taxi horns begin to honk "Brazo! Brazo!" The captain signals to the lieutenant and they hurry up the staircase. Felicia watches, bright-eyed as an arsonist at the first crackle of a forest fire. The action ceases to be literal. The cafe folds away, the sign and the grillwork fly. Felicia and Portero hurry off. Two huge arc lamps are wheeled on, and their blue-white beams sweep erratically about the theatre.*)

VOICES. (*Swelling in volume, joined by taxi horns, rhythmically.*) Brazo! Brazo! *Bra*-zo! *BRA*-zo!

ACT ONE
SCENE 8

The Plaza. Pre-dawn.

The entire cast is right down at the footlights, staring up as if to a high building. Behind them, the arc lights crisscross against the sky.

VOICES. Brazo! Brazo! Brazo! (*They are chanting as if by rote, but their faces are skeptical, squinting up to see who is atop the building. A microphone crackles alive from a loudspeaker on the balcony rail, or high in the back of the theatre. The voices quiet down to listen.*)

FELICIA'S VOICE. (*On P.A., from the back of the house.*) Citizens! Fellow workers! Listen to me!

MAN. (*Insolently.*) Why???? Who are you?

FELICIA'S VOICE. (*A slight hesitation, then a blast of bravado.*) Nobody!

2ND MAN. (*Hooting.*) Who?

FELICIA'S VOICE. Nobody at all. Except—I'm the most important person in the country. Because I'm *you*. We're a rich country. But do *I* have any of it? No! Do you have any of it?

ALL. No!

FELICIA'S VOICE. Brazo will give it to us. You, old man. Did you have an egg for breakfast?

OLD MAN. What's an egg? (*The crowd, warming to her, roars with laughter.*)

FELICIA'S VOICE. (*More confident.*) Brazo will see that you have an egg every morning. Where did *you* go to the bathroom?

WOMAN. The same place my grandmother did!

FELICIA'S VOICE. Brazo is for plumbing. Brazo is for eggs for everybody. Two eggs if you want 'em. Two toilets! (*Cheers from the crowd.*) Strong-Backs. My Strong-Backs! Why do I call you that? Because you all have strong backs—and that's *all* you've got. But Brazo will change that! Brazo will bring us justice. Not lying-lawyer justice, not Yanqui-justice. Brazo is for egg-in-your-stomach justice. Pesos-in-your-pocket justice. Perfume-for-your-wife justice. When you say "Brazo," you're saying your own name. Have you got the guts to say *your own name*?

MAN. Brazo. Brazo.

ALL. (*Joining gradually, so that it swells and swells.*) Brazo. Brazo. Brazo. (*Augment with taped voices, so that it rocks the theatre. Orton appears, shoving his way forward, trying to get their attention.*)

ORTON. Citizens! I am Maximiliano Orton. Listen to me— (*The chanting crowd shoves him back.*) —before it is too late.

FELICIA'S VOICE. (*Triumphantly.*) The Army is marching with him. The Unions are marching with him. Why aren't we *all* marching with him? March! March! March with Brazo! (*The fever has reached a peak. Drum beats begin and the intoxicated crowd swirls off, as the morning sky becomes flaming red.*)

CROWD. (*Chanting in rhythm as they fade off.*) Brazo. Brazo. Brazo. (*Orton, alone in the Plaza, a single figure against the sky, peers up at the building top.*)

ORTON. Has it tired you, child? Having intercourse with all these people?

CURTAIN

ACT TWO

SCENE 1

The Master Bedroom in the Presidential Palace. The ornate canopy of a completely covered bed is hung from the flies, but there is no practical bed. The only visible furniture is a gold-embossed chair and a small table with a silver champagne bucket filled with ice and champagne and with two glasses.

Brazo, in custom-tailored pajamas, is spinning the magnum of champagne in the ice bucket. Brazo calls apparently to a dressing room, off.

BRAZO. Felicia? (*Pause. No answer.*) Little Angel? (*Still no answer.*) You're taking longer than usual. (*Restlessly, Brazo paces, sucking in his stomach narcissistically. He does a few military deep knee bends. Then he bends over to touch his toes, and almost succeeds. With just a hint of impatience.*) Whenever you're ready, I'm ready, Little Angel. (*Felicia enters, fully dressed. Brazo is surprised and disappointed.*) You're dressed.

FELICIA. (*Preoccupied.*) Yes.

BRAZO. (*Baffled.*) I expected that—well—what have you been doing in there all that time?

FELICIA. (*Softly.*) Praying.

BRAZO. Our prayers have been answered, haven't they?

FELICIA. Some of them.

BRAZO. I know. I know what it is. You feel *strange* here in the Presidential Palace.

FELICIA. Not at all.

BRAZO. No? *I* do. So many hallways, a man could get lost. (*He laughs. She doesn't. He goes to the ice bucket, spins the champagne bottle.*) Well, here's the stuff to make us feel at home, hm? (*Popping the cork, Brazo pours two champagne glasses, spilling some of the wine on his pajamas.*) I'm launching myself. (*Brazo laughs at his own joke, but Felicia doesn't react. He lifts his glass.*) What do we drink to? To you, Little Angel. To your first night with the President of the Republic. Salud. (*Felicia doesn't drink.*) What's wrong?

FELICIA. I am not worthy.

BRAZO. Why, I might not even be here, if it weren't for you. Do you realize that?

FELICIA. (*Softly.*) Do you?

BRAZO. Chances are I'd still be in Three Rivers, if you hadn't— (*Breaking off.*) You think I'm not grateful, is that it? Little Angel, I'm the most grateful man in the world.

FELICIA. It stinks, doesn't it? Being grateful. It's like owing money.

BRAZO. What do you want me to do? Anything at all, you just tell me, and I'll do it.

FELICIA. You're tired, Senor President. You've had an exhausting day. I want you to go to bed.

BRAZO. Oh? (*Glancing at his pajamas.*) I—frankly, I fully intended to.

FELICIA. (*With a trace of intensity now, for the first time.*) And at any time, if there's anything I can do for you—ask! That's all you have to do.

BRAZO. Well, I—

FELICIA. No hesitation. Feel perfectly free, Senor President.

BRAZO. Please, *Jorge.*

FELICIA. I'll be honored if I can help in your important work. I have some very definite ideas in mind.

BRAZO. So do I.

FELICIA. I warn you, I may surprise you.

BRAZO. (*With a little chuckle.*) I don't mind being surprised.

FELICIA. But you're too tired.

BRAZO. Not at all. Couldn't feel better. Champing at the bit.

FELICIA. (*With quiet authority.*) All right. Stand on that chair.

BRAZO. Beg pardon?

FELICIA. That chair. I want you to stand on it, please.

BRAZO. Why?

FELICIA. I'm going to make love to you.

BRAZO. On a chair?

FELICIA. It's completely different from any sensation you've ever felt before. Go ahead. Go ahead. (*After some thought, Brazo climbs up on the chair and waits expectantly. But Felicia backs away.*) Now. You know where you are?

BRAZO. Standing on a chair in my pajamas. I feel like a damn fool.

FELICIA. You're on a balcony. Look down. There are ten thousand people watching you. More. Twenty thousand!

BRAZO. What an imagination!

FELICIA. You're wearing a white uniform, white for purity. (*Backing away another step.*) Look around you. Smile. Be warm. You're too stiff. Project your personality.

BRAZO. (*Starting to get down.*) Felicia, this is not the time to—

FELICIA. Stay there! (*She means it. He stays.*) Do you know who I am? A little girl, without shoes even. (*Kicking off her shoes.*) I sat up a day and a night and a day on a train-coach to come to the capital, to see you, to see my President, to stand here in the Plaza, way at the edge of the crowd. And all I want in the world is to make love to you, and have you make love to me.

BRAZO. Fine. (*He starts to get down again.*)

FELICIA. (*Sharply.*) No!!!! (*He stops, still on the chair.*) From the balcony. There are thousands of people down here. Make love to *all* of us.

BRAZO. You exaggerate my power.

FELICIA. Stretch out your hands! Take us all in your arms!

BRAZO. Little Angel, some people can do that sort of thing. It's not my gait.

FELICIA. I tell you: Jorge Salvador Brazo can do anything.

BRAZO. Fine. (*Getting down from the chair.*) But for tonight, tell these ten thousand people to get out of our bedroom. I like love on a more personal basis.

FELICIA. Heavy breathing in the dark? Is that all you think love is? You don't know anything about love.

BRAZO. (*Offended.*) Well, now, I wouldn't say—

FELICIA. (*Paying no attention to him.*) I used to think it was something that happened between a man and a woman. It isn't. That's just sex. (*Jumping up on the chair.*) Love is what happens up here. High. Alone. Except for all the people. Faces. Thousands. Looking up. At me. (*Reliving the ecstasy of the rooftop.*) With love. I can feel it. I can feel their love rising from the streets, like heat against my body! It's marvelous, Jorge. The highest kind of love. Like a holy sacrament. (*She reaches down to draw Brazo up on the chair beside her, but he resists.*) You can feel it, too, Jorge. Here, beside me. (*Reluctantly, Brazo gets up on the chair with her. He is only thinking about her closeness. But Felicia is still intoxicated with what that crowd gave her.*) All those people down there. Wanting you. Loving you. (*His arms are around her.*) When you get them to love you, they'll give you everything. Gladly. (*Slowly, she unbuttons his pajama top and slips it off, so it drops to the floor. Brazo is going crazy as she runs her fingers over the muscles of his back.*)

BRAZO. Are you going to give me everything? Tonight?

FELICIA. But it's different now. (*She gets off the chair.*)

BRAZO. Why?

FELICIA. You're the President.

BRAZO. I'm the same man I was when I wasn't the President.

FELICIA. (*Remotely.*) Why, I'd be disrespectful if I even thought of dragging you back into that shabby kind of relationship. You're the Chief of State. Everybody looks up to you. Like the flag. Oh, there mustn't be anything about you that's tawdry or undignified. (*Felicia slips on her shoes, preparing to leave. Brazo starts to get off the chair.*) No, no, stay there. So I can look up to you! All alone, up there on your pedestal. My poor lonely President! (*She starts to leave. Brazo is desperate with frustration.*)

BRAZO. Little Angel, this is the one night I wanted to celebrate with love, a victory kiss on every part of your body.

FELICIA. (*Piously.*) A man in your high position should only do things like that with his wife.

BRAZO. But I don't have a wife.

FELICIA. (*With a soft smile.*) When you do. (*Felicia pats his cheek and goes out, leaving Brazo standing on the chair in his pajama pants, frustrated and miserable. The lights go out quickly. In the darkness there is a joyous pealing of church bells, which dissolves into the ringing of a telephone. The phone is picked up.*)

SOCIAL SECRETARY'S VOICE. (*In the dark.*) Senora Brazo's social secretary speaking. The First Lady is not in.

ACT TWO
SCENE 2

The lights come up on Felicia's sanctum in the Presidential Palace. Several outré abstract paintings have been dropped from the flies. There is a low Danish-modern sofa. Upstage and up several steps is a balcony with a draped window.

A female social secretary is talking into a gold French phone.

SOCIAL SECRETARY. All I can do is put you on the appointment list. (*A male secretary, carrying a sheaf of typed memos, ushers in several servants and a liveried chauffeur, who hurry on with stacks of boxes from expensive shops. The social secretary gestures toward the couch, where they pile the boxes and go off. Into phone:*) It's difficult to say. Possibly two or three weeks. (*She hangs up.*)

MALE SECRETARY. Where's the Virgin Mary?

SOCIAL SECRETARY. Some day she's going to hear you. (*The phone rings again. The social secretary picks it up. Into phone:*) Senora Brazo's social secretary speaking. (*Closing her eyes: Oh, God!*) Postponed until when? (*Listening.*) I'll convey the Cardinal's regrets to the Senora. (*Hanging up slowly.*) Have you got today's appointment list?

MALE SECRETARY. (*Handing her a typewritten sheet.*) What's wrong with Frazzini?

SOCIAL SECRETARY. Sick.

MALE SECRETARY. I'll bet.

SOCIAL SECRETARY. (*Crossing off one line.*) Four p.m. Audience with Cardinal Frazzini. Cancelled. (*She hands the appointment list back to the male secretary, but he refuses to take it.*)

MALE SECRETARY. Oh, no. *You* tell her.

PORTERO'S VOICE. (*From off.*) I don't care. Shoot me. I'm not going to wait any longer! (*He bursts in, followed by a uniformed guard. Frantically, Portero addresses the male secretary.*)

PORTERO. She's got to see me. I'm a very important man. It's a disgrace to keep "The Wild Bull of Labor" penned up in a waiting room for three days. I want to see Senora Brazo.

SOCIAL SECRETARY. She isn't here.

MALE SECRETARY. And she certainly won't be able to see you today.

PORTERO. (*Fiercely.*) She's got to see me. Tell her promises were made—and broken!

SOCIAL SECRETARY. I wouldn't use that tone with the Senora.

MALE SECRETARY. If you phone for an appointment—

PORTERO. I've phoned. Nobody will give me an appointment. Always "two or three weeks."

FELICIA'S VOICE. (*Off.*) Did they deliver the packages? (*The guard and the male secretary try to get Portero out.*)

PORTERO. I'm going to stay right here! I'm going to talk to her! (*Felicia sweeps on, flushed with excitement. She is wearing a strikingly tailored suit; she carries a fur-piece, which she tosses aside.*)

FELICIA. Oh. Portero.

PORTERO. Senora. I've got to talk with you.

FELICIA. About what?

PORTERO. A great many things.

FELICIA. That's very nice, but I don't have time now. My mother's just arrived from the country, I'm meeting Dona Elena Rivera, and the Cardinal is waiting for me. I couldn't possibly—

PORTERO. One question, Senora. Where is Aguila?

FELICIA. Aguila?

PORTERO. Understand, he's no friend of mine. But even his wife doesn't know where he is.

FELICIA. (*Seeing the boxes, ignoring Portero.*) Is this everything?

SOCIAL SECRETARY. Yes, Senora. (*Eagerly, Felicia breaks strings and opens boxes.*)

FELICIA. (*Calling.*) In here, Mama. Come see!

PORTERO. (*Doggedly.*) All I want to know is—

FELICIA. Forty years my Mother has been waiting for a day like this. So have I. Well, not forty years, of course, but— (*Breaking off, pointing to a box.*) What's in that one?

SOCIAL SECRETARY. (*Opening the box.*) I'll see, Senora.

PORTERO. (*Looking about, desperately.*) Somebody, pay attention. In my own union, when I said "Listen," somebody listened. (*A voluptuous fur has come out of the box. Felicia examines it, ignoring Portero.*)

FELICIA. Exquisite!

PORTERO. Now, I'm *Under*secretary in the Ministry of Labor. Nobody even calls me on the telephone. (*Felicia has flung on the coat, models it.*)

SOCIAL SECRETARY. Your Mother will be overjoyed.

FELICIA. (*Thoughtfully.*) I don't think it suits her coloring. Better hang this in *my* closet. (*The social secretary goes out with the coat.*)

PORTERO. (*Dismally.*) Senora— (*Felicia edges Portero out and into the custody of the guard and male secretary.*)

FELICIA. I can't tell you how eager I am to hear all of your suggestions for the new government. But later, when I don't have so many appointments.

PORTERO. In two or three weeks.

FELICIA. No, no. Sooner. Wait. I'll try to work you in. (*Portero goes out, escorted by the guard.*)

MALE SECRETARY. (*Tentatively.*) Has the Senora checked the revised appointment list?

FELICIA. Revised? How? (*Seeing her Mother, Felicia breaks off.*) Mama! Surprises! Big surprises! All for you! (*Mama shuffles in, her face creased with sun-baked good humor. She looks like a Latin Mrs. Khrushchev. She wears rope sandals and a coarse, shapeless dress. Her hair resembles a well-used S.O.S. pad.*)

MAMA. Here. I'm right here, Baby. (*Felicia shakes out a black dress, holds up some high-heeled shoes, some lace underthings.*)

FELICIA. This is for you, Mama. And this. And these.

MAMA. Doesn't all this cost a lot of money?

FELICIA. Of course it costs a lot of money.

MAMA. Who pays?

FELICIA. It's to make people happy. I have to wear beautiful things—so they'll see the miracle that can happen to anybody in a free country! And, Mama, when you're all dressed up, and you wave to the crowds from the limousine going to the Cardinal's palace, they'll see what can happen to anybody's Mama, too! (*Handing her the clothes.*) Put these on, I want to see how you look.

MAMA. (*Mystified by the strange garments.*) I don't know how.

FELICIA. (*Calling.*) Cecile! Help my Mother get into these things. (*The social secretary hurries back in, starts gathering boxes.*)

SOCIAL SECRETARY. Yes, Senora.

MAMA. (*Picking up a corset, apprehensively.*) This is to wear?

FELICIA. To make you slim.

MAMA. (*Unbelieving.*) Slim!

FELICIA. (*Holding up a high-fashion shoe.*) All the way from Fifth Avenue in New York.

MAMA. (*Wanting to back out.*) Why don't you go see the Cardinal and tell me about it?

FELICIA. You've got to go, Mama. This is the most marvelous day of your life!

MAMA. What do I say to a Cardinal?

FELICIA. I'll talk. Just look happy. And when he holds out his hand, kiss his ring. That's all you have to do.

MALE SECRETARY. (*Cautiously.*) About the appointments—

FELICIA. And when you get back home, if that little pig-faced priest gets nasty with you in the confessional, just ask him if *he* ever had a private audience with a Prince of the Church. Ask him. Go. Get beautiful.

MAMA. (*Shaking her head.*) I'll try. (*Mama and the social secretary go off with boxes.*)

FELICIA. I'm expecting Dona Elena Rivera. Let me know the minute she arrives.

MALE SECRETARY. She got here at two.

FELICIA. (*Startled.*) And she's just been sitting out there? Since two o'clock? (*The secretary nods.*) Have her come in, for God's sake; don't leave her out there any longer.

MALE SECRETARY. Yes, Senora. (*The secretary goes off. Felicia is distressed at her faux pas. Alone, she smooths her hair, straightens her skirt. She moistens her lips, assumes a regal pose. Dona Elena enters. The two women look at each other, each waiting for the other's gambit.*)

FELICIA. Dona Elena.

DONA ELENA. Senora Brazo.

FELICIA. Please sit down. (*They both sit, at opposite ends of the couch. There is a moment of uncertain silence.*) We should have photographers. It's so rare to find two First Ladies—side by side! (*There is not a flicker of reaction from Dona Elena.*) But, naturally, I discourage any cheap publicity. The office I hold, that my *husband* holds, this very room I consider sacred.

DONA ELENA. (*Glancing around at the modern new trimmings.*) Yes.

FELICIA. It's shocking that we don't spend more time together. We're so much alike. Our husbands too. Yours was a great man. So is mine. Why, this must seem like a homecoming to you.

DONA ELENA. President Rivera and I spent many eventful years here.

FELICIA. I shall always remember that glorious evening we had together at the Case Rivera. That dear old man, Dr. Guzmano. So wise! Dona Elena, I knew instantly, that night, what good friends we were going to be. (*No response.*) You had the same feeling, didn't you? I could tell. (*An eloquent vacuum.*) That's why I feel free to ask you for advice.

DONA ELENA. Are you sure that you would welcome my advice?

FELICIA. That's why I invited you here. You must tell me. What exactly are my responsibilities? In connection with the Liberation Day Ball?

DONA ELENA. I don't understand.

FELICIA. As First Lady. What am I expected to do? I know how important tradition is to you, and oh, I share that, that solemn respect for tradition. How much it means to all your ladies.

DONA ELENA. *My* ladies?

FELICIA. Of your Society. For Benevolence. What did *you* do, when your husband took office? Did you volunteer? Or wait for the ladies to invite you?

DONA ELENA. I was already a member of the organization.

FELICIA. But the wife of the President is automatically the president of your Society.

DONA ELENA. Not automatically.

FELICIA. (*Rises, walks about energetically.*) You understand, social functions don't hold any glamour for *me*. The joy of charity for me is giving, giving. In the Hundred

Days I have—my husband and I—have been here in the Palace, I've found out what a joy it is, doing for others. The President, *our* President, works every night until midnight—until one, two, three o'clock in the morning. I am here, too, I try to help him, to be at his side. (*Softening.*) And before the few hours sleep I take, I sink to my knees by my bed to say a benediction for the "Strong-Backs" who do the work of this country. I know the poor, Dona Elena. I know how to pray for the poor.

DONA ELENA. (*After a pause.*) I also pray.

FELICIA. You see? We want the same things, we have the same high purpose. Go tell your ladies: with humility, I offer myself as your president.

DONA ELENA. With all the burden of assisting your husband, where would you find the hours to serve our organization?

FELICIA. I—

DONA ELENA. The membership might feel it is an unfair demand to press upon you.

FELICIA. (*Restraining her anger with difficulty.*) But if it's traditional—

DONA ELENA. (*With no malice.*) It is traditional for our Charity to be led by a woman of— (*Pausing, euphemizing.*) —shall we say, greater *maturity.*

FELICIA. Maturity. I see. Yes. An older woman *should* be at the head of such an ancient organization. (*Shouting.*) MAMA!!!! (*To Dona Elena.*) Naturally, your members would be embarrassed by young vigorous leadership, you want somebody of your own generation somebody you can respect— (*Yelling, with no respect whatsoever.*) Mama, get in here!!! (*Bewildered, Mama enters. Her chic black dress is unhooked up the back. She teeters on unaccustomed high heels. Her hair is half-combed.*)

MAMA. (*In pain.*) Yes, Baby?

FELICIA. Dona Elena, may I present my revered mother, Dona Rosa Jamas. Mama, Dona Elena is here to offer you a great honor. (*To Dona Elena.*) You may announce to your membership that the Mother of the First Lady is delighted to be your president, and to bring her wisdom and maturity to your Society. (*Mama doesn't follow.*) My Mother is too moved to speak. I accept for her. (*Dona Elena rises.*)

DONA ELENA. (*To Mama, with genuine kindness.*) Senora Jamas, I do not wish to see you embarrassed. May I be quite truthful? If you send out the invitations to the Liberation Day Ball, no one will come. (*A taut pause.*)

FELICIA. Why? Why won't anybody come?

DONA ELENA. (*Discreetly.*) I don't think you can change, in a hundred days, the ways things have been for a hundred years. (*Felicia stares at her with frustrated fury.*) If you'll excuse me, I shall return to my own century. What remains of it. (*To Mama.*) I hope you have a pleasant stay in the capital, Senora Jamas. (*Dona Elena goes out. Mama smiles wanly.*)

MAMA. I like her. She reminds me of your father's real wife. (*Felicia retains her hauteur until Dona Elena is gone. Then she breaks into a mixture of anger and tears.*)

FELICIA. The bitch! The god-damned bitch!

MAMA. It's my fault, Baby. If I'd been married when you were born—

FELICIA. You were.

MAMA. What?

FELICIA. Jorge had the records changed. I'm legitimate.

MAMA. (*Pleased.*) I didn't know you could do that.

FELICIA. (*Studying her Mother.*) Get out of those clothes.

MAMA. Don't you like the way I—?

FELICIA. You look like hell. (*Calling.*) Ricardo! Send all this rubbish back to the fashion faggots on the Avenida Francais. (*Both secretaries reappear.*) My Mother will wear her own clothes when we pay our respects to the Cardinal. I'm proud of you, Mama. I want His Eminence to see you the way you are. Dirt under your fingernails, no manicures. Felicia Brazo's Mama is like everybody else's. That's what makes me SPECIAL! (*Dismissing them.*) Hurry up, change. We want to be on time at the Cardinal's Palace. The courtesy of royalty. (*The secretaries exchange glances.*)

SOCIAL SECRETARY. Has the Senora checked the changes in the appointment list?

FELICIA. Changes? (*The social secretary hands her the paper. Felicia reads, then speaks softly.*) What excuse did he give?

SOCIAL SECRETARY. His secretary said he was sick.

FELICIA. He'd better be sick! He'd better be dying!

MAMA. Don't be too disappointed, Baby, on account of me.

FELICIA. *I'm* not disappointed. It's the insult. Not to you, to me. No, to the President. (*Pacing, restless, frustrated.*) Who makes the rich rich? And the cardinals holy? The poor people! But Frazzini and Dona Elena, they don't know anything about poor people. Brazo knows. *I* know! The Strong-Backs know! (*An idea is forming in her mind.*) Is Portero still out there?

MALE SECRETARY. I'll find out, Senora. (*The male secretary goes out.*)

MAMA. (*Slipping out of one shoe.*) Is it all right if—?

FELICIA. (*Preoccupied.*) Put on your sandals, Mama. Go barefoot, if you want to.

MAMA. (*Sighs, relieved.*) Thank you, Baby, you're a good girl. (*Marveling at the high heeled shoes in her hand.*) God help the Yanquis. (*Mama pads off, followed by the social secretary. Felicia quickly lights a cigarette, excited by her new idea. Portero appears.*)

FELICIA. Sit down, sit down. I want to talk with you about something. (*Portero sits uncertainly.*) You aren't happy. I can tell. You think you're wasted in your present job. You want to be more important.

PORTERO. After all, I'm not a nobody. You said it yourself: in the new army, I'm a General.

FELICIA. (*Measuring him.*) You want to be a General? Like De Santes?

PORTERO. (*Hastily.*) No, no, no, not like General De Santes.

FELICIA. He wanted to be important, too. He wanted to be more important than the President. My husband was very disappointed when De Santes took asylum in the Bolivian Embassy.

PORTERO. I don't want to be *that* important.

FELICIA. Or your friend, Aguila.

PORTERO. Not my friend, but—where is he?

FELICIA. He couldn't seem to understand President Brazo's idea of making the Labor Movement one great Union, protected by the State. So he is going to school.

PORTERO. Is this "college" at Three Rivers?

FELICIA. Don't you want to hear about my plan for you? I'm starting a great new charity, to replace the worn-out Society for Benevolence. (*Pacing.*) Oh, it's beautiful. And who is going to be in charge of fund-raising? The Wild Ox of Labor!

PORTERO. (*Correcting her.*) Bull. Wild *Bull* of Labor.

FELICIA. It'll mean handling an enormous amount of money. Can I depend on you?

PORTERO. (*Brightening for the first time.*) No question. Absolutely.

FELICIA. Senor Portero. You may contribute 25,000 pesos annually on behalf of the Butchers' Union.

PORTERO. (*As if jolted by an electric shock.*) But I don't have a union anymore.

FELICIA. But the butchers look to you as their leader. You'll want to set an example in giving.

PORTERO. (*Pale.*) But—25,000 pesos!

FELICIA. For charity. For God's work.

PORTERO. (*Weakly.*) I tithe regularly to the Church.

FELICIA. A tithe? An agent's commission. (*Growing more excited.*) Portero! You make the announcement. Through the Labor Ministry. Every working-man will voluntarily contribute two days' wages every year to my new charity. That'll give them a sense of belonging, don't you think?

PORTERO. (*Dazed.*) It'll be hundreds of millions of pesos!

FELICIA. Think of the good I'll be able to do!

PORTERO. Senora. What happened to the bottle of chili sauce? (*She doesn't answer. She seems possessed. Portero looks at her with genuine fear.*)

THE LIGHTS FADE

ACT TWO
SCENE 3

Orton's villa. Ten weeks later. Centered behind a long table is a throne-like chair. Where the tapestry had hung previously are now two huge banners: blown-up photographs of Brazo and Felicia, political posters with clenched-fist aggressiveness.

It is late at night.

Garcia comes on, much better dressed than before. He is obviously in charge, and enjoys authority. Over it all, he has assumed an air of hushed religiosity: one almost feels he wants to cross himself at the sight of Felicia. Garcia waves in two soldiers, who come on with drawn rifles, guarding Portero, who follows, carrying two heavy suitcases. Portero is wearing an overcoat. Everyone is weary.

PORTERO. Every July gets colder than last July.

GARCIA. You know why you're cold? You're selfish.

PORTERO. Don't tell me why I'm cold. I'm cold because it's cold. (*Portero places the two suitcases on the table. Garcia opens them and unpacks bundles of peso notes, which he stacks lovingly on the table. Portero stares at the money, slightly transfixed.*)

GARCIA. You just wish some of this money was yours.

PORTERO. (*Wistfully.*) It is. (*Mama wanders in. She is wearing a bright, loose-fitting peasant dress and rope sandals. She is munching some sticky candy out of a paper bag.*)

MAMA. Where's my baby?

PORTERO. Your baby is having some coffee—so she can keep us all up the rest of the night.

MAMA. Make her sleep. I tell her—but she won't listen. (*Offering candy.*) You want some?

PORTERO. Not candy.

MAMA. I've been counting the bathrooms. You know how many there are? Eleven!

GARCIA. Senator Orton used to live here. Very rich man.

MAMA. When you get rich, you gotta have eleven bathrooms? (*Felicia enters, sipping a demitasse.*)

FELICIA. How many people still waiting?

PORTERO. Thousands. The line still goes all the way around the Plaza.

FELICIA. We'll stay all night if we have to. And all day tomorrow.

GARCIA. It's not only the money they want, Senora. Mostly they want to see *you*—up close!

MAMA. Nobody can do so much, Baby.

FELICIA. *I* can, Mama. I am Felicia Brazo, First Lady of the Republic! This won't be enough. We'll need more.

PORTERO. I'll get it. (*He goes out. Garcia motions soldiers to follow.*)

FELICIA. (*Sitting.*) Have them begin again. I am ready to see more of my people.

GARCIA. (*Off.*) Single file. One at a time. State your case briefly. No pushing. (*Mama starts out.*)

FELICIA. Where are you going, Mama?

MAMA. To bed. I'm not a First Lady. I have to sleep.

FELICIA. Don't you like to see me make people happy?

MAMA. It's for such a little while.

FELICIA. What if they've never been happy at *all*? Nobody ever gave those people anything! A little gift from me, a few pesos, it makes them feel good. What if it's only for an hour? Or a minute? It's better than nothing, isn't it? Mama? (*Mama shrugs. Portero returns with two more suitcases of new bills, guarded closely by the soldiers. They pile the money high on the table.*)

MAMA. Centavos I understand. Pesos is for rich people.

FELICIA. I give them more than pesos, I listen to them. Nobody ever did that before. (*Mama watches as Garcia ushers in an old woman, bent over, with a babushka on her head.*) My dear woman. What can the Felicia Brazo Foundation do for you?

WOMAN. My husband needs to go to the hospital. He will die if nobody takes care of him.

FELICIA. *I* shall take care of him. (*She takes a generous sheaf of bills and hands them to the woman, who bows, then impulsively rushes and kisses the hem of Felicia's dress.*)

WOMAN. Bless you. You are our beloved saint. You have been sent down from heaven. (*The woman bows out. Felicia looks out and down, as through a window.*)

FELICIA. Look, Mama. All the people. (*Mama shrugs, not looking.*)

MAMA. I saw. (*Offering the sack to her daughter.*) You want some candy?

FELICIA. (*Paying no attention.*) How many do you think? A thousand? More, maybe. Like outside a theatre, to see a big movie star.

MAMA. (*Still proffering the candy.*) We never used to have candy like this except on a Feast Day, a Saint's Day. (*A white-haired old-man-with-a-crutch bobbles in. With a friendly smile, Mama offers him a piece of candy. Surprised, he likes it.*)

OLD-MAN-WITH-A-CRUTCH. (*Graciously.*) Why, thank you! (*Mama goes out. Felicia takes her post behind the money table.*)

FELICIA. You wish money for an operation.

OLD-MAN-WITH-A-CRUTCH. (*Patting his crutch.*) No. Only a mattress, a clean place to sleep, so I am not a burden to my children and grandchildren. (*Orton comes in from the opposite side. He stands, watching, arms folded. But Felicia doesn't see him.*)

FELICIA. I'm building a home for you, old man.

OLD-MAN-WITH-A-CRUTCH. (*His face brightening.*) Oh?

FELICIA. For everyone who is rich in years but not in pesos.

OLD-MAN-WITH-A-CRUTCH. (*Disappointed, his shoulders slumping.*) Oh.

FELICIA. (*Enthusing.*) Not just an old people's home. A *palace*! And every one of you will have a maid and a butler.

OLD-MAN-WITH-A-CRUTCH. Senora, that palace will never be finished before I am.

ORTON. Give him some money, Senora. Let him imagine his own heaven. (*Felicia turns, startled.*)

FELICIA. Maxo!

ORTON. (*With modulated bitterness.*) Should I have waited in line? I know other entrances to this house; I used to live here. (*This is their first vis-a-vis since the coup. Felicia doesn't know quite what to expect from Orton.*)

FELICIA. This is public property now. You are part of the public. (*Despite her outrages to him, the spark is still warm. Orton studies her.*)

ORTON. You're thinner.

FELICIA. I give myself. The joy of giving. (*She hands a wad of money to the old man.*) Take this. And bless you.

OLD-MAN-WITH-A-CRUTCH. God be praised. You are a saint. (*The old man hobbles off.*)

FELICIA. (*To Orton, her face shining.*) You hear that? You hear what he called me?

ORTON. I've always wanted to know how to be a saint. Now I can take lessons. Right in my own house.

FELICIA. I suppose you want it back?

ORTON. Naturally. But that's not why I came here.

FELICIA. What *do* you want? (*She turns, calls.*) Portero, stop the line.

ORTON. The "Wild Bull of Labor"? How did you get a ring through *his* nose?

FELICIA. A volunteer. (*Orton snorts, goes to the little table which used to contain liqueurs, opens the door and rummages among the empty bottles. She follows him.*) You don't appreciate what I've done for you. Letting you contribute this house to my glorious work!

ORTON. (*Drily.*) I doubt if a gift was ever less spontaneously made.

FELICIA. My "Strong-Backs" think you're against them. A dirty rich man. I'm trying to soap you clean. (*Orton pretends to fill two snifters.*) What are you doing? There isn't anything in there. (*He hands her an empty glass, warming his own in the palm of his hand.*)

ORTON. Air! The elemental wine. Not a good year. But we should be grateful, I suppose, for breathing. And what other luxuries your husband has left us.

FELICIA. Jorge wouldn't think that was funny.

ORTON. Neither do I. (*He lifts his glass toward the empty chair where Felicia was sitting.*) A toast. To *her*!

FELICIA. Who?

ORTON. Why, the blessed damozel behind the money table. The "Saint."

FELICIA. She *is* a Saint!

ORTON. She's a soap sales-girl!

FELICIA. You have no reverence!

ORTON. You have no sense of humor! You used to have.

FELICIA. This woman has no time for humor. Her work is too important, too serious.

ORTON. Serious! You're bright enough to see how comical this is.

FELICIA. I feel sorry for you. You didn't even see that old man, did you? The expression in his face, in his eyes.

ORTON. (*Slowly, not derisively.*) As a sponsor, I'd never have cast you in this role.

FELICIA. You're blasphemous. Watch! (*Felicia moves into the chair. Calling.*) I am ready to see more of my people. (*A man-with-a-cap enters, hesitates. Orton is both fascinated and horrified.*) Watch how they come to me like innocent children—and I am the Mother of them all! (*Stretching out her arms to the man-with-a-cap.*) Ask, my friend. What is your trouble?

MAN-WITH-A-CAP. (*Avoiding her eyes, turning his cap in his hands.*) My affliction is—unmentionable in front of the Senora. (*Jerking his thumb toward Orton.*) I could whisper it to *him.*

FELICIA. (*Hastily, forcing some bills on him.*) Go to the clinic. Buy medicine.

MAN-WITH-A-CAP. (*Starting out.*) Thank you, Senora. Thank you. (*Stopping.*) Uh—there's a girl, ten behind me in the line. She needs the same—

FELICIA. (*Waving him away.*) Everyone will be taken care of! (*The man goes out. Felicia looks at Orton's impassive face, which infuriates her. She calls out.*) No more! (*Defiantly to Orton.*) You see? Justice. Justice and charity for everybody!

ORTON. Everybody?

FELICIA. Even sinners!

ORTON. What about Guzmano?

FELICIA. (*Bluffing innocence.*) Guzmano?

ORTON. I'm not here to ask any favors for myself. Only for him.

FELICIA. If the Doctor has some complaint, why doesn't *he* come here?

ORTON. He's too old to freeze in a beggars' line!

FELICIA. He doesn't have to wait in any line. His name is even on the letterhead of the Felicia Brazo Foundation.

ORTON. Did he give you permission to use his name?

FELICIA. Did the King of Sweden ask his permission to give him the Nobel Prize? It's an honor to be part of this great work!

ORTON. Guzmano denies any connection with you, or Brazo, or this "money-dispensary"! The day he told that to a correspondent from the *New York Times* was the *last* time he got any supplies. And the next day, the *Times* man was kicked out of the country.

FELICIA. (*Evasively.*) I don't know anything about it.

ORTON. You do now. (*Taking her arm, forcefully.*) Don't withhold medicine from Dr. Guzmano.

FELICIA. (*Pulling away, pacing.*) Oh, I want to give him more than just medicine. A hospital: tall, slim, gleaming white. Rising up out of the mud of the Rio de Oro like a prayer to heaven. Inside, everything cool, clean. Spotless beds. Stainless steel. And the laboratory—anything Guzmano wants. Ten thousand white mice, if he asks for them; and all the knives and needles he needs to slice them up.

ORTON. He'll be happy if his medical requisitions are filled.

FELICIA. He has no imagination. Do you know what charity was in this country, when those old women were running it? It was dirty. Shameful. But Felicia glorifies the poor!

ORTON. Well, I am on the road to glory.

FELICIA. Tomorrow morning, I'll have a limousine call for you. To show you my "Village for Children."

ORTON. I've seen your "model orphanage."

FELICIA. Not orphanage.

ORTON. Whatever you call it.

FELICIA. Did you see the little blue post office? And the darling bank with everything just the right size for children to play like grown-ups?

ORTON. (*Nods.*) And your miniature fire department. And the swings, and the slides, and the wading pool—

FELICIA. Isn't it a perfect place for children to live?

ORTON. It's got everything. Except children.

FELICIA. What?

ORTON. Where children live, you see a few signs of children *living*: a crayon mark on the wall, a smudge of fingers on a door, a spot on the floor where oatmeal's been spilled. Not there! Just starched puppet-clothes in the closets; no child ever wore them.

FELICIA. Well, when you were there, the children must've been away—

ORTON. They've always been away. There were never any children! The whole thing's a sham, a big shiny exhibit for tourists! You think Guzmano wants a hospital like that—without patients? With an operating room like a display in a department store window?

FELICIA. I'm doing more good than Guzmano is, for God's sake.

ORTON. For *Felicia's* sake. What good are all those medicines in a warehouse where you dole them out to the jelly-brained doctors who are politically acceptable? We've got a brand-new Bible: the King Brazo version! "The meek shall inherit the penicillin, and breath belongs to the Felicia-in-heart."

FELICIA. When you go to confessional, I hope you'll ask forgiveness for that. If you ever go to confessional.

ORTON. Do you know what the church thinks of Brazo? And you?

FELICIA. Frazzini? A red hat can't make you holy! (*Pounding the table.*) *This* is religion!

ORTON. Money?

FELICIA. It's not the money, it's the *LOVE* that I give! (*She is breathless. Orton shakes his head.*)

ORTON. You used to be so good at love. But you don't really know anything about it, do you? (*Suddenly Orton takes her, turns her around to face him.*)

FELICIA. Don't touch me!

ORTON. Why not? I've touched you before.

FELICIA. Don't try to make up any stories about me. Nobody'll pay any attention. The newspapers won't be interested, I promise you. And you think you can go to the radio stations and say whatever you want to, just by *paying* for it? Well, they aren't that corrupt any more.

ORTON. (*After a pause, grimly.*) Somebody's going to stop you.

FELICIA. You're so sure you're right! Why do you think all these people shout "Viva Felicia"? Because I *do* something for them. What did you ever do? Just make soap and charge the highest price you could get. You're not even a Christian!

ORTON. (*Angrily.*) Give ten, take a hundred, is that Christianity? Give a centavo, take a peso, is that *your* holy religion? Every day a little farther, a little more. And who's left in your way? God? Or maybe He doesn't care. Maybe even He doesn't give a damn.

FELICIA. Those people out there know how holy I am. That's why they love me. They know how completely I love them.

ORTON. They don't love, they just grab. The way you do.

FELICIA. They love me because my heart is pure!

ORTON. (*Applauding with rhythmic insolence.*) That's it. Good girl. Lie! LIE!

FELICIA. Everybody in the *world* is going to know about my holy work. And one day, by God, I swear I'll go to Rome. And the Pope, the Holy Father himself, will put his hand on my head, and the Vicar of God will bless me for the sacred work I'm doing on this earth.

ORTON. (*Going out.*) Lie! Lie!

FELICIA. You'll see! The Pope will tell the whole *world* how pure and holy I am.

ORTON. Lie! Lie! (*He is gone.*)

FELICIA. (*Sinking into her chair.*) I'm pure, pure. (*Garcia has entered, and waits for her to acknowledge him.*) What is it, Garcia?

GARCIA. (*Awed.*) The President is here. (*Brazo, in a military great-coat, strides in; Garcia scoots out.*)

BRAZO. Some of my aides have told me about a woman over here who seems to be winning a popularity contest over the President. (*Pointing outside.*) In fact, my limousine had trouble getting through your crowd of admirers.

FELICIA. Oh? Did you want a wife, Jorge, to put in a closet—like a suit of cavalry dress-whites, tailored in Madrid?

BRAZO. Of course not, Little Angel. You are a part of everything I do. (*Uncertainly.*) I just hope *I* am a part of everything *you* do.

FELICIA. I am giving gifts to our people.

BRAZO. Fine. But at 3:15 in the morning, a great woman should be giving some of her great gifts to her husband.

FELICIA. What about the rest of the world? Does Brazoism stop at those mountains? (*Getting up.*) While I'm gone, I think you should plan an election.

BRAZO. (*Horrified at the word.*) An election! Where are you going?

FELICIA. To Europe. The Major Capitals of Europe. To tell them about *you*, Jorge.

BRAZO. Well, I won't stand in the way of that. But why an election?

FELICIA. So they'll know, everywhere, that Brazoism is the will of the people.

BRAZO. (*Mulling it.*) An election. Well, it might be practical—under proper military supervision. I'll look into the ramifications—

FELICIA. When Europe cheers for us, Jorge—*EUROPE!*—then everybody will have to approve. Even the United States. (*Quietly.*) Even Maximiliano Orton! (*Brazo looks at her strangely.*)

THE LIGHTS FADE

ACT TWO
SCENE 4

Brazo's office.

BRAZO'S VOICE. (*In the darkness, an irritable command.*) Run that tape back, I want to hear it again. (*There is the strident incoherent babble of a tape on fast rewind. The lights come up on Brazo's ornate desk. It is on a raised dais, so that anyone else in the room is beneath him. There are flags on poles behind him, and a rococo seal emblazoned on the front of the desk. Brazo, seated in a high-backed leather swivel chair, is oscillating angrily. The male secretary has set up a small tape recorder. Brazo glares down at it. The President wears a formal dark uniform. The male secretary, fully aware of the voltage in the room, presses the play button. There is an ecclesiastical intoning of a "Requiescat" in Latin.*)

BRAZO. (*With an impatient gesture.*) Not Frazzini. Orton! Orton! (*Nervously, the male secretary presses the forward button. The machine squawks to a stop. Then we hear the voice of Orton, in the middle of a sentence.*)

ORTON'S VOICE. (*From the tape recorder.*) —though the eyes are closed, the lips are silent, her graciousness continues to live in the memory of everyone who knew her. Dona Elena loved this country, but the country she loved died before she did. (*Bitterly, Brazo pounds his fist on the desk.*)

BRAZO. Right there. Stop it right there. (*He gestures.*) Get him. Bring him in. (*The secretary goes out immediately. Brazo picks up the telephone.*) Tell the Ministry of Information that there will be no report of remarks made by Senator Orton at the funeral this afternoon. Especially, check those bastards from Reuters and *Time* magazine. (*He starts to hang up the telephone, then he speaks into it again.*) I don't want any mention of Orton. He wasn't even there. (*Brazo turns and sees Orton being brought in between two soldiers. The Senator is dressed in the black of formal mourning. Orton stands eye-level with Brazo as he sits behind the desk still speaking into the telephone, more quietly.*) No. The Senator had been invited to speak, but he was overcome with emotion and said nothing. (*Brazo hangs up the phone. The two men stare at each other.*) Well? What do you have to say?

ORTON. (*Quietly.*) Nothing. (*Brazo waves the soldiers away. They click heels smartly and exit. The secretary is hovering hesitantly in the background, wishing he could leave. Brazo makes an effort to control and contain his anger.*)

BRAZO. I want your advice, Senator—on a matter of national security.

ORTON. (*Still very quietly.*) Not Senator. A man is a Senator only when there is a Senate. (*Brazo ignores this, shifting his weight in his chair.*)

BRAZO. I think you'd agree that it's treason to destroy a State. Isn't it also treason to say a State is dead? (*Brazo gestures to the secretary to turn on the tape again. He does so.*) Listen. I want you to listen to this. Listen.

ORTON'S VOICE. (*From the tape.*) Who is responsible for the death of a nation?

The people who *can* do, but *don't*! The men who *should* speak, but who commit instead the sin of silence!

BRAZO. (*Gesturing to cut the tape.*) That is a completely inappropriate remark at the funeral of the wife of an ex-president. In my opinion.

ORTON. (*Quietly.*) Some people in this country are still entitled to an opinion. A *few* people. One or two.

BRAZO. (*Pointing a finger at Orton.*) Would you have said these things if Senora Brazo had been at that funeral?

ORTON. In what capacity? (*Brazo stands, wanting to strike Orton, but the unwavering defiance of Orton, so vastly the President's superior in wit and intelligence, frustrates his impulse of animal violence.*)

BRAZO. (*With controlled fury.*) You intellectual pig! My wife is touring the major capitals of Europe. In triumph! Spreading the glory of Brazoism, telling the world what we have accomplished here! (*He leans forward on the desk now.*) But an old man, at the edge of a grave, spits at the saintly achievements of Senora Brazo. I choose to ignore the insult to what *I*, myself, have accomplished. Are you trying to get this country back into the democratic quicksand? A new government every two months? (*Brazo's gestures become more staccato. He turns to the male secretary.*) Play some more. Go ahead. Play it, play it, play it!

ORTON'S VOICE. (*Through the tape recorder.*) We mourn today not merely the death of a great lady, but our *own* deaths. We have committed collective suicide. We are pallbearers at our own funerals. (*Orton faces Brazo proudly and defiantly. At a gesture from Brazo, the male secretary clicks off the tape recorder.*)

BRAZO. (*Incisively, in a measured cadence.*) That is not what I would call prudent.

ORTON. As you have reminded me, I am not a young man. What I have to lose, I have already lost. Through "prudence."

BRAZO. (*Briskly, to the secretary.*) I want a stenographic transcript of that tape immediately. Classify it. No copy to be released. But send one by diplomatic pouch to Senora Brazo in Rome. (*He turns to Orton.*) What do you think my wife's reaction will be to your remarks?

ORTON. I don't think she'll be much surprised. We've always enjoyed a fairly frank and candid relationship. (*Brazo's face twitches.*)

BRAZO. As a civilized human being, I don't much want to hang you.

ORTON. I don't much want you to.

BRAZO. I see no point in putting you in prison.

ORTON. There can't be much room left in Three Rivers.

BRAZO. (*Leaning forward, forcefully.*) Orton, you have twenty-four hours to leave the country. Permanently. You're an enemy of this government. If you ever come back, you'll be shot. On sight. (*Silence.*) If you were sitting in this chair, I wonder if you would be as generous as I am. My only concern is the good of this country!

ORTON. Then, for the good of the country—why don't you join me?

THE LIGHTS FADE

ACT TWO
SCENE 5

Felicia's Executive Suite. September, fourteen months later. A balcony upstage looks out on the Plaza below. There is the rustle of a large, impatient crowd. Servants are moving in and out, piling up a mountain of feminine luggage, all sizes and shapes, dappled with stickers and custom-stamps.

The social secretary hurries on from an inner room.

SOCIAL SECRETARY. The oval blue-leather jewel-case. The Senora wishes it immediately. (*Servants and secretary scramble unsuccessfully through the pile of bags. Mama enters.*)

MAMA. (*Looking at the pile of luggage.*) Things, things. So many things.

SOCIAL SECRETARY. I hope it wasn't on the second plane. (*Mama taps her shoulder.*)

MAMA. Excuse me. I'm the Mama.

SOCIAL SECRETARY. Of course.

MAMA. How did she eat? On the trip?

SOCIAL SECRETARY. There were banquets. Everywhere.

MAMA. Yes, but did she eat?

SERVANT. (*Holding up an oval case.*) Is this it?

SOCIAL SECRETARY. (*Taking it.*) Thank God! (*The social secretary hurries off.*)

MAMA. (*To the servant.*) How does she look to you?

SERVANT. Senora Brazo is radiant. It says so in the papers. (*Mama is unconvinced. Brazo, in crisp whites, enters with an energetic restlessness. His hair is graying slightly.*)

BRAZO. Where is she? (*Mama gestures toward the inner room. He crosses toward it, calling.*) Felicia? Little Angel?

SOCIAL SECRETARY. (*Reentering.*) The Senora asks would the President care to speak to the people until she's ready?

BRAZO. (*Glancing toward the balcony.*) Alone? God, no! *I* haven't been anyplace. Ask her to— (*But the social secretary is gone. Brazo paces, taking some deep breaths. Something is bothering him. He stops abruptly beside Mama.*) How does she look to you?

MAMA. (*After a pause.*) Radiant. (*Reassured, Brazo resumes pacing. There is a sudden sweep of silk. Felicia enters. She is changed: this rapid learner has caught quickly the style of Europe, or her interpretation of it. She is whiter, thinner, more poised, more tense. The hair is lighter, drawn back with sculptured severity. Around her neck, on a scarlet ribbon, is the glittering Cross of Isabella. Without a word, Felicia offers her arm to Brazo. They climb to the balcony. The crowd cheers.*)

CROWD. (*Off.*) Viva Felicia! Bravo Brazo! Viva Felicia! Bravo Brazo! (*But soon it is a unison: "Viva Felicia!" Mama watches as Felicia stretches out her arm in a regal benedic-*

tion to the unseen crowd. Then Mama turns, troubled, and plods off. On the balcony, Felicia and Brazo turn toward each other, and he throws his arms around her in a genuinely grateful embrace. The crowd goes wild. Brazo steps back, lets Felicia take a solo "balcony call," the star actress of a performance. More cheers. The crowd, chanting.) Viva Felicia! Viva Felicia! Viva Felicia! (*She blows kisses, pretends to recognize faces in the throng below, then backs away and the clamor subsides. Brazo leads Felicia down the steps. Escaping from the sight of the crowd, they both change instantly, dropping the grand manner. Pause. Alone together, they find a zone of awkwardness between them.*)

BRAZO. I—uh—I declared a national half-holiday. To welcome you home. (*She doesn't seem to have heard him. She sits, the rigidity of her body slackens. She half-closes her eyes, weighing the gold decoration about her neck.*) That must be heavy. Let me take it off for you. (*Brazo moves behind her, but Felicia holds on to the decoration protectively.*)

FELICIA. No, no—it's not heavy. (*Remotely.*) Only a few people living have received the Cross of Isabella. Did you know that, Jorge? Francisco insisted that I call him by his first name. He's terribly interested in what I'm doing for the poor. (*She smiles at him wanly.*) Is there something you want to tell me? Jorge?

BRAZO. (*Hesitating.*) I didn't understand exactly what you were saying on the phone from Paris. But you sounded upset.

FELICIA. (*Quickly.*) It was a bad connection, that's all. Why would I be upset?

BRAZO. I'm glad you weren't upset. (*Awkwardly, taking her hand.*) Don't go away again. Not for a long time.

FELICIA. (*Withdrawing her hand.*) But the whole tour was a marvelous success. Everywhere I went, they loved me. It made me feel so humble. (*Slight pause.*)

BRAZO. What actually happened in Rome?

FELICIA. (*Ignoring the question, looking around.*) Is there any brandy? (*Brazo is surprised; she's never been a "daytime drinker."*)

BRAZO. Of course. (*He reaches beneath a side table, pours a short snifter of cognac.*)

FELICIA. A little more. (*Felicia takes the glass, drinks it down quickly, as if it were something she needed to do.*) Now you can tell me. You do have something special to tell me. Don't you, Jorge? (*Pause.*) As a welcome home present? (*He is silent, moistening his lips.*) I've been thinking about it, while I've been traveling. The election is a marvelous gesture, Jorge. The people deserve a chance to vote for you. For us. What an inspiration to my Strong-Backs to say: "Look what can happen! Anyone—even a woman—can be Vice-President of the Republic!"

BRAZO. Beloved. (*Clearing his throat.*) We've had quite a few meetings about the election. Making plans. (*He stops. How the hell can he say this?*) At the Officers' Club—there is a feeling— (*Breaking off, starting on another tack.*) Well, the military viewpoint can't be ignored. And I can appreciate—I can understand—

FELICIA. (*Staring at him coldly.*) *What* do you understand?

BRAZO. (*Like a pilot trying to fly around a thunderstorm.*) Traditions that go back hundreds of years, and—

FELICIA. And?

BRAZO. (*Blurting it out.*) There are no women in the Army. The President is the Commander-in-Chief. And if I should die, it is inconceivable to my brother officers that their Commander-in-Chief would be a woman!

FELICIA. You're not going to die.

BRAZO. Everybody dies.

FELICIA. (*Icily.*) Who? *Who* at the Officers' Club? *Who* doesn't want me to be Vice-President? Give me the names.

BRAZO. Nobody specific—just a feeling—

FELICIA. How about *you*? What's *your* feeling?

BRAZO. (*Carefully.*) Well, I tend to see things through a soldier's eyes—

FELICIA. Soldiers. The manhood of the army. You keep sticking medals on each other—for bravery. But you're afraid of a woman!

BRAZO. Forget the Vice-Presidency.

FELICIA. I *am* the Vice-President. Why not say so? The people know.

BRAZO. I have already announced that you are not a candidate.

FELICIA. (*Very softly.*) Oh, that was a mistake, Jorge. What will my Strong-Backs say?

BRAZO. They'll love you more, when you show them you can be a good loser.

FELICIA. I hate good losers. When I get in a plane to fly across the ocean, I don't want a pilot who's a "good loser"—some happy idiot who'll drown me smiling. (*Mama appears, worried by the raised voices.*)

BRAZO. (*Firmly.*) You are *not* a candidate for the Vice-Presidency. (*Brazo strides off.*)

FELICIA. (*To Mama.*) I never get anything I want!

MAMA. Look in your closets, Baby. So many clothes. All that jewelry. Nobody in the country has so many shoes!

FELICIA. Those aren't things I *want*—just things I have to *have.*

MAMA. What do you want, Baby?

FELICIA. I want to know—Mama, was there ever a time they wouldn't let us in the church?

MAMA. (*Pale.*) What, Baby?

FELICIA. A long time ago, when I was just a little girl—did I just imagine it? Was there a time, once, when God wouldn't let us in his house?

MAMA. (*Lying.*) I don't know—

FELICIA. Tell me, Mama!

MAMA. I don't understand—

FELICIA. God and I talk, all the time. Did you know that? We're good friends, just the way people are friends. When I went to Rome, I thought I was going to visit God. To visit my friend. I asked God to wash my soul, so I could go pure, clean, before the Holy Father. (*The tears are coming down her cheeks. She speaks rapidly, compulsively.*) I'll show you the dress I wore, Mama. I spent 20,000 pesos to make sure it was proper and simple, for His Holiness. No jewelry. No jewelry at all. Except Francisco's decoration over my heart. (*Suddenly feeling the weight of it.*) This is heavy. (*Mama goes behind her, lifts the ribboned medallion from around her neck. Felicia *seems to relive the experience.*) Down that long hall, through the Sistine Chapel, I saw God, Mama, watching, pointing his long finger at me, at *me*, saying: "This is the most important hour of your life!" The Pope talked to me for three minutes. That's all. He treated me like a tourist. The least, the least he could have done was give me the Order of St. Bartholomew. Some kind of recognition for all I'm doing. He didn't even mention my Charitable Foundation. And he gave me— (*A whisper.*) —a rosary. A fifteen-peso rosary! That's not God in the Vatican, Mama, just a *picture* of God! (*Shuddering.*) I should have done what they told me in Madrid. I should've listened to the doctors— (*She breaks off abruptly.*)

MAMA. What doctors, Baby?

FELICIA. Don't believe doctors, Mama. All they do is lie and frighten you.

MAMA. What did they say?

FELICIA. I *had* to go to Paris. How could I cancel Rome? Going to Vienna was impossible, I—I had to see Schiaparelli, so she could make me beautiful for my glorious, triumphant— (*A ghostly monotone.*) —*humiliating* audience with the Holy Father. (*Crying out.*) I am better than the Pope! God has chosen *me* to do His work on earth. Because I'm pure and clean and strong. Strong enough to make liars out of doctors who say I'm *not* strong. (*Getting weaker.*) I am strong. I'm strong. I'm strong. (*Terrified.*) Oh, God. I'm afraid. I want Maxo. Where is he, Mama? I want Maxo!

THE LIGHTS FADE

ACT TWO
SCENE 6

A village in the back-country of the Rio de Oro. At one side of the stage, a dangling kerosene lamp reveals a corner of Guzmano's crude clinic. The yellow light makes the hot night even more sultry.

Guzmano sits behind a rough table, holding some x-rays up to the flickering lamp. There are some medicine bottles on the table, empty. Orton bends forward anxiously, perspiration wet on his face. Guzmano sighs, puts down the x-ray, takes a page from a folder. It seems to have been torn to shreds, then Scotch-taped together again.

GUZMANO. Is this the latest lab report?

ORTON. Yes.

GUZMANO. Who the hell pasted it together?

ORTON. I did.

GUZMANO. You'll never get into medical school.

ORTON. (*Softly.*) Can you make a diagnosis? (*Pause.*) Guzmano? (*No answer.*)

GUZMANO. (*Tossing the reports aside.*) What did Brazo do? Give you back your soap mill and your citizenship, if you'd get the old man to come and see her?

ORTON. Brazo doesn't even know I'm in the country.

GUZMANO. (*Indicating the medical reports.*) Then where'd you get these?

ORTON. The Mama came to me yesterday—

GUZMANO. (*Sharply.*) Haven't you got a safe conduct? (*No answer.*) Get the hell out, Maxo, while you've still got some blood pressure.

ORTON. Will you help her?

GUZMANO. (*Getting up.*) Why me? They want a miracle? Have 'em fly a few more geniuses from Baltimore. The mighty Brazo can afford it.

ORTON. But he can't afford you.

GUZMANO. He can't buy me.

ORTON. You know what the "mighty Brazo" is doing? He cries. He doesn't sleep. He marches, all night long, up and down the corridors of the palace, crying.

GUZMANO. Am I supposed to be *moved* by this information?

ORTON. Forget who she is.

GUZMANO. I don't have that kind of forgetting equipment. Do you?

ORTON. I think you've done a masterpiece of forgetting. You pull the jungle up over your head so you don't have to watch the country go to hell.

GUZMANO. You want me to feel guilty, is that the idea?

ORTON. I laughed at her, you ignored her. Are you and I any better than the poor son-of-a-bitch who stood in the Plaza and yelled "Viva Brazo"?

GUZMANO. What good does it do to feel guilty, Maxo? Does it wipe anything clean? Hell, guilt isn't worth a damn. *Man* invented guilt—to make his sins more interesting. (*Pouring two drinks into two soiled paper cups.*) Here, have some of this. Scotch is the only medicine I can get. (*Drinks, distastefully.*) I think this is fermented castor oil.

ORTON. (*Not drinking.*) As a doctor, it is your responsibility—

GUZMANO. Don't tell me what to do "as a doctor"!

ORTON. As a *man* then—

GUZMANO. As a man, I can do anything I please! Spit in the face of God, if I like! There's only one thing a man *has* to do. Die. And it takes a lifetime to learn to do that properly.

ORTON. As a Christian?

GUZMANO. Oh, Maxo, Christ doesn't even know who I am. I *admire* him: Jesus. I respect him. As a physician. As a rebel. And— (*More softly.*) —perhaps as the purest arch to God.

ORTON. Then in God's name, help her.

GUZMANO. (*With growing anger.*) You expect me to leave a ward full of human beings, some of them dying, because that horse's ass of a cavalryman wants me to give a pill to his whore? I won't do it. I won't go!

ORTON. You don't have to go anyplace.

GUZMANO. What?

ORTON. She's here. I brought her. She's across the road, in the church. Praying.

GUZMANO. I hope God appreciates the honor. (*Very slowly the lighting rises on the opposite side of the stage. Felicia, very pale, faces directly front, kneeling as if before an altar. Beatifically, she lights rows of votive candles, which flicker on her face. Father Modesto, an awed country priest, watches from the shadows. The action in the clinic and the church continues simultaneously.*)

ORTON. Please, my old friend— (*Guzmano hesitates, shakes his head "No." Orton is furious.*) You decide? Who lives, who dies?

GUZMANO. Sometimes a virus has a vote.

ORTON. And you have a veto? (*Having lit the candles, Felicia, kneeling in the church, clasps her hands and begins to recite a pious "Hail Mary," which continues very softly in counterpoint to the action in the clinic.*)

FELICIA. (*Softly, by rote.*) "Hail Mary, Full of Grace, the Lord is with Thee . . . Blessed art Thou among women . . . "

ORTON. You only perform surgery on Saints?

GUZMANO. There aren't any. No Saints, Maxo. If there were, they wouldn't need me, they could heal themselves.

FELICIA. (*Praying in the church.*) "And blessed is the fruit of thy womb, Jesus."

ORTON. Is this a clinic, or the Judgement Seat??? *You* judge, do you, on the basis of your own bruises?

GUZMANO. Or *your* memories of a rumpled bed?

ORTON. "Judgement is mine, sayeth the Lord."

GUZMANO. (*Sarcastically.*) Scripture will now be read by the ordained soap manufacturer.

ORTON. (*Painfully, closing his eyes.*) No, no, Guzmano. The Judgement is against *me*. I made her possible. (*An exorcism.*) Would you like to wear *my* conscience for awhile? You know what Hell is, Doctor? Not brimstone. But loving what you hate, and hating what you love. (*Guzmano, deeply moved, slowly picks up the x-rays and squints at them. In the church, Felicia suddenly gestures to the priest.*)

FELICIA. (*Eyes bright in the candlelight.*) Father! I have a message for you. From God. (*Uncertainly Father Modesto takes a few steps toward her.*)

FATHER MODESTO. From God, Senora?

FELICIA. (*Simply.*) He wants me to be a nun. Will you make me a nun? Now? Right now?

FATHER MODESTO. It is not in my power—

FELICIA. But if God tells you—! I am to be a Sister of Charity. Like Sister Emilia.

FATHER MODESTO. Such things require—

FELICIA. I'll give up everything. I'll stay here with you, Father, and do the dirtiest jobs you have. (*She drops to her knees. With her lace scarf, she begins to scrub the floor.*) See? See, I'll do anything! Like Sister Emilia. (*Fiercely, Felicia scrubs at the floor. Father Modesto is wide-eyed and bewildered. He backs away from her, leaving the church to go for help. In the clinic, Guzmano scowls over the laboratory reports.*)

ORTON. (*Trying to persuade Guzmano.*) She's only a few steps away. There isn't any pride any more. Please. I'm not very good at begging— (*Guzmano is vacillating. Then, abruptly, he slams the papers down on the table.*)

GUZMANO. *I won't touch her!* (*Pointing angrily toward the ward.*) The man who was breathing in bed twenty-seven last night is in a fresh grave tonight because *she* wouldn't let me have in my hands the things that let people *live.* (*He holds out his gnarled hands, trembling and empty.*)

ORTON. All right, what's your price, what do you want? I'll get it for you—

GUZMANO. I'll tell you what I want! (*Pounding, like tympani beats.*) Antibiotics! Achromycin! Sulfanilamide! Morphine! Insulin! Dilantin! Adrenalin! Codeine! Digitalis! Probanthine! Atabrine! Cortisone! Quinine! Diphtheria vaccine! My God, a bottle of carbolic acid. Ten cc's of Merthiolate! Half a liter of ether! (*Father Modesto has entered the clinic during this tirade, and stands mute.*)

ORTON. (*After a pause.*) When you get these things, will it make any difference?

GUZMANO. (*Quietly.*) Not to my patients who have already died.

FATHER MODESTO. Please, come. I do not know what to do. The Senora—I think she is very sick.

GUZMANO. Oh? Thank you, sir—for your expert diagnosis.

ORTON. Help her! (*Guzmano turns his back on Orton and the priest. Angrily, Orton strides out toward the church. The bewildered priest is motionless. In the church, Felicia stops her symbolic scrubbing. Still on her knees, she stares front. Orton comes into the church, moves slowly toward her.*)

FELICIA. (*Swaying a little.*) Sister Emilia. You told me, when you rocked me, all I had to do was to be a good girl, and tell the truth. (*Thinking Orton is the Priest, she throws her arms around Orton's knees.*) Holy Father, I want to confess. I want to tell you the truth.

ORTON. No—! (*He reaches to touch her head, but she races on. Felicia is in physical pain, but reliving a humiliation of her childhood is even more painful.*)

FELICIA. I didn't know, I didn't understand. I was seven years old, how could I understand? I thought we were just going to Mass. I was 'way over there, just outside the door— (*Vaguely she gestures.*) Sister Emilia held me up in her arms so I could see. They wouldn't even let Mama come. And I found out for the first time that my Father belonged to another family! (*Tears flow down her cheeks, she clings to Orton's knees.*) And I watched *them*—sitting on chairs—all scrubbed and starched and so proud of their black armbands. (*Remembering the agonized words of a child.*) My Papa is dead—why can't I cry too? (*Barely a whisper.*) I hated them. I confess to you, Father, I have tried, I have tried to love the people who shut me out. But the hate has never gone away. (*Felicia has spoken the truth and dissolved her armor. Her grip *around Orton's knees grows slack and she crumples to the floor of the church. Guzmano and the priest enter and watch silently. Orton bends down, raises Felicia up by the shoulders.*)

ORTON. (*Softly.*) Child— (*Her eyes open slowly. Felicia seems surprised to see Orton; her voice has the playfulness and abandon of a ghost of their first scene together.*)

FELICIA. Maxo. Where've you been? Don't go away. Stay the rest of the afternoon with me. Please? I won't throw shoes at you— (*Her eyes close. She is motionless in Orton's arms.*)

ORTON. (*Softly.*) Felicia—? (*But she doesn't hear him. He turns to Guzmano accusingly.*) *One!* There is no number larger than one. Did you say that? Did you believe it? Don't you believe it any more? (*Guzmano is shaken by this.*)

GUZMANO. (*After a pause.*) Put her in bed twenty-seven. (*Orton carries the unconscious Felicia toward the clinic.*)

FATHER MODESTO. (*Awed, to Guzmano.*) Can you save her?

GUZMANO. (*To the priest, with faint contempt.*) What's the matter—don't you believe in miracles? (*As he moves reluctantly toward his clinic, the lights fade.*)

ACT TWO
SCENE 7

The Plaza (as in I-8). Night. The growing clamor of a crowd erupts throughout the theatre. Arc lights crisscross the sky, then blaze into the faces of a crowd which surges onto the stage like a wave breaking on a shore.

VOICES. (*Shouting.*) Abajo Brazo! Viva la Republica! (*The crowd is jubilant. A festive snake-dance twists about the Plaza. There are flags, banners, placards. Several men carry ladders and begin ripping down street signs and putting up hastily painted new ones.*)

MAN-ON-LADDER. (*Shouting, mocking.*) How do I get to the Plaza Brazo?

VOICE. Never heard of it! (*The crowd laughs. The man-on-ladder rips down a street sign which reads "Plaza Brazo" and throws it to the crowd. Eagerly, hands reach up and tear it to pieces. There is much laughter and cheering as they toss the bits back and forth. Silhouetted figures boil against the backdrop, giving the impression that the entire city is in turmoil.*)

LOUDSPEAKER VOICE. (*Booming.*) The crisis is over. President Brazo has left the country. (*A huge cheer from the crowd. A man-on-another-ladder has pried loose a second street sign and waves it above the heads of the crowd.*)

MAN-ON-ANOTHER-LADDER. (*Shouting.*) And where do we find the Avenida de Felicia Brazo???

STUDENT. In hell! (*The street sign is flung across the stage. The crowd runs to stamp on it, demolishing it under their feet. A working man comes on with a huge framed photograph of the idealized Felicia. He waggles the picture before the crowd.*)

WORKING MAN. Ole! For the Whore of the Rio de Oro! (*They crowd around to spit at the picture. Somebody throws a stone at the enormous photograph, shattering the benign face.*)

OLD WOMAN. (*Prayerfully.*) Forgive them, Santa Felicia in Heaven—!

STUDENT. (*Jeering.*) You sure you've got the right address? (*Hands reach up to tear shreds out of the photograph. Now there is a fresh burst of cheers. Orton comes on, accompanied by two soldiers with rifles as bodyguards. The crowd greets Orton jubilantly.*)

CROWD. (*Chanting.*) Orton! Orton! Viva Orton! Viva Orton! (*Orton raises both arms sternly, trying to silence them.*)

ORTON. (*Thundering.*) Kindly do not shout "Viva Orton!" It makes me vomit! (*Raggedly the crowd become still.*) I have come back to this country to form a government. But not a government of "Viva *Any*body"—least of all myself. (*He sees the ripped photograph of Felicia.*) What's that? (*The working man proudly holds the picture aloft. The Student spits at what's left of the face, and grins.*) Ohhhh, you're a brave man. Can you get rid of her that easily—with fingernails and spit? Change the street signs, change the history books. Is it that simple to get clean? (*Commandingly to the student.*) Remember her!

STUDENT. (*Sullenly.*) Brazo-Lover! (*One of the soldiers moves as if to take the student into custody. But Orton stops him.*)

ORTON. Wait. (*Orton takes the rifle from the soldier and tosses it to the startled student, who catches it.*) If you believe that, shoot me. (*Utter silence.*) Go ahead. Puncture the gasbag. Free. The government pays for the bullet. (*Gingerly, the student passes the rifle back to the soldier. Orton shrugs.*) I am a failure. I am so unpopular no one will even shoot me. (*Uncertainly, the crowd begins to disperse. Orton leans down, picks up a jagged shred of Felicia's picture, staring at it silently. Suddenly a young girl, barefoot, wearing a babushka, rushes up to Orton. She half kneels in front of him. We cannot see her face.*)

YOUNG GIRL. (*In a flood of youthful fervor.*) You are going to be our President, I know you are. (*Orton looks down at her, startled.*) You don't know me. I'm nobody. I sat up a day and a night and a day in a train coach, to come here. To see you. To see my future President. It's too marvelous! Am I actually kneeling at the feet of such a great man—? (*Orton reaches down and turns the young girl's face into the light. Is it Felicia? No. But it is the same voice, the same face. Is she with us always?*)

CURTAIN

THE NIGHT
THOREAU
SPENT IN
JAIL

Introduction

In *The Night Thoreau Spent in Jail,* Lawrence and Lee continued to explore the historic past through fiction in order to comment on the present, using Henry David Thoreau's own name and the names of his friends and fellow citizens of Concord. The play is based on Thoreau's actual incarceration when he refused to pay taxes that would go to support the Mexican-American War of 1846–48. Lawrence and Lee began work on the first draft of the play—originally titled *A Different Drummer*—in July 1966.[1] Unlike their earlier collaborations, *A Different Drummer* initially was Lawrence's project alone. The first outline opens with the exchange that was eventually to conclude act 1:

> VOICE [Emerson]: Henry, what are you doing in jail?
> HENRY (*Clutching the bars and shouting back, like a whiplash*) Waldo! What are you doing out of jail???[2]

This first version of the play employs a mock trial as the organizing focus, with figures from Thoreau's life being summoned to testify as Thoreau attempts to justify his actions. Lee's initial work on *The Night Thoreau Spent in Jail* was to serve as an editor, reacting to Lawrence's rough outline. The playwrights met to discuss the play in July 1967, but did not turn their full attention to the script until April 1969.

As a result of the playwrights' consultations, *A Different Drummer* was rethought entirely, emerging not only with a new title, but with an entirely new structure.[3] The jail setting remained as the focal point of the play, but the trial convention was abandoned, as was any pretense at strict chronology. Rather, Lawrence and Lee embraced a fluid structure reminiscent of expressionist theatrical experimentation earlier in the twentieth century.

Once the decision was made to adopt the new format, Lawrence and Lee's work on *The Night Thoreau Spent in Jail* progressed rapidly during the summer of 1969, and the finished and revised text was completed by early October. Submitted to the American Playwrights Theatre (APT), the play was quickly accepted for production. The pilot production opened at Ohio State University on 21 April 1970—fifteen years to the day after the triumphal New York opening of *Inherit the Wind.*

The Night Thoreau Spent in Jail comments on contemporaneous events, as do most of Lawrence and Lee's plays. The parallels between Thoreau's passive resistance to the Mexican-American War, and the protests erupting across the United

States in the late 1960s to the Vietnam War were obvious; and the playwrights fully intended the parallels to be seen. As early as 1967, they had noted that "the whole theme of the Thoreau piece should be the obligation to rebel non-violently. Not merely the right to rebel. But the necessity."[4]

With Thoreau as the play's constant center, the events that shaped his political and intellectual growth swirl together as he attempts to understand what brought him to the Concord jail. Thoreau's memories climax in the phantasmagoric nightmare sequence that forms the heart of act 2. Ralph Waldo Emerson serves as an appropriate foil for Thoreau: the established intellectual leader with the moral power to provide leadership against the war who instead waffles, preferring ineffectually procrastinating discussion to direct action.

The contrast between Thoreau's activism and Emerson's failure to lead is doubled by the play's other characters, who provide different sorts of contrasts. Thoreau's cellmate, Bailey, is clearly a dramatic device, allowing Thoreau to explain his beliefs to a new person and to demonstrate his abilities as a teacher when, early in the play, he teaches Bailey to write his name. Henry's brother, John, doubles Thoreau in several ways, most significantly as Henry's surrogate in the unsuccessful wooing of Ellen.

Ellen herself is a foil for Thoreau. Not only does she articulate the comfortable bourgeois philosophy Thoreau rejects (particularly early in the play), she also displays the ability to learn and grow when she is able to articulate the key elements of Transcendentalism after John's death. Each of the minor figures reverses some element of Thoreau's character, whether it be the authoritarian pedagogical style insisted upon by Deacon Ball or Sam's unquestioning acceptance of the government's dictates.

Lawrence and Lee dramatized events in Thoreau's life that illustrated their central concerns. A brief analysis of the first act will demonstrate that it is carefully constructed to lead the audience through Thoreau's development. The play's structure appears casual and loose, although each detail carries a purpose and meaning.

Waldo's apparent age and confusion in the opening sequence establishes that the play's events will take place in fluid time; Waldo's self-centeredness, which motivates his reluctance to act, is also indicated here. Henry's exchange with his mother, which follows and overlaps the Waldo-Lydian scene, sets up immediately Thoreau's independence and self-reliance.

Thoreau's insistence upon being true to himself despite the conforming drive of society, is, of course, the central theme of the play. Henry's refusal to accept the traditional order of the alphabet, followed immediately by Waldo's "Cast Conformity behind you," reinforces his individuality. The short scene that follows with his brother, John, establishes Waldo's influence on Thoreau, as well as setting up his parallel reliance upon his brother. Both the intellectual and familial support will be wrenched away from Thoreau as the play progresses. Having Waldo's moment of self-doubt follow immediately after Henry's "I want to be as much as possible like Ralph Waldo Emerson" undercuts Henry's hero worship, letting the audience know instantly that Emerson will prove ineffective.

The play's first extended scene, Thoreau in the jail cell with Bailey, follows. Thoreau is on his own here. Although the audience does not yet know that John will be dead by the time Henry is jailed or that Waldo will have failed Thoreau as well, the first Bailey scene shows the mature Thoreau. He fuses an awareness of the world of nature heightened by the Walden experience with a rejection of the political world of "a President who went out and boomed up a war all by himself—with no help from Congress and less help from me." The scene ends with Thoreau teaching Bailey to write his name and leap-frogs into Thoreau in his Concord classroom, where Deacon Ball forces Thoreau to face another consequence of the individual's freedom: the responsibility to refuse morally unsupportable orders. Thoreau's resignation as a teacher is paralleled directly by Lawrence and Lee with Emerson's resignation of his pulpit, also on a matter of conscience.

Henry and John's own school, in the following sequence, reinforces Henry's growing awareness of the natural world and also introduces Ellen and permits Henry to explain his self-directed teaching philosophy. Henry's rejection of learning in the jail cell sounds the first note of the Thoreau school's failure, which becomes clearer in the following long scene, in which Henry explores the possibility of traditional fulfillment through marriage. The rowing sequence with Ellen gives a further chance to explore his personal philosophy, while providing a sharp contrast between his behavior and the expected behavior of a polite middle-class suitor.

The jail cell, with Bailey's snore-response to Henry's question about marriage, provides the bridge to the next scene, the church service ultimately interrupted by Henry and his wheelbarrow working on Sunday, having taken the rest of the week off. John's recounting of Ellen's refusal is followed quickly by John's death and burial. Ellen's awareness of Transcendentalism demonstrates Henry's success as a teacher; but bereft of both John and Ellen, he turns to his second source of support, the Emersons, in the third major scene of the act. Walden is fully introduced in this scene, and the relationships between Henry and each of the Emersons are suggested. After a brief return to the cell, and Henry's mature reflection on what Walden has meant to him, the act's last major scene shows Henry's actual arrest and full explanation of why he refuses to pay his taxes. The act ends with the Henry/Waldo exchange that had opened the first version of *A Different Drummer* in Jerome Lawrence's original outline.

Although the structure of the first act of *The Night Thoreau Spent in Jail* is fluid, each of the elements dramatized has a specific purpose, culminating in Thoreau's arrest and then his challenge to Emerson, which ends the act. What appears on first viewing to be casual is, in fact, quite carefully plotted. The playwrights' success in capturing the mood of the late 1960s is clear not only in their use of the parallels between the Mexican-American and Vietnam Wars, but also in their contrast of the restrictive (and restricting) educational system represented by Deacon Ball to Thoreau's nature-centered approach. Thoreau's educational philosophy, as presented by the playwrights, is quite close to the alternative educational theories most forcefully articulated in the 1960s by A. S. Neill, Ivan Illich, and Jonathan Kozol.[5]

The play also contributed significantly to the then-burgeoning regional theatre movement by its production through the American Playwrights Theatre, resulting in more than one hundred forty separate productions from 1970 through 1971.[6] *The Night Thoreau Spent in Jail*'s message of individual responsibility remains current: the Hong Kong Repertory Theatre performed it in the autumn of 1989 as a memorial to the Chinese students massacred in Beijing's Tiananmen Square when the People's Army brutally crushed the freedom movement in early June 1989.

Although widely produced across North America, *The Night Thoreau Spent in Jail* was deliberately never performed either on or off Broadway, as the playwrights demonstrated that the theatre could be born and continue to live elsewhere than on a few blocks of Manhattan real estate. Even though the play is frequently produced, there has been little critical comment on the script. It many ways, *The Night Thoreau Spent in Jail* has fallen victim to the cultural dominance of the American theatre by the New York stage: scripts receive little critical attention unless they have been successfully produced in full view of the national media, centered in New York City. Although there are some indications that this bias may be lessening, it remained strongly in place when *The Night Thoreau Spent in Jail* was first produced in 1970. Lawrence and Lee's examination of individual consciousness has gone virtually unremarked other than in newspaper accounts of the (literally) hundreds of individual productions.

The Night Thoreau Spent in Jail remains in the world repertory. The play has historic significance as the greatest success of the American Playwrights Theatre, the organization founded by Lawrence and Lee in 1965 as a means of bypassing the harshly commercial conditions then beginning to dominate the Broadway stage. Headquartered at Ohio State University, where *The Night Thoreau Spent in Jail* was premiered, APT created the first truly national theatrical production mechanism seen in the United States. In significant ways, it fostered the growth of professional theatres outside New York City, helping to diminish the sole power of the Broadway stage. *The Night Thoreau Spent in Jail* was widely produced and highly successful across the country, with more than two thousand performances at APT-member theatres during its first two years alone. One scholar did note that "more people saw that play in one season than had seen . . . *Inherit the Wind* and *Auntie Mame* in their total combined runs."[7] That *The Night Thoreau Spent in Jail* still has not attracted much scholarly attention must be seen as an ironic comment on the scholarly community's lack of awareness of changes in theatrical production patterns during the past two decades, as well as on scholars ignoring evidence beneath their very noses. More than twenty years after its premiere, the Bantam edition of *The Night Thoreau Spent in Jail* has almost a half-million copies in print.[8]

NOTES

1. The process by which *The Night Thoreau Spent in Jail* was created is fully detailed in Lawrence E. Fink's "From Thought to Theatre: Creation, Development, and Production of *The Night Thoreau Spent in Jail* by Jerome Lawrence and Robert E. Lee" (master's thesis, Ohio State University, 1988).

2. Jerome Lawrence and Robert E. Lee, *A Different Drummer,* typescript, Lawrence and Lee Collection 15:1, Jerome Lawrence and Robert E. Lee Theatre Research Institute, The Ohio State University.

3. See Fink, 31–73.

4. Lawrence and Lee, "Memo 4-A: Notes on 'A Different Drummer,' July 1967," Lawrence and Lee Collection 15:1; as cited by Fink, 32.

5. See, for example, A. S. Neill, *Summerhill* (New York: Hart, 1960), Ivan Illich, *Celebration of Awareness* (Garden City, N.Y.: Doubleday, 1970), and Jonathan Kozol, *Free Schools* (Boston: Houghton Mifflin, 1972).

6. Fink provides a complete listing of APT productions in his appendix A, 94–103.

7. Gerald Berkowitz, *New Broadways: Theatre across America, 1959–1980* (Totowa, N.J.: Rowan and Littlefield, 1982), 80.

8. Telephone conversation, Susanna Porter, Bantam Press, with Charles Schlessinger, Brandt & Brandt, September 1991.

Foreword

The man imprisoned in our play belongs more to the moment than to the age in which he lived.

For more than a century, Henry David Thoreau was dismissed as a gifted weirdo. Only a rebel like Emerson's handyman would dare to question the benefits of technology! Why, it is obvious to any educated mind that technological advancement and progress are synonymous. To create a better world, all we have to do is make things bigger, faster, stronger, or cheaper.

BUT THOREAU KNEW THAT.

He smelled the smog before we saw it.

It smarted his soul before it smarted our eyes.

He spoke out; but in those television-less days men were slow to listen. He sang out in nonviolent defiance, but how few men since could carry the tune: Gandhi, Count Tolstoi, Martin Luther King.

It was the material-mindedness of his government which drove the mystic Thoreau to the shores of Walden. His outrage is closely akin to the anger of many young people today. Young Thoreau was disgusted by the lies and confusion which clouded the bloody conflict with a smaller nation, Mexico.

The President of the United States (James Polk) had made a pretense of trying to settle differences at the conference table. Then, without a declaration of war or Congressional approval, U.S. forces plunged into Mexico. An inaccurate and incomplete report from the President (which has been lamely explained by the lack of electrical communication) brought authorization from Congress.

Hawks and white supremacists of the day cheered. But the intellectual community gasped in horror.

The text of the play contains a denunciation of the war actually made by a young Whig Congressman from Illinois—who was not reelected because of his stand, but who later became the first Republican President of the United States.

American secret agents smuggled in a puppet president from Havana. Overwhelmed by U.S. armor, the Mexicans resisted all the way to the gates of their capital, which fell only when their ammunition ran out. On the side of the invaders, there was hot friction between secret envoys from the White House, an alarmed Congress, and the ambitious military leaders—two of whom became Presidents of the United States and one of the Confederacy.

A captain in the army of General Winfield Scott reported that the American troops acted like savages. They shot noncombatants on trivial pretexts. "Their conduct toward the poor inhabitants has been horrible and their coming is dreaded like death in every village."

Another eyewitness, Ulysses S. Grant, wrote in his memoirs: "I do not think there was ever a more wicked war than that waged by the United States on Mexico. I thought so at the time, when I was a youngster, only I had not the moral courage to resign." Grant had the option of resignation, which has not been granted to youngsters of later wars.

According to Santayana, "Those who do not remember the past are condemned to relive it." Perhaps this play will jog our memories as we relive the poetic protest of one of America's greatest men.

Time is awash in this jail cell. We are not trapped in happenings past. The explosive spirit of Thoreau leaps across the years, addressing with power and clarity the perils of his own time and, prophetically, of ours as well. Thoreau is a fascinating paradox:

A man who was—and is.

A self-effacing giant.

A wit who rarely laughed.

A man who loved so deeply and completely that he seemed, sometimes, not to have loved at all.

Thoreau's decision to return to the human race is the shape, the parabola of the play: his evolution from withdrawal to return, the journey from hermitizing to social conscience. This is the subtext of the play: the director and the actor must evolve it surely, slowly, so it is like the opening of a flower.

His night in jail is a mystical experience for this highly sensitive man. Confined, he has the liberty to explore what he really *is*, the composite of his experiences, past and *future*. It is an ecstasy, a "passion," a revelation, a summing up of his life in the curve of time from sunset to sunrise.

This is not the bearded, weary-eyed Thoreau of the recent postage-stamp. This is the blazing contemporary, clean-shaven, vigorous, outraged at the insanity and inanity of civilization around him. The purpose of the play is to go deeper than the words he wrote, to probe the turmoil out of which he wrote them.

If he was a revolutionary, it was in the spirit of those who, fourscore years before him, had imagined a United States—where the conserving of established order was less sacred than the hopeful helix of *change*. In the course of his night in jail, Thoreau realizes that the idyll of Walden has already worked its change upon him; and the sunrise goads him with new challenges.

This play is more than the ruminating of one man in one place in one night. We are not tied down to "flashback" or reminiscence. All the people of the play, including the audience, should be encouraged to partake in a banquet of imagining. It is eminently Thoreauvian that everyone should bring to—and take from—the play something uniquely his own.

Lawrence & Lee

EDITOR'S NOTE

The Night Thoreau Spent in Jail was published by Hill and Wang (New York) in 1971; that text is republished here. *Literary Cavalcade* serialized the play in its 1971–72 editions. Bantam's 1972 paperback edition remains in print, having gone through seventeen printings by 1989. The acting edition is available from Samuel French, Inc.

Ned Beatty and Michael Fairman in *The Night Thoreau Spent in Jail*, Arena Stage, Washington, D.C., 1970. Photo by Fletcher Drake. Jerome Lawrence and Robert E. Lee Collection, Lawrence and Lee Theatre Research Institute, The Ohio State University.

Cast

The Night Thoreau Spent in Jail was first presented through the American Playwrights Theatre in 154 different productions by resident, community, and university theatres throughout the United States. The pilot production was presented at the Ohio State University, Columbus, Ohio, on 21 April 1970 as the university's centennial play, directed by Dr. Roy H. Bowen. The scenery was designed by Russell T. Hastings, with costumes by David L. Chappell, and lighting designed by W. Alan Kirk. The cast included:

WALDO .... Donald Mauck
LYDIAN .... Dorothy Laming
MOTHER .... Irene Martin
HENRY .... David Ayers
JOHN .... Anthony B. Schmitt
BAILEY .... Burton Russell
BALL .... John W. Toth
ELLEN .... Bronwynn Hopton
SAM .... Al Converse
EDWARD .... Michael David Ayers
WILLIAMS .... Gary Easterling
PASSER-BY .... Donald Shandler
DRUNK .... Corwin Georges
FARMER .... Bruce Vilanch
WOMAN .... Jerri Aberman
TOWNSPEOPLE .. Floyd E. Hughes III, Richard Pierce, Evy Steffens, Ann Goldman, Sandra Kalenik, Dorothy Konrad, Robert Segall

Original music was composed by J. A. Huff, with percussion music by Charles Spohn. The war scene was staged by Lynn Dally.

The first production to combine professional and academic theatre took place at the University of California at Los Angeles during the summer and fall of 1970. Guy Stockwell starred as Henry, with True Boardman as Waldo, Ralph Freud as the Farmer, Dorothy Foulger as the Mother, and Larry Simpasa as Williams. Robert E. Lee directed.

Robert E. Lee giving notes to Christopher Walken and Lu Ann Post in *The Night Thoreau Spent in Jail*, Goodman Theatre, Chicago, 1971. Photo by David H. Fishman. Jerome Lawrence and Robert E. Lee Collection, Lawrence and Lee Theatre Research Institute, The Ohio State University.

THE NIGHT THOREAU SPENT IN JAIL

ACT ONE

Center is the skeletal suggestion of a prison cell: two crude cots, a chair, a wooden box which serves as a clothes locker. An imaginary window downstage looks out on Concord Square.

A thrust extends forward, not part of the cell—nor are the playing areas at either side. The cell itself is raked. The cell door, imaginary, is upstage center.

Surrounding the cell is the sky over Concord. There are night bird sounds, distant. Two men lie on the cots, motionless. Striped moonlight through the prison bars falls across Henry, but the man on the other cot is in shadow.

Time and space are awash here.

Into a weak winter light, unrelated to the cell, an old man enters on the arm of his wife. He walks with studied erectness, using an umbrella as a cane. The wife is handsomely patrician. The old man has a shawl over his shoulders, a muffler around his neck. He stops.

WALDO. (*Suddenly, as if somebody had stolen his wallet.*) What was his name?

LYDIAN. Whose name?

WALDO. I've forgotten the name of my best friend!

LYDIAN. Did you ever have a best friend?

WALDO. The boy. Who put the gloves on the chickens.

LYDIAN. Henry?

WALDO. (*Vaguely.*) I keep thinking his name was David. (*Light strikes Henry's Mother as she comes into another area, also apart from the cell. She is distressed, piling disheveled hair onto the top of her head.*)

MOTHER. David Henry! What have you gone and done? (*Henry rises on the cot. He is 29, clean-shaven, with liquid eyes. His clothes are simple, the colors of the forest. This is a young man—with a knife-like humor, fierce conviction and devastating individuality.*)

HENRY. I have not gone and done anything, Mother. I have gone and *not* done something. Which very much needed the *not* doing.

MOTHER. Oh, good heavens! (*Calling offstage.*) Louisa! David Henry's gone and *not* done something again.

HENRY. (*Correcting her.*) Henry David.

MOTHER. David Henry, you're being strange again.

WALDO. (*Distantly.*) He was strange. I almost understood him.

LYDIAN. Sometimes.

MOTHER. Sometimes I don't know who you are.

HENRY. I'm myself, Mother. (*He lifts himself and sits on the edge of the cot.*) If I'm not, who will be?

MOTHER. When you're baptized, they tell you who you are.

HENRY. I wasn't listening.

MOTHER. At the christening you didn't cry once, not once. Reverend Ripley said how remarkable it was for a baby not to cry at a christening.

HENRY. You think I knew what they were doing to me?

MOTHER. I suppose not.

HENRY. That's why I didn't cry.

WALDO. He was the saddest happy man I ever knew.

LYDIAN. The happiest sad man, I think.

WALDO. He worked on Sundays, and took the rest of the week off. (*Staring at his umbrella, puzzled.*) Who's this?

LYDIAN. It's your umbrella.

WALDO. Oh, yes. (*He studies the umbrella affectionately, as if it were a lost old friend.*) Yes, my . . . uh . . . my . . . (*But again he's lost the name.*) Yes. (*Lydian helps the vague Waldo off, as the lights fall away on them.*)

MOTHER. I wouldn't mind your being peculiar. But do you have to *work* at it so hard, David Henry?

HENRY. Henry David.

MOTHER. Getting everything backward. How did you learn your letters?

HENRY. *Must* the alphabet begin with A? (*He stands.*) Why not with Z? Z is a very sociable letter. Like the path of a man wandering in the woods. A is braced and solid. A is a house. I prefer Z. Z–Y–X–W–V–U–T–S—(*He makes a zigzag course out of the cell into the thrust area.*)

MOTHER. Oh, dear—!

HENRY. Or mix them up. Start with H. Start with Q. (*Waldo, younger and straighter, has moved to a lectern where the light makes his face glow with an inner radiance. He is at the climax of an address.*)

WALDO. (*Projecting.*) Cast Conformity behind you. (*Henry sees Waldo, and sinks to the floor, sitting squat-legged as a youthful admirer at the feet of an idol.*)

HENRY. (*As if memorizing a Commandment.*) "Cast . . . Conformity . . . Behind You . . . !" (*John enters, stands beside his disturbed Mother. Both look at Henry, as he sits in a Yoga-esque fixation, staring up into empty air. John is taller than his brother—affable, more extroverted. John moves smoothly, easily, in contrast to the explosively erratic movements of his younger brother.*)

MOTHER. You know what David Henry's trouble is, John?

JOHN. What?

MOTHER. He keeps casting conformity behind him!

JOHN. (*Shrugging.*) What the hell, he's been to Harvard.

MOTHER. (*Offended.*) *Never* say—

JOHN. Harvard? I'm sorry, Mother, I'll never say it again. (*Mother goes off, and John saunters toward his brother, who still sits transfixed. He looks at Henry with some amusement.*) Now here's a rare specimen—

WALDO. (*The vital glow still upon his face.*) There is an infinitude in the private man! If a single man plants himself indomitably on his instincts, and there abide, the huge world will come round to him . . . (*The light falls away on Waldo as he goes off. The light intensifies on Henry and John—the amber of sunny fields.*)

HENRY. (*Still squatting; to himself.*) . . . and there abide! (*John circles Henry playfully, as if examining a specimen.*)

JOHN. Hm! Is this one wild or tame? Wild, I think. Known to haunt the woods and ponds. Dull plumage. But a wise bird. Americanus something-or-other. I have it! It is the species—BROTHER!!! (*This joshing has broken Henry's near-trance. He leaps up.*)

HENRY. (*Embracing him.*) John!

JOHN. Welcome home. How's your overstuffed brain?

HENRY. I've forgotten everything already.

JOHN. At least you've got a diploma!

HENRY. No, I don't.

JOHN. Why not?

HENRY. They charge you a dollar. And I wouldn't pay it.

JOHN. But think how Mama would love it—your diploma from Harvard, framed on the wall!

HENRY. Let every sheep keep his own skin. (*John gives him a disparaging shove on the shoulder, and they tussle like boys. Breathless, they sit side by side.*) John, I got more from one man—not even a professor—than I learned in four years of academic droning and snorting at Cambridge. And the strangest thing—he wasn't a stranger. I knew him, I'd seen him. You know him. You walk by him on the street, you say hello; he's just a man, just a neighbor. *But* this man speaks and a hush falls over all of Harvard. And there's a light about him—that comes out of his face. But it's not the light of *one* man. I swear to you, John, it's the light of all Mankind!

JOHN. (*Askance.*) Idolator! (*Henry slaps the ground with the palm of his hand.*)

HENRY. Is this the Earth?

JOHN. I hope so.

HENRY. (*Coming slowly to his feet.*) No. It's you. And I. And God. And Mr. Emerson. And the Universal Mind!

JOHN. And Aunt Louisa?

HENRY. Yes, Aunt Louisa, too—false teeth and all. (*Scratching his head.*) It isn't easy to think of Aunt Louisa, swimming in the Milky Way. But that's the way of things, I'm sure of it.

JOHN. And if she can't keep afloat, you can dive in and save her! (*They laugh. John gets up, speaks more seriously.*) Now that you've turned your backside on Harvard, what do you plan to do?

HENRY. (*Pacing about.*) Well, I think I'll *think* for a while. That'll be a change from college!

JOHN. But what do you want to *be*? Do you have any idea?

HENRY. Yes, I know exactly. I want to be as much as possible like Ralph Waldo Emerson. (*The two brothers look at each other gravely. Light falls away from them. The light rises on Waldo and Lydian. He has the stature of a younger man, but he seems confused as he leafs through a manuscript.*)

LYDIAN. Your lecture was splendid, dear.

WALDO. I think I read one paragraph twice. I lost my place.

LYDIAN. Nobody noticed, dear.

WALDO. If nobody notices, then nobody was listening!

LYDIAN. They thought you did it for emphasis. (*Waldo looks at his wife uncertainly. There is snoring from the other cell cot. Henry, during the Waldo-Lydian action, has returned to his own cot in the cell.*)

WALDO. (*Starts off, then turns to his wife again.*) Did you see that one fellow? In the third row? With his eyes closed. You don't think he was sleeping, do you?

LYDIAN. Concentrating, dear. (*Almost reassured, Waldo moves off with his wife. The snoring grows to a crescendo as the key of moonlight rises in the prison cell. Henry rises to a sitting position on his cot, looks at his sleeping cell partner.*)

HENRY. (*Gently.*) My friend— (*His fellow prisoner snorts, comes groggily awake.*)

OTHER COT. Huh? Why—

HENRY. Every human being has an inalienable right to snore. *Provided* it does not interfere with the inalienable right of *other* men to snore. (*The man on the other cot stares at him.*) I couldn't hear what's going on.

OTHER COT. Nothin' goes on in here. Night half the time. Then day. Then night again. Don't make much difference.

HENRY. Sshh! (*Henry hears with every pore. There is a distant sound of a nightbird.*) Did you hear that? (*He comes to the imaginary downstage window.*)

OTHER COT (BAILEY). I didn't hear nothin'. Just a bird.

HENRY. (*Indignantly.*) "Just a bird"! Can *you* make a cry like that? Or feed on flowers? Or carry the sky on your wings? Friend, you and I can't even fly. (*There is a pause. Bailey rubs his eyes.*)

BAILEY. (*Foggily.*) I missed part of that. Guess I'm not full awake.

HENRY. (*Studying him.*) Nobody is. If I ever met a man who was completely awake, how could I look him in the face?

BAILEY. What you do to get yourself locked up?

HENRY. What do you think?

BAILEY. Well-l-l—a man who talks educated like you—he can't 'a' done something small. Must be murder or worse.

HENRY. That's what I've done by their lights, out there in the dark: murder or worse. (*Change.*) I refuse to commit murder. That's why I'm here.

BAILEY. Who they want you to kill?

HENRY. Mexico.

BAILEY. Who's that?

HENRY. That's where the war is.

BAILEY. What war?

HENRY. (*Amazed, pacing.*) Friend, this cell may be the only place in the United States that's at peace.

BAILEY. Who's fighting who?

HENRY. I'm not fighting anybody.

BAILEY. Neither'm I.

HENRY. But we've got a President who went out and boomed up a war all by himself—with no help from Congress and less help from me.

BAILEY. First I heered of it. (*Warily.*) Which side you on? (*Pointing emphatically downstage, toward Concord.*) Are you agin' *them*?

HENRY. "Them" . . . ?

BAILEY. Or are you *one* of them?

HENRY. (*Thinks.*) I'm one of Me.

BAILEY. That don't make no sense. (*Far off, there is another bird-cry, forlornly wise. Again Henry comes to the downstage imagined window.*)

HENRY. Hear that? Old friend of mine. He's a night flyer. Doesn't have to see where he's going—or maybe he can see what we can't. Or hear . . . (*The bird cries again. Bailey looks at Henry as if he were a bit daft.*) He's headed for the pond. Did you ever make friends with a loon? (*There is a pause.*)

BAILEY. Not till tonight.

HENRY. Any time you hear a man called "loony," just remember that's a great compliment to the man and a great disrespect to the loon. A loon doesn't wage war, his government is perfect, being nonexistent. He is the world's best fisherman and completely in control of his sense, thank you. (*Bailey is still not sure about his new cellmate.*) What are you here for, friend?

BAILEY. I'm waitin' trial.

HENRY. What did you do?

BAILEY. Nothin'.

HENRY. What do they *say* you did?

BAILEY. (*Grudgingly.*) Burned down a barn. (*Defiantly.*) But I didn't do it. All I did was snuck in to get some sleep and I guess the sparks from my pipe fell in the hay and—

HENRY. Tell 'em that.

BAILEY. The tellin' time is the trial. That's what I've been waitin' here for for three months.

HENRY. (*Rising in a fury.*) You've been locked up here for three entire months, waiting for a chance to say you're innocent?

BAILEY. That's about it.

HENRY. It's outrageous! (*Calling.*) Staples! Sam Staples! (*Bailey stops him.*)

BAILEY. Now don't make a ruckus. I'm not a troublemaker. I just want to earn my keep, make a little tobakky money, and get along.

HENRY. "Get along"! Those words turn my stomach. Mister—what's your name?

BAILEY. Bailey. (*A figure crosses the Village Square pompously. Henry hears with animal keenness.*)

HENRY. Mr. Bailey, listen! What do you hear?

BAILEY. Nothing—'cept footsteps.

HENRY. Footsteps of what?

BAILEY. A man, I guess.

HENRY. Where's he walking?

BAILEY. How would I know?

HENRY. I know where he's going. He's going where he's *supposed* to go. So he can *be* where he's supposed to be, at the time he's supposed to be there. Why? So he'll be *liked*. My God, a whole country of us who only want to be liked. (*Jutting his face squarely at Bailey.*) But to be *liked* you must never disagree. And if you never disagree, it's like only breathing *in* and never breathing *out*! A man can suffocate on courtesy. (*He paces.*) What if God wanted to be *liked* instead of loved? What if the Almighty delayed every decision until He was sure it would please the majority? Great whales might have offended some legislature, which God knew would rise up some day to speak endlessly of the Common Good! (*Vehemently.*) Common Good be damned! Give me something magnificently *un*common!

BAILEY. I don't understand what you're sayin', but it's a marvel to hear the way the words roll out!

HENRY. I'll put it in plain Anglo-Saxon, Mr. Bailey: you're an uncommon man. You were protesting against the barn-builder who shut you in with clapboard and daily working hours.

BAILEY. Don't say that to no judge! If I burned down a barn, they'd throw me in jail.

HENRY. Friend, where do you think you are? You might as well have done the deed you didn't do!

BAILEY: But I'm not a man who goes around burning things down.

HENRY. (*Thoughtfully.*) Good for you. Fire *in*side burns hotter than fire *out*side. A man's conviction is stronger than a flame or a bullet or a rock. (*Sinking onto the cot, thoughtfully.*) I wonder if they'll keep *me* here three months, waiting trial! Who'll weed my bean patch? (*A little laugh.*) Of course, I might get some brain work done.

BAILEY. It feels good to talk to a smart fella. I bet you can even write.

HENRY. Sometimes.

BAILEY. I wish I was a writer. If I could write my name, I'd die happy.

HENRY. Then you'd do better than most writers. *Bailey's* not a hard name.

BAILEY. I know the start of it. It's the start of the alphabet backwards.

HENRY. (*Stooping to the floor.*) I'll teach you the rest! (*A light comes up briefly on Henry's Mother.*)

MOTHER. Oh, David Henry's an expert at getting things backward! (*The light on *her falls away. Henry writes with his finger on the dust of the floor. Bailey eagerly kneels beside him.*)

HENRY. B . . . A . . .

BAILEY. That's as far as I know.

HENRY. Who's Bailey?

BAILEY. *I* am.

HENRY. That's your next letter. I! I am I.

BAILEY. How do you write it?

HENRY. (*Making a stroke in the dust.*) Simple as a beanpole. Straight up and down. "B-A-I"—there, you're halfway through your name already. So you *turn the corner*—like this: (*He draws an "L."*) That's an "L"—B-A-I-"turn the corner." Now. Here's a rough one. (*He squints up at the goggle-eyed Bailey.*) How much hair have you got?

BAILEY. Enough to comb.

HENRY. That's it. Bailey needs a comb to comb his hair! (*Drawing in the dust.*) There it is: "E"! And when you're all through, you want a nice tree to sit under. So you make a beanpole with branches on the top: that's "Y"! (*He draws it.*) And there's your name.

BAILEY. Jehosophat! You make it simple! (*As he traces the letters in the dirt floor, turning to Henry for approval.*) "B–A–Beanpole–Turn the Corner–Comb–Tree."

HENRY. You've got it! Now you can write your name! "Bailey"!

BAILEY. I'll leave this jail an educated man! (*Abruptly.*) You must be a teacher!

HENRY. Being a teacher is like being in jail: once it's on your record, you can never get rid of it. (*Henry takes the chair from the cell and places it at the foremost edge of the thrust. Bailey sinks into shadows on his cot, rehearsing his name from the letters on the floor.*

Henry becomes the young schoolmaster, addressing the audience as if they were a classroom full of unseen children.) Students, hold your hand up in front of you, like this. (*He looks about to see that they are all doing just as he is: holding the open palm of the hand eighteen inches in front of the nose.*) Is there anything between my nose and my fingers? Nothing? My young friends, there are millions of tiny, dancing particles, whizzing back and forth, running into each other, and bouncing off! Stars, worlds, planets, universes. Right here! (*He blows a puff of breath into the empty space, then claps his hands together. Ball, a pompous townsman with a silver-topped cane, stalks in, listening to the end of Henry's remarks to the schoolroom.*) And now—I give you a mystery! How do we *know* that these particles are there? (*Henry flicks his other hand through the seeming emptiness in front of him.*)

BALL. How indeed? (*Henry is startled, turns, sees the pompous visitor—then addresses the class.*)

HENRY. Ah, we have a surprise guest in the classroom today. The Chairman of the Concord School Committee, Deacon Nehemiah Ball.

BALL. I am not here to interrupt your scheduled curriculum. (*He pronounces it English-style: "sheduled."*)

HENRY. Thank you, sir. These particles—

BALL. Just an observer, that's all I am. (*Henry is getting irritated. Ball folds his arms behind his back, his cane dangles tail-like behind him; Henry starts to speak again, but Ball interrupts.*)

HENRY. Scientists have—

BALL. Try to forget I'm in the room.

HENRY. (*Clearing his throat.*) We'll try, sir. (*To his class.*) Now. In recent years, scientists have discovered that—

BALL. How is it that I see no school books open here?

HENRY. We're . . . huckleberrying, sir.

BALL. You're *what*?

HENRY. We're scrambling for ideas the way we hunt for huckleberries in the woods.

BALL. That's no way to learn anything. All they need to know is clearly spelled out in the approved school texts.

HENRY. All, Deacon Ball? Young Potter, here—(*Pointing to a student in the first row.*)—just asked me if I really think there is a God.

BALL. Young heathen!

HENRY. He simply asked why, since we never *see* God, should we believe He exists?

BALL. (*Addressing Potter.*) Matters of theology, boy, are discussable with our spiritual leader.

HENRY. Potter has already asked his "spiritual leader"—but the Reverend Whoever-It-Is called him an atheist! For committing the primary sin of *doubt.* (*To the student.*) Mr. Potter, I'll try to answer you just as I once replied to the same question put to me by an annoying, inquisitive young man—myself.

BALL. (*Narrowly.*) Will this be a *theological* opinion?

HENRY. (*Slowly.*) It will be a *human* opinion. (*Again to the student, reasonably.*) If I go into a shop and see all the nicely finished wheels, gears, pinions, springs of a *watch* lying spread out on a bench, then later find them put together exactly and working in unison to move the hands across a dial and show the passage of time, do I believe that these pieces have been flung together by blind chance? Certainly not. I believe that somebody with *thought* and plan and power has been there. An INTELLIGENCE! (*WALDO, in academic robes, has come to a pulpit in his area.*)

WALDO. An Intelligence governs the universe. And in this worship service we shall celebrate our gratitude to that Intelligence. Let us pray. (*He lowers his head, praying silently.*)

HENRY. Nor do I think that the sun rising above Concord this morning was an accident. I hope you saw it, Mr. Potter. And you, too, Deacon Ball. It was a brilliant sunrise. (*Emphatically.*) We are all related, Mr. Potter—and interrelated to a *Universal Mind.*

BALL. That's atheism! (*It is not easy for HENRY to restrain himself.*)

HENRY. I've often wondered, Deacon Ball, if atheism might even be popular with God himself.

BALL. (*Shocked.*) Transcendental blasphemy!

WALDO. The Universal Mind is the divine part of all of us; and we partake, knowingly or not, in the wonder of that Universal Mind. (*The light falls away on WALDO, but he remains at the pulpit in meditation.*)

HENRY. (*Softly.*) Does all this make any sense to you, Potter?

BALL. It makes no sense to me. You will teach the textbooks, sir!

HENRY. I find your texts somewhat behind the century.

BALL. *You* find them so!

HENRY. Yes, sir, I do!

BALL. And you choose to ignore the books which have been *pro*scribed by the School Committee?

HENRY. My students have the ache of curiosity, which I'm afraid your *pro*scriptions will not cure! (*There are a couple of young laughs—quickly stifled. They seem to come from the class. Ball turns stern eyes toward the imagined pupils.*)

BALL. (*Imperiously.*) Silence! You will show respect for your elders! And you, Schoolmaster, will teach strictly according to text! No *huckleberrying*!

HENRY. (*After a pause.*) Class. You've heard the Deacon. We shall stick to the approved books. Your eyes must not wander from the page—to look at a leaf, or an unauthorized butterfly. You must not listen to a cricket or smell a flower that has not been approved by the School Committee. You'd better close both ears and hold your nose—though you may have to grow an extra hand to do it. (*He pantomimes the difficulty of covering successively two ears, then his nose and one ear, then the other ear and his nose. At this point there is uninhibited laughter from the unseen classroom.*)

BALL. (*Waddling to the forestage.*) Silence! Is this the gratitude you show to the municipality which feeds your minds? (*The veins bulge in his forehead, he pounds with his silver-topped cane.*) You will show decent respect! (*The laughter continues. Ball turns to Henry.*) Make them be silent, sir! (*Henry simply lifts his hand; the laughter stops.*) The lack of order in this classroom will most certainly be reported to the full School Committee, which I intend to call into extraordinary session tonight. (*John appears, speaks as if to Henry's mind.*)

JOHN. Henry, give the man a penny apology. Two-cents-worth of humility!

HENRY. Why should I?

JOHN. So they won't cut you off from the class. If you're stubborn, what will happen when Potter asks questions? (*A pause—then Henry makes the supreme effort at contrition. He takes a deep breath, turns to face Ball.*)

HENRY. (*With much difficulty.*) Deacon Ball. I'm sorry that you've had a rather ragged time in my classroom today. I have intended no offense to you or the School Committee.

BALL. Well, we've come to expect a certain degree of unruliness from Harvard men. Your apology shows that you recognize this flaw in your character. But your students don't have Harvard as an excuse. They must be punished.

HENRY. I shall lecture them.

BALL. You will *flog* them!

HENRY. (*Stunned.*) What?

BALL. You will flog them—for showing irreverence to authority!

HENRY. (*Defiantly.*) No, sir.

BALL. I beg your pardon.

HENRY. I said "No." I do not believe in corporal punishment.

BALL. What you believe is irrelevant. Your opinion, as a teacher, has not been asked for. I direct you to FLOG! (*Henry hesitates.*)

HENRY. Why?

BALL. It is policy. Offending students are whipped.

HENRY. And what would that teach them?

BALL. Obedience. An essential quality in subordinates, whether they are pupils in a classroom or soldiers on a battlefield.

HENRY. They are not training to be soldiers. Not *my* students.

BALL. These young people are not *yours*. They have been sent to you by the tax-paying citizens of Concord, who expect you to abide by the rules laid down by the school administrators. (*Silence. Henry does not move.*) Perform your duty, Schoolmaster Thoreau, if you expect to retain your post in this community. (*Henry slowly unbuckles his belt, then whips it off, taking a short step toward Ball, who pulls back, thinking perhaps Henry is about to flog* him. *Then Henry turns front, to the class.*)

HENRY. (*Bitterly, to his class.*) *Six* of you. *Any* six. Come forward. It doesn't matter who. You are all—*all* of you—accused of the damning crimes of laughter, curiosity, and candid self-expression! Bigelow! (*Henry grabs the chair, spins it over as if he were putting a boy across his knee. Eyes closed, Henry lashes the chair fiercely and painfully with his belt.*) Coleman! (*Again he lashes the chair.*) Loring! (*Another lash.*) McClain! (*He whips the chair again, blindly, loathing what he is doing.*) Henderson. (*Another lash. Then a hesitation.*) Potter! (*This whipping is the most painful of all. He turns his head away. Now finished, breathless, Henry opens his eyes, stares at the belt as if it were something filthy and revolting. He flings it way from him, far offstage.*)

BALL. I congratulate you. I am happy to be able to report to the School Committee that Schoolmaster Thoreau—

HENRY. —has administered the Sacrament of the Schoolroom; and he resigns as a "teacher" in the Public Schools of Concord! (*Ball icily falls back into the shadows and disappears. The light on the pulpit comes up in full brilliance on Waldo.*)

WALDO. (*In the midst of an inner struggle.*) —but I cannot comply with custom! I cannot perform the rites required of me by this congregation. For I have searched the Scriptures and can find nothing which calls on us to repeat endlessly the ceremony of the Last Supper. Intellectually, emotionally, spiritually, I cannot administer this Sacrament. So I resign my position as pastor of the Second Unitarian Church of Boston. (*Henry has put the chair—his "student"—back in the jail cell. Sadly he comes down into the light.*)

HENRY. I shall never teach again.

WALDO. I shall never preach again. (*Light rises on Mother and John.*)

MOTHER. Have you ever noticed, John, how much Mr. Emerson talks like our David Henry? (*John notices the disconsolate Henry and goes to him.*)

JOHN. (*Quietly.*) A school doesn't need a School Committee. Or Trustees. Or Governors. Or Lumber. Or approved textbooks. All a school needs is a mind that sends, and minds that receive.

HENRY. Nobody can teach anybody anything.

JOHN. (*Blithely.*) Of course not. Teach them how to teach themselves.

HENRY. (*Fired with an idea.*) Our *own* school, John. No buildings. Break out of the classroom prison. All we need is *sky*! (*The cyclorama becomes ablaze with blue, and sunlit clouds. There is the screech and wheeling of birds, and a great sense of freedom.*) The *universe* can be our schoolroom, John—the great, vast world of the Concord countryside. (*Henry claps a broad straw hat on his head, sticks a notebook under his arm. There is a flood of light on the forestage. Henry seems to be marching across the open sunlit fields. John follows with a telescope.*) Students! (*The students, though imaginary, are presumably all around him.*) Watch! Notice! Observe! (*He takes the telescope from John and uses it as pointer.*) See what is happening around you. Did you ever have any *idea* so much was going on in Heywood's Meadow? I'll wager even Heywood doesn't know. (*A discovery.*) The cypripedium is already in flower! (*He leafs back through his notebook.*) *Last* year it didn't bloom until tomorrow! (*He makes an entry in his notebook.*) Do you know how few people know what we've just discovered? Stumbling on the first morning of a new flower! Most of Concord is too busy eating meals and going to the post office! (*A strikingly beautiful girl—twenty perhaps—stands at the edge of the light, watching and listening, fascinated.*) Oh, I would be so sad and sorry to remember that I once was in the world and noticed nothing remarkable. Not so much as a prince in disguise. (*Looking sideways at his brother.*) John, are you a prince in disguise?

JOHN. Of course. (*Henry paces about the meadow.*)

HENRY. Wouldn't it be dreadful if I had lived in the Golden Age as *hired man*? Or visited Olympus, and fell asleep after dinner—and completely missed the conversation of the gods. Or imagine living in Judea eighteen hundred years ago—and never knowing that Jesus was my contemporary! What are you doing? (*He has, in his peripatetic outpouring, come face-to-face with the girl, who has taken out a notebook; she is absorbed in writing, jarred by his question.*)

ELLEN. I'm writing.

HENRY. What?

ELLEN. What you've been saying. So I'll remember.

HENRY. Don't just remember what I said. Remember what I'm talking about. (*Obediently, she closes her notebook. Henry crosses to John, lowering his voice.*) Who's that?

JOHN. It's a girl. (*Both stare at her, impressed.*)

HENRY. One of ours? I mean, does she belong to us? Is she one of our students?

JOHN. (*Taking a good look at her.*) I wouldn't mind. Would you?

HENRY. (*Crossing back to her.*) Excuse me, Miss. But I think you're a little old to be a member of this class.

JOHN. Henry, a young lady is never too old for anything.

HENRY. It's just that—well—most of our students are twelve—or thereabouts. And you're—well, not exactly thereabouts. (*The girl laughs.*)

ELLEN. Does it make so much difference really? I just want to come along and listen and watch. I won't be any bother or ask any questions.

HENRY. Why not?

ELLEN. My little brother is the only one who has the right to ask questions: he's paying tuition.

HENRY. (*Pointing a finger at her.*) You're Sewell.

JOHN. How'd you know?

HENRY. If I can spot a cypripedium, I can spot a Sewell.

JOHN. There's only one rule in this class: no rules. So, of course, you're welcome to come along—any time you like.

ELLEN. How about tuition?

JOHN. You've already paid it. If you were ugly, we'd charge you. Or twelve. Or thereabouts. (*Ellen and John laugh. Henry does not. He merely looks at her.*)

ELLEN. You're John Thoreau. (*Turning.*) And you're the thundercloud. Henry. (*Henry frowns.*)

HENRY. What previous educational experience have you had?

ELLEN. Finishing school.

HENRY. Dear God.

ELLEN. I survived.

HENRY. I warn you, Miss Sewell, that John and I are not finishers. Nobody leaves us with a smooth surface. We rough up the consciousness, scrape the moss off young minds.

ELLEN. Please, Mr. Thoreau, go back to your students. I've interrupted.

HENRY. Of course you have. Every creative event that ever happened in the world was an interruption. Unexpected. Unplanned for. The only people who ever get anyplace interesting are the people who get lost. That's why the planets are so much better company than the stars—they keep wandering back and forth across the sky and you never know where you're going to find them. (*To the unseen class.*) Students. We have another Sewell. Edmund's sister. (*To the girl.*) You have a first name?

ELLEN. Ellen.

HENRY. Ellen Sewell. Our textbook, Miss Sewell, is Heywood's Meadow. Approved by the Almighty, if not by the School Committee. (*To the class.*) In this single pasture, there are *three hundred* distinct and separate varieties of grass. I know; I have catalogued them myself. You look down and you say: "That's grass. Grass is grass." Ridiculous. You have missed the splendid variety of the show. There's camel grass, candy grass, cloud grass, cow-quake, mouse-barley, fox-tail, London-lace, devil's knitting needle, feather-top, buffalo grass, timothy and barnyard grass and clovers enough to sweeten the bellies of all the lambs since creation. (*Ellen has taken down her notebook and is writing. Suddenly Henry leans down, seeing something, and plucks an imaginary blade of grass.*) John, look at this. What would you say it is?

JOHN. I've never seen it before.

HENRY. It's *Coix Lacryma-jobi*, which means Job's Tears. I've never seen a specimen here. Students, I beg your pardon. We are in the midst of three hundred and *one* varieties of God-made grasses. (*He jots this information in his notebook. Out of the corner of his eye, he sees Ellen writing.*) You're writing again.

ELLEN. Just "Job's tears."

HENRY. Why?

ELLEN. When you go to school, you're supposed to write things down, so you remember what you've been taught.

HENRY. Then it's the notebook that does the remembering, not you.

ELLEN. *You* keep a notebook.

HENRY. I also wear a ridiculous straw hat. That doesn't mean that *you* should wear a ridiculous hat. You'd look ridiculous in it. Nature didn't stuff this meadow full of identical blades of grass, each an imitation of another. They're all *different*! Follow-the-leader is not the game we're playing here! Young lady, BE YOUR OWN MAN!

JOHN. (*Low.*) Henry, don't shout at her.

ELLEN. I won't take notes. I promise you. Not one.

HENRY. Why not? If you want to take notes, go ahead. But not because I'm doing it, or because I told you to. (*Gently.*) Miss Sewell, I want you to be yourself—not your idea of what you think is somebody else's idea of yourself. (*Turning to the students.*) Perhaps, students, Miss Sewell's interruption has given us the essence of the textbook we call Heywood's Meadow. The multiple grasses beneath our feet. The infinity of the sky above us. (*Rifling through his notebook.*) And if I have jotted down a note about a cloud-flame, or about sunlight on bird-wings, don't you write, just because *I* am writing. Don't ape me, or copy me. (*Intensely, but quietly.*) If you wish merely to *listen* to the sky, or *smell* the sky, or *feel* the sky with your finger-tips, do that, too! (*With great conviction.*) Because I think there should be as many different persons in the world as possible. So—*each of you*—be careful to find out and pursue your own way! (*As the lights dim, Henry goes back into the dimly-lit cell.*)

BAILEY. (*Rapturously.*) Bailey, Bailey, Bailey! I kin write! Watch! Watch me do it all by myself—! (*Bailey starts again to trace his name in the dust on the cell floor. Henry bitterly erases the pattern of letters in the dust with his foot. Bailey looks up, puzzled.*)

HENRY. Don't learn to write your name.

BAILEY: I already learned.

HENRY. (*Splenetic.*) Unlearn it. Writing your name can lead to writing sentences. And the next thing you'll be doing is writing paragraphs, and then books. And then you'll be in as much trouble as I am!

BAILEY. (*Wonderingly.*) You write books?

HENRY. (*Wryly.*) Yes.

BAILEY. If my mother'd lived to see me sittin' in the same jail cell with a man who writ a book, ohhhh-ee, she'd be proud of me. Tell me somethin'. Do you make up all the words yourself?

HENRY. Oh, now and then I stick in a word or two that's been used before. The basic trick is to pick the right words and put 'em in the right order.

BAILEY. Must be a fortune in it. I hear some books cost more'n a dollar!

HENRY. But they haven't been perfected yet. They've gotta put legs on them. As it is now, a book just sits in a shop and has to wait for somebody with legs on to come and find it.

BAILEY. (*Blankly.*) Oh? (*Bailey has taken tobacco from his rough coat in the locker, thus freeing the box for the next scene.*)

HENRY. My first book—also my last book—was a very stationary model. The publisher brought out a thousand copies!—and gave me the privilege of paying for the printing. So all the copies that didn't sell belonged to the author. And they came running home to me, legs or not. (*Gravely.*) Right now, Mr. Bailey, I have a library of nearly nine hundred volumes!—seven hundred of which I wrote myself. (*Pointing to the scuffed-up letters in the dust of the floor.*) My friend, give up your literary career. (*Suddenly, Henry takes the locker-box from the cell, flips it over, open-side up, and drags it down onto the thrust. John comes on, helping him with the "boat."*)

HENRY. John, today I thought we'd make a complete circuit of the pond. If this boat isn't large enough for the whole class, I'll take the first trip, you take the second.

JOHN. It'll be large enough.

HENRY. We lost another pupil?

JOHN. No. We lost two.

HENRY. (*Defensively.*) Good. Education should not be a mass process!

JOHN. With us, it isn't.

HENRY. The whole idea of our school is that the size of the classroom grows larger and larger—

JOHN. —while the size of the class grows smaller and smaller.

HENRY. How many do we actually have left?

JOHN. (*Avoiding his eyes.*) Mother's got the name of a new family, just moved to Concord.

HENRY. How many children?

JOHN. Be patient, Henry. The wife is pregnant. (*John starts to leave.*)

HENRY. Where are you going?

JOHN. Back to the pencil factory.

HENRY. Why?

JOHN. It might be a little overpowering—to have twice as many teachers as pupils.

HENRY. Only one left? (*John goes off. Henry, alone, scowls, kicks at the box-boat. Ellen appears.*)

ELLEN. Mr. Thoreau—? (*Henry turns.*)

HENRY. Good morning.

ELLEN. I—I came to tell you that you shouldn't wait for Edmund. Just go ahead and start the class without him. He—uh—won't be coming today.

HENRY. I hope he's not ill.

ELLEN. No. (*Pause.*) It's my Father—

HENRY. *He's* ill?

ELLEN. Not exactly. Father's worried—because he thinks Edmund's learning too much.

HENRY. That's good news. I thought Edmund was a bit sluggish myself. Compared with the other students. That is, when we had other students to compare him with. (*Briskly.*) Well, tell your Father not to worry. I'll slow down with Edmund.

ELLEN. I'm afraid Father doesn't want him to come to your school at all any more.

HENRY. (*Bridling.*) Oh. Your Father's opposed to knowledge.

ELLEN. No. He's opposed to Transcendentalists. That's what he says you are. And your brother, too. "A whole family afflicted with Transcendentalism."

HENRY. What the devil does your Father think Transcendentalism *is*?

ELLEN. I asked him and he tried to explain it to me. And the more he explained, the less I understood it. Father has a gift that way.

HENRY. A born *non*-teacher. (*Suddenly.*) Miss Sewell. Get into the boat.

ELLEN. Oh?

HENRY. Since I find myself unexpectedly unemployed, I shall take you on a voyage of exploration. No tuition charge. (*Henry helps her into the boat.*) Keep your eyes on the line between the water and the sky. I'll row. (*He pantomimes pushing the boat off; the light narrows, the background trembles with the wavering pattern of sunlight reflected from water. With no visible oars, he rows. Suddenly, he points.*) There used to be a row of cedars on that far shore. (*Sighing.*) But we have lost that link with Lebanon.

ELLEN. Where have they gone?

HENRY. Into firewood—and up in smoke. Into houses. Do you know what we're doing, Miss Sewell? We're poisoning paradise. Shearing off the woods, making the poor earth bald before her time.

ELLEN. But we have to have houses, Mr. Thoreau. Or should we all live in caves?

HENRY. What's the use of a house if you haven't got a tolerable planet to put it on? Did you know that trees cry out in pain when they're cut? I've heard them. But what bells in town toll for them? We prosecute men for abusing children; we ought to prosecute them for maltreating nature.

ELLEN. My father says God put everything here for men to *use*.

HENRY. Oh? Did the Good Father put us here to root and snort and glut ourselves like the pigs? No, the pigs are better; pigs may be the most respectable part of the population: at least they consume the rubble instead of contributing to it. (*In the distance, the whistle of a railroad train.*) Hear that? There goes a carload of two-legged pigs, off to market . . . emasculating the landscape with their tracks . . .

ELLEN. I rather like the railroad. Far better than a horse and carriage.

HENRY. Why?

ELLEN. It's smoother, and much faster.

HENRY. And dirtier. And uglier. Thank God men haven't learned to fly: they'd lay waste the sky as well as the earth . . . chop down the clouds!

ELLEN. (*Somewhat puzzled.*) Is that in Transcendentalism, Mr. Thoreau?

HENRY. (*Laughs.*) No. Yes, it is—in a way. Take your father. Do you love the man?

ELLEN. Of course.

HENRY. Why?

ELLEN. He's my father.

HENRY. Is he beautiful?

ELLEN. Dear me, no!

HENRY. Does he create beauty? Paint? Play a musical instrument?

ELLEN. No.

HENRY. (*Pointing up, then down.*) Can he fly like that bird? Or swim, like that fellow down there?

ELLEN. He can swim a little. He used to. But not like that fish.

HENRY. Nevertheless you *love* him.

ELLEN. Of course.

HENRY. Your love *transcends* what your father is—and what he is not. Every consciousness is capable of going beyond itself. Every— (*Ellen frowns a bit.*) Dammit, I've lost you. Put your hand in the water. (*She does.*) Can you touch bottom?

ELLEN. (*Reaching down.*) It's too deep.

HENRY. For the length of your arm. Not for the length of your mind. (*He has stopped rowing.*) Miss Sewell. Why should your reach stop with your skin? When you transcend the limits of yourself, you can cease merely living—and begin to BE!

ELLEN. I don't mind *living*—

HENRY. But *being* is so much more interesting.

ELLEN. (*Taking her hand out of the "water."*) I'm a little bit afraid—just—to "be"!

HENRY. Think how free it is. If you're never afraid.

ELLEN. Aren't you ever afraid? (*He thinks, stares at her.*)

HENRY. Yes. I'm afraid that I might "live" right through this moment—and *only* live—(*He leans forward on his oars, looking into her face.*)—look at you and only *see* you. Oh, it doesn't hurt at all to look at you, believe me. But what if there's more—and I miss it?

ELLEN. Miss what?

HENRY. What if all that is beautiful, in women, in the world—or worlds—what if all of it is totaled up in this face here, in front of me—and I am empty enough to think I am merely seeing *one* face? (*Ellen doesn't follow him precisely, but she's pleased.*)

ELLEN. That's Transcendentalism? (*Henry has lost interest in Transcendentalism and is more interested in Ellen.*)

HENRY. (*Resumes rowing.*) If you like.

ELLEN. I don't think that's wicked. I think it's rather nice.

HENRY. Who says it's wicked?

ELLEN. Father. Last night at the dinner table, Edmund gave Father a sermon on the Over-Soul.

HENRY. Good for Edmund! Most dining rooms are tabernacles where only the father gets the pulpit.

ELLEN. Oh, Father got it right back. He was still shouting at breakfast. He broke off with an incomplete sentence last night, and picked it right up this morning at porridge.

HENRY. Well, I'm a little older than Edmund. But I have yet to hear the first syllable of valuable advice from my seniors. (*His eyes going to the horizon.*) We are born as innocents. We are polluted by advice. Here is life in front of us, like the surface of this pond, inviting us to sail on it. A voyage, an experiment. Waiting to be performed. Has your father tried it before? That's no help to me. Or to you. Keep your innocence, Edmund!

ELLEN. Ellen.

HENRY. Ellen, yes. You look very much alike, you know. The eyes. You both listen with your eyes.

ELLEN. I have to go back.

HENRY. Why?

ELLEN. Father expects me.

HENRY. Surprise him.

ELLEN. Edmund did. He's braver than I am.

HENRY. Stand up to your father! (*He stands. The boat rocks.*)

ELLEN. Please, Mr. Thoreau—not in the boat!

HENRY. Oh— (*He sits.*)

ELLEN. Will you row me back to shore, please?

HENRY. No. Listen to me. If I were to say, "I love You, Sewell—Miss Sewell. Ellen"—you wouldn't think much of it as a statement of fact if you knew it was just an echo, a mouthing, of something somebody *told* me to say. (*Disparagingly.*) Some *father*! (*Quietly.*) But if I say "I love you" out of myself, out of my own experience—or lack of it—out of my innocence, then you and God had better believe me. (*The light comes up on John and Mother, as Ellen turns away from Henry, staring at the water.*)

JOHN. (*Running in.*) Mother, Henry's in love.

MOTHER. (*Worried.*) Who's he in love with?

JOHN. A girl.

MOTHER. Thank God. (*Light falls away on John and Mother.*)

ELLEN. (*Icily.*) I'm not one of your fish, nor one of your birds, Mr. Thoreau. So I can neither swim nor fly back to dry land. I must simply sit here and hope you are gentleman enough to row me ashore. (*Henry doesn't move. He looks at her. She's beautiful, but he knows he's missed his chance, and it frustrates him.*)

HENRY. (*With a sigh.*) Miss Sewell. I apologize. And I'll row you to shore on one condition.

ELLEN. I have to accept it.

HENRY. Come to church on Sunday.

ELLEN. You don't go to church.

HENRY. Of course not. I can't stand sitting in a pew, having the Sabbath despoiled by a sermon.

ELLEN. But you still invite me to church?

HENRY. With John. *We* have a strong family resemblance, too. And if you find a single syllable in me worth writing in a notebook, you'll find *paragraphs* of it in John! Where I am cantankerous, he is amiable. Where I am thorns and brambles, he is a garden. Where I am a bare hill in winter, he is spring. (*He begins to row, slowly.*)

ELLEN. How do you know your brother would want to take me to church?

HENRY. Didn't you notice that day in Heywood's Meadow—when he proposed to you?

ELLEN. He barely spoke to me.

HENRY. That's why you didn't hear him. You missed the eloquence of his silence. (*The boat presumably comes to shore. Henry jumps out, pantomimes pulling it onto the bank, then helps Ellen as she steps out. Ellen, having won her point, wonders . . . have I really lost?*)

ELLEN. (*With mixed pride and regret.*) Good day, Mr. Thoreau. Thank you for making Transcendentalism so clear.

HENRY. Did I? If there's anything I missed, just ask Edmund.

ELLEN. What will happen to your school?

HENRY. (*Turning away.*) I'm going back to it. As a pupil. Maybe I can learn from Nature—and from John: a pasture can be raucous with flowers, and not make a single sound. But a man, presumably wiser than a daffodil—can beat so loudly on the eardrums that nobody hears what he's trying to say. (*Ellen is bewildered. Then, in his silence, Henry seems almost fierce to her, and she runs off, frightened. He looks wistfully toward the air where Ellen was. Then he stares down into the empty boat, kicks it. That emptiness is something of the vacancy he feels within himself.*

Slowly, Henry moves up into the area of the jail cell. The wavering pattern of light-on-water falls away. Only the long nocturnal shadows of the cell remain. Bailey is asleep on his cot, snoring lightly. Henry looks down at him.)

HENRY. Mr. Bailey, what do you think of marriage? (*Bailey gives out a derisive snore, which suggests that subconsciously he may have heard the question. Henry nods.*) That seems to be the majority opinion. (*He settles back on his own cot. The clock strikes eleven. The sound dilates, louder and louder, pulsing with standing waves.*) Bailey, did you hear that? I don't think I've ever felt those waves of sound from the clock tower. (*A laugh.*) That's ridiculous—that a man has to be put in a stone box before he can hear the music of his own village! (*Henry calls through the barred window.*) Thank you, Concord! Thank you for locking me up so I'm free to hear what I've never heard before. You put me behind iron bars and walls four feet thick! How do you know that *I'm* not the free one? The freest man in the world! And you, out there, are chained to what you have to do tomorrow morning! (*Now he whispers through the cell grating.*) Speak softly, Concord—I can hear you breathing. (*Bailey lets out a snore.*) Quiet, Bailey. We free men should listen to the cry of prisoners. (*The light falls away on the cell. There is a projection of a stained glass window. Facing upstage is a standing row of worshipers: Deacon Ball, Sam Staples, Waldo, Lydian, Mrs. Thoreau, John and Ellen beside him, and townspeople. All are dressed Sunday-best and singing the last stanza of a hymn: "Blest Be the Tie That Binds," Pilgrim Hymnal 272.*)

CHURCHGOERS. (*Singing in unison.*)

Blest be the tie that binds
Our hearts in Christian love;
The Fellowship of kindred minds
Is like to that Above.
A-men.

(*Halfway through the hymn, Edward scratches his bottom. Lydian pulls his hand away. After the "Amen" there is a swell of organ music, as the worshippers begin to file into the tree-dappled light of a Sunday noon. Ellen comes out, on John's arm. There is a cluster of conversation around the Emersons.*)

DEACON BALL. Tell me, Doctor Emerson. What is the feeling of a clergyman when he hears another pastor in the pulpit?

WALDO. Relief.

DEACON. That you don't have to give the sermon?

WALDO. (*Drily.*) That it's over. (*The Mother is beaming at John and Ellen. Suddenly she sees something which turns her soul to ice. The others look, with varying degrees of shock, as Henry, his shirt unbuttoned, pushes a wheelbarrow full of earth. Blithely he crosses directly in front of the washed and starched churchgoers. Ellen looks down, John suppresses a grin, Waldo and Lydian turn gracefully away, and Deacon Ball tries to look as much as possible like Moses on the mountain.*)

MOTHER. Oh, David Henry! *Not* on Sunday!

HENRY. (*Pleasantly.*) This *is* Sunday, isn't it. Have all of you been shut up inside? On this beautiful morning? What a pity!

DEACON. We've been feeding our souls!

HENRY. How selfish of you. (*He reaches into the wheelbarrow and sprinkles some of the unseen contents at the feet of the churchgoers.*) *I've* been feeding the flora of Concord. (*They wince at the aroma.*) Bringing loaves and fishes to the lilacs. (*Waving cheerfully, Henry trundles the wheelbarrow off. All eyes follow him.*)

DEACON. Labor on the Sabbath, and the Devil's in Massachusetts.

JOHN. Henry worships in the woods.

DEACON BALL. Then what do we have churches for?

WALDO. I sometimes wonder.

LYDIAN. (*Quickly.*) Dr. Emerson means that the Good Lord is everywhere.

DEACON BALL. The Lord *I* know rested on the Seventh Day.

WALDO. Why, Deacon Ball, you're older than I thought! (*Before Ball can really take offense, the warm-hearted Emerson pats his shoulder.*) For you and me, Deacon, the

Declaration of Independence has already been written. Young Thoreau has to declare it every day—Sundays included. (*Starts off, with Lydian.*) So what's the harm if he sweats his psalms instead of singing them? (*The worshipers disperse. John and Ellen go off together. Mrs. Thoreau is left alone. She looks off toward the vanished Henry.*)

MOTHER. Oh, David Henry—why did God and I have to make you so peculiar? (*Eyes to heaven.*) And please, dear Lord, don't let John get too strange. Perhaps, if it isn't too much trouble, you could slip the word "yes" into that young lady's mouth. Amen. (*She goes off. The stained glass window fades. The cyclorama becomes sunlit clouds. Amplified and echoing, John's laughter spills across the open field. Henry comes on, takes a triumphant stance.*)

HENRY. She said "Yes!!!" (*John burst on, almost drunk with his own laughter.*) Congratulations—I'm happy for you, John! Are you going to do it right away? Or do you have to go through those tribal rites—posting the banns, all that primitive nonsense? (*John, in a paroxysm of laughter, embraces his brother.*)

JOHN. She said—she said— (*He breaks off again, laughing.*)

HENRY. She said "Yes," naturally! (*John, laughing, can't answer.*) She didn't say "no!"?

JOHN. No, she didn't say "No!"

HENRY. What the devil *did* she say?

JOHN. (*Still laughing.*) She quoted her father.

HENRY. Heavenly or here?

JOHN. The one her mother married.

HENRY. Well, what did old Porridge-Face have to say?

JOHN. He said— (*Laughing.*) She said he said . . . that marriage to either of the Thoreau brothers was unthinkable!

HENRY. Amen! The Thoreau brothers never had any intention of marrying her father! (*Hopefully.*) But she stood up to him?

JOHN. I wasn't there—but evidently she sat down. (*He sits.*)

HENRY. So you wasted six good summer Sundays taking her to church!

JOHN. I swear to you, I didn't pray. I kept looking at that face out of the corner of my eye. Wondering what she was thinking. I finally realized she wasn't thinking at all!

HENRY. How many people do?

JOHN. (*Starts laughing again.*) When I asked her to marry me, there was a pregnant pause. Well, not pregnant, but a pause. Then she said: "Oh, dear . . ." At first, I thought she was being affectionate, then I realized she was only saying, "Oh, dear!"

HENRY. Then what?

JOHN. Then she said, "Why doesn't Henry ask me?" And I said, "If he does, will you say yes?" And she said, "No, but why doesn't he ask me anyhow?"

HENRY. It's an outrage! She wants to wear *both* of our scalps on her petticoat strings!

JOHN. She won't marry you, and she won't marry me. But I think she'd marry *us* in a minute.

HENRY. That's carrying Unitarianism too far!

JOHN. If we were Mohammedans—

HENRY. Wouldn't help. Moslems take multiple wives, not multiple husbands.

JOHN. But then, Henry, I destroyed the whole thing. I killed it. I laughed. (*Henry laughs a little.*) Not like that. Bigger! (*They both begin to laugh.*) Not at her, the dear girl; at *us*! I almost shattered the most sacred tradition of the Thoreau tribe: celibacy!

HENRY. (*Laughing.*) You're a good-hearted man, John! You saved the girl from marrying a monk.

JOHN. Or a pair of them! (*They laugh more heartily.*)

HENRY. Who in our brood has ever committed marriage?

JOHN. Mama and Papa.

HENRY. Only legally. Except for a couple of slips that brought about you and me, Papa is pure bachelor and Mama is a living pillar of spinsterhood. Thanks to your courageous inaction, the Thoreaus remain a race of maiden aunts and bachelors. All of us, December Virgins!

JOHN. Henry, I never told you about one April— (*Henry lifts one hand in mock forgiveness.*)

HENRY. Boy, if Father can falter, so can you! (*They laugh together, then grow serious.*)

JOHN. It makes for a rather lonely-looking future.

HENRY. Lonely? Never! Why, when I'm ninety and you're a mere infant of eighty-eight, you'll come around and comfort me.

JOHN. When you're ninety, Henry, I'll be a "mere infant" of ninety-two. (*Henry grasps his brother's hand.*)

HENRY. And *that's* the time we'll *both* go after the hand of Ellen Sewell! (*Henry and John leap about, laughing, as if they were a pair of nonagenarians who have been injected with "youth-juice." They fall into each other's arms, laughing helplessly.*

The light goes black. In utter darkness, the church bell tolls mournfully. Dimly the stained-glass window of the church appears. Then a cold white spot, directly above, strikes the box which was the boat and has now been turned over to become a coffin.)

VOICE OF MINISTER. Unto Almighty God we commend the soul of our brother departed, John Thoreau, and we commit his body to the ground, in the sure and certain hope of the Resurrection unto Eternal Life. Let us pray. (*Four black-coated townspeople carry off the casket. The Mother is in black. Henry comes slowly to her side. She looks into his face.*)

MOTHER. David Henry. *Pray* with me! (*Mother kneels, facing front. Almost like a sleep-walker, Henry sinks to his knees. His face is mask-like. His Mother clasps her hands. Automatically Henry does the same.*)

MOTHER. (*With difficulty.*) Our Father, which art in Heaven, hallowed be—(*She breaks off, looks at her silent son, who has lowered his hands.*)

HENRY. I can't, Mother. I can't pray.

MOTHER. It helps.

HENRY. Does it? I prayed *before*. What good did it do?

MOTHER. We should pray for John's soul.

HENRY. John's soul can take care of itself.

MOTHER. We should pray for understanding— (*Henry suddenly gets up, angrily.*)

HENRY. I understand! God has stopped listening, Mother—if He ever *did* listen! What kind of God would fail to see the godliness in John? I can't pray to Him. (*Henry turns away, then comes back, kisses his Mother's head. Quietly:*) Mother. Pray for *both* your sons. (*The Mother lowers her head, praying as she moves off. The stained-glass projection fades. Ellen hurries on.*)

ELLEN. (*Sympathetically.*) What happened?

HENRY. (*Shrugs.*) He died.

ELLEN. I was in Winthrop. I didn't even hear about it until after the funeral . . .

HENRY. We managed.

ELLEN. How did—didn't anybody know, beforehand—?

HENRY. What do you want, a medical report? To feed a morbid curiosity?

ELLEN. Even though I couldn't marry him—

HENRY. Couldn't you? Well, that's your business.

ELLEN. Henry, don't be so selfish with your sorrow! *I care too!*

HENRY. He had a glamorous death. Like the Knights of the Round Table who slashed at each other with rusty swords until they all died of blood-poisoning.

ELLEN. I don't understand.

HENRY. John, three mornings ago, happened to think of something very funny while he was shaving. He burst out laughing, and cut himself. The razor was old, and vicious, and it despised the blood in his veins. And so— (*Confronting her fiercely.*) —would you like the details? The spasms, the retching, the murderous ineptitude of doctors, the paralysis of the tongue, the choking, the clamping of the jaw, the blood-black face, the eyes pleading for oxygen, the— (*Henry suddenly is seized with the symptoms of psychosomatic lockjaw, and seems to be going through his brother's agony.*)

ELLEN. (*Aghast.*) Henry! (*He overcomes the illusion, breathes heavily, gets control of himself.*)

HENRY. (*Depleted, but intensely.*) If a lightning bolt had struck him, that might have been worthy of the size of the man. But a nick in the finger from a dull razor—what an indignity! What kind of God would drain away such youth and energy and laughter! A sneak attack from the Almighty! (*Turning his face to the sky.*) You plagued Job, but you spared him! Why couldn't you have been as fair with John? (*Ellen moves toward him, wants to touch him, to comfort him—but she doesn't.*)

ELLEN. I wonder if—if God lets us be hurt—so we can learn to *transcend* the pain . . . ? (*She speaks very softly and simply.*) In the boat, I didn't understand, really. But is it possible, Henry, that—even though he's stopped *living*, John continues to *be*? (*Henry turns and looks at her. She* did *understand! There is a strong urge in Henry to embrace her; but a stronger reserve, which prevents him. The light falls away on them. Another light picks up Waldo, seated, presumably in his study. Lydian stands behind him. Henry shifts his weight from one foot to the other as Waldo studies him thoughtfully.*)

WALDO. Well, what sort of work would you like to do?

HENRY. Anything. I wish to use my hands.

WALDO. And what about your head?

HENRY. It could be useful. For burrowing, perhaps. (*Lydian laughs.*) I could beat it into a ploughshare. It might be a better tool than it's been for thinking.

WALDO. You're giving up *thinking*?

HENRY. For this lifetime, yes.

WALDO. (*Turning to his wife.*) We could certainly use a handyman, Lydian. (*To Henry.*) Mrs. Emerson will assure you that, of all God's creatures, I am the least handy of men. My skill at carpentry stops at cutting cheese. (*They laugh, Henry a bit uneasily.*)

LYDIAN. There's a great deal that needs doing. The wall by the back meadow needs mending.

HENRY. I am a mason.

WALDO. You are?

HENRY. (*Quickly.*) No, of course I'm not a *Mason*—but I *do* masonry.

WALDO. The weeds are at war with the marigolds. And the last time I looked, the weeds were winning.

HENRY. They're doomed. Being a weed myself, I infiltrate their ranks.

WALDO. What about children, Mr. Thoreau?

HENRY. What about them?

LYDIAN. You've had experience with them?

HENRY. Well, I was a child once myself. Briefly.

LYDIAN. (*To Waldo.*) It would be so good for Edward—to have someone who could take him boating and hiking. . . . (*To Henry.*) Dr. Emerson has so little time to be a father—he's so occupied with his lectures and writing.

HENRY. When I'm with your son, Dr. Emerson, I might turn my brain back on—temporarily.

WALDO. I think this might be a very good arrangement. Of course, there's the matter of compensation.

HENRY. I've been paid. (*Waldo lifts his eyebrows, puzzled.*) With something far more extraordinary than money. And more valuable. The words you fling into an audience from the lecture platform—you never know what happens to them, do you? No more than a Roman Emperor knew what happened to the coins he scattered to the crowd as he rode through the streets.

WALDO. The Roman Emperors were trying to buy popularity.

HENRY. And the poor fellows only had gold. No wonder Rome fell! (*Growing more intense.*) But I sat on the grass at Harvard Yard and heard you speak for the first time. I was at the very edge of the assembly—but I think I caught more coins than the crowd at the wheels of your chariot.

WALDO. (*To Lydian.*) This may be interesting, having a Harvard man as a handyman. (*To Henry.*) I'm vain, you know. Of necessity. I'm not as lucky as the Caesars; I have to mint all my own coins. So a man sits at his desk and doubts constantly: is it gold or is it tin?

HENRY. I apologize. It was a faulty metaphor. Money is merely money. You can never spend a thought. It still belongs to you—though it makes other men rich!

WALDO. (*Accusingly.*) You're thinking, Mr. Thoreau. Incidentally, if we're going to have you around here—you, and your hands, and your head—I can't possibly go on calling you "Mr. Thoreau." Your mother calls you "David," I believe?

HENRY. I call myself "Henry."

WALDO. (*Drily.*) My mother called *me* "Ralph." You may call me "Waldo." (*They laugh and shake hands.*) And Lydian, of course, is "Lydian." And Edward—where's Edward? (*Calls.*) Edward!

LYDIAN. It's important, I think, for you to meet Edward. To be sure that you two are . . . companionable.

WALDO. Why shouldn't they be? (*Edward comes on. He is eight, and has the shyness and reserve of the son of a famous father.*)

EDWARD. (*Reporting to his father.*) Yes, sir?

WALDO. A firm handshake, Edward, for Mr. Thoreau. (*Edward and Henry shake hands.*) You're going to be extremely good friends.

HENRY. (*Easily, but not glibly.*) I don't see why not.

EDWARD. (*Stiffly.*) How do you do, sir. (*Edward is cautious in his friendships.*)

LYDIAN. Isn't it nice, Edward—having a new member of the family?

EDWARD. (*Obediently.*) Yes, ma'am.

LYDIAN. (*To her husband.*) But we can't expect Henry to work for the same munificent salary we pay Edward—which is nothing.

WALDO. Not true. Every Saturday morning, wet or fair, Edward gets a shiny new dime.

EDWARD. (*Surprised.*) I do?

WALDO. Which I promptly put in the bank for him.

LYDIAN. (*With a faint smile.*) *Some* weeks he's overpaid. (*The boy laughs—and it is clear that he is more at ease with his mother than with his father.*)

WALDO. (*Dismissing the boy, rather automatically.*) That will be all, Edward. Back to your studies.

EDWARD. Yes, Father. (*The boy scoots off.*)

HENRY. (*Watching the boy go.*) If it will make you feel better, I'll take the same pay as Edward—and try to be worth it.

WALDO. Henry, you're not a very good businessman.

HENRY. I'm not a businessman at all. If you don't pay me a regular salary, then I won't feel obliged to keep regular hours. I love a broad margin to my life . . . (*Quickly.*) But I assure you, the work will be done.

WALDO. Then you must have weekly wages . . .

HENRY. But must it be *money*? Could it be— (*He breaks off. There is a soft, leafy-green projection and the distant music of a flute. Henry pauses to hear it. Waldo and Lydian stare sat him strangely, as he stares way off, toward Walden, far in the back of the auditorium or beyond.*) How far does it extend, your back meadow?

WALDO. To the woods.

HENRY. Including the woods?

WALDO. A section of it. To the shore of the pond. (*The flute music rises, accelerates: the idea is accelerating inside his head.*)

HENRY. Perhaps, some day, if my work has been useful to you, and if we remain friends, I may ask you for a bit of your woods— (*Quickly.*) A small square, no bigger than this room. Not as a gift, I don't want to own it! Simply an understanding between friends—who know that the land really belongs to the woodchucks, anyhow!

LYDIAN. What will you do with it?

HENRY. I'm not quite sure. It's an idea I have . . . an "experiment" . . . (*The flute melody lingers, then falls away, as does the leafy projection.*)

WALDO. Good thinking, Henry. You're planning 'way up ahead, for your retirement.

HENRY. Retirement? What an absurd idea? Why spend the best part of your life earning money so that you can enjoy a questionable liberty during the least valuable part of it? Why work like a dog so you can pant for a moment or two before you die? (*Waldo laughs.*)

WALDO. Carlyle told me about an Englishman who went off to India—"Injah," he called it—to make a huge fortune so that he could come back to the Lake Country and live the life of a poet.

HENRY. If there was a poem in him, he should have rushed straight up to his garret.

WALDO. He should have! He died in the Punjab—immensely wealthy, but without a sonnet to his name.

LYDIAN. Can Henry have his parcel of woods? For his "experiment"?

WALDO. Well, I don't know what kind of experiment you have in mind. But if the woodchucks don't mind, why should I?

HENRY. Thank you, Doctor—uh— (*Corrects himself.*) —Waldo.

WALDO. (*To his wife.*) I don't really have time to make a list of all the things that need doing. Lydian, could you go into the details with Henry—various things that—

HENRY. Don't make a list. *Things* will tell me what needs to be done.

WALDO. Oh, what a relief! The hell of having people help you is that they are constantly completing what you gave them to do—and they come knocking on your door, saying: "What shall I do next?" Always when you are in the midst of doing what you your*self* should be doing next!

HENRY. I respect a man's privacy. I'll never knock at the door of your study.

WALDO. Don't be too much a stranger, Henry. Uh—I might interrupt *your* work now and then—and ask you to help me mend a cracked wall or pull a few weeds in a lecture I'm writing.

HENRY. I'm not a polite man. I'll be as frank with you as I am with the back meadow. (*Henry leaves. Lydian and Waldo stare after him.*)

LYDIAN. Not many people will understand that young man. He doesn't want anything.

WALDO. Perhaps he wants too much. (*All light falls away, except the moonlight glow on the jail cell. Henry walks back into the cell, stands by the barred casement and listens again to the sounds of Concord. Bailey jerks awake, sits up suddenly.*)

BAILEY. What time is it?

HENRY. Where were you planning to go?

BAILEY. Back to sleep. But I like to know how much of the night has swum by.

HENRY. In Samarkind, it is not quite noon.

BAILEY. That near Boston?

HENRY. It's as far away from Boston as you can get—before you start coming *back* to Boston again.

BAILEY. I could never figger out how it could be *one* time here and *another* time somewheres else. Isn't it *now* all over?

HENRY. You're wiser than most men who wear watches. I don't know what good it does to hang numbers on the hours. You can't count a river while it moves by you. The best thing to do is take off your clothes and go swimming in it. And when you feel the water all around you, then you're part of the total river—where it's been, where it is, where it's flowing. Plunge in!

BAILEY. I don't swim good.

HENRY. There's no trick to it. Yes, there is. One trick. You can't struggle with the water. If you fling your arms around and thrash and fight the stream, it fights back. And you go under. (*A drunk, laughing incoherently, staggers across the thrust, a mug of ale still in his hand. He drains the mug, thrashes about wildly. Bailey rises from his cot, crosses to the window beside Thoreau. They both look out.*)

BAILEY. That one's gone pretty far under. (*With the broken melody of a drinking song, the drunk weaves off.*)

HENRY. Drowned and drunk with ale and civilization.

BAILEY. Do you drink?

HENRY. Do you?

BAILEY. When I can afford it.

HENRY. It doesn't cost anything to be drunk. It needn't. It shouldn't. A man can be drunk all the time. Where I live, you can get drunk on the air.

BAILEY. (*Deliciously intrigued.*) Where's that? When they let me out, maybe I'll come get drunk with you. When they let *you* out. Where's it at?

HENRY. In the woods. By a pond. (*The flute melody drifts in with a leafy-green projection.*)

BAILEY. *Away* from everything.

HENRY. Oh, where I live, I have a great deal of company. But no people.

BAILEY. Don't you get scared? At night—in the dark?

HENRY. Why be afraid? The witches are all hung. Christianity and candles have been invented.

BAILEY. You live there all the time?

HENRY. All the time.

BAILEY. (*Wistfully.*) I wish I had a place to *belong.* It's always been a marvel to me how a man can git the money together to own himself a house that belongs to *him.*

HENRY. Want to hear how much my mansion cost me? Twenty-eight dollars, twelve and a half cents!

BAILEY. Man-a-mighty! I alwuz thought a house cost a fortune. Hundred dollars or more! How do you eat?

HENRY. Very well. I have a bean patch, some Indian corn. Now and then Walden serves me up a fish.

BAILEY. What happens in winter?

HENRY. (*Starting to take off one shoe.*) It snows. So I don't even have to go to the pond for fresh water—just reach out the door for a handful of snow. Melt it, and it's sweet as the sky. (*Flute and woods projection fade.*) Oh, there are a few things you have to get in town. So you walk into town. (*Henry pulls off his shoe, thrusts his hand into it, and pokes his finger through a hole in the sole. Then, one shoe on and one shoe off, he comes into the foreground. The light subsides on the jail cell and Bailey lies back on his cot in the shadows. It is late afternoon of a hot July day, and the thrust is the main street of Concord. Several people pass by Henry. They look questioningly at his curious condition; one shoe on and one shoe off. But Henry seems oblivious to it. He nods, saluting the passers-by with his shoe. Deacon Ball comes by, looks at Henry disdainfully.*)

BALL. You've condescended to pay a call on civilization, Mr. Thoreau?

HENRY. Briefly. And reluctantly.

BALL. How is life among the savages?

HENRY. If I'm in Concord long enough, Deacon, I may find out. (*Blithely, Henry salutes him with his shoe and limps on. Sam Staples ambles toward Henry. He has a piece of paper which he holds distastefully.*)

SAM. (*Clearing his throat.*) Hullo, Henry.

HENRY. Oh, hello, Sam.

SAM. What's wrong with your foot?

HENRY. Foot's fine. Got a sick shoe. (*He wiggles a finger through the hole in the sole.*) Cobbler'll cure it. (*Henry starts to walk down the street.*)

SAM. Henry. I—uh—got something here for ya.

HENRY. Oh?

SAM. (*Awkwardly.*) I can understand how a man could forget—bein' as busy as you are—out there—uh-writin' about them birds and talkin' to the fish and whatever else it is that you do out there by yourself. Naturally it don't occur to you to think much about *taxes.*

HENRY. No, I don't think much of taxes.

SAM. But they gotta be paid.

HENRY. Why?

SAM. It's the law. I ain't blamin' you for bein' forgetful, Henry. May surprise you to learn you ain't paid your tax for two years.

HENRY. Six.

SAM. (*Firming up.*) I got this order. And I got to serve it on ya. Here! (*He thrusts the legal paper on Henry.*)

HENRY. (*With a kind of arrogant calm.*) Why, thanks, Sam. (*He takes the document, glances at it, then folds it slowly, creasing it carefully. Then he slides it inside his shoe and pulls the shoe on. He stands on it, tests it with a few steps.*) Fits just fine! Exactly what I needed. I may not have to go to the cobbler after all.

SAM. (*Irked.*) Now, Henry. That there is an official paper. You can't walk over it like that.

HENRY. Why not? Best thing I ever got from the government. Most practical, anyhow.

SAM. Look, it don't pleasure me none, servin' a court order on you. Sometimes, this is an unpleasant job!

HENRY. Then quit. If you don't like bein' constable, Sam, resign.

SAM. Somebody's got to do the work of the people.

HENRY. Oh, you work for the people?

SAM. Yes!

HENRY. Well, I'm "people"—and you don't have to work for me. You're *free*! If it'll make you any happier, I'll fire you!

SAM. Lookee here, Henry. You gonna pay up your tax or ain't ya?

HENRY. You pay *your* tax, Sam?

SAM. If I didn't, I'd have to arrest myself.

HENRY. Are you going to arrest *me*? (*There's a long pause. The two men look at each other evenly.*)

SAM. I don't *want* to, Henry. But the government gets persnickety about taxes when we got a war goin'. (*Quietly, the blood is beginning to boil within Henry.*) After all, it ain't a big sum of money. If—if you're hard up, why *I'll* pay it.

HENRY. (*Erupting.*) Don't you dare!

SAM. A loan, just. You can pay me back when— (*Now all the molten outrage within Henry David Thoreau bursts out like lava from a live volcano.*)

HENRY. I will not pay one copper penny to an unjust government! I wouldn't pay the tithe and tariff to the church, so I signed off from the church! Well, I'm ready right now, Sam, to sign off from the government. Where do I sign? Where?

SAM. You can't do that.

HENRY. Why not?

SAM. (*Lamely.*) Well, even the President has to obey the laws!

HENRY. The poor President! What with preserving his popularity and doing his duty, he doesn't know what to do.

SAM. If the majority says—

HENRY. I'm the majority. A majority of one!

BALL. (*From the edge of the crowd.*) Arrest him!

SAM. (*Plaintively.*) I don't want to arrest him—

HENRY. Go ahead, Constable. An honest man can't come into town to have his shoes fixed. Not even a pair—one shoe— (*He tugs the shoe off his foot, yanks the paper out from inside and brandishes it.*) —without his neighbors coming around to *paw* him with their dirty institutions. (*For the first time, Henry realizes that he is surrounded by a little ring of people, so he addresses them as well as Sam.*) I'll tell you this. If one thousand . . . If one hundred . . . If ten men . . . ten honest men, only . . . If *one* honest man in this state of Massachusetts had the conviction and the courage to withdraw from this unholy partnership and let himself be locked up in the County Jail, it'd be the start of more true freedom than we've seen since a few farmers had the guts to block the British by the bridge up the road. (*He points off.*)

ANOTHER VOICE. Lawbreaker!

HENRY. What law ever made men free? Men have got to make the *law* free. And if a law is wrong, by Heaven, it's the duty of a man to stand up and say so. Even if your oddfellow society wants to clap him in a jail.

FARMER. That's revolution!

HENRY. Yes, sir, that's revolution! What do you think happened at Concord Bridge? A prayer meeting? (*Pointing emphatically.*)

SAM. What are you tryin' to do, Henry? Wipe out all the laws?

HENRY. As many as possible.

FARMER. What's the whole stew about?

SAM. He don't want to pay his tax.

FARMER. Neither do I.

SAM. (*Pointing to Henry.*) Yeah, but he ain't payin' his.

FARMER. Henry, it would upset your Maw if you run amuck ag'in society.

HENRY. Society's "run amuck" against *me*. I'm just going to the cobbler, minding my own business. I ask nothing from the government. Why should it take from me?

BALL. Throw him in jail!

HENRY. What're you waiting for, Sam? Get out the chains. Drag me off to jail.

SAM. There must be somethin' almighty wrong when a man's so willing to go!

HENRY. Sam. It's very simple. What the government of this country is doing *turns my stomach*! And if I keep my mouth shut, I'm a criminal. To my Conscience. To my God. To Society. And to *you*, Sam Staples. You want a dollar from me? If I don't approve the way that dollar's spent, you're not going to get it!

SAM. I swear I can't figger what makes you so ornery, Henry.

HENRY. Have you heard what they're doing down in Washington?

SAM. I—well, I don't have much time for newspapers. And I read slow.

HENRY. Open up your ears, then. Find out what he's up to—your Hired Man in the White House.

SAM. He's not just *my* President; he's yours, too.

HENRY. No, sir. I'm not paying his salary. He's fired!

SAM. You think high of Dr. Emerson, don't you?

HENRY. Usually.

SAM. He's paid his tax.

HENRY. That's his problem. I'm not paying mine.

SAM. All I know is, it ain't fittin' to throw a Harvard Man in jail. 'Specially a Thoreau. A honester man than you, Henry, I never knew.

HENRY. Is that a compliment, Sam?

SAM. Yes, sir.

HENRY. Well, thanks. Now clap me in your Bastille. (*Henry puts out his hands to be manacled. Sam sighs, looks around at the little cluster of townsmen. He shrugs helplessly, then leads Henry off. There is a shocked pause.*)

FARMER. Somebody better go tell his Maw.

WOMAN. But don't let his Aunt Louisa know; she'll have a conniption fit. (*Thinks—then with relish.*) I'm gonna go tell her! (*She hurries off. The cluster dissipates in various directions, and the light in the foreground falls away. Henry and Sam come into the cell. Bailey is on the cot, covered by a blanket. Henry doesn't realize at first that he has a cellmate. Sam carries a ring of keys, which he tosses on the bed, and a well-worn ledger book. Henry looks around.*)

SAM. Ain't much, but it's clean. (*Bailey emits a loud snore.*)

HENRY. Music, too. Very soothing.

SAM. (*As he wets the stub of pencil in his mouth.*) Now, Henry, I gotta put down your age.

HENRY. Twenty-nine summers.

SAM. (*Writing painfully.*) Two-nine. Occupation?

HENRY. What do you need that for, Sam?

SAM. If I don't fill this out correct, the Selectmen don't pay your board.

HENRY. (*Nodding toward the sleeper.*) What's *his* occupation?

SAM. Him? He's a vagrant.

HENRY. So am I.

SAM. (*Unhappy about the whole thing.*) Henry, that's no occupation. That's another charge! Gimme somethin' to put down. What *are* you, exactly?

HENRY. What am I? (*Thinking.*) Oh, Hoer of Beans. Fisherman. Inspector of Snowstorms . . .

SAM. (*Impatiently.*) Them won't do.

HENRY. You want *respectable* trades? Let's see. Pencil-maker—occasionally. Schoolteacher—once. Surveyor. Carpenter. Author—alleged. Huckleberry-hunter—expert . . .

SAM. (*Writing.*) Carpenter. That'll do.

HENRY. Risky, Sam. You'll shock the clergy if you lock up a carpenter.

SAM. (*After a little thought.*) It's writ. (*He slaps his ledger book shut and goes off, shaking his head. The lighting in the cell slowly, imperceptibly, turns into night. There is the urgent jangling of a bell-pull. The lights rise on the Emerson area. Lydian appears in a night-robe. She is reading a note—puzzled and concerned.*)

WALDO'S VOICE. (*From off.*) Who is it? I'll get it.

LYDIAN. I already have, dear. (*Waldo comes on in nightdress, wearing a nightcap.*)

WALDO. (*Sleepily.*) I'll get it. I've got it. Oh, Lydian—what are you doing up?

LYDIAN. (*To Waldo, indicating the note.*) It's about Henry. He's in jail.

WALDO. God help us! Why? What did he do?

LYDIAN. It isn't clear—

WALDO. He murdered Deacon Ball! One of Henry's acts of mercy.

LYDIAN. No—

WALDO. They've found Deacon Ball murdered, and they're accusing Henry!

LYDIAN. Deacon Ball hasn't been murdered.

WALDO. Oh? That's too bad. Let me look at that. (*He hands him the note. Simultaneously, the light rises on Mrs. Thoreau, distraught.*)

MOTHER. Every night, Louisa. Every night, I have this terrible nightmare. I dream that David Henry is in jail. But tonight I didn't even have to go to sleep! (*The light on Mrs. Thoreau fades. In the cell, Sam re-enters, standing at the cell door.*)

SAM. Before I take my boots off for the night, Henry, why don't you pay up an' let me let you outa here?

HENRY. (*Gently.*) Take off your boots, Sam. (*Sam still hesitates. In the Emerson area, Waldo grows fully awake.*)

WALDO. Lydian. I've got to get on my boots. Where's my coat? I've got to go down to Concord Square—! (*He sits, pulling on a pair of high-topped shoes over his naked feet. Lydian hands him a black topcoat which he puts on over his nightshirt.*)

LYDIAN. You're going to go like that?

WALDO. The boy's in trouble! (*He starts out. Lydian quickly pulls off his nightcap as Waldo hurries off. The light in the Emerson area fades.*)

SAM. (*Pleading.*) Please pay up, Henry. (*Previously, Henry has been volcanic. Now the lava has cooled but firmed.*)

HENRY. If you call on me to pay for a rifle, Sam, it's the same as asking me to fire it! You're making me as much a killer as the foot-soldier who crashes across the border into faraway Mexico, charges into his neighbor's house, sets fire to it and kills his children! (*The two men study each other. Troubled, Sam starts to leave. Henry goes to the cot, calls.*) Sam! (*Sam races back eagerly, thinking Henry may have changed his mind.*) You forgot your keys. (*He hands Sam the ring of keys.*)

SAM. (*Disappointed.*) Oh. (*He takes them, goes out, locks the door. Henry stares through the bars, listening to the night silence of the village. From the back of the theatre, as if shouting across Concord Square, a voice breaks the quiet.*)

WALDO. Henry! *Henry*! What are you doing in jail? (*Henry turns, faces front, responding to the challenge.*)

HENRY. (*Defiantly, pointing accusingly across Concord Square.*) Waldo! What are you doing *out* of jail?

THE LIGHTS FADE

ACT TWO

The light rises on the jail cell—moonlight casting shadows through the bars at a later angle. No light falls on either cot, but on the space between them. The town clock strikes two. The dim light gradually reveals the forms of the two men, each motionless, seemingly asleep. Henry stirs, coughs, gets up restlessly, paces a few times, goes to the barred casement. His hand reaches up in the white clarity of the moonlight. He touches the bars. Then, with a musical fancy, he pretends to pluck each bar as if it were a harp-string.

HENRY. (*Imitating the sound of a harp-string.*) Ting . . . ting . . . ting . . . tang. (*He riffles the bars as if he were doing arpeggios, which he vocalizes idly. Stops suddenly, looks toward his cellmate.*) In the prison of heaven, that's how the angels make music. (*He paces.*) I am told. (*Paces some more.*) Not having been there. (*Paces more.*) And not likely to be invited. (*Henry sits on his own cot and talks to the sleeping Bailey.*) You know what the government said to me, Bailey? "Your money or your life." I won't give it my money. And they think they have my life! (*Laughs a little.*) Only my body. I'm a free man. Free to touch my nose if I like. (*He touches his nose.*) Or not. (*He takes his hand down.*) Free to stand. Or not to stand. They can't lock up my thoughts! What I *believe* goes easily through these walls—as if the stones were air. (*He gestures front—where the wall, in fact, does not exist.*) The state is so afraid of us, Bailey, that it locks us up. The state is timid as a lone woman with her silver spoons! We have frightened her out of her wits. (*The light comes up on Lydian.*)

LYDIAN. Henry, you have wits enough to know that, in order to *get* along, you have to *go* along. (*Henry the volcano erupts again.*)

HENRY. (*Shouting, contemptuously.*) GO ALONG! GO ALONG! GO ALONG! (*Lydian has reached for a little straw berry-basket.*)

LYDIAN. Edward? (*The little boy comes running to her.*) Go along with Mr. Thoreau.

EDWARD. Where are we going? (*Henry saunters down from the cell onto the thrust. Rakishly he puts on the wide-brimmed straw hat which he wore before. The thrust becomes a sunny meadow.*)

HENRY. Huckleberry-hunting, my boy! Would you like to study composition with Mozart? Painting with Michelangelo? Study huckleberry-hunting with Thoreau, it's the same thing! (*Edward laughs; Lydian slips off as the huckleberry-hunters parade through the sun-drenched field.*) Now, when *I* was your age—if I was ever your age—my mother used to bake huckleberry pudding. Best in Concord. But all my Mama and my Papa and Uncle Charlie and Aunt Louisa and my brother John got—all *they* got—was the pudding. I had the glory of discovering the huckleberries! A half-day of wild adventure under the Concord sky.

EDWARD. How do you find huckleberries? *I* want to discover some!

HENRY. (*Imparting a great secret.*) Huckleberries are very difficult to find. Because most people think that . . . they're over *there*! (*He makes a dramatic gesture.*)

EDWARD. Should I go over there?

HENRY. No, sir! The *best* huckleberries have a sly way . . . of being . . . exactly . . . where . . . you . . . are . . . standing! Here! (*He bends down quickly, picks an imaginary huckleberry.*) The trick of it is: you have to know where to stand!

EDWARD. (*Plucking one.*) Can I taste one? Right now?

HENRY. (*Thinking.*) Well . . . yes. But for every one you taste, you have to take *two* home.

EDWARD. (*Tasting.*) Mmmmm . . . They're good! Where's your basket?

HENRY. I use my hat. Since my head is precisely the size of a huckleberry pudding! (*Edward runs about, seeming to gather huckleberries.*)

EDWARD. (*Shouts.*) Here's a whole patch of them!

HENRY. Ahhh, you have talent—no doubt about it.

EDWARD. (*Running from bush to bush.*) Let's race and see who can get the most first. (*But Henry is no racer. He has paused to savor a particular berry.*)

HENRY. (*Swallowing, benignly.*) *That* was a happy huckleberry. (*Little Edward is plunging about, grasping handfuls of huckleberries as fast as he can.*)

EDWARD. Look! I've got more than you have!

HENRY. Everybody does. (*With deliberate relaxation, Henry is plucking the berries, tossing them in his hat. His ease and calm is in contrast with the boy's bounding energy. Henry seems to be choosing the* precise *berry at each bush—the one which promises the best flavor.*)

EDWARD. How does a huckleberry get to be a huckleberry instead of a strawberry?

HENRY. Well, there are a number of books on the subject. But *meeting* a huckleberry makes you more of an expert than any botanist who ever wrote a dull book. (*Now Edward has completely filled his basket, and comes running joyfully to Henry to show him.*)

EDWARD. Look! Look, Henry! Mine's all the way to the top. Mama should've given me a bigger basket! (*Suddenly the running boy trips, falls—and the whole basket of berries—imaginary—spills out over the ground. Edward is aghast at the accident. His bright-eyed ecstasy turns to tears.*) They're all spilled and spoiled! (*Henry drops to his knees, puts his arms around the shoulders of the dejected boy, who sobs uncontrollably.*)

HENRY. Do you know what you've done? You have planted whole patches of huckleberries, for an entire generation of Edward Emersons!

EDWARD. I have . . . ? (*Through his subsiding tears.*) How?

HENRY. Because that's the way things are: Nature has provided that little boys

Michael Ayers and David Ayers in the premiere production of *The Night Thoreau Spent in Jail*, Ohio State University, Columbus, 1970. Jerome Lawrence and Robert E. Lee Collection, Lawrence and Lee Theatre Research Institute, The Ohio State University.

gathering huckleberries should, now and then, stumble and scatter the berries. Edward, you have been as helpful as a honeybee!

EDWARD. (*Now delighted.*) Let's pick some more—and *spill* 'em! (*With a grin, Edward wipes his sleeve across his eyes, reversing his previous misery. Henry pours his hatful of huckleberries into Edward's basket. Edward looks up into his face.*) But those are yours . . . !

HENRY. (*Solemnly.*) I surrender title.

EDWARD. What does that mean?

HENRY. Like most of the voodoo of ownership, it means absolutely nothing. (*The boy takes Henry's hand.*)

EDWARD. Henry. I wish you were my father . . . ! (*Henry looks at the boy, wishing he were, too, but not saying it. The lighting fades on them and simultaneously rises on Lydian, who is seated, writing a letter. She looks up as Henry and Edward walk into the Emerson area. Edward swings his basket of borrowed huckleberries . . . but carefully!*)

EDWARD. (*Running to his mother.*) These are for you, Mama! (*And he gives the basket to Lydian.*)

LYDIAN. My, what a present! Thank you, Edward.

EDWARD. (*The honesty forcing it out of him.*) I guess—really—you should thank Henry.

LYDIAN. (*Correcting him.*) Mr. Thoreau, dear.

EDWARD. Henry says I should call him "Henry."

HENRY. There's not too much formality in the huckleberry-hunting business. (*They laugh a little.*)

EDWARD. And, Mama, I've asked Henry to be my father. (*Lydian and Henry look at each other. Henry shrugs, a bit embarrassed.*)

LYDIAN. Oh? And what about your real father?

EDWARD. He's never here. He's always 'way on the other side of the ocean, or out somewhere making speeches, or up in his room where I can't disturb him. But Henry— (*A pause.*)

HENRY. —is here. (*Lydian hesitates, then hands the basket back to Edward.*)

LYDIAN. Take your huckleberries to the kitchen, will you, dear? (*The boy starts off, then turns, at the edge of the light.*)

EDWARD. (*With a fresh thought.*) If Henry's my father, that means you've got a husband, Mama. Not in England or someplace else all the time, but right here in our house. Wouldn't that be nicer? For you? (*Lydian and Henry exchange glances, and the boy goes off.*)

LYDIAN. I—I suppose it isn't wise. For you to keep on working here while Waldo's away.

HENRY. Please don't be afraid of me . . .

LYDIAN. Shouldn't I be? (*She gets up, restlessly.*) Oh, you're going to tell me that you have too much respect. For the Sage of Concord.

HENRY. And his wife.

LYDIAN. Respect is based on friendship. And friendship is based on love. And love is so . . . accidental. Isn't it, Henry? (*Henry moistens his lips.*)

HENRY. We love without knowing it. A man—or a woman—can't love on schedule. I don't wake up in the morning and say: "I shall start loving at nine-twenty, and continue until ten-fifteen." Yes, it *is* accidental. And it's everywhere—it's the wind, the tide, the waves, the sunshine.

LYDIAN. (*Very quietly.*) Henry. If love is all around you, like huckleberries—why do you pick loneliness? (*Edward bursts in carrying a protesting live chicken.*)

EDWARD. Mama! Henry! Look what happened to the chicken's feet! (*The boy holds up the chicken.*) He's wearing gloves!

LYDIAN. No, Edward, that's not poss—it *is* wearing gloves! (*She turns, puzzled, to Henry.*)

HENRY. (*A little sheepishly.*) The other day you said they were scratching in your garden, uprooting your rose plants. So I gave a little elegance to the ladies of the henhouse. They've scratched their last. Your roses are safe.

LYDIAN. (*Examining the chicken-gloves.*) You made these for all the chickens?

HENRY. I'm opposed to social distinctions. Once one chicken is gloved, you can't expect the other ladies to go about bare-clawed. (*They laugh.*)

EDWARD. (*Eagerly.*) Can I take him out and show him to everybody?

LYDIAN. He's a "she," dear. Yes, I suppose you can.

HENRY. But bring the lady home and latch the gate. If you want an omelette for breakfast. (*Edward scurries off with the chicken.*)

LYDIAN. My roses thank you.

HENRY. Oh, they're very welcome.

LYDIAN. Get married, Henry. Find a face—and teach yourself to love it.

HENRY. I have. (*Lydian looks at him quizzically.*) But I'm a crusty and resolute bachelor. And Nature is my mother-in-law.

LYDIAN. There are so many pretty young girls—

HENRY. I would drive them promptly into old age. I'm not that cruel.

LYDIAN. You need a brain to toss on the pillow next to you. What about Margaret Fuller? (*Henry repeats the name, as if he were rinsing it out of his mouth.*)

HENRY. Margaret . . . Fuller . . . ? Oh, I couldn't marry her.

LYDIAN. Why not?

HENRY. Two reasons. First, I'm not stupid enough to ask her. Second, *she'd* never be stupid enough to accept. (*Turning.*) You want to be a matchmaker, Lydian? Find me something innocent and natural and uncomplicated. A shrub-oak. A cloud. A leaf lost in the snow.

LYDIAN. But isn't it lonely, Henry?

HENRY. Lonely! (*He laughs.*) I am no more lonely, Lydian, than the North Star, or the South Wind, or the first spider in a new house. (*Then gently.*) What about *your* loneliness? Is it enough to go to bed each night with nothing but a letter from England? Telling about your husband's overwhelming passion . . . for Carlyle? (*She looks down. Henry reaches out, touching her sleeve.*) Isn't it a pity that you are so "safe" with me? (*In the cell, Bailey seems in the midst of a conversation.*)

BAILEY. I'm skeered of a trial. I ain't got no lawyer. 'Course the food ain't too bad here. (*Henry has crossed back into the cell and the lights have faded on Lydian.*) Would *you* be my lawyer?

HENRY. (*Stops short.*) I'm no lawyer!

BAILEY. Couldn't you be one—for me? You talk like a lawyer. And you're smart as most.

HENRY. Bailey, I would give you my coat, or my shoes, or my last peck of beans; I would chop wood for you, or push a wheelbarrow for you. But I would not stoop to being a lawyer for anyone! I think Lucifer was a lawyer; that's why the Devil still gives advice to Presidents.

BAILEY. Who'm I gonna get?

HENRY. If I were God, Bailey—instead of just a speck of Him—I wouldn't let you die away in the dark. (*Bailey is panicky. He gets up from the cot.*)

BAILEY. Tell me what to do!

HENRY. (*Rubbing his chin.*) Well, you might try getting yourself born in a more just and generous age. That's not a very practical suggestion. (*Another thought.*) I suppose you could try prayer.

BAILEY. I'm not very good at it.

HENRY. Neither am I.

BAILEY. But could you say one for me?

HENRY. Is the Lord so almighty absentminded that He needs a tap on the shoulder—to remind Him that Adam had children?

BAILEY. A prayer couldn't hurt none.

HENRY. All right. Let's send God a telegram. (*He clasps his hands in semi-solemnity.*)

"Blessed Are the Young,
    For they do not read the President's speeches.
Blessed Are They who never read a newspaper,
    For they shall see Nature and, through her, God.
And Blessed is Bailey, for he's a good fellow
    and deserves better treatment than you've been giving him—even
    though he *is* a man of letters.
Amen."

BAILEY. Amen. Do you think it got through?

HENRY. I wouldn't know. I don't usually pray with words. I prefer a flute. (*As Bailey sinks back onto his cot, the lights dip in the cell. Henry moves forward into the amber sunlight of the forestage, and the background takes on again the leaf-woven texture of the Walden woods. Henry reaches for a flute and begins to play something strange and peaceful—an unconventional forest idyll. The shadowy figure of a man climbs out of the pit as Henry plays. Crouching, the man creeps through the brush, unseen by Henry. The man is Williams, a black, in dirty, tattered clothes. He is husky but terrified. Still Henry does not notice him, although he thinks he may have been detected—so he darts behind another imaginary bush. With a sigh, Henry puts aside his flute and reaches down for something on the ground. Williams thinks he is going for a gun. He leaps onto the back of the astonished Henry, clamping a huge hand over Henry's mouth.*)

WILLIAMS. You ain't takin' no gun on me! (*Calmly Henry rotates the handle of the implement he was reaching for. It is a hoe. Williams relaxes a little, takes his hand off Henry's mouth.*)

HENRY. You thought this was a rifle? A rifle's no good for hoeing beans. (*He is gentle.*) Mind if I go ahead? (*Williams is afraid, uncertain.*) There isn't a gun within three-quarters of a mile of here. (*Henry is unhanded and begins to hoe. The black watches.*) What can I do for you?

WILLIAMS. I need vittles. Gimme some vittles!

HENRY. Well, sit down, neighbor. It'll take about three weeks for these beans to come up.

WILLIAMS. By then I'll be sleepin' wi' them beans! I gotta git to Cañada.

HENRY. To where?

WILLIAMS. Cañada. Cañada! North as I kin git! They say the Norther ya git, the *free-er* ya git!

HENRY. (*As he hoes.*) There's a quarter loaf of bread inside the hut. Help yourself. (*Williams starts to move in the direction Henry has indicated—then hesitates, turns back.*)

WILLIAMS. You trustin' me to go inside your place? Without you watchin'?

HENRY. Why not? (*Williams pauses—then darts into the shadows while Henry placidly hoes his beans. Then he calls toward the offstage hut:*) If you want to stay till supper, I'll catch us a fish. What's your name? (*Almost immediately Williams reappears with a chunk of bread which he chews on ravenously.*)

WILLIAMS. (*His mouth full.*) Williams.

HENRY. I'm Henry Thoreau. (*He reaches out his hand. Williams marvels—then reaches out tentatively for Henry's handshake, first wiping his hand on his pant-leg.*) Williams your first name or your last name?

WILLIAMS. It's all my name. (*Suddenly.*) But I ain't no slave. I ain't goin' back to bein' no slave. No man gonna take me back. (*With fire.*) I *borned* myself two weeks ago.

HENRY. Good for you, Mr. Williams.

WILLIAMS. I belonged to Mr. Williams. I was Mr. Williams' Williams. No more. (*Henry studies him. Williams is wary.*) You gonna turn me in?

HENRY. I've got no more stomach for slavery than you do. Here you're as free as I am. (*Williams begins to breathe more easily. He looks around.*)

WILLIAMS. How come you live like a black man? In a slave shack?

HENRY. (*Laughs.*) Maybe to prove that *less* is *more*. You see, I'm really very wealthy; I just don't have any money, that's all.

WILLIAMS. (*Still suspicious.*) Where's your wife? An' chillun?

HENRY. Well, my bride is this bean patch, Mr. Williams. And I've adopted several woodchucks. And a few rather unappreciative squirrels.

WILLIAMS. Nobody "Mistered" me before—not ever.

HENRY. You better get used to it. If you're going to be a free man. You'll have to have a first name, too—oh, you don't *have* to. But it's handy.

WILLIAMS. (*Tentatively.*) Henry, maybe . . . ? Could I call myself "Mr. Henry's Williams" . . . ?

HENRY. No!

WILLIAMS. (*Startled.*) Why you shoutin' at me?

HENRY. You don't belong to anybody, sir. Except yourself. Least of all to me. Watch out—or you'll run right into what you're running away from.

WILLIAMS. (*Tasting it.*) Henry . . . Williams . . .

HENRY. If you don't like the fit of that, there's a David in my name; you can have it, I don't use it much.

WILLIAMS. I like Henry Williams! That sound good! That's a *free* man's name! (*He cups his hands and shouts.*) HENRY WILLIAMS!

HENRY. But there's slavery in the North, too. Every man shackled to a ten-hour-a-day job is a *work*-slave. Every man who has to worry about next month's rent is a *money*-slave. Don't let that happen to you, Mr. Williams. Keep free!

WILLIAMS. I *do* feel free—here—now! With you. Never before. I hain't scared now.

HENRY. Why should you be?

WILLIAMS. (*Abruptly.*) You let me stay here? I'll work. Take my chances with the law. I'm good at hidin'! Nobody know I'm here!

HENRY. I welcome you here. But . . . you've got to find your *own* Walden, Henry Williams! Where they don't have sickening laws which keep black men in suppression. Here in Massachusetts, the color of your face is a flag. You can't hide blackness in blindness. If you want any light in your life, you'll have to find a place to live where men think of themselves as *men*—not as *white* men. (*Putting his hand on Williams' shoulder.*) Go to "Can*ya*da"! (*The light fades on the black man and the white man in the foreground. In the Emersons' area, the light picks up Waldo in the midst of an argument. His stance is twisted—almost a contortion—as if he were trying to stand simultaneously on opposite sides of a question—which he is.*)

WALDO. I have cast my vote! I've done it. I put it in the ballot-box. What more do you expect me to do? (*Henry moves into the scene.*)

HENRY. (*Aflame with indignation.*) Cast your whole vote. Not just a strip of paper! Your whole *influence*!

WALDO. (*Turning.*) We have to go along with the majority!

HENRY. (*Exasperated.*) "Go along!"

WALDO. (*Reasonably.*) Henry, one must consider the economic and sociological ramifications. When white people and black try to live together, it's infinitely complicated.

HENRY. (*Pounding his fist in the palm of his hand.*) Then simplify! Simplify!

WALDO. (*Shaking his head.*) You complicate things all the more by *rushing* them. You're a naturalist, Henry. You understand the slow evolving of the seasons. It's the same with human relationships. You can't rush a sunrise.

HENRY. (*With tethered anger.*) When a man leaps from a moving freight train—and tries to scramble through the woods to cross the border into Cañada—

WALDO. Where?

HENRY. (*Impatiently.*) Into Canada! A free-er country even though they still have the Crown. But they *don't* have a Fugitive Slave Law. When a man, at the border of freedom, is stopped by the rifle of a Boston policeman, he doesn't have time for Dr. Emerson's leisurely sermon on "the slow evolving of the seasons."

WALDO. Henry, I am just as shocked at the death of this man as you are. What was his name?

HENRY. (*Quietly.*) Henry Williams. A new man. With a new name. Hardly used!

WALDO. I am just as concerned—

HENRY. Are you? To you, Henry Williams is an abstraction. You may be able to use him sometime as a digression in a Lyceum lecture.

WALDO. How can you be so unpleasant to me when I'm trying to agree with you? (*The fever between the two men is rising.*)

HENRY. I expect more from you than from anybody else; that's why I'm more disappointed in you.

WALDO. Well, *what* do you expect of me?

HENRY. Speak out!

WALDO. I speak.

HENRY. It's not enough. Shout!

WALDO. I'm not a shouter.

HENRY. Not with your voice-box! With your brain! Waldo, *I* can't reach anybody. I can't catch the attention of people. Nobody listens to me. (*Passionately.*) But my God, you are EMERSON! (*There are almost tears in Henry's eyes as he experiences a mixture of admiration and contempt for his idol.*) Darling of the Lyceum, Lord of the Lecture Circuit! Every word you say from the platform is treasured like an heirloom. Stand up, Waldo, and say what you believe!

WALDO. (*Distantly.*) Sometimes I think I invented you, Henry. Or at least prophesied you. Because you *live* what I talk about. I couldn't exist the way you do, Henry; I like my warm toast and tea and soft-boiled egg brought to me on a tray in bed each morning. Whenever I even *think* of Walden, I get a cold. But I admire you, Henry, I really do. You're my walking ethic! (*Henry stares at Waldo, marveling at how he can drift off the point.*) Those are the exact words I used to describe you to Carlyle. Did you know that I told Carlyle about you?

HENRY. (*Frustrated, turning away.*) I don't care what you told Carlyle.

WALDO. I said to Carlyle: "Of all the men in Concord, Henry Thoreau is the best of the lot!" That's what I told him. (*Enjoying quoting himself.*) "A poet as full of buds of promise as a young apple tree." That's what I said.

HENRY. Waldo, don't talk *about* me—talk *to* me. Listen to me.

WALDO. (*His thoughts still in England.*) Whu—? How was that?

HENRY. (*Evenly.*) Can you lie in bed every morning? Have your breakfast brought to you—your soft-boiled egg, your toast and tea? Can you lift your right hand to your mouth while your left hand—which is also you—your government—is killing men in Mexico? How can you swallow, Waldo? How can you taste? How can you breathe? You cast your ballot with your right hand—but has your left hand killed Henry Williams, running to be free!

WALDO. Because I don't rant like Jeremiah, do you think I'm not outraged? I do what *can* be done!

HENRY. That's not enough. Do the impossible. That's what you tell people in your lectures. But you don't really believe any of it, do you? You trundle up and down New England, stepping to the lectern with that beneficent smile, accepting the handshake of mayors and the polite applause of little old ladies. You go on singing your spineless benedictions.

WALDO. What I say is not spineless! (*Lydian enters, drawn by their raised voices.*)

HENRY. Well, occasionally you've sounded a battle-cry. But you—you yourself—refuse to hear it.

WALDO. (*Squirming.*) You are a very difficult man!

HENRY. Good. The world is too full of *easy* men.

WALDO. Do you want me to go out and advocate violence and rebellion?

HENRY. I ask you to *stop* violence. As for rebellion, do you think this country was hatched from a soft-boiled egg??? (*Gesturing.*) Look around Concord; what do you see? We have *become* everything we protested against!

WALDO. And what are you doing about it, young man? You pull the woods up over your head. You resign from the human race. Could your woodchucks, with all their wisdom, have saved Henry Williams? Are your fish going to build roads, teach school, put out fires? (*For a moment, Henry is caught without a ready reply.*) Oh, it's very simple for a hermit to sit off at a distance and proclaim exactly how things should be. But what if everybody did that? Where would we be?

HENRY. Where *are* we, Waldo?

WALDO. We are at war. I am aware of it.

HENRY. Are you aware of the reasons—slave-holders grasping for more slave territory? *More* slavery and less freedom, is that what you want?

WALDO. Henry, we must work within the framework of our laws. The end to this war—the condition of the blacks—this is the business of the President. And the Congress.

HENRY. Do you really believe that? Then I guess I'm wrong. I thought you had the same disgust that I have for what the military is doing. But if it doesn't trouble you, then I must've made a mistake. (*With acid sarcasm.*) You're right to keep still. I'll go back to the woods—and leave you at peace with your war. (*Waldo is in genuine pain. He glances at his wife.*)

WALDO. (*After a pause.*) All right, my young conscience. What shall I do?

HENRY. Declare yourself! (*Another pause.*)

WALDO. I will. Absolutely. The next time the occasion arises—

HENRY. (*Fiercely.*) NOW! A year ago was too late! I'll get you an audience. This afternoon. At Concord Square! (*Henry strides out of the light. Waldo, troubled, looks at Lydian in silence. The light falls away on the Emersons. A bell-rope drops from the flies as the light comes up on the thrust. Henry springs up, grasps the rope, and swings on it. A bell from above peals, a reverberating command. People begin to assemble, curious and excited.*)

FARMER. (*Running on.*) Fire someplace?

WOMAN. What's the news? Is the war over?

SAM. What you doin' up there, Henry? What's goin' on? (*There is a growing babble of voices as the crowd gathers. Henry lets go of the rope as the swinging bell dies away.*)

HENRY. Dr. Emerson's coming. To speak. He's promised to make a statement! Now. Right here. Can't wait!

MOTHER. (*Rushing on.*) Oh, David Henry! Are you riling everybody up again?

HENRY. Emerson is going to rile up the whole country. And you're going to hear it *first*!

FARMER. Is he going to say something or give a sermon? (*Henry laughs, jubilantly.*)

HENRY. *Both*! God willing! (*Others are gathering.*)

SAM. Dr. Emerson gonna speak *now*?

HENRY. I just left him! He's on his way. (*There is a babble of anticipation. One man—probably a local newspaperman—draws out a pad and pencil, prepared to write.*)

VOICE. And no lecture charge, neither! (*There is a pause as they wait. They're getting a little restless.*)

WOMAN. Well, where *is* he? (*Several start to go. The reporter puts away his pad.*)

HENRY. (*Confidently.*) Don't worry! He's coming. He'll be here! (*Lydian enters slowly, her head down. The crowd falls back to let her through. She comes up to Henry. Silently she looks into his face. She clears her throat.*)

LYDIAN. Dr. Emerson has asked me to tell you—

HENRY. (*Gray.*) Yes?

LYDIAN. —that he wants more time to meditate on these matters. (*Henry does not move, merely stares at her.*) So that he can write a careful essay setting forth his position.

HENRY. And he gave his wife the happy job of coming here to tell us? Like a walking-written-excuse to a schoolmaster, saying: "So sorry, Johnny cannot come today, he's in bed with the croup"? (*Lydian shares Henry's feeling, but her loyalty to her husband is unshakable.*)

LYDIAN. Waldo wants to collect his thoughts.

HENRY. (*Outraged.*) What is this, the winter of our *content*? By the time he "collects his thoughts," they'll be as dead as dandelions under the snow. (*The crowd is restless and begins to disintegrate.*)

FARMER. Well, we came running to the fire, but nobody lit it. That's Henry for ya. (*As the crowd wanders off, Henry stares at Lydian. Slowly, he turns away from her and starts to go, too.*)

LYDIAN. (*Stopping him.*) Henry—my husband loves you—as much as any man can love another man . . . (*Henry stops, but his back is still to Lydian.*)

HENRY. (*Shaking his head.*) My God, he was my god! No more! If he is the Deity, I am a doubter!

LYDIAN. Why do you enjoy hurting him?

HENRY. (*Wheeling on her.*) He hurts *me*! (*They are both talking at once, their speeches overlapping.*)

LYDIAN. He cares what you think, and so he gets excited and overstates himself—

HENRY. Patronizing, that's what he is. I won't sit at the foot of his pulpit!

LYDIAN. When he talks to you—

HENRY. He never talks to me! Was he talking to me just now? (*Bitterly.*) He was in England, pontificating with Carlyle!

LYDIAN. You widen the distance—

HENRY. It's a waste of breath, talking to your husband. Trying to have a sane discussion with him. I lose my time, almost my identity—

LYDIAN. I hear you both. You wrangle and tussle like boys in a cricket match. Hitting and pushing and kicking each other—not for the sake of the idea, just playing to *win*!

HENRY. (*Coldly.*) Your husband, Mrs. Emerson, has the misfortune of being a gentleman. And famous. And he is drowning in his own success.

LYDIAN. My husband's best friend doesn't even know who my husband *is*! You've drawn some ideal in your mind, some imaginary Waldo—the way you want him to be. Please, Henry, give him the same liberty he gives you—to be what you are. (*Henry looks down, doesn't answer. Everyone has gone now. Lydian would like to say, "I'm sorry, Henry, I wish I could comfort you"—but she doesn't. Quickly, Lydian moves off. Henry looks around at the empty square which was recently so full of people.*)

HENRY. (*Shouts.*) People of Concord—! (*But he is talking to the wind. Frustrated, he casts about for some way to reach the ears of a deaf public. He sees the dangling bell-rope, leaps up to ring it—and though he swings on it with the weight of his whole body, there is no sound whatsoever! THE BELL DOES NOT RING! Stunned, he pulls more frantically. Nothing.*) How do we make a sound? How do we break the silence? (*The light falls away on the discouraged and disheartened Henry. The bell-rope vanishes in the flies. He throws himself on his cot in the cell.*

The sky goes red. Henry writhes on the cot. There is a cannon blast—and the sky seems ripped apart by psychedelic splatterings of shrapnel.

A snare drum snarls a military cadence. A drummer boy marches on, turns smartly front. The face is Edward Emerson's. A Sergeant comes on, in the Federal uniform of the 1840's. It is Sam Staples.)

SERGEANT (SAM). (*As if drilling troops.*)

Forward to Mexico . . . March!
Hate-two-three-four!
Hate-two-three-four!
Hate-two-three-four! (*The Sergeant prods Bailey awake with a rifle butt. Bailey staggers to attention. The Sergeant puts a military cap on Bailey and flings a musket into his hands. With the eternal imprecision of the civilian-soldier, Bailey marches around the thrust to the insistent beat of the snare drum. The Farmer, uniformed, becomes part of the marching company. Ball appears, in a General's epaulets and gold braid. He mounts the box, as if it were a military reviewing stand.*)

GENERAL (BALL). (*In the drum-cadence.*)

Learn to kill!
Learn to kill!
Learn to kill!
so you won't be killed! (*This entire sequence has the blurred and overlapping quality of a nightmare, Goya-esque. It is a* Walpurgisnacht, *a surrealistic mixing of hallucinations. Time, space, sound are wrenched awry.*)

BAILEY. (*Out of the rhythm.*) I ain't gonna shoot at them; they done nothin' to me! (*All turn on Bailey.*)

VARIOUS VOICES. Coward! Slacker! Traitor! Deserter!

GENERAL (BALL). Heathen!

SERGEANT (SAM). Vagrant! (*There is a great explosion of gunfire, and all drop to their bellies for cover. Shouts and confusion.*)

GENERAL (BALL). (*Pointing to Henry on his cot.*) Why doesn't that man have a gun?

SERGEANT (SAM). (*Shaking Henry's shoulder.*) Wake up, Henry. I got somethin' here for ya. Wake up!

HENRY. I don't want it! (*But the Sergeant forces a musket into his hands. Dazed, as if walking through syrup, Henry comes to his feet. He holds the musket at arm's length distastefully.*)

GENERAL (BALL). The purpose of this action is to stop the enemy from protecting themselves from the enemy.

HENRY. (*Helplessly defiant.*) I won't go—!

MOTHER. That's a good boy, David Henry. Always do the right thing. Even if it's wrong. (*The snare drum has continued, building snappishly. But Henry moves arrhythmically, his march out-of-sync with all the rest.*)

SERGEANT AND SOLDIERS. (*Whispered.*)

Hate-two-three-four!

Hate-two-three-four! (*The President appears in a morning coat and striped pants. It is Waldo.*)

GENERAL (BALL). Mr. President, the military advises that we conquer the entire territory. Level them all to rubble! Are you prepared to *go along*?

ALL VOICES. (*A kind of demonic glee.*)

Go along!

Go along!

Go along!

Go along! (*Henry rushes up to the President. He tries to talk, excitedly, urgently. But although his mouth is working, no sound comes out.*)

PRESIDENT (WALDO). (*Loftily, to the General.*) Is this man saying something? I can't hear him. (*Henry tries to stop the other marchers, one by one; but no one pays any attention.*)

GENERAL (BALL). What are your instructions, Mr. President?

PRESIDENT (WALDO). I wish more time to collect my thoughts. So I am going to appoint a committee to appoint a committee to appoint a committee. (*Cheers.*) Get to the bottom of this, so the top will know what to do! (*A swarthy Mexican Soldier [Williams] comes on with a Mexican flag.*)

SERGEANT (STAPLES). There he is, boys, there's the enemy! (*All muskets swing toward the Mexican; he is like a trapped animal.*)

HENRY. (*Shouts.*) Run, Henry Williams! Run for it! (*The Mexican Soldier [Williams] leaps into the midst of the Federal troops, darts a zig-zag path among them, brandishing his banner. Rifles crack at him, shots ring wildly, the smoke continues to rise. Then Williams jumps off the thrust and disappears.*)

VOICE. Dirty Nigger-Spic! He got away!

HENRY. (*Jubilant.*) He's safe! (*All of the Federal troops turn toward Henry accusingly. At the same time, they realize that the drum beat has stopped. The little Drummer Boy [Edward] has fallen wounded across his drum. Henry runs to the stricken boy, lifting him like the Pietà. Then he looks toward the statuesque President [Waldo].*) Mr. President! He only wanted to pick huckleberries! (*The President is still benign, impervious to the confusion and the smoke.*)

PRESIDENT (WALDO). I propose to write a careful essay, setting forth my position. (*The rumbling of cannon and the crack of muskets continue. Henry flings the musket away, then casts about, pleading to the air with his empty hands.*)

HENRY. Please! Somebody say something! Somebody speak out!

UNSEEN VOICE. Mr. Speaker. Gentlemen of the Congress! (*Everything on stage freezes, in whatever tortured position it is, as in stopped action. Henry listens with animal intentness.*) "This unnecessary war was unconstitutionally commenced by the President, who may be telling us the Truth—but he is not telling the *Whole* Truth. He has swept the war on and on, in showers of blood. His mind, taxed beyond its powers, is running about like some tortured creature on a burning surface!" (*With passion.*) Stop the war, Mr. President! For the love of God, *stop this war*! (*The figures of the battlefield begin to move again in weird, grotesque slow motion, as if mired and helpless in quicksand. But on Henry's face there is a look of vast relief: someone has spoken!*)

HENRY. I do not know you, Mr. Congressman. I doubt if the people of Illinois will re-elect you, because you refused to "go along." But *I* shall remember who you are, Congressman Lincoln. (*Deafening artillery fire peaks in volume. There are great flashes of light, the arcing of mortar shells, the staccato splattering of bullets. The Federal troops form into a ragged line of attacking infantrymen. They point their muskets front and move slowly forward, advancing on the audience as if it were the enemy. Henry wanders, aghast at the bloodshed.*

On a bellowed command from the Sergeant [Sam Staples] all the troops drop to one knee, and raise their rifles to fire. Then we see, for the first time, in the second rank of troops a familiar face: it is Henry's brother John, in full Federal uniform. When Henry sees John, he pushes his way through the troops to run to him.)

HENRY. John! John! (*And just as he reaches John, there is a fusillade of shots, a ricocheting bullet. John is hit. He flings his arms to the sky in pain, and falls. The troops crash about in all directions, scattering to clear the area, leaving Henry with the dying John on the battlefield in the stagnant smoke. Utterly shattered, Henry cradles John's head in his arms.*) Don't die! Not *again*, God—don't let him die! (*The whole stage fades into darkness.*)

(*Six chimes from the bell tower. Across the sky there is the faint gray line of dawn. Bailey is on his cot, Henry lies in twisted, restless sleep as Sam Staples—no longer a sergeant—enters with mugs and tin plates, which he puts on the box. From now on, all are in their customary clothing. Staples shakes Henry's shoulder.*)

SAM. Wake up, Henry. I got something here for ya. Wake up. (*Henry thrashes, still half-dreaming.*)

HENRY. I don't want it!

SAM. Well, the porridge ain't very good. But the cocoa's hot.

HENRY. (*Coming painfully awake.*) Oh. Morning, Sam. Is it morning?

SAM. Yeah. Here's yer pint of chocolate. Ya heard the news?

HENRY. What news?

SAM. It's finished.

HENRY. The war?

SAM. That wire they been stretchin' clean to Texas. And it works. Now a fella in New York can send words down there 'lectric—fast as he can talk.

HENRY. (*As he sips his chocolate thoughtfully.*) But Sam, what if nobody in New York has anything to say to anybody in Texas?

SAM. I just thought you'd be happy to know. Another thing—uh— (*Clearing his throat.*) —uh—you can leave, Henry. Any time you've a mind to.

HENRY. Leave?

SAM. During the night yer tax got paid up.

HENRY. Who did it?

SAM. Hain't material fer me to say.

HENRY. Waldo! Did Dr. Emerson pay it?

SAM. No sir.

HENRY. My mother.

SAM. No.

HENRY. Did you?

SAM. I offered, Henry. You flat refused.

HENRY. *Mrs*. Emerson. Did she come and pay it?

SAM. Now stop pokin' around tryin' to get me to tell. I promised your Aunt Louisa I wouldn't open my—

HENRY. (*disgusted.*) Aunt Louisa! (*Bailey is beginning to stir.*) I am cursed with the charity of my mother's sister! (*Shouting offstage to her.*) Aunt Louisa, why couldn't you leave your nose and your false teeth out of my life! I hereby EXCOMMUNICATE YOU FROM THE MILKY WAY! (*Sam swings the jail door open, hands Henry a paper.*)

SAM. Been nice havin' ya with us, Henry. Here's the receipt. (*Henry ignores the paper.*)

HENRY. I don't want it. You can't accuse *me* of paying my tax!

SAM. It's been paid!

HENRY. Not by me. I'm still guilty. (*Henry sits on the cot, doggedly.*)

SAM. Henry, a man's got no right to stay in jail if they's no charge ag'in him. I can't even bring you lunch.

BAILEY. (*A bit wistfully.*) You goin' already?

SAM. He's goin'!

HENRY. No!

SAM. Law put you in here. The law says when you're out.

BAILEY. Gonna be God-a'mighty quiet around here . . . (*Henry stares intensely at Bailey.*) What's wrong?

HENRY. (*Softly.*) Everything's wrong—when a man only thinks about himself. (*Wheeling sharply on Sam.*) Sam! You know what *quid pro quo* means?

SAM. (*Pained.*) That one of them Harvard words?

HENRY. It means if you see to it that Bailey gets his trial—not in another three months, or another three weeks, but *now*, right away—why, then maybe I'll favor your law by walking out onto the sidewalk. Not before.

SAM. It ain't in my power. I don't make decisions like that. (*Henry gets back into his cot, pulls the blanket over him.*)

HENRY. Goodnight, Sam.

SAM. (*Suffering.*) It's *morning*, Henry.

HENRY. Not for me. Not until you let Bailey out.

SAM. I'll do everything I kin. I'll talk to the Judge and the Selectmen.

HENRY. Tell them unless Mr. Bailey's trial is right away, they'll have another eating, non-paying guest in their jail—permanently! (*Sam goes out, almost wishing he were a Soldier in Mexico. Bailey is moved. Nobody in his life has ever stood up for him like this.*)

BAILEY. Thankee. I ain't ever gonna fergit this night here. And—when I'm out—I'm gonna come visit you, if you don't mind—at your pond place. (*The sound of the flute re-enters, but there is no leafy projection—only the mounting flames of dawn. Pause: Henry is making a difficult decision. He comes down, staring far off, toward Walden.*)

HENRY. I may not be there at the "pond place," Bailey. Seems to me I've got several more lives to live. And I don't know if I can spare any more time for *that* one.

BAILEY. Sounds to me like it's just about perfick.

HENRY. That's the trouble. If I live there much longer, I might live there forever. And you have to think twice before you accept heaven on terms like that. (*Abruptly.*) You ever take a boat trip, Bailey?

BAILEY. Riverboat only.

HENRY. When you buy a cabin ticket for an ocean passage, they give you the liberty of the whole ship. It's a privilege that should be *used*. Man shouldn't stay the whole voyage in just one place, below decks, no matter how dry and cozy it is. And warm. (*Simply.*) I think I'll have to roam the whole ship. Go before the mast! Stand out there on the foredeck. (*The flute melody falls away.*) Bailey, I tried to escape. But escape is like sleep. And when sleep is permanent, it's death. (*A pause. He moves closer to the imagined downstage window, so the morning sun fills his face.*) I must leave Walden. (*The words are painful to him. Bailey goes toward Henry as if to comfort him, raising a hand toward his shoulder; but Bailey is helpless.*) It's not necessary to be there in order to *be* there. (*Bailey moves to the window, prompted by the growing light on Henry's face. He looks out, awed.*)

BAILEY. Bright morning. Gonna be a fine July day out there.

HENRY. Sometimes the light gets so bright it puts your eyes out. And then it's just darkness all over again. If we stay awake, *then* it's morning. To be alive is to be awake. (*He looks up. The sky is really brilliant with the sunlight now.*) There is more day to dawn. The sun is only a morning star. (*He shakes hands with Bailey, starts out, remembers something: his shoe. He gets it from under the bed, salutes Bailey with it.*

In the doorway, Henry stops, looks up sharply.

From a distance, he hears an eccentric, non-military drummer.

He moves into Concord Square ablaze with morning light. Suddenly the drumbeat comes from a different direction, growing in volume. It is like thunder all around him.

His eyes follow the arc of the sky. He seems to grow in stature, lifted and strengthened by a greater challenge.

He waves to Bailey, who waves back warmly from the cell window.

With determination, Henry leaps from the stage and strides up the aisle of the theatre to the sound of his own different drummer.

No curtain falls. The lights do not fade, but grow brighter. During the curtain calls, and as the audience leaves the theatre, Henry's distinctive and irregular drum-cadence builds and resounds.)

FIRST
MONDAY
IN
OCTOBER

Introduction

The final play in this anthology, *First Monday in October*, reflects the changing patterns of the American theatre, while reaffirming Lawrence and Lee's usual collaborative methodology. The play's genesis was typical for the playwrights. As Lawrence recounted, "One of us called the other on the phone and said, 'What would happen if there was a woman on the Supreme Court?' And the other one said, 'That's a great idea! It's a wonderful idea.' "[1]

Through one of their lawyers, the playwrights were able to go behind the scenes at the Supreme Court, with the guidance of then-Chief Justice Earl Warren. Before visiting Washington, Lawrence said, "The second idea one of us came up with was, what would happen if this woman were a conservative from Orange County [California], and what if she met head-on with a liberal like William O. Douglas—and the whole play almost came to life at that moment."[2] Creating the play was not, of course, quite so simple.

The first version of *First Monday in October* opened the sixtieth anniversary season at the Cleveland Play House in 1975, under Lawrence's direction, with Melvyn Douglas and Jean Arthur as the politically opposed justices. The play followed the pattern of new scripts appearing at regional theatres prior to commercial production, which was becoming standard having been exemplified earlier by *The Night Thoreau Spent in Jail*. The stars were well received, although Arthur withdrew from the production shortly after the opening for health reasons.[3] Bill Doll reported in the *Cleveland Plain Dealer* that the play provided "an entertaining time watching the performances of these two disarming and enchanting professionals," and that the playwrights "serve up . . . some first-rate morsels of dialogue and even some sharp insights. It is a script that in its speeches, if not its substance, is first-rate Broadway caliber."[4] *Variety* reported that the stars were "outstanding performers demonstrating charm and effectiveness in their characterizations of highly individualistic personalities," while noting that the second act was "too talky."[5]

After the Cleveland production, the play attracted the attention of producer-actress Martha Scott, searching at the time for a script for the Plumstead Playhouse, which had earlier revived *Our Town* for Henry Fonda. Scott involved producer Roger L. Stevens and Fonda in the project; Edwin Sherin was signed to direct.[6] A rewritten *First Monday in October* was scheduled for production at the Kennedy Center's Eisenhower Theatre in Washington, D.C., where it opened at the end of December 1977, with Henry Fonda and Jane Alexander as the protagonists. The production was scheduled for only six weeks: Fonda was recuperating from major surgery. The new version of the script focused more on the two justices, and received a rave response from Richard L. Coe of the *Washington Post.* The playwrights, he wrote, "achieved a playwrighting coup" in a play "that is serious and trenchant and, at the same time, funny and richly human" with "gorgeous, sharp roles" for the stars.[7] The *Variety* reviewer, by contrast, called the play "one of the flimsiest of vehicles ever to be woven around two such attractive stars" and said that it amounted "to little more than two acts of ideological bickering, without much wit."[8]

Washington audiences agreed with Coe, not with *Variety; First Monday in October* sold out its Kennedy Center engagement, grossing well over the theatre's capacity each week, and setting two house records for straight plays.[9] After Fonda had rested for the summer, the production, with only one minor cast change, opened in New York at the Majestic Theatre for a limited run of eight weeks. The play opened in the midst of a newspaper strike and thus received limited reviews. The reviews that did appear all praised Fonda and Alexander. Jack Kroll opened his *Newsweek* review with "Watching Henry Fonda in *First Monday in October* is pure pleasure,"[10] while T. E. Kalem in *Time* told his readers to "count Fonda as a master of masters in precision timing, vocal inflection and revelatory comic gestures."[11]

In a short review printed in the *New York Times* after the strike, Walter Kerr called Alexander "attractively crisp and quick-thinking" and wrote that Fonda "holds back his resoluteness until it's time. Then the steel in him shows. More than that. It glows, creates a light around it, gives off whatever heat and whatever humor they [*sic*] play needs to keep it moving and breathing."[12] In the only full review published by a New York daily newspaper (the *New York Post* was not on strike), Clive Barnes praised the playwrights for having "caught these two people in the living flesh," but then judged that "Lee and Lawrence have found a situation, postulated two characters, and evoked an atmosphere. After that, they omitted to write a play."[13] Hobe Morrison, in business-oriented *Variety,* called the play "an entertaining light comedy" that "works well as literature, absorbing and consistently enjoyable theatre," predicting that it "is also likely to bring another royalty harvest to Lawrence and Lee."[14]

Audience response in New York, as in Washington, supported Morrison's view. *First Monday in October* set three house records during its scheduled eight weeks at the Majestic,[15] then continued for another four weeks at the ANTA Theatre, finally closing on 9 December; both Fonda and Alexander had film commitments.

With Fonda's health improving, *First Monday in October* (with Eva Marie Saint replacing Alexander) was scheduled to tour opening at the Huntington Hartford Theatre in Los Angeles on 28 February 1979. Sylvie Drake called the play "clever and witty entertainment that relies on verbal sparring for its action."[16] Again, audiences came in large numbers: two house records were set during the play's four-week run in Los Angeles.

From Los Angeles, the play moved to Chicago, where it was reviewed as "an offbeat, but on-target comedy about ideas, humanity, affection, and the talky virtues of the slim, but well-crafted play" with the conflict between the justices termed "a kind of sensual athleticism of the mind."[17] *First Monday in October* had played Chicago's Blackstone Theatre for only two weeks when Fonda, suddenly suffering hip pain, was diagnosed with cancer. The production closed.[18] The film version (with Walter Matthau and Jill Clayburgh) was released in 1980.

As had been the case with *A Call on Kuprin* seventeen years earlier, *First Monday in October* was quickly overtaken by events. Once Sandra Day O'Connor was named to the Supreme Court in 1981 by President Ronald Reagan, the confrontation between male and female justices ceased to be material for a timely comedy. Nevertheless, the play's use of liberal and conservative philosophies to debate the issues of censorship and the influence of multinational corporations on society have kept the play in frequent production and its film version in constant circulation.

Most of the reviews found the central conflict between Justices Snow and Loomis entertaining and crisply written. Only a few reviewers praised the play as well, with many dismissing it as a vehicle for its star performers. Similar critical judgments were recorded, of course, during the early years of such durable Lawrence and Lee plays as *Inherit the Wind, Auntie Mame,* and *The Gang's All Here.* Robert E. Lee indicated one possible reason for this critical misperception in a 1986 interview: "There's one problem, however. Sometimes you can be so entertaining that people miss the point. I think that's what happened with *First Monday in October.* We were having too much fun with the relationship between Henry Fonda and Jane Alexander."[19]

As with the earlier plays, *First Monday in October* centers on character, at the expense of the traditional well-made plot. Each of the plot developments builds to the confrontations between Dan and Ruth in the play's two acts, with Dan's clerk, Mason Woods, serving as a connection between the two justices. If reviewers expected a well-made play, disappointment was inevitable. In the hands of the authors of a well-made play, for example, Dan's estrangement from his off-stage wife might inevitably lead to the possibility of romance between the justices, while Dan's response to Ruth's conviction that her late husband's involvement with Omnitech requires her resignation from the Supreme Court would provide the romance's motivating event.

Any number of minor incidents in the play could well provide ways for a tightly constructed drama in the traditional mode to be written. Such speculation is, of course, pointless: Lawrence and Lee wrote a drama of character in *First Monday in October,* much as they had done in the earlier plays printed in this anthology. The demands of this type of drama are different from the well-made drama of plot and equally stringent, if frequently unrecognized by reviewers exposed to traditional structures and occasionally unwilling (or unable) to recognize different patterns.

The characters who provide the central thrust of *First Monday in October,* Dan Snow and Ruth Loomis, permit the playwrights to debate ideas. The changes in the play show the playwrights focusing on Dan and Ruth's conflict, cutting away distracting elements. The Cleveland version of the text, for example, included "a

Peter Pan–like common man who roams around the stage discoursing with Douglas,"[20] and the cast list includes several characters who have disappeared from the Washington and New York programs. Even in the later productions, Dan Snow's sinus-stricken secretary, Miss Birnbaum, is listed as a character, subsequently deleted from the published text. The changes all serve to center the play more firmly on Dan and Ruth's ideological debates.

Lawrence and Lee's earlier dramas provide many examples of polar opposites embodying diametrically conflicting viewpoints: Drummond and Brady in *Inherit the Wind,* Mame and Babcock in *Auntie Mame,* Golden and Whitmore from *Only in America,* Smith and Kuprin in *A Call on Kuprin,* Felicia and Orton of *Diamond Orchid, The Night Thoreau Spent in Jail*'s Thoreau and Emerson—all represent opposing positions on significant political and social issues. With the exception of *A Call on Kuprin,* with its plot derived from Edelman's novel, all the plays in this anthology, to greater or lesser degrees, are structured around their central character(s).

In the late 1970s, much of the interest in *First Monday in October* focused, quite naturally, on the playwrights' invention of the appointment of the first female Supreme Court justice. Many of the reviewers expected the play to include feminist diatribes and were startled by their absence. *Time*'s Kalem reacted typically: "While the play might be assumed to be pro-feminist, most of the laughter it arouses in the audience stems from trading on stereotypical masculine prejudices."[21] The issues the playwrights do emphasize, First Amendment rights in the first act and the actions of shadowy multinational corporations in the second, were dismissed by some 1978 reviewers as excuses for debate. As Edwin Wilson put it, "In the first instance we have heard the arguments before; in the multinational case, both the facts and the issues are murky."[22]

With hindsight, and efforts by the Supreme Court in the late 1980s and early 1990s to curtail the use of the First Amendment as a defense for free speech, the passionate speeches Lawrence and Lee wrote for Dan and Ruth seem far more timely than they did to some of the play's first reviewers. Likewise, scandals involving multinational businesses and banks make the issues raised in *First Monday in October* a great deal less murky than they appeared to Wilson in 1978. In both areas, the issues that exercised Lawrence and Lee enough to create the debates between Justices Snow and Loomis have withstood the test of time. They are no more dated than the evolutionist/creationist debate in *Inherit the Wind* has proven to be, or the political corruption revealingly analyzed in *The Gang's All Here.*

The playwrights also turned out to be insightful prophets in their depiction of the first woman Supreme Court justice: Sandra Day O'Connor has proven as conservative a jurist as the fictional Ruth Loomis. Although history caught up with Lawrence and Lee's fiction when Justice O'Connor was appointed, the issues raised in *First Monday in October* remain pertinent. As a result, the play remains in regular production, surviving without the star performances or the superficially trendy issues some reviewers saw as the reasons for its initial success.

NOTES

1. Jerome Lawrence, interview, 28 December 1988.

2. Lawrence, interview.

3. Jean Arthur became well known in her later years for her recurring stage fright; John Springer discussed her abrupt departure from the Cleveland *First Monday in October* in a letter to the editor, *TheatreWeek*, 6 May 1991, p. 4. Arthur's understudy was a young company intern, Dee Hoty, later nominated for Tony Awards for her performances in the musicals *City of Angels* (1990) and *The Will Rogers Follies* (1991).

4. Bill Doll, "Plenty of reasons to see 'October,' " *Cleveland Plain Dealer*, 18 October 1975, sec. C, p. 8.

5. Mark, "New Show in Stock: *First Monday in October*," *Variety*, 22 October 1975, 163.

6. Doug McClellend, "No Monday Blues for Martha Scott," *After Dark*, 11:6 (October 1978), 68–72.

7. Richard L. Coe, " 'First Monday': A Funny and Richly Human Court," *Washington Post*, 29 December 1977, sec. B, p. 1.

8. Paul, "Show Out of Town: *First Monday in October*," *Variety*, 11 January 1978, 128.

9. Box office figures are reported in *Variety*, 28 December 1977, p. 57; 11 January 1978, p. 124; 18 January 1978, p. 95; 25 January 1978, p. 87; 1 February 1978, p. 106.

10. "Mr. Justice Fonda," *Newsweek* (16 October 1978), rpt. *New York Theatre Critics Reviews* (abbrev. *NYTCR*), 39 (1978), 208.

11. T. E. Kalem, "High-Court Hokum," *Time* (16 October 1978), rpt. *NYTCR*, 39 (1978), 208.

12. *New York Times*, 6 November 1978, rpt. *NYTCR*, 39 (1978), 209.

13. "Wry, dry and funny," *New York Post*, 5 October 1978, rpt. *NYTCR*, 39 (1978), 206.

14. Hobe, "Shows on Broadway: *First Monday in October*," *Variety*, 4 October 1978, p. 98.

15. Box office figures from *Variety*, 1 November 1978, p. 87; 8 November 1978, p. 67; 15 November 1978, p. 87.

16. "Fonda and Saint in Courtroom Duel," *Los Angeles Times*, 1 March 1979, sec. 4, p. 1.

17. Linda Winter, " 'First Monday in October' is offbeat, on-target comedy," *Chicago Tribune*, 30 March 1979, sec. 4, p. 3.

18. The events surrounding Fonda's illness are recounted in Howard Teichmann's *Fonda: My Life; As Told to Howard Teichmann* (New York: New American Library, 1981), 332–37. The earlier engagements in *First Monday in October* are discussed on 326–28, 330–31. Teichmann errs in placing the Los Angeles engagement prior to the Broadway opening (330).

19. Christopher Meeks, "The Greatest Sport in the World" (interview with Jerome Lawrence and Robert E. Lee), *Writer's Digest* (March 1986), 33–34.

20. Doll, sec. C, p. 8.

21. Kalem, 208.

22. Edwin Wilson, "The Theater: 'First Monday in October,' " *Wall Street Journal*, 6 October 1978, rpt. *NYTCR*, 39 (1978), 207.

Foreword

On the third Thursday of October, 1975, Judge Ruth Loomis of the 9th Circuit Court of Appeals was sworn in as the first woman ever to sit as an Associate Justice of the Supreme Court. This historic event took place in the Drury Theatre of the Cleveland Play House in our native state of Ohio, and Judge Loomis carried a distinguished aka: Jean Arthur. Her chief opponent on the Court was Justice Daniel Snow, who bore a twin resemblance to Melvyn Douglas. The events were dramatically accurate. They simply hadn't happened yet in real life. In Washington, D.C., on the stage of the Eisenhower Theatre in Kennedy Center on 28 December 1977, Judge Loomis again took the path of office as the first woman on the Supreme Court—this time in the person of Jane Alexander, with Henry Fonda as her legal nemesis, Dan Snow. The same duo turned the Majestic Theatre on Broadway into a site for the "right to be wrong" on the first Tuesday in October, 1978. On Washington's Birthday, 1979, Eva Marie Saint became the first woman Justice, with Fonda feuding and frolicking with her. *First Monday in October* broke all B.O. records at Hollywood's Huntington Hartford Theatre, then went to the Blackstone Theatre in Chicago—where the sell-out run was aborted by Henry's sudden illness. On 15 May 1980, Jill Clayburgh was sworn in as the first lady justice; Walter Matthau became her battle-scarred and belligerent adversary in the motion picture version which we wrote for Paramount.

And finally, on the First Monday in October 1981, six years after the momentous event had begun happening in theatres and motion picture houses throughout the world, Sandra Day O'Connor took her place, along with the "Brethren" who constitute the highest court in the land and the most powerful legal tribunal in the solar system.

It was risky. Our policy as playwrights is to do more than participate in history; we try to anticipate events which will shape our lives before they happen. We skate very close to the "Now." We pursue the happenings of the day, the hour, much as a submarine scouts a convoy. We run up our periscopes and try to see what is happening along a horizon which is invisible to others who are submerged in the murky minutiae of the times. Often, in the belief that the behavior of human beings tends to be cyclical, we search out the past for clues to the future. In other instances, as in *First Monday*, we ride on pure conjecture.

In any event, we decry forensic theatre. A playwright should be more than a pathologist. Audiences should not be asked to pay for admission to a morgue where a blood-drained cadaver of the past is probed and dismembered. Such ghoulish antics are "yawn" stuff, the graffiti of neophytes who kid themselves into thinking they're breaking new ground when they're merely digging up old graves. In the guise of being "avant garde," today's clever chaps tend to dump out uncoordinated clumps of pseudo-theatrics, devoid of hope or humor.

We seek always to be the apostles of expectation. Sometimes the sport of writing clashes with the more serious material we are writing about. To some extent this happened in *First Monday*. Our intention was to show the baleful influences which can come from the irresponsible conduct of multinational corporations; also, we wanted to expose the erosion of our precious First Amendment rights.

But in the fury of cross-court volleys between the lady justice and her curmudgeon opponent, many audiences missed the intended significance in the fun of the contest. In a way, we won the point and lost the match.

Nevertheless, the play has had far more impact than a dry dissertation, touching thousands of minds. How fortunate we are! That process continues. People read and see this play (and others from our typewriters or word-processors); so maybe there's more hope in the world, the future may be infinitesimally brighter, and the process of change minutely less frightening.

For it is the purpose of the playwright to be aware, knowledgeable. He is the point-man of the platoon. Our job is to see it first, to beat the President to the punch, to put Ruth Loomis on the bench ahead of Sandra Day O'Connor.

Lawrence & Lee

EDITOR'S NOTE

First Monday in October was published, in an acting edition, by Samuel French in 1979. That text includes changes made to the script by the playwrights after the Broadway run, and is reproduced here.

Eugene Hare, Melvyn Douglas, George Brengel, Spencer McIntrye, Robert Snook, (back row) Ben Letter, Earl Keyes, John Buck Jr., and Jean Arthur in the premiere production of *First Monday in October*, Cleveland Play House, 1975. Photo by James Fry Foto Arts. Production files, Lawrence and Lee Theatre Research Institute, The Ohio State University.

Larry Gates, Eugene Stuckmann, Maurice Copeland, Earl Sydnor, Patrick McCullough, Alexander Reed, and Jane Alexander in *First Monday in October,* Washington, D.C., 1977. Photo by Richard Braaton. Jerome Lawrence and Robert E. Lee Collection, Lawrence and Lee Theatre Research Institute, The Ohio State University.

CAST

First Monday in October opened in New York at the Majestic Theatre on 3 October 1978. It was produced by the Kennedy Center (Roger Stevens) and Plumstead Theatre Society, Inc. (Martha Scott, Joel Spector, Bernard Wiesen), and directed by Edwin Sherin. The scenery was designed by Oliver Smith, with costumes by Ann Roth, and lighting designed by Roger Morgan. The cast included:

CUSTODIANS .... John Steward, P. J. Sidney
CHIEF JUSTICE JAMES JEFFERSON CRAWFORD ...... Larry Gates
ASSOCIATE JUSTICE JOSIAH CLEWES ..... Earl Sydnor
ASSOCIATE JUSTICE WALDO THOMPSON .... Maurice Copeland
ASSOCIATE JUSTICE DANIEL SNOW ..... Henry Fonda
ASSOCIATE JUSTICE HAROLD WEBB ... John Wardwell
MARSHAL .... John Newton
JUDGE RUTH LOOMIS .... Jane Alexander
MASON WOODS .... Tom Stechschulte
ASSOCIATE JUSTICE AMBROSE QUINCY .... Alexander Reed
ASSOCIATE JUSTICE RICHARD CAREY .... Eugene Stuckmann
ASSOCIATE JUSTICE CHRISTOPHER HALLORAN ..... Patrick McCullough
PHOTOGRAPHER .... John Stewart
BLAKE .... Ron Faber

First Monday in October was produced prior to its Broadway run at the Eisenhower Theatre of the John F. Kennedy Center for the Performing Arts, Washington, D.C., opening on 28 December 1977. An earlier version of the play had its world premiere at the Francis E. Drury Theatre as the sixtieth anniversary celebration of the Cleveland Play House, Cleveland, Ohio, on 17 October 1975. The production was directed by Jerome Lawrence, with scenery by Richard

Gould, costumes by Estelle Painter, lighting by Richard Coumbs, and properties by David Smith. The cast included:

JUSTICE DANIEL SNOW .... Melvyn Douglas
RUTH LOOMIS .... Jean Arthur
CHIEF JUSTICE JEFFERSON CRAWFORD ...... George Brengel
MASON WOODS .... Dennis Romer
BURTON SCHMERTZ .... Allan Leatherman
UNIVERSITY PRESIDENT .... Ralph Neeley
JUSTICE JOSIAH CLEWIS .... Spencer McIntyre
JUSTICE HAROLD WEBB .... Robert Snook
JUSTICE STANLEY MOOREHEAD .... John Buck, Jr.
OTHER JUSTICES .... Howard Renensland, Jr.
Eugene Hare
Ben Letter
Earle Keyes
PHOTOGRAPHER .... Ralph Neeley
SENATE CHAIRMAN .... John Buck, Jr.
SENATORS .... Andrew Lichtenberg
Howard Renensland, Jr.
Frederic Serino
OTHERS BEHIND THE SCENES AT THE COURT .....
David Meyer
George Simms
Dee Hoty
MARSHAL .... John Buck, Jr.
NIGHT WATCHMAN .... Andrew Lichtenberg

Scene: Backstage at the U.S. Supreme Court
Time: The imaginary now.
The people and events of the play are entirely fictional.

The term of the Court begins, by law, the first Monday in October of each year and continues as long as the business before the Court requires. . . . Judiciary Act of 1789

First Monday in October

ACT ONE

This is a behind-the-scenes view of the Supreme Court of the United States. In the distance is an impression of the impressive columns and Grecian facade of the Court building. At stage level are the chambers of two Justices, back to back. Just a hint of the partition divides the two chambers. Right are the chambers of Dan Snow: wood paneling, books, cluttered desk, leather couch. Left—another chamber, shrouded in dust covers. The thrust area foreground can be anything and everywhere. The lights rise on that area for a gathering of the Justices. There are only eight; one is missing. What we see is the daily assembling of the most select "Club" in the world. Today, the panoply has an overlay of tension and sadness.

A coffee table with an ornate silver urn has been rolled on by an attendant. Each Justice shakes hands with every other Justice. Their robes are over their arms, and ritualistically they help one another in the daily robing ceremony. All wear business suits underneath their robes, except for Justice Dan Snow, who wears a sports jacket and slacks. Dan has the rumpled look, silver hair, wrinkles in all the right places. When Dan shakes hands with Josiah Clewes, the Black Justice, he does it "soul-brother" style. The Chief Justice, a large man with warmth and humanity, prefers to be called "C.J." instead of the more stern and formal "Chief."

C.J. I don't like to shake just seven hands. I miss that eighth one very much. (*The C.J. crosses up to the urn, gets a cup of coffee.*)

JOSIAH CLEWES. C.J., any word from the White House? Any clue? (*C.J. shakes his head "no."*)

C.J. Dan—? (*Dan has turned upstage to the silver coffee urn, drawing himself some coffee.*) You've been here longer than any of us. You want to hazard a guess? Penetrate the Presidential mind? Who's going to replace Stanley? (*All turn their attention toward the Justice in the sports coat.*)

JOSIAH. A black? Possible?

WALDO THOMPSON. A woman? (*Dan cocks his head.*)

DAN. What about a black woman? (*Josiah laughs.*) What's so funny? You prejudiced? (*This releases the tension somewhat. Dan crosses to the C.J.*) Could be anybody. I never try to second-guess a President. Once a man moves into the White House, you have no idea what happens to his mind. Or his convictions. Or his campaign promises. (*Turning to the others.*) Any of you have any idea *you* were going to be appointed? Hell, when I got the nod—that was somewhere back in the Dark Ages—I was so surprised, I think it stunted my growth. (*There is laughter at this. Dan paces, restlessly, staring up at the Court facade.*) I just hope he names someone halfway sane—with an active membership card in the human race.

HAROLD WEBB. And somebody who agrees with you.

DAN. (*Wheeling.*) No! Not necessarily! You think I'm glad Stanley's dead? Hell, I don't wish *any* man dead. (*Softening.*) You think I hated Stanley because he didn't agree with me? Christ, *nobody* agrees with me. Not even my wife. *Especially* my wife. Justice Stanley Moorehead and I were like a couple of flying buttresses. Leaning against opposite sides of a Gothic cathedral, we helped to keep the roof from caving in. If we had both been on the same side all the time, we might have pushed the building over . . . !

MARSHAL. Ten o'clock, Gentlemen. (*The C.J. checks his watch, nods to the others, who line up behind him to form a procession. Dan is second, the others in order of seniority. Crisply, they go off.*)

MARSHAL'S VOICE. (*Offstage. Echoing through the marble corridors.*) The Honorable, the Chief Justice and the Associate Justices of the Supreme Court of the United States. (*The lights fade slowly on the thrust as the procession moves off, single file.*) Oyez! Oyez! All persons having business before the Honorable, the Supreme Court of the United States, are admonished to draw near and give their attention, for the Court is now sitting. God save the United States, and this Honorable Court. (*Gavel sounds. The lights fade. In the momentary black, the sound of the gavel crosses into the thump-thud of a tennis ball in a fierce volley—accompanied by the ring of racquet strings.*)

MAN'S VOICE (*Unseen.*) Oooohhh! Good shot! (*A telephone rings.*)

ATTENDANT'S VOICE. (*Unseen. Answering phone.*) Santa Ana Tennis Club. (*Listens.*) One moment, please. (*Booming over an echoing P.A. system.*) Judge Loomis, telephone. Phone call for Judge Loomis. (*Ruth Loomis enters, carrying a phone. She's in tennis gear, breathless, a towel over her shoulder. Ruth is vigorous, attractive—radiates energy and intelligence.*)

RUTH. (*Into phone.*) This is Ruth Loomis. (*Pause.*) Oh, my goodness . . . ! (*She sinks onto a bench.*) Wait just a second till I get my breath—! (*Ruth straightens her posture, trying to feel less casual, more legally regal.*) Don't put him on till—oh, Hello, Mr. President. (*She stands quickly, listens.*) Oh, I'm fine. I—I was just—I've been playing tennis. (*Pause. She grins.*) Seven six. Set point. (*With a laugh, relaxing a little.*) Well, I *did* have an idea something might be going on when the FBI started questioning my grade school teachers. (*Listens, soberly.*) No, I won't consider it. I'll save you another phone call. I'll say "yes" right now. (*Then gravely.*) It's a great honor, Mr. President. I don't know how anybody could say "no" to it. (*Faint smile.*) Of course, the Senate might say "no" to me—! (*Listens.*) That would be a great pleasure, Mr. President. I'd love to . . . when—and *if*—I get to Washing— (*A hazy thought crosses her mind.*) I was wondering . . . No, no, it's nothing important, I was just thinking— (*She starts to sit again, but stops herself.*) It might be considered unconstitutional for a Justice of the Supreme Court to play tennis with the Chief Executive. You know, Separation of Powers and all . . . (*Ruth listens, then nods, reassured.*) That's true, we would have a net between us. Thank you, Mr. President, very much. Goodbye. (*Dazed, unbelieving, she puts down the phone, sinks to the bench again. She clasps her hands in half prayer, half exultation. Lights fade, bench clears. Lights rise on the chambers. Dan is seated at his desk, which is piled high with well-organized clutter. There is a knock at the door.*)

DAN. Who's that?

MASON'S VOICE OFF. Mason Woods. May I come in, Sir? (*Mason Woods, Dan's law clerk, appears, pushing a library cart filled with law books and briefs. Mason is mid-20s, a jagged Oregonian; he is brighter than his Harvard Law School confreres, but lacks some of their slickness.*)

DAN. Of course you can come in. What the hell do you think you're here for? (*Mason wheels the cart in.*)

MASON. Thank you, sir.

DAN. I've only got one complaint about you so far. You're too goddam polite. A month is long enough to be scared of me. Relax, Mason, you've got the job. (*Leans back in his chair, stares up at Mason.*)

MASON. I found the references you wanted. I dug up a couple more, too.

DAN. Good. (*Dan takes some of the references, begins to study them. Mason lifts a teapot from the bottom shelf of the cart.*)

MASON. Would you like some tea, Mr. Justice? Or a Scotch?

DAN. It's been a long day. Maybe I'd better have both. (*Thinks.*) No, I don't want to overdo it. Forget the tea. (*Mason reaches into a drawer and comes up with a fifth of Scotch. Dan smiles, takes the bottle, pours an inch into a water tumbler—then adds a little water from a carafe.*) Why don't you have one yourself?

MASON. Thank you, but I don't drink, sir.

DAN. Oh, that's too bad. (*He lifts the glass in an aborted toast.*) Peace! (*He takes a sip, then squints up at Mason, who picks up another volume from the cart.*)

MASON. This one supports your position on Abbott vs. Omnitech.

DAN. (*With a faint frown.*) Forget Abbott.

MASON. It's due for consideration next week, isn't it?

DAN. The Chief took it off the conference list.

MASON. (*Indignant.*) You've gotta hear Abbott vee Omnitech!

DAN. I was sure we had the votes. I was counting on the C.J.—but I'm afraid he's getting scared. (*He slams the book shut and stands.*) I tell you the most dangerous thing in the world is to be cautious, Mason. The people who always fall down are the people who are afraid they'll trip over something. Take a chance!

MASON. Yes, sir.

DAN. And don't always agree with me! If you think I'm wrong, and don't say so, what the hell use are you? I like law clerks who argue with me. Otherwise, I'd be my own law clerk.

MASON. Yes, sir. No, sir. I mean—I'll try to do that, sir—uh, *not* to do that. Sir. (*Mason reaches for another brief on the cart, flips it open.*)

DAN. What's that?

MASON. Collins versus California. (*Dan takes it.*) It's the kinky one that kicked up from the 9th Circuit: the Berkeley student who wore a T-shirt that said "Fuck the White House."

DAN. (*Leafing through the pages.*) Did he have his pants off?

MASON. Doesn't say.

DAN. Then I don't see any clear and present danger that he intended to implement the opinion of his T-shirt.

MASON. The 9th Circuit held it was offensive to the public sensibility.

DAN. (*Shaking his head.*) Just being offensive isn't an offense. One man's pornography may be another man's poetry. (*Mason laughs. Dan flips a page, reading with a mix of amusement and annoyance.*) Yep, yep, yep! Lady Purity, speaking from the cloisters of California. Listen. (*Reads:*) "Free speech is not, ipso facto, filthy speech. Dirt is a splendid environment for earthworms, but it is a grave for the human mind." (*Slaps it shut.*) I just wish to hell she didn't write so goddamned well. This kind of moral dry-cleaning could be dangerous if it caught on. See, Mason? That's what this court is for: to restrain the Ruth Loomises of the world. (*Mason picks up another volume, flips it to a marked page.*)

MASON. I found this opinion on surveillance. But you won't have to read it.

DAN. Why not?

MASON. You wrote it.

DAN. Read it to me—I might have forgotten it. Or changed my mind. (*He leans back, sipping the drink as he listens.*)

MASON. (*Reading.*) "When God created the world, He did it alone, in private, all by Himself. No monitors, no hidden microphones. He made it the way *He* wanted it. But what if somebody had invaded God's privacy? Would He have put the world together the same way? I doubt it. He'd have made it a *popular* world—"

DAN. (*Picking up the quote from memory.*) "And the Garden of Eden would have turned out like Las Vegas or Forty-Second Street."

MASON. Uh—I have a question about that, sir.

DAN. Oh? Don't you agree with me?

MASON. I'm not sure *you* agree with you. In Gibbs vee Southeast Gas—uh, you said—uh— (*Fishing for another book.*)

DAN. What did I say?

MASON. "No disinfectant has the purifying power of sunlight. Whatever is hidden, kept in the dark, is suspect."

DAN. That was a case against a public corporation. What's public should be public, what's private is private. A seed needs the secrecy of the earth before it sprouts into a plant or a tree. Privacy is no luxury, Mason. It's indispensable as the quiet of the womb, where life waits, getting ready to sprout into a human being.

Rip into that mystery too soon, and what happens? Death! (*Pause. A faint smile.*) You think I'm inconsistent? (*Mason hesitates.*)

MASON. Possibly.

DAN. (*Leans back.*) Well, Mason, if you wake up every morning and you aren't any different, you can get pretty sick of yourself. (*The phone rings.*)

MASON. Do you want to take any calls, sir?

DAN. Birnbaum'll get it.

MASON. No, she won't. (*Picking up the phone.*) Chambers of Mr. Justice Snow. Oh, yes, Mrs. Snow. This is Mason Woods. (*He listens, turns to Dan.*) It's your wife, but she doesn't want to bother you.

DAN. (*Takes the phone.*) You're not bothering me. You're interrupting me, but you're not bothering me. (*Listens.*) I'm not sure what time I'll be home for dinner. What time do you want me home? (*Mason starts out, but Dan calls to him.*) Don't go, Mason. (*Back into the telephone.*) Tell me who's coming, I'll tell you what time I'll be home for dinner. (*Listens, blank-faced.*) Expect me about eleven-fifteen; they oughta be gone by then. (*Listens, then closes his eyes.*) I am *not* anti-social. I'll be charming. Just hand me a stiff drink when I come in the door. (*Dan hangs up the phone, jerks his head toward the outer office.*) What happened to Miss Birnbaum?

MASON. She left early.

DAN. What was her trouble?

MASON. Sinus.

DAN. Again? Maybe she should have it removed.

MASON. She looks terrible.

DAN. Birnbaum's been with me for twenty-three years—and she *always* looks terrible.

MASON. I thought maybe I'd better order you a substitute secretary, sir.

DAN. You wouldn't do that to me, Mason. (*He downs the rest of his drink.*) It's easier changing wives than changing secretaries. A substitute wife doesn't have to be shown where everything *is*. (*Mason laughs. Dan puts down his glass, circles his desk, then deftly, like a seagull diving for a fish, plucks one single sheet of paper out from under the tangle on his desk.*)

MASON. How do you do that, sir?

DAN. Do what?

MASON. Reach in and find exactly what you're looking for in the middle of all that—all that—

DAN. Mess? To *you* it's a mess, to *me* it's a wilderness of free association. (*Sternly.*) Don't ever straighten up my desk, Mason—I'd never be able to find anything. I've always been suspicious of neatness: if there's nothing on top of a man's desk, he's probably shoved all the clutter into the drawers. And if his drawers are empty, what the hell does he need the desk for? (*Surveying the pile in front of him.*) I like to have *my* mess right out on top where I can enjoy it! (*Mason laughs.*)

C.J. (*At the entrance.*) May I come in, Dan?

DAN. (*Projecting.*) Sure, C.J. (*Chief Justice James Jefferson Crawford enters.*)

MASON. How are you, Mr. Chief Justice?

C.J. I'm not sure. Mind if I lie down on your couch, Dan? (*He flops down without waiting for an answer. Dan hands the Collins brief to Mason.*)

DAN. Mason. See if those T-shirts are available on the open market. (*With relish.*) I'd like to wear one under my robes. (*Mason takes the certs, politely exits to the outer office.*)

C.J. What T-shirts?

DAN. None of your goddam business. Do I ask you about your underwear? Thanks to the Supreme Court of the United States, there are still a *few* zones of privacy left.

C.J. (*Sighs.*) How come your couch is more comfortable than mine?

DAN. Maybe I'll give you this couch. As a going-away present.

C.J. Who's going away?

DAN. *I* am. I might.

C.J. (*Sitting up.*) When?

DAN. Oh, after the President appoints a man to take Stanley's place. And the Senate confirms him. Think how many people would bust a gut with joy if I retired.

C.J. You wouldn't do that to me, Dan. (*Then worried.*) Does health have anything to do with it—?

DAN. Frankly—yes. (*Avoiding his eyes, solemnly.*) I was out at Bethesda for a checkup a few weeks ago.

C.J. Yes . . . ?

DAN. They think I'll last for a while yet. And I'll be damned if I'm going to waste what's left of my health writing dissenting opinions.

C.J. Don't leave, Dan.

DAN. Oh, I won't quit when you're short-handed. I'll stick around until you've got nine men on the bench again.

C.J. (*Lying back, with a gallows laugh.*) Yeah. . . .

DAN. When do you think the President'll make an announcement? (*Pause.*) Who's he going to pick? (*Pause.*) He's already been appointed? (*No answer.*) Who is he? (*Pause. The C.J. sighs.*)

C.J. Mr. Justice Snow, I'll have to ask you to rephrase that question.

DAN. (*A beat.*) A woman! He picked a woman! (*With some elation.*) Great. Good for him! It oughta be fun. (*Expectantly.*) Who is it? Who is she? Who? Who?

C.J. The President just sent up to the Senate Judiciary Committee the name of Judge Ruth Hagadorn Loomis of the 9th Circuit Court of Appeals.

DAN. (*Stunned.*) Get off my couch. I've gotta lie down. (*The C.J. gets up, but Dan can't lie down. His blood has hit the boiling point. He circles the room like a caged polar bear on a hot day.*)

C.J. Now, Dan—

DAN. (*Incredulous.*) Ruth Loomis! You're joking. It's a joke. It's a joke, isn't it?

C.J. (*Shakes his head.*) The President, I am told, thinks he has just taken a great progressive step in the history of mankind.

DAN. The Mother Superior of Orange County?

C.J. Appointing a woman—that's 21st-century stuff.

DAN. But Ruth Loomis??? Why would he do a think like that?

C.J. Well, the President gets advice from everybody. He doesn't want to rock the economy. And I guess he thinks she's safe.

DAN. Safe! What goes through a man's head when he makes an appointment like that?

C.J. I guess he's trying to be even-handed. President of *all* the people. And we've got this wave of morality sweeping the country. . . .

DAN. (*Shaking his head in disbelief.*) The Senate'll never go for it, will they? Will they . . . ? (*The phone rings—then rings again. Dan stretches out on the couch, ignoring it.*)

C.J. Where's Miss Birnbaum? (*Dan, preoccupied, doesn't answer. The phone continues to ring persistently. The C.J. picks it up. Into phone.*) Chambers of Mr. Justice Snow. (*He listens, covers the mouthpiece.*) It's a reporter. Do you have any comment for the Washington Post?

DAN. Sure. Tell 'em I think Sousa wrote 'em a helluva march.

C.J. (*Into phone.*) No comment from Mr. Justice Snow at this time. (*He hangs up the phone.*)

DAN. You're better than Miss Birnbaum. (*Dan jumps up from the sofa, irritated.*) The President wants a woman on the court, why not Miss Birnbaum?? She'd be perfect. She'd never show up. (*The cantankerous Dan stops abruptly, looks into the sad eyes of the C.J. He is now very serious, very reasonable.*) Delete that. Irrelevant. Frivolous. Jeff. I've been on this court longer than anybody. And I guess you know by now that I'm an incorrigible egomaniac. I'm bright as hell and I know it. So why in God's name do I have this sinking feeling in my gut when I think about that woman sitting on this court? It's not because she's a woman. I *like* women. I'm married to one. The bench'll smell better with a little perfume on it. At first, I wasn't too happy about *your* appointment, y'know. The way you handled some of your cases in private practice—

C.J. I was young.

DAN. But Ruth Loomis! Did you read the piece she wrote in the Hastings Law Review about school bussing—?

C.J. I read it.

DAN. Every President I've ever known—and I've known a lot of 'em—hears himself talking into that microphone and he's convinced it's the Sermon on the Mount. All those ad-libs he got from his speech-writers are headed straight into Bartlett's Quotations. He *thinks*. But it's the same damn thing that happens when he's taking off in that helicopter: just blowing manure off the White House lawn! (*Sighs.*) You know what's left after a President is put to pasture? You. Me. Ruth Loomis! (*The telephone rings. Dan stretches out on the couch again. But it is not easy for the C.J. to ignore the ringing.*)

C.J. How can you let it just ring? (*Another ring.*)

DAN. A telephone has no constitutional right to be answered. (*Another ring.*) Snow Versus Ma Bell. (*It rings again. The C.J. fidgets.*) Don't pay any attention to it. It'll go away. (*The phone stops. Dan grins.*) See?

C.J. Dan, what'm I going to say to the press?

DAN. *You're* not guilty. Why say anything?

C.J. (*Reassuring himself.*) I can't say anything. It would be improper. I might influence the Senate vote.

DAN. God forbid. (*A pause.*)

C.J. I hear she plays a great game of tennis.

DAN. Hitler played the harmonica. (*Mason appears in the doorway, hesitates.*)

C.J. She might not be so bad. She's young. We can use some young blood around here. And she isn't stupid. It's the dumb people of the world who drive me up the wall. You never know which way they're gonna jump.

MASON. (*Pale, to Dan.*) Is it true . . . ? (*No answer.*) Jack Anderson is on the phone. (*Again no answer. Turning to the C.J.*) Would either one of you care to say anything to him . . . ?

DAN. (*Clears his throat.*) Yeah. Ask him where I'm spending my vacation next year. *I* don't know, but *he* probably does.

MASON. (*Faint smile.*) I'll just tell him neither one of you is available for comment. (*Mason goes out. The C.J. is lost in thought. Dan gets up, paces.*)

DAN. Y'know, this whole thing could've been avoided if Stanley hadn't gone and died. Dying isn't something you oughta do on the spur of the moment. If a Justice kicks off at the wrong time, he can louse up civilization for fifty years! (*But the C.J. has been lost in thought.*)

C.J. How does Jack Anderson find out what happens in the Oval Office so fast . . . ?

DAN. Simple. He's got a friend in the Soviet Embassy.

C.J. Dan, I think I forgot to have lunch. Wanta join me?

DAN. (*Shrugs.*) Why not? Maybe "lunch" is too strong a word for cottage cheese. (*They start out. The C.J. stops.*)

C.J. Only one thing, Dan. Please talk to me before you make your resignation public.

DAN. (*Incredulous.*) Resignation! Who the hell is going to resign? You think I'd leave you here alone to get sprayed down by the Lysol Lady of Orange County??? And if that holy junta over at the White House would pick her to replace Stanley Moorehead, who in God's name do you think they'd send up to take *my* seat? Shirley Temple? (*Dan and the C.J. go out. Black. Crack of gavel in a Senate Hearing Room. The unseen Senators are heard over loudspeakers.*)

CHAIRMAN. Judge Loomis, I'm sorry these proceedings are taking so much time. But we're breaking ground here, setting precedent. And I trust the committee's questions aren't embarrassing to you. (*The lights come up on the very lip of the thrust. In the dark, a table and witness chair come into place. Ruth is going through the interrogation with a battery of microphones in front of her.*)

RUTH. (*Repressing a smile.*) I don't embarrass easily, Senator. (*Judge Loomis wears a smartly-tailored suit. She is tense, even a little frightened, but conceals it brilliantly. She listens with keen intelligence.*)

ANOTHER SENATOR. Judge Loomis, about your interests and equities. Would they influence your decisions on the High Court?

RUTH. The financial statement in front of you is complete, Senator. When I was appointed to the 9th Circuit, I sold or gave away anything that might possibly raise a question of conflict of interest.

SOUTHERN SENATOR. But you were still married to a very active and successful corporation lawyer.

RUTH. Yes. I—uh, (*With a faint smile.*) I didn't want to sell him. Or give him away.

HOSTILE SENATOR. According to this FBI report, you and your husband were partners in the law firm of Loomis and Loomis. And I believe your husband represented the respondent in the case of California versus Coastline Oil.

RUTH. May I respectfully remind you, Senator, that when the 9th Circuit heard the Coastline appeal, I disqualified myself. Is it necessary to keep bringing up my husband? After his death, I had no connection whatsoever with the firm. Are you challenging me for the opinions of my late husband?

CHAIRMAN. No, Judge Loomis, we're taking a measure of your own opinions.

HOSTILE SENATOR. Which have sometimes been extreme. In fact, you have been characterized as a "hanging judge."

RUTH. (*A beat.*) In Constitutional matters, I suppose I am.

HOSTILE SENATOR. (*Pouncing.*) But who gets hung??? Which is more sacred to you? Bodies created by lawyers—corporations? Or bodies created by God—men?

CHAIRMAN. (*An amplified whisper.*) And women.

RUTH. I think the LAW is sacred. It is made by men for men, and that includes women and children, governments, corporations, presidents, senators—even Justices of the Supreme Court.

CHAIRMAN. (*Clears his throat.*) Quite frankly, do you feel your decisions on the High Court might be influenced by the fact that—well, you're a woman?

RUTH. I certainly hope so. Aren't a man's decisions influenced by the fact that he's a man? For two centuries, the Court has expressed men's opinions. Perhaps it's time for the majority of the population to have one voice in nine in the rulings of the Supreme Court. (*A rustle of reactions, mumbled conference among the Senators.*)

SOUTHERN SENATOR. Just one minute, Judge Loomis. Are you implyin' that male justice is somehow *per*verted—?

RUTH. "*Per*verted?"

SOUTHERN SENATOR. That may be the wrong word—distorted, prejudiced—because it has been administered by the masculine gender?

RUTH. Oh, I don't think justice has gender. And it's certainly not exclusively male. Shakespeare's most famous lawyer is a woman. The statue of Justice, holding the balance scales, is a woman. Unfortunately, she's blindfolded.

CHAIRMAN. If you are confirmed by this committee, and the full body of the Senate, I guess we'll be taking the blindfold *off* the lady. (*Scattered laughter at this flicker of senatorial wit.*)

ANOTHER SENATOR. Having a lady on the Supreme Court—

RUTH. Excuse me, why do you keep thinking of me as a "Lady"? Haven't we outgrown those fears about the periodic instability of the female of the species? Eggs are not the seeds of insanity. A woman *can* ovulate and think at the same time.

CHAIRMAN. (*Squirming.*) We're . . . striving to be objective—

RUTH. I'm a woman. An "ex-girl." What has sex got to do with being a judge? Somebody with the capacity to bear children is *gifted*, not *crippled*. A uterus is like absolute pitch: some people have it, some don't.

SOUTHERN SENATOR. According to this fact sheet, uhhh, Judge Loomis has never had any children.

RUTH. Does the Constitution say a Supreme Court Justice has to be a mother?

CHAIRMAN. (*Aside.*) I think I'd drop that line of questioning, George. (*To the witness.*) Judge Loomis, this committee is cognizant of your notable career on the Federal bench—and it has not been our intention to probe into your personal life . . .

RUTH. Why not? My entire life is public. (*A pause—then, with almost unwilling candor.*) The FBI is wrong in reporting to you that I have no children. I've had hundreds. We're the parents of our ideas, aren't we? And so my children, my decisions, my legal opinions are the result of conception, and gestation, and the delivery is sometimes painful. You may not like my children, you may think they're ugly. But by God, your ideas and mine have equal rights to live together—to grow, to change, even to die. (*She looks from face to face of the unseen committee.*)

CHAIRMAN. If there are no further questions, the committee will consider in executive session what it will recommend to the full body of the Senate. Thank you, Judge Loomis, for your co-operation.

RUTH. Thank you, Mr. Chairman, Gentlemen. (*Ruth rises. She wonders: has she been too cocky? Has she booted it? She moves off. Gavel. Murmur of voices as the committee disbands. The lights fade. Dust covers are removed in the chambers Left. A Custodian places a large vase of red roses on the desk. Lights dim, except for a special which holds on the roses as: Lights rise in the Downstage area. It is the robing ceremony, as in the first scene. An Attendant wheels on the ornate coffee service. The Justices stream on from right; Harold helps the C.J. into his robes, Waldo helps Josiah. The air is charged with a kind of wary anticipation.*)

JOSIAH. Well, where is she?

C.J. Maybe we should sound the warning buzzer sooner. I suppose she has some things to do that we don't. After all, I don't have to do anything with my hair . . . (*He runs his hand across his bald head. Dan saunters in, robe over his arm.*)

AMBROSE. You're late, Dan.

DAN. Not as late as I intended to be.

CAREY. (*Pontifically.*) This is an historic occasion . . . !

DAN. (*Drily, pulling on his robes.*) Like the Jesuits going co-ed! (*Marshal appears.*)

MARSHAL. Nine-fifty-eight, gentlemen. (*Corrects himself.*) Ladies and gentleman. (*Coughs, embarrassed.*) I mean, *lady* and— (*Breaks off, confused, and goes off.*)

AMBROSE. You suppose she'll want to hang chintz curtains everywhere? I *hate* chintz.

HAROLD. (*Fidgeting.*) Why am *I* nervous? She's the one who should be nervous. (*C.J. moves Center, gestures for the others to gather closer.*)

C.J. Gentlemen, we should make up our minds right now that things are not going to be any different from the way they have been every two minutes of ten in the history of this court. We've got to think of her exactly as if she were one of the brothers. Oh, Justice Loomis— (*Ruth, robed, comes on from Left. C.J. crosses quickly to greet her.*) Welcome to the Court!

RUTH. Thank you, Mr. Chief Justice. And thank you for those lovely roses. (*C.J. glances toward Dan.*)

DAN. (*Wryly.*) "Exactly like one of the brothers . . . !" When was the last time you sent *me* flowers, C.J.?

MARSHAL. Nine-fifty-nine. (*The Justices come forward to take Ruth's hand. At first she is puzzled by the succession of handshakes. But Dan is not among them.*)

C.J. We shake hands like this every day, every morning, just before we take the bench.

DAN. Like nine boxers coming into the ring. We shake hands before we knock each other out. (*The Justices have formed a line, the C.J. at the head. Ruth, the most junior, takes her place last in line. Dan, normally second, stands aside, watching.*)

MARSHAL'S VOICE. Ten o'clock! (*Crisply, the Justices move off to take their places on the bench. Dan lingers and lets the line file past him. Marshal's Voice echoes through the marble courtroom.*) The Honorable, the Chief Justice and the Associate Justices of the Supreme Court of the United States! (*Ruth comes face to face with Dan. They look at each other with a full awareness of the gulf between them. Cryptic smiles cross each face: boy, are these two going to have a donnybrook! Slowly Dan extends his hand. Slowly she takes it.*) Oyez! Oyez! Oyez! All persons having business before the Honorable, the Supreme Court of the United States are admonished to draw near and give their attention . . . (*It seems for an instant that Dan intends gallantly to let the lady go first. No way! Just as she starts to move, he steps brusquely in front of her. They exit.*) . . . for the Court is now sitting. God save the United States and this Honorable Court. (*Black. Lights come up on Dan's chambers. Mason comes in with a pile of books. Tentatively, he makes room for them in the center of Dan's sacred mess. Then, with a glance back to make sure he's alone, Mason sits in Dan's chair, flicks on his dictating machine to listen.*)

DAN'S VOICE. (*On tape.*) Preliminary notes: Mahoney versus Nebraska. If this court is the keeper-of-the-conscience of this country, we can't pretend the First Amendment was never written. Doesn't it bind us to protect the right of free expression— (*Dan comes in, unnoticed by Mason. Both men listen.*) —even when we find ourselves defending acts which revolt us, repel us, disgust us, make us vomit?

DAN. Mason. (*Startled, Mason comes to his feet, stopping the machine.*) Make a note. Change the word "vomit" to "retch."

MASON. You're early, sir.

DAN. The Brethren went down to the screening room. The Brethren—and one Cistern. (*Dan surveys his desk narrowly. Dan speaks accusingly.*) Mason, did you rearrange my desk?????

MASON. Sir, your mess is intact. I just shifted everything about eight inches east. To make room for all the stuff you wanted on obscenity. (*Grins.*) I didn't have to mark the cases. The books just *fall open* to 'em!

DAN. Thanks, Mason. (*Dan sinks into his chair, begins leafing through one of the books. The C.J. enters.*)

C.J. Hey, Dan—don't you want to come down to the projection room?

DAN. What for?

C.J. Mahoney versus Nebraska. (*With a grin of anticipation.*) This film's called "The Naked Nymphomaniac." Even *you* might learn something.

DAN. (*Waving him away.*) Enjoy yourself.

C.J. (*Hesitates, a little ill-at-ease.*) Dan, I wanted you around because—well, this is the first porno screening we've had since—uh—well, it's sort of like having a nun at a stag party. (*The C.J. goes off. Dan settles down to work at his desk and a glow of light holds on him throughout the ensuing action. The Justices, not robed, begin to gather in a projection room which has been moved on the forestage. They take seats—but when Ruth comes in, they immediately come to their feet. She glances around the room with an expression which seems to say: "Who do you think I am, Queen Victoria?" Ruth and the Justices sit. The C.J. comes in, signals for the projectionist to start the film. Pretentious throb of music as the light flickers on an unseen screen.*)

MOVIE NARRATOR. (*With a clinical austerity.*) The Naked Nymphomaniac. Case history of Lois, a lonely girl whipped by storms of passion she couldn't understand. (*The Justices, their faces lit by the wavering light from the screen, attempt a judicial coolness. But their eyes cannot help wandering to the lone lady in their midst. Ruth stiffens. The air is tense. The C.J. shoots a sidelong glance at her, muttering something like "Oh, Jesus" under his breath. The music mounts.*) What began as a carefree game for Lois became all-consuming desire. To Lois, men are not people, not faces, voices, minds. They are bodies. Bare flesh. (*The music throbs. Ruth glances around.*)

RUTH. Why isn't Mr. Justice Snow here?

QUINCY. He never comes to these showings.

MOVIE NARRATOR. Let's look at the other sex as Lois sees them.

JOSIAH. (*Re-crosses his legs.*) Oh, let's not. (*Ruth glances away from the screen—then forces herself to watch, as a legal duty.*)

LOIS' VOICE. (*Through speaker.*) Oh, that's remarkable! Fantastic—! Is it all for me??? (*The Justices lean forward slightly. Ruth is grim and rigid. The musical scoring from the loudspeakers suggests the rhythm of a mounting orgasm. There are female exclamations of mixed pain and ecstasy.*)

HAROLD. C.J.—

LOIS' VOICE. (*Through speaker.*) Oh, it's so—so—oh! Oh—oh—ohhhhhhh—!

HAROLD. (*Clearing his throat.*) Chief—

C.J. Yes, Harold—?

HAROLD. Haven't we seen enough? I mean—is there any point in running it all the way to the abysmal end—?

MOVIE NARRATOR. Will Lois ever be cured?

JOSIAH. I don't know about Lois, but *I'm* cured.

C.J. Projectionist, will you hold the film, please? (*The film grinds to a stop, lights come up in the projection room.*) Now does anyone object if we don't run the rest of this masterpiece? (*Justices concur: "I certainly don't." "Neither do I." "Prurient slop!"*)

RUTH. I do. *I* object. I think you're stopping the film because you're embarrassed that there's a woman in the room.

CAREY. That's not why I'm uncomfortable.

HALLORAN. (*Standing.*) Well, I think Justice Loomis has a point—

RUTH. If at any time this court delimits the review of anything because you think *I* might be offended, well, that simply defeats our whole purpose here, doesn't it?

C.J. (*Calling.*) Projectionist, you may—

HAROLD. (*Standing, addressing the others.*) C.J.—just a moment, please. Oh, I suppose, Madam Justice Loomis, to be completely frank with you—I feel—I *do* feel some embarrassment that you have to sit here and watch that thing—

RUTH. Well, I *don't* have to. Justice Snow doesn't feel he has to. I do have a sense of responsibility—

C.J. I understand how Harold feels. I wouldn't want to sit through this with my wife. Or arrange a special showing for Mother's Day.

RUTH. But your wife and your mother have not been appointed to this court.

C.J. Not yet.

HAROLD. *Time* is the point, gentlemen—and Madam Justice. And I submit that we have a responsibility not to *waste* it! (*Voices of affirmation: "Hear, hear."*) We don't have to see every frame of this film any more than we have to scrutinize every fingerprint in a criminal case that comes up to us on cert. We'd never get anything done.

RUTH. Then may I suggest that the Chief Justice ask one of us to see the entire film? To find out if there's a shred of "redeeming social or artistic value."

C.J. I don't think that'll be necessary. The brief contends that the narration makes the whole thing educational. (*Looking around.*) Does anyone here need any *more* "education"? (*Negative reactions from the Justices.*)

CAREY. I've graduated.

C.J. As for the visual component, I gather you just see a lot more of Lois' clients. And a lot more of Lois.

THOMPSON. (*Getting up.*) I don't know how much more of Lois they can show us. (*Relieved laughter. The Justices are dispersing.*)

C.J. I guess the matinee is over. (*The Justices are moving off in clusters. The C.J. lingers to speak to Ruth.*) I do apologize, Madam Justice.

RUTH. You do? Why?

C.J. Well, some of our cases get a little raunchy.

RUTH. The lower court wasn't exactly the Sistine Chapel. (*Troubled.*) But something is very wrong here. You're all so polite to me. I'm not talking too much, am I?

C.J. Oh, no, no, no—we want you to speak up, speak right out, any time you feel like it. Raise hell, if you want to.

RUTH. (*Faint smile.*) You may be sorry you said that.

C.J. I howl in protest at regular intervals—full moon, usually.

RUTH. I break pencils. In private. When I'm frustrated.

C.J. Is it satisfying?

RUTH. Not very. There's only one real cure for frustration: getting your own way.

C.J. Which doesn't often happen on this court.

RUTH. With one exception.

C.J. Oh?

RUTH. Mr. Justice Snow does pretty much as he pleases. How can he pass judgment on something without judging it at all? (*Pointing to the screen.*) Eight Justices thought seeing that film was relevant to reaching a decision.

C.J. Some of it, anyhow.

RUTH. But if he shuts his eyes and plugs up his ears, does he have the right to cast a vote on what he's not seen nor heard? Hasn't he virtually disqualified himself on Mahoney?

C.J. (*After a pause.*) Would you care to suggest that to Justice Snow?

RUTH. I don't think that *is* one of my privileges. Or responsibilities. (*Askance.*) Isn't it yours? (*The C.J. opens his mouth, but doesn't say anything. He starts off.*) And Mr. Chief Justice, I'd like to examine the rest of this, if you don't mind. So I'll know what I'm talking about.

C.J. (*Calling.*) Projectionist, will you continue the film, please?

RUTH. Thank you.

C.J. You're welcome. (*Ruth sits to watch grimly. The lights in the projection room dip, the flickering from the screen resumes, along with the throbbing music. The C.J. can't take it. He goes off. As Ruth watches the motion picture screen, lights bump up on simultaneous action in Dan's chambers. Music and lights dim the screening room as Dan sorts his notes, then picks up a dictating microphone.*)

DAN. (*Dictating.*) Notes to myself. Type this up triple-space, Miss Birnbaum, with enough room for me to doodle over it. Mahoney versus Nebraska. Mahoney sought reversal of court-order which banned showing of "The Naked Nymphomaniac" at the Omaha Art Theatre. (*Checking his notes.*) Correction—make that Omaha Fine Arts Theatre. (*In the screening room, the duty-bound Ruth watches the screen. The sound-track is a diminuendo of ecstasy. In his chambers, Dan leans back, stares at the ceiling, rattles off cases and dates with amazingly total recall.*) Relevant cases: Green, 1931, 286 U.S., 29 at 32, footnote 2. U.S. vee Alberson, 1954. That's in Volume 348 U.S., maybe 349. (*The C.J. comes to Dan's door, a little gingerly.*) Pine Valley Elks Club Versus Ronald Reagan et al. That's in 419 U.S., 17 at 12— (*Noting the C.J., affably.*) Oh, hi, C.J. (*Putting down the microphone.*) Enjoy the movie? (*Lights have faded totally on projection room. Ruth clears, returning to her chambers.*)

C.J. Sure, sure. But—well, something unexpected happened.

DAN. To the "Naked Nymphomaniac"? What the hell could *that* be?

C.J. A question came up. Or, more accurately, a suggestion was made.

DAN. Yes?

C.J. Our newest member . . .

DAN. Yes?

C.J. Wondered . . .

DAN. Yes?

C.J. What it amounts to—should attendance be obligatory at these obscenity screenings?

DAN. Who wasn't there? Besides me?

C.J. The house was packed.

DAN. Then what's her beef?

C.J. (*Lamely.*) Well, the lady wonders if a Justice who hasn't seen any part of the film hasn't, in effect— (*Dan's eyes narrow. He is appalled. A towering rage is building.*)

DAN. She wants me to disqualify myself because I won't go down there and sit through that pile of crap?

C.J. Well . . .

DAN. Is a Justice of the Supreme Court expected to pass on this stuff like a slaughter-house inspector? Do I have to stamp it: "U.S. Prime Grade-A crap?" What if it *is* crap? That's not the point. Crap's got a right to be crap.

C.J. Drop the legal language, Dan.

DAN. Are you, as Chief Justice, suggesting that I disqualify myself from voting on Mahoney?

C.J. I'm merely suggesting that it's been suggested. (*Starting to leave.*) I shouldn't have said anything. (*Dan gets up, fuming.*)

DAN. For Christ's sake, C.J.! Maybe she'd like to have us rewrite the Constitution—and certain suspect parts of the Bible! (*Dan starts out.*)

C.J. Where're you going?

DAN. Where do you think I'm going? I've got a present for Madam Jus-tess. (*Stops, turns back.*) *Not* roses. I'm gonna give her a piece of my mind—which *I* can spare and she sure-as-hell can use!

C.J. She's got another complaint.

DAN. Yeah?

C.J. She thinks we're being too polite to her.

DAN. (*Narrowing his eyes.*) Oh, I'll help her *reverse that* opinion! (*Dan storms out.*

The C.J. shrugs, shakes his head, goes off. The lights dip slightly on Dan's area and rise on Ruth's chambers. She is scowling over a brief. Dan has crossed, unseen, upstage toward Ruth's office. Intercom buzzer sounds on Ruth's desk.)

RUTH. (*Into intercom.*) Yes?

MALE VOICE. (*Through intercom.*) Madame Justice . . . Mr. Justice Snow would like to see you.

RUTH. He would? When?

MALE VOICE. He's here.

RUTH. (*Somewhat startled.*) Oh? (*Neatness is a conditioned response for her. She stuffs the briefs into a drawer, slams it shut. Into intercom.*) Ask Mr. Justice Snow to come in, Mr. Robinson. (*Almost involuntarily, her hand goes to her head, straightening her hair. Dan saunters into the room. The coals of his anger have been banked, but the heat is probably heightened. He has sublimated his outrage into an icy politesse. He is so deferential that his manner is suspect. Ruth rises behind her desk.*)

DAN. Oh, no, no, no—please, please—! Don't get up!

RUTH. You'd stand, Mr. Justice, if I came to call on *you* in chambers . . . (*Dan weighs this for a moment.*)

DAN. Don't be too sure.

RUTH. I think you would. And I'm an egalitarian.

DAN. An egalitarian, I'm so glad to hear it. (*He's tried to keep the sarcasm out of his voice—but not very hard.*) I can't tell you how grateful I am to you for seeing me like this—on no notice whatsoever . . .

RUTH. It's my honor.

DAN. Is it? Well, I suppose it is. Let's relax. Do you feel like relaxing . . . ? (*She is very suspicious. They sit, simultaneously and very slowly, not taking their eyes off each other. Ruth is behind the desk, Dan in a leather chair across from her. He scans the expanse of her completely bare desk-top with mock-admiration.*) Say, that's quite a desk! And so *neat*! Do aircraft land here frequently? (*Both smile faintly at this—with the warmth of two adversaries examining the dueling pistols.*)

RUTH. What is it you wanted to see me about?

DAN. Nothing earth-shaking. (*Jerking his head toward the outer office.*) By George, I was a little startled to see that you have a male law clerk out there. I'm a little disappointed, actually.

RUTH. Mr. Robinson? He's not my law clerk. He's my secretary. (*This jars Dan. But it barely shows.*)

DAN. Well, well, well! What a generous gesture—letting men into a field that has previously been dominated by the other sex.

RUTH. (*With a dry smile.*) I'm glad to hear you're in favor of Men's Lib. My law clerk won't get here until next week. She's closing up my office in Santa Ana.

DAN. Oh, she is. I guess that's going to dam up the seemingly endless river of clerks pouring out of Harvard Law School.

RUTH. *She's* from Harvard.

DAN. Oh, she is. (*If Dan intended to pitch this ball game, the count is now 3–0 against him. He changes pace.*) Madame Justess, I hope you aren't finding our national capitol too dull, after the grandeur of Disneyland.

RUTH. You don't think much of California, do you?

DAN. I try not to think of it at all. Poor California, sitting out there with all the gold out of its teeth, gnawing at the unpacific Pacific.

RUTH. Why don't you try climbing some of our mountains?

DAN. Oh, I have, I have. I admire your mountains. It's your valleys that make me nervous. (*Getting down to business.*) Now, Madame Justess, you may have more recent and direct knowledge of certain areas of judicial consideration than *I* have . . .

RUTH. (*Demurely acid.*) I find that hard to believe. Everybody in the legal profession knows about your astonishing faculty for total recall. And how remarkable it is to retain that talent for so many, many, *many* years. (*Dan slumps slightly. He just walked a man to first—and it's a woman!*)

DAN. (*Clears his throat.*) I—I wanted your opinion on a point of law about that great American art form, the motion picture. I was wondering if, by any chance, you'd seen a film called— (*Breaks off.*) I suppose some men would be embarrassed to say the title out loud in mixed company.

RUTH. "The Naked Nymphomaniac."

DAN. That's the one. Now, you probably didn't even notice I wasn't there.

RUTH. I noticed.

DAN. Oh, you did? Well, I wanted to ask you—as an expert witness, you might say—if you found anything—well—*unpleasant* in the picture . . . ? Perhaps even a trifle distasteful . . . ?

RUTH. (*Thin-lipped.*) "The Naked Nymphomaniac" is a total offense against the public sensibility. (*Dan leans back in the chair.*)

DAN. My, my, my, my, my, my! As bad as that! Now, I wonder if you can put your finger on exactly what it was that offended you. Let's start at the beginning. Was it the title? Some particular *word* in the title? "Naked?" Is that it? What if they'd called it "The FULLY-CLOTHED Nymphomaniac"? Or maybe you were bothered by that *other* word: (*Tasting it.*) "Nym-pho-ma-ni-ac!" Suppose they'd called it "The Naked Methodist"? Or "The Naked Daughter of the American Revolution"? Perhaps the High Court should strike down *both* words! (*Stands.*) I personally would be tempted to pay money at a box-office to see something called: "The CENSORED!"

RUTH. Are you finished?

DAN. Madam Jus-*tess*, I am a long way from being "finished." But I am willing to pause briefly in case there's something you'd like to say.

RUTH. Let me ask you something. Would you call a female governor a "governess"? Is a woman composer a "composer-*ess*"? No, and her sex is entirely beside the point. And a justice of the Supreme Court is a Justice, not "Madam Jus-*tess*"! (*Dan takes it. The bases are loaded.*) Now. *I* still happen to believe there are some *absolutes* in this society.

DAN. (*Quizzically.*) "Absolutes . . . ?"

RUTH. Standards. To which the wise and honest may repair.

DAN. If there *are* absolute answers—

RUTH. (*Trying to interrupt.*) I didn't say "answers"—

DAN. Then you and I would be out of work. Why have a Supreme Court?

RUTH. To decide which standards apply! How else can government protect its citizens? Or should we just shut our eyes and permit anything! Violence in the streets. Kids on drugs. Graffiti on the marble. Schools falling apart—

DAN. Madam—

RUTH. I'm not finished. In the past we didn't coddle criminals—with plea-bargaining, suspended sentences, quick paroles. We *locked up* the lawbreakers! Including the smut-merchants! And we didn't hand the whole country an all-day sucker made out of filth and pornography!

DAN. Oh, the past—the *old* days. Is that your solution for the future?

RUTH. I think there is some wisdom in relating what will be to what *was*.

DAN. I look at it the other way around. Perhaps that's the difference between a conservative and a—

RUTH. (*Interrupting.*) A radical? I'm a radical. Latin. Radix! Root! I believe in beginnings, in primary causes, in sources. And, as a radical, I do not want to see this country pulled up by the roots. (*Dan looks at Ruth with unwilling admiration: the girl's no slouch—she's a worthy adversary!*)

DAN. (*Quieter.*) You think we've lost something?

RUTH. I certainly do!

DAN. May be. Maybe we've had too much progress. Suppose we move this whole Court back where it was—in the basement of the Capitol. "DOWN ONE FLIGHT—OPINIONS AT BARGAIN PRICES!" Back then the original Justices all lived in the same boarding house. At first, a couple of 'em had to share the same bed! Would that be all right with you, Madam . . . Justice? Now that we've all declared ourselves neuter, why not bring back the "good old days"?

RUTH. When I was appointed, I knew that you and I would disagree. But I did not expect a Justice of this High Tribunal to talk and act like a burlesque comic.

DAN. What's wrong with burlesque comics?

RUTH. I happen to think of the Supreme Court as the American Olympus.

DAN. And we're all *gods* sitting up here? Holy Christ, I've spent thirty-four years on this Court trying *not* to be a god, trying *not* to make this place some unscalable mountain-top—high above what's happening! I've been trying to bring this Court DOWN from the mountain.

RUTH. And on your vacations, you like to climb mountains. Why do you suppose you do that?

DAN. For the view!

RUTH. But you wouldn't look at "The Naked Nymphomaniac."

DAN. What I see from a mountain-top isn't going to be erased because I looked at it. When I stare out across the Owens Valley from Whitney Portal, I'm not passing judgment on it. I'm *enjoying* it. And if a buzzard, floating on the hot winds out of Death Valley, happens to mar the view, I'm not going to obliterate the landscape. Wipe it off the map.

RUTH. Now, Justice Snow. Is it your impression that the First Amendment denies this Court the right to rule on what may be decent or indecent?

DAN. I couldn't have put it better. I think it's unconstitutional for me to set myself up as a censor.

RUTH. Refusing to look at something is censorship.

DAN. Hell, I don't look at television, but that doesn't make it illegal.

RUTH. The content is irrelevant?

DAN. Constitutionally, yes.

RUTH. You think the First Amendment justifies what Mahoney did?

DAN. It's theatrical self-expression.

RUTH. (*Drily.*) So's vomiting into a fan.

DAN. Did Mahoney put a gun to anybody's head, tell 'em you've gotta buy a ticket to my masterpiece or I'll blow your brains out? *That* might be illegal.

RUTH. You set *no* limits on freedom of speech?

DAN. None.

RUTH. You permit any obscenity, any outrage . . . ?

DAN. Censorship is an outrage!

RUTH. How about a training film for terrorists? A free lecture: "How to Make a Nuclear Bomb in Your Basement!" Do you condone inciting to violence?

DAN. Of course not—

RUTH. How about inciting to *decadence?*

DAN. Define decay!

RUTH. That's what we're here for.

DAN. Not me.

RUTH. We'd better try. If the rule of law means anything.

DAN. Watch out! You can't turn law into a straitjacket. I think the Law's gotta be a suit of clothes a man can wear. It's got to fit easy, be comfortable. Law shouldn't strap a man in at the throat, or the brain, or the crotch!

RUTH. That's vivid. You know what you're doing? You're making Mahoney more important than the law.

DAN. He *is* more important than the law.

RUTH. Our job on this Court is to extract broad legal principles—

DAN. And what about the individual?

RUTH. He's covered in the Lower Courts.

DAN. *Buried*, more likely. Under your "broad legal principles!"

RUTH. Mahoney had his day in court—

DAN. What do you mean, "had"? He's still on trial! The case is; but the man's disappeared!

RUTH. This court isn't supposed to try men—we put their trials on trial.

DAN. That's it, lady. We're constantly examining the witness who isn't there. Cold records. Cold briefs. It's a rehash, a lot of legal leftovers. Where's the man? Where's the pain? We've got to touch flesh!

RUTH. We've got to be dispassionate.

DAN. Do we? I've got a feeling you left your feelings back in Santa Ana. And some faraway day, after you get off this truck about "broad legal principles" and begin thinking about human beings, you *might* make a damn good Justice. Until then, I've got my doubts.

RUTH. (*With perfumed sarcasm.*) You're just being sweet to me because I'm a woman.

DAN. I'm being "dispassionate."

RUTH. Watch out, we might agree on something.

DAN. I doubt it. (*Starts to go, turns.*) May I make a somewhat extra-legal observation? Fighting with you would be a helluva lot simpler if you had a beard! (*Dan goes out. Frustrated, Ruth snaps a pencil in two. But an idea is perking in her head. She gets up, starts out of her chambers. Lights fade on Ruth's chambers, rise on Dan's. Mason is on the phone.*)

MASON. (*Into phone.*) I'm afraid I can't reach him right now, Mrs. Snow. He's in conference. (*Listens.*) No, not in the conference room. He's in chambers with Madam Justice Loomis. (*Pause.*) I'll tell him as soon as he gets in. Goodbye. (*He hangs up just as Dan enters, bristling like a baited bear.*) Mrs. Snow just called. . . .

DAN. Call her back. Tell her I can't talk to her.

MASON. (*A little baffled by Dan's vehemence.*) Yes, sir. And—

DAN. (*Throwing himself angrily on his couch.*) I don't want to talk to *any*body. Hold all the calls. I don't want to see anybody, I don't want any interruptions. None! (*He stares fiercely at the ceiling.*) I've got to work! I have got to concentrate!

MASON. Yes, sir— (*Ruth has crossed upstage and now appears at the entrance to Dan's sanctum.*) He says he doesn't want to be—

RUTH. (*Bland and grand.*) Oh, I wouldn't *dream* of disturbing Mr. Justice Snow. I am looking for James G. Mahoney . . . (*Ruth seems to be seeing Dan for the first time.*) Oh!—there you are, Mr. Mahoney!

DAN. (*Propping himself up on one elbow.*) Huh . . . ?

RUTH. A respected colleague of mine feels I should get to know you—*and* your "artistic achievements." Now what was the expression he used? Oh, yes—"touch flesh!" (*Dan and Mason exchange glances.*) Would you care to take the witness stand, Mr. Mahoney? (*Nostrils twitching with anticipation, Dan gets up slowly, keeping his eyes fixed on Ruth. Mason is glued in the doorway, fascinated.*)

DAN. (*Sitting.*) Are you going to swear me in?

RUTH. Are you going to lie to me?

DAN. (*Pause.*) Maybe you'd better swear me in. (*Raises his hand.*) I, James G. Mahoney, do solemnly swear the testimony I am about to give will be the truth, the whole truth and nothing but the truth. So help me Loomis. (*Dan settles back into the "witness chair."*)

RUTH. Let's get right to the point, Mahoney. Are you aware that you broke a law?

DAN. (*As Mahoney—innocently.*) No, ma'am. (*He crosses his legs.*)

RUTH. Oh? You didn't realize that the State of Nebraska has a statute prohibiting pornography?

DAN. Doesn't the Constitution apply to people in Nebraska? Isn't the First Amendment an umbrella to keep everybody from getting wet? Or is there a *hole* in it over Omaha?

RUTH. Then how do you think you got in all this trouble?

DAN. I can't understand it, ma'am. I was just exercising my rights as an individual U.S. Citizen.

RUTH. There happen to be a few *other* people in Nebraska who want to be protected from people like you. So they passed a law.

DAN. And it's cock-eyed. That law's *against* the law. I got rights under the Constitution—

RUTH. You certainly have, Mr. Mahoney! You're a lucky man! But do your rights give you the *license* to stomp over the rights of everybody else???

DAN. (*Re-crossing his legs, thoroughly Mahoney.*) Look, lady, I'm a businessman. And I don't see where the government's got any business telling me how to run my business.

RUTH. I'm relieved. For awhile there I thought you might be thinking of yourself as an *artist.* I do recall the mention of the word "Art" somewhere in your brief. . . . Tell me. Do you honestly believe "The Naked Nymphomaniac" is *art*?

DAN. (*Shrugs.*) Sure. Why not? Who's to say it isn't? What's "Art," anyway? Artists don't even know—let alone lawyers.

RUTH. Well, I suppose that's what we have critics for . . .

DAN. I don't think *every*body should see my picture. Probably some people shouldn't see it.

RUTH. Oh? Who?

DAN. Kids. Too educational.

RUTH. Oh, education! Is that why you made this picture, Mr. Mahoney? Well— (*She shoves some of his books aside so she can sit on the edge of his desk. Dan is irked.*) Exactly what was your motivation for filming "The Naked Nymphomaniac"? (*Dan looks front. Should he tell her the unvarnished truth?*)

DAN. Money. (*Extending his hands, with unabashed frankness.*) You can't have much pursuit of happiness in this country unless you pursue a little money. Anything unconstitutional about that?

RUTH. Does the Constitution give you the right to do *any*thing for money?

DAN. Does it give *you* the right to shove me into bankruptcy??

RUTH. My colleague on this bench, Mr. Justice Snow, feels very strongly about profit-pursuing companies which pollute the air.

DAN. He's absolutely right. Fine man, Justice Snow!

RUTH. Doesn't your film pollute the minds and morals of people who see it?

DAN. Air's different. You've *got* to breathe. You don't *have* to go to the movies.

RUTH. In the trade, your picture is called an "exploitation" film, isn't it?

DAN. And you're trying to keep me from exploiting it.

RUTH. Aren't you exploiting women? The act of love? The innocence of young people?

DAN. Who'm I hurting? Has anybody died from seeing "The Naked Nymphomaniac"?

RUTH. Not bodily harm, perhaps. But what about injury to the spirit? Doesn't your celluloid poison attack all human dignity? And decency? And beauty?

DAN. (*Wounded.*) I don't think you like my picture. Okay. That's your right. Some people don't like Shredded Wheat. Matter of taste.

RUTH. Or lack of it. Have you been to New York City lately?

DAN. (*Blithely.*) Oh, is it still there?

RUTH. I used to go to Times Square and down 44th, 45th Streets; it was a blaze of culture. Unforgettable music. Powerful plays. Today, right around the corner on Eighth Avenue your movie is probably playing. Alongside a lot of other nudity, pornography and filth.

DAN. Careful, lady—watch out! Scratch me, put me out of business—and who else gets scratched? You can use the same end of the eraser to wipe out that unforgettable music and those powerful plays!

RUTH. You're sharp, Mahoney—you can pull every sleeve inside-out, can't you! (*Incisively.*) You demand the liberty to dirty up *my* liberty—my right of security against the profiteering, two-legged cockroaches of this world. My right to live in a sweet and decent society, and not some kind of a *sewer*! My right to— (*The C.J. comes in engrossed in the pages in his hand.*)

C.J. Dan, I'd like to have your opinion on this, uh— (*He pulls up short, baffled by what's going on. He glances at Mason, then sinks into the chair behind Dan's desk and listens.*)

RUTH. I've learned from Mr. Justice Daniel Snow that the legal process must reach the *man*, you see? Must translate him from paper into blood. Oh, I'm glad I met you, Mahoney. You've made me see how wrong it is to think the First Amendment is a piece of bubble-gum you can pull out until it's lost all it's stretch! (*Dan starts to say something, but she charges on.*) And if you try to shove that same stick of gum into everybody's mouth, all the flavor gets chewed out, and it won't stick to anything! Not even the bottom of a folding seat in the Omaha Fine Arts Theatre!

DAN. You think I'm a nut?

RUTH. The word is yours, Mahoney.

DAN. The First Amendment is supposed to protect our nuts, our nonconformists, our anomalies—

RUTH. Opinion! Not binding!

DAN. (*Fiercely.*) Because eccentricity is often the camouflage of genius!

RUTH. (*Lightly.*) You're safe, Mahoney. I've seen your picture. No more questions. You may step down. (*Dan gets up slowly.*)

DAN. Y'know, you make a pretty good trial lawyer. Too bad you had to give it up.

RUTH. You make a very good actor; your characterization of Mahoney is going to be hard to forget! I may always have the feeling there's a pornographic movie producer under your robes.

DAN. It makes me sick to my stomach to defend a principle as noble as the First Amendment on the basis of that can of film you found so offensive. (*The passion is rising in him.*) But by God, as long as I've got tongue and tonsils and the ability to talk, I'll defend everybody's right to speak. And every man's right to be wrong!

RUTH. I yield to you as the authority on *that*, Mr. Justice. (*She smiles rather sweetly, nods to Mason and the C.J. as she passes them and moves out.*)

DAN. She's dangerous. That woman is *dangerous*! We've got to stick together, C.J.; after all, this Court only has eight of us left—against *all* of HER! (*Dan, Mason, the C.J. stare toward the doorway where Ruth has just departed.*)

CURTAIN

ACT TWO

The time is late winter. Lights come up on Ruth's chambers, while Dan's remain in shadow. Ruth and Mason come into her chambers. The tone is easy, but Mason hesitates in the doorway.

MASON. It knocks me out.

RUTH. What does?

MASON. The way you play tennis.

RUTH. I was lucky today.

MASON. You're lucky every time we play. (*She's hung up her coat, starts to prepare tea.*)

RUTH. Come on in, Mason—have a cup of tea. What do you think this is, enemy territory?

MASON. (*Coming in.*) Does anybody ever break through your serve?

RUTH. Not if I can help it. Peppermint or Red Zinger?

MASON. The Red Zinger. (*She drops tea bags into two cups, hands one to Mason and crosses to her desk.*)

RUTH. You know, Dan Snow's done a lot for my tennis game. When I get a high one I can really kill, that isn't *you* on the other side of that net, Mason.

MASON. So that's why they go by me so fast. Where'd you learn to play like that?

RUTH. My husband taught me. In all the years we were married, I only beat him once. What does your good grey Justice do for recreation?

MASON. He climbs.

RUTH. I mean when there isn't a mountain in the neighborhood?

MASON. Well, uh . . . he dissents.

RUTH. (*With a wry expression.*) I'm going to ignore that.

MASON. Of course, there's always a mountain on his desk. Sometimes he works till three or four in the morning.

RUTH. His wife must love that. What's she like?

MASON. She's very pretty. Quiet. I've only met her a couple of times—at protocol things.

RUTH. How is he to work for?

MASON. It isn't work.

RUTH. Ohhhh, you're caught in the spider-web of Dan Snow's charm.

MASON. I think he's a great man.

RUTH. Well, *he* certainly thinks so. How does he feel about our playing tennis together?

MASON. I'm not sure. (*Reluctantly.*) I haven't told him yet. And I don't intend to—until I beat you at least once.

RUTH. And that's not going to happen. I like to win.

MASON. I've noticed.

RUTH. What's the matter? You scared of him?

MASON. Well—

RUTH. How do you stand the temperature changes? Every time I see him, he's either ice-cold or white-hot mad. Is he ever just room temperature?

MASON. He has very strong feelings. The same as you do.

RUTH. You don't think Dan Snow and I are alike?

MASON. No. No, but you *do* have . . . similar differences. You both *care* about things. Nothing is unimportant, nothing. Whether it's making a point on the bench, or on the tennis court.

RUTH. Thursday morning, seven-thirty?

MASON. (*Starting out.*) I'll be there.

RUTH. Oh—Mason . . . (*He stops in the doorway.*) Does he ever talk about me?

MASON. Oh . . . uh— (*Embarrassed.*) All the time.

RUTH. Anything quotable?

MASON. (*Suffering.*) Well, uh—

RUTH. I withdraw the question. Hearsay evidence: inadmissible!

MASON. Thanks. For the Zinger. (*Mason leaves. Lights dip on Ruth's chambers. Lights bump up on Dan's chambers. His desk-top is an antiseptic mesa, unscarred by so much as a paper clip. His cherished "mess" has miraculously evaporated. Dan comes in, hangs up his coat, then looks at the immaculate desk with dismay.*)

DAN. (*Calling off, toward the outer office.*) Miss Birnbaum! (*No answer. Dan presses an intercom alongside the desk.*) Miss Birnbaum, are you there? (*Silence. He presses another button on the intercom.*) Mason! Get on in here! There's been a robbery! (*Pause.*) Mason? (*No answer. He picks up a telephone.*) Get me the Marshal's office. (*He pulls open a drawer. Shocked by the neatness, he slams it shut. Into the phone:*) Marshal, this is Dan Snow. I have an emergency here. Somebody must've broken into my office. Some madwoman cleaning woman! And is my law clerk in the building—Mason Woods? (*Listens, incredulous.*) Going into *whose* chambers . . . ? Well, tell him— (*Mason appears.*) Never mind—he's come home. (*Dan hangs up the phone.*)

MASON. Is there some problem, Mr. Justice?

DAN. You're damned right there's a problem. (*Indicating the sterile-clean desk-top.*) Look at this mess! (*Mason stares at the desk as if it were the carnage at Hiroshima.*) My God, it's as if I'd lost my memory.

MASON. So much work was piling up that—

DAN. Let it pile. We can cut a hole in the ceiling and let it go right through the roof.

MASON. The secretary must have done it.

DAN. Birnbaum? Shoot her.

MASON. I had to get you a substitute. I didn't realize she was tidy.

DAN. Mason, get Birnbaum in here to restore the ruins. And get your tidy substitute another assignment. I suggest Albania.

MASON. Do you want Miss Birnbaum back even if she's sick?

DAN. Mason, Miss Birnbaum was *well* for three weeks in September of 1952. Her sinuses operate in two slightly overlapping six-month cycles. In the fall, the first frost attacks her right nostril. Come spring, her left sinus is open-house for pollen; she's allergic to the goddam cherry blossoms! (*Dan suddenly squints at his law clerk.*) Say, what were you doing with "Madame Jus-tess?" You're not a double-agent, are you?

MASON. We were— (*Clears his throat.*) —playing tennis.

DAN. In her *chambers*?? So *that's* what she does in there!

MASON. At the Tennis Club. We get in a set a couple of mornings a week—before breakfast. She plays very well for a—a Justice of the Supreme Court. (*Dan just looks at him.*) She's got one helluva backhand, sir.

DAN. Yeah, I know. I've seen it work.

MASON. When we found out we were both tennis players—well, I hope you don't mind, sir.

DAN. Hell, no. Go ahead, wear her out. (*The C.J. appears in the doorway.*)

C.J. Dan? Got a minute?

DAN. Sure, come on in. (*Mason nods to the C.J. as they pass in the doorway. The Chief carries a large, ringed notebook. He is jolted by the sterile desk-top.*) C.J., how about a little tennis tomorrow morning?

C.J. A little what?

DAN. Tennis. Exercise. You know— (*He gestures a flamboyant forehand.*) It's a new fad with Supreme Court Justices.

C.J. Oh, you gotta be careful with that kind of thing. Did you realize we had a gym on the top floor? I went up there once—pulled on some of those pulleys, you know, with the weights on 'em? Threw my back out for a week. (*The C.J. puts the ringed binder on Dan's desk.*)

DAN. You're messing up my desk. What's this?

C.J. Dan, I want to ask you a favor. Well, not a favor, really. I just want to share some of my thinking with you before we go into that conference this afternoon.

DAN. Shoot.

C.J. Well, we've got an opening on the calendar.

DAN. That's a novelty.

C.J. That Idaho Penitentiary case was mooted. Took so long everybody died.

DAN. Well, there's American justice for you. It's getting almost as fast as the Post Office.

C.J. That's what I want to talk to you about, Dan. We've got to cut through this backlog.

DAN. (*As he leafs through the book.*) Hey, what's this?

C.J. Abbott versus Omnitech. Again. We just got a supplement to the petition for cert.

DAN. Boy, I admire these guys. They just won't quit, will they?

C.J. I'm going to vote against hearing it.

DAN. What?!

C.J. The votes just aren't there, Dan!

DAN. So?

C.J. Do we have to waste three weeks reviewing a decision that can't possibly be reversed?

DAN. Oh, we pre-judge cases now, do we? Count noses, and if it looks as if the lower court ruling will be sustained, we just don't hear it!

C.J. I'm just trying to be practical. Take Mahoney—

DAN. My dissenting opinion—

C.J. —was brilliant, absolutely brilliant.

DAN. And it's on the record, goddammit!—even if Mahoney did lose 4–5. Someday, when we stop recruiting our judges from the jungles of Orange County, we'll get a Court where 4–5 turns into 5–4. (*With a sigh.*) C.J. I'm so goddam sick of being on the short end of every vote!

C.J. I'm trying to save you that, Dan . . .

DAN. Well, I don't want to be saved! I want to keep on going straight to hell!

C.J. But it's pointless to hash over Omnitech again. Now, if the missing Chairman of the Board, Donald Richards, could be found, if he'd come forward, we could have this remanded to the Lower Court and have another crack at it. Until then, I see no new Constitutional grounds—

DAN. (*Interrupting.*) I smell plenty of unrefrigerated fish in this case! (*Flicking a page in the notebook.*) This new petition indicates that the joker who testified for Omnitech *lied*—he admits it!

C.J. Dan, if we reviewed an action whenever a witness changed his mind, no trial would *ever* be settled. A simple traffic case could go on for 99 years! A witness could suddenly decide that the pedestrian ran over the car—

DAN. This is no traffic case. If a man's about to be executed, and somebody comes forward at the last minute and confesses, we'd better listen, by God!

C.J. Nobody's getting executed—

DAN. But somebody's getting screwed. Maybe you. And me. And the whole country!

C.J. Get off it, Dan.

DAN. You admit we've got an empty slot in the calendar.

C.J. Forget I said anything—

DAN. Move up Abbott!

C.J. You're a trouble-maker, you know that?

DAN. Only for trouble-makers. (*The C.J. sighs, shakes his head. He takes the ring-binder, slaps it shut and goes off. Dan thinks for a moment, then goes for his top-coat and hat. He flicks the intercom alongside his desk.*)

DAN. (*Into intercom.*) You out there, Mason?

MASON'S VOICE. (*Through intercom.*) Yes, Mr. Justice.

DAN. I'm going to be out of the office for a little while. If there's an emergency, you can find me at the Smithsonian.

MASON'S VOICE. The Smithsonian?

DAN. *Not* on exhibit! (*Dan claps his hat on his head, strides out. Lights dim on Dan's chambers and rise on Ruth's. Stiff from study at her desk, Ruth stretches, gets up, begins to exercise. Simultaneously, Mason comes in with a desk-blotter full of clutter, to restore the mess on Dan's desk. The mountain of disarray looms again and Mason goes out. Ruth finishes exercising and returns to her desk. Studiously, she pores over books and references, a dictating microphone in her hand.*)

RUTH. (*Dictating.*) Abbott v. Omnitech. Minority stockholders' suit. Omnitech acquired patent rights to a totally new type of automobile engine. Abbott claims failure of corporation to develop patents is deliberate mismanagement and unlawful monopolistic practice. (*Leafing to a new page, distastefully.*) Lower Court found for Abbott, Appeals Court reversed and found for Omnitech. New basis for High Court review: sworn deposition by disgruntled officer of the corporation—make that *ex*-officer of the corporation—supporting Abbott claim of mismanagement. Relevant references—uh—take 'em off my yellow pad, Robinson. (*Ruth continues to work at her desk, checking off notations on a legal-size pad, shooting glances into the open books on her desk. Lights fade somewhat on Ruth and rise again on Dan's area as he backs into his chambers.*)

DAN. Careful with it—! (*A Custodian and a Marshal follow Dan into his sanctum. They are lugging a heavy wooden crate about the size of a TV set.*)

MARSHAL. Where do you want us to put this, Justice Snow?

DAN. (*Where else?*) On my desk. (*Dan turns, pleased to see that the mountain of clutter has been restored. Marshal and Custodian look blankly at the desk. There might be room for a postage stamp. Helpfully, the Marshal moves toward the desk.*)

MARSHAL. You want me to clear off—

DAN. Stop! Put it on the library cart. (*The Marshal and Custodian slide a library cart from behind the couch and place the box on the top shelf.*) Careful—easy! Thank you, gentlemen. (*The helpers go off, a bit mystified, passing Mason in the doorway. Mason is glancing down at a pad in his hand as he enters.*)

MASON. There was only one call, Mr. Justice. From Hardin and Wheatson.

DAN. What do they do?

MASON. They're lawyers.

DAN. That's a lousy way to make a living. (*Removing pins and lifting the top off the box.*) Help me with this thing, will you?

MASON. If you don't mind my asking, sir—what is it?

DAN. Oh, just a revolution. Non-violent, I hope. (*The machine revealed is fascinating: a vertical armature culminating in an umbrella-like cluster of plastic leaves.*) What do you think it is?

MASON. I haven't the slightest idea.

DAN. A very rare reference work. Aren't more than a couple of 'em in the whole country.

MASON. (*Puzzled.*) What does it do?

DAN. Absolutely nothing. Oh, it goes around. Watch. (*Dan presses a switch. There is a whirring sound; the leaves of the plastic umbrella spread out like the rotor of a tiny helicopter.*) You know what you're looking at, Mason? Abbott versus Omnitech. That's the whole reason the minority stockholders are suing.

MASON. A momentum machine! Where'd you get it?

DAN. Friend of mine over at the Smithsonian. (*Mason watches the twirling little umbrella with fascination.*)

MASON. When does it stop?

DAN. Oh, in a couple of weeks. Air friction slows it down. Or you can do this . . . (*He touches the switch and it slows to a stop. The plastic leaves collapse like a folding umbrella.*)

MASON. Is there a judicial reason for bringing this here, sir?

DAN. No. Judicious, but not judicial. Several of my colleagues see the words, "Momentum Engine" in a brief and it conjures up absolutely no image whatsoever. Harold, for example. Brilliant man. But for him anything more mechanical than a nail-file is supernatural. (*Suddenly remembering.*) Those lawyers—Hardin and Wheatson—what did they want?

MASON. (*Glancing at his pad.*) They want to talk to your lawyer.

DAN. *I'm* my lawyer. What's it about?

MASON. (*Clearing his throat.*) They said they represent Mrs. Snow.

DAN. That doesn't sound much like High Court business.

MASON. I don't think it is.

DAN. Mason. Would it be appropriate for me to meet with my wife's attorneys in this monument to Justice?

MASON. Might intimidate them a little.

DAN. Not enough. Well, we gotta be fair. (*Glances at his watch, crosses to the closet for his hat and coat. Mason helps him.*) Call 'em back. Tell 'em I'll meet 'em in an hour. On the bench.

MASON. On the bench?

DAN. Third one north of the statue in Lafayette Park. (*As he starts downstage, he passes the machine, touches it.*) Say-ay! You know who needs to look at this? La Belle Dame Sans Merci! (*Dan jerks a finger toward Ruth's chambers.*)

MASON. You want me to roll this over to her chambers?

DAN. Without *me*? Mason, you can have her on the tennis court. I want to show her this myself! (*As the lights dim on Dan's chambers, Mason rolls off the cart. Dan moves downstage as a park bench comes into place on the forestage. The bench is empty. The light has the cast of bent winter sun. A smallish man with an attache case and a top-coat enters. He has the cheer and aplomb of a man on the way to his own execution. His charisma is about the same as Clement Atlee's. Awkward and uncomfortable, he checks his directions. Dan has ensconced himself on the bench, his hat slightly over his face.)*

ATTACHE CASE. (*Muttering under his breath.*) Let's see . . . North. (*Counting unseen benches.*) One . . . two . . . three. . . . Oh. (*Then he sees Dan on the bench, approaches him gingerly, clearing his throat.*) Are you Mr. Justice Snow . . . by any chance?

DAN. (*His face still hidden by his hat.*) No, not by any chance. By an Act of God. (*He cocks up his hat brim.*)

ATTACHE CASE. Of course, Mr. Justice. Uh—this is a great honor.

DAN. (*Squinting at him.*) Are you Hardin?

ATTACHE CASE. No.

DAN. Wheatson?

ATTACHE CASE. I'm Blake.

DAN. Blake?

BLAKE. Blake. I'm a partner in Hardin and Wheatson. I handle contracts mostly, uh, civil matters. I—I don't often get to Court. Oh, Probate, of course—I do a lot of Probate work.

DAN. That must be fun.

BLAKE. Do you have any objection if I sit down . . . ?

DAN. Help yourself. (*Blake sits stiffly, attache case on his lap. Dan doesn't bother to make room for him.*) You know where you're sitting?

BLAKE. The third bench north of . . .

DAN. That's Barney's perch.

BLAKE. I beg pardon?

DAN. If Bernard Baruch were still alive, you'd be sitting on his lap. (*Blake starts to get up.*) Sit down, sit down, he won't mind. What do you want to talk to me about? (*Blake settles uneasily back onto the bench.*)

BLAKE. I—I hesitate to come to you in an adversary situation—because, you see, I have enormous respect for you, Mr. Justice Snow. I think you're one of the greatest legal minds in America today!

DAN. Well, so far we're in complete agreement.

BLAKE. (*Clears his throat again.*) Our law firm has been engaged by your wife, Mrs. Snow—shall we call her the party of the first part?

DAN. I rarely do. But go ahead.

BLAKE. Yes. Well. She's asked us to contact your—am I correct in my understanding that you, as party of the second part, will not be represented by counsel?

DAN. The party of the second part has one helluva counsel. You're talking to him. Go ahead.

BLAKE. I see. Well. Our firm has been engaged to file suit against your client for dissolution of the marriage bonds, and to seek support and maintenance from you—from your client—until such time as . . . (*He trails off. Dan sits up straight on the park bench. He had a pretty good idea this was coming—and yet the official words of it are painful—grating against his male vanity.*) I'm sorry that we of the legal profession sometimes have to be the bearers of—

DAN. (*Interrupts, irked.*) How come Wheatson didn't come over here to tell me? Or Hardin? Doesn't my wife deserve to be represented by a senior member of the firm?

BLAKE. This is actually just a pro forma— (*He fishes into the attache case for the papers.*)

DAN. (*Angrily.*) You know why your bosses didn't want to face me with this, don't you? Some day they may find themselves pleading a case in front of me, and they don't want to be remembered as the boys who broke up my marriage!

BLAKE. (*Timidly and unhappily.*) Well, from the affidavit I have here from the party of the first— (*Dan snatches the papers out of the attorney's hand.*)

DAN. What does my wife say about me?

BLAKE. For all intents and purposes, your—your marriage seems to have ceased to—

DAN. What do you know about it? Have you been hanging around my house, spying in my bedroom—?

BLAKE. Oh, no, sir—no, no—there's been no surveillance.

DAN. (*Reading.*) What does she mean, we don't talk to each other? I talk to her all the time.

BLAKE. I realize—it must be painful for you to—

DAN. My wife made this complaint under oath—?

BLAKE. Yes, sir. In Mr. Hardin's office.

DAN. Why didn't she ever say any of these things to *me?*

BLAKE. She says she did—but apparently you didn't—

DAN. How the hell does she have the nerve to say I'm bad-tempered? (*Shouting.*) Goddamit, I'm the sweetest-tempered sonuvabitch in the District of Columbia!

BLAKE. (*Miserable.*) I'm not really . . . in a position to . . . make any comment on . . .

DAN. (*Reading on.*) Holy Christ! (*Blake starts to say something, just as Dan snaps to the next page of the brief—and so decides to hold his silence.*) What does she mean, I don't notice her? I always notice her. I say hello to her, goodbye to her, how are you? I don't see where it's grounds for a divorce if the honeymoon doesn't drag on for twenty years!

BLAKE. That's your copy, sir. You can keep it, if you want to.

DAN. I'll have it framed.

BLAKE. There's just one other thing we ought to settle, if you don't mind. And I ask this of you not as the party of the second part but as attorney for the party of the second part—

DAN. Yeah? What do you want to know?

BLAKE. Do you intend to contest this action?

DAN. What the hell business is that of yours? I'm going to talk this over with my wife.

BLAKE. (*Suffering.*) Mrs. Snow asked us to tell you that, to avoid unnecessary unpleasantness, all communications should take place through the lawyers—not face to face.

DAN. She doesn't want to see me? Or talk to me?

BLAKE. Those . . . uh . . . were her instructions. She says if you want the house, for the time being she's prepared to move in with friends down in Virginia. Or maybe you'd rather stay somewhere in town. . . . (*Now this is beginning to hit Dan, hard.*)

DAN. I didn't realize . . . She really means this, doesn't she?

BLAKE. It would be helpful to know if you plan to take this to court. . . .

DAN. I dunno, I dunno. (*Dan gets up, starts off—then turns.*) I doubt it. Only a damn fool goes to court unless he *has* to. (*Blake looks sadly at the dispirited Dan. The high-flying eagle has had some of his pinfeathers plucked. The lights fade. The lights come up on Ruth's chambers. She is hard at work; her desk is more cluttered than usual. The buzzer sounds.*)

RUTH. (*Into intercom.*) Robinson, I don't want to be disturbed. (*She turns back to her work. The buzzer sounds again. She slams a book shut, turns to the intercom.*) Yes?

ROBINSON'S VOICE. (*Through intercom.*) Mr. Justice Snow wonders if you'd make an exception. . . . (*A beat pause. She sighs.*)

RUTH. Of course. Have him come in. (*A little preoccupied, Dan ambles in.*) What can I do for you, Justice Snow? (*Dan looks at the confusion on her desk with mock surprise.*)

DAN. My, my, my! What happened to your desk? Has somebody been using it?

RUTH. I happen to have a great deal of work to do.

DAN. Oh? (*Shrugs.*) Okay. Sorry. (*Dan turns to go out. Ruth is surprised that he has wilted so quickly.*)

RUTH. Excuse me. I didn't mean to be so—

DAN. That's all right. I know how busy the brain of an Associate Justice can be.

RUTH. Are you all right—?

DAN. If I'm not, I don't want to know about it.

RUTH. What was it you wanted?

DAN. I've got a little present for you. Not actually a present. Since I only borrowed it, I can't exactly give it away. But we can *share* it—as we do so many things. Okay? (*Ruth nods. Dan calls off.*) Mason, wheel it in! (*Mason pushes in the library cart containing the momentum engine model.*)

RUTH. What's *that*?

DAN. In Mahoney, I know you thought it was important to see that movie he made. (*Gesturing toward the engine.*) I'm about to show you what might be called the "Naked Multinational." Just sit there and watch. We don't even have to lower the lights.

RUTH. Just a minute. You're aren't going to ask me to *censor* anything, are you?

DAN. Nothing about this machine is even faintly "offensive to the public sensibility. . . ." What they *did* to it makes rape look like calisthenics. Mason, give her a spin!

MASON. Yes, sir. (*Mason presses the button, the plastic vanes whirl up to speed; they spread out and spin as before. Ruth gets up, studies the machine.*)

RUTH. (*Skeptically.*) What does it do?

DAN. What it does, it's doing. It's an energy bank. Just like a storage battery, or a tankful of gas. Put a little gizmo like this under the hood of a car and you can wave goodbye to internal combustion.

RUTH. *This* is the invention that Omnitech bought?

DAN. Nobody invented momentum; it's been going on for quite awhile.

RUTH. You expect me to believe that thing has enough energy to drive a car?

DAN. Of course not. But imagine a fly-wheel like this—twenty times heavier—rotating a thousand times as fast. Sealed in a vacuum, no sticky air to slow it down. That's what these patents were about! (*Ruth strides to her desk, goes through blueprints, flips through the pages of a brief, looking for something.*)

RUTH. But it says here—someplace—here! The Vice-President of Omnitech testified under oath it was *not* practical or feasible.

DAN. That's the witness who wants to change his testimony.

RUTH. (*Glancing at the spinning wheel.*) Doesn't that thing make you nervous?

DAN. I'd be more nervous if I owned oil stock. (*Mason turns off the machine.*)

RUTH. How can it replace oil? Something's got to make it go.

DAN. Of course. But it can get juice anyplace, any time: a windmill, solar panels on the roof.

RUTH. (*Folding her arms.*) Why'd you bring this thing in here?

DAN. Thomas Jefferson said an educated electorate is the basis of democracy. I go further. We should even try to educate Justices. Mason, wheel this over to Harold Webb's chambers.

MASON. Just leave it?

DAN. Don't explain anything. Just let it worry him a little. (*Mason exits, pushing the cart and the momentum engine.*)

RUTH. (*Drily.*) Doesn't it strain your humility, being an expert on everything?

DAN. Well, I'm *interested* in everything. I may even take up the law.

RUTH. Do you expect to change anybody's vote with that contraption?

DAN. Think of me as an angel of enlightenment.

RUTH. I can read a brief.

DAN. I'm just changing dead words on a page into a visual image.

RUTH. Is the implication that I'm incompetent? Or stupid?

DAN. Dear lady, if I thought you were stupid, I'd ignore you.

RUTH. Now, factually, what happened? Omnitech bought up a lot of patents—

DAN. On a new power plant that could drive every car in America.

RUTH. That's not how *I* read the brief. Abbott and a handful of stockholders started screaming: "Why don't you develop this thing? Clean up the air, end the gas shortage!"

DAN. Well, why didn't they?

RUTH. There's nothing to develop. That toy you just rolled in here doesn't look anything like these blueprints. (*Brandishing some blueprints.*)

DAN. In theory, it's exactly the—

RUTH. Theory, fine. But it isn't *practical*! The momentum engine is a dandy idea that just doesn't work.

DAN. They didn't want it to work. You know what I think happened? Donald Richards looked around the table at the Board of Directors of Omnitech, and all of a sudden he said: "Hey, fellas—what the hell have we got here? This gizmo could make every car on the road as obsolete as the surrey with the fringe on top!"

RUTH. You amaze me. You absolutely amaze me . . . !

DAN. I do?

RUTH. (*Leveling at him.*) You don't think anybody in the country is honest—except *you*. I doubt if you really believe in anything!

DAN. Yes, I do. I believe in *doubt*.

RUTH. And where does that get you?

DAN. A little nearer the truth.

RUTH. Your notion of the truth. Your bias!

DAN. Just let me explain a rather fine legal point—

RUTH. (*Flaring.*) Don't you treat me like some first-year law student!

DAN. I'm trying—

RUTH. You're trying to change my mind!

DAN. I just want to show you something; then you can change your mind all by yourself.

RUTH. Would you go to all this trouble if I were a *man*? One of the "brothers"?

DAN. Sex has nothing to do with it.

RUTH. Because I'm a woman, your resplendent male ego wants to win me over! You know what you are? You're an *intellectual heterosexual*!

DAN. (*Echoing her previous jab at him.*) You're just being sweet to me because I'm a man.

RUTH. But I wouldn't dream of proselytizing *you*, or anybody. I think it's beneath the dignity of this court for Justices to act like lobbyists. Aren't we supposed to conduct ourselves on a higher plane?

DAN. Oh, one of these days you'll get used to the high altitude stuff. It's been my experience that a Justice of the Supreme Court needs five or six years just to get over the holy honor of being appointed.

RUTH. (*With conviction.*) I don't want to get over the honor. I hope I never do! I'm *proud* to be here.

DAN. Okay. You go right on being proud. I'll go right on being humble—in my usual arrogant way. (*Ruth and Dan look at each other. In a curious way, the fierceness of their disagreement is a bond.*)

RUTH. You know what *I* believe in? Fervently? Something you said.

DAN. Oh?

RUTH. From the bench. On this court. This is a verbatim quote—

DAN. And you memorized it?

RUTH. Sometimes I think you may have forgotten you said it. (*Pause. She looks at him evenly.*) "The noblest purpose of this High Court is to keep the government off the backs of the people." Do you still believe that?

DAN. Sure. But I also think it applies to *quasi*-governments.

RUTH. "Quasi-governments." Is that some new legal concept that just sprang from your forehead?

DAN. I'll try not to sound like a law-school professor. But isn't Omnitech a kind of government *beyond* government? And doesn't Donald Richards head up his own bureaucracy and foreign service? With more actual power than the man sitting in the White House?

RUTH. That simply isn't true.

DAN. Lady, the head of a multinational, unlike the fella in the White House, can hang in there for life. He rules by divine right of stock manipulation.

RUTH. *We* serve for life.

DAN. But in a blaze of light! Donald Richards lives in a closet someplace. He doesn't even show up for his own trial, for God's sake!

RUTH. He doesn't want the courts to put him out of business.

DAN. You put Mahoney out of business, didn't you?

RUTH. Mahoney broke a law. What's Donald Richards done?

DAN. Nothing visible.

RUTH. Rule against Omnitech and down goes the whole corporate system!

DAN. Only the abuses.

RUTH. In your isolated opinion! (*Both are talking at once.*)

<table>
<tr>
<td>DAN. Not so isolated! The first judge found for Abbott, didn't he? All I'm asking is: "What's fair???"</td>
<td>RUTH: (Simultaneously.) We've got statutes that define the abuses. If we try to extend our jurisdiction into legislative areas—</td>
</tr>
</table>

RUTH. (*Continues.*) Don't you see? Abbott can't win!

DAN. Oh, you know that, do you? For a certainty? Seems to me anything can happen—no matter how long the odds are. (*He moves toward the door.*) No horse ever won a race by staying in the stable. Even if he comes in last, at least he gets a little fresh air. Eventually, *everything* gets out in the open. (*A happy snort.*) God, I love the way this country works! (*He waves impudently.*) See ya in court! (*Dan leaves. The lights fade. Lights rise on the forestage as the Custodian and Marshal bring on a low bench. A Photographer is setting up his camera, tripod and strobe light in the aisle of the theatre. The Justices, robed, gather on the thrust. The C.J. and Dan enter from left, as Harold and the others come on from right. Harold glares at Dan, then moves away in a huff.*)

C.J. (*Chiding Dan.*) You shouldn't have done that to Harold.

DAN. (*Blankly.*) Done what?

C.J. That whirligig you left outside his chambers. He leaned over to see what it was, and caught his necktie in it. (*Dan is surprised, then amused. He crosses to the New England Justice.*)

DAN. (*Undoing his tie.*) Here, Harold.

HAROLD. (*Loftily.*) No apology is necessary.

DAN. I'm not apologizing. I hear you lost a necktie. (*He offers his tie to the New England Justice.*)

C.J. You're gonna need that, Dan.

DAN. (*Pointing to the bench.*) What's all that for?

C.J. Annual rites of spring.

DAN. Another group portrait? Already? (*Starting out.*) Paste me in from last year!

C.J. That would be tampering with the evidence.

RUTH. The only time I feel helpless is when I'm having a picture taken. You can't over-rule a camera.

C.J. You realize this is the first time the Nine Old Men will include a pretty face.

DAN. Please, C.J.! You'll hurt William Howard Taft's feelings. (*The Justices fall into their proper places, five seated, four standing. Dan scrunches up his tie. Ruth moves tentatively in position farthest left.*) Hey, should the lady be standing while five of us are sitting?

RUTH. This is where the newest member of the Court is supposed to be, isn't it?

DAN. I'm just worried about your making five old gentlemen look as if they weren't gentlemen.

C.J. Shut up, Dan. Let's get this over with. (*Dan raises an eyebrow; he has rarely seen the C.J. so testy.*)

PHOTOGRAPHER. Ready, everybody? Please don't look directly into the camera. I think if you seem to be looking out into space . . .

HAROLD. Into the future?

JOSIAH. I can't see that far. I didn't bring my glasses.

C.J. You'll need more than glasses.

RUTH. Should we smile . . . a little?

DAN. Good God, no. Who'd trust a *happy* Justice? The best trick is just to look blank.

PHOTOGRAPHER. Ready— (*The Photographer's flash goes off, but Ruth was straightening her robe.*)

RUTH. I didn't feel ready. (*Composing herself.*) Go ahead, shoot.

THOMPSON. My wife always hates these pictures. She says we all look stuffed.

DAN. Why not take a real picture of this Court? A snap-shot of all our convictions.

CAREY. It'd have to be a *moving* picture, if convictions mean anything.

HAROLD. *My* convictions don't move.

PHOTOGRAPHER. Ready—

DAN. (*Half-kidding.*) That's why you'll never amount to anything, Harold. (*A couple of snickers at this. Harold bridles, starts to rise. The flashbulb pops.*)

C.J. No, no. Tear that one up.

JOSIAH. I concur. I sure as hell didn't look dignified.

HAROLD. (*Icily, thin-lipped.*) Would somebody suggest to our "Great Dissenter" that he curb his celebrated sense of humor? He'll need all his wits to write the *minority* opinion.

DAN. Well, a man's gotta decide whether to be on the right side or the winning side. Once in a while they're the same. (*The New England Justice stands, tense with anger.*)

HAROLD. This Court isn't going to reverse the 7th Circuit on Omnitech!

DAN. We sure as hell aren't if we don't even hear it!

C.J. Gentlemen, save it for the conference room.

HAROLD. The whole economy of the United States—of the Western World—is at stake here. We can wreck the entire establishment of enlightened capitalism!!!

PHOTOGRAPHER. Ready—

HAROLD. (*Thrusting a finger at Dan.*) *You* can, Mr. Justice Snow, with your damn socialist ideas— (*Dan's anger rises slowly, and so does he.*)

DAN. I'm about as much of a socialist as Barbara Frietche—and you know it, you brain-washed Brahmin. (*C.J. half comes to his feet, stretching out his arm to placate the Justices.*)

C.J. Please, gentlemen—! (*Click—the Photographer's flash goes off as fists are waved in the air. C.J. looks straight at the camera, appalled.*) Destroy that negative!

DAN. Why? I'm tired of looking like an Associate Delegate to an Undertakers' Convention. Let the public see what it's really like—behind the drapes, behind the robes!

C.J. Sit down, Daniel.

DAN. (*Amiably.*) All right. (*Dan sits.*) But why do we keep on lying to the people—letting 'em think we're some superannuated boys' choir singing "God Bless America" in unison!?

RUTH. Exception.

DAN. (*Correcting himself.*) A boys' choir—augmented by the cadenzas of a brilliant coloratura from California.

C.J. That's enough, Dan. Settle down, Harold, and try to remember what you did with your face last year. You looked pretty good. (*The breeze of flattery cools his anger.*)

HAROLD. What if I cross my legs—?

DAN. It won't do a thing for you.

HALLORAN. Perhaps Mr. Justice Snow has a point: we shouldn't all look too bland and homogenized.

C.J. Trustworthy is enough. Just look trustworthy.

JOSIAH. *Somebody* in Washington better look that way. (*It is the precise moment: the Justices form that familiar frozen frieze of nobility which characterizes most portraits of the Court.*)

PHOTOGRAPHER. Ready— (*Flashbulb pops, camera clicks.*) Perfect! (*The Justices start to break ranks, but the Photographer stops them.*) Hold for one more! (*Another flash and click.*) Thank you. (*The portrait sitting breaks up. The Photographer moves off with his equipment. Custodial Personnel carry off the bench. The Justices scatter in clusters to either side. Dan moves with the C.J. down onto the thrust.*)

DAN. I'd like to have a couple copies of that one you wanted to tear up.

C.J. What for?

DAN. I dunno—irreverence, I guess. Wouldn't it be great if we had a couple of snapshots backstage at Independence Hall? The Founding Fathers scrapping with each other? Instead of all those touched-up oil paintings with everybody sitting around looking rosy and honorable— (*Pointedly raising his voice.*) —just like the Board of Directors of Omnitech International? (*Ruth has started off—but stops when she hears this, which was obviously aimed at her ears. Ruth turns, moves back toward the C.J. and Dan.*)

RUTH. Oh, Chief—

C.J. Yes . . . ?

RUTH. I don't know whether this is in order or not, but if we *do* hear Abbott v. Omnitech, I'd be very honored if you asked me to draft the majority opinion.

DAN. (*With insolent innocence.*) Oh, is it all over? And you're in the majority, are you? Well, well, well. I guess I must've missed something. (*Ruth flushes, both embarrassed and angry.*)

RUTH. I'm sorry, it was an improper request—

C.J. Not at all. A little premature, maybe. I'll certainly give it consideration.

RUTH. (*A little grimly.*) I happen to feel very strongly on this issue. Of course, I couldn't hope to match the ringing rhetoric of Justice Snow's brilliant dissent. . . .

DAN. But you can try.

RUTH. (*Evenly.*) I can try. (*The C.J. looks from one adamant adversary to the other. The lights fade. Ruth and C.J. go off left. Dan goes off right. The lights come up on Ruth's chambers. She comes on carrying an open law volume. It is very late—long past midnight. She looks up as if she heard something, sensitive to that peculiar hush which fills a public building late at night. She takes another law book, slips markers in each. Slinging a cloth coat over her arm and clutching the two volumes like a schoolgirl, she goes out, snapping out the light as she leaves. Dan's chambers are empty and dark. Rather wistfully, Dan enters, switching on the light at the entrance. He is in shirtsleeves, the cuffs rolled back, his necktie askew. He has a law volume and some papers in his hand, which he adds to the mess on his desk. The late-night chill makes him shiver. He crosses to the closet, takes down a cardigan sweater with patched elbows, pulls it on. Then he returns to his desk. A Night Watchman appears at the entrance to Dan's chambers. He sweeps a flashlight around, is about to turn out the light when he sees Dan.*)

NIGHT WATCHMAN. Oh, excuse me, Mr. Justice Snow. I noticed there was a light on—I didn't know you were still here.

DAN. (*Flatly.*) I'm still here.

NIGHT WATCHMAN. Is everything all right, sir?

DAN. *That* may be an overstatement, Jim. But there's nothing for you to worry about.

NIGHT WATCHMAN. (*Still troubled.*) Well, good night, Mr. Justice. (*Glancing at his watch.*) I guess it's good morning. (*The Night Watchman waves vaguely, goes out. Dan scrawls notes on a yellow pad. Ruth, carrying the two books, appears at the entrance to Dan's chambers. She stops, surprised to find him there. She pauses, silently to watch him. He doesn't realize she's there. Dan looks up suddenly, slightly startled.*)

DAN. How long have *you* been here?

RUTH. (*Gently.*) Since October. (*A crooked smile crosses Dan's face.*)

DAN. (*Nodding toward the books.*) Are those for me? You brought me a midnight snack.

RUTH. More like a 4 A.M. snack. What are you doing in chambers so late?

DAN. Studying for finals. What about you?

RUTH. (*Indicating the books.*) I brought you a few opinions of mine from the lower court, so you could— (*Breaks off.*) Well, I didn't have any idea you'd still be here. And I thought you'd find these first thing tomorrow morning.

DAN. I'm getting them last thing last night. It's earlier than you think. (*Ruth starts out, the books still in her arms.*) You going to leave them?

RUTH. Do you want them?

DAN. I'll read them. (*She hesitates, then puts the books on the couch.*) Thank you. (*Is he being sarcastic? Apparently not.*)

RUTH. You're welcome. (*She starts out.*)

DAN. May I ask you a question? Exactly how repulsive do you think I am? (*She turns, looks at him.*)

RUTH. You want my opinion as a Justice of the Supreme Court?

DAN. No. As a woman.

RUTH. Well—

DAN. You want to take the Fifth?

RUTH. Maybe one of us better.

DAN. Do you ever feel like wallpaper—when I'm talking to you?

RUTH. Wallpaper?

DAN. My wife does; that's one of her complaints. She claims I don't really pay any attention to her—that I treat her like some repetitive pattern that's been hanging on the wall since we moved in.

RUTH. What do you tell her when you've been in chambers working all night . . . ?

DAN. I tell her I've been in chambers working all night.

RUTH. Does she believe you?

DAN. (*Shrugs.*) It doesn't really matter too much. Things are pretty cool around the Snow household these days. (*Ruth drifts back into the room.*)

RUTH. Do you argue?

DAN. *I* argue. My wife knows how to argue without saying a word.

RUTH. Who wins?

DAN. She doesn't tell me. I think she thinks I spend so much time being furious at you I don't have enough energy left to be furious at *her*. You know—love-hate, hate-love. And I suspect she's got a hunch that I find you attractive.

RUTH. Well, there's no evidence to support *that* contention.

DAN. I wouldn't be too sure.

RUTH. I hope you'll assure Mrs. Snow that the mere fact one of your colleagues happens to be a woman . . .

DAN. That's no "mere" fact—it's a *towering* fact! But I've never been prejudiced by sex. Entertained, yeah. Prejudiced, never.

RUTH. You mystify me. . . .

DAN. I do? Well, *you* mystify *me*. (*Crossing from his desk toward Ruth.*) Sometimes I mystify myself! (*As Dan advances toward her, she is baffled, uneasy. When she realizes that Dan is merely crossing to the couch to pick up the books she has brought, Ruth is embarrassed at her own presumption. Dan leafs through one of the books.*) Yup, yup—this is a dandy, I remember it well. I don't agree with a word of it, but it's damn well written. How can you be so goddam logical and so goddam wrong?

RUTH. How can it be wrong to encourage the economy? (*Earnestly.*) I've heard you talk about "improving the quality of life on this planet." Oh, I agree with you, Dan— (*Hastily correcting herself.*) —uh—Justice Snow.

DAN. (*Very faint smile.*) "Dan" is fine.

RUTH. Look at how your life—and mine—have been improved by the achievements of the business community. Are we going to throw those benefits away? Shall I take my weekly wash down to the banks of the Potomac and beat it with rocks?

DAN. You won't get it very clean.

RUTH. Why should "multinational" be a dirty word?

DAN. Look, where do you get the idea I'm against *all* corporations? Some of 'em work fine—little family corporations, for instance. Like a cat. Friendly, clean, catches mice, purrs when you stroke it. But when the cat starts making deals with the mice to take over the house . . . !

RUTH. If we reverse the 7th Circuit on Omnitech, it'll be a crippling blow to *all* business.

DAN. Or has business crippled itself by its own self-interest? Right after Pearl Harbor, we were so scared, it only took eighteen months for American industry to turn itself around and grind out enough ships, tanks, planes to win a war. But these days Detroit wants an extra ten years to get a millionth part of the stink from the smoke that pours out of my car.

RUTH. They're trying.

DAN. Not hard enough. (*Pacing, irritably.*) Why won't Donald Richards stand trial? He's the only one with the answers.

RUTH. What do you want to know?

DAN. You're not Donald Richards. (*She looks at him steadily, then raises her right hand.*)

RUTH. Swear me in.

DAN. Oh, you want to do that again. (*With relish.*) You're sworn. (*Ruth sits. Dan begins to circle the chair, like a prosecuting attorney.*) Mr. Richards, would you state your occupation, please?

RUTH. I am President and Chairman of the Board of Omnitech, International.

DAN. Why did you refuse to testify in the suit against your company?

RUTH. I never received a subpoena.

DAN. A subpoena was issued.

RUTH. It wasn't served.

DAN. They have to know where to serve it. But you deliberately made yourself unavailable. Remained in hiding—

RUTH. An American citizen has rights of privacy. May I quote the eminent jurist, Daniel Snow? "When God created the world, he did it alone, in private—"

DAN. I know the quote.

RUTH. I hold that Justice Snow's opinion reinforces my own claim to privacy. (*She smiles.*)

DAN. Well, I thank you, Mr. Richards, for coming forward—even without a subpoena. Now. (*Circling Ruth's chair.*) I suppose you have stock in Omnitech International . . . ?

RUTH. Yes.

DAN. In fact, you're the majority stockholder, aren't you?

RUTH. (*Reluctantly.*) Yes.

DAN. I kinda thought you were. But what if you were just a little bitty stockholder—like Abbott and the others? Would *you* have faith, Mr. Richards, in a management that bought up something and then just sat on it? Dug a hole in the ground and buried it? Isn't that like *un*inventing an invention? *Un*borning a child? *Un*thinking a thought?

RUTH. It would have been dishonest to the stockholders for our company to spend any more money on an unworkable idea.

DAN. Then why did you buy it in the first place?

RUTH. The inventor was a free agent; he didn't have to sell.

DAN. Answer my question! Why did you buy it?

RUTH. We were . . . hopeful.

DAN. You were hopeful all right! That it wouldn't work! You deliberately suppressed the momentum engine! Killed it!

RUTH. You buy a corner lot, you have no obligation to put a house on it.

DAN. You just let it grow up in weeds?

RUTH. I can do what I please—as long as I've got clear title.

DAN. I sure as hell don't want *you* for a neighbor.

RUTH. As a corporation executive, I don't believe that the government has any right to interfere in the policy-making decisions of my company, as long as we remain within the law. Again—may I quote that respected patriarch of American justice, Mr. Daniel Snow. In the case of Mahoney versus Nebraska, his dissenting opinion contained this memorable sentence: "The government has no business telling James Mahoney how to run his business." Now, does James G. Mahoney, with his filthy mind, have more rights than—

DAN. (*Interrupting.*) Than Donald Richards with his filthy money?

RUTH. In the same opinion, the good Justice affirmed that "the pursuit of happiness does not preclude the pursuit of money."

DAN. You know, you've got a mind like a steel trap.

RUTH. Keep right on putting your paw in it.

DAN. Mr. Richards. You mentioned "remaining within the law." But aren't you guilty of depriving the rest of us of an idea that could enhance the quality of life for everybody?

RUTH. Is that concept anywhere in the Constitution?

DAN. That's what the Constitution is all about! (*Pounding his palm against his head.*) There is a right of eminent domain in *grey matter*! (*Ruth frowns.*) Thomas Edison dreamed up an electric light bulb. The law gave him a patent so he could profit from his invention. Fine! But the LIGHT itself belongs to everybody! And nobody, NOBODY has the right to turn on the darkness! (*Dan reaches for a blue-backed deposition on his desk.*) Now, in this deposition by your infidel vice-president—

RUTH. I seem to hear my attorney saying: "Objection."

DAN. I seem to hear the Judge saying: "Overruled!" (*The paper is in his fist.*) The vice-president who testified for Omnitech in the lower court now admits that he lied! That the momentum engine *is* workable. That it was deliberately *dumped*!

RUTH. That doesn't make any sense. If it worked, it would make millions.

DAN. But Omnitech has *billions* committed to the internal combustion engine. You have one noble purpose, Mr. Richards—to keep things just the way they are, like bronzed baby shoes!

RUTH. No! My purpose is to make things better. Look, an idea doesn't just happen. Something's got to *make* it happen. Somebody has to build a plant, grind out a product, advertise it, sell it. You know what it takes?

DAN. Capital.

RUTH. Right. And nobody's come up with an invention for raising money to beat the buck-on-the-line effectiveness of a corporation! Three cheers for private enterprise! Except it's really public enterprise—because anybody in the world can buy stock in Omnitech.

DAN. But nobody makes decisions except Donald Richards.

RUTH. If you don't like the way I run Omnitech, sell your stock—at a profit probably. Why do you insist on seeing me as a Gropper cartoon—with a bloated belly and a big black cigar? This is the day of enlightened capitalism. (*A sudden aura seems to come over Dan. His voice has a distance, a strangeness.*)

DAN. Then let there be LIGHT! Come out of the dark, Donald Richards! Who are you really? What do you look like? Where have you been? A subpoena can't find you and— (*The full realization hits him.*) Holy Christ!!! You know what I think??? Donald Richards, I think you're *dead*! (*He waves his hand in front of her face.*) I think you've been dead for a long time. Maybe eight, ten years. It's been that long since anybody saw you in public, identified you. (*Indicating deposition.*) Even that poor son-of-a-bitch of a vice-president, who's sorry now he lied for you in court, admits that he never sat in the same room with you—only saw memos, heard a voice over the telephone.

RUTH. Irresponsible fiction, fantasy.

DAN. And if you're dead, who *is* running Omnitech? Who actually holds all that power? Some cabal of faceless men—without names, or fingerprints, or Social Security numbers . . .

RUTH. Why would anybody concoct such a morbid hoax?

DAN. A helluva lot of reasons. Dodge inheritance taxes. Hang onto government contracts. Avoid a power struggle. (*Impassioned.*) *YOU* aren't Omnitech. It's not a human being. It's a *phantom government*! We can't see it. We didn't elect it! It never dies! And who knows what's going on in the sterile sanctity of those board rooms? Why, right now, maybe they're hiring some Betsy Ross to sew us up a new flag: the Star-Spangled Omnitech! Omnitech Rules the Waves! Omnitech Über Alles! Omnitech— (*He breaks off, freezes, his arm raised. But she is not looking at him.*)

RUTH. Or maybe they're planning some new— (*Ruth turns, watches in horror as Dan sways slightly, then crumples unconscious across his desk. Ruth gasps.*) Dan!!! What is it? What's the matter? Oh, my God! (*She rushes toward the door, shouting.*) Marshal! Marshal!!!! (*The lights fade. Black. An ambulance siren, far-off, approaching then whining away into the distance. Then silence. Lights rise on Ruth's chambers. She is asleep in her desk chair, dozing fitfully after a sleepless night. The intercom buzzer awakens her. Ruth switches on intercom.*) Yes?

ROBINSON'S VOICE. (*On intercom.*) Ready on your California call, Justice Loomis. The party is on the line.

RUTH. (*Picking up phone.*) Hello, Bill. Thank you for getting back to me so promptly. I know how early it is out there. What's I'm trying to find out is— (*Frowning.*) I remember my husband telling me once that you and Donald Richards were friends. (*Pause.*) Dartmouth, yes. (*She gets up, restlessly.*) Tell me: after I left the firm, did you—or my husband—or anybody at Loomis and Loomis—have any connection whatsoever with Omnitech, or with Donald Richards personally? (*Breaks off, listens.*) I need to know. It affects whether I can properly sit in judgment on this case. (*Pause, frustrated.*) Well, who *would* know, if you don't? Certainly there must be records, correspondence— (*More frustrated.*) At least you can *try* to find out. (*Pause.*) I need full documentation. If the firm did any business with him, or with Omnitech, at any time. . . . (*Pause.*) All right, all right. Thank you. Yes. Good-bye. (*She hangs up, but stares at the telephone. Then she takes a deep breath, reaches to press the intercom.*) Robinson, find out if there's any word on Justice Snow, will you?—and let me know on the bench.

ROBINSON'S VOICE. (*On intercom.*) Yes, Madame Justice. (*Troubled, Ruth goes off.*)

MARSHAL'S VOICE. (*From upstage.*) Nine fifty-nine! (*The lights rise as eight Justices, robed and grave, gather around the silver coffee urn. Ruth, especially troubled, enters.*)

HAROLD. What do the doctors say?

C.J. They don't know; they're making tests.

JOSIAH. Is he in any pain—?

C.J. I don't think so.

WALDO THOMPSON. I don't ever remember Dan being sick before.

RICHARD CAREY. He considers it unconstitutional.

AMBROSE QUINCY. But at four in the morning! What was he doing here?

CHRISTOPHER HALLORAN. Working. As usual.

JOSIAH. (*Marveling, sadly.*) I've never walked into that Court chamber without Dan there . . .

C.J. Who has? (*Solemnly, the Justices shake hands, moved by the absence of their senior member.*)

RUTH. A mind like that can't just stop. You've all had years with Dan Snow; I've only had a few months. (*All the Justices turn, look at Ruth.*)

MARSHAL'S VOICE. Ten o'clock! (*Ruth retreats to the end of the line. The C.J. leads the Justices in their solemn procession into the Court.*) The Honorable, the Chief Justice and the Associate Justices of the Supreme Court of the United States. (*As the lights begin to fade.*) Oyez! Oyez! Oyez! All persons having business before the Honorable, the Supreme Court of the United States, are admonished to draw near and give their attention, for the Court is now sitting. God save the United States and this Honorable Court. (*The lights sink to black. Lights rise on Dan's chambers. Concerned, Mason stands behind the cluttered desk. He starts to rearrange a few things—then, with the guilty air of a man who has violated the sanctum, he puts things back as they were. He picks up Dan's eyeglasses, looks at them sadly. The C.J. hurries in, alarmed.*)

C.J. Mason, has Justice Snow been in here?

MASON. (*Startled.*) No—!

C.J. How can a hospital just *lose* people???

MASON. What happened?

C.J. He's disappeared.

MASON. Good God—!

C.J. Nobody knows where he is.

MASON. (*Picking up the telephone.*) Get me the Marshal's office—

C.J. I've already talked to the Marshal. (*C.J. throws himself down on Dan's couch.*) Apparently the damn fool just got up out of bed and walked out of the hospital!

MASON. (*Frantic, floundering.*) Should we call the police? The FBI? (*Tentatively.*) The CIA?

C.J. I don't trust any of 'em! (*Dan appears—still in his crumpled cardigan sweater, but wearing a homburg. The C.J. and Mason are startled. Dan looks pale and a little weak. The Marshal trails him, worried.*)

DAN. (*Grinning sheepishly.*) Hi! (*Turning to the Marshal.*) Don't worry about me, Marshal. Go back to the lobby and check briefcases for bombs. (*The Marshal exits.*) Hi, Mason. (*The C.J., stunned, still lies on the couch.*) What's the matter, C.J.? Don't you feel good? (*Dan takes off the homburg, examines it.*) Now *that's* a stupid invention. I haven't worn a homburg for thirty years. (*Handing it to Mason.*) Get this back to my doctor, will you? I borrowed it from him. He probably hasn't even missed it.

C.J. (*Sitting up.*) Dan. What in God's name are you doing here?

DAN. I work here. (*Crossing to the spot by his desk where he collapsed.*) A couple of days ago—no, I guess it was a couple of nights ago—I was standing right here saying something moderately profound. And the next think I knew I was under an oxygen tent. And that's a damned poor place to get any work done.

C.J. What did you do? Just get up and walk out?

DAN. No, I got dressed first.

MASON. But they said you're still under observation. They aren't even sure yet what happened to you—

DAN. Well, they'll have to figure out without me. I can't give 'em any more of my time. They've got about five miles of electrocardiograms—and more of my blood than *I* have.

C.J. If it was a coronary—

DAN. My heart wouldn't dare attack me. What time's the meeting on Abbott?

C.J. Ten o'clock.

DAN. I'll be there— (*He seems to go blank, as if a wave of unreality had swept over him.*) I *think*—! (*He puts his hand to his forehead.*)

MASON. Are you all right, sir?

C.J. Dan, you'd better lie down. . . .

DAN. I will . . . if you'll get off my couch. . . . (*Mason and C.J. help Dan to the couch. Ruth comes into her own chambers. She seems preoccupied. Crossing to her desk, she finds a large, sealed envelope.*)

RUTH. (*Into intercom.*) Robinson, did you leave this envelope on my desk?

ROBINSON'S VOICE. (*Through intercom.*) Yes, ma'am. It came by hand, about fifteen minutes ago; I signed for it.

RUTH. (*As she opens the envelope.*) What's the word on Justice Snow today, Robinson?

ROBINSON'S VOICE. (*Intercom.*) I'll call the hospital. (*Intercom clicks off. Ruth looks at the contents—puzzled at first, then shocked. In his chambers, Dan has stretched out on his couch. He shivers slightly.*)

MASON. Would you like a pillow, sir?

DAN. Why not? (*Mason goes out.*)

C.J. Stick around, Dan—

DAN. I intend to. Y'know what they say—it's not how good you are, it's how long you last. (*C.J. snorts.*) Besides, I wanta climb one more mountain. I mean a *rock* mountain. I expect to get up on my feet again, climb above the timberline, and feel the sweep of wind on my varicose veins. (*Waving the C.J. away.*) Now, get in that conference room, start up the meeting.

C.J. You feel well enough to join us—?

DAN. Hell, what do you think I came back here for? I'll be there— (*Takes a deep breath, as if reaching for strength.*) Just—gimme a minute. (*Reluctantly, the C.J. leaves. Dan lies back, closes his eyes. In her chambers, Ruth reads something startling.*)

RUTH. Oh, my God—! (*She gets up, paces. Mason re-enters Dan's chambers, carrying a pillow.*)

MASON. (*Softly, tentatively.*) Are you asleep, Mr. Justice?

DAN. What would you do if I said "yes"?

MASON. (*Placing the pillow under Dan's head.*) Your doctor's coming.

DAN. For me, or for his hat? (*The buzzer sounds in Ruth's chambers. She crosses up to her intercom, presses it.*)

RUTH. Yes, Robinson?

ROBINSON'S VOICE. (*Through intercom.*) Mr. Justice Snow is in the building.

RUTH. (*Astonished.*) What!

ROBINSON'S VOICE. He's back in his chambers . . . (*Abruptly, Ruth hurries out, clutching the envelope.*)

DAN. (*Squinting at the ceiling.*) You know what's wrong with this place, Mason? The roof leaks.

MASON. (*Glancing up.*) I haven't noticed.

DAN. I have. It's as bad as Karnak.

MASON. I beg your pardon?

DAN. The Temple of Karnak. The Pharaohs were afraid the roof would cave in. So they built this forest of huge columns to support it. So many columns that a man gets lost. Dwarfed by them! You know what's left after four thousand years? No roof. Just the columns. (*Scrutinizing the ceiling again.*) Sometimes I think the Court is Karnak. So many laws you can't find the man. And he still gets rained on. (*Ruth, pale, appears in the doorway; she has the large envelope in her hand.*)

RUTH. (*Hushed.*) Mason. How is he . . . ?

DAN. Pay no attention to the vultures circling above the building; I'm fine. (*Hesitantly, she moves to the couch, looks down into Dan's face.*)

RUTH. You shouldn't be here . . .

DAN. Why not? I gave myself permission. (*Shifting his weight on the couch.*) Oh, I suppose some people will be disappointed that I didn't take the Big Trip. It may be a blow to Harold; I'll bet he already has a first draft of a eulogy.

RUTH. Do you feel well enough to talk?

DAN. I even feel well enough to listen.

MASON. I'll be standing by, if you need me . . . (*Mason goes out. Dan senses from Ruth's face that something is bothering her.*)

DAN. What's wrong?

RUTH. The other night you made an outrageous statement.

DAN. That's the root of my charm . . . what's left of it.

RUTH. You said you didn't think Donald Richards was still alive.

DAN. So? (*Ruth rotates the envelope as if it were burning her fingers.*)

RUTH. I shouldn't be talking to you about this—

DAN. (*Rising on one elbow.*) Why not?

RUTH. Lie back. You're sick. (*He reaches for the envelope.*)

DAN. What's this? A "Get Well" card? (*He takes the envelope from her. Ruth surrenders it reluctantly.*)

RUTH. I—I started to get worried about something. So I made a phone call.

DAN. Oh, that's always a mistake.

RUTH. I called up a man who used to be a law partner of my husband's. He joined the firm after I left, I didn't know him very well. But I did know he went to college with Donald Richards. And I had to be absolutely sure that Loomis and Loomis was in no way involved with Omnitech. (*Sighs.*) A few minutes ago, *that* arrived . . . (*Ruth moves away, restlessly, as Dan takes a letter out of the envelope, reads it, scowls. He reaches in again, pulls out a certificate.*)

DAN. Holy God! Has the C.J. seen this?

RUTH. No.

DAN. This makes Abbott a whole new ball game! Boy, this is going to shake up the brothers. (*Getting up, squinting at her.*) Why the hell did this lawyer send this stuff to you?

RUTH. I suppose he thought if I knew about it, I'd shut up about it.

DAN. He doesn't know you very well, does he? Hey! Watch Harold's face when he finds out. (*Starting toward the door.*) Come on, let's get in the conference room.

RUTH. I'm not going in.

DAN. Why not?

RUTH. I have to resign from the Court.

DAN. Why would you do a damn fool thing like that?

RUTH. (*With frustrated indignation.*) He knew! My husband knew about this.

DAN. (*Flipping pages, scowling.*) That Donald Richards died in Costa Rica in 1973? You've gotta admit, that's a surefire way for a guy to avoid a subpoena! Come on.

RUTH. The *real* guilt lies with the men who knew he was dead and covered it up. And my husband was part of that conspiracy.

DAN. Did *you* know? Did your husband ever tell you anything about it?

RUTH. No.

DAN. Then you're not resigning from the Court!

RUTH. The firm of Loomis and Loomis *was* involved . . . !

DAN. One Loomis is dead, the other Loomis hasn't been part of the firm for twelve years.

RUTH. (*Painfully.*) If there's any suspicion, any shadow on a member of this Court . . .

DAN. Did Ruth Loomis do anything improper . . . ?

RUTH. No. But I won't hide anything.

DAN. Don't.

RUTH. The newspapers'll scream.

DAN. Let 'em scream. It's good for their circulation.

RUTH. What's protocol? Do I write the President—?

DAN. You don't write anybody. You get the Olympian advice of Associate Justice Daniel Snow, and you do exactly what he tells you. (*Passionately.*) Keep your robes on and let the mud fly. It won't stick to you. It seems to me the most important qualification for a Justice of this Court is compassion. That includes compassion for yourself. Resigning is suicide. Taking your own life is an insult to the God who gave it to you. Quitting this Court without good reason is spitting in the face of the government that put you here.

RUTH. (*With bitterness and fire.*) "Without good reason"? I've *got* good reason!

DAN. Because of something your husband did? (*She doesn't answer. He hammers away at her resistance.*) Are you the same person who was married to your husband? Hell, no! This Court changes people. It changes men. I think it's changing a woman, too. (*Softens, summing up his whole existence.*) When they measure you for that leather chair you're going to sit in for the rest of your life— (*Slaps his thigh.*) — by God, something happens! (*Holding out his hands, staring at them strangely.*) You look down at the end of those long robed sleeves, and you say: "Hey whose hands are these? Is this anybody I know? Whose head is this? Whose thoughts?" (*Ruth is moved. She wants to believe him, but can she? Dan half-closes his eyes.*) "In a moment, in the twinkling of an eye, this corruption shall put on incorruption."

RUTH. (*Softly, recognizing the quote.*) St. Paul versus the Corinthians.

DAN. Et al. Interesting case. You have pretty good recall, too.

RUTH. But what if incorruption puts on corruption . . . ?

DAN. (*Pause.*) Ruth Loomis isn't corrupt; she's probably the most honorable human being I've ever known.

RUTH. (*Taking a deep breath.*) I thought you'd be happy to have me off the Court!

DAN. That was before you were *on* the Court. (*Moving closer to her.*) Look. I'll make a deal with you. You don't resign, I don't die. There's plenty of precedent for longevity around here. Hell, when Oliver Wendell Holmes was my age, he was still a kid. (*Starting toward the door.*) Well, let's get in that conference room. And let's keep on fighting each other.

RUTH. I can't just go in there and pick up from where I left off—

DAN. (*Moving back toward her.*) Hell, no. That's not the way this place works. Every day is different. You're different. I'm different. Every morning: a fresh start, a beginning—!

RUTH. First Monday in October . . . ?

DAN. Always. (*He turns back to his desk.*) You know what's on the calendar after we dispose of Abbott? (*Plucks a brief from the stack on his desk, with relish, reading the cover.*) "The First Atheist Church versus the City of Waco, Texas." (*Looking up at her.*) You ain't gonna miss that one, are ya????

RUTH. Obviously, community standards should prevail.

DAN. What about religious freedom?

RUTH. *Atheism* is a religion????

DAN. God, yes!

RUTH. Oh, Dan! What about Cook County Diocese versus John Doe?

DAN. What about Smith vee U.S.?

RUTH. Miller versus Moon!!!

DAN. Dalton vee Utah!

RUTH. Ohhhh—we're gonna have a battle on *that* one.

DAN. Count on it!

RUTH. You know something? You and I make each other possible.

DAN. You're damn right we do.

RUTH. That's the first time we ever agreed on anything.

DAN. I'll be a son-of-a-bitch. (*Dan holds out his hand. Is it a deal? She pauses for a second then walks slowly toward him and shakes his hand. She starts to walk toward the door, assuming "ladies first." But, as at their first meeting on the Court, he brushes in front of her, asserting his seniority, moving out of the room and into the Highest Court in the land ahead of her. Hands on her hips, she shakes her head, and follows him into the Court.*)

CURTAIN

Lawrence and Lee Chronology

14 July 1915	Jerome Lawrence born, Cleveland, Ohio
15 October 1918	Robert E. Lee born, Elyria, Ohio
1938–39	Jerome Lawrence at KMPC, Beverly Hills; writer-director for programs including *Junior Theatre of the Air, Let's Have a Party, Sunday Morning Maniacs, Through the Years,* and *Musical Portraits* (dramatic biographies of composers).
1938	Robert E. Lee writer for *Empire Builders,* radio series, WGAR, Cleveland.
1939–42	Jerome Lawrence at CBS, Hollywood, writer for programs including *Nightcap Yarns* (also released as *One Man Theatre* and *Armchair Adventures), Columbia Workshop, I Was There, Under Western Skies, Man about Hollywood, Stories from Life, Hollywood Showcase.* At CBS, New York, *They Live Forever* (in collaboration with Howard Teichmann).
1940	Robert E. Lee writer-director for *Opened by Mistake,* KMPC, Los Angeles.
1941	Robert E. Lee writer for *Flashbacks,* radio series, WGAR, Cleveland.
1941, 1942	Jerome Lawrence at NBC, Hollywood, during 12 weeks each summer to write *A Date with Judy.*
1942	Lawrence and Lee begin as a writing team for radio, television, theatre, films: 23 January 1942, New York. Initial radio scripts include: *Columbia Workshop, Manhattan at Midnight, Lincoln Highway, Stars over Hollywood,* broadcast simultaneously with *The March of Time* (major contributions by Lee during writing conferences at Young and Rubicam) and Lawrence's scripts for *They Live Forever.*

1942 — Robert E. Lee writer for "Three Sheets to the Wind," NBC radio, with John Wayne; "Task Force," Kate Smith Hour, CBS, with Paul Muni; *Ceiling Unlimited,* CBS, with Orson Welles; *Meet Corliss Archer,* CBS, with Janet Waldo.

1942–45 — Lawrence and Lee two of the founders of Armed Forces Radio Service, where they wrote during World War II:

Mail Call (60 scripts)
Command Performance
Yarns for Yanks (162 scripts)
English-American Amity Dramas
Official Army-Navy Programs for
D-Day
VE-Day
VJ-Day
Globe Theatre
Know Your Ally
Know Your Enemy
Personal Albums
New York Salute to the Armed Forces
The Army Hour
"Death of President Roosevelt," narrated by Spencer Tracy
Armed Forces information and education programs

1943 — *The World We're Fighting For;* 26 half-hour radio dramas, KFI.

1944 — *Living Newspaper: The Soviet G.I.* written and directed by Jerome Lawrence, Washington and Lee University, Lexington, Virginia.

1945–46 — *Request Performance;* 29 variety radio programs, CBS.

1946 — *Screen Guild Theatre;* radio, CBS.

1946–48 — Dramatic record albums, dramatized and directed by Lawrence and Lee:

Rip Van Winkle, starring Walter Huston; *A Cask of Amontillado,* starring Sydney Greenstreet; *A Tale of Two Cities,* starring Ronald Colman (Decca Records); *One God,* with Eddie Albert (Kapp Records).

1946–49	*Favorite Story;* 117 half-hour radio dramas, starring Ronald Colman, syndicated by Ziv Productions. Written and directed by Lawrence and Lee.
January–June 1947	*Frank Sinatra Show;* radio, CBS.
29 January 1948	*Look, Ma, I'm Dancin'!* opens, Adelphi Theatre, New York; Lawrence and Lee's first produced Broadway play, produced and codirected by George Abbott,conceived, choreographed and codirected by Jerome Robbins, music and lyrics by Hugh Martin, book by Lawrence and Lee. Closed 10 July 1948; 188 performances.
1948	*Dinah Shore Program;* radio, NBC.
1948–54	*The Railroad Hour;* 239 radio re-creations of famous works of the musical theatre, starring Gordon MacRae and guest stars plus 60 new musical theatre works; NBC radio. Librettos and lyrics by Lawrence and Lee.
1949–50	United Nations broadcasts, NBC: "The Journey of Trygvie Jones" (directed by Lee); "The Birthday Party," starring Ronald Colman. *Young Love;* 45 half-hour radio episodes; CBS.
1950–51	*Halls of Ivy;* radio, NBC.
1950–51	*Hallmark Playhouse;* radio series hosted by James Hilton, then Lionel Barrymore; CBS.
1951	*The Unexpected* (also called *Times Square Playhouse);* 39 half-hour television films, starring Herbert Marshall. Syndicated through Ziv Productions.
1952–53	*Favorite Story;* 78 half-hour television plays, syndicated by Ziv Productions.
1954–56	Musiplays published by Harms: *Annie Laurie: A Story of Robert Burns; Roaring Camp; The Familiar Stranger.*
10 January 1955	*Inherit the Wind* opens, Theatre '55, Dallas, Texas. Broadway version opens, National Theatre, New York, 21 April 1955. Closed 22 June 1957; 806 performances. Text included in this volume.

13 June 1956	*Shangri-La* opens, Winter Garden Theatre, New York. Musical, book and lyrics by James Hilton, Lawrence and Lee. Music by Harry Warren. Based on Hilton's novel *Lost Horizon*. Produced by Robert Fryer and Lawrence Carr, directed by Albert Marre, choreographed by Donald Saddler. With Dennis King, Martyn Green, Jack Cassidy, Shirley Yamaguchi. Closed 30 June 1956; 21 performances.
31 October 1956	*Auntie Mame* opens, Broadhurst Theatre, New York. Closed 28 June 1958; 639 performances. Text included in this volume.
1 October 1959	*The Gang's All Here opens,* Ambassador Theatre, New York. Closed 23 January 1960; 132 performances. Text included in this volume.
19 November 1959	*Only in America* opens, Cort Theatre, New York. Closed 12 December 1959; 28 performances. Then Ivar Theatre, Hollywood, starring Herschel Bernardi, 25 December 1960. Closed 17 November 1961; 312 performances. Text included in this volume.
25 May 1961	*A Call on Kuprin* opens, Broadhurst Theatre, New York. Closed 3 June 1961; 12 performances. Text included in this volume.
24 October 1961	*Shangri-La* broadcast on *Hallmark Hall of Fame,* NBC-TV, directed by George Schaefer. With Richard Basehart, Marissa Pavan, Claude Rains, Alice Ghostley, Helen Gallagher, Gene Nelson.
10 February 1965	*Diamond Orchid* opens, Henry Miller's Theatre, New York. Closed 13 February 1965; 5 performances. Text included in this volume.
18 November 1965	*Inherit the Wind* broadcast on *Hallmark Hall of Fame,* NBC-TV. Directed by George Schaefer. With Melvyn Douglas, Ed Begley.
3 December 1965	*Sparks Fly Upward* opens, McFarlin Auditorium, Dallas. This revised version of *Diamond Orchid* was produced by Southern Methodist University, directed by Burnet Hogood. With Nan Martin and Alexander Scourby.

14 January 1966 — *Live Spelled Backwards,* by Jerome Lawrence, opens, Beverly Hills Playhouse, Beverly Hills, California. Produced by Ray Stricklyn, directed by Bob Richards.

24 May 1966 — *Mame* opens, Winter Garden Theatre, New York. Musical based on the book by Patrick Dennis and the play by Lawrence and Lee. Music and lyrics by Jerry Herman, book by Lawrence and Lee. Produced by Fryer, Carr & Harris. Directed by Gene Saks, choreography by Onna White. With Angela Lansbury, Beatrice Arthur, Jane Connell, Willard Waterman, and others. Closed 3 January 1970; 1,508 performances.

6 February 1969 — *Dear World* opens, Mark Hellinger Theatre, New York. Musical based on Giraudoux's *The Madwoman of Chaillot,* as adapted by Maurice Valency. Music and lyrics by Jerry Herman, book by Lawrence and Lee. Produced by Alexander H. Cohen, directed and choreographed by Joe Layton. With Angela Lansbury, Milo O'Shea, Jane Connell, Carmen Matthews. Closed 31 May 1969; 132 performances.

21 April 1970 — *The Night Thoreau Spent in Jail* opens, The Ohio State University Centennial Play. Then 154 productions through American Playwrights Theatre. Text included in this volume.

August 1970 — *The Crocodile Smile* opens, State Theatre of North Carolina, Flat Rock, North Carolina. Produced by Robroy Farquhar, in association with Marty Bronson Productions. Directed by Marty Bronson and Jerome Lawrence. With David Ayers, Harry Carlson, Jay North. Previous versions produced as *The Laugh Maker* (The Players Ring, Hollywood, California, August 1952); *Turn on the Night* (Playhouse-in-the-Park, Philadelphia, Pennsylvania, August 1961).

19 October 1971 — *The Incomparable Max* opens, Royale Theatre, New York. Based on Sir Max Beerbohm's stories. Produced by Michael Abbott, Rocky H. Aoki, Jerry Hammer. Directed by Gerald Freedman. With Richard Kiley, Clive Revill, Constance Carpenter, Martyn Green. Closed 6 November 1971; 23 performances.

18 November 1972 — *Jabberwock: Improbabilities Lived and Imagined by James Thurber in the Fictional City of Columbus, Ohio* opens the Thurber Theatre, The Ohio State University; then multiple productions through American Playwrights Theatre. Directed by Roy H. Bowen. With Robert Isenhart, Rose-

mary Thurber Sauers, David Graf, David Ayers, Suzanne Shaner, and others.

31 May 1973	*Ten Days That Shook the World,* by Robert E. Lee, opens, Freud Playhouse, University of California at Los Angeles. Based on the book by John Reed. Directed by Robert E. Lee. With Ralph Freud, Gavan O'Herlihy, Bob Mitchell, and others.
3 September 1975	*Lincoln, The Unwilling Warrior,* source material from Sandburg's *Lincoln,* NBC-TV; Directed by George Schaefer. With Hal Holbrook.
13 November 1975	*Sounding Brass,* by Robert E. Lee, opens, Reformed Church, Bronxville, New York. A chancel drama, produced by Robert McIntyre and the 7 Arts Society. Directed by Hugh McPhillips. With Ray Owens, Martin Copenhaver, Kip McCardle, and others.
1977	*Actor,* musical adapted from Jerome Lawrence's *Actor, The Life and Times of Paul Muni,* with music by Billy Goldenberg. Book and lyrics by Lawrence and Lee. Broadcast on *Hollywood Television Theatre.* With Herschel Bernardi, Georgia Brown.
3 October 1978	*First Monday in October* opens, Majestic Theatre, New York. Closed after extended limited run, 10 December 1978; 78 performances. Toured to Huntington Hartford Theatre, Hollywood, and Blackstone Theatre, Chicago. Previously produced at the Cleveland Play House and the Kennedy Center, Washington, D.C. Text included in this volume.
1981	*First Monday in October.* Screenplay by Lawrence and Lee. Paramount Pictures.
29 January 1990	Lawrence and Lee inducted into national Theatre Hall of Fame.
22 April 1990	Lawrence and Lee named Fellows of the American College Theatre Festival, Kennedy Center, Washington, D.C.
4 October 1990	*Whisper in the Mind* opens, Arizona State University, Tempe. With E. G. Marshall, Michael York, and Michael Learned. Directed by Marshall W. Mason.

2 May 1994	*Whisper in the Mind* opens in revised version, Missouri Repertory Theatre, Kansas City. With Theodore Swetz, Daniel Oreskes, and Cynthia Hyer. Directed by George Keathley.
8 July 1994	Death of Robert E. Lee, Los Angeles, California.